THE
ALL ENGLAND
LAW REPORTS
1994

Volume 2

Editor
PETER HUTCHESSON LLM
Barrister, New Zealand

Assistant Editor
BROOK WATSON
of Lincoln's Inn, Barrister
and of the New South Wales Bar

Consulting Editor
WENDY SHOCKETT
of Gray's Inn, Barrister

London
BUTTERWORTHS

UNITED KINGDOM	Butterworth & Co (Publishers) Ltd, Halsbury House, 35 Chancery Lane, **London** WC2A 1EL and 4 Hill Street, **Edinburgh** EH2 3JZ
AUSTRALIA	Butterworths Pty Ltd, **Sydney**, **Melbourne**, **Brisbane**, **Adelaide**, **Perth**, **Canber**ra and **Hobart**
CANADA	Butterworths Canada Ltd, **Markham** and **Vancouver**
IRELAND	Butterworth (Ireland) Ltd, **Dublin**
MALAYSIA	Malayan Law Journal Pte Ltd, **Kuala Lumpur**
NEW ZEALAND	Butterworths of New Zealand Ltd, **Wellington** and **Auckland**
PUERTO RICO	Butterworths of Puerto Rico Inc, **San Juan**
SINGAPORE	Butterworths Asia, **Singapore**
USA	Butterworth Legal Publishers, **Austin**, Texas, **Clearwater**, Florida, **Orford**, New Hampshire, **St Paul**, Minnesota and **Salem**, New Hampshire

ISBN for the complete set of volumes: 0 406 85159 X
for this volume: 0 406 031738 X

© Butterworth & Co (Publishers) Ltd 1994

Published by Butterworths, Halsbury House, 35 Chancery Lane, London WC2A 1EL. All rights reserved. No part of this publication may be reproduced in any material form (including photocopying or storing it in any medium by electronic means and whether or not transiently or incidentally to some other use of this publication) without the written permission of the copyright owner except in accordance with the provisions of the Copyright, Designs and Patents Act 1988 or under the terms of a licence issued by the Copyright Licensing Agency Ltd, 90 Tottenham Court Road, London, England W1P 9HE. Applications for the copyright owner's written permission to reproduce any part of this publication should be addressed to the publisher.

Warning: The doing of an unauthorised act in relation to a copyright work may result in both a civil claim for damages and criminal prosecution

Printed and bound in Great Britain by William Clowes Ltd, Beccles and London

REPORTERS

House of Lords

Celia Fox Barrister

Privy Council

Celia Fox Barrister

Court of Appeal, Civil Division

Frances Rustin Barrister
Carolyn Toulmin Barrister
Wendy Shockett Barrister
Dilys Tausz Barrister
Celia Fox Barrister
Raina Levy Barrister
L I Zysman Esq Barrister

Court of Appeal, Criminal Division

N P Metcalfe Esq Barrister
Kate O'Hanlon Barrister

Chancery Division

Jacqueline Metcalfe Barrister
Hazel Hartman Barrister
Celia Fox Barrister
Paul Magrath Esq Barrister

Queen's Bench Division

K Mydeen Esq Barrister
Dilys Tausz Barrister

Family Division

Bebe Chua Barrister

Admiralty

N P Metcalfe Esq Barrister

Revenue Cases

Susan J Murphy Barrister

Courts-Martial Appeals

N P Metcalfe Esq Barrister

SUB-EDITORS
Louise Wong LLB
Erica Kendall MA Solicitor

MANAGER
Eric W Spalding Esq

EDITORIAL STAFF
Margaret Froome
Christine Stone

House of Lords

The Lord High Chancellor of Great Britain: Lord Mackay of Clashfern

Lords of Appeal in Ordinary

Lord Keith of Kinkel
Lord Bridge of Harwich
Lord Templeman
Lord Goff of Chieveley
Lord Jauncey of Tullichettle
Lord Browne-Wilkinson

Lord Mustill
Lord Slynn of Hadley
Lord Woolf
Lord Lloyd of Berwick
Lord Nolan

Court of Appeal

The Lord High Chancellor of Great Britain

The Lord Chief Justice of England: Lord Taylor of Gosforth
(President of the Criminal Division)

The Master of the Rolls: Sir Thomas Henry Bingham
(President of the Civil Division)

The President of the Family Division: Sir Stephen Brown

The Vice-Chancellor: Sir Donald James Nicholls

Lords Justices of Appeal

Sir George Brian Hugh Dillon
Sir Brian Thomas Neill
Sir Martin Charles Nourse
Sir Iain Derek Laing Glidewell
Sir Alfred John Balcombe
Sir Ralph Brian Gibson
  (retired 11 April 1994)
Sir Thomas Patrick Russell
Dame Ann Elizabeth Oldfield Butler-Sloss
Sir Murray Stuart-Smith
Sir Christopher Stephen Thomas Jonathan
  Thayer Staughton
Sir Michael Mann
Sir Donald Henry Farquharson
Sir Anthony James Denys McCowan
  (Senior Presiding Judge for England and
  Wales)
Sir Alexander Roy Asplan Beldam

Sir Andrew Peter Leggatt
Sir Richard Rashleigh Folliott Scott
Sir Johan Steyn
Sir Paul Joseph Morrow Kennedy
Sir David Cozens-Hardy Hirst
Sir Simon Denis Brown
Sir Anthony Howell Meurig Evans
Sir Christopher Dudley Roger Rose
Sir Leonard Hubert Hoffmann
Sir John Douglas Waite
Sir John Ormond Roch
Sir Peter Leslie Gibson
Sir John Stewart Hobhouse
Sir Denis Robert Maurice Henry
Sir Mark Oliver Saville
Sir Peter Julian Millett
  (appointed 12 April 1994)

High Court of Justice

The Lord High Chancellor of Great Britain
The Lord Chief Justice of England
The President of the Family Division
The Vice-Chancellor
The Senior Presiding Judge for England and Wales
The puisne judges of the High Court

Chancery Division

The Lord High Chancellor of Great Britain
The Vice-Chancellor

Sir John Evelyn Vinelott
Sir Jean-Pierre Frank Eugene Warner
Sir Jeremiah LeRoy Harman
Sir John Leonard Knox
Sir Peter Julian Millett
  (appointed Lord Justice of Appeal
  12 April 1994)
Sir Robert Andrew Morritt
  (Vice-Chancellor of the County Palatine
  of Lancaster)
Sir William Aldous
Sir Donald Keith Rattee

Sir John Frank Mummery
Sir Francis Mursell Ferris
Sir John Murray Chadwick
Sir Jonathan Frederic Parker
Sir John Edmund Fredric Lindsay
Dame Mary Howarth Arden
Sir Edward Christopher Evans-Lombe
Sir Robin Raphael Hayim Jacob
Sir William Anthony Blackburne
Sir Gavin Anthony Lightman
  (appointed 18 May 1994)

Queen's Bench Division

The Lord Chief Justice of England

Sir Haydn Tudor Evans
Sir Ronald Gough Waterhouse
Sir Frederick Maurice Drake
Sir Christopher James Saunders French
Sir Iain Charles Robert McCullough
Sir Oliver Bury Popplewell
Sir William Alan Macpherson
Sir Philip Howard Otton
Sir Michael Hutchison
Sir Swinton Barclay Thomas
Sir Richard Howard Tucker
Sir Robert Alexander Gatehouse
Sir Patrick Neville Garland
Sir Michael John Turner
Sir Harry Henry Ognall
Sir John Downes Alliott
Sir Konrad Hermann Theodor Schiemann
Sir John Arthur Dalziel Owen
Sir Francis Humphrey Potts
Sir Richard George Rougier
Sir Ian Alexander Kennedy
Sir Nicholas Addison Phillips
Sir Robin Ernest Auld
Sir Malcolm Thomas Pill
Sir Stuart Neill McKinnon
Sir Mark Howard Potter

Sir Henry Brooke
Sir Thomas Scott Gillespie Baker
Sir Igor Judge
Sir Edwin Frank Jowitt
Sir Michael Morland
Sir Mark Waller
Sir Roger John Buckley
Sir Anthony Brian Hidden
Sir John Michael Wright
Sir Charles Barrie Knight Mantell
Sir John Christopher Calthorpe Blofeld
Sir Peter John Cresswell
Sir Anthony Tristram Kenneth May
Sir John Grant McKenzie Laws
Dame Ann Marian Ebsworth
Sir Simon Lane Tuckey
Sir David Nicholas Ramsay Latham
Sir John William Kay
Sir Christopher John Holland
Sir Richard Herbert Curtis
Sir Stephen John Sedley
Dame Janet Hilary Smith
Sir Anthony David Colman
Sir Anthony Peter Clarke
Sir John Anthony Dyson
Sir Thayne Forbes

[continued on next page]

Queen's Bench Division (continued)

Sir Michael Alexander Geddes Sachs
Sir Stephen George Mitchell
Sir Rodger Bell
Sir Michael Guy Vicat Harrison
Sir Bernard Anthony Rix
Dame Anne Heather Steel

Sir William Marcus Gage
Sir Jonathan Hugh Mance
Sir Andrew Centlivres Longmore
Sir Thomas Richard Atkin Morison
Sir Richard Joseph Buxton

Family Division
The President of the Family Division

Sir Anthony Bruce Ewbank
Sir Anthony Barnard Hollis
Sir Mathew Alexander Thorpe
Sir Edward Stephen Cazalet
Sir Alan Hylton Ward
Sir Robert Lionel Johnson
Sir Douglas Dunlop Brown
Dame Joyanne Winifred Bracewell

Sir Michael Bryan Connell
Sir Jan Peter Singer
Sir Nicholas Peter Rathbone Wall
Sir Nicholas Allan Roy Wilson
Sir Andrew Tristram Hammett Kirkwood
Sir Christopher Stuart-White
Dame Brenda Hale

CITATION

These reports are cited thus:

[1994] 2 All ER

REFERENCES

These reports contain references to the following major works of legal reference described in the manner indicated below.

Halsbury's Laws of England

The reference 26 *Halsbury's Laws* (4th edn) para 577 refers to paragraph 577 on page 296 of volume 26 of the fourth edition of *Halsbury's Laws of England*.

The reference 7(1) *Halsbury's Laws* (4th edn reissue) para 267 refers to paragraph 267 on page 177 of reissue volume 7(1) of the fourth edition of *Halsbury's Laws of England*.

Halsbury's Statutes of England and Wales

The reference 40 *Halsbury's Statutes* (4th edn) 734 refers to page 734 of volume 40 of the fourth edition of *Halsbury's Statutes of England and Wales*.

The reference 19 *Halsbury's Statutes* (4th edn) (1990 reissue) 499 refers to page 499 of the 1990 reissue of volume 19 of the fourth edition of *Halsbury's Statutes of England and Wales*.

The Digest

(formerly *The English and Empire Digest*)

The reference 37(2) *Digest* (Reissue) 424, *2594* refers to case number 2594 on page 424 of the reissue of green band volume 37(2) of *The Digest*.

The reference 27(1) *Digest* (2nd reissue) 330, *2849* refers to case number 2849 on page 330 of the second reissue of green band volume 27(1) of *The Digest*.

Halsbury's Statutory Instruments

The reference 17 *Halsbury's Statutory Instruments* 305 refers to page 305 of volume 17 of the grey volumes series of *Halsbury's Statutory Instruments*.

The reference 14 *Halsbury's Statutory Instruments* (1991 reissue) 195 refers to page 195 of the 1991 reissue of volume 14 of the grey volumes series of *Halsbury's Statutory Instruments*.

Cases reported in volume 2

	Page
A, ex p, R v Canons Park Mental Health Review Tribunal [CA]	659
A-G's Reference (No 3 of 1992) [CA]	121
Ackman v Policyholders Protection Board (Nos 1 and 2) (note) [HL]	37
Aeakos Cia Naviera SA, Continental Bank NA v [CA]	540
Alliance and Leicester Building Society v Edgestop Ltd [Ch D]	38
Ananthanarayanan, R v [CA]	847
Arab Bank plc v Merchantile Holdings Ltd [Ch D]	74
Balfour v Foreign and Commonwealth Office [CA]	588
Berry, R v (No 3) [CA]	913
Bijela, The [HL]	289
Bolton v Law Society [CA]	486
British Steel plc, Rastin v [CA]	641
Brooks v DPP of Jamaica [PC]	231
Cain, R v [CA]	398
Cambridge, R v [CA]	760
Central Criminal Court, R v, ex p Guney [QBD DC]	423
Chan-Fook, R v [CA]	552
Chief Constable of North Wales, Davidson v [CA]	597
Chief Constable of South Wales, R v, ex p Merrick [QBD DC]	560
Clowes, R v (No 2) [CA]	316
Collett, R v [CA]	372
Continental Bank NA v Aeakos Cia Naviera SA [CA]	540
Coppée-Lavalin SA/NV v Ken-Ren Chemicals and Fertilizers Ltd (in liq) [HL]	449
Crickmore, Restick v [CA]	112
Crozier v Crozier [Fam D]	362
Customs and Excise Comrs v Schindler (Case C-275/92) [CJEC]	193
D, ex p, R v South East Hampshire Family Proceedings Court [QBD]	145
Dalia, Deposit Protection Board v [HL]	577
Davidson v Chief Constable of North Wales [CA]	597
Debtor, Re a (No 64 of 1992) [Ch D]	177
Debtor, Re a (No 22 of 1993) [Ch D]	105
Debtor, Re a (No 415/SD/93), ex p the debtor v IRC [Ch D]	168
Dent (a bankrupt), Re [Ch DC]	904
Dent, Trustee of the property of the bankrupt v [Ch DC]	904
Deposit Protection Board v Dalia [HL]	577
Dollar Land Holdings plc, El Ajou v [CA]	685
DPP of Jamaica, Brooks v [PC]	231
Duport Harper Foundries Ltd, Singh v [CA]	889

	Page
Edgestop Ltd, Alliance and Leicester Building Society v [Ch D]	38
EE Caledonia Ltd, McFarlane v [CA]	1
Ejaz, ex p, R v Secretary of State for the Home Dept [CA]	436
El Ajou v Dollar Land Holdings plc [CA]	685
ELS Ltd, Re [Ch D]	833
Epping Forest DC, Good v [CA]	156
Euston Centre Investments Ltd, Secretary of State for the Environment v [Ch D]	415
Foreign and Commonwealth Office, Balfour v [CA]	588
Franklin, Pearson v [CA]	137
Frenchay Healthcare NHS Trust v S [CA]	403
Furneaux, ex p, R v Secretary of State for Health [CA]	652
Goldcorp Exchange Ltd (in receivership), Re [PC]	806
Good v Epping Forest DC [CA]	156
Guney, ex p, R v Central Criminal Court [QBD DC]	423
H, R v [CA]	881
Harris, R v [CA]	354
Hunt v Severs [HL]	385
IRC, A Debtor v (No 415/SD/93), ex p, Re the debtor[Ch D]	168
Keane, R v [CA]	478
Kearley, R v (No 2) [CA]	354
Kelt, R v [CA]	780
Ken-Ren Chemicals and Fertilizers Ltd (in liq), Coppée-Lavalin SA/NV v [HL]	449
Ken-Ren Chemicals and Fertilizers Ltd (in liq), Vooest-Alpine AG v [HL]	449
KH Enterprise (cargo owners) v Pioneer Container (owners) [PC]	250
Lamb, Peggs v [Ch D]	15
Law Society, Bolton v [CA]	486
Liverpool City Magistrates' Court, R v, ex p Pender (No 2) [QBD DC]	897
M, Oxfordshire CC v [CA]	269
McFarlane v EE Caledonia Ltd [CA]	1
McFarlane, R v [CA]	283
Mallinson v Secretary of State for Social Security [HL]	295
Manchester City Council v T [CA]	526
Mandair, R v [HL]	715
Mansour, Showlag v [PC]	129
Marchant v Onslow [Ch D]	707
Marida Ltd v Oswal Steel [HL]	289
Martin v Watson [CA]	606
Martinez-Tobon, R v [CA]	90
Mehari, ex p, R v Secretary of State for the Home Dept [QBD]	494
Merchantile Holdings Ltd, Arab Bank plc v [Ch D]	74

	Page
Merrick, ex p, R v Chief Constable of South Wales [QBD DC]	560
Onslow, Marchant v [Ch D]	707
Oswal Steel, Marida Ltd v [HL]	289
Oxfordshire CC v M [CA]	269
Pearson v Franklin [CA]	137
Peggs v Lamb [Ch D]	15
Pender, ex p, R v Liverpool City Magistrates' Court (No 2) [QBD DC]	897
Pioneer Container (owners), KH Enterprise (cargo owners) v [PC]	250
Pioneer Container, The [PC]	250
Policyholders Protection Board, Ackman v (Nos 1 and 2) (note) [HL]	37
Policyholders Protection Board, Scher v (Nos 1 and 2) (note) [HL]	37
Powdrill v Watson [CA]	513
Practice Direction (costs: taxation: value added tax) [SC Taxing Office]	57
Practice Direction (costs: taxation: value added tax) [SC Taxing Office]	61
Practice Direction (hearing dates) [Ch D]	384
Practice Direction (judicial fees: security money) [HL]	176
Practice Note (persistent vegetative state: withdrawal of treatment)	413
Presentaciones Musicales S/A v Secunda [CA]	737
R v Ananthanarayanan [CA]	847
R v Berry (No 3) [CA]	913
R v Cain [CA]	398
R v Cambridge [CA]	760
R v Canons Park Mental Health Review Tribunal, ex p A [CA]	659
R v Central Criminal Court, ex p Guney [QBD DC]	423
R v Chan-Fook [CA]	552
R v Chief Constable of South Wales, ex p Merrick [QBD DC]	560
R v Clowes (No 2) [CA]	316
R v Collett [CA]	372
R v H [CA]	881
R v Harris [CA]	354
R v Keane [CA]	478
R v Kearley (No 2) [CA]	354
R v Kelt [CA]	780
R v Liverpool City Magistrates' Court, ex p Pender (No 2) [QBD DC]	897
R v McFarlane [CA]	283
R v Mandair [HL]	715
R v Martinez-Tobon [CA]	90
R v Rossiter [CA]	752
R v Ryder [CA]	859
R v Secretary of State for Health, ex p Furneaux [CA]	652
R v Secretary of State for the Home Dept, ex p Ejaz [CA]	436
R v Secretary of State for the Home Dept, ex p Mehari [QBD]	494
R v Secretary of State for the Home Dept, ex p Schmidt [QBD DC]	784
R v Shepherd [CA]	242

	Page
R v South East Hampshire Family Proceedings Court, ex p D [QBD]	445
R v W [CA]	872
R v Wernet [CA]	242
R, Yip Chiu-cheung v [PC]	924
R (a minor) (contempt: sentence), Re [CA]	144
Rastin v British Steel plc [CA]	641
Redferns (a firm), Target Holdings Ltd v [CA]	337
Restick v Crickmore [CA]	112
Rhone v Stephens [HL]	65
Rossiter, R v [CA]	752
Ryder, R v [CA]	859
S, Frenchay Healthcare NHS Trust v [CA]	403
Safe Carrier, The [HL]	99
Scher v Policyholders Protection Board (Nos 1 and 2) (note) [HL]	37
Schindler, Customs and Excise Comrs v (Case C-275/92) [CJEC]	193
Schmidt, ex p, R v Secretary of State for the Home Dept [QBD DC]	784
Seaboard Offshore Ltd v Secretary of State for Transport [HL]	99
Seagull Manufacturing Co Ltd (in liq), Re (No 2) [Ch D]	767
Secretary of State for the Environment v Euston Centre Investments Ltd [Ch D]	415
Secretary of State for Health, R v, ex p Furneaux [CA]	652
Secretary of State for the Home Dept, R v, ex p Ejaz [CA]	436
Secretary of State for the Home Dept, R v, ex p Mehari [QBD]	494
Secretary of State for the Home Dept, R v, ex p Schmidt [QBD DC]	784
Secretary of State for Social Security, Mallinson v [HL]	295
Secretary of State for Transport, Seaboard Offshore Ltd v [HL]	99
Secunda, Presentaciones Musicales S/A v [CA]	737
Severs, Hunt v [HL]	385
Shepherd, R v [CA]	242
Showlag v Mansour [PC]	129
Singh v Duport Harper Foundries Ltd [CA]	889
Smithers, Willowgreen Ltd v [CA]	533
South East Hampshire Family Proceedings Court, R v, ex p D [QBD]	445
Stephens, Rhone v [HL]	65
T, Manchester City Council v [CA]	526
Target Holdings Ltd v Redferns (a firm) [CA]	337
Trustee of the property of the bankrupt v Dent [Ch DC]	904
Villiers v Villiers [CA]	149
Vooest-Alpine AG v Ken-Ren Chemicals and Fertilizers Ltd (in liq) [HL]	449
W, R v [CA]	872
Watson, Martin v [CA]	606
Watson, Powdrill v [CA]	513
Wernet, R v [CA]	242
Willowgreen Ltd v Smithers [CA]	533
Yip Chiu-cheung v R [PC]	924

Digest of cases reported in volume 2

AGENT – Ratification – Solicitor – Proceedings commenced by solicitor without authority – Ratification after expiry of limitation period – Plaintiff entitled to adopt action after expiry of limitation period
Presentaciones Musicales S/A v Secunda .. .. CA 737

ARBITRATION – Costs – Security for costs – Arbitration under ICC rules in London – Insolvent claimant funded by third party – Jurisdiction of court to make order for security for costs
Coppée-Lavalin SA/NV v Ken-Ren Chemicals and Fertilizers Ltd (in liq), Voest-Alpine AG v v Ken-Ren Chemicals and Fertilizers Ltd (in liq) .. .. HL 449

— —Leave to appeal against award – Delay – Striking out – Failure to conduct and prosecute appeal with proper despatch
Secretary of State for the Environment v Euston Centre Investments Ltd .. .. John Cherryman QC 416

ARREST – Warrant issued before indictment preferred – Validity of warrant
Brooks v DPP of Jamaica .. .. PC 231

BAILMENT – Liability of sub-bailee to owner – Freight carriers having owners' authority to subcontract carriage 'on any terms' – Whether owner only bound by terms of sub-bailment to which he expressly or impliedly consented
KH Enterprise (cargo owners) v Pioneer Container (owners) .. .. PC 250

BANK – Deposit protection scheme – Insolvent bank – Assignment of part of deposit before bank wound up – Claim by assignee for compensation from deposit protection fund
Deposit Protection Board v Dalia .. .. HL 577

BANKRUPTCY – Avoidance of settlement – Application to set aside deed of gift made subsequent to donor's discharge from bankruptcy
Re Dent (a bankrupt), Trustee of the property of the bankrupt v Dent .. .. .. Ch DC 904

CHARITY – Charitable trust – Public benefit – Rights of commonage – Whether rights arising under charitable trust
Peggs v Lamb .. .. Morritt J 15

COMPANY – Administration order – Effect of order – Administrators continuing to employ company's staff to keep company in operation with view to sale as going concern – Adoption of employees' contracts of employment – Employees' entitlement to salary in lieu of notice
Powdrill v Watson .. .. CA 513

— —Director – Company receiving improperly obtained money – Whether director's knowledge to be attributed to company – Directing mind and will of the company
El Ajou v Dollar Land Holdings plc .. .. CA 685

— —Distress – Unpaid business rates – Whether distress can be levied over company's goods after floating charge has crystallised
Re ELS Ltd .. .. Ferris J 833

— —Shares – Purchase of shares with financial assistance of company – Foreign subsidiary company providing assistance – Whether unlawful
Arab Bank plc v Merchantile Holdings Ltd .. .. Millett J 74

CONFLICT OF LAWS – Jurisdiction – Exclusive jurisdiction clause in contract – Foreign proceedings initiated in breach of exclusive jurisdiction clause – Injunction restraining continuation of foreign proceedings
Continental Bank NA v Aeakos Cia Naviera SA .. .. CA 540

xiii

CONFLICT OF LAWS – Stay of proceedings – Agreement to refer to foreign court – Exclusive jurisdiction clause in bill of lading

    KH Enterprise (cargo owners) v Pioneer Container (owners) .. .. PC 250

CONTEMPT OF COURT – Committal – Maximum sentence – Whether 18 months' imprisonment for breach of injunction plus activation of 12-month suspended sentence for previous breach exceeding two-year statutory maximum sentence for contempt 'on any occasion'

    Villiers v Villiers .. .. CA 149

— —Committal – Maximum sentence – Whether two-year sentence imposed after giving credit for admitting certain breaches exceeding two-year statutory maximum sentence for contempt 'on any occasion'

    Re R (a minor) (contempt: sentence) .. .. CA 144

COSTS – Taxation – Value added tax – Civil proceedings and non-contentious business

    Practice Direction .. .. SC Taxing Office 57

— —Taxation – Value added tax – Crown Court

    Practice Direction .. .. SC Taxing Office 61

COUNTY COURT – Practice – Service of summons – Service by post – Service at premises owned by defendant – Defendant not residing at premises

    Willowgreen Ltd v Smithers .. .. CA 533

— —Practice – Striking out – Failure to request hearing date within time prescribed – Extension of time for requesting hearing date

    Rastin v British Steel plc .. .. CA 641

CRIMINAL EVIDENCE – Character of accused – Defendant of good character jointly tried with defendant of bad character – Direction to jury of relevance of defendant of bad character's previous convictions

    R v Cain .. .. CA 398

— —Corroboration – Similar fact evidence – Long delay between alleged offence and complaint – Possibility of contamination or collusion – Direction to jury on whether evidence capable of mutual corroboration

    R v W .. .. CA 872

— —Corroboration – Similar fact evidence – Possibility of collusion – Circumstances in which similar fact evidence should not be permitted to be lead

    R v Ryder .. .. CA 859

— —Corroboration – Similar fact evidence – Risk of contamination – Direction to jury – Real risk that complainant's evidence contaminated by another complainant

    R v Ananthanarayanan .. .. CA 847

— —Corroboration – Similar fact evidence – Risk of contamination – Whether contamination going to admissibility or quality of evidence

    R v H .. .. CA 881

— —Disclosure of police sources of information to defence – Public interest immunity – Confidentiality of police sources

    R v Keane .. .. CA 478

— —Intimate sample taken from defendant – Use as evidence in unrelated trial – Sample taken from defendant in course of criminal investigation admissible as evidence at trial of defendant on unrelated charge

    R v Kelt .. .. CA 780

CRIMINAL LAW – Appeal – Death of appellant before appeal heard – Whether right of appeal against conviction and sentence personal to appellant – Whether remission by House of Lords to Court of Appeal disposing of appeal to House of Lords

    R v Kearley (No 2), R v Harris .. .. CA 354

– –Appeal – Right of appeal – Effect of House of Lords decision – Further appeal on other grounds – Conviction restored by House of Lords – Whether open to Court of Appeal to set aside order made by House of Lords

    R v Mandair .. .. HL 715

– –Appeal to House of Lords – Powers of House of Lords in disposing of appeal – House of Lords having power not only to exercise all powers of Court of Appeal but also to remit case to Court of Appeal

    R v Mandair .. .. HL 715

– –Assault occasioning actual bodily harm – Actual bodily harm – Psychiatric injury – Psychiatric injury can amount to actual bodily harm – Appropriate direction to jury on psychiatric injury amounting to actual bodily harm

    R v Chan-Fook .. .. CA 552

– –Bail – Recognisance – Forfeiture – Effect of defendant's arraignment – Whether surety's liability continuing after defendant arraigned – Whether surety discharged on arraignment

    R v Central Criminal Court, ex p Guney .. .. QBD DC 423

– –Conspiracy – Mens rea – Mens rea of co-conspirator – Co-conspirator an undercover drug enforcement agent acting to break up drug ring

    Yip Chiu-cheung v R .. .. PC 924

– –Damage to property – Attempted aggravated arson – Intent

    A-G's Reference (No 3 of 1992) .. .. CA 121

– –Defence – Defence of superior orders or Crown or Executive fiat – Defence not available in English or Hong Kong criminal law – Executive having no power to authorise breach of law

    Yip Chiu-cheung v R .. .. PC 924

– –Grievous bodily harm – Causing and inflicting – Whether causing grievous bodily harm wide enough to include inflicting grievous bodily harm

    R v Mandair .. .. HL 715

– –Inducement to invest money – Scheme for investment of investors' funds in gilts – Manager of scheme having discretion to place uninvested funds elsewhere – Manager diverting funds for own use

    R v Clowes (No 2) .. .. CA 316

– –Living on earnings of prostitution – Woman offering sexual services and taking money from client without intending to provide services offered

    R v McFarlane .. .. CA 283

– –Making explosive substance for unlawful object – Mens rea – Necessary to prove mens rea of maker of explosive substance

    R v Berry (No 3) .. .. CA 913

– –Murder – Provocation – Direction to jury – Provocation not raised as defence at trial – Facts implying possible loss of self-control – Issue of provocation should be left to jury whenever there is material, however tenuous, capable of amounting to defence of provocation

    R v Rossiter .. .. CA 752

– –Murder – Provocation – Direction to jury – Provocation not raised by defence – Circumstances in which provocation must be left to jury – Evidence required before provocation can be left to jury

    R v Cambridge .. .. CA 760

CRIMINAL LAW – Prostitution – Whether a 'clipper' a prostitute
    R v McFarlane .. .. CA   283

– –Theft – Dishonesty – Judge directing as matter of law that defendant's conduct amounted to appropriation of property and leaving issue of dishonesty to jury
    R v Clowes (No 2) .. .. CA   316

– –Trial – Defendant's right to silence – Direction to jury – Guidelines
    R v Martinez-Tobon .. .. CA   90

DAMAGES – Personal injury – Cost of future care – Multiplier – Basis for choosing multiplier when amount and timing of future payments is known or assumed to be known
    Hunt v Severs .. .. HL   385

– –Personal injury – Nervous shock – Off-duty employee witnessing explosion and destruction of oil rig – Liability of oil rig owner
    McFarlane v EE Caledonia Ltd .. .. CA   1

– –Personal injury – Services rendered and to be rendered by defendant tortfeasor in caring for plaintiff – Whether plaintiff entitled to recover cost of services voluntarily rendered by defendant
    Hunt v Severs .. .. HL   385

DISCOVERY – Legal professional privilege – Family proceedings – Reports relating to children in care proceedings – Court's power to order disclosure
    Oxfordshire CC v M .. .. CA   269

– –Production of documents – Privilege – Disclosure alleged to be injurious to public interest – Certificate signed by Secretary of State claiming immunity from disclosure on ground of national security
    Balfour v Foreign and Commonwealth Office .. .. CA   589

DISQUALIFICATION OF DIRECTOR – Unfit conduct – Jurisdiction – Territorial limitation on jurisdiction – Jurisdiction extending to activities by director conducted overseas
    Re Seagull Manufacturing Co Ltd (in liq) (No 2) .. .. Mary Arden QC   767

DIVORCE – Financial provision – Variation of order – Appeal from consent order – Leave to appeal
    Crozier v Crozier .. .. Booth J   362

EDUCATION – School – Conveyance under School Sites Act – Reverter – Cesser of use for purposes of Act – Whether reverting to original grantor and successors
    Marchant v Onslow .. .. David Neuberger QC   707

ESTOPPEL – Res judicata – Foreign judgment – Precedence of competing foreign judgments each pronounced by court of competent jurisdiction
    Showlag v Mansour .. .. PC   129

EUROPEAN ECONOMIC COMMUNITY – Freedom of movement – Services – National legislation prohibiting holding of lotteries – Whether obstacle to freedom to provide services
    Customs and Excise Comrs v Schindler (Case C-275/92) .. .. CJEC   193

EXTRADITION – Judicial review – Authority to proceed – Applicant tricked by police into returning to jurisdiction – Whether Secretary of State's decision to issue authority to proceed subject to judicial review
    R v Secretary of State for the Home Dept, ex p Schmidt .. .. QBD DC   784

FALSE IMPRISONMENT – Elements of tort – Cause of false imprisonment – Information leading to wrongful arrest – Informant not liable for false imprisonment
    Davidson v Chief Constable of North Wales .. .. CA   597

FAMILY PROCEEDINGS – Care order – Guardian ad litem – Disclosure of information to guardian ad litem – Guardian ad litem entitled to see case record prepared by local authority in respect of proposed adoption
    Manchester City Council v T .. .. CA 526

– –Orders in family proceedings – Application for transfer of private law proceedings from magistrates' court to county court – Criteria for transfer of proceedings from magistrates' court to county court
    R v South East Hampshire Family Proceedings Court, ex p D .. .. .. Ewbank J 445

– –Specific issue order – Jurisdiction to make specific issue order excluding father from matrimonial home in interests of children
    Pearson v Franklin .. .. CA 137

HOUSE OF LORDS – Judicial fees – Security money – Increase
    Practice Direction .. .. HL 176

IMMIGRATION – British citizen – Citizenship obtained by naturalisation – Naturalisation based on husband's passport – Husband obtaining British passport fraudulently – Whether naturalisation as British citizen a nullity
    R v Secretary of State for the Home Dept, ex p Ejaz .. .. CA 436

– –Refugee – Refusal of asylum – Deportation back to third country in which no fear of persecution – Claim for asylum without foundation if safe removal to third country possible
    R v Secretary of State for the Home Dept, ex p Mehari .. .. Laws J 494

INSOLVENCY – Statutory demand – Grounds on which demand may be set aside – Debtor contending creditor's refusal of offer to secure or compound for debt unreasonable – Whether debtor entitled to have demand set aside
    Re a debtor (No 415/SD/93), ex p the debtor v IRC .. .. Jacob J 168

– –Statutory demand – Grounds on which demand may be set aside – Demand not specifying figures used to calculate liquidated sum – Validity
    Re a debtor (No 64 of 1992) .. .. Colin Rimer QC 177

– –Statutory demand – Grounds on which demand may be set aside – Unsatisfied default judgment – Application for stay of execution of judgment – Whether creditors entitled to present petition
    Re a debtor (No 22 of 1993) .. .. Mummery J 105

– –Voluntary arrangement – Creditor not receiving notice of creditors' meeting – Whether creditor bound by voluntary arrangement
    Re a debtor (No 64 of 1992) .. .. Colin Rimer QC 177

INSURANCE – Protection of policyholders – United Kingdom policy – Liquidation of insurer – Policyholder – Indemnity from Policyholders Protection Board
    Scher v Policyholders Protection Board (Nos 1 and 2), Ackman v Policyholders Protection Board (Nos 1 and 2) (note) .. .. HL 37

JAMAICA – Criminal law – Magistrate dismissing information – Director of Public Prosecutions applying for voluntary bill of indictment
    Brooks v DPP of Jamaica .. .. PC 231

JUDICIAL REVIEW – Delay – Refusal of relief – Grant of relief likely substantially to prejudice rights of another person
    R v Secretary of State for Health, ex p Furneaux .. .. CA 652

LEGAL AID – Criminal cases – Revocation of legal aid for non-payment of contributions – Fresh application for legal aid to trial court after revocation of legal aid order – Pre-trial proceedings
    R v Liverpool City Magistates' Court, ex p Pender (No 2) .. .. QBD DC 897

MALICIOUS PROSECUTION – Essentials to action for malicious prosecution – Setting law in motion – Defendant providing false information to police – Defendant not liable for malicious prosecution of plaintiff

    Martin v Watson .. .. CA   606

MEDICAL TREATMENT – Withdrawal of treatment – Insensate patient – Patient in persistent vegetative state – Practice – Sanction of High Court judge required – Consultation with Official Solicitor

    Practice Note   413

– –Withdrawal of treatment – Insensate patient – Patient in persistent vegetative state with no hope of recovery – Whether in patient's best interests to allow patient to die

    Frenchay Healthcare NHS Trust v S .. .. CA   403

MENTAL HEALTH – Discharge of patient from hospital – Whether patient suffering from psychopathic disorder entitled to be discharged if condition not able to be alleviated by treatment

    R v Canons Park Mental Health Review Tribunal, ex p A .. .. CA   659

MORTGAGE – Sale – Power to authorise sale – Court's discretion to sanction sale where mortgagee having full power to affect sale without order

    Arab Bank plc v Merchantile Holdings Ltd .. .. Millett J   74

NEGLIGENCE – Contributory negligence – Employee acting outside scope of employment – Deceit

    Alliance and Leicester Building Society v Edgestop Ltd .. .. Mummery J   38

PRACTICE – Chancery Division – Hearing dates – Target dates

    Practice Direction .. .. Ch D   384

– –Striking out – Action wrongly brought in High Court – Discretion to transfer action to county court

    Restick v Crickmore .. .. CA   112

RESTRICTIVE COVENANT AFFECTING LAND – Enforceability against vendor's successors in title – Positive covenant to repair demised property – Covenant to maintain common roof in good repair

    Rhone v Stephens .. .. HL   65

ROAD TRAFFIC – Causing death by careless or dangerous driving – Sentence – Guidelines – Aggravating features

    R v Shepherd, R v Wernet .. .. CA   242

SALE OF GOODS – Title – Unascertained goods – Generic goods – Whether contract for sale of unascertained goods conferring equitable title to goods

    Re Goldcorp Exchange Ltd (in receivership) .. .. PC   806

SHIPPING – General average – Vessel damaged shortly after commencing voyage – Whether shipowner entitled to claim general average contribution in respect of temporary repairs

    Marida Ltd v Oswal Steel, The Bijela .. .. HL   289

– –Offence – Failing to operate ship in safe manner – Whether offence of strict liability – Whether company vicariously liable for all acts of its employees

    Seaboard Offshore Ltd v Secretary of State for Transport, The Safe Carrier .. .. HL   99

SOCIAL SECURITY – Attendance allowance – Frequent 'attention' throughout day in connection with bodily functions – Blind man – Assistance in walking in unfamiliar surroundings

    Mallinson v Secretary of State for Social Security .. .. HL   295

SOLICITOR – Authority – Action begun without authority – Ratification by or on behalf of plaintiff – Plaintiff entitled to adopt action after expiry of limitation period
    Presentaciones Musicales S/A v Secunda .. CA 737

——Disciplinary proceedings – Solicitor misusing funds but subsequently making good shortage in client account – Appropriate penalty
    Bolton v Law Society .. CA 486

——Right of person in custody to have access to solicitor – Validity of police policy to regulate access by solicitors to remand cells – Police imposing visiting hours for solicitors
    R v Chief Constable of South Wales, ex p Merrick .. QBD DC 560

TOWN AND COUNTRY PLANNING – Agreement regulating development or use of land – Agreement containing covenants which could not have been imposed as conditions on grant of planning permission – Validity
    Good v Epping Forest DC .. CA 156

——Enforcement notice – Use of land in contravention of enforcement notice – Whether absolute offence
    R v Collett .. CA 372

TRUST AND TRUSTEE – Breach – Payment of trust moneys to stranger – Mortgage security released without authority before execution
    Target Holdings Ltd v Redferns (a firm) .. CA 337

WRIT – Extension of validity – Discretion – Failure to serve writ – Exercise of discretion to extend validity of writ – Principles on which discretion to be exercised
    Singh v Duport Harper Foundries Ltd .. CA 889

House of Lords petitions

This list, which covers the period 21 March to 23 June 1994, sets out all cases which have formed the subject of a report in the All England Law Reports in which an Appeal Committee of the House of Lords has, subsequent to the publication of that report, refused leave to appeal. Where the result of a petition for leave to appeal was known prior to the publication of the relevant report a note of that result appears at the end of the report.

Presentaciones Musicales SA v Secunda [1994] 2 All ER 737, CA. Leave to appeal refused 20 June 1994 (Lord Keith of Kinkel, Lord Mustill and Lord Woolf)

R v Martinez-Tobon [1994] 2 All ER 90, CA. Leave to appeal refused 4 May 1994 (Lord Goff of Chieveley, Lord Mustill and Lord Nolan)

Seagull Manufacturing Co Ltd (in liq), Re [1993] 2 All ER 980, CA. Leave to appeal refused 23 May 1994 (Lord Goff of Chieveley, Lord Slynn of Hadley and Lord Nolan)

CORRIGENDA

[1994] 2 All ER

p 130. **Showlag v Mansour.** Line *j* 3: for 'Adrian Hamilton QC' read 'Arthur Hamilton QC'. Page 133, line *a* 4: for 'Adrian Hamilton QC' read 'Arthur Hamilton QC'

p 156. **Good v Epping Forest DC.** Line *h* 1: for 'allowed' read 'dismissed'

p 540. **Continental Bank NA v Aeokos Cia Naviera SA.** The appellants were 'Aeakos Cia Naviera SA' not 'Aeokos Cia Naviera SA'

McFarlane v EE Caledonia Ltd

COURT OF APPEAL, CIVIL DIVISION
RALPH GIBSON, STUART-SMITH AND McCOWAN LJJ
9, 29 JULY 1993

Damages – Personal injury – Nervous shock – Bystander or witness – Massive explosion on oil rig – Plaintiff off duty on support vessel witnessing explosion and destruction of rig – Support vessel attempting to assist burning oil rig – Plaintiff suffering nervous shock – Whether owners of oil rig owing duty of care to plaintiff – Whether plaintiff a rescuer – Whether duty of care owed to mere bystander or witness of horrific event.

The plaintiff was employed as a painter on an oil rig in the North Sea owned and operated by the defendants. On the night of 6 July 1988, while the plaintiff was off duty and lying on his bunk on a support vessel some 550 metres away from the oil rig, a series of massive explosions occurred on the rig. Over the next hour and three-quarters the plaintiff witnessed the explosions and consequent destruction of the rig before he was evacuated by helicopter. The explosions and fire on the rig caused the death of 164 men. The closest the plaintiff came to the fire was 100 metres when the support vessel moved in towards the rig in an attempt to fight the fire and render assistance. The plaintiff brought an action against the defendants claiming damages for psychiatric illness suffered as the result of the events he had witnessed. On the trial of a preliminary issue whether the defendants owed the plaintiff a duty to exercise reasonable care to avoid causing him psychiatric injury, the judge held that the plaintiff was owed such a duty, on the ground that he was a participant in the event who had been reasonably in fear for his life and safety and that his injury had resulted from the shock caused by his fear. The judge rejected an alternative submission that he was a rescuer and consequently even if he had not been reasonably in fear for his safety he was entitled to recover because the impact of the horrifying events had caused his shock. The judge expressed no opinion on a further alternative submission that even if he was only a bystander or witness to the events, they were so horrific that it was reasonably foreseeable that they would cause psychiatric injury in such a person. The defendants appealed.

Held – For the purpose of recovering damages for nervous shock caused by fear of physical injury to himself in a horrific event, a person was a participant in the event if (i) he was in the actual area of danger created by the event, even though he escaped physical injury by chance or good fortune, or (ii) although not actually in danger he reasonably thought he was because of the sudden and unexpected nature of the event, or (iii) although not originally within the area of danger he came into it later as a rescuer. However, a person who was a mere bystander or witness of horrific events could not recover damages for psychiatric illness resulting from the experience unless there was a sufficient degree of proximity, which required both nearness in time and place and a close relationship of love and affection between plaintiff and victim. On the facts, the plaintiff was not a rescuer and it could not be said that the defendants ought reasonably to have foreseen that the plaintiff and other non-essential personnel on board the rescue vessel would suffer psychiatric injury, since the plaintiff could have taken shelter if he felt himself to be in any danger. Furthermore, it had not been shown that it was reasonably foreseeable that a man of ordinary fortitude and phlegm in the plaintiff's position would be so affected by what he saw that he would suffer psychiatric injury. It followed that the plaintiff was not entitled to succeed. The appeal would therefore be allowed (see p 9 *b* to *d*, p 10 *a b e f*, p 11 *a* to *f*, p 12 *h j*, p 13 *b c* and p 14 *c f* to *j*, post).

Alcock v Chief Constable of the South Yorkshire Police [1991] 4 All ER 907 applied.

Notes
For liability for nervous shock, see 34 *Halsbury's Laws* (4th edn) para 8, and for cases on the subject, see 17 *Digest* (Reissue) 145–147, 377–391.

Cases referred to in judgments
Alcock v Chief Constable of the South Yorkshire Police [1991] 4 All ER 907, [1992] 1 AC 310, [1991] 3 WLR 1057, HL; *affg* sub nom *Jones v Wright* [1991] 3 All ER 88, [1992] 1 AC 310, [1991] 2 WLR 814, CA.
Bourhill v Young [1942] 2 All ER 396, [1943] AC 92, HL; *affg* 1941 SC 395, Ct of Sess.
Chadwick v British Transport Commission [1967] 2 All ER 945, [1967] 1 WLR 912.
Dulieu v White & Sons [1901] 2 KB 669, [1900-3] All ER Rep 353, DC.
Hambrook v Stokes Bros [1925] 1 KB 141, [1924] All ER Rep 110, CA.
Powell v Streatham Manor Nursing Home [1935] AC 243, [1935] All ER Rep 58, HL.
Watt (or Thomas) v Thomas [1947] 1 All ER 582, [1947] AC 484, HL.
Yuill v Yuill [1945] 1 All ER 183, [1945] P 15, CA.

Cases also cited or referred to in skeleton arguments
Bell v Great Northern Rly Co of Ireland (1890) 26 LR Ir 428, Ir Ex D.
Donoghue v Stevenson [1932] AC 562, [1932] All ER Rep 1, HL.
Galt v British Railways Board (1983) 133 NLJ 870.
Hughes v Lord Advocate [1963] 1 All ER 705, [1963] AC 837, HL.
Galt v British Railways Board (1983) 133 NLJ 870.
Jaensch v Coffey (1984) 15 CLR 549, Aust HC.
McLoughlin v O'Brian [1982] 2 All ER 298, [1983] 1 AC 410, HL; *rvsg* [1981] 1 All ER 809, [1981] QB 599, CA.
Schneider v Eisovitch [1960] 1 All ER 169, [1960] 1 QB 430.
Wigg v British Railways Board (1986) Times, 4 February.

Appeal
The defendant, EE Caledonia Ltd, formerly Occidental Petroleum (Caledonia) Ltd, appealed from the judgment of Smith J dated 22 December 1992 whereby, on the trial of a preliminary issue in an action brought by the plaintiff, Francis Mcfarlane, against the defendant by writ dated 5 December 1989 claiming damages for psychiatric injury suffered as the result of the defendant's negligence in connection with an explosion and fire on the Piper Alpha oil rig on 6 July 1988, the judge held that the defendant owed the plaintiff a duty to

exercise reasonable care to avoid causing the plaintiff's psychiatric illness. The facts are set out in the judgment of Stuart-Smith LJ.

Adrian Hamilton QC and *Alistair Schaff* (instructed by *Ince & Co*) for the defendant.
Nigel Wilkinson QC and *Anna Guggenheim* (instructed by *Levinson Gray*) for the plaintiff.

Cur adv vult

29 July 1993. The following judgments were delivered.

STUART-SMITH LJ (giving the first judgment at the invitation of Ralph Gibson LJ). On the night of 6 July 1988 a disastrous fire broke out on the oil rig Piper Alpha in the North Sea. The fire spread and over the next hour or so totally engulfed the rig. One hundred and sixty four men lost their lives and many more were seriously injured. Vessels in the area went to assist in the fire fighting and rescue operations. One of these was the Tharos; the plaintiff was on board the Tharos. He sustained no physical injury; but as a result of his experiences that night he suffered psychiatric injury for which he claims damages.

The matter came before Smith J on a preliminary issue as to whether the defendants, who were the owners and operators of the Piper Alpha, owed the plaintiff a duty to exercise reasonable care to avoid causing him psychiatric injury. For the purpose of the trial of that issue, two assumptions were to be made:

'(a) That the defendant was in breach of a duty owed to those persons on board the Piper Alpha at the time of the explosion to exercise reasonable care to avoid causing physical injury or death to such persons and were thereby liable for damages in negligence to those persons on the Piper Alpha at the time of the explosion who were killed or injured as a result of the explosion; and (b) That the plaintiff has suffered psychiatric injuries which were caused as a result of the explosion of the Piper Alpha and the breach by the defendant of its duty of care owed to those persons on board the Piper Alpha at the time of the explosion.'

The judge answered the question in favour of the plaintiff. Although the preliminary issue does not extend to the question of breach of the duty of care to the plaintiff, I think it must follow or have been assumed that if the duty was owed to the plaintiff, the defendants were in breach of it. The defendants now appeal the judge's decision.

At the trial counsel for the plaintiffs advanced three bases on which it was submitted that the plaintiff was entitled to succeed. First on the ground that he was reasonably in fear for his life and safety and the fear had caused the shock which led to his injury. He was therefore a participant in the event. The judge accepted the submission. Secondly that he was a rescuer and consequently even if he was not reasonably in fear for his safety, he could recover because the impact of the horrifying events had caused his shock. The judge rejected this submission. Thirdly, it was submitted that even if he was only a bystander or witness to the events, they were so horrendous that it was reasonably to be foreseen that they would cause psychiatric injury in such a person. The judge expressed no opinion on this. By his respondent's notice the plaintiff submits that the judge's decision should, in the event that the appeal is allowed, be upheld on one of these grounds.

The defendants were the owners and operators of the Piper Alpha, an off-shore oil and gas platform situated about 120 miles north-east of Aberdeen. The platform was a huge structure whose main function was to pump ashore oil and gas brought in by pipelines from adjacent fields. There were four pipelines leading into the platform; these were from the Tartan, Claymore, MCP-01 and Chanter fields, although this last was not operative at the date of the disaster.

At the end of the horizontal section of each incoming pipeline, close to the platform there was a vertical section of piping known as a riser, which carried the oil or gas up into the pumping equipment. The platform also had a drilling rig, an accommodation section, a helideck and other ancillary facilities. At any one time, between two and three hundred men would work on the platform. Not all had living accommodation on the platform itself; some lived in quarters on board the Tharos.

The Tharos is a semi-submersible multi-function vessel designed to provide support for off-shore installations. It provides living accommodation, well-killing equipment and construction support, machine shop, fabrication shop and diving facilities. The equipment on board includes fire monitors, an hydraulically operated gangway for platform access, a heavy-duty crane, a helicopter and helideck. The vessel is also equipped to shield itself from fire or heat hazard by means of a water spray which is thrown up close to the vessel itself.

In the summer of 1988 the Tharos was stationed in the vicinity of Piper Alpha for the purpose of fitting a riser to the Chanter pipeline. However, at all times the vessel had a secondary function, which was to offer assistance in emergencies. In such emergencies the extendable gangway could be used for the evacuation of personnel. The helicopter could be used for rescue purposes. There were medical and hospital facilities on board. The vessel was not designed to respond rapidly in emergencies as when ballasted she could travel at only 2·5 knots. She was intended to provide assistance in the later stage of an emergency when her fire-fighting capabilities could be used to kill a burning well.

The vessel's standing procedures provided that all non-essential personnel should be evacuated before any fire-fighting or rescue operation began. Non-essential personnel included men like the plaintiff who were not members of the Tharos crew.

On the evening of 6 July 1988 the Tharos was lying partially anchored about 550 metres south-west of the Piper Alpha platform.

In July 1988 the plaintiff was nearly 40 years old, a married man with five children. He had been employed as a painter almost all his working life. He had worked for various off-shore employers for about seven years and had undergone regular medical examinations as required. He did a strenuous job and was in good physical condition.

He had in the past suffered from two episodes of depressive illness. The first had occurred in 1978 following the death of his father, to whom he had been very close. His medical records indicate that this episode had lasted for about six weeks. The second episode, which occurred in 1980 and 1981, had lasted about five months and had had no obvious cause. It seems there had been matrimonial problems and the plaintiff had been drinking to excess. However, the plaintiff had suffered no recurrence of psychiatric illness since 1981.

The judge found that the plaintiff was probably not a person of average fortitude or customary phlegm and that he was probably more susceptible to psychiatric injury than the average man.

The plaintiff first began work on the Piper Alpha platform in June 1988. He was employed by the Wood Group Engineering (Off-Shore) Ltd. On 6 July he was on his second tour of duty on the Piper Alpha. He completed his shift at about 1830 hrs and was transferred to his living accommodation on board the Tharos soon afterwards. By 2200 hrs he was lying on his bunk, reading.

The first explosion and fire on Piper Alpha occurred at 2200 hrs. It was readily visible on the Tharos. Within a few minutes the Tharos began to move towards Piper Alpha to give assistance. Being ballasted and partially anchored, she was only able to move slowly. As she went, preparations were made to operate the hydraulic gangway and fire-fighting equipment. The helicopter took off and the rescue boat was launched. The obvious urgency was such that the Tharos did not wait to evacuate her non-essential personnel before going to the rescue.

At 2220 hrs a huge explosion occurred on the platform. This is now known to have been caused by the rupture of the Tartan gas riser. A massive high pressure gas fire ensued. The Tharos was about 250 metres away but was still approaching the platform.

The plaintiff had gone onto the walkway of the accommodation block soon after the alarm was sounded. The Tharos was proceeding stern first. The accommodation walkway, which was the nearest point that the plaintiff got to the fire is about 50 metres from the stern of the Tharos. He said that this explosion caused him to be very afraid, he was shaking and retched.

At about 2231 hrs the fire monitors on the Tharos began to deliver water, although they were still out of range of the platform. Ten minutes later the heat shield was operating. By 2245 the Tharos was about 60 to 70 metres west of the platform and still moving closer. By 2250 hrs she was about 50 metres from the platform; this was the closest she came.

At 2252 a second major explosion occurred caused by the rupture of the MCP-01 riser. Flames shot high into the air. A fast rescue vessel from the Sandhaven, which had moved in close to one of the legs of the platform was engulfed in a fireball, causing the death of most of the occupants.

This explosion caused men to attempt to escape from the platform by jumping from the helideck and other parts of the structure. This must have entailed, in some cases, the jumping of a distance in excess of 100 feet. The structure of the platform began to collapse in the heat.

Soon after this explosion, the Tharos withdrew to a position about 100 metres from the platform, still operating her fire monitors, but by now spraying water onto the sea in front of the platform.

At about 2305 hrs the Tharos began to move back towards the Piper Alpha until she again reached a distance of about 70 metres from it. She remained in that position until about 2319 hrs. At 2314 the Piper Alpha drilling derrick collapsed inwards onto the platform. At about 2318, having been advised of danger from the escape of hydrogen sulphide gas, the master of the Tharos decided to withdraw his vessel. Within a minute or two and before that withdrawal had been effected, a third major explosion occurred. This is now known to have been due to the rupture of the Claymore gas riser and was the

largest of all the explosions. It caused further structural collapse of the
platform, which tilted towards the east. The withdrawal of the Tharos then
continued and the vessel thereafter operated at a distance of about 200 metres
from the platform.

At about 2338 hrs the evacuation by helicopter of non-essential personnel
from the Tharos was commenced. It is likely that the plaintiff was taken off at
about 2345.

The plaintiff was therefore on board the Tharos for about one and
three-quarter hours during the fire. For about half that time the vessel was
within 100 metres of the platform; of which 40 minutes were within 70 metres
and a few minutes as close as 50 metres. At no time was the plaintiff closer than
100 metres from the platform.

The judge summarised the plaintiff's evidence of what he did and how he
felt after the initial major explosion as follows:

> 'Soon afterwards he returned to his earlier position and asked members
> of the crew if there was anything he could do to help. He was told to
> collect blankets from a store and to help prepare the helihangar for the
> reception of the casualties which were expected. He says that he did this
> for some time and when that was finished the Tharos had moved in close
> to the fire. He said he was very afraid at this time as there were things
> exploding on the platform and debris was being thrown off. He was
> fearful that there could be further explosions coming perhaps from under
> the sea, where he knew there were pipelines. He said he was praying and
> thinking of his family. He could see men on the platform trying to escape,
> some climbing the derrick, some trying to climb down the platform
> supports, some on the decks waving for help, some were on fire, some
> were jumping into the sea. He could not identify these men but the sight
> caused him distress. He saw a lifeboat suspended before it fell into the sea,
> throwing the occupants out. He spoke of the temperature and the
> deafening noise, which he said was terrifying. He recalled at one stage
> meeting two survivors who had just come aboard the Tharos. They were
> able to walk but were confused and their faces were blackened. He helped
> them to the hospital area, where they were taken in. Soon after that he
> saw another explosion. He saw a fireball come towards the Tharos and
> said that he ducked in fear. He claimed to have seen the destruction of the
> Sandhaven rescue boat engulfed in a fire. He said that a while later he saw
> the sea on fire. He went to a radio room as he wanted to suggest that the
> Tharos's Clyde crane should be used to pick up survivors rather than
> trying to fight the fire, which he thought was hopeless. Then, he said,
> there was another massive explosion. That must have been the rupture of
> the Claymore riser. He thought that was not long before he was lifted off
> by helicopter. He recalled that by that time the Tharos had pulled back
> from the fire. He claimed that he knew that this was because of the danger
> from gas. He spoke of his friends and colleagues on the platform and of
> the distress, anger and grief that he had felt at what had happened.'

The defendants made a strong attack on the plaintiff's credibility, not so
much that he had deliberately said things he knew to be untrue, but rather that
because of his illness and the fact that he had read and discussed the events of
the night at great length he was confused and was unable to distinguish
between what he had experienced and what he had subsequently learnt. The

judge accepted this criticism. In particular she did not believe that the plaintiff had seen combustible materials being transferred by the overhead crane on the Tharos to a place of safety as she approached the fire; she did not accept that the plaintiff appreciated that the reason why the Tharos withdrew at 2318 was because of the danger of hydrogen sulphide gas or that he had seen the rescue boat from the Sandhaven consumed by a fireball. She said that she approached his evidence with extreme caution and was prepared to accept it only where it was supported by evidence from other sources or was inherently likely to be true.

The plaintiff called no other evidence. The defendants called two witnesses, Captain Letty, the master of the Tharos whose evidence the judge accepted, and Mr Robinson, the barge clerk and helicopter landing officer on the Tharos whose duties included mustering and evacuating the non-essential personnel. The judge was not impressed by his evidence. In addition there were photographs taken from the Tharos which do not really assist in conveying a picture of conditions as seen from that vessel, and two video films. The longer of the two was taken from the vessel Maersk Leader. This was taken throughout the fire, though not continuously, from various positions as the vessel moved about. The judge was obviously much impressed by the film. I think she plainly must have relied upon it to reach the conclusion which she did that many, probably most of the men on board the Tharos must have been afraid for their own safety, at least while the vessel was close to the platform. The judge summarised her impression thus:

'The evidential value of this film is that it conveys vividly the colossal size and the awesome power and intensity of the conflagration. It gives some impression of the noise, which although by no means deafening on the soundtrack is reminiscent of the sound of a Bunsen burner magnified many times. The film also shows the billowing smoke, mercifully being blown away from the Tharos. Had there been a sudden change in the direction of the wind, it is easy to see how the Tharos could have been enveloped in smoke and flame. Even on film, even four years after the event this is a profoundly disturbing spectacle.'

The defendants criticise the judge's speculation about the change in wind direction. I think there is force in the criticism. There was no evidence that anyone thought a change of wind direction likely. The wind was blowing from south to north, the Tharos was opposite the side of the platform which faced south-west. The shifting of the wind by a few points would have been quite immaterial; it would have had to change at least 90 degrees and probably more before it affected the Tharos. Not even the plaintiff said he feared this.

Each member of this court has seen the videos. Mr Wilkinson QC accepted that if our reaction was not the same as that of the judge, he might be in difficulty. I must therefore summarise what this video film shows. The sight of the fire on the platform is awesome and horrendous. The flames are obviously going a substantial distance into the sky. The size and intensity of the fire increases with the ruptures of the risers and at any rate after 2252 with the explosion of the MCP-01 riser the whole platform appears to be engulfed. On the other hand the smoke and flame is being blown away from the Tharos, the wind evidently being quite strong. There is no sign of a fireball approaching the Tharos, still less engulfing it. There is no evidence of flying debris, and certainly none coming near the Tharos. Other vessels are shown considerably nearer to the fire, even at times on the leewards side. When the Maersk Leader is on the far side of the platform to the Tharos, there is foreshortening and she appears closer to the platform than she is. The heat screen from the Tharos can clearly be seen, as can the high level jet or spray coming from the crane which is spraying water towards the platform and the sea between it and the Tharos.

The second video film was taken by an ITN news team who were on an RAF rescue helicopter. It is of little assistance. The helicopter lands on the helideck of the Tharos at about 2345, near the time when the plaintiff was evacuated. Operations appear to be being conducted in an orderly and controlled manner. For my part I do not think that these films provide any evidence that a man of reasonable fortitude would be in reasonable fear of his life and safety in the position in which the plaintiff was.

The judge summarised Captain Letty's evidence as follows:

'He said that no one on board the Tharos suffered any physical injury that night and that the vessel itself was undamaged save for some blistering of paint on the end of the Clyde crane, which had projected further towards the fire than any other part of the vessel. Nor, he said, had any debris from the fire been found on board. He himself was in the aft control room for virtually the whole period in question. That control room was the part of the vessel closest to the burning platform. He did not consider that his vessel was in danger. It was his duty to do what he could for Piper Alpha without endangering his vessel. He said: "We came very close to being in danger, but we did not cross the line." That was his professional judgment based upon a high degree of skill and many years of experience. He was not worried that there might be a major explosion from under the sea. He knew where the pipelines were and knew that they were not directly under the Tharos. However, he did accept that this had been the most horrifying spectacle that he had ever seen. He did not rule out the possibility of further unforeseen explosions occurring during the course of the night. Indeed, he accepted that after the Tartan riser had exploded he continued his advance in Tharos, not realising that another riser might rupture. When it did, it took him by surprise. He agreed that the heat, glare and noise from the fire might be frightening to some. He acknowledged that after one of the explosions a fireball had come towards the Tharos. He said that his entire field of vision became orange and that other officers in the control room had fallen to the floor at that moment. Even the helmsman had dropped to his knees. He had seen the sea on fire, although not immediately adjacent to the Tharos. He said that he himself had not been affected by fear during the emergency, but he had been affected afterwards by a sense of great relief that the Tharos had escaped unscathed. He agreed that he had probably been less fearful than others because of his experience and knowledge and also because he was so busy during the emergency. When giving evidence to the Cullen inquiry, he had said: "It must be remembered that on the night of the disaster all those who witnessed it experienced the disaster first-hand as it was unfolding, without knowledge of what was to happen next." He continued: "I personally do not believe that anybody who was not there on that night can imagine the magnitude and speed at which events took place".'

The judge posed the question of law that she had to answer in these terms:

'The question to be determined is whether the defendant owed the plaintiff a duty to exercise reasonable care to avoid causing the plaintiff psychiatric injury. The existence of a duty of care depends upon the tests of foreseeability of harm and a proximity of relationship between the plaintiff and the defendant.'

Although this formulation is correct so far as it goes, the judge does not specifically remind herself that it is the foreseeability of the reasonable man in the position of the defendant that is material. The question is an objective one. What ought the reasonable owner and operator of a drilling rig and platform in the position of the defendants to have foreseen in the light of the facts which were known or ought to have been known to the defendants? Specifically should he have foreseen that a person of ordinary fortitude in the position of the plaintiff would reasonably be in such fear of his life and safety as to suffer psychiatric shock? The way in which the judge answered the question she had posed, leads me to the conclusion that she did not correctly apply the test. She reached her conclusion by a three-stage process. First, she held that the plaintiff had a fear for his own safety. This was a subjective fear. She said:

'In my judgment, given the plaintiff's limited understanding of the circumstances, the heat, the noise and his proximity to an apparently uncontrollable fire, his fear for his life was entirely understandable and therefore reasonable. In my view, the test of whether the plaintiff's fear was reasonable must be a subjective one, based on what he knew and believed at the time. It cannot be based on a rational and objective appraisal made with the benefit of hindsight.'

Although the plaintiff, in order to succeed, had to establish that he in fact had such a fear, something which the defendants challenge in this appeal, it was irrelevant to the foresight of the reasonable man in the defendant's position. Secondly, that because of his limited knowledge and understanding his fear was understandable and therefore reasonable and that the presence of such a person was foreseeable; accordingly his subjective fear resulting from those circumstances was also foreseeable. But this does not answer the question which I have set out in the previous paragraph.

The final stage of the judge's reasoning was to hold that it was plainly foreseeable that a man of reasonable fortitude may suffer psychiatric injury if exposed to the shock of being put in fear of his life. But this takes the matter no further. It is true that the judge had earlier held that most men on the Tharos must have been afraid for their own safety, at least when the vessel was close to the platform and that for non-essential personnel who had no specific tasks to perform and a lesser understanding of what was involved, it must have been a very frightening experience. This is a finding that Mr Hamilton QC criticises, but even if correct, it still does not answer the question of what the defendants ought reasonably to have foreseen.

In *Alcock v Chief Constable of South Yorkshire Police* [1991] 4 All ER 907 at 923, [1992] 1 AC 310 at 407 Lord Oliver of Aylmerton identified two categories of those who suffered nervous shock through fear of injury. First, those involved mediately or immediately as a participant in the event who feared injury to themselves and secondly, those who are no more than passive and unwilling witnesses of injury caused to others. In the present case the judge held that the plaintiff was a participant.

There are I think basically three situations in which a plaintiff may be a participant when he sustains psychiatric injury through fear of physical injury to himself. First, where he is in the actual area of danger created by the event, but escapes physical injury by chance or good fortune. Such a person would be one who while actually on the Piper Alpha rig at the time of the fire, escaped physical injury, but might well be in fear for his life or safety.

Secondly, where the plaintiff is not actually in danger, but because of the sudden and unexpected nature of the event he reasonably thinks that he is. An example of this is *Dulieu v White & Sons* [1901] 2 KB 669, [1900-3] All ER 353 where the plaintiff was put in fear for her safety when the defendants' runaway vehicle burst into the public house where she was serving behind the bar. She was not in fact at risk of physical injury; but she naturally was put in fear for her own safety. This was something that plainly ought to be in the contemplation of the defendant who negligently allows his vehicle to career out of control. It is not only those who may be able to fling themselves out of its path and so escape physical injury (who would fall into category 1), but those in the agony of the moment who reasonably believe they are in danger.

A case on the other side of the line is *Bourhill v Young* [1942] 2 All ER 396, [1943] AC 92. The plaintiff was too far from the scene of the crash and it was held that the defendant could not reasonably foresee that she might be injured by his failure to exercise care. She was not within the area of potential danger arising as a result of the motorcyclist's negligence.

Thirdly, the situation may arise where the plaintiff who is not originally within the area of danger comes into it later. In the ordinary way, such a person, who is a volunteer, cannot recover if he has freely and voluntarily entered the area of danger. This is not something that the tortfeasor can reasonably foresee, and the plaintiff may also be met with a defence of volenti non fit injuria. However, if he comes as a rescuer, he can recover. This is because a tortfeasor who has put A in peril by his negligence must reasonably foresee that B may come to rescue him, even if it involves risking his own safety.

A rescuer is entitled to put his own safety at risk, but not that of others, unless they too consent to be part of the rescue. I agree with Mr Hamilton that Captain Letty's duty was to ensure the safety of his vessel and those on it. If he acted negligently and in breach of this duty, he and the defendants who employed him would be liable. There is no suggestion of this in this case and no criticism has been made of the handling or operation of the Tharos. In my judgment this is an important consideration. The analysis can be tested by assuming that the Tharos had no connection with the defendants. If Captain Letty had negligently and in breach of his duty taken the vessel into a position of danger where those on board were injured or reasonably feared injury this would be a novus actus interveniens and not something for which the defendants would be liable.

But what is the position if the captain of a rescue vessel takes what seems to be a justified risk, and in doing so his vessel comes into actual danger with the result that it is damaged and personal injury sustained by those on board? In such circumstances the owners of the rig would be liable to an injured plaintiff on the rescue vessel in respect of both physical injury and psychiatric injury resulting from a reasonable fear of personal injury. But in these circumstances the captain, although with hindsight it will be seen that he committed an error of judgment, is not negligent. A reasonable man in the position of the defendant should foresee that if his negligence caused such a catastrophic emergency, those in charge of rescue vessels may not be able to judge to a nicety exactly how near it is safe to bring their vessels.

The plaintiff does not come into either of the first two categories, and Mr Hamilton submits that he does not come into the third. The Tharos never was in actual danger. This was Captain Letty's appreciation at the time and it is borne out by events. She sustained no damage, save minimal paint blistering on the crane which projected nearest the platform; no debris fell on her; although there was one incident when a fireball may have approached fairly near, her heat shield was never turned to steam. No one sustained any physical injury, and there is no evidence that anyone other than the plaintiff sustained psychiatric injury. In my judgment it cannot be said that the defendants ought reasonably to have foreseen that the plaintiff or other non-essential personnel on board her would suffer such injury. The Tharos was a well-found vessel, equipped with a heat shield, and under the control of an experienced and competent captain. If indeed the plaintiff had felt himself to be in any danger, he could have taken refuge in or behind the helicopter hangar, which was where non-essential personnel were required to muster. The judge thought it was entirely understandable that the plaintiff and other non-essential personnel should wish to see what was happening on the Piper Alpha. I agree with this. What I do not agree with, is that someone who was in truth in fear of his life from spread of the fire and falling debris should not take shelter. Only someone who is rooted to the spot through fear would be unable to do so. The plaintiff never suggested that; he accepted that he had moved about quite freely and could have taken shelter had he wished.

Mr Hamilton strongly criticised the judge's finding that the plaintiff was actually in fear for his safety or that such fear was reasonable, even on a subjective basis.

The plaintiff associated his fear with certain specific events. The first was the explosion of the Tartan riser. The Tharos was then 250 metres from the rig. No one has suggested that he reasonably thought he was in danger at that stage. Then he attributed his fear to the transportation of combustible materials overhead by the crane on the Tharos, and at a later stage when she drew back from the platform, he said he was afraid of the hydrogen sulphide gas. But the judge did not accept the factual basis of these fears. The plaintiff said he was frightened of debris from the platform falling on him. But he accepted that he never saw any falling on the Tharos; there is no evidence that any was falling near it and the absence of damage or debris afterwards confirms that there was no danger from this source. He said he was worried about subsea explosions. It is far from clear what he meant by this. There could not be explosions in the pipelines running under the sea. Mr Wilkinson submitted that what he was really afraid of was large explosions from the ruptured risers, which were not under the sea, and that this would give rise to an uncontrollable fire which might engulf the Tharos in what was described in argument as Armageddon. But the plaintiff never said this as appears from a comment of the judge in argument. She said:

> 'In a sense the most remarkable thing about his evidence was the fact that he never said, I think, that he was simply terrified at being so close to such a huge fire, which I think perhaps would have been my own reaction, but I have already said I do not think my own reaction is very germane.'

Her recollection was not dissented from by Mr Wilkinson and it is borne out by the evidence.

Mr Hamilton submits that the factual basis of his professed fears does not exist and his case is not based upon what he actually saw and felt but on ex post facto rationalisation. Much force is given to this submission by the complete absence of any allegation in the statement of claim of fear for his own safety. The whole case was pleaded on the basis of his witnessing the terrible events happening to others on the Piper Alpha. That pleading was served in December 1989; it was amended in June 1991, but no relevant amendment was made as to the cause of his injury. It is true that in further and better particulars, served in May 1991, there is a reference to the plaintiff feeling in danger at 22·20 when the Tartan riser ruptured and he saw combustible materials being transported overhead and there is later a brief reference to being exposed to danger himself. In cross-examination the plaintiff accepted that he had not told his lawyers about these fears for his own safety in 1989; he said this was due to confusion. I cannot therefore accept Mr Wilkinson's suggested explanation, namely that the plaintiff's lawyers chose to base the case initially on the ground of the plaintiff witnessing the suffering of others and inadvertently or wrongfully omitted to plead the case that the shock was due to fear for his own safety and that it was only after the decision of the Court of Appeal in *Alcock v Chief Constable of the South Yorkshire Police* (sub nom *Jones v Wright*) [1991] 3 All ER 88, [1992] 1 AC 310 that it was realised that the case as then pleaded was not so robust as it was at first thought and the scope should be widened. No attempt was made by production of a statement dated in 1989 to show that this had all the time been the plaintiff's case. A statement, undated, was exchanged shortly before trial, in which the plaintiff does speak of fears for his own safety, linked as I have said to specific factual matters.

The judge recognised the force of this criticism. But she negatived the effect of it because she said that it was inherently likely that the plaintiff would have been afraid. With all respect to the judge I cannot see how this probability can make good what is obviously an afterthought in the plaintiff's evidence derived from the very process of discussion and rationalisation which the judge herself recognised the plaintiff had indulged in.

Mr Hamilton also submitted that the plaintiff's failure to seek the protection available to him strongly suggests that he was not genuinely in fear of his safety. As I have already said, I agree with this submission.

This court is always slow to differ from the trial judge on findings of fact, especially where they are based on the judge's assessment of the credibility of the witness: see *Powell v Streatham Manor Nursing Home* [1935] AC 243, [1935] All ER Rep 58, *Yuill v Yuill* [1945] 1 All ER 183, [1945] P 15 and *Watt (or Thomas) v Thomas* [1947] 1 All ER 582, [1947] AC 484. But in this case the judge found the plaintiff's evidence was unreliable; she was only prepared to accept it in so far as it was supported by other evidence or was inherently likely to be true. For the reasons I have given I do not think it was supported by other evidence nor was it inherently likely to be true on this point. Accordingly, I do not think her judgment can be supported on these grounds.

I turn then to the matters raised in the respondent's notice.

It is submitted by Mr Wilkinson that the plaintiff was a rescuer and that even if his injury did not result from fear for his own safety he was entitled to recover because it was due to his experiences in rescuing the survivors. In *Chadwick v British Transport Commission* [1967] 2 All ER 945, [1967] 1 WLR 912 the plaintiff's deceased husband had gone to the assistance of those involved in the Lewisham train disaster. For 12 hours he gave valuable help at very close quarters to those injured in the carnage. He was entitled to recover damages in respect of the psychoneurotic condition that resulted from his experiences. But the judge held that the plaintiff was not a rescuer even though he was on board the Tharos which went to assist in rescue operations. I agree with the judge's conclusions. The plaintiff was never actively involved in the operation beyond helping to move blankets with a view to preparing the heli-hangar to receive casualties and encountering and perhaps assisting two walking injured as they arrived on the Tharos.

This is no criticism of him, he had no role to play, and there is no reason to doubt that he would have given more help if he could. But since the defendant's liability to a rescuer depends upon his reasonable foreseeability, I do not think that a defendant could reasonably foresee that this very limited degree of involvement could possibly give rise to psychiatric injury.

Secondly, it is submitted that the plaintiff was obliged to witness the catastrophe at close range and that it was of such a horrendous nature that even as a bystander the defendants owed him a duty of care. Mr Wilkinson relies on dicta of three of their Lordships in *Alcock v Chief Constable of the South Yorkshire Police*. Lord Ackner said ([1991] 4 All ER 907 at 919, [1992] 1 AC 310 at 403):

> 'I respectfully share the difficulty expressed by Atkin LJ in *Hambrook v Stokes Bros* [1925] 1 KB 141, 158-159, [1924] All ER Rep 110 at 117—how do you explain why the duty is confined to the case of parent or guardian and child and does not extend to other relations of life also involving intimate associations; and why does it not eventually extend to bystanders? As regards the latter category, while it may be very difficult to envisage a case of a stranger, who is not actively and foreseeably involved in a disaster or its aftermath, other than in the role of rescuer, suffering shock-induced psychiatric injury by the mere observation of apprehended or actual injury of a third person in circumstances that could be considered reasonably foreseeable, I see no reason in principle why he should not, if in the circumstances, a reasonably strong-nerved person would have been so shocked. In the course of argument your Lordships were given, by way of an example, that of a petrol tanker careering out of control into a school in session and bursting into flames. I would not be prepared to rule out a potential claim by a passer-by so shocked by the scene as to suffer psychiatric illness.'

Lord Oliver said ([1991] 4 All ER 907 at 930, [1992] 1 AC 310 at 416):

> 'Equally, I would not exclude the possibility envisaged by my noble and learned friend Lord Ackner, of a successful claim, given circumstances of such horror as would be likely to traumatise even the most phlegmatic spectator, by a mere bystander.'

Lord Keith said ([1991] 4 All ER 907 at 914, [1992] AC 310 at 397):

> 'The case of a bystander unconnected with the victims of an accident is difficult. Psychiatric injury to him would not ordinarily, in my view, be within the range of reasonable foreseeability, but could not perhaps be

entirely excluded from it if the circumstances of a catastrophe occurring very close to him were particularly horrific.'

Mr Wilkinson submits that it is hardly possible to imagine anything more horrific than the holocaust on the Piper Alpha, especially to the plaintiff who knew that some of his mates were on board.

I share Lord Keith's difficulty. The whole basis of the decision in *Alcock v Chief Constable of the South Yorkshire Police* is that where the shock is caused by fear of injury to others as opposed to fear of injury to the participant, the test of proximity is not simply reasonable foreseeability. There must be a sufficiently close tie of love and affection between the plaintiff and the victim. To extend the duty to those who have no such connection, is to base the test purely on foreseeability.

It seems to me that there are great practical problems as well. Reactions to horrific events are entirely subjective; who is to say that it is more horrific to see a petrol tanker advancing out of control on a school, when perhaps unknown to the plaintiff none of the children are in the building but are somewhere safe, than to see a child or group of children run over on a pedestrian crossing? There must be few scenes more harrowing than seeing women and children trapped at the window of a blazing building, yet many people gather to witness these calamities.

In my judgment both as a matter of principle and policy the court should not extend the duty to those who are mere bystanders or witnesses of horrific events unless there is a sufficient degree of proximity, which requires both nearness in time and place and a close relationship of love and affection between plaintiff and victim.

Even if I am wrong in this view, I think the plaintiff faces insuperable difficulty in this case. Not only is there no finding that it was reasonably foreseeable that a man of ordinary fortitude and phlegm would be so affected by what he saw, a finding which I would certainly decline to make on the evidence, but there is the finding that the plaintiff was probably not such a person. I think this is fatal to this submission.

I would therefore allow the appeal.

McCOWAN LJ. I agree.

RALPH GIBSON LJ. I also agree.

Appeal allowed. Leave to appeal to the House of Lords refused.

10 February 1994. The Appeal Committee of the House of Lords (Lord Templeman, Lord Woolf and Lord Nolan) refused leave to appeal.

Raina Levy   Barrister.

Peggs v Lamb

CHANCERY DIVISION

MORRITT J

23–26 FEBRUARY, 12 MARCH 1993

Charity – Charitable trust – Public benefit – Rights of common – Freemen of borough having rights of common since time immemorial – Income from commons increasing and class of freemen entitled to benefit decreasing – Whether freemen having statutory right to income –Whether freemen's rights arising under charitable trust – Nature of charitable trust – Whether class of persons entitled to benefit could be enlarged to inhabitants of borough as a whole – Municipal Corporations Act 1835, ss 2, 92 – Charities Act 1960, s 13(1)(d).

From time immemorial the freemen and widows of the ancient borough of Huntingdon had enjoyed pasturage and grazing rights over certain commons adjoining the borough. In the course of time the rights were converted to monetary benefits and from 1910 the Charity Commissioners and from 1915 the Inland Revenue regarded the rights over the commons as being held for a charity. In 1961 particulars of two charities for the payment of income from the commons for the benefit of freemen and their widows were entered in the register of charities maintained pursuant to the Charities Act 1960. In each case the charity was presumed to arise from a grant to the borough subject to a trust or condition in favour of the freemen or their widows in order to give a lawful origin to rights which had been exercised from time immemorial. A freeman of the borough was a person who was born in the borough, was the son of a freeman, was over 21, was enrolled as a freeman, resided in the borough and paid rates. By 1991 the class of freemen entitled to benefit from the charities had been so reduced and the income from the property had so increased that the annual benefit to a freeman was more than the Charity Commissioners considered to be consistent with the application of charitable funds. The trustees of the charities, at the suggestion of the commissioners and with a view to the income from the charities being applied cy-près for the relief of only freemen in need with the surplus being applied to help the poor and sick of the borough, issued an originating summons for the determination by the court of the issues (1) whether the freemen and widows of former freemen had a statutory right originating in s 2[a] of the Municipal Corporations Act 1835 to share the whole of the income of the commons equally between them, (2) if there was no such statutory right, whether they were entitled to the income in equal shares under a charitable trust, (3) whether the original purposes of the presumed trust ought to be altered pursuant to s 13[b] of the 1960 Act, which provided that a charitable gift could be applied cy-près if, inter alia, 'the original purposes were laid down ... by reference to a class of persons ... which has for any reason since ceased to be suitable, regard being had to the spirit of the gift, or to be practical in administering the gift'. Section 2 of the 1835 Act provided that freemen of boroughs had 'the same Share and Benefit ... of Common Lands ... as he or she by any Statute, Charter, Bye Law, or Custom in force at

---

a   Section 2, so far as material, is set out at p 23 *b* to *f*, post
b   Section 13, so far as material, is set out at p 35 *j* to p 36 *c*, post

the Time of passing this Act might or could have had, acquired, or enjoyed in case this Act had not been passed', while s 92^c of the 1835 Act provided that any surplus on the borough fund 'shall be applied, under the Direction of the Council for the public Benefit of the Inhabitants and Improvement of the Borough'. The freemen contended that their rights did not arise out of a charitable trust but was a statutory right and therefore the question of applying the income under a cy-près scheme did not arise.

Held – (1) The rights of the freemen to the commons, in so far as they arose at all, arose out of a charitable trust and not by reason of s 2 of the 1835 Act. Although s 2 made pre-existing rights, including customary rights, actionable at law, s 2 could not be applied to create a right where none previously existed or to create a right out of a pre-existing precarious usage. Prior to 1835 the commons were held on a charitable trust, which the 1835 Act did not affect, and in so far as any beneficial interest remained in the borough after 1835 it became and still was subject to charitable trusts by virtue of s 92 of the 1835 Act. The trust so created could only have been a charitable trust because of the rule against perpetuities. Furthermore, it was well established that a lawful origin for the long usage and enjoyment by the freeman should, if reasonably possible, be presumed and the only lawful origin which could be found was in a charitable trust. Accordingly, the freemen and widows did not have a statutory right to take the whole of the income of the commons equally between them (see p 25 h j, p 26 d to j, p 27 a b and p 29 d e, post); *R v Watson* (1804) 5 East 480 and *Goodman v Saltash Corp* [1881–5] All ER Rep 1076 applied.

(2) The charitable trust for the benefit of the freemen and widows could not be simply a trust for the public benefit under which the freemen and widows were entitled to divide the whole of the income of the commons equally between them, since the purpose of a trust to distribute income equally amongst a class however large the income or however small the class did not fall within the spirit and intendment of the preamble to the Charitable Uses Act 1601. If the trust was to be charitable it had also to be beneficial in a way in which the law regarded as charitable and the purpose of the trust had to fall within the spirit and intendment of the preamble to the 1601 Act. Usage since time immemorial was not enough to justify the presumption that the trust existed for the purpose of benefiting the freemen individually. Instead it was to be inferred that whatever gave rise to the limitations on a gift for the benefit of a specified parish or town which rendered it a gift for exclusively charitable purposes applied equally to a gift for the benefit of a particular class of such inhabitants. It followed that the property available by virtue of the trust was and always had been applicable for exclusively charitable purposes for the benefit of freemen and their widows who qualified to share in the income from the commons (see p 33 c to e j to p 34 b f g and p 35 b to e, post); *Goodman v Saltash Corp* [1881–5] All ER Rep 1076 applied; *Re Christchurch Inclosure Act* (1888) 38 Ch D 520 and *Re Norwich Town Close Estate Charity* (1888) 40 Ch D 298 considered.

(3) The original basic intention or spirit of the trust was the benefit of the borough and, having regard to the dwindling number of the class, ie qualifying freemen and their widows, entitled to benefit and the liklihood that the class would soon cease to be a section of the public at all, the cy-près doctrine could

---

c   Section 92, so far as material, is set out at p 23 h, post

be applied and a scheme made under s 13(1)(d) of the 1960 Act to benefit the inhabitants of the borough as a whole (see p 36 c to j, post); *Re Lepton's Will Trusts, Re Lepton's Charity, Ambler v Thomas* [1971] 1 All ER 799 applied.

Notes
For the presumption of a charitable trust from usage, see 5(2) *Halsbury's Laws* (4th edn reissue) paras 103–104, and for cases on the subject, see 8(1) *Digest* (2nd reissue) 532–534, 3906–3932.

As from 1 August 1993 the Charities Act 1960, s 13 was replaced by the Charities Act 1993, s 13. For s 13 of the 1993 Act, see 5 *Halsbury's Statutes* (4th edn) (1993 reissue) 886.

The provision made by s 2 of the Municipal Corporations Act 1835 is now given effect in s 248(4) of the Local Government Act1972. For s 248 of the 1972 Act, see 25 *Halsbury's Statutes* (4th edn) (1990 reissue) 364.

Cases referred to in judgment
A-G v Aspinall (1837) 2 My & Cr 613, [1835–42] All ER Rep 525, 40 ER 773, LC.
A-G v De Winton [1906] 2 Ch 106.
A-G v Dublin Corp (1827) 1 Bli NS 312, 4 ER 888.
A-G v Heelis (1824) 2 Sim & St 67, 57 ER 270.
A-G v Mayor of Carlisle (1828) 2 Sim 437, 57 ER 851.
A-G v Wax Chandlers' Co (1873) LR 6 HL 1.
A-G v Webster (1875) LR 20 Eq 483, MR.
Barrs v Bethell [1982] 1 All ER 106, [1982] Ch 294, [1981] 3 WLR 874.
Christchurch Inclosure Act, Re (1887) 35 Ch D 355; rvsd in part (1888) 38 Ch D 520, CA; affd sub nom A-G v Meyrick [1893] AC 1, HL.
Goodman v Saltash Corp (1882) 7 App Cas 633, [1881–5] All ER Rep 1076, HL.
Hopkins v Swansea Corp (1839) 4 M & W 621, 150 ER 1569.
Howse v Chapman (1799) 4 Ves 542, 31 ER 278, LC.
Hulls v Estcourt (1863) 2 H & C 47, 159 ER 21.
Income Tax Special Purposes Comrs v Pemsel [1891] AC 531, [1891–4] All ER Rep 28, HL.
IRC v Baddeley [1955] 1 All ER 525, [1955] AC 572, [1955] 2 WLR 552, HL.
IRC v McMullen [1980] 1 All ER 884, [1981] AC 1, [1980] 2 WLR 416.
Jones v Williams (1767) Amb 651, 27 ER 422, LC.
Lepton's Will Trusts, Re, Re Lepton's Charity, Ambler v Thomas [1971] 1 All ER 799, [1972] Ch 276, [1971] 2 WLR 659.
Norwich Town Close Estate Charity, Re (1888) 40 Ch D 298, CA.
Parr v A-G (1842) 8 Cl & Fin 409, 8 ER 159, HL.
Prestney v Colchester Corp (1882) 21 Ch D 111.
R v Watson (1804) 5 East 480, 102 ER 1154.
Smith, Re, Public Trustee v Smith [1932] 1 Ch 153, [1931] All ER Rep 617.
Stanley v Norwich Corp (1887) 3 TLR 506.
Strakosch (decd), Re, Temperley v A-G [1949] 2 All ER 6, [1949] Ch 529.
Thomson v Shakspeare (1859) 1 De GF & J 399, 45 ER 413.
Williams's (Sir Howell Jones) Trustees v IRCs [1947] 1 All ER 513, [1947] AC 447, HL.
Wilson v Barnes (1886) 38 Ch D 507, CA.
Wright v Hobert (1723) 9 Mod Rep 64, 88 ER 318.

Cases also cited
Faversham Free Fishermen's Co, Re (1887) 36 Ch D 329, CA.
Houston v Burns [1918] AC 337, [1918–19] All ER Rep 817, HL.
Lincoln Corp v Holmes Common Overseers (1867) LR 2 QB 482.
Nash v Coombs (1868) LR 6 Eq 51.
Norton's Will Trusts, Re [1948] 2 All ER 842.
St Botolph Without Bishopsgate Parish Estates, Re, Lighfoot v Goldson (1887) 35 Ch D 142.
St Bride's, Fleet Street (Church or Parish Estate) Re (1877) 35 Ch D 147n.
Verge v Somerville [1924] AC 496, [1924] All ER Rep 121, PC.

Originating summons
By an originating summons issued on 9 October 1991 the plaintiffs, Kenneth Peggs, Edward Thomson Lees, Winifred Mary Price, James McKay, Norman Frank Boyes, Joseph Markham Johnson and Colin Aitken Moore, being the trustees of two charities known as the Huntingdon Commons for the benefit of Freeman and the Widows of Freeman in the Ancient Borough of Huntingdon and the Lammas Rights in the Ancient Borough of Huntingdon, sought, inter alia, the following relief: (1) the determination (i) whether by virtue of s 2 of the Municipal Corporations Act 1835 or otherwise the indefinite and fluctuating body of persons comprising the freemen and their widows, alternatively the individual freemen and their widows, had any, and if any what, interest adversely to the estate and interest of the plaintiffs as the respective trustees of the charities in (a) the commons and Lammas rights respectively in the charities, (b) the proceeds of compulsory and voluntary sales of the commons and Lammas rights, (ii) upon what trusts the commons, Lammas rights, lands, investments, moneys and other property (if any) vested in the plaintiffs as trustees or in the Official Custodian for Charities on their behalf were held, (iii) without prejudice to the generality of (ii), whether by virtue of s 2 of the 1835 Act or otherwise the indefinite and fluctuating body of persons comprising the freeman and their widows, alternatively the individual freemen and their widows for the time being, had any, and if any what, interest under the trusts in (a) the commons and Lammas rights or (b) the proceeds of compulsory or voluntary sales of the commons or Lammas rights, (iv) whether the trusts were properly registered as charities, (v) whether a scheme ought to be settled to define the charitable objects of the charities or to regulate the same and (vi) whether the property or any part of it ought to be applied cy-près on the ground that the original purposes of the charitable gifts had, since they were laid down, ceased, as being useless or harmful to the community or for other reasons, to be in law charitable or ceased in any other way to provide a suitable and effective method of using the property available by virtue of the gift, regard being had to the spirit of the gift, or on some other, and if so what, ground; (2) that, if necessary, a scheme or schemes be directed in accordance with paras (1)(v) and/or (vi) above, or alternatively that all necessary directions be given for such a scheme or schemes to be prepared and settled by the Charity Commissioners. The defendants to the summons were John Craven Lamb, Albert Plowman Bradshaw and Sidney Charles Bradshaw, representing the class of freemen interested in each of the charities, and the Attorney General, representing the interests of charity in general. The facts are set out in the judgment.

Timothy Lloyd QC and Malcolm Waters (instructed by Greenwoods, Peterborough) for the trustees.
Hubert Picarda QC (instructed by Bates Wells & Braithwaite) for the freemen.
James Munby QC and Peter Crampin (instructed by the Treasury Solicitor) for the Attorney General.

Cur adv vult

12 March 1993. The following judgment was delivered.

MORRITT J. At all material times since 1 January 1961 there have been entered in the register of charities maintained pursuant to s 4 of the Charities Act 1960 particulars respecting the two ancient institutions at Huntingdon with which this originating summons is concerned. The first is known as the 'Huntingdon Commons for the benefit of Freemen and the Widows of Freemen in the Ancient Borough of Huntingdon'. The second is called the 'Lammas Rights in the Ancient Borough of Huntingdon'. I shall refer to them as 'the commons charity' and 'the Lammas charity' respectively.

In the case of the commons charity the object as registered is described as 'provision of income for the freemen and freemen's widows of Huntingdon granted by charter'. The governing instrument is said to be 'Ancient Borough Charter (lost)'. In the case of the Lammas charity the object as registered is described as 'general benefits of the Freemen and Freemen's Widows of the former borough of Huntingdon', of which the governing instrument is the abstract of title.

In each case, it is to be inferred, the charity was presumed to arise from a grant to the ancient borough of Huntingdon subject to a trust or condition in favour of the freemen and their widows, as exemplified in the decision of the House of Lords in *Goodman v Saltash Corp* (1882) 7 App Cas 633, [1881–5] All ER Rep 1076, in order to give a lawful origin to rights which had been exercised from time immemorial.

By March 1991 the class of freemen entitled to benefit had so reduced and income from the proceeds of sale of much of the property comprised in the charities had so increased that the annual benefit to a freeman was more than the Charity Commissioners considered to be consistent with the application of charitable funds. They suggested that the plaintiffs, the trustees of both charities, ought to apply for a scheme to ensure that income is only paid to freemen in need and the surplus applied to help the poor and sick of the borough. The trustees sought the advice of leading counsel, in consequence of which the originating summons now before me was issued on 9 October 1991. The first three defendants are representatives of the class of freemen interested in each of the trusts. The fourth defendant, the Attorney General, was joined to represent the interest of charity generally. Huntingdonshire District Council indicated to the Treasury Solicitor that it did not wish to participate in the proceedings whether as successor to the ancient borough or otherwise.

In its original form the originating summons asked that it might be determined whether any part of the property of the charities ought, in accordance with s 13 of the Charities Act 1960, to be applied cy-près and if so for directions for a suitable scheme to be settled. However the researches of counsel gave rise to amendments which have substantially increased the area of dispute. The issues raised by the amended originating summons may be summarised as follows.

(1) Whether the freemen and the widows of former freemen for the time being qualified to benefit have a statutory right to take equally between them the whole of the income of the property whether in the form of land comprised in the original presumed grant or the proceeds of sale of that land or the investments for the time being representing the same. The alleged origin of the right is s 2 of the Municipal Corporations Act 1835 and the statutes subsequently repealing but re-enacting the same.

(2) If there is no such statutory right whether pursuant to the charitable trust presumed in accordance with *Goodman v Saltash Corp* the freemen are entitled to the income in equal shares and whether such right is limited to the income from what remains of the land comprised in the original presumed grant so that a scheme is necessary to clarify and declare the trusts applicable to the income arising from the proceeds of sale of such land.

(3) Whether the original purposes of the presumed trust ought to be altered pursuant to s 13 of the 1960 Act.

(4) If a scheme is required under (2) or (3) above, what directions should be given as to the principles to be observed in any scheme.

Counsel agreed that I should hear argument on and decide the first three issues first. They considered that in so doing some answers to the fourth issue would emerge, but that I should give an opportunity to the parties to present further argument on the fourth issue after I have decided the first three. This seemed to me to be a sensible way to proceed. Thus this judgment is confined to the first three issues I have described. But before I can deal with any of them it is necessary to set out the history of the charities and of the land in question in some detail.

The land comprised in the commons charity consisted of three commons known as Cow or Mill Common, Sheep or Views Common and Horse or Spring Common. These commons adjoined the ancient borough of Huntingdon on the south, west and north sides. To the east was low-lying land so that expansion of the medieval town was restricted to the north-east. It is not possible now to identify all the land over which the grazing rights comprised in the Lammas charity existed. But the rights were to the grazing on such land from 1 August to 25 March in each year. With the change of calendar the dates later became 12 August to 6 April in each year. In argument no distinction was drawn between the Lammas land and the commons or the two charities. Accordingly I will not trace their origins separately.

A charter of King John dated August 1205 addressed to the burgesses of Huntingdon confirmed unspecified rights and privileges. In 1484 the borough of Huntingdon was incorporated in the name of 'the bailiffs and burgesses of Huntingdon' by a charter of Richard III.

Such evidence as there is indicates that until 1630 the management of the lands was in the hands of the chamberlain of the borough. From 1630 to 1825 the management of the lands was delegated by the borough to a leet jury which met twice a year and was presided over by the mayor. In 1680 the borough in common council promulgated certain 'laws, ordinances and constitutions' for, inter alia, regulating the commons. The twenty-sixth recited that 'the free burgesses of this corporation when they have attained the age of 21 years and become housekeepers and none else have time out of mind had common of pasture'. It then referred to certain exchanges and ordained that 'every one of such sworn burgesses and widows of such burgesses shall and may every year for such long time as they shall continue housekeepers and pay scot and lot to the said borough keep three milch cows or heifers' on specified commons and for particular periods and forty sheep and two geldings or mares on other specified commons for particular periods. The twenty-eighth entitled the mayor to dispose of four cow commons and the chamberlain six cow commons to poor inhabitants who had no right of common.

Further 'constitutions and byelaws' were promulgated by the borough in common council in 1737, inter alia, for regulating the commons. Such regulations dealt with the lopping of willows and other trees, the extraction of gravel, clay or sand and the stocking of the commons. Byelaw 26 provided:

> 'Whereas by the constitution of this borough ... the free burgesses ... when they have attained the age of 21 years and become housekeepers and pay scot and lot within the said borough and the widows of such burgesses and none else have had time out of mind common of pasture for commonable cattle within the waste grounds ... and whereas the number of burgesses within the said borough having been since increased and whereas the common is now found by experience to be insufficient to support such a number of cattle as three cows, two geldings or mares and forty sheep ... now the common council upon due consideration ... do believe that it will be more for the benefit of the burgesses in general having a right of common that the number of each sort of cattle be reduced it is therefore constituted and ordained that ... everyone of the said several burgesses and the widows of such burgesses shall and may every year so long as they are residing in the said borough and are housekeepers and pay scot and lot there keep only two milk cows or heifers and no steers.'

Byelaw 27 reduced to two and four respectively the number of cow commons which the mayor and chamberlain might dispose of amongst the poor inhabitants.

In a case stated contemporaneous with these byelaws the purpose of the right of pasture was said to be to benefit the families of the freemen and to supply the neighbourhood with milk as occasion might require.

In 1804 the question arose whether the borough was liable to be rated in respect of the commons. The justices confirmed the rate and stated a case for the opinion of the court: see *R v Watson* (1804) 5 East 480 at 481–482, 102 ER 1154 at 1155. Such case recorded:

> 'That the Mayor, Aldermen, and Burgesses of the borough of Huntingdon are the owners or proprietors of certain large tracts of land within the said borough, used as a common of pasture, and stocked by such resident burgesses of the said borough in right of their burgerships as think proper to stock, according to a stint annually fixed by the leet jury, who are burgesses of the borough, under the control of the mayor for the time being; part of which lands, namely the Mill Common and Pitts mentioned in the notice, are in the parish of Saint Mary, and part in other parishes in the said borough. That no part of the said common was ever assessed to the poor's-rate. That there are about 80 resident burgesses who have rights of common, some of whom stock to the full of their rights, others partially, and some do not stock at all; but in the latter case receive an annual payment of 19s. 4d. in lieu thereof, which is paid by those who do stock.'

In 1825 the court leet was discontinued. The management of the lands was entrusted to a committee of freemen who appointed a foreman, in each case subject to the approval of the council. New byelaws were adopted and all former byelaws repealed in January 1826. The fourteenth prescribed that the freemen and their widows might pasture only such number of beasts as the common council might direct. In default of any such direction the byelaw laid down how many beasts might be pastured and when and where. The description of the freemen and widows entitled to such rights was the same as in the byelaws of 1680 and 1737.

Annual regulations were thereafter made. Those made on 29 April 1829 are a good example. They ordained how many cows, horses or sheep might be pastured by a freeman or his widow and when and where. Those who exercised the right paid a rate from which was paid management expenses and an allowance to those who did not exercise the right. The net balance was carried forward as a credit for the opening of the account for the next ensuing year. This practice is shown for the years from 1828 to 1836 and beyond by the foreman's account book which was produced during the course of the hearing.

In March 1835 the report of the commissioners into municipal corporations was published. In relation to Huntingdon it recorded that freedom of the corporation was acquired by birth, purchase or grant and that all sons of freemen born within the town were entitled to their freedom. There were then 87 resident and 70 non-resident burgesses. The commissioners recorded that burgesses were entitled to graze cows, horses and sheep on certain commons on payment of a rate levied on all commoners, those who chose not to stock being entitled to an annual sum. They considered that the conflicting claims of the corporation and the freemen were due to the fact that the corporation's accounts were not published.

By this time, as the evidence shows, there had been a number of occasions on which the freemen had obtained monetary benefits from their rights. First there were the headage payments made to those who did not themselves exercise their right to pasture. Second there is evidence of the freemen receiving rent from the use of the commons otherwise than for pasture. Thus in 1813 a building lease was granted for a school at a rent of £2 per annum and in 1832 another lease was granted for a gasometer at an annual rent of £6. In each case the rent was credited to the account maintained by the foreman to which I have referred rather than paid to the borough. Likewise in March 1835 the foreman received and credited his account with money from the sale of gravel.

The Municipal Corporations Act 1835 came into effect on 9 September 1835. I shall have to consider its effect in detail later, but at this stage it is only necessary to refer to some of its provisions in order to explain the history. Its purpose was to separate the freemen or burgesses from the corporation and to vest in the reconstituted or new corporation the property of the old but to preserve certain rights of the freemen. Section 1, after reciting that it was expedient that the charters constituting cities, towns and boroughs as bodies corporate should be altered, enacted that—

> 'so much of all Royal and other Charters, Grants, and Letters Patent now in force relating to the several Boroughs named in the Schedules (A.) and (B.) to this Act annexed, or to the Inhabitants thereof, or to the several Bodies or reputed Bodies Corporate named in the said Schedules, or any

of them, as are inconsistent with or contrary to the Provisions of this Act shall be and the same are hereby repealed and annulled.'

Huntingdon was referred to in Sch B. Section 2, so far as material, provided:

'And whereas in divers Cities, Towns, and Boroughs the Common Lands and Public Stock of such Cities, Towns, and Boroughs, and the Rents and Profits thereof, have been held and applied for the particular Benefit of the Citizens, Freemen, and Burgesses of the said Cities, Towns, and Boroughs respectively, or of certain of them, or of the Widows or Kindred of them, or certain of them, and have not been applied to public Purposes; be it therefore enacted, That every Person who now is or hereafter may be an Inhabitant of any Borough, and also every Person who has been admitted or who might hereafter have been admitted a Freeman or Burgess of any Borough if this Act had not been passed, or who now is or hereafter may be the Wife or Widow or Son or Daughter of any Freeman or Burgess, or who may have espoused or may hereafter espouse the Daughter or Widow of any Freeman or Burgess, or who has been or may hereafter be bound an Apprentice, shall have and enjoy and be entitled to acquire and enjoy the same Share and Benefit of the Lands, Tenements, and Hereditaments, and of the Rents and Profits thereof and of the Common Lands and Public Stock of any Borough or Body Corporate, and of any Lands, Tenements, and Hereditaments, and any Sum or Sums of Money, Chattels, Securities for Money, or other Personal Estate, of which any Person or Body Corporate may be seised or possessed in whole or in part for any charitable Uses or Trusts, as fully and effectually, and for such Time and in such Manner, as he or she by any Statute, Charter, Bye Law, or Custom in force at the Time of passing this Act might or could have had, acquired, or enjoyed in case this Act had not been passed ...'

The last of several provisos stated that nothing in the Act—

'shall be construed to ... strengthen, confirm, or affect any Claim, Right or Title of any Burgesses or Freemen of any Borough or Body Corporate, or of any Person, to the Benefit of any such Rights as are herein-before reserved, but the same in every Case may be brought in question, impeached, and set aside in like Manner as if this Act had not been passed.'

Section 3 abolished the ability to acquire the freedom of a borough by gift or purchase. Section 5 required the town clerk to maintain a roll of all those then or thereafter admitted to the freedom. Section 92 provided that any surplus on the borough fund 'shall be applied, under the Direction of the Council, for the public Benefit of the Inhabitants and Improvement of the Borough'. Section 94 provided, in effect, that no sale contracted after June 1835 might be carried out except with the consent of the Treasury.

Between 1836 and 1847 an account 'common land sold' was credited with the proceeds of sale of the site for a new workhouse and the foreman's account was credited with the proceeds of sale of some willow lop and the rent under a 99-year building lease. The rest of the nineteenth century and much of this saw the compulsory acquisition of substantial parts of the commons and Lammas land and disputes between the borough and the freemen as to the destination of the proceeds of sale.

Thus between 1847 and 1851 the Great Northern Railway Co acquired parts of the commons for approximately £7,850. In May 1850 a committee consisting of representatives of the borough and the freemen agreed that 13/14ths of the purchase money should be paid to the freemen, the remaining 1/14th being retained by the borough until the legal entitlement to the whole had been decided. But the principals of the committee members did not adopt this agreement. On 1 August 1851 Knight Bruce V-C directed that the moneys lodged in court by the railway company be invested and the interest thereon paid to the Huntingdon Corporation treasurer to be applied by him 'for such purposes as the rents and profits of the lands and hereditaments sold were properly applicable before the sale'.

In 1851 further parcels of the commons were sold to the East Anglian Railway Co for £560, which was lodged in court. In 1853 the trustees of the Huntingdon County Hospital sought to purchase a site for an infirmary. The freemen agreed to support the application to the Treasury if the remaining 1/14th of the income from the proceeds of the sales to the railway companies was released to them. This was done.

In 1861 part of the commons was sold to the Huntingdon and Godmanchester Gas and Coke Co. The freemen petitioned in respect of the purchase moneys paid into court but the evidence does not disclose what order was made.

At a special meeting of the town council held on 15 April 1868 it was decided that the borough should claim 1/20th of the principal moneys arising on sales of the commons past or future. This proposal was agreed by the freemen subject to conditions and was pursued in a memorial to the Treasury in 1884 and a private Bill which was promoted in 1885 but never passed. Since then the whole of the income of the proceeds of sale of commons land or Lammas rights has been paid to the freemen.

In 1898 the borough promoted a private Bill which would have vested the commons in the borough free from any rights of the freemen in return for a perpetual annuity. The Bill was defeated. From 1910 the commissioners and from 1915 the Revenue have regarded the commons and the Lammas rights as being held for a charity. At about that time at the latest the annual income surplus on the foreman's charity accounts was divided equally between the freemen or their widows qualified to benefit. The evidence does not show when this practice started, save that it was well after the 1835 Act was passed.

Between the 1914–18 and 1939–45 wars the commons were mostly let. From 1958 onwards there were a series of compulsory purchase orders for road construction or the provision of housing for London 'overspill' and most recently parts of the commons or Lammas land have been sold for development. This has given rise to a substantial increase in income. At the same time the numbers of freemen or widows qualified to benefit has declined. Thus in 1900 34 received about £17 each. In 1981 each received about £1,980. But in 1990 each received £31,750. There are now 15 qualified to benefit. The aggregate income has fallen because of the reduction in interest rates and because the trustees have invested capital moneys in agricultural land, thereby reducing the yield. If free to do so they would propose to continue to invest in agricultural land. As at 30 April 1992 the trustees had an income of £550,000, investments representing the proceeds of sale of land with a market value of £500,000 and capital cash of £3·8m as well as part of the original commons land

and Lammas rights and some 700 acres of agricultural land in which other proceeds of sale have been reinvested.

It is common ground that to qualify for benefit the freeman must be (1) the son of a freeman, (2) born in the ancient borough, (3) over 21, (4) sworn and enrolled as a freeman, (5) resident in the ancient borough, (6) paying scot and lot. This last condition has been interpreted as requiring the payment of rates or the community charge for the time being in force.

Prior to 1835 freedom of the borough might be obtained by purchase or grant. Thus at that time the first and second conditions were not essential so long as the person in question had obtained the freedom of the borough by some means. But a consequence of the abolition of purchase or grant as methods by which the freedom of a borough might be obtained was that after 1835 the freeman must have complied with the first and second conditions.

It is not in dispute that both before and after 1835 the qualifying conditions were such as to render the acquisition by the class of qualifying freemen of a profit à prendre by prescription impossible in law: see *Goodman v Saltash Corp* (1882) 7 App Cas 633, [1881–5] All ER Rep 1076. Nor was it disputed that a trust for such a class in perpetuity would be void on that account unless it was a charitable trust or authorised by statute: see *A-G v Webster* (1875) LR 20 Eq 483 at 491.

It was also common ground that a lawful origin for the long usage and enjoyment which the evidence demonstrates ought if reasonably possible to be presumed: see *Goodman v Saltash Corp*. The first issue arises from the claim of the freemen that such an origin may be found in s 2 of the 1835 Act.

The case for the freemen is that the evidence shows a long and consistent pattern of the freemen sharing equally between them the enjoyment of the land in specie and any income derived from it. I interpose to say that there is no evidence that the net income was distributed to the freemen in equal shares until well after the passing of the Act. This usage, the argument continues, in 1835, even if permissive only, was converted into a statutory right by s 2 of the 1835 Act. Because the right was conferred by statute it could not be invalidated by the perpetuity rule. Such a lawful origin is sufficient so that, in particular, it is not necessary to apply the principle of *Saltash* and presume a charitable trust in favour of the class. It is argued that neither institution is a charity with the consequence that each of them is wrongly registered. It is submitted that this argument has the support of the decision of Hall V-C in *Prestney v Colchester Corp* (1882) 21 Ch D 111 and of Kekewich J in *Stanley v Norwich Corp* (1887) 3 TLR 506.

The Attorney General disputes these propositions. He accepts that s 2 made pre-existing rights actionable at law when previously they may not have been so enforceable, but denies that the section was capable of creating a right out of a pre-existing precarious usage. He submits that the position prior to 1835 was that the land in question was held on charitable trusts which the 1835 Act did not affect. In this context all s 2 did was to confirm the continuation of any formal qualifications required by a freeman; it could not and did not alter the substance or enlarge the quantum of the rights enjoyed prior to 1835. He points out that in so far as any beneficial interest in the land remained in the borough at least after 1835 it became and still is subject to charitable trusts by virtue of s 92 of the 1835 Act and the various Acts repealing and re-enacting the same. He contends that the decisions in *Prestney* and *Stanley* were in substance overruled by the decision of the Court of Appeal in *Re Norwich Town Close Estate Charity* (1888) 40 Ch D 298.

In his reply counsel for the freemen contended that s 92 of the 1835 Act and the subsequent legislation did not have the effect for which the Attorney General contended. I propose to deal with this last point first to get it out of the way.

In *A-G v Aspinall* (1837) 2 My & Cr 613 at 618, [1835–42] All ER Rep 525 at 527 Lord Cottenham LC referred to the effect of s 92 as devoting the funds in question to 'public, or in other words, charitable purposes'. It is said that the reference to charitable purposes went beyond what was necessary for the decision of the case, was not repeated by Lord Cottenham LC in *Parr v A-G* (1842) 8 Cl & Fin 409, 8 ER 159 and was merely quoted by Farwell J without further comment in *A-G v De Winton* [1906] 2 Ch 106 at 115. In my view the statement of Lord Cottenham LC was not mere obiter and even if it was it has been accepted as correctly stating the law ever since under the successor legislation contained in the Act 45 & 46 Vict c 50 (municipal corporations (1882)): see *A-G v De Winton* per Farwell J, Local Government Act 1972, Warner J in *Barrs v Bethell* [1982] 1 All ER 106 at 114–115, [1982] Ch 294 at 306 and generally, and 5 *Halsbury's Laws* (4th edn) para 709.

There are several reasons why I prefer the submissions for the Attorney General on this issue. First there is the actual decision in *R v Watson* (1804) 5 East 480, 102 ER 1154. The question in that case was whether the borough was in rateable occupation of the commons. I have already quoted the passage in the case stated which described the actual method of enjoyment of the land at the time. The decision was that the freemen to whom the land had been meted out for the year in question were tenants in common of the land occupied by them and liable to be rated therefor to the exclusion of the borough. All four judges held that the borough owned the land. Lord Ellenborough CJ, Grose and Lawrence JJ held that the freemen occupiers were rateable. Le Blanc J decided in addition that the fee was vested in the corporation for the benefit of the resident burgesses. He said (5 East 480 at 488, 102 ER 1154 at 1157):

> 'It is improper therefore to call it a right of common; because it is holden in fee by the corporation for the benefit of the resident burgesses ... for this is a case of persons having an equitable right to the land, the fee of which is vested in the corporation for their benefit.'

Such a trust could only have been a charitable trust because of the rule against perpetuities.

The same result is reached by applying one of the principles established by the *Saltash* case, namely that a lawful origin for the long usage and enjoyment by the freemen should, if reasonably possible, be presumed. In my judgment it is necessary to decide what was the quality of the freemen's use and enjoyment in and before 1835 for the purpose of seeing what effect the Act might have had thereon. By then the use and enjoyment had existed for over 600 years, so that a lawful origin ought to be presumed as at 1835 if it is reasonably possible to do so. For all the reasons given by the House of Lords in the *Saltash* case, which were equally applicable in 1835, such lawful origin could only be found in a charitable trust.

Moreover the wording of s 2 predicates a right before 1835 which was more than merely precarious. The section preserves—

> 'the same Share and Benefit ... as he or she by any Statute, Charter, Bye Law, or Custom in force at the Time of passing this Act might or could have had, acquired, or enjoyed in case this Act had not been passed.'

A statute, charter or byelaw is a source of rights enforceable by the appropriate procedure. Custom being more than mere usage may be too. The section treats all four in the same way and regards them all as being capable of being 'in force'. Both the proviso and decided cases such as *Hopkins v Swansea Corp* (1839) 4 M & W 621, 150 ER 1569 and *Hulls v Estcourt* (1863) 2 H & C 47, 159 ER 21 all show that the section cannot be applied to create a right where none previously existed. The only authority to the contrary is the decision of Hall V-C in *Prestney v Colchester Corp* (1882) 21 Ch D 111 at 120, where he said:

> 'The words are "statute, charter, byelaw, or custom;" and though it is not said that it was by custom that they were entitled, I think it is sufficiently averred that such was the customary mode of applying the property. I do not consider the word "custom" in the Act to be used in the technical sense, but as meaning that such was the usage; the word is only equivalent to "usage;" and means, not that you are obliged in such a case as this to allege and prove a custom, but that you are only to allege what may be taken to be the usage and the ordinary mode of applying the property. And I think this view is somewhat fortified by the circumstance that Baron Parke ... seems to consider the word "custom," an equivalent to "or otherwise"—i.e., that in some other way, or from some other cause, the property has in fact been so applied, and that therefore such application is to go on.'

Nevertheless I am not bound by that decision, which seems to me to be inconsistent with the words of the Act and the other cases to which I have referred. In any event it was, in my judgment, effectively overruled by the decision of the Court of Appeal in *Re Norwich Town Close Estate Charity*, to which I have referred.

In *Prestney v Colchester Corp* the freemen of a borough sought to establish a right for their private benefit to share in the proceeds of sale of property vested in the corporation. Their statement of claim alleged that the property was held by the corporation in trust for them since time immemorial and that the rents and profits had been applied for their benefit at the time the 1835 Act was passed and at all times previously. The defendant corporation demurred to the entire statement of claim. The *Saltash* case had not been decided by the House of Lords and Hall V-C concluded that no trust or charity was established. His decision was (21 Ch D 111 at 119–120):

> 'What I do say is this: this right is under the Act of Parliament; it is not a right by reason of their being a charity, but because the *Municipal Corporations Act* has established that right, and has said they are to have that right; nor do I wish to save the rights of these parties from any illegality in reference to perpetuity, or otherwise, by sheltering them under this being a charity. I consider the statute ought to be read as applying to all property vested in a municipal corporation, subject only to this, that the Legislature, in passing the *Municipal Corporations Act*, had found that certain property of corporations had been applied in a particular way, and that, as I read the Act and think it ought to be read, this state of things is to go on without reference to any question as to whether it would be legal or illegal if it had been created by some private donation or grant. That is not the test. The test is one of fact. The property has been applied in the way specified; and the Legislature says that it shall continue so to be applied. And I do not think that by reason of the words,

"as fully and effectually, and for such time and in such manner as he or she, by any statute, charter, byelaw, or custom in force at the time of passing this Act, might or could have had, acquired or enjoyed, in case this Act had not been passed," I should hold upon this demurrer that this cannot go on at all because it is in itself illegal on the ground of perpetuity;—that if it be not a charity, it would be illegal, and therefore those words limit the operation of the section. I am satisfied that this section was intended to treat the interests which the freemen had got in that way as effectual and binding, whether they had got them legally or illegally, so far as regards any such consideration as that it would be a perpetuity and therefore could not be effectually given in that way. I cannot, upon any ground that I can see, consider that this is a case in which it is necessary to say that the parties, if they are to have their rights protected upon any ground, can only sue by information, that is, in the name of the Attorney-General.'

In *Stanley v Norwich Corp* (1886) 3 TLR 506 freemen of the city of Norwich claimed that the corporation held certain land over which they had exercised a right of pasture since time immemorial in trust for them. This was denied by the corporation. Kekewich J decided (at 507):

'The manner in which the rents and profits had been applied was quite consistent with the previous user of the land itself, and in each case the right of enjoyment belonged to the freemen. His Lordship did not decide this case on the doctrine laid down in Goodman v. Mayor of Saltash ((1882) 7 App Cas 633, [1881–5] All ER Rep 1076), but founded his judgment on the Municipal Corporations Act, 1835, the rights recognised by which were not taken away by the Municipal Corporations Act of 1883. The freemen were entitled by custom, and were within the saving of rights in sec. 2 of the Act of 1835. His Lordship was himself of this view, and his opinion was strongly supported by the decision of Vice-Chancellor Hall in Prestney v. Mayor of Colchester ((1882) 21 Ch D 111) which decision would, whatever his Lordship's own opinion had been, have been binding on him. The plaintiffs were therefore, entitled to the declaration claimed by them in respect of the Town Close and the rents and profits thereof. No declaration would be made in the present proceedings as to the persons entitled to be freemen, as the Corporation were prepared to give an undertaking not to admit to the freedom on the ground of servitude any person who was not entitled to be admitted by a seven years' servitude. With reference to the contention on behalf of the Attorney-General that there was a charitable trust and that a scheme should be settled, the Attorney-General was entitled to take such steps as he might be advised to take with reference to having a scheme settled, but his Lordship did not think fit to direct a scheme.'

In the subsequent proceedings of *Re Norwich Town Close Estate Charity* (1888) 40 Ch D 298 the Attorney General had issued a summons for the approval of a scheme on the footing that the trust declared by Kekewich J was a charity. The freemen contended that there was no charity, relying on the judgment which I have quoted, and that the procedure adopted was not the proper one in which to determine a dispute as to whether or not a trust was charitable. Kekewich J decided that the wrong procedure had been adopted and the Attorney General appealed. In the Court of Appeal each of the Lords Justices dealt with the merits of the dispute. Cotton LJ held (at 307):

> 'If this trust for the freemen of *Norwich* were not a charitable trust, it would undoubtedly be exposed to the objection of the rules against perpetuity, and if this trust in favour of the freemen for the time being can be supported, it can only be on the ground that it is a charitable trust. In my opinion, the declaration of Mr. Justice *Kekewich* determines that this is a charity, and that being so there is no question that there is jurisdiction under the Act in question to give any direction which may be right as to the mode of administering this charity and carrying it into effect, of course, having regard to the trusts directed by the grant which is established, and as to which a declaration is made by Mr. Justice *Kekewich*.'

Both Lindley and Bowen LJJ said that the trust declared by Kekewich J could only be a charitable trust. The Court of Appeal recognised that in so doing it had gone beyond the narrow question which had been argued by counsel for the freemen and agreed to allow further argument on the merit of the dispute. But when it came to it the freemen bowed to the inevitable and conceded that the trust was charitable.

In my judgment the decision of the Court of Appeal, which is binding on me, is necessarily inconsistent with the judgments of Hall V-C in *Prestney v Colchester Corp* and Kekewich J in *Stanley v Norwich Corp*. Thus in those two cases the interests of the freemen arose under charitable trusts of the *Saltash* type and not under private trusts based on precarious usage by virtue of s 2 of the 1835 Act. In my judgment the answer to the first issue I set out earlier in this judgment is in the negative.

On this basis it is common ground that the rights and interests of the freemen arise from a charitable trust of the *Saltash* type but the nature of such a trust and of the rights and interests of the freemen is disputed. The freemen contend that they are entitled to share equally the entire income of the land, proceeds of sale and investments for the time being representing the same.

In *Goodman v Saltash Corp* (1882) 7 App Cas 633, [1881–5] All ER Rep 1076 the plaintiffs were the corporation, which sought to prevent the defendants from trespassing on the corporation's several fishery in the river Tamar by dredging therein for oysters. The defendants claimed that they and other free inhabitants of ancient tenements in the borough of Saltash were entitled to do so during a particular period of the year. The form of the proceedings was a special case for the opinion of the court. Paragraph 9 of that case stated (7 App Cas 633 at 634):

> 'The free inhabitants of ancient tenements in the borough of Saltash have from time immemorial, without interruption and claiming as of right, exercised the privilege of dredging for oysters in the locus in quo mentioned in the statement of claim from the 2nd day of February in each year to Easter eve in each year both inclusive, and of catching and carrying away the same without stint for sale and otherwise. The acts complained of were done in exercise of the privilege.'

The corporation was successful in the High Court and the Court of Appeal and the appeal in the House of Lords was argued twice. The ground of the decision was, in each case, that the free inhabitants were a fluctuating body of persons and therefore unable in law to hold a profit à prendre in the property of another. The decision on this point was affirmed by the House of Lords. But the point on which the appeal was decided by the House of Lords in favour of the defendant freemen was not raised in any of the courts below. The conclusion, as summarised in the headnote, was that in applying the principle that if reasonably possible a lawful origin for the usage should be presumed it should be presumed that the original grant to the corporation of the several fishery was subject to a trust or condition in favour of the free inhabitants of ancient tenements in the borough in accordance with the usage. It was fundamental to the decision, though not recorded in the headnote, that such trust or condition was charitable.

Lord Selborne LC said (7 App Cas 633 at 642–643, [1881–5] All ER Rep 1076 at 1081):

> 'But it appears to me to be consistent with all the facts and documents stated or referred to in the special case, that the fishery may have been originally granted to the free burgesses of Essa, subject to a condition or proviso that the free inhabitants of ancient messuages within the borough should be entitled to fish, as they have been accustomed to do, in every year from Candlemas to Easter. I am unable to discover any reason why this should not be a good foundation in law for the right which the appellants claim. If an actual grant, so qualified, were produced, it would be immaterial, whether the word used in it were "trust," "intent," "purpose," "proviso" or "condition," or whether the trust or duty, imposed on the mayor and free burgesses, were cognizable in equity only, or also at law. In such a grant there would be all the elements necessary to constitute what, in modern jurisprudence, is called a charitable trust. "If I give" (said Lord Cairns in [*A-G v Wax Chandlers' Co* (1873) LR 6 HL 1 at 21])"an estate to A. upon condition that he shall apply the rents for the benefit of B., that is a gift in trust to all intents and purpose." A gift subject to a condition or trust for the benefit of the inhabitants of a parish or town, or of any particular class of such inhabitants, is (as I understand the law) a charitable trust: and no charitable trust can be void on the ground of perpetuity. (*Jones* v. *Williams* ((1767) Amb 651, 27 ER 422); *Attorney-General* v. *Mayor of Carlisle* ((1828) 2 Sim 437, 57 ER 851); *Howse* v. *Chapman* ((1799) 4 Ves 542, 31 ER 278); and see *Attorney-General* v. *Heelis* ((1824) 2 Sim & St 67, 57 ER 270); and *Attorney-General* v. *Mayor, &c. of Dublin* ((1827) 1 Bli NS 312, 4 ER 888). In a case cited during the argument of this appeal (*Wright* v. *Hobert* ((1723) 9 Mod Rep 64, 88 ER 318)), Lord Macclesfield established, as a charitable trust, an ancient grant of land for the pasture, during three months of the year, of the cows of "as many of the inhabitants" of a certain village "as were able to buy three cows," and during seven months of the rest of the year, "to be in common for all the inhabitants;" saying, "that if this manner of grazing had been by prescription or usage, no person but the inhabitants of ancient messuages could be entitled to it, but it is otherwise appointed by the grant of the donors".'

Lord Cairns said (7 App Cas 633 at 650–651, [1881–5] All ER Rep 1076 at 1085):

> 'Then I come to the question, Is there any difficulty, in that state of things, in supposing what we are bound to suppose if it is possible, an ancient grant to the corporation of Saltash which would explain and reconcile the whole of the practice which we have thus laid before us? It appears to me that there is no difficulty at all in supposing such a grant, a grant to the corporation before the time of legal memory of a several fishery, a grant by the Crown, with a condition in that grant in some terms

which are not before us, but which we can easily imagine—a condition that the free inhabitants of ancient tenements in the borough should enjoy this right, which as a matter of fact the case tells us they have enjoyed from time immemorial. A grant of that kind, it appears to me, would be perfectly legal and perfectly intelligible, and there would be nothing in it which would infringe any principle of law. Such a condition would create that which in the very wide language of our courts is called a charitable, that is to say a public, trust or interest, for the benefit of the free inhabitants of ancient tenements. A trust of that kind would not in any way infringe the law or rule against perpetuities, because we know very well that where you have a trust which, if it were for the benefit of private individuals or a fluctuating body of private individuals, would be void on the ground of perpetuity, yet if it creates a charitable, that is to say a public, interest, it will be free from any obnoxiousness to the rule with regard to perpetuities. That is a principle of the courts which was very well explained in a well-known case in the Court of Chancery which was decided when Lord Campbell was Lord Chancellor, a case with regard to Shakspeare's house, *Thompson v. Shakspear* ((1860) 1 De GF & J 399, 45 ER 413). Indeed it is a principle which has been established in many cases.'

Lord Watson said (7 App Cas 633 at 665):

'I am of opinion that it ought to be presumed, that the original grant of the fishery to the corporation was made subject to the condition that the class of inhabitants, which the appellants represent, should, in all time coming, possess and enjoy the right which is now claimed for them. Having regard to the relative positions of the corporation, and of these inhabitants, I can see no good reason why a qualification of the grant, expressed in these terms, should not have been held sufficient to constitute what, in the law of England, is known as a charitable trust, in the corporation for their benefit. And having regard to the facts proved or admitted in the present case, I can see no good reason for refusing to give effect to the presumption that the title of the corporation is and always has been, qualified by such a condition.'

Lord Blackburn dissented and Lord Fitzgerald added nothing of his own on this point.

It is apparent from the passages I have quoted that the grant presumed was a grant of the several fishery by the Crown to the borough of Saltash on condition that the free inhabitants of certain specific ancient messuages within the borough of Saltash should forever thereafter have the right to fish within the several fishery from Candlemas to Easter in each year. Such trust or condition was regarded as a valid charitable trust because it was for the benefit of the inhabitants of a specific locality or a particular class of such inhabitants.

The principle of the *Saltash* case has been applied in two subsequent cases to which I should refer for such light as they throw on the ambit of the principle. The first is *Re Christchurch Inclosure Act* (1888) 38 Ch D 520. In that case the occupiers of certain cottages within a manor claimed rights of turbary over the commonable and waste lands. An Inclosure Act passed in 1802 (42 Geo 3 c xliii) provided for the allotment of lands to the lord of the manor in trust for the occupiers of the cottages for a turf common. Four hundred acres was so allotted, part of which was subsequently acquired by a railway company which paid the purchase money into court. The question was who was entitled to it.

The relevant claimants were the lord of the manor, the owners of the cottages, the occupiers of the cottages, or charity represented by the Attorney General. The Attorney General argued that there was a charitable trust on the basis of the *Saltash* case. This was rejected by Stirling J, who held that the only persons interested were the lord of the manor and the occupiers, the latter being a private and therefore non-charitable class. He said ((1887) 35 Ch D 355 at 370):

> 'I am, nevertheless, unable to regard it [the *Saltash* case] as an authority for the proposition that, wherever benefits are conferred on the occupiers of a class of houses, a charitable trust is necessarily created.'

The order directed that the fund in court be apportioned between what was compensation for the rights of turbary and compensation for the soil, the former to be held for the occupiers the latter for the lord of the manor.

The Attorney General appealed, contending that the fund to be apportioned to the occupiers was held on a charitable trust for the benefit of the occupiers of the cottages. He was successful. Lindley LJ, giving the judgment of the court, said (38 Ch D 520 at 530):

> 'Had it not been for the decision of the House of Lords in *Goodman* v. *Mayor of Saltash* we should have felt great difficulty in holding this trust to be a charitable trust. For, although the occupiers of these cottages may have been, and perhaps were, poor people, the trust is not for the poor occupiers, but for all the then and future occupiers, whether poor or not. Moreover, the trust is not for the inhabitants of a parish or district, but only for some of such persons. The trust is for a comparatively small and tolerably well-defined class of persons. The class consists of all the then and future occupiers of the cottages; and there may be several occupiers of one cottage. The class, however, though limited, is as to its members uncertain, and is liable to fluctuation, and the trust for the class is perpetual. This being the case, we are unable to distinguish this case from the trust which both Lord *Selborne* and Lord *Cairns* held to be a charitable trust, and therefore valid, in *Goodman* v. *Mayor of Saltash*.'

After quoting extensively from the speeches of Lord Selborne LC and Earl Cairns in the *Saltash* case Lindley LJ continued (at 532):

> 'Mr. Justice *Stirling* considered that the trust for the occupiers was a trust for them as private individuals; but if a trust for all the free inhabitants of ancient tenements in a borough is a trust capable of being upheld as a charitable trust, we are unable to see why a trust for the occupiers for the time being of certain ancient and other cottages more than fifteen years old in a manor, or in several adjoining manors, or in some other specified district, should not be upheld on the same principle.'

There was a subsequent appeal to the House of Lords (see sub nom *A-G v Meyrick* [1893] AC 1) but not on the question of whether there was any charitable trust.

The second is *Re Norwich Town Close Estate Charity* (1888) 40 Ch D 298 to which I have already referred. The facts of the case are to be found in the report of the earlier proceedings, namely *Stanley v Norwich Corp* (1886) 3 TLR 506. The claim was that the freemen of Norwich had since before 1204 exercised rights to pasture over the Town Close. After various disputes had been settled due to the mediation of Cardinal Wolsey a particular area was set aside. From 1524 to 1699 the right to pasture had been enjoyed by the freemen exclusively. From 1700 to 1883 the land was let and the net rent divided amongst the freemen. Then the corporation claimed that the freemen had no right to the rent and sought to apply it for the public purposes of the corporation. It was in these circumstances that Kekewich J made the declaration to which I have referred which, in the subsequent proceedings, the Court of Appeal concluded must be a declaration as to the existence of a charitable trust. Cotton LJ, with whom Lindley and Bowen LJJ agreed, considered 'that the question whether such a trust is charitable was decided by the House of Lords in *Goodman* v. *Mayor of Saltash*' (see 40 Ch D 298 at 306). After quoting from the speeches of Lord Selborne and Earl Cairns, Cotton LJ reached the conclusion which I have already quoted (see 40 Ch D 298 at 307).

The problem how to reconcile the *Saltash* case with general principles of the law relating to charitable trusts is apparent from the judgment of Lindley LJ in *Re Christchurch Inclosure Act* (1888) 38 Ch D 520 at 530, the speeches of Viscount Simonds in *Sir Howell Jones Williams's Trustees v IRC* [1947] 1 All ER 513 at 521, [1947] AC 447 at 460 and in *IRC v Baddeley* [1955] 1 All ER 525 at 533, [1955] AC 572 at 591 and the discussion in *Tudor on Charities* (7th edn, 1984) pp 112ff. The point, quite simply, is that it is not enough that the trust should be for the public benefit: it must also be beneficial in a way which the law regards as charitable: see *Williams's Trustees'* case. To be beneficial in a way which the law regards as charitable the purpose of the trust must fall within the spirit and intendment of the preamble to the Act 43 Eliz 1 c 4 (charitable uses (1601)), which, nowadays, is treated as synonymous with Lord Macnaghten's classification in *Income Tax Special Purposes Comrs v Pemsel* [1891] AC 531 at 583, [1891–4] All ER Rep 28 at 55–56.

For the freemen it was submitted that the only solution is that suggested in *Tudor on Charities* p 113, namely that the particular purpose must be deemed in each case to fall within the spirit and intendment of the preamble to the 1601 Act, whether or not it does so in fact. It was contended that the purpose in this case was the provision of income and general benefits for the freemen and their widows.

This was disputed by the Attorney General. He submitted, first, that the rights of the freemen were confined to enjoyment of the land in specie which was justifiable as a charity under the fourth head of Lord Macnaghten's classification, namely other purposes beneficial to the community not falling under any of the preceding heads. He submitted, second, that the trust was one for the benefit of the community in a particular area without the specification of any particular purpose, with the consequence that the permitted purposes are limited to those within the spirit and intendment of the preamble: cf *Re Smith, Public Trustees v Smith* [1932] 1 Ch 153, [1931] All ER Rep 617 and *Re Strakosch (decd), Temperley v A-G* [1949] 2 All ER 6, [1949] Ch 529.

I have no hesitation in rejecting the submission for the freemen that the purpose of the trust is merely the provision of income and general benefits for the freemen and their widows. Until the beginning of the twentieth century there was no question of the freemen dividing between themselves the whole of the income of the land and of the proceeds of sale of the land. They benefited either from exercising a right to pasture their own cattle or from receipt of the head money if they chose not to. The gross income was used to defray expenses and any balance was carried forward. The exercise of the rights of pasture was controlled by the borough and, in earlier times, limited rights were available for disposal to the poor inhabitants. I do not think that the usage since time immemorial justifies the presumption that the trust existed for the purpose of benefiting the freemen individually, though the provision of such benefits might in suitable circumstances be the way in which the purpose is achieved. There is a difference between the purpose of a trust and the means by which the purpose may be achieved: cf *IRC v McMullen* [1980] 1 All ER 884 at 889, [1981] AC 1 at 14. Counsel for the freemen and for the Attorney General knew of no case in which a trust to distribute the income equally amongst a class however large the income or small the class had been held to be charitable. Nor do I. The reason must be that the purpose of such a trust could not come within the spirit and intendment of the preamble.

This consideration also, I think, provides the answer to the first submission for the Attorney General. It was submitted that the provision of grazing rights to the freemen was charitable as being for an 'other purpose beneficial to the community'. The suggested purpose was the stimulation of local agriculture and the provision of food and other necessaries for the community at large in time of need. This is certainly ingenious and if right as a matter of law a possible explanation for the *Saltash*, *Christchurch* and *Norwich* cases.

The limitation to a charitable purpose is inferred from the particular method of achieving it operated over a long period of time. But fisheries could only sensibly be used for fishing and pastures could only be used for grazing. I see no reason why the purpose should be limited by reference to the normal if not the only way of enjoying the trust property at (and after) the time the trust is presumed to have been created. Why, for example, should the purpose of an ancient trust to permit the freemen of the borough for the time being to take and use the wood of a specific plantation be regarded as the encouragement of silviculture rather than the provision of fuel or building material for the construction of churches or bridges or even of sea dykes? Cf *Wilson v Barnes* (1886) 38 Ch D 507.

There is, as I read them, nothing in the speeches of Lord Selborne LC or Earl Cairns in *Goodman v Saltash Corp* to suggest that the limitation to or inference of exclusively charitable purposes was arrived at by this route. The emphasis is on 'the inhabitants of a parish or town or of any particular class of such inhabitants' and 'a public, trust or interest, for the benefit of the free inhabitants'. The inference seems to be that whatever gives rise to the limitations on a gift for the benefit of a specified parish or town which renders it a gift for exclusively charitable purposes applies equally to a gift for the benefit of a particular class of such inhabitants. Indeed I think that it is clear from the passage I have already quoted from the judgment of the Court of Appeal in *Re Christchurch Inclosure Act* (1888) 38 Ch D 520 at 530 that they thought so too.

The principle on which such gifts are treated as being for exclusively charitable purposes is clear from the judgment of Lord Hanworth MR in *Re Smith* [1932] 1 Ch 153 at 169, [1931] All ER Rep 617 at 625–626. After referring to, inter alia, *Saltash* and *Christchurch* he said:

> 'The result is that I come to the conclusion that there is a definitive purpose—namely, that the bequest is to be for England. That is good in the same sense that, although general, when the sum bequeathed comes to be used it is to be applied to charitable purposes, as in *Attorney-General v. Webster* ((1875) LR 20 Eq 483). There is no area or purpose of distribution suggested which is not charitable. Why not then give effect to the plain meaning that it is for the advantage, within the meaning of the

rule as to the interpretation of the word "charitable," of the inhabitants of England?'

As was made plain in *Re Strakosch* [1949] 2 All ER 6 at 10, [1949] Ch 529 at 541, there is no scope for the application of that principle where the purpose of the trust is expressed. In that event the question will depend on whether that purpose is charitable in law or not. But it is inherent in a case such as the present that there is no trust deed setting out the purposes of the trust. Accordingly, in my judgment, the principle of *Re Smith* applies, for there is nothing to exclude it, and the property available by virtue of the gift is and always has been applicable for charitable purposes for the benefit of the freemen and their widows possessing the qualifications to which I have referred.

In the case of the Lammas charity such property has been confined to the Lammas rights. But this gives rise to no problem because, I was told, there is in the area a well-recognised formula by which the value of land is divided between those who are entitled to the Lammas rights and others interested in the land. In the case of the commons charity it seems to me that the only proper inference is that the whole interest in the land was given for charitable purposes for the benefit of the freemen even though at the time the only way the charitable purpose could be achieved was by the exercise of grazing rights. This accords with the evidence that there seems to be no instance in which the corporation obtained and retained for itself any benefit from the land, the income from the land or from the proceeds of sale or the income thereof.

Accordingly in relation to the second issue the answer is in the negative. In my judgment the income of the land or of the Lammas rights as the case may be and of the proceeds of sale of the same is held by the trustees to be applied for exclusively charitable purposes for the benefit of qualifying freemen or their widows.

Thus the question now arises whether a scheme is necessary. For the freemen it was submitted that there was no need for or jurisdiction to order the settlement of a scheme. But this submission was on the basis that the freemen were entitled to divide the annual income between them. In my judgment and for the reasons I have already given that is not so. Moreover I do not think that the settlement of a scheme would be necessary merely to make plain that the income was to be applied for the original, namely general charitable, purposes only amongst the freemen. The declaration of the court should be sufficient. If the trustees wanted a scheme they could always apply to the Charity Commissioners.

The real issue is whether in the circumstances there is jurisdiction to order the settlement of a scheme for the cy-près application of the income. This depends on s 13 of the Charities Act 1960, which provides as follows:

(1) Subject to subsection (2) below, the circumstances in which the original purposes of a charitable gift can be altered to allow the property given or part of it to be applied cy-près shall be as follows:—(a) where the original purposes, in whole or in part,—(i) have been as far as may be fulfilled; or (ii) cannot be carried out, or not according to the directions given and to the spirit of the gift; or (b) where the original purposes provide a use for part only of the property available by virtue of the gift; or (c) where the property available by virtue of the gift and other property applicable for similar purposes can be more effectively used in conjunction, and to that end can suitably, regard being had to the spirit of

the gift, be made applicable to common purposes; or (d) where the original purposes were laid down by reference to an area which then was but has since ceased to be a unit for some other purpose, or by reference to a class of persons or to an area which has for any reason since ceased to be suitable, regard being had to the spirit of the gift, or to be practical in administering the gift; or (e) where the original purposes, in whole or in part, have, since they were laid down,—(i) been adequately provided for by other means; or (ii) ceased, as being useless or harmful to the community or for other reasons, to be in law charitable; or (iii) ceased in any other way to provide a suitable and effective method of using the property available by virtue of the gift, regard being had to the spirit of the gift ...'

In *Re Lepton's Will Trusts, Re Lepton's Charity, Ambler v Thomas* [1971] 1 All ER 799 at 803, [1972] Ch 276 at 285 Pennycuick V-C construed the phrase 'spirit of the gift' as meaning the basic intention underlying the gift, such intention being ascertainable from the terms of the relevant instrument read in the light of admissible evidence. I do not think that the absence of any founding document precludes the existence of any 'spirit of the gift'. Accordingly such spirit must likewise be inferred.

For the freemen it was contended that the spirit of the gift was the benefit of the freemen.

I have concluded that the original purposes were and are general charitable purposes for the benefit of qualifying freemen and their widows. These are presumed to be the purposes laid down in the Middle Ages. In those days there can be little doubt that the freemen of a borough were a substantial section of the public both numerically and in their social, economic and political importance. As such the class of freemen was then and for several centuries thereafter entirely suitable as a class by reference to which the charitable purposes should be laid down. But I am satisfied that that is no longer so. The effect of the 1835 Act was to destroy the political importance of the freemen and thereby to undermine their social and economic importance too. But, of more importance, membership of the class was thereby restricted, in the case of these charities, to those who were the sons of freemen and born in the ancient borough. The inevitable consequence after over 150 years is that the class has dwindled very considerably. There will come a time, if it has not arrived already, when the class of freemen ceases to be a section of the public at all. It is not necessary to decide whether that time has passed so that a case for a scheme can be made out under s 13(1)(e)(ii) because I think it is clear that a sufficient case is made out under para (d).

The original basic intention or spirit of the gift was the benefit of the borough of Huntingdon. It would, in my judgment, be entirely consistent with that that in 1993 the class of persons by reference to which the charitable purposes are laid down should be enlarged from the freemen to the inhabitants as a whole. Accordingly I will direct the settlement of a scheme. I will hear further argument on what other provisions it should contain or principles it should observe.

In summary therefore and, subject to further argument on any points of detail, by reference to the amended originating summons, question 1(i) is answered in the negative. In answer to question 1(ii) and (iii) I will make an appropriate declaration. Questions 1(iv) and (v) are answered in the affirmative. Question 1(vi) is answered in the affirmative by reference to para

(b) and s 13(1)(d) of the 1960 Act. I will hear such further argument on para 2 as any party wishes to advance.

Declarations accordingly.

Hazel Hartman   Barrister.

Note

Scher and others v Policyholders Protection Board and others (Nos 1 and 2)

Ackman and others v Policyholders Protection Board and others (Nos 1 and 2)

HOUSE OF LORDS
LORD TEMPLEMAN, LORD GRIFFITHS, LORD ACKNER, LORD GOFF OF CHIEVELEY AND LORD MUSTILL
10 FEBRUARY 1994

On further consideration of the cause *Scher and ors v Policyholders Protection Board and ors (Nos 1 and 2), Ackman and ors v Policyholders Protection Board and ors (Nos 1 and 2)* [1993] 3 All ER 384, [1993] 4 All ER 840, [1993] 3 WLR 357, 1030 the Appellate Committee of the House of Lords ordered that the third and fourth of the conjoined appeals be dismissed but that the declaration incorporated in the order of the Court of Appeal of 9 July 1992 be varied so that: (1) para 2(ii) (set out in the judgment of Lord Donaldson MR at [1993] 3 All ER 397 *a b*, [1993] 2 WLR 494 F G) should read: 'A person who is not the legal holder of the policy may, nevertheless, be a policyholder if a sum is due to him under the policy. A person is only a person to whom a sum is due within the meaning of the definition of "policyholder" in s 96 of the Insurance Companies Act 1982 if all the preconditions to the liability of the insurance company have been satisfied'; (2) para 3(c) (set out in the judgment of Lord Donaldson MR at [1993] 3 All ER 398 *a b*, [1993] 2 WLR 495 G H) should read: 'Being in partnership with a PC does not disqualify an individual from being a private policyholder if he contracts with the insurance company in a capacity other than as a partner'; and (3) the following additional declaration should be made: 'A person who is not a policyholder within the meaning of s 96(1) of the Insurance Companies Act 1982 at the beginning of the liquidation but becomes a policyholder subsequent to that date does not qualify as a policyholder entitled to claim under s 8(2) of the Policyholders Protection Act 1975'.

Celia Fox   Barrister.

Alliance and Leicester Building Society v Edgestop Ltd and other appeals

CHANCERY DIVISION
MUMMERY J
23, 26, 28, 30 APRIL 1993

Negligence – Contributory negligence – Employer and employee – Employee acting outside scope of employment – Deceit – Whether contributory negligence a defence to action for deceit – Law Reform (Contributory Negligence) Act 1945.

L, an employee of the defendant estate agents and valuers, was convicted of four offences of procuring the execution of a valuable security by deception, contrary to s 20[a] of the Theft Act 1968. In each case the valuable security consisted of documents authorising the telegraphic transfer of substantial sums of money from the plaintiffs, a building society and a finance company, to a client account of a firm of solicitors. The plaintiffs brought actions against the defendants alleging that L, in the course of his employment with the defendants, had fraudulently overvalued certain hotels in order to procure the plaintiffs to make substantial loans for the purchase and on the security of the hotels. It was alleged that the defendants were vicariously liable for the actions of L, who was their servant and agent acting within the scope of his actual or ostensible authority and on the defendants' behalf, and therefore the defendants were liable in deceit. The defendants pleaded contributory negligence to the finance company's claim and applied for leave to amend their defence to the society's claim to plead contributory negligence to that claim pursuant to s 1(1)[b] of the Law Reform (Contributory Negligence) Act 1945. The particulars of contributory negligence alleged were that the plaintiffs had failed to act according to their own lending polices and guidelines and had thereby failed to ascertain that L was not qualified to make the valuations and had acted outside the scope of his authority. The defence of contributory negligence to the finance company's claim was struck out and leave to amend the defence to the society's claim was refused. The defendants appealed.

Held – Contributory negligence was not a defence to an action for deceit at common law and nothing in the 1945 Act affected that position. Accordingly, a person liable for deceit, whether personally or vicariously, was not entitled to deny, by way of a plea of contributory negligence, that his deceit was the sole effective cause of the damage suffered by the victim. It followed that the defendants were not entitled to plead contributory negligence to the plaintiffs' claims. Furthermore, the defendants were not entitled to plead that the plaintiffs did not rely or were not entitled to rely on the valuations made by L because they had been made outside the scope of his authority, since L's conviction of offences of deception under s 20 of the 1968 Act had been based on the fact that the plaintiffs had relied on L's valuations. The defendants'

---

a Section 20, so far as material, is set out at p 53 *j*, post
b Section 1(1), so far as material, is set out at p 49 *h j*, post

appeal would therefore be dismissed (see p 50 f g, p 53 c d, p 54 e f and p 57 e, post).

Redgrave v Hurd (1881) 20 Ch D 1 applied.

Murphy v Culhane [1976] 3 All ER 533 and Gran Gelato Ltd v Richcliff (Group) Ltd [1992] 1 All ER 865 distinguished.

Notes

For contributory negligence, see 34 Halsbury's Laws (4th edn) paras 68–76, and for cases on the subject, see 36(1) Digest (2nd reissue) 415–463, 3346–4004.

For the Law Reform (Contributory Negligence) Act 1945, s 1, see 31 Halsbury's Statutes (4th edn) 185.

For the Theft Act 1968, s 20, see 12 Halsbury's Statutes (4th edn) (1989 reissue) 500.

Cases referred to in judgment

Armages Ltd v Mundogas SA, The Ocean Frost [1986] 2 All ER 385, [1986] AC 717, [1986] 2 WLR 1063, HL.

Attwood v Small (1838) 6 Cl & Fin 232, 7 ER 684, HL.

Dellabarca v Northern Storemen and Packers Union [1989] 2 NZLR 734, NZ HC.

Forsikringsaktieselskapet Vesta v Butcher (No 1) [1988] 2 All ER 43, [1989] AC 852, [1988] 3 WLR 565, CA.

Gran Gelato Ltd v Richcliff (Group) Ltd [1992] 1 All ER 865, [1992] Ch 560, [1992] 2 WLR 867.

Hoebergen v Koppens [1974] 2 NZLR 597, NZ SC.

K v P (J, third party) [1993] 1 All ER 521, [1993] Ch 140, [1992] 3 WLR 1015.

Lloyd v Grace, Smith & Co [1912] AC 716, [1911–13] All ER Rep 51, HL.

Murphy v Culhane [1976] 3 All ER 533, [1977] QB 94, [1976] 3 WLR 458, CA.

Quinn v Leathem [1901] AC 495, [1900–3] All ER Rep 1, HL.

Redgrave v Hurd (1881) 20 Ch D 1, CA.

Uxbridge Permanent Benefit Building Society v Pickard [1939] 2 All ER 344, [1939] 2 KB 248, CA.

Williams & Humbert Ltd v W & H Trade Marks (Jersey) Ltd [1986] 1 All ER 129, [1986] AC 368, [1986] 2 WLR 24, HL.

Cases also cited

Allan v Gotch (1883) 9 VLR (L) 371, Vict SC.

Apperson v US Fidelity and Guaranty Co (1963) 318 F 2d 438, US Ct of Apps (5th Cir).

Cload v Ferguson (1953) 10 WWR (NS) 426, Alta DC.

Directors of Central Railway Co of Venezuela v Kisch (1867) LR 2 HL 99.

Dobell v Stevens (1825) 3 B & C 623, 107 ER 864.

Dyer v Hargrave (1805) 10 Ves 505, 32 ER 941.

Edwards v M'Leay (1818) 2 Swanst 287, 36 ER 625.

Gipps v Gipps [1978] 1 NSWLR 454, CA.

Holund Holdings Ltd v Lewicky (1970) 12 DLR (3d) 398, BC SC.

Mathias v Yetts (1882) 46 LT 497, CA.

Mureprine Properties Ltd v Adhill Properties Ltd [1990] 36 EG 114.

Oudaille v Lawson (1922) 41 NZLR 259, NZ SC.

Sagar v Closer Settlement Ltd (1929) 29 SR (NSW) 199, NSW SC.

Smith v Chadwick (1884) 9 App Cas 187, HL.

Smith v Kay (1859) 7 HL Cas 750, 11 ER 299.

Variety Homes Inc v Postal Life Insurance Co (1961) 287 F 2d 320, US Ct of Apps (2nd Cir).
Wilkinson v Detmold (1890) 16 VLR 439, Vict SC.
World Insurance Co v Pipes (1958) 255 F 2d 464, US Ct of Apps (5th Cir).

Appeals

Hamptons Residential, a private unlimited company and the defendant in four actions brought by the Alliance and Leicester Building Society and Mercantile Credit Co Ltd claiming that Hamptons were vicariously liable for the deceit of an employee, James Lancaster, who had been convicted of procuring the execution by the plaintiffs of a valuable security by a deception, appealed from the orders of Master Gowers made on 12 February 1993 refusing Hamptons' application by summons to amend its defence to the building society's claim to plead contributory negligence and on 19 March granting Mercantile Credit's application by summons to strike out Hamptons' defence of contributory negligence. The facts are set out in the judgment.

Charles Purle QC and *Christopher G Russell* (instructed by *Mackenzie Mills* in the first three appeals and by *Mackenzie Mills*, agents for *Shoosmiths & Harrison*, Northampton, in the fourth appeal) for the plaintiffs.
John Slater QC and *Dominic Dowley* (instructed by *Davies Arnold Cooper*) for the defendant.

Cur adv vult

30 April 1993. The following judgment was delivered.

MUMMERY J. Hamptons Residential (Hamptons) is a private unlimited company carrying on the business of estate agents, valuers and auctioneers. In about March 1988 Hamptons acquired a firm of estate agents in Maidenhead, Messrs Giddy & Giddy, whose employees included Mr James Lancaster. Mr Lancaster became an employee of Hamptons. He remained so until 30 April 1989.

On 16 April 1992 Mr Lancaster was convicted in the Crown Court at Winchester of four offences of procuring the execution of a valuable security by deception contrary to s 20(2) of the Theft Act 1968. He was sentenced to 15 months' imprisonment. The valuable security consisted in each case of a document authorising the telegraphic transfer of a very substantial sum of money from the Alliance and Leicester Building Society (the society) to the client account of a firm of solicitors in Southall, Messrs W P Duckney, by making false representations to the society.

The deception in each case included false representations made in early 1989 in a loan application form as to the purchase price of a hotel to be acquired with the assistance of the loan from the society and also in a written valuation prepared by Mr Lancaster as to the value of the hotel.

This was all part of a massive mortgage fraud by Mr Lancaster and others who are defendants to three actions brought by the society, actions nos 193, 1041 and 1043, and a fourth action brought by Mercantile Credit Co Ltd, action no 7925, for repayment of loans, for reimbursement and for damages for deceit. The society's claim totals about £25m. The claim of Mercantile Credit is for about £4m. Hamptons is a defendant in each action. The claim against Hamptons is that it is vicariously liable for the deceit of Mr Lancaster.

The trial of the four actions was fixed to start on 20 April. The estimated length of hearing is three months. During the morning of the first day, it became clear that Hamptons would be the principal defendant, resisting the claims of the society and Mercantile Credit. Most of the other defendants are not represented. Some consented to judgment, others did not consent to judgment, but stated that they were not in a position to defend the claims and would not contest them.

The daily cause list sets out not only the four actions but twenty-two summonses and adjourned summonses. They relate to interlocutory disputes concerning preparations for the trial. Fortunately, through the good sense of the parties and their advisers and with the encouragement of the court, most of the disputes have been resolved by agreement. This judgment is concerned with one substantial pleading application made by Hamptons and opposed by the society and Mercantile Credit. Over three days were spent on argument.

The essential question is whether Hamptons is entitled in law to plead contributory negligence as a defence to the claims against it for vicarious liability for Mr Lancaster's deceit. In my judgment, it is not entitled to plead that defence. It would be possible to state the reasons for my decision briefly and in normal circumstances I would have preferred to do just that. I have, however, decided that I should set out reasons for my decision in greater detail than would normally be appropriate, as the point of law involved is one of some general interest and importance. There are other mortgage fraud cases waiting to be heard in these courts.

I have also had the benefit of full and careful argument from leading counsel on the pleadings and the relevant law. I understand that the parties may regard the point as sufficiently significant to justify an appeal to the Court of Appeal, possibly before the case proceeds to an opening on behalf of the society. A summary of the background to the litigation and of the pleadings will increase the length of this judgment, but it may make it more intelligible and save time and costs in the Court of Appeal.

The main action is no 193. The society and Mercantile Credit are the only active plaintiffs. The case brought by them against 15 defendants is best explained by taking as an example the claim made in respect of one of the hotels, the Webbington Hotel, Axbridge, Somerset. That was put up for sale in 1989 by its then owners, the Mendip Conference Centre Ltd, and Webbington Ltd. The society's case on this hotel can be summarised as follows.

Early in March 1989 the society received a written application for a loan from a private limited company incorporated in 1988 called Edgestop Ltd. The directors of Edgestop, the first defendant, are Mr Kumar and Mr Panchal, who are the second and third defendants. They signed the application form requesting a loan of £4,975,900 for the purchase of the Webbington Hotel at a price of £5,850,000 and also a further payment for the business, making a total of £6·3m.

On 16 March 1989 a written valuation of the hotel in the sum of £5,850,000 was supplied by Mr Lancaster, the sixth defendant. At that time he was an employee of Hamptons, the fifteenth defendant. The valuation also purported to be signed by a Mr R Sloan ARICS. On 23 March 1989 the application form and the written valuation were submitted to the society by the seventh defendant, Mr Robson, an insurance salesman. Edgestop retained a firm of solicitors, W P Duckney, to act in the purchase and mortgage of the hotel to the society. The partners in that firm, Mr William Duckney, Mr Mark

Duckney and Mr Kulvinder Dhaliwal, are the eighth, ninth and tenth defendants. The eleventh defendant, Mr Saldanha, was employed by that firm. He made a written report on title to the hotel to the society on 5 May 1989. The society also retained W P Duckney to act as its solicitors in the loan and mortgage.

On 11 May 1989 the society offered to Edgestop an advance of £5·5m to be secured on the hotel. The offer was accepted. On 12 May 1989 the society sent £4,947,116 to W P Duckney. The initial contract for the sale of the hotel by the vendors had not, however, been made with Edgestop. It had been made on 14 April 1989 with another company, Alfaro Investments Ltd, the fifth defendant. Alfaro is an Isle of Man company which agreed to purchase the hotel for £3·9m.

On the same day Alfaro agreed to sell the hotel for £4·2m to Tournay Ltd, the fourth defendant. Tournay is a Jersey company controlled or owned by Mr Kumar and Mr Panchal. W P Duckney acted as solicitors for Tournay. On the same day, Tournay agreed to sell the hotel to Edgestop for £6·125m. On 12 May 1989 Edgestop granted a legal charge over the hotel to the society. The excess of the loan over the purchase price paid to the initial vendors was divided between various defendants and others, including a company called Malvern Securities Ltd, the twelfth defendant, an Isle of Man company (since dissolved). Subsequently, there were defaults in payment under the legal charge, receivers were appointed by the court and these proceedings were started. Faced with these claims, the position taken by the various defendants is as follows. (1) Mr Kumar and Mr Panchal have consented to judgment. Both were convicted at the Winchester Crown Court of dishonestly procuring the execution of a valuable security, namely, a document authorising the telegraphic transfer of £4,947,116 from the society to the client account of Messrs W P Duckney by deception, ie false representations that they, or Edgestop, had agreed to purchase the Webbington Hotel from the existing owners for £6·3m in a genuine and arm's length transaction, that they intended to provide the balance of the purchase price from their own resources and that the hotel had been valued for and on behalf of Hamptons by R Sloan and Mr Lancaster at £5·85m. (2) Mr Lancaster was convicted of the same offence. He served a defence. His legal aid was revoked. He does not intend to take part in the trial, but does not consent to judgment. (3) Mr Saldanha was convicted of the same offence. He takes the same position as Mr Lancaster. (4) The partners in W P Duckney have consented to judgment in agreed terms, while reserving their position on the question of contribution and costs to a later stage. (5) No defences have been served by Tournay, Alfaro or Malvern Securities. (6) The case against the Bank of Credit and Commerce International SA, the fourteenth defendant, has been discontinued. That leaves (1) Mr Robson, who is legally aided, and denies personal liability for deceit and (2) Hamptons, contesting the claim of vicarious liability for Mr Lancaster's deceit.

Before I consider the claims against Hamptons, I should briefly summarise the position regarding other hotels subject to similar claims in action no 193 and the other actions. In action no 193 there are claims by the society against Hamptons in respect of the Kistor Hotel, Torquay, the Russell Hotel, Harrogate and the Yarborough Hotel, Grimsby. There are claims by the society in action no 1041 in respect of the Haseley House Hotel, Haseley in Warwickshire and in action no 1043 by the society in respect of the Regency Hotel, Leicester.

In the fourth action, no 7925, brought by Mercantile Credit, there are claims in respect of the Royal Hotel, Clacton-on-Sea, and the Grand Hotel, Clacton-on-Sea. Although I shall concentrate in my judgment on action no 193 and leave certain aspects of action no 7925 for further argument, I mention these hotels now for several reasons.

Mr Lancaster was convicted in the Crown Court at Winchester of offences in relation to only four of the hotels: Haseley House Hotel, Webbington Hotel, Yarborough Hotel and Regency Hotel. Those convictions are not contested by Hamptons. Hamptons has now taken the decision to admit the fraud by Mr Lancaster in relation to all eight hotels. In those circumstances the society and Mercantile Credit have decided not to pursue claims for negligence against Mr Lancaster and against Hamptons in relation to the valuation of the hotels. The only claim against Hamptons now is for deceit on the basis of vicarious liability.

I now turn to the way in which the case is put against Hamptons in the rerereamended statement of claim and amended particulars thereunder. The case is briefly this.

Mr Lancaster was employed by Hamptons until 30 April 1989. He signed written valuations of hotels for and on behalf of Hamptons. By those valuations Mr Lancaster, and, by him, Hamptons, represented to the society that the valuations were his honest opinion as to the true value of the hotel in question and that, where another signature appeared, for example, R Sloan ARICS or V Evans FRICS, in those cases it was a joint valuation by himself and Mr Sloan or Mr Evans and that the signature of Mr Sloan and Mr Evans was genuine.

It is alleged that the purchase of the hotels and the sales through creature companies, such as Tournay, were made in performance of a common fraudulent enterprise to which Mr Lancaster was a party. The enterprise was to procure loans by fraud from the society. The valuations were false and fraudulently made by Mr Lancaster and, through him, by Hamptons, in that the valuations stated did not represent his honest opinion of the value of the hotel and that it was not a joint valuation of himself and Mr Sloan, but was his valuation, and the signature purporting to be that of R Sloan was a forgery.

It is alleged that Hamptons is vicariously liable for the actions of Mr Lancaster, its servant and agent, who acted within the scope of his authority and on its behalf and that it is therefore liable in deceit to the society. More details are given in the pleadings on the authority point.

It is alleged that Mr Lancaster had express or implied authority to value commercial properties of all types, size and value, including hotels, for clients, including lending institutions. He had such authority originally on behalf of Giddy & Giddy and subsequently on behalf of Hamptons, who submitted invoices to its clients for Mr Lancaster's services in respect of such valuations and reports.

Alternatively, Mr Lancaster had ostensible authority on behalf of Hamptons to value the hotels. Hamptons represented that Mr Lancaster had authority to value hotels on its behalf by its conduct in placing Mr Lancaster, or permitting him to be placed, in a position of authority to value commercial properties, including hotels, on behalf of its clients, including lending institutions. Having regard to the conduct of Hamptons, it is alleged that it was reasonable for the society to rely upon such representations. Finally, it is alleged that Mr Lancaster also had actual or ostensible authority not only to make representations concerning his opinion of the value of the hotels but also to represent to the society that he had carried out a joint valuation and to make representations to the society concerning the genuineness of any signature and to receive on behalf of Hamptons fees for valuations and other payments for services rendered on behalf of Hamptons.

I turn to the defence Hamptons originally served to those claims. It was a 14-page document served on 19 October 1990. It was later amplified by particulars which are proposed to be amended.

In summary the case raised in that defence was that Hamptons employed Mr Lancaster as a land buyer until about 30 April 1989. He was employed in the land department. He was concerned with residential property, with proposed residential developments and with advising prospective vendors and purchasers of the value of land for residential development. Neither the land department in general nor Mr Lancaster in particular was authorised to have involvement with any commercial property, except to comment on the potential of such property for residential development. He was not authorised to survey or value hotels or other commercial premises.

It is alleged that Mr Lancaster was not at any time authorised by Hamptons to carry out surveys or valuations on behalf of lending institutions or to make reports for building societies on the value of property. It is denied that he was authorised to receive money on behalf of Hamptons. He was never a qualified chartered surveyor or otherwise professionally qualified as a valuer.

Hamptons, it is alleged, was unaware of his activities at the material time. Those activities relied on in the statement of claim were not within the scope of his authority from Hamptons. Hamptons are not vicariously liable to the society for his activities. The valuations in question, although signed by Mr Lancaster, were not given on behalf of Hamptons and were not authorised by it. Mr Lancaster was not authorised to make joint valuations or to represent to the society that he had done so or to make any representations concerning the genuineness of any signature.

It is alleged that the society did not rely on and was not entitled to rely on any representations concerning the value of the hotels made by Mr Lancaster. Hamptons, in brief, did not make any representations to the society and is not liable to the society in deceit or to reimburse it or to make any payments to it.

I now consider briefly the procedural position surrounding the application for leave to make the amendments.

Hamptons wishes to make amendments to its defence to raise the defence of contributory negligence. The applications for amendment came before me in a procedurally confused state. Rather than waste time and money trying to untie the procedural knots in an action which must be costing thousands of pounds a day, I promptly acceded to Hamptons' application to take a shortcut. I should briefly explain the position, in case comment or complaint is made at a later stage.

In December 1992 Hamptons' solicitors provided the society's solicitors with a draft amended defence. The draft sought to raise, inter alia, the defence of contributory negligence to the claim for deceit. The society objected to the proposed amendments. Hamptons took out summonses seeking leave to amend its defences in actions nos 193, 1041 and 1043 to raise the plea of contributory negligence.

Hamptons had already pleaded contributory negligence in its defence to the Mercantile Credit claim in action no 7925 in response to claims against it both in negligence and in deceit. Mercantile Credit applied to strike out that defence of contributory negligence on the same grounds that it and the society objected to the application for leave to amend the defences in the other actions.

On 12 February 1993 Master Gowers decided that the plea of contributory negligence to the claim based in deceit, although not to the claim based in negligence in action no 7925, was demurrable. He refused leave to amend to raise that plea. On 19 March 1993 he went on to strike out that part of the defence in action no 7925 which pleaded contributory negligence to deceit. Hamptons appealed against those orders.

Unfortunately, after the master's order, Hamptons served a defence amended in red, to the extent that it had been allowed by the master. The defence also apparently contained amendments consequential on the society's earlier service of an amended statement of claim. When I came to hear the appeals against the master's orders there was put before me a draft reamended defence coloured in both red and green. The society objected that the draft was not the same draft as had been put before the master on the application for leave to amend. It contained further amendments.

It was quite obvious after I started to hear the application that it was difficult, if not impossible, to disentangle the amendments originally proposed from those new amendments made after leave had been sought from the master. I resolved the matter by acceding to an application made on behalf of Hamptons to withdraw the amended defence and to serve the new pleading in its present form. This is without prejudice to the right of the society to comment on the extent to which the amendments now proposed were made at different times since last December.

It is common ground that in dealing with the summons for leave to amend and the appeal against the striking-out order in action no 7925 I should adopt the approach of Lord Templeman in *Williams & Humbert Ltd v W & H Trade Marks (Jersey) Ltd* [1986] 1 All ER 129, [1986] AC 368.

That case concerned a motion by plaintiffs to strike out part of a defence which pleaded Spanish law. The judge at first instance made a striking-out order and refused leave to amend a defence in a related action, the purpose of the amendment being also to plead matters of Spanish law. The judge at first instance spent seven days hearing the striking-out application. His order was upheld on appeal. Lord Templeman said ([1986] 1 All ER 129 at 139, [1986] AC 368 at 436):

> 'My Lords, if an application to strike out involves a prolonged and serious argument the judge should, as a general rule, decline to proceed with the argument unless he not only harbours doubts about the soundness of the pleading but, in addition, is satisfied that striking out will obviate the necessity for a trial or will substantially reduce the burden of preparing for trial or the burden of the trial itself.'

Adopting this approach, the society opposed Hamptons application for leave to amend and the appeal against the striking-out order, to plead contributory negligence on the ground that such a plea is not available in law to Mr Lancaster and is, therefore, not available in law to Hamptons, if it is established that it is vicariously liable for his acts.

It was argued on behalf of the society that the decision on the legal point should be made now. The court should keep the new allegations off the pleadings. It should not put off a decision on the legal point until after the court had heard all the documentary evidence and the oral evidence relating to allegations about the society's negligence. It was argued that the effect of allowing the amendment would be to increase the length and cost of the trial to no purpose, because the point was doomed to failure.

Further, it was submitted that, if the amendments were allowed, the society would require an adjournment in order to prepare for trial on these new matters. Such an adjournment in consequence of these new matters might also result in an application for discovery of further documents arising out of the amendment.

Against that background I consider the extensive amendments proposed. The defence served by Hamptons on 19 October 1990 was 14-pages long. The defence Hamptons now wishes to serve, which has been evolving since last December, is 65-pages long. No useful purpose would be served and much time would be wasted by tracing the various stages through which the defence has gone since last December or by setting out in this judgment the details of the amendments. Some of those amendments are not contentious. The amendments objected to are principally in para 53B and other paragraphs which contain cross references to it.

The objections of the society are to amendments proposed in the following paragraphs or parts of them: paras 7, 10, 15B, 18, 21, 26B, 29, 33, 39A, 42, 46, 52B and 53B. In order to avoid extensive and unnecessary repetition, I shall attempt to summarise the proposed amendments.

The essence of the principal amendment is stated in para 53B of the draft defence, following a summary of a series of valuations of the hotels made by Mr Lancaster and submitted to the society between late January 1989 and late April 1989 in support of applications for lending. The pleading alleges:

> 'For the reasons set out in the following sub-paragraphs, the society was negligent in failing to discover, in the case of each of the above valuations, that Mr Lancaster was acting outside the scope of his employment and dishonestly in providing the valuations and in failing to detect the dishonesty of the applications for finance. Had the society discovered these matters in the case of any of the valuations or applications, that and all subsequent valuations and applications would have been rejected and all losses which are now alleged to have resulted from them would have been avoided.'

The next 40 pages or so contain six main sub-paragraphs under which detailed particulars are given. I shall attempt to summarise each relevant paragraph.

(1) The society's panel valuers (para 53B(2))

It is alleged that the society kept lists of surveyors and valuers whom it was prepared to use to carry out valuations of property on the security of which it was considering lending money. Prior to admitting a valuer or firm of valuers to that list, the society required to be satisfied as to the competence and good standing of the valuer or firm in question. The society kept separate lists of surveyors and valuers for residential property and of surveyors and valuers for commercial property. Valuations of commercial properties by surveyors and valuers who were on the residential panel only were not acceptable to the society. None of the valuations purported to come from any name used by Hamptons which was on the society's list of commercial surveyors and valuers or on the society's list of residential surveyors and valuers. The society had no grounds for believing that Hamptons practised as surveyors experienced in commercial valuations or, in particular, in valuing hotels.

In these circumstances neither Hamptons nor Mr Lancaster was authorised to carry out valuations of commercial property or of any property for the society and the society at all times was aware of this.

The sub-paragraph pleads that the society had internal office instructions providing that valuers should normally only be used in towns against which their names were listed and that care should be taken not to instruct valuers outside the normal area.

None of the properties valued by Mr Lancaster were within the geographical area of any of the offices of Hamptons from which Mr Lancaster sent, or purported to send, his reports to the society.

It is alleged that it would have been a simple matter for the society to check its list of panel surveyors and valuers. Any reasonably prudent lender would have done so, particularly where the valuations had not been commissioned by the lender but by the applicant for the loan. Had a check been made, in accordance with the society's own internal procedures, it would have been apparent that the valuations had not been carried out by one of the society's panel firms.

That having been discovered, a check could easily have been made with Hamptons' offices in Maidenhead or London as to the relevant firm's expertise in valuing properties, particularly hotels and commercial properties, outside the locality of the firm in question. Such a check was necessary for the society to satisfy itself that the property had been properly valued by a competent person and that the society had complied with its statutory obligations under s 13 of the Building Societies Act 1986. A reasonably prudent lender would have made such a check on receipt of the first of a series of valuations. Had such a check been made, Mr Lancaster's lack of authority and/or dishonesty would have been discovered and each of the frauds would have been avoided.

The names of R Sloan, V Evans and J Lancaster did not appear on the society's list of surveyors and valuers. The society ought to have taken steps to ensure that these individuals were properly qualified, competent and of good standing, for example, by checking in the current Royal Institute of Chartered Surveyors (RICS) handbook. A check would have disclosed that there was no member of the RICS called R Sloan who practised as, or was associated with, Hamptons; that there was no V Evans listed as a Fellow or Associate of the RICS and that Mr Lancaster did not feature anywhere in the handbook. These discoveries would have led a reasonably prudent lender to make inquiries at Hamptons. Had those inquiries been made, each fraud would have been prevented.

(2) *Qualifications of valuers (para 53(3))*

According to its office instructions, the society required valuations to be undertaken by a qualified person, for example, an associate or fellow of the RICS. It should have been apparent to the society from the first valuation submitted to it by Mr Lancaster in respect of the Kistor Hotel that the valuation had not been carried out by a properly qualified person but had, at best, been countersigned by such a person. Had the society insisted on compliance with its own requirements, which were also the requirements of s 13 of the Building Societies Act 1986, that valuation and/or subsequent valuations would not have been accepted and all the frauds would have been prevented. Since the society knew that Mr Lancaster was not qualified to carry out a valuation for a building society the society knew that he was not and would not be authorised to do so.

(3) Lending standards (para 53B(4))

It is alleged that no reasonably prudent lender would have lent money for the purchase of an hotel unless satisfied as to the continuing ability of the borrower to be able to meet the loan repayments throughout the period of the loan. A reasonably prudent lender would, regardless of the valuation, have declined to advance money for the purchase of an hotel unless the hotel had competent management in situ and the business had sustained an ample capacity to service the loan being sought.

The society's own internal procedures required data to be sought in the case of each loan by way of references, CVs, certified accounts, business projections, and so on. The society did not comply with its own criteria for loans.

It was apparent to the society, or would have been apparent to a reasonably prudent lender, that the business in question was unlikely to produce sufficient profit to service the loan and that the applicants were unlikely to be experienced in the running of an hotel or even a business in general and/or were dishonest. Any reasonably prudent lender would have declined each application. Extensive particulars are given of the allegations in relation to each hotel.

(4) Lending authorities (para 53B(5))

It is alleged that the society's policy was that lending in excess of £5m required the approval of the board of the society. In breach of this requirement, the society agreed the loan for the purchase of the Webbington Hotel which brought the society's total lending to Mr Kumar and Mr Panchal to £8·8m and then agreed to a further loan in respect of the Yarborough Hotel, in each case without reference to the board.

(5) Basis of valuation (para 53B(6))

It is alleged that the society required valuations for mortgage purposes to be exclusive of valuations attributable to goodwill, stock, fixtures and fittings. In the case of Mr Lancaster's valuations, their true basis was not apparent from the valuations themselves nor did the society take any, or adequate, steps to clarify the basis of the valuations in order to determine whether the valuations were in accordance with the society's own requirements.

(6) Features of individual transactions (para 53B(7))

It is alleged that the individual valuations themselves and the circumstances in which they were given had numerous other unusual features which would have put any reasonably prudent lender on inquiry and ought to have led the society to make inquiries of Hamptons as to the authority and expertise of Mr Lancaster, Mr Sloan and Mr Evans. The applications from prospective borrowers would, similarly, have put any reasonably prudent lender, and ought to have put the society, on inquiry as to the honesty of the applications for the loans in relation to the first valuation, the Kistor Hotel, were sufficient in themselves to put the society on inquiry and would have led any reasonably prudent lender to the discovery of Mr Lancaster's lack of authority and/or his dishonesty and the lack of honesty in the applications.

Thereafter, in the case of each subsequent transaction, there were further irregular or suspicious features of the valuations and the applications for loans which should have added to the society's concern and would have led any reasonably prudent lender to decline to provide any finance. There follow very detailed particulars in respect of each hotel.

On reading the original pleadings and comparing them with the proposed amendments, I quickly formed the view that, first, I had a serious doubt about the soundness of the parts struck out of the pleading in action no 7925 and about the amendments which the master had refused leave to make. Secondly, I formed the view that, if the allegations remain on the pleading in action no 7925 and are allowed to be pleaded in the other actions, there would be a substantial increase in the length and cost of the trial. There would be more witnesses (including experts), more documents, more law and more argument.

I therefore allowed argument to proceed over three-and-a-half days. At the end of it, I reached the conclusion that the master was right in refusing leave to amend in action no 193 and the other actions.

I deal now with the various points made on behalf of Hamptons in justification of the proposed amendments. The first is the contributory negligence point.

In reliance on all the matters summarised above, Hamptons states its position briefly in the proposed amended pleading:

> 'The society's lending in the case of each of the loans was unresearched, contrary to its own lending policies and guidelines, imprudent and negligent amounting to fault within the meaning of s 1(1) of the Law Reform (Contributory Negligence) Act 1945 and in the premises the society was the sole or part author of its own misfortune in suffering the loss and damage alleged.'

This repeats a point made earlier in the pleading that, so far as the society suffered any loss and damage following deceit or fraud on the part of Mr Lancaster, such loss or fraud resulted from the society's own fault and the society was wholly or partly responsible for such loss and damage.

It was submitted on behalf of Hamptons that it is, at the very least, reasonably arguable that there is a defence of contributory negligence on the part of the society and Mercantile Credit to the claims made against Hamptons as vicariously liable for the admitted deceit of Mr Lancaster. In order to test that submission, it is necessary to look at the 1945 Act. Section 1(1) is in these terms.

> 'Where any person suffers damage as the result partly of his own fault and partly of the fault of any other person or persons, a claim in respect of that damage shall not be defeated by reason of the fault of the person suffering the damage, but the damages recoverable in respect thereof shall be reduced to such extent as the court thinks just and equitable having regard to the claimant's share in the responsibility for the damage ...'

It is provided by s 4 that damage 'includes loss of life and personal injury'. It is not in dispute that damage may include financial loss. This certainly seems to have been assumed to be so in cases concerned with professional negligence where there may also be a concurrent liability in contract.

Section 4 also defines 'fault':

'"fault" means negligence, breach of statutory duty or other act or omission which gives rise to a liability in tort or would, apart from this Act, give rise to the defence of contributory negligence ...'

There is judicial authority on the interpretation of this definition. It was held by the Court of Appeal in the case of *Forsikringsaktieselskapet Vesta v Butcher (No 1)* [1988] 2 All ER 43 at 48ff, [1989] AC 852 at 862ff that both limbs of the definition of fault apply when considering the conduct of the plaintiff who suffers damage. If the plaintiff's fault is within the first limb of the definition it will also be within the second limb. The second limb is, however, necessary because the plaintiff's conduct amounting to contributory negligence may or may not involve a tort or other breach of duty owed to the defendant.

The defendant, however, cannot be at 'fault' unless he has committed a breach of duty which he owes to the plaintiff, ie unless the first limb of the definition is satisfied. Damages recoverable by the plaintiff from the defendant in respect of that breach of duty are liable to be reduced where the damage is also partly the result of the plaintiff's own fault, whether within the first or second limb.

The important point for present purposes is that, if the plaintiffs' conduct does not fall within the first limb, it is only caught by the second limb if it amounts to the sort of conduct which would, apart from the Act, give rise to a defence of contributory negligence. In the present case it is not argued by Hamptons that the society's alleged conduct gives rise to any liability in tort to Mr Lancaster or to Hamptons. The crucial question is, therefore, whether it would give rise to the defence of contributory negligence, apart from the Act, within the second limb of the definition.

There is no decision precisely on the point whether contributory negligence could be a defence to a claim for deceit. In principle, however, the position, before and apart, from the Act is clear. The contributory negligence of a plaintiff suing in deceit could not be pleaded as a defence. There are at least three reasons for this. (1) At common law contributory negligence of a plaintiff is no defence in the case of an intentional tort. As Lord Lindley said in *Quinn v Leathem* [1901] AC 495 at 537, [1900–3] All ER Rep 1 at 17: 'The intention to injure the plaintiff negatives all excuses ...' See also *Clerk and Lindsell on Tort* (16th edn, 1989) paras 1-115, 1-139, pp 79, 98. Deceit is a tort intentionally committed. (2) At common law a successful plea of contributory negligence would have startling consequences in the context of deceit. Before and apart from the Act, contributory negligence of a plaintiff would defeat the plaintiff's entire claim. Apart from the case of property damage at sea, governed by s 1 of the Maritime Conventions Act 1911, there was no power to apportion liability on the grounds of blameworthiness. If the plea of contributory negligence were available to a person against whom deceit was established he would escape all liability for his fraud. That result would be even more absurd and unjust than that in negligence cases where a plaintiff who had suffered serious damage, mainly as a result of the defendant's negligence, could recover nothing if he were partly to blame for the damage he had suffered. (3) That result would also have offended against the general principle stated by Jessel MR in *Redgrave v Hurd* (1881) 20 Ch D 1. He laid down general principles applicable in misrepresentation cases. Although that case was decided in the context of the equitable remedies of specific performance and rescission, his statements have been treated for over a century as applicable to claims for damages for misrepresentation. He said (at 13–14):

> 'Nothing can be plainer, I take it, on the authorities in equity than that the effect of false representation is not got rid of on the ground that the person to whom it was made has been guilty of negligence.'

He said of a person who had made a material representation to another inducing him to enter into a contract (at 21):

> 'If it is a material representation calculated to induce him to enter into the contract, it is an inference of law that he was induced by the representation to enter into it, and in order to take away his title to be relieved from the contract on the ground that the representation was untrue, it must be shewn either that he had knowledge of the facts contrary to the representation, or that he stated in terms, or shewed clearly by his conduct, that he did not rely on the representation.'

It was argued before Jessel MR, and was faintly argued before me, that the legal position is different on a true reading of the earlier decision of the House of Lords in *Attwood v Small* (1838) 6 Cl & Fin 232, 7 ER 684. I reject that submission since I am bound by the decision in *Redgrave v Hurd* rejecting the contention that *Attwood v Small* supported the proposition that a representee is at fault if he has had the opportunity to investigate the truth of the representation but does not avail himself of it or if he makes his own inquiries but does so carelessly.

That, in my view, was the position before 1945. Has it been changed by the 1945 Act? Mr Slater QC, on behalf of Hamptons, submitted that it has. The statute confers on the court in wide terms a power to reduce damages for tort to such extent as the court thinks just and equitable having regard to the claimant's share in the responsibility for the damage.

Mr Slater accepted that, in exercising that power of apportionment, the court might well regard it as just and equitable that a successful plaintiff in an action for fraud should not have his damages substantially reduced on the grounds of his negligence, thereby relieving the defendant from some of the consequences of the fraudulent conduct for which he is personally or vicariously liable. Mr Slater said that in a claim of this size, totalling almost £30m, even a 10% reduction would involve a substantial sum. He argued that the amendments should be allowed so that the court can consider at a later stage whether it is appropriate to exercise the power.

He submitted that the position had been altered from the common law position by the terms of the 1945 Act and that this is recognised in the following authorities.

First, the defence of contributory fault had been allowed since the Act in a case where the plaintiff's claim was for damages for a tort intentionally committed. *Murphy v Culhane* [1976] 3 All ER 533, [1977] QB 94 is a decision of the Court of Appeal. In that case, the deceased's widow claimed damages for the death of her husband. She alleged unlawful assault and manslaughter against the defendant. The defence pleaded that the assault occurred during a criminal affray in which the deceased had participated. Lord Denning MR said that the widow's claim for damages might fall to be reduced under the 1945 Act because 'the conduct of [the deceased man] may well have been such as to make him liable in tort' (see [1976] 3 All ER 533 at 536, [1977] QB 94 at 99).

Lord Denning MR regarded the case as potentially falling within the first limb of the definition of 'fault' in s 4 of the 1945 Act.

The case is not on all fours with the present case for two reasons. First, it is not a case of deceit, to which different considerations applied before the Act and may well continue to apply. Secondly, the conduct of the plaintiff against whom contributory negligence was pleaded might have made him liable in tort and, therefore, liable to a counterclaim or action for damages. That is not the case here. It is no part of Hamptons' case that the society is liable to it for damages in negligence or for breach of duty. The society's conduct, if it amounts to fault at all, is only within the second limb of s 4 which requires the court to look at the position apart from the Act.

For completeness I add a reference to two New Zealand cases which show that there may be doubt whether the 1945 Act ever applies to torts intentionally committed.

In *Dellabarca v Northern Storemen and Packers Union* [1989] 2 NZLR 734 at 757, a decision of the High Court of New Zealand, Smellie J held that contributory negligence is not available as a defence to an intentional tort. In that case the torts were inducement of breach of contract and conspiracy. An attempt was made, unsuccessfully, to plead that the plaintiff was at fault in having made corrupt payments to a number of members of the first defendant's firm.

In reaching that decision, he did not follow an earlier decision of the New Zealand Supreme Court, a decision of Moller J in *Hoebergen v Koppens* [1974] 2 NZLR 597 at 601–602. In that case Moller J held that, in an action for assault brought by a plaintiff, a defendant was entitled to plead by way of contributory negligence that the plaintiff had provoked him by abusive language to commit the assault sued upon.

Mr Slater contended that a recent decision of Sir Donald Nicholls V-C, *Gran Gelato Ltd v Richcliff (Group) Ltd* [1992] 1 All ER 865, [1992] Ch 560, supported the submission that contributory negligence is available as a defence to deceit. In my view, that case does not give Hamptons the support counsel sought to extract from it. Sir Donald Nicholls V-C held that the defence of contributory negligence could be raised as a defence to concurrent claims for misrepresentation for breach of a common law duty of care and for breach of s 2(1) of the Misrepresentation Act 1967. It is true that that section makes a reference to fraud. It refers to a situation 'had the misrepresentation been fraudulently made'.

Sir Donald Nicholls V-C held, however, after citing the section, that liability under s 2(1) was 'essentially founded on negligence' (see [1992] 1 All ER 865 at 875, [1992] Ch 560 at 573). He added that it would be very odd if the defence of contributory negligence were not available to a claim made under that Act when it was available to a claim for breach of the common law duty.

That approach is consistent with earlier decisions which held that the defence of contributory negligence can be pleaded to a claim in tort where there is a concurrent claim for breach of contract in respect of the same conduct: see *Forsikringsaktieselskapet Vesta v Butcher (No 1)* [1989] 1 All ER 402, [1989] AC 852.

In my judgment, *Gran Gelato* is not authority for the proposition that the defence is available where the claim is for a tort intentionally committed. It is available because the claim under s 2(1) of the 1967 Act is essentially one of negligence.

Sir Donald Nicholls V-C declined to make any reduction in the plaintiff's damages on the ground that, in principle, carelessness in not making inquiries provides no answer to a claim that the plaintiff has done that which the representor intended that he should do.

Mr Slater relied on a decision of Ferris J in *K v P (J third party)* [1993] 1 All ER 521, [1993] Ch 140. That was a case on the Civil Liability (Contribution) Act 1978. Ferris J refused to strike out a contribution claim for negligence sought to be made by the defendant sued for conspiracy to defraud. He rejected the application to strike out, which was founded on the argument that such a claim was ex turpi causa. That decision does not assist Hamptons in this case.

In my judgment, neither the 1945 Act nor any decision on it affects the general principles laid down by Jessel MR on the unavailability of the defence of negligence to an action for deceit. That view is taken in the textbooks. In my opinion, it is correct: see *Winfield and Jolowicz on Tort* (13th edn, 1989) p 159 and *Clerk and Lindsell on Torts* (16th edn, 1989) para 1-143, p 100. In brief, a person liable for deceit, whether personally or vicariously, is not entitled as a matter of law to deny, by a plea of contributory negligence, that his deceit was the sole effective cause of the damage suffered by his victim. Nothing in the Act in principle or on authority entitles a person liable for deceit to plead contributory negligence.

Another facet of the amendments is concerned with reliance. Relying on many of the facts and matters pleaded in para 53B of the proposed amended defence, Hamptons pleads that the society did not rely, and was not entitled to rely, on any representations made by Mr Lancaster (see para 53B(b) of the pleading).

This point is expressly pleaded in earlier paragraphs in which Hamptons denies that the society relied on, or was entitled to rely upon, any representation concerning the value of the hotels made by Mr Lancaster. It is averred that what the society, in fact, relied on were Mr Lancaster's representations that a valuation for mortgage advance had been performed and/or signed by a qualified member of Hamptons' staff, that the signature of the named valuer was genuine, and that both Mr Lancaster and the valuer were acting for and on behalf of Hamptons.

It is pleaded that, in making those representations, Mr Lancaster was acting fraudulently and for his own purpose and was not acting within the scope of any actual or ostensible authority given by Hamptons and that he was not acting in the course of his employment by Hamptons. These matters are pleaded in paras 10, 21, 33 and 46.

Hamptons submitted that the matters raised in the amendments to these paragraphs and in para 53B are relevant to the question whether the society in fact relied upon, or was entitled to rely on, Mr Lancaster's representations and, if so, which representations. The amendments should be allowed on that point, even if disallowed on the question of contributory negligence.

I do not accept this argument. The offences for which Mr Lancaster was convicted were contrary to s 20(2) of the Theft Act 1968. That provides:

> 'A person who dishonestly, with a view to gain for himself or another or with intent to cause loss to another, by any deception procures the execution of a valuable security shall on conviction on indictment be liable to imprisonment for a term not exceeding seven years ...'

The obtaining must be 'by' deception. This is clear from the commentary by Professor J C Smith in *The Law of Theft* (6th edn, 1989) p 84. He says: 'It must be proved that the false statement actually deceived P and caused him to do whatever act is appropriate to the offence charged.' So if P does not rely on the false statement, D is not guilty of obtaining. 'The onus is on the prosecution to prove that the representation operated on P's mind.'

Under s 11 of the Civil Evidence Act 1968 the fact of conviction is admissible in evidence in civil proceedings for the purpose of proving, where to do so is relevant to any issue in the proceedings, that he committed the offence. By s 11(2) it is provided:

> 'In any civil proceedings in which by virtue of this section a person is proved to have been convicted of an offence by or before any court in the United Kingdom ... (a) he shall be taken to have committed that offence, unless the contrary is proved ... [I pause there to state that Hamptons does not seek to prove the contrary] (b) without prejudice to the reception of any other admissible evidence for the purpose of identifying the facts on which the conviction was based, the contents of any document which is admissible as evidence of his conviction, and the contents of the information, complaint, indictment or charge-sheet on which the person in question was convicted, shall be admissible in evidence for this purpose.'

Mr Lancaster was convicted of offences under s 20(2) on charges on indictment in respect of four hotels. Hamptons does not seek to prove that he did not commit those offences. In those circumstances, the question of reliance by the society on Mr Lancaster's representations to the society has already been determined and cannot be reopened. The same applies to the other four hotels in respect of which Hamptons now admits that Mr Lancaster committed fraud. Those admissions preclude any point that the society did not rely on Mr Lancaster's representations.

I now consider the question of authority. Relying on matters in para 53B and other paragraphs of the pleading, Hamptons pleads that the society knew or had constructive knowledge of Mr Lancaster's lack of authority: see para 53B(a) of the pleading. It is pleaded specifically in earlier paragraphs, by reference to the matters pleaded in para 53B, that the society was, or ought reasonably to have been aware, of Mr Lancaster's lack of authority (see paras 7, 18, 29, and 42).

It was argued on behalf of Hamptons that the matters raised in the amendments, in particular para 53B, are not exclusively referable to the plea of contributory negligence. No time would be saved by disallowing the plea of contributory negligence, because the facts pleaded are all relevant to another aspect of the case, namely, circumstances going to authority, ie whether the society knew or had constructive knowledge of Mr Lancaster's lack of authority and whether, therefore, a plea of ostensible authority was open to the society.

For this part of its argument, Hamptons relied strongly on the statement of Lord Keith at the end of his speech in *Armagas Ltd v Mundogas, The Ocean Frost* [1986] 2 All ER 385 at 394, [1986] AC 717 at 782:

> 'In the end of the day the question is whether the circumstances under which a servant has made the fraudulent misrepresentation which has caused loss to an innocent party contracting with him are such as to make it just for the employer to bear the loss. Such circumstances exist where the employer by words or conduct has induced the injured party to believe

that the servant was acting in the lawful course of his employer's business. They do not exist where such belief, although it is present, has been brought about through misguided reliance on the servant himself, when the servant is not authorised to do what he is purporting to do, when what he is purporting to do is not within the class of acts that an employee in his position is usually authorised to do and when the employer has done nothing to represent that he is authorised to do it.'

In his very able submissions on behalf of Hamptons, Mr Slater focused on the expressions, whether the circumstances 'make it just for the employer to bear the loss', and 'misguided reliance on the servant himself'. He submitted that, even when the cause of action is fraud, an investigation into the justice of all the circumstances in general, and into the society's misguided reliance in particular on Mr Lancaster's representations is permissible. I do not accept the submission that this passage in Lord Keith's speech requires or justifies a broad 'justice in the circumstances of the case' approach to the question of ostensible authority, giving rise to liability of an employer for the fraudulent representations of his employees.

The passage cited is not a formulation or re-formulation of the rules or principles regarding ostensible authority and vicarious liability for an employee's fraud. It is simply a general explanation of the reasons why the courts in such cases reach different decisions in different circumstances.

The passage cited must be read in context, and the speech of Lord Keith must be read as a whole. In that case it was accepted by the plaintiffs that the defendant's vice-president and chartering manager did not have actual or ostensible general authority to enter into a three-year charterparty on behalf of his principal (see [1986] 2 All ER 385 at 389, [1986] AC 717 at 776). The plaintiff's case was that he had ostensible specific authority to enter into the particular contract. Lord Keith went out of his way to say that such a case was very rare and unusual, especially where the contractor knew that the agent had no general authority to enter into the transaction. It is also clear from Lord Keith's speech that the fundamental principles governing vicarious liability in the field of intentional wrongdoing, such as dishonest conduct, were regarded as well settled by him 'in a line of authority of peculiar application' (see [1986] 2 All ER 385 at 391–394, [1986] AC 717 at 779–782). According to that line of authority, the question of ostensible authority in the contractual field is closely intertwined with that of vicarious liability for the fraud of the servant. The law was settled by the House of Lords in *Lloyd v Grace Smith & Co* [1912] AC 716, [1911–13] All ER Rep 51 and by the Court of Appeal in *Uxbridge Permanent Benefit Building Society v Pickard* [1939] 2 All ER 344 at 346–348, [1939] 2 KB 248 at 252–254. The essential principle is that stated by Lord Keith ([1986] 2 All ER 385 at 393, [1986] AC 717 at 781):

'The essential feature for creating liability in the employer is that the party contracting with the fraudulent servant should have altered his position to his detriment in reliance on the belief that the servant's activities were within his authority, or, to put it another way, were part of his job, this belief having been induced by the master's representations by way of words or conduct.'

What Lord Keith said in the later passage cited by Mr Slater, must be read in the context of his earlier statement of the fundamental principle or rule relating to ostensible authority. I conclude that Mr Slater's submissions on this aspect of the case state the approach of the court too widely. On the question of actual or ostensible authority, it is not permissible to plead a whole mass of allegations and particulars relating to the alleged negligence or carelessness of the society in dealing with the applications for loans.

I add this, however. It appears from *Chitty on Contracts* (26th edn, 1989) vol 2, p 36, para 2545, that there may be cases in which a third party cannot hold the principal liable on the grounds of ostensible authority if he, the third party, did not rely on the representation by the principal or if he knew or must be taken to have known of the agent's lack of authority or if he neglected to take the opportunity of ascertaining the agent's authority or if he was put on inquiry by the facts of the transactions.

It also appears from *Bowstead on Agency* (15th edn, 1985) p 303, art 77 that no act by an agent in excess of his actual authority is binding on the principal with respect to persons having notice that, in doing the act, the agent is exceeding his authority.

It may be possible in this case to salvage material from the present draft amendments and use that material to frame an amendment which goes to these points.

The amendments on this application are not so framed. They are overambitious in their attempt to embrace too many of the circumstances surrounding the applications for loans and the conduct of the society. The pleading runs together a whole mass of matters relating to contributory negligence with matters which might relate to lack of actual or ostensible authority.

If Hamptons wishes to plead the point on ostensible authority, it should do so separately from allegations of the society's negligence or carelessness which pervade the whole of the proposed amendment. It is not appropriate for the court to formulate or help to formulate a different form of amendment by picking over parts of the proposed amendments which might be allowed in a re-formulated form.

The fourth aspect of the amendments relied on by Mr Slater related to credit. It was submitted on behalf of Hamptons that the whole history of the transactions involving Mr Lancaster and the society would be relevant, if on nothing else, as to credit. This is an unsound submission. The purpose of pleadings is to set out material facts on which each party relies for his claim or defence and, thereby, define the issues in the case. Subject to certain immaterial exceptions, every pleading must contain, and contain only, a statement in summary form of the material facts on which the party relies for his claim or defence, as the case may be, and not the evidence by which those facts are to be proved: RSC Ord 18, r 7. If matters of evidence should not be on the pleadings, a fortiori matters going only to credit should not be pleaded.

There is a separate point relating to damages. On 19 February 1993 Master Gowers made an order under RSC Ord 33, r 3 and r 4(2), that at the trial the issues of liability (if any) of the defendants to the plaintiffs and the basis of the amount of damages, compensation and/or interest should be tried before any such assessment. He ordered that, subject to the resolution of those issues, the assessment of damages should be determined after the trial, subject to the directions of the trial judge on points of claim and defence and in such manner as the trial judge should direct.

At various points in the draft amended defence Hamptons raises the question of the society's duty to mitigate—for example, para 13(A) is in this form:

> 'For the avoidance of doubt, Hamptons reserves the right to plead further, if so advised, to the society's damages claim in relation to matters concerning the final quantification of the society's claim, including but not limited to questions of any failure by the society to mitigate its losses, pursuant to the order of Master Gowers made in this action on 19th February 1993'.

A similar pleading appears in para 15A(iii), 24A, 26(A), 36(A) and 49(A).

The society objected to these amendments. After some argument, it was agreed that questions of mitigation should be dealt with after liability, if any, has been established, and when considering the basis of assessment of damages. At that later stage it may be necessary to direct further pleadings in relation to matters, such as the duty to mitigate; there may arise further applications for discovery. It is sufficient to say now that the point has been raised. It is not necessary for it to be pleaded further at this stage.

Conclusions

The position in brief is as follows. (1) I reject the application for leave to amend to plead contributory negligence in actions no 193, 1041 and 1043. (2) The master was right to strike out the plea in relation to action no 7925, but there may be further argument in relation to that action which raises some special features that do not appear in the other three actions. (3) Mitigation of damages is to be left over for further pleadings and possible interlocutory measures after the question of liability has been argued and decided.

Order accordingly.

Hazel Hartman   Barrister.

Practice Direction
(No 1 of 1994)

SUPREME COURT TAXING OFFICE

Costs – Taxation – Value added tax – Civil proceedings and non-contentious business – Bills lodged for taxation which include charge for work done or services rendered – VAT registration number – Action before taxation – Form of bill of costs – Change in rate of taxation – Apportionment – Disbursements – Legal aid – Tax invoice – Vouchers – Certificate or allocatur – Solicitors and other litigants in person – Procedure where government department involved – Value Added Tax Act 1983, ss 14, 41(1)(2) – Sheriffs' Fees (Amendment No 2) Order 1977.

This Practice Direction is issued with the concurrence of the Senior District Judge of the Family Division and the Admiralty Registrar after consultation with HM Customs and Excise, the General Council of the Bar and the Law

Society in order to comply with the law and regulations relating to value added tax (VAT).

Every taxable person as defined by the Value Added Tax Act 1983 must be registered and in general terms (subject to the exceptions set out in that Act) whenever a taxable person supplies goods or services in the United Kingdom in the course of business a liability to VAT arises.

Responsibility for making a charge to VAT in a proper case and for accounting to Customs and Excise for the proper amount of VAT is totally that of the registered person concerned or the person required to be registered.

The following directions will apply to all bills of costs lodged for taxation after the date hereof. The Practice Directions listed in Pt 1 of the schedule hereto are hereby withdrawn.

VAT registration number

1. The number allocated by Customs and Excise to every person registered under the 1983 Act (except a government department) must appear in a prominent place at the head of every bill of costs, fee sheet, account or voucher on which VAT is being included as part of a claim for costs.

Action before taxation

2. VAT should not be included in a claim for costs in an inter partes bill of costs if the receiving party is able to recover the VAT as input tax. Where the receiving party is able to obtain credit from Customs and Excise for a proportion of the VAT as input tax, only that proportion which is not eligible for credit should be claimed in the inter partes bill.

3. The responsibility for ensuring that VAT is claimed in an inter partes bill of costs only when the receiving party is unable to recover the VAT or a proportion thereof as input tax is upon the receiving party.

4. Where there is a dispute as to whether VAT is properly claimed in an inter partes bill of costs the receiving party must provide a certificate signed by the solicitors or the auditors of the receiving party in the form in Pt 2 of the schedule hereto. Where the receiving party is a litigant in person who is claiming VAT, reference should be made by him to Customs and Excise and wherever possible a statement to similar effect produced on taxation.

5. Where there is a dispute as to whether any service in respect of which a charge is proposed to be made in the bill is zero-rated or exempt, reference should be made to Customs and Excise and wherever possible the view of Customs and Excise obtained and made known on taxation. In the case of an inter partes bill such application should be made by the receiving party. In the case of a bill from a solicitor to his own client such application should be made by the client.

Form of bill of costs where VAT is included as part of the costs claimed; form of bill of costs where VAT rate changes

6. Where there is a change in the rate of VAT, suppliers of goods and services are entitled by s 41(1) and (2) of the 1983 Act in most circumstances to elect whether the new or the old rate of VAT should apply to a supply where the basic and actual tax points span a period during which there has been a change in VAT rates.

7. It will be assumed, unless a contrary indication is given in writing, that an election to take advantage of the provisions mentioned in para 6 above and

to charge VAT at the lower rate has been made. In any case in which an election to charge at the lower rate is not made, such a decision must be justified in accordance with the principles of taxation which are applicable to the basis upon which the costs are ordered to be taxed.

Apportionment

8. All bills of costs, fees and disbursements on which VAT is included must be divided into separate parts so as to show work done on a day-to-day basis before, on and after the date or dates from which any change in the rate of VAT takes effect. Where, however, a lump sum charge is made for work which spans a period during which there has been a change in VAT rates, and paras 6 and 7 above do not apply, reference should be made to paras 8 and 9 of App F to the *VAT Guide* (Customs and Excise notice 700 (1 August 1991 edn) or any revised edition of that notice), a copy of which is in the possession of every registered trader. If necessary, the lump sum should be apportioned. The totals of profit costs and disbursements in each part must be carried separately to the summary.

9. Should there be a change in the rate between the date of taxation and the signing of the certificate of taxation, any interested party may apply for the taxation to be varied so as to take account of any increase or reduction in the amount of tax payable. Once the certificate of taxation has been signed, no variation will be possible.

Disbursements

10. VAT attributable to any disbursement must (except in the case of an inter partes bill where VAT is not claimed) be shown stating if it has been paid. This will consist of VAT which has been paid at the time the bill is drawn and an amount in respect of any unpaid disbursement. These amounts must be indicated in a separate VAT column inserted to the left of the normal disbursement column.

11. (1) Petty (or general) disbursements such as postage, fares etc which are normally treated as part of a solicitor's overheads and included in his profit costs should be charged with VAT even though they bear no tax when the solicitor incurs them. The costs of travel by public transport on a specific journey for a particular client where it forms part of the service rendered by a solicitor to his client, eg charged in his bill of costs, attract VAT.

(2) With effect from 3 January 1978 VAT is added to sheriffs' fees (see the Sheriffs' Fees (Amendment No 2) Order 1977, SI 1977/2111).

12. Reference is made to the criteria set out in the *VAT Guide* (Customs and Excise notice 700 (1 August 1991 edn)) para 83, or any revised edition of that notice), as to expenses which are not subject to VAT. Charges for the cost of travel by public transport, postage, telephone calls and telegraphic transfers where these form part of the service rendered by the solicitor to his client are examples of charges which do not satisfy these criteria and are thus liable to VAT at the standard rate.

Summary

13.1. The summary at the end of the bill must include additional columns for VAT on profit costs as allowed on taxation and VAT on disbursements so that the VAT can be cast separately. The taxing fee will be calculated on the total profit costs and disbursements as taxed and the VAT thereon.

13.2. In legal aid cases the legal aid summary must be drawn so as to show the total VAT on counsel's fees as a separate item from the VAT on other disbursements and the VAT on profit costs.

Legal aid

14. VAT will be payable in respect of every supply made pursuant to a legal aid certificate provided only that the person making the supply is a taxable person. Neither the status for VAT purposes nor the place of residence of the legally aided party affects the position.

Tax invoice

15. The taxed bill lodged for certificate is always retained in the Supreme Court Taxing Office so that where a solicitor waives his solicitor and own client costs and accepts taxed costs payable by the unsuccessful party in settlement it will be necessary for a short statement as to the amount of the taxed costs and the VAT thereon to be prepared for use as the tax invoice.

Vouchers

16. Where receipted accounts for disbursements made by the solicitor or his client are retained as tax invoices a photostat copy of any such receipted account may be produced and will be accepted as sufficient evidence of payment when disbursements are vouched.

Certificate or allocatur

17. In non legal aid cases the total VAT allowed will be shown in the certificate or allocatur as a separate item. In legal aid cases the VAT on counsel's fees will be shown separately from the remaining VAT.

Solicitors and other litigants acting in person

18. Where a litigant acts in litigation on his own behalf he is not treated for the purposes of VAT as having supplied services and therefore no VAT is chargeable on that litigant's inter partes bill of costs.

19. Similarly, where a solicitor acts in litigation on his own behalf even on a matter arising out of his practice he is not treated for the purposes of VAT as having supplied services and therefore no VAT is chargeable on the bill of that solicitor.

20. Consequently where such a bill as is described in the preceding two paragraphs is presented for agreement or taxation VAT should not be claimed and will not be allowed on taxation.

Government departments

21. On a taxation inter partes where costs are being paid to a government department in respect of services rendered by its legal staff, VAT should not be added since such services do not attract VAT.

8 February 1994

P T HURST
Chief Master.

SCHEDULE

Part 1

Practice Directions withdrawn (save in so far as they relate to work done before 18 June 1979)

Practice Direction [1973] 1 All ER 974, [1973] 1 WLR 438
Practice Direction [1974] 1 All ER 847, [1974] 1 WLR 217

Practice Direction [1974] 3 All ER 177, [1974] 1 WLR 1107
Practice Direction [1979] 2 All ER 1008, [1979] 1 WLR 927
Practice Direction [1981] 1 All ER 828, [1981] 1 WLR 327
Practice Direction [1991] 2 All ER 923, [1991] 1 WLR 314

Part 2

Form of certificate

To: The [Master] [District Judge]
Address:

A v BC Ltd

With reference to the pending taxation of the defendant's [*or as the case may be*] costs and disbursements herein which are payable by the plaintiff [*or as the case may be*], we the undersigned, as [solicitors to] [the auditors of] the above-named defendant [*or as the case may be*] company, hereby certify that the defendant [*or as the case may be*] on the basis of its last completed VAT return would [not be entitled to recover] [be entitled to recover only   % of the] value added tax on such costs and disbursements, as input tax pursuant to s 14 of the Value Added Tax Act 1983.

[Signed]
[Solicitors to] [Auditors of] [Defendant] [Plaintiff] [*or as the case may be*]
Registered no

Practice Direction
(No 2 of 1994)

SUPREME COURT TAXING OFFICE

Costs – Taxation – Value added tax – Crown Court – Bills lodged for taxation which include charge for work done or services rendered – VAT registration number – Action before taxation – Form of bill of costs – Change in rate of taxation – Apportionment – Disbursements – Legal aid – Tax invoice – Vouchers – Solicitors and other litigants in person – Procedure where government department involved – Value Added Tax Act 1983, ss 14, 41(1)(2) – Sheriffs' Fees (Amendment No 2) Order 1977

This Practice Direction is issued with the concurrence of the Lord Chief Justice after consultation with HM Customs and Excise, the General Council of the Bar and the Law Society in order to comply with the law and regulations relating to value added tax (VAT).

Every taxable person as defined by the Value Added Tax Act 1983 must be registered and in general terms (subject to the exceptions set out in that Act) whenever a taxable person supplies goods or services in the United Kingdom in the course of business a liability to VAT arises.

Responsibility for making a charge to VAT in a proper case and for accounting to Customs and Excise for the proper amount of VAT is totally that of the registered person concerned or the person required to be registered.

The following directions will apply to all bills of costs lodged for taxation after the date hereof. The Practice Directions listed in Pt 1 of the schedule hereto are hereby withdrawn.

VAT registration number

1. The number allocated by Customs and Excise to every person registered under the 1983 Act (except a government department) must appear in a prominent place at the head of every bill of costs, fee sheet, account or voucher on which VAT is being included as part of a claim for costs.

Action before taxation

2. VAT should not be included in a claim for costs in an inter partes bill of costs if the receiving party is able to recover the VAT as input tax. Where the receiving party is able to obtain credit from Customs and Excise for a proportion of the VAT as input tax, only that proportion which is not eligible for credit should be claimed in the inter partes bill.

3. The responsibility for ensuring that VAT is claimed in an inter partes bill of costs only when the receiving party is unable to recover the VAT or a proportion thereof as input tax is upon the receiving party. On a taxation of costs payable out of public funds the taxing officer or determining officer as the case may be must continue to satisfy himself as to the tax position.

4. Where there is a dispute as to whether VAT is properly claimed in an inter partes bill of costs the receiving party must provide a certificate signed by the solicitors or the auditors of the receiving party in the form in Pt 2 of the schedule hereto. Where the receiving party is a litigant in person who is claiming VAT, reference should be made by him to Customs and Excise and wherever possible a statement to similar effect produced on taxation.

5. Where there is a dispute as to whether any service in respect of which a charge is proposed to be made in the bill is zero-rated or exempt, reference should be made to Customs and Excise and wherever possible the view of Customs and Excise obtained and made known on taxation. In the case of an inter partes bill such application should be made by the receiving party. In the case of a bill from a solicitor to his own client such application should be made by the client.

Form of bill of costs where VAT is included as part of the costs claimed; form of bill of costs where VAT rate changes

6. Where there is a change in the rate of VAT, suppliers of goods and services are entitled by s 41(1) and (2) of the 1983 Act in most circumstances to elect whether the new or the old rate of VAT should apply to a supply where the basic and actual tax points span a period during which there has been a change in VAT rates.

7. It will be assumed, unless a contrary indication is given in writing, that an election to take advantage of the provisions mentioned in para 6 above and to charge VAT at the lower rate has been made. In any case in which an election to charge at the lower rate is not made, such a decision must be justified in accordance with the principles of taxation which are applicable to the basis upon which the costs are ordered to be taxed.

Apportionment

8. Where a lump sum charge is made for work which spans a period during which there has been a change in VAT rates, and paras 6 and 7 above do not apply, reference should be made to paras 8 and 9 of App F to the *VAT Guide* (Customs and Excise notice 700 (1 August 1991 edn) or any revised edition of that notice), a copy of which is in the possession of every registered trader. If necessary, the lump sum should be apportioned.

Disbursements

9. VAT attributable to any disbursement, e g an expert's report, must (except in the case of an inter partes bill where VAT is not claimed) be shown as a separate item in the receipt or voucher.

10. (1) Petty (or general) disbursements such as postage, fares etc which are normally treated as part of a solicitor's overheads and included in his profit costs should be charged with VAT even though they bear no tax when the solicitor incurs them. The costs of travel by public transport on a specific journey for a particular client where it forms part of the service rendered by a solicitor to his client, e g charged in his bill of costs, attract VAT.

(2) With effect from 3 January 1978 VAT is added to sheriffs' fees (see the Sheriffs' Fees (Amendment No 2) Order 1977, SI 1977/2111).

11. Reference is made to the criteria set out in the *VAT Guide* (Customs and Excise notice 700 (1 August 1991 edn)) para 83, or any revised edition of that notice), as to expenses which are not subject to VAT. Charges for the cost of travel by public transport, postage, telephone calls and telegraphic transfers where these form part of the service rendered by the solicitor to his client are examples of charges which do not satisfy these criteria and are thus liable to VAT at the standard rate.

Legal aid

12. VAT will be payable in respect of every supply made pursuant to a legal aid certificate provided only that the person making the supply is a taxable person. Neither the status for VAT purposes nor the place of residence of the legally aided party affects the position.

13. Where costs are payable out of legal aid or central funds pursuant to any authority the tax invoice in the case of counsel will consist of his fee note and in the case of a solicitor his bill of costs as taxed together with the payment advice supplied by the court as to the fees allowed on taxation.

Where the fees or costs as taxed are varied on appeal the VAT charged will be amended as appropriate by the taxing officer or determining officer as the case may be.

Vouchers

14. Where receipted accounts for disbursements made by the solicitor or his client are retained as tax invoices a photostat copy of any such receipted account may be produced and will be accepted as sufficient evidence of payment when disbursements are vouched.

Solicitors and other litigants acting in person

15. Where a litigant acts in litigation on his own behalf he is not treated for the purposes of VAT as having supplied services and therefore no VAT is

chargeable on that litigant's inter partes bill of costs unless VAT has been charged on disbursements, when the normal rules will apply.

16. Similarly, where a solicitor acts in litigation on his own behalf even on a matter arising out of his practice he is not treated for the purposes of VAT as having supplied services and therefore no VAT is chargeable on the bill of that solicitor.

17. Consequently where such a bill as is described in the preceding two paragraphs is presented for agreement or taxation VAT should not be claimed and will not be allowed on taxation unless tax has been paid on disbursements.

Government departments

18. On a taxation inter partes where costs are being paid to a government department in respect of services rendered by its legal staff, VAT should not be added since such services do not attract VAT.

P T HURST
Chief Master.

8 February 1994

SCHEDULE

Part 1

Practice Directions withdrawn (save in so far as they relate to work done before 18 June 1979)

Practice Direction [1973] 1 All ER 971, [1973] 1 WLR 441
Practice Direction [1974] 1 All ER 848, [1974] 1 WLR 218
Practice Direction [1979] 2 All ER 1008, [1979] 1 WLR 927

Part 2

Form of certificate

To: The Chief Clerk
        Crown Court
Address:
Date:

Regina v A

With reference to the pending taxation of the [prosecutor's] [defendant's] costs and disbursements herein which are payable by the [defendant] [the prosecutor] [public funds], we the undersigned [solicitors to] [the auditors of] the [prosecutor] [defendant] hereby certify that he on the basis of his last completed VAT return would [not be entitled to recover] [be entitled to recover only   % of the] value added tax on such costs and disbursements, as input tax pursuant to s 14 of the Value Added Tax Act 1983.

[Signed]
[Solicitors to] [Auditors of] [Defendant] [Prosecutor]
Registered no

Rhone and another v Stephens

HOUSE OF LORDS

LORD TEMPLEMAN, LORD OLIVER OF AYLMERTON, LORD WOOLF, LORD LLOYD OF BERWICK AND LORD NOLAN

7, 8 FEBRUARY, 17 MARCH 1994

Restrictive covenant affecting land – Enforceability – Enforceability against vendor's successors in title – Repairing covenant – Positive covenant to repair demised property – Owner of house and contiguous cottage selling cottage and covenanting to maintain common roof in good repair – Whether covenant binding vendor's successors in title – Whether rule that positive covenants not running with freehold still applying – Law of Property Act 1925, s 79.

In 1960 the owners of a house and adjoining cottage, which were under the same roof, sold the cottage. Under cl 3 of the conveyance the vendor covenanted for himself and his successors in title as the owners of the house to maintain that part of the roof of the house which was above the cottage in good condition to the reasonable satisfaction of the purchasers and their successors in title. Since 1960 both properties had been sold. In 1986 the plaintiffs, who then owned the cottage, brought an action against the defendant, representing the estate which then owned the house, claiming that the roof above the cottage was leaking and that the estate was in breach of the covenant to repair the roof contained in cl 3. The judge held that the defendant was bound by the covenant contained in cl 3, but on appeal by the defendant the Court of Appeal reversed his decision. The plaintiff appealed to the House of Lords, contending, inter alia, that the rule that positive covenants did not run with freehold land had been reversed by s 79[a] of the Law of Property Act 1925, which provided that 'A covenant relating to any land of a covenantor or capable of being bound by him, shall ... be deemed to be made by the covenantor on behalf of himself his successors in title and the persons deriving title under him or them'.

Held – A positive covenant was not enforceable at common law because a successor in title was not a party to the contract containing the covenant, and, although breach of a negative covenant which restricted the user of land or the exercise of other rights in connection with land could be prevented or punished in equity, the burden of positive covenants did not run with the freehold and was not enforceable in equity. Furthermore, the rule that positive covenants did not run with the freehold was not affected by s 79 of the 1925 Act, which merely made it unnecessary to refer to successors in title in a covenant in a conveyance and did not have the effect of making the burden of positive covenants run with the land. It followed that the covenant by the vendor to keep the roof the cottage in good repair was not enforceable against his successors in title. The appeal would accordingly be dismissed (see p 67 *j*, p 68 *c j* to p 69 *a*, p 71 *h*, p 72 *g h* and p 73*b d* to *j*, post).

Tulk v Moxhay [1843–60] All ER Rep 9, *Haywood v Brunswick Permanent Benefit Building Society* (1881) 8 QBD 403 and *London and South Western Rly Co v Gomm* [1881–5] All ER Rep 1190 applied.

---

[a] Section 79, so far as material, is set out at p 72 *f*, post

Austerberry v Oldham Corp (1885) 29 Ch D 750 approved.

Notes
For the enforceability of a covenant against a successor in title, see 16 *Halsbury's Laws* (4th edn reissue) para 791, and for cases on the burden and benefit of covenants, see 40 *Digest* (Reissue) 445–458, *3937–3997*.

For the Law of Property Act 1925, s 79, see 37 *Halsbury's Statutes* (4th edn) 184.

Cases referred to in opinions
Austerberry v Oldham Corp (1885) 29 Ch D 750, CA.
Cooke v Chilcott (1876) 3 Ch D 694, V-C.
Cox v Bishop (1857) 8 De GM & G 815, 44 ER 604.
Federated Homes Ltd v Mill Lodge Properties Ltd [1980] 1 All ER 371, [1980] 1 WLR 594, CA.
Halsall v Brizell [1957] 1 All ER 371, [1957] Ch 169, [1957] 2 WLR 123.
Haywood v Brunswick Permanent Benefit Building Society (1881) 8 QBD 403, CA.
Jones v Price [1965] 2 All ER 625, [1965] 2 QB 618, [1965] 3 WLR 296, CA.
London and South Western Rly Co v Gomm (1882) 20 Ch D 562, [1881–5] All ER Rep 1190, CA.
Morland v Cook (1868) LR 6 Eq 252, MR.
Nisbet and Potts's Contract, Re [1905] 1 Ch 391; *affd* [1906] 1 Ch 387, [1904–7] All ER Rep 865, CA.
Sefton v Tophams Ltd [1966] 1 All ER 1039, [1967] 1 AC 50, [1966] 2 WLR 814, HL.
Smith v River Douglas Catchment Board [1949] 2 All ER 179, [1949] 2 KB 500, CA.
Spencer's Case (1583) 5 Co Rep 16a, [1558–1774] All ER Rep 68, 77 ER 72.
Tito v Waddell (No 2) [1977] 3 All ER 129, [1977] Ch 106, [1977] 2 WLR 496.
Tulk v Moxhay (1848) 2 Ph 774, [1843–60] All ER Rep 9, 41 ER 1143, LC.
Williams v Unit Construction Co Ltd (1951) 19 Conv NS 262.

Appeal
The plaintiffs, Ronald John Rhone and Hazel Grace Rhone, appealed with the leave of the Appeal Committee of the House of Lords given on 28 July 1993 from the decision of the Court of Appeal (Nourse and Steyn LJJ) on 15 January 1993 allowing the appeal of the defendant, Jean Stephens, who was sued as the executrix of May Ellen Barnard deceased, from the decision of Judge Cotterill sitting in the Bridgwater County Court on 1 July 1991 by which the judge held that the defendant's failure to maintain the roof of Walford Cottage, Combwich, Somerset, in a weatherproof condition was an actionable nuisance and a breach of cl 3 of a conveyance dated 1 April 1960 and awarded damages to the plaintiffs. The Court of Appeal ordered that the plaintiffs' action be dismissed. The facts are set out in the opinion of Lord Templeman.

James Munby QC and *John Virgo* (instructed by *Gregory Rowcliffe & Milners*, agents for *Pardoes*, Bridgwater) for the plaintiffs.
David Spens (instructed by *Alletsons*, Bridgwater) for the defendant.

Their Lordships took time for consideration.

17 March 1994. The following opinions were delivered.

LORD TEMPLEMAN. My Lords, this appeal raises the question of the enforceability of positive covenants between owners of freehold estates and involves consideration of the rule in *Austerberry v Oldham Corp* (1885) 29 Ch D 750.

The roof which covers Walford House also covers part of Walford Cottage. Both properties were in common ownership until by a conveyance dated 27 August 1960 Walford Cottage was sold. The conveyance contained the following provisions:

'2. IT IS HEREBY AGREED AND DECLARED between the Vendor and the Purchasers that all easements quasi-easements or rights in the nature of easements as now existing between the property hereby conveyed and the adjoining property of the Vendor known as Walford House aforesaid shall continue for the benefit of the respective properties

3. THE VENDOR HEREBY COVENANTS for himself and his successors in title owner or occupiers for the time being of the property known as Walford House aforesaid to maintain to the reasonable satisfaction of the Purchasers and their successors in title such part of the roof of Walford House aforesaid as lies above the property conveyed in wind and water tight condition.'

Clause 2 of the 1960 conveyance had the effect, inter alia, of conferring and confirming on Walford House the right to be supported by the contiguous Walford Cottage. The 1960 conveyance also had the effect of conferring and confirming on Walford Cottage the right to be supported by Walford House. Clause 3 of the 1960 conveyance did not confer any rights on Walford Cottage but by its express terms it appears to confer on the owners for the time being of Walford Cottage the right to sue the owner for the time being of Walford House for damages if the roof is not kept wind- and watertight.

Since 1960 both properties have been sold. The appellant plaintiffs are now the owners of Walford Cottage. The respondent defendant is the executrix of the last owner of Walford House. The trial judge ordered the owner of Walford House to pay damages to the owners of Walford Cottage for breach of the covenant contained in cl 3 of the 1960 conveyance to keep the roof of Walford House which lies above Walford Cottage in wind- and watertight condition. The Court of Appeal reversed the judge and dismissed the action.

Mr Spens, who appeared for the defendant, says that the covenant has never been breached because the part of the roof which is out of repair belongs to Walford Cottage. Examination of the plans attached to the conveyance however show that the covenant to repair must refer to the roof which protects both properties. So upon the true construction of the 1960 conveyance the owner of Walford House was in breach of the covenant to repair.

At common law a person cannot be made liable upon a contract unless he was a party to it. In *Cox v Bishop* (1857) 8 De GM & G 815, 44 ER 604 a lease was assigned to a man of straw and it was held that the covenants in the lease could not be enforced against an equitable assignee of the lease who had entered into possession. The covenants were not enforceable because there was no privity of contract or estate between the lessee and the assignee. The rigours of the common law which do not allow covenants to be enforced by and against successors in title were relaxed first by the doctrines laid down in *Spencer's Case* (1583) 5 Co Rep 16a, [1558–1774] All ER Rep 68 and then by statutory extensions of those doctrines introduced by the Act 32 Hen 8 c 34 (grantees of reversions (1540)), the Conveyancing Act 1881 and the Conveyancing Act 1911, now repealed and reproduced in ss 141 and 142 of the Law of Property Act 1925. In the result, as between landlord and tenant both the burden and the benefit of a covenant which touches or concerns the land demised and is not merely collateral run with the reversion and the term at law whether the covenant be positive or restrictive. As between persons interested in land other than as landlord and tenant, the benefit of a covenant may run with the land at law but not the burden: see the *Austerberry* case.

Thus cl 3 of the 1960 conveyance, despite its express terms, did not confer on the owner for the time being of Walford Cottage the right at common law to compel the owner for the time being of Walford House to repair the roof or to obtain damages for breach of the covenant to repair. In this appeal, Mr Munby QC, on behalf of the plaintiffs, contends that equity will compel the owner of Walford House to comply with the covenant to repair the roof or to pay damages in lieu.

My Lords, equity supplements but does not contradict the common law. When freehold land is conveyed without restriction, the conveyance confers on the purchaser the right to do with the land as he pleases provided that he does not interfere with the rights of others or infringe statutory restrictions. The conveyance may however impose restrictions which, in favour of the covenantee, deprive the purchaser of some of the rights inherent in the ownership of unrestricted land. In *Tulk v Moxhay* (1848) 2 Ph 774, [1843–60] All ER Rep 9 a purchaser of land covenanted that no buildings would be erected on Leicester Square. A subsequent purchaser of Leicester Square was restrained from building. The conveyance to the original purchaser deprived him and every subsequent purchaser taking with notice of the covenant of the right, otherwise part and parcel of the freehold, to develop the square by the construction of buildings. Equity does not contradict the common law by enforcing a restrictive covenant against a successor in title of the covenantor but prevents the successor from exercising a right which he never acquired. Equity did not allow the owner of Leicester Square to build because the owner never acquired the right to build without the consent of the persons (if any) from time to time entitled to the benefit of the covenant against building. In *Tulk v Moxhay* 2 Ph 774 at 777–778, [1843–60] All ER Rep 9 at 11 the judgment of Lord Cottenham LC contained the following passage:

> 'It is said, that the covenant being one which does not run with the land, this Court cannot enforce it; but the question is, not whether the covenant runs with the land, but whether a party shall be permitted to use the land in a manner inconsistent with the contract entered into by his vendor, and with notice of which he purchased.'

Equity can thus prevent or punish the breach of a negative covenant which restricts the user of land or the exercise of other rights in connection with land. Restrictive covenants deprive an owner of a right which he could otherwise exercise. Equity cannot compel an owner to comply with a positive covenant entered into by his predecessors in title without flatly contradicting the common law rule that a person cannot be made liable upon a contract unless he was a party to it. Enforcement of a positive covenant lies in contract; a positive covenant compels an owner to exercise his rights. Enforcement of a negative covenant lies in property; a negative covenant deprives the owner of a right over property. As Lord Cottenham LC said in *Tulk v Moxhay* 2 Ph 774 at 778, [1843–60] All ER Rep 9 at 11:

> '... if an equity is attached to the property by the owner, no one purchasing with notice of that equity can stand in a different situation from the party from whom he purchased.'

Following *Tulk v Moxhay* there was some suggestion that any covenant affecting land was enforceable in equity provided that the owner of the land had notice of the covenant prior to his purchase. In *Morland v Cook* (1868) LR 6 Eq 252 lands below sea level were partitioned by a deed containing a covenant that the expense of maintaining the sea wall should be borne by the owners of the lands and payable out of the lands by an acre-scot. Lord Romilly MR enforced the covenant against a subsequent purchaser of part of the lands on the grounds that he had purchased with notice of the covenant. In *Cooke v Chilcott* (1876) 3 Ch D 694 a covenant by the purchaser of land with a well to erect a pump and reservoir and to supply water from the well to all houses built on the vendor's land was enforced against a subsequent purchaser of the land burdened with the covenant on the grounds that the covenant ran with the land but that in any event the defendant took with notice of the obligation. Malins V-C said (at 701):

> '... I think that when a contract is entered into for the benefit of contiguous landowners, and one is bound by it, and the other entitled to the benefit of it, the covenant binds him for ever, and also runs with the land. But it is equally clear that he is bound by taking the land with notice of the covenant.'

These last two cases did not survive the decision of the Court of Appeal in *Haywood v Brunswick Permanent Benefit Building Society* (1881) 8 QBD 403. In that case land had been conveyed in consideration of a rent charge and a covenant to build and repair buildings; a mortgagee of the land was held not to be liable on the covenant either at law or in equity although the mortgagee had notice of the covenant. Brett LJ said that *Tulk v Moxhay*—

> 'decided that an assignee taking land subject to a certain class of covenants is bound by such covenants if he has notice of them, and that the class of covenants comprehended within the rule is that covenants restricting the mode of using the land only will be enforced. It may be also, but it is not necessary to decide here, that all covenants also which impose such a burden on the land as can be enforced against the land would be enforced ... it is said that if we decide for the defendants we shall have to overrule *Cooke* v. *Chilcott* ((1876) 3 Ch D 694). If that case was decided on the equitable doctrine of notice, I think we ought to overrule it.' (See 8 QBD 403 at 408.)

Cotton LJ said (at 409):

> 'Let us consider the examples in which a Court of Equity has enforced covenants affecting land. We find that they have been invariably enforced if they have been restrictive, and that with the exception of the covenants in *Cooke* v. *Chilcott*, only restrictive covenants have been enforced.'

Cotton LJ also said that *Tulk v Moxhay*—

> 'lays down the real principle that an equity attaches to the owner of the land ... The covenant to repair can only be enforced by making the owner put his hand into his pocket, and there is nothing which would justify us in going that length.'

In *London and South Western Rly Co v Gomm* (1882) 20 Ch D 562, [1881–5] All ER Rep 1190 an option to purchase land on the happening of an uncertain event was held to be void for remoteness. It was argued that the covenant was enforceable in equity. Jessel MR said (20 Ch D 562 at 582–583, [1881–5] All ER Rep 1190 at 1194–95):

> 'With regard to the argument founded on *Tulk* v. *Moxhay* ((1848) 2 Ph 774, [1843–60] All ER Rep 9), that case was very much considered by the Court of Appeal at *Westminster* in *Haywood* v. *The Brunswick Permanent Benefit Building Society* ((1881) 8 QBD 403), and the Court there decided that they would not extend the doctrine of *Tulk* v. *Moxhay* to affirmative covenants, compelling a man to lay out money or do any other act of what I may call an active character, but that it was to be confined to restrictive covenants. Of course that authority would be binding upon us if we did not agree to it, but I most cordially accede to it. I think that we ought not to extend the doctrine of *Tulk* v. *Moxhay* in the way suggested here. The doctrine of that case ... appears to me to be either an extension in equity of the doctrine of *Spencer's Case* ((1583) 5 Co Rep 16a, [1558–1774] All ER Rep 68)to another line of cases, or else an extension in equity of the doctrine of negative easements ... The covenant in *Tulk* v. *Moxhay* was affirmative in its terms, but was held by the Court to imply a negative. Where there is a negative covenant expressed or implied ... the Court interferes on one or other of the above grounds. This is an equitable doctrine, establishing an exception to the rules of Common Law which did not treat such a covenant as running with the land, and it does not matter whether it proceeds on analogy to a covenant running with the land or on analogy to an easement. The purchaser took the estate subject to the equitable burden, with the qualification that if he acquired the legal estate for value without notice he was freed from the burden.'

Lindley LJ said that because in *Haywood v Brunswick Permanent Benefit Building Society* it was sought to extend the doctrine of *Tulk v Moxhay*—

> 'to a degree which was thought dangerous, considerable pains were taken by the Court to point out the limits of that doctrine ... The conclusion arrived at ... was that *Tulk* v. *Moxhay*, when properly understood, did not apply to any but restrictive covenants.' (See 20 Ch D 562 at 587–588, [1881–5] All ER Rep 1190 at 1197.)

In the *Austerberry* case the owners of a site of a road covenanted that they and their successors in title would make the road and keep it in repair. The road was sold to the defendants and it was held that the repair covenant could not be enforced against them. Cotton LJ said (29 Ch D 750 at 773–774):

> '... undoubtedly, where there is a restrictive covenant, the burden and benefit of which do not run at law, Courts of Equity restrain anyone who takes the property with notice of that covenant from using it in a way inconsistent with the covenant. But here the covenant which is attempted

to be insisted upon on this appeal is a covenant to lay out money in doing certain work upon this land; and, that being so ... that is not a covenant which a Court of Equity will enforce: it will not enforce a covenant not running at law when it is sought to enforce that covenant in such a way as to require the successors in title of the covenantor, to spend money, and in that way to undertake a burden upon themselves. The covenantor must not use the property for a purpose inconsistent with the use for which it was originally granted; but in my opinion a Court of Equity does not and ought not to enforce a covenant binding only in equity in such a way as to require the successors of the covenantor himself, they having entered into no covenant, to expend sums of money in accordance with what the original covenantor bound himself to do.'

In *Re Nisbet and Potts's Contract* [1905] 1 Ch 391 it was held that a title acquired by adverse possession was not paramount to and did not destroy the equitable right of persons entitled to the benefit of prior restrictive covenants to enforce them against the land. Farwell J said (at 396–397):

'Covenants restricting the enjoyment of land, except of course as between the contracting parties and those privy to the contract, are not enforceable by anything in the nature of action or suit founded on contract. Such actions and suits alike depend on privity of contract, and no possession of the land coupled with notice of the covenants can avail to create such privity: *Cox* v. *Bishop* ((1857) 8 De GM & G 815, 44 ER 604). But if the covenant be negative, so as to restrict the mode of use and enjoyment of the land, then there is called into existence an equity attached to the property of such a nature that it is annexed to and runs with it in equity: *Tulk* v. *Moxhay* ((1848) 2 Ph 774, [1843–60] All ER Rep 9). This equity, although created by covenant or contract, cannot be sued on as such, but stands on the same footing with and is completely analogous to an equitable charge on real estate created by some predecessor in title of the present owner of the land charged ... effect is given to the negative covenant by means of the land itself. But the land cannot spend money on improving itself, and there is no personal liability on the owner of the land for the time being, because there is no contract on which he can be sued in contract.'

For over 100 years it has been clear and accepted law that equity will enforce negative covenants against freehold land but has no power to enforce positive covenants against successors in title of the land. To enforce a positive covenant would be to enforce a personal obligation against a person who has not covenanted. To enforce negative covenants is only to treat the land as subject to a restriction.

Mr Munby, who argued the appeal persuasively on behalf of the plaintiffs, referred to an article by Professor Sir William Wade, 'Covenants—"a broad and reasonable view"' (1972) 31 CLJ 157, and other articles in which the present state of the law is subjected to severe criticism. In 1965 the *Report of the Committee on Positive Covenants Affecting Land* (Cmnd 2719), which was a report by a committee appointed by the Lord Chancellor and under the chairmanship of Lord Wilberforce, referred to difficulties caused by the decision in the *Austerberry* case and recommended legislation to provide that positive covenants which relate to the use of land and are intended to benefit specified other land should run with the land. In *Transfer of Land: Appurtenant Rights* (Law

Commission working paper no 36, published on 5 July 1971) the present law on positive rights was described as being illogical, uncertain, incomplete and inflexible. The Law Commission Report *Transfer of Land: The Law of Positive and Restrictive Covenants* (Law Com no 127) laid before Parliament in 1984 made recommendations for the reform of the law relating to positive and restrictive obligations and submitted a draft Bill for that purpose. Nothing has been done.

In these circumstances your Lordships were invited to overrule the decision of the Court of Appeal in the *Austerberry* case. To do so would destroy the distinction between law and equity and to convert the rule of equity into a rule of notice. It is plain from the articles, reports and papers to which we were referred that judicial legislation to overrule the *Austerberry* case would create a number of difficulties, anomalies and uncertainties and affect the rights and liabilities of people who have for over 100 years bought and sold land in the knowledge, imparted at an elementary stage to every student of the law of real property, that positive covenants affecting freehold land are not directly enforceable except against the original covenantor. Parliamentary legislation to deal with the decision in the *Austerberry* case would require careful consideration of the consequences. Moreover, experience with leasehold tenure where positive covenants are enforceable by virtue of privity of estate has demonstrated that social injustice can be caused by logic. Parliament was obliged to intervene to prevent tenants losing their homes and being saddled with the costs of restoring to their original glory buildings which had languished through wars and economic depression for exactly 99 years.

Mr Munby submitted that the decision in the *Austerberry* case had been reversed remarkably but unremarked by s 79 of the Law of Property Act 1925, which, so far as material, provides:

'(1) A covenant relating to any land of a covenantor or capable of being bound by him, shall, unless a contrary intention is expressed, be deemed to be made by the covenantor on behalf of himself his successors in title and the persons deriving title under him or them, and, subject as aforesaid, shall have effect as if such successors and other persons were expressed ...'

This provision has always been regarded as intended to remove conveyancing difficulties with regard to the form of covenants and to make it unnecessary to refer to successors in title. A similar provision relating to the benefit of covenants is to be found in s 78 of the 1925 Act. In *Smith v River Douglas Catchment Board* [1949] 2 All ER 179, [1949] 2 KB 500, followed in *Williams v Unit Construction Co Ltd* (1951) 19 Conv NS 262, it was held by the Court of Appeal that s 78 of the 1925 Act had the effect of making the benefit of positive covenants run with the land. Without casting any doubt on those long-standing decisions I do not consider that it follows that s 79 of the 1925 Act had the corresponding effect of making the burden of positive covenants run with the land. In *Jones v Price* [1965] 2 All ER 625 at 630, [1965] 2 QB 618 at 633 Willmer LJ repeated that: '... a covenant to perform positive acts ... is not one the burden of which runs with the land so as to bind the successors in title of the covenantor; see *Austerberry* v. *Oldham Corpn.*'

In *Sefton v Tophams Ltd* [1966] 1 All ER 1039 at 1048, 1053, [1967] 1 AC 50 at 73, 81 Lord Upjohn and Lord Wilberforce stated that s 79 of the 1925 Act does not have the effect of causing covenants to run with the land. Finally, in *Federated Homes Ltd v Mill Lodge Properties Ltd* [1980] 1 All ER 371 at 380, [1980] 1 WLR 594 at 605–606 Brightman J referred to the authorities on s 78 of the 1925 Act and said:

> 'Section 79, in my view, involves quite different considerations and I do not think that it provides a helpful analogy.'

Mr Munby also sought to persuade your Lordships that the effect of the decision in the *Austerberry* case had been blunted by the 'pure principle of benefit and burden' distilled by Megarry V-C from the authorities in *Tito v Waddell (No 2)* [1977] 3 All ER 129 at 291–292, [1977] Ch 106 at 301–303. I am not prepared to recognise the 'pure principle' that any party deriving any benefit from a conveyance must accept any burden in the same conveyance. Megarry V-C relied on the decision of Upjohn J in *Halsall v Brizell* [1957] 1 All ER 371, [1957] Ch 169. In that case the defendant's predecessor in title had been granted the right to use the estate roads and sewers and had covenanted to pay a due proportion for the maintenance of these facilities. It was held that the defendant could not exercise the rights without paying his costs of ensuring that they could be exercised. Conditions can be attached to the exercise of a power in express terms or by implication. *Halsall v Brizell* was just such a case and I have no difficulty in whole-heartedly agreeing with the decision. It does not follow that any condition can be rendered enforceable by attaching it to a right nor does it follow that every burden imposed by a conveyance may be enforced by depriving the covenantor's successor in title of every benefit which he enjoyed thereunder. The condition must be relevant to the exercise of the right. In *Halsall v Brizell* there were reciprocal benefits and burdens enjoyed by the users of the roads and sewers. In the present case cl 2 of the 1960 conveyance imposes reciprocal benefits and burdens of support but cl 3 which imposed an obligation to repair the roof is an independent provision. In *Halsall v Brizell* the defendant could, at least in theory, choose between enjoying the right and paying his proportion of the cost or alternatively giving up the right and saving his money. In the present case the owners of Walford House could not in theory or in practice be deprived of the benefit of the mutual rights of support if they failed to repair the roof.

In the result I would dismiss the appeal and make the usual order for costs against the plaintiffs subject to the usual appropriate legal aid reservations.

LORD OLIVER OF AYLMERTON. My Lords, for the reasons given by my noble and learned friend Lord Templeman I, too, would dismiss the appeal.

LORD WOOLF. My Lords, I have benefited from reading in draft the speech of my noble and learned friend Lord Templeman. I agree with it and for the reasons he gives I would dismiss this appeal.

LORD LLOYD OF BERWICK. My Lords, I have read the speech of my noble and learned friend Lord Templeman in draft. I agree that for the reasons he gives this appeal should be dismissed.

LORD NOLAN. My Lords, for the reasons given by my noble and learned friend Lord Templeman I, too, would dismiss the appeal.

Appeal dismissed.

Celia Fox   Barrister.

Arab Bank plc v Merchantile Holdings Ltd and another

CHANCERY DIVISION

MILLETT J

23, 24, 27, 29 SEPTEMBER 1993

Company – Shares – Purchase of shares with financial assistance of company – Subsidiary company providing assistance – Foreign subsidiary – Whether unlawful for foreign subsidiary of English parent company to give financial assistance for acquisition of shares in parent company – Whether mere giving of financial assistance by subsidiary ipso facto constituting giving of such assistance by parent company – Companies Act 1985, s 151.

Mortgage – Sale – Power to authorise sale – Jurisdiction – Whether court should sanction sale where mortgagee having full power to affect sale without order and purchaser having statutory protection – Law of Property Act 1925, ss 91(2), 104.

The plaintiff bank granted a loan facility of £15·4m to the second defendant for the express purpose of enabling it to acquire the share capital of Q Ltd, the parent company of the first defendant which owned a valuable leasehold property in the City of London. By a fixed and floating charge the first defendant charged the property and assigned the rental income from it to the bank to secure the moneys advanced to the second defendant under the loan facility. Q Ltd and the second defendant were both incorporated in England and registered under the English Companies Acts. The first defendant was incorporated in Gibraltar, but it maintained a place of business in Great Britain and was an 'oversea company' and a 'subsidiary' of Q Ltd for the purposes of the Companies Act 1985 but was not itself a 'company' for the purposes of that Act. Subsequently, the bank wished to exercise its power of sale by entering into a contract to sell the property for £12m, and it sought a declaration that the power of sale had arisen and was exercisable and an order pursuant to s 91(2)[a] of the Law of Property Act 1925 directing that the property be sold, that conduct of the sale be given to the bank and that the bank be at liberty to sell the property for £12m. The defendants contended, inter alia, that the bank's security was void as having been granted in contravention of s 151[b] of the 1985 Act, which prohibited a company or any of its subsidiaries from giving financial assistance for the purpose of the acquisition of its shares. It was common ground that if the first defendant had been incorporated in England and registered under the English Companies Acts the security provided by it to the bank would have constituted the unlawful giving of financial assistance contrary to s 151 of the 1985 Act. The defendants further contended that, although the court had jurisdiction under s 91 to make the order sought, it would be an improper exercise of the court's discretion to make such an order since the bank had full power to affect the sale without an order and any purchaser would have the statutory protection afforded by s 104(2)[c] of the 1925

---

a   Section 91(2) is set out at p 83 e f, post
b   Section 151, so far as material, is set out at p 78 a b, post
c   Section 104(2), so far as material, provides that: 'Where a conveyance is made in exercise of the power of sale conferred by [the 1925 Act] the title of the purchaser shall not be impeachable on the ground ... that the power was otherwise improperly or irregularly exercised ...'

Act. The questions arose (1) whether s 151 of the 1985 Act made it unlawful for a foreign subsidiary of an English parent company to give financial assistance for the purpose of the acquisition of shares in the parent company, and (2) whether the mere giving of such assistance by the foreign subsidiary also constituted the unlawful giving of financial assistance by the parent company contrary to s 151.

Held – (1) Applying the presumption that in the absence of a contrary intention s 151 of the 1985 Act was not intended to have extra-territorial effect, the term 'any of its subsidiaries' in s 151 was to be construed as limited to those subsidiary companies which were English companies. Accordingly, s 151 did not prohibit a foreign susidiary of an English parent company from giving financial assistance for the purpose of the acquisition of shares in its parent company. Moreover, the mere giving of financial assistance by the subsidiary did not ipso facto constitute the unlawful giving of financial assistance by the parent company contrary to s 151, since the prohibition was directed to the assisting company, not to its parent company (see p 80 c d and p 82 c to p 83 c, post).

(2) The court had jurisdiction in exceptional circumstances to sanction a sale under s 91(2) of the 1925 Act and thereby render the sale unimpeachable in circumstances where the mortgagee had full power to affect the sale without an order and where the purchaser had the statutory protection afforded by s 104(2) of the 1925 Act. In doing so the court had to be satisfied not only that there was sufficient evidence to enable it to exercise the jurisdiction but also that it was a proper case for the jurisdiction to be invoked. The court had to strike a balance between the interests of the mortgagor and the mortgagee and it would only be in exceptional cases that the balance would come down in favour of making an order. However, where the court was satisfied (i) that the prospects of the mortgagor successfully impeaching the sale were utterly remote, (ii) that the mortgagor's conduct, during the application as well as before it, justified the mortgagee's apprehension that the mortgagor would not hesitate to threaten proceeding against the purchaser if that would spoil the sale and (iii) that the mortgagee's fear that the sale would be lost unless an order was obtained was not unreasonable, there would be sufficient grounds for exercising the jurisdiction. On the facts, the court would make the order directing a sale sought by the bank (see p 89 c to p 90 a, post); *Marley v Mutual Security Merchant Bank and Trust Co Ltd* [1991] 3 All ER 198 applied.

Notes

For prohibition of financial assistance by a company for acquisition of its own shares, see 7(1) *Halsbury's Laws* (4th edn reissue) paras 267–268, and for cases on the subject, see 9(2) *Digest* (2nd reissue) 32–36, 3610–3613.

For the jurisdiction of the court to order sale of mortgaged land, see 32 *Halsbury's Laws* (4th edn) paras 849, 963, and for cases on the subject, see 35 *Digest* (Reissue) 444–445, 3909–3912.

For the Law of Property Act 1925, ss 91, 104, see 37 *Halsbury's Statutes* (4th edn) 205, 229.

For the Companies Act 1985, s 151, see 8 *Halsbury's Statutes* (4th edn) (1991 reissue) 249.

Cases referred to in judgment

Astor v Perry (Inspector of Taxes), Duncan v Adamson (Inspector of Taxes) [1935] AC 398, [1935] All ER Rep 713, HL.
Collco Dealings Ltd v IRC [1961] 1 All ER 762, [1962] AC 1, [1961] 2 WLR 401, HL.
Drummond v Collins (Surveyor of Taxes) [1915] AC 1011, HL.
International Tin Council, Re [1987] 1 All ER 890, [1987] Ch 419, [1987] 2 WLR 1229; affd [1988] 3 All ER 257, [1989] Ch 309, [1988] 3 WLR 1159, CA.
Marley v Mutual Security Merchant Bank and Trust Co Ltd [1991] 3 All ER 198, PC.

Cases also cited

Carl-Zeiss-Stiftung v Herbert Smith & Co (a firm) (No 2) [1969] 2 All ER 367, [1969] 2 Ch 276, CA.
Davies Jenkins & Co Ltd v Davies (Inspector of Taxes) [1967] 1 All ER 913, [1968] AC 1097, HL.
Musgrave v Dashwood (1688) 2 Vern 63, 23 ER 650.
Palk v Mortgage Services Funding plc [1993] 2 All ER 481, [1993] Ch 330, CA.
Pritchard v Briggs [1978] 1 All ER 886, [1980] Ch 338; rvsd [1980] 1 All ER 294, [1979] 3 WLR 868, CA.
Union Bank of London v Ingram (1882) 20 Ch D 463, CA.
Wallersteiner v Moir [1974] 3 All ER 217, [1974] 1 WLR 991, CA.
Waring (Lord) v London and Manchester Assurance Co Ltd [1935] Ch 310, [1934] All ER Rep 642.
Woolley v Colman (1882) 21 Ch D 169.

Summons

By a summons dated 24 August 1993 the plaintiff, Arab Bank plc, the mortgagee under a debenture dated 9 April 1990 made between the plaintiff, the first defendant, Merchantile Holdings Ltd, and the second defendant, Shelfco (No 488) Ltd, sought (i) a declaration that the power of sale conferred upon the plaintiff under the terms of the debenture had arisen and was exercisable and (ii) an order pursuant to s 91(2) of the Law of Property Act 1925 directing that the property owned by the first defendant known as Queens Quay and Queensbridge House, 58 Upper Thames Street, London EC4, be sold, that conduct of the sale be given to the plaintiff and that the plaintiff be at liberty to sell the property to Ibis (232) Ltd at the price of £12m and on such other terms as might be agreed between Ibis and the plaintiff. The facts are set out in the judgment.

Michael Briggs (instructed by *Frere Cholmeley Bischoff*) for the plaintiff.
Martin Mann QC and *Elspeth Talbot Rice* (instructed by *Leslie Hyman*) for the first defendant.
Alan Steinfeld QC and *Adrian Francis* (instructed by *Ince & Co*) for the second defendant.

MILLETT J. I will first give judgment under para 1 of the originating summons.

This case illustrates the dangers which are inherent in any attempt to recast statutory language in more modern and direct form for no better reason than to make it shorter, simpler and more easily intelligible. It raises two questions: (1) whether s 151 of the Companies Act 1985 (which prohibits a company or any of its subsidiaries from giving financial assistance for the purpose of the acquisition of shares in the company) makes it unlawful for a company incorporated outside Great Britain (a foreign subsidiary) which is a subsidiary of a parent company registered under the English Companies Acts (an English company) to give financial assistance for the purpose of the acquisition of shares in its parent company; (2) whether the mere giving of such assistance by the subsidiary ipso facto and without more necessarily also constitutes the unlawful giving of financial assistance by the parent company contrary to s 151.

The facts

On 9 April 1990 the plaintiff, Arab Bank plc (the bank), granted a loan facility of £15·4m to the second defendant, Shelfco (No 488) Ltd (Shelfco), for the express purpose of enabling it to acquire the entire share capital of Queensbridge Estates Ltd (Queensbridge). Queensbridge was the parent company and owned the entire share capital of the first defendant, Merchantile Holdings Ltd (Merchantile), which was the owner of a leasehold property, Queensbridge House and Queens Quay, Upper Thames Street in the City of London (the property). By a fixed and floating charge also dated 9 April 1990 Merchantile, inter alia, charged the property and, by a separate memorandum of the same date, it assigned the rental income of the property to the bank to secure the moneys advanced to Shelfco under the loan facility.

Queensbridge and Shelfco are both companies incorporated in England and registered under the English Companies Acts. It is common ground that, if Merchantile were also such a company, the security which it provided to the bank would constitute the unlawful giving of financial assistance contrary to s 151 of the 1985 Act. Merchantile, however, was incorporated in Gibraltar. It maintains a place of business in Great Britain, and accordingly is an 'oversea company' within the meaning of the 1985 Act (see s 744); but it is not a 'company' within the meaning of the 1985 Act (see s 735). It is, however, a 'subsidiary' of Queensbridge within the meaning of the 1985 Act, since the word 'company' in s 736 (which sets out the circumstances in which one company may be deemed to be a subsidiary of another) includes any 'body corporate'; and 'body corporate' is defined by s 740 to include a company incorporated elsewhere than in Great Britain.

The bank now wishes to realise its security by entering into a contract of sale to sell the property for £12m. The defendants, however, have long maintained that the bank's power of sale has not yet arisen and is not exercisable, and that its security is void as having been granted in contravention of s 151 of the 1985 Act. The purchaser has notice of these contentions and has refused to enter into a contract of purchase until the bank obtains a court order which will quieten the title. Hence the present application by originating summons, para 1 of which seeks a declaration that the bank's power of sale has arisen and is now exercisable.

I am satisfied on the evidence (and for the purpose of these proceedings only the defendants have conceded) that, if the bank's security is valid, its power of sale has arisen and is exercisable. The only question, therefore, is whether the security was lawfully granted.

Both defendants received legal advice at the time of the granting of the security that, Merchantile being a foreign subsidiary, the transaction was not caught by s 151. They entered into the transaction honestly and in good faith in reliance on that advice. Now, however, it suits them to maintain that the transaction was in fact unlawful; and they have so contended before me.

The current legislation

Section 151 of the 1985 Act provides:

> '(1) Subject to the following provisions of this Chapter, where a person is acquiring or is proposing to acquire shares in a company, it is not lawful for the company or any of its subsidiaries to give financial assistance directly or indirectly for the purpose of that acquisition before or at the same time as the acquisition takes place ...
>
> (3) If a company acts in contravention of this section, it is liable to a fine, and every officer of it who is in default is liable to imprisonment or a fine, or both.'

'Financial assistance' is defined by s 152.

Section 153 exempts certain transactions from the operation of s 151. Subsection (1) opens with the words:

> 'Section 151(1) does not prohibit a company from giving financial assistance for the purpose of an acquisition of shares in it or in its holding company ...'

Some of the transactions listed in s 153 are transactions which could be entered into by a foreign subsidiary: for example, a transaction where the company's principal purpose in giving the assistance was not to give it for the purpose of the acquisition of the shares, or the giving of the assistance was only an incidental part of a larger transaction; or where it took the form of a distribution of the company's assets by way of a payment of a lawful dividend or was made in the course of the company's winding up. (This would involve reading the word 'company' in the opening words of s 153 as including a foreign company, but if s 151 applies to such a company, so must s 153 so far as possible. The exemptions must, so far as possible, be co-extensive with the prohibition.) Other transactions, however, listed in s 153 could not be entered into by a foreign subsidiary: for example, where it involves a reduction of a company's capital confirmed by the court under s 137 of the 1985 Act, or a redemption or purchase of shares in accordance with Ch VII of Pt V of the 1985 Act.

Sections 155 to 158 relax the operation of s 151 for private companies provided that the provisions of those sections are complied with and the procedures there laid down are followed. The term 'private company' is defined by s 1(3) of the 1985 Act and, unless the contrary intention appears, does not include a foreign company. The contrary intention does not appear in ss 155 to 158. On the contrary, the provisions of those sections could not be complied with by a foreign subsidiary, even if it hived down its assets into an English sub-subsidiary.

The earlier legislation

The prohibition of a company from giving financial assistance in connection with the purchase of its own shares was introduced by s 45 of the Companies Act 1929. The prohibition was naturally limited to English companies. A corresponding provision in similar terms was enacted in Gibraltar in relation to companies incorporated there. The prohibition was extended by s 73 of the Companies Act 1947 to the giving of financial assistance in connection with the purchase of shares in the company's holding company. It did so by enacting that s 45 of the 1929 Act should apply to shares in a company's holding company as it applied to shares in the company itself. No similar extension has ever been introduced into the law of Gibraltar.

Section 45 of the 1929 Act as amended by s 73 of the 1947 Act was repealed and replaced by s 54 of the Companies Act 1948. That section was in the following terms:

'(1) Subject as provided in this section, it shall not be lawful for a company to give, whether directly or indirectly ... any financial assistance for the purpose of or in connection with a purchase or subscription made or to be made by any person of or for any shares in the company, or, where the company is a subsidiary company, in its holding company ...'

The 1948 Act contained certain limited exemptions but it did not contain all those contained in s 153 of the 1985 Act, nor did it contain any provisions corresponding to the provisions of ss 155 to 158 of the 1985 Act. It did, however, contain definitions of 'company' and 'subsidiary', which in all material respects were the same as those in the 1985 Act.

It is to be observed that the prohibition contained in s 54 of the 1948 Act, like that in the statutory provisions which it replaced, was directed to the company which provided the financial assistance (the assisting company). It was unlawful for that company to provide financial assistance in connection with the acquisition of its own shares or shares in its holding company. But the assisting company must be 'a company'. In the absence of a context to the contrary, and there was none, the section did not extend to a foreign subsidiary of an English holding company. On the other hand, because of the definition of 'subsidiary', it did extend to an English subsidiary of a foreign holding company (curiously, and probably inadvertently, the 1947 Act appears not to have done so).

Section 151 of the 1985 Act

Section 54 of the 1948 Act was repealed and replaced by ss 42 to 44 of the Companies Act 1981, which have in turn been re-enacted in similar terms by ss 151 to 158 of the 1985 Act. The language of s 54 of the 1948 Act has been completely recast. The whole perspective of the section has been altered. The prohibition is still directed to the assisting company. But the section no longer starts with the assisting company and prohibits it from giving financial assistance for the purchase of its own shares or shares in its holding company. Instead, it starts with the company whose shares are to be acquired (the target company) and prohibits it or 'any of its subsidiaries' from giving financial assistance for the purchase of its own shares.

It is difficult to believe that this change, which is primarily one of style, was intended to make any alteration in the substantive law, particularly when the opening words of s 153 refer back to s 151 as if it were still cast in the old form; and in an entirely domestic situation it does not do so. But because of the statutory definitions of 'company' (which prima facie means an English company) and 'subsidiary' (which does not) it appears to have made at least one change and may have made two. Formerly, the assisting company had to be 'a company', ie an English company; but the target company did not: it was sufficient if it was the assisting company's holding company. Now, however, it is the target company which has to be 'a company'; the assisting company does not: it is sufficient if it is one of the target company's subsidiaries. The new requirement that the target company must be 'a company' means that the giving of financial assistance by the English subsidiary of a foreign parent company for the acquisition of shares in that company appears to be no longer prohibited. On the other hand, the removal of the former requirement that the assisting company must be 'a company', coupled with the use of the words 'any of its subsidiaries' instead of 'any of its subsidiary companies' in place of the cumbersome and ungainly phrase 'where the company is a subsidiary company', if taken literally, extends the prohibition for the first time to the case where the prohibited act, ie the giving of financial assistance, is committed by a foreign company.

Before considering whether it does so or not, I shall deal with the second of the two questions which has been argued before me.

Does the mere giving of financial assistance by the subsidiary ipso facto also constitute the giving of such assistance by the parent company?

In my judgment the answer is plainly No. The prohibition is, and always has been, directed to the assisting company, not to its parent company. If the giving of financial assistance by a subsidiary for the acquisition of shares in its holding company necessarily also constituted the giving of financial assistance by the holding company, s 73 of the 1947 Act would not have been necessary. Moreover, ss 153 to 158 of the 1985 Act are clearly predicated on the assumption that it is the conduct of the subsidiary alone which needs statutory authorisation.

This is not to say that the giving of financial assistance by the subsidiary may not involve unlawful conduct on the part of the parent. If the acts of the subsidiary are in breach of s 151, the conduct of the parent in procuring them will constitute an offence. And even if the section does not apply to foreign subsidiaries, the hiving down of an asset by an English company to such a subsidiary in order to enable it to be made available to finance a contemplated acquisition of shares of the English company would clearly contravene the section: it would constitute the indirect provision of financial assistance by the English company.

Does s 151 of the 1985 Act make it unlawful for a foreign subsidiary of an English parent company to give financial assistance for the purpose of the acquisition of shares of its parent company?

Read literally and with the assistance of the statutory definition of 'subsidiary', s 151 clearly purports to make it unlawful for a foreign subsidiary of an English parent company to give financial assistance for the purpose of the acquisition of shares of its parent company. The result, however, is to give the section an extra-territorial effect contrary to the general principles of private international law, for the capacity of a corporation, the regulation of its affairs, the maintenance of its capital and the protection of its creditors and shareholders are generally recognised to be matters for the law of the place of incorporation. But there have been many cases in which the words of a statute have been given a more limited meaning than they are capable of bearing where there is a proper ground for concluding that this was the intention of Parliament: see, for example, *Drummond v Collins (Surveyor of Taxes)* [1915] AC 1011 at 1017, *Astor v Perry (Inspector of Taxes), Duncan v Adamson (Inspector of Taxes)* [1935] AC 398 at 417, [1935] All ER Rep 713 at 723, *Collco Dealings Ltd v IRC* [1961] 1 All ER 762, [1962] AC 1 and *Re International Tin Council* [1987] 1 All ER 890 at 901–902, [1987] Ch 419 at 450; *affd* [1988] 3 All ER 257 at 360, [1989] Ch 309 at 329. The consideration that the more limited meaning is necessary in order to avoid the creation of a jurisdiction wider than that generally recognised by international law has often been recognised as such a ground.

The defendants submit that a literal construction is necessary in order effectively to deal with the mischief which it is the object of the section to prevent. That mischief, it is submitted, is by means of the forbidden assistance to circumvent the rule which forbids an English company from distributing its assets to shareholders otherwise than by the lawful distribution of profits, reduction of capital or distribution of surplus assets on a winding up. Subsidiaries are included in the prohibition since the distribution of its assets to the shareholders in its holding company is tantamount to a distribution of the assets of the holding company itself. The same consideration applies whether the subsidiary is incorporated in Great Britain or abroad. If foreign subsidiaries were outside the prohibition, the defendants submit, a coach and horses could be driven through the section by the simple expedient of taking the precaution of always interposing a wholly-owned foreign subsidiary between a company and its assets.

I am not impressed by the 'coach and horses' argument. As I have already observed, the hiving down of the assets by an English company to a foreign subsidiary in order that they may be available for the purpose of assisting in the financing of a contemplated purchase of the parent company's own shares would, in my judgment, constitute the indirect provision of financial assistance by the parent company; while the presence of ss 155 to 158 of the 1985 Act makes it unnecessary to interpose a foreign subsidiary in advance as a matter of routine forward strategic planning. Bearing in mind that the provision of financial assistance for the purchase will almost invariably be at the request and instigation of the purchaser rather than the target company, and that it can easily and lawfully be provided where this can be done without prejudice to the interests of creditors and minority shareholders, the interposition of a foreign subsidiary where no purchase was yet in contemplation would seem to require a combination of legal acumen, foresight and dishonesty which is most unusual.

Nor am I satisfied that the mischief which the section is designed to prevent is the extraction of the assets of the target company rather than those of its subsidiary. This was not the case before 1981, when the prohibition was limited to English subsidiaries even when the target company was an English company. The defendants submit that, if the mischief sought to be prevented was the extraction of assets from the subsidiary, then the section would have prohibited an English subsidiary of a foreign parent company from giving financial assistance for the purchase of shares of the parent company. This would be a formidable argument if I were persuaded that the failure to cover this case, covered in the 1948 Act, was deliberate; but I am not. The primary class of persons which the section was designed to protect must, in my judgment, be the creditors of the assisting company; and they are equally prejudiced by the extraction of its assets for the purpose of financing the acquisition of shares in its parent company whether that parent company is English or foreign. I can see no possible reason or justification for excluding such a case from the prohibition and, if this was indeed the result of the recasting of the statutory language in 1981, I think that it must have been inadvertent.

Whether the section is intended primarily for the protection of the creditors of the assisting company or for the protection of the creditors of its parent company, however, it is directed to the conduct of the assisting company.

Where that company is a subsidiary, it is directed to the subsidiary, not to its parent company. The section operates by regulating the conduct of the subsidiary and depriving it of the capacity to enter into transactions of the kind specified. The capacity of a corporation, the regulation of its conduct, the maintenance of its capital, and the protection of its creditors and shareholders are all matters for the law of the place of its incorporation, not the law of the place of incorporation of its parent company.

Conclusion

I have reached the firm conclusion that 'any of its subsidiaries' in s 151 of the 1985 Act must be construed as limited to those subsidiaries which are subsidiary companies, that is to say, English companies. My reasons for this conclusion are as follows.

(1) The recasting of the language of the section, and in particular the change from 'subsidiary company' to 'any of its subsidiaries', was almost certainly a matter of style and not intended to make a substantive change in the law.

(2) There is a presumption that, in the absence of a contrary intention express or implied, United Kingdom legislation does not apply to foreign persons or corporations outside the United Kingdom whose acts are performed outside the United Kingdom. Some limitation of the general words of s 151 is necessary in order to avoid imputing to Parliament an intention to create an exorbitant jurisdiction which is contrary to generally accepted principles of international law.

(3) In relation to the maintenance of the capital of a corporation and the protection of its creditors and shareholders the place where its assets are depleted or put at risk by the giving of the forbidden assistance is irrelevant. To limit the section to the giving of the forbidden assistance in the United Kingdom, as the defendants contend, would be misdirected legislation which would be wholly inadequate to protect the creditors of the subsidiary and would still be at variance with generally accepted principles of international law.

(4) Section 151 is directed at the assisting company. It renders particular acts on the part of the assisting company unlawful. Whether the section is intended primarily for the protection of the creditors of the assisting company or for the protection of creditors of its parent company, where the assisting company is a subsidiary the section is directed at the subsidiary and not at the parent company. It operates by regulating the conduct of the subsidiary and depriving it of the capacity to enter into transactions of the kind specified.

(5) The capacity of a corporation, the regulation of its conduct, the maintenance of its capital and the protection of its creditors and shareholders are all matters for the law of the place of its incorporation, not the law of the place of incorporation of its parent company.

(6) Section 54 of the 1948 Act, which the 1981 and 1985 Acts replaced, did not prohibit a foreign subsidiary from providing financial assistance for the acquisition of shares in its parent company.

(7) Section 151 does not prohibit a partly-owned foreign subsidiary from providing financial assistance for the purchase of its own shares.

(8) The penalties for contravention of s 151 do not extend to foreign subsidiaries or their officers.

(9) A number of the more important exemptions in s 153 do not apply to a foreign subsidiary, which could not take advantage of the relaxation of s 151

provided by ss 155 to 158. One would expect the exemptions and relaxations to be coextensive with the prohibition.

(10) If s 151 applies to foreign subsidiaries, such a subsidiary may be prevented from entering into a transaction which is lawful under the law of its incorporation, not only where that law is less stringent than our own, but even where it is in similar or even identical terms to our own. That cannot have been the intention of Parliament.

In my judgment s 151 does not prohibit a foreign subsidiary of an English parent company from giving financial assistance for the acquisition of shares in its parent company and I will so declare. I will also make a declaration under para 1 of the originating summons that the power of sale has arisen and is now exercisable.

I will now give judgment under para 3 of the originating summons.

Paragraph 3 of the originating summons seeks an order pursuant to s 91(2) of the Law of Property Act 1925 directing that the property be sold by the bank to Ibis (232) Ltd (Ibis) on the terms of a draft contract between the bank and Ibis or on such other terms as the court shall direct and as shall be acceptable to Ibis. After argument the bank now seeks an order directing that the property be sold, that conduct of the sale be given to the bank, and that the bank be at liberty to sell the property to Ibis at a price of £12m and on such other terms except as to price as may be agreed between Ibis and the bank.

Section 91(2) of the Law of Property Act 1925 reads as follows:

'In any action, whether for foreclosure, or for redemption, or for sale, or for the raising and payment in any manner of mortgage money, the court, on the request of the mortgagee, or of any person interested either in the mortgage money or in the right of redemption, and, notwithstanding that—(a) any other person dissents; or (b) the mortgagee or any person so interested does not appear in the action; and without allowing any time for redemption or for payment of any mortgage money, may direct a sale of the mortgaged property, on such terms as it thinks fit, including the deposit in court of a reasonable sum fixed by the court to meet the expenses of sale and to secure performance of the terms.'

The property

The property is held on three headleases from three different freeholders for terms all of which will expire in 2075. The major part of the property consists of an office building (Queensbridge House) which is held under a headlease from the City of London Corporation. The ground rent of Queensbridge House is calculated at 30·5% of the full rack rental value with an upwards only rent review every seven years. It was last reviewed in 1990 and the amount currently payable is £580,000 per annum. Since then the rental value of office property in the City of London has fallen dramatically and the ground rent is now considered to be 'far in excess' of the current rental value. The defendants concede that without a tenant of Queensbridge House the property has a negative value.

Queensbridge House was constructed in the early 1970s. Although satisfactory at the time of construction, it is now regarded as well below the standard provided by new and highly specific modern office accommodation currently available in the City of London. It is let to Wilde Sapte for a term expiring in 2012 with a mutual break option in 2007. The rent currently payable by Wilde Sapte is £2m per annum with five-year rent reviews. The most recent review was in June of this year. According to all the evidence there is no realistic prospect of an increase in the rent payable by Wilde Sapte being obtained at the reviews in 1998 or 2003.

It is widely known that Wilde Sapte intends to vacate Queensbridge House as soon as it can, and there is no prospect of its remaining in occupation after the year 2007. It has in fact been actively seeking to move from Queensbridge House since November 1991. It is, however, of paramount importance to Wilde Sapte that it should achieve a surrender of its lease of Queensbridge House upon its removal from those premises.

With its advisers (St Quintin), Wilde Sapte has met all the principal developers and prospective landlords who could provide Wilde Sapte with the accommodation which it needs upon the relocation of its offices. In every instance, with only one exception, an assignment of Wilde Sapte's lease of Queensbridge House or the purchase of the headlease of the building has been rejected out of hand by prospective landlords. The grounds for their rejection were based upon the excessive risk of taking on substantially over-rented, secondhand accommodation in the particular location.

Wilde Sapte's requirements have been well known in the market for nearly two years and St Quintin have held discussions with over 20 parties, including many who approached Wilde Sapte, but none has made an offer for Wilde Sapte's lease or the headleases.

The present proposal

Wilde Sapte has recently reached agreement in principle with Broadgate Developments plc (Broadgate) to take a lease of a new London headquarters building at 1 Fleet Place, which forms part of the Ludgate development. During the negotiations between Wilde Sapte and Broadgate, Broadgate or its officers have continuously made it plain to Wilde Sapte that Broadgate will require the lease documentation to be exchanged on or before 30 September 1993, failing which Broadgate reserves the right to withdraw from the present negotiations and to be free to seek other tenants. Wilde Sapte is unwilling to consider entering into contractual terms with Broadgate until such time as it has secured a release of its existing obligations in respect of Queensbridge House. Wilde Sapte has made arrangements to achieve such a release by arranging for Ibis, a 50% subsidiary of Ex-Lands Ltd and an independent company in which Wilde Sapte has no interest or representation on the board, to purchase the property from the bank under arrangements which Wilde Sapte has been negotiating with Broadgate, Ibis and the bank.

The proposal, in summary, is as follows. (1) The bank will sell the property to Ibis for £12m subject to and with the benefit of Wilde Sapte's lease. (2) Wilde Sapte will surrender its lease of Queensbridge House to Ibis and pay Ibis a reverse premium of £12m (which Ibis will use to fund the purchase of the lease from the bank). (3) Wilde Sapte will take a lease of 1 Fleet Place from Broadgate. (4) If Ibis should subsequently realise a profit on the sale of the property, Ibis will pay Wilde Sapte a sum equal to 25% of the net profit.

This last element of the proposal emerged at a late stage during the present hearing, being disclosed by evidence put in by Wilde Sapte. The bank was previously unaware of it.

Although the proposed purchaser is Ibis, its purchase is to be funded entirely by Wilde Sapte, and negotiations with the bank have been conducted almost entirely by Wilde Sapte. For present purposes it is appropriate to regard Wilde Sapte as the purchaser no less than Ibis.

Wilde Sapte regards itself as in a unique position to pay a premium, whether for the surrender of its lease of Queensbridge House or for the purchase of the headleases of the property, and to pay a premium in excess of a value of the property. This is because the new accommodation at 1 Fleet Place offers Wilde Sapte the opportunity to participate in a prestigious development which, in its view, suits its requirements exactly. Wilde Sapte has waited for some time for an opportunity such as the present and, if it disappears, it is unlikely that Wilde Sapte would be prepared or able to pay such a high price again to obtain its release from its obligations in respect of Queensbridge House.

The reasons for the application

The bank's statutory power of sale has arisen and is exercisable, as I have just declared under para 1 of the originating summons and the bank, therefore, is at liberty to conclude the proposed sale to Ibis without the assistance of the court. The bank, however, seeks an order from the court sanctioning the sale under s 91(2) of the Law of Property Act 1925. It does so because it fears (rightly or wrongly) that the sale may be lost unless such an order is obtained. It is not clear whether it is Wilde Sapte or Ibis which is insisting on the sale being sanctioned by the court; but Wilde Sapte has stated in an affidavit before the court that 'it is vital from Wilde Sapte's point of view that such orders be obtained before 30th September 1993' and, in the context, the phrase 'such orders' must include the order sought by the bank under s 91(2) of the 1925 Act.

If this is indeed the purchaser's attitude, it is easily understandable. Receivers were appointed by the bank of the income of the property in October 1991. The appointment was immediately challenged by Merchantile which informed the receivers that if they took any steps to dispose of the property they would do so at their peril. In 1992 the bank commenced proceedings against Merchantile in respect of events which occurred before the receivers were appointed. In those proceedings Merchantile alleged that the bank's demand for payment was premature and, inferentially, that the appointment of receivers was invalid. Merchantile has mentioned that allegation in correspondence throughout 1992. Those proceedings are due to be heard in January 1994. Even if any apprehension on the part of Ibis or Wilde Sapte that a sale would be challenged by the defendants on the ground that the price was inadequate was unsupported by evidence when the bank's application was made, it has since been shown to be well founded by the attitude which the defendants have adopted in the course of the application. They have adduced evidence asserting, without foundation, that the proposed sale is in bad faith and at an undervalue, and have taken every conceivable point on the evidence which could be taken against the proposed sale.

The bank's purpose in making the application was not to obtain protection for itself but to satisfy Ibis and Wilde Sapte that they would obtain an unimpeachable title. Accordingly, at an early stage of the application I offered to dismiss the application on the defendants' undertaking not to seek to set the transaction aside against Ibis or Wilde Sapte. This would have left them free to pursue a purely monetary remedy against the bank, which has abundant resources to satisfy any judgment. This was rejected out of hand by the defendants. It is difficult to avoid the conclusion that the defendants place a greater value on their ability to spoil a good sale than in their claim that it is a bad one.

The value of the property

The bank's application is supported by two valuations. (1) DTZ Debenham Thorpe (Debenhams) dated 13 August 1993. This contained no formal valuation of the property but described the offer of £12m to be 'very attractive and one which we recommend the Bank to accept'. It advised the bank 'to capitalise on what may be a narrow window of opportunity while Wilde Sapte wish to vacate the premises and investor demand exists'.

(2) Hillier Parker also dated 13 August 1993. Hillier Parker were asked to express their views of the proposed sale in case the defendants criticised Debenhams as not independent: the receivers appointed by the bank were apparently members of the firm, though they were not the partners who gave the valuation. The fear was justified: the criticism duly materialised. Hillier Parker gave it as their opinion that £12m was 'the best price reasonably obtainable in the open market'. They described Wilde Sapte's offer in the following terms:

> 'In the unusual circumstances of the move by Wilde Sapte to new offices in weak market conditions so that they are able to secure very advantageous terms for their new premises, the proposed transaction which has been arranged by Wilde Sapte reflects an offer from a special purchaser who is prepared to pay a higher price, that is showing a lower yield, than would be achieved in the open market.'

They added that it was extremely rare for large commercial properties in the City of London to be sold by auction and that this was not an appropriate method of sale for the property. Furthermore, they expressed the opinion that a full marketing campaign would be 'highly unlikely to produce a higher offer'.

Both firms confirmed their opinions in later correspondence. Debenhams stated that they did not believe that the best price could be achieved by auction; and that, while they had not carried out a formal valuation, they had carried out valuation exercises and were satisfied that the value of the property was less than £12m. Hillier Parker stated that 'the price of £12 million is in excess of the price which would be paid on the open market' and added:

> 'The special circumstances of Wilde Sapte's occupation cannot be given any proper or reliable valuation. At the end of the day the amount of the premium is simply a matter of negotiation. It is therefore highly speculative to value the Property purely on the basis of an arithmetical extrapolation of Wilde Sapte's obligations. The only way to value the Property is to determine what it would be worth in the open market and that is what we have done. Another key factor is that Wilde Sapte will only remain a special purchaser while they can afford to pay a capital sum to buy out their future liabilities. This situation is only likely to continue in the current weak occupational market when tenants can secure inducements when negotiating leases of new accommodation. This window of opportunity, however, is closing as the supply of the new accommodation is gradually reduced, assisted by the impact of the two IRA bombs, and tenants wake up to the fact that the position of almost unlimited choice maybe about to change.'

These two valuations were in line with three other valuations copies of which were in evidence: (1) a valuation by Wetherall Green & Smith (who advised Wilde Sapte) in January 1993 which valued the property at £9,750,000;

(2) a valuation by Richard Ellis (who advised the only other prospective purchaser who has shown any interest) that 'it would be difficult to value the head leases at more than £10 million'; (3) a 'desk top' valuation by Bernard Thorpe (now part of Debenhams but made by different partners) relied upon by the defendants. This valued the property at £15·5m. However, the valuer was under the impression that the ground rent was £180,000. Had he known that it was £580,000 he would have valued it at £12m. He also was unaware of the break clause. Had he known about this, he too would have valued the property at less than £12m.

All these valuations were criticised for the failure to take account of the redevelopment potential of Queensbridge House. However, there is in evidence a further valuation by St Quintin (Wilde Sapte's advisers); despite their belief that there were reasonable prospects of redeveloping the property in 1996–98, they valued it at only £8m.

In the present state of the market any value attributable to the future prospects of redeveloping the property must be highly speculative and, in so far as it adds anything to the value, must have been taken account of by Wilde Sapte in making its offer of £12m. I am not prepared to assume that five other reputable valuers overlooked the prospects of redevelopment or their value (if any).

The negotiations

Faced with the indisputable fact that Wilde Sapte is a special purchaser and the overwhelming evidence that its offer is in excess of the market value of the property, the defendants asserted that the bank had simply snatched at Wilde Sapte's opening offer and had failed to explore its willingness to improve upon it. This led to further evidence by the bank of the course of the negotiations, accompanied by discovery and cross-examination. The defendants' allegation turned out to be without foundation.

It is not necessary to rehearse the details of the negotiations. It is sufficient to say that Wilde Sapte approached the bank in January 1993 and asked the bank to state the 'maximum price' which it would expect to receive for the property. The bank indicated informally that it would want about £16m.

In May 1993 Wilde Sapte returned to the bank with an offer of £10m together with 25% of the net profit on any redevelopment of the property. The bank described this in evidence as an offer of £10·5m, which gives some indication of the value which the bank may have placed at the time on the value of the property's redevelopment.

The bank was not interested in a share in the profit on the redevelopment of the property, but it approached Broadgate's lenders in an attempt to see whether there was room for some further funding to enable the offer of £10m to be improved. It is not clear whether the bank was seeking some payment by Broadgate or its bankers to Wilde Sapte which would enable Wilde Sapte to pay an increased price for the property or an interest for itself in 1 Fleet Place or both; but the attempt came to nothing.

The bank rejected Wilde Sapte's offer in June. It made no counter-offer of its own. It has been criticised by the defendants for this. But the bank was under no pressure to sell. The net rents and profits of the property were sufficient to keep down the interest on the loan (though only just) and the bank was not desperate for a sale. The boot was on the other foot. It was Wilde Sapte which was desperate for the sale. The bank was criticised for its failure to make a counter-offer but, in the circumstances, its tactics appear to me to have been entirely appropriate: sit back and wait for the special purchaser, in increasing desperation, to make an increased offer.

Such an offer duly came on 9 August 1993. Wilde Sapte then offered £12m, £9m to be paid on completion and £3m to be deferred for 18 months. Wilde Sapte stated that:

> 'The price of £12 million for the property will represent a very heavy burden to this partnership which we would in no way see our way to increase.'

Despite this, on 11 August, Wilde Sapte offered to pay the whole £12m on completion provided that it was satisfied that its cash flow and resources would allow it to do so.

The bank then obtained the valuations from Debenhams and Hillier Parker and applied to its own head office for approval. Formal approval for a sale at £12m was given, but head office asked the bank to try to increase the price to £13m. Wilde Sapte was duly informed that head office had 'set a price of £13 million for the Property'. This drew the immediate response from Wide Sapte that—

> 'no offer above the £12 million already on the table is possible. We have stretched our resources and cash flow to the utmost to meet what we understood was an acceptable figure. There is, quite frankly, no more money available from us.'

Wilde Sapte gave the bank until 1 pm on the following day to accept the £12m, failing which Wilde Sapte would notify Broadgate of the position.

Summary

On this evidence, I am completely satisfied (i) that Wilde Sapte is a special purchaser, (ii) that the figure of £12m represents significantly more than the value of the property on the open market, (iii) that the bank was under no pressure to sell, (iv) that the figure of £12m represents less than the amount owed to the bank, so that it has throughout been in the bank's interest, as well as in that of the defendants, to obtain a greater price if possible, (v) that the bank tried to obtain an increase in the offer and failed and (vi) that the bank has no reason to disbelieve and does not disbelieve Wilde Sapte's protestations that there is simply no more money on the table.

It was properly conceded on behalf of the defendants that on this evidence the bank's conduct cannot be impugned. I would go further and say that the prospects of any further facts emerging hereafter which might enable the defendants to impugn the bank's conduct are remote; and that the prospects of the defendants ever having the sale set aside against the purchaser are simply fanciful. The defendants would have to prove not only that the sale was at a gross undervalue and that the bank had failed to take reasonable steps to obtain the best price but that the purchaser was aware of this. Proof that, despite Wilde Sapte's protestations, it would have paid more would be insufficient. The defendants would have to prove that the bank was aware of this and that Wilde Sapte knew that the bank was aware of it. In the absence of such knowledge, the bank had to make a commercial decision whether to accept the offer or to insist upon more and risk losing the sale altogether. The court will not second guess the exercise by the bank of its commercial judgment.

The jurisdiction

The defendants concede that the court has jurisdiction under the section to make the order but submit that it would not be a proper exercise of the discretion to make it. They rightly submit that the issue is not whether the proposed sale is one which it would be proper for the bank to enter into in the exercise of its statutory power of sale; nor whether, on the present evidence, such a sale would be capable of being impugned either as against the bank or as against the purchaser. The issue is whether the court should take the exceptional and unprecedented step of sanctioning a sale and thereby rendering the sale unimpeachable in circumstances where the mortgagee has full power to affect the sale without an order and where the purchaser has the statutory protection afforded by s 104(2) of the Law of Property Act 1925.

I accept that the application breaks new ground, though it is none the worse for that. It means only that the bank must make out a proper case not only for the proposed sale but for the court to lend its assistance by making the sale unimpeachable. I also accept that in both respects it is for the bank to make out its case. In *Marley v Mutual Security Merchant Bank and Trust Co Ltd* [1991] 3 All ER 198 where a trustee sought an order from the court authorising it to sell the trust property the Privy Council held that the question was not whether the trustee had exercised due diligence but whether there was sufficient evidence before the court to enable it to exercise its jurisdiction. The analogy is far from exact; but I agree that a similar approach ought to be adopted in the present case. Where a mortgagee seeks the assistance of the court in order to allay the fears of its purchaser, the court must be satisfied that it has sufficient evidence to enable it to exercise the jurisdiction. On the evidence before me I am completely satisfied of that. But I would go further than that. The court must also be satisfied that it is a proper case for the invocation of its jurisdiction; it must be satisfied that it should exercise its discretion rather than leave it to the mortgagee to exercise his own power of sale. The court must strike a balance between the interests of the mortgagor and those of the mortgagee. It will, I think, only be in exceptional circumstances that the balance will come down in favour of making the order. The court ought not lightly or unnecessarily to take the step of rendering a transaction unimpeachable where a party with an adverse interest wishes to impeach it. But where the court is satisfied, as I am satisfied (i) that the prospects of the mortgagor's successfully impeaching the sale are utterly remote, (ii) that the mortgagor's conduct, during the application as well as before it, justifies the apprehension that it will not hesitate to threaten proceedings against the purchaser if that will spoil the sale and (iii) that the mortgagee's fear that the sale will be lost unless an order is obtained is not unreasonable, then, in my judgment, there are sufficient grounds for exercising the jurisdiction. In such circumstances, the mortgagee's statutory power of sale is of no practical use to him. He might just as well have no such power.

Accordingly, I will make the order as asked. I have carefully considered whether, notwithstanding the defendants' rejection of my offer to dismiss the application on an undertaking by them not to bring proceedings against the purchaser, I should achieve the same result by inserting in the order a proviso to preserve Merchantile's right to impugn the transaction against the bank. I have, however, come to the conclusion that I should not do so in the absence of the slightest evidence that the bank's conduct could ever be successfully impugned.

Order accordingly.

Celia Fox Barrister.

R v Martinez-Tobon

COURT OF APPEAL, CRIMINAL DIVISION
LORD TAYLOR OF GOSFORTH CJ, SCHIEMANN AND WRIGHT JJ
25 OCTOBER, 26 NOVEMBER 1993

Criminal law – Trial – Summing up – Adverse comment – Silence of accused – Direction to jury – Defence case involving alleged facts at variance with prosecution evidence or additional to it or exculpatory and which if true within defendant's knowledge – Comment by judge on defendant's failure to give evidence – Guidelines on directing jury when defendant fails to give evidence.

D, a co-defendant of the appellant, was arrested on his arrival at Heathrow Airport when 2·48 kg of cocaine was found in his briefcase. He was charged with and later pleaded guilty to being knowingly concerned in the fraudulent evasion of the prohibition on the importation of cocaine. The appellant was arrested and charged with the same offence. At the trial the prosecution case was that the appellant was involved in arranging the drug run for D and was to be involved in the receipt of the drugs on D's arrival. The appellant's defence was that he was expecting and had discussed with D a consignment of emeralds, not cocaine. D denied that version of events and the appellant did not give evidence to support it. In his summing up the judge directed the jury that they were not to conclude from the fact that the appellant had not given evidence that he was guilty but added that, if in fact the appellant had thought D was bringing in emeralds and not cocaine, it might be thought that he would be very anxious to say so. The appellant appealed on the ground that the judge had misdirected the jury.

Held – In summing up to the jury where the defendant failed to give evidence the judge should give the conventional direction that the defendant was under no obligation to testify and the jury ought not to assume that he was guilty because he had not given evidence. However, provided such a direction was given, a stronger comment might be appropriate where the defence case involved alleged facts which were at variance with the prosecution evidence or additional to it, or exculpatory, and which, if true, had to be within the knowledge of the defendant. The nature and strength of such comment was a matter for the judge and depended on the circumstances of the individual case but could not be such as to contradict or nullify the essentials of the conventional direction. Applying those principles, the judge had been entitled to make the comment he did since the appellant had made an assertion of fact in conflict with the prosecution evidence going to the heart of the case and in respect of which, if true, the appellant could clearly have given evidence, and the jury for their part were entitled, in considering whether the suggestion concerning emeralds might possibly be true, to take into account the fact that there had been no evidence from the appellant to support what therefore remained a bare assertion. Accordingly, the appeal would be dismissed (see p 98 g to j and p 99 b c, post).

Dicta of Lord Parker CJ in *R v Bathurst* [1968] 1 All ER 1175 at 1179 and of Lawton LJ in *R v Sparrow* [1973] 2 All ER 129 at 136 applied.

Dicta of Lord Russell CJ in *R v Rhodes* [1899] 1 QB 77 at 83–84 and of Lord Alverstone CJ in *R v Corrie and Watson* (1904) 20 TLR 365 at 365 considered.

Notes

For the failure of the accused to give evidence, see 11(2) *Halsbury's Laws* (4th edn reissue) paras 1123, 1180, and for cases on the subject, see 15(2) *Digest* (2nd reissue) 203–204, 19991–20001.

Cases referred to in judgment

R v Bathurst [1968] 1 All ER 1175, [1968] 2 QB 99, [1968] 2 WLR 1092, CCA.
R v Bernard (1908) 1 Cr App R 218, CCA.
R v Berry (1992) Times, 20 May, CA.
R v Bridgen [1973] Crim LR 579, CA.
R v Brocket (12 October 1970, unreported), CA.
R v Corrie and Watson (1904) 20 TLR 365, CA.
R v Fisher [1964] Crim LR 150, CCA.
R v Fullerton [1994] Crim LR 63, CA.
R v Harris (1987) 84 Cr App R 75, CA.
R v Mutch [1973] 1 All ER 178, CA.
R v Pratt [1971] Crim LR 234, CA.
R v Rhodes [1899] 1 QB 77, CCR.
R v Sparrow [1973] 2 All ER 129, [1973] 1 WLR 488, CA.
R v Squire [1990] Crim LR 341, CA.
R v Taylor [1993] Crim LR 223, CA.
R v Voisin [1918] 1 KB 531, [1918–19] All ER Rep 491, CCA.
R v Walsh (15 May 1990, unreported), CA.
Waugh v R [1950] AC 203, PC.

Cases also cited

R v Davison [1972] 3 All ER 1121, [1972] 1 WLR 1540, CA.
R v Fleming (18 May 1988, unreported), CA.
R v Hubbard (11 December 1990, unreported), CA.
R v Marsh (18 March 1992, unreported), CA.
R v Matthews (1990) 91 Cr App R 43, CA.
R v Storey (1968) 52 Cr App R 334, CA.

Appeal against conviction

Wilson Martinez-Tobon appealed against his conviction on 29 November 1991 in the Crown Court at Isleworth before Judge Miller and a jury of being concerned in the fraudulent evasion in the prohibition on the importation of a class A drug, cocaine, for which he was sentenced to ten years' imprisonment and a confiscation order under the Drug Trafficking Offences Act 1986 was made in the sum of £2,000, with 42 days' imprisonment consecutive in default. The facts are set out in the judgment of the court.

James Montgomery (assigned by the *Registrar of Criminal Appeals*) for the appellant.
David Radcliffe (instructed by the *Solicitor for the Customs and Excise*) for the Crown.

Cur adv vult

26 November 1993. The following judgment of the court was delivered.

LORD TAYLOR OF GOSFORTH CJ. This appeal is brought upon one ground only. Indeed, it is based upon one sentence only in the learned judge's summing up. The question raised has been considered many times in this court against varying factual backgrounds, but the answers have not all been consistent. What is the scope of a judge's discretion in commenting on the defendant's failure to give evidence?

On 29 November 1991 in the Crown Court at Isleworth the appellant was convicted of being knowingly concerned in the fraudulent evasion of a prohibition on importing cocaine. He was sentenced to ten years' imprisonment, a confiscation order under the Drug Trafficking Offences Act 1986 was made in the sum of £2,000 and a sentence of 45 days' imprisonment consecutive to the ten-year sentence was imposed in default of payment. A recommendation for deportation was also made.

There were two co-accused. Hector Jose Diaz-Martinez (Diaz) had pleaded guilty on 13 August 1991 to the same offence and was sentenced at the same time as the appellant to four years' imprisonment. He gave evidence for the prosecution. Umberto Valencia was acquitted of the same offence.

The appellant was refused leave to appeal against conviction and sentence by the single judge. However, on 4 March 1993 the full court granted him leave to appeal against conviction whilst refusing leave in relation to sentence.

It was not disputed that on 30 March 1991 Diaz had knowingly brought in 2·48 kg of cocaine in his briefcase and had been arrested with it on his arrival at Heathrow Airport. In brief the prosecution case was that the appellant was deeply involved in arranging the drug run for Diaz and was to be involved in the receipt of the drugs upon Diaz's arrival. The defence case at trial was that the appellant was expecting and had discussed with Diaz a consignment of emeralds not cocaine. Diaz denied that and the appellant did not give evidence in support of it.

The prosecution case fell under three heads: (1) transactions in early 1991; (2) the events of 30 March and 1 April 1991; and (3) evidence of events during the criminal proceedings.

(1) *Transactions in early 1991*

In January 1991 Diaz came to London from Colombia. He stayed at the St Giles and Bedford Hotels. He used the false name 'Abelleira'. He said in evidence he had come to Europe to collect some money. He met the appellant. Although there was no discussion about drugs at first, he later saw a suitcase containing cocaine whilst with friends of the appellant. A few days later the appellant told him to move to the Bedford Hotel because one of those friends had been arrested with drugs. Diaz wrote certain details on a piece of the Bedford Hotel notepaper and gave it to the appellant. It was later found in the appellant's bedroom when his house was searched on 2 April 1991. The appellant gave him £4,000 to send to his wife and required him to go to São

Paulo and return to London via Copenhagen and Brussels with a suitcase containing drugs. Diaz bought an airline ticket for Caracas on 21 January and sent the £4,000 to his wife in Colombia. On 24 January a further sum of over £1,000 was sent to her. On the document detailing that payment there were typed the words 'Remite: Tony'. Diaz testified that Tony was the appellant. A receipt for the sum of £1,000 was subsequently found in the appellant's bedside cabinet.

On 12 February 1991 the appellant bought a ticket to travel from Panama to Brussels via São Paulo and Copenhagen. The name of the traveller was given as 'Abelleira', and the ticket was addressed to Hector Diaz in Bogota. The ticket details were given to the travel agent by the appellant. He saw Diaz off at Victoria Station and gave him for contact purposes his sister's telephone number. Diaz was told to call the appellant 'Tony'. Diaz claimed he had not wanted to go to São Paulo or to carry the drugs. When he was in Colombia the appellant had telephoned him at his mother's home and given him instructions. In São Paulo he was given the briefcase containing the drugs for transport to London.

(2) *30 March to 1 April 1991*

On 30 March Diaz arrived at Heathrow using the name 'Abelleira'. On arrest he was found to have, in addition to the cocaine, an airline ticket routed São Paulo/Copenhagen/Brussels, a piece of the Bedford Hotel notepaper with various entries, including the name 'Tony', the appellant's sister's telephone number in code, and another piece of the hotel's notepaper showing calculations similar to those written on the headed notepaper found at the appellant's address. Finally, he had a piece of paper detailing his false identify and route. He agreed to assist the Customs & Excise authorities and was taken to the St Giles Hotel, room 857. On the afternoon of 31 March the appellant and Valencia (acquitted by the jury) were seen looking through a window into the hotel. On 1 April two calls were put through to Diaz's room. On each occasion he was out, and a message was left that 'Tony' had called. Later that day the appellant Valencia and another were seen in the foyer of the hotel. They left, returned and were arrested. The appellant was searched. A diary was found referring to the Giles Hotel, its telephone number, and Diaz's room number 857. Another entry referred to the route Panama/Rio/Geneva/Brussels. The items found on the appellant were put in a bag. Later, he grabbed the bag from an officer and smashed it against a window in his attempt to throw it out.

Next day, the search of the appellant's home revealed a document bearing the name 'Hector J Diaz', a Bogota telephone number, the name 'Abelleira', and an airline route São Paulo/Copenhagen/Brussels. The telephone numbers of Diaz's mother and wife in Colombia were also found, together with the Bedford Hotel notepaper bearing the calculations. The appellant was interviewed. He denied knowing Diaz, denied being known as Tony, denied knowing anyone staying at the hotel, denied attempting to throw the bag away, and could not remember why he had put 'Giles Hotel 857' and its telephone number in his diary.

(3) *The evidence of Nino Sua*

Evidence was given by one Nino Sua that during the trial the appellant had approached him in the cells at the back of the court with a view to getting a message to Diaz to give a version of events favourable to the appellant. Nino Sua was himself serving a sentence of five years' imprisonment for smuggling drugs. The learned judge in summing up suggested the jury might not find his evidence very helpful.

The judge's direction

After reviewing the evidence for the Crown, and before reviewing that given by Valencia, the learned judge referred to the appellant's absence from the witness box. He began with a conventional direction as follows:

> 'Now Tobon. He did not give evidence; that is his choice. He does not have to; he may or may not—entirely as he pleases—and obviously because he has a choice you do not say: "Well, the reason he hasn't given evidence is because he is guilty." The fact that he has not given evidence adds nothing to the prosecution case and it adds nothing to the defence case, but it does have this effect: that he has done nothing to rebut, contradict or explain the prosecution case, and so, except in so far as his counsel had established various points in cross-examination, it means that the prosecution evidence stands uncontradicted.'

No criticism was made or can be made of that passage as being in any way unfair or unusual. The learned judge then went on as follows:

> 'As you have been told, perfectly correctly, suggestions by counsel are not evidence ... Evidence is what I described to you at the beginning as what you hear from the witness box, admissions, the documents, not suggestions by counsel ... So suggestions are not evidence, and the comment I make—and that I am entitled to make—is that if in fact Tobon thought it was emeralds and not drugs, one might have thought that he would be very anxious to say so.'

It is the final sentence of that passage which is said to be improper and a misdirection.

The case law

The question, what comment may the judge make when a defendant does not give evidence? only arose after the Criminal Evidence Act 1898, since the defendant had no right to give evidence before that. The statute expressly prohibited comment by the prosecution, but no such prohibition was imposed on the judge. We have been shown by counsel the many reported decisions since 1898, and it is right to say that they have not all been in agreement. The first reported case was *R v Rhodes* [1899] 1 QB 77. Lord Russell of Killowen CJ said (at 83):

> '... the only question that we have to consider is whether the chairman of quarter sessions had a right to comment on his absence from the witness-box. It seems to me that he undoubtedly had that right. There is nothing in the Act that takes away or even purports to take away the right of the Court to comment on the evidence in the case, and the manner in which the case has been conducted. The nature and degree of such comment must rest entirely in the discretion of the judge who tries the case; and it is impossible to lay down any rule as to the cases in which he ought or ought not to comment on the failure of the prisoner to give evidence, or as to what those comments should be. There are some cases in which it would be unwise to make any such comment at all; there are others in which it would be absolutely necessary in the interests of justice

that such comments should be made. That is a question entirely for the discretion of the judge ...'

In two cases shortly after that it was held on appeal that judges are entitled to direct the jury that they could draw an adverse inference against the accused in cases where the uncontested or clearly established facts pointed so strongly to guilt as to call for an explanation. The first of them was *R v Corrie and Watson* (1904) 20 TLR 365 in which Lord Alverstone CJ said (at 365):

> 'No inference should be drawn in support of a weak case from the fact that the defendants were not called; but when transactions were capable of an innocent explanation, then, if the defendants could have given it, it was not improper, once a *prima facie* case had been established, for the jury to draw a conclusion from their not being called.'

In the second case, *R v Bernard* (1908) 1 Cr App R 218, Lord Alverstone CJ had been the trial judge and had referred to the accused's failure to enter the witness box, telling the jury they must draw their own conclusions from the absence of his explanation. Darling J, giving the judgment of the appeal court, said (at 219):

> 'It is right that the jury should know, and, if necessary, be told, to draw their own conclusions from the absence of explanation by the prisoner. Here he failed to give any explanation of the circumstances in which he signed letters containing false statements ... There was abundant evidence of his guilt, and the jury were justified, in the absence of explanation by him, in convicting him.'

In *R v Voisin* [1918] 1 KB 531, [1918–19] All ER Rep 491 the Court of Criminal Appeal held that the exercise of the judge's discretion whether and how to comment was not susceptible to review on appeal, but that is no longer good law as subsequent cases show.

In *Waugh v R* [1950] AC 203, a Privy Council case, one of the grounds of appeal was that the trial judge had commented nine times in the course of his summing up on the appellant's failure to give evidence. The case for the prosecution was not strong. Lord Oaksey, giving the opinion of the Board, said:

> 'It is true that it is a matter for the judge's discretion whether he shall comment on the fact that a prisoner has not given evidence; but the very fact that the prosecution are not permitted to comment on that fact shows how careful a judge should be in making such comment ... In such a state of the evidence the judge's repeated comments on the appellant's failure to give evidence may well have led the jury to think that no innocent man could have taken such a course.'

The appeal was allowed.

However, in *R v Fisher* [1964] Crim LR 150, comment by the judge on ten occasions during the summing up as to the defendant's failure to give evidence did not lead to his appeal being allowed. The court held that none of the comments conveyed that his failure to give evidence was inconsistent with innocence or that the only reasonable inference was that he was guilty. He had, however, told a medical expert that he had taken 60 Purple Heart tablets, and this was relied upon as to the issue of intent and diminished responsibility. The court held that it was fair comment to point out that he had not gone into the witness box to say how many tablets he had taken, and the jury had not had an opportunity of forming their own opinion of him at first hand.

In *R v Bathurst* [1968] 1 All ER 1175, [1968] 2 QB 99 Lord Parker CJ gave guidance, albeit obiter, on the appropriate comments open to a judge where a defendant does not give evidence. He said ([1968] 1 All ER 1175 at 1178, [1968] 2 QB 99 at 107–108):

> '... the accepted form of comment is to inform the jury that, of course, the accused is not bound to give evidence, that he can sit back and see if the prosecution have proved their case, and that, while the jury had been deprived of the opportunity of hearing his story tested in cross-examination, the one thing they must not do is to assume that he is guilty because he has not gone into the witness box.'

That formula has been adapted by the Judicial Studies Board in its specimen directions, which are in the following terms:

> 'The defendant does not have to give evidence. He is entitled to sit in the dock and require the prosecution to prove its case. You must not assume that he is guilty because he has not given evidence. The fact that he has not given evidence proves nothing one way or the other. It does nothing to establish his guilt. On the other hand, it means that there is no evidence from the defendant to undermine, contradict, or explain the evidence put before you by the prosecution.'

But although the guidance deriving from *R v Bathurst* has generally been regarded as embodying the basic direction applicable in most cases, the judge's right to go somewhat further in appropriate cases has been asserted in some of the decisions of this court.

In *R v Sparrow* [1973] 2 All ER 129 at 135, [1973] 1 WLR 488 at 495 Lawton LJ reviewed the authorities and commented particularly on two of those cited above:

> 'In our judgment *Waugh v R* ([1950] AC 203) establishes nothing more than this: it is a wrongful exercise of judicial discretion for a judge to bolster up a weak prosecution case by making comments about the accused's failure to give evidence; and implicit in the report is the concept that failure to give evidence has no evidential value. We can find nothing in it which qualifies the statement of principle in *R v Rhodes* ([1899] 1 QB 77).'

Lawton LJ quoted the guidance given in *R v Bathurst* and went on as follows ([1973] 2 All ER 129 at 136, [1973] 1 WLR 488 at 496):

> 'In many cases, a direction in some such terms as these will be all that is required; but we are sure that Lord Parker CJ never intended his words of guidance to be regarded as a judicial directive to be recited to juries in every case in which an accused elects not to give evidence. What is said must depend on the facts of each case and in some cases the interests of justice call for a stronger comment. The trial judge, who has the feel of a case, is the person who must exercise his discretion in this matter to ensure that a trial is fair. A discretion is not to be fettered by laying down rules and regulations for its exercise ... What, however, is of the greatest importance in Lord Parker CJ's advice to judges is his reference to the need to avoid telling juries that absence from the witness box is to be equated with guilt.'

R v Mutch [1973] 1 All ER 178, was decided by this court a month before *R v Sparrow* [1973] 2 All ER 129, [1973] 1 WLR 488, and Lawton LJ presided in both.

The issue in *R v Mutch* was identity. After giving, in effect, a *Bathurst* direction the learned trial judge had added ([1973] 1 All ER 178 at 179):

> '... but, at the same time, I have to tell you this: the jury are entitled to draw inferences unfavourable to the prisoner where he is not called to establish an innocent explanation of facts proved by the prosecution, which, without such explanation, tell for his guilt.'

In quashing the conviction Lawton LJ said (at 181):

> 'The words he used might have been permissible if the evidence had established had situation calling for "confession and avoidance"; they were not proper for one of flat denial as this case was.'

Thus, the court sought to draw a distinction between a case of simple denial where the defendant puts the prosecution to proof, the burden being on them, and on the other hand a case in which the defence put forward a positive account (the 'avoidance') and the defendant fails to give evidence in support of it.

We were referred to a number of decisions of this court, both reported and unreported, in which comments going further than the conventional *Bathurst* direction have been considered. In a number the judge's directions have been disapproved. For example, in *R v Pratt* [1971] Crim LR 234, a conviction was quashed where the judge's direction plainly suggested that the jury could draw the inference of guilt because the appellant had not given evidence. Likewise, in *R v Berry* (1992) Times, 20 May a direction suggesting that an innocent man would have given evidence was disapproved, although the proviso was applied.

On the other hand, this court has approved comments going beyond the conventional direction in a number of cases. In *R v Brigden* [1973] Crim LR 579, the police were accused in cross-examination of planting glass in the appellant's shoe and papers in his car so as to incriminate him. He did not go into the witness box to support these allegations. The learned judge did not suggest his failure to testify might lead the jury to infer he was guilty. However, he did say the fact that the jury had not heard from him might help them to decide whether there was any truth in the allegation of planting. That was approved. Again, in *R v Brocket* (12 October 1970, unreported) this court held that if facts established by evidence entitled the jury to draw inference adverse to the accused in the absence of some innocent explanation, it is not improper to remind the jury in cases where the accused could obviously provide such an explanation by his own evidence that he has not, in fact, done so. This applies particularly when the jury has to decide what weight to give to purely theoretical innocent explanations which the defence has asked them to consider.

In *R v Harris* (1987) 84 Cr App R 75 this court declined to rule that whenever an accused fails to testify the judge must always direct the jury that it is wrong for them to assume he is guilty. Lawton LJ said (at 81):

> 'In our judgment, although in most cases it probably is advisable for the judge to make some comment, we are not prepared to say that judges must make a comment; indeed that would be changing the law as it has stood ever since the court first started to consider the consequences of the Criminal Evidence Act 1898. We are not prepared to make new law.'

In *R v Squire* [1990] Crim LR 341 the court reiterated that it was a matter of discretion for the judge as to whether any direction is given at all when the defendant fails to testify. However, in *R v Walsh* (15 May 1990, unreported)

Farquharson LJ, after referring to *R v Bathurst* [1968] 1 All ER 1175, [1968] 2 QB 99, said:

> 'Thus, it is the clear duty on the part of the judge to state in an unqualified and unambiguous way that there is no obligation on the part of an accused to give evidence and the fact that he has not done so must in no circumstances be regarded as any admission of guilt.'

That passage was cited in *R v Taylor* [1993] Crim LR 223, where McCullough J, giving the judgment of the court, said:

> 'This court has now said, and it is the law, that a judge is under a duty in a case where a defendant gives no evidence to state not only that there is no obligation to give evidence, but also that his failure to do so must in no circumstances be taken as any indication of guilt.'

In *R v Fullerton* [1994] Crim LR 63 Waterhouse J referred to *R v Harris* (1986) 84 Cr App R 75 and went on:

> 'The current practice appears to have moved on since 1986 and the recommended direction circulated to judges indicates that they should deal with the matter, when it arises, in words that are based broadly on Lord Parker's dicta in *R v Bathurst* ... It was plainly necessary for [the judge] when he dealt with the failure of the appellant to give evidence, to point out expressly to the jury that there was no burden of proof at all upon him and that his absence from the witness box was not to be taken in any way as an admission of guilt.'

We recognise that the decisions on this subject are not easily reconcilable and that the dividing line between permissible and impermissible comment is, under the present law, not easily discernible. We also recognise that there are presently proposals for altering the law relating not only to comment on a defendant's failure to testify, but also to his failure to answer questions put by the police. However, we consider for the present that the following principles apply where a defendant does not testify.

(1) The judge should give the jury a direction along the lines of the Judicial Studies Board specimen direction based on *R v Bathurst* [1968] 1 All ER 1175 at 1178, [1968] 2 QB 99 at 107. (2) The essentials of that direction are that the defendant is under no obligation to testify and the jury should not assume he is guilty because he has not given evidence. (3) Provided those essentials are complied with, the judge may think it appropriate to make a stronger comment where the defence case involves alleged facts which (a) are at variance with prosecution evidence or additional to it and exculpatory, and (b) must, if true, be within the knowledge of the defendant. (4) The nature and strength of such comment must be a matter for the discretion of the judge and will depend upon the circumstances of the individual case. However, it must not be such as to contradict or nullify the essentials of the conventional direction.

Applying those principles to the present case, it is clear and indeed accepted, that the learned judge, in his summing up quoted above, gave the essentials of the conventional direction. He then went on correctly to explain that suggestions made by counsel are not evidence. That was because it had been put as part of the appellant's case that his dealings and negotiations with Diaz had been concerned with emeralds not cocaine. That suggestion had been flatly denied. There followed the one sentence upon which this appeal is based and which we repeat:

> 'So suggestions are not evidence, and the comment I make—and that I am entitled to make—is that if in fact Tobon thought it was emeralds and not drugs, one might have thought that he would be very anxious to say so.'

This was a classic example of an assertion of fact in conflict with the prosecution evidence and going to the heart of the case; fact of which, if true, the appellant could clearly have spoken. In our view the learned judge was, as he said, entitled to make the comment he did. For their part the jury were entitled, in considering whether the suggestion concerning emeralds might possibly be true, to take into account the fact that there was no evidence from the defendant to support what therefore remained a bare assertion.

This appeal is dismissed.

Appeal dismissed.

20 January 1994. The court refused leave to appeal to the House of Lords but certified, under s 33(2) of the Criminal Appeal Act 1968, that the following point of law of general public importance was involved in the decision: where the defence case put in cross-examination involves exculpatory assertions of fact which are apparently within the knowledge of the defendant and no evidence is led by the defence in support of such assertions, is the judge entitled to comment that the jury may take account of the defendant's silence, provided he gives the direction recommended by the Judicial Studies Board and his comments are not inconsistent with that direction?

N P Metcalfe Esq   Barrister.

Seaboard Offshore Ltd v Secretary of State for Transport
The Safe Carrier

HOUSE OF LORDS

LORD KEITH OF KINKEL, LORD BRIDGE OF HARWICH, LORD JAUNCEY OF TULLICHETTLE, LORD BROWNE-WILKINSON AND LORD NOLAN

2, 3, 23 MARCH 1994

Shipping – Offence – Failure to operate ship in safe manner – Shipowner's liability – Company chartering ship – Engine failure on ship – Failure due to fault by someone in company – Whether company vicariously liable for all acts of its employees – Nature of offence – Merchant Shipping Act 1988, s 31.

The respondent company, the charterers of a vessel, was charged with failing to take all reasonable steps to secure that the vessel was operated in a safe manner, contrary to s 31[a] of the Merchant Shipping Act 1988. The vessel's engine had broken down three times within a period of 24 hours, leaving her drifting at sea. The justices found that the chief engineer, who was responsible for the mechanical running of the ship, had boarded the vessel for the first time less than three hours before the vessel had set sail, when the minimum time necessary for

---

a   Section 31, so far as material, is set out at p 101 *g j*, post

him to familiarise himself with the machinery was three days. Having concluded that somebody in the company was at fault, and that failure by anybody in the company to take all reasonable steps to secure that the vessel was operated in a safe manner amounted to an offence by the company under s 31, the justices convicted the company. On appeal by the company, the question arose whether s 31 of the 1988 Act imposed vicarious liability on a shipowner for all its employees. The Court of Appeal allowed the appeal on the ground that, assuming that s 31 created an offence of strict liability, it did not impose vicarious liability on the shipowner for the defaults of every employee. The Secretary of State appealed to the House of Lords, contending that there had been a failure by those entrusted with the exercise of the powers of the company to discharge the duty laid on them by s 31, in that they had failed to establish any system for securing that the ship did not go to sea before the chief engineer had had sufficient opportunity to familiarise himself with its machinery and equipment.

Held – The appeal would be dismissed for the following reasons—

(1) In order to secure a conviction under s 31 of the 1988 Act the prosecution had to prove beyond reasonable doubt that the accused owner, charterer or manager of a ship had himself failed to take to take all reasonable steps to secure that the ship was operated in a safe manner. The offence under s 31 consisted of a failure to take steps which objectively were held to be reasonable steps to take in the interests of the safe operation of a ship, and the duty which s 31 placed on the owner, charterer or manager was a personal one, since, on the true construction of s 31, Parliament could not have intended that the owner of a ship should always be criminally liable for any act or omission by any officer of the company or member of the crew which resulted in unsafe operation of the ship. The owner, charterer or manager was accordingly criminally liable if he failed personally in the duty, but he was not criminally liable for the acts or omissions of his subordinate employees if he had himself taken all such reasonable steps. Where the owner, charterer or manager was a corporation which could act only through natural persons, in law the natural persons who were to be treated as being the corporation for the purpose of acts done in the course of its business were those persons who by virtue of its constitution or otherwise were entrusted with the exercise of the powers of the corporation (see p 103 *j* to p 104 *c* and p 105*b* to *f*, post); dictum of Lord Diplock in *Tesco Supermarkets Ltd v Nattrass* [1971] 2 All ER 127 at 155 applied.

(2) Moreover, it was not open to the Secretary of State to contend on the appeal that those in charge of the company had failed to discharge their duty under s 31 of establishing a system for securing that the ship did not go to sea before the chief engineer had had sufficient opportunity to familiarise himself with its machinery and equipment, since the prosecution had not been presented to the justices in that way, so that they were not in a position to apply their minds to the question whether those were reasonable steps to be taken by the company to secure the safe operation of the ship and whether there had been a failure to take such steps (see p 104 *g* to p 105 *a d* to *f*, post).

Decision of the Divisional Court of the Queen's Bench Division [1993] 3 All ER 25 affirmed.

Notes

For criminal liability for the acts of others, see 11(1) *Halsbury's Laws* (4th edn reissue) paras 52–56, and for cases on the subject, see 14(1) *Digest* (2nd reissue) 147–153, 1199–1249.

HL   Seaboard Offshore Ltd v Secretary of State (Lord Keith)

Case referred to in opinions
Tesco Supermarkets Ltd v Nattrass [1971] 2 All ER 127, [1972] AC 153, [1971] 2 WLR 1166, HL.

Appeal
The Secretary of State for Transport appealed with the leave of the Appeal Committee of the House of Lords given on 18 October 1993 from the decision of the Divisional Court of the Queen's Bench Division (Staughton LJ and Buckley J) ([1993] 3 All ER 25, [1993] 1 WLR 1025) on 2 February 1993 allowing the appeal of the respondents, Seaboard Offshore Ltd, by way of a case stated by the justices for Newcastle upon Tyne sitting at Market Street on 20 August and 18 September 1991 in respect of their decision whereby on an information laid by the Secretary of State they convicted the respondents, the charterers of the mv Safe Carrier, of failing to take all reasonable steps to secure that the vessel was operated in a safe manner whilst sailing from the Tyne for Aberdeen on 6 September 1990, contrary to s 31 of the Merchant Shipping Act 1988. The Divisional Court had refused leave to appeal to the House of Lords but had certified, under s 1(2) of the Administration of Justice Act 1960, that a point of law of general public importance (set out at p 103 *a b*, post) was involved in the decision. The facts are set out in the opinion of Lord Keith.

R Alun Jones QC and Clare Montgomery (instructed by the Treasury Solicitor) for the Secretary of State.
Andrew Rankin QC and Nicholas Saunders (instructed by Wilkinson Maughan, Newcastle upon Tyne) for the respondents.

Their Lordships took time for consideration.

23 March 1994. The following opinions were delivered.

LORD KEITH OF KINKEL. My Lords, this appeal from the Divisional Court is concerned with the proper construction and application of s 31(1) of the Merchant Shipping Act 1988, which provides:

> 'It shall be the duty of the owner of a ship to which this section applies to take all reasonable steps to secure that the ship is operated in a safe manner.'

By virtue of sub-s (2) the section applies, inter alia, to any ship registered in the United Kingdom, and sub-s (3) provides that if the owner of a ship to which the section applies fails to discharge the duty imposed on him by sub s (1) he shall be guilty of an offence. Subsection (4) enlarges the meaning of 'owner' in sub-s (1) by providing that the word shall be construed as including a charterer under a charter by demise and a person other than the owner managing the ship under a management agreement. Subsection (4) concludes:

> '... and accordingly the reference in subsection (1) to the taking of all reasonable steps shall, in relation to the owner, the charterer or any such manager, be construed as a reference to the taking of all such steps as it is reasonable for him to take in the circumstances of the case.'

In September 1990 the respondents, Seaboard Offshore Ltd, were managers of the mv Safe Carrier, which had recently been converted for use as an offshore standby safety vessel. At 1950 hrs on 6 September 1990 the ship set sail from the River Tyne, bound for Aberdeen. The chief engineer was a Mr Carrigan. He had 27 years' experience. He had boarded the ship 2 hours and 50 minutes before she put to sea. Early in the morning of 7 September the main engines and the generators broke down. The ship was plunged into darkness. Even the engine-room emergency lighting failed to come on. The reason for the breakdown was that an incorrect gravity feed disc had been fitted to the fuel oil purifier, with the result that the throughput to the service tanks was inadequate to meet the engine demand. Mr Carrigan managed to restart the engine twice by hand-pumping fuel into the service tanks, and then, thinking that the settling and service tanks were almost empty, he opened a valve on one of the bunker tanks, which had the effect of releasing its contents directly into the starboard service tank, instead of through the settling tank. As a result the engines were flooded by water, the ship came to a halt and remained drifting in the North Sea from the evening of 7 September until 1100 hrs on 8 September, when she was towed back to the River Tyne.

The respondents were charged at the instance of the Secretary of State for Transport with a contravention of s 31 of the 1988 Act before the magistrates' court of Newcastle upon Tyne. On 20 September 1991 the justices convicted the respondents and at their request stated a case for the opinion of the High Court. The findings in the case included, in addition to the facts summarised above, (1) that it was an error of judgment on Mr Carrigan's part to release fuel directly from the bunker tank into the service tanks instead of through the settling tank, (2) that the ship was at no time in any danger, (3) that the respondents did not pressurise the master of the ship to put to sea and it was not their policy to do so, (4) that Mr Carrigan knew that he was responsible to the master for the safe mechanical operation of the ship and that he owed a duty to the master to inform him if he considered it unsafe to put to sea, (5) that Mr Carrigan was content for the ship to put to sea when she did and considered it was safe to do so, although he was aware it was not the best practice, and (6) that the minimum time necessary for a chief engineer to familiarise himself with a converted ship was three days. The case stated recorded the principal contention of the Secretary of State as being:

> 'The evidence showed the Company had failed to take the step of allowing the Chief Engineer more time to familiarize himself with the vessel M.V. "Safe Carrier" and that this was a reasonable step which could have been taken by the [respondents] to secure that the ship was operated in a safe manner.'

The reasons stated by the justices for their decision to convict the respondents included the following:

> '3. For a limited company to be convicted of an offence under S. 31 it is necessary for the prosecution to prove beyond reasonable doubt that there was some particular step that it was reasonable to expect the Company to have taken in the circumstances.
> 4. In this case, we found the Company had caused the ship to be operated in an unsafe manner by only allowing the Chief Engineer two hours fifty minutes in which to familiarize himself with the Ship before sailing, and were therefore unanimously and firmly of the opinion that the information was proved.'

The questions for the opinion of the High Court were stated to be:

> '(a) Does the principle of law governing the criminal responsibility of corporations confirmed by the House of Lords in *Tesco Supermarkets Limited v Nattrass* ([1971] 2 All ER 127, [1972] AC 153) apply to S. 31 of the Merchant Shipping Act 1988?

(b) Was there any or sufficient evidence before the Magistrates to support a finding by them that there was some particular step that it was reasonable to expect the [respondents] to have taken in the circumstances of the case to secure that the Ship was operated in a safe manner that the company failed to take?

(c) Was such a finding one that a reasonable Magistrates' Court could have made?'

The case stated came before the Divisional Court, consisting of Staughton LJ and Buckley J ([1993] 3 All ER 25, [1993] 1 WLR 1025), which on 2 February 1993 quashed the conviction. The court regarded question (a) as raising the point whether or not s 31 of the 1988 Act imposed on a shipowner vicarious liability for the acts or omissions of all its employees and expressed the opinion that it did not. As regards question (b) Staughton LJ observed that the justices had not in terms made a finding of some particular step which the defendant company should have taken, and added ([1993] 3 All ER 25 at 35, [1993] 1 WLR 1025 at 1035):

'They merely found that somebody had allowed the chief engineer only 2 hours and 50 minutes with which to familiarise himself with the ship before sailing. It is not proved that that somebody was one who engages the liability of the company.'

It was accordingly unnecessary to answer question (c).

At the request of the Secretary of State the Divisional Court certified under s 1(2) of the Administration of Justice Act 1960 that the following points of law of general public importance were involved in the case:

'1. Whether Section 31 of the Merchant Shipping Act 1988 creates an offence of strict liability

2. Whether a manager is or may be vicariously liable for a breach of duty under section 31 of the Merchant Shipping Act 1988 which arises from any act or omission by any of the manager's servants or agents.'

The Divisional Court refused leave to appeal to your Lordships' House, but on a subsequent petition by the Secretary of State the Appeal Committee granted leave on the basis of these points of law.

The statement of facts and issues agreed for the purposes of the appeal stated the issue to be—

'whether a manager is vicariously liable for a breach of duty under section 31 of the Merchant Shipping Act 1988 which arises from any act or omission by any of the manager's servants or agents'

and in the printed case for the Secretary of State it was contended that that question should be answered in the affirmative.

However, when leading counsel for the Secretary of State started his argument before your Lordships he abandoned that contention and accepted that to secure a conviction under s 31 the prosecution must prove beyond reasonable doubt that the accused owner, charterer or manager of a ship had himself failed to take to take all reasonable steps to secure that the ship was operated in a safe manner. This abandonment of the contention is not to be accepted by your Lordships as correct without any further consideration. Such consideration does, however, lead me to the conclusion that it was indeed correct. As Staughton LJ observed in the course of his judgment in the Divisional Court, it would be surprising if by the language used in s 31 Parliament intended that the owner of a ship should be criminally liable for any act or omission by any officer of the company or member of the crew which resulted in unsafe operation of the ship, ranging from a failure by the managing director to arrange repairs to a failure by the bosun or cabin steward to close portholes (see [1993] 3 All ER 25 at 33, [1993] 1 WLR 1025 at 1033). Of particular relevance in this context are the concluding words of s 31(4), referring to the taking of all such steps as are reasonable for *him* (my emphasis) to take, ie the owner, charterer or manager. The steps to be taken are to be such as will secure that the ship is operated in a safe manner. That conveys to me the idea of laying down a safe manner of operating the ship by those involved in the actual operation of it and taking appropriate measures to bring it about that such safe manner of operation is adhered to. Where the owner, charterer or manager is a corporation which can act only through natural persons, the natural persons who are to be treated in law as being the corporation for the purpose of acts done in the course of its business are those who by virtue of its constitution or otherwise are entrusted with the exercise of the powers of the corporation: see per Lord Diplock in *Tesco Supermarkets Ltd v Nattrass* [1971] 2 All ER 127 at 155, [1972] AC 153 at 199–200.

The argument for the Secretary of State then sought to make out that there had indeed been a failure by those entrusted with the powers of the respondent company to discharge the duty laid on them by s 31, in respect that they failed to establish any system for securing that the ship did not go to sea before the chief engineer had had sufficient opportunity to familiarise himself with its machinery and equipment. Reliance was placed upon the ICS/ISF (International Chamber of Shipping/International Shipping Federation) *Code of Good Management Practice in Safe Ship Operation*, which was in evidence before the justices. Paragraph 3.2 provides:

> 'Specifically, management should ensure that the crew members ... 3 have a proper knowledge of the technical aspects of the ship and its operation as necessary for the performance of their duties ...'

Reference was further made to the respondents' standing instructions, also in evidence before the justices, and it was observed that nowhere was there any stated requirement that the engineer officers should be thoroughly familiar with a ship's machinery and equipment before it put to sea.

It may very well be that in pursuance of the duty imposed by s 31 a system such as desiderated on behalf of the Secretary of State ought to be laid down by an owner, charterer or manager, and that appropriate measures should be taken to see that it is adhered to. The problem for the Secretary of State is that this does not appear to be the way in which the case was presented to the justices, so that they were not in a position to apply their minds to the question whether these were reasonable steps to be taken by the respondents to secure the safe operation of the ship and whether they failed to take them. The justices say that they found that the respondents caused the ship to be operated in an unsafe way by only allowing the chief engineer 2 hours and 50 minutes in which to familiarise himself with the ship before sailing. They make no finding as to how it came about that the ship sailed while that was the situation, nor as to who it was who gave the instruction to sail. They had expressed the opinion that *Tesco Supermarkets Ltd v Nattrass* had no application to s 31 of the 1988 Act. That was in response to a contention by the respondents that since no evidence had been adduced of any decisions taken or failed to be taken by their senior management the information ought to be dismissed. It seems, therefore, that the justices took the view that the respondents were criminally liable even though the putting to sea by the ship with a chief engineer insufficiently familiar with the engines was the fault of some employee of the company other than the senior management. That view was erroneous, and in the circumstances the conviction cannot stand.

In the judgment of the Divisional Court there is some discussion as to whether or not the offence provided for by s 31 is one of strict liability, involving no necessary element of mens rea. It is not, however, helpful to seek to categorise the offence as either being or not being one of strict liability. It consists simply in failure to take steps which by an objective standard are held to be reasonable steps to take in the interests of the safe operation of a ship, and the duty which it places on the owner, charterer or manager is a personal one. The owner, charterer or manager is criminally liable if he fails personally in the duty, but is not criminally liable for the acts or omissions of his subordinate employees if he has himself taken all such reasonable steps.

My Lords, for these reasons I would dismiss the appeal.

LORD BRIDGE OF HARWICH. My Lords, I have had the advantage of reading in draft the speech prepared by my noble and learned friend Lord Keith of Kinkel. I agree with him and for the reasons he gives I too would dismiss this appeal.

LORD JAUNCEY OF TULLICHETTLE. My Lords, I have had the advantage of reading in draft the speech by my noble and learned friend Lord Keith of Kinkel, and for the reasons he gives I too would dismiss the appeal.

LORD BROWNE-WILKINSON. My Lords, for the reasons given by my noble and learned friend Lord Keith of Kinkel, I too would dismiss the appeal.

LORD NOLAN. My Lords, I agree that, for the reasons given by my noble and learned friend Lord Keith of Kinkel, this appeal should be dismissed.

Appeal dismissed.

Celia Fox   Barrister.

Re a debtor (No 22 of 1993)

CHANCERY DIVISION
MUMMERY J
7, 8 JUNE 1993

Insolvency – Petition – Conditions for presentation   Expedited bankruptcy petition – Statutory demand – Debtor applying to set aside statutory demand – Creditors presenting expedited bankruptcy petition on ground of serious possibility of jeopardy to debtor's property – Petition presented within three weeks of statutory demand – Whether petition valid – Insolvency Act 1986, ss 267(2)(c)(d), 268(1), 270 – Insolvency Rules 1986, rr 6.8(2)(b)(ii), 7.55.

If there is a serious possibility that the debtor's property or the value thereof will be significantly diminished, and notwithstanding that there is an outstanding application under rr 6.4 and 6.5 of the the Insolvency Rules 1986 to set aside a statutory demand on which the bankruptcy petition is based, a petitioning creditor may present a petition under s 270[a] of the Insolvency Act

---

a   Section 270 is set out at p 109 *g h*, post

1986 before the end of the three weeks stipulated by s 268(1)[b]. Although the precondition in s 267(2)(c)[c] for presenting a petition on the ground of the debtor's 'inability to pay' is defined in s 268 by reference to his failure to comply with a statutory demand within three weeks of it being served and although s 267(2)(d) expressly provides that it is a further precondition for presenting a petition that there is no outstanding application to set aside a statutory demand served under s 268 in respect of the debt, that provision is expressly subject to s 270. Furthermore, non-compliance with the requirement in r 6.8(2)(b)(ii)[d] of the 1986 rules that the petition state that no application to set aside the demand is outstanding does not automatically or necessarily invalidate the petition since that requirement can be waived under r 7.55[e] if the court is satisfied that the debtor has not suffered substantial injustice or prejudice as a result of non-compliance (see p 110 g to p 111 c, post).

Notes
For expedited creditor's petitions, see 3(2) *Halsbury's Laws* (4th edn reissue) para 119.

For the Insolvency Act 1986, ss 267, 268, 270, see 4 *Halsbury's Statutes* (4th edn) (1987 reissue) 910, 911, 913.

For the Insolvency Rules 1986, rr 6.4, 6.5, 6.8, 7.55, see 3 *Halsbury's Statutory Instruments* (1991 reissue) 375, 376, 378, 459.

Cases referred to in judgment
Clark (C & J) Ltd v IRC [1973] 2 All ER 513, [1973] 1 WLR 905; affd [1975] 1 All ER 801, [1975] 1 WLR 413, CA.
Johnson v Emerson and Sparrow (1871) LR 6 Ex 329.

Appeal
The debtor appealed from the refusal of Judge Clegg sitting in the Colchester and Clacton County Court on 22 June 1993 to dismiss the expedited bankruptcy petition presented against him on 20 May by David E W Lines and Peter C B Mitchell, the joint liquidators of the creditor, Focus Insurance Co Ltd (in liq), of Hamilton, Bermuda. The facts are set out in the judgment.

The debtor appeared in person.
David Ashton (instructed by *D J Freeman*) for the joint liquidators.

Cur adv vult

8 June 1993. The following judgment was delivered.

MUMMERY J. This is an appeal from the refusal of Judge Clegg, sitting in the Colchester and Clacton County Court on 2 June 1993, to make a number of orders on the application of the debtor. On the hearing of the application and

---
b Section 268(1), so far as material, provides: 'For the purposes of section 267(2)(c) the debtor appears to be unable to pay a debt if, but only if, the debt is immediately payable and ... (a) the petitioning creditor to whom the debt is owed has served on the debtor a ... statutory demand ... requiring him to pay the debt ... at least three weeks have elapsed since the demand was served and the demand has been neither complied with nor set aside in accordance with the rules ...'
c Section 267(2), so far as material, is set out at p 108 *f*, post
d Rule 6.8(2), so far as material, is set out at p 108 *j* to p 109 *a*, post
e Rule 7.55, so far as material, is set out at p 110 *e*, post

of the appeal the debtor appeared in person. The only point pursued by him was the appeal against the refusal of the judge to make an order that the bankruptcy petition presented against him on 20 May 1993 should be dismissed immediately without any investigation of the grounds stated in the petition. He submitted that the petitioning creditors were not legally entitled to present the petition and had committed an abuse of the process of the court in so doing.

The background to the dispute is this. It is alleged that the debtor was a director of a Bermudan company, Focus Insurance Co Ltd, which is in liquidation. The joint liquidators are members of the firm of Cork Gully, Mr Lines and Mr Mitchell. They claim to have obtained a default judgment in the courts in Bermuda on 15 January 1993 for a sum of $US19,714,142, plus interest. The debtor made an unsuccessful application on 11 March 1993 to set aside the judgment based on alleged breach of duty and negligence on the part of the debtor as a director of Focus. On 8 April 1993 a statutory demand was signed by the petitioning creditors in the sum of $US20,386,583, the judgment debt plus interest. In sterling that amounts to £13,478,732. The statutory demand was served on the debtor on 30 April.

On 4 May 1993 the debtor issued an application to set aside the statutory demand. The application was supported by an affidavit. In the affidavit the debtor set out various grounds of his application. In brief, they are that the judgment in the Bermudan courts is not a final judgment. It is a default judgment, which is subject to a pending appeal to the Judicial Committee of the Privy Council. The affidavit alleges that there is a pending application for a stay of execution of the judgment, and that the debtor has a counterclaim for $US90m which overtops the amount of the debt demanded. The grounds of that claim are alleged fraud and conspiracy. There are various other allegations about the conduct of the joint liquidators and their advisors in Bermuda and here. It is not necessary to examine those for the purposes of this appeal.

The court fixed 9 June 1993 as the date for the hearing of the application. On 20 May 1993 the joint liquidators presented a petition for a bankruptcy order. That is also fixed to be heard on 9 June.

The petition is based on the debt described in the statutory demand. The petition states that the debt is due and owing and is unsecured, and that the debtor appears to be unable to pay it. The statutory demand is referred to and it is stated that since the demand was served on 30 April 1993 it has not been and will not be complied with nor set aside in accordance with the rules. The petition does not contain any reference to the outstanding application by the debtor to set aside the statutory demand. Paragraph 9 of the petition states:

> 'There is a serious possibility that the debtor's property and/or the value of his property will be significantly diminished within the three week period following the date of service of the statutory demand, and that it is just and proper that this petition be presented in respect of the debt which is the subject of the statutory demand before the end of the three-week period referred to in section 268 of the Insolvency Act 1986.'

That paragraph reads a little oddly in a petition presented on 20 May based on a statutory demand served just under three weeks previously. The debtor disputes the correctness of the assertion in para 9, but that is not a matter which arises upon his appeal.

On the appeal, which came on in the vacation as a matter of urgency in view of the pending hearing on 9 June, the debtor confined his argument to the question of the construction of the relevant provisions of the Insolvency Act 1986 and the Insolvency Rules 1986, SI 1986/1925, governing the procedure for the presentation of a bankruptcy petition. It will only be necessary to deal with the jeopardy aspects of the case if the debtor fails in his application to set aside the statutory demand and the petitioning creditors then ask for an immediate bankruptcy order to be made on the petition already presented.

Before I refer to the relevant statutory provisions I should state briefly what happened in the court below. After the presentation of the petition on 20 May the debtor took out an application asking for a number of orders, including an injunction to restrain publication of the petition, redress for contempt and an application to strike out the petition or have it dismissed as an abuse of the process of the court. Those applications were heard by Judge Clegg on 2 June. He dismissed the debtor's applications. On the matter of abuse of the process of the court Judge Clegg held that the joint liquidators were entitled to present the petition: they had not committed any breach of the statutory provisions or the rules and there had been no abuse of process.

As the case turns on the construction of the provisions of the 1986 Act and the 1986 rules I shall refer next to the relevant sections of that Act. Sections 267 and 268 of the 1986 Act state the grounds on which a creditor may present a bankruptcy petition. A creditor's petition may be presented to the court in respect of a debt owed by the debtor to the petitioning creditor, but only if certain conditions are satisfied at the time when the petition is presented. Those conditions are set out in s 267(2)(a), (b), (c) and (d). Only the latter two of the four conditions are relevant to this appeal. They provide:

'(c) the debt, or each of the debts, is a debt which the debtor appears either to be unable to pay or to have no reasonable prospect of being able to pay, and (d) there is no outstanding application to set aside a statutory demand served (under s 268 below) in respect of the debt or any of the debts.'

Section 268 defines 'inability to pay' a debt by reference to failure to comply, within a period of three weeks of it being served, with a prescribed form of statutory demand which has not been set aside in accordance with the rules.

The procedure for setting aside a statutory demand is laid down in rr 6.4 and 6.5 of the 1986 rules. The debtor may apply to the court to set the statutory demand aside within a period of 18 days from the date of service on him of the statutory demand. As from the date on which the application is filed in court, the time limited for compliance with the statutory demand ceases to run, subject to any order of the court under r 6.5(6). Under that rule it is provided:

'If the court dismisses the application, it shall make an order authorising the creditor to present a bankruptcy petition either forthwith, or on or after a date specified in the order.'

The 1986 rules require that the creditors petition should identify the debt in the manner specified in r 6.8. Rule 6.8(2) is of particular relevance. It provides:

'Where the debt is one for which, under s 268, a statutory demand must have been served on the debtor ... (b) it shall be stated that, to the best of the creditors' s knowledge and belief (i) the demand has neither been complied with nor set aside in accordance with the Rules, and (ii) no application to set it aside is outstanding.'

Having regard to those statutory provisions and rules the debtor's complaints in this case can be stated as follows.

(1) He has, in accordance with the 1986 rules, applied to the court to have the statutory demand set aside. The application is fixed for hearing before the district judge on 9 June. When he filed his application the court did not exercise the power under r 6.5(1) to dismiss his application without giving notice to the creditor on the ground that it did not show sufficient course. There will, therefore, be an inter partes hearing of his application on Wednesday.

(2) At a time when his application to set aside was outstanding, the petitioning creditors presented a petition. They were not entitled to do this because the precondition set in s 267(2)(d) of the 1986 Act was not satisfied.

(3) The petition also fails to comply with the requirements of the rules, in particular r 6.8(2)(b)(ii), because it does not state, as the rule requires, that no application to set aside the demand is outstanding. Indeed, the petitioners could not truthfully make such an assertion in the petition. The petitioners have, therefore, adopted a course which has deprived the debtor of the opportunity of avoiding the immediate presentation of the petition. If his application to set aside the demand were successful, then no petition would be presented.

In those circumstances he submits that the petition is an abuse of the process and should be dismissed immediately. The judge in the county court did not accept that submission.

In my judgment, the debtor's submissions do not take sufficient account of the terms of s 270 of the 1986 Act, read in the context of the opening words of sub-s 267(2) laying down the conditions which must be satisfied at the time when a bankruptcy petition is presented. The opening words of s 267(2) state: 'Subject to the next three sections, a creditor's petition may be presented to the court in respect of a debt or debts only if, at the time the petition is presented', the conditions in (a), (b), (c) and (d) are satisfied. One of the three sections to which s 267(2) is subject is s 270, which provides:

> 'In the case of a creditor's petition presented wholly or partly in respect of the debt which is the subject of a statutory demand under s 268, the petition may be presented before the end of the 3-week period there mentioned if there is a serious possibility that the debtor's property or the value of any of his property will be significantly diminished during that period and the petition contains a statement to that effect.'

That provision should be read with s 271(2), which provides:

> 'In a case in which the petition contains such a statement as is required by s 270, the court shall not make a bankruptcy order until at least 3 weeks have elapsed since the service of any statutory demand under s 268.'

The question raised by the debtor's submissions on this appeal is whether a petition may be presented under s 270 at a time when there is an outstanding application to set aside a statutory demand on which the petition is based.

The following points should be noted as matters not seriously disputed.

(1) A petition may be presented under s 270 in the circumstances specified in the section, even though the three week period has not expired, and the condition in s 267(2)(c) is not satisfied at the time of presentation.

(2) A petition may be presented under s 270 even before the debtor has been given an opportunity to issue an application to set aside the statutory demand on which the petition is based. The petition may be presented before the end of the three week period. It may be presented immediately after the statutory demand has been served. If a petition may be presented within the three week period, and even before the debtor has had an opportunity to apply to set the demand aside, it is difficult to see why the creditor should not be entitled to present such a petition after the application has been issued. What matters is whether the presentation is justified by a serious possibility that the debtor's property, or the value of it, will be significantly diminished during that period. That possibility may exist in a case where the debtor has issued an application to set aside the demand, as well as in a case where he has not done that or where he has not even had the opportunity to do that.

(3) None of the Insolvency Rules 1986 makes specific provision for the contents of the creditor's petition presented under s 270. It is to be noted that the general requirements in r 6.8(2) are reflected in the forms set out in Sch 4 to the 1986 rules to be used in and in connection with insolvency proceedings (see in particular form 6.7, para 4). But those forms are, according to r 12.7(2), to be used 'with such variations as the circumstances may require'.

(4) I note the provisions of r 7.55:

'No insolvency proceedings shall be invalidated by any formal defect or by any irregularity, unless the court before which objection is made considers that substantial injustice has been caused by the defect or irregularity, and that the injustice cannot be remedied by any order of the court.'

With these four points in mind I turn to the question whether this petition should be dismissed on the ground that, at the time it was presented, there was an outstanding application by the debtor to set aside the statutory demand. In my judgment, Judge Clegg was right to reject the debtor's application for this order.

In my view the legal position is as follows. (1) The requirement in s 267(2) that a creditor's petition may be presented to the court only if, at the time when it is presented, there is no outstanding application to set aside a statutory demand does not necessarily apply to every case. That requirement is expressly made 'subject to' s 270. (2) Where a statutory provision is expressed to be 'subject to' another statutory provision, the latter (the master provision) prevails over the former (the subject provision) if there is any conflict between them: see the decision of Megarry J in *C & J Clark Ltd v IRC* [1973] 2 All ER 513, [1973] 1 WLR 905; *affd* [1975] 1 All ER 801, [1975] 1 WLR 413. (3) Section 270 relaxes the requirements of s 267(2) by enabling a petition to be presented in respect of a debt demanded before the expiration of the three week period referred to in s 268. The reason for the relaxation is that the creditor may require protection against the serious possibility of jeopardy to the debtor's property during that period. (4) If the debtor's submissions to this court are correct, the provision for expedition in s 270 would operate capriciously. A creditor would be entitled to present such a petition, which I can describe as an expedited petition, if he acted so swiftly after the service of the statutory demand that the debtor had no time to issue an application to set the demand aside. But, on the debtor's construction, the creditor would not be entitled to present a petition, even if there was a serious possibility of jeopardy, if the debtor had issued his application to set aside the demand *before* the creditor had presented the expedited petition. In my view, such a consequence is unlikely to have been the parliamentary intention. (5) Non-compliance with r 6.8(2)(b)(ii) does not automatically or necessarily invalidate a petition. If the application to set aside the statutory demand succeeds, the petition will then be dismissed. If the application to set aside the statutory demand fails, the debtor will still be entitled to challenge the assertion in the expedited petition that there was a serious possibility of jeopardy to his property. If the court is not satisfied on jeopardy it may dismiss that petition. If, however, it is satisfied on that point the court may, in its discretion, waive any irregularity under r 7.55, if satisfied that the debtor has not suffered substantial injustice or prejudice as a result of non-compliance and then proceed to make a bankruptcy order on that petition. (6) I should state that I am concerned by the debtor's argument that, if the construction I have adopted is correct, the procedure under s 270 may be abused. He points out that the presentation of a petition is very damaging to a debtor's credit and standing, even though that petition is later dismissed. He submits that there is a risk that there may be cases where a petition is presented and damage is done to the debtor who ultimately succeeds on his application to set aside, even to the extent of showing that there is no question of any sum of money owing by him to the petitioning creditor.

I think that the answer to the anxieties of the debtor was provided by Mr Ashton, who appeared for the petitioning creditors. He pointed out that the statement as to the serious possibility of jeopardy in the petition cannot simply be made without foundation; it has to be verified by an affidavit which justifies the allegation made. He also points out that no order can be made until it has been established that a debt is owing. No bankruptcy order would be made until the application to set aside the statutory demand has been heard. It is also provided by s 271(2) that at a least three weeks must have elapsed since the service of the statutory demand before a bankruptcy order can be made.

I would add that if the debtor succeeds in having a statutory demand set aside, and then succeeds in having the petition dismissed, he may have redress for any damage that he has suffered if he can show that there has been an abuse of legal process by the presentation of a petition against him maliciously and without reasonable cause: see *Johnson v Emerson and Sparrow* (1871) LR 6 Exch 329.

For those reasons the debtor's concerns about the possible abuse of the expedited petition procedure are not sufficient to cause me to depart from what, in my view, is the true construction of the relevant provisions and rules. I shall dismiss the appeal.

Appeal dismissed. Leave to appeal refused.

Hazel Hartman   Barrister.

Restick v Crickmore and other appeals

COURT OF APPEAL, CIVIL DIVISION
BUTLER-SLOSS, STUART-SMITH LJJ AND SIR TASKER WATKINS
2, 3, 17 NOVEMBER 1993

Practice – Striking out – Action – Action brought in wrong court – Action wrongly brought in High Court – Transfer of action to county court – Exercise of discretion – Whether High Court judge having discretion to transfer to county court action wrongly brought in High Court – Whether action required to be struck out – Exercise of discretion to strike out action wrongly brought in High Court – County Courts Act 1984, s 40(1).

In five separate actions the plaintiffs' personal injury claims were wrongly commenced in the High Court. In each case the action was struck out under s 40(1)[a] of the County Courts Act 1984, which provided that where the High Court was satisfied that any proceedings were required to be in a county court 'it shall—(a) order the transfer of the proceedings to a county court; or (b) if the court is satisfied that the person bringing the proceedings knew, or ought to have known, of that requirement, order that they be struck out'. The judge in each case held that where the court was satisfied that the proceedings before it were required to be in a county court and that the plaintiff or his solicitor knew or ought to have known of that requirement it was obliged to strike the proceedings out and had no discretion under s 40 to transfer the case to a county court. The plaintiffs appealed to the Court of Appeal.

Held – On the true construction of s 40(1) of the 1984 Act, once the court was satisfied that the proceedings should have been brought in the county court and not the High Court it had an unfettered choice or discretion of either transferring the proceedings to the county court or striking them out, but it could only strike them out if additionally the plaintiff knew or ought to have known that they should have been brought in the county court. In exercising the power to strike out, the well-established policy of the court was that, provided the proceedings were started within the limitation period, were not frivolous, vexatious or an abuse of the process of the court and disclosed a cause of action, they would not normally be struck out because of a mistake in procedure on the part of the plaintiff or his advisers. The usual sanction for failing to comply with the requirement to start an action in the right court was in costs. It followed that the judges had erred in holding that they had no discretion to transfer the plaintiffs' cases to the county court and accordingly the plaintiffs' appeals would be allowed (see p 116 e to p 117 a j to p 118 c and p 120 h j, post).

Groome v Norman Motors (Wallisdown) Ltd [1993] PIQR P215 overruled.

Per curiam. Where an action should plainly have been started in a county court and the failure to do so was not due to a bona fide mistake but can be seen as an attempt to harass a defendant or a deliberate attempt to run up unnecessary costs or was taken in defiance of a warning by the defendant as to

---

a   Section 40(1) is set out at p 114 b c, post

the proper venue or where a party or his solicitor persistently starts actions in the wrong court or in a particularly blatant case where the value of the plaintiff's claim was obviously below the county court limit and there are no extenuating circumstances the court might well apply the sanction of striking out (see p 119 *a* to *c* and p 120 *h j*, post).

Notes

For striking out High Court proceedings that ought to have been brought in a county court, see 37 *Halsbury's Laws* (4th edn) para 66.

For the County Courts Act 1984, s 40, see 11 *Halsbury's Statutes* (4th edn) (1991 reissue) 631.

Cases referred to in judgments

Chief Adjudication Officer v Foster [1993] 1 All ER 705, [1993] AC 754, [1993] 2 WLR 292, HL.
Groome v Norman Motors (Wallisdown) Ltd [1993] PIQR P215.
Pepper (Inspector of Taxes) v Hart [1993] 1 All ER 42, [1993] AC 593, [1992] 3 WLR 1032, HL.
Practice Direction [1991] 3 All ER 352, [1991] 1 WLR 642.
Walkley v Precision Forgings Ltd [1979] 2 All ER 548, [1979] 1 WLR 606, HL.

Cases also cited

Clarke v Cush (2 November 1992, unreported), QBD at Winchester.
Hopkins v Rees & Kirby Ltd [1959] 2 All ER 352, [1959] 1 WLR 740.

Interlocutory appeals

In a number of appeals, namely (1) *Restick v Crickmore*, (2) *Nisbet v Granada Entertainment Ltd*, (3) *Reed v Dept of Employment*, (4) *Warren v Hinchcliffe and anor* and (5) *Kazmi v Wali*, the plaintiffs appealed against orders made in the High Court striking out their actions for damages for personal injury. The facts are set out in the judgment of Stuart-Smith LJ.

Michael Hosford-Tanner (instructed by *Roger Green & Co*, Pitsea) for the plaintiff in *Restick v Crickmore*.
Michael Pooles (instructed by *Budd Martin Burrett*, Chelmsford) for the defendant in *Restick v Crickmore*.
Daniel Brennan QC and Elizabeth Anne Gumbel (instructed by *David Saunders*, Ashford, Kent) for the plaintiff in *Nisbet v Granada Entertainment Ltd*.
Dermod O'Brien QC (instructed by *Argles & Court*, Maidstone) for the defendant in *Nisbet v Granada Entertainment Ltd*.
Kieran May (instructed by *Philip Hamer & Co*, Leeds and *Disken & Co*, Dewsbury) for the plaintiffs in *Reed v Dept of Employment* and *Warren v Hinchcliffe*.
Ian Burnett (instructed by the *Treasury Solicitor*) for the defendant in *Reed v Dept of Employment*.
The parties in *Kazmi v Wali* and the defendants in *Warren v Hinchcliffe* did not appear.

Cur adv vult

17 November 1993. The following judgments were delivered.

STUART-SMITH LJ (giving the first judgment at the invitation of Butler-Sloss LJ). These five appeals raise the same point as to the construction of s 40(1) of the County Courts Act 1984 as amended by s 2(1) of the Courts and Legal Services Act 1990. The amended section provides:

> 'Where the High Court is satisfied that any proceedings before it are required by any provision of a kind mentioned in subsection (8) to be in a county court it shall—(a) order the transfer of the proceedings to a county court; or (b) if the court is satisfied that the person bringing the proceedings knew, or ought to have known, of that requirement, order that they be struck out ...'

The question is this: if the court is satisfied with the condition specified in the opening words of the subsection and that in para (b) are fulfilled, is the court obliged to strike the proceedings out, or does it have a discretion or choice to transfer the case to the county court? Each of the judges in these appeals held that there was no discretion and that they had no alternative but to strike the action out. In so doing they followed the decision of Turner J in *Groome v Norman Motors (Wallisdown) Ltd* [1993] PIQR P215.

The provisions referred to in s 40(1) of the 1984 Act are those made under s 1 of the 1990 Act (see s 40(8) of the 1984 Act). Section 1 of the 1990 Act provides:

> '(1) The Lord Chancellor may by order make provision— (a) conferring jurisdiction on the High Court in relation to proceedings in which county courts have jurisdiction ... (e) specifying proceedings which may be commenced only in a county court ...
>
> (2) Without prejudice to the generality of section 120(2), any such order may differentiate between categories of proceedings by reference to such criteria as the Lord Chancellor sees fit to specify in the order.
>
> (3) The criteria so specified may, in particular, relate to—(a) the value of the action (as defined by the order); (b) the nature of the proceedings ...'

The order made pursuant to ss 1 and 120 of the 1990 Act is the High Court and County Courts Jurisdiction Order 1991, SI 1991/724. In so far as it is relevant, the 1991 order provides:

> '4. Subject to articles 5 and 6, proceedings in which both the county courts and the High Court have jurisdiction may be commenced either in a county court or in the High Court.
>
> 5.—(1) Proceedings in which county courts have jurisdiction and which include a claim for damages in respect of personal injuries shall be commenced in a county court, unless the value of the action is £50,000 or more ...
>
> 7.—(1) Subject to the following provisions of this article, proceedings in which both the High Court and the county courts have jurisdiction may be tried in the High Court or in a county court ...
>
> 9.—(1) For the purposes of articles 5 and 7—(a) the value of an action for a sum of money, whether specified or not, is the amount which the plaintiff or applicant reasonably expects to recover ...'

By RSC Ord 6, r 2(1)(f), before a writ is issued it must be indorsed where the action is an action for personal injuries with a statement that the action is not one which by virtue of art 5 of the 1991 order must be commenced in the county court. And by a practice direction issued by the Senior Master on 21 June 1991 ([1991] 3 All ER 352, [1991] 1 WLR 642), the form of the indorsement is to be in the following terms:

> 'This writ includes a claim for personal injury but may be commenced in the High Court because the value of the action for the purposes of art 5 of the High Court and County Courts Jurisdiction Order 1991 exceeds £50,000.'

That is the background to s 40(1) of the 1984 Act to be found in the statutory provisions and the rules. I turn to the construction of the subsection. The argument which prevailed with the judges in the courts below was that the word 'shall' is mandatory and governs para (b) of s 40(1); accordingly if the condition set out in that paragraph is satisfied, as it usually will be where a solicitor is issuing a writ and will often be so with a litigant in person, the court has no option but to strike out the action.

Counsel for the plaintiffs submit that the meaning is clear and there is no ambiguity and that the judges were plainly correct. Mr O'Brien QC supported this contention by a number of submissions.

First, he pointed to the contrast in the use of the word 'shall' in s 40(1) of the 1984 Act to the word 'may' in sub-s (2); that subsection provides that, subject to any provision referred to in sub-s (1), 'the High Court may order the transfer of any proceedings before it to a county court'.

Secondly, he contrasted the wording of s 34 of the 1984 Act before it was repealed by the 1990 Act. That section provided:

> '(1) Subject to subsection (2), where any proceedings are commenced in a county court in which a county court has no jurisdiction, the court shall, unless it is given jurisdiction by a jurisdiction agreement, order that the proceedings be transferred to the High Court.
> (2) Where, on the application of any defendant, it appears to the court that the plaintiff or one of the plaintiffs knew or ought to have known that the court had no jurisdiction in the proceedings, the court may, if it thinks fit, instead of ordering that the proceedings be transferred, order that they be struck out ...'

That section, says Mr O'Brien, shows how Parliament will legislate if it wishes to make a direction to the court to strike out.

Prior to 1991, the county court in a personal injury case had no jurisdiction to award damages in excess of £5,000. That is now changed. The county court has unlimited jurisdiction so there is no risk, if a plaintiff starts an action in the county court, that he can recover no more than £50,000 if his original estimate proves too low or events subsequently show a deterioration in prognosis.

Thirdly, he submits that, if the construction contended for by the appellants is correct, it could easily have been achieved by rewriting the section so that para (b) of s 40(1) was introduced by the word 'but' as opposed to 'or', or had the word 'may' before the words 'order that they be struck out'.

Fourthly, he submits that the courts will have to evolve a body of law to define or circumscribe the circumstances in which the discretion is to be exercised to strike out, if the mere satisfaction of the condition contained in para (b) is not enough.

Then he submits that, although the power is draconian, it is clearly given to achieve the purpose of the legislation, which is to remove all cases under £50,000 from the High Court. A sanction in costs alone, he submits, is an insufficient sanction to achieve this purpose, being confined to the costs of the summons, which may well be a consent summons, and such difference, if any, as there may be, and at present there is none, between the cost of issuing a writ in the High Court and a plaint note in a county court.

He submits that the defendants' construction provides a watertight system; which I take to mean that everyone knows exactly where they stand and if the solicitor makes an error, so that an applicant loses his action, there is a cast iron claim for negligence against him. He points out that it is only in those cases where the statute of limitations has run at the time of the application to strike out that there is any difficulty, since in such a case the plaintiff cannot issue fresh proceedings in the county court (see *Walkley v Precision Forgings Ltd* [1979] 2 All ER 548, [1979] 1 WLR 606). In all other cases, the plaintiff can simply start again in the county court.

Finally, he submits that it is unreasonable that by breaking the rules a solicitor should effectively gain an additional four and half months beyond the limitation point, before he has to serve a statement of claim, together with a medical report and schedule of loss. This comes about because the writ does not have to be served for four months after issue; there is then a further fourteen days after acknowledgment of service for delivery of the statement of claim. In the county court, however, the particulars of claim, medical report and schedule of loss must be served before the expiry of the limitation period.

These considerations cannot affect what in my judgment is the plain meaning of the section. With all respect to them, the judges' construction ignores the word 'or' in combination with the word 'shall' when applied at the end of the introductory words of the subsection.

Once the conditions set out in the opening words of s 40(1) are fulfilled, the court is required to do one of two things, to transfer the proceedings to the county court or strike it out. It plainly has a choice between the two courses of action. For my part, I cannot see that the use of the word 'shall', positioned where it is, requires the court to adopt one course rather than the other, simply because the necessary precondition for exercising choice (b) is also fulfilled. What the court cannot do is retain the action in the High Court. In this respect the discretion is different from that in sub-s (2), where the court has a discretion whether to retain or transfer the action. In my judgment, the meaning of the section is plain and not ambiguous. The court is required to make a choice between the two alternatives, but it can only strike out if the additional condition is satisfied, namely that the person bringing the proceedings knew, or ought to have known, of the requirement. But otherwise the choice or discretion is unfettered.

To construe the section in the sense contended by the defendants would, in my view, require different language. For example, after the opening condition 'the court may order a transfer to the county court, but if satisfied that the person bringing the proceedings knew or ought to have known of that requirement, shall order that they be struck out'. Or alternatively, 'the court shall strike out the proceedings if it is satisfied that the person knew or ought to have known of the requirement, otherwise it shall transfer them to the county court'.

For my part, I do not think there is any ambiguity in the subsection. Accordingly, I do not think it is necessary to invoke the doctrine in *Pepper (Inspector of Taxes) v Hart* [1993] 1 All ER 42, [1993] AC 593, which entitles the court to look at the debate in Parliament during the passage of the Bill. But perhaps it may be said that the difference of judicial opinion between the judges in the courts below and this court shows that there is an ambiguity (see *Chief Adjudication Officer v Foster* [1993] 1 All ER 705 at 717, [1993] AC 754 at 772 per Lord Bridge of Harwich).

But if one does look at the debate as recorded in Hansard for 16 January 1990 (514 HL *Official Report* (5th series) cols 595–628), it is plain that the Lord Chancellor intended the section to be construed as I have indicated. The Bill being considered was in these terms:

'**40.**—(1) Where the High Court is satisfied that any proceedings before it are required by any procedure provision to be in a county court, it shall—(a) order the transfer of the proceedings to a county court; or (b) order that they be struck out.'

It is plain that this section gives the court an unfettered discretion to choose (a) or (b). The Lord Chancellor, when dealing with an amendment concerning the words 'procedure provision', said (col 624):

'The point is that if, by virtue of an enactment made by or under any statutory provision, the proceedings are to be in a county court, then the High Court has two possibilities: either it may transfer the case to the county court—in other words it may deal with the case by transferring it to the county court—or, if it wishes, it may strike the case out. That is all that it says. It seems to me to be simple.'

The House then considered amendments 17 and 18; amendment 18 introduced the words in para (b) 'if the court is satisfied that the person bringing the proceedings knew, or ought to have known, of that requirement'. Lord Hacking was concerned that the power to strike out might be used too often; he wished to delete para (b) altogether. Lord Donaldson MR pointed out the power to strike out was useful to retain, for example in a case where a plaintiff persisted in starting in the wrong court when he knew perfectly well he should not. It was in this context that the Lord Chancellor said (at col 627):

'I am extremely grateful to the noble Lord, Lord Meston, and my noble and learned friend the Master of the Rolls. Originally I intended that the court would have fairly wide discretions as regards subsection (1)(b). However, on reconsidering the matter, and seeing that in Section 34(2) of the County Courts Act, which is a good precedent, there appears the phrase used in Amendment No. 18, I thought that it may be as well to express it. The object is to prevent people abusing the possibility and in that case giving the court the power to adopt a draconian remedy in the belief that it will prevent such an event happening again. The remarks made by my noble and learned friend suggest that the power given under the County Courts Act has been effective in that respect. As far as I can judge, it has been seldom used. I hope that this power will be used even less because I hope that such events will not occur too often.'

It seems to me to be plain that by introducing amendment no 18 the Lord Chancellor intended to introduce a fetter upon the power to strike out or a further hurdle which has to be overcome before the power is exercised. It is inconceivable that he was making it mandatory to strike out whenever the condition was satisfied.

The construction I prefer accords with the well-established policy of the courts, which is this: provided proceedings are started within the time permitted by the statute of limitations, are not frivolous, vexatious or an abuse of the process of the court and disclose a cause of action, they will not as a rule be struck out because of some mistake in procedure on the part of the plaintiff or his advisers. Save where there has been a contumelious disobedience of the court's order, the draconian sanction of striking out an otherwise properly constituted action, simply to punish the party who has failed to comply with the rules of court, is not part of the court's function. No injustice is involved to the defendant in transferring an action which has been started in the wrong court to the correct court.

The ordinary sanction for failure to comply with the requirements will be in costs. Moreover, the Supreme Court Act 1981, s 51, as amended by the 1990 Act, deals with costs in the High Court and county courts. Subsections (6) and (7) provide for wasted costs awards to be given against legal advisers in respect of costs incurred as a result of their improper, unreasonable or negligent acts or omissions.

Section 51(8) and (9) provides as follows:

'(8) Where—(a) a person has commenced proceedings in the High Court; but (b) those proceedings should, in the opinion of the court, have been commenced in a county court in accordance with any provision made under section 1 of the Courts and Legal Services Act 1990 or by or under any other enactment, the person responsible for determining the amount which is to be awarded to that person by way of costs shall have regard to those circumstances.

(9) Where, in complying with subsection (8), the responsible person reduces the amount which would otherwise be awarded to the person in question—(a) the amount of that reduction shall not exceed 25 per cent; and (b) on any taxation of the costs payable by that person to his legal representative, regard shall be had to the amount of the reduction.'

These subsections permit the taxing officer, in an appropriate case, to reduce the costs otherwise payable by up to 25% in the case of a person who started the case in the wrong court. The provision appears to apply both to actions which remain in the High Court because they have not been transferred under s 40(1)(a) of the 1984 Act and to those which are transferred. This is a formidable sanction; and, if taxing masters apply it, it is likely to have an electrifying effect on the solicitors' profession. I do not think they will improperly sign certificates for the purpose of RSC Ord 6, r 2 a second time. Furthermore, this provision, being introduced as it was in the 1990 Act, seems to me to be a clear indication that the court would normally transfer the action to the county court, even if the condition in para (b) of s 40(1) is satisfied.

The construction contended for by the defendants could give rise to very great injustice. If, for example, an action falling within the section is started well within the three-year period and is nearly ready for trial, by which time three years have passed from the accident, the defendant could then apply to strike out. If the defendants are right, this court has no alternative but to accede to the application. Such an unjust result is patently absurd.

It may be asked in what circumstances should the court exercise the power to strike out? I would be reluctant to attempt to lay down any guide lines which might be thought to fetter the undoubted discretion of the judge. Where the action should plainly have been started in the county court, and the failure to do so was not due to a bona fide mistake, but can be seen as an attempt to harass a defendant, deliberately run up unnecessary costs, be taken in defiance of a warning of the defendants as to the proper venue or where a party, or more likely his solicitor, persistently starts actions in the wrong court, it may well be desirable for the court to apply the more draconian order of striking out. These are merely examples and are not intended to be an exhaustive list. It may also be in a particularly blatant case where the value of the plaintiff's claim is so obviously of a very low order the action should be struck out if there are no extenuating circumstances.

Since none of the judges in these cases considered that they had any discretion to transfer, it is necessary for this court to exercise the discretion. In all the cases I am satisfied that the two conditions in s 40(1) are satisfied.

Restick v Crickmore

The accident occurred on 10 December 1989; the writ was issued on 16 November 1992; it did not bear the indorsement required by RSC Ord 6, r 2. According to the plaintiff's solicitor, this was due to an oversight. The claim was clearly not worth £50,000 or anything like it. The value of the claim was never properly considered by the plaintiff's solicitors. This might be a case for striking out, but on the other hand it seems to have been a bona fide mistake; perhaps more importantly liability was not in dispute, an interim payment had been made and the writ was issued simply to preserve the action. Had the proceedings been issued in the county court, as they should have been, additional costs of settling particulars of claim and any medical reports and schedule of loss would have been incurred in a case where it seems likely a settlement might be reached. I would not strike it out, but order a transfer. But I would draw the taxing officer's attention to s 51(8) and (9).

Nisbet v Granada Entertainment Ltd

The accident was on 14 May 1989. The writ was issued on 8 May 1992 and bore the indorsement required by RSC Ord 6, r 2. The plaintiff sustained a serious injury to her knee. Mr Patrick Bennett QC, sitting as a deputy judge of the High Court, who has great experience in these cases, considered that the case was worth no more than £35,000 in total. In his affidavit, the plaintiff's solicitor says that the claim might have been as high as £48,000 in total, that is £33,000 for loss of amenity, pain and suffering, £5,000 for loss of earning capacity and £10,000 for loss of earnings. He then adds this: 'In my submission, neither the plaintiff, nor her advisers, should be criticised for keeping this option open [ie to claim more than £50,000] however speculative it may appear to be at the moment by commencing this action in the High Court.'

I agree with Mr O'Brien that this shows a fundamental misunderstanding of the new provisions. There was nothing to prevent the plaintiff recovering more than £50,000 in the county court and the action ought to have been started there. But here again there was a bona fide mistake; the claim is a substantial one, though liability is very much in dispute. In my opinion, costs are a sufficient sanction here. I would not strike out, but transfer the case to the county court. Here too I would draw the taxing officer's attention to s 51(8) and (9) of the Supreme Court Act 1981.

Reed v Dept of Employment
On 20 July 1988 the plaintiff suffered a serious injury to his left, non-dominant thumb, while he was a trainee working with woodworking machinery. Some time after the accident he tried to go back to work, but he was nervous of working with power tools because he could not properly control them. So he gave up this work and sought training in clerical work. If the inability to work as a joiner was due to the accident, then there might well be a substantial continuing loss of earnings, although surprisingly enough the statement of claim said there was no special damage. The writ was issued on 19 July 1991 and served, together with the statement of claim, shortly afterwards. A defence was served on 27 April 1992. The summons to strike out was issued in March 1993. Mr Burnett, on behalf of the respondent, concedes that, if the court has a discretion to transfer, it should exercise it in this case. I agree; the action had progressed a considerable way beyond the writ and this is obviously a consideration which weighs against striking out. It was also a borderline case, if the loss of earnings materialised.

Warren v Hinchcliffe and anor
This is a claim under the Fatal Accident Act 1976. It is clear that the dependency is well below £50,000. The accident happened on 30 January 1990. The writ was issued on 6 November 1992 and the statement of claim served shortly afterwards. The two defences were served by 21 December. The summons to strike out was served on 14 April 1993. This is clearly not a case where the action should be struck out; it would be an example of the injustice to which I have referred, though there is no suggestion that the defendant deliberately waited until after the expiry of the Limitation Act 1980 to ambush the plaintiff. An application to strike out, if it is to succeed, should certainly be made promptly. I would order transfer to the county court and draw the taxing officer's attention to s 51(8) and (9) of the Supreme Court Act 1981.

Kazmi v Wali
There is no evidence before this court relating to this case. The matter was dealt with as one of principle before Dyson J, where it was conceded that the plaintiff's solicitor ought to have known that the claim was worth less than £50,000. I would direct that the action be transferred to the appropriate county court; in this case the order should not be drawn up for 28 days; if within this time the defendant applies to a district judge to exercise his discretion to strike out the action, the order will be of no effect. It will be a matter for the district judge to determine.
For these reasons, I would allow all the appeals.

SIR TASKER WATKINS. I agree.

BUTLER-SLOSS LJ. I also agree.

Appeals allowed. Leave to appeal to House of Lords refused.

Carolyn Toulmin   Barrister.

Attorney General's Reference (No 3 of 1992)

COURT OF APPEAL, CRIMINAL DIVISION
LORD TAYLOR OF GOSFORTH CJ, SCHIEMANN AND WRIGHT JJ
2, 12 NOVEMBER 1993

Criminal law – Damage to property – Arson – Attempted aggravated arson – Recklessness – Whether sufficient to establish specific intent to cause damage by fire and that defendant was reckless as to whether life would thereby be endangered – Whether necessary to establish that defendant intended that lives of others would be endangered by damage intended – Criminal Damage Act 1971, s 1(2).

Following previous attacks on their property the complainants maintained a night-time watch over their premises from a motor vehicle. In the early hours of the morning another car containing the respondents approached and a petrol bomb was thrown from it towards the complainants, four of whom were inside their car and two of whom were on the pavement outside. The petrol bomb passed over the complainants' vehicle and smashed against a nearby garden wall. The respondents' car then accelerated away but crashed soon after. Inside their car a milk crate containing a number of petrol bombs, matches, a petrol can and some rags were found. The respondents were arrested and charged with two counts of attempted aggravated arson contrary to s 1(2)[a] of the Criminal Damage Act 1971, count 1 alleging intent to endanger life and count 2 alleging recklessness as to whether life would be endangered. At the conclusion of the Crown's case the judge directed an acquittal. On count 1 the judge ruled that there was no evidence of the necessary intent. On count 2 the judge ruled that (i) an attempt to commit the offence could not be committed unless there was an intention to commit the offence, (ii) there was no evidence that the respondents intended by the destruction of the complainants' car to endanger the life of its occupants or the bystanders, (iii) it was impossible to intend to be reckless as to whether the life of another would be endangered by damage to property, and therefore (iv) it was impossible in law for a person to be convicted of an attempt to commit aggravated arson if all that could be proved was that the defendant intended to damage property being reckless as to whether the life of another would be endangered by such damage. The Attorney General referred to the Court of Appeal under s 36(1) of the Criminal Justice Act 1972 the question whether on a charge of attempted aggravated arson, in addition to establishing a specific intent to cause damage by fire, it was sufficient to prove that the defendant was reckless as to whether life would thereby be endangered.

Held – On a charge of attempted aggravated arson contrary to s 1(2) of the 1971 Act, it was sufficient for the Crown to establish a specific intent to cause damage by fire and that the defendant was reckless as to whether life would thereby be endangered, because if the state of mind of the defendant was that he intended to damage property and was reckless as to whether the life of another would thereby be endangered, and while in that state of mind he did an act which was more than merely preparatory to the offence, he was guilty of attempting to commit that offence. It was not necessary that he intended

---

a   Section 1(2) is set out at p 124 *d*, post

that the lives of others would be endangered by the damage which he intended (see p 126 j to p 127 b and p 128 c d g h, post).
R v Khan [1990] 2 All ER 783 applied.

Per curiam. In circumstances where the damaged property (the first property) was not the same as the property intended to be damaged (the second property), the offence of attempted aggravated arson is committed if, in addition to specific intent to cause damage by fire to the first property being established, it is proved that the defendant was reckless as to whether the second property was damaged and reckless as to whether the life of another would be endangered by the damage to the second property (see p 128 h j, post).

Notes
For destroying or damaging property, see 11(1) *Halsbury's Laws* (4th edn reissue) para 594, and for cases on the subject, see 14(2) *Digest* (2nd reissue) 517–521, 10679–10696.

For mental element in attempt, see 11(1) *Halsbury's Laws* (4th edn reissue) para 73, and for cases on the subject, see 14(1) *Digest* (2nd reissue) 23–27, 32, 82–101, 151.

For the Criminal Damage Act 1971, s 1, see 12 *Halsbury's Statutes* (4th edn) (1994 reissue) 548.

For the Criminal Justice Act 1972, s 36, see ibid 561.

Cases referred to in judgment
R v Caldwell [1981] 1 All ER 961, [1982] AC 341, [1981] 2 WLR 509, HL.
R v Khan [1990] 2 All ER 783, [1990] 1 WLR 813, CA.
R v Millard [1987] Crim LR 393, CA.
R v Steer [1987] 2 All ER 833, [1988] AC 111, [1987] 3 WLR 205, HL.

Cases also cited
Cuncliffe v Goodman [1950] 1 All ER 720, [1950] 2 KB 237, CA.
R v Hancock [1986] 1 All ER 641, [1986] AC 455, HL.
R v Mohan [1975] 2 All ER 193, [1976] QB 1, CA.
R v Moloney [1985] 1 All ER 1025, [1985] AC 905, HL.
R v Nedrick [1986] 3 All ER 1, [1986] 1 WLR 1025.
R v O'Toole [1987] Crim LR 739, CA.
R v Pearman (1985) 80 Cr App R 259, CA.
R v Pigg [1983] 1 All ER 56, [1983] 1 WLR 6, HL.
R v Rafique [1993] 4 All ER 1, [1993] QB 843, CA.
R v Satnam (1983) 78 Cr App R 149, CA.
R v Shivpuri [1986] 2 All ER 334, [1987] AC 1, HL.
R v Whybrow (1951) 35 Cr App R 141, CCA.

Reference
The Attorney General referred to the Court of Appeal under s 36 of the Criminal Justice Act 1972 for the consideration of the court the question whether on a charge of attempted arson in the aggravated form contemplated by s 1(2) of the Criminal Damage Act 1971, in addition to establishing a specific intent to cause damage by fire, it was sufficient to prove that the defendant was reckless as to whether life would thereby be endangered. The facts are set out in the opinion of the court.

David Spens (instructed by the Crown Prosecution Service, Headquarters) for the Attorney General.
Philip R Noble (assigned by the Registrar of Criminal Appeals) for the respondent A.
Jonathan Whitfield (assigned by the Registrar of Criminal Appeals) for the respondent B.
Francis Moraes (assigned by the Registrar of Criminal Appeals) for the respondent C.
Charles Briefel (assigned by the Registrar of Criminal Appeals) for the respondent D.

Cur adv vult

12 November 1993. The following opinion of the court was delivered.

SCHIEMANN J. The court has heard a reference made under s 36(1) of the Criminal Justice Act 1972. The point of law which has been referred to us was formulated as follows:

'Whether on a charge of attempted arson in the aggravated form contemplated by Section 1(2) of the Criminal Damage Act 1971, in addition to establishing a specific intent to cause damage by fire, it is sufficient to prove that the defendant was reckless as to whether life would thereby be endangered.'

Summary of the relevant facts

The acquittals which have given rise to this reference had the following background according to the prosecution evidence. Following previous attacks upon their property the complainants maintained a night-time watch over their premises from a motor car (a Ford Granada). In the early hours of the morning the defendants came upon the scene in a vehicle. Inside this car (a Sierra) was a milk crate containing a number of petrol bombs, matches, a petrol can and some rags. As the Sierra approached the complainants (four inside their car and two persons on the pavement talking to them) a lighted petrol bomb was thrown towards them from the Sierra. The Crown's case was that it was thrown at the Granada and its occupants. The petrol bomb in fact passed over the top of the Granada and smashed against the garden wall of a house a pavement's width away from the car. The Sierra accelerated away but crashed, and the defendants were arrested.

At the trial count 1 of the indictment alleged attempted aggravated arson, specifying in the particulars of offence, inter alia, an intent to endanger life. Count 2 alleged attempted aggravated arson, specifying in the particulars of offence, inter alia, recklessness as to whether life would be endangered. At the conclusion of the Crown's case the learned judge ruled that there was no evidence upon which the jury could find the necessary intent to endanger life required in count 1, and accordingly directed the jury to return 'not guilty' verdicts in respect of that count. This reference is not concerned with that ruling, but with her directing an acquittal in relation to count 2. In essence her reasoning was that (1) there can be no conviction of an attempt to commit an offence unless the defendant intends to commit that offence; (2) the evidence could not support an allegation that the defendants intended by the destruction of the car to endanger the life of its occupants, or the bystanders;

(3) it is impossible to intend to be reckless as to whether the life of another would be endangered by damage to property; and therefore (4) it is impossible in law to convict of an attempt to commit aggravated arson if all that can be proved is that the defendant intended to damage property being reckless as to whether the life of another would be endangered by such damage.

The substantive offences

Before considering the law of attempt it is necessary to set out the law in relation to the substantive offence. The relevant statutory provisions are found in the Criminal Damage Act 1971, s 1 of which provides:

> '(1) A person who without lawful excuse destroys or damages any property belonging to another intending to destroy or damage any such property or being reckless as to whether any such property would be destroyed or damaged shall be guilty of an offence.
>
> (2) A person who without lawful excuse destroys or damages any property, whether belonging to himself or another—(a) intending to destroy or damage any property or being reckless as to whether any property would be destroyed or damaged; and (b) intending by the destruction or damage to endanger the life of another or being reckless as to whether the life of another would be thereby endangered; shall be guilty of an offence.
>
> (3) An offence committed under this section by destroying or damaging property by fire shall be charged as arson.'

It is worth noting that by virtue of s 4 an offence under s 1(2) carries a maximum penalty of imprisonment for life, whereas in general an offence under s 1(1) carries a maximum penalty of ten years, albeit that in the case of arson even the lesser offence under s 1(1) also carries a maximum penalty of imprisonment for life.

There are three further preliminary matters which need to be mentioned in this context as background, although none is contentious. First, it is common ground that the recklessness here referred to is what has become known as *Caldwell* recklessness (see *R v Caldwell* [1981] 1 All ER 961, [1982] AC 341). That was a case dealing with a substantive offence under the 1971 Act and Lord Diplock, whose opinion prevailed with the majority, said ([1981] 1 All ER 961 at 967, [1982] AC 341 at 354):

> 'In my opinion, a person charged with an offence under s 1(1) of the 1971 Act as "reckless as to whether or not any property would be destroyed or damaged" if (1) he does an act which in fact creates an obvious risk that property will be destroyed or damaged and (2) when he does the act he either has not given any thought to the possibility of there being any such risk or has recognised that there was some risk involved and has none the less gone on to do it ... Where the charge is under s 1(2) the question of the state of mind of the accused must be approached in stages, corresponding to paras (a) and (b).'

The second preliminary matter is this. It is clear that the prosecution are required to prove that the danger to life resulted from the destruction of or damage to property; it is not sufficient for the prosecution to prove that it resulted from the act of the defendant which caused the destruction or damage (see *R v Steer* [1987] 2 All ER 833, [1988] AC 111).

The third preliminary matter is that although in the present reference the question is posed in relation to arson it has not been submitted that the presence or absence of fire makes any difference to the answer to the question posed, which applies to any form of attempted criminal damage. So we omit any further reference to the element of fire in this judgment.

With those three preliminary matters out of the way, we turn to consider what again is uncontentious, namely what the prosecution need to prove in each case in order to secure a conviction for the completed offence of arson and aggravated arson.

So far as the completed simple offence is concerned, the prosecution needs to prove (1) property belonging to another was damaged by the defendant and (2) the state of mind of the defendant was one of the following: (a) he intended to damage such property or (b) he was reckless as to whether any such property would be damaged.

In the case of the completed aggravated offence the prosecution needs to prove (1) the defendant in fact damaged property, whether belonging to himself or another; and (2) that the state of mind of the defendant was one of the following, (a) he intended to damage property, and intended by the damage to endanger the life of another or (b) he intended to damage property and was reckless as to whether the life of another would be thereby endangered or (c) he was reckless as to whether any property would be damaged and was reckless as to whether the life of another would be thereby endangered.

It is to be noted that the property referred to under (1) (to which we shall hereafter refer as 'the first-named property') is not necessarily the same property as that referred to in (2) (to which we shall refer as 'the second-named property'), although it normally will be. Thus a man who (1) owns a crane from which is suspended a heavy object and (2) cuts the rope (the first-named property) which holds the object with the result that (3) the object falls and hits the roof of a passing car (the second-named property) which roof (4) collapses killing the driver would be guilty if it could be shown that he damaged the rope, was reckless as to whether this would damage the car, and was reckless as to whether the life of the driver of the car would be endangered by the damage to the car.

All the foregoing is common ground. The problem which has given rise to this reference relates to an attempt to commit the aggravated offence in circumstances where the first-named property is the same as the second-named property—in the instant case a car. It amounts to this: whether, if the state of mind of the defendant was that postulated in (2)(b) above, namely that he intended to damage property and was reckless as to whether the life of another would thereby be endangered, and whilst in that state of mind he did an act which was more than merely preparatory to the offence, he is guilty of attempting to commit that offence.

We turn to the law of attempt. The law of attempt is now governed by the Criminal Attempts Act 1981, which provides in s 1:

'(1) If, with intent to commit an offence ... a person does an act which is more than merely preparatory to the commission of the offence, he is guilty of attempting to commit the offence.

(2) A person may be guilty of attempting to commit an offence ... even though the facts are such that the commission of the offence is impossible ...'

Turning from the general to the particular, it is convenient to consider, first, attempting to commit the simple offence, which causes no problem, and then to pass on to attempting to commit the aggravated offence, which is what has given rise to this reference.

So far as attempting to commit the simple offence is concerned, in order to convict on such a charge it must be proved that the defendant (a) did an act which was more than merely preparatory to the commission of the offence and (b) he did an act intending to damage any property belonging to another.

One way of analysing the situation is to say that a defendant, in order to be guilty of an attempt, must be in one of the states of mind required for the commission of the full offence, and did his best, as far as he could, to supply what was missing from the completion of the offence. It is the policy of the law that such people should be punished notwithstanding that in fact the intentions of such a defendant have not been fulfilled.

If the facts are that, although the defendant had one of the appropriate states of mind required for the complete offence, but the physical element required for the commission of the complete offence is missing, the defendant is not to be convicted unless it can be shown that he intended to supply that physical element. This was the state of affairs in *R v Millard* [1987] Crim LR 393, of which we have seen the transcript. There the defendants were convicted of attempting to damage property. The particulars of the offence were that they 'attempted to damage a wooden wall at the ... stadium ... intending to damage the ... wall or being reckless as to whether the ... wall was damaged'. The trial judge directed the jury that recklessness was sufficient. Mustill LJ, delivering the judgment of the Court of Appeal, stated:

> 'The result which would have been achieved if the offence had been taken to fruition was damage to the stand ... the prosecution had to show ... that it was this state of affairs which each appellant had decided, so far as in him lay, to bring about.'

In consequence, mere recklessness was not sufficient and the convictions were quashed.

We turn finally to the attempt to commit the aggravated offence. In the present case, what was missing to prevent a conviction for the completed offence was damage to the property referred to in the opening lines of s 1(2) of the 1981 Act, what in the example of a crane, which we gave earlier in this judgment, we referred to as 'the first-named property'. Such damage is essential for the completed offence. If a defendant does not intend to cause such damage he cannot intend to commit the completed offence. At worst he is reckless as to whether the offence is committed. The law of attempt is concerned with those who are intending to commit crimes. If that intent cannot be shown, then there can be no conviction.

However, the crime here consisted of doing certain acts in a certain state of mind in circumstances where the first-named property and the second-named property were the same, in short where the danger to life arose from the damage to the property which the defendant intended to damage. The substantive crime is committed if the defendant damaged property in a state of mind where he was reckless as to whether the life of another would thereby be endangered. We see no reason why there should not be a conviction for attempt if the prosecution can show that he, in that state of mind, intended to damage the property by throwing a bomb at it. One analysis of this situation is to say that although the defendant was in an appropriate state of mind to render him guilty of the completed offence the prosecution had not proved the physical element of the completed offence, and therefore he is not guilty of the completed offence. If, on a charge of attempting to commit the offence, the prosecution can show not only the state of mind required for the completed offence but also that the defendant intended to supply the missing physical element of the completed offence, that suffices for a conviction. That can not be done merely by the prosecution showing him to be reckless. The defendant must intend to damage property, but there is no need for a graver mental state than is required for the full offence.

The learned trial judge in the present case, however, went further than this and held that not merely must the defendant intend to supply all that was missing from the completed offence—namely damage to the first-named property—but also that recklessness as to the consequences of such damage for the lives of others was not enough to secure a conviction for attempt, although it was sufficient for the completed offence. She held that before a defendant could be convicted of attempting to commit the offence it had to be shown that he intended that the lives of others should be endangered by the damage which he intended.

She gave no policy reasons for so holding, and there is no case which bound her so to hold. The most nearly relevant case is *R v Khan* [1990] 2 All ER 783, [1990] 1 WLR 813. There the defendant was charged with attempted rape. He did not in fact penetrate the girl, but he did acts which were more than merely preparatory. The jury must have found that the girl did not in fact consent to sexual intercourse. The trial judge directed the jury that it sufficed if either the defendant knew the girl was not consenting or if he was reckless as to whether she consented or not. He was convicted and appealed, arguing that it was impossible to have an attempted reckless rape. This submission was rejected by the court. Russell LJ said ([1990] 2 All ER 783 at 787–788, [1990] 1 WLR 813 at 818–819):

'In our judgment an acceptable analysis of the crime of rape is as follows: (1) the intention of the offender is to have sexual intercourse with a woman; (2) the offence is committed if, but only if, the circumstances are that (a) the woman does not consent *and* (b) the defendant knows that she is not consenting or is reckless as to whether she consents. Precisely the same analysis can be made of the offence of attempted rape: (1) the intention of the offender is to have sexual intercourse with a woman; (2) the offence is committed if, but only if, the circumstances are that (a) the woman does not consent *and* (b) the defendant knows she is not consenting or is reckless as to whether she consents. The only difference between the two offences is that in rape sexual intercourse takes place whereas in attempted rape it does not, although there has to be some act which is more than preparatory to sexual intercourse. Considered in that way, the intent of the defendant is precisely the same in rape and in attempted rape and the mens rea is identical, namely an intention to have intercourse plus a knowledge of or recklessness as to the woman's absence of consent. No question of attempting to achieve a reckless state of mind arises; the attempt relates to the physical activity; the mental state of the defendant is the same ... Recklessness in rape and attempted rape arises not in relation to the physical act of the accused but only in his state of mind when engaged in the activity of having or attempting to have sexual intercourse ... the attempt does not require any different intention on the part of the accused from that for the full offence of rape.' (Russell LJ's emphasis.)

An attempt was made in argument to suggest that *R v Khan* was wrongly decided. No policy reasons were advanced for that view and we do not share it. The result is one which accords with common sense, and does no violence to the words of the statute.

What was missing in *R v Khan* was the act of sexual intercourse, without which the offence was not complete. What was missing in the present case was damage to the first-named property, without which the offence was not complete. The mental state of the defendant in each case contained everything which was required to render him guilty of the full offence. In order to succeed in a prosecution for attempt, it must be shown that the defendant intended to achieve that which was missing from the full offence. Unless that is shown the prosecution have not proved that the defendant intended to commit the offence. Thus in *R v Khan* the prosecution had to show an intention to have sexual intercourse, and the remaining state of mind required for the offence of rape. In the present case, the prosecution had to show an intention to damage the first-named property, and the remaining state of mind required for the offence of aggravated arson.

The learned judge in the instant case was faced, as we have been faced, not only with citations of views held by the Law Commission at one time on what should be the law of attempt, but also with various articles in legal journals and books commenting on those views. It is right to say that at one time it was proposed that intention should be required as to all the elements of an offence, thus making it impossible to secure a conviction of attempt in circumstances such as the present. However, this proposal has not prevailed, and has been overtaken by *R v Khan*, and a formulation of the draft code which does not incorporate the proposal.

While the learned judge in the instant case opined that *R v Khan* was distinguishable she did not indicate any policy reasons for distinguishing it. We see none, and none have been submitted to us directly.

We now remind ourselves of the precise question posed by the reference:

'Whether on a charge of attempted arson in the aggravated form contemplated by Section 1(2) of the Criminal Damage Act 1971, in addition to establishing a specific intent to cause damage by fire, it is sufficient to prove that the defendant was reckless as to whether life would thereby be endangered.'

We answer it in the affirmative. We add that, in circumstances where the first-named property is not the same as the second-named property, in addition to establishing a specific intent to cause damage by fire to the first-named property, it is sufficient to prove that the defendant was reckless as to whether any second-named property was damaged and reckless as to whether the life of another would be endangered by the damage to the second-named property.

Opinion accordingly.

N P Metcalfe Esq   Barrister.

Showlag v Mansour and others

PRIVY COUNCIL

LORD KEITH OF KINKEL, LORD JAUNCEY OF TULLICHETTLE, LORD BROWNE-WILKINSON, LORD WOOLF AND LORD NOLAN

14, 15 FEBRUARY, 15 MARCH 1994

Estoppel – Res judicata – Foreign judgment – Competing foreign judgments – Precedence of competing foreign judgments each pronounced by court of competent jurisdiction – Whether earlier judgment should be recognised and given effect to exclusion of later judgment.

Following the death in May 1989 of a Saudi Arabian money-broker and money-changer who had accumulated a very large fortune, his heirs discovered that two deposits, together worth about £17·5m, held by the deceased in London banks had some months prior to his death been transferred to an account at a bank in Switzerland in the name of a Panamanian company wholly owned by the respondent, who had been employed by the deceased in connection with his business affairs in London. Most of the money from the company's account had been dispersed by the respondent to a number of different countries, including Jersey and Egypt. The respondent claimed that the money in the deposits had been given to him by the deceased at the end of November 1988 but the deceased's heirs believed that the money had been stolen by the respondent, and they instituted proceedings against him in various jurisdictions, including England and Egypt. On 5 December 1990 the judge in proceedings brought by the heirs in England claiming a declaration that the respondent was a constructive trustee of the money gave judgment for the heirs in which he wholly rejected the respondent's claim that the money was a gift. On 31 December 1990 a court in Egypt adjudicating on a criminal prosecution brought against the respondent, to which the heirs were joined as civil parties, found the respondent guilty of having stolen the deposits in the two London banks but declined to deal with the heirs' civil claim and ordered that it be referred to the competent civil court. On 23 May 1991 the Misdemeanours Court of Appeal in Egypt allowed an appeal by the respondent and set aside the judgment of the lower court and ordered that the heirs' civil claim be dismissed on the ground that the respondent had received the money in the two deposits as a gift from the deceased. That judgment was under appeal by the heirs. In earlier proceedings in October 1989 the heirs had brought two actions in Jersey alleging that part of the misappropriated deposits had on the respondent's instructions been placed with two financial institutions in Jersey and seeking injunctions freezing the deposits, a declaration that they were held in trust for the deceased's estate, delivery up of the moneys to the heirs and damages for fraud. The respondent in his defence pleaded that the money in the deposits was given to him by the deceased and the proceedings were stayed pending the outcome of the English proceedings. When judgment in the English proceedings was given the heirs moved to strike out the respondent's defence on the ground that the question whether there had been a gift had become res judicata for the purpose of the Jersey proceedings, and on 12 June 1991 the Judicial Greffier granted the motion. However, following the decision of the Egyptian Misdemeanours Court of

Appeal on 23 May 1991 the respondent applied to the Royal Court of Jersey for reversal of the order of the Judicial Greffier and for leave to amend his defence so as to plead that the decision of 23 May 1991 constituted res judicata as regards the issue of gift or no gift in the Jersey proceedings. On 23 December 1991 the Royal Court allowed the respondent's appeal. The heirs appealed to the Court of Appeal of Jersey, which dismissed the appeal on the ground, inter alia, that if the Egyptian judgment qualified for recognition in Jersey as that of a court of competent jurisdiction the heirs, having taken proceedings against the respondent in two different jurisdictions, ie England and Egypt, and having obtained judgment in their favour in one but not in the other, could not insist on the favourable judgment being applied in Jersey irrespective of whether that judgment was the first or the second to be delivered. The heirs appealed to the Privy Council.

Held – Where there were two competing foreign judgments each of which was pronounced by a court of competent jurisdiction and each of which was final and not open to impeachment on any ground, the general rule was that the earlier of them in time was to be recognised and given effect to the exclusion of the later. However, the rule being part of the doctrine of res judicata, the party holding the earlier judgment could be estopped from relying on it if there were circumstances, such as an estoppel by representation, connected with the obtaining of the second judgment which made it unfair for the party founding on the first to seek to enforce it. On the facts the English judgment could not have been capable of being founded on as res judicata for the purpose of the proceedings in Egypt, since those proceedings were primarily of a criminal character, and therefore, applying the general rule, the English judgment was entitled to recognition in Jersey as being the first judgment in time. The appeal would therefore be allowed (see p 134 b c g h and p 136 j to p 137 a, post).

Owens Bank Ltd v Bracco [1992] 2 All ER 193 and *The Indian Endurance* [1993] 1 All ER 998 considered.

Notes
For the doctrine of res judicata and issue estoppel, see 16 *Halsbury's Laws* (4th edn reissue) paras 974–983, and for cases on the subject, see 21 *Digest* (Reissue) 56–62, 368–390.

Cases referred to in judgment
Indian Endurance, The, Republic of India v India Steamship Co Ltd [1993] 1 All ER 998, [1993] AC 410, [1993] 2 WLR 461, HL.
Owens Bank Ltd v Bracco [1992] 2 All ER 193, [1992] 2 AC 443, [1992] 2 WLR 621, HL; *on reference* Case C-129/92 [1994] 1 All ER 336, CJEC.

Appeal
Abdul Rahman Showlag, the plaintiff, suing on his own behalf as the son and authorised representative of the heirs of the estate of Sheikh Abdul Ahmed Showlag, appealed with special leave granted by the Board on 12 May 1993 from the decision of the Court of Appeal of Jersey (Sir Patrick Neill QC, Robert Harman QC and Adrian Hamilton QC) delivered on 28 October 1992 dismissing the appellant's appeal from the decision of the Royal Court of Jersey (Commissioner Hamon, Jurats Blampied and Herbert) delivered on 23 December 1991 allowing the appeal of the first and second defendants against

the decision of the Judicial Greffier delivered on 12 June 1991 whereby he struck out the first and second defendants' answers in two actions brought by the plaintiff against (1) Abdel Moneim Mansour, First Union Corp SA (a Virgin Islands company controlled by the first defendant) and Bank of America National Trust and Savings Assn and (2) Abdel Moneim Mansour, First Union Corp SA, Eaglesfield Ltd, Bankamerica Trust Corp (Jersey) Ltd and Midland Bank Trust Corp (Jersey) Ltd, to recover the sum of approximately $US12m held to the order of the first defendant by those defendants which were financial institutions in Jersey. The facts are set out in the judgment of the Board.

John Thomas QC, Geraldine Andrews and *Advocate Richard Michel* (Jersey) (instructed by *Trowers & Hamlins*, agents for *Crills*, St Helier, Jersey) for the plaintiff.

Christopher Carr QC and *Advocate Alan Binnington* (Jersey) (instructed by *Baker & McKenzie*, agents for *Mourant du Feu & Jeune*, St Helier, Jersey) for the defendants.

15 March 1994. The following judgment of the Board was delivered.

LORD KEITH OF KINKEL. The late Sheikh Abdul Ahmed Showlag died on 27 May 1989. He had carried on a business as money-broker and money-changer in Saudi Arabia and had accumulated a very large fortune, estimated at between $US200m and $US300m. This had included two deposits, together worth about £17.5m, held in London banks. The first was a deposit of 1,533,173,358 Spanish pesetas held at the Banco Hispano Americano and the second was one of $US11,719,540·50 at the Bank of Tokyo. After the sheikh's death his representatives discovered that these deposits no longer existed, having been transferred in late November and early December 1988 to an account at Banque Paribas, Switzerland, in the name of a company called Showlag SA. This company had been incorporated in Panama by Abdel Moniem Mansour and was wholly owned by him. The respondent, Mr Mansour, an Egyptian national, had been employed by the sheikh in connection with his business affairs in London. Mr Mansour claimed that the money in the deposits had been gifted to him by the sheikh at the end of November 1988.

Most of the money from the account of Showlag SA was dispersed by Mr Mansour to a number of different countries, including Jersey and, as to the bulk of it, Egypt. The sheikh's heirs believed that the money had been stolen by Mr Mansour, and they instituted proceedings against him in various jurisdictions including England, where he was ordinarily resident, claiming a declaration that he was a constructive trustee of the money and other assets representing the money, and an accounting. Steps were taken to obtain interim freezing measures over assets in Jersey and Switzerland, as well as England. As regards Egypt, it was necessary in order to obtain a freezing order to secure the institution by the Attorney General there of a criminal prosecution against Mr Mansour, who had by this time removed himself to Egypt, and this was done, the heirs being joined as partie civile. After sundry procedures the English action, to which Mr Mansour had entered defences, was put down for trial on 26 November 1990. Mr Mansour sought an adjournment but this was refused by Hoffmann J for reasons which need not be gone into. Mr Mansour then withdrew instructions from the solicitors and counsel who had up to that point represented him, and the trial took place in his absence. On 5 December 1990 Hoffmann J, having heard evidence which included affidavits furnished by Mr Mansour for the purpose of earlier interlocutory proceedings, gave judgment for the plaintiffs in the action. The judgment contains a devastating destruction of Mr Mansour's claim that the money was a gift.

The next developments took place in the Egyptian proceedings. On 31 December 1990 the Muharram Bey Court in Alexandria found Mr Mansour guilty of having stolen the deposits in the two London banks and sentenced him to three years imprisonment with labour. The court declined to deal with the heirs' civil claim and ordered that it be referred to the competent civil court. However, Mr Mansour appealed against that decision to the Misdemeanours Court of Appeal of East Alexandria, and on 23 May 1991 that court allowed the appeal and set aside the judgment of the lower court. It appears that the heirs had also appealed against the refusal of the lower court to deal with their civil claim, and that appeal was rejected and the civil claim dismissed. The ground of the Misdemeanours Court of Appeal's decision was that Mr Mansour had indeed received the money in the two deposits as a gift by the sheikh. The heirs and the public prosecutor appealed to the Court of Cassation to set aside the decision of the Misdemeanours Court of Appeal, inter alia, on the ground, so it appears, that one of the judges who had heard the argument had not been present at the deliberation of the judges nor signed the judgment whereas a judge who had not heard the argument had taken part in the deliberation and been party to the judgment. That appeal is still pending.

The two actions out of which the present appeal arises were commenced by the heirs in the Royal Court of Jersey in October 1989. There were two actions because sums alleged to be part of the misappropriated deposits had on instructions emanating from Mr Mansour been placed with two different financial institutions in Jersey, but the same issues arise in both actions, so that it is unnecessary to consider them separately. The remedies sought, in addition to injunctions of a holding character, were (1) a declaration that the relevant moneys were held in trust for the estate of the late sheikh, (2) an order for delivery up of the moneys to the plaintiffs, with interest, and (3) damages for fraud. The Jersey proceedings were stayed pending the outcome of the litigation in England. Mr Mansour in his original defence pleaded that the money in the deposits was gifted to him by the sheikh. Following the judgment of Hoffmann J the plaintiffs moved to strike out the defences on the ground that the question whether or not there had been a gift was now res judicata for the purpose of the Jersey proceedings, and on 12 June 1991 the Judicial Greffier granted the motion. However, following the decision of the Egyptian Misdemeanours Court of Appeal on 23 May 1991 Mr Mansour on 2 December 1991 applied to the Royal Court for reversal of the order of the Judicial Greffier and for leave to amend his defences so as to plead that the decision of 23 May 1991 constituted res judicata as regards the issue of gift or no gift in the Jersey proceedings. On 23 December 1991 the Royal Court allowed Mr Mansour's appeal, apparently on the ground that it was uncertain as to the effect of the decision of the Egyptian Misdemeanours Court of Appeal and desired further argument about that. It is not clear whether the Royal Court allowed Mr Mansour to amend his defence so as to plead that the decision of the Egyptian Misdemeanours Court of Appeal represented res judicata in Jersey. It may be that the question whether the amendment should be allowed was intended to await decision in the light of the further argument contemplated.

The heirs appealed to the Court of Appeal of Jersey. On 28 October 1992 that court (Sir Patrick Neill QC, Robert Harman QC and Adrian Hamilton QC) dismissed the appeal. The grounds for the decision appear to have been that the court was uncertain whether the Egyptian judgment qualified for recognition in Jersey as that of a court of competent jurisdiction and further that, if it did, the heirs having taken proceedings against Mr Mansour in two different jurisdictions (England and Egypt) and obtained judgment in their favour in one but not in the other could not insist upon the favourable judgment being applied in Jersey, irrespective of whether that judgment was the first or the second to be delivered. The Jersey Court of Appeal concluded its own judgment by suggesting that instead of further proceedings directed to establishing the status of the Egyptian decision and the correct application of the doctrine of res judicata the parties might prefer the merits of the case to be litigated afresh in Jersey. The Court of Appeal of Jersey refused leave to the heirs to appeal to Her Majesty in Council on the ground that it had no power to do so in an interlocutory matter. However, on report by the Board Her Majesty granted special leave to appeal on 12 May 1993.

It is common ground between the parties that the doctrine of res judicata forms part of the law of Jersey and that it applies to foreign judgments. In *Owens Bank Ltd v Bracco* [1992] 2 All ER 193 at 198, [1992] 2 AC 443 at 484 Lord Bridge of Harwich said:

'A foreign judgment given by a court of competent jurisdiction over the defendant is treated by the common law as imposing a legal obligation on the judgment debtor which will be enforced in an action on the judgment by an English court in which the defendant will not be permitted to reopen issues of either fact or law which have been decided against him by the foreign court.'

That statement holds good in Jersey as it does in England.

However, here the Jersey court is faced with the unusual situation that there are two incompatible foreign judgments, each of which is accepted by the unsuccessful party to it as being for present purposes that of a court of competent jurisdiction and not open to challenge in Jersey on any of the traditional grounds such as fraud. The respondent takes no point upon the circumstance that the trial before Hoffmann J took place in his absence. The appellant, representing the heirs, contends that the judgment of Hoffmann J, being earlier in time, should prevail over the decision of the Egyptian court. The respondent on the other hand maintains that if either of the judgments is to be treated as creating an estoppel per rem judicatam it should be the later one. In their Lordships' opinion the choice must indeed lie between these alternatives. The course taken by the Court of Appeal of Jersey was to afford the appellant an opportunity to adduce argument and perhaps evidence, including expert evidence, directed to establishing that the Egyptian judgment had characteristics such as might persuade the court that it should not be recognised. It was further suggested that the preferable course might be to have the relevant issues on the merits relitigated in Jersey. It is hard to see that the first course could produce any useful result, since no indication is given as to the kind of considerations which a Jersey court might regard as sufficient to result in a denial of recognition to the Egyptian judgment, and if no such considerations emerged the problem would still remain of deciding whether to give effect to the judgment of Hoffmann J or to that of the Egyptian court. A trial of the merits of the case in Jersey would involve that multiplication of litigation which the doctrine of res judicata is designed to avoid.

In their Lordships' opinion the correct general rule is that where there are two competing foreign judgments each of which is pronounced by a court of competent jurisdiction and is final and not open to impeachment on any ground then the earlier of them in time must be recognised and given effect to the exclusion of the later. At the same time it is to be kept in mind that there may be circumstances under which the party holding the earlier judgment may be estopped from relying on it. In Spencer Bower and Turner *Res Judicata* (2nd edn, 1969) p 331 it is said:

> '385 ... where an estoppel *per rem judicatam* meets an estoppel by representation, there is a genuine cross-estoppel, in the strictest sense of the word. For here, A. having established a good estoppel by *res judicata* against B., B. confesses and avoids such estoppel by alleging and proving that A., by representation, has precluded himself from relying upon the *res judicata*. B. does not deny that he is estopped, but insists that A. is estopped from saying so ...'

In *The Indian Endurance* [1993] 1 All ER 998, [1993] AC 410 one of the questions at issue was whether the plaintiffs, consignees of a cargo of artillery shells carried in the defendants' vessel, who had obtained a judgment in their favour in an action in India for non-delivery of a small number of shells, were entitled to bring an action in England claiming damages for total loss of the cargo due to overheating as a result of a fire. The defendants pleaded that the plaintiffs were barred from bringing the action by s 34 of the Civil Jurisdiction and Judgments Act 1982. It was held that that would ordinarily be the position, but that the plaintiffs were entitled to plead that the defendants were estopped by representation from invoking s 34. In reaching that conclusion Lord Goff of Chieveley, who delivered the leading speech, referred to the passage from *Spencer Bower and Turner* which is quoted above.

The Indian Endurance was, of course, a case where a foreign judgment was founded on as creating a bar per rem judicatam to proceedings in England by a plaintiff relying on the same cause of action. But similar principles must fall to be applied where the domestic court is dealing with two competing foreign judgments. If there are circumstances connected with the obtaining of the second judgment which make it unfair for the party founding on the first to seek to enforce it, then it may be proper to refuse to allow him to do so. It is not alleged by the respondent in the present case that there are any such circumstances here.

The view that where there are competing foreign judgments the earlier in time should receive effect to the exclusion of the later finds support from a consideration of the Judgments (Reciprocal Enforcement) (Jersey) Law 1960, which is for all practical purposes in identical terms to the corresponding 1933 United Kingdom Act. The Act provides for the registration in Jersey of any money judgment of a superior court originating in a country which affords reciprocal facilities and for its enforcement by execution. Article 6 deals with cases in which registered judgments must, or may, be set aside. Article 6(1)(a) provides that such a judgment shall be set aside if the court is satisfied of various grounds, being those upon which traditionally a foreign judgment may be impeached, such as that the courts of the country in question had no jurisdiction, that the judgment was obtained by fraud, or that enforcement of it would be contrary to public policy in Jersey. Article 6(1)(b) provides that the registration of the judgment—

'may be set aside if the Royal Court is satisfied that the matter in dispute in the proceedings in the original court had previously to the date of the judgment in the original court been the subject of a final and conclusive judgment by a court having jurisdiction in the matter.'

This indicates, at the lowest, a preference for the earlier in date of two foreign judgments. It is true that the sub-paragraph does not exclusively contemplate that the two judgments will be incompatible, but it certainly covers that case. It is argued for the respondent that a complete discretion is given to the court whether or not to set aside a registered judgment which is later in time than the other one. It is not, however, reasonable that such should have been the intention. The discretion must be exercised in the light of certain recognised principles, so that the court will not refuse to set aside the registered judgment unless there exists some good ground for so refusing. Such grounds would no doubt be present if the earlier judgment was vulnerable to impeachment by virtue of one of the matters specified in art 6(1)(a), or if there were present an estoppel by representation the possibility of which was recognised in *The Indian Endurance*.

Article 9 of the 1960 Act deals with the general subject of the recognition of foreign judgments. It provides:

'(1) Subject to the provisions of this Article, a judgment to which Part II of this Law applies or would have applied if a sum of money had been payable thereunder, whether it can be registered or not, and whether, if it can be registered, it is registered or not, shall be recognised in any court in the Island as conclusive between the parties thereto in all proceedings founded on the same cause of action and may be relied on by way of defence or counterclaim in any such proceedings.

(2) This Article shall not apply in the case of any judgment—(a) where the judgment has been registered and the registration thereof has been set aside on some ground other than—(i) that a sum of money was not payable under the judgment; or (ii) that the judgment had been wholly or partly satisfied; or (iii) that at the date of the application the judgment could not be enforced by execution in the country of the original court; or (b) where the judgment has not been registered and it is shown, whether the judgment could have been registered or not, that if it had been registered the registration thereof would have been set aside on an application for that purpose on some ground other than one of the grounds specified in sub-paragraph (a) of this paragraph.

(3) Nothing in this Article shall be taken to prevent any court in the Island recognising any judgment as conclusive of any matter of law or fact decided therein if that judgment would have been so recognised before the coming into force of this Law.'

The effect of this article is to make applicable for the purpose of regulating the recognition of foreign judgments as a general question the principles contained in art 6. Thus, where a judgment, had it been a registered judgment, would have been liable to have its registration set aside either under art 6(1)(a) or under art 6(1)(b), then it is not to receive recognition. So a judgment which is later in date than another foreign judgment which dealt with the same disputed matter is not to be recognised unless there exists some such ground as discussed above which would have led to refusal to set aside the later judgment had it been registered. Article 9(3), it would seem, has the purpose of preserving any common law rule as to the recognition of foreign judgments which prevailed before the coming into force of the law. However, there is no authority nor any other basis for holding that before the coming into force of the law there existed in Jersey any common law rule inconsistent with art 9(2)(b). If any such rule did exist, it would give rise to extreme difficulties in connection with the application of art 6(1)(b) to registered judgments. If, on the other hand, there were no such rule, no problem would arise.

It is of some significance to note that in the 1968 Brussels Convention on Jurisdiction and Enforcement of Judgments in Civil and Commercial Matters there appears art 27(5), which provides that a judgment (which means a judgment of another contracting state) shall not be recognised—

'if the judgment is irreconcilable with an earlier judgment given in a non-Contracting State involving the same cause of action and between the same parties, provided that the latter judgment fulfils the conditions necessary for its recognition in the State addressed.'

Jersey is not one of the parties to the convention, but the circumstance that this rule finds its place in this important international convention must be of some persuasive effect in the consideration of whether a similar preference for an earlier judgment in time may appropriately form part of Jersey law, in the absence of any contrary authority.

Some reference was made in the course of argument to the position in United States law, where the last-in-time rule appears to be applied in the case of conflicting judgments, at least when the matter arises in an inter-state context where the 'full faith and credit' clause of the Constitution applies. In an article 'Judgments in search of full faith and credit: the last-in-time rule for conflicting judgments' (1969) 82 Harv LR 798 Professor Ruth B Ginsburg (now a Justice of the United States Supreme Court) examines the basis of the rule, and suggests that it is not applicable in the international area. The rationale of the rule appears to be that the second judgment has the effect of deciding that the first judgment does not constitute res judicata so that the second constitutes res judicata of that issue as well as of any others that may have been raised. This is so whether or not the issue of res judicata was argued in the second proceeding by the party who was successful in the first, because on ordinary principles a party is not entitled to raise in a later proceeding a point which was open to him in an earlier one but which he did not take. Their Lordships do not consider that the position in the United States is of assistance for present purposes, but they observe that there would clearly have been no question of Hoffmann J's judgment being capable of being founded on as res judicata for the purpose of the proceedings in Egypt, considering that these proceedings were primarily of a criminal character.

For these reasons their Lordships will humbly advise Her Majesty that the appeal should be allowed, that the orders of the Court of Appeal of Jersey and of the Royal Court should be set aside and that the order of the Judicial Greffier should be restored. The appellant is entitled to his costs both before the Board and in the courts below and their Lordships invite representations in writing from the parties regarding the status of the second and third respondents.

Appeal dismissed.

Celia Fox   Barrister.

Pearson v Franklin

COURT OF APPEAL, CIVIL DIVISION
NOURSE LJ AND THORPE J
17, 19 NOVEMBER 1993

Family proceedings – Orders in family proceedings – Specific issue order – Exclusion of party from matrimonial home – Unmarried parents joint tenants of home – Mother moving out of home with children – Father continuing to live in home – Mother's accommodation less suitable for children than home – Mother seeking specific issue order to live in home with children and for father to be excluded – Order having effect of ouster order – Whether court having jurisdiction to make specific issue order excluding father from home in interests of children – Whether appropriate remedy for mother being for father to transfer joint tenancy to her – Supreme Court Act 1981, s 37 – Children Act 1989, ss 8, 15, Sch 1, para 1.

The parties, who were not married, were joint tenants under a tenancy granted by a housing association of a house in which they lived with their two children, twins born in January 1992. In September 1992 the mother left, taking the children with her, and went to live with her parents. The father continued to live in the house. In March 1993 the mother applied for a specific issue order to allow her to reside with the children at the house but specifically in the absence of the father. The judge found that the parties' relationship had irretrievably broken down and that it was not disputed that the children should live with the mother but held that he had no power to make the order sought and dismissed the application. The mother appealed, contending that since the statutory powers to oust a partner where there had been violence did not apply because there had been no violence, the judge had had jurisdiction to make the order sought either under s 8[a] of the Children Act 1989 or under the inherent jurisdiction of the court on the ground that it was manifestly in the interests of the children to reside in the more suitable accommodation afforded by the house.

Held – Although a specific issue order under s 8 of the 1989 Act was suitable for determining where a child should live, it was not appropriate to make an order

---

a   Section 8, so far as material, is set out at p 140 *h j*, post

under that section where a right of occupation was involved since such an order would have the effect of an ouster order and it had not been Parliament's intention for the section to be used for the purpose of making ouster orders under the guise of specific issue orders. Nor was the mother entitled to an ouster order to remove the father from the house under the inherent jurisdiction or s 37 of the Supreme Court Act 1981 because, as joint tenants, neither party had a right to occupy the property to the exclusion of the other. The appropriate remedy for the mother to seek was an order under s 15(1) of and para 1(2)(e)(i)[b] of Sch 1 to the 1989 Act requiring the father to transfer to her, for the benefit of the children, his interest in the joint tenancy of the house. It followed that the judge had been right to hold that he had no jurisdiction to entertain the mother's application. The appeal would therefore be dismissed (see p 141 *d e g* to *j* and p 143 *h j*, post).

Ainsbury v Millington [1986] 1 All ER 73 followed.

Per curiam. The rights of the parties when an application is made for an ouster order will differ according to whether the parties are spouses, former spouses, cohabitees or former cohabitees (see p 142 *b* to *f*, post).

Notes

For jurisdiction to grant ouster orders, see 13 *Halsbury's Laws* (4th edn) para 1001.

For the Supreme Court Act 1981, s 37, see 11 *Halsbury's Statutes* (4th edn) 792.

For the Children Act 1989, ss 8, 15, Sch 1, see 6 *Halsbury's Statutes* (4th edn) (1992 reissue) 400, 408, 529.

Cases referred to in judgments

Ainsbury v Millington [1986] 1 All ER 73, CA; *affd* [1987] 1 All ER 929, [1987] 1 WLR 379, HL.
G v J (ouster order) [1993] 1 FLR 1008, CA.
Gibson v Austin [1992] 2 FLR 437, CA.
Hennie v Hennie [1993] 1 FCR 886, CA.
K v K (minors: property transfer) [1992] 2 All ER 727, [1992] 1 WLR 530, CA.
Lucas v Lucas [1991] FCR 901, CA.
M v M (custody application) [1988] 1 FLR 225, CA.
Quinn v Quinn [1983] 4 FLR 394, CA.
Richards v Richards [1983] 2 All ER 807, [1984] AC 174, [1983] 3 WLR 173, HL.
Webb v Webb [1986] 1 FLR 541, CA.
Wilde v Wilde [1988] 2 FLR 83, CA.
Wiseman v Simpson [1988] 1 All ER 245, [1988] 1 WLR 35, CA.

Case also cited

Nottinghamshire CC v P [1994] Fam 18; *affd in part* [1993] 3 All ER 815, [1994] Fam 18, CA.

---

b   Paragraph 1, so far as material, provides: '(1) On an application made by a parent ... of a child ... the court may ... make ... (2) ... (e) an order requiring either or both parents of a child—(i) to transfer to the applicant, for the benefit of the child ... such property to which the parent is, or parents are, entitled ...'

Interlocutory appeal

The mother of two children appealed from that part of the decision of Judge Marcus Edwards sitting in the Brentford County Court on 19 July 1993 whereby he dismissed her application for a specific issue order requiring the father to vacate the property at Acton, London W5 in which the parties had formerly resided together to enable the mother and the two children to return thereto. The facts are set out in the judgment of Nourse LJ.

Rosina Hare QC (instructed by *Leslie Oliver & Co*) for the mother.
Paul Coleridge QC and *Giles Powell* (instructed by *Bruce Weir Webber & Co*) for the father.

Cur adv vult

19 November 1993. The following judgments were delivered.

NOURSE LJ. In this case an unmarried mother seeks an order excluding the father of their two young children from the home where they formerly lived together and of which they are the joint tenants under a tenancy granted by a housing association. The parties being unmarried and separated for some months and there having been no violence, neither the Matrimonial Homes Act 1983 nor the Domestic Violence and Matrimonial Proceedings Act 1976 is applicable. Instead the mother claims to be entitled to the relief sought by way of a specific issue order under s 8 of the Children Act 1989; alternatively, by way of an injunction granted under the general jurisdiction of the court.

The parties met in 1988 or 1989 and their relationship started in December 1990. In April 1991 the mother became pregnant and in July of that year she moved in to live with the father in the studio flat in Acton of which he then had a tenancy granted by a housing association. On 29 January 1992 twins, a boy and a girl, were born to them. They will soon be two years old. In July of that year the family moved to a brand new two-bedroom house with a garden at another address in Acton, of which the housing association had granted the parents a joint tenancy. Early in September 1992 the mother left the home and took the twins to her parents' house, where they have lived ever since. The father has continued to live in the home. It is plain that the relationship has irretrievably broken down.

On 17 March 1993 the mother applied in the Brentford County Court for a specific issue order that she—

'be allowed to reside with the children of the family at [the home] of which I am a joint tenant with the [father] but specifically in the absence of the [father].'

The father applied for a defined contact order. The applications came on for an effective hearing before Judge Marcus Edwards on 19 July 1993. Having heard the evidence of the parties and submissions from counsel on each side, the learned judge refused to grant the relief sought by the mother, holding that he had no power to do so in the circumstances of the case. He made a defined contact order in favour of the father. The mother now appeals against the judge's refusal to grant the order sought by her. By her notice of appeal she seeks an order that:

'The [father] do vacate [the home] and allow the [mother] to return there to live with the two children of the parties in the absence of the [father].'

The material facts found by the judge were as follows. He observed that there were no allegations on either side of violence, that there were arguments, serious at times, that the mother had said that the father behaved aggressively and that he probably did, though not excessively so. Having stated that it was plain that, despite subsequent efforts at reconciliation, the relationship had broken down permanently and that there was no prospect of the mother and father living together again, the judge continued:

'It will, in my judgment, be wholly contrary to the interests of the children to expect the mother to go back to live with the father after this long period of time in the circumstances of this case. There would be bound to be serious rows and possibly something even worse.'

The judge recorded that there was no dispute that the twins should reside with the mother. He said that the present accommodation for the father in the home was plainly more than satisfactory. If he were to leave, he would have to rent somewhere, probably for a lot more than the £52 per week which he now pays. Having referred to the father's occupation as a driver earning £165 per week net, out of which he paid £30 per week maintenance for the twins, the judge said:

'The present accommodation for the mother is wholly unsatisfactory. Her parents have a four-bedroom house, with two reception rooms, kitchen, dining room and bathroom. Both her parents live there, together with her teenage sister ... The mother is in a bedroom with bed and two cots for the twins. It is very cramped. All her belongings are there, mostly in "umpteen black bags". It is plainly very hard work for the mother there. She can get no housing benefit, because she lives with her family. She lives on £40 per week income support, with £30 per week from the father, and £69 per month child benefit. The council refuse to rehouse her, because she is a joint tenant in respect of [the home]. It is obvious that the property would be a far more suitable place for her and the children.'

In this court the mother has been represented by Miss Rosina Hare QC and the father by Mr Paul Coleridge QC and Mr Giles Powell, none of whom appeared in the court below.

The basis of Miss Hare's argument that the order sought by the mother can be granted by way of a specific issue order is the paramountcy of the children's welfare under s 1(1)(a) of the Children Act 1989 and the mother's sole parental responsibility for them under s 2(2)(a), neither of which is in dispute. By s 8(1):

'"a specific issue order" means an order giving directions for the purpose of determining a specific question which has arisen, or which may arise, in connection with any aspect of parental responsibility for a child.'

By s 3(1):

'In this Act "parental responsibility" means all the rights, duties, powers, responsibilities and authority which by law a parent of a child has in relation to the child and his property.'

In reference to these provisions, the children's welfare being our paramount consideration, Miss Hare submits that the real question with which we are concerned is where, in their best interests, the children should live; that that is just as much a specific question that has arisen in connection with the mother's duties and responsibilities in relation to the children as, for example, the question where they should in due course go to school; and that the relief the mother seeks is therefore of a kind which may properly be made the subject of a specific issue order. Miss Hare submits that this is not a straightforward ouster application: the ouster would only be a consequence of an order made in the best interests of the children.

These submissions must be rejected. It is correct to say, on the facts found by the judge, that it is in the children's best interests that they should return to live in the home with the mother in the absence of the father. It is also correct to say that, in a case where the order would not interfere with a right of occupation, the question where a child should live, for example in flat A or house B, will usually be suitable for determination on an application for a specific issue order. But that cannot be so where a right of occupation would be interfered with. However you were to dress it up, for whatever reason it was made, it would in substance be an ouster order. Such orders having become very familiar to Parliament by 1989, it cannot have been intended that they should be capable of being made under the guise of specific issue orders. The judge's decision of this question was entirely correct.

Alternatively, Miss Hare argues that the mother is entitled to an injunction under the inherent jurisdiction of the court or, if it is something different, the jurisdiction conferred by s 37 of the Supreme Court Act 1981. The jurisdiction of the High Court, whatever it may be, is effectively conferred on the County Court by s 38(1) of the County Courts Act 1984.

This is a new point, not taken below, but taken without objection before us. As Thorpe J will demonstrate, there are decided cases in this court which make distinctions between couples who are or have been married and unmarried couples who are or have been living together which may not, on a long view, be satisfactorily explicable. However, we are bound by them for what they have decided. Here it is enough to say that *Ainsbury v Millington* [1986] 1 All ER 73, decided on facts indistinguishable for any relevant purpose from those of the present case, requires us to reject Miss Hare's alternative argument.

It follows that Judge Marcus Edwards's decision to dismiss the mother's application was right. However, Mr Coleridge has pointed out that she is not without a potential remedy under the Children Act. She could have made, no doubt she could still make, an application under s 15 and Sch 1, para 1(2)(e)(i), for an order requiring the father to transfer to her, for the benefit of the twins, his interest in the joint tenancy of the home: cf *K v K (minors: property transfer)* [1992] 2 All ER 727, [1992] 1 WLR 530. Such an order would give the mother, as against the father, an exclusive right to occupy the home. Mr Coleridge says that that remedy is tailor-made for the mother in this case. He does not make any concessions as to her entitlement to such an order, it being clear that the considerations to be taken into account are not the same as those of which account has been taken so far. But he does say, and I agree with him, that the availability of a remedy under s 15 is confirmation of the unavailability of a remedy under s 8.

I would dismiss this appeal.

THORPE J. I agree with all that has been said by Nourse LJ. It is not surprising that the proceedings in the county court became confused since the Court of Appeal authorities in this field are not easy to reconcile even if clearly presented. In various respects counsel's submissions increased rather than minimised the complexities.

Since the all important decision of the House of Lords in *Richards v Richards* [1983] 2 All ER 807, [1984] 1 AC 174 there have been nine reported cases in this court where ouster orders have been either upheld or set aside in litigation between men and woman whose relationship has broken down. In their chronology they are *Ainsbury v Millington* [1986] 1 All ER 73, *Webb v Webb* [1986] 1 FLR 541, *M v M* [1988] 1 FLR 225, *Wiseman v Simpson* [1988] 1 All ER 245, [1988] 1 WLR 35, *Wilde v Wilde* [1988] 2 FLR 83, *Lucas v Lucas* [1991] FCR 901, *Gibson v Austin* [1992] 2 FLR 437, *G v J (ouster order)* [1993] 1 FLR 1008 and *Hennie v Hennie* [1993] 1 FCR 886.

It has been submitted that these cases are in some respects inconsistent and irreconcilable. I believe that there is a rational reconciliation, depending on whether the parties are spouses, former spouses, cohabitees or former cohabitees.

If they are spouses then manifestly their rights are determined by the decision in *Richards v Richards* [1983] 2 All ER 807, [1984] AC 174. If they are former spouses whose marriage has been dissolved by decree absolute then their rights are determined by the decisions in *Webb v Webb* [1986] 1 FLR 541, *Wilde v Wilde* [1988] 2 FLR 83 (following and applying *Quinn v Quinn* [1983] 4 FLR 394, which of course had been decided prior to the decision in *Richards v Richards*), *Lucas v Lucas* [1991] FCR 901 and *Hennie v Hennie* [1993] 1 FCR 886. If they are cohabitees then their rights are determined by the decisions in *Wiseman v Simpson* [1988] 1 All ER 245, [1988] 1 WLR 35, *Gibson v Austin* [1992] 2 FLR 437 and *G v J* [1993] 1 FLR 1009. If they are former cohabitees litigating after final separation then their rights are determined by the decision in *Ainsbury v Millington* [1986] 1 All ER 73.

In his judgment in *Gibson v Austin* [1992] 2 FLR 437 at 441 Nourse LJ said:

> 'Mr Creaner's second argument is based primarily on the decision of this court in *Wilde v Wilde* [1988] 2 FLR 83. He says that that decision is authority for the proposition that even in a case which is governed by the 1976 Act there is still an inherent jurisdiction in the court to make an ouster order against one or other parent, if it is in the best interests of the children that such an order should be made. As to that argument, it is only necessary to observe that *Wilde v Wilde* was a case which concerned parties whose marriage had already been dissolved, on which footing neither the 1976 Act nor the Matrimonial Causes Act 1983 could apply. That means that in a case where the marriage or cohabitation has come to an end the powers of the court may be different from those which are available where it still subsists.'

As well as agreeing with that distinction I would draw the further distinction that in a case where the marriage has ended in dissolution the powers of the court may be different from those which are available where cohabitation has come to a final end.

The only case in this court which does not fall comfortably within this rationalisation is the decision in *M v M* [1988] 1 FLR 225. In that case an order had been made at first instance restraining the former husband from returning to the former matrimonial home. This court allowed his appeal. The leading judgment included this passage (at 235):

> 'By 19 November 1986 the parties were manifestly not living in the same household as man and wife. Therefore, in my view, there was no jurisdiction in the court under the 1976 Act. The question then arose as to whether the court could make such an order under an inherent jurisdiction stemming from its power to do what is best for the welfare of the children. That matter was considered in *Ainsbury v Millington* ([1986] 1 All ER 73). I refer to the judgment of Dillon LJ. The Court of Appeal in that case applied the principle of the House of Lords decision in *Richards v Richards* ([1983] 2 All ER 807, [1984] AC 174) ... In this case it is quite clear, and Mr Blyth has not sought to argue to the contrary, that the mother cannot make out a proprietary right under the Supreme Court Act 1981. Therefore, there is no jurisdiction on that basis to grant the relief she seeks.'

From that it seems that the mother's counsel did not refer to the decision in *Quinn v Quinn* [1983] 4 FLR 394 and draw attention to the inherent jurisdiction which had been described by Ormrod LJ in these terms:

> 'It has always subsisted and the court has always exercised the jurisdiction to exclude one parent, no matter what the proceedings, if that was desirable in the interests of the children.'

Thus, upon the analysis that I offer, since *M v M* [1988] 1 FLR 225 was a dispute between ex-spouses their rights in 1988 were to be determined by the decision of this court in *Quinn v Quinn* [1983] 4 FLR 394 rather than the decision in *Ainsbury v Millington* [1986] 1 All ER 73, a case determining the rights of former cohabitees.

Since the foundation of the inherent jurisdiction reaffirmed in *Quinn v Quinn* is the protection of the interests of children it seems questionable that children of parents who have been divorced should be any better protected than children of parents who have ceased to cohabit. But my concern in this is allayed by Mr Coleridge's valuable contribution to the development of this appeal by his argument that the appellant's application under s 8 of the Children Act 1989 was misconceived. Her real target was exclusive possession of 11 Sycamore Close to enable her to carry out her unchallenged responsibility to parent the twins. The appropriate remedy was an application under s 15 of that Act and Sch 1, paras (1) to (4). The right to apply for the transfer or settlement of the property, including tenancies, is the effective remedy for a parent who has not married and who needs the only available home to enable him or her to care for child or children after the final separation of the couple. Once a s 15 application has been lodged I would suggest that the court seised of the issue control by injunctive order the use of the premises pending final determination.

I too would dismiss this appeal.

Appeal dismissed.

Carolyn Toulmin   Barrister.

Re R (a minor) (contempt: sentence)

COURT OF APPEAL, CIVIL DIVISION

SIR THOMAS BINGHAM MR, RUSSELL AND SIMON BROWN LJJ

10 NOVEMBER 1993

Contempt of court – Committal – Breach of injunction – Maximum sentence – Maximum sentence which may be imposed 'on any occasion' two years' imprisonment – Appellant guilty of number of breaches of injunctions and undertaking relating to female ward of court – Judge giving appellant credit for admitting breaches and sparing ward necessity of giving evidence – Judge then imposing total sentence of two years' imprisonment, made up of consecutive individual sentences in respect of each breach – Whether judge imposing maximum sentence permissible and not making any reduction – Contempt of Court Act 1981, s 14(1).

The appellant, a married man aged 33, formed a relationship with a girl aged 14 which resulted in her being accommodated by the local authority. In May 1992 the girl was made a ward of court on the application of the local authority and injunctions were granted preventing contact between the appellant and the ward and preventing the appellant from coming within half a mile of the ward's home. In June 1992 the appellant gave an undertaking to the court that in the event of the ward contacting him he would notify the police forthwith and remove himself from her company. The appellant committed a number of breaches of both the injunctions and the undertaking and in July 1993 appeared again before the court on an application for his committal. The judge held that although the maximum sentence that could be imposed for any contempt was two years there was no bar to imposing consecutive sentences. The judge decided that, taking into account and giving credit for the fact that the appellant had admitted various of the breaches and had spared the ward the necessity of giving evidence, a total sentence of two years should be imposed, made up of two concurrent 18-month sentences and two concurrent 6-month sentences to run consecutively, together with other concurrent 3-month sentences. The appellant appealed, contending that the judge had in fact imposed the maximum sentence which could be imposed under s 14(1)[a] of the Contempt of Court Act 1981, which provided that a term of imprisonment for contempt of court 'shall not on any occasion exceed two years', and therefore, despite his remarks, the judge had not imposed a reduced sentence to take into account the mitigating factors.

Held – Section 14(1) of the 1981 Act did not enable the court on any occasion to impose consecutive sentences which cumulatively exceeded the statutory maximum of two years' imprisonment. Since the sentence which the judge had imposed was in fact the maximum, he had not made the reduction which he had promised the contemnor that he would. The appeal would therefore be allowed and the total sentence reduced to 18 months (see p 147 *g* to p 148 *a* and p 149 *a* to *c*, post).

---

a   Section 14(1) is set out at p 147 *b c*, post

Notes
For committal to prison for contempt, see 9 *Halsbury's Laws* (4th edn) para 101 and 37 *Halsbury's Laws* (4th edn) para 1025.
For the Contempt of Court Act 1981, s 14, see 11 *Halsbury's Statutes* (4th edn) (1991 reissue) 196.

Cases cited or referred to in skeleton arguments
C (a minor) (wardship: contempt), Re [1986] 1 FLR 578, CA.
Lee v Walker [1985] 1 All ER 781, [1985] QB 1191, CA.
Mesham v Clarke [1989] 1 FLR 370, CA.

Appeal
The second defendant, Mohammed Jalil, appealed, the court granting him an extension of time to do so, from the order of Judge Farnworth sitting as a judge of the High Court in the Family Division at Luton sitting at Bedford made on 30 July 1993 on the application of the Bedfordshire County Council, committing him to prison for a total period of two years for breaches of (i) the order of Judge Hamilton dated 15 May 1992 granting injunctions preventing contact between the second defendant and R, a female ward of court, and preventing the second defendant from coming within half a mile of the ward's home, and (ii) the undertaking given by the appellant on 25 June 1992 that in the event of the ward contacting him he would notify the police forthwith and remove himself from her company. The facts are set out in the judgment of Sir Thomas Bingham MR.

Justin Shale (instructed by *Austin Allen & Co*, Luton) for the appellant.
Jonathan Bennett (instructed by *J C Atkinson*, Bedford) for the council.
Stella Reynolds (instructed by *David Barney & Co*, Stevenage) for the ward.

SIR THOMAS BINGHAM MR. This is an application for extension of time to appeal and it is made by Mohammed Jalil, the second defendant in these proceedings. The case arises out of a relationship between the second defendant and a girl born on 25 November 1976. The second defendant himself is 33 years of age, married, with six children. At a time when the girl was aged 14 a relationship developed between the second defendant and her which led to her being accommodated by the local authority. The relationship continued and in May 1992 the local authority issued an originating summons which resulted in the girl becoming a ward of court.

On 15 May 1992 Judge Hamilton granted an injunction which prevented contact between the second defendant and the ward (as I shall call her) and a further injunction preventing the second defendant from coming within half a mile of the home at which the ward was then living. He was duly served with that order and on 25 June 1992 gave an undertaking to the court that in the event of the ward contacting him he would notify the police forthwith and remove himself from her company. That was an undertaking which he did not observe any more than he observed the judge's order. He committed a number of breaches of both with the result that he appeared before the court on 6 October 1992 when he was sentenced to six months' immediate imprisonment for breaches of the order and his undertaking. The breaches occurred between 2 June and 4 July 1992 and were either eight or ten in number.

Unhappily the sentence of imprisonment does not appear to have done very much to bring the second defendant to his senses, or to make him understand the requirement that the court's orders should be obeyed. As early as 19 October the ward visited him in prison and a little bit after that he was writing letters asking that they should be handed on to the ward. He sometimes wrote directly to her. Then on 11 January 1993, the very day that he was released from prison after serving his sentence of six months less remission, he met the ward in Luton and spent the night with her in a hotel.

Following that incident he continued to meet her at various locations on more than one occasion within a short distance of the place where she was living. They went to the prison together to visit various acquaintances of his who were still in prison. On one occasion he took the ward overnight on a trip to Sheffield despite the fact that she was at that stage very heavily pregnant. When she went into hospital to have the baby he visited her on more than one occasion and both before and after the birth of the child was with her in hospital. Those incidents gave rise to a number of other breaches.

After the birth of the child, and when the child was still very, very young, he met the ward and took her off on a picnic during which both of them, but particularly the second defendant, had a very great deal to drink. The circumstances of this party were in every way unsuitable for the very young baby who was with them. That incident also gave rise to a breach of the order and the undertaking.

Following that there was a further incident when he contacted the ward at the foster home where she was then living. Not surprisingly these breaches led to an application on behalf of the county council that the second defendant show cause as to why he should not be committed for breaches of the order and the undertaking. Certain of these accusations of breach were not pursued, and some of them were dismissed, but most of them were substantially admitted and findings of contempt were made, and are not challenged, on no fewer than 13 different counts. These counts, as the story I have made clearly demonstrates, follow a period during which the second defendant had already served a sentence of imprisonment for breach of the court's orders.

The matter came back before Judge Farnworth sitting as a judge of the High Court, on 31 July 1993 and then, without very much evidence needing to be given, the breaches were either established or admitted. Not surprisingly, the learned judge took an extremely serious view of this matter, attaching particular importance to the night which the second defendant spent with the ward at the hotel on the night that he was released from prison, the occasion when he took her to Sheffield, and the occasion when she and the very young baby were taken to the picnic and a quite excessive consumption of drink took place. The learned judge imposed various sentences for these contempts, the more minor contempts earning sentences of three months' imprisonment, two of the more serious contempts earning sentences of six months' imprisonment and two of the very most serious, that is the trip to Sheffield and the picnic, earning sentences of 18 months' imprisonment. He ordered that the respective periods of 6 months each should be concurrent, and that the periods of 18 months should be concurrent with one another, but that the period of 18 months should be consecutive to the period of 6 months and that the period of 3 months should be concurrent so that the total of 24 months was made up.

The first ground which is urged by Mr Shale, who appears on behalf of the second defendant, is that in imposing a sentence of 24 months in total the learned judge imposed the maximum sentence that he could impose in the circumstances, that this was unfair and wrong since the learned judge indicated that he was giving credit to the second defendant for the fact that he had admitted various of the breaches and had spared the ward the necessity of giving evidence, and that in the circumstances he had not done so.

The governing provision for present purposes is s 14(1) of the Contempt of Court Act 1981, which provides:

> 'In any case where a court has power to commit a person to prison for contempt of court and (apart from this provision) no limitation applies to the period of committal, the committal shall (without prejudice to the power of the court to order his earlier discharge) be for a fixed term, and that term shall not on any occasion exceed two years in the case of committal by a superior court, or one month in the case of committal by an inferior court.'

It appears to be clear that the term of imprisonment which can be imposed on any occasion may not exceed two years.

In the course of his judgment, in which the learned judge reviewed the facts and gave his reasons for regarding this case as a very serious one, he responded to submissions made by Mr Shale on behalf of the second defendant. Among other things he said:

> 'I was addressed on behalf of the second defendant by Mr Shale and it is right to say that the second defendant in coming before the court has admitted a substantial amount of the allegations against him. So it is said on the second defendant's behalf that I should give credit and I do. I also give credit for the fact that although it did not become apparent until today the action of the second defendant in admitting matters made it unnecessary for the ward herself to give evidence and I do attach value to that. I determine sentence to take that into account ... for any contempt it is two years. As far as I am aware there is no bar to imposing consecutive sentences. I have, however, decided in the light of overall sentencing policy to have regard to the totality. I therefore have determined to impose sentences which total two years, determined as follows ...'

The learned judge then gave the breakdown of the sentences. The short point which is taken by Mr Shale is that since two years was the maximum the learned judge did not duly give effect to that, as he said that he would, to reflect the fact that the second defendant had acknowledged the breaches, apologised to the court and spared the ward the need to give evidence. In my judgment that submission has very considerable force.

Counsel for the mother has submitted that the learned judge did give credit in that he did not impose sentences of two years for any single one of the breaches and that by reducing the period of imprisonment imposed for breaches below the maximum of two years the learned judge did give credit as he had said that he would. That contention is in my view plainly misconceived. The section regulates the maximum which can be imposed on any one occasion and the learned judge did impose the maximum on this occasion and, therefore, it appears to me incorrect to suppose that he can be taken to have given the second defendant any credit, certainly any credit that went to the reduction of his sentence which is what one is concerned with. Accordingly it appears to me that on that ground Mr Shale is entitled to criticise the total sentence which was imposed and some reduction accordingly falls to be made.

Mr Shale goes on to make a series of points directed to the facts of the case. He points to the fact that the second defendant admitted the breaches; to the fact that it was unnecessary for the ward to give evidence; to the facts I have already referred to. He refers also to the fact that to some extent the second defendant may have been encouraged or incited to behave as he did by the ward. He refers to the fact that there was a period when the ward and he were out of contact; to his protestation that the relationship was over; to his apology; to the fact that he moved away from Luton; and to points relating to the effect on the child of discovering what had happened to the second defendant, her father. There is to my mind little or no force in any of those points. The ward herself may have been at fault in encouraging the second defendant but these orders were made for her protection as must have been very clearly explained to the second defendant more than once and he knew extremely well, particularly after serving his first sentence of imprisonment, that the court meant its orders to be obeyed and was determined that they should be obeyed. It was inherent in the orders, whether the ward encouraged him or not, that he was to have absolutely nothing to do with her and that order he disobeyed in the most flagrant way possible. So far as the interlude in their relationship was concerned it appears that it may have had a good deal to do with the fact that the second defendant was in Pakistan. There is, as I consider, very little in any of this mitigation which strengthens in any way the first submission which I have already acknowledged as having force.

There is a further and different submission which has been made by Mr Shale, which is that the learned judge was not directed to, and did not take into account, the fact that pursuant to s 45 of the Criminal Justice Act 1991 a contemnor committed to prison for 12 months or more is required to serve two-thirds of the sentence and s 33 of the Criminal Justice Act 1991 does not apply to contemnors. Accordingly, it is pointed out that a person committed to prison for a criminal offence of four years or less will only have to serve half that sentence whereas a contemnor committed to prison for 12 months or more serves two-thirds. This is a matter upon which no submission was addressed to the judge and speaking for myself I entirely decline to accept the submission made by counsel that the learned judge in any way misconceived the matter. There is nothing whatever in his judgment to suppose that he was proceeding upon wrong principles. Whether he had these considerations in mind or not one simply does not know. It does appear that they were not drawn to his attention. That is not a matter of which the second defendant is in a position to complain. More significant in my mind is the overriding policy which governs this matter. Plainly Parliament has intended that a contemnor committed to prison for 12 months or more should serve two-thirds of the sentence and plainly the judge was in no doubt whatever but that this called for a sentence of 12 months or more. It may very well be that the difference of treatment is attributable to the fact that a contemnor has the right to return to the court to purge his contempt and seek that he should be released, which is a procedure not open to the criminal defendant. For my part, however, I see no reason to interfere with the learned judge's decision on this ground and I certainly, as I say, find no reason to suppose that he was proceeding under any misapprehension.

The question, therefore, arises as to what reduction should be made to reflect the submission which Mr Shale has correctly made that the learned judge did not give the deduction which he intended to, and said that he would. In my judgment the appropriate course to adopt in the present circumstances is to reduce the two sentences of 18 months to 12 months, otherwise leaving the order as it is with the result that the total of the 24 months will be reduced to 18 months. I would add that the application for an extension of time is granted. To that extent the appeal is allowed.

RUSSELL LJ. I agree.

SIMON BROWN LJ. I agree.

Appeal allowed.

L I Zysman Esq   Barrister.

Villiers v Villiers

COURT OF APPEAL, CIVIL DIVISION
SIR THOMAS BINGHAM MR, HOFFMANN AND HENRY LJJ
10, 22 NOVEMBER 1993

Contempt of court – Committal – Breach of injunction – Maximum sentence – Maximum sentence which may be imposed 'on any occasion' two years' imprisonment – Judge activating prior suspended sentence of 12 months' imprisonment and also imposing sentence of 18 months' imprisonment making total sentence of two and a half years' imprisonment – Whether sentence exceeding statutory maximum sentence for contempt of court – Contempt of Court Act 1981, s 14(1).

In August 1992 a judge imposed a suspended 12 months' committal order on the appellant for breaches of a non-molestation order granted to his wife. The appellant subsequently committed further breaches of the order and in January 1993 he again appeared before the court. The judge imposed a sentence of 18 months' imprisonment in respect of the further breaches and also activated the suspended sentence of 12 months, making a total sentence of two and half years' imprisonment. The appellant appealed on the ground that the sentence was in excess of the maximum sentence provided for by s 14(1)[a] of the Contempt of Court Act 1981, which provided that a term of imprisonment for contempt of court 'shall not on any occasion exceed two years'.

Held – The court could not on the same occasion both activate a sentence and impose a new sentence for contempt of court which together exceeded the maximum sentence of two years' imprisonment provided for by s 14(1) of the 1981 Act, since the 'occasion' when the order was made for the purposes of

---

a   Section 14(1) is set out at p 153 *c d*, post

s 14(1) was that on which it was made, regardless of whether it related to one or more applications, and the contemnor actually left the court to go to prison. The appeal would therefore be allowed and a sentence of two years' imprisonment substituted (see p 154 *e* to *h* and p 155 *b c e g* to *j*, post).

Re R (a minor) (contempt: sentence) [1994] 2 All ER 144 considered.

Notes

For committal to prison for contempt, see 9 *Halsbury's Laws* (4th edn) para 101 and 37 *Halsbury's Laws* (4th edn) para 1025.

For the Contempt of Court Act 1981, s 14, see 11 *Halsbury's Statutes* (4th edn) (1991 reissue) 196.

Cases referred to in judgments

Lee v Walker [1985] 1 All ER 781, [1985] QB 1191, [1985] 3 WLR 170, CA.
Morris v Crown Office [1970] 1 All ER 1079, [1970] 2 QB 114, [1970] 2 WLR 792, CA.
R (a minor) (contempt: sentence), Re [1994] 2 All ER 144, [1994] 1 WLR 487, CA.
W (B) (an infant), Re [1969] 1 All ER 594, [1969] 2 Ch 50, [1969] 2 WLR 99, CA.

Cases also cited or referred to in skeleton arguments

Castro v R (1881) 6 App Cas 229, [1881–5] All ER Rep 429, HL; *affg* (1880) 5 QBD 490, CA.
Linnett v Coles [1986] 3 All ER 652, [1987] QB 555, CA.
M v P (contempt: committal), Butler v Butler [1992] 4 All ER 833, [1993] Fam 167, CA.
Mason v Lawton [1991] 2 All ER 784, [1991] 1 WLR 322, CA.
R v Blake [1961] 3 All ER 125, [1962] 2 QB 377, CCA.
R v Selby Justices, ex p Frame [1991] 2 All ER 344, [1992] QB 72, DC.
S & A Conversions Ltd, Re (1988) 4 BCC 384, CA.
Verrier v DPP [1966] 3 All ER 568, [1967] 2 AC 195, HL.

Appeal

Joseph William Villiers appealed from the order of Judge Morton Jack made in the Slough County Court on 18 January 1993 whereby the judge imposed a total sentence of two and a half years' imprisonment on the appellant for breaches of a non-molestation order granted to be appellant's wife by activating a suspended sentence of 12 months' imprisonment imposed against the appellant by Judge Holden on 18 August 1992 for breaches of the order and in addition imposing a sentence of 18 months' imprisonment for further breaches by him of the order. The facts are set out in the judgment of Sir Thomas Bingham MR.

The appellant appeared in person.
James Munby QC (instructed by the Treasury Solicitor) as amicus curiae.
The appellant's wife did not appear.

SIR THOMAS BINGHAM MR. This is an appeal by Mr Villiers against an order made by Judge Morton Jack in the Slough County Court on 18 January 1993 when the learned judge activated a suspended sentence of 12 months' imprisonment which had been imposed on 18 August 1992, and in addition imposed a consecutive sentence of 18 months' imprisonment, both those sentences being for contempt of court.

The appeal is founded on the contention that that sentence was excessive, being a sentence which the judge was not entitled under the relevant statute to impose. Before discussing the legal basis of this appeal it is necessary quite briefly to recount the history which gives rise to it.

On 13 July 1985 Mr Villiers was married to Anna Elizabeth Villiers. It is apparent from a chronology with which we have been supplied that before his marriage Mr Villiers had, on a number of occasions, been in trouble with the law as a result of drink-driving offences. It may be that the underlying problem in this case has something to do with the consumption of alcohol. That, however, is not something that is immediately before us, although it is apparent that after the date of the marriage there were various difficulties and Mr Villiers found himself in trouble for further drink-driving offences.

It is possible, however, for present purposes to come to 1 August 1991 when, on the wife's application, Judge Marder made an ex parte non-molestation order, taking the usual form, namely that Mr Villiers was not to molest his wife, and containing the additional term that he was to vacate the former matrimonial home. That order was fortified by a power of arrest, and a return date of 14 August was fixed.

Before 14 August the parties filed evidence, and on that date the order was, in effect, confirmed. The non-molestation order was repeated, a prohibition on communication by Mr Villiers with his wife was imposed, and he was ordered to keep away from the former matrimonial home until further order. That order was also reinforced by a power of arrest.

Unhappily the power of arrest was exercised only four days later on 18 August 1991. On the following day Mr Villiers was brought before Judge Marcus Edwards on that account. The learned judge on that occasion imposed a sentence of three months' imprisonment on six proven breaches, but he suspended the activation of those sentences for a period of 12 months. He continued the order and the power of arrest for just under a further year. That, therefore, was the first sentence of imprisonment imposed on Mr Villiers for contempt, although it was, as I have said, suspended.

Before August was over, however, Mr Villiers had been arrested for a second time for breaches of the order. On this occasion he came before Judge Roberts, when the breaches were proved, but the learned judge thought it unnecessary to impose any sentence. The order of 14 August accordingly remained in force and Mr Villiers was prohibited from going within two miles of his wife's address, and the power of arrest was continued; but he was not ordered to serve any sentence of imprisonment immediately.

On 19 September 1991 there was another incident when Mr Villiers entered the former matrimonial home and caused a great deal of damage, and that was quite a serious fracas. That led to his return before Judge Marcus Edwards on 20 September 1991. On this occasion, not surprisingly, the learned judge activated the suspended sentences, imposed sentences of six months for the new breaches and nine months for the damage which Mr Villiers had caused the day before. The effect therefore was that on this occasion, it being the second sentence of imprisonment, Mr Villiers was sent to prison for a total of 15 months (the total of 6 months and 9 months).

On 11 November 1991 Mr Villiers appeared before Judge Marcus Edwards again and successfully persuaded the judge that he would abide by the order and purged his contempt. The judge accordingly ordered his release, but made certain additional orders restraining Mr Villiers from assaulting, otherwise interfering with or molesting his wife, communicating with his wife save through solicitors and venturing within one mile of the former matrimonial home.

Later in November the wife gave Mr Villiers notice to show cause why he should not be committed to prison again for further breach of the injunction. On this occasion the hearing took place before a different judge, Judge Morton Jack, on 22 November 1991. He found that seven breaches were established against Mr Villiers and he ordered him to go to prison for two years. He fixed a return date of 7 January 1992, presumably because Mr Villiers was not present on that occasion. Mr Villiers was, however, taken into custody very shortly thereafter. On 7 January 1992 the order was affirmed. That, therefore, was the third sentence of imprisonment imposed on Mr Villiers.

Meanwhile, I should mention that in November 1991 a decree nisi of divorce had been pronounced, and in May 1992 that became absolute. I mention that as a fact of some relevance, because it does appear that Mr Villiers has had considerable difficulty in accepting that his marriage is over.

Having been sent to prison on that occasion Mr Villiers applied on several occasions to purge his contempt, and those applications were unsuccessful, the judges no doubt bearing in mind that on the previous occasion when he had successfully purged his contempt he had broken the order again almost immediately. However, eventually Mr Villiers was successful; on 18 June 1992 Judge Oppenheimer did order Mr Villiers to be discharged. He did so on Mr Villiers' undertaking to see a psychiatrist. The other clauses of the previous order remained in force.

Unhappily, even at that stage Mr Villiers was unable to abide by the strict letter of the order in July. He telephoned the petitioner three times again in August 1992. The petitioner gave notice for the respondent to show cause why he should not be committed to prison again for contempt. That matter came before Judge Holden on 18 August 1992, when, I think, there were three breaches before him. On that occasion he ordered that Mr Villiers be committed to prison for 12 months, but he suspended that order on the terms set out in the order. That, accordingly, was the fourth sentence of imprisonment arising out of this matter which was imposed on Mr Villiers. It was an order of 12 months suspended. Even that was not the end of the story.

On 18 January 1993 Mr Villiers appeared again before Judge Morton Jack, further breaches being established against him. The learned judge referred to five admitted breaches recorded over the last few days and said:

'What is lacking, sadly, is your ability to control yourself. Everything has been tried and none of it has worked. I must enforce the order and protect the petitioner. With regard to the serious and recent breaches you will serve 18 months' imprisonment. With regard to the breach of the suspended sentence passed on 18 August 1992, I note that you have repeated those breaches. That order comes into effect consecutively and you will serve 12 months. You must learn self-control. You have only yourself to blame. The existing order of 11 November 1991 continues as amended by the order of 19 June 1992.'

Mr Villiers left the court subject to a sentence of two and a half years' imprisonment, 18 months having been imposed for these new breaches and the suspended sentence of 12 months having been activated.

It was in that situation that Mr Villiers's application for an extension of time came before the court on 10 November 1993. He was, on that occasion as today, unrepresented. The court was concerned on two counts: first, for guidance as to the basis and principles upon which the court acts in activating suspended sentences in the field of contempt; and, secondly, as to whether, in circumstances such as the present, a total sentence of two and a half years was permissible. That question arises because s 14 of the Contempt of Court Act 1981, which is the governing section for present purposes, provides in sub-s (1):

'In any case where a court has power to commit a person to prison for contempt of court and (apart from this provision) no limitation applies to the period of committal, the committal shall (without prejudice to the power of the court to order his earlier discharge) be for a fixed term, and that term shall not on any occasion exceed two years in the case of committal by a superior court, or one month in the case of committal by an inferior court.'

On the previous occasion the court invited the assistance of the Official Solicitor in order to guide the court as to the proper approaches to these questions. I would wish to give my personal thanks both to the Official Solicitor and to Mr Munby QC, who has appeared on instructions by the Official Solicitor, and who has made submissions of the utmost helpfulness.

So far as the court's power to suspend sentences for contempt is concerned, it is apparent that those are contained in RSC Ord 52, r 7. Guidance as to the origin and basis of the practice is to be found in authorities which have been drawn to our attention, in particular *Morris v Crown Office* [1970] 1 All ER 1079, [1970] 2 QB 114 and *Lee v Walker* [1985] 1 All ER 781, [1985] QB 1191. It emerges quite clearly from those cases that the court does have the power expressed in the Rules of the Supreme Court to suspend sentences for contempt, and that in exercising that power the court is not constrained by the limitations which are imposed on the imposition of suspended sentences on the commission of criminal offences. In other words, limitations as to the imprisonment of young offenders and first offenders do not apply.

Mr Munby has also, however, and most helpfully, drawn our attention to *Re W (B) (an infant)* [1969] 1 All ER 594, [1969] 2 Ch 50 in which the activation of suspended sentences was the subject of decision by this court. It emerges clearly from the judgments of Lord Denning MR and Russell LJ with which Winn LJ agreed that the court is not obliged to activate a suspended sentence upon mere proof of breach of the suspensory condition. The judge has a discretion, taking into account both the past and the current situation and the gravity of the breach, either to activate the original sentence or to impose a reduced sentence or a fine or not to punish at all. In other words, there is nothing automatic about the activation of a suspended sentence, and it involves an exercise of judicial judgment on the occasion when the issue of activation arises.

I pass then to the question: what is the maximum sentence which the court may pass on any occasion under the section? In this context it is relevant to refer to my judgment in *Re R (a minor) (contempt: sentence)* [1994] 2 All ER 144, [1994] 1 WLR 487. On that occasion the contemnor had been found guilty of

13 breaches of an order of the court, and the learned judge imposed a term of two years' imprisonment. They were very serious breaches. There was or may well have been nothing wrong in itself with the sentence which he imposed. The problem, however, was this. In the course of submissions on behalf of the contemnor the learned judge was urged to reduce the sentence from what would otherwise have been imposed because the contemnor had admitted the breaches and expressed regret and because, by his admission, he had spared the mother of his child the need to go into the witness box and give evidence. In answer to these submissions the learned judge indicated that he would reduce the sentence which he would impose in recognition of these points, but the sentence which he imposed of two years was, as it appeared to the court, the maximum which he could impose under the section which I have quoted. He proceeded on the basis that he could have imposed consecutive sentences amounting to more than two years in total, and that therefore the sentence of two years did represent a reduction. This court held that the maximum that could be passed on any occasion was two years, and that therefore he had not made the reduction which he had promised the contemnor that he would. That case establishes that s 14 does not enable the court on any occasion to impose consecutive sentences which cumulatively exceed the statutory maximum of two years.

That, however, does not resolve the present problem, which is whether on a single occasion the court may both activate a sentence and impose a new sentence so as together to exceed the maximum sentence of two years provided by the statute. Speaking for myself, and in the light of the submissions made by Mr Munby, I am in no doubt that the 'occasion' for the purposes of s 14(1) is the occasion on which the order of committal is made, whether or not it relates to one application or more than one application, and, furthermore, that the relevant occasion is that on which the contemnor actually leaves the court to go to prison. The effect of the section, in my view, is that whether a previously suspended sentence is activated or not a contemnor must not, on any single occasion, leave court subject to a new sentence of more than two years' imprisonment for contempt. By 'new' I mean a sentence which the contemnor was not actually serving before. If a contemnor had been sentenced to an immediate term of 12 months, and on a later occasion was brought from prison to answer a further charge of contempt for which he was sentenced to a consecutive term of 18 months, there would be no breach of the section.

Accordingly, in my judgment, the appeal against the sentence which was imposed by Judge Morton Jack succeeds.

Mr Munby, in the course of his submissions, has drawn attention to a number of situations which could give rise to argument and difficulty. For example, he has indicated that a learned judge might sentence for one contempt in the morning and another in the afternoon, or for one contempt one day and another contempt the next day in the belief that by doing so he would not be imposing the sentences on one occasion. I could imagine circumstances in which this court would have little hesitation in holding that there had been a manipulation of the timetable such as to amount to an abuse of process. On the other hand, where, in the ordinary course, different contempts came before the court on different occasions and without any manipulation of the timetable it may be that cumulative sentences of more than two years could be justified. But it is, I think, clear, as I have suggested, that a contemnor must not, on any occasion, leave the court subject to a sentence of more than two years. If in doubt as to whether an occasion is to be treated as a single occasion or more than a single occasion it is incumbent on any judge in such a position to bear in mind the statutory provision and the obvious object of the statutory provision and bear in mind also the duty of fairness which is owed to any contemnor.

Accordingly, in this case I am satisfied that the sentence that was imposed did exceed by six months the maximum sentence. It would appear to me clear that it is open to this court to quash that sentence and substitute a lawful sentence. I would myself grant the extension of time for which Mr Villiers makes application, allow the appeal, quash the order of two and a half years and substitute a sentence of two years as the maximum open to the learned judge.

I substitute the sentence of two years for two main reasons. First, that these were, on any showing, most serious and repeated contempts, so that the learned judge would have been fully entitled to regard this as a case calling for the maximum, as I do. Secondly, because if any reduction from two years is to be sought then it is, in my judgment, a reduction to be sought by Mr Villiers from the county court judge. He has a pending application to purge his contempt, and if he is able, despite his record of non-compliance in the past, to persuade the judge that he really will comply with the order this time then no doubt the learned judge will make an appropriate order. If, on the other hand, he is unable to persuade the judge of that it would seem to me wrong for this court to interfere with the period of two years, which seems appropriate in all the circumstances.

That accordingly is the extent to which I would allow the appeal.

HOFFMANN LJ. Mr Munby QC's lucid submissions have satisfied me that there is no construction of s 14(1) of the Contempt of Court Act 1981 which will avoid every possibility of anomaly. But, in my view, it should be possible in practice to give effect to the general intention of that Act.

I agree with Sir Thomas Bingham MR that the occasion in s 14(1) is the hearing at which the sentence is imposed or a suspended sentence is activated, irrespective of the number of contempts or applications with which the court is dealing. In order to make this principle work it is necessary to try to ensure that all the allegations of contempt which could at any time be brought before the court, are so far as possible, considered on a single occasion. Otherwise the maximum sentence will depend on the choice of the applicant as to whether to make a single application or multiple applications and the vagaries of the listing system as to when those applications are heard. This means that it may, for example, be prudent for a defendant charged with contempt to invite the applicant to move at the same time or not at all in respect of any other contempt which he thinks that he may have committed. The application of the principle will be very much a matter for the discretion of the judge at the hearing; but I have no doubt that, with common sense, it should be possible to give effect to the general intention.

HENRY LJ. I agree with both judgments.

Appeal allowed.

L I Zysman Esq   Barrister.

Good v Epping Forest District Council

COURT OF APPEAL, CIVIL DIVISION
RALPH GIBSON, HIRST AND PETER GIBSON LJJ
28, 29 OCTOBER, 5 NOVEMBER 1993

Town and country planning – Agreement regulating development or use of land – Permission for development – Condition – Agreement containing covenant which could not have been imposed as condition on grant of planning permission – Whether local planning authority entitled to require land owner to enter into agreement containing covenant which could not have been imposed as condition on grant of planning permission – Town and Country Planning Act 1971, ss 29(1), 52(1).

A district council when granting planning permission to erect a house for a farm worker on a farm in a green belt imposed a condition that the house would only be occupied by a person wholly or mainly employed in agriculture and his spouse or other dependants and required the owner of the farm to enter into an agreement under s 52(1)[a] of the Town and Country Planning Act 1971 which contained a covenant that the house would be so occupied and would not be sold or otherwise alienated separately from the farm. The agreement under s 52 was registered as a local land charge. Under s 52 a local planning authority had power to 'enter into an agreement ... for the purpose of restricting or regulating the development or use of ... land' and under s 29(1)[b] of the 1971 Act the authority had power when determining an application for planning permission to grant permission 'subject to such conditions as they think fit'. However, whereas the imposition of a condition under s 29 was subject to appeal to the Secretary of State, there was no right of appeal against a s 52 covenant. The plaintiffs subsequently bought the farm with knowledge of the covenant but wished to be free to sell the house apart from the rest of the farm and without the restriction on occupation by a person wholly or mainly employed in agriculture. They accordingly applied for a declaration that the covenant was void. The judge refused the declaration sought. The plaintiffs appealed to the Court of Appeal, contending that the terms of the s 52 agreement could not lawfully have been imposed as conditions to the grant of permission under s 29 and that the authority could not achieve by way of a s 52 agreement that which it could not attain by imposing a condition under s 29.

Held – The appeal would be allowed for the following reasons—
(1) The powers given to a local planning authority by s 52 of the 1971 Act were to be used by the authority in good faith having regard to material considerations but if, taking into account its knowledge of local circumstances and having proper regard to all material considerations, it seemed to the authority desirable or necessary to enter into an agreement under s 52 'for the purposes of restricting or regulating the development or use of land' it was clearly entitled, and probably obliged, to seek such an agreement. Although

---

a   Section 52(1), so far as material, provides: 'A local planning authority may enter into an agreement with any person interested in land in their area for the purpose of restricting or regulating the develpment or use of the land ...'
b   Section 29(1), so far as material, is set out at p 163 c d, post

the fact that the Secretary of State would, under his declared policy, have set aside on appeal a particular requirement in a s 52 agreement if it had been imposed as a condition on the grant of planning permission under s 29, was a material fact for consideration by the authority, that fact did not render unlawful the decision to make the requirement or, if the land owner consented, the making of the agreement. In fact, the district council would have been acting within its powers as a local planning authority if it had imposed, as conditions attached to the planning permission pursuant to s 29, obligations in the terms of the s 52 agreement since they would have been imposed for a planning purpose, and their lawfulness as conditions could not depend on whether the Secretary of State in the exercise of his statutory powers would or would not have upheld them on appeal. Furthermore, by choosing to require the landowner to enter into the s 52 agreement, in order deliberately to bypass the right of appeal to the Secretary of State, the council had not acted for an improper purpose and had not been activated by a non-planning consideration (see p 160 *g* to p 161 *a j* to p 162 *c* and p 167 *h j*, post); dictum of Lord Scarman in *Newbury DC v Secretary of State for the Environment* [1980] 1 All ER 731 at 754 applied.

(2) On the true construction of s 52 of the 1971 Act the powers of a planning authority under that section were not controlled by the nature or extent of its powers under s 29 of that Act, since the two statutory powers were distinct and the exercise of either power had separate consequences and was subject to different procedures. Section 52 empowered a planning authority to enter into an agreement with the owner of land for the purpose of restricting or regulating the development or use of the land and if such an agreement was required by a planning authority and the requirement was made for such a purpose, with due regard to relevant considerations and was not unreasonable, it was not ultra vires merely because the purpose could not be validly achieved by the imposition of a condition under s 29. The validity of the agreement depended instead on the primary test of whether it was made 'for the purpose of restricting or regulating the development or use of the land' (see p 166 *h* to p 167 *b h j*, post); dictum of Lord Scarman in *Newbury DC v Secretary of State for the Environment* [1980] 1 All ER 731 at 754 applied; *R v Gillingham BC, ex p Parham Ltd* (1989) 58 P & CR 73 approved; dicta of Lloyd LJ in *Bradford City Metropolitan Council v Secretary of State for the Environment* (1987) 53 P & CR 55 at 64–66 and of Kerr LJ in *R v Westminster City Council, ex p Monahan* [1989] 2 All ER 74 at 100 explained.

Notes

For the material consideration to which local planning authorities must have in dealing with applications for the grant of planning permission for development, see 46 *Halsbury's Laws* (4th edn reissue) para 422, and for cases on the subject, see 47(1) *Digest* (Reissue) 100–108, *377–409*.

For agreements regulating the development or use of land, see 46 *Halsbury's Laws* (4th edn reissue) para 172, and for cases on the subject, see 47(1) *Digest* (Reissue) 86–89, *338–344*.

As from 24 August 1990 ss 29(1) and 52(1) of the Town and Country Planning Act 1971 were replaced by ss 70 and 106(1) and (2) of the Town and Country Planning Act 1990. For ss 70 and 106 of the 1990 Act, see 46 *Halsbury's Statutes* (4th edn) (1990 reissue) 600, 639

Cases referred to in the judgments

Associated Provincial Picture Houses Ltd v Wednesbury Corp [1947] 2 All ER 680, [1948] 1 KB 223, CA.
Bradford City Metropolitan Council v Secretary of State for the Environment (1987) 53 P & CR 55, CA.
Hazell v Hammersmith and Fulham London BC [1991] 1 All ER 545, [1992] 2 AC 1, [1991] 2 WLR 372, HL.
Jones's and White & Co's Application, Re (1989) 58 P & CR 512, Lands Tribunal.
London CC v Allen [1914] 3 KB 642, CA.
McCarthy & Stone (Developments) Ltd v Richmond upon Thames London BC [1991] 4 All ER 897, [1992] 2 AC 48, [1991] 3 WLR 941, HL.
Martins's Application, Re (1989) 57 P & CR 119, CA.
Newbury DC v Secretary of State for the Environment [1980] 1 All ER 731, [1981] AC 578, [1980] 2 WLR 379, HL.
Padfield v Minster of Agriculture Fisheries and Food [1968] 1 All ER 694, [1968] AC 997, [1968] 2 WLR 924, HL.
Pioneer Aggregates (UK) Ltd v Secretary of State for the Environment [1984] 2 All ER 358, [1985] AC 132, [1984] 3 WLR 32, HL.
Pyx Granite Co Ltd v Ministry of Housing and Local Government [1958] 1 All ER 625, [1958] 1 QB 554, [1958] 2 WLR 371, CA; rvsd [1959] 3 All ER 1, [1960] AC 260, [1959] 3 WLR 346, HL.
R v Gillingham BC, ex p Parham Ltd (1989) 58 P & CR 73.
R v Tower Hamlets London BC, ex p Chetnik Developments Ltd [1988] 1 All ER 961, [1988] AC 858, [1988] 2 WLR 654, HL.
R v Wealden DC and Federated Homes Ltd, ex p Charles Church South East Ltd (1990) 59 P & CR 150.
R v Westminster City Council, ex p Monahan [1989] 2 All ER 74, [1990] 1 QB 87, [1989] 3 WLR 408, CA.
Windsor and Maidenhead Royal BC v Brandrose Investments Ltd [1983] 1 All ER 818, [1983] 1 WLR 509, CA.

Cases also cited

R v Plymouth City Council, ex p Plymouth and South Devon Co-op Society Ltd [1993] JPL 81.
R v Tunbridge Wells DC, ex p Blue Boys Development Ltd (1989) 59 P & CR 315.
Wandsworth London BC v Winder [1984] 3 All ER 83, [1985] AC 461, CA; affd [1984] 3 All ER 976, [1985] AC 461, HL.

Appeal

The plaintiffs, Colin Geoffrey Good and Rita Good, appealed from the order of Sir Donald Nicholls V-C dated 14 April 1992 dismissing their claim as against the defendants, Epping Forest District Council, for a declaration that an agreement, dated 22 January 1987 made between the council and a previous owner of the plaintiffs' farm, Ashlings Farm in High Ongar, Essex, was null and void. The previous owner had been granted planning permission by the council to build a house on a farm within the Metropolitan Green Belt on condition that it was occupied by persons wholly or mainly employed in agriculture and had entered into a covenant under s 52 of the Town and Country Planning Act 1971 which had the effect of binding successive owners. The facts are set out in the judgment of Ralph Gibson LJ.

Barry Payton and Lady Ponsonby (instructed by Moss Beachley & Mullem) for the plaintiffs.
R M K Gray QC and Murray Hunt (instructed by Philip Cunliffe-Jones, Epping) for the council.

Cur adv vult

5 November 1993. The following judgments were delivered.

RALPH GIBSON LJ. This is an appeal by the plaintiffs, Mr Colin Geoffrey Good and Mrs Rita Good, in an action brought by them against Epping Forest District Council in which they claim a declaration that an agreement dated 22 January 1987 and made between Mr Alan Elves and the council under s 52 of the Town and Country Planning Act 1971 is void in law. On 14 April 1992 Sir Donald Nicholls V-C dismissed the plaintiffs' claims. By their appeal the plaintiffs seek an order for that declaration in this court.

The plaintiffs in June 1987 bought Ashlings Farm. The farm, in High Ongar in Essex, is in the Metropolitan Green Belt. In 1985 the then owner, Mr Elves, applied to the council for planning permission to erect a house on the farm for a farm worker. On the farm there were then 1,000 pigs. Mr Elves needed a house for a pig man and, because of difficulty in getting a man to do the work, Mr Elves wanted to be able to offer the attraction of a house for husband and wife instead of accommodation in the farmhouse for an unmarried person.

For the reasons explained by Sir Donald Nicholls V-C in his judgment, and in order to protect the green belt from abuse, the council took two precautions when granting planning permission to Mr Elves on 22 January 1987. The first was to impose a condition to the effect that occupation of the new house should be limited to persons wholly or mainly employed, or last employed, locally in agriculture or a dependant of such a person residing with him but including a widow or widower of such a person.

The second precaution taken by the council was to require from Mr Elves that he enter into a covenant under s 52 of the Town and Country Planning Act 1971, of which cl 3 provided:

'(a) that the said dwelling house when erected shall only be occupied by a person wholly or mainly employed in agriculture together with the spouse or other dependants of that person and (b) that the said dwelling house ... shall not be sold away or otherwise alienated from the remainder of the Application Site.'

The effect of the covenant, if valid in law, is to bind Ashlings Farm in the hands of successive owners. The covenant was registered as a local land charge so that the existence of it would be known to any subsequent buyer and the plaintiffs were aware of the terms of the covenant when they bought the farm in June 1987.

The plaintiffs wish to be free to sell the house for occupation by a person not 'wholly or mainly employed in agriculture' and to sell it apart from the rest of the farm. If the s 52 covenant is held to be void, the plaintiffs can apply to the council for removal or variation of the condition, which was imposed upon the grant of planning permission, as to occupation by persons so employed, and, if the council refuse that application, the plaintiffs could then appeal to the Secretary of State for the Environment. There is, however, no provision for appeal to the Secretary of State against a refusal by the council to waive or vary the terms of a s 52 covenant. An application to the Lands Tribunal under s 84 of the Law of Property Act 1925 is the only route provided by statute by which the plaintiffs can seek an order for the discharge or modification of the covenant if it was valid in law when made.

The provisions of s 52 of the Town and Country Planning Act 1971 are now contained in s 106 of the Town and Country Planning Act 1990 as amended by s 12 of the Planning and Compensation Act 1991. A person against whom a planning obligation as there defined is enforceable may, after the expiry of the relevant period, apply to the planning authority for modification or discharge of it. That period is five years from the entering into the obligation or any other prescribed period of time. By s 106B provision is made for appeal to the Secretary of State against a refusal by the planning authority to modify or discharge the obligation. These new provisions are not retrospective and the procedure is not open to the plaintiffs.

At the hearing before Sir Donald Nicholls V-C the case for the plaintiffs presented by Mr Payton of counsel was based primarily upon the proposition that the terms of the s 52 agreement could not lawfully be imposed as conditions, and the power of the council to enter into a s 52 covenant was limited to the taking of such covenants from any land owner seeking planning permission as could properly be imposed by the council as conditions upon the grant of planning permission. He relied for that proposition upon passages in the judgment of Lloyd LJ in *Bradford Metropolitan Council v Secretary of State for the Environment* (1987) 53 P & CR 55 and of Kerr LJ in *R v Westminster City Council, ex p Monahan* [1989] 2 All ER 74, [1990] 1 QB 87. Further, it was submitted for the plaintiffs that the council, by the course taken in imposing the conditions and in requiring the s 52 agreement in different and more stringent terms, demonstrated that to its knowledge the terms of the s 52 agreement were contrary to the policy declared by the Secretary of State, that those terms if imposed as conditions would be struck down by the Secretary of State on appeal and that to seek by means of a s 52 agreement rights which could not be got by means of planning conditions was to act for an improper ulterior purpose and in breach of the high standard of conduct required of a local authority.

As appears from his judgment, Sir Donald Nicholls V-C held: (i) that the council would have been acting within its powers as a local planning authority if it had imposed, as conditions attached to the planning permission pursuant to ss 29 and 30 of the 1971 Act, obligations in the terms of cl 3 in the s 52 agreement. They would have been imposed for a planning purpose and would have been valid within the threefold test stated by Lord Scarman in *Newbury DC v Secretary of State for the Environment* [1980] 1 All ER 731 at 754, [1981] AC 578 at 618. The lawfulness of those obligations as conditions could not depend upon whether the Secretary of State in the exercise of his statutory powers of discretion would or would not have upheld them on appeal; (ii) by choosing to require Mr Elves to enter into the s 52 agreement, in order deliberately to 'bypass the minister', if Mr Elves should consent to enter into the agreement, the council had taken a course in which there was 'a certain lack of attractiveness' but it did not reveal any improper purpose which could vitiate in law the s 52 agreement entered into by Mr Elves. In choosing the route provided by s 52 the council was not activated by a non-planning consideration and the council was entitled to follow it; (iii) since the cl 3 obligations could have been imposed as valid conditions, the issue raised by the council as to the scope of s 52 did not require to be decided.

By their notice of appeal the plaintiffs contended that Sir Donald Nicholls V-C (i) was wrong in law because, since the purpose of the council was deliberately to bypass the jurisdiction of the Secretary of State, the taking of the s 52 covenant from Mr Elves was not within the powers of the council under s 52 because it was not 'for the purpose of restricting or regulating the development or use of the land' and (ii) wrongly declined to find that the requiring of the s 52 covenant from Mr Elves was unlawful under *Wednesbury* principles (see *Associated Provincial Picture Houses Ltd v Wednesbury Corp* [1947] 2 All ER 630, [1948] 1 KB 223) upon the grounds argued before him; reference was made to cases including *Pioneer (UK) Aggregates Ltd v Secretary of State* [1984] 2 All ER 358, [1985] AC 132 and to *Tower Hamlets London BC v Chetnik Developments Ltd* [1988] 1 All ER 961, [1988] AC 961.

By its respondent's notice the council again contended that the powers granted to a local planning authority under s 52 enabled the authority to enter into a statutory agreement with a land owner the object of which was not attainable by the imposition of a planning condition under s 29 of the 1971 Act and, therefore, a finding of law that a covenant could not be validly imposed by way of condition under s 29 of the Act does not necessarily determine the validity of an agreement imposing that covenant made under s 52 of the Act.

In his submissions in this court, Mr Payton for the plaintiffs supported the grounds of appeal with further reference to authorities including *Hazell v Hammersmith and Fulham London BC* [1991] 1 All ER 545, [1992] 2 AC 1, *Padfield v Minister of Agriculture Fisheries and Food* [1968] 1 All ER 694, [1968] AC 977, *McCarthy & Stone (Developments) Ltd v Richmond upon Thames London BC* [1991] 4 All ER 897, [1992] 2 AC 48 and *Pyx Granite Co Ltd v Ministry of Housing and Local Government* [1958] 1 All ER 625, [1958] 1 QB 554.

The essential ground of Mr Payton's argument was that, in exercising its powers under s 52(1) of the 1971 Act to enter into an agreement 'for the purpose of restricting or regulating the development or use of the land, either permanently or during such period as may be prescribed by the agreement', the council must, upon the proper construction of the words in their statutory context, exercise its powers in accordance with the development plan and material considerations, and that must mean in accordance with the body of planning policy, ultimately decided by the Secretary of State subject to the will of Parliament. Planning control must be exercised, said Mr Payton, for purposes which are considered to be 'reasonable' by the Secretary of State because, if any other approach were permitted, a local authority would be acting outside the purposes and objectives of the statute rather than furthering those purposes and objectives. Mr Payton was constrained to accept that his proposition in effect means that a local planning authority could only lawfully exercise its powers in a way which the Secretary of State might reasonably be expected to approve.

These submissions of Mr Payton are, in my judgment, unsustainable. I agree with the conclusions of Sir Donald Nicholls V-C and with the reasons which he gave.

The powers given to the local authority by s 52 are to be used by that authority in good faith having regard to material considerations. If, with its knowledge of local circumstances and having proper regard to all material considerations, it seems to the local authority desirable or necessary to 'enter into an agreement ... for the purpose of restricting or regulating the development or use of land, either permanently or during such period as may be prescribed by the agreement' the local authority is clearly entitled, and it might be said obliged, to seek such an agreement. The probability known to the council, if that be the case, that the Secretary of State would, under his declared policy, set aside on appeal a requirement, if made as a condition on the grant of planning permission, for the obligations in the proposed s 52 agreement is a material fact for consideration by the local authority; but that fact, in my judgment, clearly does not render unlawful the decision to make the requirement or, if the landowner consents, the making of the agreement. It is, of course, common ground that the council did give consideration to that fact. The independence of judgment of the planning authority under the provisions of the planning legislation is not so restricted or puny, in my judgment, that the planning authority is required to determine what at any time is likely to be permitted in the particular circumstances in its area under the policy of Secretary of State and to make no decision which would not be upheld in the exercise of his discretion having regard to his current policy. If that had been the intention of Parliament it would have required that no s 52 agreement be entered into without the prior consent of the Secretary of State. As Mr Gray QC has demonstrated in his comprehensive examination of the history of these legislative provisions, such a requirement was contained in s 34 of the Town and Country Planning Act 1932 and in s 25 of the Town and Country Planning Act 1947; but it was removed by the Town and Country Planning Act 1968 (Sch 9, para 19) before s 52, in the form applicable to this case, appeared in the 1971 consolidation Act.

We were invited by Mr Gray to consider and to decide, as an additional ground of decision, the point raised by the council in its respondent's notice on the ground that it is of much public importance, and in particular to local planning authorities in their concern to protect against abuse land designated as green belt. We heard the submissions of the parties and, in my judgment, we should as a ground of decision state our conclusions upon this issue of law.

Mr Gray's submissions were, in summary, as follows.

(i) He identified the issue thus: can a local planning authority validly achieve by agreement any purpose which it could not validly achieve by condition, or is the test for validity the same in each case?

(ii) He described the history of the legislative provisions following the decision of the Court of Appeal in *London CC v Allen* [1914] 3 KB 642 to the effect that a local authority which took restrictive covenants from a landowner in its area for public purposes could not enforce those covenants against a successor in title of the original covenantor, because the local authority possessed no land entitled to the benefit of the covenant. Parliament passed the 1932, 1947, 1968 and 1971 Acts to which reference has been made above.

(iii) Distinct statutory provisions apply to the enforcement and to the discharge or modification of s 52 covenants. Such covenants are enforceable by the planning authority against successors in title of the original covenantor: see s 52(2). Any restriction on the use of land imposed by a s 52 agreement is registrable as a local land charge under the Local Land Charges Act 1975, s 1(1)(b). Any purchaser of land the subject of a s 52 agreement therefore has notice of the restrictive covenant and its existence is therefore reflected in the purchase price of the land. Section 52 covenants may be discharged or modified by the Lands Tribunal under s 84 of the Law of Property Act 1925.

(iv) The attaching of conditions to the grant of planning permission in the 1971 Act was governed by s 29, which provided:

'(1) ... where an application is made to a local planning authority for planning permission, that authority, in dealing with the application ... (a) ... may grant planning permission, either unconditionally or subject to such conditions as they think fit; or (b) may refuse planning permission ...'

Those provisions are now contained in s 70(1) of the 1990 Act.

(v) In *Newbury DC v Secretary of State for the Environment* [1980] 1 All ER 731 at 754, [1981] AC 578 at 618 per Lord Scarman it was accepted by the House of Lords that the law required three tests of validity for a condition imposed under s 29, namely:

'(1) the condition must fairly and reasonably relate to the provisions of the development plan and to planning considerations affecting the land, (2) it must fairly and reasonably relate to the permitted development, and (3) it must be such as a reasonable planning authority, duly appreciating its statutory duties, could have properly imposed.'

(vi) *Windsor and Maidenhead Royal BC v Brandrose Investments Ltd* [1983] 1 All ER 818, [1983] 1 WLR 509 was a case which turned upon the construction of s 52 of the 1971 Act and in which the landowner contended, in effect, that the making of a s 52 agreement, in contemplation of a planning permission not yet made, operated so as to preclude the exercise by the planning authority of certain statutory powers. Lawton LJ said ([1983] 1 All ER 818 at 822, [1983] 1 WLR 509 at 515):

'Section 52(1) empowers a local planning authority to make agreements to achieve ends which they could not achieve without the consent of an applicant for planning permission. It does not empower a local planning authority to grant planning permission otherwise than as provided by ss 26 to 29 of the Act. It follows that an agreement made pursuant to s 52 before planning permission has been granted ... may become irrelevant if planning permission is not granted or ineffective if conditions are imposed inconsistent with the agreement because circumstances may change between the time when a s 52 agreement is made and when the local planning authority comes to perform their public duty of determining a planning application ... Counsel for the defendants did not suggest that the relevant agreement in this case operated to give the defendants planning permission ... and, even if it had operated to grant planning permission, it would not have got rid of the need for consent to demolish under the conservation order unless s 52 conferred such a power. As we have already pointed out, sub-s (1) confers powers which are merely incidental to the granting of planning permission.'

(vii) In *R v Gillingham BC, ex p Parham Ltd* (1989) 58 P & CR 73 Roch J considered whether the test for the validity of a s 52 agreement is the same as the test for the validity of a s 29 condition as set out in *Newbury DC v Secretary of State for the Environment* [1980] 1 All ER 731, [1981] AC 578. Roch J held that the first and third requirements apply to s 52 agreements but the second does not. Roch J said (58 P & CR 73 at 81):

'Section 52 requires that an agreement shall be "for the purpose of restricting or regulating the development or use of the land ..." Those words allow a section 52 agreement to go beyond matters that fairly or reasonably relate to the permitted development. Section 52 agreements can encompass matters which restrict or regulate the use of the land. This is not surprising because there would be little point in enacting section 52 of the 1971 Act if section 52 agreements were confined to those matters which could be dealt with by way of conditions.'

(viii) In *R v Wealden DC and Federated Homes Ltd, ex p Charles Church South East Ltd* (1990) 59 P & CR 150 Popplewell J agreed with the reasoning of Roch J in *R v Gillingham BC, ex p Parham Ltd* (1989) 58 P & CR 73. Popplewell J said (at 162) that it was difficult to see what the purpose of s 52 is if the powers under it are no greater than the powers to impose conditions.

(ix) Mr Gray, in the course of his submission, gave examples of obligations which might be validly required by the planning authority or undertaken by the landowner as terms of a s 52 agreement which could not be imposed as conditions. One such example supposed an application by the owner of two farms, A and B, within the area of a planning authority for planning permission to construct and operate an intensive breeding establishment on farm A. Such an owner might offer, or the planning authority might require and obtain, on the grant of such planning permission, a s 52 agreement by the owner preventing the use of farm B for such use. Such an agreement would, he submitted, be made 'for the purpose of restricting or regulating the development or use of farm B' but the restriction contained in it could not be imposed as a valid condition on the grant of planning permission in respect of farm A because it would not relate to the permitted development.

(x) In *Re Martins's Application* (1989) 57 P & CR 119 this court affirmed the decision of the Lands Tribunal dismissing a s 84 application for discharge or modification of a restrictive covenant contained in a s 52 agreement where the Secretary of State, on appeal, had granted planning permission for development which would be in breach of the covenant. Fox LJ said (at 124–125):

'... it is contended that where the Minister, by his inspector, has finally determined from a planning point of view that the erection of a house on the site was acceptable, then the purpose of the section 37 [of the Town and Country Planning Act 1962, and now under s 52 of the 1971 Act] agreement has gone and the covenant should be discharged. This construction is, in my opinion, based upon a misapprehension. There are, it seems to me, two statutory regimes. One is the power of the planning authority under section 37 [and now under s 52] to enter into an agreement regulating the development and use of land by way of restrictive covenant in circumstances where, under the general law, it would be not be possible effectively to do so because of the rules as to the running of the burden and benefit of covenants. The other is the power of the planning authority under section 29 of 1971 Act ... to grant planning permission. These regimes are subject to different procedures. If a person is dissatisfied with the planning authority's refusal of planning permission, his remedy is to appeal to the Secretary of State under section 36 of the 1971 Act ... If a person who is bound by the provisions of a section 37 agreement wishes to escape from them he must go to the Lands Tribunal and persuade the Tribunal that it is a proper case to exercise its jurisdiction to discharge or modify the covenant under section 84. Nobody was obliged to enter into a section 37 agreement. If an applicant for planning permission was offered permission upon terms that he entered into a section 37 agreement he could appeal to the Secretary of State. But if he chose to enter into the agreement he (and his successors in title) must accept that he can only avoid its effect through the statutory procedure under section 84. Thus, it seems to me that, while the two regimes impinge upon each other to some extent, they constitute different systems of control and each has, and retains, an independent existence.'

Reference was also made to *Re Jones's and Whites & Co's Application* (1989) 58 P & CR 512, a decision of the Lands Tribunal.

(xi) The submission for the plaintiffs that, if an obligation could not be lawful if imposed as a condition under s 29, it could not be lawful as an obligation imposed by s 52 agreement was based upon dicta in *Bradford City Metropolitan Council v Secretary of State for the Environment* (1987) 53 P & CR 55 and in *R v Westminster City Council, ex p Monahan* [1989] 2 All ER 74, [1990] 1 QB 87. The dicta are set out in the judgment of Sir Donald Nicholls V-C. As to the *Bradford* case, Mr Gray submitted that there no question arose as to the construction of s 52 and, in particular, as to whether the powers of a planning authority under s 52 were necessarily the same in extent as those under s 29. The comments of Lloyd LJ were directed to a suggestion that a condition which required, as the price of granting the permission, the funding by the applicant of works which were the responsibility of the planning authority and which was unlawful could have been lawful as a s 52 agreement. He said (53 P & CR 55 at 64):

'In my judgment [the true principle] is neither more nor less than the third of the three requirements identified by the House of Lords in *Newbury District Council v. Secretary of State* namely, that the conditions imposed must not be manifestly unreasonable. If the proposed condition is manifestly unreasonable, then it is beyond the powers of the planning authority to impose it; and if it is beyond the powers of the planning authority to impose the condition, then it is beyond their powers to agree to impose it, even if the developer consents.'

Later in his judgment he returned to the role of the s 52 agreement in such a case. He said (at 65–66):

'Since the point does not arise directly for decision, and since it raises questions of considerable difficulty and importance on which we have heard only limited argument, I propose to confine myself to two observations, one general and one particular. The general observation is that the practice under section 52, convenient and beneficial though it undoubtedly is, may have gone beyond what the strict language of the section justifies. We were told that such agreements are now very common, much commoner than they used to be. It may be that in some future case it will be necessary for the court to consider the extent of the powers of planning authorities to enter into agreements under section 52. I am aware, of course, that such agreements are frequently entered into under combined powers, that is to say under powers contained in other statutory provisions as well as section 52. The particular observation is that I do not accept Mr Laws' submission that the present condition would have been lawful if incorporated in a section 52 agreement. If the condition was manifestly unreasonable, and so beyond the powers of the planning authority to impose it, whether or not the developers consented, it must follow that it was also beyond the powers of the planning authority to include the condition as "an incidental or consequential provision" of an agreement restricting or regulating the development or use of the land under section 52.'

That observation of Lloyd LJ did not mean, it was said, that the powers of the planning authority under s 52 were also limited by the second of the *Newbury* case requirements, namely that the obligation must fairly and reasonably relate to the permitted development.

(xii) As to the dicta of Kerr LJ in *R v Westminster City Council, ex p Monahan* [1989] 2 All ER 74 at 99–100, [1990] 1 QB 87 at 116, he declined to accept as a general proposition the submission that the view indicated by Lloyd LJ in the *Bradford* case was incorrect. He continued ([1989] 2 All ER 74 at 100, [1990] 1 QB 87 at 116–117)

'Section 52 agreements undoubtedly facilitate the formulation of qualified planning permissions in comparison with the imposition of express conditions, and no doubt they also simplify the procedural aspects of the planning process in many ways. They have the advantages of the flexibility of a negotiable agreement in contrast to a process of unilateral imposition; and they are therefore no doubt far less vulnerable to the risk of successful appeals or applications for judicial review, which is to be welcomed. But if a particular condition would be illegal, on the ground of manifest unreasonableness or otherwise, if it were imposed on an applicant for planning permission then it cannot acquire validity if it is embodied in a s 52 agreement, whether at the instance of the applicant himself or not.'

Mr Gray pointed out that in that case there had been no reference to the relevant authorities.

Conclusion

For my part I accept the submission of Mr Gray that, upon the true construction of s 52 of the 1971 Act, the powers of a planning authority under that section are not controlled by the nature or extent of its powers under s 29 of the 1971 Act; and I reject the submission advanced for the plaintiffs that those powers are so controlled. The extent of the s 52 powers is to be determined by reference to the words there used having regard to the context. In particular, they give power to a planning authority to enter into an agreement with the owner of the land 'for the purpose of restricting or regulating the development or use of the land'. If such an agreement is required by a planning authority, and the requirement is made for such a purpose, with due regard to relevant considerations, and is not unreasonable (see the first and third requirements stated in *Newbury DC v Secretary of State for the Environment* [1980] 1 All ER 731 at 754, [1981] AC 578 at 618), such a requirement is not ultra vires merely because the purpose could not be validly achieved by the imposition of a condition under s 29 of the 1971 Act. The two statutory powers are distinct and the exercise of either of these distinct powers has separate consequences and is subject to different procedures.

If such an agreement is required, and the landowner agrees to enter into it, the validity of the agreement depends upon the same primary test, namely whether it was made 'for the purpose of restricting or regulating the development or use of the land'.

Mr Payton pointed to the fact that the word 'development' is defined in s 22(1) and the word 'use' in s 290(1) of the 1971 Act. Nothing of any relevance to this issue is to be derived from these definitions. The word 'use' is defined as not including 'the use of land for the carrying out of any building or other operations thereon'. The word therefore, subject to the exclusion, has its ordinary meaning in the English language.

This construction is not, I think, in conflict with the substance of the dicta of Lloyd LJ in *Bradford City Metropolitan Council v Secretary of State for the Environment* (1987) 53 P & CR 55 or of Kerr LJ in *R v Westminster City Council, ex p Monahan* [1989] 2 All ER 74, [1990] 1 QB 87. Lloyd LJ in the *Bradford* case was commenting upon a requirement which was, whether as a condition or as a s 52 obligation, held to be manifestly unreasonable. It is not necessary to decide in what circumstances an obligation might be manifestly unreasonable as a condition but not manifestly unreasonable as a term of a s 52 agreement. Lloyd LJ was not considering that possibility but rather the suggested effectiveness of consent by the developer as a cure for manifest unreasonableness in a s 52 agreement.

The reasoning of Roch J in *R v Gillingham BC, ex p Parham Ltd* (1989) 58 P & CR 73 appears to me, with all respect, clearly to be right. In particular, I agree with his comment that it is not surprising that a s 52 agreement may go to matters beyond those that fairly or reasonably relate to the permitted development (the second requirement stated in the *Newbury* case [1980] 1 All ER 731 at 754, [1981] AC 578 at 618) because there would be little point in enacting s 52 of the 1971 Act if s 52 agreements were confined to those matters which could be dealt with by way of conditions.

It is not clear that the statement of Kerr LJ in *R v Westminster City Council, ex p Monahan* [1989] 2 All ER 74, [1990] 1 QB 87 was intended to do more than to approve the dicta of Lloyd LJ in *Bradford City Council v Secretary of State for the Environment* (1987) 53 P & CR 55. If his statement is to be read as meaning that, if a provision would be illegal as a condition not only because of breach of requirements (1) or (3) stated in the *Newbury DC v Secretary of State for the Environment* [1981] 1 All ER 731 at 754, [1981] AC 578 at 618, but also 'otherwise', that is to say for breach only of requirement (2), then I respectfully do not agree with the statement.

I would dismiss the appeal of the plaintiffs.

HIRST LJ. I agree.

PETER GIBSON LJ. I also agree.

Appeal dismissed. Leave to appeal to the House of Lords refused.

Frances Rustin   Barrister.

Re a debtor (No 415/SD/93), ex parte the debtor v Inland Revenue Commissioners

CHANCERY DIVISION

JACOB J

10, 16 NOVEMBER 1993

Insolvency – Statutory demand – Setting aside statutory demand – Grounds on which statutory demand may be set aside – Other grounds – Creditor refusing debtor's offer to secure or compound for debt – Debtor contending creditor's refusal unreasonable – Whether debtor entitled to have statutory demand set aside – Whether court will consider reasonableness of creditor's refusal of offer – Whether court will not consider reasonableness of creditor's refusal of offer until it comes to consider bankruptcy petition – Insolvency Act 1986, s 271(3)(c) – Insolvency Rules 1986, r 6.5(4)(d).

Although the court may, pursuant to s 271(3)(c)[a] of the Insolvency Act 1986, dismiss a bankruptcy petition if it is satisfied that an offer made by the debtor to secure or compound for the debt in respect of which the petition was presented has been unreasonably refused, a debtor cannot apply to have a statutory demand set aside by the court on 'other grounds' within r 6.5(4)(d)[b] of the Insolvency Rules 1986 merely because he has made an offer of security which he contends the creditor ought reasonably to have accepted, since on its true construction r 6.5(4)(d) is concerned with cases in which the statutory demand ought to be set aside because it was either defective to the point of being unfair to the debtor or because, for some other reason, it is shown that (in the case of an immediately payable debt) there is evidence that the debt will in substance be immediately paid. It is not until the hearing of the bankruptcy petition under s 271 of the 1986 Act that the court will consider the reasonableness or otherwise of an offer to secure or to compound for a debt in respect of which the petition was presented (see p 172 *g h*, p 173 *g j* and p 174 *c f j* to p 175 *d*, post).

Dicta of Nicholls LJ in *Re a debtor (No 1 of 1987, Lancaster), ex p the debtor v Royal Bank of Scotland plc* [1989] 2 All ER 46 at 50 and of Morritt J in *Re a debtor (No 51/SD/91), ex p Ritchie Bros Auctioneers v The debtor* [1993] 2 All ER 40 at 46 explained.

Notes

For setting aside a statutory demand, see 3(2) *Halsbury's Laws* (4th edn reissue) paras 148–149, and for cases on the subject, see 4(2) *Digest* (2nd reissue) 27–28, 3719–3721.

For the Insolvency Act 1986, s 271, see 4 *Halsbury's Statutes* (4th edn) (1987 reissue) 913.

For the Insolvency Rules, 1986, r 6.5, see 3 *Halsbury's Statutory Instruments* (1991 reissue) 376.

---

a   Section 271, so far as material, is set out at p 170 *g* to *j*, post
b   Rule 6.5, so far as material, is set out at p 171 *d* to *j*, post

Cases referred to in judgment

Debtor, Re a (No 1 of 1987, Lancaster), ex p the debtor v Royal Bank of Scotland plc [1989] 2 All ER 46, [1989] 1 WLR 271, CA.
Debtor, Re a (No 51/SD/91), ex p Ritchie Bros Auctioneers v The debtor [1993] 2 All ER 40, [1992] 1 WLR 1294.
Debtor, Re a (No 960/SD/1992), ex p the debtor v IRC [1993] STC 218.

Appeal

A debtor appealed from the order of Mr Registrar Scott dated 15 April 1993 dismissing the debtor's application for an order to set aside a statutory demand dated 11 March 1993 in the sum of £896,887·76 served on the debtor by the respondents, the Commissioners of Inland Revenue, in respect of capital gains tax for the years 1988 and 1989. The facts are set out in the judgment.

John Briggs (instructed by *Masons*) for appellant.
Christopher Tidmarsh (instructed by the *Solicitor for Inland Revenue*) for respondent.

Cur adv vult

16 November 1993. The following judgment was delivered.

JACOB J. This is an appeal from an order of Mr Registrar Scott of 15 April 1993 whereby he refused a debtor's application for the setting aside of a statutory demand.

The statutory demand was dated 11 March 1993 and was in the sum of £896,887·76. It was in respect of capital gains tax for the years 1988 and 1989 and interest. There is no dispute as to the amount owing or that the debt was due immediately. Nor was it in dispute that the debtor was unable to pay the debt immediately. The circumstances giving rise to the debtor's position were that he held some shares which were once worth a lot and had intended to pay the tax on the basis of those shares but that they had unfortunately become almost worthless. However, he says, he holds some other shares which are worth, he says, between £4m and £18m, but owing to the peculiarities of his holding he is not able to realise those shares (and some loan stock) for the present. In December 1992 he made an offer to the creditor, the Inland Revenue, to give security over these shares and also an offer in any event to pay the money by the end of 1993. The Revenue took the view they were entitled to immediate payment, and did not have to consider this offer. They had earlier accepted an offer to pay in instalments but the debtor defaulted after the first instalment because his bank no longer supported him. Accordingly they issued the demand. The appellant says that he is in a position to show that the Revenue were unreasonable in failing to consider his offer, that they were obliged to do so and that accordingly the statutory demand ought to be set aside.

Before me the point was argued as one of principle. Can a debtor faced with a statutory demand apply to have it set aside on the grounds that he has made an offer of security which the creditor ought reasonably to have accepted? I have not been asked to consider whether the offer was reasonable. If that is a matter which ought to be considered at this stage it was agreed that the matter should go back to the registrar.

I turn to the relevant provisions, beginning with the primary legislation contained in the Insolvency Act 1986. The relevant provisions so far as material are:

'**267.**—(1) A creditor's petition must be in respect of one or more debts owed by the debtor, and the petitioning creditor or each of the petitioning creditors must be a person to whom the debt or (as the case may be) at least one of the debts is owed.

(2) Subject to the next three sections, a creditor's petition may be presented to the court in respect of a debt or debts only if, at the time the petition is presented ... (c) the debt, or each of the debts, is a debt which the debtor appears either to be unable to pay or to have no reasonable prospect of being able to pay ...

268.—(1) For the purposes of section 267(2)(c), the debtor appears to be unable to pay a debt if, but only if, the debt is payable immediately and either—(a) the petitioning creditor to whom the debt is owed has served on the debtor a demand (known as "the statutory demand") in the prescribed form requiring him to pay the debt or to secure or compound for it to the satisfaction of the creditor, at least 3 weeks have elapsed since the demand was served and the demand has been neither complied with nor set aside in accordance with the rules, or (b) execution or other process issued in respect of the debt on a judgment or order of any court in favour of the petitioning creditor, or one or more of the petitioning creditors to whom the debt is owed, has been returned unsatisfied in whole or in part.

(2) For the purposes of section 267(2)(c) the debtor appears to have no reasonable prospect of being able to pay a debt if, but only if, the debt is not immediately payable and—(a) the petitioning creditor to whom it is owed has served on the debtor a demand (also known as "the statutory demand") in the prescribed form requiring him to establish to the satisfaction of the creditor that there is a reasonable prospect that the debtor will be able to pay the debt when it falls due, (b) at least 3 weeks have elapsed since the demand was served, and (c) the demand has been neither complied with nor set aside in accordance with the rules ...

271.—(1) The court shall not make a bankruptcy order on a creditor's petition unless it is satisfied that the debt, or one of the debts, in respect of which the petition was presented is either—(a) a debt which, having been payable at the date of the petition or having since become payable, has been neither paid nor secured or compounded for, or (b) a debt which the debtor has no reasonable prospect of being able to pay when it falls due.

(2) In a case in which the petition contains such a statement as is required by section 270, the court shall not make a bankruptcy order until at least 3 weeks have elapsed since the service of any statutory demand under section 268.

(3) The court may dismiss the petition if it is satisfied that the debtor is able to pay all his debts or is satisfied—(a) that the debtor has made an offer to secure or compound for a debt in respect of which the petition is presented, (b) that the acceptance of that offer would have required the dismissal of the petition, and (c) that the offer has been unreasonably refused; and, in determining for the purposes of this subsection whether the debtor is able to pay all his debts, the court shall take into account his contingent and prospective liabilities ...'

That is the relevant primary legislation. It sets up a two-stage process for a bankruptcy petition. There is first the statutory demand or failure of execution of a judgment debt. Either of these establishes an inability to pay. Given that, the next question follows after the petition: should a bankruptcy order in fact be made (s 271)?

I now turn to the secondary legislation, namely the relevant provisions of the Insolvency Rules 1986, SI 1986/1925. Rule 6.1 sets out some formal requirements of the statutory demand. There is a Form 6.1, which is prescribed by r 12.7. I shall return to this form. There are detailed requirements as to what should be in the statutory demand, and rules as to service. Then there is a procedure concerned with setting aside a statutory demand. It is the scope of that procedure which is in issue.

Under r 6.4(1) there is an 18-day period in which the application should be made. The application has to be supported by an affidavit and there is a prescribed form for that called Form 6.5. The procedure prescribed is intended to be brief. In my view it is aimed at establishing an inability to pay and no more. It is not a general coarse sieve where the court considers generally whether the petition will succeed or fail.

The key rule is r 6.5 which reads as follows:

'(1) On receipt of an application under Rule 6.4, the court may, if satisfied that no sufficient cause is shown for it, dismiss it without giving notice to the creditor. As from (inclusive) the date on which the application is dismissed, the time limited for compliance with the statutory demand runs again.

(2) If the application is not dismissed under paragraph (1), the court shall fix a venue for it to be heard, and shall give at least 7 days' notice of it to— (a) the debtor or, if the debtor's application was made by a solicitor acting for him, to the solicitor, (b) the creditor, and (c) whoever is named in the statutory demand as the person with whom the debtor may enter into communication with reference to the demand (or, if more than one person is so named, the first of them).

(3) On the hearing of the application, the court shall consider the evidence then available to it, and may either summarily determine the application or adjourn it, giving such directions as it thinks appropriate.

(4) The court may grant the application if—(a) the debtor appears to have a counterclaim, set-off or cross demand which equals or exceeds the amount of the debt or debts specified in the statutory demand; or (b) the debt is disputed on grounds which appear to the court to be substantial; or (c) it appears that the creditor holds some security in respect of the debt claimed by the demand, and either Rule 6.1(5) is not complied with in respect of it, or the court is satisfied that the value of the security equals or exceeds the full amount of the debt; or (d) the court is satisfied, on other grounds, that the demand ought to be set aside ...'

What 'other grounds' can the court take into account at this stage of the procedure? The question has important practical consequences. A creditor entitled to immediate payment of a sum of money would be required at this stage to consider the security offered. He would very likely have to get involved in his own valuation. There could be conflicts of valuers. The whole procedure of whether the statutory demand should or should not be set aside would turn into an elaborate affair. If in the end it was decided that the demand should not be set aside the critical date, namely that of presentation of the petition, would have been considerably delayed.

The argument for the appellant was based upon four grounds. The first of these is based upon Form 6.1, the form of the statutory demand itself. This form is of course to be treated as part of the rules, being annexed to them. The form on its first page includes the statement:

'The creditor demands that you pay the above debt or secure or compound for it to the creditor's satisfaction.'

On its last page it says:

'If you wish to avoid a bankruptcy petition being presented against you, you must pay the debt shown on page 1, particulars of which are set out on page 2 of this notice, within the period of **21 days** after its service upon you. Alternatively, you can attempt to come to a settlement with the creditor. To do this you should:

• inform the individual (or one of the individuals) named in part B above immediately that you are willing and able to offer security for the debt to the creditor's satisfaction; or

• inform the individual (or one of the individuals) named in part B immediately that you are willing and able to compound for the debt to the creditor's satisfaction.

If you dispute the demand in whole or in part you should:

• contact the individual (or one of the individuals) named in part B immediately.

If you consider that you have grounds to have this demand set aside or if you do not quickly receive a satisfactory written reply from the individual named in part B whom you have contacted you should **apply within 18 days** from the date of service of this demand on you to the appropriate court shown in part A above to have the demand set aside.'

It is argued that the form contemplates that the debtor may not 'quickly receive a satisfactory written reply' and that means a reply satisfactory to the debtor. So, the argument runs, if the debtor has made an offer to compound, for instance by giving security, he can then apply to have the demand set aside. I do not read the document in that way. The primary requirement is either 'pay or settle'. The suggestion in the form is no more than that the debtor can apply, indeed must apply, within 18 days of the date of service to have the demand set aside. I do not think that there is, as was suggested, a right vested in the debtor to obtain 'a satisfactory written reply'.

The second argument was founded on the 'other grounds' of r 6.5(4)(d). It was argued that these words confer upon the court a general discretion to consider what might happen if the petition were presented. Putting the point another way the court should ask the general question: is it unjust to allow the creditor to present the petition? It was sought to reinforce the argument by reference to what was said by Nicholls LJ in *Re a debtor (No 1 of 1987, Lancaster), ex p the debtor v Royal Bank of Scotland plc* [1989] 2 All ER 46 at 50, [1989] 1 WLR 271 at 276. The case was concerned with a very different question namely what happens if there is a defective or perplexing statutory demand which none the less in no way prejudices the debtor. In that context Nicholls LJ said:

'The question arising on this appeal concerns the exercise by the court of its power to set aside a statutory demand "on other grounds" within sub-para (d). In my view, the right approach to para (4) of r 6.5 is this. Under the 1986 Act, a statutory demand which is not complied with founds the consequence that the debtor is regarded as being unable to pay the debt in question or, if the debt is not immediately payable, as having no reasonable prospect of being able to pay the debt when it becomes due. That consequence, in turn, founds the ability of the creditor to present a bankruptcy petition because, under s 268(1), in the absence of an unsatisfied return to execution or other process a debtor's inability to pay the debt in question is established if, but only if, the appropriate statutory demand has been served and not complied with.

When therefore the rules provide, as does r 6.5(4)(d), for the court to have a residual discretion to set aside a statutory demand, the circumstances which normally will be required before a court can be satisfied that the demand "ought" to be set aside, are circumstances which would make it unjust for the statutory demand to give rise to those consequences in the particular case. The court's intervention is called for to prevent that injustice.'

In his first paragraph Nicholls LJ refers to the consequence that the debtor is regarded as being unable to pay the debt in question and then says that that consequence founds the ability of the creditor to present a bankruptcy petition. In his second paragraph he refers to a 'residual discretion' and refers to 'circumstances which would make it unjust for the statutory demand to give rise to those consequences in the particular case'.

The appellant argues that by the use of the words 'those consequences' Nicholls LJ was intending to indicate a general power of the court to intervene to prevent any injustice. By implication that includes a case where the creditor refuses to accept security reasonably by way of compounding the debt.

I do not think Nicholls LJ was considering anything like the question before me. I do not think he was indicating in his use of the expression 'residual discretion' at the stage of an application to set aside a statutory demand that the court should in effect conduct a mini-trial into whether or not at a later stage the court would make a bankruptcy order under s 271. I think he was referring to whether or not the demand itself produced injustice, which was the point in issue before him. Where the debtor admits he cannot pay, the purpose of the demand is satisfied.

Mr Briggs, who mustered the argument for the appellant as powerfully as it could possibly be, shrank from urging that any ground which might defeat a petition (eg lack of any contact with this country) could be used to set aside a statutory demand. Logically I think his argument involves such a consequence. Why should an offer of security be treated differently from any other ground under which a petition might be refused?

I think the true view is that r 6.5(4)(d) is concerned with a case in which the statutory demand ought to be set aside because it was either defective to the point of being unfair to the debtor (as was suggested to be the case in Nicholls LJ's case) or if, for some other reason, it is shown that (in the case of an immediately payable debt) there is evidence that the debt will in substance be immediately paid.

Such an instance is, I think, what Morritt J was contemplating in his obiter discussion of s 271(3) and r 6.5(4)(d) in *Re a debtor (No 51/SD/91), ex p Ritchie*

Bros Auctioneers v The debtor [1993] 2 All ER 40 at 46, [1992] 1 WLR 1294 at 1301. He said (in a case concerned with payment of a debt in a foreign currency):

> 'If the debtor makes genuine attempts to satisfy the demand by paying what reasonably appears to be the sterling equivalent at the time of payment, that will probably be regarded as compounding the debt in a manner which the creditor could not reasonably refuse (see s 271(3)) and a good reason to set aside the statutory demand under r 6.5(4)(d) if the creditor declines to accept such alternative performance.'

I do not think that Morritt J was in that case saying that any ground which could be used to defeat a petition was a matter which could be raised by the debtor at the statutory demand stage of the process. The reality of the situation he was contemplating is that the debtor can pay. I think what he said has been inappropriately taken out of its context.

The next point taken on behalf of the debtor related to the prescribed form (Form 6.5) of the affidavit in support of an application to set aside a statutory demand. In a sidenote the debtor is invited to:

> 'Insert one of the 8 following alternatives or if none of them are applicable state grounds on which you consider the statutory demand should be set aside.'

The fourth of these is:

> '"Admit the debt and am prepared to secure or compound for it to the creditor's satisfaction by ..." [state nature of satisfaction].'

It was said this contemplates a case where the debtor is offering to secure or to compound. The difficulty with the argument is that it refers to securing or compounding to the '*creditor's satisfaction*'. Whilst that may be as it were a kind of offer to the creditor, it does not seem to me that the prescribed form is suggesting that there should be an investigation by the court as to whether the offer is or is not reasonable at this stage of the process.

The fourth point argued on behalf of the appellant relates to s 268(2). This relates to a case where the debt is not immediately payable but there is none the less no reasonable prospect of the debtor being able to pay it. Then the statutory demand calls upon the debtor 'to establish to the satisfaction of the creditor that there is a reasonable prospect that the debtor will be able to pay the debt when it falls due'. What was said was that this contemplates a reasonable offer by the debtor and that, if the creditor behaves unreasonably by not accepting the offer, it would be nonsense for the procedure to carry on. Thus, it was argued, suppose there was a debt due in three months and the debtor was able to provide a banker's draft for the sum concerned payable on the due date. It would be wholly unreasonable for the creditor to say that he is not satisfied. So, it must be the case that in s 268(2)(a) the expression 'to the satisfaction of the creditor' means 'to the reasonable satisfaction of the creditor'. And if it means that in sub-s (2) then the same expression 'satisfaction of the creditor' in sub-s (1) must take the same meaning, namely 'reasonable to the satisfaction of the creditor'.

I think Mr Tidmarsh provided the answer to this. The supposed instance would be a case where if the creditor behaved unreasonably there would be a ground which would satisfy the court that the demand ought to be set aside because in the circumstances the debtor would have shown that there was a reasonable prospect of the debtor being able to pay the debt. He says, I think rightly, that the only inquiries which the court is called upon to make at the statutory demand stage is whether or not it is shown that the debtor is, in the case of s 268(1), 'unable to pay a debt' or, in the case of s 268(2), 'has no reasonable prospect of being able to pay a debt'. The 'other ground' of the rule relates and relates only to that question and ancillary matters such as whether the demand is fair. Once it is shown or admitted that the debt cannot or will not be paid (as the case may be) then the case proceeds to the next stage of bankruptcy proceedings.

At the next stage, s 271, the court may consider the reasonableness or otherwise of an offer to secure or to compound (as required by s 271(3)). It is worth noting that at that stage the court looks at whether the debtor is able to pay all his debts and looks at the debtor's contingent and prospective liabilities. If all that comes in also at the application to set aside a statutory demand then the court is looking at the whole question twice. It is not expressly directed to do so in the statute. Indeed, as Mr Tidmarsh submitted, if Parliament wanted to spell that out it could have done so. The contrast between s 271(3) and r 6.5(4) could not be more marked. The latter could have adopted the provision of the former but did not do so.

It was also argued that that rule clearly refers to the case where the creditor already holds security. It was said that it is illogical that where a creditor holds security sufficient for the debt the petition can be set aside but that this is not so when the debtor is prepared to offer such security. I think there is a world of difference. Bankruptcy is primarily concerned with unsecured debts. Where a creditor has taken a secured debt he looks to his security if a debtor fails to pay. In the case of an unsecured debt he has no such security and is not obliged to take the security offered by the debtor however good that security may be. If indeed the debtor has indeed got good security then his route to avoid a petition is to borrow against that security and pay off his creditor, who is entitled to his money forthwith.

I am comforted in reaching this conclusion by the decision of Mummery J in *Re a debtor (No 960/SD/1992), ex p the debtor v IRC* [1993] STC 218. In that case Mummery J clearly considered that an offer of security was not the same as an existing security. True it is that the case may not have been fully argued because the debtor was in person but none the less I think Mummery J was correct in drawing the distinction between r 6.5(4)(c) (where there is existing security) and the case under r 6.5(4)(d). It is fair to say that he did not refer to sub-para (d), but that cannot have been far from his mind when the provisions are so closely allied.

I think Mr Registrar Scott put the matter pithily and accurately in his decision. He said:

'Security or compounding to the satisfaction of the creditor is a means of compliance with a demand, and not a ground for setting aside.'

In the result I dismiss the appeal.

Appeal dismissed. Leave to appeal granted.

Hazel Hartman   Barrister.

Practice Direction

HOUSE OF LORDS

House of Lords – Fees and security money – Judicial fees – Security money – House of Lords Practice Directions applicable to Civil Appeals (1992), App H.

The following amendments to the *House of Lords Practice Directions applicable to Civil Appeals* (the Blue Book, 1992) have been agreed.

Appendix H

Fees and security money

(1) JUDICIAL FEES

As from 12 April 1994 the judicial fees will be increased. The new figures will be as follows:

	£
Petition of appeal..	68
Appearance	8
Waiver of security for costs	17
Petition not referred to Appeal Committee (incidental petition to conjoin or consolidate)	34
Petition referred to Appeal Committee (including report thereon)	40
Joint petition (from each party thereto).	17
Application to set down for hearing	363
Final judgment.	40

(3) SECURITY MONEY

The sum to be lodged as security for costs by appellants in appeals to the House of Lords presented on or after 12 April 1994 will be increased to £18,000.

[*Agents are reminded that in accordance with Direction 11.2 'No interest is payable on security money'.*]

8 March 1994

M A J WHEELER-BOOTH
Clerk of the Parliaments.

Re a debtor (No 64 of 1992)

CHANCERY DIVISION
COLIN RIMER QC SITTING AS A DEPUTY JUDGE OF THE HIGH COURT
13 OCTOBER, 5 NOVEMBER 1993

Insolvency – Statutory demand – Setting aside statutory demand – Grounds on which statutory demand may be set aside – Debt for liquidated sum – Whether statutory demand which did not specify figures used to calculate liquidated sum valid – Insolvency Act 1986, s 267 – Insolvency Rules 1986, r 6.1(5).

Insolvency – Voluntary arrangement – Approval by creditors – Notice of creditors' meeting sent but not received by creditor – Whether creditor deemed to have received constructive notice of meeting – Whether creditor bound by voluntary arrangement – Insolvency Act 1986, ss 257, 260(2) – Insolvency Rules 1986, r 12.16.

In 1989 the debtor entered into a mortgage with a building society under which the debtor covenanted to pay the building society the sum of £675,250 together with interest, costs and expenses by monthly instalments. It was a term of the mortgage that the mortgage debt became immediately due and payable if there was any default in paying the monthly instalments. On 21 May 1991 the society obtained an order for possession of the property. On 8 June 1992 the debtor entered into a voluntary arrangement at a creditors' meeting held under s 257[a] of the Insolvency Act 1986. A notice of the meeting had been posted to the society but was not received by it with the result that it had not attended the meeting. On 9 October the society served on the debtor a statutory demand under s 268 of the 1986 Act alleging that the debtor owed the society the sum of £411,501·18 which was payable immediately and was unsecured. The demand stated that the society's anticipated loss based upon professional advice from independent valuers was £411,501·18. The debtor applied to have the demand set aside on the grounds (i) that the sum claimed was not a 'liquidated sum' within s 267[b] of the 1986 Act, since, although the demand stated the amount of the original loan to the debtor, it had failed to state either the amount of the total debt due at the date of the demand or the value which the society put upon the security, as required by r 6.1(5)[c] of the Insolvency Rules 1986, and (ii) that the society was bound by the voluntary arrangement under s 260(2)[d] of the 1986 Act, which provided that any arrangement which had been approved at a creditors' meeting bound anyone who had notice of, and was entitled to vote at, the meeting whether present or not. The debtor further contended that since notice of the meeting had been sent to, albeit not received by, the society it had constructive notice of the meeting and under r 12.16[e] of the 1986 rules the meeting was deemed as having been duly summoned and held. The district judge accepted the debtor's contentions and set the demand side. The society appealed, contending (i) that the amount of £411,501·18 qualified as 'a liquidated sum' since if the exact figures been

a   Section 257, so far as material, is set out at p 186 c d, post
b   Section 267, so far as material, is set out at p 182 d to f, post
c   Rule 6.1(5) is set out at p 180 j to p 181 a, post
d   Section 260, so far as material, is set out at p 187 e, post
e   Rule 12.16 is set out at p 189 f g, post

disclosed, so that it could be seen how the debt claimed had been arrived at, the resulting figure would have been 'a liquidated sum' for the purposes of the 1986 Act and rules, and (ii) that, since the society had not been given notice of the proposed voluntary arrangement and therefore did not attend the meeting of creditors, it was not bound by the arrangement.

Held – The appeal would be allowed for the following reasons—

(1) Under r 6.1(5) of the 1986 rules it was competent for a secured creditor to put a value on his security and to serve a statutory demand for the amount of the total debt less such value, and the net figure resulting from such an arithmetical calculation, even though the amounts used to arrive at the net figure were unspecified, was in the nature of 'a liquidated sum' for the purposes of s 267(2)(b) of the 1986 Act provided that the net figure represented the calculation of the debt less the value put by the creditor on the security. It was also within the contemplation of r 6.1(5) that the value which the creditor put on his security would be a value with which the debtor might disagree but any such discrepancy would not provide a basis for challenging the validity of the statutory demand. Accordingly, the given net figure of £411,501·18 was in the nature of 'a liquidated sum' for the purposes of s 267(2)(b) of the 1986 Act, since although the society had not specified the exact figures used to calculate the sum stated in the statutory demand, the amount had been calculated by the formula stated in r 6.1(5), ie the debt less the amount specified as the value of the security (see p 183 *g* to p 184 *e* and p 192 *e*, post).

(2) Although a creditors' meeting under s 257 of the 1986 Act had been duly summoned and held under r 12.16 of the 1986 rules, a creditor who did not have actual notice of it was not bound by any arrangement which was approved by the creditors, since s 260(2)(b) of the 1986 Act provided that the arrangement bound only those persons who had received notice of the meeting. Since the society had not received the notice of the meeting that had allegedly been sent to it, it could not be said that the society had constructive notice of the convening of the meeting. Rule 12.16 did not deem a creditor to have had notice of the meeting but merely provided that non-receipt by him of a notice duly sent was not by itself sufficient to enable him to say that the meeting had not been duly summoned and held. Under s 260(2)(b) of the Act the society was not deemed to be one of the debtor's creditors which was bound by the voluntary arrangement and it was therefore entitled to serve a statutory demand on the debtor with a view to the subsequent presentation of a bankruptcy petition (see p 189 *g* to p 190 *d* and p 191 *h* to p 192 *c e*, post).

Notes

For setting aside a statutory demand, see 3(2) *Halsbury's Laws* (4th edn reissue) paras 148–149, and for cases on the subject, see 4(2) *Digest* (2nd reissue) 27–28, *3719–3721*.

For summoning of creditor's meetings see 3(2) *Halsbury's Laws* (4th edn reissue) para 90, and for cases on the subject, see 4(1) *Digest* (2nd reissue) 178–180, *1550–1567*.

For the Insolvency Act 1986, ss 257, 260, 267, see 4 *Halsbury's Statutes* (4th edn) (1987 reissue) 902, 904, 910.

For the Insolvency Rules 1986, rr 6.1, 12.16, see 3 *Halsbury's Statutory Instruments* (1991 reissue) 374, 473.

Cases referred to in judgment

Debtor, Re a (No 1 of 1987, Lancaster), ex p the debtor v Royal Bank of Scotland plc [1989] 2 All ER 46, [1989] 1 WLR 271, CA.
Debtor, Re a (No 106 of 1992) (1992) Independent, 20 April.
McKeen, Re (1 April 1992, unreported), Ch D.

Appeal

The Bradford and Bingley Building Society appealed against the order made by District Judge Willers sitting in the Hertford County Court on 18 February 1993 setting aside the statutory demand in the sum of £411,501·18 served by the society on the debtor on 9 October 1992. By their notice of appeal the appellants sought an order that (i) the district judge's order of 18 February be set aside, (ii) that the debtor's application dated 23 October 1992 to set aside the statutory demand be dismissed, (iii) that the society be granted leave to present a bankruptcy petition against the debtor. The grounds of appeal were that (i) the district judge was wrong in law and fact in holding that the sum of £411,501·18 claimed in the statutory demand was an unliquidated sum and accordingly the statutory demand should be set aside, (ii) the district judge was wrong in law and fact in holding that the discrepancy of between £200,000 to £250,000 in the valuation evidence before the court rendered the sum claimed in the statutory demand so uncertain as to fail to bring it within the concept of a liquidated sum, (iii) the district judge was wrong in law in holding that the defects in the statutory demand were such that it should be set aside, (iv) the district judge was wrong in law and fact in holding that the appellant had received notice within the meaning of the Insolvency Rules, SI 1986/1925 of the debtor's proposal for a voluntary arrangement with her creditors, such proposal having been approved on 8 June 1992, (v) the district judge was wrong to hold that the society was bound by the voluntary arrangement and therefore was not entitled to claim the sum £411,501·18 or any part thereof, from the debtor by way of statutory demand, (vi) the order of the district judge was wrong and ought to be set aside.

James Barker (instructed by *Hammond Suddards*, Manchester) for the society.
Jill Johnston (instructed by *Tringhams*) for the debtor.

Cur adv vult

5 November 1993. The following judgment of the court was delivered.

COLIN RIMER QC. This is an appeal by Bradford and Bingley Building Society (which I shall call 'the society') against an order of District Judge Willers made on 18 February 1993 at the Hertford County Court. By that order the district judge set aside a statutory demand which had been served by the society on Mrs G ('the debtor') and ordered the society to pay the debtor's costs of her successful application. The outline facts are as follows.

On 9 October 1992 the society served on the debtor a statutory demand under s 268(1)(a) of the Insolvency Act 1986. The demand alleged that the debtor owed the society the sum of £411,501·18 and that such sum was payable immediately and was unsecured. Particulars of the debt were set out in the demand. In view of one of the issues which I have to decide it is necessary to set out those particulars in full. They read:

'By a mortgage dated 27th day of November 1989 the debtor, together with [her husband] covenanted to pay to Leamington Spa Building Society (the lender) the sum of £675,250·00 together with interest thereon, costs and expenses. The debt was secured on a [described property].

By Clause 5 of the said mortgage it is a term of the loan that if the Borrower shall make default in payment of any monthly instalment then in such case the mortgage debt shall become immediately due and payment on 21st May 1991 [sic].

On 21st day of May 1991 the Society obtained an Order for Possession of the property in the High Court Chancery Division.

The Society's anticipated loss based upon professional advice from independent valuers is £411,501·18.

By an Instrument of Transfer of Engagements dated the 19th day of March 1991, Leamington Spa Building Society transferred all its property assets and liabilities to [the society] who are now entitled to the monies demanded hereunder.'

On 23 October 1992 the debtor issued her application to have the demand set aside. It was supported by two affidavits sworn by her husband and herself. Those affidavits raised two arguments as to why the demand should be set aside.

The first argument was to the effect that the sum claimed in the demand was not 'a liquidated sum', and that therefore it was not competent for the society to base a statutory demand on it. It was asserted that the demand was instead for what was described as 'an inchoate anticipated loss' based on an undisclosed valuation. It was pointed out that, although the demand stated the amount of the original loan to the debtor and her husband, it did not state either the amount of the total debt due at the date of the demand or the value which the society put upon the security. It was said that what the society had done was to claim a sum equal to its estimate of the likely shortfall it would suffer in the event of a sale of the security, and that its estimate was made on the basis of an unidentified valuation.

The second argument was that the debtor was subject to a voluntary arrangement made pursuant to Pt VIII of the 1986 Act. The debtor asserted that the society was bound by such arrangement and that, in consequence, it ought not to have served the statutory demand.

The district judge accepted both arguments and set the demand aside. For the society, Mr Barker submitted that the district judge was in error on both grounds. For the debtor, Miss Johnston sought to uphold the district judge's judgment on both grounds. I will deal with each ground in turn.

(1) *The 'no debt for a liquidated sum' point*

In at least two respects the particulars of the debt set out in the statutory demand are unhappily formulated. First, something has obviously gone wrong with the drafting of the latter part of the second paragraph. Secondly, although the society held a security for its debt, the demand failed to specify either the full amount of the debt at the date of the demand or the value which the society had put on its security at such date. The demand thus failed to comply with r 6.1(5) of the Insolvency Rules 1986, SI 1986/1925, which provides:

'If the creditor holds any security in respect of the debt, the full amount of the debt shall be specified, but—(a) there shall in the demand be specified the nature of the security, and the value which the creditor puts upon it as at the date of the demand, and (b) the amount of which payment is claimed by the demand shall be the full amount of the debt, less the amount specified as the value of the security.'

Rule 6.1(5) is in apparently mandatory terms; and r 6.5(4) provides that the court may grant an application to set aside a statutory demand if, inter alia—

'(c) it appears that the creditor holds some security in respect of the debt claimed by the demand, and either Rule 6.1(5) is not complied with in respect of it, or the court is satisfied that the value of the security equals or exceeds the full amount of the debt ...'

In view of r 6.5(4)(c), it might perhaps be thought that the society's non-compliance with r 6.1(5) might justify the setting aside of the statutory demand. However, Miss Johnston, who also appeared before the district judge, made clear that an argument along those lines formed no part of the debtor's case, and, if I may say so, I consider that the debtor was probably right in not so arguing. I should, however, explain why.

In this connection I was referred to *Re a debtor (No 1 of 1987, Lancaster), ex p the debtor v Royal Bank of Scotland plc* [1989] 2 All ER 46, [1989] 1 WLR 271, a decision of the Court of Appeal. It is unnecessary to refer to the case in any detail, but the principle of its decision is that deficiencies in the form and contents of a statutory demand, even including errors involving the overstatement of the debtor's indebtedness to the creditor, will not automatically entitle the debtor to have the demand set aside. The question in every case is whether, on the facts, injustice would be caused to the debtor by allowing the particular demand to stand (see [1989] 2 All ER 46 esp at 50, 52–53, [1989] 1 WLR 271 esp at 276, 279 per Nicholls LJ).

In this case the debtor does not claim that the form of the statutory demand has confused or perplexed her. She understood the route taken by the society in arriving at the sum claimed of £411,501·18, namely that it had deducted an unspecified valuation of the property from the, also unspecified, total debt due. It may be that both figures used by the society in its calculation are disputed by the debtor. However, she does not contend that the value of the security at the date of the demand either equalled or exceeded the full amount of the debt. She recognises that her indebtedness to the society at that date exceeded the amount of the security by a substantial margin, being probably well into six figures, and that the excess remains unpaid.

With regard to the last point, various valuations obtained by the debtor and her husband were put in evidence, suggesting that the security was worth, in May 1992, between £600,000 and £700,000 and, in August 1992, from £550,000 to £600,000. There was also exhibited a letter of 4 September 1992 from the society stating that the society's valuations of the property showed it to be worth only about £400,000 to £450,000. However, as against this range of valuations, the unchallenged evidence from the society is that as at 30 September 1992 the total debt due to it was £942,758·66, with interest accruing at a daily rate of £279·13. I add that I was told by Mr Barker that the property was eventually sold in May 1993 for £500,000, but nothing turns on that for present purposes.

In these circumstances, even though it may be that the debtor regards the statutory demand as overstating her indebtedness, after giving credit for the value of the security, she does not claim that the deficiencies in the form of the demand are, by themselves, such as to merit its being set aside. In particular, she does not suggest that the non-compliance with r 6.1(5) was fatal to the demand. On this particular point I was referred to *Re a debtor (No 106 of 1992)* (1989) Independant, 20 April, a decision of Mr Evans-Lombe QC, sitting as a deputy judge of the High Court in the Chancery Division. The summary is very brief, but is to the effect that it was not fatal to the statutory demand that it did not refer to the security held by the creditor or specify the value which the creditor put upon it, the debtor not having been prejudiced by such defects.

The point which the debtor does take, and which the district judge accepted, is this. It is that a bankruptcy petition can only be founded on a debt which is for 'a liquidated sum' payable to the creditor and that therefore it follows that the sum demanded by a statutory demand must also be for such a sum. The debtor's contention is that the sum demanded by the statutory demand in the present case is not such 'a liquidated sum'.

The requirement for a debt founding a bankruptcy petition to be 'a liquidated sum' is contained in s 267(2)(b) of the 1986 Act. The material parts of s 267(1) and (2) read:

'267. *Grounds of creditor's petition.*—(1) A creditor's petition must be in respect of one or more debts owed by the debtor, and the petitioning creditor or each of the petitioning creditors must be a person to whom the debt or (as the case may be) at least one of the debts is owed.

(2) Subject to the next three sections, a creditor's petition may be presented to the court in respect of a debt or debts only if, at the time the petition is presented—(a) the amount of the debt, or the aggregate amount of the debts, is equal to or exceeds the bankruptcy level, (b) the debt, or each of the debts, is for a liquidated sum payable to the petitioning creditor, or one or more of the petitioning creditors, either immediately or at some certain, future time, and is unsecured ...'

Mr Barker did not dispute, and I accept, that those provisions show that the society's demand can only have been a valid one if, inter alia, the £411,501·18 claimed can correctly be characterised as 'a liquidated sum'. Is it such a sum?

In support of the appeal Mr Barker submitted that it is. He referred me to *The Supreme Court Practice 1993* vol 1, para 6/2/4:

'"*Debt or liquidated demand*" A liquidated demand is in the nature of a debt, i.e. a specific sum of money due and payable under or by virtue of a contract. Its amount must either be already ascertained or capable of being ascertained as a mere matter of arithmetic. If the ascertainment of a sum of money, even though it be specified or named as a definite figure, requires investigation beyond mere calculation, then the sum is not a "debt or liquidated demand", but constitutes "damages".'

He submitted that that provides a sufficient guide as to the indebtedness which will qualify as 'a liquidated sum' for the purposes of s 267(2)(b) and that the amount of £411,501·18 claimed by the society duly qualified as such a sum. It was not in dispute that the society had arrived at the sum by deducting an unspecified valuation of the security (£X) from the, also unspecified, total debt (£Y). If, as it should have done, the society had disclosed on the face of the demand both the £X and £Y figures, so that it could be seen how it had arrived at the debt claimed, then it could not be argued that the resulting figure was not 'a liquidated sum' for the purposes of s 267(2)(b), since that is the very exercise which r 6.1(5) required the society to perform. It can therefore make no difference that the society has taken a short cut, and merely asserted that the debtor is indebted to it in a particular sum, without also specifying the two figures, £X and £Y, which it has used to arrive at such sum.

Miss Johnston did not question that the passage cited from *The Supreme Court Practice* provided a sufficient guide as to the meaning of 'a liquidated sum' for the purposes of s 267(2)(b). But she submitted that the identification of the sum said to be due from the debtor to the society for the purposes of supporting a statutory demand involved not just a mere matter of arithmetical calculation, but also the investigation of the two unspecified figures, £X and £Y, which it was essential to know before the sum said to be due to the society could be arrived at. Therefore the sum claimed was not 'a liquidated sum'.

Miss Johnston advanced a similar argument to the district judge, who accepted it. The relevant part of the notes of the district judge's judgment read:

'The arguments put forward by [the society] that where part of the debt is disputed and the balance is not paid the demand can still be relied upon, can only arise where the debt in which part is disputed is a liquidated sum. It is evident from [the society's] evidence on valuation and from [the debtor's] evidence on valuation, that there is enormous discrepancy between the parameters. On the one hand [the society] contends £450,000 at the most and on the other hand [the debtor] contends that the most which would be realised is £650,000. That is a discrepancy between £200,000–250,000 and even on the basis of what is outstanding to the society in September 1992 is potentially a quarter of the whole indebtedness. I have to accept the argument and do, that that renders the figure so uncertain as to fail to bring it within the concept of a liquidated sum. The failure to recite the effects of the security is to render the claim one for an unliquidated sum. In accordance with the rules and the Act a bankruptcy petition could not be founded on the debt claimed in this demand and therefore the demand should not succeed and in this form should never have been served. The application should succeed on that ground.'

With all respect to her, I do not agree with the district judge's reasoning. First, r 6.1(5) recognises that it is competent for a secured creditor to put a value on its security and to serve a statutory demand for the amount of the total debt less such value. It appears to me therefore that the net figure resulting from that exercise must be in the nature of 'a liquidated sum' for the purposes of s 267(2)(b); if it is not, I do not see how a demand prepared in purported compliance with r 6.1(5) could ever be a valid demand. Secondly, it appears to me to be within the obvious contemplation of r 6.1(5) that the value which the creditor puts on his security will be a value with which the debtor may disagree. The range of disagreement may be wide or narrow, but its consequence in either case will be that there will in turn be a difference as to the correct amount of the 'liquidated sum' due to the creditor after deduction from the full amount of the debt of the value attributed to the security. Thirdly, in my view the emergence of any such disagreement cannot by itself, and without more, provide a basis for a challenge to the validity of the statutory demand. In particular, it cannot by itself result in the sum claimed in the demand ceasing to be a demand for 'a liquidated sum' and becoming one for an 'unliquidated' sum. Further, the mere fact that there is a wide range between the competing valuations cannot in principle make any difference: the 'liquidated sum' does not become an 'unliquidated sum' merely because the parties are far apart as to whether or not it represents the true amount of the debtor's unsecured indebtedness. Fourthly, one circumstance in which any such disagreement might be of important significance, and might even justify the setting aside of the demand, would be where the debtor was able to claim by credible evidence that the creditor had undervalued the security and that its true value either equalled or exceeded the full amount of the debt. This is the type of case to which r 6.5(4)(c) is directed. However, in such a case the demand would be set aside, not because the debt claimed was not for 'a liquidated sum', but because there was a real issue as to whether, after giving proper credit for the value of the security, the debtor was indebted to the creditor at all. Fifthly, although the society did not specify in the demand the two figures, £X and £Y, which it used in order to arrive at the sum claimed to be due, the debtor does not question that that sum does represent the society's calculation of the debt less the value put by it on the security. Accordingly, I cannot see how the sum so arrived at can be any less 'a liquidated sum' than it would have been if the society had correctly complied with r 6.1(5) and had duly specified both the £X and £Y figures. In the result, I have concluded that the sum claimed in the statutory demand is 'a liquidated sum' and that the first ground upon which the debtor relied in support of her application to set aside the demand is not well founded. In my judgment the district judge was in error in accepting the argument.

(2) The debtor's voluntary arrangement

The evidence relating to this aspect of the matter is as follows. In her affidavit in support of her application to set aside the statutory demand the debtor deposed that she was subject to a voluntary arrangement which was approved by a meeting of creditors held on 8 June 1992 and that it was still in force. In answer to that, Heather Wolstenholme, a partner in the society's former solicitors, deposed that the society had not been given notice of the proposed voluntary arrangement and that therefore it did not attend the meeting of creditors. Miss Wolstenholme went on to make the point that in these circumstances the society was not bound by the arrangement.

The debtor put in some evidence in reply, including an affidavit sworn by Angela Quait. Miss Quait deposed that she was employed by a firm called Sorskys Specialised Financial Services (Sorskys) as an 'individual voluntary arrangement supervisor'. She said that the debtor attended Sorskys' offices on about 18 April 1992 when she was advised by Mr H J Sorsky, a partner, that she should enter into a voluntary arrangement. In response, the debtor provided Sorskys with a list of her creditors, including the society, and on 21 April 1992 Mr Sorsky was appointed her 'nominee' (ie pursuant to s 253(2) of the 1986 Act).

Miss Quait deposes that on 18 May 1992 Mr Sorsky instructed her to notify all the debtor's known creditors of a proposed meeting (ie the s 257 meeting) and that on the same day she sent a notification to each creditor convening it. She exhibited copies of the documents sent to each creditor, and says that the copy bundle sent to the society 'was sent to its head office situate at Bradford and Bingley Building Society, PO Box 88, Crossflats, Bingley, West Yorkshire

BD16 2UA, and has not been returned to me or my employers by the Post Office undelivered'.

The documents said to have been sent to each creditor included, inter alia, (i) a notice pursuant to s 257 of the 1986 Act convening a meeting of creditors on 8 June 1992 for the purpose of considering and, if thought fit, passing the resolution that the debtor's proposed voluntary arrangement be approved and that Mr Sorsky be appointed its supervisor; (ii) the debtor's statement of affairs: that disclosed that she had an interest in three properties (including the society's security), but that each was fully mortgaged, that there was no equity in any of them, and that she had no other assets. The society's debt was shown as £871,570 and its security was shown as being subject also to a second charge in favour of Barclays Bank plc for £68,430. The statement showed that there was a deficiency as regards unsecured creditors of £125,063. That sum represented the total indebtedness due to 13 specified creditors, described as 'non-preferential creditors', not including the society; and (iii) a proposed scheme of arrangement under which the debtor would pay the supervisor £25,000 for the benefit of her creditors over a period of five years, at the rate of £5,000 a year. The source of these moneys was the fee income (forecast at £20,000 a year) expected to be earned by the debtor as a director of a company which she and her husband had formed in 1991.

The meeting of creditors took place on 8 June 1992, when the debtor's voluntary arrangement was approved, although Mr Wessley of Cape and Dalgliesh was appointed supervisor, not Mr Sorsky.

The society's evidence does not in terms challenge Miss Quait's evidence, but is to the effect that it did not receive the notice which Miss Quait says she posted to it and that it was thus ignorant that the s 257 meeting had been convened. Of particular significance for the purposes of Mr Barker's argument before me is the evidence of Mr Andrew Hiller on behalf of the society. He deposes that the Crossflats address (to which Miss Quait says she posted the documents) was not the society's head office until 1 June 1992. Those premises were new premises, which were constructed for the society, and from which it was not fully operational until that date. He also says that the society's mortgage and administration department has never operated from the Crossflats premises, and that until 1 June 1992 the society's head office was at PO Box 2, Main Street, Bingley. He says that at all times, and as known by the debtor, the administration of the relevant mortgage account had been handled by the society's office at PO Box 1, Leamington House, Milverton Hill, Leamington Spa. He adds that, had any correspondence relating to a mortgage been received at the Crossflats address, it would have been sent immediately to the head office at Main Street, Bingley. However, he says that this did not happen in this case, and that the inquiries he has made indicate that no notice of the s 257 meeting was received by the society.

There was no cross-examination of the deponents before the district judge, and the position on the affidavit evidence is that there is in fact no factual conflict between the witnesses: in particular, there is no necessary inconsistency between Miss Quait's evidence that she posted the relevant documentation to the society and the society's evidence that it did not receive it. I understand the district judge to have approached the evidence on the basis that each deponent's evidence must be regarded as correct, and in my view that was the right approach. In the light of that evidence, and for reasons which I shall detail later, the district judge held that the society was bound by the voluntary arrangement which was approved on 8 June 1992 and that it was in consequence precluded from serving the statutory demand.

Mr Barker's submissions in support of this aspect of the society's appeal were as follows. He referred first to r 5.13 of the 1986 rules, which relates to the convening of the meeting of creditors to consider a proposed voluntary arrangement. Rule 5.13(2) provides:

> 'Notices calling the meeting shall be sent by the nominee, at least 14 days before the day fixed for it to be held, to all the creditors specified in the debtor's statement of affairs, and any other creditors of whom the nominee is otherwise aware.'

Mr Barker submitted, and it was not disputed, that notice of the meeting was thus required to be given to the society. In this respect the rule essentially mirrors the requirement of s 257(2) of the 1986 Act, which provides:

> 'The persons to be summoned to the meeting are every creditor of the debtor of whose claim and address the person summoning the meeting is aware.'

Mr Barker referred next to r 12.4(1), to the effect that (subject to immaterial exceptions) notice of the meeting was required to be given in writing; and to r 12.11(1), which provides:

> '(1) Subject to Rule 12.10 and as follows, Order 65 of the Rules of the Supreme Court applies as regards any matter relating to the service of documents and the giving of notice in insolvency proceedings.'

In this case, as to the 'as follows', the remaining provisions of r 12.11 are not material. Mr Barker submitted that nor was r 12.10; and that there had been a non-compliance with the service requirements of RSC Ord 65.

Taking RSC Ord 65 first, the relevant rule is r 5. The material parts of it provide as follows:

> '(1) Service of any document, not being a document which by virtue of any provision of these rules is required to be served personally or a document to which Order 10, rule 1, applies, may be effected—(a) by leaving the document at the proper address of the person to be served, or (b) by post ... (2) For the purposes of this rule ... the proper address of any person on whom a document is to be served in accordance with this rule shall be the address for service of that person, but if at the time when service is effected that person has no address for service his proper address for the purposes aforesaid shall be ... (d) in the case of a body corporate, the registered or principal office of the body.'

Mr Barker submitted that this was a case where proper service could only be effected by posting the notice to, or leaving it at, either the registered or principal office of the society. However, the evidence was to the effect that the Crossflats address to which Miss Quait posted the documents was neither the registered nor the principal office of the society at the time of posting. Therefore, he said, proper notice of the proposed meeting was not sent to the society in accordance with r 12.11 (incorporating RSC Ord 65). He further submitted that r 12.10 does not assist the debtor. That deals with the manner in which postal service can be effected, and with when (unless the contrary is shown) a posted document is to be treated as being served. Its only provision of possible relevance for present purposes is r 12.10(1A), which reads: 'A document to be served by post may be sent to the last known address of the person to be served.' As to that, Mr Barker submitted that, even assuming that the paragraph is capable of applying to postal service on a body corporate such as the society, nevertheless, in the light of Mr Hiller's evidence, the Crossflats address to which the documents were posted cannot then have been regarded as the society's 'last known address'.

Thus, submitted Mr Barker, not only is the evidence to the effect that the society did not receive notice of the s 257 meeting, it also shows that the manner in which notice was purportedly given to it did not comply with the requirements of the 1986 rules. In these circumstances he submitted further that (save perhaps to the limited extent to which I shall refer in a moment) the society is not bound by the voluntary arrangement and was accordingly at liberty to serve a statutory demand on the debtor with a view to the subsequent presentation of a bankruptcy petition against her. He relied on the provisions of s 260 of the 1986 Act, in particular sub-s (2)(b):

'260. *Effect of approval.*—(1) This section has effect where the meeting summoned under section 257 approves the proposed voluntary arrangement (with or without modifications).

(2) The approved arrangement—(a) takes effect as if made by the debtor at the meeting, and (b) binds every person who in accordance with the rules had notice of, and was entitled to vote at, the meeting (whether or not he was present or represented at it) as if he were a party to the arrangement ...'

Mr Barker submitted that the society did not have notice of the meeting, either 'in accordance with the rules' or at all. Therefore it is not one of the persons who, under s 260(2)(b), is bound by the arrangement 'as if he were a party to' it, and it is accordingly entitled to serve a statutory demand and pursue bankruptcy proceedings against the debtor.

If Mr Barker is right thus far in his submissions, then in my view this is as far as he needed to go in order to succeed on this aspect of the appeal. If the society is not bound by the arrangement, then in principle I consider that it must be at liberty to serve a statutory demand with a view, if it is not complied with, to the subsequent presentation of a bankruptcy petition. I did not understand Miss Johnston to dispute this.

However, Mr Barker also submitted that a course which might also have been, or might perhaps still be, open to the society would be to seek an extension of time for applying to the court for the purposes of challenging the voluntary arrangement (see ss 262 and 376 of the 1986 Act); but that, absent any successful such challenge, the society either would or might be bound by the voluntary arrangement at least to the extent (i) that it could not question that it was a valid arrangement at any rate as between the debtor and those creditors who were bound by it under s 260(2)(b) as if they were parties to it; and (ii) that any assets of the debtor which fell to be administered in accordance with the arrangement would, or might, not be assets which would be available to be distributed in a bankruptcy between those creditors (including the society) who were not so bound by the arrangement. In short, he submitted that the assets subject to the voluntary arrangement would, or might, only vest in any trustee in bankruptcy subject to such arrangement.

In support of, in particular, points (i) and (ii) above he referred me to the unreported decision of Morritt J in *Re McKeen* (1 April 1992). That case is distinguishable on its facts from the present one, in that, inter alia, there the creditor on whose petition a bankruptcy order was made was not a creditor at the date when notice of the s 257 meeting was given, but only became such subsequently (in this respect the summary of the case in *Muir Hunter on Personal Insolvency* (1987) p 3024 appears to me to be inaccurate). However, Mr Barker submitted that that distinction did not affect the points of principle to be found in *Re McKeen* relevant to his submissions.

These last submissions of Mr Barker appeared to me to lead to potentially difficult territory; further, they raised questions of an essentially future nature, and also having a potential impact on persons not before the court. In view of this, and having regard also to the relatively narrow front on which Miss Johnston argued this aspect of the appeal, I have concluded that it is both unnecessary and inappropriate for me to express any view on these particular submissions. In so concluding I make clear that I intend no discourtesy to Mr Barker, and I am grateful to him for his arguments.

Turning now to the submissions in support of the district judge's judgment, Miss Johnston did not join issue with most of the steps in Mr Barker's argument. In particular, she did not seek to argue that, on the evidence, I should conclude that proper notice of the s 257 meeting was given to the society in accordance with the 1986 rules, although she made no express admission that it was not. In this connection, I should perhaps comment that whilst there is evidence as to where the society's head office was at the material times, there is, I think, no evidence as to where, if different, its registered office was at such times. Thus, there is no evidence that the Crossflats address (to which Miss Quait posted the documentation) was not in fact the society's registered office at the time of posting. However, the argument proceeded before me on the silent assumption that it was not.

Miss Johnston's principal point was instead that, even though the society had no actual notice of the s 257 meeting, it nevertheless had constructive notice of it; it was therefore bound in all respects by the voluntary arrangement as if it were a party to it and it was therefore precluded from serving the statutory demand, since to do so would be to flout the arrangement by which it was so bound: there was no evidence of any default in connection with the voluntary arrangement and therefore no basis for the making of a bankruptcy order against the debtor (see ss 264(1)(c) and 276(1) of the 1986 Act). Her argument was, in its essentials, a repeat of the argument which had found favour with the district judge. The notes of the relevant part of the district judge's judgment are as follows:

'[The debtor] also brings the application on the basis that she is protected by a voluntary arrangement. [The society] argues that it did not receive notice of the creditors meeting. There is no doubt that for a creditor to be bound by a voluntary arrangement there must have been notice given. I have to accept that the postal rule on service must be relevant. It is not an absolute protection as unless one is satisfactorily satisfied otherwise, service is deemed to have taken place. Postal service has never allowed the person claiming the benefit to rely upon the same when there is proof to the contrary. This does not entirely help [the society] because there is also the principle of constructive notice and in this regard I rely upon the observations contained in *Muir Hunter* at p 3024, namely, "Furthermore, if that creditor had received 'constructive notice' of the summoning of the meeting of creditors, in other words, if the notice was sent to him, although he did not receive it, it is submitted that in accordance with this section [ie s 260 of the 1986 Act] and Rule 12.16 ... not only would the meeting have been duly summoned and held, but the creditor concerned would be bound by the meeting's decision". I cannot find any observation which causes me to doubt that it is right. To disregard the principle of postal service and the concept of constructive notice would then be to place on the rules and on the Act an unworkable interpretation. It would enable potentially an unscrupulous creditor, and I do not intend for a moment to impute that to [the society], as Miss Johnston puts it "to throw over the democratic process". There must be provision to contend with that and there is so within the concept of constructive notice. [The society] would have failed on the second ground—I find on the basis of the situation as it presents itself that the voluntary arrangement binds the creditor.'

As I understand it, the reasoning adopted by the district judge was therefore as follows: (i) the society had rebutted any presumption which might otherwise have arisen that it had received notice of the convening of the s 257 meeting in the ordinary course of the post; (ii) therefore it did not have actual notice of the meeting; (iii) nevertheless, it did have constructive notice of it, because notice of the meeting had been posted to it, albeit not received; (iv) therefore it was bound by the voluntary arrangement as if it were a party to it and was thus precluded from serving the statutory demand. Is this reasoning correct?

One of the material considerations which apparently formed part of the district judge's reasoning leading to step (iii) above was r 12.16 of the 1986 rules, which provides:

'*Non-receipt of notice of meeting.* Where in accordance with the Act or the Rules a meeting of creditors or other persons is summoned by notice, the meeting is presumed to have been duly summoned and held, notwithstanding that not all those to whom the notice is to be given have received it.'

I comment first that, in my view, for the presumption under that rule to apply, it is a necessary precondition that those convening the meeting should have taken proper steps to summon it in accordance with the Act and the Rules. Thus, in the present case, the nominee's duty pursuant to r 5.13(2) was to give or send notice to each creditor referred to in the statement of affairs, or otherwise known to him, and to do so in compliance with the provisions of r 12.11. The giving of such notice did not have to be by way of personal service, but could be by post. However, provided that notice was duly sent or given to all creditors entitled to receive it, then, even if any creditor did not actually receive it, r 12.16 raises a presumption that the meeting has nevertheless been 'duly summoned and held'.

I shall assume first, without deciding, that in the circumstances of the present case, the meeting of 8 June 1992 would be presumed by r 12.16 to have been duly summoned and held, an assumption which is the most favourable to the debtor for present purposes. On this assumption, but accepting (as is admitted) that the society had no actual notice of the meeting, is it nevertheless open to the society to deny that it is one of the persons whom s 260(2)(b) provides are bound by the arrangement approved at the meeting? The district judge appears to have answered 'No' to this question. However, I respectfully disagree. I draw attention to the fact that, in specifying whether or not a creditor is bound by the arrangement, s 260(2)(b) focuses on whether or not he 'had notice of' the meeting (ie, in my view, had received notice of it). By contrast, the presumed validation of a meeting under r 12.16 depends essentially on whether or not the notice was duly sent, whether or not actually received. Further, the only presumption that r 12.16 in terms raises is as to the validity of the summoning and holding of the meeting: it does not purport also to raise a presumption that a creditor had notice of the meeting when in fact he had none.

In my judgment, these considerations point to the conclusion that, even though a s 257 meeting may be presumed by r 12.16 to have been duly summoned and held, nevertheless a creditor who had no actual notice of it will not be bound by any arrangement which was approved at it. The reason why he is not so bound is that s 260(2)(b) provides that the arrangement binds those persons (and, in my view, only those persons) who, inter alia, had 'notice' of the meeting, whereas such creditor had none.

In coming to a different view the district judge appears to have been much influenced by the sentence which she quoted from *Muir Hunter*, a sentence which was also central to Miss Johnston's argument. Counsel were not agreed as to the nature of the point which was being made in that sentence. In my view, in order to understand the sentence, it is necessary to read it in its context, and so I shall set out the whole of the main part of the commentary (on s 260 of the Act) in which it appears. The relevant passages are as follows, starting at p 3024:

'*Clause (b)*

Persons bound by the decision Every person who had notice of the meeting, and was entitled to vote at it (whether or not he was present or represented there) is bound by the approved arrangement, as if he were himself a party to it. It appears therefore to be of the utmost importance to the debtor, and to his nominee and to their respective advisers, to ensure that all persons entitled (under the Rules) to receive such notice, so that they may attend and vote, do receive such notice. If one or more of them do not receive such a notice, then in the absence of any Rule introducing some form of "constructive notice", a "creditor" (within the very wide definition referred to in s 257(3), *ante*) who did not receive such notice, would not be bound: but *vide infra* ...

Consequences of failure to bind a creditor by the arrangement The question arises, what will be the consequences of the failure, through lack of, or defective, notice, to bind a creditor, and whether this may expose the arrangement to a destructive "challenge" (whether or not in the s. 262 sense), so as to deprive the debtor, and the assenting creditors, of the security they did not enjoy under the Deeds of Arrangement Act 1914, this was the protection which was the principal objective of the enactment of the voluntary arrangements procedure. It may well be the case that the debtor will be exposed to the risk of a bankruptcy petition at the suit of a 'non-bound' creditor; but it does not follow that any such bankruptcy proceedings could invalidate the arrangement, so far as concerns the creditors' interest therein, and profit therefrom. Any such bankruptcy petition by a non-bound creditor with a suitable provable debt will no longer (as it would have done under the Act of 1914, *ipso facto*) upset the arrangement as constituting an act of bankruptcy; for in view of the elimination of the acts of bankruptcy doctrine, the arrangement, once approved, will have become complete without the participation of that creditor. There seems to be no machinery to set aside the approved proposal constituting the arrangement, in so far as it affects a disposition of the debtor's property. Furthermore, if that creditor had received "constructive notice" of the summoning of the meeting of creditors, in other words, if the notice was sent to him, although he did not receive it, it is submitted that in accordance with this section and r. 12.16, *post*, not only would the meeting have been duly summoned and held, but the creditor concerned would be bound by the meeting's decision.'

If the last sentence, the one relied on by the district judge, is taken in isolation, and out of context, then its natural interpretation is that, provided notice of a s 257 meeting has been duly sent in accordance with the rules, a creditor to whom notice was so sent will be bound by the voluntary arrangement approved at the meeting as if he were a party to it, even though he did not actually receive such notice, and therefore had no actual notice of the meeting. Miss Johnston submitted that this is what the sentence means, and that in this respect it is correct as a matter of law. It appears to me that the district judge also interpreted the sentence in this sense.

Mr Barker submitted that the sentence ought not to be interpreted in this way, and drew attention to the fact that it appears in a passage under the sub-heading 'Consequences of failure to bind a creditor by the arrangement' and that (but subject, as it seems to me, to the effect of the 'vide infra') the authors had expressed a view to the contrary effect in the preceding passage under the sub-heading 'Persons bound by the decision'. He submitted that the intended sense of the sentence in the context in which it appears is that, where an arrangement has been approved at a meeting which is presumed by r 12.16 to have been duly summoned and held, a creditor who had no actual notice of the meeting may nevertheless be bound by it at any rate to the extent that he may not be able to set the decision of the meeting aside: but that it is not also intended to mean that such creditor will be bound by the arrangement in the further sense that he is to be treated as a party to it.

I do not propose to express a view on these rival submissions as to the intended meaning of the sentence. If, however, it is intended to bear the wider meaning which the district judge appears to have attached to it, then I would respectfully disagree with it. I, in any event, respectfully disagree with the suggestion in it that a creditor who does not receive, and remains in ignorance of, the notice of a meeting which is sent to him can (in the bare circumstances apparently envisaged by *Muir Hunter*) nevertheless still have 'constructive notice' of such meeting. A person ordinarily only has 'constructive notice' of a fact when he is put on notice of matters whose investigation would lead him to discover it, an investigation which he abstains from making; or where he anyway deliberately or carelessly fails to make inquiries which a prudent person in his position ought to have made and which, if made, would have led him to discovery of the fact. However, a creditor, such as the society, which never received a notice of a meeting which is said to have been sent to it, cannot in my view, and without more, be said to have 'constructive notice' of the convening of the meeting. In particular, and as I have earlier pointed out, r 12.16 does not deem the creditor to have had notice of the meeting: it merely provides (in effect) that the non-receipt by him of a notice duly sent will not by itself be sufficient to enable him to say that the meeting had not been duly summoned and held.

In the result I conclude that the district judge misdirected herself as to the law with regard to this limb of the debtor's application. In my judgment she should instead have concluded that the society had no notice of the s 257 meeting; that s 260(2)(b) therefore showed that it was not one of the debtor's creditors which was bound by the voluntary arrangement; and that it was entitled to serve a statutory demand on the debtor with a view, if the same was not complied with, to the subsequent presentation of a bankruptcy petition.

Having reached this conclusion, it is not necessary for me to express any view on whether, on the facts which emerge from the evidence before the court, the s 257 meeting held on 8 June 1992 would in fact be presumed by r 12.16 to have been duly summoned and held. Whether or not it would is a matter which may have consequences affecting other creditors who are not before the court and therefore I regard it as inappropriate to say any more about it.

Conclusion

I have therefore come to the conclusion that the district judge was in error on both the grounds on which she acceded to the debtor's application. I allow the society's appeal.

Appeal allowed.

Hazel Hartman Barrister.

Customs and Excise Commissioners v Schindler and another
(Case C-275/92)

COURT OF JUSTICE OF THE EUROPEAN COMMUNITIES

JUDGES DUE (PRESIDENT), MANCINI, MOITINHO DE ALMEIDA, DÍEZ DE VELASCO (PRESIDENTS OF CHAMBERS), KAKOURIS, SCHOCKWEILER, RODRÍGUEZ IGLESIAS, GRÉVISSE (RAPPORTEUR), ZULEEG, KAPTEYN AND MURRAY

22 SEPTEMBER, 16 DECEMBER 1993, 24 MARCH 1994

European Economic Community – Freedom of movement – Services – Lottery – Advertisements, application forms and tickets – Whether importation of advertisements, applications and tickets for lottery activities relating to 'goods' – Whether activities 'services' – Whether national legislation prohibiting holding of lotteries an obstacle to freedom to provide services – Whether national legislation justifiable on grounds of social policy and prevention of fraud – Revenue Act 1898, s 1(ii) – Lotteries and Amusements Act 1976, s 2 – EEC Treaty, arts 30, 36, 56, 59, 60.

The defendants were independent agents of a public body (SKL) which was responsible for organising 'class' lotteries on behalf of four Länder of the Federal Republic of Germany and as such they promoted and sold tickets for SKL lotteries. The defendants dispatched from the Netherlands to United Kingdom nationals envelopes which each contained an invitation to participate in one of the SKL lotteries, an application form for participating in it and a preprinted reply envelope. The envelopes were confiscated by the Customs and Excise on the ground that they had been imported in breach of s 1(ii)[a] of the Revenue Act 1898 and s 2[b] of the Lotteries and Amusements Act 1976, which prohibited the importation for publication in the United Kingdom of advertisements or other notices relating to lotteries in contravention of any Act relating to lotteries. In proceedings brought by the Commissioners of Customs and Excise for the condemnation of the items seized the defendants contended that s 1 of the 1898 Act and s 2 of the 1976 Act were incompatible with art 30[c] or alternatively art 59[d] of the EEC Treaty since they prohibited the importation into a member state of the European Communities of tickets, letters and application forms relating to a lottery lawfully conducted in another member state. The commissioners contended that tickets and advertisements for a lottery did not constitute 'goods' within the meaning of the Treaty, that neither art 30 nor art 59 applied to the prohibition on importation in the United Kingdom legislation since that legislation applied to all large-scale lotteries whatever their origin and that in any event the prohibition was justified by the United Kingdom government's concern to limit lotteries for social policy reasons and to prevent fraud. The Queen's Bench Division stayed the

---

a Section 1 is set out at p 223 g, post
b Section 2, so far as material, is set out at p 223 j to p 224 b, post
c Article 30, so far as material, provides: 'Quantitative restrictions on imports and all measures having equivalent effect shall ... be prohibited between Member States.'
d Article 59, so far as material, provides: '... restrictions on freedom to provide services within the Community shall be ... abolished ... in respect of nationals of Member States who are established in a State of the Community other than that of the person for whom the services are intended ...'

proceedings and referred to the Court of Justice of the European Communities for a preliminary ruling under art 177 of the Treaty the questions, inter alia, whether tickets in or advertisements for a lottery lawfully conducted in another member state constituted goods for the purposes of the prohibition on quantitative restrictions on imports between member states contained in art 30, whether the provision of tickets in or the sending of advertisements for a lottery lawfully conducted in another member state constituted the provision of services for the purposes of the abolition of restrictions on freedom to provide services within the Community provided for in art 59 and whether the concerns of the United Kingdom to limit lotteries for social policy reasons and to prevent fraud constituted legitimate public policy or public morality considerations, whether under art 36[e] or art 56[f] or otherwise, which justified the restrictions of which complaint was made.

Held – (1) Although the activity pursued by the defendants appeared to be limited to sending advertisements, application forms and possibly tickets on behalf of SKL, those activities were only specific steps in the organisation or operation of a lottery and could not, under the EEC Treaty, be considered independently to the lottery to which they related, their sole purpose being to enable residents of the member states where those objects were imported and distributed to participate in the lottery. It followed, therefore, that lottery activities were not activities relating to 'goods' for the purposes of art 30. They were, however, 'services' within the meaning of the Treaty, being the services provided by the lottery operator to enable purchasers of lottery tickets to participate in the lottery, and were cross-border services when they were in a member state other than the one in which the lottery operator was established. Consequently, the importation of lottery advertisements and tickets into a member state with a view to the participation by residents of that state in a lottery operated in another member state related to a 'service' within art 60[g] of the EEC Treaty and accordingly fell within the scope of art 59 of the Treaty (see p 226 c e g h, p 227 j and p 231 a, post).

(2) National legislation could fall within the ambit of art 59 of the Treaty, even if it was applicable without distinction, when it was liable to prohibit or otherwise impede the activities of a provider of services established in another member state where he lawfully provided similar services, as did the United Kingdom legislation on lotteries, which precluded lottery operators from other member states from promoting their lotteries and selling their tickets, whether directly or through independent agents, in the United Kingdom. Accordingly, national legislation which, like the United Kingdom legislation on lotteries, prohibited, subject to specified exceptions, the holding of lotteries in a member state was an obstacle to the freedom to provide services (see p 228 d to f and p 231 b, post); *Säger v Dennemeyer & Co Ltd* Case C-76/90 [1991] ECR I-4221 applied.

---

e   Article 36, so far as material, provides: 'The provisions of Articles 30 to 34 shall not preclude prohibitions or restrictions on imports ... on grounds of public morality, public policy ...'
f   Article 56, so far as material, provides: '1. The provisions of [inter alia, art 59: vide art 66 of the EEC Treaty] and measures taken in pursuance thereof shall not prejudice the applicability of provisions laid down by law ... providing for special treatment for foreign nationals on grounds of public policy ...'
g   Article 60, so far as material, is set out at p 226 f, post

(3) On the facts, the United Kingdom legislation did not discriminate on the basis of the nationality of the economic agents concerned or of the member state in which they were established. Furthermore, the objectives of that legislation, which were to prevent crime and ensure that gamblers were treated honestly, to avoid stimulating demand in the gambling sector which had damaging social consequences when taken to excess and to ensure that lotteries could not be operated for personal and commercial profit but solely for charitable, sporting or cultural purposes, concerned the protection of the recipients of the service and, more generally, of consumers as well as the maintenance of order in society and justified restrictions, as regarded art 59 of the Treaty, which might go so far as to prohibit lotteries in a member state. Accordingly, the provisions of the Treaty relating to freedom to provide services did not preclude legislation such as the United Kingdom lotteries legislation, in view of the concerns of social policy and of the prevention of fraud which justified it (see p 228 *h j*, p 229 *c d h* to p 230 *h* and p 231 *b*, post); *Société Générale Alsacienne de Banque SA v Koestler* Case 15/78 [1978] ECR 1971 at 1981 (para 5), *Ministère Public v Van Wesemael* Joined cases 110 and 111/78 [1979] ECR 35 at 52 (para 28) and *EC Commission v France* Case 220/83 [1986] ECR 3663 at 3709 (para 20) applied.

Notes

For the freedom to provide services within the European Community and derogations from the Treaty provisions relating thereto, see 52 *Halsbury's Laws* (4th edn) paras 16·01, 16·05, 16·23, and for cases on the subject, see 21 *Digest* (Reissue) 270–271, *1753–1758*.

For the Revenue Act 1898, s 1, see 13 *Halsbury's Statutes* (4th edn) (1991 reissue) 60.

For the Lotteries and Amusements Act 1976, s 2, see 5 *Halsbury's Statutes* (4th edn) (1993 reissue) 214.

For the EEC Treaty, arts 30, 36, 56, 59, 60, 177, see 50 *Halsbury's Statutes* (4th edn) 276, 278, 286, 287, 288, 325.

As from 21 December 1993 the National Lottery etc Act 1993 amended s 1 of the 1898 Act and s 2 of the 1976 Act so as to relax the importation and exportation restrictions therein.

Cases cited

Bachmann v Belgium Case C-204/90 [1992] ECR I 249.
Bond van Adverteerders v Netherlands Case 352/85 [1988] ECR 2085.
Champion v Ames (Lottery Case) (1903) 188 US 321, US SC.
Cinéthèque SA v Fédération nationale des cinémas français Joined cases 60 and 61/84 [1985] ECR 2605.
Cowan v Trésor public Case 186/87 [1989] ECR 195.
Donà v Mantero Case 13/76 [1976] ECR 1333.
EC Commission v France Case 220/83 [1986] ECR 3663.
EC Commission v France Case C-154/89 [1991] ECR I-659.
EC Commission v Germany Case 205/84 [1986] ECR 3755.
EC Commission v Greece Case C-198/89 [1991] ECR I-727.
EC Commission v Italy Case C-180/89 [1991] ECR I-709.
EC Commission v Italy Case C-272/91 (pending), CJEC.
EC Commission v Netherlands Case C-353/89 [1991] ECR I-4069.
Einberger v Hauptzollamt Freiburg Case 294/82 [1984] ECR 1177.

196   All England Law Reports   [1994] 2 All ER

GB-INNO-BM v Confédération du commerce luxembourgeois Case C-362/88 [1990] ECR I-667.
Keck, Criminal proceedings against Joined cases C-267/91 and C-268/91 (1993) Times, 25 November 1993, CJEC.
Ministère Public v Van Wesemael Joined cases 110 and 111/78 [1979] ECR 35.
Procureur du Roi v Dassonville Case 8/74 [1974] ECR 837.
Procureur du Roi v Debauve Case 52/79 [1980] ECR 833.
R v Bouchereau Case 30/77 [1981] 2 All ER 924, [1978] QB 732, [1978] 2 WLR 250, [1977] ECR 1999, CJEC.
R v Thompson Case 7/78 [1980] 2 All ER 102, [1980] QB 229, [1980] 2 WLR 521, [1978] ECR 2247, CJEC.
Säger v Dennemeyer & Co Ltd Case C-76/90 [1991] ECR I-4221.
Société Générale Alsacienne de Banque SA v Koestler Case 15/78 [1978] ECR 1971.
Society for the Protection of Unborn Children Ireland Ltd v Grogan Case C-159/90 [1991] ECR I-4685.
Steymann v Staatssecretaris van Justitie Case 196/87 [1988] ECR 6159.
Stoke-on-Trent City Council v B & Q plc Case C-169/91 [1993] 1 All ER 481, [1993] AC 900, [1993] 2 WLR 730, [1992] ECR I-6635, CJEC.
Walrave and Koch v Association Union Cycliste Internationale Case 36/74 [1974] ECR 1405.
Webb, Criminal proceedings against Case 279/80 [1981] ECR 3305.

Reference
By an order dated 3 April 1992 the Queen's Bench Division of the High Court of Justice referred to the Court of Justice of the European Communities for a preliminary ruling under art 177 of the EEC Treaty six questions (set out at p 224, post) on the interpretation of arts 30, 36, 56 and 59 of the Treaty in order to determine whether national legislation prohibiting the holding of certain lotteries in a member state was compatible with those provisions. The questions were raised in the course of proceedings between the Commissioners of Customs and Excise, the plaintiffs in the main proceedings, and Gerhart and Jörg Schindler, the defendants in the main proceedings, concerning the dispatch of advertisements and application forms for a lottery organised in the Federal Republic of Germany to United Kingdom nationals. Written observations were submitted on behalf of the defendants, by Mark Brealey, barrister, the Belgian government, by Jan Devadder, Principal Director in the Ministry of Foreign Affairs, Foreign Trade and Co-operation with Developing Countries, acting as agent, and Ph Vlaemminck, of the Ghent Bar, the Danish government, by Jørgen Molde, Legal Adviser at the Ministry of Foreign Affairs, acting as agent, the German government, by Ernst Röder, Ministerialrat in the Federal Ministry of Economic Affairs, acting as agent, the Greek government, by Vassileios Kontolaimos, Assistant Legal Adviser, and Ioannis Chalkias, legal representative, of the State Legal Service, acting as agents, the Spanish government, by Alberto Navarro González, Director General for Community Legal and Institutional Co-ordination, and Miguel Bravo-Ferrer Delgado, State Attorney in the Legal Department for Matters before the Court of Justice, acting as agents, the French government, by Philippe Pouzoulet, Deputy Director in the Legal Affairs Directorate of the Ministry of Foreign Affairs, and Hélène Duchène, Secretary of Foreign Affairs, acting as agents, the Luxembourg government, by Charles Elsen, Principal Government Adviser, acting as agent, assisted by René Diederich, of the Luxembourg Bar, the Netherlands government, by A Bos, Legal Adviser in the

Ministry of Foreign Affairs, acting as agent, the United Kingdom, by Susan Cochrane, Treasury Solicitor's Department, acting as agent, and David Pannick QC, of the Bar of England and Wales, and the Commission of the European Communities, by Richard Wainwright, Legal Adviser, and Arnold Ridout, a United Kingdom civil servant on secondment to the Legal Service of the Commission, acting as agents. Oral observations were presented to the court by the defendants, the Belgian government, the German government, represented by Mrs Bargmann-Huber, Ministerialrätin at the Interior Ministry for Bavaria, acting as agent, the Greek government, the Spanish government, the French government, the Irish government, represented by Mary Finlay, Senior Counsel, acting as agent, the Luxembourg government, the Netherlands government, represented by J W de Zwaan, Assistant Legal Adviser at the Ministry of Foreign Affairs, acting as agent, the Portuguese government, represented by Luis Fernandes, Director of the Legal Service of the Directorate General of the European Communities of the Ministry of Foreign Affairs, and Rogério Leitão, Professor at the Institute of European Studies of the University of Lusíada, acting as agents, the United Kingdom, represented by John Collins, Assistant Treasury Solicitor, acting as agent, and Stephen Richards, barrister, and the Commission of the European Communities. The language of the case was English. The facts are set out in the judgment of the Court of Justice.

16 December 1993. **The Advocate General (C Gulmann)** delivered the following opinion[1].

Mr President, Members of the Court,
1. In the legal systems of all the member states there is a fundamental prohibition on lotteries and other forms of games of chance. The reasons for the prohibitions are broadly the same. Lotteries and games of chance are activities which, for ethical and social reasons, should not be permitted. Citizens should be protected against the dangers that may stem from the urge to gamble and there is a significant risk of criminality in this field.

But at the same time in all member states there are to a greater or lesser extent exceptions from that prohibition. That is because it may be appropriate to permit some measure of gambling, partly to meet the citizens' desire to gamble and partly to prevent unlawful gambling. It is possible to lay down requirements concerning permitted forms of gambling in such a way as to limit the risk of criminality. In addition a significant factor in all the member states is that it is possible to make authorisation subject to conditions whereby the revenue from gambling is used for public-interest purposes or accrues to the state exchequer.

2. The lotteries sector, with which the present case is concerned, is characterised by the fact that in most of the member states there is one or more large country-wide lottery which is either operated directly by the public authorities or is subject to tight public controls and there are also rules under which small local lotteries are permitted subject to certain conditions, in particular as regards their revenue. Moreover, according to the information given, there are prohibitions or far-reaching restrictions on the activities of foreign lotteries in the member states[2].

---

1 Translated from the Danish
2 See point 41 of the order for reference.

The internal market has thus not been achieved in the lotteries sector. The large country-wide lotteries have been given exclusive rights and they are to a large extent protected against competition from foreign lotteries.

3. In the present case the Court of Justice is called on to determine whether the rules in the EEC Treaty are applicable in this sector and if so whether the restrictions which apply to the activities of foreign lottery operators are compatible with the Treaty.

The case is thus of considerable practical and fundamental interest and all the member states except Italy have submitted their observations.

4. The questions referred to the Court of Justice for a preliminary ruling have been raised in a case in which an English court must rule on the compatibility with Community law of the seizure of advertising material for a foreign lottery pursuant to United Kingdom legislation which at the material time prohibited lotteries apart from specified local lotteries, that is to say at a time when there was no large country-wide lottery in the United Kingdom.

Gambling and the regulation of gambling in the member states

5. It may be appropriate to supplement these introductory remarks by a short overview of the various forms of gambling in the member states and the regulations applying thereto.

6. This information is largely taken from a report published by the Commission on gambling in the internal market[3]. The Report, which points out that the figures used therein relate to 1989 and are to be treated with caution, sub-divides the gambling market into a number of product sectors with the following market shares at Community level:

national lotteries and the like	36%
horse-racing and the like	31%
casinos	17%
gaming machines	11%
bingo etc	5%

Total turnover, that is to say the sums staked in the legal gambling sector, was estimated at just over ECU 45,000 million.

7. The report shows that there are major differences between the gambling markets in the various member states.

As a result of those national differences in the market for horse-racing betting, for example, the United Kingdom and France had 55% and 30% respectively of the total market at Community level while the lottery market[4]—in respect of which the Report includes only figures for the large country-wide lotteries but on the other hand includes figures from betting on football and other sports (Toto/football pools)—was distributed as follows amongst the national markets:

---

3 *Gambling in the Single Market: A study of the Current Legal and Market Situation* vols 1, 2 and 3 (June 1991) (the 'Commission report'). The report was prepared for the Commission by the accountants Coopers & Lybrand and it is stated that the report 'does not necessarily represent the Commission's official position'. Underlying the report is a distinction between betting and gaming. Betting is defined as a game where a financial stake is wagered against the outcome of an event. Betting involves an element of knowledge of the event concerned. Gaming, on the other hand, is defined as the wagering of a stake against the outcome of an event in which no skill element is involved. That form of gaming is thus called games of chance. Lotteries are games of chance.

Germany	28·5%
Spain	26·0%
France	16·0%
Italy	11·0%
United Kingdom (presumably only football pools)	6·0%
The other member states	12·5%

8. The Commission report thus emphasises that the gambling market is made up of highly differentiated national markets and that that reflects different national traditions and preferences and differing national regimes[5].

9. The Report also states that the gambling market today must not least be seen as an important source of state revenue.

That is striking in the lottery sector too. It is apparent from the Commission Report and also from the observations submitted in this case that the states either retain revenues from lotteries for themselves (and pay them into the public exchequer) or require that revenues be used for purposes in the public interest (in some cases after deduction from the revenue of taxes for the public exchequer). In some member states winners have to pay tax on their winnings. According to the information that has been given, no country-wide lotteries operated on a commercial basis, by private undertakings which may decide on the use of revenue themselves, are permitted.

The proportion of the total turnover which, as revenue, is to be paid into the state exchequer or used for purposes in the public interest varies somewhat from one member state to another but in all cases it is a relatively high proportion of total turnover, typically between 25% and 40%.

10. Even if the basic principle is the same in all the member states, namely that lotteries are prohibited unless they have been specifically authorised or comply with general conditions for specified, normally local, operators, there are considerable differences as regards the operators who are given authorisation. As mentioned above, in most member states the large country-wide lotteries are operated by the public authorities themselves or by state companies. It is also possible for lottery concessions to be granted to companies which are responsible for holding lotteries on behalf of the state. Finally, there are instances in many member states of lotteries being held at national level by benevolent organisations which finance part of their operations with the revenues from the lotteries they organise.

11. It is apparent from the Commission report[6] that to a certain limited—but, because of technical developments, increasing—extent there is to be found cross-border sale of lottery tickets. In particular, lottery tickets for the German Class Lotteries are sold in Belgium, Denmark, the Netherlands and

---

4   Lotteries are characterised by a pooling of all the stakes and a high win/low stake ratio. The lottery market today is dominated by lotto. Class lotteries, like lotteries in general, consist of the sale of numbered tickets from which one or more winning numbers are subsequently drawn. In class lotteries players take part in several draws (classes) with a single ticket. The various class lotteries have adopted specific rules on the number of draws in each class. There are also other forms of lotteries. One example is the 'instant lottery', where the 'draw' is carried out immediately in that the player for example can scratch part of the lottery ticket and immediately see whether he has won. According to the Commission report the breakdown of the market for lotteries and the like was as follows: 'classic' lotteries—25%, lotto—46%, the toto (betting on sport)—22%, and 'instant lotteries'—6%.

5   See vol 1, p 3 of the report.
6   Volume 1, pp 3, 18.

Luxembourg. The Commission report points out that the United Kingdom market is particularly interesting for foreign lottery operators since there has hitherto been no possibility there of taking part in large lotteries. It is presumed that cross-border gambling is a 'market-driven phenomenon' since consumers are primarily attracted by the size of prizes.

12. The United Kingdom lottery market has hitherto differed from the lottery markets in the other member states.

The United Kingdom legislation lays down a general prohibition on the organisation of lotteries. Exceptions are made from that prohibition only in respect of certain specified local lotteries promoted either by local authorities or by organisations or the like where the profit is destined for 'good causes'.

One consequence is that it has not been possible for country-wide lotteries to be held and a prohibition has also applied to the sale of lottery tickets in or the marketing of foreign lotteries[7].

13. That legal position, which obtained at the material time in this case (April 1990), has now been altered in key respects. On the basis of a White Paper in March 1992[8] a law was adopted on 21 October 1993 on the establishment of a national lottery (National Lottery etc Act 1993) to be operated by a concession-holder under public control, the profit from which is destined for purposes in the public interest. The legislation has also been amended to allow the import of lottery tickets from lotteries in other member states but the prohibition on at least certain forms of promotion of foreign lotteries remains.

It is apparent from the White Paper that those amendments should be seen in the light of the technical developments which at one and the same time open up the possibility of extensive cross-border lottery operations and render difficult the maintenance of the ban on such operations[9].

The background to the questions referred for a preliminary ruling and their content

14. Gerhart Schindler acts, together with his brother Jörg Schindler, as an independent agent for the Süddeutsche Klassenlotterie. In 1990 they sent as a mass mailshot from the Netherlands some 20,000 individually addressed envelopes to persons resident in the United Kingdom. Each envelope contained a letter inviting the addressee to participate in the 87th issue of the Süddeutsche Klassenlotterie, application forms and a reply envelope on which was printed an address in the Netherlands[10].

---

7   The United Kingdom stated at the hearing that there is no ban on private individuals buying lottery tickets and importing them into the United Kingdom for their own use.
8   *A National Lottery: Raising Money for Good Causes* (Cm 1861 (1992)).
9   According to the White Paper: '8. Recently, concern about the potential impact of lotteries from other European Community countries following the completion of the Single European Market on 1 January 1993 has given a new stimulus to the debate about a national lottery ... 9. However, even if our prohibition on foreign lotteries is maintained in law, the Government recognises that it would become increasingly difficult to enforce in practice. Without a national lottery of our own, the United Kingdom market would continue to be attractive to lotteries from other EC countries and elsewhere. 10. It is undoubtedly true that modern technology will make it increasingly difficult to prevent our citizens seeing advertising for, and participating in, foreign lotteries ... Many foreign broadcasts are already available on satellite television. Cheaper telecommunications, and new means of payment, might in due course make participation in a foreign lottery as easy as a phone call. The British public might therefore be able to participate in lotteries benefiting the citizens of other countries but not their own.'

15. Her Majesty's Customs seized all the letters and application forms on the grounds that they had been imported into the United Kingdom in breach of the law. The customs authorities subsequently brought an action against Gerhart and Jörg Schindler for a declaration that the seizure, which had been contested by the brothers, was lawful.

16. The High Court of Justice (Queen's Bench Division) has asked six questions pursuant to art 177 of the EEC Treaty.

Questions 1 and 4 seek to ascertain whether tickets in, or advertisements for, a lottery which is lawfully conducted in another member state constitute goods for the purposes of art 30 of the EEC Treaty or whether the provision of tickets in, or the sending of advertisements for, such a lottery constitutes the provision of services for the purposes of art 59 of the EEC Treaty.

Questions 2 and 5 seek to ascertain whether either art 30 or art 59 applies 'to the prohibition by the United Kingdom of the importation of tickets or advertisements for major lotteries, given that the restrictions imposed by United Kingdom law on the conduct of such lotteries within the United Kingdom apply without discrimination on grounds of nationality and irrespective of whether the lottery is organised from outside or within the United Kingdom'.

If the answer is affirmative, questions 3 and 6 seek a ruling on whether 'the concerns of the United Kingdom to limit lotteries for social policy reasons and to prevent fraud constitute legitimate public policy or public morality considerations to justify the restrictions of which complaint is made, whether under Article 36' or 'under Article 56 read with Article 66 or otherwise.'

17. The observations that have been submitted in this case show the need to examine the following questions:

(1) To what extent is the establishment and operation of lotteries an 'economic activity' falling within the scope of the Treaty?

(2) Do tickets and advertising for lotteries constitute goods within the meaning of art 30 or services within the meaning of art 59?

(3) Is the ban on imports discriminatory?

(4) If not, does it constitute a restriction on the free movement of goods or services which is in principle incompatible with the Treaty?

(5) Can the grounds which are relied on justify such a restriction?

(6) Is the restriction necessary and proportionate to the objects that are being pursued?

---

10 The Süddeutsche Klassenlotterie is a public institution established by the four German Länder of Bavaria, Hessen, Baden-Württemberg and the Rheinland Palatinate and has an annual turnover of some DM700m. The management of the lottery is supervised by a state lottery committee which has to approve the budget and the annual accounts. Agents, who must meet specified requirements as to personal and professional qualifications, are expected to promote the lottery but under the rules of the Süddeutsche Klassenlotterie may not promote the lottery in states where that is prohibited. The agents receive a commission for every ticket sold. The Süddeutsche Klassenlotterie is a lottery in which players buy whole tickets or fractions of tickets which are entered in several draws in each class. There are two lotteries a year. Each lottery runs for a period of 26 weeks. The draws are spread over six classes, with four draws in classes 1 to 5 and six draws in class 6. In practice there is one draw each week throughout the year. Tickets are issued for each class separately. Class 6 offers the highest prize (in the lottery in question in the main proceedings, the highest prize was DM4m). The attraction of the class lottery lies in the very high main prize and also the relatively high chance of recovering the stake. See also paras 34 to 38 of the report for the hearing (not reproduced in this report but is available in English, as a public document, in the registry of the Court of Justice) and the Commission report vol 2, p 93.

Are lotteries covered by the Treaty?

18. Several of the member states have argued either that lotteries fall wholly outside the scope of the Treaty or that in any event they are not covered by the Treaty rules on the free movement of services. Some of those member states have, however, confined that view to lotteries which can be characterised as public undertakings providing services.

19. The underlying common argument for that view is that the Treaty applies only to economic activities with a view to attaining the objectives set out in art 2 of the Treaty and that a lottery does not constitute such an economic activity. Reference is made in this respect inter alia to the case law of the Court of Justice to the effect that non-economic activities fall outside the scope of the Treaty, in particular the judgments in *Walrave* and *Donà*[11], in which it was held that certain sporting activities were not covered by the Treaty because they were not of an economic nature. Reference was also made to the provision in art 58 of the Treaty under which the Treaty applies only to companies or firms which operate for profit and that it is apparent from the Treaty definition of the provision of services that it refers to services which are normally carried out for payment (see art 60).

It is also argued that support for that view can be drawn from the fact that gambling is in principle unlawful in all the member states and that gambling debts cannot be enforced since the underlying agreements are regarded as invalid. It is said that such agreements constitute a threat to public order and that they do not pursue any aim meriting protection. Further support is to be found in the fact that in some member states, and in any event in Germany, gambling is regarded as a matter of public law.

20. I do not consider that view tenable. The circumstances stressed by the member states show that gambling has a special position in society in comparison with most common economic activities. They are circumstances which are clearly relevant to the assessment of the significance of the rules of the Treaty in this field but they do not entail that the Treaty as such or the Treaty rules on services are fundamentally inapplicable.

21. There is no basis in the Treaty rules, as interpreted by the Court of Justice[12], for giving the Treaty a narrow scope. It is clear from this case that

---

11 *Walrave and Koch v Association Union Cycliste Internationale* Case 36/74 [1974] ECR 1405 and *Donà v Mantero* Case 13/76 [1976] ECR 1333.

12 See in this connection the judgments in *Steymann v Staatssecretaris van Justitie* Case 196/87 [1988] ECR 6159 concerning the application of the Treaty rules to the economic activities of religious organisations, *Cowan v Trésor public* Case 186/87 [1989] ECR 195 concerning the application of the Treaty to national rules on compensation for victims of acts of violence, and *Society for the Protection of Unborn Children Ireland Ltd v Grogan* Case C-159/90 [1991] ECR I-4685 concerning the application of the Treaty to rules regarding information on abortion. Reference may also be made in this connection to *EC Commission v Italy* Case C-272/91 (pending) in which the Court of Justice has been asked to rule on the compatibility with the Treaty and Council Directive (EEC) 77/62 on public supply contracts of an Italian public tendering procedure for computerisation of the Italian lottery. The Italian government contends that the tendering procedure relates to a concession of the right to hold the lottery and that it is therefore covered by arts 55 and 66 of the Treaty. As far as the present case is concerned, it is worth observing that neither the Italian government nor the Commission was prompted to consider whether the holding of a lottery is covered by the Treaty rules at all. In my opinion of 14 July 1993 in Case C-272/91 I concluded that the tendering procedure did not concern the right to operate the lottery since I considered that the procedure related to an agreement to carry out services for and the supply of goods to the public administration with a view to the latter's holding of lotteries. If the Court of Justice follows that view, the question whether lotteries as such are covered by the Treaty rules will not directly be at issue in that case.

the economic significance of gambling, including lotteries, is considerable in all the member states. It is a quite particular form of economic activity inasmuch as, at least in so far as lotteries are concerned, the revenue, after payment of the often considerable expense of holding the lottery and the prizes, either accrues to the state exchequer or is used for public-interest purposes. However, that does not signify that the activity falls outside the scope of the Treaty. Such activities are also economic activities within the meaning of the Treaty. The services in question, participation in a lottery with the consequent possibility of winning, are provided for payment and the revenue from the activity is economic, irrespective of the use to which it is put. Article 90 of the Treaty shows that the Treaty also applies to public undertakings and undertakings to which member states grant special or exclusive rights, including undertakings which have the characteristics of fiscal monopolies.

22. No cogent grounds have been put forward for gambling, including lotteries, to be in principle outside the scope of the Treaty[13]. It should be plain in my view that, in so far as they authorise gambling, the member states must observe the fundamental prohibition in the Treaty of discrimination on grounds of nationality.

23. In connection with the question of the scope of the Treaty, reference has been made to Council Directive (EEC) 75/368 of 16 June 1975 on measures to facilitate the effective exercise of freedom of establishment and freedom to provide services in respect of various activities (ex ISIC Division 01 to 85) and, in particular, transitional measures in respect of those activities[14]. That directive, one of the so-called transitional directives, applies inter alia to lotteries conducted by private persons in certain member states but does not cover lotteries organised by public bodies (public services)[15]. It can in any event be concluded from that directive that lotteries are not as such excluded from the scope of the Treaty. In so far as concerns lotteries operated by public bodies, the only conclusion that may be drawn is that the Council did not consider it appropriate for the rules in that directive to apply to them.

Do the facts in the main proceedings relate to goods or services within the meaning of the Treaty (questions 1 and 4)?

24. As mentioned above, the court has been expressly asked to rule on how certain activities relating to lotteries are to be classified with regard to the concepts of goods and services under the Treaty.

Such a classification under the Treaty is in any event necessary even though it is at least to some extent correct, as certain member states point out in their observations, that the question whether the United Kingdom rules are to be assessed on the basis of the Treaty rules on the free movement of goods or the

---

13 No weight can be attached to the view that the activity in question is not regarded as a private-law economic activity in one or more member states. The scope of the Treaty must necessarily be determined on the basis of an independent interpretation of the Treaty which cannot be bound by the definition of terms in one or more member states.
14 OJ 1975 L167, p 22.
15 According to the preamble 'lottery and similar activities which come under ISIC Group 859 often belong to the field of public services, either directly or through public bodies, or are prohibited, and some of these activities do not therefore come within the scope of this Directive ... however, in certain Member States such activities can be conducted by private persons and should be included in this Directive'.

Treaty rules on the free movement of services is not determinative for a decision on their lawfulness (see also point 56).

25. I do not consider that such classification gives rise to any major problems.

26. That lotteries as such constitute services within the meaning of the Treaty has not been contested in this case and is probably indisputable. That is in any event also clearly presupposed by the directive referred to in point 23.

It is Gerhart and Jörg Schindler alone who contend that lottery tickets must be regarded as goods within the meaning of the Treaty and that advertising material connected to the sale of lottery tickets is covered by the Treaty rules on the free movement of goods.

The member states which have commented on the issue and the Commission agree that the activities in question in this case relating to a lottery must be regarded as part of the provision of those services.

27. There can be no doubt to my mind that that view is correct. There is no particular reason for treating lottery tickets as goods. They represent the evidence that the owner of the lottery ticket has paid for the right to take part in the lottery, that is to say, has paid for the chance of being drawn as the winner of one of the prizes in the lottery in question. The purchase of a lottery ticket corresponds in that context to the signing of an insurance contract or the purchase of personal travel services where the documents issued by the provider of the services for the purchase of the services—the policy and the travel ticket—are not good within the meaning of the Treaty. The factual and legal differences that may exist as regards the transferability of such documents are not material in this instance.

28. The court has held that advertising material relating to trade in goods is to be treated as goods under the Treaty rules[16]. I consider that there can be no doubt that advertising material relating to the provision of services must be treated as services under the Treaty rules.

29. It follows that lotteries and related activities, including the sale of lottery tickets and advertising for lotteries, constitute services within the meaning of the Treaty and that national rules regulating such activities fall within the Treaty rules on the freedom to provide services.

The right of the member states to regulate lotteries

30. No rules have been adopted at Community level on lotteries and other forms of gambling that are relevant in the present instance. The above-mentioned Directive 75/368/EEC on transitional provisions only lays down a limited obligation for member states to accept specified evidence of the good repute and other qualifications of foreign undertakings and the member states' obligations in this regard are also limited in so far as concerns lotteries conducted by private individuals.

It has also been stated in the course of the proceedings that the Commission has informed the European Council that in view of the principle of subsidiarity, as embodied in the new art 3b inserted in the EC Treaty by the Treaty on European Union, it has decided not to submit proposals for Community rules in this field[17].

31. There can be no doubt that the member states regulate this sector in an intensive and fairly restrictive manner.

---

16   See judgment in *GB-INNO-BM v Confédération du commerce luxembourgeois* Case C-362/88 [1990] ECR I-667.

The question is not whether the member states may undertake such regulation. The Treaty does not affect the member states' fundamental competence to lay down rules on the access to and exercise of occupations. The only question is what limitations are to be inferred from the Treaty rules for the member states' regulatory power in this sector.

32. As stated above, the present case concerns the significance in this context of the Treaty rules on services. But it may be useful, before considering the rules on services, to make more general observations regarding the member states' general competence to regulate the access to and exercise of activities in the lottery sector.

33. The starting point in all the member states is, as mentioned above, that gambling is prohibited and that legal position cannot be contrary to the Treaty. In practice certain forms of gambling are, however, allowed in all member states under certain specified conditions. There are quite considerable differences between the member states as regards the forms of gambling that are permitted and as regards the conditions for such authorisation. As a result, one form of gambling may be prohibited in one member state but permitted in another.

34. If gambling is permitted, the member states may undoubtedly lay down rules regarding the qualifications to be met in order for operators to be allowed access to the activity and as regards the way in which the activity must be carried out in order to ensure that it is not abused to the detriment of the individual players and of society as a whole.

There may be differences in the intensity and scope of the protection against abuse afforded by the legislation of the various countries.

35. In practice a frequent requirement in the member states, and one laid down in all major cases in the lotteries sector[18], is that revenue from the activity in question accrues to the state exchequer or is applied to public-interest purposes. It must be possible for the member states to lay down such requirements.

36. The practice in member states where lotteries are permitted is that major national lotteries must generally be administered by the public sector or subject to public supervision. That is apparently because it is regarded as an appropriate means of protecting against abuse and because it is regarded as natural in view of the fact that the revenue is to accrue to the state exchequer or to be used for public-interest purposes.

37. Finally, in practice the member states regulate, at least to a certain extent, lotteries in such a way that the 'supply' is restricted. The purpose is said to be to protect consumers against the dangers inherent in excessive participation in gambling by individuals (gambling fever) and the means used include, in particular, restricting the number of undertakings which may operate lotteries, restricting the number of lotteries that may be offered and restricting the number of draws.

---

17 See the conclusions of the Presidency of the European Council Meeting in Edinburgh on 11 and 12 December 1992, Annex 2 to Pt A: 'Subsidiarity—Examples of the Review of Pending Proposals and Existing Legislation', published in the *Bulletin of the European Communities* No 12-1992, pp 16ff.

18 However, examples are to be found under national legislation where revenue from certain lotteries can accrue to private individuals. Typical conditions are that the sums involved are small (both as regards the price of each lottery ticket, the total turnover and the prizes offered, which commonly may not be cash prizes) and the activity is conducted as part of other entertainments, for example travelling funfairs and the like.

38. Provided that the fundamental requirement of equal treatment of undertakings laid down in art 52 of the Treaty is observed, I believe it may be presumed that member states may, without coming into conflict with the Treaty, lay down rules on lotteries which: prohibit lotteries altogether or in part; lay down requirements regarding responsible operation of an authorised activity; require revenue to be used solely for public or public-interest purposes; and restrict the supply of lotteries, at least to some extent.

39. It is perhaps more doubtful whether the member states may restrict supply as they do in practice, by confining the activity in question exclusively to one or more undertakings or, in some cases, by reserving it to the state itself.

Such doubts arise both with regard to the Treaty rules on establishment and the Treaty rules on services.

It is plain from the rules on establishment under the Treaty and the case law of the court that there is no absolute prohibition on confining certain forms of commercial activity to one or more undertakings, including possibly public undertakings or undertakings under public control. But the Treaty does require that there be general criteria which are acceptable under the scheme of the Treaty and which necessitate such derogation from the principle of equal access to trades or occupations (see point 75 below).

40. The question is whether the member states can restrict access to the exercise of lottery activities on the basis of what might be called an assessment of needs, that is to say on the basis of determining what supply there should be on the market for the services in question. In other words, the question is whether member states can in this field set aside the general mechanisms of the market.

41. There must be good reasons for not allowing the general mechanisms of the market to function. In an open market economy it is market forces and not public regulation which should in principle determine what supply of certain goods or services there should be.

42. But in this particular field cogent grounds have been put forward for such interference with the mechanisms of the market. All member states have in any event taken two key measures: first, either no lotteries are allowed at national level at all or only one or a few lotteries are allowed, and secondly, no ordinary commercial undertaking may be operated in this sector.

There is certainly no call in these proceedings to examine from the right of establishment aspect the lawfulness of such restrictions on the right of undertakings to engage in the business of lotteries. But, as will be seen below, there can be no real doubt that member states may lawfully regulate the market in the above-mentioned respects provided that they comply with the obligation of equal treatment under art 52 of the Treaty and so long as the Community has not adopted relevant rules on the matter.

43. Those considerations are not conclusive but they are relevant to a decision on the nub of this case, namely what are the limits applying to the right of states to extend the scope of their legislation to apply to foreign providers of services.

44. Those considerations are not conclusive because it is apparent from the case law referred to in point 54 below that the prohibition under art 59 against restricting the free movement of services is more extensive than the prohibition which under art 52 applies to the possibility for member states to regulate the right of establishment of undertakings.

The considerations are relevant because the factors which underlie the member states' regulation of the right of establishment are the same factors that may form the basis for limitations on the free movement of services and it may well be that the object pursued in regulating the right of establishment can only be achieved if the rules on establishment, that is to say the rules on access to and exercise of the activity in question, must be complied with both by national and by foreign undertakings.

45. In deciding on the fundamental issue in these proceedings it is important to appreciate clearly the consequences of the court's possible answers.

46. The most far-reaching impact of application of the Treaty rules on services to the member states' rules on foreign lotteries would be that the state of destination would have to admit unreservedly services from undertakings operating lotteries lawfully under the legislation of their own state. That would entail in principle full mutual recognition amongst the member states of their rules on lotteries.

47. It would of course be necessary to consider to what extent the state of destination could, in that event, also require of foreign providers of services that their activities were exercised in compliance with rules affording sufficient guarantees of responsible operation with a view to the protection of the interests of consumers and society.

48. It is also necessary to consider whether the state of destination would be able to apply to foreign providers of services in the same way as to its own undertakings the requirements that profits must in any event be applied to public or public-interest purposes.

49. The court must finally consider, and this is the key issue in the case, whether the state of destination must in addition be given the possibility of restricting the supply of lotteries.

If they were not given such a possibility, there would exist in each member state a market situation in which the state's own lottery or lotteries would offer their services and, at the same time, all lotteries operating lawfully in other member states (and if appropriate complying with the above-mentioned requirements regarding responsible operation and the like) would be able to do the same.

In such a situation it would be substantively impossible for an individual state to restrict supply since the total supply on the market would depend on the supply that was permitted in other states and at the same time a situation would arise on the market in which the large lotteries—first and foremost those with a large home market—would have significant competitive advantages because they were in a position to offer consumers the biggest prizes (see point 113 below).

In short a situation would arise in which there would be no real possibility of restricting supply in order to protect consumers against the dangers of excessive gambling and competition would not be between private commercial undertakings, with the ensuing advantages regarding the allocation of resources, but between public funds and public-interest purposes in the various member states.

50. It is that result which the member states find fundamentally wrong and which, they claim, cannot result from the Treaty.

Observations on questions 5 and 6

51. As mentioned above, these questions relate to the significance of the rules on services as regards the application to foreign lotteries of the United

Kingdom rules laying down a general prohibition on the operation of large lotteries in the United Kingdom.

52. In principle I believe that the court should confine its answer to those questions to the legality of such rules under the Treaty.

None the less I have also considered it appropriate to include observations regarding the significance of the Treaty to the situation applying in most of the member states where the market for large lotteries is confined to one or more lottery undertakings which are operated by the public sector itself under public control. In interpreting the Treaty rules in the context of this case the court must, of course, take account of the implications of its interpretation for the legal positions in the other member states. Moreover, the United Kingdom has rightly pointed out that the rules that applied at the material time in the main proceedings cannot be assessed without regard to the fact that a decision has finally been taken in the United Kingdom to introduce a legal situation which in principle corresponds to that in the other member states. Furthermore, the other member states in their observations have largely expressed views which are relevant to an assessment of the legal positions in those countries.

Question 5

53. As indicated above, question 5 asks:

'... does Article 59 apply to the prohibition by the United Kingdom of the importation of tickets or advertisements for major lotteries, given that the restrictions imposed by the United Kingdom law on the conduct of such lotteries within the United Kingdom apply without discrimination on grounds of nationality and irrespective of whether the lottery is organized from outside or within the United Kingdom?'

54. The court has always stressed in its case law that the Treaty rules on services primarily prohibit overt and covert discrimination against foreign services but it has further stated that the prohibition can also affect restrictions other than those stemming from discriminatory rules. In its judgments in 1979 in *Van Wesemael* and in 1981 in *Webb*[19] the court held that the rules on services can also limit the possibility for member states to apply non-discriminatory rules to foreign services. That was stated still more clearly in the 1986 judgments in the so-called 'Co-insurance cases', which related to non-discriminatory requirements regarding establishment and authorisation in the insurance sector[20]. It has been reiterated most recently in the 1991 judgment in the so-called 'Tourist guide cases'[21] and in the 1991 judgment in *Säger* on patent renewal services[22]. In *Säger* (at 4243 (para 12)) the court held:

'... Article 59 of the Treaty requires not only the elimination of all discrimination against a person providing services on the ground of his nationality but also the abolition of any restriction, even if it applies without distinction to national providers of services and to those of other Member States, when it is liable to prohibit or otherwise impede the

---

19 *Ministère Public v Van Wesemael* Joined cases 110 and 111/78 [1979] ECR 35 and *Criminal proceedings against Webb* Case 279/80 [1981] ECR 3305.
20 See in particular *EC Commission v Germany* Case 205/84 [1986] ECR 3755.
21 *EC Commission v France* Case C-154/89 [1991] ECR I-659, *EC Commission v Italy* Case C-180/89 [1991] ECR I-709 and *EC Commission v Greece* Case C-198/89 [1991] ECR I-727.
22 *Säger v Dennemeyer & Co Ltd* Case C-76/90 [1991] ECR I-4221.

activities of a provider of services established in another Member State where he lawfully provides similar services.'

55. An important proviso for a proper understanding of the court's case law on this point is of course the possibility that still exists that restrictions, whether or not they stem from discriminatory rules, may be justified and therefore lawful.

As regards 'national rules which are not applicable to services without discrimination as regards their origin', they 'are compatible with Community law only if they can be brought within the scope of an express exemption, such as that contained in Article 56 of the Treaty'[23]. In so far as concerns other restrictions the court has held[24]:

'Having regard to the particular characteristics of certain provisions of services, specific requirements imposed on the provider, which result from the application of rules governing those types of activities, cannot be regarded as incompatible with the Treaty. However, as a fundamental principle of the Treaty, the freedom to provide services may be limited only by rules which are justified by imperative reasons relating to the public interest and which apply to all persons or undertakings pursuing an activity in the State of destination, in so far as that interest is not protected by the rules to which the person providing the services is subject in the Member State in which he is established. In particular, those requirements must be objectively necessary in order to ensure compliance with professional rules and to guarantee the protection of the recipient of services and they must not exceed what is necessary to attain those objectives ...'

56. As will be seen, there is a large degree of correspondence between the court's case law concerning art 30 and art 59 of the Treaty.

It should, however, be pointed out that the court has not held with regard to art 59, in the same way as it has with regard to art 30, that any restriction capable of hindering, directly or indirectly, actually or potentially, the free movement of services is covered by the prohibition under the Treaty[25].

The area of services is at least to some extent different from that of goods in particular because of the important personal element in many services and the consequent importance of distinguishing between conditions applying to access to the activity in question (personal qualifications and the like) and the conditions applying to the exercise of that activity.

57. On that basis the court's case law regarding art 59 can perhaps most accurately be summarised as follows: all discriminatory measures are caught by art 59; and some, but not necessarily all, other measures that restrict the activities of foreign providers of services in the host country may be caught by art 59[26].

---

23 See for example judgment in *EC Commission v Netherlands* Case C-353/89 [1991] ECR I-4069 at 4093 (para 15).
24 See judgment in *Säger v Dennemeyer & Co Ltd* Case C-76/90 [1991] ECR I-4221 at 4244 (para 15).
25 See the judgment in *Procureur du Roi v Dassonville* Case 8/74 [1974] ECR 837.
26 The principle that within the context of art 30 too there may also exist limitations on the free movement of goods which do not constitute restrictions within the meaning of art 30 has been laid down in the judgment in *Criminal proceedings against Keck* Joined cases C-267/91 and C-268/91 (1993) Times, 25 November 1993.

58. A finding that the rules at issue constitute a non-discriminatory limitation on the activities in the United Kingdom of foreign providers of services does not, therefore, answer the High Court's fifth question.

It is necessary to determine whether the limitation constitutes a restriction within the meaning of art 59.

59. Most of the observations that have been submitted in these proceedings, including those of the United Kingdom, contend that this question must be answered in the affirmative.

60. However, some governments have defended the contrary view. They refer to the judgments of the court in *Société Générale Alsacienne de Banque*[27] and in *Debauve*[28] which can both be read as signifying that the national rules at issue were not caught by the prohibition under art 59 simply because they were non-discriminatory[29].

61. It seems to me that strong grounds can be put forward for holding that national rules which contain a general prohibition of a specified activity and which are neither overtly nor covertly discriminatory are not incompatible with art 59 of the Treaty. Such rules are equally burdensome for national and foreign providers of services and it is not immediately clear why foreign providers of services should be able to exercise an activity which is prohibited for nationals merely because those foreign providers lawfully exercise that activity in their own state.

62. But that cannot be conclusive in the present case. The two above-mentioned judgments can be relied on in support of that result only up to a point. In *Debauve* the court in fact carried out an assessment of whether the prohibition at issue was disproportionate to the objective pursued and the fact must not be overlooked that the court in its subsequent decisions has stated, as mentioned above, that non-discriminatory restrictions can also be caught by art 59.

63. There is, moreover, one ground which in the circumstances of this case suggests that rules like those at issue must also be regarded as restrictions within the meaning of art 59. The prohibition at issue is being applied in a situation in which the United Kingdom has stated that it is to be abolished because the view has been taken that it is appropriate to set up a national lottery. A legal position under which foreign providers of services cannot operate in the same way as national providers is in any event a restriction

---

27 *Société Générale Alsacienne de Banque SA v Koestler* Case 15/78 [1978] ECR 1971.
28 *Procureur du Roi v Debauve* Case 52/79 [1980] ECR 833.
29 *Société Générale Alsacienne de Banque SA v Koestler* Case 15/78 [1978] ECR 1971 concerned a provision of services, specifically stock exchange time-bargains carried out by a bank on instructions from a customer, which under German law were regarded as not being legally binding. The court held (at 1981 (para 5)): 'The fact that debts arising out of a wagering contract or other similar debts are not actionable cannot be regarded as discrimination against a person providing services established in another Member State if the same limitation applies to any person providing services established within the territory of the same State whenever that person claims payment of a debt of the same kind, and this has not been disputed in the present case.' *Procureur du Roi v Debauve* Case 52/79 [1980] ECR 833 concerned a Belgian prohibition on the transmission on cable television of foreign advertisements. The court held (at 857 (para 16)): '... Articles 59 and 60 of the Treaty do not preclude national rules prohibiting the transmission of advertisements by cable television—as they prohibit the broadcasting of advertisements by television—if those rules are applied without distinction as regards the origin, whether national or foreign, of those advertisements, the nationality of the person providing the service, or the place where he is established'.

CJEC Customs and Excise Comrs v Schindler (Advocate General) 211

within the meaning of art 59, even if in this case it was to be regarded as non-discriminatory.

64. On those grounds the following answer should be given to question 5: art 59 of the Treaty applies to the rules at issue even if they apply without discrimination on grounds of nationality and irrespective of whether the lottery is organised within or outside the United Kingdom.

Are the United Kingdom rules substantively discriminatory?

65. Nobody in this case seems to have challenged the correctness of the premise underlying question 5, namely that the United Kingdom rules at issue, in so far as their actual content is concerned, apply without discrimination on grounds of nationality and irrespective of whether the lottery is organised within or outside the United Kingdom.

66. However, the Commission and Gerhart and Jörg Schindler contend that the rules are in fact discriminatory since they deny a lottery like the Süddeutsche Klassenlotterie access to a market on which similar gambling activities by competing undertakings are permitted.

They point primarily to the activities that may be carried out by local lotteries and the activities carried out by private undertakings which organise football pools. According to the Commission and Gerhart and Jörg Schindler, those competing undertakings are thus afforded indirect protection and the rules at issue are therefore discriminatory.

67. I do not consider that the view is correct.

68. The starting point must be the fact that the United Kingdom legislation lays down a general prohibition on the holding of lotteries that is only subject to a number of specified and prima facie objectively well-founded exceptions for the benefit of local lotteries whose objects are well-defined and whose turnover cannot exceed specified limits[30].

There is nothing in this case to indicate that the direct or indirect object of that legal situation is to protect British lotteries against competition from other lotteries organised outside the United Kingdom. There is an apparently objectively-founded delimitation of the United Kingdom lottery market to admit only local lotteries with a limited turnover. The fact that that limitation signifies that large foreign lotteries cannot exercise their activities in competition with the authorised local lotteries does not make the rules in question discriminatory.

69. The United Kingdom legislation does permit football pools as a form of gambling. Authorisation is even given for private undertakings to engage in this activity for profit since regulation by the state is confined to ensuring that

---

30 Under the Lotteries and Amusements Act 1976 the exceptions are for small lotteries incidental to certain entertainments (s 3), private lotteries confined to a restricted group (s 4), lotteries promoted on behalf of certain societies (s 5), lotteries promoted by local authorities (s 6) and lotteries promoted and conducted in accordance with the Art Unions Act 1846. In practice it is the lotteries referred to in ss 5 and 6 of the 1976 Act that are the most significant. The following details of such lotteries are set out in Annex A to the 1992 White Paper on a national lottery: 'There are three types of lotteries which may be promoted by a society or local authority. A short-term lottery can be promoted within a month of a previous lottery. The maximum turnover (ie value of tickets sold) is £45,000 and the maximum prize is £6,000. A medium-term lottery can be promoted between one and three months of a previous lottery. The maximum turnover is £90,000 and the maximum prize is £9,000. The largest public lotteries are promoted quarterly with turnover of £180,000 and a maximum single prize of £12,000. In all cases, the maximum price of a ticket is £1.' The United Kingdom has stated that those limits have been raised in connection with the establishment of the national lottery.

the activity is conducted in a responsible manner and that a proper proportion of the profit flows into the exchequer as tax[31].

There has been nothing to suggest that the current United Kingdom rules on football pools taken on their own are incompatible with the Treaty rules, nor has there been anything to indicate that the United Kingdom's rules applying to the gambling market in question here might have been adopted in order to protect the British gambling market against competition from foreign lottery undertakings.

Those regulations must be regarded as a legitimate manifestation of the United Kingdom legislature's views on how the gambling market should be organised. They may reflect historical experience and take account of what is regarded as socially most acceptable (for example there is an element of skill in football pools which is lacking in lotteries) and they may reflect a simple choice between two possible forms of gambling as the legislature considers that it is desirable to allow only one because otherwise the total supply of gambling would be too great.

70. The United Kingdom legislation treats different forms of gambling in different ways and the fact that there are to some extent competing activities does not in itself signify that there exists covert discrimination. Moreover, acceptance of the view put forward by the Commission and Gerhart and Jörg Schindler could in fact be said to rest on the premise that because a member state has authorised one form of gambling it is obliged for that reason alone to accept corresponding forms of gambling conducted by foreign undertakings.

Is the existence of a large national lottery significant with regard to the question of discrimination?

71. It may be claimed that the decision to set up a national lottery shows that there is in fact discrimination against corresponding foreign lotteries.

72. But it would be wrong in my view when assessing the possible discriminatory effect of the rules in question in this case to attach any

---

31 The court has heard that there are currently three pools undertakings: Littlewoods, with more than 76% of the market, Vernons with some 20% of the market and Zetters with some 3%. According to a Mintel survey, *Special Report, Gambling* (1991) pp 32ff, those undertakings pay more than 40% of their turnover to the state while their own net revenue amounts to some 4·4% of turnover. In its 1992 White Paper the United Kingdom described the effects that the establishment of the national lottery would have on other forms of gambling as follows: '29. The football pools are the form of gambling most likely to be affected by the national lottery. They offer a "small stake/large win" form of gambling and have expressed concern that a national lottery would eventually drive them out of business. In some countries a national lottery has had an adverse effect on the pools but in others they co-exist. More work will be needed to establish the impact of the national lottery on the pools in this country. 30. Other forms of gambling are less likely to be affected than the pools. They offer a product which differs substantially from a national lottery either in the nature of the gamble or the circumstances in which it is made, or both. For example, those who bet on horse or greyhound racing are unlikely to be attracted by the "long-odds/no skill" gamble of a national lottery. Bingo is a social activity for which the purchase of a lottery ticket is no substitute. Similarly, casinos offer a type of gambling and other facilities quite different from participation in a lottery. Gaming machines most readily available to the public provide amusement rather than the chance to win a major prize ... 33. One of the concerns most frequently voiced about the impact of a national lottery is that charities will lose income from existing small lotteries and from charitable donations generally. The level of income which charities at present obtain from small lotteries is unclear because figures for all lotteries are not collected centrally ... Charities will be specifically singled out as one of the categories to benefit from the national lottery ...'

importance to the fact that those rules have subsequently been amended. The rules in question in the main proceedings do not become discriminatory because at the time in question consideration may have been given to amending those rules and that may subsequently have resulted in amendments.

73. But I am also inclined to hold that it would not be right to classify as discriminatory a legal position like that which applies in the United Kingdom following the adoption of the National Lottery Act 1993 and which, according to what we have been told, applies in the other member states.

74. It is quite possible for rules to apply in a country which prevent foreign service undertakings from providing their services—even if that is permitted for national undertakings—without such rules falling to be classified as discriminatory. Typical examples are national rules which provide that a specified occupation can only be exercised by undertakings which are established in that country. Such rules constitute 'the very negation' of the freedom to provide services in the words of the court's judgment in the Co-insurance cases[32]. The court did not classify that legal position as discriminatory but held that 'if such requirement is to be accepted, it must be shown that it constitutes a condition which is indispensable for attaining the objective pursued' and it thus accepted that factors other than those referred to in art 56 of the Treaty might justify such a significant restriction on the free movement of services.

75. The situation in this instance differs from a general requirement regarding establishment in so far as the activity in question, after an assessment of needs, is permitted only for one or a few undertakings. That in itself does not make the rules discriminatory. The most appropriate assumption is still that they do not embody discriminatory treatment on grounds of nationality or the origin of the undertakings.

It is not in itself incompatible with the Treaty for the member states to give one or a few undertakings exclusive rights (see in this respect art 90 of the Treaty). In such a situation the member states are under a duty to comply with the general rules of the Treaty, that is to say in the present context in particular the Treaty rules on establishment and services. That signifies inter alia that the limitations which the exclusive rights in question entail for the free movement of services must be capable of being justified under the general case law of the court.

If the very fact that exclusive rights have been granted is seen as constituting discrimination, exclusive rights would be lawful only if they were on the grounds of one of the factors referred to in art 56, namely public policy, public security or public health.

Such a result would not, in my view, be correct.

76. On the one hand, I consider that it would be inappropriate to give a broad scope to the concept of discrimination in a context such as this and, on the other, I do not consider that it is of conclusive importance for the effective application of art 59 of the Treaty whether or not the situation is classified as discriminatory.

77. Article 56 provides that the provisions of the chapters on establishment and service do not prejudice the applicability of national 'provisions ...

---

32   *EC Commission v Germany* Case 205/84 [1986] ECR 3755 at 3809 (para 52).

providing for special treatment for foreign nationals' on grounds of one of the factors referred to in that provision.

The very wording of art 56 shows that there must be special rules for foreign undertakings and it does not seem reasonable to me in cases where exclusive rights are given to certain undertakings without regard to nationality or the undertakings' origin to describe such rules as 'special treatment for *foreign*' undertakings.

Moreover, the court has given a restrictive interpretation to art 56 and stressed that the grounds referred to in that article may be invoked only if there exists 'a genuine and sufficiently serious threat to ... one of the fundamental interests of society'[33]. Such a restrictive interpretation is undoubtedly apposite with regard to national rules which, whether overtly or covertly, take account of nationality or the undertakings' origin. But it would be out of place if any discriminatory effects of disputed measures were a practical consequence of delimiting criteria which may be objectively well founded.

I can see a danger in applying a broad concept of discrimination and at the same time interpreting art 56 restrictively. It might lead to an unintended limitation of the regulatory powers which, under the scheme of the Treaty, the member states must necessarily enjoy so long as the Community institutions have not undertaken a harmonisation of the national rules on the matter.

78. Nor do I consider that the question of classification is of any great practical importance in this case. However the situation is classified with regard to the concept of discrimination, there is a significant restriction, a real negation of the right to the free movement of services, which can be justified only if the measures at issue are objectively necessary to take account of fundamental interests of society.

79. The decisive questions are thus in my view in any event whether the interests of society invoked by the states are so fundamental that in the area in question they can justify the existing restriction and whether the rules in question are objectively necessary in order to achieve the objective pursued and are also reasonable in relation to that objective.

Does the restriction resulting from the United Kingdom prohibition on the import of lottery tickets and advertising for large lotteries comply with the conditions of legality under the Treaty?

80. Question 6 asks:

'do the concerns of the United Kingdom to limit lotteries for social policy reasons and to prevent fraud constitute legitimate public policy or public morality considerations to justify the restrictions of which complaint is made, whether under Article 56 read with Article 66 or otherwise, in the circumstances of the present case?'

81. The 11 member states which have submitted observations all proposed that this question should be answered in the affirmative. Gerhart and Jörg Schindler and the Commission disagree.

---

33   Judgment in *R v Bouchereau* Case 30/77 [1981] 2 All ER 924 at 940, [1978] QB 732 at 760 (para 35).

What interests do the existing restrictions seek to protect?

82. The member states essentially contend that three interests underlie the strict regulation of lotteries and the ensuing restrictions on free movement of services.

83. The first is the need to protect consumers, that is players in the lottery, against fraud and other forms of illegal conduct of lotteries[34].

84. Reference is also made to the need more generally to combat by regulation and controls the real danger of lotteries being taken over by criminal elements and used for criminal purposes, including money laundering.

85. It is contended that there are special risks with cross-border lotteries[35]. Some member states have referred in this connection to the increased risk of tax evasion. The Commission does not deny that there is an increased risk of abuse with cross-border lotteries but has stated that, on the basis of the information given, that has not caused the member states any insurmountable problems.

86. Second, all the member states contend that for the sake of consumers it is necessary to limit the overall supply of gambling and to regulate the manner in which gambling is offered. They point to the real danger that certain persons can gamble to excess with serious social and health consequences for themselves and their families, and thus for society.

87. Third, reference is made to the need to ensure that revenues from lotteries are used for specified purposes approved by society in connection with which it may be necessary to regulate what proportion of the lottery's turnover may be applied to the operating expenditure of the lottery, what proportion may be used as prizes, and what proportion must be used for public purposes or other purposes in the public interest.

88. It is in my view undeniable, and as far as can be seen it has not seriously been disputed in these proceedings, that each one of those aims could in appropriate circumstances justify limitations on the free movement of services. They are aims which are so important that the court could if it saw fit classify them as aims falling within art 56 of the Treaty.

89. The decisive point remains therefore whether the restrictions considered here are necessary in order to achieve the aims in question, whether those aims could be achieved by other, less restrictive means, and whether those restrictions are in general reasonable in relation to those aims.

Do they comply with the principle of proportionality?

90. The answer given by Gerhart and Jörg Schindler and the Commission to that question is clearly negative while the member states are unanimous in giving an affirmative answer.

---

34 It is pointed out that lotteries are a form of gambling which is especially vulnerable to fraud. That is because the participant has no ready and independent means of ascertaining either the total amount paid in or that the promised prizes have been paid out. Without adequate controls, it would be possible for the operator of a lottery to skim off part of the proceeds, or, in the case of instant lotteries, to withhold, perhaps for his own use, the winning tickets (see point 30 of the order for reference).

35 Examples of complaints of such alleged abuses are given in the observations of the Belgian government.

91. It was contended in these proceedings that those factors cannot be taken in isolation one from another. In essence I agree with that. While it is necessary to consider each factor separately, that does not, however, rule out the possibility that the factors taken together may justify the restrictions even if, considered separately, they cannot do so.

Are the restrictions necessary in order to protect consumers and society against fraud and the like?

92. It has not been disputed in these proceedings that the concern to protect consumers against the obvious dangers of abuse in lotteries and also against the use of lotteries for criminal ends may justify even very stringent regulation of and controls over lotteries.

93. It is, however, argued that at least in the present case that factor cannot justify the relevant restrictions, in particular because it can only be invoked in so far as the lottery undertaking providing the services in question is not already subject in its home state to adequate rules concerning its activities and to adequate controls corresponding to the rules and controls applying in the state of destination.

94. It follows from the case law of the court that the state of destination cannot insist that its own rules be complied with by foreign providers of services if the considerations underlying those requirements are already taken into account by the provider's own legislation (principle of equivalence)[36].

95. In this instance it can certainly be argued that the principle of equivalence is difficult to apply because large lotteries were prohibited in the United Kingdom at the material time in the main proceedings and because there was therefore no prescribed level of protection with which the level of protection applying to the foreign provider of services can be compared.

However that objection is merely one of form. First of all, it is possible in this respect to make a comparison with the protection afforded by the United Kingdom to consumers in connection with local lotteries and similar gambling activities such as football pools and also now with the protection that will be afforded to consumers in connection with the new national lottery.

Second, it is established that the rules applying to and the controls exercised over the Süddeutsche Klassenlotterie offer a high degree of protection against abuse[37].

It has, moreover, not been argued in the course of these proceedings that there is a greater risk of abuse in connection with the Süddeutsche Klassenlotterie than is considered acceptable for comparable gambling activities in the United Kingdom.

96. Nor, finally, is there any real basis, in my view, in the assertions of the member states in general terms regarding the increased risk in connection with cross-border lotteries for holding that that alleged risk in itself could justify the United Kingdom authorities' application of the rules at issue.

97. If the aforementioned factor cannot be relied on in the present instance as a basis for the exclusion of the Süddeutsche Klassenlotterie's activities in the United Kingdom, that does not of course signify that the member states are

---

36 See the judgments in the Co-insurance cases, in particular *EC Commission v Germany* Case 205/84 [1986] ECR 3755 at 3804–3808 (paras 34–47).
37 See footnote 10.

prevented in other instances from refusing foreign lotteries access to their markets if the rules applying to those lotteries in their home states and the controls to which they are there subject are not adequate by comparison with the level of protection which the state of destination wishes to ensure.

Are the restrictions necessary in order to limit the supply of gambling in the state of destination?

98. If it is accepted—and all the member states have proceeded on this basis—that it is necessary to limit the overall supply of gambling, it would at first sight also appear necessary for the member states to be able to limit the right of foreign undertakings to provide their services.

The fact is, as mentioned above, that the gambling markets in the various countries differ. What is permitted in one country may be prohibited in another. If a state cannot ban services from countries where they are permitted, its possibility of limiting the total supply of gambling will be sharply reduced.

99. Against that, Gerhart and Jörg Schindler and the Commission argue that such factors cannot reasonably be invoked in this instance by the United Kingdom in view of the following: the total gambling market in the United Kingdom in 1990 amounted to more than £stg13,000m; a comprehensive range of gambling is available, including football pools (which are private commercial undertakings which in principle can be operated by anybody who meets the relevant general requirements); the United Kingdom has decided to establish a large national lottery; and the United Kingdom has also acknowledged that lotteries are the least dangerous form of gambling[38].

100. However, those arguments, which at first sight appear very cogent, must be rejected for the following reasons.

101. Acceptance of the view argued for by Gerhart and Jörg Schindler and the Commission would, as mentioned above, have the result that a member state with relatively liberal gambling laws would no longer be able to maintain limitations on the supply of gambling, at least not with regard to the form of gambling which the authorities of that country regard as the least harmful form of gambling in relative terms.

Quite apart from making difficult discretionary decisions necessary, acceptance of that point of view would entail the rejection of a central part of

---

38 See the 1992 White Paper, in which it is stated: '14. The Rothschild Royal Commission recognised two principles for gambling policy. First, that gambling should be properly regulated to ensure that it is conducted honestly and fairly. Second, that the demand for gambling should not be positively encouraged because, if taken to excess, it can cause misery for the individual and his family, and have damaging consequences for society as a whole. Although these general principles underlie all gambling controls, they have been applied in different degrees to different forms of gambling. 15. For example, casino gaming is more vulnerable to abuse by criminals and large amounts of money may be lost very quickly. It represents the "hardest" form (in the sense of vulnerability to abuse and of its danger to the individual) of gambling and so it is the most tightly regulated ... By contrast, lotteries have long been considered to be the "softest" form of gambling. The amounts staked are usually small and there is not the same incentive to chase losses. They are subject to a lighter regulatory regime because the sums of money involved are more modest. Because they offer modest prizes and support good causes, they can be advertised quite freely. In particular, they can be advertised on TV and radio whereas the broadcast advertising of all betting and gaming is prohibited by a mixture of statutory controls and the broadcasting authorities' advertising codes.'

the member states' arguments for being able to regulate gambling, namely the necessity of being able to limit overall supply.

In view of what is now known of the dangers associated with gambling for certain people, I do not consider it possible to dismiss the consensus of the member states that there is a real need to limit the supply of gambling and that such limitation—in the absence of Community rules on the matter—must necessarily be undertaken by each member state separately.

102. If the individual member states must admit lotteries which are held in a lawful and proper manner in all other member states, they are denied the possibility of controlling the number of lotteries held, the number of draws, and the amount of the authorised turnover. The supply in the member states will in fact be determined by overall supply in all the member states.

103. The Commission itself indicated at the hearing that there presumably must be some possibility for the individual member states to limit supply by means of a non-discriminatory system of authorisations.

104. That view shows the difficulty of opening the national markets to foreign services by means of the direct application of the Treaty rules on services.

I do not consider it possible to interpret the Treaty rules on services—or the Treaty rules on the right of establishment—as meaning that the member states are precluded from prohibiting certain forms of gambling on an objective basis.

No duty can therefore be inferred on the basis of the Treaty for member states to introduce a system of authorisations in a field where they consider that the form of gambling in question should be prohibited.

However, as mentioned above, it is undoubtedly possible on the basis of the Treaty to require the member states, in so far as they authorise a limited supply of a certain form of gambling, to implement that in a non-discriminatory manner.

On the other hand I consider it impossible to infer from the Treaty rules on services directly applicable obligations for the member states to issue authorisations to a specified number of lotteries. In other words, it is not possible on the basis of the Treaty to infer criteria for determining how large a supply of a certain form of gambling there should be.

If it is accepted that the member states may limit the supply, the question of the extent of that supply must be left to the member states, whose decisions will reflect choices that are largely determined by the social and cultural circumstances prevailing in those countries[39].

105. In short, I believe that on the basis of the Treaty rules on services and in the absence of harmonisation at Community level, an intermediate solution can be found between, on the one hand, accepting the possibility for the member states to limit supply on a non-discriminatory basis, including by means of prohibiting or limiting the provision of services by foreign lotteries, and, on the other, total acceptance of the right of foreign lotteries to provide their services if they are subject to proper control and the like in their home state.

106. If it is thus accepted that the member states must be able to regulate the supply of gambling, and in particular lotteries, it must also be accepted that

---

39 See judgment in *Stoke-on-Trent City Council v B & Q plc* Case C-169/91 [1993] 1 All ER 481 at 518, [1993] AC 900 at 947 (para 11).

limitation of the services provided by foreign undertakings is a necessary and proportionate measure.

Are the restrictions necessary in order to maintain the member states' ability to lay down rules regarding the use of lottery revenues?

107. The last of the factors invoked by the member states, namely the possibility of ensuring that revenues from lotteries are used for public or public-interest purposes, is also relevant as a basis for accepting the possibility for member states to limit the provision of services by foreign lotteries.

108. The contention that a main underlying reason for allowing gambling at all is that the revenues from it can be used for 'good causes' is undoubtedly both historically correct and still a reality.

109. There are certainly some grounds for scepticism today as to the motives behind member states' regulation of the gambling market. As already mentioned above, the disapprobation of gambling as such and the concern to reduce the risk of excessive gambling amongst their citizens have, in a number of member states at least, lost ground to the concern to exploit people's desire to gamble as a source of funds for the state exchequer (with the revenue either accruing directly to the exchequer or being subject to high levels of taxation) or for public-interest purposes. The liberalisation of the gambling market in many of the member states and the acceptance of often quite aggressive advertising for gambling are indications of that trend.

110. But even if that is so, it remains true that the revenues are used for non-commercial purposes. I consider it immaterial whether the revenues accrue to the state exchequer or public-interest purposes. If the revenues are devoted to public-interest purposes that will to some extent at least relieve the public purse of expenditure on those purposes.

111. A number of factors are relevant in this regard.

It is probably right, as is mentioned in many of the observations, that participants in lotteries do to some extent decide to participate because the revenues accrue to a purpose which is of particular concern to them. But on the basis of the foregoing it may also be presumed that, in so far as the large lotteries are concerned, the use to which the revenues are put has only a limited bearing on the participants' decision to take part. It seems to be accepted that it is not least the size of the prizes that is decisive[40].

112. It is therefore reasonable to suppose, as has moreover been claimed by many of the member states, that the opening of the national markets would probably lead to intensive competition between the large lotteries for market shares throughout the whole Community.

A not unlikely development would be that the lotteries which are the largest to start with—those that today have the largest 'home market'—would be able

---

40 According to the Commission report on *Gambling in the Single Market* vol 1, p 44: 'The player's main interest is to participate in an attractive game. A game's attractiveness is reflected in the size of the prizes, the chances to win and in the fact that no or only little tax is levied on the winnings. Where a foreign lottery seems more attractive than a domestic game, some players will participate either by ordering the tickets by mail or by crossing the border to buy them at an agent's abroad. Mail order is particularly viable in class lotteries as deadlines for accepting tickets can be many weeks in the future.'

to out-compete not just the small local lotteries (which face difficulties from the outset) but also the national lotteries of the smaller member states[41].

113. The competition would, presumably, as mentioned above, also be conducted on the basis of the size of prizes. These essentially depend on turnover, the amount of administrative costs, and the proportion of revenues that must be devoted to public or public-interest purposes. A major parameter for competition would therefore be what proportion may be used for prizes and what proportion must be devoted to public or public-interest purposes. The lotteries which devote the greatest proportion to prizes would have a competitive advantage. It seems to me that it ought to be permissible for the member states to prevent such forms of competition on this very special market.

114. It is undoubtedly also important for the member states to be able to prevent free competition arising between lotteries at European level as the main practical result would be that the exchequers or public-interest purposes of the various countries would compete for the money which European citizens spend on lotteries.

On that basis it is certainly not impossible that one potential consequence of the opening of the national markets would be that the large German Class Lotteries would come to have such a dominant share of the market that it would become uneconomic to operate the small national lotteries in neighbouring countries. That would signify that the funds that have hitherto accrued to public-interest purposes in those countries would henceforth flow into the public funds of the German Länder which operate those lotteries.

115. The Commission disputes that any weight can be attached to that factor in connection with the application of one of the fundamental principles of the Treaty which is one of the cornerstones of the attainment of the internal market.

That view is supported by the case law of the court to the effect that economic aims cannot justify derogations from the Treaty rules on the free movement of services[42].

116. It might perhaps at first sight appear contrary to the principles for such an 'economic aim' to serve to justify limitations on the free movement of services.

But I believe that closer examination shows that that aim can be taken into account in the present context. It does not constitute an economic aim within the meaning attributed to that term in the case law of the court.

---

41 According to the Commission report vol 1, p 18: 'Cross-border betting is a market-driven phenomenon. The agents of certain Klassenlotteries are the most active promoters of illegal cross-border betting. "Mail-shot" marketing has been organized throughout the twelve Member States. The smaller lottery markets, with correspondingly small prizes, are clearly the most vulnerable ... The big prizes of the German Klassenlotterie are very attractive to consumers who normally play on the small national lotteries which have small first prizes. In this regard, diagram 8 shows the vulnerability of Denmark, Belgium and the Netherlands ... Cross-border betting which occurs out of convenience resulting from nearness to a neighbouring Member State or similar language and culture is of an osmotic nature. Osmotic cross-border betting is more likely to occur if there is a disproportionate size of population and therefore larger lotteries with bigger prizes next to smaller national lotteries or lottos.'
42 See for example *Bond van Adverteerders v Netherlands* Case 352/85 [1988] ECR 2085 at 2135 (para 34), in which the court held: 'It must be pointed out that economic aims, such as that of securing for a national public foundation all the revenue from advertising intended especially for the public of the Member State in question, cannot constitute grounds of public policy within the meaning of Article 56 of the Treaty.'

CJEC Customs and Excise Comrs v Schindler (Advocate General) 221

a
117. The Treaty is founded on the principle that turnover in economic goods can be taxed in the state of consumption (see art 95 of the Treaty).

The Commission pointed out at the hearing that a member state cannot ban the sale of tobacco and spirits from other member states if the sale thereof is permitted in the state in question. That is of course right. But it does not alter the fact that the member states may tax the imported goods in the same way as national goods.

b

It seems to me not unreasonable to regard the position relating to lotteries as also involving a form of taxation. If the Commission's view that under the Treaty the member states are under a duty to open their markets to foreign lotteries is upheld, that will mean that the 'tax' on lottery tickets—that is that proportion of the payment for the lottery ticket which must be paid into the state exchequer (or be applied for public-interest purposes)—will be paid to the 'state of production' and not the 'state of consumption.'

c

118. That it is not unreasonable to view the position in that light is borne out by the information given regarding the arrangements between the Luxembourg Government and two German lotteries under which those two lotteries have been authorised to carry on their activities in Luxembourg in return for the Luxembourg State receiving a certain percentage of their turnover in Luxembourg.

d

119. I find support for the view that this factor may in appropriate circumstances justify restrictions on cross-border services in the judgment in *Bachmann* in which the court held that the serious restrictions on the free movement of workers and services at issue in that case could be justified by the aim of protecting the states' tax revenues by ensuring the cohesion of tax systems[43].

e

120. What is more important, however, in my view, is that the court in the present case is considering a market of a very special nature where the rules of all the member states show that the general mechanisms of the market cannot and should not apply. So far as I can see, not one of the member states considers it appropriate to have free competition in this area with the consequences that are detailed above.

f

121. There would be competition that could hardly fail to have far-reaching consequences for a number of lotteries of long-standing which are a major source of finance for important benevolent and public-interest organisations. Acceptance of the competition that would result from the opening of the markets might curtail national diversities and cannot, in my view, be regarded as a necessary consequence of the attainment of the internal market.

g

122. It is hard to point to any effects of the opening of the markets that would merit protection. So far as I can see it would not serve to further any of the aims referred to in art 2 of the Treaty.

h

123. The appropriate allocation of resources which from an economic point of view is the most important basis for the Treaty rules on the free movement of services is not, in my view, of any relevance as regards lotteries[44].

j
124. The Commission does indeed point out that the opening of the markets would mean that consumers would have a wider range of choice

---

43 Judgment in *Bachmann v Belgium* Case C-204/90 [1992] ECR I-249.
44 See art 102a of the EC Treaty as amended by the Treaty on European Union, the second sentence of which provides: 'The Member States and the Community shall act in accordance with the principle of an open market economy with free competition, favouring an efficient allocation of resources, and in compliance with the principles set out in Article 3a.'

between the public-interest purposes they wish to support and would also offer
consumers bigger prizes. As regards the former, it is possible that the
Commission is right in the short-term. But, as mentioned above, it is not
unlikely that one long-term effect of the opening of the markets would be that
a number of lotteries would be driven from the market which would thus
narrow the range of choice available to consumers.

The Commission is perhaps also right as regards the latter point. However,
I do not consider that that can be one of the aims which the Treaty seeks to
achieve. An increase in the size of the prizes might on the one hand increase
the desire to gamble and on the other result in a reduction in the proportion of
the turnover of lotteries which accrues as revenue for public or public interest
purposes.

125. It may therefore be concluded, in my view, that there are no cogent
reasons which must be taken into account pursuant to the aims of the Treaty
militating against the member states continuing to be able to limit the free
movement of services; on the other hand considerable importance must attach
to the grounds invoked by all the member states against opening the markets.
It is an area in which there are good grounds for continuing to uphold the
regulatory powers of the member states so long as it is established that the
Community does not intend to exercise its regulatory powers in this area.

126. It must also be concluded in my view that it is not possible on the basis
of the foregoing to identify less restrictive means of achieving the aims
underlying the existing limitations on the free movement of services[45].

127. I therefore consider that it is appropriate to hold, in answer to the High
Court's questions, that there is nothing in the Treaty rules on services to
preclude the application of national rules which prohibit the import of lottery
tickets and advertising material for large foreign lotteries in a situation in
which large national lotteries are also prohibited.

It is of no significance in this respect that a decision has been taken to set up
a large national lottery, if only because, in my view, even where such lotteries
exist, the member states may maintain limitations on the free movement of
services[46].

Conclusion

128. For those reasons I propose that the court give the following answer to
the High Court's questions:

'Rules on the import of lottery tickets and advertisements for large
lotteries are within the scope of art 59 of the Treaty of Rome but that does
not preclude those rules from prohibiting services from large foreign

---

45 In the United States of America, Congress, acting pursuant to the commerce clause in the
Federal Constitution, has laid down a fundamental prohibition on the free movement of services
between the states in the field of lotteries. The constitutionality of that legislation was
confirmed by a 1903 judgment of the Federal Supreme Court in the Lottery case (*Champion v
Ames* (1903) 188 US 321).
46 I have considered whether the second paragraph of art 55 of the Treaty may be of any relevance
to the interpretation of art 59 of the Treaty in the context of this case. Article 55, in conjunction
with art 66, provides that the provisions of the chapter on services are not to apply to certain
activities. There has been nothing in these proceedings to suggest that the Council and
Commission might have considered applying that provision to exempt lotteries from the Treaty
rules on services. It is clearly of importance in any event that that provision cannot apply unless
the Commission has submitted a proposal regarding its application. The result of my analysis is
that that provision is not of any relevance in the context of this case.

lotteries where such a prohibition is part of a general prohibition of the conduct of large lotteries.'

24 March 1994. THE COURT OF JUSTICE gave the following judgment.

1. By order of 3 April 1992, received at the court on 18 June 1992, the High Court of Justice of England and Wales (Queen's Bench Division) referred to the court for a preliminary ruling under art 177 of the EEC Treaty six questions on the interpretation of arts 30, 36, 56 and 59 of the Treaty in order to determine whether national legislation prohibiting the holding of certain lotteries in a member state was compatible with those provisions.

2. Those questions were raised in the course of proceedings between the Commissioners of Customs and Excise (hereinafter 'the commissioners'), plaintiffs in the main proceedings, and Gerhart and Jörg Schindler concerning the dispatch of advertisements and application forms for a lottery organised in the Federal Republic of Germany to United Kingdom nationals.

3. Gerhart and Jörg Schindler are independent agents for the Süddeutsche Klassenlotterie (hereinafter 'SKL'), a public body responsible for organising what are known as 'Class' lotteries on behalf of four Länder of the Federal Republic of Germany. As such agents, they promote SKL lotteries and unquestionably sell tickets for those lotteries.

4. Gerhart and Jörg Schindler dispatched envelopes from the Netherlands to United Kingdom nationals. Each envelope contained a letter inviting the addressee to participate in the 87th issue of the SKL, application forms for participating in that lottery and a preprinted reply envelope.

5. The envelopes were intercepted and confiscated by the commissioners at Dover postal depot on the ground that they had been imported in breach of s 1(ii) of the Revenue Act 1898 in conjunction with s 2 of the Lotteries and Amusements Act 1976, before their amendment by the National Lottery etc Act 1993.

6. Section 1 of the Revenue Act 1898 as then in force provided:

'The importation of the following articles is prohibited, that is to say:—
(ii) Any advertisement or other notice of, or relating to, the drawing or intended drawing of any lottery, which, in the opinion of Commissioners of Customs, is imported for the purpose of publication in the United Kingdom, in contravention of any Act relating to lotteries.'

7. Section 1 of the Lotteries and Amusements Act 1976 prohibits lotteries which do not constitute gaming within the meaning of the United Kingdom legislation on gaming (in particular the Gaming Act 1968), namely the distribution of winnings in money or money's worth on the basis of chance where money has been staked by the players. However, by way of exception to that prohibition, the law permits certain types of lottery, mainly small-scale lotteries for charitable and similar purposes.

8. According to the order for reference, the 87th issue of the SKL was prohibited by virtue of those provisions.

9. Section 2 of the Act of 1976 as then in force provided:

'(1) ... every person who in connection with any lottery promoted or proposed to be promoted either in Great Britain or elsewhere ... (d) brings, or invites any person to send, into Great Britain, for the purposes of sale or distribution any ticket in, or advertisement of, the lottery; or (e) sends or attempts to send out of Great Britain any money or valuable thing received in respect of the sale or distribution, or any document recording the sale or distribution, or the identity of the holder, of any ticket or chance in the lottery; or ... (g) causes, procures or attempts to procure any person to do any of the above-mentioned acts, shall be guilty of an offence.'

10. In proceedings brought by the commissioners for condemnation of the items seized, Gerhart and Jörg Schindler, defendants in the main proceedings, argued before the High Court of Justice that s 1(ii) of the Revenue Act 1898 and s 2 of the Lotteries and Amusements Act 1976 were incompatible with art 30, or in the alternative art 59, of the Treaty since they prohibited the importation into a member state of tickets, letters and application forms relating to a lottery lawfully conducted in another member state.

11. The commissioners contended that tickets and advertisements for a lottery did not constitute 'goods' within the meaning of the Treaty, that neither art 30 nor art 59 of the Treaty applied to the prohibition on importation in the United Kingdom legislation since that legislation applied to all large-scale lotteries whatever their origin and that in any event the prohibition was justified by the United Kingdom government's concern to limit lotteries for social policy reasons and to prevent fraud.

12. Considering that resolution of that dispute required an interpretation of Community law, the High Court of Justice stayed the proceedings and referred the following questions to the court:

'(1) Do tickets in, or advertisements for, a lottery which is lawfully conducted in another Member State constitute goods for the purposes of Article 30 of the Treaty of Rome?

(2) If so, does Article 30 apply to the prohibition by the United Kingdom of the importation of tickets or advertisements for major lotteries, given that the restrictions imposed by United Kingdom law on the conduct of such lotteries within the United Kingdom apply without discrimination on ground of nationality and irrespective of whether the lottery is organized from outside or with the United Kingdom?

(3) If so, do the concerns of the United Kingdom to limit lotteries for social policy reasons and to prevent fraud constitute legitimate public policy or public morality considerations to justify the restrictions of which complaint is made, whether under Article 36 or otherwise, in the circumstances of the present case?

(4) Does the provision of tickets in, or the sending of advertisements for, a lottery which is lawfully conducted in another Member State constitute the provision of services for the purposes of Article 59 of the Treaty of Rome?

(5) If so, does Article 59 apply to the prohibition by the United Kingdom of the importation of tickets or advertisements for major lotteries, given that the restrictions imposed by United Kingdom law on the conduct of such lotteries within the United Kingdom apply without discrimination on grounds of nationality and irrespective of whether the lottery is organized from outside or within the United Kingdom?

(6) If so, do the concerns of the United Kingdom to limit lotteries for social policy reasons and to prevent fraud constitute legitimate public

policy or public morality considerations to justify the restrictions of which complaint is made, whether under Article 56 read with Article 66 or otherwise, in the circumstances of the present case?'

13. Read in the light of the arguments adduced before it by the parties to the main proceedings and the reasons given in its order for reference, the question put by the national court is essentially whether arts 30 and 59 of the Treaty preclude the legislation of a member state from prohibiting, subject to exceptions, lotteries in its territory—as does the United Kingdom legislation— and consequently the importation of material intended to enable its residents to participate in foreign lotteries.

14. The first and fourth questions are put by the national court to ascertain whether the importation of lottery advertisements and tickets into a member state with a view to the participation by residents of that state in a lottery operated in another member state constitutes an importation of goods and falls under art 30 of the Treaty or whether such an activity amounts to a provision of services which as such comes within the scope of art 59 of the Treaty.

15. In those circumstances, those two questions should be considered together.

The first and fourth questions

16. In assessing whether arts 30 and 59 of the Treaty apply, the Belgian, German, Irish, Luxembourg and Portuguese governments argue that lotteries are not an 'economic activity' within the meaning of the Treaty. They submit that lotteries have traditionally been prohibited in the member states, or are operated either directly by the public authorities or under their control, solely in the public interest. They consider that lotteries have no economic purpose since they are based on chance. In any case, lotteries are in the nature of recreation or amusement rather than economic. The Belgian and Luxembourg governments add that it is clear from Council Directive (EEC) 75/368 of 16 June 1975 on measures to facilitate the effective exercise of freedom of establishment and freedom to provide services in respect of various activities (ex ISIC Division 01 to 85) and, in particular, transitional measures in respect of those activities (OJ 1975 L167, p 22) that lotteries fall outside the scope of the Treaty except where they are operated by individuals with a view to profit.

17. The Spanish, French and United Kingdom governments and the Commission argue that operating lotteries is a 'service' within the meaning of art 60 of the Treaty. They submit that such an activity relates to services normally provided for remuneration to the operator of the lottery or to the participants in it, but not covered by the rules on the free movement of goods.

18. Finally, the defendants in the main proceedings argue that their activity comes within the scope of art 30 of the Treaty. They submit that the advertisement and documents announcing or concerning a lottery draw are 'goods' within the meaning of the Treaty, that is to say in accordance with the court's definition in *Cinéthèque SA v Fédération nationale des cinémas français* Joined cases 60 and 61/84 [1985] ECR 2605 they are manufactured material objects.

19. Since some governments argue that lotteries are not 'economic activities' within the meaning of the Treaty, it must be made clear that the importation of goods or the provision of services for remuneration (see on the latter point the judgments in *Donà v Mantero* Case 13/76 [1976] ECR 1333 at 1340 (para 12) and *Steymann v Staatssecretaris van Justitie* Case 196/87 [1988]

ECR 6159 at 6172 (para 10)) are to be regarded as 'economic activities' within the meaning of the Treaty.

20. That being so, it will be sufficient to consider whether lotteries fall within the scope of one or other of the articles of the Treaty referred to in the order of reference.

21. The national court asks whether lotteries fall, at least in part, within the ambit of art 30 of the Treaty to the extent that they involve the large-scale sending and distribution, in this case in another member state, of material objects such as letters, promotional leaflets or lottery tickets.

22. The activity pursued by the defendants in the main proceedings appears, admittedly, to be limited to sending advertisements and application forms, and possibly tickets, on behalf of a lottery operator, SKL. However, those activities are only specific steps in the organisation or operation of a lottery and cannot, under the Treaty, be considered independently of the lottery to which they relate. The importation and distribution of objects are not ends in themselves. Their sole purpose is to enable residents of the member states where those objects are imported and distributed to participate in the lottery.

23. The point relied on by Gerhart and Jörg Schindler, that on the facts of the main proceedings agents of the SKL send material objects into Great Britain in order to advertise the lottery and sell tickets therein, and that material objects which have been manufactured are goods within the meaning of the court's case law, is not sufficient to reduce their activity to one of exportation or importation

24. Lottery activities are thus not activities relating to 'goods', falling, as such, under art 30 of the Treaty.

25. They are however to be regarded as 'services' within the meaning of the Treaty.

26. The first paragraph of art 60 of the Treaty provides:

'Services shall be considered to be "services" within the meaning of this Treaty where they are normally provided for remuneration, in so far as they are not governed by the provisions relating to freedom of movement for goods, capital and persons.'

27. The services at issue are those provided by the operator of the lottery to enable purchasers of tickets to participate in a game of chance with the hope of winning, by arranging for that purpose for the stakes to be collected, the draws to be organised and the prizes for winnings to be ascertained and paid out.

28. Those services are normally provided for remuneration constituted by the price of the lottery ticket.

29. The services in question are cross-border services when, as in the main proceedings, they are offered in a member state other than that in which the lottery operator is established.

30. Finally, lotteries are governed neither by the Treaty rules on the free movement of goods (see para 24 above), nor by the rules on the free movement of persons, which concern only movements of persons, nor by the rules on free movement of capital, which concern only capital movements though not all monetary transfers necessary to economic activities (see the judgment in *R v Thompson* Case 7/78 [1980] 2 All ER 102, [1980] QB 229).

31. Admittedly, as some member states point out, lotteries are subject to particularly strict regulation and close control by the public authorities in the various member states of the Community. However, they are not totally

prohibited in those states. On the contrary, they are commonplace. In particular, although in principle lotteries are prohibited in the United Kingdom, small-scale lotteries for charitable and similar purposes are permitted, and, since the enactment of the appropriate law in 1993, so is the national lottery.

32. In these circumstances, lotteries cannot be regarded as activities whose harmful nature causes them to be prohibited in all the member states and whose position under Community law may be likened to that of activities involving illegal products (see, in relation to drugs, the judgment in *Einberger v Hauptzollamt Freiburg* Case 294/82 [1984] ECR 1177) even though, as the Belgian and Luxembourg governments point out, the law of certain member states treats gaming contracts as void. Even if the morality of lotteries is at least questionable, it is not for the court to substitute its assessment for that of the legislatures of the member states where that activity is practised legally (see the judgment in *Society for the Protection of Unborn Children Ireland Ltd v Grogan* Case C-159/90 [1991] ECR I-4685 at 4739 (para 20)).

33. Some governments stress the chance character of lottery winnings. However, a normal lottery transaction consists of the payment of a sum by a gambler who hopes in return to receive a prize or winnings. The element of chance inherent in that return does not prevent the transaction having an economic nature.

34. It is also the case that, like amateur sport, a lottery may provide entertainment for the players who participate. However, that recreational aspect of the lottery does not take it out of the realm of the provision of services. Not only does it give the players, if not always a win, at least the hope of a win, it also yields a gain for the operator. Lotteries are operated by private or public persons with a view to profit since, in most cases, not all the money staked by the participants is redistributed as prizes or winnings.

35. Although in many member states the law provides that the profits made by a lottery may be used only for certain purposes, in particular in the public interest, or may even be required to be paid into the state budget, the rules on the allocation of profits do not alter the nature of the activity in question or deprive it of its economic character.

36. Finally, in excluding from its ambit lottery activities other than those conducted by individuals with a view to profit, Directive 75/368, mentioned above, did not thereby deny those activities the character of 'services'. The sole object of that directive is to make it easier, by way of transitional measures, for nationals of other member states to pursue specified activities as self-employed persons. Thus, neither the object nor the effect of the directive is, or indeed could have been, to exclude lotteries from the scope of arts 59 and 60 of the Treaty.

37. Consequently, the reply to be given to the first and fourth questions should be that the importation of lottery advertisements and tickets into a member state with a view to the participation by residents of that state in a lottery operated in another member state relates to a 'service' within the meaning of art 60 of the Treaty and accordingly falls within the scope of art 59 of the Treaty.

The second and third questions

38. It is clear from their wording that the national court's second and third questions are put only if the activity in issue in the main proceedings falls

within the scope of art 30 of the Treaty. Since that is not the case, those questions do not call for a reply.

The fifth question

39. The essence of the national court's fifth question is whether national legislation which, like the United Kingdom legislation on lotteries, prohibits, subject to specified exceptions, the holding of lotteries in a member state constitutes an obstacle to the freedom to provide services.

40. The Commission and the defendants in the main proceedings argue that, on any view of the matter, such legislation, being in fact discriminatory, restricts the freedom to provide services.

41. The Spanish, French, Greek and United Kingdom governments accept that such legislation may restrict freedom to provide services even though it is applicable without distinction.

42. The Belgian and Luxembourg governments submit that legislation such as the United Kingdom legislation does not restrict freedom to provide services because is it applicable without distinction.

43. According to the case law of the court (see the judgment in *Säger v Dennemeyer & Co Ltd* Case C-76/90 [1991] ECR I-4221 at 4243 (para 12)) national legislation may fall within the ambit of art 59 of the Treaty, even if it is applicable without distinction, when it is liable to prohibit or otherwise impede the activities of a provider of services established in another member state where he lawfully provides similar services.

44. It is sufficient to note that this is the case with national legislation such as the United Kingdom legislation on lotteries which wholly precludes lottery operators from other member states from promoting their lotteries and selling their tickets, whether directly or through independent agents, in the member state which enacted that legislation.

45. Accordingly, the reply to the fifth question should be that national legislation which, like the United Kingdom legislation on lotteries, prohibits, subject to specified exceptions, the holding of lotteries in a member state is an obstacle to the freedom to provide services.

The sixth question

46. The national court's sixth question raises the issue whether the Treaty provisions relating to the freedom to provide services preclude legislation such as the United Kingdom lotteries legislation, where there are concerns of social policy and of the prevention of fraud to justify it.

47. First, as the national court states, legislation such as the United Kingdom legislation involves no discrimination on the basis of nationality and must consequently be regarded as being applicable without distinction.

48. It is common ground that a prohibition such as that laid down in the United Kingdom legislation, which applies to the operation of large-scale lotteries and in particular to the advertising and distribution of tickets for such lotteries, applies irrespective of the nationality of the lottery operator or his agents and whatever the member state or states in which the operator or his agents are established. It does not therefore discriminate on the basis of the nationality of the economic agents concerned or of the member state in which they are established.

49. The Commission and the defendants in the main proceedings argue, however, that legislation such as the United Kingdom lotteries legislation is in fact discriminatory. They submit that, although such legislation prohibits

large lotteries in the United Kingdom in an apparently non-discriminatory
manner, it permits the simultaneous operation by the same person of several
small lotteries, which is equivalent to one large lottery and further the
operation of games of chance which are comparable in nature and scale to large
lotteries, such a football pools or bingo.

50. It is true that the prohibition in question in the main proceedings does
not apply to all types of lottery, small-scale lotteries not conducted for private
gain being permitted in the national territory and the prohibition being set in
the more general context of the national legislation on gambling which permits
certain forms of gambling similar to lotteries, such as football pools or bingo.

51. However, even though the amounts at stake in the games so permitted
in the United Kingdom may be comparable to those in large-scale lotteries and
even though those games involve a significant element of chance they differ in
their object, rules and methods of organisation from those large-scale lotteries
which were established in member states other than the United Kingdom
before the enactment of the National Lottery etc Act 1993. They are therefore
not in a comparable situation to the lotteries prohibited by the United
Kingdom legislation and, contrary to the arguments of the Commission and
the defendants in the main proceedings, cannot be assimilated to them.

52. In those circumstances legislation such as the United Kingdom
legislation cannot be considered to be discriminatory.

53. That leads to the question whether art 59 of the Treaty precludes such
legislation which, although not discriminatory, nonetheless as stated above (at
para 45) restricts freedom to provide services.

54. All the governments which have submitted observations consider that
legislation such as that at issue is compatible with art 59 of the Treaty. They
argue that the legislation must be regarded as justified by overriding public
interest considerations of consumer protection, prevention of crime,
protection of public morality, restriction of demand for gambling and the
financing of public interest activities. They consider, furthermore, that such
legislation is proportionate to the objectives pursued thereby.

55. In contrast the Commission considers that although it is based on
overriding public interest considerations a prohibition on lotteries such as that
provided under United Kingdom law is not compatible with art 59 of the
Treaty since the objectives it pursues may be achieved by less restrictive
measures.

56. The defendants in the main proceedings argue for their part that the
reasons invoked to justify the prohibition at issue cannot constitute overriding
considerations of public interest since legislation such as the United Kingdom
legislation does not contain an equivalent prohibition of gambling of the same
nature as large-scale lotteries.

57. According to the information provided by the referring court, the
United Kingdom legislation, before its amendment by the 1993 Act establishing
the national lottery, pursued the following objectives: to prevent crime and to
ensure that gamblers would be treated honestly; to avoid stimulating demand
in the gambling sector which has damaging social consequences when taken to
excess; and to ensure that lotteries could not be operated for personal and
commercial profit but solely for charitable, sporting or cultural purposes.

58. Those considerations, which must be taken together, concern the
protection of the recipients of the service and, more generally, of consumers as
well as the maintenance of order in society. The court has already held that
those objectives figure among those which can justify restrictions on freedom

to provide services (see judgments in *Ministère Public v Van Wesemael* Joined cases 110 and 111/78 [1979] ECR 35 at 52 (para 28), *EC Commission v France* Case 220/83 [1986] ECR 3663 at 3709 (para 20) and *Société Générale Alsacienne de Banque SA v Koestler* Case 15/78 [1978] ECR 1971 at 1981 (para 5)).

59. Given the peculiar nature of lotteries, which has been stressed by many member states, those considerations are such as to justify restrictions, as regards art 59 of the Treaty, which may go so far as to prohibit lotteries in a member state.

60. First of all, it is not possible to disregard the moral, religious or cultural aspects of lotteries, like other types of gambling, in all the member states. The general tendency of the member states is to restrict, or even prohibit, the practice of gambling and to prevent it from being a source of private profit. Secondly, lotteries involve a high risk of crime or fraud, given the size of the amounts which can be staked and of the winnings which they can hold out to the players, particularly when they are operated on a large scale, Thirdly, they are an incitement to spend which may have damaging individual and social consequences. A final ground which is not without relevance, although it cannot in itself be regarded as an objective justification, is that lotteries may make a significant contribution to the financing of benevolent or public interest activities such as social works, charitable works, sport or culture.

61. Those particular factors justify national authorities having a sufficient degree of latitude to determine what is required to protect the players and, more generally, in the light of the specific social and cultural features of each member state, to maintain order in society, as regards the manner in which lotteries are operated, the size of the stakes and the allocation of the profits they yield. In those circumstances, it is for them to assess not only whether it is necessary to restrict the activities of lotteries but also whether they should be prohibited, provided that those restrictions are not discriminatory.

62. When a member state prohibits in its territory the operation of large-scale lotteries and in particular the advertising and distribution of tickets for that type of lottery, the prohibition on the importation of materials intended to enable nationals of that member state to participate in such lotteries organised in another member state cannot be regarded as a measure involving an unjustified interference with the freedom to provide services. Such a prohibition on import is a necessary part of the protection which that member state seeks to secure in its territory in relation to lotteries.

63. Accordingly, the reply to be given to the sixth question must be that the Treaty provisions relating to freedom to provide services do not preclude legislation such as the United Kingdom lotteries legislation, in view of the concerns of social policy and of the prevention of fraud which justify it.

Costs

64. The costs incurred by the Belgian, Danish, German, Greek, Spanish, French, Irish, Luxembourg, Netherlands, Portuguese and United Kingdom governments and the Commission of the European Communities, which have submitted observations to the court, are not recoverable. Since these proceedings are, for the parties to the main proceedings, a step in the action pending before the national court, the decision on costs is a matter for that court.

On those grounds, the court, in answer to the questions referred to it by the High Court of Justice (Queen's Bench Division, Commercial Court) by order of 3 April 1992, hereby rules: (1) the importation of lottery advertisements and tickets into a member state with a view to the participation by residents of that state in a lottery operated in another member state relates to a 'service' within the meaning of art 60 of the Treaty and accordingly falls within the scope of art 59 of the Treaty; (2) national legislation which, like the United Kingdom legislation on lotteries, prohibits, subject to specified exceptions, the holding of lotteries in a member state is an obstacle to the freedom to provide services; (3) the Treaty provisions relating to freedom to provide services do not preclude legislation such as the United Kingdom lotteries legislation, in view of the concerns of social policy and of the prevention of fraud which justify it.

Carolyn Toulmin   Barrister.

Brooks v Director of Public Prosecutions of Jamaica and another

PRIVY COUNCIL
LORD MACKAY OF CLASHFERN LC, LORD TEMPLEMAN, LORD ACKNER, LORD SLYNN OF HADLEY AND LORD WOOLF
7, 8 DECEMBER 1993, 24 JANUARY 1994

Jamaica – Criminal law – Bill of indictment – Information charging defendant dismissed by resident magistrate on ground of no case to answer – DPP applying to judge for voluntary bill of indictment against defendant for same offence – Defendant not given notice of DPP's application – Warrant issued before indictment preferred – DPP having power to prefer bill of indictment without applying to judge – Whether judge having jurisdiction to prefer indictment – Whether defendant entitled to notice of application – Whether abuse of process for bill of indictment to be preferred where defendant discharged after preliminary inquiry in absence of fresh evidence – Whether warrant for arrest valid – Constitution of Jamaica, s 94(6) – Criminal Justice (Administration) Act (Jamaica), s 2(2).

After a 16-day hearing a resident magistrate in Jamaica dismissed an information charging the appellant, a registered medical practitioner, with carnal abuse of a girl under the age of 12, on the ground that no prima facie case had been made out. The Director of Public Prosecutions (the DPP) disagreed with that decision and on his application by summons under s 2(2)[a] of the Criminal Justice (Administration) Act, a Supreme Court judge ordered that a voluntary bill of indictment be preferred against the appellant for the same offence and that a warrant be issued for his arrest. The appellant was not given notice of the summons. The bench warrant for the appellant's arrest was signed by the judge and an indictment charging the appellant with the same offence was signed on behalf of the DPP. The appellant was arrested and later granted bail. The appellant applied to the Full Court for redress under s 25 of

---

a   Section 2(2), so far as material, is set out at p 236 j, post

the Constitution of Jamaica on the grounds (i) that, since s 2(2) conferred exclusively on the DPP the power to prefer an indictment and since by virtue of s 94(6)[b] of the Constitution the power to institute or continue criminal proceedings was vested in the DPP to the exclusion 'of any other person or authority', the DPP should not have sought an order from the judge to do that which he could lawfully have done without an order, (ii) that the rules of natural justice required the appellant to be given a fair hearing before the indictment was preferred, (iii) that, in the absence of fresh evidence, it was an abuse of process for the DPP or the judge to direct or consent to the preferral of an indictment when the appellant had been discharged by the resident magistrate after a complete and regular preliminary inquiry and (iv) that the warrant on which the appellant was arrested was not valid or lawful since it had been issued before the indictment was preferred. The Full Court dismissed his application and the Court of Appeal dismissed the appellant's appeal against that decision. The appellant appealed to the Privy Council.

Held – The appeal would be dismissed for the following reasons—

(1) On the true construction of s 2(2) of the Criminal Justice (Administration) Act the DPP was entitled, in the exercise of his unfettered discretion, to seek the directions or consent of a judge as to whether an indictment should be preferred, notwithstanding that in certain circumstances the power to prefer an indictment was exclusively available to the DPP or those acting on his behalf. The primary purpose of s 94(6) of the Constitution was to protect the DPP from any political interference and it was not intended to apply to judicial control of the conduct of proceedings, particularly where that control was imposed not against the wishes of the DPP but at his request. There were certain situations where it would be sensible for the DPP not to exercise his own power to prefer an indictment but to take advantage of the power of a judge to direct or consent to an indictment being preferred, eg where the DPP adopted the exceptional course of seeking to prefer a bill of indictment without relying on any additional evidence after a resident magistrate had concluded that there was no prima facie case to answer, since he would thereby be putting the proceedings under the control of the judge from the outset rather than later. Furthermore, the judge in exercising his discretion under s 2(2) to direct the preferral of the indictment had merely given his indorsement of the initiation of proceedings, which was a procedural step, and neither principles of fairness, the common law nor the Constitution required the person subject to the proceedings to be given prior notice of the DPP's application or to be present when the judge made his direction (see p 237 h j, p 238 d to g and p 239 a to e g to j, post); *Grant v DPP* [1982] AC 190 applied; *R v Phillips, Lucas and Gibson* (1764) 3 Burr 1564 and *R v Phillips* (1767) 4 Burr 2090 considered.

(2) In deciding whether or not a indictment should have been preferred where it had been held in committal proceedings that there was no prima facie case, the DPP and/or the judge had to balance the interests of the Crown acting on behalf of the community against the interests of the defendant. In so doing the DPP and/or the judge were required to treat the decision of the resident magistrate with the greatest respect and to regard their jurisdiction as one to be exercised with great circumspection. There had to be exceptional

---

b   Section 94(6) is set out at p 236 c d, post

circumstances to warrant prosecuting a defendant after it had been found in committal proceedings that there was no case to answer but in all the circumstances it could not be said that it would be an abuse of the process to allow the trial of the appellant to proceed (see p 240 *f* to *j* and p 241 *a b*, post); *R v Horsham Justices, ex p Reeves* (1980) 75 Cr App R 236 and *Barton v R* (1980) 147 CLR 75 applied.

(3) In order to decide the validity of the indictment the time at which the warrant was executed was critical. The judge was entitled, once he had reached his decision that an indictment could be preferred, to sign the warrant. The warrant was not effective until the indictment had been preferred but as long as that had happened before the warrant was executed the execution of the warrant was lawful (see p 241 *h*, post).

Notes

For the Constitution of Jamaica, see 6 *Halsbury's Laws* (4th edn reissue) paras 933–934.

For voluntary bills of indictment, see 11(2) *Halsbury's Laws* (4th edn reissue) paras 918–920, and for cases on the subject, see 15(1) *Digest* (2nd reissue) 215–216, 13624–13627..

Cases referred to in judgment

Barton v R (1980) 147 CLR 75, Aust HC.
Grant v DPP [1982] AC 190, [1981] 3 WLR 352, PC.
IRC v Rossminster Ltd [1980] 1 All ER 80, [1980] AC 952, [1980] 2 WLR 1, HL.
R v Crown Court at Derby, ex p Brooks (1984) 80 Cr App R 164, DC.
R v Horsham Justices, ex p Reeves (1980) 75 Cr App R 236, DC.
R v Raymond [1981] 2 All ER 246, [1981] QB 910, [1981] 3 WLR 660, CA.
R v Phillips (1767) 4 Burr 2090, 98 ER 90.
R v Phillips, Lucas and Gibson (1764) 3 Burr 1564, 97 ER 983 .
Wiseman v Borneman [1969] 3 All ER 275, [1971] AC 297, [1969] 3 WLR 706, HL.

Cases also cited

Commonwealth Life Assurance Society v Smith (1938) 59 CLR 527, Aust HC.
Githunguri v Republic of Kenya [1986] 3 LRC (Const) 618, Kenya HC.
McBean v R [1977] AC 537, [1976] 3 WLR 482, PC.
R v Brentford Justices, ex p Wong [1981] 1 All ER 884, [1981] QB 445, DC.
R v Epping and Harlow Justices, ex p Massaro [1973] 1 All ER 1011, [1973] QB 433, DC.
R v Governor of Pentonville Prison, ex p Alves [1992] 4 All ER 787, [1993] AC 284, I IL.
Bennett v Horseferry Road Magistrates' Court [1993] 3 All ER 138, [1994] AC 42, HL.
R v Morais [1988] 3 All ER 161, CA.
R v Spilsbury [1898] 2 QB 615.
Roberts, Re [1967] 1 WLR 474, Assizes.
Williams and Salisbury, Re (1978) 26 WIR 133, Guyana CA.

Appeal

Lloyd Brooks appealed with the leave of the Court of Appeal of Jamaica from the decision of that court (Carey and Wright JJA (Downer JA dissenting in part)) on 9 April 1992 dismissing his appeal from the judgment of the Full Court of the Supreme Court (Rowe ACJ, Clarke J and James AJ) on 16 September 1991

dismissing his motion against the respondents, the Director of Public
Prosecutions of Jamaica and the Attorney General of Jamaica, for redress under
s 25 of the Constitution of Jamaica. The facts are set out in the judgment of the
Board.

Lord Gifford QC, Ian Ramsay and *Jacqueline Samuels-Brown* (both of the Jamaican
Bar) with him, (instructed by *Edwin Coe*) for the appellant.
The Director of Public Prosecutions of Jamaica (*Glen Andrade QC*), the *Senior Deputy
Director of Public Prosecutions of Jamaica* (*Lloyd Hibbert*) with him, (instructed
by *Charles Russell*) in his own behalf.
The Senior Assistant Attorney General of Jamaica (*Lennox Campbell*) and the
Assistant Attorney General of Jamaica (*Lackston Robinson*) (instructed by
Charles Russell) for the Attorney General.

At the conclusion of the argument the Board announced that it would advise
that the appeal be dismissed for reasons to be given later.

24 January 1994. The following judgment of the Board was delivered.

LORD WOOLF. The appellant is a registered medical practitioner. After a
16-day hearing between 4 December 1990 and 1 May 1991, the resident
magistrate for the parish of St Andrew, Jamaica, dismissed an information
charging the appellant with an offence of carnal abuse of a girl under the age of
12 years, contrary to s 48(1) of the Offences against the Person Act. The
resident magistrate decided that no prima facie case had been made out. The
Director of Public Prosecutions of Jamaica (the DPP) disagreed with this
decision.

The sequence of subsequent events is important and is as follows. On 4 June
1991 the DPP applied by summons to a judge of the Supreme Court for a
voluntary bill of indictment against the appellant for the same offence; on 6
June 1991, without the appellant being given prior notice, the representative of
the DPP appeared before Courtenay Orr J in chambers, who made an order
that a voluntary bill of indictment be granted against the appellant and that a
warrant be issued for his arrest; on 10 June 1991 the order of the judge was
signed by the registrar and filed with the registry of the Supreme Court; on 11
June 1991 a bench warrant for the arrest of the appellant was signed by
Courtenay Orr J; subsequently, on 13 June 1991 an indictment charging the
appellant with the same offence was signed on behalf of the DPP; and on 17
June 1991 the appellant was arrested and later granted bail.

The appellant challenged what had happened, initially, before the Full Court
and then by way of appeal to the Court of Appeal. He was unsuccessful before
both courts. The Court of Appeal gave the appellant leave to appeal to the
Board. That appeal was heard on 7 and 8 December 1993. At the conclusion
of the hearing their Lordships announced that they would humbly advise Her
Majesty to dismiss the appeal for reasons to be delivered later. This judgment
sets out those reasons.

As the appellant will probably stand trial in Jamaica in the near future, their
Lordships consider that they should limit their description of the evidence
which was before the resident magistrate in so far as this is possible.

The girl referred to in the charge was a patient of the appellant. At the time
of the alleged offence she was about 10 years old and lived with her

grandparents. On 26 May 1990, according to her grandmother, she left home with the appellant at about 11.00 am and did not return until about 3.00 pm. The appellant had said that he was taking her to see a child psychologist. However it was alleged that while the girl was with the appellant she went with him to an apartment where he had sexual intercourse with her. Afterwards the appellant did take her to the office of the child psychologist, but no appointment had been made and the psychologist was not there.

When the child returned home, she made a complaint to her grandmother which was broadly consistent with her evidence that the appellant had sexual intercourse with her. A report was made to the police and on 28 May 1990, two days after the alleged incident, she was examined by a doctor who found signs of recent sexual intercourse and was of the opinion that the girl's hymen had been ruptured within a period of three days prior to the examination. There was also corroborative evidence from a forensic analyst.

If the girl's evidence was credible, the case was reasonably strong. However there were two particularly worrying features revealed as a result of the extensive cross-examination which took place before the resident magistrate. The first was that the girl was probably suffering from gonorrhoea. The second was that there was evidence given by the girl which suggested that she may have had a relationship involving another man.

In support of this appeal Lord Gifford QC identified the following four issues on which the outcome of the appeal depended.

(1) *The jurisdiction issue* Whether a judge of the Supreme Court has power to make an order that a voluntary bill of indictment should be preferred at the instance of the DPP.

(2) *The fair hearing issue* Whether, in cases where a judge has power to direct the preferral of an indictment, the provisions of s 20 in Sch 2 to the Jamaica (Constitution) Order in Council 1962, SI 1962/1550 (the Constitution), and/or the rules of natural justice require a fair hearing at which the proposed defendant has the right to appear and be heard.

(3) *The abuse of process issue* Whether it is an abuse of process for the DPP and/or for a judge of the Supreme Court to direct or consent to the preferral of an indictment in circumstances where the proposed defendant has been discharged by a resident magistrate after a complete and regular preliminary inquiry in the absence of fresh evidence.

(4) *The validity of warrant issue* Whether the warrant on which the appellant was arrested was a valid and lawful warrant, since it was issued before the indictment was preferred.

The four issues will be examined in turn.

The jurisdiction issue

The powers of the DPP are set out in the Constitution. The relevant section is s 94, which also deals with his important status within the Jamaican criminal justice system. Section 94(1) provides that the office of DPP is a public office and s 94(2) indicates that in order to become DPP it is necessary to have the same qualifications as are required for an appointment as a judge of the Supreme Court. In accordance with s 94(3) the DPP—

'shall have power in any case in which he considers it desirable so to do—(a) to institute and undertake criminal proceedings against any person before any court other than a court-martial in respect of any offence against the law of Jamaica; (b) to take over and continue any such criminal proceedings that may have been instituted by any other person or authority; and (c) to discontinue at any stage before judgment is delivered any such criminal proceedings instituted or undertaken by himself or any other person or authority.'

Section 94(4) gives the DPP a power to delegate and s 94(5) provides that the powers referred to in paras (b) and (c) of sub-s (3) are vested in the DPP to the exclusion 'of any other person or authority':

'Provided that where any other person or authority has instituted criminal proceedings, nothing in this subsection shall prevent the withdrawal of those proceedings by or at the instance of that person or authority and with the leave of the court.'

Section 94(6) is the critical subsection for the purposes of this issue since it provides:

'In the exercise of the powers conferred upon him by this section the Director of Public Prosecutions shall not be subject to the direction or control of any other person or authority.'

Lord Gifford submits, on behalf of the appellant, that 'authority' in s 94(6) must include a court so the DPP cannot be 'subject to the direction or control' of a judge when deciding whether an indictment should be preferred. In support of this submission he relies on s 1(9), which he submits confirms that an 'authority' includes a court. Section 1(9) provides:

'No provision of this Constitution that any person or authority shall not be subject to the direction or control of any other person or authority in exercising any functions under this Constitution shall be construed as precluding a court from exercising jurisdiction in relation to any question whether that person or authority has performed those functions in accordance with this Constitution or any other law.'

The circumstances in which an indictment can be preferred are set out in s 2(2) of the Criminal Justice (Administration) Act. The subsection sets out five different situations in which an indictment may be preferred (see per Lord Diplock in *Grant v DPP* [1982] AC 190 at 201). The first is where the prosecutor or other person has been bound by recognisance to prosecute or give evidence against the person accused, the second is where the accused has been committed to or detained in custody and the third is where the accused has been bound by recognisance to appear to answer to an indictment. It is however the fourth and fifth situations which are relevant for present purposes. As to those situations s 2(2) provides that no indictment shall be preferred—

'unless such indictment for such offence be preferred by the direction of, or with the consent in writing of a judge of any of the courts of this island, or by the direction or with the consent of the Director of Public Prosecutions, or of the Deputy Director of Public Prosecutions, or of any person authorised in that behalf by the Director of Public Prosecutions.'

Section 2(2) makes it clear that the position in Jamaica is different from that which now exists in England and Wales since the counterpart of the DPP in England has no personal power to prefer an indictment. In England and Wales it is a judge of the High Court alone who has the power to prefer a voluntary bill.

Basing himself upon the statutory provisions which have been set out, Lord Gifford submits that it would be repugnant to justice if the DPP were able to seek from a judge an order to do that which he could lawfully do without such an order. For this contention Lord Gifford was able to obtain support from the judgment of Downer JA, who, on this point, took a different view from that of the other members of the Court of Appeal (Carey and Wright JJA). Downer JA regarded the application to the judge as 'superfluous' and 'constitutionally impermissible'. This was because for the DPP to be 'directed or controlled' by a judge would be contrary to the principle of the separation of powers and would contravene s 94(6). He considered that his approach was strongly supported by two decisions of Lord Mansfield CJ, the first in *R v Phillips, Lucas and Gibson* (1764) 3 Burr 1565, 97 ER 983 and the second in *R v Phillips* (1767) 4 Burr 2090, 98 ER 90. At the time those cases were decided, the Attorney General was entitled himself to sign an information and in this situation Lord Mansfield CJ made it clear that he strongly disapproved of the Attorney General seeking the approval of the court to do something which he could do without that approval. In the earlier case Lord Mansfield CJ declared (3 Burr 1565, 97 ER 983):

'... the *court* would never grant an information upon the application of the *attorney general*, in cases prosecuted *by the crown*; because the attorney general has a right himself, *ex officio*, to exhibit one: and he may, if he thinks proper, summon the parties, to shew cause ...'

In the later case Lord Mansfield CJ declared, in the course of argument (4 Burr 2090, 98 ER 90):

'... he would never grant a motion for an information applied for *by the Attorney General* on behalf of the Crown; because the Attorney General has himself power to grant it, if he judges it to be a proper case for an information; and it would be a strange thing for the Court to direct *their officer* to sign an information which the Attorney General might sign *himself*, if he thought proper; and if he did not think it a proper case, it would equally be a reason why the Court should not intermeddle.'

Lord Mansfield CJ stated the position even more clearly in his short judgment which followed by saying (4 Burr 2090, 98 ER 90):

'If it appears to the King's Attorney General to be right to grant an information, he may do it himself; if he does not think it so, he cannot expect us to do it.'

The problem with adopting this approach to the issue under consideration, unless Lord Mansfield CJ is to be regarded as doing no more than giving a robust indication of how he would exercise his discretion, is that it is quite contrary to the language of s 2(2), which is perfectly clear and sets out five distinct powers for preferring an indictment. The fact that one of those powers is exclusively available to the DPP or those acting on his behalf does not mean that the DPP is not entitled to avail himself of the other methods of obtaining the preferment of an indictment. It is interesting to note that in *Grant v DPP* [1982] AC 190 at 201 Lord Diplock, in giving the opinion of the Board, regarded the meaning of s 2(2) as being clear and free from any ambiguity and, after setting out the 'five different circumstances in which an indictment may lawfully be preferred', went on to say:

'... as a matter of construction it is as plain as plain can be that the Director of Public Prosecutions is empowered to prefer an indictment at a circuit court without the necessity for there having been any preliminary examination of the accused before a resident magistrate. The words being plain and unambiguous it is not, in their Lordships' view, legitimate to have recourse to legislative history in the hope of finding something to cast doubt upon their plain and unambiguous meaning. The office of the Director of Public Prosecutions was a public office newly-created by section 94 of the Constitution. His security of tenure and independence from political influence is assured. In the exercise of his functions, which include instituting and undertaking criminal prosecutions, he is not subject to the direction or control of any other person. There would be nothing surprising if he were given less fettered powers to prefer indictments than had previously been bestowed on anyone other than a judge.'

On the language of s 2(2) their Lordships regard it as being equally clear that the DPP is entitled, if he chooses to do so in his unfettered discretion, to seek the directions or consent of a judge as to whether an indictment should be preferred. Lord Diplock was not intending to indicate the contrary. If Lord Gifford's submission is correct it would mean that s 94 of the Constitution does not alter the situation. Section 94(6) prevented a judge from exercising any control over the manner in which the DPP was supposed to 'undertake' proceedings. Lord Gifford appreciated the force of this point and sought to meet it by submitting that such a remarkable position is avoided by the language of s 1(9) of the Constitution, which he submitted did not apply to the initiation of proceedings but did apply to the way they were undertaken. However s 1(9) is primarily designed to make it clear that provisions of the nature to which it refers do not restrict the court's powers of judicial review. Its purpose is not to authorise a judge to exercise the continuing control which obviously needs to exist over the way the parties to criminal proceedings conduct those proceedings. While the word 'authority' is capable of being interpreted as including a judge, other provisions of the Constitution, for example s 20, indicate that usually where the draftsman of the Constitution intends to refer to a court this is made clear. Section 94(6) does not refer to a court because its primary purpose is to protect the DPP from the type of objectionable political interference referred to in the passage of the speech of Lord Diplock already cited. It is not intended to apply to judicial control of the proceedings.

In giving effect to s 94(6) it must be remembered that until s 2(2) was amended in 1962 by the Constitution (Transfer of Functions) (Attorney General to the Director of Public Prosecutions) Order 1962, on the creation by the Constitution of the office of the DPP, the powers of preferring an indictment, which the DPP now has, were exercised by the Attorney General. In performing those powers, the Attorney General, as is the case with his English counterpart, would not be operating in his governmental role but in his role as the guardian of the public interest. In 1962 it would not have been contemplated that the courts would or could exercise any control over the Attorney General against his wishes in circumstances now being considered. It is, however, one thing to impose control over the appropriate law officer against his wishes and another to impose control at his request.

There are obviously situations where it can be sensible for the DPP not to exercise his own power to prefer an indictment but to take advantage of the power of a judge to direct or consent to an indictment being preferred. The DPP with reason says that this case falls within that category. He recognises that to seek to prefer a bill of indictment after a resident magistrate has concluded that there is no prima facie case, without relying on any additional evidence, is an exceptional course to adopt. It was in the interests of the appellant and it demonstrates a proper respect for a decision by a member of the judiciary if, before such an exceptional course is taken, the DPP seeks the approval of a more senior judge than the resident magistrate to the course which he was proposing to take.

By seeking that approval, the doctrine of separation of powers was not offended in any way. The DPP is not a part of government, or a government official. If he wishes to bring proceedings inevitably there must come a stage when the manner in which he undertakes those proceedings is subject to control by the court. If he had not adopted the course of seeking the authority of a judge for the initiation of the proceedings, but had initiated the proceedings himself, the proceedings would become subject to the control of the court in due course, and in the event that they were held to constitute an abuse they would be dismissed. The only difference, which would result from the DPP initiating the proceedings himself, without going to a judge, is that the control by the court would be exercised at a later stage of the proceedings. That is normally at the commencement of the trial.

The DPP, by taking the course that he did, was at risk that he would come before a judge who would harshly adopt the same robust attitude as did Lord Mansfield CJ and not consent to the preferment of a bill. If this happened that judge would not be declining jurisdiction, but exercising the jurisdiction and declining to give consent as a matter of discretion. In the circumstances of this case, the judge did not exercise his discretion in that way.

The natural justice issue

The judge in exercising his powers under s 2(2) is doing no more than giving his indorsement of the initiation of proceedings. This is a procedural step which is not required by principles of fairness, the common law or the Constitution to be the subject of prior notice to the person who is to be subject to the proceedings. If guidance as to the position at common law is required, then it is provided by the decisions of the House of Lords in *Wiseman v Borneman* [1969] 3 All ER 275, [1971] AC 297 and *R v Raymond* [1981] 2 All ER 246, [1981] QB 910. The Constitution adds nothing to the position at common law.

The judge has a residual discretion which he can exercise in exceptional circumstances to require a defendant to be notified and to consider any representations which a defendant may wish to make, but this case is certainly far from being a case where such action was necessary or even desirable. The judge in order to come to his decision could do no more than study the depositions of the proceedings before the resident magistrate. These were placed before the judge as an exhibit to the affidavit of Crown counsel in the office of the DPP and the judge no doubt had proper regard to them. No more was required. There is nothing in this issue.

The abuse of process issue

This is the issue which has caused their Lordships the greatest concern. The resident magistrate came to her decision after a long hearing during which she had ample time to form an assessment as to the credibility of the witnesses. Her decision is therefore entitled to be treated with considerable respect. There was however ample evidence on which she would have been entitled to find that there was a prima facie case which justified the appellant being committed for trial. The resident magistrate's decision must therefore have been based on the lack of credibility of the prosecution witnesses and in particular of the girl who is alleged to have been raped.

Questions of credibility, except in the clearest of cases, do not normally result in a finding that there is no prima facie case. They are usually left to be determined at the trial. Nevertheless there are features of the evidence of the complainant which make her decision understandable and their Lordships accept Lord Gifford's submission that an application for certiorari to quash the resident magistrate's decision would have failed.

This does not, however, mean that the decision of the DPP to decide to apply for a bill of indictment to be preferred was an abuse of the process of the court. He could point to the existence of corroboration and the complaint by the girl which showed consistency on her part. The case, particularly having regard to the appellant's profession, was an important one from the appellant's and the public's point of view.

In *R v Crown Court at Derby, ex p Brooks* (1984) 80 Cr App R 164 at 168 the Divisional Court adopted, as one category of abuse of process, the fact that the prosecutor 'can be said to have manipulated or misused the rules of procedure'. In *Barton v R* (1980) 147 CLR 75 Gibbs and Mason JJ, in a judgment with which other members of the court agreed, pointed out that committal proceedings are an important element for the protection of an accused in the criminal justice systems of England and Australia, and that it is for the court, not the Attorney General, to decide in the last resort whether a trial should proceed in the absence of committal proceedings. However the court made clear that, in deciding whether a trial should proceed in the absence of preliminary examination, the court 'must have regard to the interests of the Crown acting on behalf of the community as well as to the interests of the accused' (at 101).

This balanced approach is also appropriate where, after there have been committal proceedings in which it has been decided that there is no prima facie case, the DPP, in Jamaica, decides that an indictment should be preferred. In such a situation the DPP, or, if his consent is sought, the judge, is in a better position than was the court in *Barton v R* to say whether it would be an abuse to initiate proceedings, in so far as the depositions were already in existence and their contents could be taken into account at the time of the decision. In coming to his decision the DPP or the judge should treat the decision of the resident magistrate with the greatest respect and regard their jurisdiction as one to be exercised with great circumspection. There have to be exceptional circumstances to warrant prosecuting a defendant after it has been found in committal proceedings that there is no case to answer (see the judgment of Ackner LJ in *R v Horsham Justices, ex p Reeves* (1980) 75 Cr App R 236).

On an appeal, the decision as to whether or not there is an abuse of process is one which the appeal court must itself determine. In doing so the court is not merely reviewing the decision of the DPP or the judge but deciding for itself whether, in all the circumstances and having regard to the considerations to which reference has already been made, the proceedings are an abuse. On the issue coming before the Board, as here, their Lordships have the additional advantage of being able to take into account the decisions of both the Full Court and the Court of Appeal. In this case, having done so, their Lordships have come to the conclusion that it cannot be said that it would be an abuse of the process to allow the trial to proceed. The circumstances do not justify interfering with the decision of the DPP, the judge and the courts below.

The validity of warrant issue

Lord Gifford argues that because the warrant was issued before the indictment was actually preferred this meant that the warrant was invalid. This issue is being raised by the appellant not because it affects the validity of the indictment, but because, if Lord Gifford's submissions are correct, he will be entitled to compensation for the contravention of s 15 of the Constitution, which forbids a person being deprived of his personal liberty except in the specified cases authorised by law. In support of his contention that the validity of a warrant must be tested 'at the date of its birth and not the date on which it is put into effect' Lord Gifford refers to a passage in *Archbold's Pleading, Evidence and Practice in Criminal Cases* (36th edn, 1966) para 1971 which states:

'Any court of record before which an indictment is preferred and signed may *forthwith* issue a bench warrant for arresting the party charged, and bringing him immediately before such court, to answer such indictment.' (My emphasis.)

Lord Gifford refers to that edition of *Archbold* because it was published prior to the law of England being changed by s 13(2) of the Courts Act 1971 (now s 80(2) of the Supreme Court Act 1981). He also seeks to draw support from the statements made as to search warrants in the speeches of the House of Lords in *IRC v Rossminster Ltd* [1980] 1 All ER 80, [1980] AC 952.

The point which is being taken is a technical one since, at the time when the warrant was executed, the indictment had certainly been preferred. However, where the liberty of the subject is at stake, technicalities are important and if the contentions made on behalf of the appellant were valid their Lordships would give effect to them. However this is not the case. It is the time at which the warrant is executed which is critical. In this case it was perfectly in order for the judge, having reached his decision that an indictment *could* be preferred, to sign the warrant. The warrant would not then be effective until the indictment had been preferred, but when this happened it would become effective and as long as this happened before the warrant was executed the execution would be lawful.

It is for these reasons that their Lordships have advised Her Majesty that the appellant's appeal should be dismissed.

Appeal dismissed.

Celia Fox   Barrister.

R v Shepherd
R v Wernet

COURT OF APPEAL, CRIMINAL DIVISION
LORD TAYLOR OF GOSFORTH CJ, POPPLEWELL AND SCOTT BAKER JJ
16, 17 DECEMBER 1993

Road traffic – Causing death by careless or dangerous driving – Sentence – Guidelines – Aggravating features – Careless driving when under influence of drink or drugs – Road Traffic Act 1988, ss 1, 3A – Criminal Justice Act 1993, s 67.

For the purpose of sentencing for the offences of causing death by dangerous driving under s 1[a] of the Road Traffic Act 1988 and causing death by careless driving when under the influence of drink or drugs under s 3A[b] of that Act, the consumption of alcohol or drugs is an aggravating feature which generally necessitates the imposition of a custodial sentence. The offence under s 3A, although requiring proof only of careless rather than of dangerous driving, has built into it the aggravating feature of the consumption of alcohol or drugs and thus where a driver is over the limit and kills someone as a result of his careless driving a prison sentence is usually appropriate, the length depending on the circumstances but especially on the extent of the carelessness and the amount by which the defendant was over the limit. Killing more than one person is an aggravating feature which the court should take into account. Having regard to the fact that s 67[b] of the Criminal Justice Act 1993 has increased the maximum sentence for offences under ss 1 and 3A of the 1988 Act from five to ten years, in bad cases drivers should lose their liberty for upwards of five years and in the very worst cases, if contested, sentences should be in the higher range of permitted sentences. Only exceptionally will a non-custodial sentence be possible (see p 244 *j* to p 245 *d g* to *j*, post).

R v Boswell [1984] 3 All ER 353 considered.

Notes
For causing death by careless driving when under the influence of drink or drugs, see 40 *Halsbury's Laws* (4th edn) para 472.

For sentencing principles, see 11(2) *Halsbury's Laws* (4th edn reissue) paras 1187–1189.

For the Road Traffic Act 1988, s 1, see 38 *Halsbury's Statutes* (4th edn) 830.

As from 1 July 1992, s 1 of the 1988 Act was substituted and s 3A was inserted therein by ss 1 and 3 of the Road Traffic Act 1991.

Cases referred to in judgment
R v Boswell [1984] 3 All ER 353, [1984] 1 WLR 1047, CA.
R v Newton (1982) 77 Cr App 13, CA.
R v Pettipher (1989) 11 Cr App R (S) 321, CA.

---

a Section 1 provides: 'A person who causes the death of another person by driving a menchanically propelled vehicle dangerously on a road or other public place is guilty of an offence.'
b Section 3A, so far as material, is set out at p 244 *c d*, post

Cases also cited or referred to in references
A-G's Reference (No 15 of 1990) (1990) 12 Cr App R (S) 510, CA.
R v Holmes (1990) 12 Cr App R (S) 32, CA.
R v Mawson (1992) 13 Cr App R (S) 218, CA.
R v Miah (1992) 13 Cr App R (S) 278, CA.
R v Morgan (1988) 10 Cr App (S) 192, CA.
R v Reardon (1993) 14 Cr App R (S) 275, CA.
R v Robson (1989) 11 Cr App R (S) 78, CA.
R v Turner (1990) 12 Cr App R (S) 472, CA.

References

R v Shepherd
On 21 June 1993 the defendant, Peter James Shepherd, pleaded guilty at the Crown Court at Norwich before Judge Binns to two counts of causing death by careless driving after having consumed alcohol above the prescribed limit contrary to s 3A of the Road Traffic Act 1988, as inserted by s 3 of the Road Traffic Act 1991, and was fined £250 and disqualified from driving for a period of two years. Pursuant to s 36 of the Criminal Justice Act 1988 and with leave of the Court of Appeal the Attorney General referred the case to that court (Reference No 14 of 1993) on the ground that the sentence was too lenient. The facts are set out in the judgment of the court.

R v Wernet
On 5 July 1993 the defendant, Robert Stewart Wernet, pleaded guilty at the Crown Court at Norwich before Judge Harris QC to causing death by driving without due care and attention after having consumed alcohol above the prescribed limit contrary to s 3A of the Road Traffic Act 1988, as inserted by s 3 of the Road Traffic Act 1991. The court accepted his plea of not guilty of causing death by dangerous driving contrary to s 1 of the Road Traffic Act 1988 and he was sentenced to nine months' imprisonment and disqualified from driving for two years on 3 September 1993 at the Crown Court at Oxford after a *Newton* hearing (see *R v Newton* (1982) 77 Cr App R 13). Pursuant to s 36 of the Criminal Justice Act 1988 and with leave of the Court of Appeal the Attorney General referred the case to that court (Reference No 24 of 1993) on the ground that the sentence was too lenient. The facts are set out in the judgment of the court.

The cases were argued seriatim and raised the same question relating to the sentence of an offender under s 3A of the 1988 Act.

John Nutting (instructed by the *Crown Prosecution Service*, Headquarters) for the Attorney General.
Roger D Harrison (instructed by *Taylor Vinters*, Cambridge) for Shepherd.
Anthony McGeorge (instructed by *Simms & Co*, Oxford) for Wernet.

Cur adv vult

17 December 1993. The following opinion of the court was delivered.

LORD TAYLOR OF GOSFORTH CJ. These are two applications by Her Majesty's Attorney General pursuant to s 36 of the Criminal Justice Act 1988 for leave to refer to this court for review sentences which he regards as unduly lenient. We have granted leave.

The Road Traffic Act 1991 created two new offences by way of amendment of the Road Traffic Act 1988. Section 1 of the 1991 Act substituted for ss 1 and 2 of the 1988 Act the new offence of causing death by dangerous driving, thereby replacing the offence of causing death by reckless driving. At one time earlier in the somewhat chequered history of road traffic offences there had been an offence of causing death by dangerous driving. However, s 3 of the 1991 Act inserted an entirely new offence by creating a s 3A of the 1988 Act. That offence is of causing death by careless driving when under the influence of drink or drugs.

The terms of s 3A are as follows:

'(1) If a person causes the death of another person by driving a mechanically propelled vehicle on a road or other public place without due care and attention, or without reasonable consideration for other persons using the road or place, and—(a) he is, at the time when he is driving, unfit to drive through drink or drugs, or (b) he has consumed so much alcohol that the proportion of it in his breath, blood or urine at that time exceeds the prescribed limit, or (c) he is, within 18 hours after that time, required to provide a specimen in pursuance of section 7 of this Act, but without reasonable excuse fails to provide it, he is guilty of an offence ...'

It is not necessary to read the rest of the section.

Those two new offences came into existence on 1 July 1992. The maximum sentence in respect of each was then five years' imprisonment. However, within a year Parliament, by s 67 of the Criminal Justice Act 1993, increased the maximum sentence for each of the two offences from five years to ten years. That change came into effect on 16 August 1993. In our judgment that increase of sentence was not retrospective, so that neither of the cases before us is directly affected by it.

These reforms show an intention by Parliament to strengthen the criminal law, to reduce death on the roads by increasing the punishment available to the courts, and by specifically targeting those who cause death whilst driving with excess alcohol. The five-year maximum sentence for causing death by dangerous driving has been doubled. In tandem with that, causing death by the less serious form of culpable driving, characterised as careless, carries the same maximum sentence if coupled with driving whilst unfit through drink or over the limit. The latter offences do not require proof of a causal connection between the drink and the death. Thus, under s 3A, whoever drives with excess alcohol does so at his or her peril, and even if the driving is merely careless but death results, the courts' powers to punish are the same as for causing death by dangerous driving.

Guidelines for sentencing in respect of the pre-1991 offence were laid down in the well-known case of *R v Boswell* [1984] 3 All ER 353, [1984] 1 WLR 1047 at a time when the maximum sentence for that offence was five years' imprisonment. For offences committed before the sentence was increased to ten years, we consider that the criteria laid down in that case applied equally to the new offence of causing death by dangerous driving. In *R v Boswell* [1984] 3 All ER 353 at 356–357, [1984] 1 WLR 1047 at 1051–1052 Lord Lane CJ listed a number of aggravating features. The first was the consumption of alcohol or drugs. He said that where an aggravating feature was present a custodial sentence was generally necessary. The offence under s 3A, although requiring proof only of careless driving rather than of dangerous driving, also has built into it the aggravating feature which was the first in the list in *Boswell*, namely consumption of alcohol or drugs. Thus, where a driver is over the limit, and kills someone as a result of his careless driving, a prison sentence will ordinarily be appropriate. The length of sentence will of course depend upon the aggravating and mitigating circumstances in the particular case, but especially on the extent of the carelessness and the amount the defendant is over the limit. In an exceptional case, if the alcohol level at the time of the offence is just over the borderline, the carelessness is momentary, and there is strong mitigation, a non-custodial sentence may be possible. But in other cases a prison sentence is required to punish the offender, to deter others from drinking and driving, and to reflect the public's abhorrence of deaths being caused by drivers with excess alcohol.

In regard to that final element of public perception, as has been said before in *Boswell* and in *R v Pettipher* (1989) 11 Cr App R (S) 321, although it may be fortuitous and therefore strictly illogical, the fact that the offence caused more than one death is itself an aggravating feature which the court should consider. It was put in this way in *R v Pettipher* (at 323):

'... more than one person was killed. It is rather illogical in some ways, it might be thought, that a given piece of driving which causes three deaths should be punished more heavily than the identical piece of driving causing one death, or indeed causing no death at all, given that no one suggests this appellant was deliberately driving so as to kill people. The fact is that in the public estimation it is a factor which people in general do take into account. People do regard killing three as more criminal than killing one. That is a fact of life which this court recognises.'

Having said that, we wish to stress that human life cannot be restored, nor can its loss be measured by the length of a prison sentence. We recognise that no term of months or years imposed on the offender can reconcile the family of a deceased victim to their loss, nor will it cure their anguish.

Since Parliament has thought it right and necessary not merely to increase, but to double the maximum sentence for offences under ss 1 and 3A of the 1988 Act (as amended) the guidelines in *Boswell* need to be reconsidered. Clearly the statements of principle in that case, and the examples of aggravating and mitigating circumstances still stand, but there appears the following statement ([1984] 3 All ER 353 at 357, [1984] 1 WLR 1047 at 1052):

'Drivers who for example indulge in racing on the highway and/or driving with reckless disregard for the safety of others after taking alcohol should understand that in bad cases they will lose their liberty for two years or more.'

In our judgment the phrase 'two years or more' should now read 'upwards of five years', and in the very worst cases, if contested, sentences will be in the higher range of those now permitted by Parliament.

With those principles in mind we turn to the instant applications by the Attorney General. In the first, the offender's name is Peter James Shepherd. He is 29 years of age. On 21 June 1993, in the Crown Court at Norwich, he pleaded guilty to two counts of causing death by careless driving, having consumed alcohol above the prescribed limit, contrary to s 3A of the 1988 Act (as amended). The learned judge sentenced him to be fined £250, disqualified him from driving for two years, and ordered that he pay costs of £100.

The offender had spent the weekend of Saturday, 14 to Sunday, 15 November staying with friends in Cambridgeshire. Also staying at the same house was a young woman called Tracy Fairhead and her ten-month-old baby daughter. On the evening of Sunday, 15 November Miss Fairhead decided to return home to Ealing with her baby because of a domestic problem. The offender had been drinking lager during the afternoon. It is fair to say that he had probably not expected or intended to drive. However, he offered Miss Fairhead a lift in his vehicle. Shortly before 10 pm they embarked on their journey. It seems that neither the offender nor his passenger fastened their safety belts. Miss Fairhead had her baby on her lap.

Meanwhile, a very large articulated lorry had broken down on the A142 road. The driver pulled into the roadside and kept his lorry illuminated in front and rear. He also switched on his hazard lights. He contacted a garage and waited for assistance. It was dark. Although it was not raining, the road surface was wet. However, the road was level. Visibility was good and stretched for half a mile in each direction. Other drivers approaching the parked lorry from the rear managed to negotiate the obstruction without difficulty. Either they passed it straight away, or, when traffic was approaching from the opposite direction, they waited before pulling out to pass. The offender's route took him along this road shortly before 10.15 pm. It is clear that he failed to see the lorry ahead of him. He only applied his brakes when he was approximately 30 m from it. He was unable to stop in time. Nor was he able to pass the lorry because of oncoming traffic. In the result his vehicle collided at some speed with the rear of the lorry. Miss Fairhead and her baby were killed instantly by the force of the impact. At the scene the offender said: 'I did not see the lorry until it was too late.'

At 12.30 am, over two hours after the event, the offender provided a specimen of blood for analysis. That specimen was found to contain 82 mg of alcohol in 100 ml of blood. On 18 November he was interviewed about the accident. He estimated that he had consumed four cans of lager beer during the afternoon. He emphasised that he had not intended to drive, and had only done so because, having learned that Miss Fairhead wished to go home, he offered her a lift. His explanation for having failed to see the lorry was that he was 'engrossed in conversation with Miss Fairhead'.

There was a pre-sentence report before the learned judge which emphasised the remorse which the offender felt for what had happened, and also his sense of helplessness as to how he could make amends.

On behalf of the Attorney General attention is drawn to certain aggravating features. One starts with the built-in element which is an ingredient in the offence that he was over the limit. But on top of that, reliance is placed upon two additional matters: first, what is submitted to be the high degree of carelessness in failing to see the lorry, although there was every opportunity to do so; and secondly, the fact that more than one person was killed.

On behalf of the offender, it is right to point out that he pleaded guilty, that he had, and probably always will have, a genuine feeling of remorse, the more so because the victims were his friends.

Mr Harrison, on behalf of the offender, sought to persuade the court that the blood/alcohol figure in this case was only marginally over the limit of 80, and that it was not the cause of the accident. The cause, he submits, was momentary inattention while talking to his passenger. We cannot accept those submissions. The blood sample taken from the appellant was not taken until over two hours after the accident. It is clear that at the time of the accident the offender must have been substantially over the limit. As the learned trial judge pointed out, it was not possible to quantify what the blood/alcohol figure would have been at the time of the impact, but it must have been substantially over the 82 which was recorded two hours later. Secondly, this was more than momentary inattention. The parked lorry with its hazard lights flashing was visible from half a mile distance, and to fail to see it whilst proceeding over that distance indicates a substantial failure to attend to the road in front. Moreover, it is not easy to see how conversation with a passenger can amount to any excuse for failing to look ahead. It is perfectly possible to converse whilst keeping one's eye upon the road. Causation of the death by the drink taken is not, as we have already pointed out, a necessary ingredient in this offence, but it is hard in the circumstances of the present case to reach any other conclusion than that there was some nexus between the drink taken and the inattention.

We accept that despite the two deaths the conduct of the offender in the present case was not of the worst type. But we do not agree that this was the sort of marginal case where a custodial sentence could be avoided. To fine the offender was to do no more than would have been appropriate had he simply been found guilty of driving with excess alcohol. Parliament has clearly indicated that this offence is to be treated much more punitively than that. We bear in mind that this offence preceded the increase in the maximum sentence. We recognise that, this offence apart, the offender had a good record with no previous convictions; he had not intended or expected to drive, but was trying to do his passenger a favour. Instead, he has on his conscience their deaths for which he is remorseful. He pleaded guilty. He was pursuing a university course, and, had he been given a short sentence at first instance, Mr Harrison points out that he would have been able to resume that course two months ago in October.

All of those are cogent and even poignant mitigating factors. However, we consider that the sentence passed by the learned judge was unduly lenient. A custodial sentence was required. We bear in mind the maximum sentence at the time, and we have particular regard to the element of double jeopardy which is involved when someone is sentenced, particularly if a non-custodial sentence is imposed and then he is brought back to this court on the application of the Attorney General, with all the anxiety that impending possibility of custody must create, coupled with the appearance here and the resentencing. Bearing all those matters in mind, we consider that the appropriate sentence here is one of three months' imprisonment on each count concurrently, and that is what we impose. We see no reason to interfere with the two-year disqualification.

We turn to the second application. Robert Stewart Wernet is 26 years old. On 5 July 1993 he appeared in the Crown Court at Oxford. He there pleaded guilty to causing death by driving without due care and attention, contrary to s 3A of the 1988 Act (as amended). There was on the indictment also a count of causing death by dangerous driving, contrary to s 1 of that Act. The court accepted his plea of not guilty to that offence. A *Newton* hearing (see *R v Newton* (1982) 77 Cr App R 13) was conducted on 3 September 1993 in order to reach a conclusion as to the speed at which the offender had been driving at the time of the accident. He contended (it is right to say on the basis of a theoretical opinion by an expert) that he had only been driving at about 37 to 38 mph. Eye witnesses put the speed very much higher. The learned judge determined that he had been driving, making all due allowances and taking the most favourable view, at 60 mph at the time of the accident. He then imposed a sentence of nine months' imprisonment and disqualified the offender from driving for a period of two years.

The facts of the matter were as follows. At 5 pm on Tuesday, 8 September 1992 the offender, who was uninsured at the time, drove his Ford Orion motor car to a public house called the Albion, Hollybush Road, Oxford. There he met two friends, John McCallam and Jackie Dollomore. He drank a pint of lager. At about 6 pm he drove Miss Dollomore home so that she could get some more money and a change of shirt for the other member of the party, Mr McCallam. On the return journey to the Albion, the offender left his car outside his own house and walked the rest of the way back with Miss Dollomore. They arrived at the Albion at about 7 pm and the offender drank a second pint of lager. At about 7.30 pm the offender arranged by telephone to meet another friend at the Prince of Wales public house, Iffley Road. He collected his car and drove Miss Dollomore and Mr McCallam to the Prince of Wales. They arrived there at about 8 pm, and the offender drank another pint of lager. He and his friends decided to go to yet another public house, the Monmouth, Abingdon Road. The offender drove Miss Dollomore, Mr McCallam and the other friend, Mr Croft, to the Monmouth. There, he drank two more pints of lager. Towards closing time, the offender suggested that the four of them should take a taxi home. However, Mr McCallam protested that, as the offender had 'dragged him out to the Monmouth', he should be given a lift home. Accordingly, the offender agreed to drive the others in the party back to their respective homes. Miss Dollomore got into the front passenger seat, Mr McCallam and Mr Croft into the rear passenger seats. Mr McCallam was not wearing a safety belt.

The driving conditions were good. The offender drove along Donnington Bridge Road towards Iffley Road. He exceeded the speed limit of 30 mph along that stretch of road, but there is no suggestion that his passengers were raising any protest about his manner or speed of driving. He turned into Iffley Road and dropped off Mr Croft. He then proceeded farther along Iffley Road towards the city centre. That length of roadway is controlled by a 30 mph limit. At about 11.20 pm the offender approached the crossroads with Jackdaw Lane, which was on the nearside, and Bullingdon Road on the offside. That section of Iffley Road is flanked by Victorian terraced houses and is illuminated by sodium street lights. Just beyond the crossroads the road begins to bend steadily to the right before straightening out towards the city centre. Drivers are forewarned of the crossroads' presence by illuminated 'keep left' bollards. Despite that, the offender drove in the middle of the road at an excessive speed through the crossroads. One eye witness estimated his speed at being more than 80 mph. Others certainly put it over 50 mph. As indicated, the learned judge concluded, taking any error in the offender's favour, as 60 mph. After driving over the crossroads, the offender suddenly found himself confronted by an illuminated 'keep left' bollard. To avoid the bollard he steered sharply to the left, but in doing so he noticed his car was about to collide with the kerb. He therefore pulled the steering wheel over to the right. The car began to slip sideways and, after veering across to the other side of the road, it careered into the offside kerb, struck a pillar box and demolished a garden wall. The impact of the collision forced the car to roll over on to its side, facing in the direction of the city centre. The car was a write-off, and the offence resulted in damage to two other vehicles. The offender, Mr McCallam and Miss Dollomore were all trapped. Rescue services finally managed to remove them from the wreckage. Mr McCallam, who was 27 years old at the time of the offence, sustained serious head injuries and was found to be dead on arrival at hospital at 12.20 am. He had a high blood/alcohol figure of 129 mg of alcohol per 100 ml of blood. Miss Dollomore also sustained serious head injuries which rendered her comatose for three weeks.

At 3.15 am, some four hours after the incident, a specimen of blood was taken from the offender. It was found, even at that remove of time, to contain 86 milligrams of alcohol in 100 ml of blood.

The offender was interviewed by the police one month later. He admitted that he had drunk five pints of lager in three different public houses between 5 pm and 11 pm. He also admitted to having been uninsured at the time of the offence. He claimed to know very little else about the accident. He said that he had wanted to call a taxi, but Mr McCallam persuaded him to drive the friends home. He said that he knew Iffley Road very well as he had lived nearby some years previously.

The offender had been unemployed for some time before the offence. In mitigation before the learned judge he claimed he had recently found work. He had one relevant previous conviction for driving whilst uninsured, for which he had been fined on 4 September 1987.

In this case, as in the last one, one starts with the built-in aggravating feature as an ingredient of the offence of driving over the limit. However, on behalf of the Attorney General further aggravating features are pointed out. Firstly, the driving was at a grossly excessive speed, 60 mph, as the learned judge found, in a 30 mph residential area. Secondly, the offender knew that he was uninsured and that his car was untaxed at the relevant time. That was aggravated further by the fact that he had previously been convicted of an offence of that kind.

On behalf of the offender, the mitigating features put forward were that he had previous good character, save for the one offence of driving uninsured. He had pleaded guilty and, as in the previous case, he felt deep remorse, particularly as the person killed was a close friend of his.

Clearly this was a case which demanded a custodial sentence, and the learned judge imposed one. However, on behalf of the Attorney General it is submitted that the sentence of nine months' imprisonment in respect of this offence was unduly lenient. With that submission we agree. This was a bad offence. The offender was clearly well over the limit, if one takes into account the blood/alcohol figure and allows for the four hours that had passed between the last drink taken and the sample being obtained. He was driving at a grossly excessive speed, and he was doing so whilst uninsured, despite having been previously convicted of an offence of that kind. In our judgment, bearing in mind the element of double jeopardy, bearing in mind the maximum sentence of only five years at that time for this offence, we consider that the least sentence which could properly be imposed, and the one which we substitute, is one of 18 months' imprisonment. Furthermore, we consider that having regard to this man's record and the quality of the driving on this occasion that the disqualification of two years was inadequate. We substitute for that a disqualification of five years.

Orders accordingly.

N P Metcalfe Esq Barrister.

The Pioneer Container
KH Enterprise (cargo owners) v Pioneer Container (owners)

PRIVY COUNCIL
LORD GOFF OF CHIEVELEY, LORD LOWRY, LORD SLYNN OF HADLEY, LORD LLOYD OF BERWICK AND SIR THOMAS EICHELBAUM
15, 16, 17 NOVEMBER 1993, 21 MARCH 1994

Bailment – Sub-bailment for reward – Liability of sub-bailee to owner of goods bailed – Relationship between owner of goods and sub-bailee – Goods shipped by shipowners under sub-contract made with freight carriers – Freight carriers having authority of owners of goods to sub-contract carriage 'on any terms' – Bill of lading issued to freight carriers containing exclusive jurisdiction clause – Owners of goods not party to bill of lading – Vessel and cargo lost at sea – Whether owner of goods bound by terms on which goods sub-bailed – Whether owner only bound by terms of sub-bailment to which he expressly or impliedly consented – Whether owners of shipped goods bound by exclusive jurisdiction clause in bill of lading.

Conflict of laws – Stay of proceedings – Agreement to refer to foreign court – Exclusive jurisdiction clause in bill of lading – Agreement to refer disputes to foreign court – Stay of proceedings to be granted unless strong cause for not doing so shown – Clause in bill of lading that disputes to be determined in Taiwan – Vessel and cargo lost at sea – Plaintiff cargo owners deciding not to bring action against shipowners in Taiwan – Time limit for bringing action in Taiwan expiring – Cargo owners bringing action in Hong Kong – Whether cargo owners acting unreasonably in allowing time limit for bringing action in Taiwan – Whether Hong Kong proceedings should be stayed.

The plaintiffs contracted with freight carriers for the carriage of the plaintiffs' goods by container from Taiwan to Hong Kong either as a complete voyage or as part of through carriage to other ports. The carriers issued the plaintiffs with bills of lading which provided that the carrier was entitled to sub-contract 'on any terms' the whole or any part of the handling, storage or carriage of the goods. The carriers sub-contracted the carriage to the defendant shipowners, who issued two feeder bills of lading acknowledging receipt of the plaintiffs' containers for shipment. The feeder bills of lading incorporated an exclusive jurisdiction clause (cl 26) which provided that the bills of lading were governed by Chinese law and that any claim or other dispute arising under the 'bill of lading contract' was to be determined in Taiwan unless the carrier otherwise agreed. The vessel on which the plaintiffs' containers were being shipped from

Taiwan to Hong Kong sank with the loss of all cargo following a collision with another vessel during the voyage. The plaintiffs commenced proceedings in Hong Kong by the issue of a writ in rem against a sister ship of the vessel, claiming damages for the loss of their cargo. The shipowners applied to have the proceedings stayed on the grounds that the plaintiffs had, by cl 26 of the bills of lading, agreed that any claim or other dispute thereunder should be determined in Taiwan, or alternatively that in all the circumstances the courts of Taiwan were the natural and appropriate forum for the trial of the action. The judge held that cl 26 was a valid and effective exclusive jurisdiction clause which was binding on the plaintiffs, but he dismissed the shipowners' motion, holding that the plaintiffs had shown strong cause why their claims should not proceed in Taiwan, since their claims had become time-barred there and the plaintiffs had not acted unreasonably in failing to commence proceedings there before the expiry of the time bar because they would have had to put up a percentage of their claim as advance costs. The Court of Appeal of Hong Kong allowed an appeal by the shipowners and granted a stay, on the grounds that the plaintiffs were bound by the exclusive jurisdiction clause and that the judge had erred in exercising his discretion to decline to grant a stay of the proceedings. The plaintiffs appealed to the Privy Council, contending, inter alia, that cl 26 was not binding on them because there was no contractual relationship between them and the shipowners

Held – The appeal would be dismissed for the following reasons—

(1) Where a bailee sub-bailed goods with the authority of the owner the relationship between the owner of the goods and the sub-bailee was that of bailor and bailee and the owner was bound by the terms on which the goods were sub-bailed if he expressly or impliedly consented to the bailee making a sub-bailment containing those conditions, but not otherwise. Thus, if the sub-bailee voluntarily received into his custody the goods of the owner and so assumed towards the owner the responsibility of a bailee, the effect of the sub-bailment was that the owner was taken to have authorised, to the extent that he consented to the terms of the sub-bailment, the bailee to regulate the duties of the sub-bailee in respect of the goods entrusted to him, not only towards the bailee but also towards the owner. Conversely, the sub-bailee, by voluntarily taking the owner's goods into his custody, ipso facto became the bailee of those goods vis-à-vis the owner and the owner's rights against the sub-bailee were only subject to the terms of the sub-bailment if the owner consented to them, ie if he authorised the bailee to entrust the goods to the sub-bailee on those terms. The underlying principle was that a sub-bailee could only be said to have voluntarily taken into his possession the goods of another if he had sufficient notice that a person other than the bailee was interested in the goods so that it could properly be said that (in addition to his duties to the bailee) he had, by taking the goods into his custody, assumed towards that other person the responsibility for the goods which was characteristic of a bailee. On the facts, on receipt of the plaintiffs' goods the shipowners became the bailees of the goods for reward. However, the plaintiffs had contracted with the freight carriers that they were entitled to sub-contract the carriage 'on any terms', which was wide enough to be express consent to the application of an exclusive jurisdiction clause to the sub-bailment, since an exclusive jurisdiction clause was not so unusual or unreasonable as to be excluded from the wide consent given by the plaintiffs

(see p 258 *b c g*, p 259 *e f*, p 261 *g h*, p 262 *b* to *e*, p 264 *e*, p 265 *e j* to p 266 *d j* to p 267 *a*, post).

(2) Applying the principle that the court should exercise its discretion by granting a stay of proceedings brought in breach of an agreement to refer disputes to a foreign court unless strong cause for not doing so was shown, the expiry of the time limit in Taiwan was not sufficient reason for refusing a stay since the plaintiffs had advisedly but unreasonably gambled on being permitted to litigate in their preferred forum of Hong Kong rather than Taiwan, which was where they were bound to litigate, and had let time run out in Taiwan without taking the trouble even to issue a protective writ there. In so doing, the plaintiffs had acted unreasonably. The appeal would therefore be dismissed (see p 267 *b c* and p 268 *c d h* to p 269 *a*, post).

Notes

For sub-bailment, see 2 *Halsbury's Laws* (4th edn reissue) para 1841, and for cases on the subject, see 3(2) *Digest* (2nd reissue) 35–36, 52, 278–279, 380.

For stay of proceedings, see 37 *Halsbury's Laws* (4th edn) paras 437–446, and for cases on the subject, see 37(3) *Digest* (Reissue) 53–67, 3247–3292.

Cases referred to in judgment

Aratra Potato Co Ltd v Egyptian Navigation Co, The El Amria [1981] 2 Lloyd's Rep 119, CA.
Blue Wave, The [1982] 1 Lloyd's Rep 151.
Cap Blanco, The [1913] P 131, [1911–13] All ER Rep 365.
Cia Portorafti Commerciale SA v Ultramar Panama Inc, The Captain Gregos (No 2) [1990] 2 Lloyd's Rep 395, CA.
Elder Dempster & Co Ltd v Paterson Zochonis & Co Ltd [1924] AC 522, [1924] All ER Rep 135, HL.
Forum Craftsman, The [1985] 1 Lloyd's Rep 291, CA.
Foulkes v Metropolitan District Rly Co (1880) 5 CPD 157.
Gilchrist Watt & Sanderson Pty Ltd v York Products Pty Ltd [1970] 3 All ER 825, [1970] 1 WLR 1262, PC.
Hispanica de Petroleos SA v Vencedora Oceanica Navigacion SA, The Kapetan Markos (No 2) [1987] 2 Lloyd's Rep 321, CA.
Hooper v London and North Western Rly Co (1881) 50 LJQB 103.
Johnson Matthey & Co Ltd v Constantine Terminals Ltd [1976] 2 Lloyd's Rep 215.
Makefjell, The [1976] 2 Lloyd's Rep 29, CA; affg [1975] 1 Lloyd's Rep 528.
Midland Silicones Ltd v Scruttons Ltd [1962] 1 All ER 1, [1962] AC 446, [1962] 2 WLR186, HL.
Morris v C W Martin & Son [1965] 2 All ER 725, [1966] 1 QB 716, [1965] 3 WLR 276, CA.
New Zealand Shipping Co Ltd v A M Satterthwaite & Co Ltd [1974] 1 All ER 1015, [1975] AC 154, [1974] 2 WLR 865, PC.
Singer Co (UK) Ltd v Tees and Hartlepool Port Authority [1988] 2 Lloyd's Rep 164.
Skips A/S Nordheim v Syrian Petroleum Co Ltd, The Varenna [1983] 3 All ER 645, [1984] QB 599, [1984] 2 WLR 156, CA.
Spiliada Maritime Corp v Cansulex Ltd, The Spiliada [1986] 3 All ER 843, [1987] AC 460, [1986] 3 WLR 972, HL.
Thomas (T W) & Co Ltd v Portsea Steamship Co Ltd [1912] AC 1, HL.
Wilson v Darling Island Stevedoring and Lighterage Co Ltd (1955) 95 CLR 43, Aust HC.

Appeal

The plaintiffs, who were the owners of cargo lately laden on board the vessel KH Enterprise, appealed with leave granted by the Court of Appeal of Hong Kong on 6 May 1992 from the decision of that court (Cons V-P, Power JA and Godfrey J) on 10 April 1992 allowing the appeal of the defendants, who were the owners of the vessel Pioneer Container, from the judgment of Sears J in the High Court on 14 May 1991 dismissing the shipowners' application to stay the Admiralty action in rem brought by the plaintiffs against the Pioneer Container arising out of the loss on the high seas of the KH Enterprise, a sister ship of the Pioneer Container, with all her cargo on 11 March 1987. The Court of Appeal ordered the proceedings to be stayed on the ground that the plaintiffs were bound by an exclusive jurisdiction clause in the bills of lading issued by the shipowners for the carriage of the cargo to refer their claims to the courts of Taipei in Taiwan. The facts are set out in the judgment of the Board.

Sydney Kentridge QC and *George Leggatt* (instructed by *Clyde & Co*) for the plaintiffs.

Michael Thomas QC and *Anthony Dicks* (instructed by *Holman Fenwick & Willan*) for the shipowners.

21 March 1994. The following judgment of the Board was delivered.

LORD GOFF OF CHIEVELEY. The appellants (whom their Lordships will refer to as 'the plaintiffs') were the owners of goods laden on board the respondents' Taiwanese container ship KH Enterprise (which their Lordships will refer to as 'the vessel'), which sank with all her cargo off the coast of Taiwan on 11 March 1987, following a collision in fog with another larger ship, the Oriental Faith. The plaintiffs commenced the present proceedings in Hong Kong by the issue of a writ in rem dated 10 March 1988 against the respondents' ship Pioneer Container, a sister ship of the vessel, claiming damages in respect of the loss of their cargo. The Pioneer Container was arrested in Hong Kong on 29 October 1988, but was released on 5 December 1988 against a P & I club guarantee in the sum of $US1·6m. On 8 September 1989 the respondents (whom their Lordships will refer to as 'the shipowners') issued a notice of motion in the High Court of Hong Kong, asking that the proceedings be stayed on the grounds (1) that the plaintiffs had, by cl 26 of the relevant bills of lading, agreed that any claim or other dispute thereunder should be determined at Taipei in Taiwan or alternatively (2) that in all the circumstances the courts of Taipei were the natural and appropriate forum for the trial of the action.

Clause 26 provided as follows:

'This Bill of Lading contract shall be governed by Chinese Law. Any claim or other dispute arising thereunder shall be determined at Taipei in Taiwan unless the carrier otherwise agrees in writing.'

The matter came before Sears J in September 1990. On 26 September he made a preliminary ruling under which he held, first, that the exclusive jurisdiction clause (cl 26) on which the shipowners relied was a valid and effective clause under Taiwanese law, and, second that the agreement contained in the clause was binding on all the plaintiffs. Subsequently however, on 14 May 1991, he dismissed the shipowners' motion, holding that the plaintiffs had shown strong cause why their claims should not proceed in

Taipei, since their claims had become time-barred there and, in the opinion of
the judge, the plaintiffs had not acted unreasonably in failing to commence
proceedings there before the expiry of the time bar. However, on 10 April
1992, the Court of Appeal of Hong Kong allowed the shipowners' appeal from
that decision. They agreed with Sears J that all the plaintiffs were bound by the
exclusive jurisdiction clause; but it held that he had erred in the exercise of his
discretion in declining to grant a stay of the proceedings, which it, exercising
its own discretion afresh, held should be granted. It is from that decision that
the plaintiffs now appeal to the Privy Council.

The plaintiffs fall into three groups, which have become known as 'the Kien
Hung plaintiffs', 'the Hanjin plaintiffs' and 'the Scandutch plaintiffs'.

(1) The Kien Hung plaintiffs shipped goods on board the vessel at
Taiwanese ports for carriage to Hong Kong under bills of lading issued in
Taiwan and signed on behalf of the shipowners. There was therefore a direct
contractual relationship between the Kien Hung plaintiffs and the shipowners,
and there is no doubt that the exclusive jurisdiction clause contained in the bills
of lading is binding upon these plaintiffs. There are 213 claims under the bills
of lading in this category. In virtually all cases, the shippers were in Taiwan,
and the receivers in Hong Kong.

(2) The Hanjin plaintiffs shipped goods on board another vessel in the
United States under bills of lading issued by Hanjin Container Lines (Hanjin),
a Korean company, in respect of the carriage of the goods from the United
States to Hong Kong. Each bill of lading contained the following provision:

'6. The Carrier shall be entitled to sub-contract on any terms the whole
or any part of the handling, storage or carriage of the Goods and any and
all duties whatsoever undertaken by the Carrier in relation to the Goods
...'

Hanjin in turn sub-contracted to the shipowners the carriage of the goods over
the last stage of the voyage, from Taiwan to Hong Kong. The goods were
trans-shipped onto the vessel in Taiwan, and in respect of all the goods of the
Hanjin plaintiffs the shipowners issued a single feeder bill of lading (Feeder
103) in the same form as those issued to the Kien Hung plaintiffs (and so
incorporating cl 26) acknowledging receipt of 41 containers for shipment from
Keelung in Taiwan to Hong Kong. There are 15 claims in this category, of
which one has a Taiwanese connection and 14 have a Hong Kong connection.

(3) The goods of the Scandutch plaintiffs were shipped on board the vessel
in Taiwanese ports. Each plaintiff was issued with a bill of lading issued on
behalf of Scandutch I/S (Scandutch) covering the carriage of the goods from a
Taiwanese port to an ultimate destination in Europe or the Middle East. Each
bill of lading contained the following provision:

'4(1) The Carrier shall be entitled to sub-contract on any terms the
whole or any part of the carriage, loading, unloading, storing,
warehousing, handling and any and all duties whatsoever undertaken by
the Carrier in relation to the Goods ...'

For the carriage of the goods from Taiwan to Hong Kong, which was
sub-contracted by Scandutch to the shipowners, the latter issued a single
feeder bill of lading (Feeder 104), again in the same form (including cl 26),
acknowledging receipt of 140 containers for shipment from Taiwan to Hong

Kong, with a view to the containers being transshipped in Hong Kong. There are 214 claims in this category, of which five have a Hong Kong connection.

The difficulty which has arisen with respect to the Hanjin plaintiffs and the Scandutch plaintiffs is that, on ordinary principles of law, there was no contractual relationship between them and the shipowners, and accordingly these two classes of plaintiff have claimed that the exclusive jurisdiction clause, cl 26, is not binding upon them. However, that contention was rejected, both by Sears J and by the Court of Appeal, on the ground that there was a bailment to the shipowners on terms (including cl 26) which these plaintiffs had expressly or impliedly authorised and that, on the principles stated by Lord Denning MR in *Morris v C W Martin & Son* [1965] 2 All ER 725, [1966] 1 QB 716, these plaintiffs were bound by cl 26. Whether the courts below were correct in so holding is the principal issue which falls for consideration on this appeal; but the further question arises whether, if the plaintiffs were bound by the exclusive jurisdiction clause, the Court of Appeal was justified in interfering with the exercise by the judge of his discretion to refuse a stay of proceedings and, if so, whether the Court of Appeal was entitled, exercising its discretion afresh, to order a stay.

The central problem

Their Lordships turn immediately to the central problem in the case, which is whether the shipowners can rely, as against the Scandutch and Hanjin plaintiffs, on the exclusive jurisdiction clause (cl 26) in the feeder bills of lading to which these plaintiffs were not parties. They think it right to observe, at the outset, that in commercial terms it would be most inconvenient if these two groups of plaintiffs were not so bound. Here is a ship upon which goods are loaded in a large number of containers; indeed, one container may contain goods belonging to a number of cargo owners. One incident may affect goods owned by several cargo owners, or even (as here) all the cargo owners with goods on board. Common sense and practical convenience combine to demand that all of these claims should be dealt with in one jurisdiction, in accordance with one system of law. If this cannot be achieved, there may be chaos. Much expense may be wasted on litigation in a number of different jurisdictions, as indeed happened in the present case, where there was litigation in eight other countries as well as Hong Kong and Taiwan. There is however no international regime designed to produce a uniformity of jurisdiction and governing law in the case of a multiplicity of claims of this kind. It is scarcely surprising therefore that shipowners seek to achieve uniformity of treatment in respect of all such claims, by clauses designed to impose an exclusive jurisdiction and an agreed governing law, as in the present cl 26 in the shipowners' standard form of bill of lading. Within reason, such an attempt must be regarded with a considerable degree of sympathy and understanding.

However, so far as English law and the law of Hong Kong are concerned, a technical problem faces shipowners who carry goods, for example under the feeder bills of lading in the present case, where there is no contractual relationship between the shipowners and certain cargo owners. This is because English law still maintains, though subject to increasing criticism, a strict principle of privity of contract, under which as a matter of general principle only a person who is a party to a contract may sue upon it. The force of this principle is supported and enhanced by the doctrine of consideration, under which as a general rule only a promise supported by consideration will be enforceable at common law. How long these principles will continue to be maintained in all their strictness is now open to question. But, in the middle of this century, judges of great authority and distinction were in no doubt that they should be so maintained. Their Lordships refer in particular to the speech of Viscount Simonds in *Midland Silicones Ltd v Scruttons Ltd* [1962] 1 All ER 1 at 6–7, [1962] AC 446 at 467–468. The present case is concerned with the question whether the law of bailment can here be invoked by the shipowners to circumvent this difficulty.

Bailment and sub-bailment

Their Lordships are here concerned with a case where there has been a sub-bailment—a bailment by the owner of goods to a bailee, followed by a sub-bailment by the bailee to a sub-bailee—and the question has arisen whether, in an action by the owner against the sub-bailee for loss of the goods, the sub-bailee can rely as against the owner upon one of the terms upon which the goods have been sub-bailed to him by the bailee. In the case of the Hanjin plaintiffs, the goods were received for shipment by Hanjin Container Lines from the shippers, for through carriage from a North American port to Hong Kong, and then sub-bailed to the shipowners for the last leg of the voyage, viz from Taiwan to Hong Kong. In the case of the Scandutch plaintiffs, the goods were received for shipment by Scandutch for through carriage from Taiwan to the Middle East or Europe, and sub-bailed to the shipowners for the first leg of the voyage, again from Taiwan to Hong Kong. The question is whether the shipowners can in these circumstances rely upon the exclusive jurisdiction clause in the feeder bills of lading as against both groups of plaintiffs, notwithstanding that the plaintiffs in neither group were parties to the contract with the shipowners contained in or evidenced by such a bill of lading, having regard to the fact that the plaintiffs are seeking to hold the shipowners liable for failing to care for the goods so entrusted to them or failing to deliver them to the plaintiffs—in other words, for committing a breach of duty which is characteristic of a bailee.

The question whether a sub-bailee can in circumstances such as these rely upon such a term, and if so upon what principle he is entitled to do so, is one which has been considered in cases in the past, but so far neither by the House of Lords nor by the Privy Council. It has been much discussed by academic writers. Their Lordships are grateful to counsel for the citation to them of academic writings, especially *Palmer's Bailment* (1991), and *Bell's Modern Law of Personal Property in England and Ireland* (1989), to which they have repeatedly referred while considering the problems which have arisen for decision in the present case.

In approaching the central problem in the present case, their Lordships wish to observe that they are here concerned with two related questions. The first question relates to the identification of the relationship between the owner and the sub-bailee. Once that question is answered, it is possible to address the second question, which is whether, given that relationship, it is open to the sub-bailee to invoke as against the owner the terms upon which he received the goods from the bailee.

The relationship between the owner and the sub-bailee

Fortunately, authoritative guidance on the answer to the first question is to be found in the decision of the Privy Council in *Gilchrist Watt & Sanderson Pty*

Ltd v York Products Pty Ltd [1970] 3 All ER 825, [1970] 1 WLR 1262, an appeal from the Court of Appeal of New South Wales. There two cases of clocks were shipped from Hamburg to Sydney. On arrival of the ship at Sydney the goods were unloaded, sorted and stacked on the wharf by the defendants, who were ships' agents and stevedores. The plaintiffs were the holders of the relevant bills of lading. When their agents sought delivery of the two cases from the defendants, one was missing and was never found. The plaintiffs sought to hold the defendants responsible as bailees of the goods. The Privy Council proceeded on the basis that there was a bailment to the shipowners, and a sub-bailment by the shipowners to the defendants and that the defendants as sub-bailees received possession of the goods for the purpose of looking after them and delivering them to the holders of the bills of lading, who were the plaintiffs. Accordingly, the defendants 'took upon themselves an obligation to the plaintiffs to exercise due care for the safety of the goods, although there was no contractual relation or attornment between the defendants and the plaintiffs' (see [1970] 3 All ER 825 at 829, [1970] 1 WLR 1262 at 1267 per Lord Pearson). In support of that conclusion, the Privy Council relied in particular on *Morris v C W Martin & Son* [1965] 2 All ER 725 at 733, 734, 739–740, [1966] 1 QB 716 at 729, 731, 738, and on the statements of principle by Lord Denning MR, Diplock and Salmon LJJ in that case. There a mink stole, sent by the plaintiff to a furrier for cleaning, was sub-bailed by the furrier to the defendants, who were cleaning specialists, under a contract between them and the furrier. The stole was stolen by a servant of the defendants, and the plaintiff claimed damages from them. Both Diplock and Salmon LJJ held that the defendants, by voluntarily receiving into their possession goods which were the property of another, became responsible to the plaintiff as bailees of the goods. Lord Denning MR invoked an authoritative statement of the law in *Pollock and Wright on Possession* (1888) p 169, where it is stated as follows:

'If the bailee of a thing sub-bails it by authority, there may be a difference according as it is intended that the bailee's bailment is to determine and the third person is to hold as the immediate bailee of the owner, in which case the third person really becomes a first bailee directly from the owner and the case passes back into a simple case of bailment, or that the first bailee is to retain (so to speak) a reversionary interest and there is no direct privity of contract between the third person and the owner, in which case it would seem that both the owner and the first bailee have concurrently the rights of a bailor against the third person according to the nature of the sub-bailment.'

In addition, Lord Pearson invoked two nineteenth century cases concerned with the liability of railway companies where the plaintiff buys a ticket from one railway company, and claims liability from another which has undertaken responsibility for part of the services to be rendered to the plaintiff under the contract evidenced by the ticket: see *Foulkes v Metropolitan District Rly Co* (1880) 5 CPD 157 and *Hooper v London and North Western Rly Co* (1881) 50 LJQB 103. He also relied on the duty imposed by law on the finder of goods who takes them into his possession. He concluded as follows ([1970] 3 All ER 825 at 832, [1970] 1 WLR 1262 at 1270):

'Both on principle, and on old as well as recent authority it is clear that, although there was no contract or attornment between the plaintiffs and the defendants, the defendants by voluntarily taking possession of the plaintiffs' goods, in the circumstances assumed an obligation to take due care of them and are liable to the plaintiffs for their failure to do so (as found by the trial judge). The obligation is at any rate the same as that of a bailee, whether or not it can with strict accuracy be described as being the obligation of a bailee. In a case such as this, the obligation is created by the delivery and assumption of possession under a sub-bailment.'

In this passage, Lord Pearson was cautious about describing the obligation of the defendants as bailees vis-à-vis the plaintiffs. Even so, both Diplock and Salmon LJJ described the relationship between the owner of the goods and the sub-bailee in *Morris v C W Martin & Son* as that of bailor and bailee, and their Lordships are generally in agreement with this approach. However, Diplock LJ restricted his statement of the law to those circumstances where the sub-bailee is *aware* that the goods are the property of a person other than the bailee (see [1965] 2 All ER 725 at 734, [1966] 1 QB 716 at 731). This is a point to which their Lordships will return at a later stage. However, the point does not directly arise in the present case, in which their Lordships understand the shipowners to have had sufficient notice that persons other than Hanjin or Scandutch were the owners of the goods. It was doubtless for this reason that no argument on the point was addressed to their Lordships.

Their Lordships pause to observe that the statement of the law by *Pollock and Wright* is restricted to those circumstances in which the bailee has sub-bailed the goods with the authority of the owner. As will appear, such is the position in the present case. Their Lordships are not therefore concerned with the position where the bailee sub-bails the goods to another without the authority of the owner, and so they do not think it appropriate to consider that situation, about which they heard no argument.

The terms of the collateral bailment between the owner and the sub-bailee

On the authority of the case of *Gilchrist Watt & Sanderson Pty Ltd v York Products Pty Ltd* [1970] 3 All ER 825, [1970] 1 WLR 1262 their Lordships have no difficulty in concluding that, in the present case, the shipowners became on receipt of the relevant goods the bailees of the goods of both the Hanjin plaintiffs and the Scandutch plaintiffs. Furthermore, they are of the opinion that the shipowners became the bailees of the goods for reward. In *Pollock and Wright on Possession* it is stated that both the owner of the goods and the bailee have concurrently the rights of a bailor against the sub-bailee according to the nature of the sub-bailment. Their Lordships, like Lord Denning MR in *Morris v C W Martin & Son* [1965] 2 All ER 725 at 733, [1966] 1 QB 716 at 729, consider that, if the sub-bailment is for reward, the obligation owed by the sub-bailee to the owner must likewise be that of a bailee for reward, notwithstanding that the reward is payable not by the owner but by the bailee. It would, they consider, be inconsistent in these circumstances to impose on the sub-bailee two different standards of care in respect of goods so entrusted to him.

But the question then arises whether, as against the owners (here the two groups of plaintiffs), the sub-bailees (here the shipowners) can invoke any of the terms on which the goods were sub-bailed to them, and in particular the exclusive jurisdiction clause (cl 26).

In *Morris v C W Martin & Son* [1965] 2 All ER 725 at 733, [1966] 1 QB 716 at 729 Lord Denning MR expressed his opinion on this point in clear terms, though on the facts of the case his opinion was obiter. He said:

'The answer to the problem lies, I think, in this: the owner is bound by the conditions if he has expressly or impliedly consented to the bailee making a sub-bailment containing those conditions, but not otherwise.'

His expression of opinion on this point has proved to be attractive to a number of judges. In *Morris v C W Martin & Son* [1965] 2 All ER 725 at 741, [1966] 1 QB 716 at 741 itself, Salmon LJ expressed himself to be strongly attracted by it: see also *Cia Portorafti Commerciale SA v Ultramar Panama Inc, The Captain Gregos (No 2)* [1990] 2 Lloyd's Rep 395 at 405 per Bingham LJ (delivering the judgment of the court). Furthermore, on this point Lord Denning MR's statement of the law was applied by Steyn J in *Singer Co (UK) Ltd v Tees and Hartlepool Port Authority* [1988] 2 Lloyd's Rep 164. It was not however followed by Donaldson J in *Johnson Matthey & Co Ltd v Constantine Terminals Ltd* [1976] 2 Lloyd's Rep 215, a decision to which their Lordships will revert at a later stage.

In order to decide whether, like Steyn J, to accept the principle so stated by Lord Denning MR, it is necessary to consider the relevance of the concept of 'consent' in this context. It must be assumed that, on the facts of the case, no direct contractual relationship has been created between the owner and the sub-bailee, the only contract created by the sub-bailment being that between the bailee and the sub-bailee. Even so, if the effect of the sub-bailment is that the sub-bailee voluntarily receives into his custody the goods of the owner and so assumes towards the owner the responsibility of a bailee, then to the extent that the terms of the sub-bailment are consented to by the owner, it can properly be said that the owner has authorised the bailee so to regulate the duties of the sub-bailee in respect of the goods entrusted to him, not only towards the bailee but also towards the owner. (Their Lordships add in parenthesis that for this purpose it is not, in their opinion, necessary to have recourse to the doctrine of estoppel (cf *Hispanica de Petroleos SA v Vencedora Oceanica Navigacion SA, The Kapetan Markos (No 2)* [1987] 2 Lloyd's Rep 321 at 336, 340 per Nicholls and Dillon LJJ). Even where there is express or implied consent to the relevant terms by the owner of the goods, there can be no estoppel without some holding out on his part. Estoppel may however be relevant if recourse is to be had to the doctrine of ostensible authority.)

Such a conclusion, finding its origin in the law of bailment rather than the law of contract, does not depend for its efficacy either on the doctrine of privity of contract or on the doctrine of consideration. That this may be so appears from the decision of the House of Lords in *Elder Dempster & Co Ltd v Paterson Zochonis & Co Ltd* [1924] AC 522, [1924] All ER Rep 135. In that case, shippers of cargo on a chartered ship brought an action against the shipowners for damage caused to the cargo by bad stowage, for which the shipowners were responsible. It is crucial to observe that the cargo was shipped under charterers' bills of lading, so that the contract of carriage contained in or evidenced by the bills of lading was between the shippers and the charterers. The shipowners nevertheless sought to rely, as against the shippers, upon an exception in the bill of lading which protected the charterers from liability for damage due to bad stowage. It was held that the shipowners were entitled to do so, the preferred reason upon which the House so held (see *Midland Silicones Ltd v Scruttons Ltd* [1962] 1 All ER 1 at 8, [1962] AC 446 at 470 per Viscount

Simonds, following the opinion of Fullagar J In *Wilson v Darling Island Stevedoring and Lighterage Co Ltd* (1955) 95 CLR 43 at 78) being found in the speech of Lord Sumner where he said ([1924] AC 522 at 564, [1924] All ER Rep 135 at 155):

'... in the circumstances of this case the obligations to be inferred from the reception of the cargo for carriage to the United Kingdom amount to a bailment upon terms, which include the exceptions and limitations of liability stipulated in the known and contemplated form of bill of lading.'

Of course, there was in that case a bailment by the shippers direct to the shipowners, so that it was not necessary to have recourse to the concept of sub-bailment. Even so, notwithstanding the absence of any contract between the shippers and the shipowners, the shipowners' obligations as bailees were effectively subject to the terms upon which the shipowners implicitly received the goods into their possession. Their Lordships do not imagine that a different conclusion would have been reached in the *Elder Dempster* case if the shippers had delivered the goods, not directly to the ship, but into the possession of agents of the charterers who had, in their turn, loaded the goods on board; because in such circumstances, by parity of reasoning, the shippers may be held to have impliedly consented that the sub-bailment to the shipowners should be on terms which included the exemption from liability for bad stowage.

The Johnson Matthey case

At this stage, their Lordships turn to the decision of Donaldson J in *Johnson Matthey & Co Ltd v Constantine Terminals Ltd* [1976] 2 Lloyd's Rep 215. In that case, the plaintiffs sought to hold sub-bailees of their goods liable to them as bailees; and the sub-bailees in their turn sought to rely, as against the plaintiffs, on certain clauses in the contract of sub-bailment. Donaldson J cited the relevant passage from the judgment of Lord Denning MR in *Morris v C W Martin & Son* [1965] 2 All ER 725 at 733, [1966] 1 QB 716 at 729 and held that, on the facts of the case, the plaintiffs had consented to a sub-bailment on the conditions of Constantine Terminals, the sub-bailees. It was however his opinion that the consent of the plaintiffs was not relevant in the case before him. He nevertheless held that the sub-bailees were entitled to rely on the clauses in question. He said ([1976] 2 Lloyd's Rep 215 at 222):

'But the plaintiffs cannot prove the bailment upon which, in my judgment, they must rely, without referring to terms upon which the silver was received by Constantine Terminals from International Express. These terms establish (a) that Constantine Terminals were bailees for reward but also (b) that the implied duties of such a bailee were qualified by exceptions. And, despite [counsel's] vigorous argument to the contrary, I really do not see how the plaintiffs can rely upon one part of the contract while ignoring the other. Consent seems to me to be relevant only between the bailor and head bailee. If the sub-bailment is on terms to which the bailor consented, he has no cause of action against the head bailee. If it was not, the sub-bailee is still protected, but if the bailor is damnified by the terms of the sub-bailment he has a cause of action against the head bailee.'

The reasoning of Donaldson J (if correct) is, of course, highly relevant to the present case, since it leads to the conclusion that, if (as here) the plaintiffs seek to hold the shipowners liable as bailees, they will ipso facto be bound by the terms of the sub-bailment under which the shipowners received the goods into their possession, including cl 26 (the exclusive jurisdiction clause). However their Lordships are, with respect, unable to accept this reasoning which (related, as it was, to an authorised sub-bailment) is, in their opinion, inconsistent with the decision of the Court of Appeal in *Morris v C W Martin & Son* (by which Donaldson J was bound) and also with the decision of the Privy Council in *Gilchrist Watt & Sanderson Pty Ltd v York Products Pty Ltd* [1970] 3 All ER 825, [1970] 1 WLR 1262. Both these decisions proceeded on the basis that the voluntary taking by a sub-bailee of the owner's goods into his custody of itself results in his owing to the owner the duties of a bailee—as Diplock LJ put it in *Morris v Martin* [1965] 2 All ER 725 at 734, [1966] 1 QB 716 at 731, it brings into existence 'the relationship of bailor and bailee by sub-bailment'. It is therefore from these facts that the owner can prove the bailment upon which he relies when he proceeds directly against the sub-bailee. He does not for this purpose have to rely upon the contract of sub-bailment as between the bailee and the sub-bailee. Moreover, the reasoning of Donaldson J leads to the conclusion that the owner who holds an authorised sub-bailee responsible to him as bailee of his goods has to accept all the terms of the contract of sub-bailment, apparently without limit; indeed logically it leads to the further conclusion that a sub-bailee under an unauthorised sub-bailment which he knew to be unauthorised would likewise be able to invoke all such terms against the owner who sought to hold him responsible as bailee. Their Lordships do not find these conclusions attractive. Furthermore, in their opinion, the approach of Donaldson J cannot be rescued by resort to the doctrine of ratification; for if, as the authorities demonstrate, the owner is able to hold the sub-bailee responsible to him as bailee without reliance on the contract of sub-bailment, it cannot be said that his so doing amounts to ratification of the terms of that contract if unauthorised by him.

In addition, the conclusion of Donaldson J that consent is relevant *only* between the owner and the bailee is inconsistent with the reasoning of Lord Denning MR in *Morris v C W Martin & Son* when he expressed the opinion that the bailor is bound by the terms of the sub-bailment to which he has consented but not otherwise. Their Lordships have already expressed their agreement with the approach of Lord Denning MR on this point. Indeed, as they see it, once it is recognised that the sub-bailee, by voluntarily taking the owner's goods into his custody, ipso facto becomes the bailee of those goods vis-à-vis the owner, it must follow that the owner's rights against the sub-bailee will only be subject to terms of the sub-bailment if he has consented to them, ie if he has authorised the bailee to entrust the goods to the sub-bailee on those terms. Such consent may, as Lord Denning MR pointed out, be express or implied; and in this context the sub-bailee may also be able to invoke, where appropriate, the principle of ostensible authority.

In truth, at the root of this question lies a doctrinal dispute of a fundamental nature, which is epitomised in the question—is it a prerequisite of a bailment that the bailor should have consented to the bailee's possession of the goods? An affirmative answer to this question (which is the answer given by Bell *Modern Law of Personal Property in England and Ireland* (1989) pp 88–89) leads to the conclusion that, if the owner seeks to hold a sub-bailee responsible to him as bailee, he has to accept all the terms of the sub-bailment, warts and all; for either he will have consented to the sub-bailment on those terms or, if not, he will (by holding the sub-bailee liable to him as bailee) be held to have ratified all the terms of the sub-bailment. A negative answer to the question is however supported by other writers, notably by *Palmer's Bailment* pp 31 ff, where Professor Palmer cites a number of examples of bailment without the consent of the owner, and by Professor Tay in her article 'The essence of bailment' (1966) 5 Syd LR 239. On this approach, a person who voluntarily takes another person's goods into his custody holds them as bailee of that person (the owner); and he can only invoke, for example, terms of a sub-bailment under which he received the goods from an intermediate bailee as qualifying or otherwise affecting his responsibility to the owner if the owner consented to them. It is the latter approach which, as their Lordships have explained, has been adopted by English law and, with English law, the law of Hong Kong.

Their Lordships wish to add that this conclusion, which flows from the decisions in *Morris v C W Martin & Son* and the *Gilchrist Watt* case, produces a result which in their opinion is both principled and just. They incline to the opinion that a sub-bailee can only be said for these purposes to have voluntarily taken into his possession the goods of another if he has sufficient notice that a person other than the bailee is interested in the goods so that it can properly be said that (in addition to his duties to the bailee) he has, by taking the goods into his custody, assumed towards that other person the responsibility for the goods which is characteristic of a bailee. This they believe to be the underlying principle. Moreover, their Lordships do not consider this principle to impose obligations on the sub-bailee which are onerous or unfair, once it is recognised that he can invoke against the owner terms of the sub-bailment which the owner has actually (expressly or impliedly) or even ostensibly authorised. In the last resort the sub-bailee may, if necessary and appropriate, be able to invoke against the bailee the principle of warranty of authority.

The facts of the case

Their Lordships turn to the application of these principles to the facts of the present case. They start with the fact that, under cll 6 and 4(1) of the Hanjin and Scandutch bills of lading respectively, it was provided that 'The Carrier shall be entitled to sub-contract on any terms the whole or any part of the ... carriage of the Goods ...' It is necessary to consider whether the consent of these two groups of plaintiffs contained in this provision is effective to entitle the shipowners to invoke the exclusive jurisdiction clause contained in cl 26 of their form of bill of lading.

However, before addressing this question directly, their Lordships have first to consider certain threshold points raised on behalf of the plaintiffs.

(1) *'This bill of lading contract'*

First, cl 26 applies to any claim or dispute arising under 'This bill of lading contract', and it was submitted on behalf of the plaintiffs that, since none of their claims are contractual in nature, they do not fall within cl 26. Here they rely not only on the fact that there is no contractual relationship between the Hanjin and Scandutch plaintiffs on the one hand, and the shipowners as sub-bailees on the other; but also on the fact that the claims of the Kien Hung plaintiffs (who are parties to bill of lading contracts with the shipowners containing cl 26) have been framed not in contract but in bailment or in tort.

A similar point was taken in *Kitchens of Sara Lee (Canada) Ltd v A/S Falkefjell, The Makefjell* [1975] 1 Lloyd's Rep 528 but was rejected by Brandon J at first instance, and his decision on the point was affirmed by the Court of Appeal (see [1976] 2 Lloyd's Rep 29). There the clause in question, which like cl 26 in the present case was concerned with both governing law and jurisdiction (there Norwegian), applied to 'any claim ... arising under this bill of lading'. It was held, to adopt the words of Cairns LJ ([1976] 2 Lloyd's Rep 29 at 33), that there could be no doubt that 'the parties intended that any claims in respect of damage to the goods carried under the bill of lading should be decided in Oslo and according to Norwegian law, however they were framed'. In so holding Cairns LJ (like Brandon J) relied on the statement of Evans P in *The Cap Blanco* [1913] P 131 at 136, [1911–13] All ER Rep 365 at 368, where he said that 'effect must be given, if the terms of the contract permit it, to the obvious intention and agreement of the parties'.

In the present case, however, the clause in question refers to any claim or other dispute arising under 'This Bill of Lading *contract*'; and Mr Kentridge QC for the plaintiffs submitted that this wording compelled the conclusion that the clause applied only to contractual claims. Arguments of this kind can lead to reasoning of some technicality, far removed from the spirit of the dictum of Evans P; and Mr Thomas QC for the shipowners sought to build upon that dictum in order to advance an argument that cl 26 should be read broadly, to embrace not only claims which are contractual in nature, but also claims in bailment or in tort where the liability of the shipowners was governed by the contractual terms set out in a bill of lading in the shipowners' form.

However, Mr Thomas also referred to the fact that the bills of lading were expressed to be governed by Chinese law, and he complained that the point here relied on by the plaintiffs had not been taken by them below, and as a result the expert witnesses on Chinese law who gave evidence before Sears J were not, as they should have been, examined on the point, although there were indications (but no more) in the evidence of both experts favourable to his clients on this issue. Their Lordships have come to the conclusion that Mr Thomas's objection to this point being taken for the first time before the Board was no mere technical point, but one of substance. In their opinion, it would not be right in these circumstances to allow the plaintiffs to pursue the point before the Board, and they so rule.

Even so, their Lordships wish to dwell for a moment upon the extreme technicality of the point here taken on behalf of the plaintiffs. This is a case where goods have been shipped under bills of lading. Bills of lading are documents which operate as receipts for the goods, and which contain or evidence the terms of the contract of carriage. Such terms include provisions relating to the shipowners' obligations in respect of the goods while in their care, and so regulate their responsibility for the goods as bailees. In these circumstances, their Lordships find it difficult to believe that a clause providing for the governing law and for exclusive jurisdiction over claims should be held not to be apt to cover claims by the cargo owners against the shipowners framed in bailment rather than in contract, simply because the clause refers to claims under the bill of lading contract as opposed to claims under the bill of lading. Furthermore, if this view is correct, it must follow that shipowners who are sub-bailees of the goods may similarly be able to invoke such a clause against owners of the goods who are seeking to hold them liable as bailees and who have consented to the inclusion of the clause in the bill of lading. Their Lordships cannot help feeling that any other conclusion would not merely offend against the spirit of the statement of Evans P in *The Cap Blanco*, but would lead to refinements and inconsistencies which are unacceptable in a commercial context.

(2) *Superimposition of terms*

The next point taken on behalf of the plaintiffs was that the shipowners' form of bill of lading, like many others, contained a 'Himalaya' clause which, following the decision of the Privy Council in *New Zealand Shipping Co Ltd v A M Satterthwaite & Co Ltd* [1974] 1 All ER 1015, [1975] AC 154, may be effective to provide protection for sub-contractors of carriers by enabling them to take advantage of exceptions in the bill of lading on the basis that the carrier has contracted for the exceptions not only on his own behalf but also as agent for the sub-contractors. The submission of the plaintiffs in the present case was that the 'Himalaya' clause gives sufficient effect to the commercial expectations of the parties, and that to allow a sub-bailee to take advantage of the terms of his own contract with the bailee was not only unnecessary but created a potential inconsistency between the two regimes. In their Lordships' opinion, however, this argument is not well founded. They are satisfied that, on the legal principles previously stated, a sub-bailee may indeed be able to take advantage, as against the owner of goods, of the terms on which the goods have been sub-bailed to him. This may, of course, occur in circumstances where no 'Himalaya' clause is applicable; but the mere fact that such a clause is applicable cannot, in their Lordships' opinion, be effective to oust the sub-bailee's right to rely on the terms of the sub-bailment as against the owner of the goods. If it should transpire that there are in consequence two alternative regimes which the sub-bailee may invoke, it does not necessarily follow that they will be inconsistent; nor does it follow, if they are inconsistent, that the sub-bailee should not be entitled to choose to rely upon one or other of them as against the owner of the goods (see A P Bell's paper in *Interests in Goods* (1989) Ch 6, pp 178–180). Their Lordships are therefore satisfied that the mere fact that a 'Himalaya' clause is applicable does not of itself defeat the shipowners' argument on this point.

(3) *Quasi-bailment*

The third point invoked by the plaintiffs affected only the Scandutch plaintiffs. It was based on the proposition that in their case the shipowners were not sub-bailees at all. The submission was that there was no evidence that Scandutch ever obtained actual possession of the goods; if that was the case, it was said, the shipowners were not sub-bailees but quasi-bailees, and there was no authority that the doctrine of sub-bailment on terms extended to quasi-bailments. Their Lordships feel bound to say that they view this point with some concern. There is no trace of it in the judgments in the courts below. Not only that, but Sears J expressly found that the shipowners were sub-bailees of the goods of the Scandutch plaintiffs, a conclusion which was inconsistent with the proposition that Scandutch never had possession of the goods; and this conclusion of fact appears to have been challenged neither in the plaintiffs' respondent's notice, nor in their argument, before the Court of Appeal. If the point had been taken and pursued, the first question to be explored would have been whether it was right that the goods were never in the possession of Scandutch or their agents. As it was, the form of bill of lading issued by Scandutch in respect of these goods represented that Scandutch had received the goods for transportation from the place of receipt; and no evidence was adduced to contradict this statement. In these circumstances, their Lordships do not think it right for the plaintiffs to be allowed to raise the point for the first time before the Board. They wish to add however that, on the limited argument on this point which took place before them, it is difficult to see why the shipowners should not, when they received the goods of the Scandutch plaintiffs into their possession, have become responsible as bailees to the owners of the goods even if the goods were never in the possession of Scandutch (see *Palmer on Bailment* (2nd edn, 1991) pp 34, 1292) and, if so, it is not easy to see why they should not be able to invoke against the owners any terms upon which the intermediary (Scandutch), with the owners' consent, entrusted the goods to them. This point can, however, await decision, after consideration in greater depth, on another occasion.

Having disposed of these three threshold points, their Lordships turn to the basic question which arises on this aspect of the case which is whether, in the case of a sub-bailment, the owners of the goods who seek to hold the sub-bailee liable to them as a bailee will be bound by an exclusive jurisdiction clause which forms part of the contract governing the sub-bailment. Their Lordships start, of course, with the position that, under cll 6 and 4(1) of the Hanjin and Scandutch bills of lading respectively, there was vested in both Hanjin and Scandutch a very wide authority to sub-contract the whole or any part of the carriage of the goods 'on any terms'. Since the sub-contracting of any part of the carriage to another will ordinarily involve a bailment (or sub-bailment) to that carrier, it must follow that both the Hanjin and Scandutch plaintiffs had expressly consented to the sub-bailment of their goods to another carrier on any terms. It further follows that no question arises in the present case of implied consent, the only question relating to the scope of the express consent so given.

At first sight, the words used are wide enough to authorise consent to the application of an exclusive jurisdiction clause to the sub-bailment. However, it was the submission of the plaintiffs that this was not so. They submitted that the exclusive jurisdiction clause should be excluded from such incorporation because it was not a clause directly germane to the subject matter of the bill of lading, viz the shipment, carriage and delivery of the relevant goods. In support of this submission, they relied on the well known line of authority concerned with the incorporation of charterparty terms into bills of lading, of which *T W Thomas & Co Ltd v Portsea Steamship Co Ltd* [1912] AC 1 is perhaps the most familiar. However, the present context is by no means identical with that in the *Thomas v Portsea* line of cases, which have been described as a special corner of the law (see *Skips A/S Nordheim v Syrian Petroleum Co Ltd, The Varenna* [1983] 3 All ER 645 at 648–649, [1984] QB 599 at 616–617 per Donaldson MR). In this line of cases, the question is whether general words incorporating the terms of a charterparty into a bill of lading contract are effective to incorporate, for example, an arbitration clause in the charterparty; and it is readily understandable that, in so transporting terms from one contract of carriage to another, some limit should be placed on the incorporation by relating it to the subject matter of the receiving contract. Here, however, the question is whether consent given by the owner of goods to his bailee to bail the goods to a sub-bailee on any terms is wide enough to embrace an exclusive jurisdiction clause in the contract governing the sub-bailment; and their Lordships do not

perceive a similar need to limit the terms so consented to. Nor do their
Lordships consider that the mere fact that the relevant clause may (as here) be
regarded as, in a sense, imposing a positive obligation on the owner is of itself
sufficient to exclude it from the scope of the consent so given. In such a case,
it seems to them, the element of control must be derived from the scope of the
owner's consent; and where, as here, the consent is very wide in its terms, only
terms which are so unusual or so unreasonable that they could not reasonably
be understood to fall within such consent are likely to be held to be excluded.
Bearing this in mind, their Lordships perceive a number of considerations
which militate in favour of the incorporation of the exclusive jurisdiction
clause in the present case. First, by way of introduction, it is common in the
present context for an exclusive jurisdiction clause to be coupled with an
express choice of law clause, often contained (as here) in the same contractual
provision, and usually providing for the law of the chosen forum to be the law
governing the contract. Second, a provision in this form is by no means
uncommon in shipowners' standard forms of bill of lading; indeed such a
provision must, their Lordships imagine, be very common in the case of
shipowners engaged in the container trade. Third, their Lordships do not
consider that it can possibly be said that the incorporation of such a clause in a
bill of lading is per se unreasonable. In this connection, they refer again to the
difficulties, described earlier, which may arise if bill of lading holders are free
to pursue their claims in various jurisdictions throughout the world; and they
do not overlook the fact that, in common law countries, a stay of proceedings
to enforce an exclusive jurisdiction clause is a matter for the court's discretion.

In support of their argument, the plaintiffs invoked the decision of the Court
of Appeal in *The Forum Craftsman* [1985] 1 Lloyd's Rep 291. But their Lordships
are satisfied that that case is not in pari materia with the present. There the
shippers (the owners of the goods) sought to invoke against the shipowners
(the sub-bailees) an exclusive jurisdiction clause in the relevant bills of lading.
But the case was concerned with a chartered ship, and the bills of lading, issued
by the charterers, contained an exclusive jurisdiction clause (providing for the
contract to be governed by Japanese law, and for the exclusive jurisdiction of
the Tokyo District Court). It was not therefore a case where sub-bailees were
seeking to enforce against the owners of the goods an exclusive jurisdiction
clause in the contract governing the sub-bailment which had been consented
to by the owners. It was a case in which the owners of the goods were seeking
to enforce against the sub-bailees an exclusive jurisdiction clause in their
contract (the bill of lading contract) with the bailees (the charterers), a contract
to which the sub-bailees (the shipowners) were not party, and to which they
had never consented. It was scarcely surprising that, in these circumstances,
the Court of Appeal declined to hold that the shipowners were bound by the
clause. In their Lordships' opinion, the case provides no useful guidance in the
very different circumstances of the present case.

For these reasons, their Lordships do not feel able to accept the argument of
the plaintiffs on this point. On the contrary, they consider that the
incorporation of the relevant clause in the sub-bailment would be in
accordance with the reasonable commercial expectations of those who engage
in this type of trade, and that such incorporation will generally lead to a
conclusion which is eminently sensible in the context of the carriage of goods
by sea, especially in a container ship, in so far as it is productive of an ordered
and sensible resolution of disputes in a single jurisdiction, so avoiding wasted

expenditure in legal costs and an undesirable disharmony of differing consequences where claims are resolved in different jurisdictions. On this point, therefore, their Lordships find themselves to be in agreement with the conclusion reached both by Sears J and the Court of Appeal.

The application for a stay of proceedings

It is common ground between the parties that, in a case such as the present, the applicable principles are those set out in the judgment of Brandon LJ in *Aratra Potato Co Ltd v Egyptian Navigation Co, The El Amria* [1981] 2 Lloyd's Rep 119. According to those principles, the court has a discretion whether to grant a stay of proceedings brought in breach of an agreement to refer disputes to a foreign court; but the discretion should be exercised by granting a stay, unless strong cause for not doing so is shown. One of the matters to be taken into account in the exercise of the discretion is whether the plaintiff would be prejudiced by having to sue in the foreign court because, for example, he would be faced with a time bar not applicable in the domestic jurisdiction, here Hong Kong.

In considering the exercise of his discretion, Sears J was satisfied that, apart from one matter, ie the time bar applicable in Taiwan, the connection with Taiwan was so strong that he would have had no doubt that he should grant a stay. So far as the time bar was concerned, the applicable limitation period in Taiwan was two years with an optional extension of six months. The casualty occurred on 11 March 1987, and the time bar must have expired at the latest on 11 September 1989. The writ in rem in the Hong Kong proceedings against the Pioneer Container was issued on 10 March 1988 and served on 29 October 1988. On 8 September 1989 the shipowners issued their notice of motion for a stay. The matter did not come before Sears J until September 1990. After a preliminary ruling on 26 September 1990 on the issue of bailment on terms, Sears J decided on 14 May 1991 that the shipowners' application for a stay should be dismissed.

On the question of the time bar, Sears J approached the matter on the principles set out by Sheen J in *The Blue Wave* [1982] 1 Lloyd's Rep 151 at 156 and by Lord Goff of Chieveley in *Spiliada Maritime Corp v Cansulex Ltd, The Spiliada* [1986] 3 All ER 843, [1987] AC 460. In the latter case Lord Goff said ([1986] 3 All ER 843 at 860, [1987] AC 460 at 483–484):

> 'But, in my opinion, this is a case where practical justice should be done. And practical justice demands that, if the court considers that the plaintiff acted reasonably in commencing proceedings in this country, and that, although it appears that (putting on one side the time-bar point) the appropriate forum for the trial of the action is elsewhere than England, the plaintiff did not act unreasonably in failing to commence proceedings (for example by issuing a protective writ) in that jurisdiction within the limitation period applicable there, it would not, I think, be just to deprive the plaintiff of the benefit of having started proceedings within the limitation period applicable in this country. This approach is consistent with that of Sheen J in *The Blue Wave* ...'

However, in an earlier passage Lord Goff said ([1986] 3 All ER 843 at 860, [1987] AC 460 at 483):

> '... suppose that the plaintiff allowed the limitation period to elapse in the appropriate jurisdiction, and came here simply because he wanted to

take advantage of a more generous time-bar applicable in this country; or suppose that it was obvious that the plaintiff should have commenced proceedings in the appropriate jurisdiction, and yet he did not trouble to issue a protective writ there; in cases such as these, I cannot see that the court should hesitate to stay the proceedings in this country, even though the effect would be that the plaintiff's claim would inevitably be defeated by a plea of the time-bar in the appropriate jurisdiction.'

Sears J concluded that the plaintiffs had not acted unreasonably in allowing the time bar to elapse in Taiwan. In so holding, he appears to have been influenced in particular by two factors, viz that the plaintiffs would have had to put up a percentage of their claim (either 1% or 3%) as advance costs, and that, if an arrest had been made, counter-security for the full amount of the claim would have had to be provided. However, as Cons V-P pointed out in the Court of Appeal, the truth of the matter was (as was indeed conceded before the Court of Appeal) that the plaintiffs had deliberately and advisedly allowed the time limit to expire in Taiwan; and the Court of Appeal did not see that the two matters relied upon by Sears J provided sufficient justification for so doing. The amount of costs required to be put up in advance (about $HK1m) was by no means large in the context of modern commercial litigation. As to security, there was no evidence that the defendants would not be able to satisfy any judgment given against them in Taiwan. In these circumstances, Godfrey J described the position as follows:

'If you find yourself bound to litigate in a forum which is more expensive that the one you would prefer, deliberately to choose the latter rather than the former seems to me (although the judge thought otherwise) to be forum shopping in one of its purest and most undesirable forms. And if in pursuance of your deliberate decision to litigate here instead, you let time run out in the jurisdiction in which you are bound to litigate, without taking the trouble (because of the expense) even to issue a protective writ there, you are not, as I think, acting reasonably at all; you are gambling on the chance of a stay being refused here and you cannot complain if you then lose that gamble. That may seem to you at the time a justifiable commercial risk to take. But that, in the context of the litigation, does not make your decision a reasonable one.'

Accordingly, the Court of Appeal concluded that Sears J had erred in the exercise of his discretion. Their Lordships cannot fault that conclusion.

When the Court of Appeal came to exercise its own discretion in place of that of the judge, it was faced with the simple fact that the plaintiffs had deliberately allowed the time bar to elapse in Taiwan. The Kien Hung plaintiffs were well aware of cl 26. It was true that the other two groups of plaintiffs had their argument that they were not bound by the clause, but there was nothing to indicate that uncertainty in the application of the clause was present to the minds of those representing them at any time before the issue of the motion for a stay—indeed such indications as there were pointed the other way. In these circumstances, the Court of Appeal decided in the exercise of its discretion to order that all proceedings in the action be stayed. Their Lordships are of the opinion that it was fully entitled so to do.

For these reasons, their Lordships will humbly advise Her Majesty that the appeal should be dismissed. The plaintiffs must pay the shipowners' costs before their Lordships' Board.

Appeal dismissed.

Celia Fox   Barrister.

Oxfordshire County Council v M and another

COURT OF APPEAL, CIVIL DIVISION
SIR STEPHEN BROWN P, STEYN AND KENNEDY LJJ
26, 27 OCTOBER 1993

Discovery – Legal professional privilege – Family proceedings – Production of documents – Privilege – Reports containing material adverse to client's interests but relevant to determination of case – Reports relating to children in care proceedings – Whether court having power to order disclosure of privileged material in family proceedings.

Proceedings under the Children Act 1989 are not adversarial and the court's duty is to investigate and to seek to achieve a result which is in the interests of the welfare of the child or children the subject of the proceedings. Such proceedings are not similar to ordinary civil litigation in cases between party and party in which the doctrine of professional privilege applies but fall into a special category where the court is bound to undertake all necessary steps to arrive at an appropriate result in the paramount interests of the welfare of the child. Accordingly, the court has power to override legal professional privilege and order disclosure where a party wishes not to disclose an unfavourable expert's report obtained with the leave of the court (see p 278 *c g* to *j*, p 279 *b* to *d*, p 281 *j* to p 282 *e*, post).

Re R (a minor) (disclosure of privileged material) [1993] 4 All ER 702 approved.
Barking and Dagenham London BC v O [1993] 4 All ER 59 overruled.

Notes

For legal professional privilege in general, see 13 *Halsbury's Laws* (4th edn) paras 71–85, and for cases on the subject, see 18 *Digest* (Reissue) 154–163, 1379–1428.

For the Children Act 1989, see 6 *Halsbury's Statutes* (4th edn) (1992 reissue) 387.

Cases referred to in judgments

A (minors: disclosure of material), Re [1991] 2 FLR 473.
B v Derbyshire CC [1992] 1 FLR 538.
Barking and Dagenham London BC v O [1993] 4 All ER 59, [1993] Fam 295, [1993] 3 WLR 493.
Causton v Mann Egerton (Johnsons) Ltd [1974] 1 All ER 453, [1974] 1 WLR 162, CA.

Comfort Hotels Ltd v Wembley Stadium Ltd (Silkin and ors, third parties) [1988] 3 All ER 53, [1988] 1 WLR 872.
E (SA) (a minor) (wardship), Re [1984] 1 All ER 289, [1984] 1 WLR 156, HL.
Humberside CC v DPR (an infant) [1977] 3 All ER 964, [1977] 1 WLR 1251, DC.
M (a minor) (disclosure of material), Re [1990] 2 FLR 36, CA.
Official Solicitor v K [1963] 3 All ER 191, sub nom *Re K (infants)* [1965] AC 201, [1963] 3 WLR 408, HL.
R v Barton [1972] 2 All ER 1192, [1973] 1 WLR 115.
R v Birmingham Juvenile Court, ex p G, R v Birmingham Juvenile Court, ex p R (a minor) [1989] 3 All ER 336, [1990] 1 QB 573, [1989] 3 WLR 1024, CA; affg [1988] 3 All ER 726, [1988] 1 WLR 950.
R v Hampshire CC, ex p K [1990] 2 All ER 129, [1990] 2 QB 71, [1990] 2 WLR 649, DC.
R v Secretary of State for the Home Dept, ex p Leech [1993] 4 All ER 539, [1994] QB 198, [1993] 3 WLR 1125, CA.
R (a minor) (disclosure of privileged material), Re [1993] 4 All ER 702, sub nom *Essex CC v R* [1994] 2 WLR 407.
Saxton (decd), Re, Johnson v Saxton [1962] 3 All ER 92, [1962] 1 WLR 968, CA.
Scott v Scott [1913] AC 417, HL.
Worral v Reich [1955] 1 All ER 363, [1955] 1 QB 296.
X (a minor) (wardship: restriction on publication), Re [1975] 1 All ER 697, [1975] Fam 47, [1975] 2 WLR 335, CA.

Cases also cited
B (minor) (disclosure of evidence), Re [1993] 1 FLR 191
C (a minor: irregularity of practice), Re [1991] 2 FLR 438
E (SA) (a minor) (wardship), Re [1984] 1 All ER 289, [1984] 1 WLR 156, HL.
H v H (minors) (child abuse: evidence), Re [1989] 3 All ER 740, [1990] Fam 86, [1989] 3 WLR 933, CA.
W v Egdell [1990] 1 All ER 835, [1990] Ch 359, [1990] 2 WLR 471, CA.
Waugh v British Railways Board [1979] 2 All ER 1169, [1980] AC 521, [1979] 3 WLR 150, HL.

Appeal
In care proceedings initiated by the respondent local authority in respect of the two younger children of the appellant mother by different fathers, Judge Paul Clark, at a directions hearing on 28 September 1993 in the Oxford County Court, gave leave to the appellant and second respondent, the father of one of the children, to disclose a video recording of an interview of the two older children and certain documents to the consultant psychiatrist instructed on their behalf on condition that the report was filed and served by 29 November 1993. On 11 October at a directions hearing before Judge Harold Wilson the appellant and second respondent applied to amend the order of 28 September by the removal of the condition that the psychiatrist's report be filed and disclose to the court and the other parties. Judge Wilson refused the application to amend the order. The appellant and second respondent appealed against the judges' refusal to amend the order. The facts are set out in the judgment of Sir Stephen Brown P.

Jonathan Baker (instructed by *Bower & Bailey*, Oxford) for the appellant.
Georgina Middleton (instructed by *Linnells*, Oxford) for the second respondent.
Leo Curran (instructed by *Colin S Rowland*, Oxford) for the local authority.

Joanna Hall (instructed by Richard Pooler & Co, Oxford) for the guardian ad litem.
Sally Max (instructed by Hedges & Son, Didcot) for the third respondent.

SIR STEPHEN BROWN P. The court has before it appeals from interlocutory orders made by Judge Harold Wilson at Oxford County Court on 11 October 1993. The relevant orders were made at a hearing for directions in care proceedings brought by the Oxfordshire County Council pursuant to s 31 of the Children Act 1989. The chronological history of this matter can be briefly stated. I am grateful for the assistance of a chronology prepared by the first respondent to the care proceedings, the principal appellant. The proceedings concern two girls aged four and two years of age. Their mother is the first respondent to the care proceedings. They are the children of different fathers. The father of the younger child, T, is the second respondent in the care proceedings. The father of the older girl, L, is the third respondent. The girls themselves are parties to the proceedings and are represented by a guardian ad litem. The mother has two older children, both boys, now aged nine and eight years respectively. They were both born to her and to her former husband, whom she divorced in 1987. The older girl, L, is the child of the mother by her second husband, the third respondent, from whom she separated in 1990. The younger daughter, T, is the child of her association with the second respondent. The mother presently lives in the same household as the second respondent with the two girls.

In 1992 the Oxfordshire County Council commenced care proceedings in respect of the two older boys on the ground that they were suffering, and were likely to suffer significant harm, as a result of neglect. In February 1993 care orders were made in respect of both boys by a family proceedings court and the boys were placed with foster parents. In June 1993 the older boy disclosed to his foster mother that he had been sexually abused, inter alia, by his mother. She reported this, and both boys were subsequently interviewed separately by a child protection investigation team. The older boy repeated the allegations at a disclosure interview which was video recorded. In July both boys were examined by a paediatrician, instructed by the social services department.

On 22 July 1993 the Oxfordshire County Council began care proceedings in respect of the two girls on the ground that they were likely to suffering significant harm, having regard to the matters which were alleged to have taken place with regard to the older boys. On 22 July 1993 a family proceedings court made interim supervision orders in respect of both girls, and meanwhile they remained at home in the care of their mother, subject to the supervision order. In September 1993 the family proceedings court transferred the care proceedings to the Oxford County Court.

At a directions hearing held on 28 September 1993 Judge Paul Clark made a number of orders by consent, including, the following direction:

'The first and second respondent do have leave to disclose the video recording of the interview with [the older boys] dated 30 June 1993 and copies of documents in the matter held by the Court to the consultant psychiatrist instructed on behalf of the First and Second Respondent whose report shall be filed and served by 29 November 1993.'

At the same hearing, the judge gave directions that the guardian ad litem should also have leave to disclose copies of documents in the matter held by the court to a consultant psychiatrist to be instructed by her on behalf of the two girls. He directed that the guardian should file her report by 6 December 1993. He finally ordered that the matter should be listed for further directions on 11 October.

On 11 October the directions hearing came before Judge Harold Wilson at the Oxford County Court. On that occasion, the first respondent, the mother, and the second respondent, the father of T, applied to the judge for a direction that cl 4 of Judge Paul Clark's order, which I have cited, should be amended by removing the requirement to disclose and file the consultant psychiatrist's report. Counsel for the mother also sought leave to consult a child psychiatrist with a view to commenting on the allegations made by the boys and also to commenting on evidence filed by the consultant child psychiatrist instructed by the county council. Counsel also sought leave for the mother to be allowed to disclose that material to an adult psychiatrist whom she proposed to consult, and further leave to disclose the case material to a paediatrician, whom she wished to consult. The second respondent joined in the mother's application to amend cl 4 of the order made by Judge Paul Clark on 28 September. He also joined in the application for leave to disclose material to a paediatrician. These applications were all made upon the basis that if the leave sought were to be granted and reports consequently obtained, the respondents should not then be under any obligation to disclose the report. In other words, they would be at liberty to withhold them, if they should prove to be unfavourable to their cases.

The learned county court judge was confronted with two conflicting decisions of judges of the Family Division of the High Court. They were, firstly, a decision of Douglas Brown J in *Barking and Dagenham London BC v O* [1993] 4 All ER 59, [1993] Fam 295 and a decision of Thorpe J made subsequently, *Re R (a minor) (disclosure of privileged material)* [1993] 4 All ER 702, [1994] 2 WLR 407. Douglas Brown J was faced with applications very similar to those which were being made to Judge Harold Wilson. The headnote reads as follows ([1993] Fam 295 at 295–296):

> 'In September 1992, the local authority instituted care proceedings under the Children Act 1989 relating to two half-brothers, then aged six and two, who were then in the care of the mother. Interim care orders were made and the substantive hearing date fixed. On the summons for directions, orders were made, inter alia, that the mother file and serve medical reports from three named doctors which related to her and which had been commissioned on her behalf on the advice of her legal advisers. A further order was made that the mother file and serve hospital reports relating to the boys. The orders were made by consent. Ten days before the substantive hearing the mother applied to amend the order requiring her to file and serve the medical reports relating to her by the addition of the words, "if the mother intends to rely on them." On the question whether disclosure could be ordered by the court:—*Held*, granting the application, that since proceedings under the Children Act 1989 were adversarial in the sense that each party was entitled to be heard, be represented by an advocate and challenge opposing evidence in cross-examination they were proceedings in which legal professional privilege could not be overridden; that in the absence of waiver by the party concerned, the court had no power to order disclosure of legally professionally privileged documents and that therefore the mother was not obliged to disclose medical reports obtained by her solicitor unless she wished to do so.'

There has been no appeal directly from that decision. The decision was cited
to Judge Harold Wilson. In the course of his judgment, Douglas Brown J
referred to cases dealing with legal privilege where he said ([1993] 4 All ER 59
at 62, [1993] Fam 295 at 298):

> 'In these circumstances, says Mr Rippon [counsel for the mother], the
> law is clear. Medical reports made on behalf of a party to litigation on the
> advice of legal advisers are privileged documents and, in the absence of a
> waiver, no order for disclosure can be made. He relied on *Causton v Mann
> Egerton (Johnsons) Ltd* [1974] 1 All ER 453, [1974] 1 WLR 162. He drew my
> attention in particular to the judgment of Roskill LJ, who, in the course of
> his judgment, made reference to the passage from the judgment of Lord
> Denning MR in *Re Saxton (decd), Johnson v Saxton* [1962] 3 All ER 92 at 94–
> 95, [1962] 1 WLR 968 at 972, where he said: "The court would not *order* the
> report of either expert to be shown to the other side before the trial. That
> could only be done by agreement. This is the familiar practice in all cases
> where experts are called, such as patent cases and Factory Act cases (where
> engineers are employed) or personal injury cases (where doctors are
> employed). The reports of experts are often exchanged by agreement, but
> no compulsion on either side is exercised; see *Worral v. Reich* ([1955] 1 All
> ER 363, [1955] 1 QB 296). The reason is because, to our way of thinking,
> the expert should be allowed to give his report fully and frankly to the
> party who employs him, with all its strength and weakness, and not be
> made to offer it beforehand as a hostage to the opponent, lest he take
> unfair advantage of it. In short, it is one of our notions of a fair trial that,
> except by agreement, one side is not entitled to see the proofs of the other
> side's witnesses.'

The learned judge, Douglas Brown J, then continued his judgment as follows:

> 'Mr Rippon referred to other passages in the judgment, which I do not
> need to refer to, which carry the matter really no further. He properly
> drew my attention to *Re A (minors: disclosure of material)* [1991] 2 FLR 473,
> a decision of Johnson J expressed to be obiter where the facts are rather
> similar to the present case. The judge in that case drew a distinction
> between ordinary litigation where the rule illustrated in *Causton v Mann
> Egerton (Johnsons) Ltd* applied and wardship cases. Because the jurisdiction
> in wardship was parental, administrative and non-adversarial in character,
> there was, at any rate in legal theory, an unrestricted jurisdiction to do
> whatever was necessary for the welfare of the ward. That included the
> power in appropriate cases to override legal professional privilege. The
> power should only be exercised rarely and only when the court is satisfied,
> and conducting a balancing exercise, that it was necessary for it to be
> exercised in order to achieve the best interests of the child's welfare. Mr
> Rippon made three submissions about that case. First of all, it was a
> decision obiter; secondly, that I am not sitting in wardship and paternal
> aspects of wardship have not been transferred to the Children Act
> jurisdiction. The decision of Johnson J, if correct, has no application when
> the judge is concerned with a Children Act application. Thirdly, if there
> was jurisdiction to override legal professional privilege this was not a case
> where it should be done.'

In his conclusion the judge said ([1993] 4 All ER 59 at 63–64, [1993] Fam 295 at 300):

> 'In my judgment this mother, in the absence of waiver, is not bound to disclose medical reports obtained by her solicitor unless she wishes to do so, and I will amend the order to add the words suggested by Mr Rippon. It may be (and I express no concluded view as to the correctness of Johnson J's decision in *Re A (minors: disclosure of material)* that in wardship proceedings there is power to order disclosure of material governed by legal professional privilege. Children Act proceedings are not wardship proceedings. They are not paternal, they are not administrative and they are not in reality non-adversarial, although they should be conducted in a non-adversarial spirit. Johnson J's justification for the view he took, based in part on *Re M (a minor) (disclosure of material)* was that he would have been exercising the wide powers of the wardship judge. Those powers are not available to me giving interlocutory directions on a s 31 care order application. Miss Bradwell argued that the welfare paramountcy principle was common to both wardship and to the Children Act 1989, and so it is, but the justification for taking the highly unusual step of overriding legal professional privilege was the particular nature of the wardship jurisdiction which has not been inherited by the Children Act jurisdiction. Children Act proceedings are adversarial in the sense that each party is entitled to be heard and to challenge opposing evidence by cross-examination and entitled to representation by an advocate. In this context I refer to the judgment of Roskill LJ in *Causton v Mann Egerton (Johnsons) Ltd* [1974] 1 All ER 453 at 460, [1974] 1 WLR 162 at 170: "As counsel for the defendants said, so long as we have an adversary system, a party is entitled not to produce documents which are properly protected by privilege if it is not to his advantage to produce them, and even though their production might assist his adversary if his adversary or his solicitor were aware of their contents and might lead the court to a different conclusion from that to which the court would come in ignorance of their existence. Some may regret this; but the law has always allowed it and it is not for us to change the law in this respect."'

Douglas Brown J then continued:

> 'I respectfully agree, and if it be the case that the court ought to have the power to direct disclosure of legal professionally privileged documents in children's cases then it will have to be given that power by legislation ... '

In the result, he ordered that the application to amend the order would be granted. His judgment was delivered on 12 March 1993. It was reported on 13 August 1993. It had, I think, previously been reported in the All England Reports, because it was available when Thorpe J considered *Re R (a minor) (disclosure of privilege material)* [1993] 4 All ER 702, [1994] 2 WLR 407 on 23 July 1993. Thorpe J, in the course of a care hearing, was faced with a similar problem. It had not occurred in the same way at a directions hearing, but nevertheless it was the same matter in principle. The learned judge in his judgment said ([1993] 4 All ER 702 at 704, [1994] 2 WLR 407 at 408):

> 'In relation to this issue, what was the professional responsibility of the mother's legal team? Obviously the report was the subject of legal professional privilege. Was it discoverable, or were the mother's advisers

in any event entitled to conduct the case as though the report had never been made? The professional responsibility in these circumstances is not clear on the authorities as they now stand. On one view the decision of Johnson J in *Re A (minors: disclosure of material)* [1991] 2 FLR 473 establishes that the court in wardship had the power to order a party to disclose a report to which legal professional privilege attaches if containing material relevant to the determination of the case and even if that material is adverse to the party's cause. A subsequent judgment of Douglas Brown J in *Barking and Dagenham London BC v O* [1993] 4 All ER 59, [1993] Fam 295 declines to extend that principle, seemingly established in wardship, into Children Act applications. The decision makes it plain that legal professional privilege is not to be displaced in Children Act cases other than by legislative process. If there was such a power in wardship, it rested upon the parens patria jurisdiction and is not to be extended into Children Act cases. I find myself in disagreement with that decision. It is relevant to observe that the point came to Douglas Brown J as the applications judge, he being asked to vary as a matter of urgency a direction that had been made by another judge of the Family Division for the filing of reports by a deadline which was expiring that day. The argument presented to Douglas Brown J rested partly upon the basis that the decision of Johnson J in *Re A* was obiter. Technically it might have been said to be an obiter decision, in the sense that the report was ultimately proffered voluntarily by leading counsel for the mother before the court order compelled that. But Johnson J was asked to rule on the point and he heard full argument from leading counsel before giving a considered judgment. It is quite plain to me that the judge in wardship held a responsibility to investigate any material relevant to the determination of the welfare issue, whether put before him by the parties in adversarial range or not. There is clear authority to that effect in the House of Lords: see *Re E (SA)* [1984] 1 All ER 289, [1984] 1 WLR 156. I do not accept that the investigative powers and responsibilities of a Family Division judge have been curtailed now that his principal jurisdiction is under the Children Act 1989. It follows in my judgment that all that is said by Johnson J in *Re A* is of equal application in Children Act cases decided by a judge of the Family Division. Legal professional privilege is the creature of case law and, where limitations by exception have seemed necessary, those limitations have equally been developed by case law. In my judgment, where the court considers the welfare of a child, the power that it holds, allied to its responsibility, enables it to override a legal professional privilege which is set up to preserve or enhance the adversarial position of one of the parties.'

Those two decisions were drawn to the attention of Judge Harold Wilson. He was faced with the difficult task of having to make a decision in the knowledge that there were conflicting rulings of two High Court judges of the Family Division. He heard argument, of course, from counsel who appeared then and who appear before this court in this appeal for the various parties. Having referred to those two decisions, he said of his judgment:

'I prefer to follow the guidance contained in Thorpe J.'s decision because it seems to me to accord far more closely to the spirit which lies within the Children Act. It is an Act which puts the child first without any qualification of any sort, and is the first piece of legislation so to do. In those circumstances it seems to me that the court is concerned from beginning to end and overwhelmingly with doing everything possible to come to the right conclusion for the future of the child with which the court is concerned. The game of adversarial litigation has no place when one is trying to deal with fragile and vulnerable people like small children. Every other consideration must come second to the need to reach the right conclusion if possible. Accordingly, I decline to amend the wording of Clause 4 and insofar as I grant leave as sought by Mr. Baker with regard to the other experts that leave is conditional upon the reports which are furnished being filed with the court and served upon the other parties, including, of course, the Guardian.'

The judge then proceeded to grant the leave sought by both the mother and the father of L for leave to disclose documents to experts, but he ordered that any consequential reports should be filed by a specific date and served on the other parties. It is against that decision of Judge Harold Wilson that the mother and the father of L now appeal to this court. The appeal is very properly brought to this court on this point, because there is at present the embarrassment of two conflicting decisions of the High Court.

We are indebted to the careful argument which Mr Baker has developed in advancing the appellant's case. He submits that this court should prefer Douglas Brown J's reasoning and decision to that of Thorpe J. Without any disrespect to Mr Baker, it is not necessary to recite in this judgment each of the points which are clearly set out in his careful skeleton argument and which he developed orally in his submissions to us, because in point of fact his submissions follow very closely the points made in the judgment of Douglas Brown J, to which I have already referred. In short, Mr Baker, supported by Miss Middleton (counsel for the second respondent) submits that legal professional privilege is not to be set aside by a judge hearing a Children Act case where a care order is sought. Although the privilege derives from case law, it is nonetheless entrenched in our law and can only be set aside or overridden in extreme circumstances. Mr Baker did, of course, invite the court's attention to the judgment of Johnson J in Re A (*minors: disclosure of material*) [1991] 2 FLR 473. The headnote to that report reads:

'After a hearing in wardship proceedings of the local authority's application for two children to be placed with long-term foster-parents with a view to adoption, the judge was asked to give a ruling on the question whether the court would have had the power, if it was thought necessary, to order the disclosure of a report by a paediatric pathologist, made at the request of the mother's solicitors but not submitted on her behalf nor placed in the agreed bundle of medical evidence. Held – in ordinary litigation, the court normally had no power to override the privilege of material produced for a party by expert witnesses. The situation was different, however, in the wardship court, where jurisdiction was parental, administrative and non-adversarial in character and where there was, at any rate in legal theory, an unrestricted jurisdiction to do whatever was necessary for the welfare of the ward. The court sitting in wardship did have the power, in appropriate cases, to override the legal professional privilege which attached to a report such as that obtained by the mother's solicitors from the paediatric pathologist, though that power should be exercised rarely, giving due consideration to the need for parties not to feel inhibited from obtaining such reports and not to be left with a feeling of injustice, and only in the interests of the child so required.'

The judge reviewed a number of cases including *Causton v Mann Egerton (Johnsons) Ltd* [1974] 1 All ER 453, [1974] 1 WLR 162, *Scott v Scott* [1913] AC 417, *Re Saxton, Johnson v Saxton* [1962] 3 All ER 92, [1962] 1 WLR 968 and *Official Solicitor v K* [1963] 3 All ER 191 at 210, [1965] AC 201 at 240, where Lord Devlin made the following observation:

'The jurisdiction regarding wards of court which is now exercised by the Chancery Division is an ancient jurisdiction deriving from the prerogative of the Crown as parens patriae. It is not based on the rights of parents, and its primary concern is not to ensure their rights but to ensure the welfare of the children.'

The learned judge, having cited that passage, continued ([1991] 2 FLR 473 at 476):

'So, as is well known, prior to the power being incorporated in s.33 of the Family Law Act 1986, the court sitting in wardship had power to order a solicitor to disclose the whereabouts of the ward, notwithstanding that his means of knowledge derived from his position as solicitor for a party. Of course, the jurisdiction in wardship is to be exercised on a judicial basis. In *Re X (A Minor) (Wardship: Jurisdiction)* ([1975] Fam 47) Roskill LJ said at p. 60: "For my part I would agree with Mr Anns that no limits to that jurisdiction have yet been drawn and it is not necessary to consider here what, if any, limits there are to that jurisdiction."'

At the conclusion of his judgment the learned judge said (at 477):

'I hold that the court sitting in wardship does have power, in appropriate cases, to override the legal professional privilege which attaches to a report such as that obtained by the mother's solicitors from the paediatric pathologist. That power should, I consider, be exercised only rarely, and only when the court is satisfied that it is necessary for it to be exercised in order to achieve the best interest of the child involved.'

That decision formed the basis of Thorpe J's decision in *Re R (a minor) (disclosure of privileged material)* [1993] 4 All ER 702, [1994] 2 WLR 407, to which I have referred. The argument addressed to this court by the two appellants is that because the doctrine of legal professional privilege appertaining to experts' reports, having been established by case law, is so well entrenched in the common law of this country it should not be overridden in cases involving children brought under the provisions of the Children Act 1989.

Mr Baker emphasises that the Children Act is a statute. It contains no specific provision for the overriding of legal professional privilege in any circumstances. In the absence of any specific provision either by Act of Parliament or statutory instrument the court has no jurisdiction to override that privilege.

On behalf of the county council and on behalf of the guardian and indeed on behalf of the third respondent, the submission made is that Thorpe J's exposition of the position is to be preferred, and that the learned county court judge was correct in following his judgment rather than that of Douglas Brown J. The submission is made by the guardian in a helpful skeleton argument and expanded by oral submissions is that the jurisdiction in care cases under the

Children Act is not in essence different in spirit from that exercised by the court under its wardship jurisdiction. Wardship is not in fact abolished by the Children Act, although the ability of local authorities to seek relief in wardship is restricted. Further, s 1 of the Children Act 1989 provides:

> 'When a court determines any question with respect to (a) the up-bringing of a child ... the child's welfare shall be the court's paramount consideration.'

That provision governs the entire application of the 1989 Act to children's cases. It is a provision which overrides every other consideration in the application of the Act to this area of the law. The child's welfare is paramount and the duty of the court when considering a care case is to arrive at a conclusion which is in the overriding interests of the welfare of the child.

Attention has been drawn, to a number of cases in which comment has been made by learned judges of the Court of Appeal and indeed by myself at the first instance in a case, *R v Birmingham Juvenile Court, ex p G* [1988] 3 All ER 726, [1988] 1 WLR 950, which then went to the Court of Appeal (see [1989] 3 All ER 336, [1990] 2 QB 573) and was cited by the guardian ad litem. There judicial observations were to the effect that children cases, including those considered under the earlier legislation were not adversarial. Miss Hall, on behalf of the guardian, drew attention to the words of Lord Widgery CJ in *Humberside CC v DPR (an infant)* [1977] 3 All ER 964, [1977] 1 WLR 1251 in which he deprecated the idea that children's welfare should be dealt with on an adversarial basis. I find that in *B v Derbyshire CC* [1992] 1 FLR 538 at 546 I said:

> 'On 14 October 1991 the Children Act 1989 is going to become effective and, when that takes place, I very much hope that the adversarial approach to care proceedings will disappear to a very large extent. What has happened in this case is symptomatic of the adversarial approach, where technical points are taken in order to secure a particular result. What will become more apparent from 14 October 1991 is that what the court is concerned with is the whole welfare of the child and that its task is to investigate, in an inquisitorial manner if necessary, the interests of the child.'

I then dealt with the particulars of that case. I reiterate what I then said. The proceedings under the Children Act 1989 are not adversarial, although an adversarial approach is frequently adopted by various of the parties. However, so far as the court is concerned, its duty is to investigate and to seek to achieve a result which is in the interests of the welfare of the child. In my judgment, Douglas Brown J erred in following too closely the procedures of civil litigation which had given rise to the application of the doctrine of professional privilege in cases between party and party. Children's cases are not similar cases. They fall into a special category where the court is bound to undertake all necessary steps to arrive at an appropriate result in the paramount interests of the welfare of the child. If a party, having obtained the leave of the court, were to be able to conceal, or withhold from the court, matters which were of importance and were relevant to the future of the child, there would be a risk that the welfare of the child would not be promoted as the Children Act 1989 requires. In my judgment, the court must have power to override legal professional privilege in these circumstances.

Judge Harold Wilson was perfectly correct in the course which he took. In my judgment, he made a correct decision. I agree with Thorpe J that the investigative powers and responsibilities of Family Division judges have not been curtailed now that the principal jurisdiction of the court in children's cases arises under the Children Act 1989. It may not have escaped notice that on the coming into force of the Children Act in 1991, orders which had been made in wardship, committing children to the care of local authorities under the provisions of s 7(2) of the Family Law Reform Act 1969, were automatically converted into care orders under s 31 of the Children Act. Children's cases are to be regarded as being in a special category. In these circumstances, the court has power to override legal professional privilege in relation to expert's reports when it gives leave to parties to obtain them. Relevant information should be made available to the court in order that it can arrive at a conclusion which is in the overriding interests of the welfare of the child.

For these reasons, I would dismiss both these appeals. They have, in fact, followed a similar course and they should, in my judgment, be dismissed.

STEYN LJ. I agree with the order proposed by my Sir Stephen Brown P, and I agree with the reasons given in his judgment. In care proceedings under the Children Act 1989 the appellants claim the right to be able to suppress experts' reports, if those reports turn out to be unfavourable, in the same way as a party in ordinary civil litigation is entitled to suppress unfavourable proofs of evidence or experts' reports. The judge's order in effect denies the appellants the benefit of legal professional privilege. In my judgment, the principal question is whether this privilege does attach to experts' reports obtained in care proceedings under the Children Act 1989. This is an important question of law which has considerable implications for the way in which litigation under the 1989 Act is conducted. It is also a difficult question, as is evident from the fact that in careful judgments two experienced judges of the Family Division have come to opposite conclusions, as Sir Stephen Brown P, has already explained.

In the present case the judge came to the conclusion that a note in *The Family Court Practice* (1993) p 1124, para 4.18 correctly summarises the approach to be adopted. The editors conclude that legal professional privilege does attach to experts' reports and that 'there is no obligation to volunteer disclosure and that what would be material evidence can, in effect, be kept from the court.' But they consider that the problem can be solved in an oblique fashion. They state:

'The court can avoid this rather undesirable state of affairs, where an examination or assessment of the child is to take place and leave is required, by granting leave only on condition that the expert's report (or if there is no report, the substance of his opinion) be disclosed to the court and, if appropriate, to the other parties, and it is suggested that this should be the routine approach. It will also be possible to achieve a similar result in other cases by attaching the same condition when granting leave to disclose the documents in the case to an expert.'

The judge in this case thought Thorpe J shared this view. It does not seem to me that Thorpe J approached the matter in this way. But, in any event, the suggested approach does not seem to me to be a satisfactory way of dealing with the matter. The power to attach conditions to the grant of the required leave does not derive from the 1989 Act. It is an implied power in the Family Proceedings Rules 1991, SI 1991/1247. Given that the power to grant the

required leave does not expressly contain a power to attach conditions, I
readily accept that by necessary implication the power to grant leave
comprehends the right to attach conditions to the grant of leave. But, if it be
the case legal professional privilege attaches to experts' reports in care
proceedings, it seems to me to follow that it would be wrong to exercise the
power to attach conditions in order to destroy the privilege. If the privilege
applies, it must be respected. Moreover, it seems to me axiomatic that a strong
privilege, such as legal professional privilege, cannot be taken away pursuant
to subordinate legislation: see *Comfort Hotels v Wembley Stadium Ltd* (*Silkin and
ors, third parties*) [1988] 3 All ER 53, [1988] 1 WLR 872 and *R v Secretary of State
for the Home Dept, ex p Leech* [1993] 4 All ER 539, [1994] QB 198. But that is
exactly what the judge purported to do. He relied on the implied power to
attach conditions to the grant of leave contained in the subordinate legislation.
Much as I sympathise with the result which the judge sought to achieve, I
cannot support that part of his reasoning. In my view, the answer to the
problem must be sought in the primary legislation, viz the 1989 Act.

That brings me to the question whether the privilege does apply in care
proceedings under the 1989 Act. The rationale of the privilege is that without
it a party's access to justice will be undermined. It is therefore an auxiliary
principle buttressing the constitutional right of access to justice. On the other
hand, the privilege contemplates that relevant evidence will sometimes be
withheld from the court. It must be therefore kept in justifiable bounds.
Leaving aside statutory exceptions and waiver, Matthews and Malek *Discovery*
(1993) p 181, para 8.51 points out that there are at least eight established
exceptions to legal professional privilege. An instructive exception is the rule
that the privilege will not justify withholding documents which, if produced,
would perhaps enable a man to establish his innocence or to resist an allegation
made by the Crown in a criminal trial: see *R v Barton* [1972] 2 All ER 1192 at
1194, [1973] 1 WLR 115 at 118. In such a case the rationale of legal professional
privilege must yield to the higher value society attaches to the liberty of the
subject. It demonstrates the point that there may be countervailing policy
considerations which militate against the privilege. But there are other
exceptions and even closer analogies. In *Re A* (*minors: disclosure of material*)
[1991] 2 FLR 473 Johnson J held that in wardship proceedings the court has the
power to exercise legal professional privilege. It is true that Johnson J
expressed himself in cautious terms in saying that the power should only be
exercised in rare circumstances. The reason for the judge's caution may be the
fact that discovery is practically unknown in wardship proceedings. In any
event, the reason for the rule in wardship proceedings is not a technical one but
the broad consideration that the court has a plenary jurisdiction to do what is
necessary for the welfare of the child. Making due allowance for a
jurisdictional differences between wardship proceedings and care proceedings
under the 1989 Act, one is immediately struck by the fact that a common
feature in both adjudicative processes is the paramountcy of the welfare of the
child. Rhetorically, I would ask: why should there be a difference on this point
between the two jurisdictions? There is another close analogy. Even before
the 1989 Act, a local authority did not have the benefit of legal professional
privilege in respect of experts' reports in care proceedings. It was obliged to
disclose to all parties *all* relevant documents and experts' reports which were
within its possession: see *R v Hampshire CC, ex p K* [1990] 2 All ER 129 at 133,
[1990] 2 QB 71 at 77 per Watkins LJ. The only qualification to these

propositions is the necessarily rare case when public interest immunity will justify withholding such reports. It is important to note the reason for this exception to legal professional privilege. The reason is to ensure the court will make properly informed decisions in the best interests of the child. I accept, of course, that other parties to care proceedings, such as a father or mother of the child, are interested parties in a more direct or immediate sense. On other hand, in the theory of the law such interested parties must be credited with the objective of seeking to promote the best interests of the child, albeit their perspectives are coloured by subjective considerations. In my view, *R v Hampshire CC, ex p K* throws light on the problem before us: it established that the legal professional privilege of the local authority had to yield to the paramount consideration of the welfare of the child.

That brings me directly to the question before us. Is an interested party in care proceedings, who has obtained an unfavourable expert's report, entitled to suppress the report and to maintain through counsel and solicitors a case at variance with it? If the answer is Yes, the spectre cannot be avoided that judges will sometimes decide cases affecting children in ignorance of material facts and in a way detrimental to their best interests. In *Barking and Dagenham London BC v O* [1993] 4 All ER 59, [1993] Fam 295 Douglas Brown J squarely confronted this problem. He emphasised the adversarial character of care proceedings. He relied on dicta of Roskill LJ in *Causton v Mann Egerton (Johnsons) Ltd* [1974] 1 All ER 453, [1974] 1 WLR 162. Roskill LJ made reference to a judgment of Lord Denning MR in *Re Saxton (decd), Saxton v Saxton* [1962] 3 All ER 92 at 94, [1962] 1 WLR 968 at 972, in which Lord Denning MR, in effect, said that it was one of our notions of a fair trial that a party should not see the proofs of the other side's witnesses, including their experts.

Much has happened in our system of civil justice since 1962. Today there is a comprehensive system for exchange of experts' reports and witnesses' statements. Our system of civil justice has become more open. Judges have had to become more interventionist. But it is of particular importance to note that in the Family Division, care proceedings do not have an essentially adversarial character: see *R v Birmingham Juvenile Court, ex p G* [1989] 3 All ER 336 at 345, 348, 352, [1990] 2 QB 573 at 584, 589, 597 per Purchas and Russell LJJ. In practice, judges dealing with directions hearings in such cases adopt an interventionist style. And at the substantive hearing the judge has substantially greater control over the deployment of evidence and argument than a judge sitting in, for example, the Queen's Bench Division. In any event, it seems to me that the fact that care proceedings under the 1989 Act still have some vestigial adversarial characteristics does not by itself answer the question before us. After all, exceptions to this common law privilege have been established in the context of a largely adversarial system, the reason being that the interest served by the privilege had to yield to an interest to which the law attached a higher value.

The countervailing factor to be considered in the present case is the fact that under the Children Act 1989 the child's welfare is the paramount consideration. This objective is spelled out explicitly in s 1(1). The welfare check list in s 1(3) underpins it. And the Act contains a framework designed to achieve that purpose. The 1989 Act was a watershed. Subject to the threshold criteria set out in s 31 of the Act having been made out, the Act established the paramountcy of the child's welfare as the governing principle in care proceedings. Like Thorpe J in *Re R (a minor) (disclosure of privileged material)* [1993] 4 All ER 702, [1994] 2 WLR 402 I take the view that this legislative

objective would be defeated if a party in care proceedings is entitled to
suppress an available expert's report. I accept that, if interested parties do not
have the benefit of legal professional privilege in experts' reports, they may
occasionally be less inclined to seek expert advise. Some might say fewer
experts would be a blessing in this corner of law. However, giving full weight
to this potentially inhibiting factor, it seems to me that it is outweighed by the
paramountcy principle enunciated in s 1(1). The general legal professional
privilege attaching to an expert's report must therefore yield to the greater
value to be attached to the particular legislative purpose of making the child's
welfare the sole criterion in care proceedings. I would, therefore, rule that in
care proceedings under the 1989 Act a judge is empowered to make the orders
which are challenged on this appeal. But I restrict my conclusion to the point
before us. It does not mean that legal professional privilege has no role to play.
For example, the promotion of the welfare of the child does not require that
communications between a client and a lawyer should be disclosed; such
advice is not material which could arguably affect the judgment of the court.

For reasons somewhat different from those given by the judge in his helpful
judgment, I conclude that the judge's orders were properly made and I would
dismiss both appeals.

KENNEDY LJ. I agree the appeals should be dismissed and with what has
fallen from Sir Stephen Brown P. I do not share entirely the misgivings of
Steyn LJ as to the approach adopted by the judge. Normally in civil litigation
conducted on adversarial lines a medical report obtained by one party is
privileged. The party need only disclose it if he or she wishes to call the
particular witness. However, if the party desiring to obtain a medical report
needs the assistance of another party, or in this instance of the court, that other
party or the court, as it seems to me, may make it a condition of providing the
necessary assistance that the report when obtained shall be disclosed. I, for my
part, see nothing in the leave provisions of the statute which makes that course
objectionable. That approach received some approval from the Court of
Appeal in *Causton v Mann Egerton (Johnsons) Ltd* [1974] 1 All ER 453 at 458,
[1974] 1 WLR 162 at 168, where Lord Denning MR, although in the minority,
said:

'... I hope that in future the solicitors for every plaintiff will refuse to
allow any defendants to have any medical examination of the plaintiff
except on the terms that the defendants will disclose the medical reports
following the examination.'

Stamp LJ, in majority, said ([1974] 1 All ER 453 at 458, [1974] 1 WLR 162 at 168):

'However desirable it may be that there should be agreements between
the parties for the disclosure and exchange of such documents, in the
absence of an agreement or waiver of the privilege which would otherwise
attach to them, they remain in my judgment privileged.'

That was the route by which he came to the conclusion at which he arrived.
But it will be noted that he, like Lord Denning MR, countenanced the
possibility of there being such an agreement or waiver. In effect, that is, as it
seems to me, what happened in this case. Judge Paul Clark made his order, as
it happened, by consent. The order was in the form that the report, when
obtained, should be disclosed. The parties went back before Judge Harold

Wilson in order to delete the requirement of disclosure. It seems to me that in the context of the Children Act 1989 it is quite impossible to say that the conclusion at which Judge Harold Wilson arrived was in any way erroneous. He was entitled to maintain, as he did, that if this report was to be produced, which required the leave of the court in order to allow access to documents and video tape recordings, then the condition should be imposed which he imposed. Accordingly, for somewhat different reasons to those ventilated so far, I arrive at the conclusion that this appeal must be dismissed.

Appeal dismissed. Leave to appeal to the House of Lords refused.

Bebe Chua   Barrister.

R v McFarlane

COURT OF APPEAL, CRIMINAL DIVISION

LORD TAYLOR OF GOSFORTH CJ, POPPLEWELL AND SCOTT BAKER JJ

20 DECEMBER 1993

Criminal law – Prostitution – Living on earnings of prostitution – Earnings of prostitution – Clipping – Woman offering sexual services and taking money from client without intending to provide services offered – Whether 'clipper' a prostitute – Whether man who knowingly lives on earnings of clipper guilty of living on earnings of prostitution – Sexual Offences Act 1956, s 30(1).

The appellant was charged with living on the earnings of prostitution, contrary to s 30(1)[a] of the Sexual Offences Act 1956. He lived with the woman in question as man and wife. The woman gave evidence that she was not a prostitute but a 'clipper', ie a woman who offered sexual favours for reward and took the money without intending to provide the favours. The judge ruled that the woman was a prostitute, albeit a dishonest prostitute, because she had 'offered her body for lewdness for reward', and that there was no difference between a prostitute and a clipper. The appellant was convicted. He appealed on the ground that being a clipper did not amount to being a prostitute and that therefore he could not be guilty of the offence charged.

Held – The crucial feature in defining prostitution was the making of an offer of sexual services for reward. The difference between a prostitute and a clipper was immaterial and accordingly living on the earnings of a woman who offered sexual services and then reneged on the offer amounted to living on the earnings of prostitution. The judge's ruling had been correct and the appellant had been properly convicted. The appeal would therefore be dismissed (see p 288 *c g* to *j*, post).

R v De Munck [1918–19] All ER Rep 499, *R v Webb* [1963] 3 All ER 177 and *R v Morris-Lowe* [1985] 1 All ER 400 considered.

---

a   Section 30(1) is set out at p 286 *c*, post

Notes

For prostitution and living on the earnings of prostitution, see 11(1) *Halsbury's Laws* (4th edn reissue) paras 386, 390, and for cases on the subject, see 14(2) *Digest* (2nd reissue) 214–216, 7327–7345.

For the Sexual Offences Act 1956, s 30, see 12 *Halsbury's Statutes* (4th edn) (1994 reissue) 258.

Cases referred to in judgment

R v De Munck [1918] 1 KB 635, [1918–19] All ER Rep 499, CCA.
R v Morris-Lowe [1985] 1 All ER 400, [1985] 1 WLR 29, CA.
R v Webb [1963] 3 All ER 177, [1964] 1 QB 357, [1963] 3 WLR 638, CCA.

Appeal against conviction

Eric McFarlane appealed against his conviction on 16 December 1991 in the Crown Court at Knightsbridge before Judge Hordern QC and a jury of living on the earnings of prostitution for which he was sentenced to four months' imprisonment. The facts are set out in the judgment of the court.

Roger Carne (assigned by the *Registrar of Criminal Appeals*) for the appellant.
Jeremy Carter-Manning QC and *Christopher Amis* (neither of whom appeared below) (instructed by the *Crown Prosecution Service*) for the Crown.

LORD TAYLOR OF GOSFORTH CJ delivered the following judgment of the court. On 16 December 1991 in the Crown Court at Knightsbridge, the appellant was convicted of living on the earnings of prostitution. He was sentenced to four months' imprisonment. This appeal involves a point of law as to the meaning of prostitution which surprisingly has not been the subject of judicial decision with any finality prior to this.

The appellant lived as man and wife with Miss Josephs who, on the judge's ruling, was a prostitute. She maintained she was not a prostitute but a clipper—one who offers sexual services for reward and pockets the reward in advance never intending to provide the service. She said that she engaged in this occupation four or five nights a month, earning up to £400 on a good night. There was evidence, and it was accepted by the appellant and Miss Josephs, that he lived at least partly on her earnings in that they shared their living expenses. The main issue in the case was whether he was thus living on the earnings of prostitution knowingly. The prosecution pointed to the fact that he had lived with her for eleven years, the past five of which she had on her own account been engaged on this business. It was pointed out that he must have been aware of the pattern of her life, the fact that she had more money than could be accounted for by the £50-a-week job as a cloakroom attendant which she said she told him she did.

Further, on 16 January 1990 the appellant was seen taking Miss Josephs and her sister into the court at Bow Street where they both appeared on charges of loitering for the purposes of prostitution. There was also evidence from two police officers who kept observation on the appellant between 29 January and 6 February 1991. Those observations tended to show that he assisted her in her occupation. At 10 pm on 30 January he drove Miss Josephs in his car to the West End of London. Later that night, in the same area, Miss Josephs offered one of the police officers sexual intercourse for £40 (which of course was not accepted). On 4 February the appellant drove Miss Josephs to Rupert Street and left her there. In Wardour Street she offered the other officer in the case sexual intercourse for £40. He too did not accept it. At 11.30 pm on 5 February the appellant drove Miss Josephs to the top end of Rupert Street and left her there. He met her an hour later in Shaftesbury Avenue. She took something from her shoe which she gave to the appellant. At 10.15 pm on 6 February the appellant again drove Miss Josephs to the same area and waited in the car in Rupert Street. At 10.40 pm she went off with someone in a taxi, returning to the appellant an hour later. Whether or not that was an occasion of 'clipping' or the real thing is a matter which we need not consider in any depth.

The defence case was that the appellant knew nothing of Miss Josephs's activities. She gave evidence that she told him she worked as a cloakroom girl and also behind the bar at a club. She kept her real occupation secret from him. She used to go out to make it look as if she was at the job which she told him she did. She told him the money for items she bought for the home came from her mother. As regards the attendance at Bow Street Magistrates' Court, the appellant said that he had not stayed for the hearing, and Miss Josephs told him that it concerned a deception charge of which she was acquitted. As regards the observation evidence, essentially the appellant and Miss Josephs, together with her sister, challenged the evidence of observations, maintaining that it was all lies.

A submission was made to the learned judge that acting as a clipper did not amount to acting as a prostitute. Although at that stage counsel both for the prosecution and the defence supported that view, the learned judge rejected it. When the appeal came on before another constitution of this court, counsel then appearing for the Crown (not counsel who has appeared for the Crown today) again supported the appellant's submission that the learned judge's ruling was wrong. However, the court itself took the view that the matter should be fully argued, saying:

'There was a substantial argument in favour of the view taken by the trial judge.'

It is most convenient therefore to deal first with what the learned judge said both in giving his ruling and in directing the jury. In his ruling he said:

'The question of whether someone offering themselves, but intending— and it has to be intending—firmly never, ever to make good that offer—it has to go that far—it has never, so far as I can see, been adjudicated upon. My view is that the indications in the textbooks—and I have looked at Blackstone's Criminal Practice and it is not so obvious, but again it speaks of offering—the dictionary, and decided cases say that as soon as you are offering yourself for lewdness for reward, you are indulging in prostitution and that is how I propose to direct the jury.'

When it came to the summing up, the learned judge said this to the jury:

'She has told you she is not a prostitute, she is a clipper. But, a prostitute is a person who offers her body for lewdness for reward. Put in slightly more "with it" words, such as Sarah Tuckey [that is the sister] used, "offers sexual services". I am bound to say that I prefer the directness of the old Anglo-Saxon, but there it is. Miss Josephs said, "Yes, I do offer sexual services, but I do not mean to make that offer good." And she suggests to you that for that reason she is not a prostitute. But, members of the jury, she has made the offer. It is at that point that she is a prostitute. The fact that the offer is bogus, rather than genuine, if it was, is neither here nor there. There are not two categories—a clipper and a prostitute. There are prostitutes who are honest and prostitutes who are dishonest. Miss Josephs tells you that she is a dishonest prostitute. But she is a prostitute, members of the jury.'

The issue on this appeal is whether, as a matter of law, the judge was correct to rule and direct the jury that a woman who offers herself for sexual services, takes the money and fails to provide the services, is engaging in prostitution within the meaning of s 30 of the Sexual Offences Act 1956. Section 30, so far as is relevant, provides as follows:

'(1) It is an offence for a man knowingly to live wholly or in part on the earnings of prostitution ...'

Mr Carne for the appellant submits that to be a prostitute a woman must not only offer sexual services, but must provide them, or be prepared to do so. For the Crown, Mr Carter-Manning QC submits the essence of the offence is the offer of the sexual services in return for reward.

The words 'prostitute' and 'prostitution' are not defined in any statute. Our attention was drawn to dictionary definitions and to three decided cases. The Concise Oxford Dictionary defines a prostitute as:

'A woman who offers her body to promiscuous sexual intercourse esp. for payment ...'

The Shorter Oxford English Dictionary defines a prostitute as:

'A woman who is devoted, or (usu.) [who] offers her body to indiscriminate sexual intercourse, esp. for hire; a common harlot ...'

Mr Carne points to the definition of 'offer' in The Shorter Oxford English Dictionary, and to one meaning given there:

'To give, make presentation of ... To tender for acceptance or refusal ...'

However, another meaning within the same dictionary is:

'To make the proposal, suggest ... To propose, or express one's willingness (to do something), conditionally on the assent of the person addressed.'

The first of the three cases cited is *R v De Munck* [1918] 1 KB 635, [1918–19] All ER Rep 499. The issue there was whether prostitution was concerned only with sexual intercourse, or whether other sexual activity would suffice. Darling J, giving the judgment of the court, said ([1918] 1 KB 635 at 637–638, [1918–19] All ER Rep 499 at 500):

'We have to decide what is a prostitute or what is prostitution. The argument advanced on behalf of the appellant practically was that the offering by a woman of her body for the gratification of the sexual passions of men, even if it is done as a regular trade, indiscriminately and for gain, is not prostitution unless the men's passions are gratified by the act of sexual connection and not otherwise. We have come to the conclusion that that contention was not well founded. It was advanced before the learned commissioner at the Central Criminal Court and he laid down the law practically as we are now going to lay it down, and we, therefore, uphold his decision. The Court is of opinion that the term "common prostitute" in the statute is not limited so as to mean only one who permits acts of lewdness with all and sundry, or with such as hire her, when such acts are in the nature of ordinary sexual connection. We are of opinion that prostitution is proved if it be shown that a woman offers her body commonly for lewdness for payment in return.'

In *R v Webb* [1963] 3 All ER 177, [1964] 1 QB 357 the issue was whether girls employed in a massage parlour were acting as prostitutes if they masturbated male customers. In other words, did the definition depend upon whether the female was physically active or passive? Lord Parker CJ said ([1963] 3 All ER 177 at 179–180, [1964] 1 QB 357 at 366):

'From a purely practical point of view, it would be artificial, to say the least, to draw a distinction between the case of a woman who takes a passive role and one in which she takes an active role. Indeed, it can be said with some force that some activity on her part is of the very essence of prostitution. It cannot matter whether she whips the man or the man whips her; it cannot matter whether he masturbates himself on her or she masturbates him. In our judgment the explanation used by DARLING, J., "a woman offers her body for purposes amounting to common lewdness" means no more and was intended to mean no more than "offers herself", and it includes at any rate such a case as this, where a woman offers herself as a participant in physical acts of indecency for the sexual gratification of men.'

That case was not concerned with a situation where the woman makes the offer but does not deliver the service. It was concerned with what part a woman needs to play in admitted sexual activity in order to render herself a prostitute. Mr Carne, however, relies on one sentence in the passage quoted:

'... it can be said with some force that some activity on her part is of the very essence of prostitution.'

It is of course true that prostitution most frequently, at any rate in the past, has meant the actual indulgence of a woman in sexual intercourse for reward, and so activity in the sexual sense has been regarded as being of the very essence of the full extent of prostitution. But in that single sentence taken in the context of the passage quoted, and indeed taken in the context of the issue in *R v Webb*, we do not think Lord Parker CJ was seeking to provide an answer to the question which is raised in this case.

The third authority to which we were referred was *R v Morris-Lowe* [1985] 1 All ER 400, [1985] 1 WLR 29. There, the issue was whether it was sufficient to constitute a woman a 'common prostitute' if she indulged in sexual activity for reward with one man on one occasion. That is again a totally different issue from that which faces this court. Lord Lane CJ said ([1985] 1 All ER 400 at 402, [1985] 1 WLR 29 at 32):

'A common prostitute is any woman who offers herself commonly for lewdness for reward. This appellant on his own version plainly attempted to persuade the woman in each case to offer herself for lewdness for reward. What about the word "common" or its adverbial form? Is it a meaningless word which adds nothing to the word "prostitute", or does it have some effect? That really is the only point in this appeal. It is clear to us that the word is not mere surplusage. We do not pause to consider whether the performance by a woman of a single act of lewdness with a man on one occasion for reward constitutes the woman a prostitute. But we are of the view that it does not make her a woman who offers herself commonly for lewdness. That must be someone who is prepared for reward to engage in acts of lewdness with all and sundry, or with anyone who may hire her for that purpose.'

Again in that passage Mr Carne seeks to pick out one sentence, the final sentence, to support his argument. However, the court did not have in contemplation in that case the instance of a woman making an offer she did not intend to fulfil. To read the last sentence of the passage quoted as support for the appellant's argument here would be in conflict with the first sentence of the passage where Lord Lane CJ defined 'common prostitute' as 'any woman who offers herself commonly for lewdness for reward'.

In our judgment both the dictionary definitions and the cases show that the crucial feature in defining prostitution is the making of an offer of sexual services for reward. Mr Carne submits that the true offence here was not one of living off immoral earnings, and that the woman in question, Miss Josephs, was not acting by way of prostitution. She was acting dishonestly and she could have been proceeded against, he submits, for obtaining money by false pretences. It may be that the appellant could have been proceeded against for conspiring with her to do so, or for aiding and abetting her. But it is submitted that the offence of living off immoral earnings is not made out. Mr Carne also submits that the mischief against which s 30 of the Sexual Offences Act 1956 is directed is the exploitation of women. Here, the appellant was not exploiting Miss Josephs sexually, only dishonestly. However, if Mr Carne's argument were right, the mischief aimed at in other statutes requiring proof of prostitution would not be defeated. There have been a number of statutes, from the Vagrancy Act 1824 through the Town Police Clauses Act 1847, up to and including the Street Offences Act 1959, whose object has been to prevent the nuisance of women soliciting and offering sexual favours in public places. If it were a defence to soliciting for prostitution under s 1 of the 1959 Act that the accused woman was acting as a 'clipper' and not as a 'hooker', proof of such offences would be extremely difficult. It would be necessary to prove not merely the offer of sexual services in a public place, but that the services were actually provided, or were at the time of the offering intended to be provided. The mischief being simply the harassment and nuisance to members of the public on the streets, the distinction between 'clippers' and 'hookers' is immaterial.

We have no doubt that the ruling of the learned judge was both robust and correct (to adopt the phrase used by Mr Carter-Manning in his submission). For a man to live off the earnings of a woman who offers sexual services, takes the money and then reneges on the offer, if she does, is in our view to live off the earnings of prostitution, or, as it used to be termed, immoral earnings. Indeed, most people would consider such earnings doubly immoral. This appeal is dismissed.

Appeal dismissed.

N P Metcalfe Esq   Barrister.

Marida Ltd and others v Oswal Steel and others
The Bijela

HOUSE OF LORDS

LORD TEMPLEMAN, LORD JAUNCEY OF TULLICHETTLE, LORD SLYNN OF HADLEY, LORD WOOLF AND LORD LLOYD OF BERWICK

9, 10 MARCH, 21 APRIL 1994

Shipping – General average – General average expenditure – Temporary repairs – Vessel damaged shortly after commencing voyage – Owners carrying out temporary repairs to enable vessel to continue voyage – Temporary repairs costing much less than permanent repairs – Owners claiming cost of temporary repairs as general average – Whether shipowner entitled to claim general average contribution in respect of temporary repairs – York-Antwerp Rules 1974, rr X(b), XIV.

In the course of a vessel's voyage from Providence, Rhode Island to India with a cargo of scrap iron under a charterparty which provided that general average was to be settled according to the York-Antwerp Rules 1974, the vessel touched bottom and put into Jamestown, the nearest anchorage, where the owners decided that temporary repairs should be effected so that the vessel could proceed with the voyage. The alternative was to discharge and store the cargo, put the vessel into the nearest dry dock, which was at New York, for permanent repairs, and then reload and proceed with the voyage. The temporary repairs cost $282,606. Discharging, storing and reloading the cargo while permanent repairs were undertaken at New York would have cost more than $535,000. The owners claimed that the cost of the temporary repairs should be allowed as general average because the saving in expense which would have been allowed in general average if the vessel had undergone permanent repairs in New York exceeded the actual cost of the temporary repairs. Under r X(b)[a] of the York-Antwerp Rules the cost of discharging cargo necessary to enable damage to the vessel to be repaired was to be admitted as general average 'if the repairs were necessary for the safe prosecution of the voyage'. Rule XIV[b] provided that where temporary repairs were effected in order to enable the voyage to be completed the cost of such repairs was to be admitted as general average but only 'up to the saving in expense which would have been incurred and allowed in general average if such repairs had not been effected'. The owners issued a writ against the cargo owners claiming $402,364, being the amount calculated by average adjusters which the shipowners were entitled to receive on general average when the whole of the cost of the temporary repairs was taken into account. The judge dismissed the owners' claim on the ground that permanent repairs in New York were not necessary for the safe prosecution of the voyage and his decision was affirmed by the Court of Appeal. The owners appealed to the House of Lords.

Held – Rule XIV of the York-Antwerp Rules was to be construed on the assumption that temporary repairs had not been carried out, from which it was

---
a Rule X(b) is set out at p 292 *f g*, post
b Rule XIV is set out at p 291 *h j*, post

to be further assumed that it would have been necessary for the vessel to have undergone permanent repairs to enable it to continue the voyage safely, which in turn would have required the cargo to be discharged, stored and reloaded, in which case the costs of doing so would have been admitted as general average under r X(b). Accordingly, an owner was entitled to claim general average contribution in respect of temporary repairs which enabled the vessel to complete its voyage if they effected a saving in expense which would have been incurred and allowed in general average if such repairs had not been effected. The owners had discharged the burden on them of showing that the cost of discharging, storing and reloading the cargo would have been allowable in general average if repairs had been carried out in New York instead of Jamestown, since such repairs would, on the assumption that the vessel had not already undergone temporary repairs, have been necessary for the safe prosecution of the voyage within the meaning of r X(b) and therefore they were entitled to have the cost of the temporary repairs allowed as general average. The appeal would accordingly be allowed (see p 290 *j* to p 291 *c d f* to *j* and p 294 *j* to p 295 *a*, post).

Notes
For general average, see 43 *Halsbury's Laws* (4th edn) paras 742–758, and for cases on the subject, see 43 *Digest* (Reissue) 508–530, 10364–10572.

Appeal
Marida Ltd, Dabinovic (International) SA and Dabinovic (Monaco) SAM, the owners of the vessel Bijela, appealed with the leave of the Appeal Committee of the House of Lords given on 1 July 1993 from the decision of the Court of Appeal (Neill and Mann LJJ (Hoffmann LJ dissenting)) ([1993] 1 Lloyd's Rep 411) on 3 February 1993 dismissing their appeal from the decision of Hobhouse J ([1992] 1 Lloyd's Rep 636) on 7 February 1992 disallowing their claim for the cost of temporary repairs to the vessel carried out at Jamestown between November 1985 and January 1986 in the course of a chartered voyage from Providence, Rhode Island to India to be allowed in general average. The respondents to the appeal were Oswal Steel, Rathi Alloys and Steel Ltd, Muzaffarnagar Steels Ltd, Steel Strips Ltd, Mohta Ispat Ltd and Rathi Ispat Ltd, who were owners of cargo shipped on board the vessel. The facts are set out in the opinion of Lord Lloyd.

Bernard Eder QC and *Simon Gault* (instructed by *Lloyd & Co*) for the appellants.
Stewart Boyd QC and *Steven Berry* (instructed by *Ince & Co*) for the respondents.

Their Lordships took time for consideration.

21 April 1994. The following opinions were delivered.

LORD TEMPLEMAN. My Lords, for the reasons to be given by my noble and learned friend Lord Lloyd of Berwick, I would allow this appeal.

LORD JAUNCEY OF TULLICHETTLE. My Lords, I have had the advantage of reading in draft the speech by my noble and learned friend Lord Lloyd of Berwick. For the reasons he gives I, too, would allow the appeal.

LORD SLYNN OF HADLEY. My Lords, I have had the advantage of reading in draft the speech by my noble and learned friend Lord Lloyd of Berwick. For the reasons he gives I, too, would allow the appeal.

LORD WOOLF. My Lords, I have had the advantage of reading in draft the speech by my noble and learned friend Lord Lloyd of Berwick, and for the reasons he gives I, too, would allow the appeal.

LORD LLOYD OF BERWICK. My Lords, the issue in this appeal is whether the owners of the Bijela can claim general average contribution in respect of the cost of temporary repairs carried out in the course of a voyage from Providence, Rhode Island to Kandla in India. The question turns on the construction of the second paragraph of r XIV of the York-Antwerp Rules 1974. There is no dispute as to the relevant facts.

The vessel completed loading a cargo of scrap iron at Providence at 1400 hrs on 14 November 1985. She sailed at 1500 hrs. At 1605 hrs she touched bottom, sustaining heavy damage to her double bottom tanks. She put into Jamestown, the nearest anchorage, at 1745 hrs. She could not proceed on her voyage without repairs. There were two alternatives. Either she could discharge part of her cargo into barges, return to Providence, and there discharge the rest of her cargo. She would then be able to proceed under her own power to New York, where she could undergo permanent repairs in dry dock. The alternative was to carry out temporary repairs where she lay anchored at Jamestown, in the hope that they would be sufficient to enable her to complete the voyage to India. Hobhouse J ([1992] 1 Lloyd's Rep 636 at 639) described the decision as difficult. In the event the shipowners chose the latter course, and their choice was justified. For although the temporary repairs proved troublesome, and took longer than expected, they were eventually completed and approved by Lloyd's Register on 30 January 1986, at a cost of $US282,606. The vessel sailed on 3 February. She arrived in India without further incident on 8 March 1986. After completing discharge she proceeded to Singapore for permanent repairs.

It is accepted that the cost of entering Jamestown, as a port of refuge, and her detention there, is allowable in general average under rr X and XI of the York-Antwerp Rules. The question is whether the cost of the temporary repairs should also be admitted. This depends, as I have said, on the second paragraph of r XIV. That rule provides:

> 'Where temporary repairs are effected to a ship at a port of loading, call or refuge, for the common safety, or of damage caused by general average sacrifice, the cost of such repairs shall be admitted as general average.
> Where temporary repairs of accidental damage are effected in order to enable the adventure to be completed, the cost of such repairs shall be admitted as general average without regard to the saving, if any, to other interest, but only up to the saving in expense which would have been incurred and allowed in general average if such repairs had not been effected there.
> No deductions "new for old" shall be made from the cost of temporary repairs allowable as general average.'

The shipowners say that, if temporary repairs had not been effected at Jamestown, certain expenses would have been incurred in effecting permanent repairs in New York, which would have been allowed in general average.

Thus, in order to effect repairs in New York, it would first have been necessary to discharge the cargo in Providence, store the cargo during repairs and then reload. The cost of these operations, all of which would, say the owners, have been allowable in general average under r X, would have amounted to more than $535,000. Accordingly, the saving in expense which would have been allowed in general average if the vessel had undergone permanent repairs in New York far exceeds the actual cost of temporary repairs. It follows, if the owners are right, that the whole of the cost of the temporary repairs should be allowed.

The initial adjustment was prepared by Messrs William Elmslie & Son. Contrary to the owners' expectation, the adjusters disallowed the cost of temporary repairs. Accordingly the shipowners instructed Messrs Richards Hogg Ltd to prepare a second adjustment. They took a different view from Messrs William Elmslie. They allowed the whole of the cost of temporary repairs. The difference in result was that, whereas according to the first adjustment the shipowners were to receive $141,175, according to the second adjustment they were to receive $402,564.

On 22 June 1989 the shipowners issued a writ claiming the amount due to them under the second adjustment. The case came before Hobhouse J in February 1992. He dismissed the shipowners' claim (see [1992] 1 Lloyd's Rep 636). He held that permanent repairs in New York were not necessary for the safe prosecution of the voyage. All that was necessary were the temporary repairs which were in fact carried out at Jamestown.

In order to understand Hobhouse J's reasoning it is convenient at this stage to set out the relevant provisions of r X(b):

'The cost of handling on board or discharging cargo, fuel or stores whether at a port or place of loading, call or refuge, shall be admitted as general average, when the handling or discharge was necessary for the common safety or to enable damage to the ship caused by sacrifice or accident to be repaired if the repairs were necessary for the safe prosecution of the voyage, except in cases where the damage to the ship is discovered at a port or place of loading or call without any accident or other extraordinary circumstance connected with such damage having taken place during the voyage.'

Since, in Hobhouse J's view, repairs in dry dock were not 'necessary for the safe prosecution of the voyage' (see [1992] 1 Lloyd's Rep 636 at 644), the cost of discharging, storing and reloading the cargo at Providence would not have been allowed in general average.

The shipowners appealed. The Court of Appeal, by a majority, dismissed the appeal ([1993] 1 Lloyd's Rep 411). Neill and Mann LJJ adopted the same reasoning as Hobhouse J. They held that the permanent repairs in New York had not been shown to be necessary, because of the alternative of temporary repairs at Jamestown. Hoffmann LJ would have agreed with the majority that repairs in New York were not necessary, if the only assumption required by r XIV were that temporary repairs had not been carried out in Jamestown. But he went on to hold that a further assumption must be implied in r XIV, namely that the temporary repairs not only were not, but *could not* have been, carried out at Jamestown (at 423). Such further assumption was necessary, he said, in order to give r XIV business efficacy. For without such further assumption the second paragraph of r XIV would be devoid of all practical effect. On that ground Hoffmann LJ held that permanent repairs at New York were 'necessary' for the purpose of r X(b). He would therefore have allowed the appeal.

Before your Lordships, Mr Boyd QC, on behalf of the cargo owners, was unable to suggest any circumstances in which the second paragraph of r XIV could be given practical effect if his construction of r X(b) were correct. In every case temporary repairs would, ex hypothesi, have been carried out. It would follow, on Mr Boyd's construction, that permanent repairs could *never* be 'necessary' under r X(b), and owners could never recover the cost of temporary repairs under the second paragraph of r XIV. Mr Boyd did not go so far as to concede that the second paragraph of r XIV would be wholly ineffective if his construction were correct, since it might, he said, have effect by some unspecified foreign law. But in any event, even if the paragraph is wholly devoid of effect, the rules must be given their plain meaning. On the plain meaning of r X(b) repairs in New York were not, he submitted, necessary for the safe prosecution of the voyage. The vessel could have been (and was) repaired in Jamestown.

With deference to Hobhouse J and the Court of Appeal, I find no difficulty in giving full effect to rr X(b) and XIV, as they stand, without, as Hoffmann LJ thought necessary, implying anything in either rule. On the facts of the present case, Hobhouse J found that the delay in carrying out permanent repairs in New York would have been no greater than the delay in fact resulting from carrying out temporary repairs in Jamestown. Accordingly, he was not prepared to hold that the shipowners would have been in breach of contract if they had adopted that alternative. In your Lordships' House, the point was expressly conceded by the cargo owners in their printed case. It is unnecessary to consider what would have been the position if the nearest place for effecting permanent repairs had been, as Mr Boyd asked us to envisage, on the other side of the world.

The second paragraph of r XIV obliges us to suppose that the temporary repairs had not been effected at Jamestown. What then would have happened? The answer is simple. She would have gone into dry dock in New York. Was the discharge of the cargo necessary to enable the damage to the ship to be repaired in dry dock? The answer is clearly Yes. Were those repairs necessary to enable the vessel to proceed safely from New York to India, always assuming that she had not already been repaired in Jamestown? The answer, again, is clearly Yes. The assumption required by r XIV must be carried through when applying r X. It is not necessary to assume that the vessel *could not* have been repaired in Jamestown in order to give effect to the two rules. It is necessary only to assume that she was not so repaired, as r XIV requires. In this way effect can be given to the clear intention of the opening words of the second paragraph of r XIV, that the cost of temporary repairs of accidental damage are admissible in general average, subject only to the limit imposed by the second half of the paragraph.

I hope it is not discourteous to Hobhouse J and the Court of Appeal to leave the matter there. Like most questions of construction, the point is a short one and incapable of much elaboration. In particular, I do not find it necessary to trace the gradual evolution of r XIV, as to which there is an interesting account in Hoffmann LJ's judgment (see [1993] 1 Lloyd's Rep 411 at 420–422), nor to consider what would have been the position if the York-Antwerp Rules had not been incorporated. I will only say that although rr X(b) and XIV have been in much the same form since 1890 and 1924 respectively, it was not until 1955, in the first edition of Lowndes and Rudolf's *Law of General Average and the York Antwerp Rules* (8th edn) for which Mr J F Donaldson (as he then was) and Mr C T Ellis were responsible, that any doubt as to the meaning of these two interlocking rules emerged.

In addition to the point so far considered, Hobhouse J detected a further difficulty, which he regarded as insuperable. There was only one port of refuge, namely Jamestown. If expenses incurred at any other port or place were to be admitted as general average (in this case the expenses of discharging, storing and reloading the cargo at Providence) it would be necessary to bring the case within the second paragraph of r X(a), which provides:

> 'When a ship is at any port or place of refuge and is necessarily removed to another port or place because repairs cannot be carried out in the first port or place, the provisions of this Rule shall be applied to the second port or place as if it were a port or place of refuge and the cost of such removal including temporary repairs and towage shall be admitted as general average. The provisions of rule XI shall be applied to the prolongation of the voyage occasioned by such removal.'

Hobhouse J considered that the present case could not be brought within r X(a) since all necessary repairs could be, and were, carried out at Jamestown. But your Lordships need not be concerned with that objection. For the point is covered by a concession in para 13(3) of the cargo owners' printed case, which reads:

> 'The [cargo owners] no longer contend that the expenditure which would have been incurred on the notional voyage in discharging and reloading the cargo at Providence is irrelevant on the additional ground that Providence was not a port of loading, call or refuge for the purpose of rule X(b).'

By this I understand it to be accepted that the expenditure at Providence would have been allowable in general average subject only to Mr Boyd's point that repairs at New York were not 'necessary for the safe prosecution of the voyage'.

Finally, Mr Boyd drew our attention to a supposed difference in viewpoint between the European and American delegates to the Amsterdam Conference in 1949: Proceedings of the CMI International Sub-committee on General Average. The European delegates put forward an amendment to the second paragraph of r XIV to make clear that the cost of temporary repairs at a port of refuge is only allowable where it would have been possible to carry out permanent repairs at that port or place: see *Lowndes and Rudolf* (11th edn, 1990) para 14.31, footnote 32. In the event r XIV was left as it was. The point would have had to be decided in the present appeal if it had not been conceded by the cargo owners in their printed case. It was not revived by Mr Boyd in oral argument. He mentioned it only to show that r XIV is a rule on which different views have been, and will no doubt continue to be, held. I would allow the appeal on the simple ground that the owners have shown (the burden of proof being upon them) that the cost of discharging, storing and reloading cargo at Providence would have been allowable in general average, if repairs had been carried out in New York instead of Jamestown, since such repairs would, on that assumption, have been necessary, within the meaning of r X(b), for the safe prosecution of the voyage. I would confirm the adjustment of Messrs Richards Hogg Ltd.

Appeal allowed.

Celia Fox   Barrister.

Mallinson v Secretary of State for Social Security

HOUSE OF LORDS
LORD TEMPLEMAN, LORD BROWNE-WILKINSON, LORD MUSTILL, LORD WOOLF AND LORD LLOYD OF BERWICK
20 JANUARY, 21 APRIL 1994

Social security – Attendance allowance – Frequent attention throughout day in connection with bodily functions – Attention – Blind man requiring assistance in bathing, eating and walking in unfamiliar surroundings – Whether assistance in walking in unfamiliar surroundings 'attention required in connection with .... bodily functions' – Social Security Act 1975, s 35(1)(a)(i).

The appellant, who was aged 48, was blind. He was able to walk about his flat and in familiar surroundings without hurting himself but he was at risk of injury when walking in unfamiliar surroundings. He also required assistance in taking a bath and cutting up food. He applied for an attendance allowance under s 35(1)(a)[a] of the Social Security Act 1975, which provided that a severely disabled person was entitled to attendance allowance if, inter alia, he required from someone else '(i) frequent attention throughout the day in connection with his bodily functions, or (ii) continual supervision throughout the day in order to avoid substantial danger to himself or others'. A delegated medical practitioner, acting on behalf of the Attendance Allowance Board, decided that the appellant did not qualify for the allowance because although severely disabled by his blindness the fact that he could walk about his flat and in familiar surroundings without hurting himself meant that he did not require 'continual supervision throughout the day'. The appellant appealed to a social security commissioner, who dismissed his appeal. He appealed to the Court of Appeal, which dismissed his appeal. He appealed to the House of Lords, contending that he required 'frequent attention throughout the day in connection with his bodily functions'.

Held (Lord Mustill and Lord Lloyd dissenting) – Assistance provided to a blind person in connection with his bodily functions of bathing, eating and walking in unfamiliar surroundings could amount to 'attention' for the purposes of s 35(1)(a)(i) of the 1975 Act, and if that assistance amounted to 'frequent attention throughout the day', which was a question of fact, the person

---

[a] Section 35(1) is set out at p 298 *e f*, post

receiving the assistance was entitled to an attendance allowance under s 35(1). In particular, assistance required by a blind person while walking out of doors in unfamiliar surroundings was 'attention required' by the blind person 'in connection with his bodily functions' within s 35(1)(a) since the act of guiding a blind person had the active and close, caring, personal qualities characteristic of 'attention' and was provided 'in connection with his bodily function' of seeing. Although a blind person's walking ability and mobility might be unimpaired, he had the problem of not knowing where and when to walk when in unfamiliar surroundings and the only attention which could be given to a person 'in connection with' a sight handicap was to provide assistance to enable that person to do what he could physically do for himself if he had sight. It followed that, subject to the appellant satisfying an adjudication officer that he required 'frequent attention throughout the day', he was entitled to an attendance allowance in connection with his bodily functions of bathing, eating and walking in unfamiliar surroundings. The appeal would therefore be allowed (see p 297 g to p 298 a, p 301 j, p 304 h to p 305 c e g h, p 306 a b d e j and p 307 j, post).

R v National Insurance Comr, ex p Secretary of State for Social Services [1981] 2 All ER 738 and Woodling v Secretary of State for Social Services [1984] 1 All ER 593 considered.

Per Lord Templeman, Lord Browne-Wilkinson and Lord Woolf. 'Attention' and 'supervision' are not mutually exclusive concepts for the purposes of s 35(1) of the 1975 Act. There can be situations where supervision is taking place with the object of the person supervising being in the position to give attention which falls within s 35(1)(a)(i) if and when an incident occurs, e g in the case of a person suffering from epilepsy: if the person does not have an epileptic attack, there will be 'supervision' which is capable of falling within s 35(1)(a)(ii) if it is constant but if the person does have an attack assistance rendered to him may amount to 'attention' for the purposes of s 35(1)(a)(i) (see p 297 j to p 298 a and p 303 j to p 304 b, post).

Notes
For attendance allowance, see 33 *Halsbury's Laws* (4th edn) para 448.
As from 1 July 1992 s 35(1) of the Social Security Act 1975 was replaced by s 64 of the Social Security Contributions and Benefits Act 1992. For s 64 of the 1992 Act, see 40 *Halsbury's Statutes* (4th edn) 581.

Cases referred to in opinions
Moran v Secretary of State for Social Services [1987] CA Transcript 244.
Puhlhofer v Hillingdon London BC [1986] 1 All ER 467, [1986] AC 484, [1986] 2 WLR 259, HL.
R v National Insurance Comr, ex p Secretary of State for Social Services [1981] 2 All ER 738, [1981] 1 WLR 1017, CA.
Woodling v Secretary of State for Social Services [1984] 1 All ER 593, [1984] 1 WLR 348, HL.

Appeal
Eric Mallinson appealed with leave of the Court of Appeal from the decision of that court (Ralph Gibson and Mann LJJ (Nolan LJ dissenting)) delivered on 1 April 1993 dismissing the appellant's appeal from the decision of the Social Security Commissioner (Mrs R F M Heggs) given on 25 September 1991

dismissing the appellant's appeal from a determination on review by a delegated medical practitioner, acting on behalf of the Attendance Allowance Board, on 12 December 1990 whereby the delegated medical practitioner decided that the appellant's blindness did not entitle him to an attendance allowance under s 35(1) of the Social Security Act 1975. The facts are set out in the opinion of Lord Woolf.

Richard Drabble (instructed by *David Thomas*) for the appellant.

Duncan Ouseley QC and *Paul Stinchcombe* (instructed by the *Solicitor to the Department of Social Security*) for the Secretary of State.

Their Lordships took time for consideration.

21 April 1994. The following opinions were delivered.

LORD TEMPLEMAN. My Lords, by s 35(1)(a)(i) of the Social Security Act 1975 attendance allowance is payable to a severely disabled person if he requires from another person 'frequent attention throughout the day in connection with his bodily functions'.

The courts have given a wide meaning to the expression 'bodily functions' and your Lordships were not asked to quarrel with the definition given by Lord Denning MR in *R v National Insurance Comr, ex p Secretary of State for Social Services* [1981] 2 All ER 738 at 741, [1981] 1 WLR 1017 at 1022 (*Packer's* case) when he said:

'"Bodily functions" include breathing, hearing, seeing, eating, drinking, walking, sitting, sleeping, getting in or out of bed, dressing, undressing, eliminating waste products, and the like, all of which an ordinary person, who is not suffering from any disability, does for himself. But they do not include cooking, shopping or any of the other things which a wife or daughter does as part of her domestic duties, or generally which one of the household normally does for the rest of the family.'

In the present case the appellant, Mr Mallinson, is severely disabled by blindness. It is conceded that, though Mr Mallinson can wash himself when he is in the bath, he requires attendance in connection with his bodily function of bathing in the form of assistance in getting into and out of the bath. It is also conceded that, although Mr Mallinson can feed himself, he requires attention in connection with his bodily function of eating in the form of assistance in cutting up his food. Mr Mallinson can walk but he requires attention in connection with his bodily function of walking in the form of assistance to guide and help him when he is outdoors. True it is that Mr Mallinson can walk within the confines of his flat without attention but this facility is only a factor which the adjudication officer will bear in mind in deciding whether the aggregate attention required by Mr Mallinson in connection with his bodily functions of bathing, eating and walking amount to 'frequent attention throughout the day'.

For these reasons and for the reasons given by my noble and learned friend Lord Woolf I would allow this appeal.

LORD BROWNE-WILKINSON. My Lords, for the reasons given in a speech to be delivered by my noble and learned friend Lord Woolf I too would allow the appeal.

LORD MUSTILL. My Lords, I have found this a difficult case, but have come to the conclusion that the appeal should be dismissed for the reasons given by my noble and learned friend Lord Lloyd of Berwick. I will add only this, that whilst s 35(1)(a)(i) and (b)(i) are aimed at the relationship between the disability and the performance of the bodily functions themselves, the focus of s 35(1)(a)(ii) and (b)(ii) is the danger which the continued supervision is intended to avert. Since the problem faced by Mr Mallinson is not that he cannot walk but that in some outdoor situations he cannot walk without risk, it is the continued supervision called for by para (b) rather than the frequent attention demanded by para (a) which one would expect to find as the touchstone of the right to an attendance allowance; and which for the reasons given by Lord Lloyd I believe one does find.

LORD WOOLF. My Lords, the issue raised on this appeal is a short one. However, as indicated by Ralph Gibson LJ in the Court of Appeal, it is by no means easy to resolve. The issue is whether the assistance required by a blind person while walking out of doors in unfamiliar surroundings is 'attention' 'required' by the blind person 'in connection with his bodily functions' within s 35(1)(a) of the Social Security Act 1975. The terms of that subsection are:

> 'A person shall be entitled to an attendance allowance if he satisfies prescribed conditions as to residence or presence in Great Britain and either—(a) he is so severely disabled physically or mentally that, by day, he requires from another person either—(i) frequent attention throughout the day in connection with his bodily functions, or (ii) continual supervision throughout the day in order to avoid substantial danger to himself or others; or (b) he is so severely disabled physically or mentally that, at night, he requires from another person either—(i) prolonged or repeated attention during the night in connection with his bodily functions, or (ii) continual supervision throughout the night in order to avoid substantial danger to himself or others.'

The answer to the issue can also be of relevance to a carer of a severely disabled person. This is because under s 37 of the 1975 Act invalid care allowance was payable, subject to certain requirements, to a person who cared for a severely disabled person and the definition of a severely disabled person included 'a person in respect of whom there is payable either an attendance allowance or such other payment out of public funds on account of his need for attendance as may be prescribed'. While ss 35 and 37 of the 1975 Act are no longer in force the outcome of this appeal is of relevance to the similar requirements that have to be fulfilled to qualify for allowances under the current Social Security Contributions and Benefits Act 1992.

The appellant Mr Mallinson is blind. He suffers from no mental disability but requires assistance with getting in and out of the bath and with cutting up food. He can walk about his flat and outside in familiar surroundings without risk of danger to himself, but, because he cannot see, when walking in unfamiliar surroundings he risks injury to himself unless he is guided by someone else.

Mr Mallinson first claimed attendance allowance on a form dated 22 August 1989. On 6 October 1989 a delegated medical practitioner, acting on behalf of the Attendance Allowance Board, decided that Mr Mallinson did not satisfy any of the attendance conditions set out in s 35(1) of the 1975 Act. That decision was subsequently reviewed on 2 March 1990 and again on 12 December 1990 without the decision being altered. There was then an appeal, with leave, to Mrs Heggs, a social security commissioner, which was dismissed on 25 September 1991. A further appeal, with leave, against her decision to the Court of Appeal was dismissed by a majority (Ralph Gibson and Mann LJJ (Nolan LJ dissenting)). However, the Court of Appeal gave leave for this appeal.

On analysis of the section it is apparent that in order to satisfy the conditions prescribed by s 35(1)(a) a claimant must establish (a) that he is severely disabled, (b) that his disablement is so severe that he requires from another person frequent attention throughout the day, and (c) that the frequent attention is in connection with his bodily functions.

As Mr Mallinson is blind it has always been accepted that he fulfils condition (a). It is part of requirement (b) and requirement (c) which have given rise to the difficulty.

In his decision announcing the result of the second review, on 12 December 1990, the third delegated medical practitioner, in a determination which was upheld by the commissioner as being correct, said:

'DAY ATTENTION

4. The examining doctor in the medical report of 20 September 1990 was of the opinion that Mr Mallinson required assistance to bathe and to cut up food. The medical evidence indicates that Mr Mallinson uses a white stick.

5. I appreciate that Mr Mallinson is blind but he has suffered from blindness for a number of years and it is clear from the evidence before me that he has adjusted well to disability.

6. Your letter dated 31 July 1990 [ie from Mr Rathfelder, a hospital welfare rights officer] indicates that Mr Mallinson regularly needs assistance with the bodily function of walking but this is not borne out by the medical evidence. The examining doctor in the medical report of 20 September 1990 was of the opinion that Mr Mallinson could walk without assistance from another person and having considered the clinical picture I agree with his opinion.

7. Mr Mallinson has no physical disorder of mobility and, therefore, he should be able to walk and to get about within his familiar surroundings without assistance.

8. Mr Mallinson requires assistance to bathe and to cut up food but this does not amount to frequent attention throughout the day. Consequently, my conclusion is that Mr Mallinson does not satisfy the day attention condition.

DAY SUPERVISION

9. The examining doctor in the medical report of 20 September 1990 was of the opinion that Mr Mallinson was aware of common dangers both inside and outside the house but he went on to indicate that Mr Mallinson cannot see dangers outside the house. He further indicated that Mr

Mallinson could safely be left unsupervised all day. Mr Mallinson is described as having normal mental ability.

10. Mr Mallinson has been blind for a number of years but he is stated to be mentally normal. I can see no medical reason why he should not be aware of his surroundings. He has no physical disorder of mobility and I consider that he should be able to find his way around in the familiar surroundings of his home.

11. I accept that supervision is required when he [is] out in traffic or in unfamiliar surroundings but such supervision is limited in time and frequency and can be arranged in advance.

12. Taking an overall view my conclusion is that this condition is not satisfied.'

The medical report of 20 September 1990 referred to in the decision sets out Mr Mallinson's description of his condition as being:

'I do not go out into unfamiliar surroundings without someone with me as I have walked into lamp posts and broken glasses and knocked teeth out in the past',

and it includes the opinion of the doctor that—

'[Mr Mallinson] is relatively safe in the familiar surroundings of his own home but he would need supervision outdoors in view of his previous injuries (knocked out front teeth on lamp post).'

To a question on the form, 'In your opinion can the disabled person's condition give rise to danger to himself or someone else?' the doctor answers: 'Needs supervision in unfamiliar surroundings.'

The medical report is silent as to what form of 'supervision' in unfamiliar surroundings was required. However, in the course of argument before your Lordships and, it appears, in the Court of Appeal, it was sensibly accepted that what Mr Mallinson required in unfamiliar surroundings was to have a person to accompany him. That person would act as his guide. He would guide Mr Mallinson either physically, perhaps by linking arms, or orally by describing to Mr Mallinson what he should do. Both methods involve the guide, in unfamiliar surroundings, acting as Mr Mallinson's eyes, doing for Mr Mallinson what he could not do for himself, which was to see where he was going.

The commissioner stated that Mr Mallinson 'is able to walk and even does so out of doors. However he does risk injury when walking in unfamiliar surroundings because he cannot see'. She indorsed the delegated medical practitioner's classification of the assistance required by Mr. Mallinson when walking as 'supervision' rather than 'attention'. If this classification is justified then it is conceded by Mr Drabble, on behalf of Mr Mallinson, that he cannot qualify for attendance allowance under s 35(1)(a)(ii) because any such supervision would not be 'continual ... throughout the day', which is the standard set by the second limb of s 35(1).

In the Court of Appeal, Ralph Gibson LJ in stating his conclusions indicated that his initial impression was favourable to Mr Mallinson and that 'the act of guiding a blind man or woman, when walking, could be held to be something involving care, consideration and vigilance for the blind person and a service of a close and intimate nature, in connection with the bodily function of

walking', all of which, on the authorities to which I will have to refer, suggest
that 'attention' rather than 'supervision' was provided by the guide. However,
he then stated that he had changed his view because of the difficulties which
could arise if different blind persons were not treated in the same way: that is,
if some are to be treated as qualifying and others not doing so. The allowance
is not on a sliding scale increasing with the attention you need. He considered
that the bodily function in connection with which assistance is given was that
of walking and could not accept the alternative contention made on behalf of
Mr Mallinson that it was in connection with seeing since, according to Ralph
Gibson LJ, 'Mr Mallinson cannot see and he cannot require or receive attention
with seeing'. Mann LJ was also influenced by the undesirability of reaching a
decision which 'would result in fine adjudications as to the need for
accompanied walking amongst claimants who could not readily understand
distinctions between themselves'. However, he appears to have taken the
view that while guiding constituted 'attention' it was not 'attention' in
connection with a bodily function since it only arose as a result of a 'physical
need or desire which Mr Mallinson may have to walk outside his familiar
surroundings for therapeutic or recreational reasons'. This Mann LJ regarded
as being 'an immaterial consideration'. Nolan LJ took a different view because
he considered that it was inevitable that results will differ from case to case and
'the suggestion that a blind person walking on or across the highway needs
only passive supervision coupled with a readiness to intervene in an
emergency seems to me to be unrealistic'.

Assisted by the extremely able argument of Mr Drabble on behalf of Mr
Mallinson and Mr Ouseley QC on behalf of the Secretary of State, it is apparent
that the judgments of the majority of the Court of Appeal seek to give effect to
what has been said which is of general application in the earlier authorities.
Those authorities were dealing with claims for attendance allowance which
were made in different circumstances from those of this appeal but which
contain valuable guidance as to the proper approach to the application of
s 35(1). The earliest of those cases is *R v National Insurance Comr, ex p Secretary
of State for Social Services* [1981] 2 All ER 738, [1981] 1 WLR 1017 (*Packer's* case).
That case involved an 83-year-old lady who had numerous disabilities
associated with advancing years. The activity which it was sought to take into
account was the assistance which she received with cooking. In the course of
giving the first judgment in that case, Lord Denning MR said ([1981] 2 All ER
738 at 741–742, [1981] 1 WLR 1017 at 1022):

'In order to qualify at all, the person must be "so severely disabled
physically or mentally" that he requires attention. This conveys the
thought that the attention must be required so as to enable him to cope
with his disability, whatever it is.'

This is surely just what the guide does for Mr Mallinson in unfamiliar
surroundings—helps him to cope with his disability of being unable to see.
Lord Denning MR added that 'attention' is different from 'activity' or
'attendance' and he continued:

'"Bodily functions" include breathing, hearing, seeing, eating, drinking,
walking, sitting, sleeping, getting in or out of bed, dressing, undressing,
eliminating waste products, and the like, all of which an ordinary person,
who is not suffering from any disability, does for himself. But they do not

include cooking, shopping or any of the other things which a wife or daughter does as part of her domestic duties, or generally which one of the household normally does for the rest of the family.'

Lord Denning MR's reference to the role of different members of the family, as he perceived them to be, are not in contemporary circumstances of any real assistance. He did, however, correctly point out that it was 'in connection with' which give rise to difficulty, and he went on to say that—

'ordinary domestic duties such as shopping, cooking meals, making tea or coffee, laying the table or the tray, carrying it into the room, making the bed or filling the hot water bottle, do not qualify as "attention ... in connection with [the] bodily functions" of the disabled person. But that duties that are out of the ordinary, doing for the disabled person what a normal person would do for himself, such as cutting up food, lifting the cup to the mouth, helping to dress and undress or at the toilet, all do qualify as "attention ... in connection with [the] bodily functions" of the disabled person.'

In this later passage Lord Denning MR correctly focuses on the close connection required between the activity and the bodily function if it is to qualify as 'attention ... in connection with his bodily functions'.

This is a feature to which Dunn LJ also drew attention when he said ([1981] 2 All ER 738 at 742, [1981] 1 WLR 1017 at 1023):

'I look first at the section without regard to authority. To my mind the word "functions" in its physiological or bodily sense connotes the normal actions of any organs or set of organs of the body, and so the attention must be in connection with such normal actions. The word "attention" itself indicates something more than personal service, something involving care, consideration and vigilance for the person being attended. The very word suggests a service of a close and intimate nature. And the phrase "attention ... in connection with ... bodily functions" involves some service involving personal contact carried out in the presence of the disabled person.'

In that passage Dunn LJ adopts an approach which I would commend subject to one minor caveat and that is that 'contact' need not be physical contact: it can be the contact established by the spoken word in the type of situations to which I will refer later.

The next decision is that of this House in *Woodling v Secretary of State for Social Services* [1984] 1 All ER 593, [1984] 1 WLR 348, when this House came to the same conclusion as to cooking as in *Packer's* case. Lord Bridge of Harwich, in a speech with which the other members of the House agreed, approved the observations of Dunn LJ in *Packer's* case which I have already cited (see [1984] 1 All ER 593 at 596, [1984] 1 WLR 348 at 352). Lord Bridge also, in giving general guidance as to the correct approach to the section, indicated that the section should be considered as a whole, that the phrase 'bodily function' is restrictive and precise, narrower than, for example, 'bodily needs' and that when read as a whole the provision 'connotes a high degree of physical intimacy between the person giving and the person receiving the attention'. Lord Bridge doubted that—

'the construction of the relevant words can be more accurately or more concisely expressed than in the passage from the decision of Mr Commissioner Monroe in 1974 (decision CA 60/74), cited by Dunn LJ (([1981] 2 All ER 738 at 744, [1981] 1 WLR 1017 at 1025): "I consider that the words of the section refer to a person who needs the relevant degree of attention in connection with the performance of his bodily functions and that they are directed primarily to those functions which the fit man normally performs for himself."' (See [1984] 1 All ER 593 at 596, [1984] 1 WLR 348 at 352–353.)

These words of Mr Commissioner Monroe which received such a strong endorsement of this House in 1984 are not wide enough to cover 'domestic chores'. Nonetheless, they mean that attention qualifies if it is 'in connection with the performance' of the many 'functions which the fit man normally performs for himself'.

The third case to which I should refer is the unreported decision of the Court of Appeal in *Moran v Secretary of State for Social Services* [1987] CA Transcript 244, which is an appendix to a commissioner's decision (No R(A) 1/88). In that case, the judgment was given by Nicholls LJ. The case concerned supervision of rather than attention to someone who suffered from epileptic fits. In the course of his judgment Nicholls LJ pointed out that 'attention' and 'supervision' are intended to denote two different concepts. 'Attention' denotes a concept of some personal service of an active nature, such as helping the disable person to wash or eat. 'Supervision' denotes a more passive concept, such as being in the same room with the disabled person so as to be prepared to intervene if necessary but not actually intervening save in emergency. That is a helpful guide as to the way in which to draw the distinction between supervision and attention. The vital contrast is between activity and a state of passivity coupled with a readiness to intervene.

Before examining the actual circumstances of this appeal, it is necessary to deal with two general submissions of Mr Ouseley. The first was that the two limbs of s 35(1)(a)(i) and (ii) are mutually exclusive and at least involve the fact-finding body being required, if a claim is to succeed, having examined the circumstances of a particular case, placing it in one or other category, that is, as being either 'attention' or 'supervision' and then deciding whether it complies with the other requirements of the relevant limb. The consequence of this approach is that if the situation is one which primarily involves supervision then there can be no attention to be taken into account under s 35(1)(a)(i). Likewise, if the situation is one which primarily involves attention, the fact that continual supervision is also involved will not result in the case qualifying for attendance allowance under s 35(1)(a)(ii). According to this argument, a case must only be assessed against the requirements of its dominant category. In the circumstances of this appeal Mr Ouseley submits that this involves primarily 'supervision' and that if this is so it cannot involve 'attention'.

This is a mistaken approach to the application of s 35(1). There can be situations where supervision is taking place with the object of the person supervising being in the position to give attention which falls within s 35(1)(a)(i) if, and when, an incident occurs. A good example is provided by the supervision which is given to an epileptic which was considered in *Moran's* case. If the person suffering from epilepsy does not have an attack, there will be supervision which is capable of falling within s 35(1)(a)(ii) alone but only if it is constant. If the claimant does have an attack then there can be assistance which will amount to 'attention' for the purposes of s 35(1)(a)(i). The attention during the incident can then be aggregated with other incidents where attention is given and in the result there may be 'frequent attention'. Here it is to be noted that the allowance is payable under s 35(2)(a) during 'a period throughout which he has satisfied or is *likely* to satisfy the condition mentioned in subsection (1)(a)'.

The other submission of Mr Ouseley was based on *Puhlhofer v Hillingdon London BC* [1986] 1 All ER 467, [1986] AC 484. That case involved an application for judicial review of a decision by a local authority under the Housing (Homeless Persons) Act 1977. Lord Brightman in giving a speech with which the other members of this House agreed, indicated that the question of what is accommodation for the purpose of that Act was a question of fact and that considerable restraint should be exercised by the courts in giving leave to proceed by judicial review as to decisions of the local authority of this nature. He concluded his remarks on this subject by saying ([1986] 1 All ER 467 at 474, [1986] AC 484 at 518):

'Where the existence or non-existence of a fact is left to the judgment and discretion of a public body and that fact involves a broad spectrum ranging from the obvious to the debatable to the just conceivable, it is the duty of the court to leave the decision of that fact to the public body to whom Parliament has entrusted the decision-making power save in a case where it is obvious that the public body, consciously or unconsciously, are acting perversely.'

Similarly here, Mr Ouseley contends, the courts should exercise the same restraint and not intervene with the decision of the delegated medical practitioner or the commissioner unless the court is satisfied that they have acted perversely. I do not accept that it is appropriate to apply Lord Brightman's approach to the present issue. This is a statutory appeal on a point of law. The court on such an appeal does not have the residual discretion which it has on an application for judicial review to limit the circumstances in which it grants leave or relief. It is contended on Mr Mallinson's behalf that there have been errors made in the adjudication of his claim for attendance allowance in that what in law constitutes attention in connection with bodily functions has been treated as supervision. If he is right as to this, then this constituted an error of law which on appeal the courts are required to rectify. Other issues in other circumstances, for example, as to whether acts which are attention constitute *frequent* attention, will normally be questions of fact and therefore findings which cannot be disturbed on appeal.

I turn now to consider whether Mr Mallinson can establish that the assistance which he requires in unfamiliar surroundings in connection with his bodily functions amounts to attention for the purposes of s 35(1). I consider first whether the guiding he requires in unfamiliar surroundings constitutes 'attention' and not 'supervision'. In my opinion it does. The process of guiding has the active and the close, caring, personal qualities referred to in the authorities which I have cited. The position is different from that which would exist in the case of, for example, a mother coming out to watch her child cross the road. She would, no doubt, be in a position to intervene if there was a situation of danger but until she did intervene she would be supervising, not attending to, her child. No doubt there will be cases which are borderline as to whether they are supervision or attention. If, however, the situation is one where, as here, the function cannot take place without assistance, that assistance is likely to constitute attention.

For the purpose of this appeal, the remaining part of requirement (b), the frequency of the attention, need not be considered. Mr Drabble recognises that the quantum of assistance which Mr Mallinson receives in unfamiliar surroundings cannot, by itself, amount to '*frequent* attention throughout the day'. He accepts that if he is to succeed on this appeal, the case will have to be remitted so that the appropriate fact-finding tribunal can consider whether, when the attention Mr Mallinson admittedly receives in cutting his food and with bathing is aggregated with the attention which he receives when walking in unfamiliar surrounds, the aggregation as a matter of fact fulfils the requirement that there should be 'frequent attention throughout the day'. This could prove a formidable hurdle for Mr Mallinson to surmount on this appeal. The requirement of frequency of attention throughout the day is a significant control on the circumstances in which the allowance is payable.

There remains, therefore, the final requirement, requirement (c), which creates the most difficulty in this case. Is the attention Mr Mallinson receives when walking 'in connection with his bodily functions'? In order to answer this question it is necessary to identify the bodily function or functions to which the attention relates. So far the suggestion that this could be in connection with Mr Mallinson's bodily function of seeing has been rejected out of hand. This approach I believe to be wrong.

The problem that Mr Mallinson has is that because he cannot see he does not know, in unfamiliar surroundings, *where* to walk or, for example, when crossing the road, *when* to walk. His walking ability itself is unimpaired and if he can overcome his inability to see his mobility is also unimpaired. He overcomes the lack of the bodily function of seeing which restricts his mobility in his home by memorising his surroundings and in surroundings with which he is unfamiliar by having the attention of a guide who can see the surroundings for him. Mr Ouseley submitted that, as Ralph Gibson LJ concluded, that the attention cannot be with the bodily function of seeing because Mr Mallinson cannot see. I confess that initially I was attracted by this approach but on further consideration I am satisfied it is mistaken. The only attention which can be given to a person 'in connection with' a sight handicap is to provide the assistance to enable that person to do what he could physically do for himself if he had sight. If, for example, a person with a sight handicap receives correspondence, someone has to read their contents to him if he cannot read them for himself. That I would regard as being the active personal assistance which constitutes the attention which a normal person does not require which the subsection demands. It would be inconceivable that Parliament intended that in those circumstances, a partially sighted person should qualify for an allowance but in the same circumstances a totally blind person should not qualify. Consistently with his submission, Mr Ouseley argued that, while a one-legged man who was supported when walking or standing if he received assistance from someone else would be receiving attention, the person who had lost the use of both his legs and was therefore pushed in a wheelchair rather than supported would not be receiving attention in respect of his bodily function of walking because he was incapable of performing the function of walking. Such a result is obvious nonsense and does not cease to be nonsense because there is a different allowance which can be payable for lack of mobility. The fact that your disability is so severe that you are incapable of exercising a bodily function does not mean that the attention you receive is not in connection with that bodily function. The attention is in connection with the bodily function if it provides a substitute method of providing what the bodily function would provide if it were not totally or partially impaired.

Whether the result of a sight defect is partial loss or total loss of vision, the function impaired, namely that of seeing, is the same although the degree of impairment differs. Thus reading to or guiding of a man with a sight defect remains attention in connection with bodily functions even if it replaces a total rather than a partial incapacity. If the position were otherwise, this would disqualify not only the person receiving the attention from receiving the care allowance under what was previously s 35 but also the person providing the attention from receiving invalid care allowance under what was previously s 37.

Then it might be suggested that the section requires a 'disability' which differs from the loss of 'function' and that that is why in the present case you have to treat the inability to walk as the loss of function and the loss of sight as the disability. Again I do not agree. If a man loses his leg and cannot walk, the loss of the leg is the disability and the inability to walk is the bodily function which is impaired. If a man's eyes are injured (he could lose one or both eyes), the disability is partial or total blindness and the bodily function which is impaired is the ability to see.

I note that s 35 refers to bodily functions, in the plural, and I recognise that the same result can be achieved by treating the assistance with walking required due to blindness as being in connection with both the bodily function of seeing and that of walking. This is a possible approach. But take the cutting of Mr Mallinson's food or the assistance with bathing which, correctly, in accordance with earlier decisions, are treated as attention. There is nothing wrong with Mr Mallinson's hands. They function satisfactorily and still perform many functions without assistance but he still cannot use them for these functions because they require sight. In time he may well be able to do so but for the time being he needs help. Therefore where, as is the case with blindness and other disabilities, such as deafness or paralysis, the function which is primarily impaired as a result of the disability can be readily identified, I suggest that it is preferable to focus on that function. So here, the assistance with cutting of food, with bathing and guiding would all be attention, which should be aggregated as being required in connection with Mr Mallinson's totally impaired sight. This is a more straightforward approach than seeking to link the attention with those different functions which he could perform perfectly but for his loss of sight.

In the case of mental, as opposed to physical, disabilities the position would usually be different. If a mental disability is not serious it will be a case for supervision, which if it is to qualify must meet the requirements in the second limb of the subsection. However, a severe case of mental disability may well require attention with a wide range of independent bodily functions as opposed to primarily one function.

If guiding a person who is blind can be attention in connection with the bodily functions, then it does not cease to be attention because the attention is only required in limited circumstances as, for example, when the blind person is walking in unfamiliar as opposed to familiar surroundings. It will usually be the case that, as a person who has the misfortune to lose his sight learns to cope with his disability, the circumstances in which he may need attention will progressively diminish. Initially, he will probably need attention both inside his home and in public with walking, and likewise with reading until he learns to 'read' Braille. As he learns to cope with his disability his needs will be less. However, in those situations when he is still dependent upon help he will require attention. This may mean that he no longer receives 'frequent attention throughout the day' and if this is the case he will not qualify for the allowance because the attention is infrequent, not because the nature of the attention has changed. The section in its first limb provides two safeguards against being applied too broadly: the need for the attention to be frequent throughout the day; and the need for it to be in connection with bodily functions. The safeguards are perfectly adequate without adopting a restrictive approach to the other requirements.

It is possible to imagine extreme situations where a blind person would require assistance which is unlikely to have been intended to qualify for aggregation in order to establish that the person concerned required 'frequent attention throughout the day'. Those extreme situations would not have to be taken into account because either they would not result from the severity of the disability or the attention would not be reasonably required. Although the section does not make any reference to the attention having to be reasonably required, as Mr Drabble concedes on behalf of Mr Mallinson, it is only attention which is reasonably required by the person subject to the disability which qualifies for the purposes of s 35(1)(a)(i).

Concern has been expressed that to allow attention to qualify which relates to walking in unfamiliar surroundings would lead to a situation which is difficult to administer or enforce. I do not believe that this will be the result. The delegated medical practitioner already has the task of applying the relevant statutory formula to a multiplicity of factual situations. But this usually involves doing no more than looking, as in this case, at the claimant's account of what he can and cannot do together with the relevant medical report and asking four simple questions. (1) Has the claimant a serious disability? (2) If so, what bodily functions does it impair? (3) Does he reasonably require attention in connection with those functions? (4) Is that attention frequent? For a doctor having to answer such questions should not be an over-demanding task. While there are always going to be a minority of cases where it is difficult for him to decide on which side of the line a case falls, in the majority of cases the answer will be straightforward and a result should be achieved without creating any sense of justified grievance between one claimant and another.

For these reasons I consider that this appeal should be allowed and so that the frequency of the attention throughout the day can be reassessed the case should be remitted for reconsideration and a second-tier adjudication by an adjudication officer.

LORD LLOYD OF BERWICK. My Lords, the appellant Mr Eric Mallinson has been a registered blind person since 1974. On 22 August 1989 he made a claim for an attendance allowance under s 35(1) of the Social Security Act 1975. That subsection (now repealed by s 3(1) of and Sch 1 to the Social Security

(Consequential Provisions) Act 1992 and replaced by s 64 of the Social Security Contributions and Benefits Act 1992) provides:

'A person shall be entitled to an attendance allowance if he satisfies prescribed conditions as to residence or presence in Great Britain and either—(a) he is so severely disabled physically or mentally that, by day, he requires from another person either—(i) frequent attention throughout the day in connection with his bodily functions, or (ii) continual supervision throughout the day in order to avoid substantial danger to himself or others; or (b) he is so severely disabled physically or mentally that, at night, he requires from another person either—(i) prolonged or repeated attention during the night in connection with his bodily functions, or (ii) continual supervision throughout the night in order to avoid substantial danger to himself or others.'

On 23 September 1989 he was seen by an examining medical officer. On 6 October 1989 the delegated medical practitioner acting on behalf of the Attendance Allowance Board rejected Mr Mallinson's claim. In his view Mr Mallinson did not satisfy any of the four conditions set out in s 35(1) of the Act. Mr Mallinson asked for a review. In his letter dated 28 November 1989 he said that he needed frequent attention throughout the day with his bodily functions and also continuous supervision throughout the day in order to avoid substantial danger to himself. Under the heading 'bodily functions' he listed cutting up food, drinking, bathing, washing his hair, shaving, and cutting his fingernails and toenails. Under the heading 'supervision' he said:

'Outdoors I require supervision and guidance to get from A to B. Crossing roads is extremely hazardous for me and there have been a few incidents where I have been in danger from oncoming traffic ... Obstacles, such as lampposts, are a danger to me. In the past I have walked into them, one of these incidents resulted in two of my teeth being knocked out. Indoors I require help and supervision when dealing with hot liquids and cooking as I have suffered many burns in the past ... Although I can move around my own flat adequately I cannot do so in unfamiliar surroundings. I also require constant supervision whilst bathing.'

On 2 March 1990 another delegated medical practitioner upheld the previous decision.

Mr Mallinson's case was then taken up by Mr Martin Rathfelder, a hospital welfare rights officer employed by Manchester City Council. On 31 July 1990 Mr Rathfelder wrote on behalf of Mr Mallinson to the Attendance Allowance Unit, asking for a further review. I quote from his letter:

'Mr. Mallinson tells me he regularly needs assistance with the bodily function of walking. Because he does not generally have access to such assistance he tells me he walks into trees, lamp posts and similar obstructions, and has knocked teeth out and broken his glasses on a number of occasions. He also needs supervision when cooking or making a drink because he is in danger of burning himself.'

On 20 September 1990 Mr Mallinson was seen by another examining medical officer, Dr Woodhouse. Dr Woodhouse's report is set out on a form (DS4) issued by the Department of Social Security. In answer to question 3, Dr Woodhouse described Mr Mallinson's general state as follows:

'He can get around the flat well, using furniture and familiar objects to guide him. He was able to walk up and down the stairs to let me in. He can get on and off the toilet and in and out of bed ... He is relatively safe in the familiar surroundings of his own home but he would need supervision outdoors in view of his previous injuries (knocked out front teeth on lamp post).'

In answer to question 4 Dr Woodhouse considered that Mr Mallinson's condition was such as to give rise to danger to himself. He concluded that he needed supervision in unfamiliar surroundings. In a supplementary report dealing specifically with supervision, Dr Woodhouse repeated his view that Mr Mallinson needed supervision out of doors, but added that he could be safely left unsupervised all day.

In another part of the main form there is a list of functions which may be of some importance. The list is as follows:

'Move position in bed, get out of bed, get into bed, rise from usual chair, walk, use stairs, dress and undress, wash, bath, get to the toilet, cut up food, eat, drink, use wheelchair.'

Dr Woodhouse considered that Mr Mallinson was able to perform all these functions without assistance, except having a bath, for which he needed help getting in and out, and for cutting up food. In the light of that report Mr Mallinson's case was considered by yet another delegated medical practitioner. His decision is dated 12 December 1990. He upheld the previous decisions. Since it is the decision of 12 December 1990 which is attacked as being erroneous in law, it is necessary to set out the relevant paragraphs verbatim:

'DAY ATTENTION

4. The examining doctor in the medical report of 20 September 1990 was of the opinion that Mr Mallinson required assistance to bathe and to cut up food. The medical evidence indicates that Mr Mallinson uses a white stick.

5. I appreciate that Mr Mallinson is blind but he has suffered from blindness for a number of years and it is clear from the evidence before me that he has adjusted well to disability.

6. Your letter dated 31 July 1990 indicates that Mr Mallinson regularly needs assistance with the bodily function of walking but this is not borne out by the medical evidence. The examining doctor in the medical report of 20 September 1990 was of the opinion that Mr Mallinson could walk without assistance from another person and having considered the clinical picture I agree with his opinion.

7. Mr Mallinson has no physical disorder of mobility and, therefore, he should be able to walk and to get about within his familiar surroundings without assistance.

8. Mr Mallinson requires assistance to bathe and to cut up food but this does not amount to frequent attention throughout the day. Consequently, my conclusion is that Mr Mallinson does not satisfy the day attention condition.

DAY SUPERVISION

9. The examining doctor in the medical report of 20 September 1990 was of the opinion that Mr Mallinson was aware of common dangers both inside and outside the house but he went on to indicate that Mr Mallinson cannot see dangers outside the house. He further indicated that Mr Mallinson could safely be left unsupervised all day. Mr Mallinson is described as having normal mental ability.

10. Mr Mallinson has been blind for a number of years but he is stated to be mentally normal. I can see no medical reason why he should not be aware of his surroundings. He has no physical disorder of mobility and I consider that he should be able to find his way around in the familiar surroundings of his home.

11. I accept that supervision is required when he [is] out in traffic or in unfamiliar surroundings but such supervision is limited in time and frequency and can be arranged in advance.

12. Taking an overall view my conclusion is that this condition is not satisfied.'

There is an appeal from a decision of the Attendance Allowance Board to a social security commissioner, but only on a question of law. In the present case there was an oral hearing before Mrs R F M Heggs, at which Mr Mallinson was represented by Mr Rathfelder. Mr Rathfelder argued that the decision of 12 December 1990 was erroneous in law in two respects; first, because the delegated medical practitioner had failed to deal explicitly with the question whether the help needed with walking was to be considered as supervision or attention, and that he had therefore given inadequate reasons for his decision; and, secondly, because the help which he needed with walking should have been considered under the 'attention condition', and not under the 'supervision condition'. The commissioner rejected both submissions. I quote from para 6 of her decision:

'It is not in dispute that the claimant is physically capable of walking. What is contended is that he requires assistance when walking in unfamiliar surroundings so that he does not injure himself. Section 35(1)(a)(i) relates to assistance without which the person with severe disabilities would not be able to perform his bodily functions. The [delegated medical practitioner] makes this clear in paragraphs 6 and 7 of his determination. The claimant in the present case is able to walk and even does so out of doors. However he does risk injury when walking in unfamiliar surroundings because he cannot see. In my view, the [delegated medical practitioner] correctly considered the assistance required by the claimant when walking as "supervision" rather than "attention". It follows that I cannot accept Mr Rathfelder's argument that the aggregate of the "attention" required by the claimant throughout the day when bathing, cutting up his food and walking satisfy the conditions contained in section 35(1)(a)(ii) of the Act.'

The commissioner concluded that the delegated medical practitioner decision was not erroneous in point of law.

Mr Mallinson appealed with leave to the Court of Appeal. The grounds of appeal consist of a single paragraph. It is said that the commissioner erred in law in holding that the assistance required by the appellant while walking out of doors in unfamiliar surroundings was not 'attention ... in connection with his bodily functions' for the purpose of s 35(1)(a)(i). The case was argued by junior counsel instructed by the Child Poverty Action Group. The appeal was dismissed by a majority. Ralph Gibson LJ held that the decision of the delegated medical practitioner contained no error of law. He accepted, as indeed is obvious, that walking is a bodily function within the meaning of the section. But Mr Mallinson could walk without assistance. The only assistance he needed was when he was walking in unfamiliar circumstances. No doubt Mr Mallinson enjoyed getting out of his flat. But walking in unfamiliar circumstances was not a bodily function within the concept of the section.

Mann LJ defined the question as being whether Mr Mallinson required attention in connection with his walking. He answered that question in the negative:

'Mr Mallinson could walk but his blindness prevented him enjoying the exercise of that bodily function outside a familiar area. Outside it he required an attender. However, an attendance in order to enlarge the practical enjoyment of an unimpaired bodily function is [not] in my judgment a required attendance in connection with that bodily function.'

Mann LJ could find no error of law in the delegated medical practitioner's decision.

Nolan LJ dissented. He held that Mr Mallinson suffers from a 'physical disorder of mobility', since he cannot see to walk. The delegated medical practitioner was wrong in law to hold otherwise. Secondly, he was wrong in law to hold that Mr Mallinson required supervision rather than attention.

There was an alternative argument that Mr Mallinson required attention in connection with his bodily function of seeing. Ralph Gibson LJ dealt with that argument as follows:

'As to the bodily function in connection with which the assistance is given, it has, I think, been correctly identified throughout this case at all its stages as being that of walking. I cannot accept the alternative contention now made that the relevant bodily function is that of seeing. Mr Mallinson cannot see and he cannot require or receive attention with seeing.'

Paragraph 1 of the appellant's printed case reads:

'As the statement of issue and facts makes clear, Mr Mallinson is blind. Although he can move in familiar surroundings without a guide, he cannot do so in unfamiliar surroundings. He contends that the assistance given to him by a guide is "attention" that he requires in connection with the "bodily function" of walking, and accordingly that this attention can be considered in deciding whether he met the condition in section 35(1)(a)(i) of the Social Security Act 1975.'

So Mr Drabble, a most experienced advocate in this field, was accepting that the relevant bodily function in this case is walking. Nowhere in the printed case is it suggested that the relevant bodily function is seeing, or a combination of the two bodily functions of seeing and walking. It appears, therefore, that at that stage Mr Drabble did not intend to resurrect the alternative argument which had failed in the court below.

The thrust of the printed case and of Mr Drabble's oral argument was that the activity of guiding a blind man involves attention rather than supervision, and that such attention was required in this case in connection with Mr

Mallinson's bodily function of walking in unfamiliar surroundings. I take each of these matters in turn.

The distinction between attention and supervision has long been recognised. In a case involving an epileptic (Decision CA 6/72) Mr Comr Lazarus QC pointed out that attention and supervision are intended to denote two separate concepts. Attention denotes a concept of some personal service of an active nature, such as helping the disabled person to wash or eat. Supervision denotes a more passive concept, such as being in the same room with the disabled person so as to be prepared to intervene if necessary, but not actually intervening save in emergencies.

In a later case (Decision 2/75) it was stated that the object of supervision is—

'to avoid substantial danger which may or may not in fact arise; so supervision may be precautionary and anticipatory, yet never result in intervention, or may be ancillary to and part of active assistance given on specific occasions to the claimant.'

These two decisions were cited with approval by Nicholls LJ in giving the judgment of the Court of Appeal in *Moran v Secretary of State for Social Services* [1987] CA Transcript 244. The question in *Moran's* case, which also involved an epileptic, was whether a person who requires assistance in the event of an attack could be said to require continual supervision *between* attacks. Not surprisingly, the answer was yes. It was not suggested that the assistance given *during* an attack was other than 'supervision' within the meaning of s 35(1)(a)(ii).

On which side of the line does the present case come? Mr Drabble urges us to hold that guiding the blind involves active intervention all the time, and should therefore be classed as attention, rather than supervision. Supervision is, he says, passive by nature, such as the supervision which parents provide for their children. But the concept of supervision is not confined to the nursery or the sick room. Young children may also require supervision in the street or when crossing a busy road, in case they get run over. So may the blind. The dangers for the blind are greater, since they may also walk into stationary obstacles, as happened most unfortunately to Mr Mallinson in the present case. But the service provided is essentially the same in both cases and both are correctly described as supervision. Mann and Nolan LJJ regarded the distinction between attention and supervision as unrealistic. But the distinction is embedded in the section itself. Of course there may be cases which could fall on either side of the line. But such cases should be left to be decided by the delegated medical practitioner as a question of fact. Mr Drabble has failed to persuade me that the delegated medical practitioner erred in law when he found, as he did in para 11, that what Mr Mallinson required was supervision when he was out in traffic, or in unfamiliar surroundings. It was a view that he was entitled to take. If that is right, then Mr Drabble concedes that Mr Mallinson cannot qualify under this head, since the supervision required was not continual throughout the day.

I turn to the second half of the argument, which assumes that what Mr Mallinson requires when walking in unfamiliar surroundings is attention, and not supervision. The question turns on the delegated medical practitioner's finding in para 6. Mr Drabble submits that Mr Mallinson requires attention in connection with his bodily function of walking, even though he only requires that attention when walking in unfamiliar surroundings, and that the delegated medical practitioner was wrong in law to find otherwise.

The meaning of 'bodily function' has been considered in two cases, in both of which it was argued that cooking for a disabled person was attention which he required in connection with his bodily functions. The first of these cases was *R v National Insurance Comr, ex p Secretary of State for Social Services* [1981] 2 All ER 738, [1981] 1 WLR 1017, commonly known as *'Packer's* case'. Forbes J at first instance appears to have held that bodily functions included 'every mode of action of which the fit body is capable at the dictate of the normal brain': see [1981] 2 All ER 738 at 740, [1981] 1 WLR 1017 at 1020. Since the intention of the section was to help maintain a particular quality of life, cooking was itself to be regarded as a bodily function.

This was clearly far too wide. The Secretary of State appealed and his appeal was allowed. The Court of Appeal held that the relevant bodily function was not cooking, but eating; and that while cutting up food for a person was sufficiently closely connected with the bodily function of eating to come within the section, cooking was not. Lord Denning MR said ([1981] 2 All ER 738 at 741, [1981] 1 WLR 1017 at 1022):

'"Bodily functions" include breathing, hearing, seeing, eating, drinking, walking, sitting, sleeping, getting in or out of bed, dressing, undressing, eliminating waste products, and the like, all of which an ordinary person, who is not suffering from any disability, does for himself.'

A little later he said:

'I would hold that ordinary domestic duties such as shopping, cooking meals, making tea or coffee, laying the table or the tray, carrying it into the room, making the bed or filling the hot water bottle, do not qualify as "attention ... in connection with [the] bodily functions" of the disabled person. But that duties that are out of the ordinary, doing for the disabled person what a normal person would do for himself, such as cutting up food, lifting the cup to the mouth, helping to dress and undress or at the toilet, all do qualify as "attention ... in connection with [the] bodily functions" of the disabled person.'

Lord Denning MR pointed out that the section had to be applied day in and day out by delegated medical practitioners all over the country. The section should, so far as possible, be applied uniformly. Dunn LJ added that, if the claimant's construction were correct, it would be necessary for the delegated medical practitioner to ascertain in each case whether the claimant usually cooked for himself, because, if he did not, the attention would not be required because of his disability.

The second case was *Woodling v Secretary of State for Social Services* [1984] 1 All ER 593, [1984] 1 WLR 348. The appellant in that case argued that *Packer's* case had been wrongly decided. The appeal was dismissed. Lord Bridge of Harwich said ([1984] 1 All ER 593 at 595–596, [1984] 1 WLR 348 at 352):

'... it is clear that the policy underlying s 35 of the 1975 Act stops short of providing an attendance allowance for all who are incapable of looking after themselves without some outside help even if that help is frequently required. Very large areas of domestic work in respect of which the disabled are necessarily dependent on others are deliberately excluded. If cooking is the one domestic chore which qualifies, it is, in a sense, the odd man out.'

Lord Bridge went on to emphasise three points ([1984] 1 All ER 593 at 596, [1984] 1 WLR 348 at 352):

'First, the disablement must be severe. Second, the phrase "bodily functions" is a restricted and precise one, narrower than, for example, "bodily needs". Third, the phrase "attention ... in connection with bodily functions", which must, I think, be read as a whole, connotes a high degree of physical intimacy between the person giving and the person receiving the attention.'

Lord Bridge quoted a sentence from a decision of Mr Commissioner Monroe (in Decision CA 60/74):

'I consider that the words of the section refer to a person who needs the relevant degree of attention in connection with the performance of his bodily functions and that they are directed primarily to those functions which the fit man normally performs for himself.'

Lord Bridge concluded:

'This criterion has the great merit of being clear and easily applied. I would find it very difficult to formulate any alternative criterion which would not give rise to difficulties in practice. This is not an additional reason for construing the section in the restricted rather than the broad sense. It is perhaps an additional ground for satisfaction in reaching the conclusion that the restricted construction is the correct one.'

It will be noticed that Lord Bridge in *Woodling*'s case and Lord Denning MR MR and Dunn LJ in *Packer's* case all stressed the need for a test which can be easily and uniformly applied.

I return to the facts of the present case. Mr Drabble argued that the relevant bodily function was walking. It was common ground that Mr Mallinson can walk without assistance. That was the finding of the examining medical officer. So if walking per se is the relevant bodily function, Mr Mallinson requires no attention. But Mr Drabble submits that walking as a bodily function includes walking in unfamiliar surroundings. If so, then walking in unfamiliar surroundings can be aggregated with cutting up food and getting in and out of the bath. By failing to take account of Mr Mallinson's need to walk in unfamiliar surroundings, the delegated medical practitioner erred in law.

I regret that I cannot agree. The distinction between 'walking' and 'walking in unfamiliar surroundings' may seem a narrow one. But it is typical of the sort of distinction which Lord Bridge had in mind when he said that bodily functions is a restricted and precise phrase, narrower than, for example, bodily needs. The point can be illustrated by referring again to the list of functions set out in Form DS4. The list does not, of course, have statutory force. But it is a helpful pointer, nonetheless, and seems to be based at least in part on Lord Denning MR's judgment in *Packer's* case. One of the functions is 'rise from usual chair'. A disabled person who is so crippled with arthritis that he cannot rise from his usual chair without assistance would in that respect require attention in connection with his bodily functions. But suppose he could rise from his usual chair, but could not rise, for example, from a deck-chair? Could rising from a deck-chair be regarded as a separate bodily function? Clearly not. As Dunn LJ and O'Connor LJ both said in *Packer's* case, the line has got to be drawn somewhere.

The same applies to 'walking in unfamiliar surroundings'. It is much too vague and imprecise to count as a separate bodily function. It would mean that the examining medical officer would have to inquire how often the disabled person needed to walk in unfamiliar surroundings, and for what purpose. Fine distinctions would spring up between one case and another, and the delegated medical practitioner's task would never be done. In my opinion Ralph Gibson LJ was right to hold that walking in unfamiliar circumstances is not a bodily function within the concept set out in the section. The only relevant bodily function (apart from getting in and out of bed and cutting up food) is walking. No doubt Mr Mallinson's enjoyment of that function is limited. But the function itself is unimpaired. The delegated medical practitioner was entitled to take the view that Mr Mallinson can walk without assistance. I can find no error of law in para 6 of his decision.

Lastly, I should mention again the alternative argument which failed in the court below. As Ralph Gibson LJ pointed out in the Court of Appeal, the case has been fought all the way up on the basis that the relevant bodily function is walking. I should be very reluctant at this stage to accept an argument that the relevant bodily function is seeing, or a combination of the two.

Blindness is, of course, the disability from which Mr Mallison suffers. But it is not enough that he requires attention by reason of that disability. He must require attention in connection with some bodily function. Is seeing then a bodily function? In one sense it is. Thus Lord Denning MR included breathing, hearing and seeing in his list of bodily functions in *Packer's* case as well as the more obvious bodily functions such as eating and drinking. But I have some difficulty in regarding hearing and seeing as bodily functions within the meaning of the section. It will be remembered that Mr Comr Monroe's test (in Decision CA 60/74), expressly approved by the House of Lords in *Woodling's* case, refers to functions which a fit man normally performs for himself. It would not be right to attach too much importance to a single word. But whereas eating, drinking, walking and washing, to take a few examples, are all bodily functions which a fit man *performs* for himself, it would not be a normal use of language to say that seeing is a function which a fit man *performs*. So even if the case had been fought on the basis that the relevant bodily function is seeing and not walking, I do not think Mr Mallinson's chances of success would have been any greater. If you were to ask a blind man's guide what his purpose was he would reply 'I am helping him walk because he cannot see'; he would not say 'I am helping him see to walk'.

For all the above reasons I would dismiss this appeal.

Appeal allowed.

Celia Fox   Barrister.

R v Clowes and another (No 2)

COURT OF APPEAL, CRIMINAL DIVISION
WATKINS LJ, SCOTT BAKER AND AULD JJ
10, 11 JUNE, 8 JULY 1993

Criminal law – Inducement to invest money – Arrangement – Purpose or pretended purpose – Scheme for investment of investors' funds in gilts – Manager of scheme having discretion to place uninvested funds elsewhere – Manager of scheme diverting funds for own use – Whether relationship between investors and manager contractual or whether akin to trust – Whether discretion to place uninvested funds elsewhere freestanding authority or merely incidental or ancillary power to place moneys temporarily pending investment or re-investment in gilts or return to investors – Whether manager of scheme dishonestly misappropriating investors' funds to his own use – Theft Act 1968, s 5.

Criminal law – Theft – Dishonesty – Direction to jury that as matter of law defendant's conduct amounted to appropriation of property – Property belonging to another – Possession or control of another – Scheme for investment of investors' funds in gilts – Manager of scheme diverting funds for own use – Trustee's money mixed with trust money of investors – Judge directing jury that as matter of law defendant's conduct amounted to appropriation of investors' funds and leaving it to jury to determine as question of fact whether defendant had acted dishonestly – Whether issue of appropriation should have been kept separate from issue of dishonesty – Whether judge correctly directing jury – Theft Act 1968, s 5.

The appellants C and N were charged with a number of offences of dishonesty, including theft and making a false statement to induce investment, following the collapse of a group of companies (the BC group) of which C was the guiding light and N his second in command in the management of the companies. The BC group marketed off-shore investment schemes, known as portfolios, for investment in gilt-edged stock and between 1983 and 1988 millions of pounds were received from investors, most of whom were induced to invest by misrepresentation that their moneys would be securely invested in gilts. Brochures issued by the BC group represented that the portfolios offered security by the investment of clients' money in gilts. The brochures stated that investors' cheques were to be made payable to the BC group's international clients account, that 'All moneys received are held in a designated clients account and the clients are the beneficial owners of all securities purchased on their behalf' and that the BC group was authorised to buy and sell British government stock on investors' behalf on a fully discretionary basis 'and to place any uninvested funds with any bank, local authority or other body on such terms and conditions as [the BC group saw] fit whether bearing interest or not'. Very little of the investors' money was used to buy gilts or kept in the designated clients account. Instead, all investors' money was mingled together in deposit accounts from which large sums were withdrawn by C for his own personal use. At their trial C and N's defence was that neither the brochures nor the portfolios contained false representations and that there was nothing dishonest about transfers of money from clients accounts to other accounts because the relationship between the BC group and each investor was not that of a trustee and beneficiary but simply that of a creditor and debtor and that, therefore, there had been no appropriation of property for the purposes of s 5ª of the Theft Act 1968. The judge ruled that C and N held the investors' funds on trust and had misappropriated the funds. C and N were both convicted of theft and C was convicted of making a false statement to induce investment. They appealed, contending, inter alia, that the BC group was not a trustee of investors' funds but beneficially entitled to them, subject only to a contractual obligation to pay the guaranteed rate of return and to pay back on demand equivalent sums to those invested, that on a proper construction of the brochures the relationship between the BC group and its investors was akin to that of a bank and depositor or creditor and debtor rather than that of trustee and beneficiary, and that the investment clause in the application form in the brochures did not limit the BC group to investing funds in gilts, but also authorised it to invest the funds by, inter alia, purchasing shares in any public or private company or by lending them to any body or person in the discretion of the BC group without restriction as to the terms of the loan and with or without security. C also appealed on the ground that the judge's disclosure to the jury of his ruling that the brochures only authorised the investment of investors' funds in gilts or the placing of money on deposit pending investment in gilts might have prejudiced the defence that C had not acted dishonestly because he believed he was entitled to use the funds without restriction, since the jury in considering that defence would have been aware that as a matter of law C had no justification for making the transfers.

Held – The appeals would be dismissed for the following reasons—

(1) It was clear from the brochures and the terms of the portfolio investments, construed as a whole, that the BC group had received funds from investors on trust to invest them in British government stocks. The BC group was not authorised to treat investors' funds as its own, since the nature of the investment scheme stated in the brochures was investment in and the management of British government securities for the purpose of capital gain and the BC group's role was to act as a trustee of funds invested with it for that purpose and for that purpose only. No other form of investment was mentioned. The power to place uninvested funds elsewhere was not an investment authority but merely an incidental or ancillary power to place any such moneys elsewhere temporarily pending investment or reinvestment in gilts or return to investors and was in any event merely a power of placement, not investment. Accordingly, the brochures constituted the BC group a trustee for investors who invested funds for the purchase and management of British government stock and, since it was admitted that if the BC group was a trustee C had dishonestly misappropriated investors' funds to his own use, C had been properly convicted of theft (see p 327 *d* to p 328 *c h j*, p 329 *d e j* to p 330 *b*, post).

(2) The legal relationship which was created between the BC group and investors when they invested moneys with it under the portfolios, which were contractual documents, was a question of law, not of fact. It was therefore open to the judge to direct the jury that as a matter of law C's conduct amounted to the appropriation of the property of the investors and then to leave it to the jury to determine as a question of fact whether he had acted dishonestly. Since the judge had kept separate the matter of appropriation, on

---

a Section 5, so far as material, is set out at p 322 *e* to *g*, post

which he had directed the jury as a matter of law, and the question of
dishonesty, which he had left for the jury to decide subjectively, ie to consider
C's own state of mind as to what he could do with the invested funds and the
legal advice he had received which was relevant to that belief, it followed that
the jury had been correctly directed (see p 330 d e h, p 331 g to j and p 333 g to
j, post); *Stephens v R* (1978) 139 CLR 315 followed.

Notes
For theft generally, see 11(1) *Halsbury's Laws* (4th edn reissue) paras 541–549,
for property belonging to another, see ibid para 548, and for cases on the
subject, see 14(2) *Digest* (2nd reissue) 258–268, *7813–7852*..
For the Theft Act 1968, s 5, see 12 *Halsbury's Statutes* (4th edn reissue) 488.

Cases referred to in judgment
Barclays Bank Ltd v Quistclose Investments Ltd [1968] 3 All ER 651, [1970] AC 567,
 [1970] 1097 WLR, HL.
Barlow Clowes International Ltd (in liq) v Vaughan [1992] 4 All ER 22, CA.
Burdick v Garrick (1870) LR 5 Ch App 233, LC and LJ.
Diplock's Estate, Re, Diplock v Wintle [1948] 2 All ER 318, [1948] Ch 465, CA.
Douglas' Wills Trusts, Re [1959] 3 All ER 785, [1959] 1 WLR 744, CA.
Foley v Hill (1848) 2 HL Cas 28, [1843–60] All ER Rep 16, 9 ER 1002.
Hallett's Estate, Re, Knatchell v Hallett (1880) 13 Ch D 696, [1874–80] All ER Rep
 793, CA.
Harari's Settlement Trusts, Re, Wordsworth v Fanshawe [1949] 1 All ER 430.
Henry v Hammond [1913] 2 KB 515.
Hunter v Moss [1993] 1 WLR 934.
Kayford Ltd, Re [1975] 1 All ER 604, [1975] 1 WLR 279.
Kolb's Will Trusts, Re [1961] 3 All ER 811, [1962] Ch 531, [1961] 3 WLR 1034.
Nanwa Gold Mines Ltd, Re [1955] 3 All ER 219, [1955] 1 WLR 1080.
Neste Oy v Lloyds Bank plc [1983] 2 Lloyd's Rep 658.
New Zealand and Australian Land Co v Watson (1881) 7 QBD 374, CA.
Oatway, Re, Hertslet v Oatway [1903] 2 Ch 356.
Prenn v Simmonds [1971] 3 All ER 237, [1971] 1 WLR 1381, HL.
R v Adams (1993) Times, 28 January, CA.
R v Ghosh [1982] 2 All ER 689, [1982] QB 1053, [1982] 3 WLR 110, CA.
R v Lightfoot (1992) Times, 3 November, CA.
R v Spens [1991] 4 All ER 421, [1991] 1 WLR 624, CA.
Ross v Lord Advocate [1986] 3 All ER 79, [1986] 1 WLR 1078, HL.
Sinclair v Brougham [1914] AC 398, [1914–1915] All ER Rep 622, HL.
Stanley, Re, Tennant v Stanley [1906] 1 Ch 131.
Stephens v R (1978) 139 CLR 315, Aust HC.
Tilley's Will Trusts, Re, Burgin v Croad [1967] 2 All ER 303, [1967] 1 Ch 1179,
 [1967] 2 WLR 1533.

Cases also cited or referred to in skeleton arguments
Andrabell Ltd (in liq), Re [1984] 3 All ER 407.
Bond Worth Ltd, Re [1979] 3 All ER 919, [1980] Ch 228.
Life Assurance Co of Australia Ltd v Phillips (1925) 36 CLR 60, Aust HC.
London Wine Co (Shippers) Ltd, Re [1986] PCC 121.
SCF Finance v Masri (No 2) [1986] 1 All ER 175, [1987] 1 QB 1002, CA.

Appeals against conviction

Peter Clowes appealed with leave of the single judge against his conviction on 10 February at the Central Criminal Court before Phillips J and a jury on ten counts of theft, for which he was sentenced on 11 February 1992 to a total of five years' imprisonment. He did not appeal against his conviction on eight counts of making a false statement to induce investment for which he was sentenced to a total of five years' imprisonment, consecutive to the sentence on the theft counts, making his total sentence ten years' imprisonment. He was also disqualified from being a company director for 15 years. His co-defendant, Peter John Naylor, appealed as of right on a point of law against his conviction on 10 February 1992 at the Central Criminal Court before Phillips J and a jury of one count of theft for which he was sentenced on 11 February 1992 to 18 months' imprisonment. The facts are set out in the judgment of the court.

Anthony Glass QC and *Francis Barlow* (instructed by *Kingsley Napley*) for the appellant Naylor.
Anthony Hacking QC and *Geoffrey Vos QC* (instructed by *Burton Copeland*, Manchester) for the appellant Clowes.
Alan Suckling QC, *Robin Hollington* and *Mark Lucraft* (instructed by the *Serious Fraud Office*) for the Crown.

Cur adv vult

8 July 1993. The following judgment of the court was delivered.

WATKINS LJ. On 10 February 1992, following a trial which lasted for 112 days in the Central Criminal Court before Phillips J, Peter John Naylor, who is 37 years of age, and Peter John Clowes, who is 50 years of age, were convicted of a number of offences of dishonesty. The next day Naylor was sentenced to 18 months' imprisonment for an offence of theft (count 11). Clowes was sentenced to an overall term of 10 years' imprisonment for 8 offences of making a false statement to induce investment (counts 2 to 9) and 10 offences of theft (counts 10 and 12 to 20). Clowes was disqualified from being a company director for the next 15 years.

Both appellants were acquitted of conspiring to contravene s 13(1) of the Prevention of Fraud (Investments) Act 1958. Naylor was also acquitted of a further three offences of theft and a number of yet further counts of theft and of conspiracy to steal were ordered to lie on the file upon the usual terms A number of other counts in the indictment affecting Clowes, alleging theft, conspiracy to steal, conspiracy to make use of false documents, conspiring to defraud and doing acts tending to pervert the course of public justice were also ordered to lie on the file upon the usual terms.

There were four co-accused. Three of them, Guy von Cramer, Christopher Frank Newman and David Campbell Mitchell, were acquitted of the charges against them, and the other, Haim Judah Michael Levy, was discharged when that part of the indictment affecting him was quashed.

Naylor appeals against conviction upon a point of law. He did not, therefore, require leave. Clowes appeals against conviction upon the counts of theft with the leave of Rattee J, and he renews his application for leave to appeal against sentence after refusal by that learned judge.

In June 1988 the Barlow Clowes companies and partnership collapsed, and soon afterwards the Securities and Investment Board closed the UK Barlow Clowes company, Barlow Clowes Gilt Managers Ltd.

The Crown alleged that the indictment against the appellants was a mirror of an investment fraud of massive proportions. Between October 1983 and May 1988 companies operated by Clowes obtained millions of pounds from investors, the vast majority of whom were induced to invest by misrepresentation that their moneys would be securely invested in gilts. In fact, very little, if any, of that money was invested in gilts. Investors' moneys were stolen and used to buy houses, farms, yachts, cars, antique furniture, a vineyard and shares in private and public companies.

At the end of 1987 the Department of Trade became alerted to the fact that a fraud on a grand scale lay within the facade of the Barlow Clowes group of companies.

There is no doubt that Clowes masterminded the activities of what became a very large organisation. He brought that into existence, operated the very involved ramifications of it and, in a most determined way, encouraged the receipt of moneys by one or more of his companies from many thousands of people who were led to believe that they would receive from their investments a return which was higher than could be expected from other investment sources in the United Kingdom. He soon gave the appearance of being a millionaire, if only because he lived like one.

Naylor joined Barlow Clowes and Partners in 1982. He very soon became Clowes's right-hand man and second in command of the Barlow Clowes group. He played an active part in the management of companies within the group and was a signatory on the principal accounts of the businesses. The group spread its wings out of the United Kingdom into Jersey, Switzerland and Gibraltar.

Barlow Clowes marketed investment schemes. They were called portfolios and were said to be based on investment in gilts. Some of the portfolios were administered in the United Kingdom, whilst others were administered off-shore. The case presented to the jury concerned off-shore portfolios, in particular Portfolios 28 and 68, which were sold mainly in the United Kingdom through intermediaries, but sometimes directly by Barlow Clowes. Some, if not all, of the administration for these portfolios was conducted either in Geneva or in Gibraltar. Moneys received from investors were paid into designated clients accounts in Jersey and other off-shore places. It was represented that the portfolios offered security, seeing that investment of clients' money was to be in gilts or cash with a high-guaranteed return which would be wholly or partly tax-free. Brochures were issued which contained the terms of the investments which gave the plain indication that each investor's cheque was to be made payable to Barlow Clowes International Clients Account and that Barlow Clowes was to be authorised to buy and sell British government stock on the investors' behalf on a fully discretionary basis. One of the terms, of very great importance, was 'and to place any uninvested funds with any bank, local authority or other body on such terms and conditions as you see fit whether bearing interest or not'. The Crown acknowledged that this term permitted Barlow Clowes to invest in things other than gilts, but only upon a temporary basis pending re-investment in gilts.

A rate of return was declared each month. It was fixed by comparing rates of other investment bodies and it was paid by money put in by other investors and not from any gains on buying and selling gilts.

From July 1985 to March 1987 the bulk of investors' funds were put into either Lloyds Bank or the Midland Bank in Jersey. From March 1987 onwards they were credited to BCI Clients Call Deposit Account and BCI Jersey Clients Call Account at Barclays Bank, Gibraltar, which were comprised wholly of clients' funds. One of the arms of Barlow Clowes in the City of London received funds by way of transfer from other client accounts. In none of the various accounts kept in the United Kingdom and overseas were individual investors' payments kept segregated. In fact, all investors' moneys were mingled together.

Misappropriation of investors' moneys from a large number of accounts took place over a considerable period of time before the responsible authorities began to realise that Barlow Clowes was operating a fraud largely for the benefit of the appellant Clowes. The convictions for theft demonstrate that at various times sums between in excess of £1m and £3·5m were being taken out of accounts supposedly holding investors' moneys securely.

Clowes' defence, generally speaking, was that neither the brochures nor the portfolios contained false representations and that he used techniques for encouraging investment which were generally well known and commonly practised. There was nothing dishonest, moreover, about transfers of money from clients accounts to other accounts for what was involved in that was payment of fees properly charged and other perfectly proper capital transfers.

Naylor took £19,000 from one of the client accounts, namely JER 54, and covered his tracks by using in computer records the name of a fictitious investor called Dr Patel. It is unnecessary to recount the machinations of Naylor in that respect. Suffice to say that the jury were persuaded that, although not in the same class as Clowes as a fraudsman, he was no mean deceiver. That £19,000 was paid into Naylor's own account and then transferred to his wife's account.

Naylor's defence was simply that the moneys he was accused of stealing he removed from the appropriate account because Clowes had agreed to pay him a bonus of £25,000, of which the £19,000 was part. Furthermore, his use of the name Dr Patel was a matter known to Clowes, who had done some such thing as that himself. Clowes denied Naylor's account of this matter.

From time to time legal argument was addressed to the trial judge who was, therefore, called upon to give rulings. Some of these have been criticised and are reflected in the grounds of appeal relied upon by Clowes. Those grounds of appeal are that the judge wrongly construed the meaning of the relevant clause in the brochures or Portfolios 28 and 68; he should have held that there was a·contractual relationship between each investor and Barlow Clowes, the relationship between investor and Barlow Clowes was not consistent with the existence of a trust; if the judge had decided that the relationship was contractual the theft counts were without foundation. The judge wrongly ruled that the authorities only permitted investment in gilts or the placing of money on deposit whilst waiting to invest in gilts, he should have held that the terms of the brochures meant that Barlow Clowes had an absolute discretion to invest with any corporation they thought fit, if he had done so there would have been no case to go to the jury that the property belonging to the investors had been stolen. Alternatively, having made the ruling, he was wrong to tell the jury what his ruling was; he ought to have said that the question of investment powers was very difficult in law, one that a layman would not necessarily be expected to have correctly decided and one that it was not necessary for them to know the answer to in order to decide the questions before them; by telling them of his ruling he removed the meaning of the relevant clause as an issue between the Crown and the defence; thus, the jury may have been prejudiced in considering the defence by knowing that, as a matter of law, Clowes had no justification for having made the transfers. The judge should have made it clear to the jury that there was room for genuine doubt as to the proper construction of the material documents. Finally, he wrongly ruled as inadmissible answers to a questionnaire of Clyde & Co which was, or may have been, very helpful to the defence.

Naylor's ground of appeal is that the judge wrongly ruled that the Crown had established an equitable charge in favour of investors sufficient to satisfy the requirements of s 5(1) of the Theft Act 1968. We shall examine Clowes's ground of appeal first.

Section 1(1) of the 1968 Act defines theft as follows:

'A person is guilty of theft if he dishonestly appropriates property belonging to another with the intention of permanently depriving the other of it ...'

Section 5(1), (2) and (3) of the 1968 Act, so far as material, provides:

'(1) Property shall be regarded as belonging to any person ... having in it any proprietary right or interest ...

(2) Where property is subject to a trust, the persons to whom it belongs shall be regarded as including any person having a right to enforce the trust, and an intention to defeat the trust shall be regarded accordingly as an intention to deprive of the property any person having that right.

(3) Where a person receives property from or on account of another, and is under an obligation to the other to retain and deal with that property or its proceeds in a particular way, the property or proceeds shall be regarded (as against him) as belonging to the other.'

The first and main issue arising from Clowes's appeal against conviction of the charges of theft is whether in each case he appropriated the property of another. It is admitted for the purpose of this appeal that if he did so, the other ingredients of the offence, in particular dishonesty, are present. If Barlow Clowes was a trustee of funds invested with it under its Portfolios 28 and 68 investment schemes, the funds remained the investors' property by virtue of s 5(1), (2) and (3) and Clowes, in diverting the funds to his own use, appropriated property belonging to another and is guilty in each case of theft. If, on the other hand, Barlow Clowes was not a trustee of those funds but beneficially entitled to them, and subject only to a contractual obligation to pay the guaranteed rate of return and to pay back on demand equivalent sums to those invested, he, as the authorised agent of Barlow Clowes, did not appropriate property belonging to another and is, therefore, not guilty of any of the charges of theft. The outstanding question in this appeal is, therefore, whether Barlow Clowes was a trustee of funds invested with it under its Portfolio 28 and Portfolio 68 investment schemes.

The answer to it is one of law and is to be determined as a matter of construction of the contract to be found in the brochure, including the application form, for each investment scheme.

At the close of the Crown's case counsel for Clowes, Mr Hacking QC, and counsel for Mr Naylor, Mr Glass QC, submitted to the judge that the charges of theft should be withdrawn from the jury. They argued that on a proper construction of the brochure the relationship between Barlow Clowes and each investor was not that of a trustee and beneficiary but simply of a creditor and debtor and that, therefore, there had been no appropriation of property. Their principal argument on the question of construction was that the investment clause in the application form in each brochure did not limit Barlow Clowes to investing funds in British government stock, but also authorised it to invest the funds in, inter alia, the purchase of shares of any public or private company or by lending it to any body or person in the discretion of Barlow Clowes without restriction as to the terms of the loan and with or without security.

The judge rejected that submission, ruling that the pre- and post-April 1986 brochure created a relationship of trustee and beneficiary between Barlow Clowes and its investors and that any authority to place moneys other than in British government stock was merely for purposes ancillary to investment in such stock. He said:

'The wording of the brochure is only consistent with an agreement on the part of Barlow Clowes to hold investors' funds in trust and to manage their funds by investment in gilt edged securities. The most significant clause is that which states: "All moneys received are held in a designated clients account and the clients are the beneficial owners of all securities purchased on their behalf." This wording is unequivocal and wholly incompatible with the defendants' case that the investors retained no proprietary interest in their money or the securities purchased with it. Also of particular significance is the investment clause in the application form itself. This has to be construed having regard to its context. It does not give Barlow Clowes a mandate to invest clients' funds in alternative investments to gilts. It authorises Barlow Clowes to buy and sell gilts on the investors' behalf—a further indication that the gilts belong beneficially to the investors. The clause goes on to deal with what Barlow Clowes are entitled to do with the investors' funds pending investment in gilts— "invested funds". The authority to place funds with the specified bodies "whether bearing interest or not" cannot be read as giving a power to make such placements by way of alternative investment to gilt edged securities. The authority is only given to make such placements as action ancillary to using the funds to buy and sell gilts. There is scope for debate as to the precise nature of the bodies with whom funds could be placed pending investment in gilts, but that question is not of relevance in the present context. What is relevant is that the wording of the investment clause and, in particular, the provision limiting Barlow Clowes's authority to buying and selling gilts on behalf of the investors, and incidental placement of the funds, reinforces the conclusion that the agreements made provision for the management by Barlow Clowes of investments in which investors would retain a beneficial proprietary interest. This conclusion is further reinforced by reference elsewhere in the brochure to

Barlow Clowes being specialists in and providing the service of
management of gilts to investors making capital investment and to
investors' returns being paid in the form of realised capital gains.'

As to the pre-May 1986 brochure and application form (for investment in
Portfolio 28), the judge held that the indications of a trust were even stronger
in that the application form contained an authority from the investor only 'to
purchase British government stock on my behalf and thereafter manage the
said stock on a fully discretionary basis'; and the brochure assured absolute
security because 'your portfolio will always be a British government stock or
cash'.

Mr Hacking, assisted in this court on Chancery aspects by Mr Vos QC,
challenged that ruling here, arguing that on a proper construction of the
brochure the relationship between Barlow Clowes and its investors was more
akin to that of a bank and depositor or creditor and debtor, than to that of
trustee and beneficiary. Such relationships are not mutually exclusive: see
Barclays Bank Ltd v Quistclose Investments Ltd [1968] 3 All ER 651, [1970] AC 567,
but where the bank is not a trustee the relevance of the distinction is that
money deposited with a bank becomes the property of the bank, and the
depositor has a personal, not a proprietary, remedy against the bank in respect
of any failure to repay an equivalent sum to that deposited: see for example
Lord Cottenham LC in *Foley v Hill* (1848) 2 HL Cas 28 at 35–37, [1843–60] All
ER Rep 16 at 18–19; and Lord Templeman at *Ross v Lord Advocate* [1986] 3 All
ER 79 at 85, [1986] 1 WLR 1077 at 1084.

Counsel for Clowes argued that the terms of the contract between Barlow
Clowes and each investor were to be found only in the application form at the
end of the brochure, not in the brochure as a whole. They submitted that the
remainder of the brochure contained, at most, non-contractual representations
to the potential investor, which could not be used as aids to construction of the
contract. They contended that the application form in the post-April 1986
brochures, read on its own, contained wide powers of investment which
should not be regarded as having been cut down by more restrictive passages
in the remaining part of the brochure. They relied in particular upon the words
immediately following the initial authorisation to Barlow Clowes to buy and
sell British government stock on the investor's behalf, namely:

> 'and to place any uninvested funds with any bank, local authority,
> corporation or other body on such terms and conditions as you see fit
> whether bearing interest or not.'

However, and somewhat inconsistently, they sought to rely on the brochure
as a whole as an aid to construction of the terms of the application form for the
purpose of showing that there was an inherent inconsistency in the nature of
the scheme as represented with one that restricted Barlow Clowes to
investment of funds placed with it in British government stock. They argued
that the representation that Barlow Clowes provided an investment service
offering capital gains from the management of British government stock was
inconsistent and made impossible by the undertakings of a guaranteed rate of
monthly return with a higher expected rate. A feature of British government
stock is that its value before maturity fluctuates and that its return, measured
against its par value, does not fluctuate, and it is not payable monthly. Counsel
submitted, therefore, that it was plain to the reader of the brochure that these

investment schemes could only work if Barlow Clowes was not limited to investment of funds in British government stocks or at least was able to mingle the individual investors' funds to ensure the return to any investor, at the expense of others, of his invested capital and to meet the individual guaranteed returns of interest.

Mr Suckling QC for the Crown argued that whether the terms of the contract are to be found in the brochure as a whole or are confined to the application form at the end of it, their effect was to make Barlow Clowes a trustee of the moneys placed with it for investment. He submitted that in fact the contract was to be found in the brochure as a whole.

On the question of the approach that the court should take in the construction of the contractual documents here, counsel for Barlow Clowes argued first that the authorities indicate an unwillingness by the courts to construe a relationship of trust in commercial transactions, and, second, that it is unusual for there to be a trust of funds where the transaction in question does not require segregation of such funds. The starting point for both of these propositions is the following passage from the judgment of Channell J in *Henry v Hammond* [1913] 2 KB 515 at 521:

'It is clear that if the terms upon which the person receives the money are that he is bound to keep it separate, either in a bank or elsewhere, and to hand that money so kept as a separate fund to the person entitled to it, then he is a trustee of that money and must hand it over to the person who is his cestui que trust. If on the other hand he is not bound to keep the money separate, but is entitled to mix it with his own money and deal with it as he pleases, and when called upon to hand over an equivalent sum of money, then, in my opinion, he is not a trustee of the money, but merely a debtor. All the authorities seem to me to be consistent with that statement of the law. I agree with the observation of Bramwell L.J. in *New Zealand and Australian Land Co. v. Watson* ((1881) 7 QBD 1053) when he said that he would be very sorry to see the intricacies and doctrines connected with trusts introduced into commercial transactions.'

Those propositions of Channell J have stood the test of time. As to commercial transactions, Bingham J applied them in *Neste Oy v Lloyds Bank plc* [1983] 2 Lloyd's Rep 658, where the issue was whether a shipowner's agent was a trustee of moneys remitted to it by the shipowner for the discharge of harbour expenses. In the course of ruling that the agent was not a trustee, he said (at 665):

'I start from a general disinclination, shared with Lord Justice Bramwell and Mr. Justice Channell, to see the intricacies and doctrines connected with trusts introduced into everyday commercial transactions. Sometimes, of course, those principles clearly apply to the commercial transactions in question.'

As to segregation of funds, the effect of the authorities seems to be that a requirement to keep moneys separate is normally an indicator that they are impressed with a trust, and that the absence of such a requirement, *if there are no other indicators of a trust,* normally negatives it. The fact that a transaction contemplates the mingling of funds is, therefore, not necessarily fatal to a trust.

Thus, in *Burdick v Garrick* (1870) LR 5 Ch App 233 an agent, who was entrusted by his principal with funds for the purchase of land or stock, was held to be a trustee of the funds and required to keep them separate from his own money: see also *Re Nanwa Gold Mines Ltd* [1955] 3 All ER 219, [1955] 1 WLR 1080 where a company which invited subscriptions for an issue of capital on terms that moneys subscribed would be held in a separate account pending issue of stock or refunding, was held to be a trustee of such moneys.

Neste Oy v Lloyds Bank is an example of a case which, on its facts, was on the other side of the line. Bingham J cited *Henry v Hammond* and a number of authorities as establishing the proposition that—

> 'where money was with the consent of the principal paid by agents into a general account containing their own funds the proper inference was that the relationship was one of debtor and creditor, not trustee and beneficiary.' (See [1993] 2 Lloyd's Rep 658 at 664.)

He went on to hold, on the facts of the case, that there was no indication of a trust, whether by way of a requirement on the agent to keep funds separate or otherwise.

However, there are other cases which demonstrate that the essential question is to determine, in all the circumstances of the transaction in question, not just the express arrangements as to how money is to be held, but whether it is held on trust: see for example *Re Kayford Ltd* [1975] 1 All ER 604, [1975] 1 WLR 279, and *Hunter v Moss* [1993] 1 WLR 934.

On the question of the claimed inconsistency of the scheme as offered and represented in the brochure with a restriction of Barlow Clowes's investment authority to British government stocks, we recognise that the discerning reader should have been alerted by it. However, it does not seem to us that the proper construction of the document is affected by what were in effect false representations as to constancy in value of investors' capital and of high-guaranteed returns, or by the fact that Barlow Clowes might have had difficulty in honouring those representations. Moreover, as Mr Suckling observed in argument, the inconsistencies relied upon disappear or lose their sharpness if the trust was to hold government stock for investors in a common fund rather than to hold particular stock on trust for each investor. In support of this observation he relied upon the decision of the Court of Appeal in *Barlow Clowes International Ltd (in liq) v Vaughan* [1992] 4 All ER 22, where the court held that the 'first in, first out' rule did not apply to Barlow Clowes investors claiming return of their respective funds since they were to be presumed in the circumstances to have intended to participate in a collective investment scheme by which their money would be mixed together and invested through a common fund. That authority has, we think, to be approached with some caution in these criminal proceedings since it was assumed for the purpose of those civil proceedings that Barlow Clowes held the invested funds on trust. In addition, Dillon LJ and Woolf LJ expressly stated that their decision had no relevance to the criminal proceedings against Clowes and others (see [1992] 4 All ER 22 at 26, 34). However the court's disclaimer was essentially with regard to the facts giving rise to the criminal proceedings. It examined with some care and was impressed by the inconsistencies of the investment schemes, if regarded as imposing an obligation to return fixed capital and to guarantee a high return to each individual investor in respect of his own individual investment. Its conclusion that what was intended was a common fund held under trust is at least highly persuasive in these proceedings, notwithstanding that it was based on an assumption or concession between the parties that Barlow Clowes was a trustee of investors' funds. Dillon LJ put his conclusion in this way ([1992] 4 All ER 22 at 30–31):

'I find the wording of the documents issued by or on behalf of BCI ambiguous in relation to the nature of the arrangements envisaged under the labels Portfolio 28 and 68. It matters not for present purposes whether the ambiguity was intentional, as a result of a fraudulent desire to confuse investors, or was merely the result of muddleheadedness and confusion in the mind of the draftsman. My conclusion is, however, that what was envisaged was some form of common fund in which all investors would in some way participate. I attach particular importance to the factor of the "expected" as well as the "guaranteed" rate of interest ...'

Woolf LJ expressed a similar view ([1992] 4 All ER 22 at 41):

'With some hesitation I have come to the conclusion that, while it is difficult on the documentation to decide whether the investments were to be made subject to a collective scheme or not, the better view is that they were.'

See also per Leggatt LJ (at 44–46).

It should be noted that the Court of Appeal, in reaching its conclusion that there was a common trust fund, construed the brochures as a whole, not just the application form. We respectfully agree with that approach. For example, para 5 of the brochure, which provides the means by which the investor may receive his income or capital growth, and para 6 of it, which provides for him to receive monthly statements of the performance of his investment, are plainly contractual terms. In our judgment, the judge was correct to regard the whole brochure in the case of each portfolio investment as a contractual document. However, we agree with Mr Suckling that even if the contract were confined to the application form alone it constituted Barlow Clowes a trustee of moneys invested pursuant to it.

As to the application form itself, we regard the following features of it as clear indicators that Barlow Clowes received investment funds on trust to *invest* them in British government stocks and was authorised to *place* any such moneys elsewhere only temporarily and pending such investment or re-investment or return to the investors. (1) It required the investor's cheque to be made payable to an account designated as a 'Client Account' of Barlow Clowes. (2) It authorised Barlow Clowes to buy and sell British government stock 'on my [ie the investor's] behalf' on a fully discretionary basis. (3) It did not expressly include in that authorisation the buying and selling of any other form of investment. (4) The ensuing words 'and to place any uninvested funds with any bank, local authority, corporation or other body on such terms and conditions as you see fit whether bearing interest or not' are distinguishable from the opening part of the authority as to buying and selling British government stock in the use of the terms 'to place' and 'uninvested funds'.

In our view, the use of these terms makes plain that the purpose of this provision was, as the judge ruled, only to authorise Barlow Clowes 'to make such placements as action ancillary to using the funds to buy and sell gilts'. The connecting word 'and' at the beginning does not, in our view, act conjunctively to add a second and almost unlimited category of investment to that of buying and selling British government stocks on the investor's behalf.

In particular, it did not authorise the lending of investors' funds to Clowes personally as a 'mini-merchant bank' to treat as his own. Apart from the broader question of construction, neither Barlow Clowes, which was a partnership, nor Clowes, was a corporate body for the purpose of the provision.

As to the remainder of the brochure, the following passages, in highlighting the nature of the investment scheme as one for investment in and the management of British government securities for the purpose of capital gain, underline the role of Barlow Clowes as a trustee of funds invested with it for that purpose and for that purpose only. Again, no other form of investment is mentioned:

'Portfolio 68 has been created by Barlow Clowes one of the leading specialists in the management of British government securities for private investors. This portfolio provides investors with a high secure income tax efficiency and access to capital at all times.

1. A High Return—Portfolio 68 is an investment service offering capital gains from the management of British government securities ...

2. Security—Security and quality of service are hallmarks of Barlow Clowes. The Group ... has become a recognised leader in the development of investment programmes based on British government stock ...'

The following passage in para 2 of the brochure, also under the heading 'Security', goes to the heart of the relationship proposed, expressly committing Barlow Clowes to placing investors' funds in a separate, 'designated', account and to treating the investors as beneficial owners, and hence Barlow Clowes as trustees, of such funds:

'All moneys received are held in a designated clients account and clients are the beneficial owners of all securities purchased on their behalf ...'

The following provision as to tax efficiency and tax-free capital gains would be of no effect unless investors' moneys were invested in British government stocks. Investment in other stocks did not attract such tax benefit:

'3. A Tax Efficient Investment—The actual return will be paid in the form of realised capital gains, without the deduction of any tax ... UK residents enjoy a personal exemption and, from 2nd July 1986, gains on gilt edged securities are free of capital gains tax.'

See also the various references in paras 4, 5 and 6 of the brochure to 'your investment', 'your capital investment', 'capital gains' and 'our management fee'.

In our judgment, the brochure as a whole, not just that part of it containing the application form, constituted the contract.

Even if the brochure as a whole were not a contractual document, the contract as contained in the application form fell to be construed by reference to it: see per Lord Wilberforce in *Prenn v Simmonds* [1971] 3 All ER 237 at 239–242, [1971] 1 WLR 1381 at 1383–1386.

The pre-May brochure and application form were, as the judge ruled, even more restrictive in form and, a fortiori, constituted Barlow Clowes a trustee for investors who invested funds before that date in the purchase and management of British government stock.

The ground of appeal involving the scope of the investment authority relates only to the post-April 1986 brochures and to counts 12 to 16 and 19 to 20 where Clowes's defence was that his use of investors' funds was within his investment authority. In the case of counts 10, 17 and 18 his defence was that he was entitled to the moneys as commission or fees. The contention is that if the judge was right to hold that Barlow Clowes was a trustee of the invested moneys, its investment authority was nevertheless not confined to the purchase of British government stocks. Counsel on behalf of Clowes have submitted that the judge was wrong so to construe the contract. They maintained that the judge has incorrectly treated the term 'uninvested funds' in the application form as meaning that Barlow Clowes could only place such funds elsewhere temporarily while waiting to invest in British government stocks. They submitted that when the two parts of the authority in the application form are read together it is clear that it gave Barlow Clowes authority to invest in British government stocks or in any body on such terms as it saw fit. In formulating the argument in that way, counsel have themselves misstated the effect of the authority. As we have already pointed out, its scheme is to authorise Barlow Clowes 'to buy and sell', ie invest in, British government stocks on behalf of the investor and 'to place', not to invest, 'any uninvested funds' elsewhere.

An important part in our reasoning thus far is that Barlow Clowes received investment funds for the specific purpose of purchasing British government stock and that the judge was correct in construing the authority as entitling the placement of funds elsewhere only temporarily and as incidental or ancillary to investment in such stock.

However, counsel for Clowes pointed for the liberal interpretation now given to trustees' powers of investment. They have referred us to a passage to that effect in *Snell's Principles of Equity* (29th edn, 1990) p 225, and have cited as examples of that approach *Re Harari's Settlement Trusts* [1949] 1 All ER 430 per Jenkins J, *Re Douglas' Will Trusts* [1959] 3 All ER 785, [1959] 1 WLR 744 per Vaisey J, *Re Kolb's Will Trusts* [1961] 3 All ER 811, [1962] 1 Ch 531 per Cross J and ss 1(3) and 3(1) of the Trustee Investments Act 1961, which widened the investment powers of trustees.

In support of their contention for a broader interpretation than that of limiting the investment authority to British government stocks, counsel for Clowes focused on the words 'corporation or any other body' in the second part of the authority in the application 'and to place any uninvested funds with any bank, local authority, corporation or other body on such terms and conditions as you see fit . . .' Their submission was that those words were wide enough to encompass any incorporated body, including those companies in which Barlow Clowes used the moneys to buy shares (as in the transactions the subjects of counts 13 to 16), and any unincorporated body such as the partnership of Barlow Clowes itself.

In so submitting, they also relied upon an indication of Buckley J in *Re Stanley* [1905] 1 Ch 131, in construing an investment clause referring to 'any corporation or company', that the two terms were indistinguishable. They also referred to definitions of the word 'corporation' in *Words and Phrases Legally Defined* (3rd edn, 1988) vol 1, pp 353–354.

In our view, the words 'corporation or other body' in the second part of the post-April 1986 authority cannot be construed under a spotlight in this way. They have to be considered in the context of the whole authority which, as we have said, makes plain that its sole purpose was for the investment of funds in British government stocks with authority, as ancillary to that purpose to place any uninvested funds temporarily elsewhere. The purchase of shares in companies fits neither the nature of investment authorised nor the ancillary function of temporary placement of uninvested funds. In our judgment, this ground of appeal also fails.

We now turn to the issue of dishonesty. It was said that the judge should not have directed the jury as a matter of law that Barlow Clowes held the invested moneys on trust, but should have left it to the jury to determine whether a reasonable and honest person could reasonably have thought that there was no trust. We are told that counsel for Clowes did not suggest to the judge that he should not so direct the jury in the course of his summing up. We are also told that the judge, before doing so, submitted the passages of his proposed direction to all counsel for comment, and that counsel for the appellants did not object.

Counsel for Clowes, in argument, elaborated upon this complaint in the following way. They said that Clowes's belief in his entitlement to use the invested moneys in a variety of ways was fundamental to his defence and that the judge prejudiced that defence by directing the jury that he was not, in law, entitled to use the moneys in that way.

In our judgment, this submission is unsound. It was a question of law, not a question of fact, what legal relationship was created between Barlow Clowes and its investors when they invested moneys with it under its Portfolios 28 and 68 investment schemes: see for example *Stephens v R* (1978) 139 CLR 315, a decision of the High Court of Australia, in particular the judgment of Barwick CJ (at 322), cited with approval by Watkins LJ, giving the judgment of the court, in *R v Spens* [1991] 4 All ER 421, [1991] 1 WLR 624 at 632, a criminal case concerning the construction of the City Code on Take-Overs and Mergers. In *R v Spens* the Court of Appeal held that the construction of a contractual document is a matter of law for the judge, not a question of fact for the jury, to decide. Watkins LJ said ([1991] 4 All ER 421 at 428, [1991] 1 WLR 624 at 632):

'... the construction of documents in the general sense is a matter of fact for determination by the jury. From that generality there must of course be excluded binding agreements between one party and another and all forms of parliamentary and local government legislation, in respect of which the process of construction by the judge is indispensable.'

Here, the answer to the question of law whether Barlow Clowes was a trustee of the invested funds depended on one, but only one, of the constituents of each charge of theft against Clowes, namely whether he had appropriated property belonging to another. The central question of fact for the jury was whether, in dealing with funds in such a way that in law amounted to appropriating investors' funds, he acted dishonestly.

Now in one sense it might be argued that whether he was dishonest depended upon whether he knew that in law he was a trustee of the investors' funds and had appropriated their funds. Where, as here, the question of law was open to argument among lawyers it could have been very difficult, if not impossible, to make a jury sure that Clowes, a layman, had reached such a conclusion of law.

However, dishonesty is an ingredient of many offences and does not necessarily depend upon a correct understanding by an accused of all the legal implications of the particular offence with which he is charged. The test is that laid down by this court in *R v Ghosh* [1982] 2 All ER 689, [1982] QB 1053, namely whether the accused was acting dishonestly by the standards of ordinary and decent people and, if so, whether he himself must have realised that what he was doing was, by those standards, dishonest.

In the recent case of *R v Lightfoot* (1992) Times, 3 November this court emphasised the clear distinction between an accused's knowledge of the law and his appreciation that he was doing something which, by the ordinary standards of reasonable and honest people, would be regarded as dishonest. The fact that he did not know what was criminal and what was not or that he did not understand the relevant principles of the civil law could not save him from conviction if what he did, coupled with his state of mind, satisfied the elements of the crime of which he was accused.

In the Australian case of *Stephens v R*, a case of criminal conversion, the issue for the jury was very similar to that before the jury here, namely whether there had been an 'entrusting' of money to the appellant. Jacobs J distinguished between the judicial task of deciding the legal effect of the transaction and the factual task for the jury in deciding fraud or dishonesty. He said (1978) 139 CLR 315 at 336–337):

'... once it was established that the moneys the subject of the charge were paid pursuant to the terms of the written contract the question whether or not there was an "entrusting" depended upon the construction of that written contract. This was a question of law for the presiding judge. However, this does not mean that guilt or innocence turned substantially upon the construction of an obscurely worded instrument. The real question for the jury was whether the applicant had fraudulently converted the money. For him to be guilty of fraud knowledge that he was not entitled to treat the money as his own was a necessary element. The jury clearly found that he had the knowledge and belief. He would not have been guilty of fraudulent conversion if he had not had that knowledge and belief but once it is held that in law he was entrusted with the moneys and it having been found that in fact he knew and believed that this was so the offence was duly proved to have been committed.'

Counsel for Clowes sought to distinguish *R v Spens* [1991] 4 All ER 421, [1991] 1 WLR 624. They submitted, in reliance on *R v Adams* (1993) Times, 28 January, a decision of this court, that where the meaning of a contractual document is central to the question of guilt or innocence it is a matter for construction by the jury. This line of argument is misconceived for two reasons: first because *R v Adams* concerned an alleged false representation in an application to hire a car, not, as here, the meaning and legal consequence of a contractual document; and second, because the construction of the contractual document here, though critical to establishing one of the ingredients of theft, was not central to the issue which the judge left to the jury, namely whether Clowes had been dishonest. The two issues were quite distinct and, as will appear, the judge kept them distinct.

It was for the judge to direct the jury as a matter of law, as he did, that Clowes's conduct amounted to the appropriation of the property of the investors, and for the jury to determine as a question of fact whether, whatever his own legal interpretation of the relationship between Barlow Clowes and its investors, he was acting dishonestly.

The judge first referred to the issue of dishonesty towards the beginning of his summing up in his directions on the law as to the constituents of the various charges of theft in the indictment. He gave them the classic *Ghosh* direction in the following passage:

'... The first hurdle that the prosecution have to cross in proving that a defendant was dishonest is to satisfy you that the defendant knew that the funds he was helping to transfer were in whole or in part investors' funds. That is funds sent in to Barlow Clowes by investors in P28 or P68. If the prosecution get over that hurdle, they then have to satisfy you that the defendant knew that the investors' funds were being transferred in a way that according to the ordinary standards of reasonable and honest people was dishonest and that the defendant was aware of this. If the prosecution satisfy you of both those matters, then it will [be] open to you to conclude that the defendant was acting dishonestly. Let me just illustrate how that works in the case of the defendants. Mr Clowes has told you that he knew about and authorised most of the transfers. He has told you that he knew that the funds had come from investors in P28 and P68. So, in his case the prosecution have no difficulty in getting over their first hurdle.'

It is plain that, in his reference in this passage to 'investors' funds' and in his description of them as 'funds sent in to Barlow Clowes by investors in P28 and P68', the judge was not inviting the jury to approach the question of dishonesty by first forming a view as to Clowes's state of knowledge as to the beneficial ownership of the funds. That is also plain from the way in which the judge continued with his illustration:

'But Mr Clowes has told you that he believed that each transfer that he authorised was a proper transfer. He has told you that he believed that the contracts authorised him to take over the funds as a mini merchant bank and invest them as he pleased. In some cases he has told you that he believed he was personally entitled to the funds transferred as commission. If Mr Clowes genuinely held these beliefs, he was not dishonest in authorising the transfers and he was not guilty of theft. You are not guilty of theft if you take someone else's property in the mistaken belief that he has authorised you to do so. It is not for Mr Clowes to satisfy you that he believed he was entitled to make transfers. It is for the prosecution to satisfy you that he had no such belief.'

The judge first referred to his ruling on the issue of appropriation while dealing with the allegations in counts 1 to 9 that the brochures were misleading so as to contravene s 13(1) of the Prevention of Fraud (Investments) Act 1958. He said:

'Mr Clowes told you that he believed that [the post-April 1986] investment clause entitled him to use investor's money in the way that he did. I have ruled that, as a matter of law, it did not. But what that clause did or did not permit as a matter of law is not the question that you have to consider when looking at counts 2 to 9.'

He returned to the matter again at the start of his treatment of the respective cases of the Crown and the defence on the counts of theft, though he did so only shortly and in the course of his direction on the issue of dishonesty. He said:

'The important question you are going to have to consider so far as Mr Clowes is concerned in relation to each count is: did he act dishonestly in procuring the transfer in question? ... You can only convict Mr Clowes of theft if you are sure he knew very well he could not use investors' funds in the way that he did. How do you decide that question? How do you decide what Mr Clowes believed he was entitled to do? Well, the starting point, I suggest, is to consider precisely what it was that Mr Clowes said he thought he was entitled to do and why and ask yourselves how likely is it that any reasonable intelligent businessman could hold such a belief. The second stage is to examine how Mr Clowes behaved—what he said and did—and see whether that is the behaviour of a man who honestly held the belief that Mr Clowes says he did. What was it that Mr Clowes said he was entitled to do with investors' money? He recognised, did he not, that what he was entitled to do with the money depended upon the legal effect of the brochures, depended on the legal contracts spelt out in the brochures? *I have told you what the legal effect was—the contracts required Barlow Clowes to use investors' money to buy and sell gilts. The investors would own the gilts and the investors would be entitled to any gains made by buying and selling the gilts. In between selling and buying the gilts, Barlow Clowes could hold the investors' funds on deposit but only as an incidental step to dealing in gilts.* What was it Mr Clowes said he thought the contracts entitled Barlow Clowes to do? He said they entitled Barlow Clowes to take a policy decision not to buy any gilts at all, but to place the investors' money permanently on deposit ... His evidence was, I think, that [the post-April 1986 wider investment clause] was put in to remove any possible doubt as to the right of Barlow Clowes to lend investors' money and to lend it to himself. *I have told you that as a matter of law that wider investment clause did not confer on Barlow Clowes any such right.* The question you have to consider is whether it is possible that Mr Clowes honestly believed that this clause entitled him to use investors' money for the purpose of his investment policy.' (Our emphasis.)

In our judgment, the judge, in these passages kept quite separate the matter of appropriation, upon which he had directed them as a matter of law, and the question of dishonesty which he left for them to decide in accordance with his direction based on *Ghosh*. The jury can have been in no doubt that the central question for it on the counts of theft was one of dishonesty and that the answer to that question did not depend upon who was the beneficial owner of the invested funds or the ambit of the investment authority or on the judge's ruling on those matters in the trial.

Counsel for Clowes suggested that even if the judge was entitled to direct the jury as to the effect in law of the brochures, he did so in such a way as to undermine Clowes's case as to his understanding of what they entitled him to do with the invested moneys. In our view, it is plain from the passages from the judge's summing up that we have set out that there is no substance in this complaint. As we have already said, he kept the two issues distinct and did not suggest that they should decide the question of dishonesty against Clowes on the basis of his, the judge's, interpretation of the contracts. He properly and accurately directed the jury how they should approach the question of dishonesty. As to the subjective part of the test, he directed them carefully to consider Clowes's own state of mind as to what he could do with the invested funds and the legal advice that he had received which was relevant to that belief.

We must now deal with the Clyde & Co questionnaire. The judge's refusal to permit to be put in evidence before the jury the response to a questionnaire sent by Clyde & Co, solicitors for the Department of Trade acting on their behalf in civil proceedings against Barlow Clowes, is the subject of complaint. Question 42 of that questionnaire read:

'What advice, if any, did your financial advisor provide as to the extent of Barlow Clowes's discretion to invest your money? [In some portfolios, Barlow Clowes had a discretion to place money in any body they chose and not simply in government gilt-edged stocks.]'

Counsel for Clowes submitted to the judge that the fact that Clyde & Co, as solicitors, had expressed in that question the view that Barlow Clowes had not been confined to investing funds in government stocks was relevant to the objective part of the *Ghosh* test for the jury's decision, namely whether a reasonable person could have held that belief. The judge refused to admit the evidence, saying that the issue of the legal effect of the documents was a matter of law for him and that the opinion of another lawyer on that issue was not, therefore, admissible as a matter of evidence.

Counsel for Clowes now argue that, in the light of the objective part of the *Ghosh* direction that the judge later gave to the jury in his summing-up, for example, whether 'any reasonable intelligent businessman' could have believed that he was contractually entitled to act as he did, his refusal to admit that evidence was wrong.

In our view, that submission is misconceived. As counsel for the Crown observed in their skeleton argument, the issue for the jury was the state of mind of Clowes at the time of the alleged thefts. The evidence of a lawyer of his understanding of the investment powers of Barlow Clowes would have been relevant and admissible, albeit not in the form of a questionnaire, if he had so advised Clowes at the time of the transactions in question. However, the understanding of a lawyer drafting a questionnaire after the events, which may or may not have been a considered or reasonable view of the matter, could not assist the jury, and certainly not in the form of the questionnaire. In any event, the understanding of the draftsman of the questionnaire as to Clowes's investment powers clearly did not extend to his lending investors' funds to himself. Further, regardless of Clowes's exact views as to his investment powers, there was overwhelming evidence before the jury that he did not honestly believe that he was entitled to make the transfers, the subjects of the charges of theft. Accordingly, we also reject this ground of appeal. The appeal of Clowes against conviction therefore fails.

We now proceed to examine the appeal of Naylor. Put precisely, the accusation against him, count 11, was that on 17 April 1985 he stole a chose in action, namely a debt constituted by a credit in the sum of £19,000 held upon an account in the name of Barlow Clowes and Partners Funding Clients Premium Deposit Account at the Midland Bank, Threadneedle Street belonging to the clients of Peter Clowes trading as Barlow Clowes and Partners.

For the purposes of this appeal, Mr Glass, who was assisted upon Chancery aspects in this court by Mr Barlow, did not dispute that Naylor had acted dishonestly.

JER 54 was a mixed account, consisting in part of money contributed by clients of Barlow Clowes (the investors' funds) and in part of money coming from other sources (the non-investors' funds). It was common ground at the trial that the non-investors' funds were funds belonging to Barlow Clowes. The distinction between count 11 and other counts was that at the time Naylor withdrew the £19,000 from JER 54 the non-investors' funds exceeded £19,000. It was submitted on behalf of Naylor that the £19,000 withdrawn by him was not, in the circumstances, property belonging to clients of Barlow Clowes but to Barlow Clowes itself and that Naylor could not, therefore, be guilty of the offence with which he was charged.

In the course of his ruling the judge referred to *Chitty on Contracts* (26th edn, 1990) para 2093, p 1370 where it is stated:

'*Identifying property in equity*. Equity may trace property beyond "the verge of actual identification" [*Sinclair v Brougham* [1914] AC 398 at 459, [1914–1915] All ER Rep 622 at 652] into any specific asset purchased with it, or into a bank account even when it is mixed with other moneys; "... equity regarded the amalgam as capable, in proper circumstances, of being resolved into its component parts." [See *Re Diplock's Estate, Diplock v Wintle* [1948] 2 All ER 318 at 346, [1948] Ch 465 at 520, CA.] Accordingly, if the trustee mixes his own money with the trust money, the beneficiary can claim a first charge on the mixed fund, or on any asset purchased with the mixed fund. If the trustee mixes the trust funds of two separate trusts, there is an equal equity in each beneficiary, so that the separate beneficiaries can trace and share *pari passu*, or enjoy *pari passu* any equitable lien or charge on an asset purchased with the mixed fund. (Any equitable charge may be enforced ultimately by sale of the assets.) If the trust money is received by a volunteer who then mixes it with his own money, the beneficiary may again trace the property, claiming a declaration of charge if necessary, but he must share the fund (or any asset purchased therewith) *pari passu* with the volunteer.'

Having referred to the principal authorities in support of that passage he then continued:

'It follows on the application of these principles, that investors had equitable interests in both the accounts and the withdrawals made from those accounts. Those interests, in my judgment, constituted proprietary rights or interests within s 5(1) of the Theft Act 1968. Difficult problems arise in practice in identifying which investors had interests in which accounts, and the extent of their interests, but those are problems for the civil court, not the criminal court. The prosecution have to prove simply that investors had an interest in the relevant funds. They do not have to identify those investors. I was at one time concerned with whether the complex rules of equity as to tracing might, on the evidence adduced by the prosecution, leave open the possibility that the withdrawal alleged to have been made by Dr Naylor, which forms the subject matter of count 11, could be deemed to be withdrawal exclusively of non-investors' funds in which investors had no equitable interest. I am satisfied, however, having particular regard to the case of *Re Oatway* [1903] 2 Ch 356, that if the prosecution establishes that Dr Naylor dishonestly made the withdrawal in question the withdrawal will have been subject to an equitable charge in favour of investors which constituted a sufficient interest on their part to satisfy s 5(1) of the Theft Act 1968.'

On the 68th day of the trial counsel for the Crown, foreseeing an argument that if the £19,000 belonged to Barlow Clowes rather than the investors, Naylor would not be guilty of the offence as charged, applied for leave to amend count 11 to allege ownership in the alternative. Mr Glass opposed the amendment and the judge refused to allow it. His reason was that the whole thrust of the Crown's case had throughout been that Naylor and Clowes were acting in unison in stealing investors' money.

We can see why the judge took this view but he might well have allowed the amendment which would have caused no prejudice to Naylor, and thereby avoided the issue that has arisen on this count.

Mr Glass advanced an interesting argument based on the decision in *Re Hallett's Estates* (1880) 13 Ch D 696, [1874–80] All ER Rep 793 contending that where, as here, a trustee adds his own money to an account containing trust money and makes a withdrawal from that account for his own purposes he is deemed to draw out his own money first leaving the trust money intact. This authority, he contended, rather than *Oatway*, which was relied on by the judge, was to be followed in the present case.

In our view, however, there is much force in Mr Suckling's response that *Hallett* and *Oatway* and similar cases are concerned with tracing assets and the enforcement of beneficiaries and interests. They illustrate that equity assists a beneficiary against a defaulting trustee. As Ungoed-Thomas J pointed out in *Re Tilley's Will Trusts* [1967] 2 All ER 303 at 306, [1967] 1 Ch 1179 at 1183C, if a trustee mixes trust assets with his own, the onus is on the trustee to distinguish the separate assets, and to the extent that he fails to do so they belong to the trust. In the present case the court is concerned not with tracing assets and the enforcement of beneficial interests but with the meaning of s 5(1) of the 1968 Act.

Where a trustee mixes trust money with his own, as was the case with the money in account JER 54, the beneficiaries are entitled to a first charge on the mixed fund: see *Snell's Principles of Equity* (29th edn, 1990) p 303 and the passage from *Chitty on Contracts* that was cited by the judge in his ruling. Thus at the moment Naylor removed the £19,000 he was taking something in which the investors had an equitable interest. What was taken falls in our view four square within the definition of property belonging to another under s 5(1) of the 1968 Act. The judge's ruling at the close of the Crown case was correct and, because Naylor took the money dishonestly, he was guilty of theft. His appeal also against conviction fails.

Appeals dismissed.

Kate O'Hanlon   Barrister.

Target Holdings Ltd v Redferns (a firm) and another

COURT OF APPEAL, CIVIL DIVISION
RALPH GIBSON, HIRST AND PETER GIBSON LJJ
14, 15 OCTOBER, 8 NOVEMBER 1993

Trust and trustee – Breach – Payment of trust moneys to stranger – Compensation for breach – Trustee's duty to make immediate restitution of loss to trust estate subject only to giving credit for benefit subsequently received from trustee's actions – Solicitor acting for mortgagor and mortgagee releasing mortgage moneys without authority before mortgage security executed – Mortgage security executed some days later – Whether solicitor in breach of trust – Whether solicitor under immediate duty to make restitution of mortgage moneys subject to mortgagee giving credit for moneys recovered from sale of property.

A company, C Ltd, incorporated by the defendant solicitors for clients of the defendants, agreed to purchase two properties for £775,000 and then approached the plaintiffs for a loan of £1,525,000 to be secured by a mortgage on the properties. The 'estimated value/purchase price' of the properties was stated to be £2m, having been valued at that figure, allegedly negligently, by a firm of estate agents. The plaintiffs were not informed that the properties were being purchased for £775,000. The defendants' clients had in the meantime acquired another company, P Ltd, through the defendants and it was proposed that P Ltd would purchase the properties from the vendor for £775,000, that P Ltd would sell the properties on to K Ltd, another company owned by the clients, for £1.25m and that K Ltd would sell it on to C Ltd for £2m. In that way the purchase price would be uplifted from the original £775,000 to the £2m 'estimated value/purchase price'. The plaintiffs approved the loan of £1,525,000 and made a mortgage offer of that amount to C Ltd. The plaintiffs also instructed the defendants to act for them as the mortgagees in the transaction. Prior to completion the plaintiffs paid the £1,525,000 to the defendants, who before completion paid the moneys, less fees and stamp duty, to P Ltd and K Ltd. The defendants then notified the plaintiffs that the purchase and the plaintiffs' charge had been completed although those transactions had not at that stage taken place. Some days later the defendants' clients arranged for £775,000 to be paid to the vendor of the properties and the various transfers and the plaintiffs' charge were in fact completed. The balance of the loan advanced by the plaintiffs was to the knowledge of the defendants retained by K Ltd. The plaintiffs subsequently repossessed the properties and entered into a contract to sell them for £500,000. The plaintiffs brought an action against the defendants for breach of trust. In proceedings for summary judgment the defendants accepted that they had received the loan moneys from the plaintiffs as agents for the plaintiffs and until authorised by the plaintiffs to release the moneys they held them on trust for the plaintiffs and that they had committed a breach of trust when they transferred the moneys to P Ltd and K Ltd before the contract for the purchase of the properties by C Ltd and the mortgage were executed but claimed that the breach of trust was technical only and the plaintiffs had not suffered any loss because the defendants had obtained the mortgages to which the plaintiffs were entitled.

The judge gave the defendants leave to defend upon condition that they made interim payment of £1m to the plaintiffs. The defendants appealed to the Court of Appeal, contending that since the plaintiffs had suffered no loss as a result of the breach of trust they were entitled to unconditional leave to defend and no interim payment should have been ordered. The plaintiffs cross-appealed on the ground that the judge should have given final judgment on the claim for breach of trust.

Held (Ralph Gibson LJ dissenting) – The obligation of a trustee who had committed a breach of trust was to put the trust fund in the same position as it would have been if no breach had taken place and where the breach consisted in the wrongful paying away of trust moneys to a stranger so that there was an immediate loss it was not necessary that there should be an inquiry as to whether the loss would have happened if there had been no breach, since there was an obvious causal connection. The remedy afforded to the beneficiary by equity was compensation in the form of restitution of that which had been lost to the trust estate and the trustee's duty to make immediate restitution was qualified only by the requirement that a beneficiary who subsequent to the loss received a benefit from the trustee's actions should give credit for that benefit. The release of the mortgage moneys by the defendants to persons not authorised by the plaintiffs constituted a breach of trust for which the defendants were under an immediate duty to make restitution, subject only to the plaintiffs giving credit for moneys recovered from the sale of the properties. Accordingly the appeal would be dismissed and the cross-appeal allowed (see p 348 j to p 349 a, p 350 b c, p 351 b f g, p 353 g to j and p 354 a, post).

Bishopsgate Investment Management Ltd (in liq) v Maxwell (No 2) [1994] 1 All ER 261 applied.

Re Dawson (decd), Union Fidelity Trustee Co Ltd v Perpetual Trustee Co Ltd [1966] 2 NSWR 211 considered.

Notes

For the exercise of the powers of trustees generally, see 48 *Halsbury's Laws* (4th edn) paras 837–840, and for the extent of liability for breach of trust, see ibid paras 951, 954, and for cases on the subject, see 48 *Digest* (Reissue) 657–661, 6044–6072.

Cases referred to in judgments

Adamson, Ex p, re Collie (1878) 8 Ch D 807, CA.
Alliance and Leicester Building Society v Edgestop Ltd (18 January 1991, unreported), Ch D.
Bartlett v Barclays Bank Trust Co Ltd (No 2) [1980] 2 All ER 92, [1980] Ch 515, [1980] 2 WLR 430.
Bishopsgate Investment Management Ltd (in liq) v Maxwell (No 2) [1994] 1 All ER 261, CA; affg [1993] BCLC 814.
Caffrey v Darby (1801) 6 Ves 488, [1775–1802] All ER Rep 507, 31 ER 1159.
Canson Enterprises Ltd v Boughton & Co (1991) 85 DLR (4th) 129, Can SC.
Clough v Bond (1838) 3 My & Cr 490, 40 ER 1016, LC.
Dawson (decd), Re, Union Fidelity Trustee Co Ltd v Perpetual Trustee Co Ltd [1966] 2 NSWR 211, NSW SC.
Miller's Deed Trusts, Re [1978] LS Gaz 454.

Nestle v National Westminster Bank plc [1994] 1 All ER 118, [1993] 1 WLR 1260, CA.
Nocton v Lord Ashburton [1914] AC 932, [1914–15] All ER Rep 45, HL.

Case also cited
British and Commonwealth Holdings plc v Quadrex Holdings Inc [1989] 3 All ER 492, [1989] QB 842, CA.

Interlocutory appeal
The first defendants, Redferns, a firm of solicitors, appealed from that part of the order of Warner J made on 30 November 1992 in an action brought by the plaintiffs, Target Holdings Ltd, against the first defendants and the second defendants, Alexander Stevens & Co Ltd (trading as Alexander Stevens Druce), on the hearing of a motion for summary judgment, whereby the judge gave leave to the first defendant to defend the plaintiffs' claim for breach of trust on condition that the first defendants pay the sum of £1m by way of interim payment to the plaintiffs. By a respondent's notice dated 8 January 1993 the plaintiffs cross-appealed from the judge's order in so far as it was not an order for final judgment. The facts are set out in the judgment of Ralph Gibson LJ

Anthony Mann QC and *Grant Crawford* (instructed by *Wansbroughs Willey Hargrave*) for the appellants.
Nicholas Patten QC and *Thomas Leech* (instructed by *Rosling King*) for the respondents.
The second defendants were not represented.

Cur adv vult

8 November 1993. The following judgments were delivered.

RALPH GIBSON LJ. This an appeal by Redferns, a firm of solicitors, who are the first defendants in an action brought by Target Holdings Ltd (Target), against the order of Warner J made on 30 November 1992 in Ord 14 proceedings. The order made was that Redferns have leave to defend Target's claim against them for breach of trust upon condition that Redferns bring into court the sum of £1m on or before 17 December 1992. Upon provision of a guarantee for repayment of the £1m, if such repayment should be ordered by the court, the sum of £1m was to be paid to Target as an interim payment. As to the claim by Target against Redferns for damages for professional negligence, there was an order for unconditional leave to defend.

In brief summary, Target's case is that in June 1989 a mortgage fraud was carried out against Target by Mr Ajit Kohli and Mr Baboo Musafir in the acquisition by Crowngate Developments Ltd (Crowngate) of 60–64 Great Hampton Street, Hockley, Birmingham (the properties). Redferns, by Mr Bundy, a senior partner, were instructed by Kohli and Musafir on 12 May 1989 to act in the purchase of the properties. The vendor was Mirage Properties Ltd (Mirage). Mirage was to be paid £775,000. The sale was to be effected through a Jersey company, Panther Ltd, incorporated on the instructions of Kohli and Musafir. Crowngate applied to Target for loans in the amount of £1,694,000 for the purchase of the property on the basis of valuations of the properties in the total sum of £2m, the price which Redferns were told by Mr Kohli was to be paid by Crowngate. In addition to Panther Ltd, there was another

intermediate purchaser, namely Kohli & Co Ltd, a company controlled by Mr
Kohli. Redferns were also instructed to act for Target.

The valuations were provided by Alexander Stevens & Co Ltd, estate agents
of Birmingham, the second defendants. Target has obtained judgment in
default against the second defendants, who are in liquidation. Little, if
anything, will be recovered from them.

Warner J stated the facts on which Target's claims are based. I set out his
account substantially in his words.

(i) Until 30 June 1989 the property was owned by Mirage. Mirage was
registered as proprietor of it under two titles, one of which comprised nos 61–
63 Great Hampton Street and part of the other which comprised nos 60–64. On
or about 15 May 1989 Mirage agreed, subject to contract, to sell the property to
Crowngate at the price of £775,000. On that day the draft contract for that sale
was sent by Mirage's solicitors, Edge & Ellison of Birmingham, to Redferns. It
was received by Redferns on 17 May. By that time Mr Bundy had put in train
the acquisition of Panther through agents in Jersey, Reeds Ltd. Reeds were
told that the beneficial owner of Panther would be a Mrs Jasdeep Chadha with
an address in New Jersey. On 24 May 1989 Mr Bundy wrote to Mr Kohli saying
that 'the vehicle' for the acquisition of the property, namely Panther, was now
available to trade.

(ii) On 9 June 1989 Target received two completed loan application forms
signed by Mr Kohli on behalf of Crowngate. One was an application for a loan
of £990,000 on the security of 60–63 Great Hampton Street, of which 'the
estimated value/purchase price' was stated to be £1·2m. The other was an
application for a loan of £704,000, later amended to £716,000, on the security of
64 Great Hampton Street, of which 'the estimated value/purchase price' was
stated to be £800,000. In each application, Crowngate was stated to be
purchasing the property in question and in each its solicitors were stated to be
Redferns, Mr Bundy. In each, a box in which particulars of the vendor were to
be given was struck through. The applications referred to, and were
accompanied by, valuations dated 9 June 1989 of nos 60–63 Great Hampton
Street at £1·2m and no 64 at £800,000. The valuations were by Alexander
Stephens Druce, the second defendants. Those valuations were expressed to
be made for Target and are alleged by Target to have been negligent. The way
in which the loan applications and the valuations divided the property between
60–63 Great Hampton Street on the one hand, and 64 on the other, did not
exactly correspond to the way in which the title to the property was divided on
the register. At all events, the loan applications and valuations showed an
aggregate estimated value and purchase price of £2m.

(iii) On 15 June 1989 Target approved each loan, knowing nothing of the
agreement for sale by Mirage to Crowngate at £775,000. On 21 June 1989
Target wrote two letters to Mr Bundy, one in respect of each loan, asking him
to act for Target in the matter. With each letter Target enclosed copies of the
relevant loan application and valuation and of its own mortgage offer and
standard mortgage deed. In each mortgage offer, there was mention of the
'Stated purchase price: £1,200,000' in one case, '£800,000' in the other. In its
letters Target said that it proposed to take a first charge on the property
concerned. Those letters were received by Redferns on 23 June 1989, and on
that day Mr Quinn of Redferns wrote two letters to Target implicitly accepting
its instructions and reporting on various points. In particular he mentioned the
way in which the title to the property was divided and asked Target to confirm

that this would not affect the amount to be borrowed in respect of each part of the property. He did not mention the purchase price of £775,000. In the meantime—Mr Bundy says that it was on 21 June 1989—Mr Kohli instructed Mr Bundy that Panther, having purchased the property from Mirage for £775,000, was to sell it on to Kohli & Co for £1·25 m and that Kohli & Co was in its turn to sell it on to Crowngate for £2m.

(iv) On 28 June 1989, pursuant to a request made by Mr Bundy by fax the previous day, Target transferred to Redferns' client account sums of £885,000 and £640,000 making a total of £1,525,000. Those sums represented the net amount of the two loans after deduction of certain premiums. Target gave no express instructions to Redferns as to the release of those sums.

(v) On 29 June 1989 Mr Bundy transferred the sum of £1·25m from Redferns' client account to a banking account in Jersey which had been opened for Panther by Reeds on Mr Bundy's instructions. Mr Bundy saw that sum as representing the price payable by Kohli & Co to Panther and as part of the price of £2m payable by Crowngate to Kohli & Co.

(vi) On 30 June 1989 contracts were exchanged between Mirage and Panther for the sale and purchase of the property at the price of £775,000. The contract provided for completion to take place on the same day. In fact the contract had not yet been signed on behalf of Panther, but that matter was covered by a solicitor's undertaking given by Redferns to Edge & Ellison.

(vii) On 3 July 1989 Redferns received from Edge & Ellison transfers of the two parts of the property executed by Mirage in favour of Panther. Also on 3 July 1989 Mr Bundy paid £240,000 out of Redferns' client account to Kohli & Co. He saw that sum as representing a further part of the £2m payable by Crowngate to Kohli & Co and as leaving £510,000 so payable. He was told by Mr Kohli on the telephone on 30 June 1989 that that £510,000 was being paid direct by Crowngate to Kohli & Co and by a letter dated 12 July 1989 Mr Kohli confirmed to him that it had been so paid.

(viii) The payments out of Redferns' client account of £1·25m on 29 June and of £240,000 on 3 July resulted in there being only £35,000 left of the money provided by Target. That £35,000 was later expended by Mr Bundy on stamp duty and fees.

(ix) On 30 June 1989 Mr Bundy faxed instructions to Reeds to transfer a sum of £772,787 from Panther's bank account to the account of Edge & Ellison. That was the amount due on completion of the sale by Mirage after adjustments relating to leases of parts of the property. By the same fax he instructed Reeds to arrange for a number of other payments, totalling £300,000, to be made out of Panther's bank account by way of transfer or of banker's draft to a number of persons, some at least of whom appear from evidence very recently obtained by Target to have been directors of Mirage. Instructions for those payments to be made had been given to Mr Bundy by Mr Kohli and Mr Musafir or one of them. The instructions were complied with by Reeds. Further sums of £80,000 and £85,000 were paid out of Panther's bank account to persons having no obvious connection with the transactions, pursuant to similar instructions faxed by Mr Bundy to Reeds on 4 and 11 July 1989 respectively.

(x) Contracts for the sales by Panther to Kohli & Co and by Kohli & Co to Crowngate, transfers by Panther to Crowngate in completion of those sales, and mortgages by Crowngate in favour of Target were not executed until dates in July 1989. Of those documents, those that required to be executed by Kohli & Co and by Crowngate were sent by Mr Bundy to Mr Kohli on 4 July and were executed by those companies some days later. Those required to be executed by Panther were sent by Mr Bundy to Reeds on 6 July, executed on 10 July and returned to Redferns on 11 July. However, all those documents appear to have been dated 30 June 1989, except the mortgages to Target, which were dated 30 July 1989.

(xi) On 4 July 1989 Mr Bundy faxed to Target a letter dated 30 June 1989, in which he said:

'I write to confirm that the purchase of the property and charge to the Group [he meant by that the Target group] has today been successfully completed and I am now proceeding with the appropriate stamping and H.M. Land Registry formalities in the usual way.'

Mr Bundy admits in an affidavit that that was inaccurate. It was plainly untrue.

(xii) Registration of Crowngate's title to the property and of Target's mortgages was effected on 26 November 1989. In May 1990 Panther was dissolved on instructions given to Reeds by Mr Bundy. On 27 May 1992 Target entered into a contract for the sale of the property at the price of £500,000. At the time of the hearing before Warner J that contract had not been completed. The writ in this action was issued on 25 June 1992.

Warner J considered first the claim by Target based on breach of trust. His conclusion was that Target's claim for restitution of the sums of £1·2m and £240,000 was very nearly strong enough to justify summary judgment in Target's favour, even though Target had not pleaded fraud in connection with those claims, and therefore this was a proper case for leave to defend conditional upon bringing into court an appropriate sum of money. He determined the amount of the payment at £1m. If the ground of the order was properly based there is no issue on this appeal as to the amount of the payment.

Warner J reached that conclusion by the following steps.

(a) Redferns, as Target's solicitors, received £1,525,000 on 28 June 1989 as agents for Target and, until authorised by Target to release that money, they held it on trust for Target.

(b) There were no express instructions from Target to release the money. It was common ground that Redferns had implied authority to pay the money to Crowngate or at their directions only upon receipt of executed transfers of the properties to Crowngate and of executed charges made between Crowngate and Target in the required form.

(c) It was also common ground that Redferns committed a breach of trust when Mr Bundy transferred £1·25m to Panther's bank account on 29 June 1989 and £240,000 to Kohli & Co on 3 July 1989 because there was not then a contract for the purchase of the properties by Crowngate nor were there transfers or mortgages.

(d) The contention for Target was that that breach of trust imposed on Redferns at once a liability to restore the sums so paid to Target and that nothing thereafter absolved Redferns from that liability save for the obligation of Target to give credit for any sum obtained by Target on sale of the properties.

(e) The contention for Redferns was that the breach of trust was technical only. It resulted in no loss to Target because Mr Bundy obtained the mortgages to which Target was entitled.

(f) That contention for Redferns was answered on behalf of Target by a submission, based on a passage in Underhill and Hayton *Law Relating to Trusts and Trustees* (14th edn, 1987) pp 734, 736, that a defaulting trustee's liability to restore the trust fund cannot be limited by the application of principles relating to the causation of damage. On that contention the learned judge was 'not against' Target.

(g) The learned judge noted a further contention for Target, advanced in case the judge did not accept the proposition that causation was irrelevant, to the effect that if Target's money had not been available to pay Mirage on 30 June 1989, the deal with Mirage would have been off with the result that none of Target's money would even have been used at all. No finding upon that further contention was expressed by the judge.

Next, Warner J considered Target's claim for damages for professional negligence. The claim was advanced on three grounds. Firstly, that Redferns knew or ought to have known that the loan applications by Kohli for Crowngate contained a fraudulent misrepresentation that the total price of the properties was £2m and failed to reveal the fact; secondly, that if the first ground was not made out, Redferns had knowledge of circumstances which should have made a competent solicitor suspicious of fraud and they therefore were under a duty to inform Target of those circumstances; thirdly, that, if the loan applications were not made fraudulently, there arose between 21 and 30 June 1989 a conflict between the interests of Crowngate and those of Target of which Redferns should have informed Target and should have ceased to act for Target.

Warner J reviewed the evidence and the submissions of the parties. He began by noting that the claim in negligence was complex. He concluded that it was probable that Target would succeed at trial upon the second or third grounds of the alleged negligence but that it was not clear enough for him to give summary judgment or to hold that Redferns should on these issues have only conditional leave to defend.

By their notice of appeal of 22 December 1992 Redferns contend, as their first ground, that the judge was wrong to hold that Target's claim for restitution of the £1,490,000 was very nearly made out because the true measure of Redferns' liability for breach of trust is nil: the legal charges to Target in return for which Redferns were authorised to release the money were obtained, although some 11 days after the release.

The second ground was to this effect. If the judge relied on Target's contention that, if Redferns had not released the money before having obtained the charges, Target would never have authorised its release at all because Mirage would have withdrawn from the transaction, the judge was not entitled to do so since the evidence on that point was inconclusive and the question whether Mirage would in fact have withdrawn was a triable issue. It was therefore the contention for Redferns that they were entitled to unconditional leave to defend on the issue of breach of trust and no interim payment should have been ordered.

Target served a respondent's notice on 8 January 1993 by which they claim that the plaintiffs are entitled to summary judgment for an order that Redferns restore the full sum paid away, namely £1,525,000, less any due credits, with interest at £501 per day, together with orders for taking an account and for payment of the sums found to be due; and for payment of £1m as an interim payment. The ground of that cross-appeal is that Warner J decided that Redferns had no defence to the claim that Redferns paid the sums of £1·25m and £240,000 on 29 June and 3 July 1989 to Panther and Kolhi & Co in breach of trust and that Redferns were liable to make restitution of the total advance of £1,490,000 to Target less any credit in respect of the proceeds of sale of the properties. Accordingly the judge should have made an order for final judgment.

The submissions for Redferns

Mr Mann QC's submissions in this court, on behalf of Redferns, in brief summary, were directed to the central contention, as he described it, for Target, namely that release of the mortgage money to the borrowers before the receipt of executed transfers and charges, and therefore in breach of trust, gave rise to an immediate liability to restore the money subject only to credit for the amount of security realisations. This central contention was, it was said, wrong in law and common sense. The true principles of equity applicable in this case require that the court ascertain whether any and if so what loss was caused by the breach of trust. In fact Target got what it required, namely charges over the properties, and any loss suffered by Target has been caused by the fall in the property market or because the valuations, for which Redferns are not responsible, were negligent.

Mr Mann submitted further: (a) as to the requirement or expectation of common sense, if the main contention for Target is correct, Redferns would be liable to restore the full amount of the mortgage loans even if the charges, when taken, were full and proper security; and if the money had been released only 15 minutes before it ought to have been; and if the losses suffered by Target on sale had resulted only from a fall in the market value of the land. Such a result would be unjust in the circumstances of this sort of commercial conveyancing transaction. (b) As to principles of equity, Redferns have a triable case to the effect that no loss was caused to Target by the breach of trust. Neither *Re Dawson (decd), Union Fidelity Trustee Co Ltd v Perpetual Trustee Co Ltd* [1966] 2 NSWR 211, which provided the basis of the passage in *Underhill and Hayton* pp 734–735 to which Warner J referred in his judgment, nor the cases there considered, exclude the requirement of proof of a causal connection between the breach of trust and the loss claimed, although common law principles of causation, remoteness and foreseeability may not be applicable. (c) As to the contention for Target that, if Target's money had not been made available to pay Mirage on 30 June 1989, without authority and therefore in breach of trust, the deal with Mirage would have been off, so that Target's money would not have been used at all, the point, it was said, had not been pleaded; it had been raised before Warner J only in reply by Target's counsel, and raised at best a triable issue for Redferns. (d) There should therefore be unconditional leave for Redferns to defend.

The submissions for Target

Mr Patten QC for Target made submissions which, in brief summary, were as follows.

(i) The primary case made for Target is that Redferns were negligent and thereby caused loss to Target. In particular, Target would not have made the advances if the truth about the transactions known to Redferns had been revealed to Target on or before 29 June 1989. The grant of unconditional leave to Redferns to defend the negligence claims was, however, not under appeal.

(ii) The primary duty of a trustee who parts with trust assets in breach of trust is to replace the assets or put the trust in the same position in money terms as it was before the breach of trust occurred: reference was made to *Underhill and Hayton* pp 731–734, *Snell's Equity* (29th edn, 1990) pp 287–288, *Ex p Adamson, re Collie* (1878) 8 Ch D 807 at 819, *Nocton v Lord Ashburton* [1914] AC 932 at 952, 958, [1914–15] All ER Rep 45 at 51, 54–55, *Bartlett v Barclays Bank Trust Co Ltd (No 2)* [1980] 2 All ER 92 at 95, [1980] Ch 515 at 543, *Alliance and Leicester Building Society v Edgestop Ltd* (18 January 1991, unreported) and *Bishopsgate Investment Management Ltd (in liq) v Maxwell (No 2)* [1994] 1 All ER 261; *affg* [1993] BCLC 814.

(iii) The principles of remoteness of damage, of mitigation and causation, as applied to breaches of contract and tort, do not apply to breach of trust. In any event this breach of trust did cause a direct loss of £1,490,000 to Target. Reference was made to *Underhill and Hayton* pp 734–738 and to the cases there cited and to *Canson Enterprises Ltd v Boughton & Co* (1991) 85 DLR (4th) 129.

(iv) A trustee is not empowered to 'cure' a breach of trust (eg by later obtaining the transfers and charges) without either the fully informed consent of the beneficiary or by obtaining relief from the court under s 61 of the Trustee Act 1925.

(v) The breach of trust was not 'technical'. The advances were paid by Redferns on 29 June 1989 and 3 July 1989 to strangers with whom Target had no contractual relationship and with whom Crowngate had no contractual relationship.

(vi) If Target is not entitled to judgment for restitution of £1,490,000, subject to credit for any sums recovered, on the ground that the loss is not, at this stage, shown to have been caused by the breach of trust in releasing the money, Target is nevertheless entitled to judgment because of the separate breaches of trust committed by Redferns which did cause such loss, namely (a) the failure by Redferns, before releasing the money in furtherance of the transaction but without authority, to ask Target for their consent to the release, which consent it is clear Target would have refused; and (b) the failure by Redferns to report to Target at once their breach of trust in releasing the money on 29 June to Reeds upon receipt of which information Target would have required the return of their money.

(vii) Even if any requirement of a causal connection between the breaches of trust and the loss of Target's money is not satisfied by the foregoing, that requirement is met by the evidence that, if the money had not been made available in breach of trust on 30 June 1989, the sale would have gone off by refusal of Mirage to complete and Target would have lost nothing.

(viii) There was therefore no arguable defence and there should be judgment for the restoration by Redferns of the fund of £1,490,000 plus interest, less the proceeds of sale of the property; and the order for interim payment should stand until accounts are taken.

Conclusion

For my part, for the reasons which follow, I would dismiss both the appeal and the cross-appeal. I will consider first the cross-appeal by Target.

As to the contentions that, upon the breach of trust committed by the paying away of £1,490,000 without authority, Redferns became liable at once to restore the money, I do not accept it as applicable in this case in Ord 14 proceedings on the material before the court. Nor do I accept that Warner J made, as Mr Patten has submitted that he did, any finding to that effect. The hearing proceeded before Warner J for six days, and for part of another day, over which time he heard detailed submissions with reference to the negligence claims upon which he gave unconditional leave to defend. The passage in which Warner J expressed his conclusion upon the claim for breach of trust is short and condensed but, in my judgment, the meaning is clear. He noted the argument, based on the passage in *Underhill and Hayton*, that a defaulting trustee's liability to restore the trust fund could not be limited 'by the application of principles relating to the causation of damage'. Warner J did not hold that that principle was applicable so as to require or justify judgment for Target. He was, he said, 'not against' Mr Patten on that proposition. He noted also the point made by Mr Patten with reference to evidence showing that probably, if Target's money had not been available to pay £772,787 to Mirage on 30 June 1989, the deal would have been off. He then held that Target's claim was very nearly strong enough to justify summary judgment but Redferns were entitled to conditional leave to defend. That must have been because an arguable defence upon his view of the evidence had been established by Redferns on the material before him.

The reasons why he reached that conclusion are, I think, plain. He did not mean, when he referred to the point that 'a defaulting trustee's liability to restore the trust fund cannot be limited by the application of principles relating to the causation of damage' that no causal connection between the breach and the loss is required. I say that because, in my judgment, the requirement is unquestionably part of the law and it would be astonishing if it were not; and, in the passage in *Underhill and Hayton* to which Warner J referred, that requirement is recognised. Liability for breach of trust, it is there said, can be more extensive than liability for damage for tort or breach of contract. Then, in the passages cited from the judgment of Street J in *Re Dawson (decd), Union Fidelity Trustee Co Ltd v Perpetual Trustee Co Ltd* [1966] 2 NSWR 211 at 215–216 the following appears:

> '*Caffrey v. Darby* ((1801) 6 Ves 488, [1775–1802] All ER Rep 507) is consistent with the proposition that if a breach has been committed then the trustee is liable to place the trust estate in the same position as it would have been in if no breach had been committed. Considerations of causation, foreseeability and remoteness do not readily enter into the matter. To the same effect is the case of *Clough v. Bond* ((1838) 3 My & Cr 490, 40 ER 1016). It was argued before Lord Cottenham, L.C., that "the principle of the Court is to charge persons in the situation of trustees as parties to a breach of trust, wherever they have acted irregularly, and the irregularity, however well intended, has, in the result, enabled their co-trustees to commit a breach of trust, or has been, however remotely, the origin of the loss" ... The principles embodied in this approach do not appear to involve any inquiry as to whether the loss was caused by or flowed from the breach. *Rather the inquiry in each instance would appear to be whether the loss would have happened if there had been no breach* ... The cases to which I have referred demonstrate that the obligation to make restitution, which courts of equity have from very early times imposed on defaulting trustees and other fiduciaries is of a more absolute nature than the common law obligation to pay damages for tort or breach of contract.' (My emphasis.)

Accepting therefore that the issue on causal connection between loss and breach of trust was not limited by principles of causation of damage for breach of contract or tort, but turned upon whether the loss would have happened if there had been no breach, Warner J held, as stated above, that against Target's very strong case Redferns had raised an arguable defence, namely that the loss of Target would have happened if there had been no breach.

As I understood his submission, Mr Patten did not in fact maintain in this court the contention that a requirement of a causal connection in that sense is not part of the law. He contended that, since the breach of trust caused the paying away of the money, which, subject to recovery of part on resale, has been lost, the causal connection was clearly proved. He was constrained to accept that, if in fact Target would have proceeded with the transaction in any event in reliance upon the valuation provided by the second defendant, so that their loss would have been suffered if there had been no breach of trust, it was a very fortunate thing indeed for Target that Redferns committed the breach of trust. Warner J was right, in my judgment, not to accept Mr Patten's submission on the evidence before him. In considering whether it is open to a defendant who has committed a breach of trust by paying away without authority money held by him on trust to contend that the loss of the money would have happened if there had been no breach of trust, it is necessary for the court to examine the nature of the relationship between the plaintiff and the defendant out of which the fiduciary duty arises. If it appears just to the court, having regard to that relationship, and its purpose, and the obligations of the parties within it, and the way in which the parties would have behaved, for the court to regard the breach as having caused no loss to the plaintiff, because the loss would have happened if there had been no breach, then the court can and must so hold. I do not accept that the only route by which that conclusion can be reached is by an application for relief under s 61 of the Trustee Act 1925.

Warner J thought it probable that Target would succeed on this issue. I agree with him. I also agree with Warner J that Redferns have made out an arguable defence which entitled them to conditional leave to defend.

As to the remaining submissions advanced for Target, I do not accept that they afford any ground for varying the orders of Warner J. The alleged separate breaches of trust set out in para (vi)(a) and (b) above were not, Mr Mann has objected, pleaded as separate breaches of trust and do not appear in the respondent's notice; and he has submitted that they are not in law separate breaches of trust but are, if proved, acts of omission in respect of which any resulting loss must be proved to have been thereby caused. For my part, I do not regard it as necessary for this court to determine whether upon any set of assumed facts Redferns were, in regard to these matters, in breach of a distinct trust obligation. The questions whether on the facts known to Redferns they were, as solicitors, in breach of duty to Target in failing to inform Target of the facts of the intermediate sales and the agreed prices, or in failing to consult Target before releasing the money with the intention of obtaining in return the transfers and charges, are matters raised in the allegations of negligence upon which unconditional leave to defend was given. For the purposes of the issue of causal connection between the alleged breaches of trust and the loss claimed by Target, Redferns have, in my view, an arguable defence.

There is no greater force in the point listed in para (vii) above. Warner J referred to it and held that it did not provide on the material before him a ground for entering summary judgment. I agree with his view.

As to the plaintiff's appeal, I see no basis for varying the judge's order so as to give unconditional leave to defend on the issue of breach of trust. For the reasons which I have given, I do not accept that Warner J approached the case on the footing that no causal connection was required by the law to be proved between the loss claimed and the breach of trust alleged. If I am right, he accepted the principles of law substantially as Mr Mann has contended that they are to be derived from *Re Dawson (decd)* and the cases there cited. Applying those principles, Warner J held that Redferns have an arguable defence but of such an uncertain nature that conditional leave only to defend should be given. Again I agree with his view of the effect of the evidence before him.

I would dismiss both appeal and cross-appeal.

PETER GIBSON LJ. This appeal raises a short but important point on the measure of compensation to be allowed to a beneficiary following an admitted breach of trust by the trustee.

I gratefully adopt Ralph Gibson LJ's exposition of the facts. It is only necessary for the purpose of this judgment to pick out the following key facts.

(1) Target Holdings Ltd (Target) on 21 June 1989 instructed Redferns, and Redferns on 23 June 1989 accepted those instructions, to act as solicitors for it as the proposed mortgagee, lending a net sum of £1,525,000 to Crowngate Developments Ltd (Crowngate), the proposed mortgagor of 60–64 Great Hampton Street, Hockley, which Crowngate told Target it was purchasing and 'the estimated value/purchase price' of which was given by Crowngate as £2m, that valuation being supported by a valuation from the second defendants. Redferns also acted as solicitors for Crowngate, but at no time was Target told that Crowngate was purchasing the property for £775,000.

(2) Redferns received from Target on 28 June 1989 the two sums totalling £1,525,000 and held the same on a bare trust for Target, subject only to Redferns having implied authority to transmit the moneys to Crowngate or at Crowngate's direction, but then only upon receipt of executed transfers to Crowngate of the property to be charged to Target and of executed charges made between Crowngate and Target in respect of that property in the form of Target's standard mortgage deed.

(3) In breach of trust Redferns paid away £1,250,000 on 29 June 1989 and £240,000 on 3 July 1989 to persons not authorised by Target.

(4) The transfers whereby the property was transferred to Crowngate were executed on various dates in July and not returned to Redferns till 11 July 1989. The charges were dated 30 July 1989.

(5) On 22 May 1992 Target as mortgagee contracted to sell the property for £500,000, but at the time of the hearing before the judge that contract had not been completed.

(6) At no time have Redferns sought to justify their breach of trust or to seek relief under s 61 of the Trustee Act 1925 as persons who acted honestly and reasonably and ought fairly to be excused. Indeed on the facts it is clear that this was a conscious and deliberate breach of trust by Mr Bundy of Redferns who compounded his default by his letter dated 30 June 1989, faxed to Target on 4 July 1989, in which he untruthfully confirmed that the purchase and charges had been completed. That letter falls to be considered in the light of the fact that Target had the right to withdraw its moneys at any time before actual completion when Redferns could act pursuant to its implied authority to release the moneys.

It is not in dispute or in doubt that the obligation of a trustee who commits a breach of trust is to account for and restore to the trust fund that which has thereby been lost to it. The remedy afforded to the beneficiary by equity is compensation in the form of restitution of that which has been lost to the trust estate, not damages. Viscount Haldane LC in *Nocton v Lord Ashburton* [1914] AC 932 at 952, [1914–15] All ER Rep 45 at 51 referred to the 'more elastic' remedies of the Court of Chancery than those of the common law courts, and said:

> 'Operating in personam as a Court of conscience it could order the defendant, not, indeed, in those days, to pay damages as such, but to make restitution, or to compensate the plaintiff by putting him in as good a position pecuniarily as that in which he was before the injury.'

That is still true today (see, for example, *Bartlett v Barclays Bank Trust Co Ltd (No 2)* [1980] 2 All ER 92 at 95, [1980] Ch 515 at 543 in which Brightman LJ referred with approval to the remarks to the like effect of Street J in *Re Dawson (decd), Union Fidelity Trustee Co Ltd v Perpetual Trustee Co Ltd* [1966] 2 NSWR 211 at 214–216).

All this is trite law. A further consequence of the equitable remedy is that to which Street J drew attention (at 215):

> '... the trustee is liable to place the trust estate in the same position as it would have been in if no breach had been committed. Considerations of causation, foreseeability and remoteness do not readily enter into the matter.'

I do not thereby understand Street J to be saying, nor in my judgment would it be right to say, that considerations of causation have no part to play in the assessment of the measure of compensation where there has been a breach of trust. Thus Street J goes on to cite with approval (at 215) the summary of Lord Cottenham LC in *Clough v Bond* (1838) 3 My & Cr 490 at 496–497, 40 ER 1016 at 1018 of the earlier authorities:

> 'It will be found to be the result of all the best authorities upon the subject, that, although a personal representative, acting strictly within the line of his duty, and exercising reasonable care and diligence, would not be responsible for the failure or depreciation of the fund in which any part of the estate may be invested, or for the insolvency or misconduct of any person who may have possessed it, yet, if that line of duty be not strictly pursued, and any part of the property be invested by such personal representative in funds or upon securities not authorised, or be put within the control of persons who ought not to be entrusted with it, and a loss be thereby eventually sustained, such personal representative will be liable to make it good, however unexpected the result, however little likely to arise from the course adopted, and however free such conduct may have been from any improper motive.'

Lord Cottenham LC then gave as examples the case of an omission to sell property when it ought to have been sold, the case of leaving moneys due upon only personal security, albeit good at the time, the case of investing in an unauthorised fund and the entrusting of the trust estate to a co-executor or co-administrator, instead of keeping the trust property vested in all the executors or administrators. In each of these cases the breach of trust is not one of a wrongful disposal of trust property causing immediate loss, and one therefore waits to see whether and, if so, what loss will thereby be eventually sustained. All such loss is recoverable, even though it would not have been on the application of principles derived from the law of tort relating to causation, foreseeability and remoteness. Street J's comment on this summary of those cases was:

> 'The principles embodied in this approach do not appear to involve any inquiry as to whether the loss was caused by or flowed from the breach. Rather the inquiry in each instance would appear to be whether the loss would have happened if there had been no breach.'

But again I would observe that this was a comment on cases where it makes sense to ask whether the loss would have happened but for the breach. Where the breach consists in the wrongful paying away of trust moneys so that there is an immediate loss, no inquiry is necessary: the causal connection is obvious.

Mr Mann QC relied on the decision of this court in *Nestle v National Westminster Bank plc* [1994] 1 All ER 118, [1993] 1 WLR 1260. That was a case where the will trustee misconstrued the will's investment clause and failed to review investments regularly. A beneficiary, seeking (i) an inquiry as to what the value of the trust fund would have been if there were no such breaches and (ii) compensation measured by the results of the inquiry, failed in her action because she had not discharged the onus on her to prove that she had suffered loss as a result of the breaches. That case is not one of a breach of trust committed by the wrongful disposition of trust property.

We were also referred by Mr Mann to the decision of the Supreme Court of Canada in *Canson Enterprises Ltd v Boughton & Co* (1991) 85 DLR (4th) 129. In that case the question was the extent of a solicitor's liability for breach of his fiduciary duty while acting for the appellant in the purchase and redevelopment of land. If that breach had not occurred, the appellant would not have purchased the land. A claim by the appellant for compensation in equity for the loss occasioned by the collapse of the building erected on the developed land was dismissed as having been caused by the intervention of third parties. The majority departed from the traditional approach in deciding that equity could borrow principles from the common law in relation to damages for tort and by that route held that the solicitor's liability was limited. Mr Mann relied on certain passages in the judgment of McLachlin J (with whom Lamer CJC and L'Heureux-Dubé J agreed), who concurred with the majority in the result but reached her conclusion by applying equitable principles. McLachlin J emphasised (at 160) that the loss was limited to that which flowed from the trustee's breach. However this was not a case like that with which we are concerned when trust moneys were paid away to a stranger. Indeed La Forest J (at 146), giving the judgment of the majority, drew a sharp distinction between a situation where a person has control of property belonging to another and one where a person is under a fiduciary duty to perform an obligation, where equity's concern, he said, was simply that the duty be performed honestly and in accordance with the undertaking taken on by the fiduciary. He continued:

> 'In the case of a trust relationship, the trustee's obligation is to hold the *res* or object of the trust for his *cestui que trust*, and on breach the concern of equity is that it be restored to the *cestui que trust* or, if that cannot be done, to afford compensation for what the object would be worth. In the case of a mere breach of duty, the concern of equity is to ascertain the loss resulting from the breach of the particular duty. Where the wrongdoer has received some benefit, that benefit can be disgorged, but the measure

of compensation where no such benefit has been obtained by the wrongdoer raises different issues.'

He clearly recognised that the situation with which he was dealing was the latter rather than the former. The decision in that case is therefore not of direct relevance to the present case.

What is the position where the trustee in breach of trust pays away trust moneys to a stranger? That there is an immediate loss, placing the trustee under an immediate duty to restore the moneys to the trust fund, seems to me obvious as, I believe, it did to Warner J. He expressly stated that he was not against the proposition advanced by Mr Patten QC that a defaulting trustee's liability to restore the trust fund cannot be limited by the application of principles relating to the causation of damage. The judge plainly rejected Mr Mann's argument on causation, viz that because Redferns eventually obtained for Target the charges on the property no loss was sustained or recoverable, and that unconditional leave to defend must be given. What, with respect, the judge does not do is to explain what it was that led him to qualify his acceptance of Target's case for restitution of the moneys paid away by saying only that it was 'very nearly strong enough to justify summary judgment being given in its favour' and to hold that it was a proper case for conditional leave to defend. The only two other matters that are referred to in this part of the judgment are Mr Patten's fall-back argument if the judge had been against him on the proposition to which I have referred and the absence of a plea of fraud. Neither of those matters could be a valid reason for the judge's conclusion (although for my part I accept Mr Mann's submissions for Redferns that if the question depended on the fall-back argument, the matter would have to go to trial), and the judge does not say that either contributed to his decision.

It is with the utmost diffidence that I venture to differ from Ralph Gibson LJ as well as from so complete a master of equity as Warner J, but I can see no answer to the claim by Target in its cross-appeal that Redferns are liable to replace all the moneys paid away in breach of trust, subject only to Target giving credit for any moneys recovered on the realisation by it of its security. The elastic remedies of equity are sufficiently flexible to require that a beneficiary who subsequent to the loss receives a benefit from the trustee's actions give credit for that benefit. That a trustee or other fiduciary in breach of trust disposes of trust property to a stranger comes under an immediate duty to make restitution seems to me supported by two recent authorities.

The first is the decision of Hoffmann J in *Alliance and Leicester Building Society v Edgestop Ltd* (18 January 1991, unreported). This was another case of an alleged mortgage fraud. The plaintiff society brought an action against the solicitors who accepted instructions to act for the society and to whom moneys were paid for the purpose of the mortgage. Hoffmann J said:

'The case against them is put in various ways but the principal cause of action relied upon is misapplication of the society's funds. It is said that upon receipt of the money from the society, the solicitors held it in trust to apply it in accordance with the society's instructions and subject thereto in trust for the society. The society's instructions authorised the money to be advanced for the purposes of the purchases set out in the instructions and not for some materially different transactions. It also required that the society should, before completion, be notified of matters which ought reasonably to have been brought to its attention. The solicitors knew or ought to have known that the true nature of the transactions had been

concealed from the society and I think that there can be no doubt that if
the facts known to the solicitors had been brought to the attention of the
society before completion, it would not have made any of the advances.
Accordingly the application of the whole of each of the society's advances
was a breach of trust by the solicitors and they are liable to restore the fund
with interest, subject to being given credit for any money which the
society may recover by realisation of its security or recovery on the
shortfall policies.'

The judge accepted the society's case and said that the defendants could not
claim that any disbursement of the society's funds was within their authority,
and accordingly he acceded to the society's application that an interim
payment should be ordered.

Mr Mann rightly pointed out that that case differs from the present in that
Hoffmann J found that a fraud had been practised on the society whereas in the
present case fraud is not alleged against Redferns, and further there was a
finding that if the facts known to the solicitors had been brought to the
society's attention before completion, the lender would not have made the
advances, whereas in the present case the like question is an issue fit to be tried.
But Hoffmann J appears to have accepted that where there was a breach of
trust constituted by the wrongful application of the society's advances, the
solicitors were liable to restore the fund, subject to the society giving credit for
what it received.

The second is *Bishopsgate Investment Management Ltd (in liq) v Maxwell (No 2)*
[1994] 1 All ER 261. In that case the defendant was a director of the plaintiff
company by which he was sued for breaches of fiduciary duty. Those breaches
consisted of acts of omission by him in relation to some transactions, but in
relation to certain transfers of shares to Crédit Suisse the breaches were acts of
commission in that he had signed the transfers. On an application for
summary judgment against the director, Chadwick J refused the application in
so far as it relied on the acts of omission, but he gave summary judgment on
the claim based on breach of duty in signing the transfers (see [1993] BCLC
814). Chadwick J referred to the judgment of Oliver J in *Re Miller's Deed Trusts*
[1978] LS Gaz 454. This was a case in which trustees were sued for breach of
trust in their management of a trust fund. The fund held a controlling interest
in a private company which at one time was very valuable but which had
become valueless. Oliver J's judgment is reported as including the following:

'It was necessary to prove a causal connection between the breach of
duty and the resulting loss. No principle could be extracted from the cases
that once a breach of duty was shown the burden fell on the defaulting
trustee to show that the loss did not result from the breach.'

That again was a case of an alleged breach of trust not consisting of the
wrongful disposal of trust money giving rise to an immediate loss. Chadwick
J relied on the decision in holding that there was a triable issue in relation to
the breaches of trust consisting of omissions as it was not clear whether but for
the omissions the claimed loss would have occurred. But he found that in
relation to the breach of trust in signing the transfers, the loss resulted from the
transfers and so summary judgment would be given.

On appeal Hoffmann LJ, who gave the leading judgment in this court and
with whom Ralph Gibson and Leggatt LJJ agreed, accepted the validity of the
distinction between the acts of omission and those of commission. He referred

to the argument of Mr Rimer QC for the director that the plaintiff company had failed to show that his breaches of duty in signing the transfers had caused the loss. Hoffmann LJ commented ([1994] 1 All ER 261 at 265–266):

'This is an attempt to characterise the breach of duty as an omission equivalent to Mr Ian Maxwell's inactivity concerning the other transactions. But in my view it is fallacious. I say nothing about cases in which the breach of duty consists in doing an act without first making reasonable inquiries. Mr Rimer referred us to authorities which do not speak with one voice on whether it must be assumed that the defendant would have learnt the truth or whether he might have been told a plausible lie. In the case of breach of the fiduciary duty, it seems to me that the action is constituted not by failure to make inquiries but simply the improper transfer of the shares to Robert Maxwell Group plc. Even if Mr Ian Maxwell had made inquiries and received reassuring answers from other directors whom he was reasonably entitled to trust, he would not have escaped liability for a transfer which was in fact for a purpose outside the powers entrusted to the board. He may or may not have been entitled to relief under s 727 of the Companies Act 1985 [the equivalent provision in that Act to s 61 of the Trustee Act 1925] but since in fact he made no inquiry, no reliance has—in my view rightly—been placed on this section. The burden of justification is upon Mr Ian Maxwell and on this he has adduced no evidence to raise a triable issue. It was the improper transfer which caused the loss and the necessary causal connection is therefore established. I therefore think that the judge was right to hold there was no triable issue on the Crédit Suisse transactions and the appeal should therefore be dismissed.'

In respect of an argument on quantum Hoffmann LJ said (at 267):

'Secondly, Mr Rimer says it does not follow that the company's loss would be the full value of the shares. It might be able to get something back from Crédit Suisse. But the company held the shares as trustee for the pension funds and its liability as trustee was to restore the fund. Prima facie, therefore, its loss was its liability to make good the value of the shares.'

Similarly in my judgment the cause of action is constituted simply by the payment away of Target's moneys in breach of trust and the loss is quantified in the amount of those moneys, subject to Target giving credit for the realisation of the security it received. It was for Redferns to justify their action or otherwise to show why Target was not entitled to compensation in the sum claimed.

If this appears harsh treatment of a defaulting trustee, it has to be acknowledged that equity has always treated a defaulting trustee severely, no doubt, as was said in *Nocton v Lord Ashburton* [1914] AC 932 at 963, [1914–15] All ER Rep 45 at 57 by Lord Dunedin, in exercise of its jurisdiction 'to keep persons in a fiduciary capacity up to their duty'.

Accordingly, despite Mr Mann's admirably well-sustained arguments, I have reached the conclusion that the appeal by Redferns should be dismissed and the cross-appeal by Target allowed. I need say nothing further on the alternative arguments advanced by Mr Patten. I would order that Redferns pay Target £1,490,000 together with interest less the net proceeds of the sale of the property.

HIRST LJ. I agree with the judgment of Peter Gibson LJ

Appeal dismissed. Leave to appeal to the House of Lords refused.

14 March 1994. The Appeal Committee of the House of Lords gave leave to Appeal.

Carolyn Toulmin   Barrister.

R v Kearley (No 2)
R v Harris

COURT OF APPEAL, CRIMINAL DIVISION
LORD TAYLOR OF GOSFORTH CJ, SCHIEMANN AND WRIGHT JJ
11 NOVEMBER 1993

Criminal law – Appeal – Death of appellant – Effect – Death of appellant before appeal heard – House of Lords allowing appeal and remitting case to Court of Appeal to reconsider sentence – Death of appellant before Court of Appeal hearing remitted appeal – Whether right of appeal against conviction and sentence right of that person and no-one else – Whether death of appellant before appeal heard abating appeal – Whether remission by House of Lords to Court of Appeal disposing of appeal to House of Lords – Criminal Appeal Act 1968, ss 1, 9, 34, 35.

In two separate appeals the question arose whether the Court of Appeal had jurisdiction to continue to hear an appeal if the appellant had died before the appeal was heard or whether the appeal was abated by reason of the death of the appellant. The first appeal arose out of the conviction of one K in the Crown Court in May 1989 for drug trafficking offences. In August K was sentenced and a confiscation order was made under the Drug Trafficking Offences Act 1986 in the sum of £10,371. He appealed against conviction and sentence. The Court of Appeal dismissed his appeal against conviction but quashed certain terms of his sentence and affirmed the confiscation order. He appealed to the House of Lords, which allowed his appeal, with the result that his conviction in respect of certain counts in the indictment with which he was charged was quashed. The case was then remitted to the Court of Appeal, Criminal Division, pursuant to s 35(3)[a] of the Criminal Appeal Act 1968 to consider whether the confiscation order should be set aside or varied. Before the case could be relisted K was murdered. Under ss 1(1)[b] and 9(1)[c] of the 1968 Act a 'person' convicted of an offence could appeal to the Court of Appeal against his conviction or sentence while in the case of an appeal to the House of Lords s 34(3)[d] of that Act provided that an appeal to the House of Lords was to be 'treated as pending until ... disposed of' and s 35(3) provided that 'For the purpose of disposing of an appeal the House of Lords ... may remit the case to

---

a   Section 35(3), so far as material, is set out at p 360 *e*, post
b   Section 1(1) is set out at p 357 *g*, post
c   Section 9(1) is set out at p 357 *h*, post
d   ˡ ˈon 34(3) is set out at p360 *c d*, post

Decision of the Court of Appeal (Criminal Division) affirmed.
[1994] 3 W.L.R.
413, H.L.(E.)

the [Court of Appeal]'. The second appeal arose out a hospital order made in December 1991 in respect of one H under s 37 of the Mental Health Act 1983 with a restriction order without limit of time under s 41 following his conviction for assault occasioning actual bodily harm. He was granted leave to appeal against sentence but died in June 1992 before his appeal came before the court.

Held – (1) The plain meaning of ss 1(1) and 9(1) of the 1968 Act was that the right to appeal against conviction and sentence was the right of the person convicted and sentenced and no one else. The appeal of H was therefore abated by reason of his death although it was open to his relatives to petition the Secretary of State to refer the case to the Court of Appeal under s 17 of the 1968 Act, when the appeal would be treated as if he were notionally still alive (see p 357 j and p 359 d to g, post); *R v Jefferies* [1968] 3 All ER 238 and *R v Maguire* [1992] 2 All ER 433 applied.

(2) In the case of K, the clear meaning of s 35(3) of the 1968 Act was that the House of Lords could either exercise any powers of the Court of Appeal or remit the case to the Court of Appeal for the purpose of the Court of Appeal exercising its powers. When the House of Lords remitted the case to the Court of Appeal the House thereby disposed of the appeal to it and the appeal did not remain 'pending' for the purposes of s 34(3) until the Court of Appeal disposed of it. When the case was remitted to the Court of Appeal the court's powers were limited to those derived from the 1968 Act and accordingly the court had exactly the same powers as if the issue had come before it by way of an appeal against sentence. Therefore ss 1(1) and 9(1) of the 1968 Act applied and the appeal was abated by reason of the death of the appellant (see p 361 a to g, post); *R v Jefferies* [1968] 3 All ER 238 and *R v Maguire* [1992] 2 All ER 433 applied.

Notes

For the effect on an appeal of the death of the appellant, see 11(2) *Halsbury's Laws* (4th edn reissue) para 1463, and for cases on the subject, see 15(2) *Digest* (2nd reissue) 405, 21985–21986.

For the Criminal Appeal Act 1968, ss 1, 9, 17, 34, 35 see 12 *Halsbury's Statutes* (4th edn) (1994 reissue) 390, 398, 407, 417, 418.

For the Mental Health Act 1983, s 41, see 28 *Halsbury's Statutes* (4th edn) 684.

Cases referred to in judgment

R v Berry (No 2) [1991] 2 All ER 789, [1991] 1 WLR 125, CA.
R v Jefferies [1968] 3 All ER 238, [1969] 1 QB 120, [1968] 3 WLR 830, CA.
R v Maguire [1992] 2 All ER 433, [1992] QB 936, [1992] 2 WLR 767, CA.
R v Rowe [1955] 2 All ER 234, [1955] 1 QB 573, [1955] 2 WLR 1056, CCA.

Appeals against sentence

R v Kearley (No 2)

Alan Robert Kearley was convicted on 19 May 1989 in the Crown Court at Bournemouth before Judge Best and a jury of various offences in three indictments and sentenced to a total of five years six months' imprisonment and a confiscation order under the Drug Trafficking Offences Act 1986 was made in the sum of £10,371. He appealed against conviction and sentence and on 29 November 1990 the Court of Appeal (Lloyd LJ, Schiemann and Jowitt JJ) dismissed his appeal against conviction but varied his sentence to four years

and one month's imprisonment and affirmed the confiscation order ((1991) 93
Cr App R 222). The Court of Appeal granted leave to the House of Lords. On
8 April 1992 the House of Lords ([1992] 2 All ER 345, [1992] 2 AC 228) quashed
three counts involving drugs in the second indictment and the case was
remitted to the Court of Appeal under s 35(3) of the Criminal Appeal Act 1968
for consideration whether the confiscation order should be set aside or varied.
Before the case could be relisted, Kearley was murdered. The Registrar of
Criminal Appeals referred the case to the Court of Appeal to decide whether
the question of the confiscation order should still be considered. The facts are
set out in the judgment.

R v Harris

Lee Harris was convicted on 8 May 1991 in the Crown Court at Croydon before
Judge Tilling and a jury of assault occasioning actual bodily harm. Interim
hospital orders were made in his case and on 5 December 1991 he was made
the subject of a hospital order under s 37 of the Mental Health Act 1983, with a
restriction order without limit under s 41 of that Act. He appealed against
sentence, but died before his appeal came before the Court of Appeal. His legal
representatives sought to continue the appeal. The facts are set out in the
judgment.

The appeals were heard together.

Marion Smullen (assigned by the *Registrar of Criminal Appeals*) on behalf of the
deceased Harris.
John Aspinall (assigned by the *Registrar of Criminal Appeals*) on behalf of the
deceased Kearley.
Andrew Mitchell (instructed by the *Crown Prosecution Service*, Headquarters) for
the Crown.
James Curtis QC (instructed by the *Treasury Solicitor*) as amicus curiae.

LORD TAYLOR OF GOSFORTH CJ. These two cases raise the question of
whether an appeal to this court can be continued when the appellant dies
before it is heard. The two cases are not entirely on all fours and we shall
indicate the distinctions between them.

We deal first with the facts of the case of Kearley. On 19 May 1989 in the
Crown Court at Bournemouth Mr Kearley was convicted of offences on three
indictments, having pleaded guilty on a change of plea. On 3 August 1989 he
was sentenced to a total of five years' and six months' imprisonment, and a
confiscation order was made under the Drug Trafficking Offences Act 1986 in
the sum of £10,371. On 29 November 1990 the full court dismissed his appeal
against conviction. On his appeal against sentence the full court quashed
certain terms of the prison sentence, passing lesser terms, but affirmed the
confiscation order. The position, following the decision of this court, was as
follows: on counts 5 to 8 of the first indictment, for offences of handling stolen
goods, concurrent sentences of two years' imprisonment were imposed. On
count 5 of the second indictment, for supplying a controlled drug of class B, a
consecutive sentence of two years' imprisonment was imposed; on count 6, for
possessing a controlled drug of class B with intent, a concurrent sentence of
two years' imprisonment was imposed; and on counts 7 and 8, for possessing
a controlled drug of class B, concurrent sentences of 12 months' imprisonment

were imposed. On count 2 of the third indictment, for possessing a class B drug, a consecutive sentence of one month's imprisonment was imposed. The total sentence was four years and one month's imprisonment. The confiscation order in the sum of £10,371 was unchanged.

This court certified that a point of law of general public importance was involved. It concerned the admissibility of certain evidence. The court granted leave to appeal to the House of Lords. On 8 April 1992 the Appellate Committee of the House of Lords delivered their opinion on the point of law of public importance, answering the question posed in the appellant's favour (see [1992] 2 All ER 345, [1992] 2 AC 228). The effect of that was that the convictions in respect of counts 6 to 8 inclusive on the second indictment were quashed. The case was then remitted by the House of Lords to this court pursuant to s 35(3) of the Criminal Appeal Act 1968, to which we must return later, for determination as to whether the confiscation order should be set aside or varied. However, after the case had been so remitted to this court, but before it could be relisted, the registrar was informed that the appellant had been killed. Accordingly, the question is whether in those circumstances the matter is one with which this court still has power to deal, or whether the appeal is abated by reason of the death of the appellant.

We turn next to the facts of the case of Harris. He was convicted on 8 May 1991 at the Crown Court at Croydon of assault occasioning actual bodily harm. Interim hospital orders were made in his case, and on 5 December 1991 he was made the subject of a hospital order under s 37 of the Mental Health Act 1983, with a restriction order without limit of time under s 41. He appealed against sentence, and leave to appeal was granted by the single judge on 23 March 1992. There was then some delay in the matter proceeding because of a need for further medical reports to be obtained, and also because of the illness of the appellant. In the result he died on 17 June 1992 before his appeal came before this court. In his case, as in the case of Kearley, it is submitted that the appeal can go ahead notwithstanding his death.

We deal first with the case of Harris. Mrs Smullen has sought to persuade this court that notwithstanding the death of the appellant an appeal can still be pursued. It must be an appeal pursuant to s 9 of the Criminal Appeal Act 1968. It is convenient at this stage to deal with ss 1(1) and 9(1) of that Act. Section 1(1) provides:

'A person convicted of an offence on indictment may appeal to the Court of Appeal against his conviction.'

Section 9(1) provides:

'A person who has been convicted of an offence on indictment may appeal to the Court of Appeal against any sentence (not being a sentence fixed by law) passed on him for the offence, whether passed on his conviction or in subsequent proceedings.'

The plain meaning of the words in each of those two sections is that the right to appeal is that of the person convicted and sentenced and no one else. That view has been affirmed in judicial decisions. In *R v Jefferies* [1968] 3 All ER 238, [1969] 1 QB 120 the widow of a convict who died before his appeal could be heard sought to continue it. She had an interest in that the court had made a costs order in the sum of £1,300 and she sought to relieve his estate of the obligation under that order. The relevant statutory provisions were those

contained in the Criminal Appeal Act 1907, which were in similar terms to
those already quoted from the 1968 Act. Widgery LJ considered certain
observations by Lord Goddard CJ in *R v Rowe* [1955] 2 All ER 234, [1955] 1 QB
573 to the effect that it may be that the court would allow executors to appeal
so as to recover a fine for the benefit of the deceased convict's estate. Widgery
LJ said those observations were obiter and could not be reinforced by
authority. He continued ([1968] 3 All ER 238 at 240, [1969] 1 QB 120 at 124):

> 'Whatever may be the powers of courts exercising a jurisdiction that
> does not derive from statute, the powers of this court are derived from,
> and confined to, those given by the Criminal Appeal Act 1907. We take it
> to be a general principle that whenever a party to proceedings dies, the
> proceedings must abate, unless his personal representatives both have an
> interest in the subject-matter and can by virtue of the express terms of a
> statute (or from rules of court made by virtue of jurisdiction given by a
> statute) take the appropriate steps to have themselves substituted for the
> deceased as a party to the proceedings. Although in this case the estate
> would benefit if the widow were allowed to continue the appeal and were
> successful, there is no procedure whereby she can be substituted as an
> appellant and we do not see how there can be an inherent power in the
> court to allow this when the appeal is itself the creature of statute. We
> could add that not only the wording of s. 3 of the Act of 1907 but the
> general tenor of the statute as a whole is such as to make the right of appeal
> strictly personal to the "person convicted".'

Widgery LJ then said that he agreed with Lord Goddard CJ's observation that
there could be cases in which injustice might result to personal representatives
who have a legal interest without remedy. He said ([1968] 3 All ER 238 at 240,
[1969] 1 QB 120 at 124):

> 'It is, however, open to the personal representatives to petition the
> Secretary of State for relief and if the Secretary of State were in an
> appropriate case so minded he could seek the opinion of this court under
> s. 19(b) of the Act of 1907 as amended. This provision will shortly be
> superseded by s. 17 of the Criminal Appeal Act 1968 which provides ...'

Widgery LJ then set out the provisions of the section, which it is material for
us to quote:

> '17—(1) Where a person has been convicted on indictment, or been
> tried on indictment and found not guilty by reason of insanity, or been
> found by a jury to be under disability, the Secretary of State may, if he
> thinks fit, at any time either—(a) refer the whole case to the Court of
> Appeal and the case shall then be treated for all purposes as an appeal to
> the Court by that person; or (b) if he desires the assistance of the Court on
> any point arising in the case, refer that point to the Court for their opinion
> thereon, and the Court shall consider the point so referred and furnish the
> Secretary of State of their opinion thereon accordingly.
> (2) A reference by the Secretary of State under this section may be made
> by him either on an application by the person referred to in subsection (1),
> or without any such application.'

In *R v Maguire* [1992] 2 All ER 433 at 436, [1992] 1 QB 936 at 945 the right to
pursue an appeal upon a reference by the Home Secretary, notwithstanding

the death of the appellant, was upheld. Stuart-Smith LJ referred to s 1 of the Criminal Appeal Act 1968 and said:

'It is clear that an appeal brought under this section, which of course embraces the vast majority of appeals against conviction, is personal to the appellant and can only be brought while he is alive. Similar considerations apply to appeals brought under s 9 against sentence: see *R v Jefferies* [1968] 3 All ER 238, [1969] 1 QB 120.'

Dealing with the reference under s 17, Stuart-Smith LJ said ([1992] 2 All ER 433 at 438, [1992] 1 QB 936 at 947):

'[The point] remains a narrow one of construction of s 17(1)(a). The opening words of this subsection suggest that the case of a deceased person can be referred to the court and after referral it has to be treated as an appeal by that person. That follows from the use of the word "then". The appeal is to be treated as if he were notionally still alive, a concept that presents no real difficulty and is not inconsistent with the Criminal Appeal Rules.'

In our judgment those two authorities are clearly relevant and effective to deal with the submissions which have been made to us by Mrs Smullen. She has bravely sought to contend that where an appellant has done all that is in his power to set an appeal in motion, that is to say has made his application and if necessary has renewed it and has obtained leave, that the appeal is then effective for the purposes of a hearing in this court, and his demise before the hearing arises should not prevent the court from hearing it. We cannot accede to that submission for the reasons which are set out in the decisions which have already been cited. We consider that the statutory framework within which this court must operate provides only for an appeal by a live person so far as s 1 and s 9 are concerned. Accordingly, so far as the case of Harris is concerned we have to treat the appeal, notwithstanding that the learned single judge gave leave, as one which has been abated as a result of his death. This still leaves it open to the relatives, if they feel there is any basis or purpose which would persuade the Home Secretary to refer the case to this court under s 17, to petition him to do so, but so far as an appeal under s 9 is concerned, that cannot be pursued and it is abated.

We turn now to the case of Kearley, which has arrived before us for decision by a different and somewhat longer route. As already indicated in the history, the case proceeded to the House of Lords on a point of law of public importance. The House of Lords, having decided the point of law of public importance, remitted the case to this court pursuant to s 35(3). Mr Aspinall has argued before us that whilst an appeal under s 1 or s 9 directly to this court must be abated on the death of the appellant, different considerations apply where an appeal comes back to this court from the House of Lords by way of remission. He relies on the provisions of Pt II of the Criminal Appeal Act 1968. That is headed 'Appeal to the House of Lords from the Court of Appeal', and we should en passant refer to s 51, which is the interpretation section of the Act. It provides, so far as the word 'appeal' is concerned, as follows:

'... "appeal", where used in Part I or II of this Act, means appeal under that Part and "appellant" has a corresponding meaning.'

Accordingly, under Pt II the word 'appeal' means an appeal to the House of Lords. Section 33(1) provides:

'An appeal lies to the House of Lords, at the instance of the defendant or the prosecutor, from any decision of the Court of Appeal on an appeal to that court under Part I of this Act.'

Subsection (2) provides that such an appeal lies only with leave.

It is s 34 which is at the heart of Mr Aspinall's submission. That is a section dealing with application for leave to appeal, and with time limits. Subsection (1) provides for the time in which an application has to be made. Subsection (2) provides power to extend the time. Subsection (3) provides as follows:

'An appeal to the House of Lords shall be treated as pending until any application for leave to appeal is disposed of and, if leave to appeal is granted, until the appeal is disposed of; and for the purposes of this Part of this Act an application for leave to appeal shall be treated as disposed of at the expiration of the time within which it may be made, if it is not made within that time.'

Section 35 deals with the hearing and disposal of appeals. It is sub-s (3) of that section, together with s 34, which is relied on by Mr Aspinall. That subsection provides as follows:

'For the purpose of disposing of an appeal, the House of Lords may exercise any powers of the Court of Appeal or may remit the case to the Court.'

The argument addressed to us runs as follows. Section 34(3) requires that an appeal to the House of Lords shall be treated as pending until it is disposed of. In the present case there was an appeal to the House of Lords. The House of Lords, whilst dealing with the point of public importance, proceeded to deal with other aspects of the case. Those which had been described in *R v Berry (No 2)* [1991] 2 All ER 789, [1991] 1 WLR 125 as ancillary matters were remitted to this court under sub-s (3) of s 35. Mr Aspinall argues that the appeal is still pending whilst that matter remains to be dealt with by this court. He argues that in effect the House of Lords has merely delegated its powers to the Court of Appeal to dispose of the matter regarding the confiscation order. The House of Lords, having quashed certain of the convictions recorded against Mr Kearley, remitted the case to this court so it could consider the effect of the quashing of those convictions on the confiscation order which had originally been made. Accordingly the argument is that the appeal to the House of Lords has not been disposed of; it is still pending, and the fact that Mr Kearley has died does not prevent it from being pending until disposed of by reason of s 34(3). There was some discussion during the argument as to what would happen if an appellant were to die whilst the case was actually being heard by the House of Lords. It was suggested that because of the particular wording of s 33(1), namely that 'an appeal lies ... at the instance of the defendant', it might be that the appeal could continue before the House of Lords because 'at the instance of' might merely mean that the defendant had set the appeal in motion, but need not necessarily be extant at the time of the hearing. Mr Aspinall supported that interpretation of s 33(1) by arguing that a point of public importance, which had been referred to the House of Lords, ought not to remain undecided simply because the appellant, who was the catalyst to the appeal being heard, had died.

However that may be, we have to consider on what basis this court is to proceed when a case is remitted to this court from the House of Lords pursuant to s 35(3). The wording of that subsection begins: 'For the purpose of disposing of an appeal', and it goes on to say: 'the House of Lords may exercise any powers of the Court of Appeal ...' We ask ourselves: what are the powers of the Court of Appeal? The answer to that question is that this court's powers are those given to it by the Criminal Appeal Act 1968. This court is, as has been said many times, a creature of that statute, and the only powers it has are the powers which are afforded to it by that statute. Accordingly sub-s (3) of s 35 must mean that for the purpose of disposing of an appeal the House of Lords may exercise the powers that this court has pursuant to Pt I of the Act.

The final phrase is: 'the House of Lords ... may remit the case to the Court'. That clearly means it may remit the case to the Court of Appeal for the purpose of the Court of Appeal exercising its powers. Those powers again can only be powers which this court derives from the Act. Accordingly this court is then in the position in our judgment of having to deal with the issue referred to it as it would have done had the case come to it through the route laid down in the Criminal Appeal Act 1968, Pt I. In those circumstances we consider that our powers are exactly those which we would have had if the issue in question had come to this court directly by way of an appeal against sentence. We can see no reason why the same principle which applied in *Jefferies*, and was approved in *Maguire*, should not apply in this situation. We consider that the House of Lords, when it remitted the case to this court, was in fact disposing of the appeal under Pt II. The House of Lords had decided the point of public importance, and in remitting the case to this court it was disposing of the appeal to the House of Lords. This court was then faced with the exercise of its powers under Pt I of the Criminal Appeal Act 1968 to deal with the issue which had been remitted. In those circumstances we consider that the same situation arises as arose in the case of Harris, that the demise of the appellant Kearley caused this appeal to abate, although there could be a petition to the Home Secretary for a reference under s 17. We express no opinion on what would be the situation if an appellant were to die in the course of an appeal to the House of Lords whilst that appeal was in progress. It is not relevant to the decision we have to make in the present case. Moreover it would be inappropriate for this court to express any view on a matter which clearly, if it ever arose, would be before the House of Lords for their Lordships to decide in that instance. Accordingly we say nothing about that. The effect of what we have said is that in both these cases the appeals are abated.

Orders accordingly. The court refused leave to appeal to the House of Lords but certified in R v Kearley, under s 33(2) of the Criminal Appeal Act 1968 ,that the following point of law of general public importance was involved in the decision: where a case is remitted by the House of Lords to the Court of Appeal, Criminal Division pursuant to s 35(3) of the Criminal Appeal Act 1968 and the appellant dies before the case is heard in the Court of Appeal, has that court jurisdiction to deal with the case?

N P Metcalfe Esq   Barrister.

Crozier v Crozier

FAMILY DIVISION

BOOTH J

3 NOVEMBER, 7 DECEMBER 1993

Divorce – Financial provision – Variation of order – Consent order – Appeal from consent order – Order made in full and final settlement of all claims between parties – Husband transferring his share in matrimonial home to wife on basis that wife would have full responsibility of maintaining child in future – Wife receiving income support – Child Support Agency requiring husband to contribute towards maintenance of child – Husband applying for leave to appeal to set aside consent order to recover his share in former matrimonial home – Whether demand by Child Support Agency constituting new event which undermined basis of consent order – Whether consent order should be set aside.

The husband and wife were married in 1981 and this marriage was dissolved in 1988. There was one child of the marriage. In ancillary proceedings the parties came to an agreement that the husband would transfer to the wife his half share in the matrimonial home, which had an equity of about £16,000, the wife would take over responsibility for the mortgage of £11,862 and she would have full responsibility for maintaining the child of the marriage. The registrar approved the terms of the agreement and made a consent order in February 1989 to that effect which was expressed to be 'intended to effect a full and final settlement of all financial and property claims arising between the parties from the breakdown of the marriage whether present or future save for child maintenance', the proviso being inserted by the registrar with a view to preserving the child's entitlement in certain exigencies. The wife's earnings were insufficient to maintain herself and the child and she received income support. The husband was a self-employed joiner then earning about £50 to £60 per week. In March 1993, following a complaint by the Secretary of State under the Social Security Administration Act 1992, an order was made that the husband pay £4 per week towards the child's maintenance. The husband was subsequently notified by the Child Support Agency that, applying the formula introduced under the Child Support Act 1991, his liability for the child's maintenance would be increased to approximately £29 per week. The husband applied for leave to appeal against the consent order so that it could be set aside or varied. The husband, whose current earnings were £9,390 gross, was living with another woman and her child aged seven and their own child aged two. They wished to purchase their home for £17,800 on a 100% mortgage. The wife was living with another man whom she was shortly to marry. The child of the marriage and their own child lived with them. The wife had sold the former matrimonial home and the proceeds of £20,000 were held on deposit. If the consent order was set aside the husband's half share of the proceeds would if invested be sufficient to enable him to pay any maintenance required of him in the future for the child of the marriage. The husband contended that his increased liability for child maintenance assessed under the 1991 Act constituted a new event which had undermined the basis of the consent order, which should be set aside to enable him to recover his share of the proceeds of sale of the former home.

Held – A demand made on a husband by the Child Support Agency that he contribute towards the maintenance of the child or children of his former marriage according to the formula introduced under the 1991 Act was not a reason for setting aside a clean break consent order made on the basis that the husband would transfer his share of the matrimonial home in full and final settlement of the wife's claims for herself and the children. While the parties were free to achieve a clean break as between themselves, they had no power to do so in respect of their children since the legal liability to maintain their children remained on both parents. The continuing right of the child to be maintained had been reflected in the consent order by the registrar's proviso, 'save for child maintenance'. Although the wife had agreed to assume responsibility for the child's maintenance she had been unable to do so without state support and at the time the agreement was concluded and the order was made, the state was empowered to seek the recovery of its expenditure on benefit from a person who was liable for maintenance. Furthermore, the state was not bound by the agreement or the consent order. The fact that the 1991 Act had introduced a new administrative method, bypassing the courts' jurisdiction, by which the state could compel a parent to contribute towards the maintenance of a child did not constitute a new event in fact or law which was sufficient to invalidate the basis of the consent order. Accordingly, there were no grounds to set aside the consent order and leave to appeal would be refused (see p 370 *d* to *h*, p 371 *c* to *g* and p 372 *a b*, post).

Barder v Barder (Caluori intervening) [1987] 2 All ER 440 considered.

Notes

For the court's power to vary consent orders for ancillary relief, see 13 *Halsbury's Laws* (4th edn) para 1170, and for cases on the subject see 27(2) *Digest* (Reissue) 842, *6700–6701*.

For the Child Support Act 1991, see 6 *Halsbury's Statutes* (4th edn) (1992 reissue) 639.

Cases referred to in judgment

B (GC) v B (BA) [1970] 1 All ER 913, [1970] 1 WLR 664, DC.
Barder v Barder (Caluori intervening) [1987] 2 All ER 440, [1988] AC 20, [1987] 2 WLR 1350, HL.
de Lasala v de Lasala [1979] 2 All ER 1146, [1980] AC 546, [1979] 3 WLR 390, PC.
Minton v Minton [1979] 1 All ER 79, [1979] AC 593, [1979] 2 WLR 31 HL.
Preston v Preston [1982] 1 All ER 41, [1982] Fam 17, [1981] 3 WLR 619, CA.
Robinson v Robinson [1982] 2 All ER 699, [1982] 1 WLR 786, CA
Thwaite v Thwaite [1981] 2 All ER 789, [1982] Fam 1, [1981] 3 WLR 96, CA.

Appeal

By notice dated 20 May 1993 the husband applied under r 8(1) of the Family Proceedings Rules 1991 for leave to appeal out of time and for an order to set aside or vary an ancillary order by consent made by Mr Registrar Holloway on 8 February 1989 in the Carlisle County Court in divorce proceedings between the husband and his former wife. The appeal was transferred to the High Court on the ground that it raised a point of public importance. The facts are set out in the judgment.

Judith Fordham (instructed by *J A Coupland & Co*, Carlisle) for the wife.

Iain Goldrein (instructed by *Brabner Holden*, Liverpool) for the husband.

BOOTH J. On 8 February 1989 Mr Registrar Holloway, sitting in the Carlisle County Court, made an ancillary relief order in the divorce proceedings between the husband and the wife. It was an order made with the consent of both parties. It provided that the husband should transfer to the wife absolutely his share in the matrimonial home in full and final settlement of all her financial claims against him. The order was also made on the agreed basis that there should be a nominal order only for the maintenance of the one child of the family, a boy then aged five years who lived with the wife. It was specifically stated in the order that she would have the full responsibility of maintaining the child in the future. The wife, however, was unable to earn sufficient to maintain herself and her son and she received income support.

Early in 1993 the Secretary of State for Social Security made a complaint in the Carlisle Magistrates' Court, under the Social Security Administration Act 1992, for an order requiring the husband to contribute towards the boy's maintenance, and on 10 March 1993 an order was made that he should pay £4 a week. The husband has now received documents from the Child Support Agency. It is anticipated that, on the application of the formula introduced under the Child Support Act 1991, his liability for his son would be increased to approximately £29 per week.

It is in those circumstances that he now asks the court to set aside, or vary, the consent order, so that he may recover his share of the former matrimonial home. The wife objects to this.

Before dealing with the substantive issue between the parties, it is convenient to consider, first, the procedure taken on behalf of the husband (and I will refer to the parties as 'husband' and 'wife') to bring the matter before this court.

By notice dated 20 May 1993, the husband applied for leave to appeal out of time and for the order to be set aside or varied. In family proceedings, appeals from registrars are governed by Family Proceedings Rules 1991, SI 1991/1247, r 8(1), and in the case of an order made on an application for ancillary relief, the judge hearing the appeal may exercise his own discretion in substitution for that of the registrar.

Mrs Fordham, on behalf of the wife, submits that this was not the correct procedure and that the husband should have instead issued fresh proceedings to set aside the consent order, in accordance with CCR Ord 37, r 1.

The procedure to be followed, where it is desired to set aside or vary a consent order, has been judicially considered in a number of reported authorities. In *de Lasala v de Lasala* [1979] 2 All ER 1146 at 1155, [1980] AC 546 at 561 Lord Diplock opined that two routes were open to the applicant. He said:

'Where a party to an action seeks to challenge, on the ground that it was obtained by fraud or mistake, a judgment or order that finally disposes of the issues raised between the parties, the only ways of doing it that are open to him are by appeal from the judgment or order to a higher court or by bringing a fresh action to set it aside.'

Both these courses have been followed in subsequent cases.

In *Thwaite v Thwaite* [1981] 2 All ER 789 at 794, [1982] Fam 1 at 8, the appellate course was taken and approved. In that case, the parties to matrimonial proceedings agreed terms which were embodied in a consent order. The husband was to convey to the wife his share of the matrimonial home, on the basis that it would be used by her as a permanent home for herself and the children, and that her applications for financial relief would be dismissed. Before the conveyance had been effected, the husband discovered that the wife had no intention of remaining in England and he appealed against the consent order. Ormrod LJ, delivering the judgment of the court, applied the principle that agreements which were made the subject of consent orders derived their legal effect from the order. He went on to say:

> 'The effect of eliminating the contractual basis of these consent orders should simplify the problems. If their legal effect is derived from the court order it must follow, we think, that they must be treated as orders of the court and dealt with, so far as possible, in the same way as non-consensual orders. So, if the order is one of those listed in s 31(2) of the Matrimonial Causes Act 1973, it can be varied in accordance with the terms of that section (see *B (GC) v B (BA)* [1970] 1 All ER 913, [1970] 1 WLR 664). But if it is not within the list, it cannot be varied by the court of first instance. Similarly, as orders of the court, they must be subject to the provisions which apply to appeals from orders made at first instance, though with one important exception. Where the court of first instance has not adjudicated on the evidence, its decision cannot be challenged on the ground that the court has reached a wrong conclusion on the evidence before it. Final orders of all kinds, however, can be challenged on appeal and may be set aside on other grounds. Lord Diplock referred to two such grounds, fraud or mistake, but there are others, for example, on fresh evidence properly admitted by the appellate court.'

The appellate procedure was that which was followed in *Barder v Barder (Caluori intervening)* [1987] 2 All ER 440, [1988] AC 20, where a husband applied for leave to appeal out of time against a consent order made by a registrar, in circumstances to which I will refer in greater detail later in this judgment. There is no mention in the report that that procedure was challenged.

The second route, that of issuing fresh proceedings to set aside the order, was considered and amended by the Court of Appeal in *Robinson v Robinson* [1982] 2 All ER 699, [1982] 1 WLR 786. There, the wife appealed to the Court of Appeal against a consent order of a High Court judge, on the ground that the husband had misrepresented his financial position. Dealing with the procedural questions which had been raised during the hearing, Ormrod LJ said ([1982] 2 All ER 699 at 700, [1982] 1 WLR 786 at 786–787):

> 'From the point of view of convenience, there is a lot to be said for proceedings of this kind taking place before a judge at first instance, because there will usually be serious and often difficult issues of fact to be determined before the power to set aside can be exercised. These can be determined more easily, as a rule, by a judge at first instance. Moreover he can go on to make the appropriate order which we cannot do in this court. I think that these proceedings should normally be started before a judge at first instance, although there may be special circumstances which make it better to proceed by way of appeal.'

In my judgment two principles can be drawn from these authorities. The first is that it is open to the party who seeks to set aside or vary a consent order, to proceed either by way of appeal or to bring fresh proceedings. The second principle is that the procedure selected shall be that which is the better suited for the determination of the issues involved. In cases where issues of fact will need to be resolved, or the court will be asked to make substantive orders, then it will clearly be more convenient for the case to be heard by a judge with the appropriate jurisdiction, rather than by the Court of Appeal. There is no suggestion anywhere in the authorities that the court would apply a different approach on the basis of the procedure adopted, so that the same principles would apply in either case.

I am satisfied that the procedure followed on behalf of the husband is entirely appropriate to this case and that it would be artificial and serve no purpose whatever to require him to commence fresh proceedings. An appeal from a registrar allows a judge, who has all the necessary powers and jurisdiction, to determine facts and make orders, where necessary exercising his discretion in substitution for that of the registrar. In this case, because the appeal raised a point of public importance, it was transferred from the county court to the High Court, and in that way it comes before this court. I am in no doubt at all that the correct steps have been taken to enable the court to determine the issues which are now before it.

I turn now to the substance of the appeal.

In order to understand the gravamen of the husband's case and the impact upon him of the implementation of the Child Support Act 1991, it is necessary to consider the facts in greater detail; they are not in dispute.

The parties were married in July 1981 and lived together for almost six years. Their marriage was finally dissolved in May 1988. At the time the consent order was made the husband was a self-employed joiner with an income of about £50 to £60 a week. The wife was earning about £30 a week and received a little over £50 a week by way of income support. The matrimonial home had an agreed value of £28,000 and was subject to an outstanding mortgage of £11,862, so that the equity was in the region of £16,000. It was held in joint names. In offering to transfer his interest, worth approximately £8,000, the husband intended it to be a total settlement, with no further maintenance payable either to her or to the child. This was acceptable to the wife, who was advised by solicitors.

Accordingly, the matter came before the registrar on 8 February 1989. The application was made by the wife's solicitors and was indorsed with the consent of the husband. The learned registrar approved the agreement and exercised his discretion to make the order, with the addition, however, of some important words of his own. It is necessary now to refer to the order in full; it reads as follows:

'By consent it is ordered that (1) The respondent do pay or cause to be paid to the petitioner for the benefit of the child ... (born 31 October 1984), maintenance pending suit and thereafter periodical payments at the rate of 5p per annum until the said child shall attain the age of 17 years or until further order. (2) The petitioner's claim for maintenance for herself be dismissed. (3) The respondent do transfer to the petitioner absolutely all his legal and equitable estate in the [matrimonial home] subject to the mortgage in favour of the Cumberland Building Society, and it is recorded that the petitioner will use her best endeavours to obtain the release of the respondent from his obligations under the said mortgage. All rights of occupation of the property by the respondent shall then be terminated. (4) That the contents of the former matrimonial home shall be hereby declared to be the property of the petitioner absolutely. (5) And it is hereby agreed and declared between the parties that the respondent is transferring all his estate, share and interest in the matrimonial home to the petitioner absolutely on the basis that there is to be a nominal order for maintenance for the child only and that the petitioner will have the full responsibility of maintaining the said child in future. (6) It is recorded that this order is intended to effect a full and final settlement of all financial and property claims arising between the parties from the breakdown of the marriage, whether present or future, save for child maintenance, and upon compliance with paras 1 to 7 herein, the respective claims of the parties under ss 23, 24 and 24A of the Matrimonial Causes Act 1973 do stand dismissed and neither party shall make any application under the Married Women's Property Act, 1882. (7) Without prejudice to the generality of the foregoing, it is directed (a) neither party shall make any further application for an order under s 23(1) or s 23(b) of the Matrimonial Causes Act 1973; (b) neither party shall upon the death of the other apply for an order under s 2 of the Inheritance (Provision for Family and Dependants) Act 1975. (8) No order for costs, save that the costs of the petitioner be taxed on a standard basis, in accordance with the provisions of the Second Schedule to the Legal Aid Act 1974.'

The words which were added to the order by the registrar were those of the proviso, 'save for child maintenance', which appear in para (6). In a note of his reasons for making the order, which he has provided for the purposes of this appeal, the registrar stated that he added those words in order 'to preserve the child's entitlement in certain exigencies'.

The husband duly transferred his interest in the former matrimonial home to the wife, and was not called upon to make any further payments in respect of the mortgage. But contrary to the intention and expectation of the parties, the order was made on 10 March 1993 that he should pay periodical payments for the child at the rate of £4 a week.

The husband is presently employed as a wood machinist earning £9,390 pa gross. He lives with a lady and her child aged seven, together with the child of their union, aged two. That lady is earning some £4,800 pa. She receives maintenance in respect of her child, of £14 a week, and child benefit for both children. The couple are purchasing their home, a former council house, for £17,800, with the aid of 100% mortgage. Their monthly outgoings total £1,140.

The wife is living with another man whom she is shortly to marry. The child of the family lives with them, together with a baby of their union aged six months. It is fortuitous from the husband's point of view that, in view of the wife's forthcoming marriage, the former matrimonial home has recently been sold and the proceeds, of approximately £20,000, are being held on deposit pending the outcome of this appeal.

The husband asks that the consent order should now be set aside, to enable him to recover his half share of the proceeds of sale of the property. That sum of £10,000 or thereabouts could be invested, and from the interest the husband could pay any maintenance, now and in the future, required of him for the child of the family. It has been calculated that the interest that he could reasonably expect to receive would enable him to meet the sum which it is anticipated that he will in due course be required to pay under the child support formula.

The husband does not dispute his obligation to maintain his son. It is his case that he has already fulfilled this obligation by way of the capital payment to the wife represented by his half share of the home.

The wife accepts that the property transfer was intended for the benefit of the child and was given and accepted in lieu of periodical payments.

By reason of the intervention of the state, the husband contends that he is being required to pay twice over, no account being taken of the sum he has already paid.

Although she concedes the basis upon which she and the husband reached agreement in 1989, the wife nevertheless contests the appeal. She intends that half the proceeds of the sale, in effect the husband's half, should be invested for the benefit of their child and that the income therefrom will go towards his maintenance. On her remarriage, and with the additional income that she will have, she will no longer be entitled to income support. The result will be that the husband may not then be subject either to the present maintenance order or, perhaps more importantly, to any demands made under the Child Support Act 1991.

The initial factual premise of this judgment must be that the parties would never have reached the agreement that they did if they had thought that the husband would be required to make periodical payments for the child of the family, certainly of the magnitude of the sum calculated by formula under the Child Support Act 1991 or probably at all. His half share of the home represented the entirety of his capital assets.

The marriage was not of long duration, having subsisted for seven years at the most. There were no circumstances to suggest that a court would have been reasonably likely to have made an order giving the wife all the available capital for herself, even in full and final satisfaction of her claims. Had the parties contemplated a continuing liability for periodical payments, either for the wife or for the child, it is reasonable to suppose that the husband's half share in the property would have been preserved for the use of the wife, qua mother, for as long as she needed it as a home for herself and the child, and thereafter would have reverted to the husband. With the sale of the house and the wife's remarriage, that position would now have been reached. It is common ground between the parties that the absolute transfer of the husband's half share to the wife was intended to benefit the child, and it is her continuing intention that it should do so.

In accordance with s 25 of the Matrimonial Causes Act 1973, as substituted by s 3 of the Matrimonial and Family Proceedings Act 1984, the court, when making the order, was bound to have as its first consideration the welfare of the child, and it is clear, from the note written to this court by Registrar Holloway, that such agreements were at the time regarded as appropriate and beneficial for a child in circumstances such as these, where the husband's income was not such that he could afford to make periodical payments.

It is against that factual background that Mr Goldrein, for the husband, now seeks to set aside the order.

The primary authority in relation to such an application is the decision of the House of Lords in *Barder v Barder (Caluori intervening)* [1987] 2 All ER 440, [1988] AC 20. In that case the matrimonial home was owned jointly by the husband and wife. On the dissolution of their marriage, the wife was awarded the custody and care and control of the two children of the family, and an order was made by consent that the husband should transfer to her his interest in the property. Before the transfer had been executed, the wife killed the children and committed suicide. The husband appealed the order out of time, on the ground that it had been based on a fundamental assumption that the wife and the children would, for a substantial period of time, require a suitable home and that that assumption had been totally invalidated by their deaths.

The appeal was allowed and the order was set aside. In his speech, Lord Brandon of Oakbrook identified certain conditions which required to be satisfied before a court could properly exercise its discretion to grant leave to appeal out of time from an order for financial provision or property transfer made after a divorce on the ground of new events. He said ([1987] 2 All ER 440 at 453, [1988] AC 20 at 43):

> 'The first condition is that new events have occurred since the making of the order which invalidate the basis, or fundamental assumption, on which the order was made, so that, if leave to appeal out of time were to be given, the appeal would be certain, or very likely, to succeed. The second condition is that the new events should have occurred within a relatively short time of the order having been made. While the length of time cannot be laid down precisely, I should regard it as extremely unlikely that it could be as much as a year, and that in most cases it will be no more than a few months. The third condition is that the application for leave to appeal out of time should be made reasonably promptly in the circumstances of the case ... [The] fourth condition is that the grant of leave to appeal out of time should not prejudice third parties who have acquired, in good faith and for valuable consideration, interests in property which is the subject matter of the relevant order.'

I turn to the first of those four conditions and to consider whether the new events which have occurred since the making of the consent order in 1989 invalidate the basis or fundamental assumption on which it was made. In this case, as in *Barder v Barder*, the agreement which the parties reached was intended to operate as a clean financial break between them. The desirability of achieving a clean financial break between spouses emanates from the speech of Lord Scarman in *Minton v Minton* [1979] 1 All ER 79 at 87, [1979] AC 593 at 608. The issue there to be determined, was whether or not the provisions of the Matrimonial Causes Act 1973, empowered the court to make a second or subsequent maintenance order for a wife after an earlier application had been dismissed. Lord Scarman said:

> 'There are two principles which inform the modern legislation. One is the public interest that spouses, to the extent that their means permit, should provide for themselves and their children. But the other, of equal importance, is the principle of "the clean break". The law now encourages spouses to avoid bitterness after family breakdown and to settle their money and property problems. An object of the modern law is to encourage the parties to put the past behind them and to begin a new life which is not overshadowed by the relationship which has broken down. It would be inconsistent with this principle if the court could not make, as between the spouses, a genuinely final order unless it was prepared to dismiss the application.'

As between spouses, the 'clean break' principle now forms part of the statutory code governing the court's approach to ancillary relief applications. The court itself is required to consider the exercise of its powers in such a way as will terminate the financial obligations of each party towards the other: see s 15(a) of the Matrimonial Causes Act 1973, inserted by s 3 of the Matrimonial Proceedings and Property Act 1984.

Different considerations, however, have applied in relation to child maintenance, where the ongoing responsibility of the parents has remained a basic factor, to which the clean break principle has never applied.

In *Preston v Preston* [1982] 1 All ER 41, [1982] Fam 17 Brandon LJ expressed the view that it was neither possible nor desirable to bring about a clean break between father and son. That principle has been consistently applied and was clearly acknowledged by the learned registrar in this case, when he inserted in the order the words, 'save for child maintenance', thus emphasising the continuing right of the child to be maintained and, therefore, the continuing duty on the parents to do so.

While the parties were free to achieve a clean break as between themselves, it was outside their powers to do so in respect of their child. That position could not be changed by reason of the statement of intent which appears upon the face of the order that the wife would assume responsibility for the child's maintenance. In fact, at the time the order was made the wife was not maintaining the child, since she did not have the adequate means to do so. Accordingly, she was in receipt of income support and so, in effect, the state was assuming that liability of her behalf. In reality, the husband could only be relieved of his obligation at the expense of the state.

What was not anticipated by the parties was that the state would intervene, to relieve itself (if not rid itself) of that financial burden. Nevertheless, at the time they concluded the agreement and the order was made, the state was empowered to seek the recovery of its expenditure on benefit from a person who was liable for maintenance.

As to this, the relevant statutory provision in force in February 1989 was s 24 of the Social Security Act 1986, which enabled the Secretary of State to make a complaint to a magistrates' court for an order against a person, liable to maintain another, who was in receipt of income support. That was by no means a new statutory provision; its precursor was contained in the Supplementary Benefits Act 1976. That same provision is now to be found in ss 106 and 107 of the Social Security Administration Act 1992, under provisions of which the existing periodical payments order of March 1993 was made against the husband.

Mr Goldrein seeks to draw a distinction between the power vested in the Secretary of State to obtain an order in the magistrates' court under the longstanding legislation and an order made in accordance with the new Child Support Act 1991. In the former case, on an application to the court, the Bench will exercise a judicial discretion, being required by statute to have regard to all the circumstances of the case. No such wide discretion exists under the 1991 Act, which came fully into force on 5 April 1993. The purpose of that Act, as stated in the preamble, is—

> 'to make provision for the assessment, collection and enforcement of periodical maintenance payable by certain parents with respect to children of theirs who are not in their care.'

To this end, the Act introduces a machinery outside the jurisdiction of the
courts, whereby liability for child maintenance is assessed in accordance with
a formula which is based upon income support rates and upon prescribed
information as to the financial means of both parents.

This calculation does not admit of variation. It is a straight mathematical
computation. The result in monetary terms may be very different from the
quantum of a court order, as in the present case, where the husband's current
liability has been determined at £4 a week, as against his anticipated liability of
£29 per week. Mr Goldrein submits that it is that method of assessment,
imposed by Parliament since the making of the consent order, that constitutes
a new event which has undermined the basis of the order to the extent that it
should be set aside.

I am unable to accept that submission. The fact that Parliament has chosen
a new administrative method by which the state may intervene to compel a
parent to contribute towards the maintenance of a child, bypassing the
jurisdiction of the courts, does not fundamentally alter the position as it was in
law in February 1989. The parties were then unable to achieve a clean financial
break in respect of their son. The legal liability to maintain him remained on
them both as his parents. While the wife was prepared to assume that
responsibility as between herself and the husband, she could not in fact fulfil
that obligation without the assistance of state moneys. The state was never
bound by the agreement or the order. At any time it could have intervened,
through the Secretary of State, to seek an order through the courts, and the
parties were not entitled to assume for the purposes of their agreement that it
would not do so.

I consider that it is immaterial for this purpose that that same parental
liability will now be enforced through an agency outside the courts. That is a
difference only in the means by which the state may proceed to relieve itself of
the obligation which is the duty of the parents to discharge. The fact that the
sum required of a parent may be greater under the new procedure than under
the old is a consequence of the procedural change and not of any new and
unforeseen power vested in the state.

In my judgment, neither the existing order made in March 1993, under the
statutory machinery which existed in February 1989, nor any anticipated
liability which may be levied under the new machinery introduced by the 1991
Act, constitutes a new event, in fact or in law, sufficient to invalidate the basis
of the consent order.

That finding is sufficient to dispose of Mr Goldrein's submissions, based
upon the principles of *Barder v Barder (Caluori intervening)* [1987] 2 All ER 440,
[1988] AC 20. I do not think that it is appropriate, or that it would serve any
useful purpose for me to consider whether the alleged new event was
sufficiently proximate in time to the order to satisfy the second condition
promulgated by Lord Brandon. Mr Goldrein did, however, advance a further
argument, based upon the doctrine of frustration in the law of contract. While
it is well established that a subsequent change in the law, or in the legal
position affecting a contract, may constitute a head of frustration, in my
judgment that is not applicable to this case. As Mrs Fordham, for the wife,
correctly contends, once a financial agreement has been made the subject of a
court order, its legal effect derives from that order and not from the agreement
of the parties: see per Lord Diplock in *de Lasala v de Lasala* [1979] 2 All ER 1146,
[1980] AC 546.

In this case the agreement which the parties reached has been subsumed in the consent order to which the doctrine of contractual frustration does not apply.

In my judgment there are no grounds on which this consent order can be set aside and the husband cannot succeed on his appeal, harsh though the result may be for him.

In those circumstances I refuse leave for him to appeal out of time.

Leave to appeal refused.

Bebe Chua Barrister.

R v Collett and others

COURT OF APPEAL, CRIMINAL DIVISION
NOLAN LJ, TUCKEY AND LATHAM JJ
7, 11, 21 OCTOBER 1993

Town and country planning – Enforcement notice – Contravention – Use of land in contravention of enforcement notice – Whether absolute offence or whether proof of knowledge of enforcement notice required – Town and Country Planning Act 1990, ss 179(6), 285(2).

On the true construction of s 179(6)[a] of the Town and Country Planning Act 1990, read in conjunction with s 285(2)[b] of that Act, the offence of using, causing or permitting land to be used in contravention of an enforcement notice served by a local planning authority under s 172(1)[c] of the 1990 Act is an absolute offence which does not require the prosecution to prove that the defendant had actual knowledge of the enforcement notice, since Parliament must have intended that the burden of establishing whether any use of land is prohibited should be on the person seeking to make use of the land. Section 285(2) provides a very limited opportunity to challenge the validity of the enforcement notice, and therefore defend a charge under s 179(6), to a

---

a Section 179(6) provides: 'Where, by virtue of an enforcement notice—(a) a use of land is required to be discontinued, or (b) any conditions or limitations are required to be complied with in respect of a use of land or in respect of the carrying out of operations on it, then, if any person uses the land or causes or permits it to be used, or carries out those operations or causes or permits them to be carried out, in contravention of the notice, he shall be guilty of an offence.'

b Section 285, so far as material, provides:
'(1) ... the validity of an enforcement notice shall not, except by way of an appeal under Part VII, be questioned in any proceedings whatsoever on any of the grounds on which an appeal may be brought.
(2) Subsection (1) shall not apply to proceedings brought under section 179(6) ... against a person who—(a) has held an interest in the land since before the enforcement was issued under that Part; (b) did not have a copy of the enforcement notice served on him under that Part; and (c) satisfies the court—(i) that he did not know and could not reasonably have been expected to know that the enforcement notice had been issued; and (ii) that his interests have been substantially prejudiced by the failure to serve him with a copy of it ...'

c Section 172(1), so far as material, provides: 'Where—(a) it appears to the local planning authority that there has been a breach of planning control ... they may issue a notice requiring the breach to be remedied.'

restricted category of those who did not know that an enforcement notice had been served, and it is plain from s 285(2) that the statutory provisions are intended to encourage those who own, occupy or otherwise have interests in land to take all necessary steps to advise themselves of the planning status of land. Section 285(2) would be wholly unnecessary if the prosecution had to establish knowledge of the enforcement notice in order to prove the offence under s 172(1) (see p 381 *h j* and p 382 *b* to *g*, post).

Gammon v A-G of Hong Kong [1984] 2 All ER 503 applied.

Notes

For the offence of failing to comply with an enforcement notice, see 46 *Halsbury's Laws* (4th edn reissue) para 672, and for cases on the subject, see 47(1) *Digest* (Reissue) 147–149, 535–542.

For the Town and Country Planning Act 1990, ss 172, 179, 285, see 46 *Halsbury's Statutes* (4th edn) (1990 reissue) 709, 721, 828.

As from 24 August 1990 ss 172(1), 179(6) and 285(2) of the 1990 Act replaced ss 87(1), 89(5) and 243(2) of the Town and Country Planning Act 1971.

Cases referred to in judgment

Brend v Wood (1946) 175 LT 306, DC.
Gammon (Hong Kong) Ltd v A-G of Hong Kong [1984] 2 All ER 503, [1985] AC 1, [1984] 3 WLR 437, PC.
McDaid v Clydebank DC [1984] JPL 579, Ct of Sess.
R v Kuxhaus [1988] 2 All ER 705, [1988] QB 631, [1988] 2 WLR 1005, CA.
R v Greenwich London BC, ex p Patel [1985] JPL 851, CA.
R v Secretary of State for the Environment, ex p Kuxhaus [1985] CA Transcript 682.
Sweet v Parsley [1969] 1 All ER 347, [1970] AC 132, [1969] 2 WLR 470, HL.
Wrekin DC v Shah (1986) 150 JP 22, DC.

Cases also cited

Lim Chin Aik v R [1963] 1 All ER 223, [1963] AC 160, PC.
Maltglade Ltd v St Albans RDC [1972] 3 All ER 129, [1972] 1 WLR 1230, DC.
Moody v Godstone RDC [1966] 2 All ER 696, [1966] 1 WLR 1085, DC.
R v Tolson (1889) 23 QBD 168, [1886–90] All ER Rep 26, CCR.
White v Weston [1968] 2 All ER 842, [1968] 2 QB 647, CA.

Appeals against conviction

Michael Collett, Derek James Furminger, Hessam Nazari, Philip James Pope and Nasser Bandar appealed against their convictions on 10 September 1990 in the Crown Court at Lewes before Mr C W Byers sitting as an assistant recorder, having changed their pleas to guilty at the close of the prosecution case, on an indictment containing two counts of using land in contravention of enforcement notices dated 11 October 1979 contrary to s 89(5) of the Town and Country Planning Act 1971. On 12 September 1990 Collett, Pope and Bandar were each fined £300 and Furminger and Nazari were fined £500. Collett, Furminger and Bandar were each ordered to pay a maximum of £250 towards legal aid, and each appellant was ordered to pay £1,200 prosecution costs. The facts are set out in the judgment of the court.

Christopher Beaumont (assigned by the *Registrar of Criminal Appeals*) for Collett, Furminger and Bandar and (instructed by *Pothecary & Barratt*, Bishop's Stortford) for Nazari and Pope.

Paul Ashwell (instructed by Catherine Knight, Lewes) for the Crown.

Cur adv vult

21 October 1993. The following judgment of the court was delivered.

LATHAM J. On 10 September 1990 in the Crown Court at Lewes the first four appellants pleaded not guilty to an offence of using land for the purposes of car and body repairs with associated paint spraying in contravention of an enforcement notice dated 11 October 1979; the fifth appellant pleaded not guilty to using the same land for the storage of building materials in contravention of a further enforcement notice of the same date. Counsel acting on their behalf made legal submissions at the end of the prosecution case which were rejected by the assistant recorder. All the appellants then pleaded guilty to the charges which they respectively faced. They were each ordered to pay £1,200 towards the costs of the prosecution. The appellants Mr Collett, Mr Pope and Mr Bandar were fined £300; the appellants Mr Furminger and Mr Nazari were fined £500. Mr Collett, Mr Furminger and Mr Bandar were also ordered to pay a maximum of £250 contribution towards their legal aid. They appeal against their convictions on the grounds that the rulings made by the assistant recorder were wrong in law.

The facts were as follows. Springfield Farm, Wivelsfield, East Sussex is the land in question. At all material times it had been owned by a Mr Saunders. In 1973 planning permission was granted for the use of the land as an egg packing and distribution station and for the servic*g* *g* of vehicles used in connection with these activities. This permission in f_t validated the use to which the land had been put for some time. Howevei, during the 1970s the egg packing and distribution business declined, and by 1979 at least three different and quite distinct business activities were taking place in buildings on the land which were nothing to do with egg packing or distribution. A Mr Kuxhaus was running a vehicle repair business; a Mr Wenban and a Mr Hilder were carrying on a business of servicing and repairing vehicles, including paint spraying; and a company, Philbridge Ltd, was using the site for bulk storage of builders' materials. The Lewes District Council determined to take enforcement action, and proceeded to serve enforcement notices in respect of the land in three different forms.

As far as the use being made of the land by Mr Kuxhaus was concerned, it required him to—

'discontinue the storage and repair of motor vehicles on the said land and remove therefrom all vehicles and materials used in connection therewith.'

The land itself was described as—

'all that piece or parcel of land adjacent to Ditchling Road, Wivelsfield in the County of Sussex shown edged red on the plan attached hereto and known as Springfield Farm (formerly Hey Farm) and in particular the building known and marked "A" on the said plan.'

This enforcement notice became known thereafter as 'enforcement notice A'.

As far as the use being made of the land by Mr Wenban and Mr Hilder was concerned, the enforcement notice required them to—

'discontinue the storage repair and paint spraying of motor vehicles on the said land and remove therefrom all materials and vehicles used in connection therewith.'

It described the land in the same way as in enforcement notice A, save that it identified in particular a building marked 'B' on the plan annexed to the notice. This notice became known as 'enforcement notice B'.

As far as the use of the land made by Philbridge Ltd was concerned, the enforcement notice required it to—

'discontinue the storage of builders' materials on the said land including two portable storage huts and an oil storage tank and remove therefrom all such materials and items mentioned and used in connection therewith.'

It described the land again in exactly the same terms as in enforcement notice A, save that it identified in particular a part of a building and a storage area shown and marked 'C' on the plan annexed to that notice. This notice became known as 'enforcement notice C'.

Enforcement notices in precisely the same terms were undoubtedly drafted in respect of Mr Saunders, the owner of the land, and there is no doubt that enforcement notice C was served on him. There is an issue as to what happened in respect of enforcement notice B. We have not been told anything about the service of enforcement notice A on Mr Saunders: it is, strictly, irrelevant, as the enforcement notices referred to in the indictment are enforcement notice B as far as the first four appellants are concerned and enforcement notice C as far as the fifth appellant is concerned.

The correspondence which has been provided for this appeal but which was not before the Crown Court shows that the principal legal officer for the Lewes District Council wrote on 11 October 1979 to a firm of solicitors, Messrs Pothecary & Barratt, in the following terms:

'I enclose for your information a copy of correspondence and enforcement notices served on the alleged owners and also the occupiers of land at the above property (Springfield Farm). These are served on you as solicitors acting for Mr. Kuxhaus and also for Mr. P G Saunders and I believe for the company which still owns the land which is The Lakeside Food Wholesale Ltd.'

On 13 November 1979 the solicitors replied stating:

'Mr. Saunders has instructed us to accept service of the enforcement notices addressed to him on his behalf. He also asks us to inform you that Lakeside Food Wholesale Ltd. has no interest in Springfield farm nor does his wife Mrs. Marcia Saunders. We also acknowledge receipt of the new notice served on us as solicitors for Mr. Kuxhaus.'

These same solicitors were then instructed on behalf of Mr Wenban and Mr Hilder, and on behalf of Philbridge Ltd. They entered an appeal against enforcement notice A on behalf of Mr Kuxhaus; they entered an appeal against enforcement notice B on behalf of Mr Wenban and Mr Hilder; and they entered appeals against enforcement notice C on behalf of Philbridge Ltd and Mr Saunders. The Secretary of State for the Environment dealt with the appeals together. A local inquiry was held. On 14 January 1982 the enforcement notices were upheld, but in an amended form. Mr Kuxhaus, Mr Wenban and Mr Hilder then exercised their right of appeal to the High Court in respect of enforcement notices A and B by notice of motion dated 11 February 1982. There was no appeal against the Secretary of State's decision in respect of enforcement notice C. The Secretary of State accepted that he had failed to give sufficient reasons for his decision, and, by consent, the matter, ie the appeals against enforcement notices A and B, was remitted in January 1983 to the Secretary of State for rehearing and redetermination. On 28 February 1985 he again upheld the two enforcement notices, this time in virtually their original form. Mr Kuxhaus and Mr Wenban (Mr Hilder having disappeared from the scene) appealed that decision to the High Court. The appeal was dismissed by Forbes J on 10 July 1985. On 7 November 1985 the Court of Appeal dismissed the appeal from the decision of Forbes J (see *R v Secretary of State for the Environment, ex p Kuxhaus* [1985] CA Transcript 682), and on 30 January 1986 the House of Lords dismissed a petition for leave to appeal.

In the meantime the Lewes District Council had decided to prosecute Mr Kuxhaus, Mr Wenban, and a number of other persons in occupation of the land, including the fourth and fifth appellants in these appeals, for breaches of enforcement notices A and B. The informations were laid in August 1985, and the matter eventually reached the Crown Court at Lewes on 27 October 1986. Amongst submissions made, and rejected by the judge, was the argument that, because the appeals had not been finally determined in 1985, by reason of the outstanding appeal to the Court of Appeal, there was no breach of the enforcement notices. The defendants to that prosecution then pleaded guilty, and appealed against their convictions. The Court of Appeal held that the judge had been wrong (see *R v Kuxhaus* [1988] 2 All ER 705, [1988] QB 631). The enforcement notices did not take effect until after the process of appeal to the High Court had been concluded by the dismissal of the petition to the House of Lords.

The proceedings which are the subject matter of these appeals are therefore the culmination of a long history of frustrated attempts by the Lewes District Council to give effect to the enforcement notices. They are based on a visit to the site by Mr Hayward, the council's enforcement officer, on 16 January 1990. He saw that the first four defendants were engaged in various activities relating to the repair and spraying of vehicles, and the fifth appellant was loading tiles, which were stored on the land, into the boot of his car.

At the trial Mr Hayward gave evidence to the jury of what he saw on this visit. He also gave evidence as to the existence of an entry by Lewes District Council in the local land charges register to the effect that the land was subject to enforcement notices served on 11 October 1979, and he produced copies of enforcement notices B and C addressed to Mr Peter Saunders, c/o National Westminster Bank Ltd, Munster Green, Haywards Heath.

That was the only evidence given on behalf of the prosecution. Mr Beaumont, on behalf of the appellants, made three submissions.

First, as far as count 1 was concerned, he submitted that on the true construction of s 87 of the Town and Country Planning Act 1971 it was necessary for an enforcement notice to be served on the owner before it could have any effect, and that there was no evidence before the court that it had been so served. The assistant recorder rejected this submission, but gave no reasons.

Second, Mr Beaumont submitted that the enforcement notices, properly construed, only prohibited the non-conforming uses in the areas identified respectively as B and C on the plans annexed to the two enforcement notices, and that Mr Hayward had failed to give any evidence as to what activities took place in these areas which could be said to be in breach of the enforcement notices and to be the responsibility of these appellants. The assistant recorder ruled that the enforcement notices clearly referred to the whole of the land, and therefore rejected this submission.

Third, Mr Beaumont submitted that the offence with which the appellants were charged, ie an offence under s 89(5) of the 1971 Act, was not an absolute offence, but required the prosecution to prove, which it had not, that each appellant knew of the existence of the enforcement notice of which he was said to be in breach, and that the registration of an enforcement notice in the local land charges register was not sufficient to establish such knowledge. The assistant recorder held that the offence was an offence of strict liability, but that, if and in so far as any knowledge was required on the part of the appellants, registration in the land charges register was sufficient to establish such knowledge, as it constituted deemed knowledge of the enforcement notices. It was after these submissions had been rejected that the appellants changed their pleas to guilty and were dealt with as we have described at the beginning of this judgment.

In this court Mr Beaumont repeated the submissions that he made to the assistant recorder. In addition, he submitted that the entry in the land charges register is deficient, that it does not relate to enforcement notice C and, therefore, cannot be used to support an argument that Mr Bandar must have been deemed to have known of the existence of this enforcement notice. And he yet further submitted that in any event, in relation to enforcement notice C, the appeal process has, inadvertently, never been concluded, because the effect of the order of 21 January 1983 in the appeal by Mr Kuxhaus, Mr Wenban and Mr Hilder was that the whole decision letter, including the part which dealt with enforcement notice C, was quashed, leaving the appeal in relation to enforcement notice C still outstanding.

Before dealing with these grounds of appeal, which we will do seriatim hereafter, it is necessary to set out the relevant statutory provisions. They are contained in the Town and Country Planning Act 1971. Although this Act was amended by the Local Government and Planning (Amendment) Act 1981 and has since been replaced by the Town and Country Planning Act 1990, it is the 1971 Act in its unamended form with which we are concerned.

Section 87(1) empowers a local planning authority to serve an enforcement notice where it appears that there has been a breach of planning control, requiring the breach to be remedied. Section 87(4) provides that an enforcement notice shall be served on the owner or any other person having an interest in the land which in the opinion of the authority is materially affected by the notice.

Section 283 sets out the methods by which service can be effected.

Section 88(1) gives a right of appeal to the Secretary of State for the Environment against the enforcement notice to any person who has been served with the notice, or any other person having an interest in the land, on a number of grounds including, by para (e), that the enforcement notice has not been served as required by s 87(4). By s 88(4)(b) the Secretary of State is given a discretion to disregard the failure to serve any person required to be served, if neither the person appealing nor the person who should have been served has been substantially prejudiced by the failure to be served. Section 88(3) provides that where an appeal has been brought the enforcement notice shall be of no effect pending the final determination or the withdrawal of the appeal.

By s 89(1) the owner of land upon whom an enforcement notice has been served is guilty of an offence if the steps required by the notice to be taken (other than the discontinuance of a use of land) have not been taken within the period specified in the enforcement notice. By s 89(5):

'Where, by virtue of an enforcement notice, a use of land is required to be discontinued ... if any person uses the land or causes or permits it to be used ... in contravention of the notice, he shall be guilty of an offence ...'

This is the subsection under which these appellants were convicted.

Section 91(1) provides that, if steps (other than the discontinuance of the use of the land) have not been taken within the period specified by an enforcement notice, the local planning authority may enter the land and take those steps and recover the cost from the owner of the land.

Section 110(2) provides that if a person has appealed against an enforcement notice to the Secretary of State no one can claim that the enforcement notice was not duly served on that person.

Section 243(1) provides that the validity of an enforcement notice shall not be questioned in any proceedings whatsoever, other than by way of an appeal under s 88 on a number of the grounds set out in s 88(1), including the failure to serve a notice as required by s 87(4). The rigour of this provision is mitigated to some extent by s 243(2). Where proceedings are brought under s 89(5), a defendant who can establish that he held an interest in the land before the enforcement notice was served, did not have the enforcement notice served on him and can satisfy the court, firstly, that he did not know and could not reasonably have been expected to know that the enforcement notice had been served and, secondly, that his interests have been substantially prejudiced by the failure to serve him is, by this subsection, entitled to raise any of the grounds of appeal set out in s 88(1) by way of defence, including the fact that the enforcement notice was not served as required by s 87(4).

The first ground of appeal is to the effect that, so far as count 1 is concerned, the document put forward by Lewes District Council as an enforcement notice was no more than a draft which had not been served, or at least as to which there was no evidence of service. The document was addressed to Mr Saunders, the owner of the land; but there was no evidence of it ever having been served in any of the ways provided for by s 283(1). As Mr Wenban and Mr Hilder had appealed against it, the appellant was not able to argue that there was a complete failure of service: s 110(2) precludes such an argument. But, as Mr Saunders did not appeal, that section was not available in so far as service was required upon him. It should be noted that, as Mr Saunders and Philbridge Ltd appealed against enforcement notice C, the same argument is not available to Mr Bandar in respect of his conviction on count 2.

It seems to us that the evidence before the assistant recorder, that is the document addressed to Mr Saunders, was clearly sufficient to establish that an enforcement notice had come into existence. The question was whether or not it was valid, in the sense of being capable of taking effect. That depended, for the purposes of this case, upon whether or not it had been served on Mr Saunders. If it had not been so served, anyone affected by the notice could have appealed under s 88(1) and, subject to the Secretary of State's discretion, under s 88(4)(b), would have been entitled to succeed on such an appeal. In these current proceedings the appellants in respect of count 1 seek to raise that precise point. At first sight it would appear as though s 243(1) provides a complete answer, as the appellants are seeking to question the validity of the enforcement notice on one of the relevant grounds upon which an appeal could have been brought under s 88(1); and they are precluded from so doing. The only category of person who could raise this question would be a person who could bring himself within the provisions of s 243(2); and none of these appellants falls into that category.

Mr Beaumont on behalf of the appellants argues that despite its apparently clear words s 243(1) does not apply in this situation. He argued that service of a document such as an enforcement notice, which is capable of affecting a person's rights, must be a prerequisite to any proceedings based upon it, that the purported notice was a nullity and that s 243(1) could not be used to validate something which was of no legal effect, and was a required precondition for the proceedings in question.

He relied upon *McDaid v Clydebank DC* [1984] JPL 579. That was a case under the equivalent provisions of the Act which applied to Scotland (the Town and Country Planning (Scotland) Act 1972). The petitioners were the owners of a yard and garage which was allegedly used in contravention of planning conditions by one Logan, the occupier, upon whom the respondents served an enforcement notice. Although the respondents knew of the identity of the petitioners as owners, no notice was served upon them. The owners were unaware of the existence of the notice until after the period within which they could appeal to the Secretary of State. Logan, although served, failed to appeal, apparently as a result of bad legal advice. The petitioners asked the court for suspension of the enforcement notices and an interdict of the respondents from relying on the notices. At first instance it was held that the equivalent of s 243(1) precluded the petitioners from obtaining any remedy; and because they had not been prosecuted under the equivalent of s 89(5) they could not rely on the equivalent of s 243(2). On appeal it was held that the petitioners were entitled to the remedies that they sought. The respondents had deprived the petitioners, by their failure to serve the notice, of the right to appeal against the notice to the Secretary of State in circumstances where the failure was neither explained nor excused. In those circumstances the court was not prepared to conclude that Parliament had intended to deprive the petitioners of their legal right to appeal to the Secretary of State without express words. Lord Cameron said (at 582):

'It was not readily to be presumed that the legislature intended to deprive a citizen through no fault or failure on his part of all right to challenge a plainly defective exercise of executive authority, involving him it might be in a serious financial loss in the use of his own property. If that were the intention of the legislature and to exclude the jurisdiction of the court to provide a remedy, then it must be made abundantly clear.'

It should be noted that the circumstances of that case were very different from the instant case. What undoubtedly affected the court was its conclusion that for the respondents to rely on the enforcement notice would be an abuse of its powers, having by its own act deprived the petitioners of the opportunity to appeal. None the less, the language used suggested that the court considered that it was entitled to intervene on the basis that the notice was a nullity.

The question was considered subsequently by the Court of Appeal in *R v Greenwich London BC, ex p Patel* [1985] JPL 851. The applicant in that case was the owner of property which was occupied by his sister-in-law. The sister-in-law erected a shed without planning permission, and apparently without the knowledge of the applicant, who was at all material times resident in the United States of America. An application made after the event on behalf of the sister-in-law for the erection of the shed, which was treated as an application to retain it, was refused by the local planning authority, and, on appeal, by the Secretary of State. An enforcement notice was served on the sister-in-law requiring her to remove the shed. She failed to do so. She was prosecuted under s 89(1) of the Town and Country Planning Act 1971; but, as she was not the owner, she had a complete defence and was acquitted. The council then decided to take action under s 91; and at about this time the applicant discovered what was happening and sought judicial review to prohibit the council from exercising any purported powers under s 91. Glidewell LJ refused the application and the owner appealed to the Court of Appeal.

The essence of the submissions on his behalf was that because the notice had not been served on the owner as required by s 87(4) the notice was a nullity. Neill LJ held that the combined effect of ss 88(1)(e) and 88(4) and 243(2) made it plain that the failure to serve an enforcement notice could not render the notice a nullity. Parliament had expressly provided machinery to deal with circumstances where such a notice was not served: that machinery could only operate upon the premise that the notice was valid. He referred to the decision in *McDaid v Clydebank DC*, and said that, in so far as it was intended to hold that the failure to serve the notice rendered the notice a nullity, he would decline to follow it. Sir John Megaw agreed. Donaldson MR also agreed, whilst leaving over the question of whether or not the courts would intervene by way of judicial review in circumstances where injustice might otherwise arise.

In our judgment, that case is clear authority for the proposition that the failure to serve an enforcement notice in accordance with s 87(4) does not render the notice a nullity. We respectfully agree with and follow the analysis of the statutory provisions in the judgment of Neill LJ. It is in our view plain that, at least in the context of the proceedings taking place pursuant to the scheme set out in the 1971 Act (as opposed to judicial review proceedings based on abuse of power), the question of defective service can only be raised under ss 88(1) and 243(2). Otherwise, any challenge is a challenge to the validity of the enforcement notice, on the ground set out in s 88(1)(e) which is precluded by s 243(1). The assistant recorder was therefore right to reject the submission based upon the argument that the Lewes District Council had failed to prove service of enforcement notice B.

The second ground of appeal is that the assistant recorder was wrong to hold that the enforcement notices related to the whole of the site, and not to the buildings particularly identified respectively as 'B' in enforcement notice B and 'C' in enforcement notice C on the plans annexed to the notices. In our judgment this ground of appeal is unarguable. Both of the enforcement notices relate to 'all that piece and parcel of land adjacent to Ditchling Road Wivelsfield in the county of Sussex shown edged red on the plan'. The appeal to Forbes J and subsequently to the Court of Appeal was based, inter alia, on the argument that the Secretary of State had wrongly identified the planning unit as the whole site, and that the site was, in truth, a number of separate planning units which should therefore be the subject matter of individual enforcement notices. This argument was rejected. Forbes J held, and the Court of Appeal agreed, that the Secretary of State was perfectly entitled to come to the conclusion that the whole site was a single planning unit on which mixed non-conforming uses were taking place. In these circumstances it was sufficient for the Lewes District Council to establish that the particular activities alleged against these appellants took place on the site. It was not necessary to establish that they occurred in the specific areas identified as 'B' and 'C'. The assistant recorder came to a correct conclusion in this respect.

The third ground of appeal raises an important issue of general principle. The Lewes District Council did not lead any evidence to establish that the appellants had any actual knowledge of the enforcement notice. Mr Beaumont argues that s 89(5) does not create an absolute offence, and that the Lewes District Council therefore had to establish that the appellants knew of the existence of the enforcement notice in respect of which each was charged before they could be convicted. The assistant recorder held, as we have said, that it was an absolute offence, but that if and in so far as any knowledge was required it was established by reason of the entry in the local land charges register. The latter point is the subject of the fourth ground of appeal, which we deal with hereafter.

The general principle is not in doubt. Lord Goddard CJ said in *Brend v Wood* (1946) 175 LT 306 at 307:

'It is of the utmost importance for the protection of the liberty of the subject that a court should always bear in mind that, unless a statute, either clearly or by necessary implication, rules out *mens rea* as a constituent part of a crime, the court should not find a man guilty of an offence against the criminal law unless he has a guilty mind.'

In *Gammon (Hong Kong) Ltd v A-G of Hong Kong* [1984] 2 All ER 503 at 508, [1985] AC 1 at 14 Lord Scarman said:

'In their Lordships' opinion the law relevant to this appeal may be stated in the following propositions ... (1) there is a presumption of law that mens rea is required before a person can be held guilty of a criminal offence; (2) the presumption is particularly strong where the offence is "truly criminal" in character; (3) the presumption applies to statutory offences, and can be displaced only if this is clearly or by necessary implication the effect of the statute; (4) the only situation in which the presumption can be displaced is where the statute was concerned with an issue of social concern; public safety is such an issue; (5) even where a statute is concerned with such an issue, the presumption of mens rea stands unless it can be shown that the creation of strict liability will be effective to promote the objects of the statute by encouraging greater vigilance to prevent the commission of the prohibited act.'

The statute with which we are concerned in these appeals deals with issues of social concern. Whilst the concept of what is 'truly criminal' may not always be easy to determine, in our view it is in the present case, in that an offence under s 89(5) cannot be so classified. It follows that, whilst the presumption still remains that mens rea is required, the offences fall into the category of those in which the presumption can be displaced if the proper construction of the relevant statutory provisions makes it plain that Parliament did not intend that it should be necessary to establish mens rea, particularly if that would appear to promote the object of the statute.

The wording in s 89(5) itself is arguably ambiguous. The phrase 'if any person uses the land or causes or permits it to be used ... in contravention of the notice' could be said, by the conjunction of the word 'permits' and the phrase 'in contravention of', to carry the flavour of knowledge of the existence of the notice, in the same way, for example, as Lord Wilberforce in *Sweet v Parsley* [1969] 1 All ER 347 at 360, [1970] AC 132 at 161 indicated that the phrase 'concerned in the management of any premises used for any such purpose' could be said to convey the impression, as he put it, of 'purposeful management'. But it is important to note that in coming to that conclusion Lord Wilberforce was affected by the general context within which those words appeared. In the case of s 89(5) that context must include s 243(2). Whatever potential ambiguity there may in the words of s 89(5) itself, read together with s 243(2), it is quite plain that knowledge of the enforcement notice is not an essential part of the offences. This latter subsection would be wholly unnecessary if the prosecution had to establish knowledge of the enforcement notice in order to prove the offence. Section 243(2) provides a very limited opportunity to challenge the validity of the enforcement notice, and therefore defend the charge under s 89(5), to a restricted category of those who did not know that an enforcement notice had been served.

It is also plain from s 243(2) that the statutory provisions are intended to encourage those who own, occupy or otherwise have interests in land to take all necessary steps to advise themselves of the planning status of land. The subsection only provides a person whose interests have been affected by an enforcement notice an opportunity to challenge its validity if, amongst other things, he 'could not reasonably have been expected to know that the enforcement notice had been served'. No such opportunity is given to a person whose interest arises after the service of the enforcement notice. Parliament must therefore have intended that the burden of establishing whether or not any use of land is prohibited should be on the person seeking to make use of the land. That obligation must be seen against the background that enforcement notices are registrable as land charges, as was done in the present case; and since the Local Government and Planning (Amendment) Act 1981 every district planning authority is under an obligation to keep a register of enforcement notices, which is to be available for inspection by the public at all reasonable hours. These provisions underline our view that the policy of the Act was to impose absolute liability so as to encourage vigilance on the part of the land owners and users. It follows that we reject this ground of appeal.

The fourth ground of appeal is that, if the Lewes District Council had to prove that the appellants had knowledge of the enforcement notices, the fact that the notices are registered in the land charges registry was not sufficient to prove the necessary knowledge. Strictly, this ground of appeal does not arise in the light of our views in respect of the third ground of appeal, but we have heard argument in relation to it and therefore consider it would be helpful to express our views. The assistant recorder held that, if knowledge was a necessary ingredient of the offence under s 89(5), registration of the notices was sufficient to establish that knowledge. Section 198(1) of the Law of Property Act 1925 provides:

> 'The registration of any instrument or matter under the provisions of the Land Charges Act, 1925, or any enactment which it replaces, in any register kept at the land registry or elsewhere, shall be deemed to constitute actual notice of such instrument or matter, and of the fact of such registration, to all persons and for all purposes connected with the land affected, as from the date of registration or other prescribed date and so long as the registration continues in force.'

It seems to us that, whilst the fact that an enforcement notice is registered helps to determine whether or not, as we have said, the offence under s 89(5) is an absolute offence, it would be surprising if deemed knowledge could satisfy the requirement of the mens rea in a criminal offence. A similar question was raised in the Queen's Bench Divisional Court in *Wrekin DC v Shah* (1986) 150 JP 22. In that case the prosecution had argued that, where a person was charged under s 27 of the Housing Act 1957 with using premises in contravention of a closing order 'knowing that a closing order had become operative', the fact that the closing order had been registered under the Land Charges Act 1925 was sufficient to establish the element of knowledge. The Divisional Court dismissed that argument, holding that such a provision required proof of actual, not deemed, knowledge. If it were necessary for us to determine the point we would have followed the Divisional Court, and held that the fact of registration did not satisfy the requirement to establish knowledge if mens rea was required for the completion of the offence.

The fifth ground of appeal was to the effect that the land charges register did not, in any event, satisfactorily identify the enforcement notices, and in particular enforcement notices B and C. The entry suggests that the notices were originally upheld on appeal in January 1982, when in fact that decision was quashed so far as enforcement notices A and B were concerned, and also suggests that there was a further upholding on appeal on 28 February 1985, when that did not relate to enforcement notice C. None the less, we consider that the entry sufficiently identified the nature of the charge that was registered, and sufficiently informed any person reading the charge to enable that person to make the appropriate inquiries. If it were necessary for us to do so we would have rejected this ground of appeal.

Finally, by the sixth ground of appeal, which was added with our leave, it was argued that the consent order made on 27 January 1983 by Forbes J in the appeal by Mr Kuxhaus, Mr Wenban and Mr Hilder had the effect of quashing the whole of the decision letter of 14 January 1982, and that, since the only decisions thereafter were in respect of enforcement notices A and B, the process has not been concluded as far as enforcement notice C was concerned, and therefore, in accordance with s 88(3), the enforcement notice is still of no effect. In our view this argument is misconceived. There were separate appeals in respect of the three enforcement notices. As a matter of convenience the Secretary of State dealt with them in one inquiry, the inspector heard all the evidence at one hearing, and finally the Secretary of State gave his decisions in one decision letter. They still remained separate appeals. The notice of motion of 11 February 1982 referred to the appeals 'against two enforcement notices', that is enforcement notices A and B. That was 'the matter' which was dealt with at the consent hearing in January 1983. The order was that 'the matter be referred to the first respondent for rehearing and redetermination'. The order only related to enforcement notices A and B. The Secretary of State's decision in respect of enforcement notice C therefore stood, and was effective, and can properly found count 2 in this indictment. We reject this ground of appeal. For the reasons we have set out above we dismiss these appeals.

Appeal dismissed. The court refused leave to appeal to the House of Lords but certified, under s 33(2) of the Criminal Appeal Act 1968, that the following point of law of general public importance was involved in the decision: whether an offence under s

89(5) of the Town and Country Planning Act 1971 is an offence of strict liability or whether it is necessary to establish mens rea.

Kate O'Hanlon   Barrister.

Practice Direction

CHANCERY DIVISION

Practice – Chancery Division – Hearing dates – Target dates – Parties and legal representatives to be ready and available for hearing within target dates – Interlocutory applications after proceedings set down to be made to motions judge if appointment before master would delay hearing of proceedings.

From the mid-1980s there has been an enormous increase in the case load of the Chancery Division. Overall the load more than doubled. In some areas the increase has been threefold. This has led to many cases having to wait for an unacceptably long time before being heard.

In the last few months the case load has started to level out and in some areas diminish. This, coupled with an increase in the number of courts which are sitting, means that in many instances parties can now be offered much earlier hearing dates than has been possible recently.

Parties and their advisers should therefore be aware that the hearing date targets at which the Chancery clerk of the lists is aiming are as set out below. These are targets, and it will not always be possible for the court to achieve these dates, especially for longer cases in part 1 of the Witness List. However, parties and their legal representatives will be expected to be ready and available for a hearing within the target dates unless good reason is shown to the contrary.

The targets, which exclude the months of August and September, are as follows.

(1) Witness list part 1 (hearings estimated to occupy the court for more than three days), and Companies Court cases of a similar length: six months from the date of attendance upon the clerk of the lists to fix a hearing date or, if the case is estimated to last more than ten days, nine months.

(2) Witness list part 2 (hearings estimated to last three days or less), and Companies Court cases of a similar length: three months from setting down or, where appropriate, from attendance to fix a date.

(3) Non-witness list: two months from setting down.

(4) Motions by order: one month from attendance to fix a date or, if later, one month from close of evidence.

(5) Bankruptcy appeals: two months from issue of the appeal.

(6) Revenue appeals: three months from attendance to fix a date.

After proceedings have been set down applications for interlocutory directions normally made to a master should be made to the Chancery motions judge if an appointment cannot be obtained before the master in time for this not to cause delay in the hearing of the proceedings.

22 April 1994   DONALD NICHOLLS V-C.

Hunt v Severs

HOUSE OF LORDS

LORD KEITH OF KINKEL, LORD BRIDGE OF HARWICH, LORD JAUNCEY OF TULLICHETTLE, LORD BROWNE-WILKINSON AND LORD NOLAN

28 FEBRUARY, 1 MARCH, 28 APRIL 1994

Damages – Personal injury – Services rendered to plaintiff – Services rendered and to be rendered by defendant tortfeasor in caring for plaintiff – Defendant husband of plaintiff – Defendant rendering services to plaintiff voluntarily – Whether plaintiff entitled to recover cost of services voluntarily rendered by defendant.

Damages – Personal injury – Cost of future care – Multiplier – Basis for choosing multiplier when amount and timing of future payments is known or assumed to be known.

The plaintiff, who was nearly 29 years of age at the time of the trial, suffered severe injuries in 1985 in an accident when she was a pillion passenger on a motor cycle driven by the defendant. She was discharged from hospital in 1987 and thereafter lived with the defendant. They married in November 1990. The plaintiff's injuries were such that she had lost any chance of remunerative employment and her post-injury complications were such that she was at risk of developing complications in the future. She brought an action for damages against the defendant. At the trial liability was admitted and it was agreed that the plaintiff had a life expectancy of 25 years. The plaintiff was awarded a total of £617,004 damages, which included awards of £17,000 for services rendered and £60,000 for services to be rendered in the future by the defendant in caring for the plaintiff. In arriving at the award the judge adopted a multiplier for future care of 14 by taking the plaintiff's estimated expectation of life of 25 years and discounting £1 pa at 4·5%. The defendant appealed against the award for services rendered and to be rendered by him in caring for the plaintiff, contending that in so far as he had rendered or would render those services voluntarily he could not be obliged also to pay damages since that would mean that the plaintiff would be recovering twice and he would be paying twice. The plaintiff cross-appealed, contending, inter alia, that the multiplier for future care should be 15. The Court of Appeal dismissed the appeal, holding that where services were voluntarily rendered from motives of affection or duty by a defendant tortfeasor in caring for a plaintiff who had been injured as a result of the defendant's negligence, the plaintiff could recover the cost of those services by way of damages. The court allowed the cross-appeal and substituted a multiplier of 15. The defendant appealed to the House of Lords.

Held – The appeal would be allowed for the following reasons—

(1) Where services in the form of care and assistance were gratuitously rendered by a defendant tortfeasor to a plaintiff injured as a result of the defendant's negligence, the plaintiff could not recover the cost of those services by way of damages. The central objective of an award in respect of voluntary care received by the plaintiff was compensation for the voluntary carer, and where the tortfeasor had himself rendered services to the plaintiff

there was no ground in public policy or otherwise for requiring the tortfeasor to pay to the plaintiff a sum of money in respect of the services which the plaintiff then had to repay to him. It followed that the award of damages would be reduced by the amount awarded for services rendered and to be rendered in the future by the defendant in caring for the plaintiff (see p 387 f, p 393 a b, p 394 h j and p 397 f to h, post); *Donnelly v Joyce* [1973] 3 All ER 475 overruled.

(2) Before a judge's assessment of the appropriate multiplier for future loss, arrived at by the conventional method of assessment and which was not attacked as being wrong in principle, could properly be adjusted by an appellate court by reference to actuarial calculations, it was essential that the particular calculation relied on by the appellate court was precisely in point and should be seen as demonstrably giving a more accurate assessment than the figure used by the judge. The trial judge's decision to take a multiplier of 14 and apply it, subject to various adjustments, in arriving at his award for both the future cost of care and the future loss of earnings could not be faulted and therefore the Court of Appeal had not been entitled to substitute a multiplier of 15 (see p 387 f, p 396 j and p 397 d e g h, post).

Per curiam. An injured plaintiff who recovers damages under the head of recompense for services rendered by a voluntary carer is to be taken as holding them on trust for the voluntary carer (see p 387 f, p 394 g h and p 397 g h, post); dictum of Lord Denning MR in *Cunningham v Harrison* [1973] 3 All ER 463 at 469–470 approved.

Decision of the Court of Appeal [1993] 4 All ER 180 reversed.

Notes

For the measure of damages in personal injury cases, see 34 *Halsbury's Laws* (4th edn) paras 78–87, and for cases on the subject, see 36(1) *Digest* (2nd reissue) 479–504, 4159–4266.

Cases referred to in opinions

Cunningham v Harrison [1973] 3 All ER 463, [1973] QB 942, [1973] 3 WLR 97, CA.
Donnelly v Joyce [1973] 3 All ER 475, [1974] QB 454, [1973] 3 WLR 514, CA.
Edgar v Postmaster General 1965 SLT 158, Ct of Sess.
Gowling v Mercantile Mutual Insurance Co Ltd and Gowling [1980] 24 SASR 321, S Aust SC.
Griffiths v Kerkemeyer (1977) 139 CLR 161, Aust HC.
Gutkin v Gutkin [1983] 2 Qd R 764, Qld SC.
Housecroft v Burnett [1986] 1 All ER 332, CA.
Hussain v New Taplow Paper Mills Ltd [1988] 1 All ER 541, [1988] AC 514, [1988] 2 WLR 266, HL.
Janney v Gentry (1966) 110 SJ 408.
Jones v Jones [1982] Tas R 282, Tas SC.
Kirkham v Boughey [1957] 3 All ER 153, [1958] 2 QB 338, [1957] 3 WLR 626.
Lynch v Lynch (1991) 25 NSWLR 411, NSW CA.
Maan v Westbrook [1993] 2 Qd R 267, Qld SC.
Motor Accidents Insurance Board v Pulford (1993) Aust Torts Rep 81-235, Tas SC.
Parry v Cleaver [1969] 1 All ER 555, [1970] AC 1, [1969] 2 WLR 821, HL.
Roach v Yates [1937] 3 All ER 442, [1938] 1 KB 256, CA.
Schneider v Eisovitch [1960] 1 All ER 169, [1960] 2 QB 430, [1960] 2 WLR 169.
Snape v Reid (1984) Aust Torts Rep 80-620, WA SC.

Taylor v O'Connor [1970] 1 All ER 365, [1971] AC 115, [1970] 2 WLR 472, HL.
Wattson v Port of London Authority [1969] 1 Lloyd's Rep 95.

Appeal

The defendant, David Severs, appealed from the decision of the Court of Appeal (Sir Thomas Bingham MR, Staughton and Waite LJJ) ([1993] 4 All ER 180, [1993] QB 815) delivered on 12 May 1993 dismissing his appeal from the judgment of David Latham QC sitting as a deputy judge of the High Court in the Queen's Bench Division on 15 April 1992 whereby at the trial of the assessment of damages in the action, the defendant having admitted liability, the deputy judge awarded the plaintiff, Katharine Hunt (now Mrs Severs), damages of £17,000 for services rendered and £60,000 for services to be rendered in the future by the defendant in caring for the plaintiff as part of a total award of £617,004 damages for personal injuries sustained by reason of the negligence of the defendant. The facts are set out in the judgment of Lord Bridge.

John Crowley QC and *Jonathan Woods* (instructed by *E Edwards Son & Noice*) for the defendant.
Harvey McGregor QC and *Roderick Doggett* (instructed by *Wheelers*, Ash Vale) for the plaintiff.

Their Lordships took time for consideration.

28 April 1994. The following judgments were delivered.

LORD KEITH OF KINKEL. My Lords, for the reasons given in the speech prepared by my noble and learned friend Lord Bridge of Harwich, which I have read in draft and with which I agree, I would allow this appeal and make the order he proposes.

LORD BRIDGE OF HARWICH. My Lords, a plaintiff who establishes a claim for damages for personal injury is entitled in English law to recover as part of those damages the reasonable value of services rendered to him gratuitously by a relative or friend in the provision of nursing care or domestic assistance of the kind rendered necessary by the injuries the plaintiff has suffered. The major issue which arises for determination in this appeal is whether the law will sustain such a claim in respect of gratuitous services in the case where the voluntary carer is the tortfeasor himself.

The plaintiff was gravely injured on 14 September 1985 in a road accident in France when she was riding on the pillion of a motorcycle driven by the defendant. She was then 22 years of age. The defendant's liability in negligence has never been in dispute. The plaintiff's injuries caused paraplegia and unhappily she suffered many complications. The two doctors called by the plaintiff and the defendant at the trial agreed that, in terms of complications, she was the worst paraplegic case they had come across. She spent long periods in various hospitals, but whenever she was not in hospital she and the defendant were living together and in November 1990 they were married.

The action was tried in April 1992 by David Latham QC sitting as a deputy judge of the Queen's Bench Division ([1993] PIQR Q43). He delivered judgment on 15 April 1992 awarding the plaintiff a total sum of £617,004 made up as follows:

General damages for pain and suffering and loss of amenity	£90,000
Special damages	£90,094
Future loss	£412,104
Interest on general damages	£6,588
Interest on special damages	£18,218
Total	£617,004

Included in the award of special damages was a sum of £4,429 representing the defendant's travelling expenses incurred in visiting the plaintiff while she was in hospital and a sum of £17,000 representing the value of the past services rendered by the defendant in caring for the plaintiff when she was at home. Included in the award for future loss was a sum of £60,000 representing the estimated value of the services which would be rendered by the defendant in caring for the plaintiff in future. The basis on which the judge approached the assessment of the several elements which went to make up the plaintiff's estimated future loss, subject to a number of detailed adjustments which it is unnecessary for present purposes to examine, was to apply a multiplier of 14 to the estimated future annual losses.

The defendant appealed against the inclusion in the award of the sums in respect of the defendant's travelling expenses and care for the plaintiff. The plaintiff cross-appealed on various grounds. The Court of Appeal (Sir Thomas Bingham MR, Staughton and Waite LJJ) ([1993] 4 All ER 180, [1993] QB 815), in a reserved judgment delivered on 12 May 1993, dismissed the defendant's appeal and allowed the plaintiff's cross-appeal to the extent of substituting 15 for 14 as the appropriate multiplier to be used in calculating future loss which, taking account of the detailed adjustments referred to, had the effect of increasing the total award of damages by £20,013.

The defendant now appeals by leave of the Court of Appeal to your Lordships' House. Three issues arise for decision. The first relates to the award in respect of the defendant's travelling expenses, the second to that in respect of his past and future care of the plaintiff, the third to the Court of Appeal's increase in the judge's award. The first two issues are theoretically distinct, but I propose to address them together. There is no dispute that the defendant's visits to the plaintiff in hospital made a valuable and important contribution to her general well-being and were calculated to assist her recovery from the devastating consequences of the accident. But for the fact that the defendant was himself the tortfeasor, the propriety of the award under this head would be no more open to question than the award for his services as a voluntary carer. Accordingly, it seems to me that both these issues must depend upon the same considerations of principle. The third issue is, of course, quite distinct and I will consider it later.

The trial judge said of the claims now in dispute:

'It is said that these sums are irrecoverable, that they represent in effect a benefit to the defendant himself, that in so far as they reflect a loss on the plaintiff's part it has been made good by the defendant so that there is in truth no loss, and that if the incidence of insurance is put on one side it can be seen that the claim is misconceived. However, in my judgment this ignores the basis upon which the claim is made. It is merely a notional monetary figure placed on the true nature of the loss for which she is entitled to compensation. This loss is the need she now has by reason of the accident for care and support which she did not have before. This follows from the analysis of the legal basis of such claims by Megaw LJ in *Donnelly v Joyce* [1973] 3 All ER 475 at 480, [1974] QB 454 at 462. The valuation of this need remains a difficult exercise. In *Housecroft v Burnett* [1986] 1 All ER 332 O'Connor LJ made it clear that when provided by unpaid carers there remains a value to be placed on it. In my view that remains so whether provided by the tortfeasor or not. He may give his care in response to the need, but that does not make good the loss, otherwise there will be no sustainable claim in any case where the need has apparently been "met" by unpaid carers.'

In the Court of Appeal the judgment of Megaw LJ in *Donnelly v Joyce* [1973] 3 All ER 475, [1974] QB 454 again provided the main foundation for the court's reasoning. Having examined this and other authorities, Sir Thomas Bingham MR, delivering the judgment of the court expressed their conclusion ([1993] 4 All ER 180 at 191–192, [1993] QB 815 at 831):

'Where services are voluntarily rendered by a tortfeasor in caring for the plaintiff from motives of affection or duty they should in our opinion be regarded as in the same category as services rendered voluntarily by a third party, or charitable gifts, or insurance payments. They are adventitious benefits, which for policy reasons are not to be regarded as diminishing the plaintiff's loss. On the facts of the present case the judge's decision was not in our view contrary to principle or authority and it was fortified by what we regard as compelling considerations of public policy. We consider that he reached the right conclusion and would accordingly dismiss the defendant's appeal.'

The starting point for any inquiry into the measure of damages which an injured plaintiff is entitled to recover is the recognition that damages in the tort of negligence are purely compensatory. He should recover from the tortfeasor no more and no less than he has lost. Difficult questions may arise when the plaintiff's injuries attract benefits from third parties. According to their nature these may or may not be taken into account as reducing the tortfeasor's liability. The two well-established categories of receipt which are to be ignored in assessing damages are the fruits of insurance which the plaintiff himself has provided against the contingency causing his injuries (which may or may not lead to a claim by the insurer as subrogated to the rights of the plaintiff) and the fruits of the benevolence of third parties motivated by sympathy for the plaintiff's misfortune. The policy considerations which underlie these two apparent exceptions to the rule against double recovery are, I think, well understood: see, for example, *Parry v Cleaver* [1969] 1 All ER 555 at 558, [1970] AC 1 at 14 and *Hussain v New Taplow Paper Mills Ltd* [1988] 1 All ER 541 at 545, [1988] AC 514 at 528. But I find it difficult to see what considerations of public policy can justify a requirement that the tortfeasor himself should compensate the plaintiff twice over for the self same loss. If the loss in question is a direct pecuniary loss (eg loss of wages) *Hussain*'s case is clear authority that the defendant employer, as the tortfeasor who makes good the loss either voluntarily or contractually, thereby mitigates his liability in damages pro tanto. The Court of Appeal, in the judgment appealed from, readily accepted a number of examples advanced in argument for the defendant as showing that a tortfeasor may mitigate his liability by making good in kind the physical damage which his tort has caused to the plaintiff's property. In a wide-ranging argument before your Lordships, where many hypothetical examples were examined of gratuitous services rendered by a tortfeasor to an injured plaintiff in satisfaction of a need occasioned by his tort, Mr McGregor QC for the plaintiff was constrained to accept as a general rule that the tortfeasor, having provided those services, cannot also be held liable to the plaintiff in damages for their value. But he submitted that where the tortfeasor is a relative or close friend of the plaintiff and gratuitously provides services of an intimate personal or domestic character, he is required by law, as a narrow exception to the general rule, also to pay the plaintiff the value of those services.

The law with respect to the services of a third party who provides voluntary care for a tortiously injured plaintiff has developed somewhat erratically in England. The voluntary carer has no cause of action of his own against the tortfeasor. The justice of allowing the injured plaintiff to recover the value of the services so that he may recompense the voluntary carer has been generally recognised, but there has been difficulty in articulating a consistent juridical principle to justify this result.

In *Roach v Yates* [1937] 3 All ER 442, [1938] 1 KB 256 the injured plaintiff needed to be cared for day and night and his wife and sister-in-law both gave up their employment to provide that care for him and together lost wages of £3 a week. A claim for the value of their services at £3 a week was included in the special damages claimed and a similar claim made as an element in general damages related to future loss. The services were given voluntarily but the plaintiff was held entitled to recover in respect of them. Referring to the nursing services required by the plaintiff, Greer LJ said ([1937] 3 All ER 442 at 444, [1938] 1 KB 256 at 263):

'... he can get those services, and perhaps get them better, only from the attendance being given to him by his wife and his sister-in-law, but, quite naturally, he would feel that he ought to compensate them for what they have lost by giving up the work at which they were earning the sum of £3. I think that Mr. Beyfus was right in saying that we must take into account, at any rate, for the period during which he may now be expected to live, the sum of £3 a week as the minimum expense which this unfortunate man would have to incur in retaining the services of his wife and his sister-in-law.'

In *Schneider v Eisovitch* [1960] 1 All ER 169, [1960] 2 QB 430 the plaintiff and her husband were involved in a road accident in France in which the plaintiff was injured and the husband killed. The plaintiff's brother-in-law and his wife voluntarily flew out to France to assist the plaintiff back to England and to arrange the return of the husband's body for burial. The plaintiff claimed their expenses as part of her damages. Paull J said with respect to this claim ([1960] 1 All ER 169 at 174, [1960] 2 QB 430 at 440):

'Before such a sum can be recovered the plaintiff must show first that the services rendered were reasonably necessary as a consequence of the tortfeasor's tort; secondly, that the out-of-pocket expenses of the friend or friends who rendered these services are reasonable bearing in mind all the circumstances including whether expenses would have been incurred had the friend or friends not assisted, and, thirdly, that the plaintiff undertakes to pay the sum awarded to the friend or friends.'

In the event Paull J held that these conditions were satisfied and that the plaintiff was entitled to recover.

In *Wattson v Port of London Authority* [1969] 1 Lloyd's Rep 95 the plaintiff's wife had for a period given up her work and consequently lost earnings in order to look after her injured husband. Megaw J held that the wife's loss was properly included in the husband's damages. Referring to the fact that there had been no contract between husband and wife with respect to her services in caring for him, Megaw J said (at 102):

'That is not how human beings work and it would, in my judgment— and I say this because I think it ought to be said—be a blot on the law if the law were to be such that a wife who in these circumstances had held her husband to make a contract to repay her he should recover damages for that amount; but if she behaves like an ordinary decent human being and does not put construction upon the act of that service, there is financial disadvantage to the plaintiff as a result. In my judgment, this position is covered in substance in the judgment of Mr. Justice Paull in the case of *Schneider v. Eisovitch* ([1960] 1 All ER 169, [1960] 2 QB 430). The essence of the judgment appears ([1960] 1 All ER 169 at 174, [1960] 2 QB 430 at 440) and in this case I do not think it matters that there is no firm undertaking on the part of the plaintiff that if he is awarded this sum ... he will repay that money to his wife.'

In *Cunningham v Harrison* [1973] 3 All ER 463, [1973] QB 942 and *Donnelly v Joyce* [1973] 3 All ER 475, [1974] QB 454 judgments were delivered by different divisions of the Court of Appeal on successive days. In *Cunningham* the wife of a severely disabled plaintiff, who had initially looked after him, had died before the trial. Lord Denning MR said ([1973] 3 All ER 463 at 469–470, [1973] QB 942 at 951–952):

'Before dealing with [the claim for future nursing expenses] I would like to consider what the position would have been if the wife had not died and had continued to look after her husband, as she had been doing. The plaintiff's advisers seem to have thought that a husband could not claim for the nursing services rendered by a wife unless the husband was legally bound to pay her for them. So, on their advice on 11th July 1972 an agreement was signed whereby the husband agreed to pay his wife £2,000 per annum in respect of her nursing services. We were told that such advice is often given by counsel in such cases as these when advising on evidence. I know the reason why such advice is given. It is because it has been said in some cases that a plaintiff can only recover for services rendered to him when he was legally liable to pay for them: see for instance *Kirkham v Boughey* [1957] 3 All ER 153 at 156, [1958] 2 QB 338 at 342 and *Janney v Gentry* (1966) 110 SJ 408. But, I think that view is much too narrow. It seems to me that when a husband is grievously injured— and is entitled to damages—then it is only right and just that, if his wife renders service to him, instead of a nurse, he should recover compensation for the value of the services that his wife has rendered. It should not be necessary to draw up a legal agreement for them. On recovering such an amount, the husband should hold it on trust for her and pay it over to her. She cannot herself sue the wrongdoer ... but she has rendered services necessitated by the wrongdoing, and should be compensated for it. If she had given up paid work to look after him, he would clearly have been entitled to recover on her behalf, because the family income would have dropped by so much: see *Wattson v Port of London Authority* [1969] 1 Lloyd's Rep 95 at 102 per Megaw J. Even though she had not been doing paid work but only domestic duties in the house, nevertheless all extra attendance on him certainly calls for compensation.'

In *Donnelly v Joyce*, the injured plaintiff was a boy of six. His mother gave up her work for a period to provide necessary care for him and the disputed item in his claim related to the mother's loss of wages. The judgment of the court delivered by Megaw LJ contains a lengthy review of the authorities, but the key passage relied on by the trial judge and the Court of Appeal in the instant case reads ([1973] 3 All ER 475 at 479–480, [1974] QB 454 at 461–462):

"We do not agree with the proposition, inherent in counsel for the defendant's submission, that the plaintiff's claim, in circumstances such as the present, is properly to be regarded as being, to use his phrase, "in relation to someone else's loss", merely because someone else has provided to, or for the benefit of, the plaintiff—the injured person—the money, or the services to be valued as money, to provide for needs of the plaintiff directly caused by the defendant's wrongdoing. The loss *is* the plaintiff's loss. The question from what source the plaintiff's needs have been met, the question who has paid the money or given the services, the question whether or not the plaintiff is or is not under a legal or moral liability to repay, are, so far as the defendant and his liability are concerned, all irrelevant. The plaintiff's loss, to take this present case, is not the expenditure of money to buy the special boots or to pay for the nursing attention. His loss is the existence of the need for those special boots or for those nursing services, the value of which for purposes of damages—for the purpose of the ascertainment of the amount of his loss—is the proper and reasonable cost of supplying those needs. That, in our judgment, is the key to the problem. So far as the defendant is concerned, the loss is not someone else's loss. It is the plaintiff's loss. Hence it does not matter, so far as the defendant's liability to the plaintiff is concerned, whether the needs have been supplied by the plaintiff out of his own pocket or by a charitable contribution to him from some other person whom we shall call "the provider"; it does not matter, for that purpose, whether the plaintiff has a legal liability, absolute or conditional, to repay to the provider what he has received, because of the general law or because of some private agreement between himself and the provider; it does not matter whether he has a moral obligation, however ascertained or defined, so to do. The question of legal liability to reimburse the provider may be very relevant to the question of the legal right of the provider to recover from the plaintiff. That may depend on the nature of the liability imposed by the general law or the particular agreement. But it is not a matter which affects the right of the plaintiff against the wrongdoer.' (Megaw LJ's emphasis.)

With respect, I do not find this reasoning convincing. I accept that the basis of a plaintiff's claim for damages may consist in his need for services but I cannot accept that the question from what source that need has been met is irrelevant. If an injured plaintiff is treated in hospital as a private patient he is entitled to recover the cost of that treatment. But if he receives free treatment under the National Health Service, his need has been met without cost to him and he cannot claim the cost of the treatment from the tortfeasor. So it cannot, I think, be right to say that in all cases the plaintiff's loss is 'for the purpose of damages ... the proper and reasonable cost of supplying [his] needs'.

In Scotland the law on this subject has developed differently. In *Edgar v Postmaster General* 1965 SLT 158 it was held by a majority of the Inner House of the Court of Session that the injured pursuer's averment that his accident had caused his wife to give up work to look after him and thereby lose wages was irrelevant. Having pointed out that the wife, not being a party to the action, could not recover the loss, the Lord President (Clyde) continued (at 160):

'If, on the other hand, the averment is intended to form the basis for a claim for domestic assistance for which the pursuer would have had to pay if he had not been able to secure it gratuitously the claim is, in my opinion, an irrelevant one. It would have been another matter altogether if the pursuer had actually paid some third party, or had entered into a contract to pay some third party for this domestic assistance. It could then have formed a relevant item in his claim for damages. But if the assistance which he got was given gratuitously and there is no undertaking or understanding by him to pay for it (and that is the situation in the present case) then I am quite unable to see how he can claim to be reimbursed for a payment he has not and cannot be compelled to make. In Scotland, damages necessarily involves a loss either actual or prospective, and the plain fact of the matter is that the pursuer has sustained no such loss at all in regard to this item.'

The difference in this regard between Scottish and English law was examined by the Scottish Law Commission in 1978 (Scot Law Com No 51). In para 20 they adopted the view that 'the value of the services of persons who have assisted the injured person should be recoverable by the latter in his action against the wrongdoer' but considered that 'the principle should only apply as between members of the injured person's family group or circle'. In para 22 they criticised the reasoning used in the judgment of Megaw LJ in *Donnelly v Joyce* in the following terms:

'In cases where services have been rendered gratuitously to an injured person, it is artificial to regard that person as having suffered a net loss in the events which happened. The loss is in fact sustained by the person rendering the services, a point vividly illustrated in cases where he has lost earnings in the course of rendering those services. We suggest, therefore, that it is wrong in principle, in cases where services have been rendered gratuitously by another to an injured person, to regard the latter as having in fact suffered a net loss.'

They concluded (at para 23)—

'that it would be right to devise an approach which will enable the injured person to recover in his own action the value of services which have been rendered to him by relatives but which would, at the same time, enable the relative to recover, if he so wished, the value of these services from the injured person.'

The Commission's recommendations in this respect were implemented by Pt II of the Administration of Justice Act 1982, which applies to damages for personal injuries in Scotland and which by s 8 provides:

'(1) Where necessary services have been rendered to the injured person by a relative in consequence of the injuries in question, then, unless the relative has expressly agreed in the knowledge that an action for damages has been raised or is in contemplation that no payment should be made in respect of those services, the responsible person shall be liable to pay to the injured person by way of damages such sum as represents reasonable remuneration for those services and repayment of reasonable expenses incurred in connection therewith.

(2) The relative shall have no direct right of action in delict against the responsible person in respect of the services or expenses referred to in this section, but the injured person shall be under an obligation to account to the relative for any damages recovered from the responsible person under this section.'

An elaborate definition of 'relative' in s 13(1), which I need not here set out, implements the Commission's recommendation that this provision should apply only if the person rendering the services and the injured person belong to the same 'family group or circle'.

Thus, in both England and Scotland the law now ensures that an injured plaintiff may recover the reasonable value of gratuitous services rendered to him by way of voluntary care by a member of his family. Differences between the English common law route and the Scottish statutory route to this conclusion are, I think, rarely likely to be of practical importance, since in most cases the sum recovered will simply go to swell the family income. But it is nevertheless important to recognise that the underlying rationale of the English law, as all the cases before *Donnelly v Joyce* demonstrate, is to enable the voluntary carer to receive proper recompense for his or her services and I would think it appropriate for the House to take the opportunity so far as possible to bring the law of the two countries into accord by adopting the view of Lord Denning MR in *Cunningham v Harrison* that in England the injured plaintiff who recovers damages under this head should hold them on trust for the voluntary carer.

By concentrating on the plaintiff's need and the plaintiff's loss as the basis of an award in respect of voluntary care received by the plaintiff, the reasoning in *Donnelly v Joyce* diverts attention from the award's central objective of compensating the voluntary carer. Once this is recognised it becomes evident that there can be no ground in public policy or otherwise for requiring the tortfeasor to pay to the plaintiff, in respect of the services which he himself has rendered, a sum of money which the plaintiff must then repay to him. If the present case had been brought in Scotland and the claim in respect of the tortfeasor's services made in reliance on s 8 of the Administration of Justice Act 1982, it would have been immediately obvious that such a claim was not sustainable.

The case for the plaintiff was argued in the Court of Appeal without reference to the circumstance that the defendant's liability was covered by insurance. But before your Lordships Mr McGregor, recognising the difficulty of formulating any principle of public policy which could justify recovery against the tortfeasor who has to pay out of his own pocket, advanced the bold proposition that such a policy could be founded on the liability of insurers to meet the claim. Exploration of the implications of this proposition in argument revealed the many difficulties which it encounters. But I do not think it necessary to examine these in detail. The short answer, in my judgment, to Mr McGregor's contention is that its acceptance would represent a novel and radical departure in the law of a kind which only the legislature may properly effect. At common law the circumstance that a defendant is contractually indemnified by a third party against a particular legal liability can have no relevance whatever to the measure of that liability.

I add a short postscript with reference to a number of Australian authorities which were helpfully drawn to your Lordships' attention. The decision of the High Court of Australia in *Griffiths v Kerkemeyer* (1977) 139 CLR 161 adopts in substance what I may call the principle of *Donnelly v Joyce*. Since then there has been a significant number of Australian decisions, both reported and unreported, rejecting claims by injured plaintiffs to recover the value of gratuitous services rendered to them by defendants. The reported decisions to this effect by single judges are *Gowling v Mercantile Mutual Insurance Co Ltd and Gowling* (1980) 24 SASR 321, *Jones v Jones* [1982] Tas R 282, *Gutkin v Gutkin* [1983] 2 Qd R 764 and *Maan v Westbrook* [1993] 2 Qd R 267. To the like effect are the decisions of the Full Court of the Supreme Court of Western Australia in *Snape v Reid* (1984) Aust Torts Rep 80-620; and of the Full Court of the Supreme Court of Tasmania in *Motor Accidents Insurance Board v Pulford* (1993) Aust Torts Rep 81-235. The only contrary decision is that of the Court of Appeal of New South Wales in *Lynch v Lynch* (1991) 25 NSWLR 411. In this case the court's reasoning was expressly related to the circumstance that the claim arose out of an accident which was the subject of a particular statutory compulsory insurance scheme. I do not think it would be helpful to encumber this opinion with a detailed examination of the case. I am content to say that I agree with the criticism of the decision by the Full Court of the Supreme Court of Tasmania in *Motor Accidents Insurance Board v Pulford*, who declined to follow it.

I turn to the separate issue relating to the appropriate multiplier to be applied in relation to the several elements of the plaintiff's future loss. Both doctors who gave evidence at the trial estimated the plaintiff's expectation of life at 25 years. It is clear from the relevant passages of their evidence that these estimates were related solely to the plaintiff's medical condition and that there was no suggestion that the doctors had approached the problem actuarially or assessed the effect of other contingencies on the plaintiff's life expectancy. The trial judge said:

'For the future, the first question is the appropriate multiplier. With an expectation of life of 25 years from today the right multiplier is, in my judgment, 14. This is slightly lower than the 14·82 which is produced from the 4·5 per cent. discount table, but is in line with what has to be described as a spread of multipliers to be gleaned from the decisions recorded in *Kemp & Kemp* [*The Quantum of Damages*]. This will therefore be the

appropriate multiplier for all those items in respect of which life
expectancy is relevant.'

The table that the judge is referring to is that showing the present value of a
payment of £1 pa for 25 years discounted at 4·5% as £14·82821. In the Court of
Appeal the argument for the plaintiff that the multiplier should be increased
from 14 to 15 was based largely on the table which appears in *Kemp and Kemp*
vol 1, p 8028, headed 'Multipliers for loss of earnings to pension age 60
(females)' with the sub-heading 'Multiplier calculated with allowance for
population mortality and rate of interest of ...' followed by a number of
columns headed with different interest rates. The column applicable to a rate
of interest of 4·5% shows the appropriate multiplier for a woman aged 35 at
date of trial as 14.8. Referring to the *Kemp and Kemp* tables, of which this is one,
the Court of Appeal said ([1993] 4 All ER 180 at 201, [1993] QB 815 at 841):

'They contain, as the heading shows, "allowance for population
mortality". In other words, as it seems to us, there may be some allowance
for the contingency that the beneficiary of future payments may not live
long enough to receive them. Such an allowance is not appropriate in the
present case, where the agreed life expectancy of the plaintiff is 25 years.
That is a fact, or rather an agreed assumption, upon which the damages
payable for future care must be based. The *Kemp and Kemp* table could be
too favourable to the defendant, if used for that purpose. What we need
is a simple arithmetical calculation of the present value of future
payments. Counsel have provided us with a table. It shows that the
present value of £1 per annum payable for the next 25 years, discounted at
4·5%, is £14·82821. That is very little different from the figure in the *Kemp
and Kemp* table, which shows that the allowance for mortality must be very
small. It would suggest a multiplier of 15. Accordingly we think it right
to substitute the multiplier of 15 which Mr McGregor contends for in the
calculation of future costs of care.'

Subject to the same adjustments as had been made by the trial judge, the
Court of Appeal applied the same reasoning to increase the multiplier in
relation to future loss of earnings.

The assessment of damages is not and never can be an exact science. There
are too many imponderables. For this reason, the courts have been
traditionally mistrustful of reliance on actuarial tables as the primary basis of
calculation, approving their use only as a check on assessments arrived at by
the familiar conventional methods; see, for example, *Taylor v O'Connor* [1970]
1 All ER 365 at 377, [1971] AC 115 at 140 per Lord Pearson. We are told by
counsel that the practice has changed in recent years and that actuarial tables
tend to figure more prominently in the evidence on which courts rely. This
may well be so. But before a judge's assessment of the appropriate multiplier
for future loss, which he has arrived at by the conventional method of
assessment and which is not attacked as being wrong in principle, can properly
be adjusted by an appellate court by reference to actuarial calculations, it is
essential, in my judgment, that the particular calculation relied on should be
precisely in point and should be seen as demonstrably giving a more accurate
assessment than the figure used by the judge.

The passage I have cited from the judgment of the Court of Appeal appears
to show the court as treating the circumstance that both doctors in evidence

estimated the plaintiff's expectation of life at 25 years as establishing the 'fact' or 'assumption' that she would live for 25 years and thus converting the process of assessing future loss into 'a simple arithmetical calculation'. I cannot think that this was a correct approach to the evidence. A man or woman in normal health, at a given age, no doubt has an ascertainable statistical life expectancy. But in using such a figure as the basis for assessment of damages with respect to future losses, some discount in respect of life's manifold contingencies is invariably made. Moreover, when the Court of Appeal referred to the *Kemp and Kemp* table as showing 'that the allowance for mortality must be very small', they were not making an appropriate comparison of like with like. The figure of 14.8 taken from the *Kemp and Kemp* table refers, as already indicated, to a woman of 35 with an average expectation of life. From the life table, also set out in *Kemp and Kemp*, we see that this expectation is 44.6 years. Thus the fact that only a small allowance for mortality is appropriate in relation to the average woman's expectation of survival from the age of 35 to the age of 60 cannot be a reliable guide to the allowance for mortality appropriate to a severely injured woman aged 29 with a total expectation of life estimated by doctors as no more than 25 years.

I can find no fault in the trial judge's decision to take a multiplier of 14 and apply it, subject to the various adjustments he made, in arriving at his award for both the future cost of care and the future loss of earnings. The use of a discount rate of 4·5% was not and is not disputed. The judge had due regard to the full present value of £1 pa for 25 years discounted at that rate, but decided, as I think rightly, to take a slightly lower figure which he found to be in line with a spread of multipliers in comparable cases. I do not, with respect, think that the reasoning of the Court of Appeal entitled them to substitute a multiplier of 15 by rounding up the figure taken from the discount table.

I would accordingly allow the appeal, set aside the Court of Appeal's order and vary the trial judge's order by reducing the principal award by £81,429 and reducing the award of interest on special damages by so much as represents interest on the sum of £21,429 included in the principal award.

LORD JAUNCEY OF TULLICHETTLE. My Lords, for the reasons given by my noble and learned friend Lord Bridge of Harwich, I, too, would allow the appeal and make the order that he proposes.

LORD BROWNE-WILKINSON. My Lords, for the reasons given by my noble and learned friend Lord Bridge of Harwich, I, too, would allow the appeal and make the order that he proposes.

LORD NOLAN. My Lords, for the reasons given by my noble and learned friend Lord Bridge of Harwich, I, too, would allow the appeal and make the order that he proposes.

Appeal allowed.

Celia Fox   Barrister.

R v Cain

COURT OF APPEAL, CRIMINAL DIVISION
HOBHOUSE LJ, JUDGE AND BELL JJ
14, 15 OCTOBER 1993

Criminal evidence – Character of accused – Good character – Credibility and propensity to commit offence – Effect of defendant's good character on credibility and propensity to commit offence – Defendant of good character jointly tried with defendant of bad character – Evidence of defendant of bad character's previous convictions – Direction to jury as to relevance of previous convictions.

Where a defendant of good character is jointly tried with a defendant of bad character and there is positive evidence before the jury of the latter defendant's previous convictions, the requirement for appropriate directions about character applies equally to both defendants. The defendant of good character is entitled to the benefit of a direction as to the relevance of good character to credibility and propensity to commit crime and the defendant of bad character is entitled to the benefit of a direction as to the limited relevance of the evidence of his previous convictions, namely that the convictions are irrelevant to his guilt but relevant to his credibility. In the absence of any such direction the jury may assume that the convictions of the defendant of bad character are relevant to the same issues as the other defendant's good character and in particular to propensity and therefore his guilt (see p 402 *b* to *d*, post).

R v Vye [1993] 3 All ER 241 considered.

Notes

For character generally, see 11(2) *Halsbury's Laws* (4th edn reissue) para 1070.

For good character of accused, see ibid para 1073, and for cases on the subject, see 15(1) *Digest* (2nd reissue) 556–558, 17451–17484.

Case referred to in judgment

R v Vye [1993] 3 All ER 241, [1993] 1 WLR 471, CA.

Cases also cited

R v Gibson (1991) 93 Cr App R 9, CA.
R v Prince [1990] Crim LR 49.

Appeal against conviction

Jason Sylvester Cain appealed with the leave of the single judge against his conviction on 1 April 1992 in the Crown Court at Harrow before Judge Levy QC and a jury of affray for which he was sentenced to two months' imprisonment. The facts are set out in the judgment of the court.

Edward Rees (assigned by the *Registrar of Criminal Appeals*) for the appellant.
Walter Bealby (instructed by the *Crown Prosecution Service*, Harrow) for the Crown.

Cur adv vult

15 October 1993. The following judgment of the court was delivered.

JUDGE J. On 1 April 1992 in the Crown Court at Harrow before Judge Levy QC and a jury this appellant was convicted of affray. He was sentenced to two months' imprisonment. At the same time the jury returned a verdict of guilty on the same affray against a co-defendant named Wayne Hylton and a verdict of not guilty in the case of another co-defendant, Lizette Hylton. The appellant now appeals against conviction with leave of the single judge.

The only issue in the appeal concerns the way in which the judge directed the jury on the issue of character and previous convictions.

The material facts can be summarised shortly. On 29 June 1991 a social worker, Desmond Coke, was attacked by a group of men. Mr Coke was responsible for organising and distributing kit for local football teams. Earlier that same evening he had, for perfectly good reason, been unable to supply football kit to the appellant and Wayne Hylton. He also said that he would take the kit to the home of Mrs Hylton later that night. He was on his way in his van when he was attacked. The gang included Wayne Hylton and the appellant, who were identified by Mr Coke as two of those who were carrying bottles. Mr Coke was knocked to the ground. The attack on him continued as he lay there.

Later he saw Mrs Hylton at the scene. As she was acquitted by the jury we do not propose to say anything further about the part she was alleged to have played in the incident, but it is not in dispute that she was heard to order the attackers to stop what they were doing.

It was, therefore, an unpleasant incident of public violence, which created fear in those who witnessed it. Mr Coke needed stitches in a head wound and suffered bruising to his chest and feet.

The first defendant on the indictment was Lizette Hylton. After the close of the prosecution case she gave evidence about the facts and the part that she had played in the incident. She also emphasised her positive good character, which was amply supported by character witnesses. The second defendant was her son, Wayne Hylton. He also gave evidence about his involvement in this incident. Nothing at all was said to the jury about his character. The third defendant was the present appellant. He gave evidence which, put briefly, denied any criminal participation in the incident. His account was that Mr Coke had started the fight and that he, the appellant, had intervened when he saw that Mrs Hylton had been pushed to the ground. In effect, he was not acting unlawfully because he only did what he did in self-defence and, indeed, in defence of Mrs Hylton. By their verdict the jury must have rejected his account.

The appellant also volunteered evidence to the jury that he had previous convictions for theft and possession of cannabis. Counsel appearing for him on the appeal cannot now recall why this evidence was put before the jury. There had been a sustained attack on the creditworthiness of Mr Coke, but as far as counsel could recollect, the judge had not given any warning to him that he was at risk of putting his client's character before the jury. It is also possible that because there were no convictions for any offences of violence the jury might have been persuaded to take a favourable view of the absence of any known propensity to violence. In any event, however, the appellant's previous convictions were before the jury.

When the evidence was concluded the judge faced the problem of how to leave the issue of character of each defendant to the jury, when the evidence relating to the character of each was different: with the first defendant, positive good character; with the second defendant, no evidence whatever either way; with the third defendant, the appellant, previous convictions. The problem was compounded by the fact that at the time when the case was heard the principles relating to the question of character were unclear.

Accordingly, before speeches to the jury the judge invited submissions from counsel. We have studied the relevant part of the transcript. Part of it reads as follows. The judge said:

'What I was proposing to do, rather than give a direction about good character, was to say, when saying "I want to say a few words about each of the defendants", separating Mrs Hylton from each of the witnesses, separating Mrs Hylton as much as I can from her son, and stress her good character there. No doubt that is something the jury will take into account. That seems to me more appropriate than giving a pointed direction about Mrs Hylton being of good character and what the jury should make of that which has inferences which the jury may properly or improperly draw against Wayne.'

Counsel for the present appellant had this to say a few moments later:

'The only difficulty that I would anticipate is really on the question of whether your Honour seeks to deal with propensity. In my submission, the circumstances of this case are such that it is impossible to do so without one or other of the defendants suffering.'

The judge then interrupted: 'When you say "deal with propensity"—.' Counsel then continued: 'The double barrel direction that the Court of Appeal now considers it is appropriate to give in cases where a defendant has good character.' The judge said: 'I was not going to give any direction on character at all. That does not harm your client.'

Counsel for the appellant understood the judge to be saying that he would not be giving a direction to the jury about the effect of Mrs Hylton's good character. There is no purpose in considering whether in view of the overall context, part of which has just been quoted, he should have sought clarification on the point. He decided that in his speech he would not address any argument to the jury about the appellant's previous convictions, and he did not do so.

When the judge summed up the case to the jury he reminded them of Mrs Hylton's good character. He directed them as follows:

'A good character affects the position in two ways. It adds to the credibility of the evidence, more likely she is telling you the truth and, members of the jury, it is also less likely that a person of her background, of her character, it is less likely she would have behaved in the manner alleged by the prosecution. That does not mean to say that she has not.'

When setting out Mrs Hylton's account of the incident he ended it by saying:

'Well, members of the jury, no doubt, as I said, when you consider her evidence you will take very seriously indeed the fact that she is of previous good character.'

When the judge referred to the evidence of Wayne Hylton he said nothing at all about his character. When he came to deal with the appellant's evidence, he said: 'He has had paid employment with Sun Star, and he is 21. He has had a spot of trouble with the police before.'

These directions are criticised, first, because the judge acted contrary to counsel's understanding of the directions he intended to give the jury and, second, because insofar as there was any direction about the relevance of the defendant's convictions it was incomplete, as it did not direct the jury that the convictions added nothing to the Crown's case against the appellant.

If the judge had informed counsel of precisely what he intended to say in his summing up, counsel suggested in argument before this court that he might have taken one of three courses. First, he might have sought an order for severance. In reality, as counsel recognised, such an application would have been doomed. Second, he might have addressed the jury on the issue. If so, he would have dealt with the effect of the appellant's convictions, not only on propensity, but also on the effect on his client's credibility. Third, he might have persuaded the judge to provide a complete direction on the subject.

Since the conclusion of this trial the decision of the Court of Appeal in *R v Vye* [1993] 3 All ER 241, [1993] 1 WLR 471 has clarified the principles which apply, not only when the defendant of good character is tried on his own, but also when he is jointly tried with a defendant of bad character. Lord Taylor CJ, expressed the principles in this way ([1993] 3 All ER 241 at 248, [1993] 1 WLR 471 at 479):

'In our judgment a defendant A of good character is entitled to have the judge direct the jury even if he is jointly tried with a defendant B of bad character. This leaves the question as to what, if anything, the judge should say about the latter. In some cases the judge may think it best to grasp the nettle in his summing up and tell the jury that they must try the case on the evidence, that there has been no evidence about B's character, that they must not speculate and must not take the absence of information as to B's character as any evidence against B. In other cases the judge may, however, think it best to say nothing about the absence of evidence as to B's character. What course he takes must depend upon the circumstances of the individual case, for example how great an issue has been made of character during the evidence and speeches ... in our judgment the following principles are to be applied. (1) A direction as to the relevance of his good character to a defendant's credibility is to be given where he has testified or made pre-trial answers or statements. (2) A direction as to the relevance of his good character to the likelihood of his having committed the offence charged is to be given, whether or not he has testified, or made pre-trial answers or statements. (3) Where defendant A of good character is jointly tried with defendant B of bad character, (1) and (2) still apply.'

In view of these principles, therefore, the judge in the present case was correct when he referred to Mrs Hylton's good character and its possible relevance to her credibility and propensity to commit the crime alleged. She was entitled to such a direction. Furthermore, the judge had a discretion whether to say anything at all to the jury about Wayne Hylton's character. He chose not to do so, and his decision is not open to criticism.

However, as the passage from the judgment shows, the observations in *R v Vye* about the co-defendant of 'bad character' did not extend to cases where there was positive evidence on the subject, and in particular did not suggest that the defendant whose previous convictions were put before the jury should be treated in the same way as the defendant about whose character there was no evidence either way. In other words, it was not dealing with the problem which arises in the present case, where there was positive evidence before the jury that the co-defendant had previous criminal convictions.

The decision in *R v Vye* underlined that in a joint trial the defendant of good character is 'entitled' to the benefit of a direction 'as to its relevance', both to credibility and to propensity. In the absence of directions about the possible relevance of evidence of the co-defendant's previous convictions, the jury may assume that they are relevant to the same issues and, in particular, to propensity to commit crime and, therefore, to guilt.

In our judgment that risk should be avoided by directions about the limited relevance of the evidence of previous convictions and the way in which it should be approached. The requirement for appropriate directions about character therefore applies equally to the defendant with previous convictions as it does to the defendant of good character. The precise terms of the directions will be decided by the judge on his analysis of the issues in the individual case.

It follows that in the present case the judge's reference to the appellant's previous convictions was incomplete. Given the uncertainty of legal principle then current, this was understandable. The judge had to deal with the character of three different defendants, ensuring fairness between each of them. This defendant's previous convictions had been volunteered to the jury for reasons which seemed appropriate to counsel at the time; none of them involved any offence of a violent nature. No doubt the judge was deliberately dismissive when he spoke of a 'spot of trouble with the police', and he did so in order to deprive the convictions of any adverse significance.

Applying the principles to the facts of the present case, we have considered first whether the misunderstanding between counsel and the judge about the judge's intended directions had any damaging effect on the subsequent conduct of the defence. In our judgment it had none. The only possible difference might have been that counsel would have addressed the jury on the topic and the judge would, thereupon, have given complete directions on the subject.

We have, therefore, compared what the judge actually said to the jury with what, if he had given complete directions, he should have said. He would, dealing with the matter in general terms, have warned the jury to disregard the convictions as irrelevant to guilt, perhaps referring to the fact that the convictions were, in any event, for quite different offences. Although he did not give an unequivocal warning, the dismissive language he actually used went some way to reducing any adverse inferences which might otherwise have been drawn.

The judge would probably also have reminded the jury that the convictions were relevant to credibility. As one of the appellant's convictions was for dishonesty and the crucial issue in the trial was credibility, from the appellant's point of view the overall result was not less favourable than it would have been if a complete direction had been given.

Accordingly, notwithstanding the judge's omission to give appropriate directions to the jury about the appellant's previous convictions, we have concluded that this was immaterial to the outcome of the case and that no miscarriage of justice actually occurred. Accordingly, this appeal will be dismissed.

Appeal dismissed.

Kate O'Hanlon   Barrister.

Frenchay Healthcare NHS Trust v S

COURT OF APPEAL, CIVIL DIVISION

SIR THOMAS BINGHAM MR, WAITE AND PETER GIBSON LJJ

14 JANUARY 1994

Medical treatment – Withdrawal of treatment – Insensate patient – Patient in persistent vegetative state with no hope of recovery – Patient requiring operation if he was to continue to be fed – Medical opinion that in patient's best interests for no action to be taken and that he be allowed to die naturally – Hospital applying as matter of urgency for declaration authorising no action to be taken – Official Solicitor not having time to explore facts – Judge granting declaration – Whether judge right to grant declaration – Whether court should necessarily accept medical opinion as to patient's best interests – Whether in patient's best interests to take no action and allow patient to die.

In June 1991 S, a healthy young man, took a drug overdose which resulted in acute and extreme brain damage. Despite hospital treatment he remained in a persistent vegetative state. Until June 1993 he was fed through a nasogastric tube as the only practicable way of feeding him and when that became unsatisfactory an operation was performed to insert a gastrostomy tube through the stomach wall and into the stomach to permit him to be fed in that way. On 10 January 1994 the medical staff discovered that the gastrostomy tube through which S was being fed had been removed from his body, probably as a result of his own movement pulling it out of the stomach. It was not medically practicable to reinsert the tube and faced with performing a further operation to insert another gastrostomy tube into S's stomach or taking no action at all, which would cause death within a limited period, the consultant in charge of S recommended that it was in S's best interests for no action to be taken and that he be allowed to die naturally. Other medical opinions were to the effect that S had permanent and severe brain damage, that his quality of life was nil and that there was no prospect of recovery. The plaintiff hospital applied as a matter of urgency to the court for a declaration authorising the hospital not to replace the gastrostomy tube. The judge granted the declaration sought. The Official Solicitor, as S's guardian ad litem, appealed to the Court of Appeal, contending inter alia (i) that the procedure adopted had deprived the Official Solicitor of a full and fair opportunity to explore the matter fully so as to ensure that all relevant material was before the court and (ii) that the judge had attached too much importance to the judgment of the doctors as to what was in S's best interests.

Held – The question which the court had to determine when considering an application by a hospital for authority not to continue treating a patient in a persistent vegetative state who would inevitably die without life-prolonging treatment was what would be in the best interests of the patient. Although the court had the ultimate power and duty to review the medical decision in the light of all the facts and should not necessarily accept medical opinion as to what was in the patient's best interests as being in fact in the patient's best interests, the court should be reluctant to place those treating the patient in a position of having to carry out treatment which they considered to be contrary to the patient's best interests unless the court had real doubt about the reliability, bona fides or correctness of the medical opinion in question. Having regard to the facts and the material before the court, it would not be right to allow the appeal merely because there had not been an opportunity on behalf of S for the full exploration of the facts which in other circumstances would be desirable. There was no reason to question the conclusion of S's consultant that it was in his best interests for no action to be taken and for him to be allowed to die naturally. The appeal would therefore be dismissed (see p 410 *b c*, p 411 *g* to p 412 *d j* to p 413 *b*, post).

Airedale NHS Trust v Bland [1993] 1 All ER 821 applied.

Per curiam. Where a hospital seeks to discontinue treatment of a patient in a persistent vegetative state, as a general rule the hospital should apply to the court for and obtain a declaration that it was proper to do so, and such an application should be preceded by a full investigation with an opportunity for the Official Solicitor, as the representative of the patient, to explore the situation fully, to obtain independent medical opinions of his own, and to ensure that all proper material was before the court. Nevertheless, emergency situations will arise in which an application to the court is not possible, or where, although an application to the court is possible, it will not be possible to present the applicaton in the same leisurely way as in the case where there is no pressure of time (see p 409 *g* to p 410 *b* and p 413 *a b*, post).

Notes

For consent to medical treatment, see 30 *Halsbury's Laws* (4th edn reissue) para 39, and for cases on the subject, see 33 *Digest* (Reissue) 273–275, 2242–2246.

Case referred to in judgments

Airedale NHS Trust v Bland [1993] 1 All ER 821, [1993] AC 789, [1993] 3 WLR 316, Fam D, CA and HL.

Cases also cited

Bolam v Friern Hospital Management Committee [1957] 2 All ER 118, [1957] 1 WLR 582.

F v West Berkshire Health Authority (Mental Health Act Commission intervening) [1989] 2 All ER 545, sub nom *Re F (mental patient: sterilisation)* [1990] 2 AC 1, HL.

J v C (note) [1990] 3 All ER 735, [1990] 1 WLR 1248.

J (a minor) (wardship: medical treatment), Re [1990] 3 All ER 930, [1991] Fam 33, CA.

J (a minor) (wardship: medical treatment), Re [1992] 4 All ER 614, [1993] Fam 15, CA.

Appeal

The defendant S, acting by the Official Solictor as his guardian ad litem, appealed from the order of Swinton Thomas J dated 13 January 1994 whereby he declared, inter alia, that despite the inability of the defendant to consent thereto, the plaintiffs, the Frenchay Healthcare NHS Trust, and their responsible physicians could (a) lawfully refrain from renewing and/or could lawfully discontinue all life-sustaining treatment and medical support measures designed to keep the defendant alive in his persistent vegetative state including the termination of ventilation, nutrition and hydration by artifical means, and (b) lawfully discontinue and therefore need not furnish medical treatment to him except for the sole purpose of enabling him to end his life and die peacefully with the greatest dignity and the least pain, suffering and distress. The facts are set out in the judgment of Sir Thomas Bingham MR.

James Munby QC (instructed by the *Official Solicitor*) for the Official Solicitor as guardian ad litem.
Adrian Palmer QC (instructed by *Lawrence Tucketts*, Bristol) for the plaintiffs.

SIR THOMAS BINGHAM MR. This appeal comes before the court at very short notice and raises an acute dilemma. The question for decision put very shortly is whether the plaintiffs in the action, who are a hospital trust, should in effect be given leave not to embark on a surgical procedure, the result of that decision being (if they do not carry out the procedure) that a patient, a young man aged 24, will die within a couple of days.

The problem arises in this way. The patient (whom I shall call 'S') was a fit, energetic and sane young man who in June 1991 took a large overdose of drugs with the result that he suffered acute and extreme brain damage. He was taken to a hospital in the Bristol area, where this event occurred, in a state of deep unconsciousness. Various treatments were given and he received care for his condition in a general ward over a period of some months.

In October 1991 he was transferred to a rehabilitation unit, also in the Bristol area, and since that time he has been under the care of a consultant who is the main medical witness in this case. The consultant in question, whose curriculum vitae is before us, is a consultant of very wide and long experience in the treatment of the acutely disabled, including the young acutely disabled. It is apparent from his curriculum vitae that he has the most extensive and wide ranging experience in this country and abroad. He is extremely well qualified in medical terms and he has also, perhaps relevantly, engaged himself in the consideration of ethical questions.

Over the period since October 1991 he has treated S. In the course of a report which he wrote at short notice, in circumstances that I shall describe, he records that since October 1991 there has been no improvement in S's brain function and no improvement in his ability to communicate or do anything independently. He writes:

'There is no evidence that he has a conscious self and it is felt that from the time of diagnosis the technical label for his brain damage was persistent vegetative state. This term, coined by Jennet and Plum in 1972, describes a group of patients who, though having a pattern of sleeping and waking, show no meaningful responses to changes in their environment except at a reflex level. It differentiates them from patients in coma who do not open their eyes and show no reflex response to stimulation.'

It is I think unnecessary to describe the persistent vegetative state in detail since that has recently been done by a number of judges in *Airedale NHS Trust v Bland* [1993] 1 All ER 821, [1993] AC 789, to which I fear I shall make repeated reference.

The treatment which S underwent at the rehabilitation unit involved an intensive nursing regime with attention of one sort or another every two hours; toilet, bathing, relieving his bladder, emptying his bowels, turning him, and so on. Until June 1993 he was fed thorough a nasogastric tube as the only practicable way of feeding him. That became unsatisfactory because as a result of restlessness following each feed S repeatedly pulled on the tube and there was some evidence of bleeding in the stomach, probably caused by the tube itself. Accordingly the nasogastric tube was removed and a consultant surgeon performed an operation to insert a gastrostomy tube through the stomach wall and into the stomach to permit him to be fed in that way. It is of interest to note that at the time the first consultant surgeon who was invited to perform this operation declined to do so since he took the view that it was, having regard to the patient's condition, an unjustifiable operative treatment to carry out. The operation was nonetheless performed and the tube had to be changed from time to time. In October 1993, to investigate whether there was any hope of achieving any improvement in S's condition, he was transferred to the Putney Royal Hospital and Home, and there spent some six weeks during which period a new tube was inserted.

The Bristol consultant said:

'After two years, despite persistent attempts to stimulate him and encourage recovery, the doctors and nurses on the ward together with expert opinions felt that there was no chance of recovery and began to take steps to obtain legal permission to withdraw artificially given nutrition and fluid.'

In other words, they had formed the opinion that S was in the same position as Anthony Bland and that the same medical approach was justified.

The consideration of that question was interrupted when on Monday of this week, shortly before midday, it was found that the gastrostomy tube through which S was being fed, and had recently been fed, had been removed from his body, probably as a result of his own movement, pulling it out of the stomach. That of course presented the doctors with an acute and immediate problem. In the absence of the tube and without any other tube it was impossible to feed S at all. It was apparently not medically practicable simply to reinsert the tube in the orifice from which it had been pulled out, and the question which faced them was whether in those circumstances a further surgical procedure should be undertaken in order to feed a further gastrostomy tube into S's stomach. The decision that the consultant in charge of S took was that that was something that should not be done. He felt that there were two options which faced him. The first was to reinsert the gastrostomy tube so as to resume feeding. He said:

'There is no chance whatever of this being to his benefit. There is no chance whatever of it benefiting his mother who has clearly wished his body to be allowed to die for the last two years. I do not believe it is in the interest of the father for S's body to be kept artificially alive as it will probably delay his grieving and heartache. To reinsert the tube now that we have such certainty about the state of his brain, his function and prospects would, in my opinion, be a criminal act as it would be being done against the best interests of S.'

The other option which the consultant recognised was not to reinsert the tube. He accepted that this would cause death within a limited period but added that there was absolutely no reason to expect lack of food or fluid to cause suffering or ill effect.

The consultant in the course of his report refers to his experience in looking after patients in conditions such as this. He observes:

'Nearly all doctors looking after patients have been faced very many times with the problem of when to withdraw medical interference with the natural process of a patient's dying. The decision to withdraw or withhold various treatments and allow death to take place peacefully and gracefully are taken every day in the community and hospitals throughout the country. S is only different in degree. He has a fatal illness. His body is terribly ill and all our attention is focused on easing any distress and helping the relatives. I believe there is nothing good to be gained for S by further prolonging an unnatural state of affairs. My following conclusion has not been reached suddenly but over the last two years in repeated discussion with other doctors and nurses and with great difficulty because I fear I might be failing to take all aspects of the problem into consideration. I am convinced that we have proof that S is in a persistent vegetative state and cannot improve and that it is in his best interest for him to be allowed to die naturally. By not reinstating artificial feeding I am convinced that the process of his dying cannot cause him distress.'

The consultant then in the course of his report referred to the mother, who strongly favoured the course which he himself also favoured of not resuming feeding; to the position of the father, whose position was more equivocal and who was reluctant to commit himself to support that course (and indeed signed a permission for the tube to be reinserted); and to the position of the nurses on the ward who, having nursed S for a period of over two years, strongly favoured the course which commended itself to the consultant.

I should make reference also to other medical opinions which in a short period of time have been assembled. One of those is a report by a professor of neurology who had seen S from time to time over the years and who wrote a report in which he said: 'He has permanent, severe brain damage and there is no prospect of further recovery.' That was a report written in 1992. More recently the same professor wrote:

'As far as I can ascertain there has been very little change since last time. [That was a reference to September 1992.] There is still no verbalisation although he often grunts and can be noisy. He appears to suffer pain but it is not obvious where this is originating. He is restless for much of the time and throws himself around the bed which has padded sides. I understand that he has had several febrile episodes presumably due to urinary infections.'

He had no suggestion to make as to any treatment.

A further medical report was obtained from a consultant neuropsychiatrist who again has seen S from time to time over the years. Significantly, he saw him and examined him in February 1993 and concluded his clinical note by reporting:

'His current quality of life is nil and I see no prospect of this improving.'

The same message was contained in a report written since the detachment of the tube on Monday, 10 January in which the doctor said:

'S has been in a persistent vegetative state for almost three years. There is no prospect of any recovery for him at any stage. This view is backed by the current medical literature on this condition with which I am familiar.'

The last medical opinion is given by a consultant in rehabilitation medicine who is on the staff of the Putney Royal Hospital and Home, which is the hospital to which S was sent for six weeks in October and November of last year. She referred to various changes that she thought could make S more comfortable, in particular by reducing the heavy doses of medication which he was at the time receiving and by use of a chair which she thought would enable him to position himself more comfortably. She however reports:

'In summary S shows many of the features which in combination can be described as the persistent vegetative state. He has no meaningful response to changes in his environment except at a reflex level but does show a reflex response to some stimuli. However, within the six-week period of assessment we were not able to provide him with his own supportive seating system nor was it possible to reduce the high doses of sedative drugs which he has been on.'

It is fair to observe that one of her suggestions, namely a reduction in medication, had been tried by those who were treating him in Bristol but with ill effect.

Reverting then to the narrative, the doctors were confronted on Monday with this appalling decision as to whether they should authorise a further surgical procedure to insert a gastrostomy tube or whether they should desist with the prospect that the patient would shortly thereafter die. Advice was taken and late on Wednesday of this week an application to the judge sitting in Bristol was mounted. Notice was given to the Official Solicitor that the application was being made but it was very short notice, through no fault of the plaintiffs. Thus it was that the matter came before Swinton Thomas J yesterday afternoon, 13 January, in Bristol when he was invited to make a declaration, the effect of which was to authorise the plaintiff hospital trust not to replace the gastrostomy tube. The Official Solicitor was represented by counsel, but it is of course right to observe that the Official Solicitor himself had very little time to give instructions and counsel herself had very little time to prepare her submissions. However, the matter was heard before the learned judge yesterday afternoon and having heard argument on both sides, and having been referred in some detail to *Airdale NHS Trust v Bland* [1993] 1 All ER 821, [1993] AC 789, particularly the House of Lords decision, the learned judge concluded that he should in all the circumstances grant the declaration which the hospital were seeking.

Today, and still at short notice, the Official Solicitor appeals to this court against that decision and the case has been argued, with his customary skill and erudition, by Mr Munby QC on his behalf.

I am conscious that in the course of this judgment I have already referred on a number of occasions to the authority of *Airdale NHS Trust v Bland*. That is a very well-known decision, young though it is, involving a young Hillsborough victim who had been in a persistent vegetative state for a period of over three

CA   Frenchay NHS Trust v S (Sir Thomas Bingham MR)   409

years, and who gave rise to an application to the court on behalf of the hospital
trust responsible for his treatment for leave to discontinue feeding and
providing liquid to him. The case began with Sir Stephen Brown P, passed
through this court and ended in the House of Lords, Lord Keith, Lord Goff,
Lord Browne-Wilkinson and Lord Mustill at all levels, being unanimous in
their view that the leave which the hospital sought should be given. It is right
to observe that it was an extreme case of the persistent vegetative state. There
was no hope of recovery whatever. There was no division of medical opinion.
The ethical guidelines which were before the court all pointed the same way.
There was, despite this unanimity of judicial opinion, widespread and
understandable concern, both among lawyers and amongst the public, at the
implications of the decision. This is not in any way surprising since it touched
on values which are literally fundamental to our view of society and of the
world. The courts were of course alive to, and I would hope responsive to, this
concern. They were certainly anxious that their decision should not be in any
way misunderstood or misapplied. So it was that various rules and principles
were laid down in that case to try and prevent abuse and reassure the public.
First of all, it was suggested, at any rate in the short term, that those seeking to
discontinue treatment in what I may call the *Bland* situation should come to
court and obtain a declaration from the court that it was proper to do so.
Secondly, it was envisaged that such applications should be preceded by full
investigation with an opportunity for the Official Solicitor, as the
representative of the unconscious patient, to explore the situation fully, to
obtain independent medical opinions of his own, and to ensure that all proper
material was before the court before such a momentous decision was taken.
Thirdly, the courts made plain that their decisions were to be understood as
strictly applying to the *Bland* situation and no other. A number of judges were
at pains to emphasise that they should not be taken as approving anything
falling outside the factual situation which was then before the court.

It is against that background that we have heard the submissions made on
behalf of the Official Solicitor today. So far as the first of those safeguards is
concerned, namely the application to the court, that has indeed been satisfied
because despite the compressed timetable it has been possible for the plaintiff
trust to apply to the court, to put medical reports and opinions before the
court, and to enable the court to consider the matter, albeit at short notice. It
is however to be observed that cases must from time to time arise in which this
procedure simply cannot be practicable. I have in mind the acute emergency
when a decision has to be taken within a matter of minutes, or at most hours,
as to whether treatment should be given or not, whether one form of
treatment should be given or another, or as to whether treatment should be
withheld. In such situations it is of course impossible that doctors should be
obliged or able to come to the court and seek a decision. I think it is therefore
inevitable that there must be emergencies in which application to the court is
simply not possible, even though this case is not one of them. That
consideration does however lead on to Mr Munby's first major submission of
the three which he has made to us, which is that the procedure which has been
adopted in this case has in effect deprived S, and his representative, the Official
Solicitor, of a fair and full opportunity to explore the matter fully and make
sure that all relevant material is before the court. There is inevitably a measure
of truth in that. If the court were to allow the appeal and withhold a
declaration, it may be that the surgical procedure would be undertaken and
that there would then be an opportunity for a full investigation with the

prospect of an application such as was made in *Bland*'s case in some months' time. It does not however seem to me that we should regard that consideration as conclusive. Just as there will be some situations in which it will be impracticable for the plaintiff to apply to the court at all, so there will be other situations, such as the present, in which, although it is possible to come to court, it is not possible to present the application in the same leisurely way as in a case where there is no pressure of time at all. For my part, therefore, I think it important to take note of Mr Munby's submission and to look very critically at the facts and at the material which is before the court, but I do not consider that it would be right to allow the appeal simply on the basis that there has not been an opportunity on behalf of S for there to be a full exploration of the facts which in other circumstances would be desirable.

I go on then to what is Mr Munby's second major submission, which is that on the face of the plaintiff's own evidence there is reason to question the diagnosis of PVS. This is of course an important submission because, as I have emphasised, in *Bland*'s case the courts were at pains to emphasise that their decision applied only to the facts which were before them. Mr Munby raises an important question as to whether the facts of *Bland*'s case are the facts of the present case for legal purposes. He draws attention to a number of features of the evidence which in his submission raise doubts as to whether the cases are truly comparable. He draws attention, for example, to the fact that the consultant in charge of S made his original diagnosis after only four months, and he reminds us of BMA guidelines which suggest that a diagnosis of PVS should not be confirmed until 12 months has expired. For my part I see little force in that point since the initial diagnosis was clearly provisional. There is no doubt at all that it has been confirmed by the consultant with a very much more detailed knowledge of S's case. Mr Munby draws attention to the fact that rehabilitation was pursued for a period of two years and this again, he suggests, throws doubt on the confidence with which the consultant made his diagnosis, since this would have been futile had the diagnosis been made with complete confidence. Again, I cannot for my part regard that as undermining the acceptability of the consultant's diagnosis since, however sure one was that the prospects of recovery were nil one would still wish to leave no possible stone unturned and no doubt it would be necessary to satisfy members of the family that every possible chance was being explored. More significantly, attention is drawn to suggestions in the medical reports of what might be interpreted as volitional behaviour: that is, not mere spasm or reflex reaction, but voluntary behaviour on the part of the patient. There is reference at one point to pulling at the nasogastric tube and indeed to the pulling out of the gastrostomy tube on Monday of this week. There are references to the possibility that S may feel distress and may be suffering. Indeed, it is pointed out that one of the reasons why the nurses are so gravely distressed by S's condition is that they are convinced that at times he seems to suffer.

It is commented that the consultant neuropsychiatrist does little more than endorse the consultant's report and it is suggested in respect of the professor of neurology that he does not diagnose PVS. It is true, I think, that that is not an expression that he uses and he expresses doubt as to whether S can recognise his family rather than expressing a concluded opinion that he cannot. He makes a reference to S appearing to suffer pain. Again, it is pointed out that the consultant at Putney does not unequivocally diagnose PVS but refers to resistance by S on some occasions and to certain forms of response, and expresses her views on his ability to communicate in a somewhat equivocal way. In contrast again to the neuropsychiatrist, who thought that S's quality of life was nil, she thought that there were respects in which it could be improved.

I think it is plain that the evidence in this case is not as emphatic and not as unanimous as that in *Bland's* case. That certainly causes one to look critically and anxiously at the evidence that is before us. In particular we have to ask ourselves whether the respects in which the evidence is not the same throws doubt on the decision which the consultant has taken and invited the court to approve. For my part there appears to be very little doubt in the evidence, particularly the evidence of the doctors who know S best, that he is in a persistent vegetative state, that there is no prospect of recovery, and that he has no cognitive function worth the name. It is not suggested that one is dealing here with a brain-damaged patient who has some significant cognitive function. The evidence to which I have already referred in some detail presents S as a person who has no conscious being at all. That being the case it does not seem to me that in the acute emergency which has arisen the court should attach great weight to the points of distinction that have been raised between the two cases.

I come on, therefore, to the third major submission that Mr Munby has laid before the court which is this. Mr Munby is at pains to make plain that he is anything but critical of the learned judge who was faced with a difficult decision to be made at short notice and with very little opportunity for thought, certainly for prolonged thought. Mr Munby does, however, submit that the judge erred in attaching too much importance to the judgment of doctors as to what was in the patient's best interests. Mr Munby submits that the House of Lords decision in *Airedale NHS Trust v Bland* [1993] 1 All ER 821, [1993] AC 789 left open whether the judgment was finally to be made by the doctors or by the court, his submission being that in the last resort it must be made by the court, albeit with great regard to the opinions of responsible medical men. It is true that the learned judge paid close attention to what members of the House of Lords had said about the subject in the course of their speeches in *Bland's* case and did express the view that the conclusion at which S's consultant had arrived was reasonable and bona fide. He regarded the judgments which had been expressed by the doctors in this case as being fully in accord with criteria which their Lordships had laid down. It is, I think, important that there should not be a belief that what the doctor says is the patient's best interest is the patient's best interest. For my part I would certainly reserve to the court the ultimate power and duty to review the doctors' decision in the light of all the facts. But in a case such as this the question which must be asked is I think clear, and the question is: what is in the best interests of the patient? The plaintiffs' answer to that question is clear, and it is that given by the consultant to whom I have repeatedly referred. The answer given on behalf of S, through the Official Solicitor, is that a declaration should not be made. That would leave the doctors in this position: either they would feel obliged to embark upon the surgical procedure necessary to reinsert the tube, which the consultant has made quite clear is contrary in a profound sense to his judgment of what is in the patient's best interests, and which he is himself unwilling to authorise, or they would simply do nothing and persist in the course of conduct on which they have embarked, uncertain whether at the end of the day the law would condemn that decision or not. That may sometimes be the right course for the court to adopt, but it seems to me a highly unsatisfactory position into which one should be reluctant to lead doctors unless the court has real doubt about the reliability, or bona fides, or correctness of the medical opinion in question. Here we have, as it seems to me, a careful, professional and clearly very thoughtful conclusion expressed by a consultant of the highest standing with a knowledge of this patient acquired over a period of years. It is an opinion shared by other doctors who have had the opportunity of seeing the patient, again over a period of years. It is an opinion which no medical opinion contradicts. It is strictly correct, as Mr Munby points out, that there are not two independent medical opinions supporting that of the consultant who in effect makes this application. That is partly a reflection of the emergency which has given rise to the application. But we have, as I have said, two opinions, both to the same effect as the consultant's, and no contrary opinion.

Returning, therefore, to the fundamental question, what is in the best interests of the patient, I find no reason to question the answer which the consultant has given and the answer which the plaintiff hospital trust propounds. I accordingly find myself in agreement with the judge in the decision to which he came and I would for my part dismiss the appeal.

WAITE LJ. The judge had to make a finely balanced decision in circumstances of acute sadness and extreme urgency. So urgent, indeed, was the case, that it might forgivably have been thought impossible by the medical authorities to mount any application to the court at all in the very limited time which S's tragic plight has left available. The application was nevertheless made, and it thereupon became the anxious duty of the court to decide whether to grant or refuse the requested leave.

A difficult preliminary question for the judge was the need to decide whether the decision could be postponed while the case received the benefit of that full investigation which, under the procedures that have now become established for cases of this kind, would be accorded to it by the Official Solicitor and specialists instructed on his behalf. I confess, for myself, I have found this the most difficult aspect of the case.

Mr Munby's submission was that these major decisions—quite literally of life and death—ought not to be taken without due consideration of any features which may take the case out of the absolute category of PVS. There ought, in particular, to be an inquiry as to whether S's case is one where what Lord Mustill in *Airedale NHS Trust v Bland* [1993] 1 All ER 821 at 896, [1993] AC 789 at 899 called the 'glimmerings of awareness' are to be found. If such an inquiry, so Mr Munby submits, should involve leaving the doctors with a need to act now against their own medical judgment through reinsertion of the gastrostomy tube, or finding another doctor who is willing to do what they cannot bring themselves to do, then that is a disadvantage which needs to be accepted in S's interests in the short term, for the sake of ensuring a properly informed decision in the long term before the crucial and irretrievable die is cast.

That was a persuasive and a cogent argument. Nevertheless, this was a case where the decision had to be taken in S's best interests; interests which fell to be appraised by a judge who had the benefit of hearing the witnesses and reaching a conclusion in his own discretion under the pressure of extreme urgency. It was, in the last analysis, for him to decide whether S's interests required a final determination there and then, or a postponement involving further medical intervention against his own doctors' views of their patient's best medical interests. The judge clearly evaluated that issue with all the sympathy and care for which it called, as he did on all other issues in this case. I would not therefore feel justified myself in interfering with the conclusions that he reached, and for this reason, and for all the reasons which have been given by Sir Thomas Bingham MR, I too would dismiss the appeal.

PETER GIBSON LJ. For the reasons given by Sir Thomas Bingham MR, with which I am in entire agreement, I too would dismiss this appeal.

Appeal dismissed.

L I Zysman Esq   Barrister.

Practice Note

Medical treatment – Withdrawal of treatment – Insensate patient – Patient in persistent vegetative state – Practice – Sanction of High Court judge required before treatment terminated – Confirmation of diagnosis – Form of application – Parties to application – Evidence – Views of patient – Consultation with Official Solicitor.

The need for the prior sanction of a High Court judge
1. The termination of artificial feeding and hydration for patients in a persistent vegetative state (PVS) will in virtually all cases require the prior sanction of a High Court judge: *Airedale NHS Trust v Bland* [1993] 1 All ER 821 at 833, [1993] AC 789 at 805 per Sir Stephen Brown P and *Frenchay Healthcare NHS Trust v S* [1994] 2 All ER 403.

The diagnosis
2. The Medical Ethics Committee of the British Medical Association issued guidelines on treatment decisions for patients in persistent vegetative state in July 1993. According to the BMA, current methods of diagnosing PVS cannot be regarded as infallible. Such a diagnosis should not be considered confirmed until the patient has been insentient for at least 12 months. Before then, as soon as the patient's condition has stabilised, rehabilitative measures such as coma arousal programmes should be instituted (see *Airedale NHS Trust v Bland* [1993] 1 All ER 821 at 872, [1993] AC 789 at 871 per Lord Goff). For a discussion of the diagnosis of PVS and of other conditions with which it is sometimes confused, see App 4 (and paras 156–162, 251–258) of the *Report of the House of Lords Select Committee on Medical Ethics* (HL Paper (1993–94) 21-I).

Applications to court
3. Applications to court should be by originating summons issued in the Family Division of the High Court seeking a declaration in the form set out in para 4 below. Subject to specific provisions below, the application should follow the procedure laid down for sterilisation cases by the House of Lords in *F v West Berkshire Health Authority (Mental Health Act Commission intervening)* [1989] 2 All ER 545, [1990] 2 AC 1 and in the Official Solicitor's Practice Note of May 1993 ([1993] 3 All ER 222).
4. The originating summons should seek relief in the following form:

'It is declared that despite the inability of X to give a valid consent, the plaintiffs and/or the responsible medical practitioners: (i) may lawfully discontinue all life-sustaining treatment and medical support measures designed to keep X alive in his existing persistent vegetative state including the termination of ventilation, nutrition and hydration by artificial means; and (ii) may lawfully discontinue and thereafter need not furnish medical treatment to X except for the sole purpose of enabling X to end his life and to die peacefully with the greatest dignity and the least distress.

It is ordered that in the event of a material change in the existing circumstances occurring before the withdrawal of artificial feeding and hydration any party shall have liberty to apply for such further or other declaration or order as may be just.'

5. The case should normally be heard in chambers and the judgment given in open court.

The parties

6. The applicants may be either the next of kin or the relevant area health authority/NHS Trust (which in any event ought to be a party). The views of the next of kin are very important and should be made known to the court in every case.

7. The Official Solicitor should be invited to act as guardian ad litem of the patient, who will inevitably be a patient within the meaning of RSC Ord 80.

The evidence

8. There should be at least two neurological reports on the patient, one of which will be commissioned by the Official Solicitor. Other medical evidence, such as evidence about rehabilitation or nursing care, may be necessary.

The views of the patient

9. The views of the patient may have been previously expressed, either in writing or otherwise. The High Court exercising its inherent jurisdiction may determine the effect of a purported advance directive as to future medical treatment: *Re T (adult: refusal of medical treatment)* [1992] 4 All ER 649, [1993] Fam 95, *Re C (adult: refusal of medical treatment)* [1994] 1 All ER 819, [1994] 1 WLR 290. In summary, the patient's previously expressed views, if any, will always be a very important component in the decisions of the doctors and the court.

Consultation

10. Members of the Official Solicitor's legal staff are prepared to discuss PVS cases before proceedings have been issued. Contact with the Official Solicitor may be made by telephoning 071-911 7127 during office hours.

March 1994

PETER M HARRIS
Official Solicitor.

Secretary of State for the Environment v Euston Centre Investments Ltd

CHANCERY DIVISION
JOHN CHERRYMAN QC SITTING AS A DEPUTY JUDGE OF THE HIGH COURT
2, 9 DECEMBER 1993

Decision of Mr. John Cherryman Q.C. sitting as a deputy judge of the Chancery Division reversed.
[1995] Ch. 200, C.A.

Arbitration – Leave to appeal against award – Delay – Striking out – Failure to conduct and prosecute appeal with proper despatch – Applicant applying for leave to appeal against arbitrator's award on rent review – Applicant not obtaining date for hearing until more than 12 months after award – Whether application for leave to appeal should be struck out for delay – Principles applying to striking out for delay – Arbitration Act 1979, s 1(3)(b).

By a lease dated 9 May 1970 premises were demised by the landlord to the tenant for a term of 49 years from 25 March 1970 at an initial rent of £1,729,200 pa with provision for rent reviews every seven years. On the third rent review the parties were unable to agree the rent and the dispute was referred to an arbitrator who by an interim award on 28 May 1992 determined the rent at £7,760,000 pa. The tenant applied under s 1(3)(b)[a] of the Arbitration Act 1979 for leave to appeal on 17 June 1992 within 21 days after publication of the award, pursuant to RSC Ord 73, r 5. On 19 March 1993 the Commercial Court made an order transferring the proceedings to the Chancery Division, the delay of ten months being due to an administrative error by the court. The tenant's solicitor received notification of the transfer on 29 April 1993 and wrote to the solicitors for the landlord on 9 June 1993 to arrange for a date of hearing to be fixed. On 19 August 1993 the hearing was fixed for 2 December 1993. On 24 November 1993 the tenant applied under the inherent jurisdiction of the court to strike out the landlord's application for leave to appeal on the ground of want of prosecution because the landlord had failed to conduct the proceedings with proper despatch. The landlord contended that the court's jurisdiction to strike out could only be exercised if the court was satisfied either that the default had been intentional and contumelious or that there had been inordinate and inexcusable delay which gave rise to a substantial risk that it was not possible to have a fair trial of the issues or had caused or was likely to cause serious prejudice to the defendant and that in the circumstances those principles did not apply.

Held – The principles on which the court would strike out actions for intentional and contumelious default or because of inordinate and inexcusable delay which gave rise to a substantial risk that it would not be possible to have a fair trial or would cause serious prejudice to the defendant only applied to actions that had yet to be tried. Where parties aggrieved by an arbitration award utilised the appeal procedure introduced by s 1(3)(b) of the 1979 Act the court would control the procedure strictly in order to prevent abuse and would be vigilant to prevent frustration of the intention of Parliament to promote speedy finality in arbitral awards, whether or not the defendant had suffered

---

a Section 1(3)(b), so far as material, provides: 'An appeal under this section may be brought by any of the parties to the reference ... with the leave of the court.'

any prejudice from the want of prosecution. In seeking leave to appeal from an award of an arbitrator the applicant was invoking a special statutory jurisdiction which public policy required to be exercised with the utmost expedition and therefore the inherent power to strike out applications for leave was exercisable whenever there was a failure to conduct and prosecute an appeal with proper despatch since . On the facts, the delay in prosecuting the application for leave to appeal had been grossly excessive and accordingly the application would be struck out (see p 421 *b* to *f* and p 422 *a* to *h*, post).

Antaios Cia Naviera SA v Salen Rederierna AB, The Antaios [1984] 3 All ER 229 applied.

Birkett v James [1977] 2 All ER 801 distinguished.

Notes

For appeals to the High Court from an arbitrator, see 2 *Halsbury's Laws* (4th edn reissue) paras 706, 709.

For the Arbitration Act 1979, s 1, see 2 *Halsbury's Statutes* (4th edn) 651.

Cases referred to in judgment

Antaios Cia Naviera SA v Salen Rederierna AB, The Antaios [1984] 3 All ER 229, [1985] AC 191, [1984] 3 WLR 592, HL.
Birkett v James [1977] 2 All ER 801, [1978] AC 297, [1977] 3 WLR 38, HL.
Leon Corp v Atlantic Lines and Navigation Co Inc, The Leon [1985] 2 Lloyd's Rep 470.
Mebro Oil SA v Gatoil International Inc [1985] 2 Lloyd's Rep 234.
Rheinoel GmbH v Huron Liberian Co, The Concordia C [1985] 2 Lloyd's Rep 55.
Urban Small Space Ltd v Burford Investment Co [1993] 2 EGLR 120.

Originating motion

By a notice of motion dated 17 June 1992 the applicant, the Secretary of State for the Environment, applied for leave to appeal from the interim award dated 28 May 1992 made by Mr George Grover FRICS as the sole arbitrator in an arbitration between the applicant and the respondent, Euston Centre Investments Ltd, on a rent review of premises at Euston Tower, London, NW1, of which the respondent was the landlord and the applicant the tenant. The applicant sought an order remitting the award to the arbitrator. By a notice of motion dated 24 November 1993 the respondent applied for an order that the appellant's originating notice of motion dated 17 June 1992 be struck out for want of prosecution. The facts are set out in the judgment.

Jonathan Gaunt QC (instructed by the *Treasury Solicitor*) for the applicant.
Michael Barnes QC and *John Male* (instructed by *S J Berwin & Co*) for the respondent.

Cur adv vult

9 December 1993. The following judgment was delivered.

JOHN CHERRYMAN QC. There was due to be heard before me on 2 December 1993 an application under s 1(3)(b) of the Arbitration Act 1979 by the Secretary of State for the Environment for leave to appeal against an arbitration award made as long ago as 28 May 1992. However, Mr Michael Barnes QC, counsel for the respondent, Euston Centre Investments Ltd, has moved for an order to strike out the applicant's proceedings for want of prosecution and I have naturally heard argument on that motion first. As will appear, a question of general importance arises, namely whether the principles to be applied in determining the respondent's motion are those stated in *Birkett v James* [1977] 2 All ER 801, [1978] AC 297 or, because an appeal from an award is involved, some other principles.

The matter arises in the following way. By a lease dated 9 May 1970 premises at Euston Tower, London, NW1 were demised for a term of 49 years from 25 March 1970 at an initial rent of £1,729,200 pa with rent reviews every seven years. The rent was increased to £3,710,000 pa at the second review on 25 March 1984. The respondent, Euston Centre Investments Ltd, and the applicant, the Secretary of State, are respectively the present landlord and tenant of the premises. The parties were unable to agree the market rent as at 25 March 1991 for the purposes of the third rent review. Determination of the rent was referred to an arbitrator, Mr G C Grover FRICS, who was appointed on 14 March 1991. He heard evidence and argument in February and April 1992 and published his interim award on 28 May 1992, determining the market rent as at 25 March 1991 at £7,760,000 pa.

The applicant's originating notice of motion of appeal and summons for leave to appeal were duly issued served and entered in the Commercial Court on 17 June 1992, ie within 21 days after publication of the award as required by RSC Ord 73, r 5. Thereafter there has been deplorable delay. The complete chronology is as follows.

28.5.92	Interim award published.
17.6.92	Originating notice of motion and summons for leave issued.
19.3.93	Order of Commercial Court transferring these proceedings to the Chancery Division.
29.4.93	Treasury Solicitor receives notification of transfer to Chancery Division.
9.6.93	Treasury Solicitor writes to respondent's solicitors suggesting leading counsels' clerks should liaise to fix a date for the hearing of the application for leave to appeal.
15.6.93	Respondent's solicitors agree to this proposal.
21.6.93	Chancery Listing Office sends out time estimate certificate for completion by counsel.
29.7.93	Certificate signed by leading counsel for applicant.
15.8.93	Certificate signed by leading counsel for respondent.
19.8.93	Hearing of leave application fixed for 2.12.93.
24.11.93	Service of respondent's notice of motion to strike out.

The respondent's application to strike out the applicant's proceedings is made under the inherent jurisdiction of the court. Mr Jonathan Gaunt QC for the applicant submitted that this jurisdiction must be exercised in the present case in accordance with the principles stated by Lord Diplock in *Birkett v James* [1977] 2 All ER 801 at 805, [1978] AC 297 318 in the following terms:

'The power should be exercised only where the court is satisfied either (1) that the default has been intentional and contumelious, eg disobedience to a peremptory order of the court or conduct amounting to an abuse of the process of the court; or (2)(a) that there has been inordinate and inexcusable delay on the part of the plaintiff or his lawyers, and (b)

that such delay will give rise to a substantial risk that it is not possible to
have a fair trial of the issues in the action or is such as is likely to cause or
to have caused serious prejudice to the defendants either as between
themselves and the plaintiff or between each other or between them and
a third party.'

Mr Barnes has accepted that, if these principles do apply in the present case,
his application is bound to fail because he would be unable to establish the
likelihood of serious prejudice necessary to satisfy principle 2(b). However, Mr
Barnes has submitted that the *Birkett v James* principles do not apply to appeal
proceedings in the High Court pursuant to s 1 of the Arbitration Act 1979, in
particular applications for leave to appeal under s 1(3)(b). His submission was
that the court has inherent jurisdiction to stay such proceedings if there has
been failure to conduct and prosecute the appeal (or application for leave) with
proper despatch.

Mr Barnes pointed out that in *Birkett v James* the House of Lords was
concerned to state the appropriate test to be applied in actions where the
dispute between the parties had yet to be resolved. He argued that nothing
said by the House of Lords in that case bound the court to apply the same test
in a case such as the present where the arbitrator had already resolved the
dispute subject to it being possible to take a question of law to the High Court
under the special statutory procedure if leave to do so is obtained. In such a
case Mr Barnes submitted a more stringent test must be applied for striking out
purposes, otherwise the legislative intention inherent in the 1979 Act was in
danger of being thwarted. He referred me to the well-known passage in the
speech of Lord Diplock in *Antaios Cia Naviera SA v Salen Rederierna AB, The
Antaios* [1984] 3 All ER 229 at 232, [1985] AC 191 at 199:

'Unless judges are prepared to be vigilant in the exercise of the
discretions conferred on them by ss 1 and 2 of the Arbitration Act 1979,
including in s 1 the new sub-s (6A) that was added by s 148(2) of the
Supreme Court Act 1981, they will allow to be frustrated the intention of
Parliament, as plainly manifested by changes in procedure that these
statutes introduced, to promote speedy finality in arbitral awards rather
than that insistence on meticulous semantic and syntactical analysis of the
words in which businessmen happen to have chosen to express the bargain
made between them, the meaning of which is technically, though hardly
commonsensically, classified in English jurisprudence as a pure question
of law.'

He also relied on the following statement in Mustill and Boyd *Commercial
Arbitration* (2nd edn, 1989) p 611:

'It is the duty of the appellant to prosecute his application for leave to
appeal and, if leave is granted, the appeal itself with proper despatch.
Failure to do so may lead to the application or the appeal being struck out.'

Three cases are cited in support of this passage: *Rheinoel GmbH v Huron
Liberian Co, The Concordia C* [1985] 2 Lloyd's Rep 55, *Mebro Oil SA v Gatoil
International Inc* [1985] 2 Lloyd's Rep 234 and *Leon Corp v Atlantic Lines and
Navigation Co Inc, The Leon* [1985] 2 Lloyd's Rep 470.

In *The Concordia C* Bingham J determined an appeal from an arbitrator's
decision by varying the award. The judge made the following comments with

reference to the delay which had occurred in that case (15 months since the award and 11 months since leave was granted):

'In conclusion, I draw attention to the lamentable fact that it is now over 15 months since this award was made and over 11 months since leave to appeal was given. I am told that the delay over the past year has arisen from attempts to accommodate Counsel, one of whom did not in the event appear to argue the appeal. If the objects of the new Act are to be achieved, delays of this length are plainly unacceptable. I shall do my best to see that such delays do not recur. The court naturally values the assistance of Counsel who have appeared before the arbitrators, but only exceptionally could this assistance justify delay. The engagements of Counsel will not in future be permitted to prevent the prompt disposal of appeals where leave is given in the absence of very special circumstances.' (See [1985] 2 Lloyd's Rep 55 at 58.)

In the *Mebro Oil* case Gatoil applied to strike out Mebro's originating notice of motion of appeal on the ground that Mebro had not sought leave to appeal within the time prescribed by RSC Ord 73, alternatively for want of prosecution. The case was decided at a time when the only time limit expressly prescribed by the rules was 21 days for the originating motion. Mebro's originating notice of motion was served and entered within the 21 days, but the summons for leave was not issued until nearly seven weeks later. Bingham J held that Ord 73 prescribed no time limit within which the application for leave must be made. The appeal therefore could not be struck out for failure to comply with the rules. The judge decided not to exercise what he called 'the stringent power of striking out for want of prosecution' in the particular context of that case. However, he added ([1985] 2 Lloyd's Rep 234 at 238):

'Let me, however, make the position quite clear. I hope that the rules will, as a matter of urgency, be amended to apply a 21 day time limit, plain for all to see, to applications for leave. Unless or until that change is made, this court will regard 21 days as the period within which summonses seeking leave to appeal should ordinarily be issued. Where an application is not issued within that period, the originating motion will be at risk of being struck out for want of prosecution in the absence of strong and exceptional reasons for the failure to issue the appropriate summons earlier.'

In *The Leon* Hobhouse J allowed the owner's appeal and set aside an arbitration award deciding that the charterers were entitled to make certain deductions from the hire payments. However, the judge refused for two reasons to give the owners leave to amend so that an award for the full amount of the hire could be substituted. The second reason was delay. The judge said ([1985] 2 Lloyd's Rep 470 at 476):

'The second reason is that the prosecution of this motion has been attended by grossly excessive delay. The notice of motion was dated Mar. 6, 1984, I repeat, 1984. Leave to appeal was applied for and granted on June 19, 1984. Then instead of promptly applying for and obtaining a hearing date for the motion (rightly estimated at one day) owners refrained from so applying as they wished to accommodate the convenience of the Counsel to be instructed by charterers for the appeal who was not then available for many months owing to other commitments. The application was left until January, 1985, and then again the position of Counsel resulted in the date May 22, being allocated. That date had to be put back to last Wednesday through no fault of either party. This type of delay in prosecuting a motion under s. 1 of the 1979 Act has already been the subject of comment by Mr. Justice Bingham in *The Concordia C* ([1985] 2 Lloyd's Rep 55). The policy of the law as contained in the 1979 Act is that appeals under that Act must have regard to the expeditious and economical disposal of disputes which have been referred to arbitration and must not be allowed without proper warrant to delay the achievement of a final determination. The present is a particularly bad case of delay. The dispute had only arisen in January, 1984. The arbitrators had held the hearing on Feb. 18, 1984 and the umpire's reasoned interim award was dated Feb. 25, 1984. The London Maritime Arbitrators Association had provided the parties with a first class service and a prompt decision appropriate to the relative urgency of the matter submitted. I understand that pending the hearing of this appeal the arbitration has gone to sleep and the real dispute is no nearer its conclusion. Whilst any spirit of sensible co-operation between the lawyers representing the parties to a commercial dispute is to be warmly commended and encouraged, it must be remembered that the plaintiff to a motion, as to an action, has the conduct of it and the duty to prosecute it with proper despatch. Just as an appellant to the Court of Appeal must prosecute his appeal or account for his failure to do so, so must an appellant to this Court under the 1979 Act. Those who fail to recognize this duty risk prejudicing their client's rights and the same applies to respondents who are a party to any such unwarranted delay.'

Mr Barnes also referred me to *Urban Small Space Ltd v Burford Investment Co* [1993] 2 EGLR 120 at 121, where BrowneWilkinson V-C when dealing with an application for leave to appeal from an interim award of an arbitrator ordering discovery said:

'I think it is important that this kind of interim appeal should not be brought. The arbitrator should decide the substance of the matter as quickly as possible, saving delay and substantial expense. It has taken six months from the date of the interim award to get this application before this Court. That is not right.'

Mr Gaunt's argument was that the limits of the inherent jurisdiction to strike out for want of prosecution are defined for all purposes by the principles stated in *Birkett v James*. He submitted that none of the cases cited by Mr Barnes is authority for the proposition that *Birkett v James* does not apply to appeals from arbitrators.

Mr Gaunt took me through the detailed provisions of s 1 of the 1979 Act and RSC Ord 73 and pointed out that no other framework for applications for leave to appeal is prescribed than the requirement that leave must be applied for within the 21 days' time limit.

Mr Gaunt correctly described the passage I have cited from the judgment in *The Concordia C* as obiter and not made in a striking out context. He accepted that the *Mebro Oil* case was decided in such a context, but submitted that the judge's remarks emphasising the risk of late applications for leave being struck out were made in very special circumstances and, apparently, without any argument about the applicability of the principles stated in *Birkett v James*.

As to *The Leon*, Mr Gaunt emphasised that the passage I have cited was not spoken in a striking out context and in his submission did not assist in deciding whether or not the principles in *Birkett v James* apply where it is sought to strike out an application for leave to appeal due to the applicant's delay.

My own view is that the principles stated by Lord Diplock in *Birkett v James* were intended to define the inherent power to strike out actions that had yet to be tried. Nothing said by the House of Lords was intended to place strict limits on the manner in which the court should exercise the inherent jurisdiction in proceedings of a different type.

The manner in which the leave to appeal procedure introduced by s 1(3)(b) of the 1979 Act is utilised by parties aggrieved by arbitration awards is something that the court must control strictly in order to prevent abuse of the procedure. Judges must be vigilant to prevent frustration of the intention of Parliament 'to promote speedy finality in arbitral awards'. The dicta in *The Concordia C* and *The Leon* are strong expressions of judicial determination to pursue this aim. In the *Mebro Oil* case Bingham J proceeded on the basis that he had jurisdiction to strike out an application for leave for delay despite the obvious lack of prejudice to the respondent in that case. I accept that he did not mention *Birkett v James* but the tests laid down in that case can hardly have been absent from his mind. The ability to exercise the inherent jurisdiction to strike out must be one of the weapons available to the court in these cases whether or not serious prejudice is likely, and in saying this I do not draw any distinction between cases involving commercial disputes and cases involving property disputes. My conclusion therefore is that the inherent power to strike out applications for leave is not limited by *Birkett v James* principles but is exercisable whenever there has been a failure to conduct and prosecute an appeal with proper despatch. Whether such power should be exercised in any particular case is, of course, a matter for the discretion of the court.

I now turn to the factual situation in the present case. Mr Gaunt accepted that the Secretary of State's application for leave has taken far too long to come on, the reason for the delay in transfer to the Chancery Division probably being some administrative slip-up in the Commercial Court. He submitted that this was not an appropriate case for striking out because (so he put to me): (1) the applicant has not failed to comply with any rule; (2) the applicant is not to blame for the ten-month delay which occurred before the Treasury Solicitor was informed of the transfer of the proceedings to this division; (3) since then (nearly another six months), there has been no material delay because: (a) the five weeks' delay before the Treasury Solicitor wrote the letter of 9 June 1993 is not particularly significant and (b) since then, the delay has been largely for procedural reasons, including fixing the hearing for a date convenient to the respondent's leading counsel and such delay has been concurred in by the respondent; and (4) although there has been great delay, it is excusable and should not in any event lead to striking out because loss of the chance of appealing could cost the applicant annually a sum which might be between £150,000 and £200,000.

As to the initial delay of ten months, the evidence from a barrister employed by the Treasury Solicitor was that he 'telephoned the Commercial Court from time to time' but he gave no dates, nor details and produced no notes, nor apparently did he write any letters to the court. Mr Gaunt did accept that perhaps something more could have been done to see what had happened to the leave application but he refused to accept that an applicant is under any positive obligation to take steps to get something done if delay occurs at the court. In my judgment an applicant for leave under s 1(3)(b) of the 1979 Act cannot take such a relaxed attitude. It is incumbent on such an applicant to use all reasonable endeavours to get the application on as soon as practicable. In property matters, the transfer often occurs within a matter of weeks without any representation to the Commercial Court being necessary. When delay in the transfer does occur and the delay in this case was enormous it is the duty of the applicant to make representations and, if the response is unsatisfactory, to make an application to the Commercial Court. The applicant did not do this in the present case and as a result in my view cannot simply throw the blame for the delay on the Commercial Court.

I am unable to regard as insignificant the period of five weeks which elapsed between the Treasury Solicitor learning of the transfer to the Chancery Division and the writing of the letter of 9 June 1993. In isolation such delay might not be of importance, but when added to an existing grossly excessive delay of ten months it becomes a serious matter.

As to the hearing being fixed to suit the convenience of the respondent's counsel, I am afraid that, as is made plain in *The Concordia C* and *The Leon*, an applicant who accepts anything other than a tight timetable for the hearing for the convenience of counsel on either side, does so at his peril.

Moreover, in my judgment it is no good saying that the respondent by its inaction and in agreeing to fix the hearing date appear to have concurred in the delay. When leave to appeal from an award of an arbitrator is sought, the applicant invokes a special statutory jurisdiction which public policy requires to be exercised with the utmost expedition. The parties cannot dispense with this requirement and it is quite unsafe for an applicant to assume that slow progress of a leave application will not lead to trouble simply because the other side raise no objection.

Having weighed all these matters up, having taken into account the prejudice to the applicant if shut out from appealing and having taken into account the previous warnings to litigants about delay given in the authorities I have cited (as well as in *Mustill and Boyd*), I have come to the conclusion that this is a case where the court should in its discretion strike out the applicant's entire proceedings in the High Court under the inherent jurisdiction. I therefore order that the originating notice of motion herein dated 17 June 1992 be struck out for want of prosecution.

Order accordingly.

Hazel Hartman   Barrister.

R v Central Criminal Court, ex p Guney

QUEEN'S BENCH DIVISION

RALPH GIBSON LJ AND SMITH J

14, 26 JANUARY 1994

Decision of the Divisional Court of the Queen's Bench Division reversed. **[1995] 1 W.L.R. 576 C.A.**

Criminal law – Bail – Recognisance – Forfeiture – Effect of defendant's arraignment – Arraignment taking place at preparatory hearing – Defendant pleading not guilty to indictment at arraignment – Agreement between counsel that defendant not required to surrender to custody of court for arraignment – Defendant subsequently fleeing jurisdiction – Whether surety's liability continuing after defendant arraigned – Whether surety discharged on arraignment – Whether arraignment valid.

In January 1991 the applicant stood surety in the sum of £1m for a defendant charged with offences of theft and false accounting. In June 1992 at the preparatory hearing in the Crown Court the defendant was arraigned and pleaded not guilty to the indictment. On that occasion prosecution and defence counsel privately agreed that it would not be necessary for the defendant to surrender to the custody of the court. In May 1993 the defendant fled the country and in July 1993 the applicant was ordered to forfeit the sum of £650,000 within six months with two years' imprisonment in default of payment. The applicant applied for judicial review of the forfeiture order, contending (i) that the order was made without jurisdiction since the applicant's obligations under the recognisance had come to an end in June 1992 when the defendant had been arraigned and had surrendered to the custody of the court for that purpose and (ii) that the court or the prosecution had failed to inform the applicant of allegations that an attempt had been made to bribe the judge to secure variations of the conditions of the defendant's bail.

Held – It was not necessary for a defendant to surrender to the custody of the court before there could be a valid arraignment. The purpose of arraignment was to establish whether a defendant accepted the jurisdiction of the court and whether, by reason of a plea of not guilty, there would be a trial by jury and the purposes of arraignment could be fully served without injustice or risk thereof to the defendant if he pleaded to the indictment without being required to surrender to the custody of the court. Furthermore, there was nothing irregular in the agreement between counsel that neither side would invite the judge to require the defendant to surrender to custody and there was no risk of injustice to sureties if a defendant pleaded to an indictment without being required to surrender to the custody of the court since sureties were not required to be informed when the defendant would be required to attend to surrender to the custody of the court. Moreover, there had been no unfairness in the failure to report the bribery allegations to the applicant since it was reasonable to assume that he was paying due attention to the risk imposed on him by the recognisance. The application would therefore be dismissed (see p 430 *j*, p 431 *b* to *j*, p 432 *d* to *h*, p 434 *h* and p 435 *b c g h*, post).

DPP v Richards [1988] 3 All ER 406 considered.

Notes

For remand on bail in criminal proceedings, see 29 *Halsbury's Laws* (4th edn) para 349.

For the meaning of arraignment, see 11(2) *Halsbury's Laws* (4th edn reissue) para 961.

Cases referred to in judgments

DPP v Richards [1988] 3 All ER 406, [1988] QB 701, [1988] 3 WLR 153, DC.
R v Ellis (1973) 57 Cr App R 571, CA.
R v Gomez [1993] 1 All ER 1, [1993] AC 442, [1992] 3 WLR 1067, HL; *rvsg* [1991] 3 All ER 394, [1991] 1 WLR 1334, CA.
R v Horseferry Road Magistrates' Court, ex p Pearson [1976] 2 All ER 264, [1976] 1 WLR 511, DC.
R v Panel on Take-overs and Mergers, ex p Guinness plc [1989] 1 All ER 509, [1990] 1 QB 146, [1989] 2 WLR 863, CA.
R v Southampton Justices, ex p Green [1975] 2 All ER 1073, [1976] QB 11, [1975] 3 WLR 277, CA.
R v Tottenham Magistrates' Court, ex p Riccardi (1978) 66 Cr App R 150, DC.
R v Wells Street Magistrates' Court, ex p Albanese [1981] 3 All ER 769, [1982] QB 333, [1981] 3 WLR 694.
R v Williams [1977] 1 All ER 874, [1978] QB 373, [1977] 2 WLR 400, CA.

Cases also cited

R v Crown Court at Reading, ex p Bello [1992] 3 All ER 353, CA.
R v Crown Court at York, ex p Coleman (1988) 86 Cr App R 151, DC.

Application for judicial review

Ramadan Hussein Guney applied with leave of Brooke J granted on 17 November 1993 for judicial review of the decision of Tucker J on 30 July 1993 in the matter of Asil Nadir, a defendant for whom the applicant had stood surety and who had fled the jurisdiction, that the applicant pay a sum of £650,000 within six months of the date of that hearing to satisfy his obligation to the court on his recognisance or in default be committed to prison for two years. The relief sought was an order of certiorari to quash the decision on the grounds that the judge had erred in law in ruling that Nadir had not surrendered himself to the custody of the Crown Court when he had been arraigned on 22 June 1992, that the decision to estreat the applicant's recognisance was in breach of natural justice and unfair in that the court had failed to inform the applicant of matters potentially relevant to the likelihood that Nadir would not surrender to his bail, namely that Nadir, together with his leading counsel and a senior police officer, were under serious and active investigation by the police of a plot to bribe Tucker J, the trial judge. The facts are set out in the judgment of Ralph Gibson LJ.

Edmund Lawson QC and *Russell Houston* (instructed by *Kaim Todner*) for the applicant.
Robert Owen QC, David Calvert-Smith and *Cathryn McGahey* (instructed by the *Serious Fraud Office*) for the Serious Fraud Office as an interested party.
The defendant did not appear.

Cur adv vult

26 January 1994. The following judgments were delivered.

RALPH GIBSON LJ. This is an application for judicial review by Mr Ramadan Hussein Guney, a member of the Turkish Cypriot community in this country. He stood surety, in the sum of £1m, for Mr Asil Nadir, also a member of that community, when Mr Nadir was charged in December 1990 with offences of theft and false accounting and was granted bail on certain terms and conditions, including the provision of sureties. Mr Asil Nadir, who has at all times asserted his innocence, chose on 4 May 1993 not to face trial upon the charges made against him in this country but instead to run away to Northern Cyprus leaving Mr Guney to bear such burden as the law should impose upon Mr Guney in respect of his recognisance. On 30 July 1993 Tucker J ordered forfeiture in the sum of £650,000 to be paid by Mr Guney within six months and with two years' imprisonment in default of payment. Mr Guney claims that the order of forfeiture was made without jurisdiction on the ground that, as is asserted on his behalf by Mr Lawson QC, any obligation under the recognisance had, as a matter of law, come to an end on 22 June 1992 when Mr Nadir, upon being arraigned before Tucker J and pleading not guilty to the indictment, surrendered to the custody of the court. Since the recognisance was not renewed, there was, it is said, no continuing liability, and it matters not that Mr Guney and all other participants in the proceedings, including the judge, confidently supposed that Mr Nadir was on bail supported by the recognisance of Mr Guney.

Leave to apply was granted on 17 November 1993. The grounds stated were directed to the issue whether after 22 June 1992 Mr Guney was in law liable on the recognisance. In addition, the point was raised as to the amount ordered to be forfeited and, if it should be held that Mr Guney is liable at all, it was contended that the judge failed properly to take into account the means of Mr Guney. That alternative ground has not been pursued in this court. Mr Lawson, however, applied for leave to add an additional ground, namely that the court or the prosecution failed to inform Mr Guney of allegations made or discovered in October 1992 to the effect that an attempt was to be made to bribe Tucker J to secure variation of the conditions of Mr Nadir's bail. The relief sought on this alternative ground, if it should be made out, is an order remitting the Crown's application for forfeiture to the court for reconsideration of the amount to be forfeited having regard to such relevant unfairness as might be proved to have been caused by the failure to inform. Leave to amend the grounds was granted.

The facts must be stated in some detail.

(1) On 28 January 1991 Mr Guney signed the recognisance upon which forfeiture was ordered by Tucker J. It reads:

'I acknowledge my obligation to pay the court the sum specified opposite my signature [£1m] if the accused fails to surrender to the custody of the above-named court [Bow Street Magistrates' Court] on 23 April 1991 at 2 pm; and custody at every time and place to which during the course of the proceedings the hearing may from time to time be adjourned and custody of the Crown Court on such day and at such time and place as may be notified to the accused by the appropriate officer of that court.'

(2) On 28 January 1991 Mr Nadir was remanded to 23 April 1991, with one variation to the detailed conditions of his bail which included conditions such as reporting weekly to a police station, and that Mr Nadir deposit £2m with his

solicitors, to be held to the order of the clerk of the court. Miss Aysegul Nadir, the former wife of Mr Nadir, was also surety in the sum of £500,000. It is said by the Crown that 'it was agreed' that the surety should be made continuous to trial. That was not an agreement to which Mr Guney was party. It is submitted for Mr Guney that it was not within the power of the magistrates' court to make an order for bail extending beyond 'surrender to the custody' of the Crown Court.

(3) Mr Nadir appeared at Bow Street Magistrates' Court on various dates between April and 22 October 1991 when he was charged with 58 further offences of theft and remanded to 7 November 1991. The clerk at Bow Street then wrote to ask whether Mr Guney was content to continue as surety. On 1 November 1991 Mr Guney replied to the effect that he wished to continue to be bound as surety.

(4) On 7 February 1992 the charges against Mr Nadir and a co-defendant, Mr John Turner, were transferred to the Central Criminal Court under s 4 of the Criminal Justice Act 1987. The Serious Fraud Office (the SFO) was established under that Act. Transfer under s 4 is effected by a notice to the court by a designated authority, which expression includes the SFO, if the authority is of opinion that the evidence of the offence charged would be sufficient for the person charged to be committed for trial and that the evidence reveals a case of fraud of such seriousness and complexity that it is appropriate that the management of the case should without delay be taken over by the Crown Court. There was a preliminary hearing at the Central Criminal Court before Tucker J on 28 February 1992 when the preparatory hearing was fixed for 22 June 1992.

(5) On 8 June 1992 Tucker J, on the application of Mr Nadir, dismissed 46 of the charges against him on, as I understand it, the authority of the decision of the Court of Appeal, Criminal Division in *R v Gomez* [1991] 3 All ER 394, [1991] 1 WLR 1334. The charges were later reinstated in December 1992 when that decision was reversed by the House of Lords ([1993] 1 All ER 1, [1993] AC 442).

(6) On 22 June 1992 at a hearing before Tucker J in a court at Chichester Rents the 'preparatory hearing' began. There is a full transcript before this court. The purpose of a preparatory hearing, and the nature of it, and the possible consequences, are clear from the provisions of ss 7, 8 and 9 of the Criminal Justice Act 1987:

'7. *Power to order preparatory hearing.*—(1) Where it appears to a judge of the Crown Court that the evidence on an indictment reveals a case of fraud of such seriousness and complexity that substantial benefits are likely to accrue from a ... preparatory hearing ... before the jury are sworn, for the purpose of—(a) identifying issues which are likely to be material to the verdict of the jury; (b) assisting their comprehension of any such issues; (c) expediting the proceedings before the jury; (d) assisting the judge's management of the trial, he may order that such a hearing shall be held ...

(3) If a judge orders a preparatory hearing, he may also order the prosecution to prepare and serve any documents that appear to him to be relevant and whose service could be ordered at the preparatory hearing ...

(4) Where—(a) a judge has made an order under subsection (3) above; and (b) the prosecution have complied with it, the judge may order the person indicted ... to prepare and serve any documents that appear to him to be relevant and whose service could be so ordered at the preparatory hearing ...

8. *Commencement of trial and arraignment.*—(1) If a judge orders a preparatory hearing, the trial shall begin with that hearing.
(2) Arraignment shall accordingly take place at the start of the preparatory hearing.
9. *The preparatory hearing.*—(1) At the preparatory hearing the judge may exercise any of the powers specified in this section.
(2) The judge may adjourn a preparatory hearing from time to time ...
(11) An appeal shall lie to the Court of Appeal from any order or ruling of a judge under subsection (3) ... above, but only with the leave of the judge or of the Court of Appeal.'

(7) On 22 June 1992 Mr Owen QC appeared for the prosecution, Mr Anthony Scrivener QC appeared for Mr Nadir and Mr Michael Hopmeier appeared for Mr Turner before Tucker J. After various submissions and rulings, Tucker J asked whether the court could move on to the preparatory hearing. A short adjournment was ordered on the request of Mr Scrivener at a stage which the judge described as 'appropriate to mark the difference between the pre-preparatory hearing and transition into the preparatory and the start of the trial proper'. When the judge sat again at noon there was further discussion of the indictment and amendments were directed to be made to it. Counsel for the defendants did not object to arraignment taking place. There was no dock in the court and Mr Nadir and Mr Turner were sitting with solicitors and counsel. Tucker J said: 'Arraignment can take place. Would Mr Nadir and Mr Turner please stand up for the moment?' They did so in the places where they had been sitting. The counts in the indictment were then put by the clerk of the court in the usual manner, and each defendant pleaded not guilty to each count. At the conclusion, the clerk said 'Thank you. Please sit down' and they sat. The preparatory hearing continued with an application by Mr Owen to amend the indictment by introducing certain counts. There was then pending an application for judicial review of the decision of Tucker J to dismiss the 46 counts, and the outcome of that application depended upon the decision of the House of Lords in *R v Gomez* which was then awaited. Leave was granted to amend the indictment. The prosecution did not ask for arraignment on the amended indictment. There was discussion of the time which should be allowed for the statement of defence by Mr Nadir. There was discussion of the 'proposed agenda' which continued after the midday adjournment. There was reference to a possible date of trial in March 1993. The discussion of dates and of matters such as the layout of the court continued. There was no further mention of the position of Mr Nadir or Mr Turner with reference to bail or custody. A further preparatory hearing was held on 7 September 1992. Bail was not then mentioned.

(8) On 1 October 1992 information was said to have been received by the SFO—

'that a document had been discovered which purported to be signed by Safiye Nadir and Bilge Nevzat and which appeared to relate to the payment of £3·5 million in the event of Asil Nadir leaving the UK ... There was in addition to the document, an allegation that the sum of money was to be paid to Tucker J following the successful application for variation of bail conditions.'

A further preparatory hearing, which was due to be held on 2 October 1992, was, according to the SFO document of 5 November 1992, cancelled after the allegations were brought to the attention of the Lord Chief Justice. On 6 November 1992 there was a further hearing before Tucker J in open court. The prosecution stated that 'it would be inappropriate to proceed with the preparatory hearing'. Reporting restrictions were imposed under s 4(2) of the Contempt of Court Act 1981. Reference was made by counsel for the prosecution to the fact that 'those responsible for the investigation ... [state] that there is a probability that officers involved ... would wish to interview the judge'. The document, dated 5 November 1992, to which reference was made, contained the assertion that 'the matters to which it relates will be relied upon by the Crown in any application relating to the bail of the defendant as Asil Nadir made either by the Crown or by the defendant'. A copy of the document did not come into the possession of Mr Guney until after application had been made to the court.

(9) On 16 and 17 December 1992 the preparatory hearing continued before Tucker J. Application was made by Mr Nadir in chambers to vary bail conditions to facilitate his visiting Northern Cyprus in preparation of his defence. Opposition was advanced by the Crown to the application on the grounds that 'there are substantial grounds for believing that he will not come back to stand his trial and also that he will interfere with witnesses or documents'. Reference was made to the document of 5 November 1992. The judge rejected Mr Nadir's application for variation of the conditions of bail and said, inter alia, that he had 'substantial grounds for believing that if the variation were granted, the defendant would fail to surrender to custody and also that he would interfere with witnesses or otherwise obstruct the course of justice'. He therefore directed that the conditions of bail would remain as at present.

(10) On 8 March 1993 Tucker J sat in chambers to hear an application by Mr Scrivener that the judge should discharge himself from the case. Mr Alun Jones QC appeared on behalf of the DPP. He informed the court that the allegation under investigation by police was that Mr Nadir, the judge, Mr Scrivener and an assistant commissioner of police were parties to corruption. The police were pursuing inquiries. It was reasonable to conclude that the allegation was not a hoax or a prank. Mr Jones declined to reveal further details. The judge stated that he would stay with the case.

(11) On 10 March 1993 Mr Nadir was arrested and granted police bail in respect of an allegation of conspiracy to pervert the course of justice.

(12) On 12 March 1993 a further hearing was conducted by Tucker J in chambers at which Mr Scrivener applied for the judge to discharge himself. Tucker J refused to do so. In November 1993 it was announced by the DPP that a police investigation had revealed no evidence to support the corruption allegations. On 29 November 1993 Tucker J authorised the reporting of the hearings on 6 November 1992 and 8 and 12 March 1993.

(13) Mr Guney in April 1993 took certain steps with reference to his position as surety. Solicitors acting for him wrote to Bow Street giving notice of his wish to withdraw as surety. On 29 April 1993 similar notice was given to the Central Criminal Court. On 30 April 1993 his solicitors wrote to the Central Criminal Court seeking an urgent hearing. That request, however, was countermanded by later letters of the same day and the application was withdrawn. The application was said to have arisen from a 'misunderstanding'.

(14) On 4 May 1993 Mr Nadir left this country by private aircraft and went to Northern Cyprus. On 6 May 1993, at a hearing at the Central Criminal Court

before Macpherson J, upon Mr Nadir failing to attend, a bench warrant was issued.

(15) On 17 May 1993 notice was given to the applicant to show cause why his recognisance should not be forfeited. At a hearing on 30 July 1993 Tucker J made the order for forfeiture of £650,000 on the terms stated above.

The grounds of decision of Tucker J

After reviewing the submissions which had been made by Mr Batten, counsel then appearing for Mr Guney, Tucker J proceeded as follows. (i) He accepted from Mr Owen that, on 22 June 1992, Mr Owen discussed with Mr Scrivener, counsel for Mr Nadir, the necessity for Mr Nadir to surrender to his bail on that occasion because, if he had surrendered to his bail then, before he could have been released, it would have been necessary for the court to consider the terms of any further bail which should be granted. The two counsel agreed that it was not necessary for Mr Nadir to surrender to the custody of the court. (ii) Tucker J was not aware of the discussion of counsel. He had not regarded Mr Nadir as having surrendered to the custody of the court on that occasion. (iii) The trial in theory began on that preparatory hearing but the day to day control of the trial would have commenced when Mr Nadir and Mr Turner were put in charge of the jury. (iv) Having regard to the agreement between counsel that Mr Nadir should not surrender his bail on 22 June 1992, Tucker J did not regard him as having surrendered to the custody of the court on that occasion. The obligation of the surety therefore continued.

The submissions for Mr Guney

Mr Lawson's contentions were as follows.

(1) The powers of the Bow Street Magistrates' Court were limited to securing the initial 'surrender to custody' of Mr Nadir at the Crown Court and, thereafter, the Crown Court had sole jurisdiction as to the grant of bail. Mr Nadir surrendered to the custody of the Crown Court on 22 June 1992 because the effect and requirements of arraignment meant that Mr Nadir was in the custody of the court for that purpose. The private arrangement between counsel could be of no effect to prevent the consequence in law of arraignment.

(2) The fact that there was no mention of bail on 22 June 1992 was of no effect in law. The recognisance had come to an end because the condition set out in it was satisfied. No new recognisance came into existence. Although Mr Nadir clearly thought otherwise, he was on unconditional bail thereafter. The further applications for variation of the bail conditions by Mr Nadir, which were rejected by the judge, and the reference in court to 'conditions of bail remaining as present' could not reimpose any liability upon Mr Guney.

(3) Mr Lawson drew attention to the provisions of the Bail Act 1976. In particular, the words 'surrender to custody' are defined by s 2(2) of that Act to mean:

'in relation to a person released on bail, surrendering himself into the custody of the court or of the constable (according to the requirements of the grant of bail) at the time and place for the time being appointed for him to do so.'

Further, by s 2(3) of the 1976 Act:

'Where an enactment ... which relates to bail in criminal proceedings refers to the person bailed appearing before a court it is to be construed unless the context otherwise requires as referring to his surrendering himself into the custody of the court.'

Mr Lawson relied upon the decision of the Divisional Court in *DPP v Richards* [1988] 3 All ER 406 at 412, [1988] QB 701 at 711 where Glidewell LJ said:

'I take the view that if a court provides a procedure which, by some form of direction, by notice or orally, instructs a person surrendering to bail to report to a particular office or to a particular official, when he complies with that direction he surrenders to his bail. Thereafter, albeit he may not be physically restrained, albeit he may be allowed to sit in the court concourse and visit the court canteen, he is in the custody of the court. I have already suggested that he is under an implied, if not an express obligation, not to leave the building without consent until the case is called on.'

(4) The procedure of arraignment is described in *Archbold's Pleading, Evidence and Practice in Criminal Cases* (44th edn, 1993) vol 1, para 4-84:

'The arraignment of defendants, against whom bills of indictment have been preferred and signed, consists of three parts: (1) calling the defendant to the bar by name; (2) reading the indictment to him; (3) asking him whether he is guilty or not.'

It was to be inferred that Mr Nadir was requested by notice from the court to attend at the Central Criminal Court for the purposes of the preparatory hearing and of arraignment. When Mr Nadir complied with that requirement and, at the direction of the judge, stood up for the arraignment he had surrendered to the custody of the court.

The submissions for the SFO

Mr Owen submitted that the judge made no error of law. For a defendant to surrender to the custody of the court he must be present at court; the court must require him to surrender to custody; that requirement must be communicated to him by the judge, or by an officer of the court, whether orally or in writing; and the defendant must comply with the requirement. The submission was consistent with the decision of the court in *DDP v Richards*.

Next, it was submitted that there was no requirement communicated to Mr Nadir before 22 June 1992 that he surrender to the custody of the court on 22 June 1992. The fixing of the date for the preparatory hearing was not a requirement to surrender to custody.

Further, there was no requirement on 22 June 1992 by the court or by any officer that Mr Nadir surrender to the court on that date, nor was there any procedure put into effect which gave the appearance of surrendering to custody. There was no dock. There were no notices directing that any person on bail report to any person or office.

Next Mr Owen contended that there is no established principle of law or practice to the effect that arraignment by itself involves surrender to the custody of the court. The purpose of arraignment is to establish whether a defendant accepts the jurisdiction of the court and whether, by reason of a plea of not guilty, there will be a trial by jury. In almost all cases a defendant will be arraigned whilst in the dock and in the custody of the court but for the effective conduct of the arraignment it matters not whether the defendant has or has not surrendered to the custody of the court. It is common place for a defendant to be called to the bar of the court by name but not to surrender to custody, which would involve the renewal of bail, for example when a trial cannot proceed on the appointed day.

Lastly Mr Owen also advanced an alternative submission that, if the court should hold that Mr Nadir had surrendered to the custody of the court on 22 June 1992, bail was by necessary implication renewed upon the same terms.

Conclusion on the effect of the arraignment

I would refuse the application on this ground because, in my judgment, and in general acceptance of Mr Owen's primary submissions, Tucker J did not in any respect go wrong in law. No authority is cited for the proposition that arraignment can only be validly conducted if the defendant is in the custody of the court. There is, in my judgment, no consideration of substantial justice necessary for the protection of a defendant which requires the law to be so stated.

Arraignment is an important step: our law requires that, for a plea of guilty, the plea must be stated by the defendant personally. It may not be uttered on his behalf by counsel: see *R v Ellis* (1973) 57 Cr App R 571 and *R v Williams* [1977] 1 All ER 874, [1978] QB 373. But if a plea of not guilty be uttered by counsel on behalf of the defendant; or if no plea is taken at all but the trial proceeds on the basis that the accused has pleaded not guilty, the error is to be regretted but does not necessarily vitiate the trial. Such formal requirements of a criminal trial are thus essential only where the form protects a substantive right: thus to permit a vicarious plea of guilty would be fraught with danger because injustice rather than justice would be the likely product of a principle which permitted delegated confessions of guilt: per Shaw LJ giving the judgment of the court in *R v Williams* [1977] 1 All ER 874 at 876–877, [1978] QB 373 at 378.

The purposes of arraignment can, in my judgment, be fully served without injustice or risk of injustice to the defendant if the defendant pleads to the indictment without being required to surrender to the custody of the court. It is in the interests of convenience and of the saving of court time and of costs if it is possible in law for an arraignment to take place without surrender of the defendant to the custody of the court; because, as in the present case, such a rule will permit a preparatory hearing to commence under the statute without the need to obtain a new order for bail with the reinstatement of the recognisances of sureties. Such a rule, moreover, gives rise, in my judgment, to no risk of injustice to sureties. The surety does not know, unless he makes it his business to ensure that he is informed, or to find out for himself, when a defendant will be required to attend court to surrender to the custody of the court. It is not the duty of the court or of the prosecution to inform the surety.

It follows that there was, in my judgment, nothing contrary to law, or contrary to the ordinary and proper conduct of proceedings by counsel, in the arrangement or agreement made to the effect that on 22 June 1992 Mr Nadir should not be required to surrender to the custody of the court. That agreement meant, as I understand it, no more than that neither counsel would invite the judge to make any such requirement. It was obvious to all concerned that the arraignment, which was required at the commencement of the preparatory hearing under s 8 of the 1987 Act, would be followed by further adjourned preparatory hearings which would continue for many months before the hearing in the presence of the jury could commence.

There was, of course, nothing to stop a formal surrender by the defendants to the custody of the court and the renewal of bail, on the same or varied conditions, at the order of Tucker J which could have been made continuous until the full trial started. Such difficulty as there was in doing that in this case did not extend beyond the renewal of recognisances, and that, in itself, does not necessarily give rise to significant trouble. As I understand the circumstances, it was thought sensible to avoid any such difficulty or trouble and, in my judgment, counsel were acting properly in taking that course. The judge was not informed. It would have been better if he had been told on the principle that the judge should know what is agreed between counsel on such a matter. Although all concerned were of the same mind it would have been better for express reference to be made to the point so that it would have been recorded.

I accept that if what was said and done in court on 22 June 1992 amounted, as Mr Lawson submits, to a surrender by Mr Nadir to the custody of the court, then the agreement between counsel would not cause there to have been no surrender; and, if there was surrender, the condition of the recognisance was satisfied, and the recognisance was not thereafter expressly reinstated. I would prefer to express no conclusion upon the concept of implied reinstatement but I find it very difficult to see how by such a means a recognisance could be reinstated as against the surety. The agreement, however, although not mentioned was, in my judgment effective in the circumstances of this case to make it plain that there was no surrender to the custody of the court: the agreement caused Mr Nadir to know that he was not required to surrender. Neither the judge nor the clerk of the court in the circumstances existing in the court at Chichester Rents said or did anything which necessarily amounted to a requirement that Mr Nadir surrender to the custody of the court, or gave the appearance of such a requirement. Neither the judge, nor the clerk of the court, considered that there had been any such requirement and, by making no reference thereafter to the need for Mr Nadir to be released from custody, or for the grant of bail, they demonstrated that they had so understood what was done. This is not to say that, by common error of counsel, clerk, defendant and judge, that which in law is a surrender to custody can be transformed into the mere taking of a plea without surrender. It is, rather, to assert that the facts recounted show that in law no surrender took place because, in my judgment, surrender to custody, as Mr Owen has submitted, occurs when it is made known to the defendant that surrender is required and, in response to that requirement, the defendant surrenders or puts himself at the direction of the court or an officer of the court. The law does not, in my judgment, require that Mr Nadir be treated as having surrendered to the custody of the court when neither he nor the court understood him to have been required so to surrender and when that which was done in and at the end of the hearing was consistent with him not having so surrendered.

It was said that Mr Nadir, having been asked to stand up for the indictment to be put to him, must be treated as having put himself at the direction of the court, and the question was put: what would have happened if Mr Nadir had decided to walk out of the court in the course of the arraignment? The answer, if I am right in my view, is that on the facts Mr Nadir had not been required to put himself at the direction of the court, and had not done so; but, if he had attempted to leave so as to frustrate the court's intention of conducting the arraignment, so that the preparatory hearing could continue, he would have been at once required by the court to surrender to the custody of the court.

The corruption allegations: failure to inform

In *R v Southampton Justices, ex p Green* [1975] 2 All ER 1073, [1976] QB 11 the Court of Appeal (Lord Denning MR, Browne LJ and Brightman J) considered the decision of a magistrates' court under s 96 of the Magistrates' Courts Act 1952 to direct forfeiture of the whole of the sum in which a surety was bound. The provisions are now contained in s 120 of the Magistrates' Courts Act 1980. The court quashed the decision and did not remit the application for reconsideration. Lord Denning MR, in a judgment with which the other members of the court agreed, said ([1975] 2 All ER 1073 at 1077, [1976] QB 11 at 19):

'By what principles are the justices to be guided? They ought, I think, to consider to what extent the surety was at fault. If he or she connived at the disappearance of the accused man, or aided it or abetted it, it would proper to forfeit the whole of the sum. If he or she was wanting in due diligence to secure his appearance, it might be proper to forfeit the whole or a substantial part of it, depending on the degree of fault. If he or she was guilty of no want of diligence and used every effort to secure the appearance of the accused man, it might be proper to remit it entirely.'

In *R v Horseferry Road Magistrates' Court, ex p Pearson* [1976] 2 All ER 264 at 266, [1976] 1 WLR 511 at 513 and *R v Tottenham Magistrates' Court, ex p Riccardi* (1978) 66 Cr App R 150 at 153 Lord Widgery CJ referred to that passage in the judgment of Lord Denning in *R v Southampton Justices, ex p Green* and emphasised another aspect of the obligation assumed by a surety:

'... the forfeiture of recognisance is in no sense a penalty imposed on the surety for misconduct. I do not doubt that the magistrate, before forfeiting the recognisance, must consider amongst other things the conduct of the surety and see whether it was open to criticism or not. But one must, I think, start all these problems on the footing that the surety has seriously entered into a serious obligation and ought to pay the amount which he or she has promised unless there are circumstances in the case, relating either to her means or to her culpability, which make it fair and just to pay a smaller sum.'

Mr Lawson referred to *R v Wells Street Magistrates' Court, ex p Albanese* [1981] 3 All ER 769, [1982] QB 333. In that case an order of forfeiture was remitted to the magistrates' court for reconsideration of the amount which should be forfeited on the ground that the magistrate had not considered, as a result of an error in the court's records, a variation in bail conditions which the surety alleged was relevant. The court has been invited to follow that course if this alternative ground is made good by Mr Guney.

For this point Mr Lawson accepts that there was no obligation on the court or the prosecution to inform Mr Guney of the making of the allegations of corruption, and that failure to inform did not avoid the recognisance. It is submitted, however, that, when the court or prosecution receives information which is clearly relevant to the likely assessment by the surety of the risk of the accused failing to appear, the information should, because of the demands of fairness, be passed to the surety and, if it is not, the court and prosecution must contemplate that the failure will be taken into account upon any application for forfeiture. Reference was made to *R v Panel on Take-overs and Mergers, ex p Guinness plc* [1989] 1 All ER 509 at 527, 531, [1990] 1 QB 146 at 178, 184. It was

further pointed out that such a course was in fact taken in October 1991 when
Mr Nadir was charged with further offences as stated above.

Mr Lawson submitted that it was plainly unfair for the information not to
have been passed to Mr Guney. When the application was heard by Tucker J in
July 1993, Mr Guney and his advisors were unaware of the allegation which had
been made and no submissions were directed to it. By affidavit of 7 January
1994 Mr Guney has asserted:

'I should have been informed ... of what was going on. I had staked £1
million for no consideration flowing to me, on Nadir's appearance for trial.
I deserved the opportunity to decide if the now established fact that the
police were taking the matter seriously was something which could effect
my willingness to continue as surety, while Nadir was still within the
jurisdiction, and capable of being taken into custody had I decided to
withdraw. I can only address the question with hindsight, since nobody
told me what was going on until after Nadir had fled. I cannot now say
what my decision would have been. It might well have depended on the
nature and quality of the information which I was given. My point is that
by leaving me ignorant of potential material information, the court unfairly
deprived me of the chance to make an informed or any decision.'

Mr Lawson submitted that credence should be given to those assertions
having regard to the actions of Mr Guney on 28 to 30 April 1993; and that, if the
applicant had been aware of the provisions of s 7(3) of the Bail Act 1976, or if his
solicitor's letter had been passed to the police, Mr Nadir would in all probability
have been arrested. The effect of s 7(3) of the 1976 Act is that a person who has
been released on bail and is under a duty to surrender into the custody of a court
may be arrested without warrant by a constable if the constable has reasonable
grounds for believing that that person is not likely to surrender to custody; or,
in a case where that person was released on bail with one or more surety or
sureties, if a surety notifies a constable in writing that that person is unlikely to
surrender to custody and for that reason the surety wishes to be relieved of his
obligations as a surety.

For the SFO Mr Owen submitted that the information in question was
supposition only and that it would have been oppressive to Mr Nadir if such
information had been conveyed to Mr Guney before the investigations were
completed and if, in consequence, Mr Guney had withdrawn as surety. The
information could not properly have been taken into account in assessing what
sum should be forfeited.

I would reject also this ground of application. There was, in my judgment,
no unfairness on the part of anyone in failing to report the allegations to Mr
Guney. Not only was it reasonable to assume that Mr Guney was paying due
attention to the risk imposed upon him by the recognisance but it is clear that
he was in fact doing so and was in close touch with Mr Nadir.

The allegation was, in short, that some people were proposing to pay or to
offer to pay £3·5m in the event of Mr Nadir leaving the United Kingdom
following a successful application for variation of the bail conditions. It was
necessary for this bizarre allegation to be investigated, if only to discover who
were responsible for what appeared to be a mischievous intervention which
was bound to cause waste of time on the part of the police and others. It was an
unimpressive allegation even to a person able to encompass the thought of a

serious approach to Tucker J to raise the question of bribing him, because it is impossible to see why Mr Nadir, or others on his behalf, should think it worth while to pay £3·5m to secure variations in the conditions of bail when Mr Nadir, with his resources, was able to escape from this country, if willing to contemplate forfeiture of his deposit, and the recognisances of his sureties, without further expenditure in bribing the judge. The allegation in short was ridiculous even if the making of it was something which required investigation.

Mr Guney has lived in this country for many years. When he heard a rumour that, in return for a large sum of money, Mr Nadir was to receive a suspended sentence and £1m fine, he knew enough of the system of justice to disregard the rumour as completely fanciful. He would, I have no doubt, have regarded this allegation in the same way.

Mr Guney has said that, if he had known that such a matter was the subject of serious investigation into the supposed bribery plot his decision to continue as surety might have been different. In his affidavit of 29 July 1993 Mr Guney gave a long account of the rumours and threats and assertions which reached his ears about Mr Nadir and his intentions. In runs to some 15 pages. He expressed the wish that the whole story should not be made public. Much of it is unsubstantiated stories and fears. It is not necessary to set it all out in this judgment, and it is sufficient for me to state my conclusion upon consideration of it. I am persuaded that the passing to Mr Guney of the information about the allegations of the intended attempts to bribe or corrupt the judge or others, which were discovered in October 1992, would have made no difference whatever to Mr Guney and to his willingness to continue as surety for Mr Nadir or to such efforts as he made to ensure that Mr Nadir should appear at court for his trial. The one thing that Mr Guney did not do was to report to the police in writing that in his view it was unlikely that Mr Nadir would surrender to custody and for that reason he wished to be relieved of his obligations as a surety.

As stated above, with the advice of solicitors, Mr Guney first decided to apply to be released as surety and then withdrew that application. His reasons for being concerned about the intentions and good faith of Mr Nadir were, on his account, substantial. On 30 April, he met Mr Nadir and was persuaded by him to remain as surety. The addition of information about the allegation of intended attempts to bribe the judge to alter the conditions of bail could not rationally have made any difference to his decision.

For these reasons I would dismiss Mr Guney's application to this court.

SMITH J. I agree

Application dismissed.

Dilys Tausz   Barrister.

R v Secretary of State for the Home Department, ex parte Ejaz

COURT OF APPEAL, CIVIL DIVISION
BALCOMBE, STUART-SMITH AND PETER GIBSON LJJ
24 NOVEMBER, 3 DECEMBER 1993

Immigration – Illegal entrant – Husband obtaining British passport fraudulently – Appellant obtaining naturalisation as wife of British citizen – Appellant declared illegal immigrant after returning from trip abroad and not applying for leave for entry – Whether appellant's naturalisation as British citizen a nullity – Whether appellant remaining British citizen unless and until deprived of such status – British Nationality Act 1981, ss 6, 40, 42(5).

The appellant, who was born and married in Pakistan, came to the United Kingdom with her husband in 1984. Her husband had obtained a British passport in 1979 using the name of X, and had used that name to marry her and return with her to the United Kingdom. In 1986 the husband purported to change his name to Z and obtained a British passport in that name. In 1987 the appellant applied for naturalisation under s 6[a] of the British Nationality Act 1981 on the ground that she was married to a British citizen. She was granted a certificate of naturalisation in 1990 and was issued with a British passport which she used to travel abroad. When she returned to the United Kingdom in 1991 she entered without leave on the strength of her British passport. When the husband's deception in obtaining a passport using a false name was discovered the Secretary of State decided that the appellant had entered illegally when she returned to the United Kingdom in 1991, since her husband had never been a British citizen, and that her naturalisation granted on the basis that he was a British citizen was a nullity and therefore she had required leave to re-enter the United Kingdom, which she had not obtained, and therefore she was an illegal immigrant who was liable to detention and deportation. The appellant applied for judicial review of the Secretary of State's decision. It was common ground that if the appellant's naturalisation was a nullity she was an illegal immigrant but if it was not a nullity she was entitled to remain in the United Kingdom unless and until she was deprived of her British citizenship under s 40[b] of the 1981 Act, which provided, inter alia, that the Secretary of State could deprive any person of citizenship acquired by naturalisation if he was satisfied that the naturalisation had been obtained by means of fraud. The Secretary of State contended that unless an applicant was of full age and capacity and married to a British citizen (which the the appellant was not) at the date of the application he had no power to grant a certificate of naturalisation and that any certificate granted without those preconditions being fulfilled was a nullity. The judge upheld the Secretary of State's decision to treat her as an illegal immigrant and dismissed the application. The appellant appealed to the Court of Appeal on the grounds that the judge had failed to consider s 42(5)[c] of the Act, which provided that a person to whom a

---

a Section 6, so far as material, is set out at p 439 g to j, post
b Section 40, so far as material, is set out at p 440 f to j, post
c Section 42(5) is set out at p 441 c, post

CA   R v Secretary of State for the Home Dept, ex p Ejaz   437

certificate of naturalisation was granted under the Act was to be considered as a British citizen from the date on which the certificate was granted.

Held – Under s 42(5) of the 1981 Act the status of citizenship was conferred by the certificate of naturalisation and that citizenship commenced on the date of the certificate. Anyone who held such a certificate was a British citizen unless and until he was deprived of that status under s 40 because the Secretary of State was satisfied that the certificate of naturalisation had been obtained by fraud, false representation or concealment of any material fact. Since the Secretary of State had not invoked his powers under s 40 the appellant remained in possession of a valid certificate of naturalisation. The appeal would therefore be allowed (see p 441 h j, p 443 j to p 444 d g to p 445 c, post).

R v Secretary of State for the Home Dept, ex p Akhtar [1980] 2 All ER 735 applied.

Notes
For citizenship by naturalisation and registration, see 4(2) *Halsbury's Laws* (4th edn reissue) paras 22–25, and for cases on the subject, see 2 *Digest* (Reissue) 239–242, 1319–1332.

For the British Nationality Act 1981, ss 6, 40, 42(5), see 31 *Halsbury's Statutes* (4th edn) (1994 reissue) 135, 162, 167.

Cases referred to in judgments
Howell v Falmouth Boat Construction Co Ltd [1951] 2 All ER 278, [1951] AC 837, HL.
Ministry of Agriculture and Fisheries v Hunkin (1948, unreported), CA.
Ministry of Agriculture and Fisheries v Matthews [1949] 2 All ER 724, [1950] 1 KB 148.
R v Secretary of State for the Home Dept, ex p Akhtar [1980] 2 All ER 735, [1981] QB 46, [1980] 3 WLR 302, CA.
R v Secretary of State for the Home Dept, ex p Sultan Mahmood [1981] QB 58n, [1980] 3 WLR 312n, CA.

Cases also cited
Mokuolo v Secretary of State for the Home Dept [1989] Imm AR 51, CA.
Hoffmann-La Roche (F) & Co AG v Secretary of State for Trade and Industry [1973] 3 All ER 945, [1975] AC 295, CA.

Appeal
The applicant, Naheed Ejaz, appealed against the decision of Hutchison J, hearing the Crown Office list on 16 July 1993, whereby he dismissed her application for judicial review by way of a declaration that the applicant was a British citizen, an order of prohibition to prevent the Home Secretary, the respondent, from removing the applicant as an illegal entrant from the United Kingdom and an order of certiorari to quash the decision of the Home Secretary that the applicant was an illegal entrant. The facts are set out in the judgment of Stuart-Smith LJ.

Ian MacDonald QC and *Frances Webber* (instructed by *Griffiths Robertson*, Reading) for the applicant.
David Pannick QC and *Alison Foster* (instructed by the *Treasury Solicitor*) for the Secretary of State.

Cur adv vult

3 December 1993. The following judgments were delivered.

STUART-SMITH LJ (giving the first judgment at the invitation of Balcombe LJ). This appeal raises a question of general importance as to the effect of the grant by the Secretary of State of a certificate of naturalisation under the British Nationality Act 1981.

The facts, which are not in dispute, are these: the appellant was born in Pakistan in October 1964. She married there in December 1983 and came to the United Kingdom with her husband in October 1984. They have three surviving children, all born in the United Kingdom. The appellant's husband first came here in 1979 using a British passport in the name of Arshad Iqbal, and it was in that name that he married her and returned with her to the United Kingdom. In 1986 or 1987 he purported to change his name to Diwan Hashmat Kamal; he subsequently obtained a British passport in that name. On 8 October 1987, the appellant applied for naturalisation as the wife of a British citizen. On 19 June 1990, pursuant to the provisions of s 6(2) of the 1981 Act, the Secretary of State granted the appellant a certificate of naturalisation as a British citizen. She was later issued with a British passport, with which she travelled abroad with her three children in June 1991. When she later returned here she entered without leave on the strength of her British passport.

For the purpose of these proceedings it is accepted that the appellant's husband was not the holder of the British passport in the name of Arshad Iqbal, but was in truth a citizen of Pakistan named Diwan Hashmat Kamal. Accordingly, he never was a British citizen. It is unnecessary for the purpose of these proceedings to consider whether the appellant knew of her husband's false identity and the fact that he was not a British citizen. The Secretary of State asserts that she did; the appellant maintains she did not.

Following the discovery of her husband's deception the Secretary of State decided that the appellant, when she returned to the United Kingdom in June 1991, had entered illegally. The basis of this assertion is that since her husband never was a British citizen, her own naturalisation granted upon the basis that he was such a citizen is a nullity. Accordingly, she required leave to enter which she had not obtained, and by virtue of the combined effect of ss 33(1) and 3(1)(a) of the Immigration Act 1971, she was an illegal entrant. She is therefore liable to detention and deportation.

It is common ground that if the Secretary of State's contention is correct, namely that the appellant's naturalisation is a nullity, she is an illegal entrant; conversely, if it is not a nullity, she is entitled to remain here unless and until she is deprived of her British citizenship under the provisions of s 40 of the 1981 Act. Hutchison J, in a judgment delivered on 16 July 1993, upheld the Secretary of State's contention and dismissed the appellant's application for judicial review of the decision to treat her as an illegal entrant. It is against that judgment that the appellant appeals.

The statutory framework of the 1981 Act, so far as it is relevant, is this: a person may become a British citizen by birth in the United Kingdom to parents, one of whom is a British citizen or settled here (s 1(1) and (2)); by adoption, if he is adopted by a British citizen (s 1(5)); or by descent (s 2). None of these ways involve the intervention of the Secretary of State. A person may also become a British citizen by registration or naturalisation; these ways involve the intervention of the Secretary of State.

There are a number of instances in which a person can acquire British citizenship by registration. One example will suffice by way of illustration. Section 3 provides:

'(1) If while a person is a minor an application is made for his registration as a British citizen, the Secretary of State may, if he thinks fit, cause him to be registered as such a citizen.

(2) A person born outside the United Kingdom shall be entitled, on an application for his registration as a British citizen made within the period of twelve months from the date of the birth, to be registered as such a citizen if the requirements specified in subsection (3) or, in the case of a person born stateless, the requirements specified in paragraphs (a) and (b) of that subsection, are fulfilled in the case of either that person's father or his mother ("the parent in question").

(3) The requirements referred to in subsection (2) are—(a) that the parent in question was a British citizen by descent at the time of the birth; and (b) that the father or mother of the parent in question—(i) was a British citizen otherwise than by descent at the time of the birth of the parent in question; or (ii) became a British citizen otherwise than by descent at commencement, or would have become such a citizen otherwise than by descent at commencement but for his or her death; and (c) that, as regards some period of three years ending with a date not later than the date of birth—(i) the parent in question was in the United Kingdom at the beginning of that period; and (ii) the number of days on which the parent in question was absent from the United Kingdom in that period does not exceed 270.'

Acquisition by naturalisation is dealt with in s 6 of the 1981 Act which provides:

'(1) If, on an application for naturalisation as a British citizen made by a person of full age and capacity, the Secretary of State is satisfied that the applicant fulfils the requirements of Schedule 1 for naturalisation as such a citizen under this subsection, he may, if he thinks fit, grant to him a certificate of naturalisation as such a citizen.

(2) If, on an application for naturalisation as a British citizen made by a person of full age and capacity who on the date of the application is married to a British citizen, the Secretary of State is satisfied that the applicant fulfils the requirements of Schedule 1 for naturalisation as such a citizen under this subsection, he may, if he thinks fit, grant to him a certificate of naturalisation as such a citizen.'

It is s 6(2) which is relevant in this case.

The requirements set out in Sch 1, so far as s 6(1) of the Act is concerned, are: good character, a sufficient knowledge of the English, Welsh or Scottish Gaelic language, an intention to live in the United Kingdom or enter the service of the Crown, and, subject to certain exceptions, presence in the United Kingdom during the previous five years. Paragraph 3 of Sch 1 applies to applicants under s 6(2) and provides as follows:

'(a) that he was in the United Kingdom at the beginning of three years ending with the date of the application, and that the number of days on which he was absent from the United Kingdom in that period does not exceed 270; and (b) that the number of days on which he was absent from the United Kingdom in the period of twelve months so ending does not exceed 90; and (c) that on the date of the application he was not subject under the immigration laws to any restriction on the period for which he might remain in the United Kingdom; and (d) that he was not at any time in the period of three years ending with the date of the application in the United Kingdom in breach of the immigration laws; and (e) the requirement specified in paragraph 1(1)(b). [Namely, that he be of good character.]'

Paragraph 2 (in relation to s 6(1) applicants) and para 4 (in relation to s 6(2) applicants) gives the Secretary of State discretionary power to relax or waive some of these requirements.

A person who has acquired British citizenship by registration or certificate of naturalisation can however be deprived of his citizenship as a result of conduct that led to the grant of registration or naturalisation, or because of certain conduct thereafter. Subsequent conduct is dealt with in s 40(3) and consists of (a) disloyalty or disaffection to the Queen, (b) trading or communicating with the enemy in time of war or (c) imprisonment for twelve months or more within five years of the date when the person became a British citizen. We are not concerned with this subsection. So far as it is relevant to this appeal, s 40 provides:

'(1) Subject to the provisions of this section, the Secretary of State may by order deprive any British citizen to whom this subsection applies of his British citizenship if the Secretary of State is satisfied that the registration or certificate of naturalisation by virtue of which he is such a citizen was obtained by means of fraud, false representation or the concealment of any material fact.

(2) Subsection (1) applies to any British citizen who—(a) became a British citizen after commencement by virtue of—(i) his registration as a British citizen under any provision of the British Nationality Acts 1981 and 1983; or (ii) a certificate of naturalisation granted to him under section 6 ...

(5) The Secretary of State—(a) shall not deprive a person of British citizenship under this section unless he is satisfied that it is not conducive to the public good that the person should continue to be a British citizen; and (b) shall not deprive a person of British citizenship under subsection (3) on the ground mentioned in paragraph (c) of that subsection if it appears to him that that person would thereupon become stateless.'

Before making an order under s 40, the Secretary of State must give notice in writing of his intention to do so and the grounds upon which it is proposed to be made and telling the person of his right to have an inquiry. If the person applies for an inquiry, then the Secretary of State may refer the case to a committee of inquiry and there are rules governing the conduct of the inquiry enacted in the British Citizenship (Deprivation) Rules 1982, SI 1982/988 (see s 40, ss 6, 7 and 8). We are told, however, that no case has ever been referred to the committee.

Section 42 of the Act, to which the judge's attention unfortunately was not drawn, contains two further relevant provisions. A person is not to be registered as a British citizen or granted a certificate of naturalisation unless he has paid the appropriate fee and taken the oath of allegiance. This represented a change from the previous law by which British citizenship was effective from the date of registration or the certificate of naturalisation but was conditional upon the oath of allegiance being taken: (see ss 9 and 10 of the British Nationality Act 1948).

More importantly, s 42(5) provides:

'A person to whom a certificate of naturalisation as a British citizen or as a British Dependent Territories citizen is granted under any provision of this Act shall be a citizen of that description as from the date on which the certificate is granted.'

Mr Pannick QC's construction of s 6(2) has the attraction of simplicity. He submits that the opening words of the subsection lay down three matters which have to be established as precedent facts before the Secretary of State can exercise the power to consider the matters set out in Sch 1. The three matters are that the applicant is of full age, is of full capacity and, at the date of the application, is married to a British citizen. If any of the three matters are not in fact correct, then the Secretary of State has no power to grant the certificate, and any certificate which purports to have been granted by him is a nullity. The Secretary of State cannot, by mistaking his own powers, enlarge them beyond what Parliament has granted. And he cannot be estopped from asserting that he lacked the necessary power, if that be the case (see *Ministry of Agriculture and Fisheries v Matthews* [1949] 2 All ER 724 at 729, [1950] 1 KB 148 at 153 where Cassels J applied *Ministry of Agriculture and Fisheries v Hunkin* an unreported decision of the Court of Appeal in 1948 and *Howell v Falmouth Boat Construction Co Ltd* [1951] 2 All ER 278 at 280, 285, [1951] AC 837 at 845, 849).

Mr Pannick submits that there is a clear dichotomy between the two parts of s 6(2), the first part going to vires, the second being matters for the Secretary of State's judgment and discretion. It is only those matters in the second part which can form the subject of consideration under s 40, and since in this case the certificate is a nullity, s 40 cannot have any application because the subject is not a British citizen.

Mr MacDonald QC for the appellant submits that she is and remains a British citizen by virtue of the certificate of registration unless and until she is deprived of it under the provisions of s 40.

I cannot accept Mr Pannick's submission for a number of reasons.

(1) It fails to give effect to s 42(5). This subsection does two things. It makes it plain that it is the certificate of naturalisation which confers the status of citizenship and, secondly, that citizenship commences on the date of the certificate. Consequently, anyone who holds such a certificate is a British citizen and is within s 40(1). Mr Pannick submitted that s 42(5) was merely concerned with the date from which citizenship runs and is simply for the avoidance of doubt. But this fails to give effect to the words 'shall be a citizen' and, in any event, I cannot see that there could be any doubt as to the date from which citizenship runs, since fees have to be paid and the oath of allegiance taken before the grant of the certificate.

(2) I agree with Mr MacDonald that there is no logical reason why the fraud, false representation or concealment of any material fact referred to in s 40(1)

should be confined to the requirements of Sch 1 as opposed to the requirements of age, capacity or marriage to a British citizen.

(3) If Mr Pannick's submission is correct, it must apply equally to those sections of the Act dealing with registration, since s 6 must be construed in the context of the Act as a whole. One can therefore test the proposition by seeking to apply it to s 3(2) of the Act. Although Mr Pannick was perhaps understandably reluctant to say how it would apply, he did submit that all the requirements set out in this section must, if his construction is correct, be precedent facts which have to be established before the Secretary of State has the necessary vires. I think he has to make this submission. But it has bizarre consequences. First, because it means that s 40 will have nothing to bite on at all in relation to an applicant within s 3(2); and secondly, while s 3(3)(c) is in very similar words to Sch l, para 3(a), the former is a precedent fact going to vires and jurisdiction, while the latter is not. There must be something wrong with a construction that leads to this result. It is unnecessary to examine in any detail the other provisions in relation to registration; these give rise to similar problems.

(4) Mr Pannick's construction is contrary to the views expressed in this court in *R v Secretary of State for the Home Dept, ex p Akhtar* [1980] 2 All ER 735, [1981] QB 46. The facts of that case were these. In 1975 the applicant, who had been born in Pakistan, was admitted to the United Kingdom as the infant son of WA, an immigrant permanently settled here as a citizen of the United Kingdom and Colonies. WA applied for registration of his infant son as a citizen of the United Kingdom and Colonies under the provisions of the 1948 Act. The application was granted. The applicant, who purported to be WA's son, left the United Kingdom temporarily in 1978. On his return he was refused entry by the immigration officer on the grounds that he was not the son of WA named in the registration, but was AH, the son of NH, who had no right of entry into the United Kingdom. He was detained in custody pending his removal as an illegal entrant.

On his application for a writ of habeas corpus it was contended that his detention was unlawful as he was a citizen of the United Kingdom and Colonies by reason of the registration and that he remained a citizen until he was deprived of citizenship under the provisions of s 20 of the 1948 Act, which are in substantially the same form as s 40 of the 1981 Act. The Divisional Court and Court of Appeal rejected this contention on the grounds that the applicant was not entitled to rely on the registration effected on his behalf unless he proved that he was the person described in the registration, and this he failed to do. One of the submissions made on behalf of the applicant was that if the provisions of s 20 did not apply to that case, the section would serve no useful purpose. In rejecting this submission Templeman LJ gave two examples of situations where s 20 would apply. The second is this ([1980] 2 All ER 735 at 739, [1981] QB 46 at 54):

> 'Again, in the present case, if the applicant were proved to be the registered son of Waris Ali he would be entitled to the benefit of the registration and would be patrial. But, as a son of Waris Ali, he would only be entitled to be registered if Waris Ali himself was a citizen of the United Kingdom and Colonies. If Waris Ali was not a citizen of the United Kingdom and Colonies the registration of the applicant would be effective but would have been obtained by the fraudulent misrepresentation that

Waris Ali was a citizen. The Secretary of State would be obliged to deprive the applicant of citizenship by the machinery of s 20 of the British Nationality Act 1948 before anyone could treat the applicant as an illegal entrant under the Immigration Act 1971.'

Sir Patrick Browne expressly agreed with this part of Templeman LJ's judgment and his examples of the application of s 20, and added that it would similarly apply to the sections dealing with naturalisation ([1980] 2 All ER 735 at 741, [1981] QB 46 at 54). Megaw LJ also agreed.

I accept Mr Pannick's submission that the passage is strictly speaking obiter. But the example illustrates the reasoning of the court; it was a reserved judgment; and it is therefore of very great persuasive authority, even if not strictly binding upon us. I respectfully agree with the opinions there expressed.

(5) Mr Pannick's construction would lead to much greater uncertainty and could lead to great injustice. The uncertainty arises because if at any time a precedent fact is discovered to be incorrect, no matter how long after the registration or naturalisation, the effect will be as if the registration or naturalisation had never been granted. This has the inevitable consequence of affecting the status of others, such as children. This is highly undesirable where questions of status are concerned. While the construction contended for by the applicant does not eliminate all uncertainty, since the status is defeasible under s 40, such a construction gives rise to much less uncertainty since the section does not operate retrospectively.

By depriving the Secretary of State of the wide discretion that he is granted under s 40, it seems to me that great injustice could be done. For example, however innocent the mistake may have been, if there is error in relation to precedent fact such as age, the registration or naturalisation is null and void. In many instances deprivation of British citizenship may render the person stateless. Although it is only in the case of persons sentenced to 12 months' imprisonment or more that s 40(5)(b) provides an absolute bar on the Secretary of State's power to deprive a person of British citizenship on that ground if it appears to the Secretary of State that the result will be to make him stateless, it seems to me that this consequence must be one of the considerations which the Secretary of State should take into account in the exercise of his discretion under s 40.

(6) In my judgment, the opening words of s 6(1) and (2), like the opening words of those sections dealing with registration, do no more than identify the categories of persons with whom the relevant section is dealing. The section then empowers the Secretary of State to consider both whether the applicant falls within the category of persons so identified and whether the specific requirements are satisfied. Once he has been registered or granted a certificate of naturalisation, the person is a British citizen unless and until he is deprived of that status under the provisions of s 40. Jurisdiction to deprive him arises under s 40(1) if the Secretary of State is satisfied that the registration or certificate of naturalisation was obtained by fraud, false representation or concealment of any material fact. Thereupon, the Secretary of State has a discretion whether to deprive, subject only to the requirement that he must be satisfied that it is not conducive to the public good that the person should continue to be a British citizen. These provisions, of course, only apply to the person described in the registration or certificate of naturalisation. If he is not,

as in the *Akhtar* and *Sultan Mahmood* cases (reported as a note to *Akhtar's* case, *R v Secretary of State for the Home Department, ex p Akhtar* [1981] QB 46 at 58) then the registration or certificate confers nothing on that person.
I would allow the appeal.

BALCOMBE LJ. Hutchison J was obviously reluctant to adopt a construction of the British Nationality Act 1981 which required him to hold that the naturalisation certificate issued to the appellant by the Secretary of State was a nullity. It is therefore in the highest degree unfortunate that the judge was not referred to the provisions of s 42(5) of the Act, since he might well have been persuaded that the construction which he felt constrained to adopt was clearly incompatible with the provisions of that subsection. Since a certificate of naturalisation confers on its holder the status of being a British citizen, which may affect persons other than the holder of the certificate—eg his or her children—I would in any event have been reluctant to accept a construction of the statute which could result in the certificate being a nullity and its holder being deprived of his or her status without the opportunity of making representations to a committee of inquiry held under s 40; but in any event for the reasons given by Stuart-Smith LJ, with which I agree, I am satisfied that such a construction is incorrect. I agree that this appeal should be allowed.

PETER GIBSON LJ. In deference to the very experienced judge from whose decision we are differing, I add a few words of my own.

As Mr Pannick QC rightly submitted, it is an important principle of administrative law that estoppel cannot be invoked to give a minister or authority powers which he or it does not in law possess (see, for example, *Wade on Administrative Law* (6th edn, 1988) p 262). So also, he submitted, the Secretary of State cannot lawfully create the status of British citizen under s 6(2) in circumstances in which he has no lawful power to do so. As a matter of construction of s 6(2) British Nationality Act 1981 taken in isolation, I see considerable force in that submission.

However, looking at the Act as a whole, I am persuaded that the intention of Parliament was, subject to two matters, to give the act of a Secretary of State, in conferring citizenship by a certificate of naturalisation, effect, even though it is subsequently shown that that person did not satisfy what Mr Pannick has called the condition precedent for the operation of s 6(2). Those two matters are s 40 and the exception exemplified by *R v Secretary of State for the Home Dept, ex p Akhtar* [1980] 2 All ER 735, [1981] QB 46 and *R v Secretary of State for the Home Dept, ex p Sultan Mahmood* [1981] QB 58n, viz where a person who is registered or to whom a certificate of naturalisation is granted does not answer the description of the person in the registration or certificate of naturalisation. It is unfortunate that the judge did not have his attention drawn to s 42(5), which strongly supports that construction. Further, I doubt if he heard much, if any, argument based on a comparison of s 6(2) and Sch 1 with the conditions for registration under, for example, s 3 and on how s 40 operates in relation to them. These and the other considerations set out in the judgment of Stuart-Smith LJ lead me to conclude that despite the prima facie dichotomy between the two parts of s 6(2), all the matters referred to in s 6(2) can be the subject of consideration under s 40.

If one asks why Parliament should have chosen to allow a mistaken registration or certificate of naturalisation validity unless and until the

Secretary of State successfully invokes s 40, the answer would appear to lie in the fact that status is conferred by the registration or certification. Status may affect persons other than the person registered or certified to be naturalised. It may well have been thought to be intolerable that, for example, an innocent mistake as to the age or capacity of the person registered or certified to be naturalised should, when the mistake comes to light perhaps many years later, have the effect of rendering the registration or naturalisation void ab initio with dire consequences for those whose status is derived from that person.

For these reasons I too would allow this appeal.

Appeal allowed. Leave to appeal to the House of Lords refused.

Carolyn Toulmin   Barrister.

R v South East Hampshire Family Proceedings Court, ex parte D

QUEEN'S BENCH DIVISION

EWBANK J

13 JANUARY 1994

Family proceedings – Orders in family proceedings – Application for transfer of private law proceedings from magistrates' court to county court – Delay in determining question likely to prejudice welfare of child – Whether delay only criterion for transfer of proceedings from magistrates' court to county court – Whether magistrates' court required to consider which court is most appropriate and what would be in interests of child – Children (Allocation of Proceedings) Order 1991, art 8.

On the true construction of art 8[a] of the Children (Allocation of Proceedings) Order 1991, which provides that a magistrates' court may transfer private law family proceedings to a county court where, having regard to the general principle that any delay in determining the question is likely to prejudice the welfare of the child, it considers that in the interests of the child the proceedings can be dealt with more appropriately in the county court, delay is only one of the matters and not the only matter to be taken into account by the magistrates' court in deciding whether the proceedings should be transferred to the county court. Accordingly, although the magistrates' court is required to have regard to the question of delay, its main function is to consider which court is most appropriate and what would be in the interests of the child (see p 448 *d* to *f*, post).

Notes

For the transfer of proceedings from the magistrates' court to the county court generally in private law cases, see 5(2) *Halsbury's Laws* (4th edn reissue) paras 754–755, 759.

---

a   Article 8, so far as material, is set out at p 447 *j*, post

Application for judicial review

The mother of a child born on 25 May 1991 applied, with the leave of Sir Stephen Brown P granted on 16 July 1993, for judicial review of the order made on 20 April 1993 by the deputy justices' clerk of the South East Hampshire Family Proceedings Court at Portsmouth, in a directions hearing, refusing the mother's application for the hearing of the father's application for contact and parental responsibility orders to be transferred to the county court on the grounds that the matter would be more expeditiously dealt with in the Family Proceedings Court. The mother sought the following relief: (a) mandamus requiring the court to exercise its judicial duty and transfer the case to the county court; (b) alternatively, certiorari to quash the decision of the Family Proceedings Court so as to enable fresh proceedings to be taken in the county court; (c) alternatively, prohibition to restrain the Family Proceedings Court from hearing the father's application for contact any further; (d) alternatively, a declaration that the Children (Allocation of Proceedings) Order 1991, SI 1991/1677, provides for an appeal against the refusal of transfer in private law cases. The facts are set out in the judgment.

Jonathan Swift (instructed by *Saulet & Co*, Portsmouth) for the applicant
Kerry Barker (instructed by *Richard Holliday*, Portsmouth) for the respondent.

EWBANK J. This is an application for judicial review of an order made by Julia Oakford, who was a deputy clerk of the justices for the South and South East Hampshire Petty Sessional Division in Portsmouth. She had before her an application to transfer a case which had started in her magistrates' court to the county court. She refused that application. The application today is to quash her decision.

The decision she made was on 20 April 1993. The application for judicial review went before the Sir Stephen Brown P. He decided on 16 July 1993 to grant leave to make the application and he ordered that there should be expedition. It is a matter of concern, accordingly, that leave having been granted in the middle of July 1993, in a children's case, where the President has ordered expedition, that it does not come into the list until January 1994. I caused inquiries to be made why this state of affairs should have occurred.

Immediately after the Sir Stephen Brown P's decision, the long vacation took place. Legal aid was granted to the applicant to make the application for judicial review on 6 October. Meanwhile a letter had been received by the applicant on 29 September from the Crown Office saying the case should be fixed by the applicant as soon as possible. Counsel's clerk made several applications in October for the case to be fixed. These applications were made to the clerk of the rules office and were not met with any great enthusiasm. It was not until November that the case was fixed for hearing today.

On the information that I have it appears that counsel's clerk and counsel did all they could to get the case heard. The delay appears to have been in the clerk of the rules' office. No records are kept of applications for fixing dates so it is not possible to know who is responsible for the disinclination to expedite this case. Having pointed out the circumstances of this case I hope the people concerned in the clerk of the rules' office will make a point of expediting those cases which a judge has ordered to be expedited.

This case relates to a child who was born on 25 May 1991. The father and mother were not married and separated in August 1992. In December 1992 the father applied for contact and for parental responsibility. He made that application, as he was entitled to, in the Family Proceedings Court for South Hampshire. There were directions hearings in January and February of 1993 and the matter came for a further directions hearing on 20 April 1993. By this time a court welfare officer had been appointed and had made a report. Having read the report, the father and the mother took the view that the matter should be transferred to the county court. This was a course that was recommended by the court welfare officer. Accordingly, an application was made on 20 April to the deputy clerk to transfer the case to the county court. That application was refused by the deputy clerk. The mother decided to apply to the district judge to reconsider the refusal to transfer the case to the county court and the matter came on 21 May 1993 before a district judge of the Portsmouth County Court. He refused the application on the ground that he had no jurisdiction to grant it.

Up to this point, it had been thought that there was an appeal or an opportunity for reconsideration for the district judge as there is in public law cases. There is no such reconsideration available in private law cases. Accordingly, on 8 July, the mother made this application for judicial review of the decision of the deputy clerk dated 20 April 1993.

There is a distinction between public law cases and private law cases in relation to transfer from the magistrates' court to a county court. Article 7 of the Children (Allocation of Proceedings) Order 1991, SI 1991/1677 deals with public law cases and that provides, as is well known, that the magistrates' court can transfer a case to the county court on an application by a party or of its own motion if it considers it to be in the interests of the child having regard first to the principle set out in s 1(2) of the Children Act 1989, which provides:

'... the court shall have regard to the general principle that any delay in determining the question is likely to prejudice the welfare of the child',

and secondly, to a series of other questions relating to the gravity, importance or complexity of the case. The provisions relate, as I have said, only to public law cases. The provisions in relation to private law are quite different. Under the old law, before the Children Act 1989 came into force, if a private law case started in the magistrates' court the court had power not to hear the case if they thought it was more suitable that the case should be heard in the High Court. There was no provision for any particular person to make the application and sometimes the court made an order of its own motion. There was no appeal from any decision made in relation to this matter.

The present rules seem to have been derived from the old law rather than any new assessment of the situation. There is no reference in art 8, which is the regulation dealing with this matter, to who may make an application or whether the court can make it of its own motion. This is in accord with the old law. There is no reference to any appeal of an order made under art 8. This, too, seems to be following the old law. The general view on the old law was that you could choose which court you wished in dealing with children in private law cases and, once you had chosen, it was the court and only the court who could transfer the case. Article 8 provides in private law cases that a magistrates' court can transfer a case to the county court where—

'having regard to the principle set out in section 1(2), it considers that in the interests of the child the proceedings can be dealt with more appropriately in that county court.'

The deputy clerk of the magistrates took the view that the effective words of this article were 'having regard to the principle set out in section 1(2)'. She accordingly refused the transfer on the ground, as she put it, 'as having regard to the delay principle it can be more expeditiously dealt with in the Family Proceedings Court'. I am told that there are many courts in England which take the same view. There are other courts, however, who take the view that there is a wider discretion and that delay is not the only matter to be taken into account.

This application, accordingly, depends upon the correct interpretation of art 8 of the Children (Allocation of Proceedings) Order 1991. It is to be observed that the article does not read 'having exclusive regard to the principle set out in section 1(2)', it merely says 'having regard' to that principle. The wording of the article is simple and straightforward. The words, 'having regard to the principle set out in section 1(2)', are surrounded by commas which imply the same as if the words were in parenthesis. The main clause of this part are the words 'it considers that in the interests of the child the proceedings can be dealt with more appropriately in that county court'. The words, 'having regard to the principle set out in section 1(2)', form a subordinate clause.

Accordingly, it is my view that although the court has to have regard to the question of delay, its main function is to consider the interests of the child and to decide whether the proceedings can be more appropriately dealt with in the county court than in the magistrates' court. The deputy clerk precluded herself from considering the interests of the child and limited herself to the question of delay. Here she fell into error. She came to her decision based on an incorrect principle. Delay was one of the matters which had to be taken into account. It was only one of the matters. She should have considered which court was most appropriate and what would be in the interests of the child.

Accordingly, the matter will have to return to the magistrates' court for a decision to be made on the correct principle and an order for certiorari will accordingly be made. The order of 20 April 1993 is quashed. The case which started in January 1993 has still not been heard because of the application to a district judge and then the application for judicial review. If it was urgent, as Sir Stephen Brown P decided in July 1993, it is more urgent now and ought to be dealt with great expedition. I will direct legal aid taxation.

Order accordingly.

Bebe Chua   Barrister.

Coppée-Lavalin SA/NV v Ken-Ren Chemicals and Fertilizers Ltd (in liq)
Voest-Alpine AG v Ken-Ren Chemicals and Fertilizers Ltd (in liq)

HOUSE OF LORDS

LORD KEITH OF KINKEL, LORD BROWNE-WILKINSON, LORD MUSTILL, LORD SLYNN OF HADLEY AND LORD WOOLF

11, 12, 13 JANUARY, 5 MAY 1994

Arbitration – Costs – Security for costs – Claimant ordinarily resident out of jurisdiction – International arbitration in accordance with rules of International Chamber of Commerce – Parties agreeing that ICC arbitration should take place in England – Parties having no connection with England – Application by party for security for costs – Respondent insolvent – Respondent's claim financed by third party which would not be responsible for costs awarded against respondent – Whether court having jurisdiction to order security for costs in ICC arbitration conducted in England – Whether security for costs should be ordered in exceptional cases – Arbitration Act 1950, s 12(6)(a).

The appellant was a Belgian company which entered into a contract dated 18 November 1975 with the respondent for the construction and start-up of a chemical plant in Kenya. The respondent was a Kenyan company, the majority shareholder of which was the Kenyan government. Article 24 of the contract provided that disputes between the parties were to be referred to arbitration by the Court of Arbitration of the International Chamber of Commerce (the ICC) whose award was to be final and binding on the parties. Disputes arose between the parties and in 1990 the respondent lodged a request for arbitration with the ICC. It was agreed that the arbitration would take place in London. Arbitrators were appointed by the ICC which requested each party to pay half the amount fixed as the ICC's fees and costs. The respondent had by then become insolvent but it paid its half of the deposit requested by the ICC. The appellant refused to pay its half-share of the deposit on the grounds of the respondent's insolvency and instead applied to the High Court under s 12(6)(a)[a] of the Arbitration Act 1950 for security for costs on the grounds that the respondent was ordinarily resident out of the jurisdiction, it was the nominal claimant, the real claimant being the Kenyan government, and the respondent would be unable to pay the appellant's costs in the arbitration if ordered to do so. The judge refused the appellant's application. On appeal the Court of Appeal upheld the judge's decision. The appellant appealed to the House of Lords, contending that under art 8(5)[b] of the ICC rules parties were entitled in exceptional circumstances after an arbitrator had been appointed and the file referred to him to apply to a competent judicial authority 'for interim or conservatory measures' and that the facts justified an order for security for costs being made.

---

a   Section s 12(6), so far as material, is set out at p 454 b to e, post
b   Article 8(5) is set out at p 455 d, post

Held – (1) The English court could support an ICC arbitration in England by interim measures (a) which ordered purely procedural steps which the arbitrators either could not order or could not enforce, such as requiring an inspection of the subject matter immediately the dispute arose or compelling the attendance of an unwilling witness, (b) which maintained the status quo pending the making of an award, eg by an interlocutory injunction, so as to prevent one party from bringing about a change of circumstances adverse to the other which the arbitrators could not adequately remedy, and (c) which afforded remedies such as a Mareva injunction designed to ensure that the award had the intended practical effect by causing one party to provide a fund to which recourse could be had by the other party if the first party failed to honour an adverse award spontaneously. However, in determining whether to grant interim measures in support of the agreement to arbitrate under the ICC rules, the English court, as the local court, should have regard to (a) the fact that arbitration was a consensual process and that the court should strive to make the consensus effective by identifying, so far as possible, the kind of arbitrational process that the parties either expressly or impliedly indicated that they were contemplating when they entered into the arbitration agreement, (b) the fact that the choice of an ICC arbitration indicated that the parties intended that the arbitration should, as far as possible, be independent of the national legal system of the country in which the arbitration was to take place, and (c) the degree to which any interim measures would encroach on the arbitrators' function (see p 452 b c f, p 468 e f j to p 469 b d to h, p 470 c, p 471 e to g and p 472 b to d, post); *Bank Mellat v Helliniki Techniki SA* [1983] 3 All ER 428 considered.

(2) The court was not precluded by art 8(5) of the ICC rules from making an order for security for costs either under s 12(6)(a) of the 1950 Act or its inherent jurisdiction in an international arbitration conducted in England under ICC rules but such an order should only be made in exceptional cases where (per Lord Keith, Lord Slynn and Lord Woolf) the arbitration was such that an order for security for costs would support the arbitration by preventing the arbitrator's power to award costs being nullified. In determining whether to exercise its discretion under s 12(6)(a) by ordering security for costs in an ICC arbitration conducted in England, the court had to look at all the circumstances to see whether it was consistent with the nature of the arbitration agreement for an order for security for costs to be made. Mere lack of means of a party was not, in ordinary circumstances sufficient by itself to justify an order for security for costs since the parties were to be taken as having accepted the risks involved in the other party, while having the means necessary to enable him to take part in the arbitration, lacking the means, if he was unsuccessful, to meet his opponent's costs (see p 452 c d f, p 461 d, p 466 e to g, p 471 h j, p 473 d e and p 476 e to h, post); dictum of Kerr LJ in *Bank Mellat v Helliniki Techniki SA* [1983] 3 All ER 428 at 438 disapproved.

(3) (Lord Browne-Wilkinson and Lord Mustill dissenting) Since not only was the respondent insolvent but also its claim was being funded by a third party, the Kenyan government, which stood to gain if the respondent was successful in the arbitration but would bear no responsibility for costs if the respondent was unsuccessful, leaving the appellant with an empty order if costs were awarded in its favour, it was appropriate that, exceptionally, the court should make an order for security for costs. The appeal would therefore be allowed (see p 452 d to f, p 471 j, p 472 e f and p 476 j to p 477 d, post).

Notes

For the power of the court to award security for costs in arbitration proceedings, see 2 *Halsbury's Laws* (4th edn reissue) para 677 and for a case on the subject, see 2(1) *Digest* (2nd reissue) 430, *3484*.

For the Arbitration Act 1950, s 12, see 2 *Halsbury's Statutes* (4th edn) (1992 reissue) 585.

Cases referred to in opinions

Badger Chiyoda v CBI NZ Ltd [1986] 2 NZLR 599, NZ HC.
Bank Mellat v Helliniki Techniki SA [1983] 3 All ER 428, [1984] QB 291, [1983] 3 WLR 783, CA.
Bremer Vulkan Schiffbau Und Maschinenfabrik v South India Shipping Corp [1981] 1 All ER 289, [1981] AC 909, [1981] 2 WLR 141, HL.
Channel Tunnel Group Ltd v Balfour Beatty Construction Ltd [1993] 1 All ER 664, [1993] AC 384, [1993] 2 WLR 262, HL.
Hitachi Shipbuilding and Engineering Co Ltd v Viafiel Cia Naviera SA [1981] 2 Lloyd's Rep 498.
Hudson Strumpffabrik GmbH v Bentley Engineering Co Ltd [1962] 3 All ER 460, [1962] 2 QB 587, [1962] 3 WLR 758.
K/S A/S Bani and K/S A/S Havbulk I v Korea Shipbuilding & Engineering Corp [1987] 2 Lloyd's Rep 445, CA.
Mavani v Ralli Bros Ltd [1973] 1 All ER 555, [1973] 1 WLR 468.
Porzelack KG v Porzelack (UK) Ltd [1987] 1 All ER 1074, [1987] 1 WLR 420.

Appeal

Coppée-Lavalin SA/NV v Ken-Ren Chemicals and Fertilizers Ltd

Coppée-Lavalin SA/NV, a Belgian company, appealed with leave of the Court of Appeal against the decision of the Court of Appeal (Lloyd, Beldam and Roch LJJ) delivered on 29 June 1993 dismissing the the appellant's appeal against the judgment of Potter J delivered on 8 October 1992 dismissing the appellant's application for an order that the respondent, Ken-Ren Chemicals and Fertilizers Ltd (in liquidation in Kenya), provide security for its costs in defending a claim made by the appellant in an arbitration between the parties commenced on 14 November 1990 under the auspices of the International Chamber of Commerce of Paris, the agreed place of arbitration being London. The facts are set out in the opinion of Lord Mustill.

Voest-Alpine AG v Ken-Ren Chemicals and Fertilizers Ltd

Voest-Alpine AG, an Austrian company, appealed with leave of the Court of Appeal against the decision of the Court of Appeal (Lloyd, Beldam and Roch LJJ) delivered on 29 June 1993 dismissing the the appellant's appeal against the judgment of Hirst J delivered on 3 September 1992 dismissing the appellant's application for an order that the respondent, Ken-Ren Chemicals and Fertilizers Ltd (in liquidation in Kenya), provide security for its costs in defending a claim made by the appellant in an arbitration between the parties commenced on 13 November 1990 under the auspices of the International Chamber of Commerce of Paris, the agreed place of arbitration being London. The facts are set out in the opinion of Lord Mustill.

Colin Reece QC and *Dominique Rawley* (instructed by *Clifford Chance* and *Denton Hall*) for the appellants.

Peter Gross QC (instructed by *Freshfields*) for the respondents.

Their Lordships took time for consideration.

5 May 1994. The following opinions were delivered.

LORD KEITH OF KINKEL. My Lords, I have had the advantage of reading in draft the speech to be delivered by my noble and learned friend Lord Mustill and also that prepared by my noble and learned friend Lord Woolf. I agree entirely with the views expressed by Lord Mustill as to the general approach which should be adopted by the court in considering whether or not to exercise its jurisdiction under s 12(6)(a) of the Arbitration Act 1950 so as to order security for costs in an international arbitration conducted in England, in particular an arbitration under the International Chamber of Commerce (ICC) rules. Like Lord Woolf, however, I differ from him on the critical question whether the present cases fall within the exceptional category where such an order would be just and appropriate. The circumstance that not only are the claimants insolvent and thus incapable of meeting any order for costs which might be made against them should the claims fail, but also that the arbitrations are being financed on their side by an outside party standing to gain substantially from success in them, appears to me to favour most strongly the making of the order. If it is not appropriate to do so in these cases I have the greatest difficulty, as does my noble and learned friend Lord Woolf, in envisaging any case involving ICC rules in which the order would indeed be appropriate.

I would therefore allow the appeal in both cases, and make a remit to the judge to fix the amount of security.

LORD BROWNE-WILKINSON. My Lords, for the reasons given by my noble and learned friend Lord Mustill, I, too, would dismiss both appeals.

LORD MUSTILL. My Lords, these appeals raise two issues. The first is controversial, but narrow: what principles should the English court apply when considering an application for security for costs made under s 12(6)(a) of the Arbitration Act 1950 by a party to an international arbitration conducted in England under the auspices of the Court of Arbitration of the International Chamber of Commerce? The second is of great general importance: in what spirit should a national court, and in particular an English court, approach the exercise of its statutory or other powers to order interim relief in the context of an international arbitration between foreign parties conducted in accordance with the procedural rules of an arbitral institution?

Although the disputes from which these appeals arise are complex, the relevant facts may be very shortly stated. For this purpose I will concentrate on one of the appeals. Coppée-Lavalin SA/NV (Coppée) is a Belgian company. By a contract dated 18 November 1975 it agreed with Ken-Ren Chemicals and Fertilizers Ltd (Ken-Ren) to engineer, supply, deliver and supervise the erection and start-up of a plant for the manufacture of a chemical plant in Kenya. Ken-Ren is a Kenyan company, of which the majority shareholder is the government of Kenya. It is now insolvent. Article 24 of the contract provided as follows:

'ARBITRATION. If at any time any question, dispute or difference shall arise between the Seller and the Purchaser, either party shall, as soon as reasonably practicable, give to the other notice in writing of the existence of such question, dispute or difference, specifying its nature and the point at issue, and the same shall be referred to the International Chamber of Commerce in Paris. The arbitrators shall be (3) three in number, shall be appointed in accordance with the Rules of Conciliation and Arbitration of the International Chamber of Commerce in Paris and shall meet in London. The award of the arbitrators shall be final and binding on the parties and there is no recourse to the local Courts. Belgian law shall be the substantive governing law.'

Very serious disputes have arisen under the contract and heavy losses have been incurred. The parties have rightly agreed, in accordance with the observations of Browne-Wilkinson V-C in *Porzelack KG v Porzelack (UK) Ltd* [1987] 1 All ER 1074, [1987] 1 WLR 420 that it is not appropriate to enter into the merits of the underlying dispute on an application for security for costs, and the application has been conducted on the basis that arguable claims have been made and have been met with arguable defences.

On 14 November 1990 Ken-Ren lodged with the Court of Arbitration of the International Chamber of Commerce (the ICC) a request for arbitration. This was followed by an answer from Coppée. In due course arbitrators were appointed, being nationals respectively of the United States, Belgium and England. The parties and the arbitrators signed terms of reference dated 29 January 1992. Subsequently, in accordance with art 9 of the Rules of Conciliation and Arbitration of the ICC (the ICC rules) the ICC invited each party to pay one-half of the amount fixed by the Court of Arbitration as the deposit to cover the ICC's costs and the fees of the arbitrators. Coppée refused to pay, giving as one of its reasons the insolvency of Ken-Ren. The latter then paid the other half of the deposit and pursuant to art 9.4 of the ICC rules the terms of reference thereupon became operative on 30 June 1992. One week later Coppée issued a summons in the High Court seeking an order for security, giving as grounds that Ken-Ren is ordinarily resident out of the jurisdiction; it is a nominal claimant in the arbitration in so far as it is claiming on behalf of the government of Kenya; and it will be unable to pay Coppée's costs if ordered to do so (by analogy with s 726 of the Companies Act 1985 and also RSC Ord 23, r 1). On 8 October 1992 Potter J refused the application. Coppée appealed to the Court of Appeal with the leave of the full court. The argument of the appeal was dominated by the previous decision of the Court of Appeal in *Bank Mellat v Helliniki Techniki SA* [1983] 3 All ER 428, [1984] QB 291 in which the court had dismissed an application for security for costs made in respect of an ICC arbitration, Kerr LJ (with whom Waller LJ briefly agreed) and Robert Goff LJ giving different reasons for reaching the same conclusion. Since the *Bank Mellat* case was binding on the Court of Appeal, in the present case close attention was naturally given to the differences and similarities between the two judgments and to identifying the ratio decidendi of the decision. Since your Lordships' House is not bound by *Bank Mellat* it is unnecessary to enter into details and it is sufficient to say that in the result the Court of Appeal followed the reasoning of Kerr LJ and upheld the judge's refusal to order security for costs. Lloyd LJ added that his provisional view, not based on full argument, was that he would have allowed the appeal had he been free to do so. The court granted leave to appeal to this House on the ground that this was a point of major importance in arbitration law.

I THE STATUTES, ORDERS AND RULES

The jurisdiction of the High Court to order security for costs in an arbitration is created by s 12(6) of the 1950 Act as amended:

'The High Court shall have, for the purpose of and in relation to a reference, the same power of making orders in respect of—(a) security for costs ... (c) the giving of evidence by affidavit; (d) examination on oath of any witness before an officer of the High Court or any other person, and the issue of a commission or request for the examination of a witness out of the jurisdiction; (e) the preservation, interim custody or sale of any goods which are the subject matter of the reference; (f) securing the amount in dispute in the reference; (g) the detention, preservation or inspection of any property or thing which is the subject of the reference or as to which any question may arise therein, and authorising for any of the purposes aforesaid any persons to enter upon or into any land or building in the possession of any party to the reference, or authorising any samples to be taken or any observation to be made or experiment to be tried which may be necessary or expedient for the purpose of obtaining full information or evidence; and (h) interim injunctions or the appointment of a receiver; as it has for the purpose of and in relation to an action or matter in the High Court: Provided that nothing in this subsection shall be taken to prejudice any power which may be vested in an arbitrator or umpire of making orders with respect to any of the matters aforesaid.'

The addition of para (a) (amongst others) to the much shorter list of powers already created by the Arbitration Act 1889 followed recommendations in the Report of the MacKinnon Committee on the Law of Arbitration (1927, Cmd 2817). There is nothing in the published papers relating to the antecedents of this power to indicate the principles according to which Parliament intended it to be exercised.

The power of the High Court to which s 12(6)(a) is assimilated is contained in RSC Ord 23, r 1, which (omitting immaterial provisions) reads:

'(1) Where, on the application of a defendant to an action or other proceeding in the High Court, it appears to the Court—(a) that the plaintiff is ordinarily resident out of the jurisdiction, or (b) that the plaintiff (not being a plaintiff who is suing in a representative capacity) is a nominal plaintiff who is suing for the benefit of some other person and that there is reason to believe that he will be unable to pay the costs of the defendant if ordered to do so ... then if, having regard to all the circumstances of the case, the Court thinks it just to do so, it may order the plaintiff to give such security for the defendant's costs of the action or other proceeding as it thinks just.'

In the High Court an order for security for costs usually provides that proceedings shall be stayed until such provision is given. If the plaintiff makes default the action may be dismissed. According to *The Supreme Court Practice 1993*, para 23/1-3/30, the power to dismiss derives from the inherent jurisdiction of the court. It is not easy to see how a power either to stay the action pending the provision of security or to dismiss it if the order is not complied with can be similarly derived when the court makes an order under s 12(6), since it is well settled that the High Court has no inherent jurisdiction to intervene in a pending arbitration: *Bremer Vulkan Schiffbau Und Maschinenfabrik v South India Shipping Corp* [1981] 1 All ER 289, [1981] AC 909. No point was taken in argument on the nature and source of the power and I mention it only because the question is linked to one which I must emphasise at a later stage.

Mention must also be made of s 726 of the Companies Act 1985:

'(1) Where in England and Wales a limited company is plaintiff in an action or other legal proceeding, the court having jurisdiction in the matter may, if it appears by credible testimony that there is reason to believe that the company will be unable to pay the defendant's costs if successful in his defence, require sufficient security to be given for those costs, and may stay all proceedings until the security is given.'

Finally, there are the ICC rules and in particular art 8(5):

'Before the file is transmitted to the arbitrator, and in exceptional circumstances even thereafter, the parties shall be at liberty to apply to any competent judicial authority for interim or conservatory measures, and they shall not by so doing be held to infringe the agreement to arbitrate or to affect the relevant powers reserved to the arbitrator.'

Although this is by far the most important of the ICC rules for present purposes I must also quote those provisions which have been relied on in previous judgments on this question:

'*Article 1 International Court of Arbitration*

(1) The International Court of Arbitration of the International Chamber of Commerce is the arbitration body attached to the International Chamber of Commerce. Members of the Court are appointed by the Council of the International Chamber of Commerce. The function of the Court is to provide for the settlement by arbitration of business disputes of an international character in accordance with these Rules ...

Article 2 The arbitral tribunal

(1) The International Court of Arbitration does not itself settle disputes. Insofar as the parties shall not have provided otherwise, it appoints, or confirms the appointments of, arbitrators in accordance with the provisions of this Article. In making or confirming such appointment, the Court shall have regard to the proposed arbitrator's nationality, residence and other relationships with the countries of which the parties or the other arbitrators are nationals ...

Article 8 Effect of the agreement to arbitrate

(1) Where the parties have agreed to submit to arbitration by the International Chamber of Commerce, they shall be deemed thereby to have submitted ipso facto to the present Rules ...

Article 9 Advance to cover costs of arbitration

(1) The International Court of Arbitration shall fix the amount of the advance on costs in a sum likely to cover the costs of arbitration of the claims which have been referred to it. Where, apart from the principal claim, one or more counter-claims are submitted, the court may fix

separate advances on costs for the principal claim and the counter-claim or counter-claims.

(2) The advance on costs shall be payable in equal shares by the Claimant or Claimants and the Defendant or Defendants. However, any one party shall be free to pay the whole of the advance on costs in respect of the claim or the counter-claim should the other party fail to pay its share.

(3) The Secretariat may make the transmission of the file to the arbitrator conditional upon the payment by the parties or one of them of the whole or part of the advance on costs to the International Chamber of Commerce.

(4) When the Terms of Reference are communicated to the Court in accordance with the provisions of Article 13, the Court shall verify whether the requests for the advance on costs have been complied with. The Terms of Reference shall only become operative and the arbitrator shall only proceed in respect of those claims for which the advance on costs has been duly paid to the International Chamber of Commerce ...

Article 11 Rules governing the proceedings

The rules governing the proceedings before the arbitrator shall be those resulting from these Rules and, where these Rules are silent, any rules which the parties (or, failing them, the arbitrator) may settle, and whether or not reference is thereby made to a municipal procedural law to be applied to the arbitration.

Article 12 Place of arbitration

The place of arbitration shall be fixed by the International Court of Arbitration, unless agreed upon by the parties.'

II THE BACKGROUND

Since the importance of this appeal transcends the narrow question in dispute I begin by sketching the background of international doctrine and practice against which the court's undoubted discretion must be exercised. Since great stress was laid both in *Bank Mellat v Helliniki Techniki SA* [1983] 3 All ER 428, [1984] QB 291 and in the writings of informed critics on the special character of an ICC arbitration I must say something about the nature and functions of the ICC Court of Arbitration (hereafter 'the Court of Arbitration').

(1) *The Court of Arbitration and its rules*

Nowadays, international arbitration institutions are springing up throughout the world, but for many years the Court of Arbitration was unique. Institutional arbitration limited to individual trades has existed for centuries, and institutions with wider international functions were not unknown. What marked out the Court of Arbitration was its origins. When the founding national chambers of commerce came together in 1920 to create the International Chamber it was an integral part of the design that there would be rules for conciliation and arbitration and an organisation which under the wing of the new body would have a permanent function as a vehicle for the conduct of international arbitration and for the development of arbitration law and techniques. (For a full account see Dr Frederic Eisemann, 'The Court of Arbitration: Outline of its Changes from Inception to the Present Day' in *60 years of ICC Arbitration* (ICC, 1984, pp 391 ff).) Just as the national chambers, whilst retaining their own identity and aims, had conceived the International

Chamber to fulfil a wider purpose, so also was the Court of Arbitration designed to be the medium for expressing a wider and more generalised view of arbitration than was practicable for national institutions. This gave the Court of Arbitration a special standing in world commerce.

As time passed, and the volume of its business increased, the Court of Arbitration came to play three distinct roles. First, the availability of ICC arbitration gave to contracting parties, often widely separated in geography and culture, the possibility of finding a venue for dispute resolution acceptable to both. Second, and more obviously, the court and its secretariat could offer the parties an established administrative structure, a continuity of experience and a stance of proclaimed and carefully cultivated neutrality which together would reduce friction, suspicion and inefficiency. A third consequence was that at least for a time the ICC became the focus of a theory, indeed an ethos, of international arbitration called 'transnationalism', to which I must shortly return.

I now turn to the functions of the Court of Arbitration. The word 'court' is rather misleading. As art 2(1) declares: 'The International Court of Arbitration does not itself settle disputes'. Rather, its function is to provide an administrative framework within which arbitrations can be conducted, and its participation is in the main limited to the early and the concluding stages of dispute resolution, leaving the decision-making function to the arbitrators appointed pursuant to the ICC rules.

This division of roles is clear from a glance at the ICC rules themselves. At the outset the Court of Arbitration is in charge of appointing the sole arbitrator or third arbitrator; making default appointments if the agreed mechanism breaks down; ruling on challenges to arbitrators; fixing the place of arbitration; settling the administrative costs and the fees of the arbitrators and taking a deposit on account of them; supervising the preparation of terms of reference. Other rules are prescriptive of matters relating to the further end of the arbitration, such as time-limits for the award, majority awards, decisions as to costs, and deposit of the award. The court also has an important function under r 21 in scrutinising the award and directing modifications of its form. It is only in this very last respect that the Court of Arbitration performs anything resembling a judicial function.

When one turns to the business of actually deciding the dispute the Court of Arbitration is a conspicuous absentee and the arbitrators are left to their own judgment. For example, if there is an issue about the validity of the agreement to arbitrate this is decided by the arbitrator, not the Court of Arbitration (art 8(4)). Where the ICC rules and the agreement of the parties are silent, the rules governing the procedure are settled by the arbitrators (art 11). The arbitrator may decide whether to hear experts (art 14(2)). The arbitrator chooses when to summon the parties, and how to proceed in their absence (art 15), and determines the language of the arbitration. Crucially, 'The arbitrator shall be in full charge of the hearings ...' (art 15(4)).

Thus, as pointed out by Dr Eisemann (at p 397), under the current form of the ICC rules, 'the division of tasks between the arbitrators and the court is more in keeping with the nature of their respective functions—essentially administrative for the court and judicial for the arbitrators'. Moreover, not only do the ICC rules leave the widest discretion to the arbitrators as to the discharge of their functions, untrammelled either by detailed provisions in the ICC rules or by directions from the Court of Arbitration, but there are large

areas of the relationship between the parties and the arbitrators on which the
ICC rules have nothing to say. A list of instances may be found in Craig, Park
and Paulsson *International Chamber of Commerce Arbitration* (2nd edn, 1990) para
28.04. The details are immaterial. It is sufficient to say that for good practical
reasons the rule-makers have not set out to produce a complete voluntary code
of arbitration; the reasons being first that this task would be impracticable (as
the framers of the UNCITRAL Model Law on International Commercial
Arbitration (1985) (for which see Mustill and Boyd *Commercial Arbitration* (2nd
edn, 1989) App 3, p 730) tacitly acknowledged), and second that there are
several aspects of the relationship where breakdowns can only be remedied by
enlisting the coercive powers of a national court.

(2) *Transnationalism*

At this stage I must deal briefly with three concepts which though quite
different are easily confused. Each of them is commonly given a label. The
first is 'party autonomy', which emphasises that arbitration is a consensual
process, and that national courts should within very broad limits recognise and
give effect to any agreement between the parties, express or tacit, as to the way
in which the arbitration should be conducted. This is now widely recognised
as a first principle of arbitration law, and the English courts in common with
those of other nations with developed systems of arbitration law strive to give
effect to it. I will leave this aside for the moment.

The two remaining concepts have a common aim but wholly inconsistent
methods. The common aim is to make international arbitration truly
international by securing that no matter in what country the proceedings
physically take place, an arbitration conducted between the same parties under
the same agreement and with the same arbitrators will take broadly the same
procedural shape. 'Transnationalism' is a theoretical ideal which posits that
international arbitration, at least as regards certain types of contractual
disputes conducted under the auspices of an arbitral institution, is a
self-contained juridical system, by its very nature separate from national
systems of law, and indeed antithetical to them. If the ideal is fully realised,
national courts will not feature in the law and practice of international
arbitration at all and differences between national laws will become irrelevant.
By contrast, 'harmonisation' recognises that participation by the court,
however unwelcome in theory, is in certain situations inevitable, and sets out
to minimise the differences between national arbitration laws, and with them
the practical significance of the choice of *forum*. The UNCITRAL Model Law
on International Commercial Arbitration, embodied in the law of Scotland,
and an impetus for proposed legislation for the remainder of the United
Kingdom, is an important example of harmonisation, albeit of only a partial
nature.

My Lords, I think it unnecessary to enter into the controversy over
transnationalism which has been a feature of the past two decades, and would
indeed not have mentioned the term if it had not been pressed in argument. I
doubt whether in its purest sense the doctrine now commands widespread
support: as witness the recognition of court-imposed interim measures in,
amongst others, art 9 of the UNCITRAL Model Law and art 8(5) of the ICC
rules. At all events it cannot be the law of England, for otherwise this House
would have dismissed at the very outset the attempt in *Channel Tunnel Group
Ltd v Balfour Beatty Construction Ltd* [1993] 1 All ER 664, [1993] AC 384 to

procure an interim injunction during the currency of an ICC arbitration. (To avoid misunderstanding I should make it clear that I am speaking only of transnationalism in the strict sense, which is concerned with the detachment of international institutionalised arbitration from local procedural laws. There is another doctrine, sometimes given the same name, which asserts a single unified 'lex mercatoria' governing the substantive rights and duties of the parties to certain types of international transaction, to the exclusion of national substantive laws. This concept has no bearing on the present dispute which is concerned only with matters of procedure, and I say nothing about it.)

(3) Institutional arbitration and interim measures

Institutional arbitration has many advantages but speed off the mark is not usually one of them. Taking the ICC as an example, the Court of Arbitration appoints the third arbitrator or sole arbitrator, as the case may be, having first obtained the opinion of the national committee of the country from where the chosen arbitrator is to come; it forwards the request for arbitration to the defendant, and receives the latter's answer and the claimant's reply. For these steps quite generous time-limits are allowed. Under art 9 of the ICC rules the court must fix and then wait to receive the sums payable by each party by way of an advance on the costs of the arbitration. This is important because the arbitrator cannot proceed in relation to any claim which has not been the subject of an advance on costs (art 9(4)). Finally, the court transmits the file to the arbitrator whose first task, 'before proceeding with the preparation of the case' (art 13(1)), is to draw up a document defining his terms of reference which the parties must sign. All these proceedings take time. For example, in the present case 14 months elapsed between the submission of the request for arbitration and the signature of the terms of reference and because of the delay brought about by the refusal of Coppée to put up its share of the deposit another five months elapsed before the arbitrators were in a position even to make a start on their task. Within this time scale most ad hoc arbitrators would expect to make really substantial progress and in many instances the arbitration would already be completed.

My purpose in making these observations is not to criticise the ICC or to ignore the obvious fact that the kinds of dispute which go to arbitration under the auspices of the ICC and kindred bodies are by their nature liable to take longer, and often much longer, than many disputes submitted to ad hoc arbitration. Rather, I seek to emphasise that institutional arbitrations are vulnerable in their early stages when the interests of the parties and the fairness of the ultimate decision may be adversely and perhaps irrevocably affected by changes of circumstance which the Court of Arbitration and the arbitrators have no power to forestall. It is in recognition of this fact that the ICC has recently introduced a 'referee' procedure under which, if the parties have agreed to it in advance, the court appoints an independent person empowered to order 'provisional or conservatory' measures before the arbitrators take control. This procedure is available only by agreement and has no application to the present case. Absent any such procedure, if the parties and the arbitral process need protection there is nowhere to turn but the national court.

My Lords, there is plainly a tension here. On the one hand the concept of arbitration as a consensual process, reinforced by the ideal of transnationalism, leans always against the involvement of the mechanisms of state through the medium of a municipal court. On the other side there is the plain fact, palatable or not, that it is only a court possessing coercive powers which can rescue the arbitration if it is in danger of foundering, and that the only court which possesses these powers is the municipal court of an individual state. Whatever extreme positions may have been taken in the past there is, I believe, a broad consensus acknowledging that the local court can have a proper and beneficial part to play in the grant of supportive measures. Total consistency cannot be expected. Each domestic court has its own practical methods, developed in the context of litigation, which it will instinctively tend to bring to bear when similar questions arise in the context of arbitration; each country will have its own traditions of arbitration and its own traditions of the relationship between arbitration and the courts. The result is a considerable diversity from one country to another, well illustrated by an analysis of the laws of 16 countries contained in Shenton and Kuhn *Interim Court Remedies in Support of Arbitration* (International Bar Association, 1987). Nevertheless, there is emerging a general measure of agreement about the spirit in which a local court should approach a problem such as the present: that it should aim to be at the same time supportive but sparing in the use of its powers.

(4) *Article 8(5) and s 12(6)*

Two questions arise in relation to art 8(5). First, what is meant by 'interim or conservatory measures'? (The French text speaks of 'mesures provisoires ou conservatoires'). This question has arisen before both arbitrators and the courts; the former because it is from time to time suggested by a party that the act of his opponent in applying to a national court for interim measures is a waiver or breach of the arbitration agreement, and the latter because the court wishes to know whether the article purports to inhibit the grant of the particular measure in contemplation. Valuable studies of the case law of national courts and ICC tribunals by S R Bond and E A Schwartz, respectively the former and current Secretaries General of the Court of Arbitration ('The Nature of Conservatory and Provisional Measures' and 'The Practices and Experience of the ICC Court' in *Conservatory and Provisional Measures in International Arbitration* (ICC, 1993) pp 8 and 45), demonstrate both the wide diversity of such measures and the lack of consensus about the scope of art 8(5). The latter is indeed demonstrated by the fact that *Bank Mellat v Helliniki Techniki SA* [1983] 3 All ER 428, [1984] QB 291 was fought on the agreed basis that an order for security for costs was outside art 8(5) whereas *Bond* (at pp 11– 12) includes such an order in a list of typical interim or conservatory measures. For my part I tend to prefer the latter opinion, since the order is interim in the sense of being made whilst the substantive dispute is awaiting final adjudication, and conservatory in the sense of being designed to ensure that the arbitral process is not frustrated in its last stages by the refusal of the losing party to honour the award; but I do not think that anything decisive turns on this.

The second question concerns the effect of the article on applications to the national court. Although the matter was not fully explored in argument I believe that the principal aim of the article was protective rather than exclusionary: not to prohibit for the first time recourse to national courts, for this would run counter to the doctrinal writings which acknowledge the importance of the reinforcement which the courts can provide when the arbitral tribunal is powerless, but rather to ensure that the party who makes the application does not risk being held to have broken or waived the arbitration agreement. I am confirmed in this opinion both by the striking number of cases in which allegations of this kind have been made (see *Schwartz*) and also by the observations of Henry J in *Badger Chiyoda v CBI NZ Ltd* [1986] 2 NZLR 599.

Turning to s 12(6) of the 1950 Act, it is clear from the absence of the introductory words 'unless a contrary intention is expressed [in the arbitration agreement]' which are found elsewhere in s 12 that the powers under s 12(6) cannot be excluded by consent: *Mavani v Ralli Bros Ltd* [1973] 1 All ER 555 at 559, [1973] 1 WLR 468 at 473. On the other hand, if the arbitration agreement expressly stipulates that a party shall not apply to a national court for an order of the type in question the principle of party autonomy will almost always require the local court to honour the agreement and abstain from exercising its powers. (I add the words 'almost always' because in the last resort the court must act according to the justice of the case, and procedural situations are so various and unpredictable that it is preferable not to rule out in advance the possibility that special factors might combine to outweigh the parties' choice.)

Putting art 8(5) and s 12(6) together I arrive at the following conclusions. Article 8(5) does not expressly prohibit an application for interim relief, and consequently does not preclude the making of such an order by the English court under s 12(6)(a) or under its inherent jurisdiction. (This was taken for granted by your Lordships in *Channel Tunnel Group Ltd v Balfour Beatty Construction Ltd* [1993] 1 All ER 664, [1993] AC 384.) At the same time the distinction drawn between the times before and after the arbitrators receive the file shows what would in any event be obvious: that if the order is made at a later stage it is more likely to infringe the spirit of the arbitration agreement than if it had been made at a time when the arbitrators are not yet in charge. This is as much as I am able to derive from art 8(5).

III THE TWO LEADING CASES

Against this background I turn to the judgments of Kerr and Robert Goff LJJ in *Bank Mellat v Helliniki Techniki SA* [1983] 3 All ER 428, [1984] QB 291 and of Bingham LJ in *K/S A/S Bani v Korea Shipbuilding and Engineering Corp* [1987] 2 Lloyd's Rep 445. Although these are not binding on your Lordships it is obvious that the problem is greatly illuminated by the separate analyses furnished by three judges of such profound knowledge and experience in the field of international arbitration. The judgments are too long to permit the quotation of all the relevant statements of principle but I believe that the following is a fair summary of what was decided and said.

The *Bank Mellat* case arose from a joint venture between an Iranian bank, a Greek contractor and a Danish company. The contract stated that it was to be governed by the laws of Iran. It contained an ICC arbitration clause, with a stipulation that it was to be governed by the law of Iran and that the venue was to be the City of London. Proceedings were to be in the English language. The arbitration had proceeded as far as deposits by the parties on account of fees and the completion of the terms of reference. One of the parties issued a summons for an order that the other party should provide security for costs. At first instance Bingham J declined to make an order and the applicant appealed.

After setting out the general law in an entirely uncontroversial manner Kerr LJ began his detailed consideration of the problem by stating that in relation to international arbitration particular regard would be paid to the degree of connection which the parties or the arbitration have with this country and its legal system (see [1983] 3 All ER 428 at 432, [1984] QB 291 at 303). Thus if the respondent is English and the claimant is foreign, and there is no agreement that particular rules are to apply, then an order for security is likely to be the norm: cf *Hudson Strumpffabrik GmbH v Bentley Engineering Co Ltd* [1962] 3 All ER 460, [1962] 2 QB 587. But the choice of a particular set of arbitration rules may well be relevant to the exercise of the discretion. Kerr LJ went on to analyse the ICC rules beginning with the general proposition that—

'the rules provide a code which is intended to be self-sufficient, in the sense that it is capable of covering all aspects of arbitrations conducted under the rules, without the need for any recourse to any municipal system of law or any application to the courts of the forum.' (See [1983] 3 All ER 428 at 433, [1984] QB 291 at 304.)

After pointing out that the ICC rules contained no provision for the giving of security for costs as distinct from the costs of the arbitrators, Kerr LJ examined arts 9, 11, 12, 20 and 26, and proceeded to make two further points. First, that parties to arbitration agreements mainly look to the international conventions on the enforcement of arbitral awards and do not envisage any advance provision being made by way of security in relation to any of the matters to be dealt with in the award, unless they agree to arbitrate under rules that make express provision in this regard or possibly under rules governed by some municipal system of law which expressly provides for such security. Second, that the power of the courts under s 12(6) is a somewhat exceptional procedure in comparison with most systems of law. Kerr LJ then closed this part of his judgment with a 'conclusion in principle' ([1983] 3 All ER 428 at 437, [1984] QB 291 at 308–309):

'As it seems to me, the English courts should be slow in applying the jurisdiction to order security for costs in international arbitration unless, in the particular circumstances of each case, there is some more specific connection with this country, as discussed earlier in this judgment, than the mere fact that the parties have agreed that any arbitration is to take place in England. In the present case we are concerned with such an arbitration under the ICC rules. The judge's [Bingham J's] conclusion in this connection is mainly contained in the following passages of his judgment: "But what is quite clear is that the detailed provisions of the rules with respect to the giving of deposits, the payment of costs and the question of applications to local courts contain no express permission for the parties to make such application and probably by implication envisage that applications of that kind will not be made." This language may not be very precise, but I am wholly in agreement with the thought which underlies it. As I see it, the application for security for costs in the present case is one which is inconsistent with the scheme and spirit of the ICC rules, not literally inconsistent, either expressly or even by necessary implication, but sufficiently inconsistent, for the reasons explained above, to make it inappropriate in principle for the court to exercise its statutory discretion in favour of the order sought in this case.'

After discussing the financial position of the party against whom the order was sought Kerr LJ expressed his conclusion thus ([1983] 3 All ER 428 at 438, [1984] QB 291 at 309–310):

> 'Since I consider that in an arbitration under the ICC rules, which has no connection with this country other than that it had been agreed between foreign parties that any such arbitration was to take place here, it would be inappropriate in principle to make an order for security for costs on the ground that the claimant is ordinarily resident abroad, I would also regard it as wrong in principle to make any such order on the ground that the claimant may be unable to pay the other party's costs if the award requires him to do so.'

Turning to the judgment of Robert Goff LJ, his Lordship first discussed the argument that art 8(5) indicated the circumstances in which an application to the court was contemplated by the rules and that these did not include an application for security for costs (see [1983] 3 All ER 428 at 439, [1984] QB 291 at 311–312). (This argument, and the Court of Appeal's discussion, was premised on the assumption that such an order does not fall within the meaning of art 8(5), an assumption which I do not myself share.) Robert Goff LJ continued ([1983] 3 All ER 428 at 439–440, [1984] QB 291 at 312–313):

> 'It is of course true that the ICC rules, while providing for deposits to be made in equal shares covering the costs of the award, are silent on the question of either party providing security for the other party's legal costs. I cannot infer from that, or indeed from the ICC rules as a whole, any implicit agreement that neither party should be free to take advantage of any provision of the curial law of the arbitration under which security for costs may be applied for. In truth, the silence of the ICC rules on that matter in all probability reflects no more than that the experience of those who drew up the rules was of systems of law under which security of that kind is not ordered. The fact that the ICC rules provide for deposits to cover the costs of the award reflects only the intention that those persons for whom the ICC is responsible shall have their remuneration and expenses secured; and, since the outcome of the arbitration is unknown, it is obviously sensible and just that such deposits should in general be furnished by both parties in equal shares. But the fact that security in the form of deposits for costs of that kind is required by the rules is, in my judgment, in no way inconsistent with either party taking advantage of a provision of the curial law under which security for a party's legal costs may be ordered. Indeed, the readiness of the ICC, as envisaged in its own rules, to extract from the parties security (in the onerous form of a deposit) for their own costs, can arguably be regarded as entirely consistent with a party taking advantage of an opportunity available to him under the curial law to obtain, where appropriate, an order for security for his own legal costs ... The mere fact that reference is made in that article to a particular form of application to the court (which is in fact a form of application well known under continental systems of law) cannot impliedly exclude other forms of application available under the curial law; indeed, if that argument were right, it could likewise be argued that an application under s 12(6)(b) of the 1950 Act for an order for discovery of documents should

be inhibited by reason of the implied agreement of the parties not to make any such application.'

Next Robert Goff LJ discussed and dismissed the argument that an order for security was inconsistent with the ICC rules.

By this stage Robert Goff LJ had concluded that the judge had misdirected himself in his construction of the ICC rules as a complete and exclusive code, and he now went on to consider how in his judgment the discretion should be exercised. In summary his reasoning was as follows. An application for security in an arbitration should not always be approached in the same way as in the High Court. Although in the case of many arbitrations held in this country it is the practice to order security, these are in general commercial arbitrations of a type regularly held in London under standard English forms of contract governed by English law, having a very close connection with the English jurisdiction. A different kind of arbitration has now developed under a clause providing for arbitration in a neutral forum and for a neutral arbitration. Such contracts may incorporate rules such as those of the ICC. Side by side with the growth of this type of international arbitration have been developments under conventions upon which the parties rely for the enforcement of awards. London may well be chosen as a convenient neutral forum and in such an event the policy historical underlying an order for security for costs appeared to Robert Goff LJ in most cases inapplicable. It might very readily be inferred in most cases that the parties will be proceeding in reliance upon the ordinary convention procedure for enforcement of awards (including awards as to costs).

Robert Goff LJ then stated that in considering the exercise of its discretion the court must consider all the circumstances of the particular case, and continued ([1983] 3 All ER 428 at 442, [1984] QB 291 at 315–316):

'But in the case of international arbitrations of the kind I have described the court should, in my judgment, as a general rule decline to make an order for security for costs against a foreign claimant unless there are special circumstances which warrant it, because the policy underlying an order for the provision of security for costs by a foreign claimant is not generally applicable in such cases. In reaching this conclusion, I wish to state first that I should not be understood to be expressing any view about awards of security for costs in the case of ordinary commercial arbitrations of the type which have for many years been regularly held in this country, in particular arbitrations on maritime disputes and in the commodity trades ... Nor should I be understood as suggesting that there is any special barrier against parties in international arbitrations taking advantage of other provisions of English law as the curial law relating, for example, to the conduct of the arbitration (including discovery of documents) or to interim measures and orders. My observations should be understood as concerned only with the exercise of the court's discretion to award security for costs.'

It followed from what Robert Goff LJ had said that no order for costs should be made against the defendants unless there were special circumstances justifying such an order—no particular weight being attached to the fact the parties had agreed to arbitration in accordance with the ICC rules, save that it emphasised the international character of the arbitration. Robert Goff LJ continued ([1983] 3 All ER 428 at 442, [1984] QB 291 at 316):

> 'The solution to the present problem must, I consider, lie in a realistic appreciation of the character of the relevant arbitration and the circumstances in which England comes to be chosen as the forum, rather than in squeezing indications, often with great difficulty, out of rules the draftsman of which in all probability never even addressed his mind to the question of security for costs. Indeed, it is theoretically possible that there could be arbitrations under the ICC rules which are not of the character which I have described, in which it might be proper to make an award for security. But in practical terms, having regard to the character of arbitrations conducted under the ICC rules, I cannot myself conceive of any such case.'

Finally, on questions of principle Robert Goff LJ declared ([1983] 3 All ER 428 at 443, [1984] QB 291 at 316):

> 'In my judgment, if a claimant in an international arbitration held in this country is an English or foreign company as to which it appears by credible testimony that there is reason to believe that it will be unable to pay the costs of the respondent if successful in his defence, then it would be proper for the court, in an appropriate case, by virtue of s 447 of the Companies Act 1948 or by analogy with that section, to exercise its discretion to order the claimant to furnish security for the respondent's costs. The policy underlying an order for security in such a case is untouched by the considerations which I have mentioned, which in my judgment negative the policy of ordering security for costs on the ground only that the claimant is resident outside the jurisdiction.'

Turning to the evidence of insolvency, Robert Goff LJ held that it fell short of establishing the basis for an order for security for costs and so agreed with the other members of the court in dismissing the appeal.

I now turn to the decision of the Court of Appeal in *K/S A/S Bani v Korea Shipbuilding and Engineering Corp* [1987] 2 Lloyd's Rep 445. This arose from contracts for the construction of two vessels in Korea for Norwegian purchasers. The contracts contained a London arbitration clause and were expressly made subject to English law. There was provision for a default appointment of the third arbitrator by the president of the London Maritime Arbitrators Association, and for the service of English court proceedings. In the Commercial Court Hirst J refused to order security, but his decision was reversed on appeal. Delivering the only full judgment Bingham LJ analysed in some detail the two judgments in *Bank Mellat v Helliniki Techniki SA* [1983] 3 All ER 428, [1984] QB 291. Although entirely endorsing this analysis I need not set it out, since the Court of Appeal was bound, as your Lordships are not, by the judgment of the majority in *Bank Mellat*. It may however be noted that Bingham LJ could detect no criticism in the judgment of Robert Goff LJ ([1983] 3 All ER 428 at 442, [1984] QB 291 at 315) of the prevailing practice of making orders for security in 'ordinary commercial arbitrations of the type that have for many years been regularly held in this country ...' (see [1987] 2 Lloyd's Rep 445 at 451). Bingham LJ then compared the instant case with *Bank Mellat* and found the following points of difference (at 452). The arbitration was of a type which had for many years been regularly conducted in London. It was not a

quintessentially one-off arbitration of the kind which Robert Goff LJ had in
mind. On the contrary, it was 'of a kind with which any reasonably seasoned
shipping practitioner will be very familiar... [It] is to be regarded as regular
London business as the *Bank Mellat* arbitration could not'. In addition, the
proper law of the contracts was English, and the contracts were apparently
drafted with reference to English or commercial law concepts in mind; the
contracts did not incorporate a detailed code of rules; and in addition there
were the provisions for default appointment and service of proceedings. These
considerations were sufficient to distinguish the *Bank Mellat* case and to place
the instant case very firmly in the category of arbitration in which orders for
security are in general appropriate.   Finally, Bingham LJ considered the
financial position of the builders and found that it appeared to be precarious,
which fortified his view that this was an appropriate case for security (see at
454–455). Woolf and Dillon LJJ concurred.

IV THE EXERCISE OF THE DISCRETION

I now turn to consider how the discretion under s 12(6)(a) should be
exercised, and will begin with four grounds which are said to be conclusive
against, or at least very strongly opposed to, the grant of relief. The first is the
express submission to the ICC rules which are said to be material in more than
one way. In the first place, it is maintained, in line with the reasoning of Kerr
LJ in *Bank Mellat*, that the rules expressly or by implication exclude the right of
either party to apply to a national court for security for costs; and thus whilst
not formally ousting the power of the English court under Ord 23, they create
a situation in which the grant of such an order would be unjust. For my part,
I must concur with the judgments of Robert Goff LJ in *Bank Mellat* and Henry
J in *Badger Chiyoda v CBI NZ Ltd* [1986] 2 NZLR 599 at 606–607 in rejecting this
argument. (Whilst it is true that in the latter case there was a degree of
connection between the dispute and the national court which was absent from
Bank Mellat, the logic of the argument, if correct, would be just as applicable
however close or remote the link between the two.) I need not go over the
ground already covered in these two judgments. For the reasons there given I
see nothing either express or implied in the rules to inhibit the court from
deploying whatever national interim remedies may be necessary to suit the
justice of the individual case. The nearest that the rules come to such a
provision is art 8(5) and this, as already suggested, is there to facilitate the grant
of interim measures, not to rule them out. Any other conclusion would have
the most serious adverse consequences for the utility of ICC arbitration; for
since the rules do not specifically mention security for costs any more than any
other form of interim relief, if the argument is sound as regards security for
costs it must be equally sound for the remainder. Whatever view is taken
regarding the correct balance of the relationship between international
arbitration and national courts, it is impossible to doubt that at least in some
instances the intervention of the court may be not only permissible but highly
beneficial.

The alternative argument under the rules is that an order for security by the
national court would be inconsistent not with their individual terms but with
the scheme which they embody, since (so it is maintained) they comprise a
complete and self-contained procedural code which leaves no room for
recourse to the local court. I quite agree that even in the absence of a provision
such as art 26 a local court should, so far as its own laws permit, try to give

effect to what the parties have agreed; and if the court were to be confronted with a body of agreed procedural regulations clearly intended to be an exhaustive statement of all the remedies to be granted or withheld in all foreseeable situations it would be obliged so far as possible not to step outside it. I am not aware of any body of arbitral rules which even aims to have this effect, but in any event I am confident that the ICC rules are of a quite different character. Even as regards proceedings within the arbitration itself the rules are of a highly permissive nature, and concerning recourse to outside agencies it is only through art 8(5) that they have anything at all to say. Once again, if the argument is sound for security for costs it must be equally sound for other forms of supportive relief. This proves too much. The fact that the parties have chosen ICC arbitration does, as I shall suggest, have something important to say about the way in which the parties want their disputes to be resolved and hence about the spirit in which the national court should approach a request for the exercise of powers created by the local law. But it is quite another matter to suggest that the mere presence of the rules dictates a policy of total non-intervention. At least so far as concerns the English court, the tenor of the discussion in *Channel Tunnel Group Ltd v Balfour Beatty Construction Ltd* [1993] 1 All ER 664, [1993] AC 384 shows that no such policy exists.

The second ground upon which it was urged that an order for security is objectionable in principle is that international conventions provide such effective means of ensuring that an award of costs is honoured that either the parties must be taken to have contracted on the basis that they would look to the conventions alone or the court, adopting a policy of minimum intervention, should not make any order in an arbitration which is not absolutely necessary. I see great practical problems with such an argument. The reasoning, if sound, must apply equally to all forms of international arbitration to which the conventions apply, including those characteristic of the maritime and commodity trades in which orders under s 12(6)(a) have been made for many years without any hint that they might be objectionable in principle. Furthermore, the same argument would apply equally to means taken in advance to ensure that a monetary award on the merits will not be frustrated by absence of funds. This would rule out the possibility of measures such as saisie conservatoire, which would surely be a retrograde step. In any event I am with respect unable to accept the reasoning. As regards the suggestion that the parties have impliedly agreed to look to the conventions alone I do not believe that the parties, if asked, would have agreed to abandon any of the ways in which an award might be rendered fruitful; as to the other grounds argued there seems no reason why the court should abstain from adding a further means to ensure that a party in default does not escape from its obligations simply because an existing procedure may in the event serve the purpose.

The next argument is that the present is a quintessentially one-off arbitration which marks it out from the run-of-the-mill London arbitrations and demands a different treatment. I must own to some difficulties with this expression. Elsewhere in the law of arbitration, 'one-off' denotes a unique contract, situation or problem which is unlikely to recur. Evidently *Bank Mellat v Helliniki Techniki SA* [1983] 3 All ER 428, [1984] QB 291 fell into this category, although the report of the facts does not disclose precisely why. But there is nothing unique about the present case. On the contrary it appears to be a typical ICC arbitration. True, the sum involved is large and the conflicting

allegations are serious but this is no reason for special treatment so far as
security for costs is concerned. In reality, the argument is no more than a
variant of the general proposition that an order by a national court for security
for costs is out of place in an ICC arbitration.

Finally, there is the argument that security for costs is an English
idiosyncrasy which should be excluded from the cosmopolitan world of
institutional arbitration. This is correct to the extent that most national
arbitration laws do not offer such a procedure, which is not surprising since
only the common law systems (and not all of these) enable a tribunal to order
the losing party to pay its opponent's costs. Yet art 20(1) of the ICC rules
acknowledges the propriety of an order for costs, and in my judgment it goes
too far to hold that the ancillary order for security must be rejected simply
because the majority of nations do not employ it. I shall later give full weight
to the special features of an order for security for costs and to the need to
ensure that a choice of venue does not critically affect the type of arbitral
procedure which ensues, but it seems to me that if a particular feature of
national law conduces to justice it should not be rejected simply because other
nations do not employ it. Otherwise, given the wide divergences between
national laws as to the way in which arbitrations can be most effectively
protected and sustained, the capability of international arbitration to face up to
a world in which it can no longer be taken for granted that parties will conduct
their disputes in an honourable manner will be seriously diminished.

My Lords, for these reasons I reject each of the arguments which are said to
yield an immediate solution for all arbitrations falling within a particular
category. Nevertheless, much of their substance reappears when the exercise
of the discretion is approached, as I believe it should be, on a case-to-case basis
in the light of the prime consideration that arbitration is a consensual process
and that the national court and arbitrators alike should strive to make the
consensus effective. The first step must therefore be to identify, so far as is
possible, the kind of arbitral procedure which the parties have envisaged.
Mainly, this will be concerned with proceedings within the arbitration itself.
Often the answer may be given directly by the incorporation of a set of
standard arbitration rules. In other instances the combination of the choice of
venue with the nature of the subject matter will yield an implied choice. For
example, in the days before maritime arbitration became the subject of
published contractual rules, the choice in a charterparty case of London
arbitration coupled with a provision that the arbitrators were to be commercial
men would be a very strong indication that the procedures were to take that
informal shape which had been commonplace in the resolution of such
disputes in London for many years. Similarly, in the small minority of cases
where the assistance of the court is invoked because the procedures in a trade
arbitration are said to have gone amiss, the parties by choosing London as a
venue might fairly be said to have expected the court to follow the generally
permissive approach to deviations from the procedural norm which the
English courts have adopted in relation to such arbitrations for many decades.
When one turns to the present case I believe that the foreign parties to a
contract governed by a foreign law and entirely performed abroad have by
choosing an ICC arbitration given an unmistakeable signal of their intentions,
even though the ICC rules have themselves nothing useful to say on the
matter. The signal may perhaps be difficult to spell out in detail but its
meaning is clear enough. Although the rules recognise, and experience has

shown, that different arbitral tribunals faced with different types of dispute may adopt procedures which differ widely in detail, ICC arbitrations tend to take very much the same general shape; and it is a procedure so shaped that the parties who have chosen ICC arbitration may be taken to desire. More than this they have signified that although the arbitration must perforce be physically located somewhere, it is the invariable framework of the ICC rather than the diverse local laws and practices which is to form the context within which the dispute is resolved. I would go further, and assert that the choice of ICC arbitration is an indication that the parties are looking for a relationship with particular national courts which is less closely coupled than would otherwise be the case.

My Lords, this is not to adopt a transnationalist approach in the accepted sense of the term. If it were, then no national court or legal system could have a part to play. As already stated, I believe this to be impossible in practice, and not what the parties intend. Recourse to a national court may be inevitable and if it has useful powers they should not be emasculated simply because they are not universally found. At the same time I believe that a court faced with a request for interim measures arising from an arbitration in which a body such as the ICC is involved should be careful not to cut across the parties' expectation of a general homogeneity of internal and external procedures, independent of the identity of the arbitrators and of the national legal regime prevailing in the place where they perform their tasks. It is for this reason that the House should in my opinion attach significance to the fact that in the international arbitrating community security of costs is very much a minority measure.

There is however another aspect of an order for security to which I attach even greater weight.

For present purposes, interim measures may be arranged in three groups. The object of them all is to support the agreement to arbitrate, but their effects are not at all the same. With the first group the national court lends its support by ordering purely procedural steps which the arbitrators either cannot order or cannot enforce; such as requiring an inspection of the subject matter immediately the dispute has arisen or compelling the attendance of an unwilling witness. The second group seeks to maintain the status quo pending the making of an award, so as to prevent one party from bringing about a change of circumstances adverse to the other which the arbitrators cannot adequately remedy. An interlocutory injunction is the most characteristic of these remedies. The third group consists of remedies designed to make sure that the award has the intended practical effect by causing one party to provide a fund to which recourse can be made by the other party if the first fails to honour an adverse award spontaneously. Saisie conservatoire and Mareva injunctions are typical of this kind of relief.

My Lords, it is I believe clear that the frame of mind in which a national court should approach the grant of such measures must be substantially influenced by the category into which they fall. In the case of the first group the court is concerned only to fill a gap which it can do without encroaching on the agreed procedure or the substantive decision-making powers of the arbitrators. With the third group an application for relief may call for some trespassing on the arbitrators' territory, since in some legal systems the court may be required to assess the apparent strength of the claim in order to decide whether it is just to make an order which interferes with the defendant's right to make free use of his funds. The second group potentially involves the greatest encroachment, for at the lowest the court will often find it necessary to consider whether a particular state of affairs which the arbitrators are being asked to create or declare (for example whether one party is obliged to do a certain act or abstain from doing another) is likely in the event to be created or declared by the award, in order to decide whether it is just to order holding relief in the shape of an injunction; and the intrusion will of course be even greater where (as in *Channel Tunnel Group Ltd v Balfour Beatty Construction Ltd* [1993] 1 All ER 664, [1993] AC 384) the interim measure takes the shape of an order that the party shall perform in advance of an award the very obligation the existence of which the arbitrators are in the course of deciding. It is in my judgment clear that the approach of the national court to the grant of interim relief should be conditioned to an important extent by the degree to which the particular remedy encroaches on the agreement that the arbitrators shall be the sole judges of the merits.

At first sight it may appear that this general approach does no harm to Coppée's application since an order for security of costs neither awards in advance something which it is the arbitrators' function to award nor calls for any preliminary assessment of the merits. Yet there is one respect in which such an order impinges much more fundamentally on the arbitration agreement than any of those already mentioned; for the order is almost invariably accompanied by a condition, such as was imposed in the present case, that until security is provided the arbitration will be stayed. Thus, notwithstanding that the parties have agreed that the claimant can and must submit his claim to arbitration, that art II of the New York Convention on the Recognition and Enforcement of Foreign Arbitral Awards (1958), UN Treaty Series (1959) 330 (see Mustill and Boyd *Commercial Arbitration* (2nd edn, 1989) App 2, p 725) requires the United Kingdom to recognise and enforce the agreement, and that *Bremer Vulkan Schiffbau Und Maschinenfabrik v South India Shipping Corp* [1981] 1 All ER 289, [1981] AC 909 put beyond doubt the general principle that the English court has no power to interfere directly with the conduct of the reference, an order for security will prohibit the claimant from proceeding with a validly constituted arbitration until he has put up the security, and will (if he is unable or unwilling to do so) prevent him from pursuing his claim at all. This is a powerful countervailing factor. I do not say that it is conclusive, for there are many international arbitrations in which it is, and may properly continue to be, the practice to make such orders. But I believe that in any case which is out of the ordinary the court should pause and look carefully for considerations which point the other way; and, in particular, should have regard to the particular type of arbitration in the course of which the application is brought.

I come at length to the exercise of the discretion in this particular case. Coppée is in a most unenviable position. It is forced into what is likely to be a long and very expensive arbitration by an insolvent claimant whose backers are willing to fund both halves of the ICC's requirement for a deposit and also presumably the considerable fees of its own lawyers without giving any sign that they will prove equally ready to part with their money if Ken-Ren loses the arbitration and is ordered to pay the costs. The network of national laws for the mutual enforcement of awards will not help Coppée if there are no assets against which to enforce. The fact remains however that an uncorrectable miscarriage of justice is something which parties risk by agreeing to entrust their disputes to a private dispute-resolution system which has very few internal resources to deal with someone who will not play fair. The parties choose arbitration for better or for worse. They relish the better features, of which there are many. When things take a turn for the worse there are limits beyond which they cannot be allowed, consistently with their arbitration agreement, to run to the courts for help. The problem in a case such as the present is to fix those limits. I have found it very difficult. In the end, and with much hesitation, I have come to the conclusion that an order for security for costs does not conform with the type of procedure which the parties have impliedly chosen, and that an order for security should be refused notwithstanding that on a narrower view it appears to answer the justice of the case.

My Lords, I have said nothing about the second appeal, to which the parties are Ken-Ren and Voest-Alpine AG, a company incorporated in Austria. The relevant terms of the contract are a little different, but the essential issue is the same as in the case of Coppée's appeal, and the answer must in my view be the same.

Accordingly, I would dismiss both appeals.

LORD SLYNN OF HADLEY. My Lords, I have had the advantage of reading the speeches prepared by my noble and learned friends Lord Mustill and Lord Woolf. Since they have both analysed the issues involved in this appeal in depth I set out my conclusions shortly.

In my opinion there is nothing in the ICC rules which necessarily excludes the jurisdiction of a national court to order security for costs; nor is the fact that many other legal systems do not provide for such an order sufficient to indicate that in arbitrations based on a set of rules adopted by an international institution, a national court cannot exercise a general power which it has to make such an order. The parties have chosen their forum, they must take its rules unless, as far as is lawfully possible, they expressly exclude them. In so far as concerns jurisdiction I do not find it acceptable to draw an absolute or even a clear-cut distinction between the present type of arbitration and commercial arbitrations held in London where frequently orders for security for costs are made. I am satisfied that there is jurisdiction in this class of arbitration to award security for costs even if the discretion to do so may not frequently be exercised in favour of making an order.

It is plainly not sufficient to justify an order that one or both of the parties is not ordinarily resident in the jurisdiction. There must be other factors indicating that the justice of the case requires that security should be ordered. Those factors exist in the present case. The respondents will not be able to pay the appellants' costs if the respondents lose; the government supporting the respondents will not be legally bound to pay the appellants' costs. On the other hand if the respondents win the appellants will have to pay the respondents' costs, the amount of which will presumably be reimbursed to the government.

In my opinion the justice of the case requires that an order for security of the costs should be made. I would accordingly allow the appeal; the matter must be referred back to the judge for him to fix the amount.

LORD WOOLF. My Lords, I have had the advantage of reading in draft the speech prepared by my noble and learned friend Lord Mustill. Based on his experience of the area of the law with which this appeal is concerned he has been able in his speech to place the important issue which we are required to decide as to international arbitrations and their relations with the High Court in its proper context. By doing this he has made clear what should be the general approach of the High Court when deciding how it should exercise its jurisdiction to grant interlocutory relief in the form of security for costs in connection with international arbitrations which are taking place in this country in accordance with the terms of an arbitration agreement, although the arbitrations otherwise have no connection with this country.

I am in complete agreement with that general approach. In particular I agree with Lord Mustill that, while the High Court has a discretion to order security for costs in the case of such an international arbitration, when deciding how it should exercise that discretion the court should place at the forefront of its consideration the fact that arbitration is a consensual process. Accordingly the court should strive to make the consensus effective by identifying, so far as possible, the kind of arbitrational process that the parties have either expressly or impliedly indicated that they were contemplating when they entered into the arbitration agreement. However, while there is so much of Lord Mustill's speech with which I agree, it is my misfortune to find myself in disagreement with him as to the ultimate step of his analysis which determines the outcome of this appeal; that is, as to whether this is a sufficiently exceptional case to justify departing from what should be the normal approach to ordering security for costs in arbitrations of this nature. Lord Mustill, for the reasons he expresses with such force and clarity, would make no order for security, though on a narrow approach he agrees an order would appear to answer the justice of the case. I, on the other hand, because I believe that this is a case which, as strongly as any case could, demonstrates as a matter of fairness that there should be security, consider that this is the very exceptional case in which an order should be made. The extent of my agreement with the speech of Lord Mustill does, however, enable me to set out my reasons shortly for differing as to the outcome of this appeal.

The appeal does not concern the extent of the English courts' jurisdiction. The extent of the jurisdiction is clearly laid down in s 12(6) of the Arbitration Act 1950. As that section states, in relation to each of the seven categories of order which are referred to in sub-s (6), for the purpose of and in relation to an arbitration the High Court has the same power as it has for the purpose of and in relation to an action or matter in the High Court. Furthermore, this is a jurisdiction which the parties to the arbitration are not in a position to oust whether by agreement or otherwise. However, as was explained convincingly by Kerr J in *Mavani v Ralli Bros Ltd* [1973] 1 All ER 555 at 560, [1973] 1 WLR 468 at 473–474, this does not mean that the parties cannot 'incorporate into their agreement or submission to arbitration provisions which would make it obviously unjust in all the circumstances to order security' for the simple reason that 'the question whether or not there should be security for costs is one which only affects the parties inter se, not the administration of justice in general'. This is true notwithstanding the fact that s 12(1), (2) and (3) of the 1950 Act is expressly subject to a contrary intention being expressed in the arbitration agreement, whereas s 12(6) contains no such statement. The difference between s 12(6) and the earlier subsections is explicable because the existence of an expression of a contrary intention means in the case of the other subsections that they can have no application, whereas in the case of s 12(6) the contrary intention, if it can be gleaned from the arbitration agreement, does not go to the existence of the power, but only to the manner in which the power should be exercised.

Unfortunately, however, the majority of arbitration agreements, particularly where they are of an international character of the type which is being considered here, do not make clear what are the parties' intentions with regard to exercise of the power of the High Court, contained in s 12(6)(a), to make an order for security of costs. In those circumstances, the court has no alternative but to exercise the power in a manner which it deems most closely accords with what would have been likely to have been agreed to be the appropriate approach by the parties if they had been required to deal with the question. This is of particular importance in relation to an order for security of costs since it is an order which is not normally an incident of litigation in the courts in this country and a type of order which is without a counterpart in many jurisdictions. It cannot therefore be readily assumed that the power to make such an order was a power which the parties intended should be exercised when they entered into the arbitration agreement. This is so even if, as here, the parties have by electing London as the seat of the arbitration made it clear that in general English legal procedure should apply to the conduct of the arbitration. When faced with an application for security in relation to such an arbitration, the general approach of the courts has to be to look at all the circumstances and to ask whether it is consistent with the nature of the arbitration agreement for an order for security for costs to be made. This, as it appears to me, is an approach which the Court of Appeal was seeking to adopt in *Bank Mellat v Helliniki Techniki SA* [1983] 3 All ER 428, [1984] QB 291. In that case, although there was a difference, at least in emphasis, between the approach in the judgment of Robert Goff LJ from that adopted in the judgment of Kerr LJ, with whom Waller LJ agreed, as I read their judgments both Robert Goff and Kerr LJJ were seeking to perform basically the same exercise: that is, by examining all the circumstances, deciding whether this was a class of arbitration in which it would ever be appropriate to make an order for security for costs and if so whether on the particular facts of the case an order should be made. Having performed this exercise in relation to the category of arbitration which is conducted in accordance with the ICC rules where the only connection the arbitration had with this country was that it was the seat of the arbitration, Kerr LJ came to the conclusion—

> 'that in an arbitration under the ICC rules, which has no connection with this country other than that it had been agreed between foreign parties that any such arbitration was to take place here, it would be inappropriate in principle to make an order for security for costs on the ground that the claimant is ordinarily resident abroad [and] that the claimant may be unable to pay the other party's costs if the award requires him to do so.'

(See [1983] 3 All ER 428 at 438, [1984] QB 291 at 309–310.)

Robert Goff LJ, on the other hand, came to the conclusion that the parties by incorporating the ICC's rules in their contract had not given an indication which made it inappropriate in any circumstances to make an order for security for costs. The situation was one where because it was—

> 'a typical international arbitration ... prima facie no order for security for costs should be made against [the defendant] as foreign claimant unless

there are special circumstances justifying such an order.' (See [1983] 3 All ER 428 at 442, [1984] QB 291 at 316.)

The fact that the arbitration was in accordance with the ICC rules was not a matter to which Robert Goff LJ attached 'any particular weight ... save that that fact serves to emphasise the character of the international arbitration' with which the court was there concerned. Robert Goff LJ, having come to that conclusion, goes on to make apparent the real difference between his approach and that of Kerr LJ by stating that if in such an arbitration there was reason to believe that the claimant would be unable to pay the costs of the respondent if unsuccessful in his defence, then—

'it would be proper for the court, in an appropriate case, by virtue of s 447 of the Companies Act 1948 or by analogy with that section, to exercise its discretion to order the claimant to furnish security for the respondent's costs.' (See [1983] 3 All ER 428 at 443, [1984] QB 291 at 316.)

The fact that two judges, both of whom have immense experience of arbitrations of this nature, can come to a different conclusion of this nature illustrates how finely balanced the outcome of the exercise of discretion can be. (The same is true of the comments made by Lloyd LJ which indicate that he was by no means happy about the result to which the Court of Appeal in the present case was compelled by authority to come.) Their approach is very different from that which had been adopted 22 years earlier by Mocatta J in *Hudson Strumpffabrik GmbH v Bentley Engineering Co Ltd* [1962] 3 All ER 460 at 464, [1962] 2 QB 587 at 592–593 where he reflected the then attitude by saying:

'... a foreign resident who enters into a contract with an English arbitration clause, without any special procedural provisions, may not unfairly be taken to have accepted the English procedural law for better or for worse. He may find the practice as to security for costs unwelcome, but he will often find other English procedural rules, particularly as to discovery, not only novel, but also of significant assistance to his case. I can find no distinction between the circumstances of an action and an arbitration sufficient to warrant any departure in dealing with applications for security for costs in arbitrations from the rule of practice to which I have referred ... the phraseology of s. 12(6) of the Arbitration Act, 1950, strongly suggests that there is none.'

The *Bank Mellat* case was considered by Bingham LJ in a judgment with which the other members of the court agreed in *K/S A/S Bani v Korea Shipbuilding & Engineering Corp* [1987] 2 Lloyd's Rep 445. That was a case which involved disputes under two shipbuilding contracts which gave rise to international arbitrations in which the connection with this country was limited to the fact that it was stated to be the place of arbitration. As Bingham LJ pointed out (at 448):

'While the existence of any discretion necessarily means that there is an area within which the Judge's decision is final and unchallengeable, it is highly desirable that the general lines on which a familiar discretion will be exercised should be generally known and broadly predictable. The present case illustrates the point. Here are two highly experienced firms of shipping solicitors who deal with each other constantly. The arbitration is one which, however complex its peculiar facts, is of a very familiar kind. The application for security is of the most routine kind. The Commercial Judge will deal with several each week. But the argument will usually be short and relate to quantum only, and security will usually be given by agreement or not applied for. This is because practitioners have a very shrewd idea what to expect, so that expensive and time-consuming contests can be avoided. It is important that this should be so. Unless advisers are able to make a fairly accurate prediction of the likely outcome of a contested application of this kind, they can give their clients no reliable advice and the issue will be repeatedly put to the test. This would not be in the interest of litigants as a whole, let alone of other Commercial Court users. It is of course impossible to eliminate all uncertainty how a discretion will be exercised, because two cases are rarely identical and special features will strike different minds in different ways. But some general uniformity of approach and practice is in my view desirable.'

These words are very apposite to the issue now before their Lordships and it is important, if the courts are going to play a proper role in supporting international arbitrations, that the situation should not be left as a result of this appeal in a position where it is not reasonably clear what are the circumstances in which an order for security for costs is likely to be or not to be granted.

In the *Korea Shipbuilding* case Bingham LJ went on to consider the similarities and dissimilarities between the facts of that case and those in *Bank Mellat v Helliniki Techniki SA* [1983] 3 All ER 428, [1984] QB 291. It is sufficient to draw attention to the following dissimilarities which he identified (see [1987] 2 Lloyd's Rep 445 at 452). First, the proper law of the contract was English; second, unlike in the *Bank Mellat* case, the parties did not incorporate a detailed code of procedural rules other than ordinary English rules of procedure; and third, the arbitration was 'to be regarded as regular London business as the *Bank Mellat* arbitration could not'.

Having considered the similarities and dissimilarities, Bingham LJ came to the conclusion that the case was distinguishable from the *Bank Mellat* case because whether the test adumbrated by Kerr LJ or that favoured by Robert Goff LJ was applied, the differences between the circumstances of the case and those under consideration in *Bank Mellat* placed it firmly in the category of arbitrations in which orders for security are in general appropriate. That is to say, it was—

'a type of maritime arbitration which has for many years and regularly been conducted in London. It cannot accurately be described as a quintessential one-off arbitration ...' (See [1987] 2 Lloyd's Rep 445 at 453.)

Security was therefore granted in that case and Bingham LJ concluded his judgment by saying (at 456):

'It was not suggested in argument that this is a case in which we could or should undertake any radical review of the practice of awarding security for costs in arbitrations. That is a matter on which two broad views may be taken. To some the ordering of security may appear to be an unwarranted intrusion of the court into a consensual procedure. To others it may seem just that those obliged to resist claims made in arbitrations in this country should not be at risk in costs if they do so successfully. The former view may perhaps appeal more to claimants, the latter to respondents. But many commercial and maritime enterprises

find themselves sometimes in one role, sometimes in the other. Three
brief points may be worth making. First, there is not (as I think) any
evidence of general dissatisfaction with the English practice in this field as
it has been applied in recent years. Secondly, even since the *Bank Mellat*
decision, the occasions on which applications for security have been
resisted in principle have been very few indeed. Such contests remain a
rarity. Thirdly, while Lord Justice Donaldson pointed out in the *Hitachi*
case (*Hitachi Shipbuilding & Engineering Co Ltd v Viafiel Compania Naviera SA*
[1981] 2 Lloyd's Rep 498 at 505) the virtue of conferring on arbitrators a
statutory power to order security with a stay if security were not given, he
did not suggest that the power was in itself one which should be curtailed
or eliminated. All in all, there is no reason to think that the guidance
recently given in *Bank Mellat* calls for revision, even if it were open to us
to revise it.'

While I draw considerable assistance from the judgment of Bingham LJ, the
same issue having come before your Lordships, I consider that I should make
it clear that in agreement with what I believe to be the the approach of Lord
Mustill I regard Kerr LJ as overstating the situation when he indicated that it
would be inappropriate as a matter of principle to make an order for security
in the present class of arbitration. This does not, however, affect in any way
the correctness of the decision which was reached in that case.

The approach which I would adopt, not being restricted by the decision in
that case, is that with an arbitration of the class here being considered
incorporating the ICC rules, but only having very limited connection with this
country, it is not right to say that there will never be circumstances in which it
will be appropriate to order security for costs, only that it will be rarely right
to do so. In the exceptional case, however, it is important that the court should
exercise its jurisdiction. In the exceptional case, far from undermining the
nature of the arbitration the order can support it. Once it is accepted that the
arbitration is one where the arbitrator in due course will have to consider
making an order that one party has to pay the other party's costs, it is apparent
that an order which has the result of preventing that power being nullified is
one which should be regarded as supporting the arbitration. In this respect it
is as supportive of the award, so far as it relates to costs, as a Mareva injunction
will be in respect of the quantum of the award. Mere lack of means of a party
is not, however, in ordinary circumstances sufficient by itself to justify the
grant of security in this class of arbitration. The parties must be taken to accept
the risks involved in the other party in the ordinary way, while having the
means necessary to enable him to take part in the arbitration, lacking the
means, if he is unsuccessful, to meet his opponent's costs.

Turning back to the facts of this case, the conclusion that I would come to is
that it falls within the exceptional category. This is not a case in which all that
is relied upon is the insolvency of the claimant as in *Bank Mellat*. There is the
additional factor, which I regard as being critical, that the arbitration is being
funded by a third party, namely, the state of Kenya. If the proceedings are
successful, as they could well be, the state, while it will not be the sole
beneficiary, will be a principal beneficiary and if there is an order for costs the
money it has invested in the proceedings could well be reimbursed as a result
of an order that the appellants pay costs. If the proceedings are unsuccessful
the respondents will almost certainly have insufficient means to pay costs and
the state, which has the means, will have no responsibility for paying costs.

This means that the appellants will be deprived, in reality, of the advantage of having an order for costs made in their favour against the unsuccessful party, which is a feature of arbitrations, even of this character, which are by agreement conducted in this country and which the parties are regarded as having accepted. For the English courts to exercise their undoubted jurisdiction to intervene and order security for costs in this situation avoids the risk of a third party, while financing what could prove to be unfounded litigation, sheltering behind an impoverished party so as to escape what would be otherwise a normal consequence as to costs of being unsuccessful in the arbitration. This seems to me to be the sort of exceptional situation where even in a case of an arbitration conducted under the ICC rules, it could not be said that the intervention of the English court is in any way inappropriate. Indeed if it is not appropriate to make an order in this case, then I have difficulty in envisaging any case in which it would be appropriate to make an order. Dismissing this appeal would, therefore, from a practical point of view, be equivalent to confirming the approach indicated by Kerr LJ. I accept that if the order for security is not complied with this would mean that the arbitration would come to a halt but this in practice is likely to be the result where any party who initiates arbitration proceedings fails to comply with orders made under any of the provisions of s 12(6). In the special circumstances of this case, I would therefore allow the appeals and refer the matter back to the judge to assess what security would be appropriate.

The fact that I take the view that in the very exceptional circumstances which exist here it is appropriate to order security in an ICC arbitration of this sort raises two consequential problems. The first is, to what other arbitrations the same approach should be adopted. Here I find it difficult to lay down precisely any appropriate boundaries. Bearing in mind the judgment of Bingham LJ to which I have referred, this is unfortunate but the requirement of exceptional circumstances should restrict the uncertainty. I would, however, add that nothing I have said should be regarded as indicating any dissent from the present practice which is adopted in relation to the type of arbitration which is regularly heard in this country in relation to which orders for security for costs are frequently made. While it may be difficult sometimes to identify arbitrations which fall within this class, those who practice in the field, including the judges of the commercial courts, will rarely have difficulty in identifying the cases to which I refer. The distinguishing feature of those cases from the present one is that any overseas parties who choose to have that kind of arbitration conducted here should be taken to appreciate that they will be subject to the current practice with regard to security for costs applied by the Commercial Court. If they do not wish to be subject to that policy then they should indicate this in their arbitration agreement. There will remain cases which do not fall within either category. However, so far as those cases are concerned the final paragraph of the judgment of Bingham LJ in *K/S A/S Bani v Korea Shipbuilding & Engineering Corp* [1987] 2 Lloyd's Rep 445 at 456, which I have cited, leads me to believe they will not be large in numbers.

There remains the issue raised by the respondents in their respondents' notice. Mr Gross QC was anxious to persuade your Lordships to hear an argument in support of that notice but your Lordships declined to do so. The issue which Mr Gross wished to raise was that if the English courts had power to order security for costs they should decline to do so because the issue is much better dealt with in the arbitration, assuming the arbitrator had power to consider the issue. In relation to this issue, your Lordships did not have the advantage of the views of the ICC or the arbitrators or the lower courts. Although their views would only be persuasive, I consider that, on an issue of this importance to the arbitration world, it would be undesirable for your Lordships to express their opinion without having been informed of the views to which I have referred.

Appeals allowed.

Celia Fox   Barrister.

R v Keane

COURT OF APPEAL, CRIMINAL DIVISION
LORD TAYLOR OF GOSFORTH CJ, AULD AND MITCHELL JJ
15 FEBRUARY, 14 MARCH 1994

Criminal evidence – Prosecution evidence – Disclosure of police sources of information to defence – Public interest immunity – Confidentiality of sources – Weight of public interest in non-disclosure to be balanced against importance of documents to defence – Material documents to be put before court.

On 16 February 1991 the police obtained a warrant permitting them to search the appellant's home in Birmingham on the grounds that there was a reasonable suspicion that he was involved in a currency counterfeiting operation. On 19 February the appellant, while driving a car in London with two other men, was stopped by police on suspicion that a passenger in the car had assaulted a motorist in Birmingham in 1990. The three occupants of the car were arrested in connection with the assault and taken to a police station where the car, which did not belong to the appellant, was searched and counterfeit US dollar notes and counterfeiting material and implements were found. When interviewed the appellant stated that the items found in the car had nothing to do with him. When his house in Birmingham was then searched pursuant to the search warrant obtained three days earlier, the police found a white envelope with serial numbers consistent with numbers necessary to make counterfeit US bank notes. At his trial on counterfeiting charges the appellant did not give evidence and his defence was that he was merely the driver of the car, that he knew nothing of the incriminating articles, and that they had been planted in the car by one of the passengers on the instructions of undercover officers with a view to turning the passenger into an informer. The trial judge ruled that on the grounds of public interest immunity the prosecution was not required to reveal the sources of the information leading to the appellant's arrest on 19 February. The appellant was convicted. He appealed on the grounds that the judge's ruling was wrong.

Held – Where the prosecution refused, on the grounds of public interest immunity, to disclose relevant material to the defence, the court had to balance the weight of public interest in non-disclosure against the importance of the documents to the defence. In carrying out that balancing exercise the court

should always order disclosure if the disputed material might prove the
defendant's innocence or avoid a miscarriage of justice. In order to put the
court in a position to determine whether and to what extent the material which
the Crown wished to withhold was of assistance to the defence, the
prosecution was required to put before the court only those documents which
it regarded as material but wished to withhold. Material documents included
those which could be seen on a sensible appraisal by the prosecution to be
relevant or possibly relevant to an issue in the case, or which raised or possibly
raised a new issue whose existence was not apparent from the evidence the
prosecution proposed to use, or which held out a real, as opposed to fanciful,
prospect of providing a lead on evidence which went to a relevant or new issue.
Since there was undoubtedly a public interest in not disclosing the material
withheld by the Crown and the material would not have assisted the defence
no injustice had been caused to the appellant by the non-disclosure. The
appeal would therefore be dismissed (see p 483 *h j*, p 484 *e* to *g j* to p 485 *c* to *f h
j*, post).

R v Agar [1990] 2 All ER 442 and *R v Governor of Brixton Prison, ex p Osman (No
1)* [1992] 1 All ER 108 applied.

Per curiam. Ex parte applications are contrary to the general principle of
open justice in criminal trials and and should not be adopted save on the
application of the Crown to enable the court to discharge its function of testing
a claim that public interest immunity or sensitivity justifies non-disclosure of
material in the possession of the Crown (see p 483 *c d*, post).

Notes
For disclosure of unused material to defence, see 11(2) *Halsbury's Laws* (4th edn reissue) paras 1104, 1119.

For exclusion of evidence on grounds of public policy, see 11(2) *Halsbury's Laws* (4th edn reissue) para 1164, and for cases on the subject, see 15(2) *Digest* (2nd reissue) 178–179, 19771–19774.

Cases referred to in judgment
Marks v Beyfus (1890) 25 QBD 494, CA.
R v Agar [1990] 2 All ER 442, CA.
R v Davis [1993] 2 All ER 643, [1993] 1 WLR 613, CA.
R v Governor of Brixton Prison, ex p Osman (No 1) [1992] 1 All ER 108, [1992] 1 WLR 281, DC.
R v Hennessey (Timothy) (1978) 68 Cr App R 419, CA.
R v Melvin and Dingle (20 December 1993, unreported), CCC.
R v Ward [1993] 2 All ER 577, [1993] 1 WLR 619, CA.

Cases also cited
Practice Note [1982] 1 All ER 734, CA.
Makanjuola v Comr of Police of the Metropolis (1989) [1992] 3 All ER 617, DC.
R v Miller (9 February 1993, unreported), CCC.
R v Saunders (20 September 1989, unreported), CCC.
R v Smith (2 November 1993, unreported), CCC.

Appeal against conviction
Stephen John Keane appealed against his conviction on 23 October 1992 at the
Central Criminal Court before Judge Rogers QC and a jury on two counts of

having custody or control of counterfeit notes (counts 1 and 2) and one count of having custody and control of counterfeiting materials and implements (count 3) for which he was sentenced to four years' imprisonment on count 1, five years' imprisonment on count 2 and six years' imprisonment on count 3, all the terms to run concurrently. The facts are set out in the judgment of the court.

Mio Sylvester (assigned by the *Registrar of Criminal Appeals*) for the appellant.
Stephen Kramer (instructed by the *Crown Prosecution Service*) for the Crown.

Cur adv vult

14 March 1994. The following judgment of the court was delivered.

LORD TAYLOR OF GOSFORTH CJ. This case concerns the problems arising when a trial judge is invited by the defence to order disclosure of documents and is invited by the Crown to refuse such disclosure in the public interest.

On 23 October 1992 at the Central Criminal Court before Judge Rogers QC the appellant was convicted of two offences of having custody or control of counterfeit notes (counts 1 and 2—count 1 by a majority of ten to two) and one offence of having custody or control of counterfeiting materials and implements (count 3).

On 30 October 1992 he was sentenced to four years' imprisonment on count 1, five years' imprisonment on count 2 and six years' imprisonment on count 3. Those sentences were ordered to run concurrently and an order was made for the forfeiture of the counterfeit currency.

There had originally been two co-accused, Ian Shipman and John Dunbar. Shipman and Dunbar were dealt with before the appellant. All three had been committed for trial together on bail on 8 May 1991. The trial was fixed for 7 October 1991. The appellant failed to surrender on that date. The next day, 8 October 1991, the case against Shipman and Dunbar proceeded with the appellant still absent. A submission was made to the trial judge, Judge Gordon, on behalf of both Shipman and Dunbar that the prosecution should disclose the sources of their information. Having heard the nature of the defence of each of the two defendants, the learned judge ruled in favour of disclosure in Shipman's case but not in the case of Dunbar. The Crown thereupon offered no evidence against Shipman who was discharged. Dunbar changed his plea to guilty on count 1. He also pleaded guilty on a second indictment to possessing a firearm without a certificate. He was sentenced to consecutive sentences of three years' and 12 months' imprisonment. The appellant was not rearrested until 7 July 1992 and he was tried alone over five days in October 1992. His appeal against conviction is brought by leave of the single judge.

The chronology of the case was as follows: on 24 November 1990, a motorist had been assaulted in Birmingham and the assailant had driven away in a Mercedes car of which the number was recorded at the time.

On 16 February 1991 the police obtained a warrant permitting them to search the appellant's home in Birmingham on the grounds that there was reasonable suspicion that he was involved in a currency counterfeiting operation.

About 10.25 pm on 19 February 1991 the appellant was driving a Mercedes car in Edgware Road near Marble Arch with Dunbar as front seat passenger and Shipman in the rear. The car belonged to Shipman and bore the registration number recorded on 24 November 1990. Two police officers, Det Con Page and Det Sgt Watters, with others in attendance, stopped the vehicle on suspicion that one or other of the occupants may have been the assailant on 24 November. According to the police, the appellant opened the driver's door and was seen to place an envelope into the pocket on the door. The three men were arrested in connection with the assault and taken to a police station. There, the car was searched and four separate items were found. First, a white envelope containing two negatives for forging $US 100 notes was recovered from the driver's door pocket (count 3). Second, a brown envelope containing 247 forged $US 100 notes was found in the glove compartment (count 2). Third, 1504 forged US dollar notes in a brown paper bag contained in a white plastic bag were recovered from the rear seat footwell under the front passenger seat (count 1). Finally, a piece of paper with US dollar notes printed on it in a man's leather wallet was found in the front passenger footwell.

Four fingermarks on the outside of the white envelope were found to have been made by the appellant and were said by the Crown to indicate that the envelope had been handled more than once by him.

Meanwhile, a search of the appellant's address in Birmingham, pursuant to the search warrant which had been obtained three days earlier, took place at 12.45 am on 20 February. It revealed a black briefcase containing the appellant's business documents but including a white envelope with serial numbers consistent with the numbers necessary to make counterfeit US bank notes.

The appellant's immediate response was that what had been found in the car had nothing to do with him.

In interview, the appellant said he did not know how the negatives came to be in the car. He saw the envelope containing them in the pouch in the driver's door. He admitted examining the envelope. He thought it was a birthday card but on seeing that it was a dollar imprint, did not ask Dunbar about it. He said he had seen the envelope in the glove compartment at about 9 pm that night. The first thing that occurred to him was that it may have contained dollars. He denied any knowledge of the other two items found. He said he had come to London to see a girlfriend and had spent the afternoon with her in Covent Garden and in a wine bar, rejoining his two co-accused in the evening preparatory to driving home.

The appellant did not give evidence on his own behalf. The scope of the defence cross-examination of the police officers must be mentioned later. But in the result, it was put to them that they had not seen the appellant place the envelope in the car door pocket. It was suggested that the counterfeit items had been given to Dunbar by undercover officers with a view to turning Dunbar into an informer. Essentially, the case put was that the appellant was merely the driver who knew nothing of the incriminating articles and merely happened to be in the wrong place at the wrong time.

The grounds of this appeal are based solely on the learned judge's rulings as to disclosure and the scope of cross-examination he permitted. At the start of the trial, the judge was invited to order the prosecution to disclose the sources of the information leading to the appellant's arrest on 19 February. Mr Sylvester pointed to the unusual circumstances of that arrest. A number of officers were involved, some quite senior. The reason given for the arrest concerned a minor assault which had occurred some months earlier. Yet three

days before the arrest, a search warrant relating to counterfeiting had been
obtained which had not been executed before the counterfeit notes were found
in the car. Counsel accepted that the general rule was in favour of protecting
the identity of informers, but he cited *R v Hennessey* (1978) 68 Cr App R 419 and
R v Agar [1990] 2 All ER 442.

The court observed in *R v Hennessey* (1978) 68 Cr App R 419 at 425:

'The Courts appreciate the need to protect the identity of informers, not
only for their own safety but to ensure that the supply of information
about criminal activities does not dry up: see *Marks v. Beyfus* (1890) 25
QBD 494. In general this should be the approach of the Courts; but cases
may occur when for good reason the need to protect the liberty of the
subject should prevail over the need to protect informers. It will be for the
accused to show that there is good reason.'

In *R v Agar* [1990] 2 All ER 442 at 448 Mustill LJ said:

'Now it is certainly not the case that a defendant can circumvent the rule
of public policy so as to find out the name of the person who has informed
on him, for his own future reference and possible reprisal, simply by
pretending that something is part of his case, when in truth it adds nothing
to it. And it may be, and we emphasise "may", that if the defence is
manifestly frivolous and doomed to failure the trial judge may conclude
that it must be sacrificed to the general public interest in the protection of
informers. We do not see the present case in this light. There was a
strong, and absent to any contrary indication, overwhelming public
interest in keeping secret the source of information; but as the authorities
show, there was an even stronger public interest in allowing a defendant
to put forwards a tenable case in its best light.'

In reliance particularly on the latter passage, Mr Sylvester submitted that
there were in the present case various possibilities such as that the appellant
had been 'set up', and that to enable him to 'put forward a tenable case in its
best light' disclosure should be ordered. The learned judge rejected the
application and ruled that the police could be asked in cross-examination as to
the source of their information but that an officer need not answer such a
question 'unless he wishes to'.

Mr Sylvester renewed his application after the arresting officers had given
evidence and before Det Chief Insp Hose was called. This was because it had
been agreed that the arresting officers would not answer questions as to
investigations prior to 10.25 pm on 19 February, but such questions were to be
addressed to the detective chief inspector. Mr Sylvester submitted that it was
now clear there must be observation logs, and possibly other documents which
might support the appellant's case. He invited the judge to change his earlier
ruling. The judge refused to order disclosure of documents. After some
extended discussion, he ruled that Mr Sylvester could put positive assertions in
cross-examination and could ask the chief inspector about his sources of
information but it was for the witness to decide whether he could answer
without divulging that which the Crown wished to protect.

In this appeal, complaint is made that the learned judge was wrong in
refusing to order disclosure of the information sought. Further, the effect of
his rulings was wrongly to leave the police witnesses as the sole arbiters of
whether they should answer questions put in cross-examination or not.

At the time of this trial the procedural rules laid down following *R v Ward* [1992] 2 All ER 577, [1992] 1 WLR 619 had not yet been stated. Even *R v Ward* itself was not yet reported although a transcript of part of the judgment was quoted to the learned judge. *R v Davis* [1993] 2 All ER 643, [1993] 1 WLR 613, in which this court outlined the procedure to be followed where the Crown rely on public interest immunity or sensitivity to withhold material, had not yet been decided. Clearly, this case fell within para (3) of the tabulation at [1993] 2 All ER 643 at 647, [1993] 1 WLR 613 at 617. The Crown should have notified the defence before the trial began that an ex parte application was to be made to the court and such an application should have been made so that the trial judge could himself have seen the material and heard the Crown's reasons for not wishing to disclose it before making his ruling.

We wish to stress that ex parte applications are contrary to the general principle of open justice in criminal trials. They were sanctioned in *R v Davis* solely to enable the court to discharge its function in testing a claim that public interest immunity or sensitivity justifies non-disclosure of material in the possession of the Crown. Accordingly, the ex parte procedure should not be adopted, save on the application of the Crown and only for that specific purpose.

In fairness to the learned judge, not only had this procedure not been laid down, but he was not invited by either side to view the material himself. In the event, he was at a disadvantage in not knowing the precise scope of the information the Crown were seeking to protect. All he had to go on was the statement by prosecuting counsel that objection was made to disclosing this unused material 'for reasons of public policy within the Attorney General's guidelines'. Accordingly, having been apprised that the scope of the refusal was to protect sources of information, the learned judge resorted to letting the police witnesses decide how far they would answer questions. It became clear that they were not prepared to answer questions about investigations or surveillance prior to 10.25 pm on 19 February.

Before the appeal came on, no doubt conscious of the decision in *R v Davis*, the Crown gave notice to the appellant's lawyers that an ex parte application was being made to this court to look at the undisclosed material and to hear the Crown ex parte so as to decide whether disclosure should be made for the purposes of the appeal. Accordingly, each member of this court received and read that material before the appeal was opened.

Where the prosecution rely on public interest immunity or sensitivity, given that it is for the court to decide whether disclosure is to be made and the scope of cross-examination, what ought the court's approach to be? As the citations from *R v Hennessey* and *R v Agar* above show, the court has to carry out a balancing exercise. As Mann LJ put it in *R v Governor of Brixton Prison ex p Osman (No 1)* [1992] 1 All ER 108 at 116, [1991] 1 WLR 281 at 288:

> 'Suffice it to say for the moment that a judge is balancing on the one hand the desirability of preserving the public interest in the absence of disclosure against, on the other hand, the interests of justice. Where the interests of justice arise in a criminal case touching and concerning liberty ... the weight to be attached to the interest of justice is plainly very great indeed.'

It has been suggested that there are two classes of case: those in which the balancing exercise must be carried out and those in which the possibility of a miscarriage of justice dictates that disclosure must be made without any balancing exercise. To support this proposition, Mr Sylvester referred to the judgment of Lord Esher MR in *Marks v Beyfus* (1890) 25 QBD 494 at 498, as follows:

> '... if upon the trial of a prisoner the judge should be of the opinion that disclosure of the name of the informant is necessary or right to shew the prisoner's innocence, then one public policy is in conflict with another public policy, and that which says that an innocent man is not to be condemned when his innocence can be proved is the policy that must prevail.'

In *R v Governor of Brixton, ex p Osman* (*No 1*) [1992] 1 All ER 108 at 118, [1991] 1 WLR 281 at 290 Mann LJ said:

> 'In those cases, which establish a privilege in regard to information leading to the detection of crime, there are observations to the effect that the privilege cannot prevail if the evidence is necessary for the prevention of a miscarriage of justice. No balance is called for. If admission is necessary to prevent miscarriage of justice, balance does not arise.'

We prefer to say that the outcome in the instances given by Lord Esher MR and Mann LJ results from performing the balancing exercise, not from dispensing with it. If the disputed material may prove the defendant's innocence or avoid a miscarriage of justice, then the balance comes down resoundingly in favour of disclosing it.

But how is it to be determined whether and to what extent the material which the Crown wish to withhold may be of assistance to the defence?

First, it is for the prosecution to put before the court only those documents which it regards as material but wishes to withhold. As to what documents are 'material' we would adopt the test suggested by Jowitt J in *R v Melvin and Dingle* (20 December 1993, unreported). The learned judge said:

> 'I would judge to be material in the realm of disclosure that which can be seen on a sensible appraisal by the prosecution: (1) to be relevant or possibly relevant to an issue in the case; (2) to raise or possibly raise a new issue whose existence is not apparent from the evidence the prosecution proposes to use; (3) to hold out a real (as opposed to fanciful) prospect of providing a lead on evidence which goes to (1) or (2).'

As was pointed out later in that judgment, it is open to the defence to indicate to the prosecution a defence or an issue they propose to raise as to which material in the possession of the prosecution may be of assistance, and if that is done the prosecution may need to reconsider what should be disclosed.

We also wish, in passing, to indorse the observations of the learned judge in that case as to the scope of the Crown's duty. It would be an abdication of that duty for the prosecution, out of an over-abundance of caution, simply to dump all its unused material into the court's lap and leave it to the judge to sort through it all regardless of its materiality to the issues present or potential. The prosecution must identify the documents and information which are material according to the criteria set out above. Having identified what is material, the prosecution should disclose it unless they wish to maintain that public interest immunity or other sensitivity justifies withholding some or all of it. Only that part which is both material in the estimation of the prosecution and sought to be withheld should be put before the court for its decision. If in an exceptional case the prosecution are in doubt about the materiality of some documents or information, the court may be asked to rule on that issue.

Secondly, when the court is seized of the material, the judge has to perform the balancing exercise by having regard on the one hand to the weight of the public interest in non-disclosure. On the other hand, he must consider the importance of the documents to the issues of interest to the defence, present and potential, so far as they have been disclosed to him or he can foresee them. Accordingly, the more full and specific the indication the defendant's lawyers give of the defence or issues they are likely to raise, the more accurately both prosecution and judge will be able to assess the value to the defence of the material.

In the present case, the appellant had suggested in his interviews the nature of his case especially as to his own movements on the day of the arrest. Counsel, in making his application to the trial judge, was very forthcoming as to the issues he hoped that prosecution disclosure might have addressed.

Having examined the material which the Crown put before us, we are wholly satisfied of two matters. First, there was undoubtedly a public interest in not disclosing the material withheld by the Crown. Second, that material, had it been disclosed, would not have assisted the defence at all. On the contrary, it would have assisted the prosecution. We have no doubt that if the learned judge had been shown the material, he would have decided that the balance was clearly in favour of non-disclosure. We are satisfied that no injustice was done to this appellant by his not having access to the documents we have seen.

Likewise, we consider that the restriction of cross-examination and the stance the police were allowed to take in response to cross-examination resulted in no unfairness to the defendant. It would not have been possible to have allowed any significantly greater scope to defending counsel in questioning the police without putting at risk information which, on balance, clearly needed to be protected. In the event, the appellant was able to put his case as to where he was and what he was doing during the day on 19 February and what his function was in the car. The jury had to make up their minds whether they believed the police as to the appellant putting the white envelope in the pocket of the car door and the other circumstances of the arrest. It was open to them to draw inferences from the finding of the counterfeit money and equipment in the car, from the appellant's answers in interview and from the document found in the appellant's briefcase at his home. Since the appellant did not give evidence, he did nothing to cast doubt on the prosecution evidence or undermine it.

In these circumstances, we see no grounds for regarding the jury's verdict as unsafe or unsatisfactory. The appeal must be dismissed.

Appeal dismissed. Application refused.

N P Metcalfe Esq   Barrister.

Bolton v Law Society

COURT OF APPEAL, CIVIL DIVISION
SIR THOMAS BINGHAM MR, ROSE AND WAITE LJJ
6 DECEMBER 1993

Solicitor – Disciplinary proceedings – Sentence – Solicitor improperly disbursing client funds instead of placing them in client account – Solicitor subsequently making good shortage in client account – Solicitor an honest man who had not stolen client's moneys in a premeditated fashion or embarked on a deliberate course of dishonest conduct – Solicitors Disciplinary Tribunal suspending solicitor from practice for two years – Divisional Court quashing order for suspension and substituting fine – Whether court right to do so.

In 1989 a solicitor whose wife had agreed to sell a flat in her house to her brother acted for all the parties in the transaction. The brother agreed to purchase the flat with the assistance of a building society mortgage and the solicitor received a cheque for £45,000 from the building society. However, he did not place the money in his client account, as was his duty, but disbursed the whole sum. The sale was never completed and documentation in regard to the building society's security was never executed. In 1990 an accountant from the Solicitors Complaints Bureau discovered the shortage in the client account. The solicitor admitted that he had misused the building society funds and made good the shortage in full. The complaints bureau complained to the Solicitors Disciplinary Tribunal that the solicitor had misapplied funds received from the building society. The tribunal held that the solicitor's conduct was wholly unacceptable and very serious and would ordinarily have merited his being struck off the Roll of Solicitors, but since he was an honest man who had not stolen his clients' moneys in a premeditated fashion or embarked on a deliberate course of dishonest conduct, he would be suspended from practice for two years. The solicitor appealed to the Divisional Court and, pending the appeal, the tribunal's order for suspension was stayed. The Divisional Court allowed the appeal and substituted a fine of £3000 on the grounds that there was no dishonesty on the solicitor's part, that in practice there was not much difference between an order of suspension and a striking off order since the solicitor's chance of recovering a practice after two years would be virtually non-existent, that the penalty imposed by the tribunal was disproportionate to its findings, and that the court had seen testimonials which had they been seen by the tribunal might have caused it not to make an order for suspension. The Law Society appealed to the Court of Appeal.

Held – A solicitor who discharged his professional duties with anything less than complete integrity, probity and trustworthiness had to expect severe sanctions to be imposed upon him by the Solicitors Disciplinary Tribunal, and except in a very strong case, an appellate court should not interfere with the sentence imposed by the tribunal. The decision whether to strike off or to suspend involved a difficult exercise of judgment made by the tribunal as an informed and expert body on all the facts of the case, and only in a very unusual or venial case would the tribunal be likely to regard as appropriate an order less severe than one of suspension. Furthermore, because orders made by the tribunal were not primarily punitive but were directed to ensuring that the offender did not have the opportunity to repeat the offence and to maintaining the reputation of the solicitor's profession and sustaining public confidence in its integrity, considerations which would ordinarily weigh in mitigation of punishment had less effect than in criminal cases and so it could never be an objection to an order of suspension in an appropriate case that the solicitor might be unable to re-establish his practice when the period of suspension was over. Accordingly, since in making the order the tribunal was fully aware of the solicitor's honesty and the consequences of suspension, as the majority of its members were practising solicitors, since it had considered the solicitor's conduct wholly unacceptable and very serious and since it was inconceivable that it would have thought it appropriate to impose a fine even if the testimonial evidence had been before it as that evidence was of limited weight, it followed that the Divisional Court had not had good reason for interfering with the tribunal's decision and had acted contrary to settled principles in doing so. However, having regard to the time which had elapsed and the fact that as a result of being stayed the order for suspension had never taken effect, it would be oppressive to reinstate that order. The appeal would therefore be dismissed (see p 490 f g, p 491 f to p 493 b f to h and p 494 b to d, post).

McCoan v General Medical Council [1964] 3 All ER 143 applied.

Notes

For the power of the Solicitors Disciplinary Tribunal to suspend a solicitor from practice, see 44 *Halsbury's Laws* (4th edn) para 305, and for cases on the subject, see 44 *Digest* (Reissue) 502–503, 5519–5537.

For appeals against orders of the Solicitors Disciplinary Tribunal, see 44 *Halsbury's Laws* (4th edn) paras 318–321, and for cases on the subject, see 44 *Digest* (1984 reissue) 507–509, 5578–5598.

Cases referred to in judgments

McCoan v General Medical Council [1964] 3 All ER 143, [1964] 1 WLR 1107, PC.
Solicitor, Re a [1956] 3 All ER 516, [1956] 1 WLR 1312, DC.
Solicitor, Re a [1960] 2 All ER 621, [1960] 2 QB 212, [1960] 3 WLR 138, DC.

Cases also cited or referred to in skeleton arguments

A-G's Reference (No 3 of 1989) [1989] RTR 337, CA.
A-G's Reference (No 4 of 1989) [1990] 1 WLR 41, CA.
Solicitor, Re a [1969] 3 All ER 610, [1969] 1 WLR 1068, DC.
Solicitor, Re a (1976) 120 SJ 117, DC.
Solicitor, Re a (1976) 120 SJ 353, DC.

Appeal

The Law Society appealed with the leave of Leggatt LJ granted on 21 January 1993 from the order of the Divisional Court of the Queen's Bench Division (Watkins LJ, Tucker and Buckley JJ) dated 7 July 1992 whereby the court allowed in part an appeal by a solicitor, Andrew John Bolton, against the order of the Solicitors Disciplinary Tribunal dated 23 May 1991 suspending him from practice for two years, and quashed the order for suspension and substituted a fine of £3,000. The facts are set out in the judgment of Sir Thomas Bingham MR.

Charles Flint (instructed by *Marsh Ferriman & Cheale*, Worthing) for the Law Society.

Malcolm Knott (instructed by A J Bolton & Co) for the solicitor.

SIR THOMAS BINGHAM MR. This is an appeal by the Law Society against a decision of the Queen's Bench Divisional Court given on 7 July 1992. The Divisional Court then quashed an order of the Solicitors Disciplinary Tribunal that Mr Andrew John Bolton be suspended from practice as a solicitor for two years and substituted an order that he be fined £3,000. The Law Society appeal against that decision with the leave of Leggatt LJ. It is said, so far as I know correctly, that there is no precedent for such an appeal by the Law Society.

Mr Bolton is now aged 39. He was admitted as a solicitor in 1987 at the age of 33, having previously been employed in other occupations. On his admission he set up in practice in East London with one partner. The transaction that brought him to the attention of the Solicitors Complaints Bureau occurred in 1989–1990, not very long after his admission. This transaction concerned a house at 38 Studley Road, Forest Gate, London E7. The house had been bought by Mr Bolton's wife with the assistance of a mortgage advance made by the Abbey National to her of some £91,000. Mrs Bolton agreed to sell the lower ground floor flat in that house to her brother, Mr Egwu, for £65,000. Mr Bolton acted as solicitor in this transaction, apparently for his wife, his brother-in-law, and the Leeds & Holbeck Building Society, which was to advance £45,000 odd to assist Mr Egwu to buy the flat upon the security of the flat. Mr Bolton duly received a cheque for £45,000 from the building society. It was then his duty to hold that money in his client account until the conveyance of the lower ground floor flat was made to his brother-in-law and security documentation in favour of the building society was executed. He did not do that. Having received the cheque on 10 May 1989 he started, as early as 16 May, disbursing that money. In just over a month he disbursed the whole sum, partly to mortgagees and partly to the Inland Revenue and, as to £25,000, to his wife. The brother-in-law never paid the £20,000 which was due from him in addition to the building society's advance or any part of it. The sale to the brother-in-law was never completed. The security documentation was never executed. The money received from the building society was disbursed without its receiving the security which was the condition of its making any advance. None of this came to light until the Solicitors Complaints Bureau sent an investigation accountant to look at the books of the firm at the end of August 1990. The investigation accountant found an error in the book-keeping practice which was minor and irrelevant for present purposes. I shall henceforward ignore it. The accountant also learnt of this shortage on the client account which by then had existed un-rectified for a period of nearly 16 months. The matter came to light during the visit although it was not shown in the firm's books relating to the client account.

When interviewed Mr Bolton admitted, apparently without prevarication, that these payments had been made. He admitted that the moneys received from the building society had been misused and acknowledged the shortage. That shortage was, however, made good very shortly thereafter in full on 11 September 1990. That did, however, leave the building society out of pocket so far as 16 months' interest was concerned and it issued a writ for that sum which led to the entry of judgment in default for £9,000 odd on 7 January 1991. That judgment was satisfied.

Not long thereafter, on 16 January 1991, the Solicitors Complaints Bureau complained to the Solicitors Disciplinary Tribunal that Mr Bolton had misapplied funds received for the purpose indicated. A hearing took place on 26 March 1991 at which Mr Bolton represented himself and relied primarily upon an affidavit which he had sworn. The findings and order of the tribunal were delivered on 23 May 1991 and they follow the usual form. The facts were summarised and there followed a summary of the contentions made on behalf of the complaining party and on behalf of the respondent solicitor. There then followed the conclusions of the tribunal. The conclusions of the tribunal in this instance are of great importance and I should quote them in full. They read, after a reference to the subsidiary complaint about the book-keeping which I have already mentioned, in this way:

'However, the matter contained in allegation (b) was of a far more serious nature. It concerned the misuse of clients' moneys. In essence the respondent had paid money belonging to a client Building Society to his wife. That was wholly unacceptable. The respondent in anticipation of the completion of a conveyancing transaction took a deliberate risk and paid out moneys which were not available to him. The Tribunal accept that the respondent has put matters right to the extent of repaying the advance from Leeds & Holbeck Building Society. Interest and costs however remained outstanding. The conveyancing system in England and Wales depends to a very great extent upon building societies and other lending institutions being able to trust a solicitor to handle large sums of money properly and carefully. The payment out of moneys held on behalf of a client by a respondent to his wife would normally be regarded very seriously indeed. Indeed it would be unusual for a respondent in that position not to be struck off the Roll. The Tribunal are able to accept that this respondent is an honest man and he was not stealing clients' money in a premeditated fashion, he was naive and stupid and paid moneys out prematurely in anticipation of formal completion of a conveyancing transaction. He was caught out by a purchaser reneging. The Tribunal accept that the respondent's judgment might have been clouded by his relationship by marriage to that purchaser. It is because this respondent is young, relatively inexperienced, and apparently more experienced in assisting legally aided clients than dealing with conveyancing, that the Tribunal are able to consider that his behaviour was naive and foolish but did not represent a deliberate course of dishonest conduct. The Tribunal are therefore able to exercise leniency and not make a striking off order. However, they do regard the respondent's less than proper approach to the handling of clients' matters as a very serious matter indeed and they ORDER that the respondent ... be suspended from practice as a solicitor for the period of two years ...'

Three points stand out clearly from that paragraph. (1) The tribunal accepted that Mr Bolton was an honest man. The tribunal found that he had not stolen clients' moneys in a premeditated fashion and that his actions did not represent a deliberate course of dishonest conduct. (2) The tribunal considered that his conduct was wholly unacceptable and regarded this as a very serious matter indeed. (3) In the tribunal's judgment such conduct would ordinarily merit striking off but the tribunal felt able, on the facts of this case, to make the more lenient order of suspension.

I pause to observe that for my part I find no fault at all in the disciplinary tribunal's reasoning. Mr Bolton's conduct, even if accepted as honest, represented a flagrant departure from the elementary rules which bind anyone, most of all a solicitor, holding a sum of money on behalf of someone else. The fact that a close family relationship was involved made it more, not less, necessary to act with scrupulous propriety. There were a number of mitigating factors upon which Mr Bolton relied and it is plain that the disciplinary tribunal gave those the fullest weight but nothing could disguise the fact that Mr Bolton's conduct was, indeed, as the tribunal held, 'wholly unacceptable'. Mr Bolton appealed against the decision of the tribunal. During the period of appeal the order for suspension was stayed. The Divisional Court, as I have said, gave its judgment on 7 July. At the very outset of its judgment the court stated the principle which has been derived from *McCoan v General Medical Council* [1964] 3 All ER 143 at 147, [1964] 1 WLR 1107 at 1113. Where the Judicial Committee of the Privy Council said:

> 'Their lordships are of opinion that LORD PARKER, C.J., may have gone too far in *Re a Solicitor* ([1960] 2 All ER 621 at 624, [1960] 2 QB 212 at 221), when he said that the appellate court would never differ from sentence in cases of professional misconduct, but their lordships agree with LORD GODDARD, C.J., in *Re a Solicitor* ([1956] 3 All ER 516 at 517, [1956] 1 WLR 1312 at 1314) when he said that it would require a very strong case to interfere with sentence in such a case, because the Disciplinary Committee are the best possible people for weighing the seriousness of the professional misconduct.'

It is not, I think, necessary to explore the authorities which lead up to that statement of principle at any length since there is no controversy about the correctness of that principle which, for the last thirty years at least, has been very clearly understood and very regularly applied.

In its judgment the Divisional Court said that the misappropriation of money is a very serious matter. Later in the judgment the Divisional Court described the client account of a solicitor as 'sacrosanct'. With those expressions of opinion I respectfully agree. Any approach to a case such as this must start from recognition of that as a correct starting point. Why then did the Divisional Court disturb the decision of the disciplinary tribunal? There were, I think, four reasons which the Divisional Court gave in the course of its judgment. The first, set out in a number of places, is the finding of the tribunal that there was no dishonesty in this case. That was a factor to which the Divisional Court attached very great importance. Secondly, the Divisional Court drew attention to its view that there was in practice not very much difference between an order of suspension and one of striking off. The Divisional Court said this:

> 'One wonders whether there is much difference in practical effect between striking him off and suspending someone like this appellant for two years. What chance he would have of recovering a practice after two years if he were to be struck off the roll and with the reputation of having been struck off seems to us to be negligible and probably non-existent in these times. We feel bound to differ with the approach of the Disciplinary Committee in that sense. They were it seems to us effectively, slowly but surely, striking him off although they did not go so far as to say so, obviously. To do that to someone who is regarded as an honest man

makes us wonder what they would have done to a dishonest one in the circumstances.'

I think it is right that in the early sentences there the words 'struck off' are used when 'suspended' was the intended meaning.

The third reason given by the Divisional Court is that there is a disproportion between the findings of the disciplinary tribunal and the penalty exacted. The fourth reason is that the Divisional Court had seen testimonials which the tribunal had not. These came, as the Divisional Court said, from a number of sources and the Divisional Court took the view that the tribunal might very well have come to the same conclusion as the Divisional Court had it had access to that material. It is, indeed, true that the Divisional Court had much material supportive of Mr Bolton which had not been before the tribunal, although some testimonials were before it. Mr Bolton said that he did not submit this material to the tribunal because he expected another hearing at which his mitigation would be presented. For my part I find that a somewhat unconvincing submission since on his attendance before the tribunal he was in effect pleading guilty. In any event, if he was in doubt as to the procedure he had only to ask.

Before returning to the facts of this case I think it may be worth saying something in more general terms about the principles which underlie cases such as this. The correct approach to questions of this kind has been laid down in a number of authorities, in particular a number of unreported decisions of Lord Donaldson of Lymington MR exercising the jurisdiction conferred on the Master of the Rolls by ss 13 and 49 of the Solicitors Act 1974. I do not think there is anything very surprising or very novel about the principles which emerge from those decisions but I attempt a summary of them, which cannot of course be exhaustive, in the hope that it may serve to make these principles better known and dispel any misunderstanding that there may be in any quarter.

It is required of lawyers practising in this country that they should discharge their professional duties with integrity, probity and complete trustworthiness. That requirement applies as much to barristers as it does to solicitors. If I make no further reference to barristers it is because this appeal concerns a solicitor, and where a client's moneys have been misappropriated the complaint is inevitably made against a solicitor, since solicitors receive and handle clients' moneys and barristers do not.

Any solicitor who is shown to have discharged his professional duties with anything less than complete integrity, probity and trustworthiness must expect severe sanctions to be imposed upon him by the Solicitors Disciplinary Tribunal. Lapses from the required high standard may, of course, take different forms and be of varying degrees. The most serious involves proven dishonesty, whether or not leading to criminal proceedings and criminal penalties. In such cases the tribunal has almost invariably, no matter how strong the mitigation advanced for the solicitor, ordered that he be struck off the Roll of Solicitors. Only infrequently, particularly in recent years, has it been willing to order the restoration to the Roll of a solicitor against whom serious dishonesty had been established, even after a passage of years, and even where the solicitor had made every effort to re-establish himself and redeem his reputation. If a solicitor is not shown to have acted dishonestly, but is shown to have fallen below the required standards of integrity, probity and trustworthiness, his lapse is less serious but it remains very serious indeed in a member of a profession whose reputation depends upon trust. A striking-off order will not necessarily follow in such a case, but it may well. The decision whether to strike off or to suspend will often involve a fine and difficult exercise of judgment, to be made by the tribunal as an informed and expert body on all the facts of the case. Only in a very unusual and venial case of this kind would the tribunal be likely to regard as appropriate any order less severe than one of suspension.

It is important that there should be full understanding of the reasons why the tribunal makes orders which might otherwise seem harsh. There is, in some of these orders, a punitive element: a penalty may be visited on a solicitor who has fallen below the standards required of his profession in order to punish him for what he has done and to deter any other solicitor tempted to behave in the same way. Those are traditional objects of punishment. But often the order is not punitive in intention. Particularly is this so where a criminal penalty has been imposed and satisfied. The solicitor has paid his debt to society. There is no need, and it would be unjust, to punish him again. In most cases the order of the tribunal will be primarily directed to one or other or both of two other purposes. One is to be sure that the offender does not have the opportunity to repeat the offence. This purpose is achieved for a limited period by an order of suspension; plainly it is hoped that experience of suspension will make the offender meticulous in his future compliance with the required standards. The purpose is achieved for a longer period, and quite possibly indefinitely, by an order of striking off. The second purpose is the most fundamental of all: to maintain the reputation of the solicitors' profession as one in which every member, of whatever standing, may be trusted to the ends of the earth. To maintain this reputation and sustain public confidence in the integrity of the profession it is often necessary that those guilty of serious lapses are not only expelled but denied re-admission. If a member of the public sells his house, very often his largest asset, and entrusts the proceeds to his solicitor, pending re-investment in another house, he is ordinarily entitled to expect that the solicitor will be a person whose trustworthiness is not, and never has been, seriously in question. Otherwise, the whole profession, and the public as a whole, is injured. A profession's most valuable asset is its collective reputation and the confidence which that inspires.

Because orders made by the tribunal are not primarily punitive, it follows that considerations which would ordinarily weigh in mitigation of punishment have less effect on the exercise of this jurisdiction than on the ordinary run of sentences imposed in criminal cases. It often happens that a solicitor appearing before the tribunal can adduce a wealth of glowing tributes from his professional brethren. He can often show that for him and his family the consequences of striking off or suspension would be little short of tragic. Often he will say, convincingly, that he has learned his lesson and will not offend again. On applying for restoration after striking off, all these points may be made, and the former solicitor may also be able to point to real efforts made to re-establish himself and redeem his reputation. All these matters are relevant and should be considered. But none of them touches the essential issue, which is the need to maintain among members of the public a well-founded confidence that any solicitor whom they instruct will be a person of unquestionable integrity, probity and trustworthiness. Thus it can never be an objection to an order of suspension in an appropriate case that the solicitor may be unable to re-establish his practice when the period of suspension is past. If that proves, or appears, likely to be so the consequence for the individual and his family may be deeply unfortunate and unintended. But it does not make suspension the wrong order if it is otherwise right. The reputation of the profession is more important than the fortunes of any individual member. Membership of a profession brings many benefits, but that is a part of the price.

I return then to consider the four reasons given by the Divisional Court for disturbing the order of the tribunal. The first is the emphasis on the finding that Mr Bolton had not been dishonest. I have already read in full the tribunal's very carefully drafted conclusions. It has to be borne in mind that the tribunal made its order very fully aware of the conclusion that it had reached concerning Mr Bolton's honesty. It cannot sensibly be said to have overlooked its conclusions in that regard. So far as the difference between striking off and suspension are concerned, I find it difficult to think that the Divisional Court could have expected to bring more insight to bear on that question than a tribunal with a majority of practising solicitors among its members. The consequences of suspension would be something of which they would be vividly aware. Nonetheless, they concluded that suspension was the minimum sanction which they could impose in the present circumstances. Quite apart from that it is, of course, clear that there is a substantial difference between these two forms of order. At the end of a period of suspension a solicitor is able to seek employment, or seek to re-establish himself in partnership, perhaps subject to such conditions as the Law Society see fit to attach to his practising certificate. But that puts him in quite a different position from a solicitor who has been struck off, who cannot practice at all as a solicitor unless or until he is restored to the Roll.

So far as the finding of disproportion between the findings of the tribunal and the penalty are concerned, I do not for my part understand how suspension can be said to be a disproportionate order in a case of conduct described, and rightly described, by the tribunal, as 'wholly unacceptable' and 'very serious indeed'.

In my judgment, the Divisional Court was doing, no doubt unwittingly, exactly what authority says the court should not do, namely substitute its own view on penalty for that of the professional tribunal. It is true, as the Divisional Court found, that there was a good deal of material in the mitigation which it did have the opportunity to consider and the tribunal did not. That cannot, however, be of more than limited weight for reasons that I have endeavoured to explain. It seems to me inconceivable that the tribunal would have thought it appropriate to impose a fine even if all this material had been before it. In my judgment, therefore, the Divisional Court gave no good reasons for interfering with the decision of the tribunal and acted contrary to settled principles in doing so. In the ordinary way I would without hesitation allow this appeal and restore the order of the disciplinary tribunal. In the present circumstances, however, a real question arises as to what should be done now, having regard to the time which has elapsed in the course of these proceedings, none of it due, I should say, to the disciplinary tribunal itself, or to either of these parties. The fact, however, is that, as a result of the various stays that have been granted in the course of these proceedings, the order of suspension has never taken effect and it would, in my judgment, be oppressive to reinstate the tribunal's order two and a half years after the order was made, and 16 months after the Divisional Court quashed it. The Law Society acknowledge the force of this contention and are more concerned in this appeal to allay misunderstanding and obtain a clear statement of practice and principle than to achieve the suspension of Mr Bolton from practice. It was suggested that the court might allow the appeal and award the Law Society their costs in the Divisional Court where both sides were ordered to bear their own costs. That is a possible course but to my mind a rather artificial and unattractive one. I have made clear that in my judgment the Divisional Court erred but since, in the circumstances, the penalty it imposed will not be quashed I decline to allow the appeal simply in order to disturb its order for costs. I would, therefore, dismiss the Law Society's appeal, making clear that in my opinion, on the quite exceptional facts of this case, the appeal was properly brought. I observe that the Law Society have achieved their substantial objective. I would not, however, wish to give the impression that appeals by the Law Society in situations of this kind should be other than quite exceptional.

ROSE LJ. I agree with the order proposed and I also agree with the reasons given by Sir Thomas Bingham MR.

WAITE LJ. I also agree with the order proposed by Sir Thomas Bingham MR.

Appeal dismissed.

L I Zysman Esq   Barrister.

R v Secretary of State for the Home Department, ex parte Mehari and other applications

QUEEN'S BENCH DIVISION (CROWN OFFICE LIST)
LAWS J
28, 29 SEPTEMBER, 4, 8 OCTOBER 1993

Immigration – Leave to enter – Refugee – Asylum – Deportation back to third country – Home Secretary's certificate that applicant's claim that removal from United Kingdom would breach the 1951 Convention on Refugees was without foundation – Whether claim for asylum without foundation if it was unnecessary for Home Secretary to decide whether claimant a refugee because he could be removed to safe third country – Function of special adjudicators on appeal against Home Secretary's certificate – Asylum and Immigration Appeals Act 1993, Sch 2, para 5(3)(a) – Statement of changes in Immigration Rules (HC Paper (1993) No 725), para 180K.

The five applicants arrived in the United Kingdom from European countries and claimed asylum on arrival because they feared persecution in their native countries. In each case the Secretary of State decided, pursuant to para 180K[a] of the 1993 Immigration Rules (Statement of Changes in Immigration Rules (HC

---

a   Paragraph 180K is set out at p 502 c to f, post

Paper (1993) No 725)) that the applicant could be returned to the safe third country from which he had arrived and refused to give substantive consideration to the asylum claim and certified under para 5(3)(a)^b of Sch 2 to the Asylum and Immigration Appeals Act 1993 that the applicant's claim that his removal from the United Kingdom would breach the 1951 Geneva Convention on Refugees was 'without foundation'. The applicants were refused leave to enter the United Kingdom. Their appeals against that refusal were dismissed by special adjudicators. They applied for judicial review of the adjudicators' decisions.

Held – (1) For the purposes of the Secretary of State certifying under para 5(3)(a) of Sch 2 to the 1993 Act that the claim by an applicant for asylum that his removal from the United Kingdom would breach the 1951 Geneva Convention was without foundation, a claim for asylum did 'not raise any issue' and was therefore without foundation if it was unnecessary for the Secretary of State to decide whether the claimant was a refugee who ought to be admitted to the United Kingdom by virtue of its convention obligations, because he could be removed to a third country in which he did not fear persecution. Before issuing such a certificate the Secretary of State was required under para 180K of the 1993 Immigration Rules to form a view on the information known to him (i) whether the country to which he proposed to remove the claimant was a safe country as defined by para 180K, and (ii) whether he was barred by para 180K from removing the claimant by virtue of either of the specific provisions in para 180K(a) and (b), ie because the applicant had not had the opportunity in the third country of making contact with that country's authorities in order to seek their protection or because there was no clear evidence of his admissibility to a third country. If for any reason the Secretary of State was unable to issue a certificate under para 5(3)(a) of Sch 2 to the 1993 Act he had to decide the claim to refugee status on its merits (see p 504 c d, p 505 b c and p 507 f g, post).

(2) Where the Secretary of State issued a certificate under para 5(3)(a) of Sch 2 to the 1993 Act a special adjudicator hearing an appeal by the claimant could not accept it at face value but had to judge the merits of the certificate independently by deciding whether he agreed with it before going on to decide how to dispose of the appeal. The adjudicator was required to agree with the certificate, and dismiss the appeal, if on the material before him he concluded that the claimant could properly be removed to a third country under para 180K of the 1993 Immigration Rules but if he disagreed with the certificate because he concluded that removal was not justified under para 180K he could then allow the appeal or refer the case to the Secretary of State for reconsideration under para 5(6), although in practice he was likely to do the latter since ex hypothesi the claimant's substantive claim to refugee status would then have to be decided. Alternatively, he could disagree with the certificate because he was in doubt as to whether the claimant could properly be removed within para 180K in which case he was likely to refer the case to the Secretary of State for reconsideration indicating the nature of his doubts (see p 499 j to p 500 a, p 505 c to j, p 507 h and p 508 c, post).

(3) On the facts, the adjudicator in one case had wrongly held that the onus was on the applicant to show that his removal would not breach the United Kingdom's convention obligations while in another case the adjudicator had

---

b   Paragraph 5, so far as material, is set out at p 499 *a* to *d*, post

taken into account certain matters which did not bear on the issue whether the applicant could safely be returned to a third country and certiorari would be granted in those two cases. In the other cases the adjudicator had been entitled to agree with the Secretary of State's certificate and accordingly the applications would be dismissed (see p 508 *a b g* to *j*, p 509 *h j* and p 511 *j* to p 512 *a*, post).

Notes

For control of immigration with respect to refugees, see 4 *Halsbury's Laws* (4th edn) paras 981.

For refugees and stateless persons under the Geneva Convention on Reugees, see 18 ibid paras 1717–1722.

Cases referred to in judgment

Associated Provincial Picture Houses Ltd v Wednesbury Corp [1947] 2 All ER 680, [1948] 1 KB 223, CA.

Bouzeid v Secretary of State for the Home Dept [1991] Imm AR 204, CA.

Bugdaycay v Secretary of State for the Home Dept [1987] 1 All ER 940, [1987] AC 514, [1987] 2 WLR 606, HL.

Oladehinde v Secretary of State for the Home Dept [1990] 3 All ER 393, [1991] 1 AC 254, [1990] 3 WLR 797, HL.

Pepper (Inspector of Taxes) v Hart [1993] 1 All ER 42, [1993] AC 593, [1992] 3 WLR 1032, HL.

R v Secretary of State for the Home Dept, ex p Hilaludeen [1993] Imm AR 250.

Applications for judicial review

R v Secretary of State for the Home Department, ex p Mehari

Senay Mehari, a citizen of Ethiopia who arrived in the United Kingdom on 11 August 1993 from Italy where he had been resident for about a year and who was a minor applying by his next friend, Deborah Winterbourne, applied for judicial review by way of orders of certiorari to quash (i) the decision of the Secretary of State made on 16 August to refuse the applicant leave to enter the United Kingdom and to remove him to Italy, and (ii) the decision of a special adjudicator given on 27 August dismissing his appeal from the Secretary of State's decision. The facts, so far as relevant, are set out in the judgment.

R v Secretary of State for the Home Department, ex p Doreh

Mohamed Ahmed Doreh, a citizen of Somalia who arrived in the United Kingdom on 10 August 1993 from Italy where he had been since 6 August, applied for judicial review by way of a declaration that paras 180D and 180K of the Immigration Rules breached the United Kingdom's obligations under the 1951 Geneva Convention on Refugees, certiorari to quash (i) the decision of the Secretary of State made on 22 August 1993 to refuse him leave to enter the United Kingdom and his decision to certify that the applicant's application for asylum was without foundation (ii) the decision of a special adjudicator given on 2 September dismissing his appeal from the Secretary of State's decision, and (iii) the decision of the Secretary of State made on 3 September to issue directions to remove the applicant from the United Kingdom the following day to Italy. The facts, so far as relevant, are set out in the judgment.

R v Secretary of State for the Home Department, ex p Hersi
Ali Abdi Hersi, a citizen of Somalia who arrived in the United Kingdom on 14 August 1993 from Germany where he had spent six days, applied for judicial review by way of certiorari to quash the decision of a special adjudicator given on 31 August dismissing his appeal from the Secretary of State's decision on 15 August to refuse the applicant leave to enter the United Kingdom or to consider his claim for asylum because he could be returned to Germany and his application for asylum was without foundation. The facts, so far as relevant, are set out in the judgment.

R v Secretary of State for the Home Department, ex p Celik
Fuat Celik, a citizen of Turkey who arrived in the United Kingdom on 21 July 1993 from Holland where he had spent about one and a half hours after travelling overland from Turkey, applied for judicial review by way of certiorari to quash the decision of a special adjudicator given on 7 September dismissing his appeal from the Secretary of State's decision on 19 August to refuse to consider his claim for asylum because he could be returned to Holland and to certify that the applicant's application for asylum was without foundation. The facts, so far as relevant, are set out in the judgment.

R v Secretary of State for the Home Department, ex p Kuti Augusto
Massampo Kuti Augusto, a citizen of Angola who arrived in the United Kingdom on 8 August 1993 from France to where he had travelled from Angola, applied for judicial review by way of certiorari to quash the decision of a special adjudicator given on 8 September dismissing his appeal from the Secretary of State's decision on 12 August to refuse to consider his claim for asylum because he could be returned to France and to certify that the applicant's application for asylum was without foundation. The facts, so far as relevant, are set out in the judgment.

Nicholas Blake (instructed by *Winstanley-Burgess*) for the applicant Mehari.
Rambert de Melo (instructed by *White Ryland*) for the applicant Doreh.
David Abbott (instructed by *Thiru & Co*) for the applicant Hersi.
Andrew Nicol (instructed by the *Humberside Law Centre*, Hull) for the applicant Celik.
Richard Scannell (instructed by *Winstanley-Burgess*) appeared for the applicant Augusto.
David Pannick QC (instructed by the *Treasury Solicitor*) for the Secretary of State .

Cur adv vult

8 October 1993. The following judgment was delivered.

LAWS J. All these applications seek judicial review of decisions of special adjudicators given under the Asylum and Immigration Appeals Act 1993, which came into effect on 26 July 1993. Each applicant is an asylum-seeker who appealed to the special adjudicator under s 8 of the Act in effect against the Secretary of State's decision not to consider the merits of his claim that he had a well-founded fear of persecution, but rather to remove him to what the Secretary of State regards as what I may call a safe third country, being the country from which he had directly travelled to the United Kingdom. In all but one of the cases the appeal was brought under s 8(1) against the Secretary of

State's refusal of leave to enter. In the Celik case the appeal was brought under s 8(4) against removal directions. In each case the Secretary of State also issued a certificate under para 5 of Sch 2 to the 1993 Act to the effect that the applicant's claim that his removal as proposed by the Secretary of State would contravene the United Kingdom's obligations under the Convention and Protocol Relating to the Status of Refugees (Geneva, 28 July 1951, TS 39 (1954), Cmd 9171; New York, 31 January 1967, TS 15 (1969), Cmnd 3906) (which I shall refer to as 'the convention') was without foundation. All the applications raise a common question of no little importance as to the true construction of para 5 of Sch 2. Individually they raise other points.

[His Lordship then set out an outline chronology of each case which included the following: Mehari was a citizen of Ethiopia who arrived in the United Kingdom on 11 August 1993 from Italy and claimed asylum on the ground that he feared persecution in Ethiopia; Hersi and Doreh were citizens of Somalia who arrived in the United Kingdom on 14 and 20 August 1993 from Germany and Italy respectively and claimed asylum on arrival; Celik was a citizen of Turkey who arrived in the United Kingdom on 21 July 1993 from Holland and claimed asylum on arrival; Augusto was a citizen of Angola who arrived in the United Kingdom on 7 August 1993 from France and claimed asylum on arrival. His Lordship continued:] I may now turn to the 1993 Act. Section 1, inter alia, defines 'the Convention' as meaning the 1951 Geneva Convention and the Protocol. Section 2 provides:

'Nothing in the immigration rules (within the meaning of the 1971 Act [ie the Immigration Act 1971]) shall lay down any practice which would be contrary to the Convention.'

Section 8 provides in part as follows:

'(1) A person who is refused leave to enter the United Kingdom under the 1971 Act may appeal against the refusal to a special adjudicator on the ground that his removal in consequence of the refusal would be contrary to the United Kingdom's obligations under the Convention ...

(4) Where directions are given ... for a person's removal from the United Kingdom, the person may appeal to a special adjudicator against the directions on the ground that his removal in pursuance of the directions would be contrary to the United Kingdom's obligations under the Convention.'

It is worth bearing in mind that before the 1993 Act came into force, subject to certain limited exceptions a person refused leave to enter the United Kingdom could not appeal against the refusal unless he left this country first; that was the effect of s 13 of the 1971 Act. The right of appeal conferred by s 8(1) is of course exercisable within the United Kingdom, and so for the first time provides what many would regard as effective access in a port refusal case to the statutory appellate authorities for a person who has made a claim for political asylum. Section 8(6) gives effect to Sch 2 to the Act. The critical part of Sch 2 for present purposes is para 5, most of which I must set out, but it is important to see that para 4 (which is made subject to para 5) applies to s 8 appeals certain of the provisions of the 1971 Act dealing with the appellate jurisdiction and procedure of adjudicators and the Immigration Appeal Tribunal, including s 19 (dealing with the adjudicators' functions), s 20 (conferring a right of appeal from an adjudicator to the tribunal) and s 22 (which confers on the Lord Chancellor the power to make rules of procedure by statutory instrument).

Paragraph 5 in part provides:

'(1) ... this paragraph applies to an appeal by a person under sub-s (1) ... or (4) of s 8 of this Act if the Secretary of State has certified that, in his opinion, the person's claim on the ground that it would be contrary to the United Kingdom's obligations under the Convention for him to be removed from the United Kingdom is without foundation ...

(3) For the purpose of this paragraph a claim is without foundation if (and only if)—(a) it does not raise any issue as to United Kingdom's obligations under the Convention; or (b) it is otherwise frivolous or vexatious.

(4) Rules of procedure under s 22 of the 1971 Act may make special provision in relation to appeals to which this paragraph applies.

(5) If on an appeal to which this paragraph applies the special adjudicator agrees that the claim is without foundation, s 20(1) of that Act shall not confer on the appellant any right of appeal to the Immigration Appeal Tribunal.

(6) If the special adjudicator does not agree that the claim is without foundation, he may (as an alternative to allowing or dismissing the appeal) refer the case to the Secretary of State for reconsideration; and the making of such a reference shall, accordingly, be regarded as disposing of the appeal.'

New rules of procedure for the appellate authorities have been made. These are the Asylum Appeals (Procedure) Rules 1993, SI 1993/1661, which came into force on the same day as the new Act, 26 July 1993. They apply only to s 8 appeals. It is quite apparent from the provisions which I was shown that a prime purpose of these rules is to set in place a very speedy regime indeed, and a yet speedier one where the Secretary of State has certified under para 5 of Sch 2 that the claim is without foundation. Thus the time limit for giving notice of appeal is only two days in any s 8(1) case, in any case where the Secretary of State has certified under para 5 of Sch 2, and in any case where the decision in question has been personally served on the appellant (r 5(2)); in other cases it is ten days (r 5(1)); and the special adjudicator is to give notice of the date, time, and place fixed for the hearing within five days after receiving the notice of appeal—but only three days in a para 5 certificate case (r 6). There is no provision for extending these time limits. By r 9 the special adjudicator is to determine an appeal not later than 42 days after receiving notice of appeal; but only seven days in a para 5 certificate case. These latter time limits are however extendable under r 31. Other provisions exemplifying the theme of expedition include r 11(4), by which in a case where the special adjudicator agrees under para 5(5) of Sch 2 with the Secretary of State's certificate, he is to pronounce his determination and reasons at the conclusion of the hearing. The balance of r 11 imposes constraints on the time he may take with his decision in other cases.

From these materials it is at once apparent that the certification procedure is of critical significance: it conditions the time limits, and, what is I think of much greater importance, its application determines the availability or otherwise of a further appeal to the tribunal. These applications require me to construe para 5 of Sch 2, so as to ascertain the legal effects of the certification procedure as it works in practice.

In a case where the Secretary of State gives a certificate, the first task for the special adjudicator is to decide whether he agrees with it or not under paras 5(5) or (6) of Sch 2. If he does agree (as in effect he did in each of these cases) that is of course the end of the appeal; the appellant has no further relevant legal rights save that he may apply for leave to move for judicial review against the adjudicator's decision. Where the adjudicator disagrees with the certificate, he must then proceed as a separate exercise to decide whether to allow or dismiss the appeal, or refer the case back to the Secretary of State under para 5(6). It is also clear (as Mr Pannick QC accepts) that in deciding whether to agree or disagree with the certificate the adjudicator does not apply the public law *Wednesbury* test (see *Associated Provincial Picture Houses Ltd v Wednesbury Corp* [1947] 2 All ER 680, [1948] 1 KB 223), or anything akin to it, but must consider for himself whether the claim is indeed 'without foundation' as that term is defined in para 5(3). The primary question to be resolved in these proceedings is the meaning of that definition: more particularly, the words in the first part at sub-para (a):

'It [ie the claim] does not raise any issue as to the United Kingdom's obligations under the Convention.'

The arguments of the applicants before me did not all take the same position on this question, and Mr Pannick for the Secretary of State proposed two alternative constructions of para 5(3). Mr De Mello for the applicant Doreh submitted that an issue is raised within the meaning of para 5(3)(a) upon an appellant merely asserting that he is a refugee. I can say at once that this putative construction is in my judgment obviously wrong. By definition, every appellant under s 8 will assert that he is a refugee. If such an assertion is sufficient to negative the Secretary of State's certificate, there will be no case under para 5(3)(a) in which such a certificate could lawfully be upheld by the adjudicator. Paragraph 5(3)(a) becomes a dead letter.

Mr Pannick's first proposed construction, though not his preferred case, was that an issue is only raised within the meaning of para 5(3)(a) if the appellant has an arguable case that his removal would be contrary to the UK's convention obligations. On this approach, the certificate will only be proper, and the adjudicator will only agree with it, if the case on the facts is akin to one in which judicial review leave would be refused in the public law court. The analogy is plainly not exact, if only because by the time the case reaches the adjudicator it falls by definition to be determined on an inter partes basis, and it is for the Secretary of State to satisfy the adjudicator that his certificate is good, rather than for the appellant to establish that his case is arguable. But leaving aside questions as to burden of proof, the comparison with judicial review leave suffices to identify the thrust of this proposed construction: it means that the adjudicator is not to decide for himself whether in fact the appellant's removal would contravene the convention obligations, but only whether it is arguable that it might do so. If he holds it is arguable, he will disagree with the certificate.

This construction was in essence agreed to by Mr Blake for the applicant Mehari and Mr Nicol for Celik, but the difference between them and Mr Pannick is as to what constitutes an arguable claim in a third country removal case; they join issue as to the true effect of para 180K of the new Immigration Rules (Statement of Changes in Immigration Rules (HC Paper (1993) No 725)), and more generally as to the scope of the United Kingdom's convention obligations in a third country case. I shall have to return to the new rules, but need not for immediate purposes set out or construe para 180K, because in my judgment this construction of para 5(3)(a) falls to be rejected on grounds unaffected by its scope.

I do not think it can sensibly be suggested that in deciding whether to give a para 5(3)(a) certificate the Secretary of State is himself to carry out an exercise bearing any similarity to a refusal of judicial review leave. Under para 5(1), he may give a certificate if in his opinion the claim is without foundation. I cannot believe that when Parliament came to define the term 'without foundation' in para 5(3)(a), it intended by implication to provide that the Secretary of State, who of course will have made the decision to remove the appellant on his own view of the facts, and who as the respondent to any appeal has his own case to urge, should under para 5(1) don a judicial mantle and merely pronounce that the claim, which on its facts he has ex hypothesi rejected, is not an arguable one. His certificate is surely to indicate his view of the claim's final and overall merits. But if the Secretary of State's function as regards certification is to reach a view on the merits, the adjudicator's can be no different when he comes to decide whether to agree or disagree with a certificate that has been issued. I have said that Mr Pannick, correctly, accepts that the adjudicator does not conduct a judicial review of the Secretary of State's certificate. If therefore (as I have held), the certificate is to express the Secretary of State's view of the claim's overall merits, the adjudicator's agreement or disagreement with it is in principle concerned with the overall merits as well.

Moreover, I think it extremely unlikely that Parliament would have chosen to define the expression 'without foundation' in terms so distant from its ordinary meaning as are implied by the construction which I am presently considering. The words 'without foundation' are apt to describe a claim which after full examination has no merits, and not merely one which on the face of it is not arguable. Statute may, of course, define any expression as the legislature chooses. But if the intention in para 5 was to introduce the concept of an arguable case, rather than one which in the end was either good or bad, I do not believe that the formula 'without foundation' would have been chosen as the means of its introduction.

I should notice one particular argument mounted to contradict the proposition that under para 5(5) and (6) the adjudicator is himself to decide the merits of the claim. It is to the effect that upon this construction there will be no para 5(3)(a) case in which the adjudicator both disagrees with the certificate and dismisses the appeal, since, if he disagrees with it, he will ex hypothesi have accepted the merits of the appeal: yet para 5(6) would appear to contemplate that in all cases where the adjudicator does so disagree, the question of allowing or dismissing the appeal involves a separate and distinct exercise. However, as I will show in dealing with the next proposed construction of para 5, there is scope where the adjudicator disagrees with a para 5(3)(a) certificate for him to refer the matter back to the Secretary of State under para 5(6); and in addition it is clear that in the case of a para 5(3)(b) certificate the adjudicator may both disagree with the certificate and dismiss the appeal. I do not consider, therefore, that this argument should persuade me that anything like a judicial review exercise is involved in the certification procedure.

So I reject this proposed construction of para 5(3)(a). It follows that the certification process, if invoked, involves both Secretary of State and adjudicator in a judgment as to the factual merits of the appellant's claim.

To make sense of the further arguments on the construction issue it is necessary now to refer to the new Immigration Rules. They were laid before Parliament on 5 July 1993 as HC Paper (1993) No 725 under the procedure provided by s 3(2) of the 1971 Act. Most of the changes which they made, including those relevant for present purposes, took effect on 26 July 1993 which, as I have said, is also the date when the new Act and the Procedure Rules came into force. HC Paper (1993) No 725 makes some amendments to the main body

of the Immigration Rules, but its principal substance is the addition of a new Part
13 headed 'Asylum'. This is plainly intended to dovetail with the new regime
created by the Act.

Paragraph 180D of the new rules is in part in these terms:

'The Secretary of State may decide not to consider the substance of a
person's claim to refugee status if he is satisfied that the person's removal to
a third country does not raise any issue as to the United Kingdom's
obligations under the Convention and Protocol. More details are given in
paragraphs 180K and 180M.'

Paragraph 180K, to which I have referred in passing, is headed 'Third country
cases' and provides:

'If the Secretary of State is satisfied that there is a safe country to which an
asylum applicant can be sent his application will normally be refused
without substantive consideration of his claim to refugee status. A safe
country is one in which the life or freedom of the asylum applicant would
not be threatened (within the meaning of Art. 33 of the Convention) and the
government of which would not send the applicant elsewhere in a manner
contrary to the principles of the Convention and Protocol. The Secretary of
State shall not remove an asylum applicant without substantive
consideration of his claim unless: (a) the asylum applicant has not arrived
in the United Kingdom directly from the country in which he claims to fear
persecution and has had an opportunity, at the border or within the
territory of a third country, to make contact with that country's authorities
in order to seek their protection; or (b) there is other clear evidence of his
admissibility to a third country. Provided that he is satisfied that a case
meets these criteria, the Secretary of State is under no obligation to consult
the authorities of the third country before the removal of an asylum
applicant.'

I may now turn to Mr Pannick's principal case as to the construction of para
5(3)(a), which is contested by all the applicants. It contains two elements. The
first is that para 5(3)(a) is only concerned with third country cases, where the
Secretary of State has not considered the substance of the asylum application
because he proposes to remove the appellant under para 180K of the new rules.
In other cases, where the substantive application has been considered, the
Secretary of State may certify under para 5(3)(b) if he considers that the claim is
frivolous or vexatious. The second element is that as regards the certificate both
Secretary of State and adjudicator are to proceed on their view of the overall
merits of the case, and not on any basis akin to judicial review or *Wednesbury*
principles (see *Associated Provincial Picture Houses Ltd v Wednesbury Corp* [1947] 2
All ER 680, [1948] 1 KB 223).

I have already accepted, in principle, this latter element in rejecting a
construction of para 5(3)(a) by which the concept of an arguable case is made the
touchstone of the certification procedure. I must therefore address the first
element. I should notice at once that the Act makes no distinction whatever on
its face between third country cases and other cases. On Mr Pannick's
submission, however, this distinction is the linchpin of the construction of the
subparagraph. The first important point here, in my judgment, is that
Parliament manifestly proposed some distinction between para 5(3)(a) and (b).
If the intention was that there be a single criterion for 'without foundation'
claims, nothing was easier than to enact that the words meant any claim which

was frivolous or vexatious, or one which fell under any other unitary description which might be chosen. But Parliament has specified two criteria, not one. It must have been intended to isolate a particular class of case under para 5(3)(a).

Mr Pannick says that the class of case thus isolated is that of third country removals. He submits that this position is supported by the following materials: (a) para 180D of the new rules, which I have read. He draws attention to the use there of the same words as appear in para 5(3)(a): 'does not raise any issue'. These words are used specifically in the context of third country cases; (b) statements made by the responsible minister as the Bill which became the new Act passed through the committee stage in the House of Lords. Opposing a motion for an amendment proposed by Lord Ackner relating to the time limit for notice of appeal in the prospective procedure rules, Earl Ferrers, the minister, having set out the conditions which it was intended should be met for the two day limit to apply, said this (Hansard (HL Deb) 11 February 1993, col 877):

'The great majority of cases which fall within those conditions will be cases where the person has arrived from a safe third country to which it is proposed to remove him. Those cases are regarded as without foundation in the terms of para 4 [it became para 5] of Schedule 2, they do not raise any issue as to the United Kingdom's obligations under the Convention.'

The minister then described the rationale of the safe third country policy, and the need in cases to which it applied for great expedition in the appeal process. He said:

'The longer a person remains here, the less likely it is that the authorities of the other country will accept him back ... certainly, access to the full asylum appeals process which the Bill creates would mean that in virtually every case a person would stay here so long that it would be impossible to get the safe third country to accept him back. That would undermine the internationally accepted principle ... that refugees should seek asylum in the first safe country which they enter. It would make it much more difficult to prevent misuse of the asylum procedures by those who are not refugees.'

Towards the end of his speech he said (col 878):

'An effective filtering mechanism is required to prevent the new appeals system which we are providing from becoming clogged up with claims which do not involve any real issue regarding the protection of the life and freedom of refugees, but which are claims without foundation.'

I must briefly consider whether, as Mr Pannick asserted, these materials constitute a legitimate aid to the construction of the Act. In my view recourse may be had to the statements of the minister, given the House of Lords' decision in *Pepper (Inspector of Taxes) v Hart* [1993] 1 All ER 42, [1993] AC 593. The conditions there laid down for reference to such parliamentary material to be permissible are met in this case. Paragraph 5(3)(a) is unclear on its face, and so may be said to be ambiguous; the material on which Mr Pannick relies is a statement by a minister promoting the bill; and its terms are clear. As regards r 180D, Mr Nicol submitted that the new Immigration Rules are not a legitimate aid to construction if only because the time has not yet passed within which they may be disapproved by either House of Parliament under s 3(2) of the 1971 Act. He does not, I think, dissent from the proposition that if the time for Parliamentary disapproval had passed, I could have regard to the rule: and this is surely right. In my judgment the fact that that time has not yet passed goes perhaps to the weight I should attach to the rule, but cannot constitute an absolute bar against my taking it into account. At present the rule has legal effect for the administration of immigration control, and does so in the context of the new Act. There is manifestly no kind of presumption that Parliament will strike it down. Its position is analogous to (though not identical with) that of a statutory instrument which may be prayed in aid to construe main legislation, where it is clear that the two are intended to form an overall code; I do not think that in such a case the court would have to disregard entirely the statutory instrument on the ground only that it still remained open to Parliament to strike it down by negative resolution.

In my judgment para 180D of the Immigration Rules, and the statement of the minister, demonstrate that in seeking the legislation now contained in the Act the government for its part intended that the expression 'does not raise any issue' was to be taken as referring to a case where it was unnecessary for the Secretary of State to decide whether the claimant was a refugee who ought to be admitted to the United Kingdom by virtue of its convention obligations, because he could be removed to a third country in which he did not fear persecution. It was contemplated that para 5(3)(a) (as of course the provision became when enacted) should be construed in this sense. This assists Mr Pannick, but I think that in any case such a construction is supported by other considerations.

First, it is hard to see what distinction is intended between para 5(3)(a) and (b) if it is not the difference between third country cases and those where the asylum application has been substantively considered. If the potential subject-matter of the two sub-paragraphs were the same, there is no easily perceptible sense in a provision enabling the Secretary of State to certify against the claim on the alternative grounds specified. One would expect to see a single criterion, by which the Secretary of State would certify if in effect he formed the view that there was nothing in the case, whether it involved a third country removal or not.

Secondly, the convention itself is on its face silent as to the duties of a signatory state in a potential third country case. Mr Pannick disavowed the proposition that such a case does not at all involve the Secretary of State's convention obligations; and, not least given the House of Lords' decision in *Musisi's* case (reported with *Bugdaycay v Secretary of State for the Home Dept* [1987] 1 All ER 940, [1987] AC 514), I can readily understand why. Musisi was a third country case. Such a case may obviously involve questions of danger to life and limb, and the court will be concerned to review any decision bearing on such issues with what Lord Bridge called 'the most anxious scrutiny' (see [1987] 1 All ER 940 at 952, [1987] AC 514 at 531). And Lord Bridge was clearly of the view that a third country removal might involve a potential breach of art 33 of the convention (see [1987] 1 All ER 940 at 952, [1987] AC 514 at 532). He also pointed out, however, that the case before him was not one 'where the claim to refugee status itself is in issue'; and this will always be so in third country cases. The point for present purposes is that such cases only *contingently* involve consideration of the merits of a substantive asylum claim; in other cases the Secretary of State is bound to consider them. In my view the words in para 5(3)(a) 'does not raise any issue' may properly be construed as referring to those instances of the former class of case in which the contingency does not arise because there may be a safe removal to a third country.

Thirdly, it is not without significance that the certification procedure provided by para 5 does not apply to a case where the appeal is brought under s

8(2), where there will be much less urgency than in a s 8(1) case since by definition the appellant will be a person who has been granted leave to enter or remain. I recognise, as was submitted to me, that para 5 also applies to a s 8(3)(b) appeal against a refusal to revoke a deportation order; no doubt some such cases will be urgent, others not. But the point retains some force as an indicator of the intended scope of para 5(3)(a).

In my judgment, the true construction of para 5(3)(a) is this: an appellant's claim does not raise any issue as to the United Kingdom's convention obligations unless on the facts it is incumbent upon the Secretary of State to consider his substantive claim to refugee status. On that basis, para 5(3)(a) can only apply in third country cases, since in every other case where asylum is claimed, the Secretary of State will have to decide the claim to refugee status on its merits.

This reasoning identifies the class of case in which a para 5(3)(a) certificate may be issued; but the class contains three sub-classes.

The first arises where the special adjudicator may lawfully agree with the certificate, and so dismiss the appeal. In my judgment, he is to agree if on the material before him at the hearing of the appeal, he concludes that the appellant may properly be removed to a third country under para 180K of the rules. As Mr Pannick accepts, it will be for the Secretary of State to demonstrate that the appellant may be so removed.

The second sub-class arises where the adjudicator concludes on the facts that para 180K does not justify removal; then he will disagree with the certificate, and he may either allow the appeal or refer the case to the Secretary of State for reconsideration under para 5(6): in practice he is likely to do the latter since ex hypothesi the appellant's substantive claim to refugee status would then have to be decided.

The third sub-class arises where the adjudicator is in doubt as to whether, on the facts, the appellant may properly be removed within para 180K. In such a case he will also disagree with the certificate, since the Secretary of State will not have satisfied him that para 180K applies. If everything else were equal, one would expect it to be the duty of the adjudicator, like any other judicial office-holder, to make up his mind one way or the other. But the time limits are important here: the scope for resolving any proper doubt, which the adjudicator initially entertains, by an adjournment for further evidence is circumscribed by the pressure which the Procedure Rules exert to promote fast decision-making. Certainly the adjudicator is not to conduct an exhaustive enquiry involving anything like extensive adjournments. Thus there may be cases (though I emphasise in my view they will be very few) in which he may permissibly entertain substantial doubts on the material presented to him within the short timescale which is prima facie prescribed. In a case of this kind, having disagreed with the certificate, the adjudicator is likely also to refer the matter back to the Secretary of State under para 5(6) indicating the scope of his doubts for the assistance of the Secretary of State on the latter's reconsideration of the case. In contrast to the second su-class, the primary subject of the reconsideration will be the applicability of para 180K, rather than the substantive asylum claim; though if, upon the case being referred back to him, the Secretary of State concludes that the appellant would be at risk if he were removed under para 180K, he will no doubt go on to address the substantive claim.

While the conclusion I have arrived at determines, if I am right, the correct construction of para 5 of Sch 2, its application in practice will depend upon what circumstances are to count as showing, in a third country case, that it is incumbent upon the Secretary of State to consider the substantive claim to refugee status. Mr Blake submitted that a third country removal is only legally permissible where the Secretary of State has first ensured that the third country will admit the claimant to its own asylum procedures for the purpose of resolving his claim. Mr Nicol made a similar submission: he said that an asylum applicant cannot be removed to a third country unless the Secretary of State has been assured, by the authorities of the third country, that the asylum claim will be considered substantively: although he accepted that absent an express assurance, there may still be a lawful third country removal if, but only if, the Secretary of State has positive and compelling evidence that the third country will give substantive consideration to the claim.

In canvassing these arguments, counsel relied on a variety of materials, including art 35 of the convention, which imposes upon the contracting states an obligation to cooperate with the Office of the United Nations High Commissioner for Refugees (UNHCR), the Statute of the UNHCR, and certain declarations (as I think I may call them) of the High Commissioner's Executive Committee. The theme of the applicants' argument was that, not least given the incorporation into English law of the 1951 convention by the 1993 Act, removal of an asylum applicant to a third country will only be lawful if the Secretary of State has received something in the nature of a positive guarantee that the applicant will be admitted to the third country's asylum procedures and his claim there properly dealt with under the 1951 convention. I mean no disrespect to this argument (nor indeed to the UNHCR, whose representative has made submissions to special adjudicators deciding appeals under the 1993 Act) in rejecting it without canvassing the detail of the international materials which were relied on. These points seem to me to be critical:

(i) Article 35 imposes a general obligation at the international level; it is not translated by s 2 of the 1993 Act into a legal duty enforceable in the English courts by an asylum applicant. I do not of course suggest that art 35 is unimportant, or in any way to be sidelined. But it is clear in principle that statements of preferred practice, or policy aspiration, made by or on behalf of the UNHCR do not form part of the content of the legal obligations owed to, and enforceable in municipal proceedings by, an applicant for refugee status. If authority were needed for this, it is to be found in the speech of Lord Bridge in *Bugdaycay v Secretary of State for the Home Dept* [1987] 1 All ER 940 at 946, [1987] AC 514 at 524, which comments upon the status of statements made in the 'Handbook on Procedures and Criteria for Determining Refugee Status' published in 1979 by the UNHCR. I do not believe that Lord Bridge's reasoning is in some sense disapplied by the enactment of s 2 of the 1993 Act.

(ii) The position taken by the applicants was in large part based upon the premise that the extent of the Secretary of State's obligations under the convention, enforceable in the English courts, has in some way been heightened by s 2 of the 1993 Act. In my judgment this is a false premise. Manifestly the passage into law of that Act does not affect the scope of the United Kingdom's obligations at the international level. As regards domestic law, before the Act was passed, the Secretary of State had undertaken by the then current Immigration Rules in effect to abide by the convention. Section 2 of the 1993 Act merely requires that he should do the same thing in future. Under the pre-existing regime the government had created at any rate a legitimate expectation that the Secretary of State would not remove an asylum claimant from the UK where to do so would, or perhaps reasonably might, expose him to persecution: whatever the reach of the obligation not thus to remove a claimant, it is not lengthened by s 2 of the 1993 Act.

(iii) The applicants specifically submitted that it would be a breach of the United Kingdom's convention obligations were the Secretary of State to remove a claimant to a third country from which he might be returned here. In an Amnesty International document published on 26 July 1993, this scenario is, perhaps reasonably, described as 'passing the buck'. This argument is misconceived: however undesirable it might be on humanitarian or other grounds, it is no breach of the convention that a claimant be returned to the United Kingdom by a third country without consideration of his substantive claim, because such a course of action would not expose him to a convention risk; nor therefore is it any breach for the United Kingdom to send the claimant to a safe third country even if the Home Secretary appreciates that he may simply be sent back here again. This conclusion is I believe supported by the decision of the Court of Appeal in *Bouzeid v Secretary of State for the Home Dept* [1991] Imm AR 204; though, as that case indicates, there may be a sustainable legal complaint if the Secretary of State were to send a claimant back to the third country for a second time. I also reject Mr Nicol's kindred argument that it would be a breach to return an applicant to a third country which might then return him to a fourth (not being the country of feared persecution) where his claim might fall to be considered substantively, or which might even send him to a fifth, and so on. No doubt in cases where there is something like a chain of states, through which the claimant has passed, between the country of feared persecution and the United Kingdom, the Secretary of State must give careful consideration to the extent to which each state, on the facts known to him, adheres to its convention obligations; and there will be special factors for his assessment if one or more of the intervening countries is not a signatory to the convention.

In my judgment the true position is that, under para 180K, the Secretary of State is to form a view on the information known to him (a) as to whether the country to which he proposes to remove the claimant is a safe country as defined by the rule, and (b) as to whether he is barred by the rule from removing the claimant by virtue of either of the specific provisions set out in the rule at (a) and (b). The United Kingdom's convention obligations do not require any further stipulations to be written into the rule than those which it already contains. If, having formed his view, he gives a para 5 certificate, the adjudicator on any subsequent s 8 appeal must decide whether he agrees with it in light of the construction of para 5 which I have set out. The discipline which this system imposes upon the Secretary of State consists in the fact that the adjudicator must independently judge the merits of the certificate.

I heard some submissions that para 180K is repugnant to s 2 of the 1993 Act, and thus ultra vires the Secretary of State; but it follows from what I have said that this is not so.

I may now turn to the individual applications before me. It will not be necessary to travel through the reasoning of each adjudicator's decision, because the principal thrust of the applicants' complaints depends upon putative constructions of the 1993 Act which I have already rejected, and also because the remaining discrete arguments may be resolved without recourse to much in the way of detail. But I should make these observations. Some of the decisions before me suggest that, in the short time in which the 1993 Act has been in force, the special adjudicators have not always recognised the clear distinction between their function in deciding whether to agree with the Secretary of State's certificate, and their separate function of deciding whether or not to allow or dismiss an appeal or refer the case to the Secretary of State as appropriate. Because in these particular cases (save for two, Mehari and Augusto, which for reasons I will shortly explain will have to be reconsidered) I shall hold that the adjudicator was quite entitled to agree with the certificate and thus necessarily dismiss the appeal, any want of attention to this distinction is without practical significance; and I should in any case make it clear that I mean no criticism of the adjudicators, who have had to grapple with new legislation which is not altogether straightforward and in circumstances where they have had to work within the tight time limits which I have described. It is however of great importance that the adjudicators appreciate that in a para 5 case their first distinct task is to decide whether or not they agree with the certificate.

Secondly, some of the decisions betray a perception that once a certificate is given, it has to be accepted by the adjudicator. This has arisen out of a reliance placed on the decision of Schiemann J in *R v Secretary of State for the Home Dept, ex p Hilaludeen* [1993] Imm AR 250. In that case, however, the court was dealing with an application for leave to move for judicial review directly against the Secretary of State's decision to remove the applicant to France without consideration of his substantive asylum claim. The Secretary of State had given a certificate to the effect that he believed the applicant would be re-admitted to France. Schiemann J said that the court had to take such a certificate at face value unless the applicant could demonstrate that there was no basis on which the Secretary of State could be so satisfied. I see no reason to doubt Schiemann J's conclusion (and none was suggested), but the case is entirely irrelevant to the adjudicator's functions on appeals under the 1993 Act. Schiemann J had to deal with the case before him on the public law *Wednesbury* basis; an adjudicator in a para 5 case has to consider the merits of the Secretary of State's certificate. Again, however, such references as there are in the decisions before me to *Ex p Hilaludeen* do not matter, because the adjudicators decided that on the merits the appellants before them could be removed to the third country in question without breach of convention obligations, and to that extent impliedly agreed with the merits of the Secretary of State's certificate.

I should turn to the cases which will have to be reconsidered. It is accepted by Mr Pannick that the adjudicators' decisions in the cases of Mehari and Augusto should be quashed. In the case of Mehari, this is because the adjudicator seems to have held that the onus was on the appellant to show that his removal would not breach the United Kingdom's convention obligations. I agree that this vitiates her decision, although she did not put the matter in such plain terms, perhaps because (as it seems to me) she rolled together her function of deciding whether to agree or disagree with the Secretary of State's certificate and her disposal of the appeal as such: and this is a feature, not unique to Mehari's case, to which I have already referred. I will grant an order of certiorari in Mehari's case.

I should not, however, leave that case without noticing two further points taken by Mr Blake. First, he submitted that even on Mr Pannick's highest position as to the construction of para 5 (and, he would say, on the construction which I have adopted), upon the factual material before the adjudicator she was bound to disagree with the Secretary of State's certificate. Thus, if the same material is put before another adjudicator when the appeal comes to be re-determined, that adjudicator also will be bound to disagree with the certificate; and, in effect, Mr Blake invites me to say as much. I do not propose

to go into the details underlying this submission, since Mr Blake's argument is
a in reality a tacit invitation to me to give an advisory opinion as to how the next
adjudicator should respond to the evidence before him. I have no doubt that
there are circumstances in which the public law court ought to exercise the
jurisdiction (which it certainly possesses) to give advisory opinions; but this is
not one of them. I will make only the following observations. Mr Blake accepts
b that the Secretary of State's decision letter, indicating that the applicant could
properly be removed to Italy because that country would not, on the
information available to him, further remove the applicant to Ethiopia without
first considering his substantive asylum application, is material which the
adjudicator was entitled to take into account. The evidence the other way,
which was placed before the adjudicator, is summarised in Mr Blake's skeleton
c argument. It consists in large measure of documents from Amnesty
International suggesting recent failures by Italy to comply with its convention
obligations. A large part of this evidence concerned cases in which, allegedly,
refugee claimants returned to Italy had then been returned again to the United
Kingdom: and I have already held that this, however stressful or undesirable it
d may be, does not amount to breach of the convention. I am not prepared to hold
that on the evidence before the adjudicator, she was bound to disagree with the
certificate; but I am not to be taken as deciding the point, because the next
adjudicator must assess for himself whatever evidence is put before him. It may
not, of course, be identical with that put before the previous adjudicator.

Mr Blake's other point concerns the fact that his client is a minor, having been
e born on 1 December 1975. Mr Blake says that by virtue of paras 180P and 180Q
of the new Immigration Rules (which I have not set out) and a statement by the
minister in the House (which it is said gave rise to a legitimate expectation) the
Secretary of State was not entitled to return the applicant to Italy without special
safeguards, and in particular without ensuring that he would be received there.
f I heard some argument as to whether it is constitutionally permissible to found
in legal proceedings an enforceable legitimate expectation upon anything said in
Parliament. But again, I do not propose to decide the point: as Mr Blake himself
asserted in reply, the removal directions in this case have become entirely
academic since, obviously, the applicant will be permitted to stay until his appeal
has been re-determined. I decline to embark upon an excursus into the law of
g legitimate expectations and the use of Parliamentary material in a case where,
for all I know, there may not be any further removal directions at all.

In Augusto, the special adjudicator disbelieved the appellant's evidence to the
effect that at a particular stage he did not realise that he had arrived in France,
and also his evidence that he felt he was at some risk in Spain, through which he
h passed but where he did not claim asylum: but the adjudicator seems to have
treated these findings as relevant to the question whether the appellant could be
safely returned to France. However such findings do not and could not logically
bear on that issue at all. In this case also, therefore, I will grant an order of
certiorari. It is unnecessary to say any more about Augusto's case.

I propose next to take the case of Celik, because Mr Nicol advanced a greater
j weight of distinct submissions than was done in the other cases.

First I should indicate that in this case the appellant led no evidence as to what
might happen to him in Holland if he were to return there. The Secretary of
State had given a decision letter (similar to that in Mehari and indeed other cases)
indicating his view, on information available to him, that the Dutch authorities
would not further remove the appellant to Turkey without first considering his
asylum application. The adjudicator was plainly entitled to take that into

account, and there was nothing the other way. Some reference was made to a copy document, apparently emanating from the Dutch authorities, indicating that they would take Mr Celik back. Mr Nicol showed me a passage in the appeal decision where the adjudicator clearly attaches very little, if any, weight to the document, and he submitted that there is nothing in it to say for how long Holland would be prepared to take back his client, nor whether his substantive claim would be considered. But even if this document offered no real assistance to the Secretary of State's case, it certainly did nothing to advance Mr Celik's. In the result there can thus be no quarrel with the decision in Celik's case unless any of Mr Nicol's separate points ought to prevail.

The first which I will take was this. Mr Nicol submitted that the adjudicator was guilty of procedural unfairness by virtue of the way in which he rejected Mr Celik's evidence that he did not have the opportunity to claim asylum in any country through which he passed before arriving in Holland, and that in Holland he spent only one to one and a half hours at a port, and was under the direction and control of others throughout that period. If he had no such opportunity, that would go to the legitimacy of his removal having regard to the requirements of sub-para (a) of para 180K. The adjudicator, before whom the appellant gave evidence, disbelieved his account. In rejecting it, as the decision shows, he was moved by what he saw as major discrepancies between the evidence and what Mr Celik had said in interview. He found as a fact that there had been nothing in the way of Mr Celik's seeking political asylum at the port in Holland.

Mr Nicol's argument is that the discrepancies were not put to his client in the witness box, either by the Home Office representative or by the adjudicator himself. He has filed evidence which, he says, shows that if they had been put to him he would have had a good explanation. I need not rehearse the detail, because in my judgment the point is bad in principle. Mr Celik was represented at the hearing before the adjudicator by counsel. Counsel had in his possession the record of interview, and must be taken as having known what his client was going to say in the witness box. He was or should have been alive to the potential importance of any discrepancy between the two accounts. It was open to him to deal with it, either in the course of his client's evidence in chief or otherwise, and if he failed to do so, that gives rise to no imputation of unfairness by the adjudicator who was entitled to make findings of fact on the evidence as he reasonably saw fit.

The next argument with which I will deal is Mr Nicol's submission that the Secretary of State possessed a discretion within the terms of para 180K whether or not to remove his client to a third country even if it were a safe one under the rule; and that his exercise of this discretion was itself appealable to the adjudicator, who should thus have decided whether the discretion ought to have been exercised differently, but did not effectively do so. This submission was founded on s 19(1)(a)(ii) which falls within Part II of the 1971 Act; and, indeed, that sub-paragraph deals with an adjudicator's jurisdiction in discretion cases. By para 4(2)(b) of Sch 2 to the 1993 Act, s 19 is to have effect as if s 8 of the 1993 Act were contained in Part II of the 1971 Act. The submission is, however, misconceived, because a s 8 appeal is not a discretion case: the only ground which the adjudicator is to consider is the assertion that the appellant's removal as proposed would contravene the United Kingdom's convention obligations. So s 19(1)(a)(ii) can have no application in a s 8 case.

Next, Mr Nicol submitted that the Secretary of State was obliged by r 5(6) of the new Procedure Rules to serve on the appellant (and the adjudicator and the UNHCR representative) any documents supporting the reference in the decision letter to 'the information available ... about the policies and practice of Holland'. The obligation in the sub-rule is to serve certain particular documents, and 'any other document referred to in the decision which is being appealed'. This is a bad point. The decision letter did not refer to any documents. In my judgment the rule only requires service of documents specifically referred to, or, at least, necessarily identified by the terms of the decision letter.

Mr Nicol also submitted that the Secretary of State's certificate was bad, or invalid, because it was not proved that the person signing it had in fact been authorised to do so on behalf of the Secretary of State. He said that s 32(2) of the 1971 Act has no application to para 5 certificates. That subsection provides:

'Any document purporting to be an order, notice or direction made or given by the Secretary of State for the purposes of this Act and to be signed by him or on his behalf, and any document purporting to be a certificate of the Secretary of State so given and to be signed by him, shall be received in evidence, and shall, until the contrary is proved, deemed to be made or issued by him.'

Under the signature on the certificate in Celik's case appear the words 'For and on behalf of the Secretary of State', and, at the bottom left, the words 'Home Office Asylum Division'. There was, moreover, another document before the adjudicator undoubtedly put in by the Home Office, signed by Mr Ing, who also signed the decision letter, which asserts: 'The Secretary of State has certified this claim to be without foundation.' In my judgment, quite irrespective of s 32(2), the adjudicator was plainly entitled to take the certificate as having been signed on behalf of the Secretary of State—there was evidence before him to that effect; indeed it would have been perverse to do otherwise.

It was also submitted that there should have been evidence before the adjudicator of the 'Grading or experience' of the person who signed the certificate. Mr Nicol referred to *Oladehinde v Secretary of State for the Home Dept* [1990] 3 All ER 393 at 401, [1991] 1 AC 254 at 303. But that case is authority for the proposition that it is for Secretary of State to decide what level of officer is apt for the performance of a particular function. He was not, in my judgment, obliged to lead any positive evidence before the adjudicator as to the status of the officer selected to sign the certificate in support of his case that the certificate should be agreed to.

Mr Nicol next submitted that the certificate was bad because it bears no date. It must have been signed after 21 July 1993 (the date of the applicant's arrival) and no later than 19 August (the date of the decision letter). Within that period, said Mr Nicol, representations were made on the applicant's behalf which might properly have affected the Secretary of State's judgment; so that it is not possible to say precisely what material the Secretary of State had in mind when the certificate was made. I am not aware of any evidence to suggest that the question whether Holland was a safe third country could possibly have depended on anything said or done between 21 July and 19 August 1993. No doubt it will be good practice for para 5 certificates to be dated; but on the facts here I do not regard Mr Nicol's submission as disclosing any perceptible point of law going to the validity of the certificate.

The other cases in my judgment also fall to be determined adversely to the applicants in the light of my findings as to the construction of the 1993 Act and the effect of para 180K, but there are some individual points with which I must deal.

In Hersi, Mr Pannick accepts that the adjudicator, in his decision, cast the burden on the appellant to prove that he would not be re-admitted to Germany for his asylum claim to be considered; whereas it is for the Secretary of State to make good his certificate. However there was no material whatever before the adjudicator to indicate that Germany might not fulfil its convention obligations, and the Secretary of State's decision letter indicated the contrary. I accept Mr Pannick's submission that on the evidence no reasonable adjudicator could have disagreed with the certificate.

In fact much of the burden of Mr Hersi's case on the facts was that he had been given to understand that there were instances of asylum-seekers in Germany being ill-treated, sometimes seriously so. But no case was made to the effect that the German authorities might not or would not fulfil its convention obligations.

Lastly, Mr Abbott on Hersi's behalf submitted that the adjudicator was wrong to refuse his client's applications for an adjournment of the appeal, so as to obtain the services of an interpreter and/or legal assistance. But (as the adjudicator pointed out) he gave evidence in perfectly understandable English; and he had been interviewed in English, and had signed a document stating that he did not wish to be provided with an interpreter. The question of an adjournment for legal assistance was one for the adjudicator's discretion within the constraints imposed by rr 9 and 10 of the Procedure Rules. I am quite unable to detect any error in the refusal of an adjournment, for either of the reasons urged, such as to attract judicial review relief.

In Doreh's case, the only material put before the adjudicator to support the contention that Italy might not fulfil her convention obligations was evidence of instances where claimants had been returned by that country to the United Kingdom after being removed there from the United Kingdom: the Amnesty document 'Passing the Buck', which also featured in Mehari's case, was put in. I have already held that this founds no objection to a third country removal on convention grounds.

Mr Doreh claimed to have family connections in the United Kingdom, namely two cousins and certain other more distant relatives, and so it was put to the adjudicator that there were special circumstances why he should not be removed from this country. The adjudicator considered that such factors could not help the appellant. Mr De Mello on his behalf says that the adjudicator should have decided whether as a matter of discretion his client ought not to be removed from the United Kingdom. But this is the same point upon s 19(1)(a)(ii) of the 1971 Act as was taken by Mr Nicol, and falls to be rejected for the same reasons as I have given in dealing with his argument.

In the result, then, orders of certiorari will go in the cases of Mehari and Augusto; the other applications will be dismissed.

Orders accordingly.

K Mydeen Esq   Barrister.

Powdrill and another v Watson and another

COURT OF APPEAL, CIVIL DIVISION
DILLON, LEGGATT AND HENRY LJJ
21, 22 FEBRUARY 1994

Decision of the Court of Appeal varied.
[1995] 2 W.L.R. 312, H.L.(E.)

Company – Administration order – Administrator – Powers – Effect of administration order – Administrators continuing to employ company's staff to keep company in operation with view to sale as going concern – Administrators subsequently terminating employees' employment – Whether administrators adopting employees' contracts of employment – Whether employees entitled to claim salary in lieu of notice, holiday pay and interest as part of administration expenses – Insolvency Act 1986, s 19(5).

The respondents were employed as pilots by a company which operated a charter airline. Administrators of the company were appointed by court order on 7 August 1989 pursuant to s 8(1)[a] of the Insolvency Act 1986. On 14 August the administrators wrote to the employees stating that the company would continue to meet their salaries but that the administrators 'are not and will not at any future time adopt or assume personal liability in respect of your Contracts of Employment'. In September the administrators wrote a further letter to all captains and first officers stating that additional payments would be made to all captains and first officers who remained in employment and worked for the company. The administrators hoped to be able to keep the company in operation with a view to selling it as a going concern but by 30 November the administrators had been unable to find a buyer and on 5 December letters of dismissal were sent to all staff terminating their employment. The respondents issued a petition under s 27 of the 1986 Act claiming two months' salary in lieu of notice on their dismissal, holiday pay and interest. The judge made the order sought. The administrators appealed. The respondents cross-appealed contending that the bonus payments referred to in the September letter were in fact a concealed pay rise and therefore their termination payment ought to be based on a salary which included the bonus payment.

Held – If the administrators of a company continued after 14 days of their appointment substantially to employ staff and paid them in accordance with their previous contracts of employment they would be taken to have impliedly 'adopted' the contracts of employment pursuant to s 19(5)[b] of the Insolvency Act 1986 and would be liable to pay, as part of the administration expenses, salary in lieu of notice and holiday pay on dismissal of the employees of the company. The letter of 14 August was far too obscure to be construed as an offer to employees of employment on terms other than all the terms of their previous contractual entitlement and the mere assertion by the administrators that they were not adopting the contracts of employment had no legal effect because adoption was not merely a matter of words but of fact. It followed that the respondents were entitled to two months' payment of salary in lieu of

---

a   Section 8(1), so far as material, is set out at p 516 g to j, post
b   Section 19(5) is set out at p 518 b, post

notice, holiday pay and interest. However the termination payment would not be based on a salary which included the bonus payment in the September letter since the bonus payments were made under separate contracts which were brought to an end by dismissal. The appeal and the cross-appeal would therefore be dismissed (see p 520 c d h j, p 522 g to p 523 c, p 524 b to e j to p 525 c f to j, post).

Notes
For the effect of an administration order, see 7(2) *Halsbury's Laws* (4th edn reissue) para 1330, and for cases on the subject, see 10(1) *Digest* (2nd reissue) 276, 8103–8104.

For the vacation of office of an administrator, see 7(2) *Halsbury's Laws* (4th edn reissue) para 1359.

For the Insolvency Act 1986, ss 8, 19, see 4 *Halsbury's Statutes* (4th edn) (1987 reissue) 736, 745. The Insolvency Act 1986, s 19 has been amended by the Insolvency Act 1994 in relation to contracts of employment adopted on or after 15 March 1994.

Cases referred to in judgments
James, Ex p, re Condon (1874) LR 9 Ch App 609, [1874–80] All ER Rep 388, LJJ.
Salford Union Guardians v Dewhurst [1926] AC 619, HL.
Specialised Mouldings Ltd, Re (13 February 1987, unreported), Ch D.

Cases also cited
Atlantic Computer Systems plc, Re [1992] 1 All ER 476, [1992] Ch 505, CA.
Bristol Airport plc v Powdrill [1990] 2 All ER 493, [1990] Ch 744, CA.
Maxwell Communications Corp plc, Re (No 2) [1994] 1 All ER 737, [1993] 1 WLR 1402.

Appeal and cross-appeal
Roger Arthur Powdrill and Joseph Beaumont Atkinson, who were the joint administrators of Paramount Airways Ltd (the company), appealed from the decision of Evans-Lombe J made on 27 July 1993 whereby he held that the contracts of employment of the respondents, John Watson and Anthony John Unwin, had been adopted by the appellants in the course of the carrying on by them of their functions as administrators of the company within the meaning of s 19(5) of the Insolvency Act 1986. The respondents cross-appealed in respect of bonus payments offered to them by the appellants. The facts are set out in the judgment of Dillon LJ.

Michael Crystal QC and Mark Phillips (instructed by Wilde Sapte) for the administrators.
Robin Potts QC and Richard Snowden (instructed by Burrough & Co, Cardiff) for the respondents.

DILLON LJ. This is an appeal by Mr Powdrill and Mr Atkinson, who are the joint administrators of a company called Paramount Airways Ltd, from an order made by Evans-Lombe J in the Companies Court on 27 July 1993. The respondents are two former employees of the company, Captain Watson and Captain Unwin. There is a further point taken, in effect by cross-appeal by a respondent's notice to which I shall have to come.

The general question arises in the field relating to the continued employment by the company, after the appointment of the administrators, of staff previously in the company's employment and the extent of the benefits which the staff so employed are entitled to claim as administration expenses within the meaning of s 19(5) of the Insolvency Act 1986.

The basic facts are that the company operated a charter airline from Bristol Airport and certain other airports in the United Kingdom. The administrators were appointed by Warner J by an order of 7 August 1989. The administrators sent a letter to all employees on 14 August 1989 as follows:

'I write to advise you that [we] were appointed Joint Administrators of the above company by an Order of the High Court dated 7 August 1989. Under the provisions of the Insolvency Act 1986 the Joint Administrators act as agents of the Company. We are currently investigating the Company's position but as yet we are uncertain as to the true contractual position between yourself and the company. Nothing in this letter is to be taken to affect the true identity of your employer, however, we should like to take this opportunity of re-assuring you that the company will continue to pay your monthly salary during the interim period, including that payable on 31 August 1989, together with any other sums which you are contractually entitled to pursuant to the terms and conditions of your Contract of Employment. We hope that we may have your co-operation during this period. We wish to make it clear that the Joint Administrators act at all times as agents of the Company and without personal liability. The Administrators are not and will not at any future time adopt or assume personal liability in respect of your Contracts of Employment.
[signed]
R A Powdrill in his capacity as Joint Administrator of Paramount Airways Limited acting as its agent and without personal liability.'

Following that, a question arose in relation to keeping the airline captains and first officers in the employment of the company while it was in administration and it was hoped that it might be able to arrange to sell the business as a going concern. In those circumstances the administrators, in September 1989, wrote a further letter to all captains and first officers as follows:

'Further to our meeting on 21 September 1989 and following representations from Mr W B Morgan, we would propose making the following additional payments to Captains and First Officers. These payments will be made to all Captains and First Officers remaining in employment and working for Paramount Airways Limited as at 31 October 1989, or as at the date of a sale of the business if earlier; and who have not tendered their resignation by such time. Payments will be made for the period commencing 1 September 1989 and will be apportioned if foreshortened by a sale. If the Administrators remain in office after 31 October 1989, this arrangement will continue on a monthly basis until further notice with each month end date being relevant for not having tendered resignations.
The following payments are proposed:
CAPTAINS
For September—£300 For October and each subsequent months—£400

FIRST OFFICERS
For September—£250
For October and each subsequent months—£300
The first payment will be made with the October salary and will include September payments. This arrangement will not be binding upon the company following the Administrators' resignation. The Administrators are not adopting any or all terms of any contracts of employment or service you have and act only as agents of Paramount Airways Limited and without personal liability.'

On 3 November 1989 the statutory creditors' meeting was held in accordance with the scheme of the Act and it passed a resolution approving that the administrators should seek to sell the company as a going concern. From their appointment until, at any rate, the end of September the administrators had been concerned not only to work out what could be put to the creditors at the creditors' meeting but to keep the charter airline business operating through the peak holiday season of that year. Despite the approval of the meeting of 3 November, by 30 November the administrators found that they had been unable to find any buyer and, apart from a wet lease of a single plane, which for present purposes is immaterial, the operations of the company had been suspended. Accordingly, on 30 November a meeting was held when the employees were told that that was the state of affairs. On 5 December 1989 letters of dismissal were sent to all staff, except possibly the few required for the wet lease arrangement, terminating their contracts of employment summarily and, indeed, retrospectively, namely as from 30 November.

In September 1991 each of the respondents, Captain Watson and Captain Unwin, issued a petition under s 27 of the Insolvency Act 1986 claiming what they said to be their entitlement as a result of their dismissals. The very proper reaction of the administrators to that was that they issued a summons on 31 October, seeking the directions of the Companies Court on these matters and they joined the respondents as parties to the summons.

The system of administration is a new system recommended by the Cork Report (Report of the Review Committee on Insolvency Law and Practice) (Cmnd 8558 (1982)), which is introduced in the Insolvency Act 1986. The scheme is under s 8(1):

'... if the court—(a) is satisfied that a company is or is likely to become unable to pay its debts (within the meaning given to that expression by section 123 of this Act), and (b) considers that the making of an order under this section would be likely to achieve one or more of the purposes mentioned below, the court may make an administration order in relation to the company.

(2) An administration order is an order directing that, during the period for which the order is in force, the affairs, business and property of the company shall be managed by a person ("the administrator") appointed for the purpose by the court.'

The purposes for whose achievement an administration order may be made include, under s 8(3), (a) the survival of the company and the whole or any part of its undertaking as a going concern and (b) a more advantageous realisation of the company's assets than would be effected on a winding up.

I need not go in great detail into the scheme of the Act, but it is pertinent to note that under s 11 the effect of the making of an administration order is that any petition for the winding up of the company shall be dismissed and any administrative receiver of the company shall vacate office.

It is further provided by s 11(3):

> 'During the period for which an administration order is in force—(a) no resolution may be passed or order made for the winding up of the company; (b) no administrative receiver of the company may be appointed; (c) no other steps may be taken to enforce any security over the company's property, or repossess goods in the company's possession under any hire-purchase agreement, except with the consent of the administrator or the leave of the court and subject (where the court gives leave) to such terms as the court may impose; and (d) no other proceedings and no execution or other legal process may be commenced or continued, and no distress may be levied, against the company or its property except with the consent of the administrator or the leave of the court and subject (where the court gives leave) to such terms as aforesaid.'

Section 14(1) provides:

> 'The administrator of a company—(a) may do all such things as may be necessary for the management of the affairs, business and property of the company, and (b) without prejudice to the generality of paragraph (a), has the powers specified in Schedule 1 to this Act.'

He is further given power under sub-s (2) to remove any director of the company and appoint any person to be a director of it whether to fill a vacancy or otherwise and under sub-s (3) to apply to the court for directions in relation to any particular matter arising in connection with the carrying out of his functions.

It is also provided by s 14(5) that, in exercising his powers, the administrator is deemed to act as the company's agent. He is not, therefore, personally liable under contracts he makes or contracts which he adopts.

Section 15 provides:

> '(1) The administrator of a company may dispose of or otherwise exercise his powers in relation to any property of the company which is subject to a security to which this subsection applies as if the property were not subject to the security ...
>
> (3) Subsection (1) applies to any security which, as created, was a floating charge ...'

Section 18 provides for the discharge of an administration order and of the administrator at the discretion of the administrator and mandatorily if it appears to the administrator that the purpose or each of the purposes specified in the order has been achieved or is incapable of achievement, or he is required to do so by a meeting of the company's creditors.

Section 19 is concerned with the vacation of office by an administrator. Subsection (2) provides by alternative (b) that the administrator shall vacate office if the administration order is discharged. Subsections (3), (4) and (5) then provide as follows:

> '(3) Where at any time a person ceases to be administrator, the next two subsections apply.

(4) His remuneration and any expenses properly incurred by him shall be charged on and paid out of any property of the company which is in his custody or under his control at that time in priority to any security to which section 15(1) then applies.

(5) Any sums payable in respect of debts or liabilities incurred, while he was administrator, under contracts entered into or contracts of employment adopted by him or a predecessor of his in the carrying out of his or the predecessor's functions shall be charged on and paid out of any such property as is mentioned in subsection (4) in priority to any charge arising under that subsection. For this purpose, the administrator is not to be taken to have adopted a contract of employment by reason of anything done or omitted to be done within 14 days after his appointment.'

So far as sub-s (4) is concerned, the remuneration of the administrator and his expenses properly incurred are to be charged out of any property of the company which is in his custody or under his control at the time of his ceasing to be administrator and if that property was subject to a security to which s 15(1) applies, that is to say a security which was initially a floating charge, it is to be paid in priority to that charge.

We are not concerned with specific charges. In addition, we have the provision that the administrator is not to be taken to have adopted a contract of employment by reason of anything done or omitted to be done within 14 days after his appointment. That gives him a time of 14 days to endeavour to take stock, and what has been done in that period cannot be relied on as showing that he has adopted a contract of employment. After the 14 days it becomes a question whether he has or has not adopted a contract of employment by reason of anything done or omitted after the 14 days.

I should next pass, to complete the summary of the facts, to the terms of the contract of employment of the respondents which appears to have been in the company's standard form. We have a form for Captain Watson which tells us that the date of commencement is as Appendix 1, but does not include Appendix 1. Nothing, however, turns on that. It is relevant to notice certain clauses, because of the issues which are raised. One is cl 8 which is concerned with holidays and is relevant because one of the matters in issue is the entitlement of the respondents to holiday pay. Clause 8 provides:

'(a) The Company's holiday year begins on 1st April and ends on 31st March.'

The relevant year, therefore, in the present case, is the year that began on 1 April 1989. It is expressly provided by sub-cl (e):

'Except as otherwise agreed in writing ... holiday entitlement expires on 31st March annually and may not be carried forward to the next holiday year.'

Sub-cl (c) provides:

'Your holiday entitlement is 28 days plus 8 associated days off per annum or, in year of joining, pro rata from your date of commencement until 31st March next following.'

Then it is said, and it is understandable from the nature of the business:

'Except as agreed in writing with the Company's Director of Flight Operations no holiday may normally be taken between 1st May and 30th September each year ...'

Finally, and this is where holiday pay comes in, sub-para (f) provides:

'On termination of employment other than for mis-conduct your holiday entitlement will be paid on the basis of one-twelfth of the annual entitlement for each full calendar month's service from the previous 1st April or, if you commenced employment after such date, then your date of commencement, less any leave taken.'

Clause 10 is concerned with contracting out which means, in relation to the staff pensions, the company's pension scheme:

'You may, if you wish, join Holdings' pension scheme on the applicable terms and conditions ... whereupon you will become contracted out of the State Earnings Related Pension Scheme.'

The pension scheme was contributory by the employees and also by company contributions.

There is cl 12, which deals with notice of termination of employment:

'Notice of termination of employment to be given either by yourself or the Company ... shall be in writing and as follows: (a) During a probationary period comprising the first six months of your employment hereunder: two weeks (b) Thereafter: two months ...'

There is a minor point, which is not in issue on this appeal, that there was doubt at one stage whether the employing company of Captain Watson and Captain Unwin at the crucial time was the company Paramount Airways Ltd or its parent company Paramount Holdings Ltd. But the conclusion which is not challenged is that though there was talk of the holding company becoming the employer, the employment continued as employment by Paramount Airways Ltd. In the letter of 14 August the passage saying, 'Nothing in this letter is to be taken to affect the true identity of your employer ...' was merely preserving at that stage whether the employer was Paramount Airways or the holding company.

It is accepted by the administrators that during the time from their appointment on 7 August until 30 November they were bound to pay to each of the employees, whose services were used by them, his salary and to pay for him the contributions to the pension fund according to the rates appropriate under his service agreement which had been in force before the appointment of the administrators, subject to an addition in relation to bonus payments under the bonus payment scheme, which is the subject of the cross appeal by respondent's notice, which I lay on one side for the moment. It is also accepted that they would be entitled to a portion of holiday pay in respect of that year. But it is asserted for the administrators that they did not ever adopt the previous contracts because they said in the letter to each employee of 14 August 1989, apart from making it clear that they as joint administrators at all times acted as agents of the company and worked without personal liability, that they were not and would not at any future time adopt or assume personal liability in respect of the employees' contracts of employment.

In the letter of September 1989 to the captains and first officers there is a ritual incantation in the last paragraph:

'The Administrators are not adopting any or all terms of any contracts of employment or service you have and act only as agents of Paramount Airways Limited and without personal liability.'

That is said, notwithstanding that by September the administrators had been making payments to the employees, and in the September letter where the additional payments were provided for, the additional payments were said to being made to all captains and first officers remaining in 'employment' and working for Paramount Airways Ltd as at 31 October 1989 etc.

One wonders how, if they had not adopted the contracts, these employees, and particularly the captains and first officers, came to be in their employment at all.

It is submitted, however, that to adopt a contract of employment the administrators must do something positive. It is said that here, by the original August letter, they said that they would not. As I see it, that does not do. If they continue substantially after the 14 days to employ staff and pay them in accordance with their previous contracts they will be held impliedly to have adopted those contracts of employment.

The whole function of administration will normally require that the administrators carry on the business of the company concerned, with a view either, with the benefit of the moratorium, to trade out of difficulties into profit so that the directors can take over and the company can carry on as a going concern after the administrators have been discharged or, at any rate, to have time to find a buyer for the business as a going concern. They will, therefore, want employees. But if they want to use the existing staff they must, as I see it, either adopt the existing contracts or negotiate new contracts. But if they are going to negotiate new contracts they must not be sham.

In the present case it is suggested that by the letter of 14 August they have offered the employees new contracts on the basis that the employees will work as required and will be paid their monthly salary and the pension provisions together with any other sums to which the employees were contractually entitled, pursuant to the terms and conditions of the previous contracts of employment, but without adopting the contract of employment and, in particular, without adopting the terms of the contract of employment which would require the employee to be given notice of termination of his contract or paid two months' salary with other benefits in lieu of notice, and without adopting any term of the contract of employment which might require the administrators to pay at any future time any sum calculated by reference to past service of the employee, such as holiday pay, in respect of the period from 1 April 1989 to the appointment of the administrators on 7 August.

The learned judge held that the letter in question was far too obscure to be construed as an offer to employees of employment on terms other than all the terms of their previous contractual entitlement. In my judgment, he was plainly right. The letter is, understandably, pointing out that the administrators will not be personally liable to the employees for the employees' salaries and so forth. Apart from that, it is conveying the intention that they will continue to be employed under their previous contracts. It points in favour of adoption rather than against it, despite the phrase at the end about the administrators not adopting, and not at any future time adopting contracts of employment.

That phrase seems to have become, as I have said, a ritual incantation as a result of a case of Harman J, *Re Specialised Mouldings Ltd* (13 February 1987, unreported). The case is summarised in Stewart *Administrative Receivers and Administrators* (1987). That reference has been picked up by Professor Goode in his book *Principles of Corporate Insolvency Law* (1990) p 101. In that passage Professor Goode says:

> 'If the above interpretation of "adopted" be correct, [and, in my view, it is, and he is talking about an administrative receiver, not an administrator] the receiver who allows a contract of employment to continue does not escape liability merely because in doing so he makes it clear that the company remains the employer and that he, the receiver, is not adopting the contract. However, in *Re Specialised Mouldings Ltd*, Harman J. held, on an application for directions under section 35 of the Insolvency Act, that a receiver can avoid adopting an employment contract by stipulating expressly that he does not do so. In reliance on this decision it has become common practice for a receiver to write to all employees after his appointment to say that their contracts with the company will be continued on the same basis as previously, that the receiver is not adopting the contract and that he assumes no personal liability in relation to the employee's employment. The authority of the decision is somewhat weakened by the fact that the learned judge did not reduce his judgment to writing, and it is submitted that it is wrong. Adoption is not merely a matter of words but of fact. It is difficult to see how a receiver can claim not to have adopted a contract of employment if he allows the contract to remain in force and continues to make use of the employees' services. Such an interpretation drives a coach and horses through section 44(2) [I interject, that is of the Insolvency Act relating to administrative receivers] and deprives it of any significant meaning.'

With all respect to Harman J, a decision that he has given where there is no report, transcript or note of the reasons by which he reached his conclusion and no indication of what the facts were, cannot rank as a helpful authority. No doubt, he did not particularly intend something so denuded of judgment to be an authority in future times, but it does not help at all. And the mere assertion by an administrator or receiver that he is not adopting the contract is mere wind with no legal effect, because adoption is a matter not merely of words but of fact. Here all the facts point to the administrators having adopted the contracts.

We were asked to consider further whether the administrators could, if they made fresh contracts with employees, exclude some matters which would be their liabilities if they adopted the existing contracts. We were referred, in respect of that, by Mr Potts QC to the decision of the House of Lords in *Salford Union Guardians v Dewhurst* [1926] AC 619 which held that where Parliament had said that poor law officers were to have pensions, the guardians could not, and the poor law officers could not, contract out of a mandatory requirement by agreeing that the poor law officers should not have pensions. That is an important principle in relation to statutory construction and application, but I do not find it necessary to consider its application in the present case. I have expressed my clear view on adoption, as it is in this case and in any circumstances where the administrators take advantage of the services of an employee. I do not find it necessary to go further and consider what might or might not be permissible to include in a contract of employment in lieu of the contract which was subsisting at the time of the appointment of the administrators in other cases and on other facts, for instance, where there might be a contract with a managing director whose contract with the company contained 'golden handshake' provisions and so forth.

As the contract has been adopted, the first question we have to consider is whether the employees whose contracts were thus adopted are entitled to notice in accordance with the contractual terms or payment of salary in lieu of notice. We consider this as a general question. It may, of course, be that on the ordinary principles of mitigation of damages, an employee will have taken other employment during what would otherwise have been his notice period, and what they earn in the other employment must of course be set against anything to which they may claim to be entitled under s 19(5).

The crucial words in s 19(5) are:

'... sums payable in respect of debts or liabilities incurred, while he was administrator, under contracts of employment adopted by him or a predecessor of his ...'

Although strictly sums payable are under s 19(5) only payable when the administrator vacates office, it is well understood that administrators will, in the ordinary way, pay expenses of the administration including the salaries and other payments to employees as they arise during the continuance of the administration. There is no need to wait until the end, and it would be impossible as a practical matter to do that. What is picked up at the end are those matters which fall within the phrase, but have not been paid.

As I see it, the liability to pay wages in lieu of notice arose when the employee was dismissed at 30 November, or a few days later when the notices were sent out. The administrator was still the administrator then. He had not vacated the office, and it was he who terminated the contracts. He still has not vacated office because, as a practical matter, apparently, of the need to have these issues decided. It has been felt that the company which is no longer carrying on any business should remain strictly in administration until these proceedings have been disposed of, before being put into liquidation on a petition by the administrators in the usual way where administration does not lead to the sale of the business as a going concern or to trading into profit or achieving any of the other objects under s 8(3).

As I see it, one looks at the contract which is the contract that has been adopted and which was a continuing contract before that. One sees what notice was required to terminate it. The administrator could give that notice and pay the salary under the terms of the contract during the continuance of the notice or he can give, as he did in this case, summary notice of termination, in which event a liability or debt is incurred to the employee of the amount of the salary in lieu of notice which he should have received. That arises under the contract under which he was employed which had been adopted. In my judgment, the salary for the two months is carried by that clause and the employee is entitled to have it paid out of any property of the company which is in the custody or under the control of the administrator now. The same goes, as is conceded, if that result is right in respect of salary, to payments in respect of the employee's membership of the pension scheme.

I then come to holiday pay. It must follow, in my judgment, that the holiday pay is likewise to be calculated for the two months period of the notice that should have been given; the same wording applies. The question is then in respect of the holiday pay back to 1 April 1989 in the case of those employees who had not taken their full holiday allowance during the holiday year that then began. They must give credit for such holidays as they have had. But, again, in my judgment, the holiday pay is covered by the same words, '... sums payable in respect of debts or liabilities incurred'.

Holiday pay is not payable until the employee's employment has been terminated; that flows from the wording of the contract. It is not right, although it is a contingent potential liability in one sense, to say that at 1 April the company incurred a contingent liability for holiday pay for the whole of the year in respect of each of its employees which would be gradually reduced as they took their holidays during the year, and finally reduced yet further if the year expired without their having terminated their employment. The natural reading, in my judgment, is that the liability for holiday pay was incurred when the administrators terminated the employment and the whole liability in respect of the whole period from 1 April was incurred from that date and not earlier. It is also incurred under the service contract of employment which had been adopted by the administrators because it is the very contract which provides for what the holiday pay is and when it is to be paid.

There is then a question on the appeal as to interest. Should the sums which the employees are entitled to carry interest? The judge, in his order, directed that:

'The Applicants [that is the administrators] should pay to the Respondents interest on any sums falling to be paid as debts and liabilities incurred under their contracts of employment ... from 30 June 1990 until payment at the rate of interest which the Applicants have received on the funds in their hands since that date, and in any event at the rate at which interest would have been payable had the funds been paid into the Insolvency Services Account on 30th June 1990.'

That was in a supplemental judgment following discussion after delivery of the main judgment.

What the judge said after deciding that interest should be paid in principle, was that, since the insolvency estate is bound to pay those moneys into the insolvency estate's account, the appropriate rate of interest is the interest that would have been on that account. The judge is, in referring to the insolvency estate's account, referring, I think, to the insolvency services account mentioned in the order, but it appears that administrators are not required to pay the funds they hold into that account; they are entitled to leave surplus moneys on deposit in bank accounts and that is what these administrators have done. Therefore, the words in the judge's order:

'... and in any event at the rate at which interest would have been payable had the fund been paid into the Insolvency Services Account on 30 June 1990',

are inappropriate and should be deleted.

The judge dealt with the matter of principle, as to whether interest should be payable, by saying in very general terms, it seems to me, that there is no reason in principle why, where sums become due in the course of administration as an expense of that administration and they are not paid and they are ultimately held to be payable, those entitled to receive payment should not receive interest. I would not wish to support as wide a declaration as that because the circumstances in which sums may not be paid initially as they are incurred and may come to be paid much later on may vary very considerably. There may be cases of debt or damages which the administrators are liable to pay—not personally liable for but liable to pay out of the assets in their hands under s 19(5)—where the course of events may lead to an award of interest under the Supreme Court Act 1981. There may be other circumstances where interest may be payable under another heading and I do not see that it is necessary to consider in this case whether the full width of the judge's pronouncement is justified. I guard myself in that respect.

In the present case the administrators have very properly made this application to the court by summons for directions in October 1991. We are now heading for two and a half years later. The application was itself prompted by the respondents' s 27 applications made in September 1991. In those circumstances, as the administrators have had money invested and earning interest while being held until the question is resolved, it is right, and in accordance with the principle in *Ex p James, re Condon* (1874) LR 9 Ch App 609, [1874–80] All ER Rep 388, that the administrators should pay interest at the rate they have earned and pay the moneys to the respondents in respect of their entitlement. Accordingly, I would accept that basis for the order, which Mr Potts says was the basis on which the claim was put to the judge in the court below.

I see no reason, therefore, to differ from the date 30 June 1990 which was the date the judge in his discretion selected as the date from which interest should run. It is the date from which claims were made on behalf of some former employees to interest on their benefits as well as to the benefits themselves. There has been no argument about date in this court. It is said, however, that the court should not allow the benefit of this decision as to interest to enure to other employees than those who have specifically claimed interest. But we are dealing with this matter on the basis that the administrators are officers of the court and they have applied to the court for directions. In my judgment, it would not be right that the benefits of the respondents' success should not extend to all employees who have also been deprived of their benefits.

Finally, there is the point taken by way of respondents' notice in respect of the bonuses which were paid under the letter set out at the beginning of this judgment, of September 1989, to the captains and first officers. Mr Potts submits that these bonus payments, referred to as loyalty bonus payments, for those who remained in the employment of and working for Paramount Airways Ltd as at 31 October 1989, and who had not tendered their resignations by that time, and as at the end of each subsequent month if the arrangement had gone on for longer, were really a concealed pay rise and what is being done is to try and contract out of the benefits of giving a pay rise. The question, as I see it, depends entirely on the construction of this letter, and what strikes me about it is that it makes provision for the administrators remaining in office after 31 October 1989 and says that, on that basis, this arrangement will continue on a monthly basis until further notice, with each month and date being relevant for not having tendered resignations. I regard this as a genuine letter, save for the final paragraph, and not a sham for a pay rise and I do not see, taken as a genuine letter, that the bonus arrangement is made necessarily coterminous with the employment.

Of course, if the employment is terminated and they cease working for Paramount Airways, the bonus will also cease. But the bonus could be terminated at the end of a month without terminating the underlying contract of employment. The additional payment would then cease but the basic salary would continue to be payable. In these circumstances, I regard this as a separate contract and not covered by the words in s 19(5) as a contract of employment adopted by the administrator.

It follows, save in respect of the minor alteration, cutting out a few words about the rate of interest, that I agree with the judge on all points and, largely, for the reasons he gave, save that I do not put the right to interest so wide or go so far as he did into the question of contracting out.

I would, therefore, dismiss the appeal and the cross-appeal by respondents' notice.

LEGGATT LJ. Nothing has persuaded me that, as used in s 19(5) of the Insolvency Act 1986, the word 'adopted' connotes, in relation to contracts of employment, anything other than 'the continuance of which is expressly or impliedly accepted'. That is what the administrators unequivocally did by their letter of 14 August 1989 without confining the contracts of employment to rights arising after the administration order was made.

Whatever the consequences for insolvency law which Mr Michael Crystal QC may apprehend, the point is in my judgment too plain for argument. The essential question is whether the relevant debts or liabilities were incurred while administrators were acting as such. I was at first attracted by Mr Crystal's argument that the right to holiday pay constituted a contingent liability which was incurred from time to time before the administration order was made, the contingency being the termination of the contract of employment without all the holiday earned during the current year having been taken. But cl 8(f) of the contract of employment provides: 'On termination of employment, other than for misconduct, your entitlement will be paid ...'

It follows that not until termination, and so during the period of administration, will that debt have been incurred. Since s 19(5) applies to debts or liabilities, debts in respect of holiday pay have to be paid out of property of the company in the hands of the administrators in accordance with that provision. Since the rights to contractual notice and to pension contributions during the period of notice arose out of contracts of employment which the administrators adopted, the sums due in respect of those rights following dismissal must be similarly dealt with for the reasons explained by Dillon LJ.

I say nothing about contracting out since it does not arise in this case. The bonus payments that the respondents also claim were made under new contracts which were to continue on a monthly basis until further notice, but made no provision for any periods of notice. There is no warrant for regarding the contracts as coterminous with contracts of employment. The contracts for bonus payment in this case were brought to an end by dismissal. About interest, I do not wish to add anything to what Dillon LJ has said. It follows that I agree that the order should go which he has proposed.

HENRY LJ. I agree with the judgments given and do not wish to add anything to them.

Appeal and cross-appeal dismissed. Leave to appeal to the House of Lords refused.

29 March. The Appeal Committee of the House of Lords gave leave to appeal.

Celia Fox   Barrister.

Manchester City Council v T

COURT OF APPEAL, CIVIL DIVISION
BALCOMBE, STUART-SMITH, PETER GIBSON LJJ
9, 21 DECEMBER 1993

Family proceedings – Orders in family proceedings – Care order – Guardian ad litem – Disclosure of information to guardian ad litem – Local authority filing care plan in respect of minor – Local authority seeking adoptive parents for minor – Local authority preparing case record on prospective parents but refusing to disclose case record to guardian ad litem – Whether guardian ad litem entitled to see case record – Children Act 1989, ss 42(1)(b)(2)(a).

In 1992 the local authority applied for a care order in respect of a two-year-old boy, A. A guardian ad litem was appointed and an interim care order was made. The local authority filed a care plan in respect of A pursuant to which it proposed to seek adoptive parents for him. In due course the local authority found a couple who were possible adoptive parents and prepared a case record (Form F) which was shown to the guardian ad litem. It was subsequently agreed that the couple were unsuitable adoptive parents for A but in 1993 the local authority found other proposed adopters for him. However, on that occasion the authority refused to show the guardian ad litem Form F and he was unable to make any report to the court about the placement of A with those proposed adopters. The local authority applied for a care order and intended if an order was made in its favour to place A with the proposed adoptive parents. The judge held that the guardian ad litem had no right to see Form F and made the order sought. The guardian ad litem appealed on the grounds that under s 42[a] of the Children Act 1989 he was entitled to examine any records which a local authority held 'in connection with any functions ... referred to their social services committee ... so far as those records relate to [the] child [and] any records of, or held by, the local authority compiled in connection with any functions ... referred to their social services committee'. The local authority contended that Form F was a confidential document and that to allow the guardian ad litem and, through him, the court to see Form F and possibly question the desirability of placing A with the prospective adopters would amount to an unwarranted interference with the local authority's care plan.

Held – The appeal would be allowed for the following reasons—
(1) The undoubted confidentiality of a local authority case record was nevertheless subject to the guardian ad litem's right under s 42(3) of the 1989 Act to use information acquired from the case record in his report or evidence to the court considering the application for a care order 'regardless of any enactment or rule of law which would otherwise prevent the record in question being admissible in evidence' (see p 531 b to d and p 533 f, post).
(2) Since Form F, which had been prepared by the local authority in relation to the prospective adopters it had in mind for A, was a record which fell within the category of 'any records of, or held by, the local authority compiled in connection with any functions ... referred to their social services committee',

---

[a] Section 42, so far as material, is set out at p 529 e to g, post

ie which related to a child in family proceeding matters, the guardian ad litem was entitled under s 42(1)(b) of the 1989 Act to see Form F prepared by the local authority. Accordingly, the judge had been wrong in her conclusion that the guardian ad litem was not entitled to see it. Furthermore, not only was the guardian ad litem entitled to see and take copies of the form, he was also entitled under s 42(2)(a) to include the relevant information derived from it in his report to the court on the likely effect on A of living with the proposed adopters and how capable they would be of meeting A's needs. Although in the majority of cases it was most unlikely that the court would refuse to make a care order because of the identity of the persons with whom the local authority proposed to place the child, the court was not a rubber stamp and retained the right to refuse to make the order and unless the guardian ad litem had access to Form F, the court would be denied the opportunity of considering whether the proposed placement was so unsuitable that it would be better to make no order rather than a care order which would lead to an unsuitable placement. The appeal would therefore be allowed, the care order set aside and the case remitted to the High Court for reconsideration of the case after the guardian ad litem had seen the relevant Form F and prepared a further report (see p 530 c d, p 532 d to g and p 533 c d f, post).

Notes
For the right of access of guardian ad litem to local authority records, see 5(2) *Halsbury's Laws* (4th edn reissue) para 828.
For the Children Act 1989, s 42, see 6 *Halsbury's Statutes* (4th edn) (1992 reissue) 447.

Cases referred to in judgments
Adoption Application, Re [1990] 1 FLR 412.
B (minors) (care: contact: local authority's plans), Re [1993] 1 FLR 543, CA.
S (adoption application: disclosure of information), Re [1993] 2 FCR 16, CA.
W (a minor) (wardship: freedom of publication), Re [1992] 1 All ER 794, [1992] 1 WLR 100.

Cases also cited or referred to in skeleton arguments
A v Liverpool City Council [1981] 2 All ER 385, [1982] AC 363, HL.
C N (a minor) (care order), Re [1992] 2 FCR 401.
Cheshire CC v B [1992] FCR 572.
E (a minor), Re [1993] CA Transcript 0769.
M (a minor) (care order: threshold conditions), Re [1994] 1 All ER 424, [1994] 2 WLR 200, CA.
Manchester City Council v F [1993] 1 FLR 419.
R v North Yorkshire CC, ex p M [1989] 1 FLR 203, DC.
W (a minor) (residence order), Re [1993] 2 FCR 589, CA.

Appeal
The guardian ad litem of a minor, A, appealed against the order of Bracewell J made on 23 July 1993 that A be placed in the care of the respondent, the Manchester City Council, pursuant to s 31 of the Children Act 1989. The facts are set out in the judgment of Balcombe LJ.

Diana Eaglestone (instructed by *Cliffords*, Alderley Edge) for the guardian ad litem.

Ernest Ryder (instructed by Roy Ingham, Manchester) for the local authority.

Cur adv vult

21 December 1993. The following judgments were delivered.

BALCOMBE LJ. A was born on 16 June 1989. His parents separated in 1991 and A remained with his mother. She committed suicide in December 1991. A's father has never felt able to take responsibility for his care. Until March 1992 A remained in the care of his maternal grandmother but she then said she could no longer care for him and on 26 March 1992 he was 'accommodated' by the local authority and placed with a short-term foster mother. On 9 September 1992 the local authority applied for a care order in respect of A. On 18 September 1992 Mr Paul Doherty was appointed guardian ad litem for A in the application for the care order, and an interim care order was also then made. That interim order was, from time to time, renewed until the substantive hearing of the local authority's application in July 1993. On 8 October 1992 the local authority filed a care plan in respect of A pursuant to their obligations under reg 3 of the Arrangements for Placement of Children (General) Regulations 1991, SI 1991/890. Pursuant to the care plan the local authority decided to seek adoptive parents for A, and in due course found a couple in respect of whom they prepared a case record (Form F) in compliance with their obligations under reg 8(2)(a) of the Adoption Agencies Regulations 1983, SI 1983/1964. They showed this Form F to the guardian ad litem, and he and they then agreed that these prospective adopters were not suitable for A. In June 1993 the local authority found other prospective adopters for A but on this occasion they refused to allow the guardian ad litem a sight of Form F. The guardian ad litem was therefore unable to make any report to the court about the placement of A with these prospective adopters, which was the avowed intention of the local authority if a care order was made in their favour. The prospective adopters were on 16 June 1993 approved by the local authority's adoption panel as a match for A.

The application came before Bracewell J, who on 23 July 1993 ruled that the guardian ad litem had no right to see the Form F and made a care order in favour of the local authority. From that order A, by his guardian ad litem, has appealed to this court.

Proceedings on an application for a care order are within the meaning of 'specified proceedings' as defined by s 41(6)(a) of the Children Act 1989. (All future references in this judgment to sections without more are references to sections of the Children Act 1989.) So A's guardian ad litem, who was appointed under s 41(1), was under a duty to safeguard A's interests in the manner prescribed by the Family Proceedings Rules 1991, SI 1991/1247, s 41(2)(b).

Rule 4.11 of the Family Proceedings Rules 1991 is concerned with the powers and duties of the guardian ad litem. Rule 4.11(1) provides that in carrying out his duty (to safeguard A's interests) under s 41(2), the guardian ad litem shall have regard to: (i) the principle set out in s 1(2), viz that any delay in determining the question of A's upbringing is likely to prejudice his welfare; and (ii) the matters set out in s 1(3)—'the check-list'. Of these matters the following are particularly relevant to A's circumstances: (b) his emotional needs, (c) the likely effect on him of any change in his circumstances, (d) how capable any person in relation to whom the guardian ad litem considers the question to be relevant is of meeting A's needs.

Under r 4.11(4) the guardian ad litem is under a duty to advise the court on the following matters, inter alia: (e) the options available to it in respect of A and the suitability of each such option, including what order should be made in determining the application. The options available include making no order—s 1(5)—so that the guardian ad litem is under a duty to advise the court whether in the particular circumstances to make a care order would be better for A than making no order at all; (f) any other matter concerning which the guardian ad litem considers that the court should be informed.

Under r 4.11(7) the guardian ad litem has to file a written report advising on the interests of the child, and a copy of that report has to be served on the parties, who in the present case include A's father.

Rule 4.11(9) is in the following terms:

> 'The guardian ad litem shall make such investigations as may be necessary for him to carry out his duties and shall, in particular—(a) contact or seek to interview such persons as he thinks appropriate or as the court directs, (b) if he inspects records of the kinds referred to in section 42, bring to the attention of the court and such other persons as the court may direct all such records and documents which may, in his opinion, assist in the proper determination of the proceedings ...'

Section 42, so far as relevant, provides:

> '(1) Where a person has been appointed as a guardian ad litem under this Act he shall have the right at all reasonable times to examine and take copies of ... (b) any other records of, or held by, a local authority which were compiled in connection with any functions which stand referred to their social services committee under the Local Authority Social Services Act 1970, so far as those records relate to that child.
>
> (2) Where a guardian ad litem takes a copy of any record which he is entitled to examine under this section, that copy or any part of it shall be admissible as evidence of any matter referred to in any ... (a) report which he makes to the court in the proceedings in question; or (b) evidence which he gives in those proceedings.
>
> (3) Subsection (2) has effect regardless of any enactment or rule of law which would otherwise prevent the record in question being admissible in evidence.'

In the present case the guardian ad litem wishes to see the Form F which the local authority has prepared in relation to the prospective adopters it has in mind for A. This form contains detailed information relating to the prospective adopters, including an objective assessment by the social worker who has screened them. As already mentioned, the Form F is prepared by the local authority in the exercise of its functions as an adoption agency, and these are functions which stand referred to its social services committee under the Local Authority Social Services Act 1970—see s 2(1)(a) of, and Sch 1 to, the Local Authority Social Services Act 1970; Adoption Act 1976, Sch 3, para 15. In addition to the Form F relating to the prospective adopters, the local authority has to prepare a similar case record in respect of the child being considered for adoption—in this case A—under reg 7(2)(a) of the Adoption Agencies Regulations 1983. When the local authority is considering a proposal to place a particular child with particular applicants, the local authority sets up a 'matched' case record with all appropriate information relating to both the child and the applicants under reg 9(3) of the 1983 Regulations and the Form F then forms part of the matched case record. The local authority accepts, and rightly so, that such a matched case record relates to the child concerned within s 42(1)(b). Further, such a matched case record must exist in relation to A, since the prospective adopters have already been approved as a match for him.

When the local authority's application for a care order in respect of A came before the court, the judge had the option of making a care order or of making no order. If a care order were made it was the local authority's avowed intention to remove A from his short-term foster mother and place him with the prospective adopters. The guardian ad litem, in pursuance of his duty to safeguard A's interests, was therefore required to report to the court upon the likely effect on A of living with the proposed adopters, and how capable they would be of meeting A's needs. He could only fulfil this duty properly if he was able to see the Form F relating to the prospective adopters. In my judgment s 42(1)(b) gives him the right to see and take copies of the Form F, and s 42(2)(a) to include the relevant information derived from it in his report to the court.

This construction of s 42 accords with what was previously recommended good practice before the Children Act 1989 came into force. Paragraph 15 of the local authority circular, LAC(86)2, sent by the DHSS to local authorities, inter alios, provided:

> 'Access to records by the guardian ad litem
> 15. The guardian ad litem has a duty, as part of his investigation, to inspect such records as he thinks appropriate. The effect of Regulation 15 of the Adoption Agencies Regulations is to give guardians ad litem and reporting officers in adoption proceedings unrestricted access to adoption records in a particular case. In child care cases guardians ad litem have no similar right to access. Local authorities and other agencies (such as Area Review Committees) are nevertheless expected to allow guardians ad litem access to records, in view of the guardian's status as an officer appointed by the court. The Guide for Guardians ad Litem in the Juvenile Court emphasises that the guardian is to treat confidentially all information that comes into his possession during the course of his enquiries including reports, documents and records to which he gains access.'

This recommendation was confirmed in para 23 of the Appendix to LAC(88)17, another DHSS circular:

> '23. *Guardians ad litem and reporting officers.* LAC(86)2 gives guidance on access to records by guardians ad litem and reporting officers. Guardians ad litem and reporting officers in adoption proceedings have a right of access to records held by an adoption agency under Regulation 15 of the Adoption Agencies Regulations 1983. In care and related proceedings where no similar right exists, local authorities are expected to allow guardians ad litem access to records including personal information in view of the guardian's status as an officer of the court. Access to personal information should also be afforded to other court officers eg a probation officer or the Official Solicitor to assist them to discharge their duty to prepare a report for the court.'

The submissions of the local authority, which found favour with Bracewell J and were repeated before us, are: (a) that Form F is a confidential document and/or the subject of public interest immunity; (b) that to allow the guardian ad litem and, through him, the court to see Form F and possibly question the desirability of placing A with the prospective adopters would amount to an unwarranted interference with the local authority's care plan for A.

I will consider these two submissions separately.

(1) Confidentiality

Undoubtedly Form F is a confidential record under reg 14 of the 1983 regulations and the guardian ad litem in care proceedings is not one of the persons to whom access is to be given, and information disclosed, under reg 15. However, s 42(1)(b) is quite clear in its terms, and s 42(3) makes it clear that the guardian ad litem is entitled to use the information so acquired in his report or evidence to the court considering the application for a care order 'regardless of any enactment or rule of law which would otherwise prevent the record in question being admissible in evidence'. In my judgment Parliament could not have made its intentions clearer. It follows that I do not agree with the following passage from the judgment of Bracewell J:

> 'I am satisfied that under the adoption legislation the local authority does not have the power or privilege to waive confidentiality and the Children Act has not in any way affected the operation of the Adoption Act in respect of disclosure and confidentiality. I am further satisfied that if Parliament had intended to make such a fundamental change, as argued by the guardian ad litem, it would have done so expressly.'

Two cases relied upon by Mr Ryder for the local authority in support of this submission, and referred to in the judgment below, do not, upon examination, help him. *Re an adoption application* [1990] 1 FLR 412, relates to the release of information in adoption records for the benefit of a stepfather within criminal proceedings; *Re S (adoption application: disclosure of information)* [1993] 2 FCR 16 relates to the release, in adoption proceedings where the identity of the adoptive parents was being kept confidential by a serial number, of information about the adoptive parents to the natural parent. Neither case is concerned with the rights and duties conferred by statute on a guardian ad litem in care proceedings.

Mr Ryder did not develop any separate argument based on public interest immunity for Form F. Even if this immunity should exist, it would not prevail over the express provisions of s 42.

However, I must utter one word of caution. It is easy to see that to include confidential material—such as the identity of the prospective adopters, or matter which might lead to their identification—in the guardian ad litem's report, of which a copy has to be served on the other parties, might well be detrimental to the child's interests if, as is likely to happen in many cases, a care order is made and the local authority's proposals are implemented. However, the guardian ad litem is an officer of the court, chosen from a panel established under reg 2(1) of the Guardians ad Litem and Reporting Officers (Panels) Regulations 1991, SI 1991/2051, and may be relied upon to be well aware of his or her primary duty to safeguard the interests of the child. In performing that duty he or she will be fully conscious that the child's interests will often require that the identity of the prospective adopters should remain confidential and that nothing should be contained in the report which might reveal that identity to other parties, in particular the child's natural parents.

(2) *Interference with the care plan*

As Butler-Sloss LJ said in *Re B (minors)* [1993] 1 FLR 543 at 551:

'The present position of a child whose welfare is being considered under Part IV of the Act appears to me to be that he will not be placed in care unless a court has been satisfied that the threshold conditions in s 31 have been met and that it is better to make a care order than not to do so. After the care order is made, the court has no continuing role in the future welfare of the child. The local authority has parental responsibility for the child by s 33(3). However, issues relating to the child may come before the court, for instance on applications for contact or leave to refuse contact, to discharge the care order or by an application for a s 8 residence order. The making of a residence order discharges the care order (s 91(1)).'

So it is generally the case that, subject to the specific exceptions to which Butler-Sloss LJ refers in the passage just cited, the court has no power to interfere with a local authority's plan for a child in its care under a care order.

However, in this case the issue before the judge was whether or not a care order should be made. While in the majority of cases it is most unlikely that the court would refuse to make a care order because of the identity of the persons with whom the local authority proposed to place the child, the court always has the right to refuse to make the order: it is not a rubber stamp. Thus, to take a highly improbable scenario, suppose that it emerged that the local authority proposed to place the child with individuals who had convictions for indecently assaulting a child of the same age and sex as the child to be placed with them. A court might well take the view that in such a case, even though the threshold conditions in s 31 were satisfied, it would be better to make no order, even though that might have the effect of leaving the child in limbo, at least temporarily. If that example sounds far-fetched, reported cases show that not all local authority placements are free from the possibility of criticism—see eg *Re W (a minor)* [1992] 1 All ER 794, [1992] 1 WLR 100. Unless the guardian ad litem has access to Form F, the court will be denied the opportunity of considering whether the proposed placement is so unsuitable that it would be better to make no order than a care order which would lead to an unsuitable placement.

Unfortunately the judge approached this issue with the preconceived view that the option of no order was not open to her. Thus she said:

'There is no dispute in this case that ... this is a case in which the welfare of A demands an order rather than no order ... In the present case there are no realistic alternatives to a care order, that is conceded by the guardian ad litem. In such circumstances the court cannot impose conditions which might have the effect of a review of the care order.'

Then, after considering the relevant statutory provisions, regulations and case law, she concluded:

'I find that a decision by a local authority to place a child with a particular adoptive family, as opposed to having a general plan to so place, goes beyond the role of the guardian ad litem in specified proceedings under the Children Act. I find that the role of the guardian ad litem is limited to advising the court which order, if any, is appropriate and to evaluation of the proposals of the various parties in the best interests of the child, whose welfare is of paramount consideration. I do not find that the role extends to identifying and evaluating a particular family with whom the local authority intend to place a child in the event of a care order being granted.'

Thus the judge was throughout assuming that she was bound to make a care order irrespective of the suitability of the prospective adopters, about whom she had no information. On that assumption, it was fair to conclude that the only relevance of the information in Form F would be if the court were prepared to interfere with the local authority's care plan. But if the assumption was wrong— as in my judgment it was—then the conclusion was also wrong.

For the reasons I have given I am satisfied that the judge was wrong in her conclusion that the guardian ad litem was not entitled to see Form F in relation to the prospective adopters, and was wrong to make a care order without the benefit of a report from the guardian ad litem about the effect on A's interests of the making of a care order with its inevitable consequence that he would be placed with the prospective adopters. I would therefore allow the appeal, set aside the care order of 23 July 1993, and remit the case to the High Court for a reconsideration of the case after the guardian ad litem has seen the relevant Form F and has prepared his further report. We were told that, since the order of 23 July, A has in fact been placed with the prospective adopters, and it would clearly be wrong to move him again pending the re-hearing of this case. I would therefore make an interim care order under s 38 for the maximum permitted period of four weeks from today's date—see s 38(4)(b) and 5(a). No doubt that interim care order will be renewed as may be necessary until the substantive re-hearing takes place.

STUART-SMITH LJ. I agree.

PETER GIBSON LJ. I also agree.

Appeal allowed. Leave to appeal to the House of Lords refused.

Celia Fox   Barrister.

Willowgreen Ltd v Smithers

COURT OF APPEAL, CIVIL DIVISION
NOURSE LJ AND THORPE J
29 NOVEMBER, 1 DECEMBER 1993

County court – Practice – Service of summons – Service by post – Service at premises owned by defendant – Defendant not residing at premises – Defendant not receiving summons sent to him at premises owned by him – Whether summons properly served – CCR, Ord 7, r 10(1).

The defendant was the legal and beneficial owner of a flat under a 99-year lease. The plaintiff was the landlord of the flat. The defendant let his stepfather stay in the flat rent-free on condition that he would pay all the bills, including the ground rent and service charge. That arrangement was not notified to the landlord or its managing agents, nor were they given any other address to which communications should be sent. The defendant last saw his stepfather in 1986 and did not visit the flat until 1991 when he found that his stepfather had left and that someone else was in occupation. The last payment of rent and service charge was made in 1987. In 1990 the landlord filed a request in the county court for the issue of a summons against the defendant for possession of the flat. The request was made on a standard practice form and gave the defendant's address as that of the flat. The summons was sent to the defendant at the flat in accordance with CCR Ord 7, r 10(1)(b)[a], which provided that service of a summons could be effected 'by an officer of the court sending it by first-class post to the defendant at the address stated in the request for summons'. However, the summons did not reach the defendant and in his absence judgment was entered for the plaintiff for possession of the flat. The defendant applied to have the judgment set aside but the judge dismissed the application on the ground that the summons had been properly served on the defendant since the address was one with which he had a direct and immediate connection and in the circumstances, in particular since rights of innocent third parties who were occupying the flat had arisen, the judge would not exercise his discretion to set the judgment aside. The defendant appealed to the Court of Appeal on the ground that the delivery of the summons had not been properly effected pursuant to Ord 7, r 10(1)(b) since it had been sent to the defendant at premises which had never been his address.

Held – The word 'address' in CCR Ord 7, r 10(1)(b) was to be given its ordinary meaning, namely a place at which to a greater or lesser extent a person was present to receive delivery of written communications. It did not include a place at which the person was never present and at which the service of a summons did not come to his notice, albeit that it was a place which, in the circumstances, had a direct and immediate connection with him. It followed that the summons had not been properly served on the defendant and that the judgment would be set aside (see p 537 g, p 539 a to c h and p 540 d e, post).

White v Weston [1968] 2 All ER 842 followed.

Notes

For service of documents in general, see 10 *Halsbury's Laws* (4th edn) para 184, and for cases on the subject, see 13 *Digest* (Reissue) 458–460, *3800–3808*.

Cases referred to in judgments

Cooper v Scott-Farnell [1969] 1 All ER 178, [1969] 1 WLR 120, CA.
R v Appeal Committee of County of London Quarter Sessions, ex p Rossi [1956] 1 All ER 670, [1956] 1 QB 682, [1956] 2 WLR 800, CA.
Rolph v Zolan [1993] 4 All ER 202, [1993] 1 WLR 1305, CA.
White v Weston [1968] 2 All ER 842, [1968] 2 QB 647, [1968] 2 WLR 1459, CA.

Appeal

The defendant, Douglas Smithers, appealed from the decision of Judge Quentin Edwards sitting at the Central London County Court on 14 April 1993

---

a   Rule 10, so far as material, is set out at p 535 *d*, post

whereby he dismissed the defendant's application to set aside the judgment given on 6 December 1990 by Judge Martin giving possession of Flat 135, Peters Court, Paddington, London to the plaintiffs, Willowgreen Ltd, together with arrears of rent. The facts are set out in the judgment of Nourse LJ.

Beverley Lang (instructed by *Parfitt Cresswell Carnt & Mudie*) for the appellant.
Anthony Radevsky (instructed by *Finers*) for the respondent.

Cur adv vult

1 December 1993. The following judgments were delivered.

NOURSE LJ. CCR Ord 3, r 3(1) provides that a plaintiff desiring to commence a default or fixed date action shall file a request for the issue of a summons. Order 7, r 10(1) provides that service of the summons shall usually be effected (a) by the plaintiff delivering the summons to the defendant personally; or (b):

'by an officer of the court sending it by first-class post to the defendant at the address stated in the request for the summons.'

Here, in a landlord's action for forfeiture and possession of a flat, the address stated in the request for the summons was that of the flat, where the tenant had never lived or worked. The question, which may be one of some general importance, is whether, on its delivery there pursuant to Ord 7, r 10(1)(b), the summons was properly served on the tenant.

By a lease dated 30 August 1978 and made between the then landlord of the first part, a management company of the second part and the defendant Douglas Smithers and his mother of the third part, a flat known as 135 Peters Court, Porchester Road, London W2 was demised to the defendant and his mother for a term of 99 years from 25 December 1971 at a premium of £17,500 and an initial yearly ground rent of £25. The lease contained provisions for payment of service charge and a provision for re-entry in standard form. By cl 8(f) it was agreed and declared that:

'Any demand for payment notice or other document required or authorised to be given to the Tenant shall be well and sufficiently given if sent by the Lessor or the Company or its agent for the time being through the post addressed to the Tenant by name or by the general description of 'the Tenant' or it may be left for the Tenant at the Demised Premises ...'

The flat was owned by the defendant and his mother as joint tenants at law and in equity. They bought it as a home for the defendant's mother and stepfather, but she never lived there. She died on 14 September 1979, while still living at 85 Princess Court, Queensway, W2, the address stated in the lease to have been that of the defendant as well as of herself. However, since 1971 the defendant has lived at an address in another part of London, 4 Brunel House, 105 Cheyne Walk, SW10.

On his mother's death, the defendant became the sole legal and beneficial owner of the flat. He offered it to his stepfather and allowed him to live there rent-free on the understanding that he would pay all the bills, including the demands for ground rent and service charge. This arrangement was not notified to the landlord or the management company. Nor did the defendant notify them or their successors of any other address to which communications should be sent.

The last time that the defendant saw his stepfather was in 1986. He did not visit the flat between then and December 1991, when he called there and found someone else in occupation. The porter told him that his stepfather had died. The defendant's solicitors have been unable to find any recorded death between 1986 and 1990 for someone of the stepfather's name and age. But whether he be dead or alive, it is certain that there has been no trace of him since.

It appears that the last payment of rent and service charge was made in 1987, presumably by the stepfather. By that time the plaintiff, Willowgreen Ltd, had acquired the reversion immediately expectant on the determination of the lease. A letter addressed to the defendant at the flat dated 15 September 1987 and written by the plaintiff's managing agents shows that arrears of service charge and ground rent amounting to £567·08 and £12·50 respectively were then claimed. On 9 July 1990 a notice under s 146 of the Law of Property Act 1925 addressed to the defendant at the flat was served under cover of a letter from the plaintiff's solicitors similarly addressed.

On 24 September 1990, pursuant to Ord 3, r 3(1), the plaintiff filed a request for the issue of a summons against the defendant in the Bloomsbury County Court. The request was made on form N204, which is headed 'Request for Issue of Summons for Possession of Land'. It is not a form prescribed by the County Court Rules, but a practice form approved by the Lord Chancellor. At the top on the left are four boxes: the first for the 'Plaintiff's full name and address'; the second for the 'Name and address for service and payment (*if different from the above*)'; the third for the 'Defendant's name and address'; beside the fourth appear the words 'The claim is for possession of (Give the full address of the land claimed)'.

In both the third and fourth boxes the address stated was that of the flat. Curiously, the defendant's name was omitted from the third, although nothing turns on that. The plaintiff also filed particulars of claim claiming possession of the flat, together with arrears of rent and service charge, interest payable pursuant to the terms of the lease and mesne profits at the daily rate of 7 pence.

In purported pursuance of Ord 7, r 10(1)(b), an officer of the court sent the summons by first-class post to the defendant at the flat. It never came to his notice. There having been no reply or response on the part of the defendant, on 6 December 1990 Judge Martin QC, in the absence of the defendant, entered judgment for the plaintiff for recovery of possession of the flat on 3 January 1991, and for the sum of £4,464·89, together with mesne profits at the rate claimed and costs on scale 3. A warrant of possession was duly issued. It was executed on 5 February 1991. Meanwhile, on 30 July 1991, the plaintiff had sold the freehold of Peters Court to Ets Croy (Croy) and on the same day Croy granted the plaintiff a 125-year leaseback of the flat. However, on 9 May 1991 the plaintiff surrendered that lease to Croy, since when the plaintiff has had no interest in the flat. It appears that there have since been other dealings with it, although the defendant remains the registered proprietor of the lease at HM Land Registry.

Soon after he discovered the position in December 1991, the defendant instructed solicitors to act on his behalf. In due course he applied to set the judgment of 6 December 1990 aside. The application came before Judge Quentin Edwards QC on 14 April 1993, when he held, first, that the summons had been properly served on the defendant and, secondly, that in the circumstances, especially since rights of innocent third parties had arisen, he ought not in his discretion to set the judgment aside. The defendant now appeals to this court.

On the question of service the judge thought that the only obligation of the plaintiff under the rules was to state in the request an address which had 'a direct and immediate connection' with the defendant. If that was correct, I would be inclined to think that the plaintiff did what it had to do in this case. In view of the terms of cl 8(f) of the lease, the fact that demands and notices under it were always sent to or left for the defendant at the flat and the further fact that he never notified the landlord or the managing agents of any other address to which communications should be sent, I would be inclined to think that the address of the flat did have a direct and immediate connection with him. However, as Mr Radevsky, for the plaintiff, has recognised, that interpretation of the rules might, in certain circumstances, include a number of addresses, perhaps up to four or five residential addresses alone. For my part, I do not think that the judge's interpretation can be correct.

Since form N204 is not a prescribed form, neither its front nor the notes on its back can be resorted to in order to construe the rules. Thus we are left with Ord 7, r 10(1)(b), in which it is implicit that the plaintiff is obliged to state the defendant's address in the request for the summons. So far I am in agreement with the judge. But what is the defendant's 'address' for this purpose?

It is remarkable that a question seemingly so fundamental should seemingly be so free from authority. We have been referred to only four decided cases. Miss Lang, for the defendant, has referred us to *R v Appeal Committee of County of London Quarter Sessions, ex p Rossi* [1956] 1 All ER 670, [1956] 1 QB 682, *White v Weston* [1968] 2 All ER 842, [1968] 2 QB 647 and *Cooper v Scott-Farnell* [1969] 1 All ER 178, [1969] 1 WLR 120. Mr Radevsky has also referred us to *Rolph v Zolan* [1993] 4 All ER 202, [1993] 1 WLR 1305. I will say at once that I am unable to see in what way that last decision assists either side in the present dispute.

I start by considering the question apart from authority. In ordinary parlance a person's address is a place at which written communications can be delivered to him. In order that they can be delivered to him, he must, to a greater or lesser extent, be present to receive them. The extent to which his presence is necessary to make it his address may vary, and vary significantly, with the circumstances. But if he is never there at all, it cannot properly be called his address. It can, if communications will be sent on to him from there, be called a forwarding address. But that is not the same thing as an address.

In construing the word 'address' in a rule which permits service of proceedings to be made by post, it is important to remember that that mode of service involves a significant departure from the rule, which prevailed until well into this century, that an originating process should, in the absence of agreement, authority or special order, be served on the defendant or the respondent personally. As Denning LJ put it in *Ex p Rossi* [1956] 1 All ER 670 at 674, [1956] 1 QB 682 at 691:

'When construing this section, it is to be remembered that it is a fundamental principle of our law that no one is to be found guilty or made liable by an order of any tribunal unless he has been given fair notice of the proceedings so as to enable him to appear and defend them. The common law has always been very careful to see that the defendant is fully apprised of the proceedings before it makes any order against him.'

Having referred to the common law writ of capias, which required the sheriff to bring the defendant to court, Denning LJ continued ([1956] 1 All ER 670 at 674, [1956] 1 QB 682 at 691–692):

> 'That has all been done away with, but the law still insists in most cases that the defendant shall be served personally so as to be sure that he knows of the proceedings against him. In modern times there have been a few statutes and rules which allow service by registered post, and this is one of them. The merit of registered post in this regard is that the postman will only deliver the letter to the person to whom it is addressed or to someone who will take responsibility for seeing that he gets it. Otherwise he will return it to the sender, who will thus get to know, sooner or later, if the letter is not received.'

What we have here is a rule which does not even require service to be made by registered post. The postman who delivers the first-class post is expected to do no more than put it through the letterbox or leave it on the premises, a process fraught with the risk that the addressee will not receive it. The rule-making authority could hardly have intended that the risk should be increased still further by permitting first-class postal service at a place where the addressee is never present and where it does not come to his notice.

Further support for this view can be derived from *White v Weston*, where it was held by this court that a summons had not, for the purposes of Ord 8, r 8(3) of the County Court Rules 1936, been sent to the defendant by ordinary post because the letter containing it had been sent to a place at which the defendant had ceased to reside more than five months earlier; with the result that it was not 'properly addressed' as required by s 26 of the Interpretation Act 1889. Russell LJ said ([1968] 2 All ER 842 at 845, [1968] 2 QB 647 at 658):

> 'A summons addressed to an address with which the defendant has had no connexion for five months or more, however, cannot be said to be properly addressed ... The function of service is primarily to bring to the attention of the person to be served the fact that he is being sued, and particular language is in my judgment required if something short of that is to constitute service.'

Sachs LJ said ([1968] 2 All ER 842 at 847, [1968] 2 QB 647 at 661):

> 'I can find no warrant in any of the County Court Rules or in s. 26 of the Interpretation Act, 1889, for holding that service in purported pursuance of C.C.R., Ord. 8, r. 3, at an address which at the relevant time was not the abode, residence, or place of business of a defendant, is good service should the relevant document not in fact reach him.'

Mr Radevsky submits that the first of those observations of Russell LJ supports the judge's 'direct and immediate connection' view of the question. I reject that submission. I think that Russell LJ, like Sachs LJ, regarded it as essential that the defendant should have had some continuing presence there before the residence in question could properly have been called his address. It seems that that was the view of Russell LJ's observation taken by Willmer LJ in *Cooper v Scott-Farnell* [1969] 1 All ER 178 at 182–183, [1969] 1 WLR 120 at 127.

The position therefore is that the three relevant authorities to which we have been referred support the view that the word 'address' in Ord 7, r 10(1)(b) should be construed in accordance with its ordinary meaning. Thus it does not include a place at which the defendant is never present and at which the process does not come to his notice, albeit that it is a place which, in the circumstances of this case, may well have had a direct and immediate connection with him. It follows that the summons here was not properly served on the defendant.

What then should be the fate of the judgment entered by Judge Martin on 6 December 1990? The judgment having been obtained in proceedings initiated by a summons which was not properly served on the defendant, it seems plain that it must be set aside ex debito justitiae. Mr Radevsky has submitted that there is some sort of discretion in the matter, but it is clear both on principle and from *White v Weston* that that is not the case.

I would therefore allow the appeal, discharge the order of Judge Quentin Edwards and set aside the judgment of Judge Martin entered on 6 December 1990.

THORPE J. The facts and circumstances which give rise to this appeal are no doubt highly unusual. However, it is agreed between counsel that the County Court Rule that governed the service of the respondent's default summons on the appellant was Ord 7, r 10 (1)(b). That rule provides that service shall be effected—

'by an officer of the court sending it by first-class post to the defendant at the address stated in the request for summons.'

The request for issue of summons for possession of land is a practice form N204. On its face are seven numbered boxes for completion. Box 3 requires the insertion of 'Defendant's name and address'. Beside box 4 appears 'The claim is for possession of (Give the full address of the land claimed)'. In this case box 4 was accurately completed 'Flat 135 Peters Court, Porchester Road, London W2'. Precisely the same words were inappropriately typed into box 3. The defendant's name was not stated and the premises in dispute had never been his address. Had due care been given to the completion of box 3 it might have read 'Douglas Smithers whose present address is unknown to the plaintiff'. For the request for summons was dated 24 September 1990, by which date the premises had been empty for three years.

However, the question of law in the appeal is whether the judge was right to construe the words 'the address' in Ord 7, r 10 (1)(b) as 'an address which has direct and immediate connection with the defendant'. In my judgment the judge was plainly wrong in that construction. There is no authority for its adoption, and despite the submissions of Mr Radevsky it is contrary to the principles stated in the judgments in *White v Weston* [1968] 2 All ER 842 at 847, [1968] 2 QB 647 at 660. The principle is stated by Sachs LJ in these terms:

'It follows that only an explicit and clear provision in a statute, or in rules having statutory force, can operate to deprive a citizen of his right to receive notice of the commencement of process against him; and to permit service other than personal at an address which is not in fact his abode (to use the word employed, for instance, in r. 19(*b*) of the Magistrates' Courts

Rules, 1952) nor his residence, nor his business address, would be a provision clearly calculated to deprive him of that right.'

Russell LJ in his judgment had said ([1968] 2 All ER 842 at 845, [1968] 2 QB 647 at 658):

'A summons addressed to an address with which the defendant has had no connexion for five months or more, however, cannot be said to be properly addressed.'

That sentence seems to me to support the appellant's argument. Mr Radevsky claims it for his case by advancing it by corollary as the foundation for the judge's test, namely: did the address have a direct and immediate connection with the defendant? It is plain to me that far from formulating a test so wide and potentially productive of injustice, Russell LJ was upholding the principle that the function of service is to bring to the attention of the person to be served the fact he is being sued and particular language is required if anything short of that is to constitute service. I do not myself see any useful distinction between the proposed defendant's abode and the proposed defendant's residence. In most cases 'the address' in Ord 7, r 10(1)(b) will be the address at which the defendant ordinarily resides or works.

I therefore conclude that the summons was not served in accordance with the rules, and the judgment should be set aside as of right ex debito justitiae. Mr Radevsky's argument, that even if the appellant was not served in accordance with the rules he is not entitled to have the order set aside ex debito justitiae, is also precluded by the judgment of Russell LJ in *White v Weston*.

I too would allow this appeal.

Appeal allowed.

Carolyn Toulmin Barrister.

Continental Bank NA v Aeokos Cia Naviera SA and others

COURT OF APPEAL, CIVIL DIVISION
SIR STEPHEN BROWN P, STEYN AND KENNEDY LJJ
9, 10 NOVEMBER 1993

Conflict of laws – Jurisdiction – Exclusive jurisdiction – Loan agreement requiring borrowers to submit to jurisdiction of English courts – Borrowers initiating foreign proceedings against bank – Bank applying for injunction to restrain borrowers from continuing foreign proceedings – Appropriate court – Whether English courts having exclusive jurisdiction – Whether English proceedings should be stayed on ground that foreign court first seised of proceedings – Whether injunction should be granted restraining borrowers from continuing foreign proceedings – Civil Jurisdiction and Judgments Act 1982, Sch 1, arts 17, 21, 22.

The respondent bank granted a loan facility to the appellants, a group of one-ship companies managed by a Greek shipping company in Athens. The agreement provided that the loan agreement was governed by English law and that each of the appellants 'irrevocably submits to the jurisdiction of the English courts'. The appellants defaulted on the loan repayments and in November 1990 brought an action in the Athens court claiming damages against the bank for exercising its rights under the loan agreement contrary to Greek law. In April 1991 the bank issued a writ in England against the appellants seeking an injunction to restrain the appellants from continuing the Greek proceedings in breach of the exclusive jurisdiction agreement. The appellants applied to strike out or stay the English proceedings pending the outcome of the Greek action pursuant to arts 21^a or 22^b of the Convention on Jurisdiction and the Enforcement of Judgments in Civil and Commercial Matters (which had the force of law in the United Kingdom by virtue of s 2(1) of the Civil Jurisdiction and Judgments Act 1982 and was set out in Sch 1 thereto) on the grounds that the Greek and English proceedings involved the same cause of action or related actions and the Athens court was the court first seised of the action. The judge dismissed the application and granted an injunction in the bank's favour. The appellants appealed, contending that the jurisdiction clause in the agreement did not cover the Greek proceedings nor did it confer exclusive jurisdiction on the English courts, that the judge should have stayed the English proceedings under arts 21 or 22 of the 1968 convention or under the inherent powers of the court until the Athens court had decided whether or not it had jurisdiction, and that the judge should not have granted an injunction since it amounted to indirect interference in the proceedings of a foreign court and the pursuit of the remedy in the foreign court was not vexatious or oppressive.

Held – The appeal would be dismissed for the following reasons—

(1) On the proper construction of the jurisdiction clause the appellants were clearly bound to submit all disputes relating to the loan facility, including the subject matter of the Greek proceedings, to the English courts. The parties to an exclusive jurisdiction agreement were presumed to have intended that all matters in dispute would be settled by the same tribunal and that there would not be claims tried in different jurisdictions. Since there was a valid exclusive jurisdiction clause, art 17^c of the 1968 convention, which gave paramount effect to exclusive jurisdiction agreements, applied to deprive the courts of other contracting states of jurisdiction, with the result that the question of a stay of proceedings under arts 21 or 22 did not arise, since the provisions of art 17 took precedence over arts 21 and 22 (see p 545 *f* to *j*, p 546 *c* to *j*, p 547 *f*, p 549 *f* to *h*, p 550 *d* and p 552 *a*, post); dicta of Balcombe and Dingham LJJ in *Ashville Investments Ltd v Elmer Contractors Ltd* [1988] 2 All ER 577 at 588, 599 and of Hoffmann LJ in *Harbour Assurance Co (UK) Ltd v Kansa General International Assurance Co Ltd* [1993] 3 All ER 897 at 916 applied.

(2) Since an injunction was the only effective remedy for the appellants' breach of the jurisdiction agreement and since the continuation of the Greek proceedings amounted to vexatious and oppressive conduct by the appellants, the judge had exercised his discretion properly in granting the injunction (see p 551 *e f*, post).

---

a   Article 21 is set out at p 548 *d*, post
b   Article 22 is set out at p 548 *e f*, post
c   Article 17, so far as material, is set out at p 548 *a* to *c*, post

Notes
For the principles governing the grant of interlocutory injunction see 34 *Halsbury's Laws* (4th edn) paras 953–956, and for cases on the subject, see 28(4) *Digest* (2nd reissue) 156–160, 4993–5025.

For the general jurisdiction of the court under the 1968 convention and for exclusive jurisdiction conferred by contract, see supplement to 8 *Halsbury's Laws* (4th edn) para 768B(1), 768B(3).

For the Civil Jurisdiction and Judgments Act 1982, s 2, Sch 1, arts 17, 21, 22, see 11 *Halsbury's Statutes* (4th edn) (1991 reissue) 1108, 1145, 1148.

As from 1 December 1991 Sch 1 to the 1982 Act was substituted by the Civil Jurisdiction and Judgments Act 1982 (Amendment) Order 1990, SI 1990/2591, art 12(1), Sch 1.

Cases referred to in judgment
Anonima Petroli Italiana SpA v West of England Shipowners Mutual Insurance Association (London) Ltd (9 April 1990, unreported), QBD.
Antaios Cia Naviera SA v Salen Rederierna AB, The Antaios [1984] 3 All ER 229, [1985] AC 191, [1984] 3 WLR 592, HL.
Ashville Investments Ltd v Elmer Contractors Ltd [1988] 2 All ER 577, [1989] QB 488, [1988] 3 WLR 867, CA.
Austrian Lloyd Steamship Co v Gresham Life Assurance Society Ltd [1903] 1 KB 249, [1900–3] All ER Rep 604, CA.
British Aerospace plc v Dee Howard Co [1993] 1 Lloyd's Rep 368.
Cannon Screen Entertainment Ltd v Handmade Films (Distributors) Ltd (11 July 1989, unreported), QBD.
Empresa Exportadora de Azucar v Industria Azucarera Nacional SA, The Playa Larga [1983] 2 Lloyd's Rep 171, CA.
Gubisch Maschinenfabrik KG v Palumbo Case 144/86 [1987] ECR 4861.
Harbour Assurance Co (UK) Ltd v Kansa General International Assurance Co Ltd [1993] 3 All ER 897, [1993] QB 701, [1993] 3 WLR 42, CA.
IP Metal Ltd v Ruote OZ SpA [1993] 2 Lloyd's Rep 60.
Kloeckner & Co AG v Gatoil Overseas Inc [1990] 1 Lloyd's Rep 177.
Kurz v Stella Musical Veranstaltungs GmbH [1992] 1 All ER 630, [1992] Ch 196, [1991] 3 WLR 1046.
SNI Aérospatiale v Lee Kui Jak [1987] 3 All ER 510, [1987] AC 871, [1987] 3 WLR 59, PC.
Sohio Supply Co v Gatoil (USA) Inc [1989] 1 Lloyd's Rep 588, CA.

Cases also cited
Barclays Bank plc v Homan [1993] BCLC 680, Ch D and CA.
Berisford (S & W) plc v New Hampshire Insurance Co [1990] 2 QB 631, [1990] 3 WLR 688.
British Airways Board v Laker Airways Ltd [1984] 3 All ER 39, [1985] AC 58, HL.
Bushby v Munday (1821) 5 Madd 297, [1814–23] All ER Rep 304, 56 ER 908.
Castanho v Brown & Root (UK) Ltd [1981] 1 All ER 143, [1981] AC 557, HL.
Dumez France v Tracoba Case C-277/87 [1990] ECR 1-49.
Maciej Rataj, The [1992] 2 Lloyd's Rep 552.
Man (E D & F) (Sugar) Ltd v Yani Haryanto (No 2) [1991] 1 Lloyd's Rep 429, CA.
Overseas Union Insurance Ltd v New Hampshire Insurance Co Case C351/89 [1992] 2 All ER 138, [1992] QB 434, CJEC.
Owens Bank Ltd v Bracco [1992] 2 All ER 193, [1992] 2 AC 443, HL.

South Carolina Insurance Co v Assurantie Maatschappij 'De Zeven Provincien' NV [1986] 3 All ER 487, [1987] AC 24, HL.

Appeal

By a loan agreement dated 20 May 1981 the American bank, Continental Bank NA (the bank), granted loans totalling $US56m to the first 15 appellants which were one-ship companies registered in Panama and Liberia and managed by Aegis Shipping Co Ltd of Athens. The sixteenth to eighteenth appellants were guarantors of the loan. The agreement contained a clause that the borrowers would submit irrevocably to the jurisdiction of the English courts. On 20 November 1990 the appellants commenced proceedings against the bank in the First Instance Court of Athens under art 919 of the Greek Civil Code claiming damages against the bank totalling $US63m alleging that the bank had exercised its rights under the agreement contrary to business morality. By summons dated 3 June 1991 the bank sought an injunction to restrain the appellants from continuing with the Greek proceedings. By summons dated 23 July 1991 the appellants sought an order to strike out the bank's writ and points of claim under RSC Ord 18, r 19 or the court's inherent jurisdiction or that the English action be stayed under arts 21 or 22 of the 1968 Convention on Jurisdiction and the Enforcement of Judgments in Civil and Commercial Matters. On 23 August 1991 Gatehouse J dismissed the application and granted final injunctions restraining the appellants from taking any further steps in the Greek proceedings. The appellants appealed. The facts are set out in the judgment of the court.

Barbara Dohmannn QC and *Thomas Beazley* (instructed by *Constant & Constant*) for the appellants.
Christopher Clarke QC and *Mark Hapgood* (instructed by *Norton Rose*) for the bank.

STEYN LJ. This is the judgment of the court. The central question is whether Continental Bank NA is entitled by virtue of an exclusive jurisdiction agreement to an injunction restraining a group of borrowers and guarantors from bringing legal proceedings against the bank in Greece.

Continental Bank NA is an American bank. The bank had a branch in Greece. The first to the fifteenth appellants are one-ship companies registered in Panama and Liberia. They are managed as a group by Aegis Shipping Co Ltd of Athens. By a loan agreement dated 20 May 1981, as subsequently amended, the bank, through its Athens branch, granted to the first to fifteenth appellants a secured floating interest rate loan facility of $US56m. As security each borrower granted to the bank an assignment of freights and other earnings, and a mortgage over the vessel owned by it. The bank also obtained guarantees dated 3 June 1981 from three individual members of the Papalios family, who were beneficially interested in the corporate borrowers. The guarantors are the sixteenth to the eighteenth appellants. $US29·8m of the facility was used to pay off the previous mortgagee, the Bank of America, which had a mortgage over six of the vessels, and the balance was used to refinance the purchase of vessels by nine other companies.

The borrowers defaulted within a year of the grant of the loan facility. The last quarterly instalment was paid in December 1981. As early as mid-1981 there had been a downturn in the shipping cycle. By 1984 freight rates and the price of vessels had dropped markedly. The shipping cycle had entered a phase

of recession. The borrowers were substantially in arrears. On 24 December
1984 the bank and the borrowers and guarantors entered into a rescheduling
agreement. Pursuant to this agreement the bank agreed to waive certain
amounts of interest, to reschedule repayment of outstanding principal and to
limit the liabilities of the guarantors. It is the bank's case that conditions
precedent of the rescheduling agreement were never fulfilled, and that it
therefore never became effective. But, the bank argues, this issue is
unimportant because the borrowers failed to repay the second and subsequent
rescheduled payments of principal, and therefore, if the rescheduling
agreement became effective, the bank became restored to its original rights.
The bank contends that it is owed the sum of $US32,855,311 and interest.

On 4 October 1991 the bank issued a writ in an English action against the
borrowers and guarantors. But on 20 November 1990 the appellants had
commenced an action against the bank in the First Instance Court of Athens.
The borrowers claimed damages against the bank totalling about $US63m and
a declaration that the guarantors have been released. The cause of action is
based on art 919 of the Greek Civil Code, which provides:

'Whoever intentionally in a manner which violates the commands of
morality, causes damages to another is bound to make reparation to the
other for any damage this caused.'

The thrust of the appellants' claim is that the bank exercised its rights under
the loan agreement contrary to business morality. The judgment under appeal
records that the appellants 'expressly disavowed any reliance on any breach of
contract on the part of the bank'. Miss Dohmann QC for the appellants told us
that the true position is more complex. She said the claim was principally in
tort but it had contractual aspects. So be it.

In March 1991, and in Chicago, the complaint in the Greek proceedings was
served on the bank. The bank's response was to issue a writ in an English
action on 7 April 1991. In the English action the bank sought an injunction
to restrain the appellants from continuing the Greek proceedings in breach of
various jurisdiction agreements which, in the bank's submission, conferred
exclusive jurisdiction on the English courts to try the relevant disputes. Clause
21 of the loan agreement of 20 May 1981 provides as follows:

'21.01 This agreement shall be governed by and construed in
accordance with English law. 21.02 Each of the borrowers ... hereby
irrevocably submits to the jurisdiction of the English courts and hereby
irrevocably nominates Messrs Aegis (London) Ltd of 197 Knightsbridge,
London SW7, England, to receive service of proceedings in such courts on
its behalf but the bank reserves the right to proceed under this agreement
in the courts of any other country claiming or having jurisdiction in
respect thereof.'

The jurisdiction agreements contained in the amending agreements, the
rescheduling agreement and the guarantees are in somewhat different terms.
It is, however, agreed that it is only necessary for us to consider the
interpretation and effect of cl 21.02.

By a summons dated 3 June 1991 the bank sought a permanent injunction
against the appellants to restrain them from taking further steps in the Greek
proceedings, or, alternatively, the bank sought an interim injunction to the
same effect until trial or further order. The appellants took out a

cross-summons dated 23 July 1991. The appellants sought an order that the bank's writ and points of claim be struck out under RSC Ord 18, r 19, or under the court's inherent jurisdiction, or that the action be stayed under arts 21 or 22 of the Convention on Jurisdiction and the Enforcement of Judgments in Civil and Commercial Matters (Brussels, 27 September 1968; EC 46 (1978); Cmnd 7395) (which has the force of law in the United Kingdom by virtue of s 2(1) of the Civil Jurisdiction and Judgments Act 1982 and is set out in Sch 1 thereto).

On 30 July 1991 the rival summonses came before Gatehouse J for hearing. Broadly speaking there were three issues before Gatehouse J. (1) Were the appellants in breach of contract by suing in Greece? (2) If so, do arts 21 and 22 of the 1968 convention require the English court to stay the proceeding? (3) If not, ought the English court nevertheless as a matter of discretion under English law to stay the English proceedings or, in any event, to refuse to grant an injunction? In a reserved judgment, given on 23 August 1991, Gatehouse J decided all three issues in favour of the bank and granted final injunctions restraining the appellants from taking any further steps in the Greek proceedings.

On this appeal the issues can conveniently be considered under the three broad headings which we have identified.

THE ALLEGED BREACH OF THE JURISDICTION AGREEMENTS

Miss Dohmann challenges the judge's construction of cl 21.02 on two fronts. First, she submits, the Greek proceedings fall outside the scope of cl 21.02. Secondly, she submits that even if the Greek proceedings fall within the scope of cl 21.02, it is not an exclusive jurisdiction clause. If either submission is right, the appeal must succeed.

Is cl 21.02 wide enough to cover the Greek proceedings?

It is common ground that not only the loan agreement, as amended, but also the separate jurisdiction agreement are governed by English law. And the construction of cl 21.02 is, of course, a question of law. Clause 21.02 is undoubtedly elliptical. It simply provides that the borrowers and guarantors 'submit to the jurisdiction of the English courts'. In our judgment the clause should be read in a transitive sense: see *Austrian Lloyd Steamship Co v Gresham Life Assurance Society Ltd* [1903] 1 KB 249, [1900–3] All ER Rep 604. It contemplates the submission of disputes to the English courts. The correctness of this construction is reinforced by the fact that the clause contemplates service of proceedings. But what disputes does it cover? The answer is not to be found in the niceties of the language of cl 21.02. It is to be found in a common sense view of the purpose of the clause. We are emboldened to adopt this approach by the observation of Lord Diplock in *Antaios Cia Naviera SA v Salen Rederierna AB, The Antaios* [1984] 3 All ER 229 at 233, [1985] AC 191 at 201 that—

'if detailed semantic and syntactical analysis of words in a commercial contract is going to lead to a conclusion that flouts business common sense, it must be made to yield to business common sense ...'

The only sensible construction of cl 21.02 is that it is a submission of disputes in connection with the loan facility to the jurisdiction of the English courts.

Prima facie, therefore, cl 21.02 covers the Greek proceedings. But Miss Dohmann submits that the clause cannot be construed as extending to a claim in tort. It seems to us to be useful on this point to consider the approach adopted nowadays in the closely analogous field of arbitration clauses. In *Empresa Exportadora de Azucar v Industria Azucarera Nacional SA, The Playa Larga* [1983] 2 Lloyd's Rep 171 the arbitration clause covered 'any dispute arising out of this contract'. The question was whether it covered only contractual claims or also a claim in conversion. In giving the judgment of the court Ackner LJ concluded (at 183):

'... the contractual and tortious claims were so closely knitted together on the facts, that the agreement to arbitrate on one can properly be construed as covering the other.'

Moreover, if Miss Dohmann is right, it would mean that a claim for damages for a negligent misrepresentation inducing the contract (a tort) would be outside cl 21.02 but a claim seeking rescission of the contract on the ground of the same misrepresentation (a contractual claim) would be covered by it. If the appellants' contention is accepted, it follows that the two claims might have to be tried in different jurisdictions. That would be a forensic nightmare. Again, in the field of the construction of arbitration clauses the modern approach provides helpful guidance. In *Ashville Investments Ltd v Elmer Contractors Ltd* [1988] 2 All ER 577 at 599, [1989] QB 488 at 517 Bingham LJ said:

'I would be very slow to attribute to reasonable parties an intention that there should in any foreseeable eventuality be two sets of proceedings.'

In the same case Balcombe LJ adopted a similar approach. He said ([1988] 2 All ER 577 at 588, [1989] QB 488 at 503):

'(1) it may be presumed that the parties intended to refer all the disputes arising out of this particular transaction to arbitration; (2) it may also be presumed that the parties intended that all disputes should be determined finally by the same tribunal ...'

In *Harbour Assurance Co (UK) Ltd v Kansa General International Assurance Co Ltd* [1993] 3 All ER 897 at 916, [1993] QB 701 at 726 Hoffmann LJ adopted the same approach and vividly described it as 'the presumption in favour of one-stop adjudication'. We are in respectful agreement with these observations, and there is no conceivable reason why the same approach should not apply to the construction of jurisdiction agreements.

The complaint in the Greek proceedings makes clear that the thrust of the appellants' case is that the bank performed the loan agreement in a manner which is contrary to business morality. The issue in the Greek proceedings is inextricably interwoven with the contractual rights and duties of the parties. In our judgment the judge rightly concluded that all disputes in connection with the loan facility are covered by the jurisdiction clause, and, so construed, cl 21.01 is apt to cover the disputes in the Greek proceedings.

Does cl 21.02 contain an exclusive jurisdiction clause?

Clause 21.02 does not expressly make clear that the jurisdiction agreement is an exclusive one. Dicey and Morris *The Conflict of Laws* (12th edn, 1993) vol 1, p 422, submit that the question is simply whether on its true construction the clause obliges the parties to resort to the relevant jurisdiction, irrespective of whether the word 'exclusive' is used. In *Sohio Supply Co Ltd v Gatoil (USA) Inc* [1989] 1 Lloyd's Rep 588 at 591 the Court of Appeal approved this submission as contained in the previous edition of *Dicey and Morris*. In our judgment it would be a surrender to formalism to require a jurisdiction clause to provide in express terms that the chosen court is to be the exclusive forum.

We have already explained why we interpret cl 21.01 in a transitive sense as involving an agreement by the appellants to submit disputes in connection with the loan facility to the jurisdiction of the English courts. That does not necessarily mean that cl 21.02 is an exclusive jurisdiction agreement. Mr Christopher Clarke QC submits that where there is an agreement to submit disputes to the jurisdiction of a particular country, the parties are taken to have intended the chosen court's jurisdiction to be exclusive unless there are unusual or particular circumstances which indicate otherwise. He finds some comfort in *Austrian Lloyd Steamship Co v Gresham Life Assurance Society Ltd* [1903] 1 KB 249 at 251–252, [1900–3] All ER Rep 604, *Sohio Supply Co Ltd v Gatoil (USA) Inc* [1989] 1 Lloyd's Rep 588 and *British Aerospace plc v Dee Howard Co* [1993] 1 Lloyd's Rep 368. See, however, *Cannon Screen Entertainment Ltd v Handmade Films (Distributors) Ltd* (11 July 1989, unreported) per Hobhouse J. We find it unnecessary to explore this line of authority or to express any view on Mr Clarke's submission. We say that because cl 21.01 (the only jurisdiction agreement that we are asked to consider) does not contain a submission to English jurisdiction simpliciter. We regard the concluding words as significant:

'... but the bank reserves the right to proceed under this agreement in the courts of any other country claiming or having jurisdiction in respect thereof.'

The juxtaposition of a submission by the appellants to the jurisdiction of the English courts and the option reserved in favour of the bank to sue elsewhere brings into play the expressio unius exclusio alterius canon of construction. It suggests that a similar option in favour of the appellants was deliberately omitted. In our judgment the language of cl 21.02 evinces a clear intention that the appellants, but not the bank, would be obliged to submit disputes in connection with the loan facility to the English courts.

In view of this conclusion it is unnecessary to consider an alternative argument which the bank was ready to advance. It is right, however, that we should identify it. Relying on the judgment of Hoffmann J in *Kurz v Stella Musical Veranstaltungs GmbH* [1992] 1 All ER 630 at 637, [1992] Ch 196 at 203, the bank's case was that, if cl 21.01 was not an *exclusive* jurisdiction clause, art 17 of the 1968 convention nevertheless applied to it. Eminent writers are in disagreement on the correctness of the decision in *Kurz's* case. See Cheshire and North *Private International Law* (12th edn, 1992) pp 316–317, *Dicey and Morris* vol 1, p 431 and Richard Fentiman 'Jurisdiction—when non-exclusive means exclusive' [1992] CLJ 234. Since we heard no argument on the point, we express no view on it.

THE IMPACT OF THE 1968 CONVENTION

The appellants submit that the provisions of arts 21 or 22 of the 1968 convention required the judge to refuse to grant an injunction and to stay the English action. That submission is based on the undoubted fact that the proceedings in Greece were commenced before the proceedings in England. Given that we have concluded that an exclusive jurisdiction agreement obliged the appellants to sue in England, and that the appellants acted in breach of that agreement, it is necessary to consider the interaction of art 17 and arts 21 and 22. Article 17, so far as it is material, provides as follows:

> 'If the parties, one or more of whom is domiciled in a Contracting State, have agreed that a court or the courts of a Contracting State are to have jurisdiction to settle any disputes which have arisen or which may arise in connection with a particular legal relationship, that court or those courts shall have exclusive jurisdiction ... Where such an agreement is concluded by parties, none of whom is domiciled in a Contracting State, the courts of other Contracting States shall have no jurisdiction over their disputes unless the court or courts chosen have declined jurisdiction ... If an agreement conferring jurisdiction was concluded for the benefit of only one of the parties, that party shall retain the right to bring proceedings in any other court which has jurisdiction by virtue of this Convention.'

Article 21 provides as follows:

> 'Where proceedings involving the same cause of action and between the same parties are brought in the courts of different Contracting States, any court other than the court first seised shall of its own motion decline jurisdiction in favour of that court. A court which would be required to decline jurisdiction may stay its proceedings if the jurisdiction of the other court is contested.'

Article 22 provides as follows:

> 'Where related actions are brought in the courts of different Contracting States, any court other than the court first seised may, while the actions are pending at first instance, stay its proceedings. A court other than the court first seised may also, on the application of one of the parties, decline jurisdiction if the law of that court permits the consolidation of related actions and the court first seised has jurisdiction over both actions. For the purposes of this Article, actions are deemed to be related where they are so closely connected that it is expedient to hear and determine them together to avoid the risk of irreconcilable judgments resulting from separate proceedings.'

Miss Dohmann submits that the Athens court was 'the court first seised' within the meaning of arts 21 and art 22. She further submits 'the same cause of action' is involved in the Greek and English proceedings. Accordingly, she submits that the judge was obliged under art 21 to stay the English action. Alternatively, she submits that one is dealing with 'related actions' and the judge had a discretion to be exercised in accordance with art 22, as interpreted in the jurisprudence governing it, and that he was wrong not to stay the English action.

The judge dealt with this point in commendably succinct terms. He said:

> 'The defendants rely on arts 21 and/or 22. But in my judgment, the defendants' action in the Athens court and the plaintiff's action in this court do not involve the same causes of action for the purposes of art 21, as interpreted in *Gubisch Maschinenfabrik KG v Palumbo* Case 144/86 [1987] ECR 4861. Nor are they "related actions" for the purposes of art 22. The actions are totally different, as appears from the respective pleadings, and it is not enough that one issue—jurisdiction—could arise in both actions. In any case, the provisions of art 17 are conclusive. The corporate

defendants are all domiciled in Liberia or Panama; it may be arguable that they are also domiciled in Greece, where they are all managed. The individual defendants are either domiciled in Greece or in England—there is a dispute as to this, but their domicile is undoubtedly one or the other, so it is immaterial which is correct. The bank, it is admitted, is domiciled in Illinois. So either the opening sentence of art 17 applies, or alternatively the third sentence. Clause 21.02 thus confirms the exclusive jurisdiction of the English courts for any action brought by the defendants against the plaintiff bank. The Brussels Convention, therefore, does not alter the position and the bank is entitled to the injunction it seeks.'

We do not propose to consider whether arts 21 or 22 would be applicable if there were no exclusive jurisdiction clause. The fact is that there is an exclusive jurisdiction agreement. And it is common ground that art 17 applies to it.

In construing the 1968 convention it is important to put aside preconceptions based on traditional English rules. The convention is a radical new regime governing the international legal relationships of the contracting states. It is intended to eliminate obstacles to the functioning of the common market and to further the evolution of a vast single market: Jennard Report (1979) OJ C59, p 19. The genesis of the convention is the jurisprudence of the civil law rather than the common law. Since the original states were all civil law countries, and the United Kingdom played no role in the drafting of the 1968 convention, this is hardly surprising. Traditionally, English courts assert a discretion to enjoin a party by injunction from pursuing foreign legal proceedings in breach of an exclusive jurisdiction clause. The idea that a national court has discretion in the exercise of its jurisdiction does not generally exist in civilian systems: Schlosser Report (1979) OJ C59 p 97, para 76. Article 17 follows the civilian approach. Article 17 has mandatory effect. When art 17 applies it follows that the jurisdiction agreement prorogates (confers) jurisdiction on the courts of the contracting state chosen by the parties, and that the jurisdiction agreement deprives the courts of other contracting states of jurisdiction. Indeed, it is the duty of the courts of other contracting states of their own motion to consider whether art 17 applies and to decline jurisdiction if it does: Schlosser Report, para 22. There is no discretionary power *in the convention itself* to override the conclusive effect of an exclusive jurisdiction agreement, which conforms with the requirements of art 17. It follows that, if art 17 applies, its provisions take precedence over the provisions of arts 21 and 22. The structure and logic of the convention convincingly points to this conclusion. The reasons supporting this conclusion are, however, not formalistic. The consequences that would flow from the adoption of the submission of Miss Dohmann are startling. Article 21 provides that there shall be a mandatory stay of proceedings in favour of the court first seised, if courts of different contracting states are seised of proceedings involving 'the same cause of action'. If Miss Dohmann's submission is correct, it follows that a party will be able to override an exclusive jurisdiction agreement, which is governed by art 17, by pre-emptively suing in the courts of another contracting state. The courts of the latter state, which ex hypothesi have been deprived of jurisdiction, would then be 'the court first seised'. The chosen court of the parties would then be obliged to decline jurisdiction or, if the jurisdiction of the other court is contested, to stay its proceedings. In this way a party who is in breach of the contract will be able to set at naught an

exclusive jurisdiction agreement which is the product of the free will of the
parties. The principle of the autonomy of the parties, enshrined in art 17,
cannot countenance such a conclusion.

In coming to the same conclusion in *Kloeckner & Co AG v Gatoil Overseas Inc*
[1990] 1 Lloyd's Rep 177 at 195–196, Hirst J pointed to the additional policy
factor that in the 1968 convention system the best placed court to decide
questions of exclusive jurisdiction is the court chosen by the parties in their
jurisdiction agreement. It is not altogether surprising that in *Anonima Petroli
Italiana SpA v West of England Shipowners Mutual Insurance Association (London)
Ltd* (9 April 1990, unreported) Saville J described an argument similar to the one
addressed to us on behalf of the appellants as entailing 'ludicrous'
consequences. With due deference to the careful arguments of Miss
Dohmann, we find ourselves in agreement with Saville J. See also *IP Metal Ltd
v Ruote OZ SpA* [1993] 2 Lloyd's Rep 60. The critical point is that there is
nothing in the convention which is inconsistent with a power vesting in the
English court to grant an injunction the objective of which is to secure
enforcement of an exclusive jurisdiction agreement.

For all these reasons we conclude that, since art 17 applies, the question of a
stay under arts 21 and 22 of the convention does not arise.

THE EXERCISE OF DISCRETION UNDER ENGLISH LAW

On the supposition that arts 21 and 22 of the 1968 convention are
inapplicable, the appellants seek to invoke the inherent power of the court to
stay the English proceedings. They argue that the judge should have granted
a stay until the Greek court had decided whether or not it had jurisdiction. In
any event, the appellants submit that, even if a stay was inappropriate, the
judge ought not to have granted an injunction. They draw attention to the fact
that, although a stay involves the regulation of English legal proceedings, an
injunction restraining foreign legal proceedings involves indirect interference
in the procedure of a foreign court. Accordingly, the appellants submit, a court
invited to grant such an injunction ought to proceed with great caution and
ought to grant such an injunction only if the ends of justice require it: see *SNI
Aérospatiale v Lee Kui Jak* [1987] 3 All ER 510 at 518–522, [1987] AC 871 at 891–
897.

Miss Dohmann emphasised that the Greek court is the court first seised with
the substantive action. She said that it would be wrong for the English court
to decide that the Greek court does not have jurisdiction. The question
whether the Greek court has jurisdiction ought to be left to the Greek court.
The English courts ought to trust the Greek court. The injunction will operate
as an indirect interference with the workings of a Community court. Such an
injunction should only be granted if the pursuit of the remedy in the foreign
court would be vexatious and oppressive. That test is not satisfied. For these
reasons, Miss Dohmann submitted, the judge erred in not staying the English
action, but, in any event, she said, he plainly erred in exercising his discretion
in favour of the granting of an injunction.

It is necessary to bear in mind that the proper construction of the jurisdiction
agreements is governed by English law. And as a matter of English law, the
jurisdiction agreements apply to the subject matter of the Greek proceedings,
and are exclusive jurisdiction agreements. It follows that the English courts
have exclusive jurisdiction. And by virtue of art 17 the Greek courts have been
deprived of jurisdiction.

But Miss Dohmann submits that the English courts ought to defer to the Greek courts on the interpretation and effect of the exclusive jurisdiction agreement. She argues that we can safely leave it to the Greek courts to decide the art 17 issue on its merits. That is not how we understand the expert evidence on Greek law filed in this case. Mr Soufias, the bank's Greek lawyer, appears to say that the Greek court will assume jurisdiction. Mr Stephanakis, the appellants' Greek lawyer, says that the Greek court will not consider a jurisdictional issue because the bank co-operated at an early stage in asking for an adjournment. He says that in Greece that will be regarded as a submission to jurisdiction. It does not appear that the Greek court will consider the impact on its jurisdiction of the exclusive jurisdiction agreement and art 17 of the 1968 convention. But we do not rest our judgment on this point.

Under the Greek rules of civil procedure a defendant is obliged to file a defence on the merits at the same time as an objection to jurisdiction. The bank cannot therefore in practice challenge the jurisdiction of the Greek court without filing a detailed defence on the merits to the appellants' complaint, which runs to 38 pages, and the bank will in addition have to lodge at the same time all supporting documentary evidence. Legal fees will apparently amount to about $US120,000. And in addition the bank would have to serve expert evidence from an English lawyer on the effect of cl 21.02. Again, we do not rest our judgment on this point.

In our view the decisive matter is that the bank applied for the injunction to restrain the appellants' clear breach of contract. In the circumstances, a claim for damages for breach of contract would be a relatively ineffective remedy. An injunction is the only effective remedy for the appellants' breach of contract. If the injunction is set aside, the appellants will persist in their breach of contract, and the bank's legal rights as enshrined in the jurisdiction agreements will prove to be valueless. Given the total absence of special countervailing factors, this is the paradigm case for the grant of an injunction restraining a party from acting in breach of an exclusive jurisdiction agreement. In our judgment the continuance of the Greek proceedings amounts to vexatious and oppressive conduct on the part of the appellants. The judge exercised his discretion properly.

Conclusion

It follows that we would reject the submissions of the appellants under all three headings. It is right to add, however, that in relation to the link between arts 17 and 21 of the 1968 convention, the appellants applied for an order referring an appropriate question to the Court of Justice of the European Communities. It is true that, except for first instance decisions, there is apparently no authority directly in point. The more obvious the answer to a question is, the less authority there sometimes is on it. We entertain no doubt about the answer to the proposed question. We would reject the application. Somewhat tentatively, the appellants also asked for an order that the following two questions be referred to the European Court:

(a) Whether the Greek proceedings and the English proceedings involve 'the same cause of action' for the purposes of art 21 of the Convention.
(b) Whether the Greek proceedings and the English proceedings are 'related actions' for the purposes of art 22 of the convention.

In our judgment there are no relevant questions of 'interpretation' of the 1968 convention which arise in the present case. In our judgment no reference is necessary. We would also reject this application in both parts.

We would dismiss the appeal.

Appeal dismissed.

Bebe Chua Barrister.

R v Chan-Fook

COURT OF APPEAL, CRIMINAL DIVISION
HOBHOUSE LJ, JUDGE AND BELL JJ
19, 22 OCTOBER 1993

Criminal law – Assault occasioning actual bodily harm – Actual bodily harm – Psychiatric injury – No physical harm suffered – Whether psychiatric injury can amount to actual bodily harm – Whether emotion such as extreme fear or panic can amount to actual bodily harm – Appropriate direction to jury on psychiatric injury amounting to actual bodily harm – Offences against the Person Act 1861, s 47.

The appellant was told by his fiancée that she suspected that the complainant, a foreign student lodging with her family, had stolen her engagement ring. The appellant and other members of the family strongly questioned the complainant about the disappearance of the engagement ring even though there was no evidence to support the suspicion that he had taken it. The complainant was unable to explain the disappearance of the ring and the appellant then dragged the complainant upstairs and locked him in a second floor room. The complainant tried to escape through the window but was injured when he fell to the ground below. The appellant was charged with assault occasioning actual bodily harm contrary to s 47[a] of the Offences against the Person Act 1861. At his trial the Crown alleged that even if the complainant had not suffered any physical injury as a result of the assault upon him by the appellant, he had nevertheless been reduced to a mental state which in itself amounted to actual bodily harm. There was no medical evidence to support that allegation, the only evidence being that of the complainant that he had felt abused, humiliated and frightened. The judge referred to the complainant's 'mental state' and directed the jury that an assault which caused a hysterical or nervous condition was capable of being an assault occasioning actual bodily harm. The appellant was convicted. He appealed against his conviction on the grounds of a misdirection.

Held – The phrase 'actual bodily harm' in s 47 of the 1861 Act was capable of including psychiatric injury but did not include mere emotions such as fear, distress, panic or a hysterical or nervous condition, nor did it include states of

---

[a] Section 47, so far as material, provides: 'Whosoever shall be convicted upon an indictment of any assault occasioning actual bodily harm shall be liable to [imprisonment for not more than five years].'

mind that were not themselves evidence of some identifiable clinical condition. The phrase 'state of mind' was not a scientific one and should be avoided in a direction to the jury on the issue whether or not a psychiatric injury had been caused since its use was likely to create in the minds of the jury the impression that something which was no more than a strong emotion, such as extreme fear or panic, could amount to actual bodily harm when that was not the case. Similarly, the jury should not be directed that an assault which caused a hysterical and nervous condition was an assault occasioning actual bodily harm. Where there was evidence that an assault had caused some psychiatric injury the jury should be directed that the injury was capable of amounting to actual bodily harm but otherwise there should be no reference to the mental state of the complainant following the assault unless it was relevant to some other aspect of the case. Where psychiatric injury was relied on as the basis for an allegation of bodily harm which was disputed by the defence the Crown should call expert evidence and in the absence of such expert evidence the question whether psychiatric injury had been occasioned by an assault should not be left to the jury. On the facts, the direction to the jury was defective since there was no evidence to support the allegation that the complainant had been caused any psychiatric injury by the assault. The appeal would therefore be allowed and the conviction quashed (see p 559 *e* to *g j* and p 560 *c*, post).

Notes
For assault occasioning actual bodily harm, see 11(1) *Halsbury's Laws* (4th edn reissue) para 490.

For the Offences against the Person Act 1861, s 47, see 12 *Halsbury's Statutes* (4th edn) (1994 reissue) 105.

Cases referred to in judgment
Alcock v Chief Constable of the South Yorkshire Police [1991] 4 All ER 907, [1992] 1 AC 310, [1991] 3 WLR 1057, HL.
Attia v British Gas plc [1987] 3 All ER 455, [1988] QB 304, [1987] 3 WLR 1101, CA.
DPP v Smith [1960] 3 All ER 161, [1961] AC 290, [1960] 3 WLR 546, HL.
Fagan v Metropolitan Police Comr [1968] 3 All ER 442, [1969] 1 QB 439, [1968] 3 WLR 1120, DC.
McLoughlin v O'Brian [1982] 2 All ER 298, [1983] 1 AC 410, [1982] 2 WLR 982, HL.
R v Ashman (1858) 1 F & F 88, 175 ER 638.
R v Metharam [1961] 3 All ER 200, CCA.
R v Miller [1951] VLR 346, Vict SC.
R v Miller [1954] 2 All ER 529, [1954] 2 QB 282, [1954] 2 WLR 138, Assizes.
R v R— (rape: marital exemption) [1991] 4 All ER 481, [1992] 1 AC 599, [1991] 3 WLR 767, HL.
R v Roberts (1971) 56 Cr App R 95, CA.

Case also cited
R v Donovan [1934] 2 KB 498, [1934] All ER Rep 207, CCA.

Appeal against conviction
Mike Chan-Fook appealed on a reference of the Registrar of Criminal Appeals against his conviction on 24 February 1992 in the Crown Court at Inner London Sessions before Judge Bernard Charles QC and a jury of assault

occasioning actual bodily harm, for which he was ordered to pay £250
compensation and £1,000 towards prosecution costs. The facts are set out in
the judgment of the court.

Philip Sapsford QC and *Charles Salter* (assigned by the *Registrar of Criminal
Appeals*) for the appellant.
Brian Barker QC and *Rupert Overbury* (instructed by the *Crown Prosecution
Service,* Inner London) for the Crown.

Cur adv vult

22 October 1993. The following judgment of the court was delivered.

HOBHOUSE LJ. On 24 February 1992 after a trial in the Crown Court at Inner
London Sessions before Judge Bernard Charles QC and a jury the appellant,
Mike Chan-Fook, was convicted on a single count of assault occasioning actual
bodily harm contrary to s 47 of the Offences against the Person Act 1861. He
was ordered to pay £250 compensation and £1,000 costs. The particulars of the
offence were that on 30 May 1991 he 'assaulted Sidney Martins thereby
occasioning him actual bodily harm'. (No point was taken on the drafting of
these particulars.) The question raised by this appeal is whether the jury were
correctly directed upon the meaning of the words 'actual bodily harm'.

The facts of the case were unusual. Sidney Martins was a French student
who in May 1991 was attending a course in English in London. He was lodging
at the house in Lewisham of a Mrs Fox. Also living in the house were Mrs Fox's
daughter, Jackie, and her son, Peter. Jackie was engaged to marry the
appellant. On 29 May Jackie Fox apparently discovered that her engagement
ring was missing from her room. She suspected that Mr Martins had stolen it
although there was no evidence, other than opportunity, to implicate Mr
Martins in any way whatever. However the household, including the
appellant, decided that they should investigate the matter further. The
following evening they contrived by a subterfuge that Mr Martins should come
down to Mrs Fox's living room so as to give the appellant and Peter Fox an
opportunity to search his room. This they did but they neither found the ring
nor any evidence to connect Mr Martins with its loss. Undeterred, they then
carried out an interrogation of Mr Martins in the living room. The person
primarily involved was the appellant. On any view this interrogation was very
aggressively conducted and extremely disturbing and frightening for Mr
Martins, who was a stranger in this country and only had a limited familiarity
with the English language. Mr Martins was unable to offer them any
explanation for the loss of the ring and had no information to give the appellant
and the others who were interrogating him. The interrogation ended with the
appellant dragging Mr Martins upstairs to his room on the second floor and
locking him in. The appellant had already removed from Mr Martins his keys
and his personal papers.

However the evidence of Mr Martins was that things went further. He said
that the appellant struck him about the head many times with his hands, using
on some occasions the base of his palm causing bruises to Mr Martins's face and
head. He felt abused and humiliated. Mr Martins also said that during the
course of the assaults on him he had been kneed by the appellant and at one
point his head had hit the wall. He said that he had asked that the police be
called but the appellant had refused. He further said that, when locking him

into his room, the appellant had threatened him with further violence if he did not tell them where the ring was.

Having been locked in his room he was frightened that the appellant would return and assault him further. 'I thought he was going to get a weapon because he was very violent.' It was in those circumstances that Mr Martins bolted the door on the inside, made a rope out of his bed sheets knotted together, attached the sheets to the curtain rail and then sought to escape through the window to the ground below. Unfortunately the curtain rail broke under his weight and he fell into the garden below. He suffered injuries from his fall. At the trial a statement was read from a doctor at the hospital who had examined him at 8.15 that night. Mr Martins had a fractured right wrist and a dislocation of his pelvis. He further had tenderness in his right groin and bruising on his face.

The defence case at the trial was that the interrogation and other aspects of the incident had not involved any hitting of Mr Martins. It was admitted that the appellant had taken him upstairs forcibly by the collar of his jacket and that the appellant had locked him in his room. It was said that at no time had Mr Martins been struck nor had any injuries been caused to him. The injuries observed by the doctor were attributable solely to his fall from the window and were not caused by any assault by the appellant.

Although the evidence of Mr Martins, and indeed the defence case, would have justified the appellant being charged with other counts besides the count of assault occasioning actual bodily harm, the appellant was tried solely on the single count under s 47. The case was not complicated by any allegation that the injuries suffered by Mr Martins when he fell to the ground from his window were caused by the assaults which had taken place prior to his being locked in his room (cf *R v Roberts* (1971) 56 Cr App R 95). However, unfortunately, the prosecution chose to introduce into the case an allegation that even if Mr Martins had suffered no physical injury at all as a result of the assault upon him by the appellant, he had nevertheless been reduced to a mental state which in itself, without more, amounted to actual bodily harm. The only evidence to which the prosecution could point in support of this allegation was the evidence of Mr Martins that he felt abused and humiliated, that he had been threatened with further violence, and that he was very frightened. There was no medical or psychiatric evidence to support the allegation. There was no evidence that he was in a state of shock at any time prior to receiving the injuries which he suffered as a result of falling from the window. Nevertheless the trial judge directed the jury in terms of the sentence in *Archbold's Pleading, Evidence and Practice in Criminal Cases* (44th edn, 1992) vol 2, para 19-197: 'An assault which causes an hysterical and nervous condition is an assault occasioning actual bodily harm ...' He left that question to the jury in addition to the other questions in the case. The appellant's submission before us is that there was a misdirection and that in any event there was no evidence of any psychological injury which was capable of supporting the allegation of actual bodily harm and the allegation of such further harm should not have been left to the jury.

The trial judge said:

'If you are satisfied that he committed an assault, then you have to consider whether it was an assault, as the indictment says, occasioning him actual bodily harm, in other words causing Mr Martins actual bodily harm. What is meant by "actual bodily harm"? It does not have to be

permanent. It does not have to be serious. It is some actual harm which
interferes with the comfort of the individual, for the time being, described
as any hurt or injury calculated to interfere with the health or comfort of
Mr Martins, in this case. An assault that causes a hysterical or nervous
condition is capable of being an assault causing actual bodily harm ... [The
Crown] have to prove that the harm—some actual bodily harm—was
sustained and was the result of the assault. What the Crown says was the
result of the assault was, firstly, his bruising to his head or face; and a
bruise, that is temporary, interferes with one's comfort, does it not, on a
temporary basis. It is sore, it is tender, you do not have it beforehand. One
would be able to say "I have been harmed as a result, on my body I have a
bruise which I did not have before". Not the most serious thing naturally.
Equally the Crown says that his mental state, which caused him to lock the
door and take that extreme action of climbing out of a window, tying the
sheets together, indicates that he was in a nervous, maybe hysterical
condition. It is a matter for you to judge what his condition was. That in
itself is capable of amounting to actual bodily harm. Why did he go out of
the window at all? ... You have to be satisfied, before you can convict, that
some actual bodily harm was sustained by Mr Martins which was caused
by the assault. So it has to be a direct consequence, and what the Crown
puts in front of you and invites you to consider is the bruising to the face,
and the mental state of Mr Martins when he—let us break the sequence—
put his foot onto the windowsill in order to descend down the sheet, not
when he hit the ground, having tried to descend down the sheet. So
members of the jury, that, in a nutshell, is what this case is about ... [The
defendant] was asked if he could think of any reason why Mr Martins
should leave his room via the window, lock himself in his room and leave
all his property behind, and he couldn't. The Crown says that the reason
for acting in that way was he was hysterical, he was frightened. He was in
such a state that he took extreme emergency action. It is for you to decide
which is right.'

There were a number of other points during the summing up at which the judge referred to the 'mental state' of Mr Martins.

Historically, the phrase 'bodily harm' antedates the 1861 Act. It has been used for a long time in English law in connection with the definitions of aggravated assault and murder. At Bristol in 1858 Willes J in *R v Ashman* 1 F & F 88 at 88–89, 175 ER 638 at 639, on the trial of a defendant charged with shooting with intent, directed the jury:

'You must be satisfied that the prisoner had an intent to do grievous bodily harm. It is not necessary that such harm should have been actually done, or that it should be either permanent or dangerous, if it be such as seriously to interfere with comfort or health, it is sufficient.'

That phraseology was extensively used in relation to grievous bodily harm until the decision of the House of Lords in *DPP v Smith* [1960] 3 All ER 161, [1961] AC 290. That case concerned the element of mens rea necessary for the crime of murder. The trial judge had used the phrase 'intends to kill or to inflict some harm which will seriously interfere for a time with health or comfort'. Vicount Kilmuir LC with the agreement of all members of the House said ([1960] 3 All ER 161 at 171–172, [1961] AC 290 at 334):

'My Lords, I confess that, whether one is considering the crime of murder or the statutory offence, I can find no warrant for giving the words "grievous bodily harm" a meaning other than that which the words convey in their ordinary and natural meaning. "Bodily harm" needs no explanation and "grievous" means no more and no less than "really serious". In this connexion, your Lordships were referred to the judgment of the Supreme Court of Victoria in *R. v. Miller* ([1951] VLR 346 at 357). In giving the judgment of the court, MARTIN, J., having expressed the view that the directions of WILLES, J., could only be justified, if at all, in the case of the statutory offence, said: "... there does not appear to be any justification for treating the expression 'grievous bodily harm' or the other similar expressions used in the authorities upon this common law question which are cited as bearing any other than their ordinary and natural meaning." In my opinion, the view of the law thus expressed by MARTIN, J., is correct, and I would only add that I can see no ground for giving the words a wider meaning when considering the statutory offence.'

We consider that the same is true of the phrase 'actual bodily harm'. These are three words of the English language which require no elaboration and in the ordinary course should not receive any. The word 'harm' is a synonym for injury. The word 'actual' indicates that the injury (although there is no need for it to be permanent) should not be so trivial as to be wholly insignificant. The purpose of the definition in s 47 is to define an element of aggravation in the assault. It must be an assault which besides being an assault (or assault and battery) causes to the victim some injury.

The danger of any elaboration of the words of the statute is that it may have the effect, as was pointed out by the House of Lords, of altering, or at the least distracting the jury from, the ordinary meaning of the words. Further, as can be seen from the summing up in the present case, there may be an elision of the need to show some harm or injury. There will be a risk that language will be used which suggests to the jury that it is sufficient that the assault has interfered with the health or comfort of the victim, whether or not any injury or hurt has been caused. No doubt what is intended by those who have used these words in the past is to indicate that some injury which otherwise might be regarded as wholly trivial is not to be so regarded because it has caused the victim pain. Similarly an injury can be caused to someone by injuring their health; an assault may have the consequence of infecting the victim with a disease or causing the victim to become ill. The injury may be internal and may not be accompanied by any external injury. A blow may leave no external mark but may cause the victim to lose consciousness.

The dangers of departing from the simple words 'bodily harm' and the elision which may result are further illustrated by *R v Metharam* [1961] 3 All ER 200, a case of wounding with intent contrary to s 18 of the 1861 Act, in which the Court of Criminal Appeal followed and applied what had been said by Vicount Kilmuir LC in *DPP v Smith*. Ashworth J said (at 202):

'... it is a misdirection of the jury to adopt the old formula and invite a jury to find a man accused of wounding with intent to do grievous bodily harm guilty if the only intent established is one to interfere seriously with health or comfort. Reading the speech of VISCOUNT KILMUIR, L.C., as a whole, it seems to follow that certainly as applied to this case the adoption of the old formula is one that amounts to a misdirection.'

In certain cases an explanation may be required of what is involved in the word 'bodily'. The sentence we have quoted from *Archbold* and the direction which the trial judge gave in the present case derived from what was said by Lynskey J in *R v Miller* [1954] 2 All ER 529, [1954] 2 QB 282. That was a case where the defendant was charged on an indictment containing two counts. The first alleged rape and the second alleged assault occasioning actual bodily harm. Both counts related to the same incident. The alleged victim was the defendant's wife to whom he was still legally married although they had separated and she was petitioning for divorce. At the commencement of the trial the defence moved to quash the indictment. The rape count was quashed on the basis that a husband could not in law rape his wife (see now *R v R— (rape: marital exemption)* [1991] 4 All ER 481, [1992] 1 AC 599). Lynskey J declined to quash the other count. The report shows that there was evidence that the wife had suffered acute mental and emotional distress which persisted over more than one day as a result of the assaults upon her; it was said that that was capable of amounting to a hurt or injury calculated to interfere with her health and comfort. Lynskey J said ([1954] 2 All ER 529 at 534, [1954] 2 QB 282 at 292):

'The point was taken that there is no evidence of bodily harm. The bodily harm alleged is said to be the result of the defendant's actions, and they were, if the jury accept the evidence, that he threw the wife down three times. There is evidence that afterwards she was in a hysterical and nervous condition, but it is submitted by counsel for the defendant that that is not "actual bodily harm". According to ARCHBOLD'S CRIMINAL PLEADING, EVIDENCE AND PRACTICE ((32nd edn, 1949) p 959): "Actual bodily harm includes any hurt or injury calculated to interfere with the health or comfort of the prosecutor ..." There was a time when shock was not regarded as bodily hurt, but the day has gone by when that could be said. It seems to me now that, if a person is caused hurt or injury resulting, not in any physical injury, but in an injury to the state of his mind for the time being, that is within the definition of "actual bodily harm". On that point I would leave the case to the jury.'

Certain comments need to be made about this passage. First, Lynskey J was concerned with a question whether the indictment should be quashed. (The jury subsequently returned a verdict of guilty of common assault.) He was not concerned with defining the offence. Secondly, in using the phrase 'injury to the state of his mind', he was using language which, certainly today, would be capable of creating confusion. The 'state' of somebody's mind is not something which is capable of being injured on any ordinary use of language and there are today more accurate and less misleading expressions that should be used. Thirdly, the statement in *Archbold*, although drawn verbatim from the headnote in the Law Reports, distorts what Lynskey J actually said.

The first question on the present appeal is whether the inclusion of the word 'bodily' in the phrase 'actual bodily harm' limits harm to harm to the skin, flesh and bones of the victim. Lynskey J rejected this submission. In our judgment he was right to do so. The body of the victim includes all parts of his body, including his organs, his nervous system and his brain. Bodily injury therefore may include injury to any of those parts of his body responsible for his mental and other faculties. The matter was well summarised by Lord Wilberforce in *McLoughlin v O'Brian* [1982] 2 All ER 298 at 301, [1983] 1 AC 410 at 418:

'Whatever is unknown about the mind-body relationship (and the area of ignorance seems to expand with that of knowledge), it is now accepted by medical science that recognisable and severe physical damage to the human body and system may be caused by the impact, through the senses, of external events on the mind. Thus may be produced what is as identifiable an illness as any that may be caused by direct physical impact.'

As is pointed out by Lord Wilberforce earlier in his speech the conventional phrase 'nervous shock' is now inaccurate and inappropriate. Observations to the like effect are to be found in *Attia v British Gas plc* [1987] 3 All ER 455, [1988] QB 304 and *Alcock v Chief Constable of the South Yorkshire Police* [1991] 4 All ER 907, [1992] 1 AC 310. In *Attia*'s case the Court of Appeal discussed where the borderline should be drawn between on the one hand the emotions of distress and grief and on the other hand some actual psychiatric illness such as anxiety neurosis or a reactive depression. The authorities recognised that there is a line to be drawn and whether any given case falls on one side or the other is a matter for expert evidence. The civil cases are also concerned with a broader question of the boundaries of the law of negligence and the duty of care, which do not concern us.

Accordingly the phrase 'actual bodily harm' is capable of including psychiatric injury. But it does not include mere emotions such as fear or distress or panic nor does it include, as such, states of mind that are not themselves evidence of some identifiable clinical condition. The phrase 'state of mind' is not a scientific one and should be avoided in considering whether or not a psychiatric injury has been caused; its use is likely to create in the minds of the jury the impression that something which is no more than a strong emotion, such as extreme fear or panic, can amount to actual bodily harm. It cannot. Similarly juries should not be directed that an assault which causes a hysterical and nervous condition is an assault occasioning actual bodily harm. Where there is evidence that the assault has caused some psychiatric injury, the jury should be directed that that injury is capable of amounting to actual bodily harm; otherwise there should be no reference to the mental state of the victim following the assault unless it be relevant to some other aspect of the case, as it was in *R v Roberts* (1971) 56 Cr App R 95.

It is also relevant to have in mind the relationship between the offence of aggravated assault comprised in s 47 and simple assault. The latter can include conduct which causes the victim to apprehend immediate and unlawful violence (*Fagan v Metropolitan Police Comr* [1968] 3 All ER 442, [1969] 1 QB 439). To treat the victim's fear of such unlawful violence, without more, as amounting to actual bodily harm would be to risk rendering the definition of the aggravated offence academic in many cases.

In any case where psychiatric injury is relied upon as the basis for an allegation of bodily harm, and the matter has not been admitted by the defence, expert evidence should be called by the prosecution. It should not be left to be inferred by the jury from the general facts of the case. In the absence of appropriate expert evidence a question whether or not the assault occasioned psychiatric injury should not be left to the jury. Cases where it is necessary to allege that psychiatric injury has been caused by an assault will be very few and far between. It is to be observed that there has been no reported case on the point since 1953 and the present case was not, on a correct assessment, a case where such an allegation should have been made. But, if there should be such a case, the evidential difficulties will be no greater than juries often have to consider in other aspects of the criminal law, for example an issue of diminished responsibility. There is no reason for refusing to have regard to psychiatric injury as the consequence of an assault if there is properly qualified evidence that it has occurred.

Counsel referred us to a Law Commission consultation paper, *Legislating the Criminal Code: Offences against the Person and General Principles* (Law Com no 122). Whilst we found the discussion contained in that document enlightening, we do not think that it is necessary to refer to it further in this judgment.

Accordingly the appeal will be allowed. The directions to the jury were defective in law and there was no evidence to be left to the jury in support of the allegation that any psychiatric injury had been caused to Mr Martins by the assault. Since the indictment did not include any alternative count charging common assault, it follows that the conviction must be quashed.

Appeal allowed. Conviction quashed.

Kate O'Hanlon   Barrister.

R v Chief Constable of South Wales, ex parte Merrick

QUEEN'S BENCH DIVISION

RALPH GIBSON LJ AND SMITH J

17, 18 JANUARY, 9 FEBRUARY 1994

Solicitor – Access to – Right of person in custody – Remand prisoner – Validity of police policy to regulate access by solicitors to remand cells – Applicant held in cells at magistrates' court – Police policy to deny access by solicitors to cells after 10 am – Applicant's solicitor seeking access at 3.15 pm – Whether applicant having right to see solicitor – Whether policy lawful – Police and Criminal Evidence Act 1984, s 58.

On 26 April 1993 the applicant was arrested and charged with arson after allegedly setting his estranged wife's car on fire. He was detained in police custody on remand until 12 May. On that day he was represented by a solicitor, who saw the applicant early in the morning in the cells at the court prior to making a further application for bail. The applicant's case was put back until 2.15 pm. At 1.15 pm the solicitor went to the cells to see the applicant but was refused access by a police officer. The application for bail was dismissed and the applicant was remanded until 20 May. At 3.15 pm the solicitor again requested access to the applicant in order to explain the refusal of bail, to obtain instructions concerning the next steps to be taken, and to discuss the contents of papers obtained from the prosecution. Access to the applicant was refused by the police officer in charge of the cells, acting on a standing order by the chief constable prohibiting entry to the cells by solicitors after 10 am. The chief constable, supported by the clerk to the justices, had adopted a policy that it was necessary to regulate access by solicitors to the cells at the court because in his opinion they were not a police custody office but were 'a holding area for the courts' to which the provisions of the Police and Criminal Evidence Act 1984 did not apply and because of the shortage of police resources and the demands of security. Under that policy, if defendants were produced before 10 am solicitors were expected to interview them before court commenced at 10 am and if solicitors wished to interview clients after 10 am access would be allowed if there was a valid reason for not having seen the client before 10 am and security permitted. The applicant applied for judicial review by way of declarations that the decision of the chief constable and/or the clerk to the justices to refuse him access to his solicitor and the policy of the chief constable and/or the clerk to the justices to refuse access of solicitors to clients in police custody at the magistrates' court after 10 am were unlawful and that it was unlawful to refuse prisoners in custody access to their solicitors at magistrates' courts. The applicant contended that the respondents' policy was contrary to s 58[a] of the 1984 Act, which provided that 'if a person [in custody] makes such a request he must be permitted to consult a solicitor as soon as is practicable', and that they had acted unlawfully by interfering with the applicant's fundamental right of access to legal advice.

Held – A person held in custody in cells at a courthouse had a common law right, on request, to be permitted to consult a solicitor as soon as was practicable. Although a denial of access to a solicitor was, in some circumstances, unavoidable, and therefore justifiable, if it was not practicable or reasonably practicable for the police to arrange for access, if in the circumstances access was practicable or reasonably practicable there was no justification for refusing access. The chief constable and the clerk to the justices were entitled to impose a policy regulating visits by solicitors to remand prisoners but the particular policy operated by chief constable and the clerk to the justices was unlawful in so far as it it authorised or permitted the officers at the cells to refuse access to a solicitor on the sole ground that the request was made after 10 am without reference to whether it was reasonably practicable to allow access at once or within a reasonable period. The failure of the police to allow the applicant's solicitor access to the applicant at 3.15 pm on 12 May 1993 constituted a breach of the applicant's common law right and a declaration would be made to that effect (see p 572 h to p 573 a, p 574 c to f, p 575 a to c f and p 576 c h, post).

Per curiam. Section 58 of the 1984 Act does not apply to a person who is in custody after being remanded in custody by a magistrates' court except in special circumstances, eg where the defendant is the subject of continuing investigations for other offences (see p 571 e to j and p 574 g, post).

Notes

For false imprisonment as the result of arrest by a private person, see 45 *Halsbury's Laws* (th edn) para 1327.

For the Police and Criminal Evidence Act 1984, s 58, see 12 *Halsbury's Statutes* (4th edn) (1994 reissue) 906.

Cases referred to in judgments

Brind v Secretary of State for the Home Dept [1991] 1 All ER 720, [1991] 1 AC 696, [1991] 2 WLR 588, HL.

---

a   Section 58, so far as material, is set out at p 568 d e, post

Dedman v British Building and Engineering Appliances Ltd [1974] 1 All ER 520, [1974] 1 WLR 171, CA.
Golder v UK (1975) 1 EHRR 524, E Ct HR.
R v Cambridge Justices, ex p Peacock [1993] Crim LR 219, DC.
R v Jones [1984] Crim LR 357, CA.
R v Kerawalla [1991] Crim LR 451, CA.
R v Lemsatef [1977] 2 All ER 835, [1977] 1 WLR 812, CA.
R v Metropolitan Police Comr, ex p Blackburn [1968] 1 All ER 763, [1968] 2 QB 118, [1968] 2 WLR 893, CA.
R v Secretary of State for the Home Dept, ex p Anderson [1984] 1 All ER 920, [1984] QB 778, [1984] 2 WLR 725, DC.
R v Secretary of State for the Home Dept, ex p McAvoy [1984] 3 All ER 417, [1984] 1 WLR 1408.
R v Walsh (1989) 91 Cr App R 161, CA.
Raymond v Honey [1982] 1 All ER 756, [1983] 1 AC 1, [1982] 2 WLR 465, HL.

Cases also cited
Allen v Chief Constable of Cheshire Constabulary (1988) Times, 16 July, CA.
Artico v Italy (1980) 3 EHRR 1, E Ct HR.
R v Samuel [1988] 2 All ER 135, [1988] QB 615, CA.
Wynne v Secretary of State for the Home Dept [1993] 1 All ER 574, [1993] 1 WLR 115, HL.

Application for judicial review
Bryn Merrick applied with the leave of Hutchison J granted on 22 July 1993 for judicial review by way of declarations that (i) the decision of the first respondent, the Chief Constable of the South Wales Constabulary and/or the second respondent, the clerk to the justices of the Cardiff Magistrates' Court, to refuse the applicant access to his solicitor was unlawful, (ii) the policy of the first and/or second respondents to refuse access of solicitors to clients in police custody at the magistrates' courts at Cardiff after 10 am was unlawful and (iii) it was unlawful to refuse prisoners in custody access to their solicitors at magistrates' courts. The facts are set out in the judgment of Ralph Gibson LJ.

Richard Clayton (instructed by *Jonathan Brierley,* Cardiff) for the appellant.
Crispin Masterman (instructed by *Gareth Madge,* Bridgend) for the respondent.
Nicholas Hilliard (instructed by the *Treasury Solicitor*) as amicus curiae.
The clerk to the justices did not appear.

Cur adv vult

9 February 1994. The following judgments were delivered.

RALPH GIBSON LJ. This is an application by Mr Bryn Merrick for judicial review of the decision made on 12 May 1993 to refuse him access to his solicitor when the applicant was held in custody in the cells at Cardiff Magistrates' Court. The respondents are the Chief Constable of the South Wales Constabulary and the clerk to the justices at Cardiff Magistrates' Court. Leave to apply was granted on 22 July 1993. The relief sought is a series of declarations which, by their terms, demonstrate the issues raised for decision. They are (i) a declaration that the decision of the first and/or the second respondent to refuse him access to his solicitors was unlawful; (ii) a declaration that the policy of the first and/or second respondent to refuse access of solicitors to clients in police custody at magistrates' courts after 10 am is unlawful; (iii) a declaration that it is unlawful to refuse prisoners in custody access to their solicitors at magistrates' courts.

The applicant was on 12 May 1993 a defendant in criminal proceedings who had been remanded in custody, after being arrested on 26 April 1993, and charged with an offence of arson by setting on fire the car of his estranged wife. He was detained in police custody to appear before Cardiff Magistrates' Court (CMC) on 28 April. An application by a duty solicitor on his behalf for bail was rejected and he was remanded in custody until 5 May. On 5 May he was again remanded in custody to 12 May. While in custody on remand he was held at Cardiff prison which is about 100 yards from CMC. On 12 May he was represented by Mr Brierley, a solicitor in practice in Cardiff, when a further application for bail was dismissed and he was remanded until 20 May. On 13 May 1993 an application was made in chambers to Judge Crowther QC, which was rejected. On 20 May 1993 the applicant pleaded guilty to an amended charge of criminal damage and was granted conditional bail. On 21 June 1993 he appeared for sentence and was fined.

The cell complex and the policy

(i) The circumstances in which Mr Brierley, as solicitor for the applicant, was refused access to the applicant arose out of the decision of the chief constable that it was necessary to devise some suitable regulation for access by solicitors to the cells at CMC

(ii) The new building of CMC at Fitzalan Place, which was opened on 25 April 1990, has 14 court rooms and includes a cell complex of some 21 cells for holding prisoners awaiting appearance at the courts. The cells are, it is said, owned and controlled by the Magistrates' Courts' Committee of South Glamorgan as 'a holding area for the courts' and are not in the view of Mr Evans, an assistant chief constable, in any way a custody office for the constabulary. The cells are divided into two blocks each with its own secure corridor.

(iii) Prisoners in detention or on remand are brought to the CMC cells from Cardiff, or from other prisons, from about 7.30 am each day. The South Wales Constabulary agreed to provide officers to man the cell complex and to provide the service to the courts of taking prisoners to the courts and of protection and security. The officers are provided reluctantly because it is the opinion of the constabulary that it is the responsibility of the court to provide such services and not of the constabulary. There have been one sergeant and nine constables assigned to this work with a discretion to use more officers in exceptional circumstances.

(iv) The duties of these officers include collecting prisoners from the Rumney and Cardiff Central Police Stations and receiving prisoners from other police stations and from HM prison establishments. The officers have the care, including feeding, safety and security of all these prisoners while they are in the building. The officers have to convey prisoners from the cells to the courts and although there is one main custody court, it is a regular occurrence that prisoners have to be produced at two or three courts at the same time. This may involve the appearance of two or more prisoners in each court. Prisoners previously on bail who are sentenced to custody have to be taken from the courts to the cells. Prisoners, previously remanded in custody, who are released, require to have property returned to them. If there is any emergency, disturbance, damage or outbreak of violence within the confines of the CMC these officers have to respond to such events. They also have to convey remanded prisoners to prison establishments. In addition, where practicable, they facilitate visits to prisoners by legal representatives, probation officers and social services' personnel.

(v) Access by legal advisers to prisoners at CMC has been a contentious issue with solicitors in Cardiff since the new building opened. It has appeared to the police officers in charge that the solicitors were asserting a right of access to clients whenever they wished and that the police were asserting their inability to meet those demands having regard to all that is required of the police in operating the cell complex. Efforts were made through discussions with the Cardiff Law Society to find an agreed solution. Facilities were provided for interviews between 7.30 and 10 am but, in the view of the police, were not generally taken up. Incidents occurred of assaults by prisoners upon police officers in the course of providing access for interviews.

(vi) The chief constable therefore, in the interests of safety and security and having regard to the available resources, decided that as from 2 February 1993 solicitors or their representatives should not be afforded access to prisoners in custody at the cells after 10 am but that facilities would remain for such conferences between 8.30 am and 10 am each day. This decision was supported by the clerk to the justices. Notice to that effect was therefore displayed at the cells complex.

(vii) Mr Heap, the clerk to the justices of CMC, was responsible for setting up the Court Users Group which meets quarterly. A policy was adopted of controlling access to the cells complex in order to ensure the security of personnel and to enable the courts to deal efficiently with their daily work load. The policy was: (a) if defendants are produced before 10 am, solicitors are expected to interview them before the courts commence at 10 am; (b) if solicitors wish to interview their clients after 10 am then access will be allowed if there is a valid reason for not having seen the client before 10 am; and if security permits the visit, whilst the police continue their duties as escort officers to the court. Mr Heap points out in his affidavit that—

'it is open to the justices in court to direct that solicitors have access to their clients regardless of the general policy, although the result of so doing might be that other court rooms cannot continue with their cases until the police have manned the directed interview.'

(viii) Both Mr Evans and Mr Heap assert that 'the policy' has been implemented by the police at CMC with considerable 'flexibility'. Mr Evans has said that, where prisoners arrived after 10 am, or where there was a valid change in circumstances, the supervising officer would allow a visit after 10 am if there were adequate staff. As a 'long stop' solicitors have the option to apply to the magistrates to authorise a visit. After the particular dispute in this case arose, times of arrival at the cells by solicitors have been observed. Generally speaking there is no attempt to make a visit to a client before about 9.30 am. It is an extremely rare occurrence for a solicitor to arrive before 9 am. As a result the six available interview rooms are usually full but interviews in progress at 10 am are allowed to continue until 10.15 am or later.

(ix) On 7 July 1993 (ie some seven weeks after the alleged refusal of access on 12 May) the policy as described by Mr Heap was discussed at a meeting of the Court Users Group. No solicitor attended the meeting.

(x) The policy was the result of efforts, as Mr Evans has asserted, to 'satisfy the competing demands on the time of the cell officers'. In the view of Mr Heap:

'... the policy is the result of a series of compromises in which the police and prison services have agreed to lodge prisoners as early as possible, the defence solicitors arrive at an appropriate time and the court makes special arrangements to facilitate interviews.'

He expressed the hope that solicitors, wishing to see a client after the case has concluded, will take the opportunity of a professional visit at Cardiff prison if the defendant is remanded in custody. He asserts that the policy is not applied with unreasonable rigidity and a discretion is allowed to those with the difficult job of ensuring the safety of prisoners, solicitors and professional colleagues.

The refusal of access on 12 May 1993

(i) On this day Mr Brierley saw the applicant early in the morning in the cells at CMC. He observed the notice which stated that no visits would be allowed after 10 am. The applicant's case was put back to 2.15 pm. Mr Brierley went to the cells at 1.15 pm in order to see the applicant to take instructions but was refused access by the police officer who said that he was not prepared to allow Mr Brierley to see the applicant because there were only two police officers present. Mr Brierley offered to be locked into a consultation room with the applicant or to sit in a cell with him but both suggestions were rejected. He was told that the police did not have enough manpower and that some other officers were at lunch. Mr Brierley insisted that he wished to see the applicant in the interests of justice but the officers refused to allow it.

(ii) Following the unsuccessful bail application, presumably made at 2.15 pm by Mr Brierley, it seemed necessary to Mr Brierley to see the applicant to explain the refusal of bail, to obtain instructions concerning the next steps to be taken, and to discuss the contents of papers obtained through advanced disclosure of the prosecution case. His application for access to the applicant at 3.15 pm was refused on the ground of a standing order which prohibited entry to the cells after 10 am. When Mr Brierley urged the need for immediate access, acting sergeant no 1768 was called and he repeated the refusal and, in so doing, acknowledged that there was at that time no shortage of manpower.

(iii) By letter of 13 May 1993 to the chief constable Mr Brierley reported those events. He made no complaint of the refusal at 1.15 pm—he recognised the need for breaks in a working day—but pointed out that the practice was unlike that adopted in other courts. As to the refusal at 3.15 pm, he complained that it was a result of an unreasonable restriction. He asked to be told what the precise policy was. He referred to the need to institute judicial review proceedings if the present unworkable situation could not be changed.

(iv) By letter of 19 May 1993 the chief constable expressed the view that the police were not bound in law to provide a service of gaolers at the court but the constabulary had done so for many years and endeavoured to do so in order to facilitate the smooth running of the court. The cells complex was not a police station and the provisions of the Police and Criminal Evidence Act 1984 do not apply to it. The practice of allowing legal visits after the commencement of the court day at 10 am committed a proportion of the police officers to duties other than court escort duties. The practice therefore had the potential not only to frustrate the smooth running of the court but to endanger those officers left to escort prisoners to and from the courts. Further, the policy of refusing access after 10 am although agreed by the magistrates' clerk, is not strictly practised. In fact, provided that a certain ratio of police officers to prisoners exists, legal visits are allowed outside the permitted access time. He complained that some solicitors continually flout the facility by using the permitted access time as an alternative to visiting clients at prison. His letter continued:

'There will be exceptions to the general rule and occasions when in the interests of justice, access outside the permitted time must be facilitated. In such instances, discretion and common sense must be exercised. Nevertheless, practising solicitors have an implied responsibility to exercise fairplay and professionalism when operating within a working environment when many members of the public, including court officials and police officers, could be put at serious risk if dangerous criminals are not properly secured and supervised.'

The chief constable with limited resources and the growing demands on policing in South Wales, was not in a position, nor was he prepared, to deploy extra resources to facilitate continuous visits.

(v) Mr Brierley replied by letter of 25 May 1993 in which, after contentions upon the legality of the policy, he asked to be told whether the officers had been given any guidance on the circumstances in which discretion is to exercised and what circumstances are. The chief constable's reply of 27 May 1993 was to reiterate—

'the need for co-operation by all parties and confirmed his commitment to arranging a meeting of what is in effect the Court Users Group with a view to achieving a negotiated settlement.'

(vi) By letter of 22 May 1993 Mr Brierley asked the clerk to the justices to confirm whether or not the clerk had any involvement in the policy decision, apparently taken by the police. By letter of 7 June 1993 from the deputy clerk to the justices, Mr Brierley was informed that the issue of access to the cells would be discussed at the next User Group Committee on 7 July 1993.

(vii) On the particular merits of the refusal of access on 12 May 1993 Mr Evans pointed out that, on the application to Judge Crowther on 13 May, no issue was raised by Mr Brierley that his ability to make the application had been impaired by the denial of access on the preceding day; and asserted that, upon information from officer no 1768, Mr Brierley wished to see the applicant on a civil matter. In any event, it was open to Mr Brierley to see the applicant in Cardiff prison; Mr Brierley did not apply to the magistrates for an order that he be given access to his client; and there was no evidence that the applicant had asked for access to his solicitor and was refused. At the hearing in this court it was pointed out that, on 12 May 1993 when the applicant was brought to court at 2.15 pm, Mr Brierley had the opportunity of speaking to his client in court and, as we were told, he had done so.

The evidence of the solicitors

The direction of the judge was that the applicant should file any affidavits in reply 14 days after the filing of the respondents' evidence. The first affidavit of Mr Evans was served on 23 August 1993 but the further affidavits filed on behalf of the applicant by Mr Brierley were not received by the respondents until 7 January 1994. The second affidavit of Mr Evans was filed on 13 January 1994. The delay on the part of Mr Brierley is to be regretted. The substance of the further evidence of the solicitors in Cardiff was as follows.

(i) Mr Davies practises, mainly in criminal work, in Cardiff. His affidavit of 4 January 1994, after reference to the various circumstances in which persons may be detained at CMC, and the reasons why such persons require access to legal advice, states that it is unrealistic to suggest that their requirements can be met by the making of an appointment for a meeting at the prison. It is virtually impossible to gain access to an accused person on remand in prison without giving 72 hours' notice. The immediate need for access at CMC arises, for example, to discuss new developments, such as information disclosed by the CPS and, when a person is first ordered into custody, and to discuss advice on appeal and information to be given to the prisoner's family. The experience of Mr Davies had been that a rigid policy was in force of refusing contact after 10 am, save in cases where the person in custody did not arrive at court until after 10 am. He questioned any contention that access for solicitors must be restricted in the interests of safety and security. In his view, the physical facilities are adequate for safety. As to the reference to resources, Mr Davies contends that if the police assume the responsibility for those in custody at CMC, they must arrange matters so as to ensure that the legal rights of persons in custody are protected.

(ii) By an affidavit of 6 January 1994 Mr Simon D Joseph, who practises in Cardiff, in substance supports from his own experience the evidence of Mr Davies. He acknowledged that the police have shown 'flexibility' in respect of persons who arrive late at court but he has experienced real difficulty in getting access to clients, in particular when he had more than one case at the court. He asserts that it is wrong in principle for police constables to be in the position of deciding which persons in custody are entitled to see solicitors after 10 am. As to the power of the magistrates to direct that access be allowed, he has never seen magistrates make such an order. The escort officer is usually asked what can be done, and the court is told that there are insufficient police officers available; and the case is then put back and regret is expressed. He doubts whether the magistrates appreciate that they have the power to make such an order.

(iii) Mr Brierley's further affidavit was substantially to the same effect. In addition, he said that the denial of access on 12 May was not mentioned to Judge Crowther on 13 May because it was not relevant. He had not sought to see the applicant about a civil matter, as had been suggested. Further he did not know how the police officer had come to assert anything about the subject upon which discussion with the applicant was required; he objected to the process by which Mr Evans made conjectures as to the degree of urgency in the applicant's need for legal advice; and referred to the difficulties, from his obligations of professional confidence to his client, in responding to the speculations of Mr Evans. Such difficulties arose from the nature of the policy itself

(iv) By affidavit of 10 January 1994 Mr Gwyn Jones of the firm Messrs Leo Abse & Cohen, described his experiences in seeking access to clients in the cells of CMC and asserted that, as it appeared to him, the court was operating an inflexible policy of denying access to those in custody by solicitors after 10 am.

Further evidence

The applicant also provided a further affidavit in January 1994 in which he said that he was not told that Mr Brierley had tried to see him at 1.15 pm on 12 May; and that, after he was refused bail at 2.15 pm, he had asked the police officers if he could see Mr Brierley. He was told that Mr Brierley had gone. He had not been told of Mr Brierley's second attempt to see him.

In the further evidence of Mr Evans, he described limited inquiries made by him of colleagues in other forces and asserts that Cardiff is not alone in imposing restrictions. In support of his evidence that the policy is applied flexibly, he produced a record kept by Sgt Burley, who had been in charge of the cells at CMC, in which were recorded examples of occasions in June, July and August 1993 when late visits were allowed for good reason. He also produced a list of 'incidents of disorder', which described the difficulties faced by the police in maintaining order in the cell complex. He made reference to *R v Cambridge Justices, ex p Peacock* [1993] Crim LR 219, which dealt with the handcuffing of accused persons.

The submissions for the applicant

Mr Clayton, in summary, contended that the policy implemented by the respondents and their actions in pursuance of it were unlawful because: (i) the policy was based upon a misunderstanding of s 58 of the Police and Criminal Evidence Act 1984; (ii) they acted unlawfully by interfering with the applicant's fundamental right of access to legal advice; (iii) they failed to take account of relevant considerations by ignoring, inter alia, the fact that for prisoners in police custody the right of access to solicitors is no less than that of suspects on arrest under s 58 and of prisoners in prison; (iv) they took into account an irrelevant consideration by having regard to 'limited resources'; (v) the policy is so contrary to the interests of those in police custody that it is wholly irrational; and (vi) they failed to apply their discretion by considering whether the applicant should be granted access to his solicitor when request was made.

The basis of these submissions was that s 58(1) of the 1984 Act secured to the applicant the right to 'consult a solicitor privately at any time' because, in the cells at CMC, the applicant was 'a person arrested and held in custody in a police station or other premises'; and that that right was subject only to sub-s (4), which provides that 'if a person makes such a request he must be permitted to consult a solicitor as soon as is practicable except to the extent that delay is permitted by this section'. (That exception, which is described in sub-s (6) is, as is common ground, of no relevance to this case.)

The applicability of this provision to a person in custody in CMC is, it was said, made clear by sub-ss (2) and (3); since it would not be necessary to make the provision in sub-s (3) unless the section as a whole applied to a person in custody at a court. Next, s 58 distinguishes between a person being in 'police custody', which entitles him to access to legal advice under s 58(1), and in 'police detention', which permits a limited class of detainees to be denied access to legal advice under s 58(6).

If there is any doubt as to the meaning of s 58, the court should presume that Parliament intended to legislate in conformity with the European Convention on Human Rights (Convention for the Protection of Human Rights and Fundamental Freedoms (Rome, 4 November 1950; TS 71 (1953); Cmd 8969)). Reference was made to *Brind v Secretary of State for the Home Dept* [1991] 1 All ER 720, [1991] 1 AC 696. The refusal to permit to the applicant access to legal advice was contrary to art 6 of the convention. The request for access to the applicant made by Mr Brierley should be treated as made on the applicant's behalf and therefore as his request: reference was made to *R v Jones* [1984] Crim LR 357.

For the proposition that refusal of access to a solicitor constitutes breach of art 6(1) of the convention, reference was made to *Golder v UK* (1975) 1 EHRR 524.

In support of the proposition that the respondents acted ultra vires in refusing to permit the applicant to have access to his solicitor, Mr Clayton relied upon *R v Secretary of State for the Home Dept, ex p Anderson* [1984] 1 All ER 920, [1984] QB 778 in which the Divisional Court (Robert Goff LJ and Mann J) held with reference to a prisoner serving a sentence of imprisonment that—

'although it was proper to regulate the circumstances in which prisoners could have access to legal advisers, a prisoner had a right to unimpeded access to the courts and access to a legal adviser to receive advice and guidance in connection with possible future civil proceedings in the courts was an inseparable part of that right; that the simultaneous ventilation rule was an impediment to a prisoner's right of access to a legal adviser and accordingly, the standing orders, by prohibiting the visit of a legal adviser to advise on prisoners' complaints about prison treatment and restricting prisoners' correspondence with their legal advisers on such matters unless a complaint had been lodged with the prison authorities first, were ultra vires ...' (See [1984] QB 778 at 778–779.)

If the basis of the applicant's right to legal advice was not at the material time derived from s 58 of the 1984 Act, it was secured to him by the common law which, it was submitted, could be seen as declared in s 82 of the Criminal Justice Act 1991. That provision did not apply to the police officers at CMC. It imposed upon a prisoner custody officer duties which include the duty to attend to the well being of prisoners and to give effect to any directions as to their treatment which are given by a court.

Prison custody officers could not, it was submitted, lawfully deny to a person in custody at a court the right of access to legal advice because the statute confers upon them no power so to do.

The submissions for the respondents

Mr Heap, the clerk to the magistrates' court, was present in court, having provided his affidavit for the assistance of the court. The submissions for the respondents were advanced by Mr Masterman who was instructed on behalf of the chief constable. In summary his submissions were as follows.

(i) The declarations sought should be refused because the applicant had not made, on the evidence, any request which had been refused. The applicant when he asked, was told that Mr Brierley had gone. Mr Brierley could have applied to the magistrates for an order for access.

(ii) The chief constable's policy did not prevent access to legal advice: it did no more than to regulate such access. Such restriction as there was resulted from the necessary balancing of competing interests and such inconvenience as had been caused was justified in the circumstances. There was no denial of any right of access to legal advisers which was secured to the applicant at police stations under the 1984 Act, at prison under the prison rules, and at CMC under the policy stated. Reference was made to *R v Secretary of State for the Home Dept, ex p McAvoy* [1984] 3 All ER 417 at 424, [1984] 1 WLR 1408 at 1417, for support for the proposition that the court will not intervene merely because access to legal advisers is affected by the exercise of discretionary powers, properly exercised for another purpose (namely transfer of a prisoner from one prison to another) which has the effect of impeding such access.

(iii) As to the legality of the policy, it was submitted that persons on remand at CMC are in the custody of the court. Part IV of the Police and Criminal Evidence Act 1984, 'Detention—conditions and duration', ss 34 to 45, provides a code for police detention following arrest. Part V, 'Questioning and treatment of persons by police', ss 53 to 65, provides a code for the questioning and treatment of persons by the police which governs the police investigative process and initial detention including access to legal advice, before the prisoner is brought into the custody of the court. Thus, s 118(2) provides:

'A person is in police detention for the purposes of this Act if—(a) he has been taken to a police station after being arrested for an offence ... or (b) he is arrested at a police station after attending voluntarily at the station ... and is detained there or is detained elsewhere in the charge of a constable, except that a person who is at a court after being charged is not in police detention for those purposes.'

Further s 34 indicates the absence of any clear or consistent distinction in the use of the words 'detention' and 'custody':

'(1) A person arrested for an offence shall not be kept in police detention except in accordance with the provisions of this part of this Act.
(2) Subject to subsection (3) below, if at any time a custody officer—(a) becomes aware, in relation to any person in police detention, that the grounds for the detention of that person have ceased to apply ... it shall be the duty of the custody officer, subject to subsection (4) below, to order his immediate release from custody.'

It was submitted that s 58 is only intelligible upon the basis that the 1984 Act is concerned with the investigative process and not the judicial process. The phrase 'other premises', as defined by s 118 and s 23, is consistent with the limitation of s 58(1) to situations prior to the charging of an accused person. Further assistance is to be derived from s 128(7) and (8) of the Magistrates' Courts Act 1980, as added to that Act by the Police and Criminal Evidence Act 1984, in that the distinction is there emphasised between detention at a police station, where the 1984 Act applies, and detention at court or in prison where, it is submitted, it does not.
(iv) The decision not to admit Mr Brierley on 12 May 1993 to the cells in CMC did not deny to the applicant access to the courts on the principles stated in *Golder's* case, or access to legal advice. The decision was made in the course of the lawful regulation of access to legal advice, as contrasted with denial of access to the court as in *Raymond v Honey* [1982] 1 All ER 756, [1983] 1 AC 1. Further, *R v Secretary of State for the Home Dept, ex p Anderson* [1984] 1 All ER 920, [1984] QB 778 was concerned with the legality of prison rules which impeded, in the sense of prevented, access of prisoners to legal advice in connection with the possible institution of proceedings and not with administrative restrictions upon the hours of access.
(v) The policy acknowledged, it was submitted, and did not deny, the right of access to legal advice in regulating the times at which such access might be arranged. The chief constable was entitled to have regard to the other obligations of the police as gaolers at CMC, including the maintenance of order, and a proper balance was required to be struck having regard to available manpower. In striking that balance the chief constable—as the head of a constabulary providing an unpaid service to the court—was entitled to have regard to the deployment of his available resources in his area as a whole. Reference was made to *R v Metropolitan Police Comr, ex p Blackburn* [1968] 1 All ER 763 at 769, [1968] 2 QB 118 at 136.
(vi) The policy had a built in 'discretion' which was exercised in individual cases. A forum of discussion was offered at the Court Users' Group which enabled the policy to be amended in the light of representations made. The chief constable had not 'fettered his discretion'.

The court also heard submissions from Mr Hilliard as amicus instructed by the Attorney General. We are grateful for the assistance which we received. His submissions were as follows.

(a) The provisions of s 58 of the 1984 Act did not apply to the police officers at the cells in CMC with reference to the applicant on 12 May 1993. The purpose of s 58 and of the Codes of Practice issued under s 66 of the 1984 Act is to achieve fairness by preserving the legal rights of the accused and by reducing unfounded allegations against police officers. The provisions of s 58 ceased to apply with reference to the applicant on 20 April 1993, ie on his first appearance at court after charge: see s 46. Reference was also made to *R v Kerawalla* [1991] Crim LR 451.

(b) Nevertheless, the law requires that there be afforded to a person in custody at a court access to legal advice which is reasonable in order for advice to be given and for his case to be effectively presented. The arrangements for access at CMC were not unreasonable. Such access is required for a prisoner's 'wellbeing' (see s 82 of the Criminal Justice Act 1991).

(c) The policy as adopted by the chief constable at the material time did provide for reasonable access. The police would abide by any order of the court but applications were not being made. The circumstances in which the court should direct that access be allowed were, for example, following the imposition of an immediate custodial sentence and following service of documents by the prosecution after 10 am. It was not appropriate to grant relief on the facts before the court.

Conclusion

(i) The extent of the applicability of s 58(1) is, in my judgment, not easy to decide. It appears to me to be unlikely, from the words used in s 58, that Parliament intended the provisions of s 58 to apply to a person who is in custody after being remanded in custody by a magistrates' court. The section appears in Pt V of the 1984 Act, which deals with questioning and treatment of persons by the police. The wording of s 58(1) refers to a person 'arrested and held in custody in a police station or other premises' thus indicating that the circumstances contemplated are those following arrest and before remand by the court. The definition of 'premises' in s 23 as including 'any place and, in particular ... any vehicle, vessel, aircraft or hovercraft, any offshore installation, and any tent or moveable structure ...' suggests that Parliament was concerned to ensure that persons arrested and held in custody in, for example, a police car, should in the process of questioning be protected as effectively as they would be in a police station.

(ii) The only permitted ground for delay is that stated in sub-s (6), which is clearly appropriate only to the stage of investigation before charge.

(iii) Nevertheless, it is not possible to accept, I think, the submission that the provisions of s 58 always cease to apply with reference to a person in custody on his first appearance at court after charge: such an appearance may occur under s 46 and he may be committed to detention at a police station under s 128(7) of the Magistrates' Courts Act 1980 (as added by the 1984 Act), normally, as I understand it, for the purpose of allowing questioning about other offences (see: Zander *Police & Criminal Evidence Act 1984* (2nd edn, 1990)). In such circumstances, the investigative process would, of course, be continuing and, while in custody at the police station under such a commitment, the provisions of s 58(1) would clearly apply to such a person.

(iv) It is said that persons on remand at CMC are in the custody of the court. If it be the case that a person on remand in the cells at CMC is in the custody of the court, that fact alone, on the wording of s 58(1) does not preclude application of the subsection: the words refer to 'a person held in custody'. Further, while I accept that when a person on bail surrenders at the court, he surrenders to the

custody of the court (see s 7 of the Bail Act 1976) and remains in the custody of the
court until either released, or sentenced, or remanded in custody; I do not think
that this concept provides any answer to the questions raised in this case.

When a person, in custody before a court, is remanded in custody, or sentenced
to imprisonment, he is, as I understand it, committed by the court into the
custody of others. Immediately at the court, he is committed to the custody of the
dock officers or gaolers to be removed to the cells. Under a warrant of
commitment the police constable and 'authorised persons for the area' are
required to convey the accused to the prison and there to deliver him to the
governor where the governor is required to receive the accused into his custody
and (subject to bail) to keep the accused until such time as he receives another
warrant of commitment from the court. The accused, when before the court, is
in the custody of the court in the sense that the court alone is able to decide
whether he remains in custody or is released. When the accused is in the cells,
having been produced at the court from prison by the governor under a warrant
of commitment, and before appearing in court, the accused is in the custody of the
court in the sense stated above but he is also, in my judgment, in the custody of
the police officers at all times after leaving the prison on his way to court and
before appearing in court. Rule 38(2) of the Prison Rules 1964, SI 1964/388,
provides:

> 'A prisoner required to be taken in custody anywhere outside a prison shall
> be kept in the custody of an officer appointed under section 3 of the Prison
> Act 1952 or a police officer.'

The word 'prisoner' in that rule includes an unconvicted prisoner. Further,
having been remanded in custody by the court and returned to the cells in the
court in order to be conveyed to the prison under the warrant, the accused person
is in the custody of the officers who are in charge of him.

The question is raised whether, when an accused person is in custody at the
court, the court gives a direction that the accused is to be allowed access to legal
advice before the hearing of the case, or of any ancillary proceedings such as an
application for bail, or whether the court does no more than to indicate its
opinion. I do not propose to express any decision on this point because it is not
necessary to do so for the proper decision of the questions in this case. Further,
since the police officers assigned to duty at the CMC are so assigned to provide the
necessary services to the court, there is, I think, little, if any, distinction between
a direction and a request: in either case the officers are under a duty to comply,
and will comply, as soon as is reasonably practicable and could do no more.

(v) It was not necessary, in my judgment, for Parliament to apply s 58(1) to a
person on remand and held in custody in the cells of a court in order to secure to
that person the right to consult a solicitor. At common law a man in custody is
entitled to consult a solicitor at an early stage of the investigation. The only
qualification was that he could not delay the investigation by asking to see a
solicitor if the effect would be to cause 'unreasonable delay or hindrance ... to the
process of investigation or the administration of justice' (see *R v Lemsatef* [1977] 2
All ER 835, [1977] 1 WLR 812 where the decision was based upon principle (c) of
the Judges' Rules). The right of a person in custody at a court to consult a solicitor
can, in my judgment, be no less than that of a person in detention in the course of
investigation of a suspected offence under the rules of common law which
preceded the 1984 Act and which were not abrogated by that Act. That right in
my judgment is on request to be permitted to consult a solicitor as soon as is

reasonably practicable. It follows that if s 58(1) applies to a person in custody in the cells at CMC his right, when he asks, is to be permitted to see a solicitor as soon as is practicable; and, if s 58(1) does not apply, his right when he asks is to be permitted to see a solicitor as soon as is reasonably practicable. There may be cases in which such a difference would be decisive. This, for reasons which will appear, was not such a case.

(vi) The right to consult a solicitor is not, so far as concerns a person in custody, a free standing right of uniform extent irrespective of the circumstances. So far as concerns questioning of a person by the police and treatment of him after arrest, and while he is in custody before charge, the primary purpose is to ensure that the questioning is fair and that his legal rights may be preserved and protected, in particular that he should understand and, if he wishes, have resort to his right to be silent (see *R v Walsh* (1989) 91 Cr App R 161 at 163). To that end, it is necessary that the right should be secured to such a person at that stage to consult a solicitor privately at any time while the enquiry proceeds and 'as soon as is practicable'; and, subject to the exceptions listed in para 6.6 of the *Code of Practice for the Detention, Treatment and Questioning of Persons by Police Officers* (Code C) a person who wants legal advice may not be interviewed or continue to be interviewed until he has received it. After a person has been charged, and is in custody at a court on remand, the primary purpose of the right to consult a solicitor is to ensure that the trial, and all ancillary proceedings, such as applications for bail, are conducted fairly and effectively. To that end, it is necessary that the right should be secured to such a person at such time or times as will enable the proceedings to be fairly and effectively conducted by him or on his behalf. A significant difference between a person in detention or custody but before charge, whose conduct is under investigation by the police, on the one hand, and a person in custody after charge on remand in the cells of a magistrates' court, on the other hand, is that the court stands between the person in custody and the prosecutor, and the court, provided that complaint is made by or on behalf of the accused, is well able to ensure that any preceding failure to provide sufficient access for an accused to a solicitor is not permitted to prejudice the conduct of the proceedings on the behalf of the accused. The court can direct, or indicate its opinion—I have discussed the distinction above— that the accused is to be allowed sufficient access to his legal advisers before the hearing of the case, or of any ancillary proceeding, will proceed.

(vii) The right under s 58 (1) is not absolute in the sense that there is a breach of duty by any person to which s 58 applies if the requirement by a person in custody is not at once met by being enabled to consult a solicitor: the request must be met 'as soon as is practicable' apart from the permitted exception which is not here relevant. 'Practicable' in its dictionary meaning is defined as 'capable of being carried out—feasible' (*Shorter Oxford Dictionary*); or 'possible to be accomplished with known means or known resources' (*Webster*). In *Dedman v British Building and Engineering Appliances Ltd* [1974] 1 All ER 520, [1974] 1 WLR 171 the Court of Appeal considered the meaning of the word as used in the Industrial Tribunal (Industrial Relations, etc) Regulations 1972, SI 1972/38, with reference to the time for presenting a complaint. Scarman LJ said ([1974] 1 All ER 520 at 528, [1974] 1 WLR 171 at 179):

'On the point of construction of "the escape clause" I agree with Lord Denning MR. The word "practicable" is an ordinary English word of great flexibility: it takes its meaning from its context. But, whenever used, it is a call for the exercise of common sense, a warning that sound judgment will be impossible without compromise. Sometimes the context contemplates a situation rarely to be achieved, though much to be desired: the word then indicates one must be satisfied with less than perfection: see, for example, its use in s 5 of the Matrimonial Proceedings and Property Act 1970. Sometimes, as is submitted in the present case, what the context requires may have been possible, but may not for some reason have been "practicable". Whatever its context, the quality of the word is that there are circumstances in which we must be content with less than 100 per cent: and it calls for judgment to determine how much less.'

(viii) It follows, in my judgment, whether s 58(1) applies or not, that which is to be regarded as complying with the duty to permit consultation with a solicitor 'as soon as practicable' or, if s 58(1) does not apply, 'as soon as is reasonably practicable', requires consideration of the circumstances of the accused, and of the police in charge of the cells. Those circumstances include the other duties of the police and the immediate demands upon them when the request is made. It is to be noted that the word 'practicable' is not in s 58 qualified by the word 'reasonably' as it was, for example, in s 68(2) of the 1984 Act as first enacted. If the police undertake the task of controlling persons in custody at a court, it is, in my judgment, their duty to comply fully with the obligations imposed by the law upon any person performing such a task and it is irrelevant that the officers of the particular constabulary are assigned to the task 'voluntarily' and without—if it be the case—any legal duty previously imposed upon the constabulary. The law does not, however, impose a duty upon the constabulary, or upon particular officers within it, to meet a request for access to a solicitor made by a person in custody at a court forthwith or at a time when it is not 'practicable' having regard to the other immediate duties of the officers and the number of them available, provided that the resources made available are reasonably sufficient to ensure that such a request is, so far as is reasonably foreseeable, capable of being met so as to satisfy the primary purposes for which such access is required.

(ix) Accordingly, in my judgment, there is in cases such as this no significant difference, so far as concerns securing to persons in custody the substantial benefits of the right to consult a solicitor, between that specifically enacted by s 58(1) and that secured to such a person by the common law. I conclude that, upon the construction of the provisions of s 58, in its statutory context, and having regard to the substance and effect of the common law of which Parliament was aware, s 58 did not apply to the applicant in the circumstances in which he was on 12 May 1993.

(x) So far as concerns the applicant on 12 May 1993, it is shown, in my judgment, that he did make a request to consult a solicitor privately. The contention for the chief constable that there was no request by the applicant, but only by Mr Brierley, is, in my judgment, misconceived. The applicant had instructed Mr Brierley. When Mr Brierley requested access to see the applicant, that request was, as it seems to me, made by Mr Brierley on behalf of the applicant.

(xi) There was no significantly adverse consequence to the applicant as a result of failure to comply with either of his requests on 12 May so far as concerns the primary purpose of such consultation. Mr Brierley saw him in court before the hearing at 2.15 pm and did not ask for further time. The making of the application on 13 May was not adversely affected. The applicant was, however, denied the opportunity to consult with his solicitor immediately after the dismissal of his bail application. The opportunity to consult was required not only for consideration of any further step open to the applicant, such as a renewed application to the judge in chambers, but also for what in argument were called 'humanitarian purposes' of explanation, comfort and the conveying of instructions or requests to family or friends. Such denial of the opportunity may, in some circumstances, be unavoidable, and therefore justifiable, if it is not practicable, or reasonably practicable, for the police to arrange for access, but, if in the circumstances it was practicable, or reasonably practicable then, in my judgment, there was no justification for refusing it.

(xii) This brings me to the policy. It is clear that both the chief constable and the chief clerk intended to devise rules for handling access to persons in custody at CMC which gave full effect to the rights of those in custody with, so far as was practicable, due regard to the convenience of solicitors, and which did not impair the ability of the police to provide to the court the essential service of guarding and of producing persons in custody to the court and of protection and security of the court and the public. Save in one particular, the policy was, in my judgment, lawful.

There is no material upon which it could be concluded that there was any failure to assign sufficient manpower to the task so as to render it not reasonably possible to secure to those in custody effective implementation of their rights. It was both right and necessary for the chief constable to devise workable rules for regulation of the right of access of persons in custody to solicitors although, in devising such rules, it was necessary, in my view, for the chief constable to have in mind that he was not providing rules for balancing the competing interests of persons in custody, who wish to consult solicitors, on the one hand, and of the police, who have other duties to perform, on the other; but he was providing rules for the regulation of the exercise by persons in custody of the right to consult a solicitor and the duty of the police having custody of them to secure the orderly provision of facilities for the exercise of that right, subject only to the due performance of other duties imposed upon the police. The one particular defect in the policy which, in my judgment, was unlawful was that it authorised or permitted the gaolers to refuse access to a solicitor on the sole ground that the request was made after 10 am without reference to the question whether it was reasonably practicable to allow access at once or within a period of time.

(xiii) The arranging and announcing that facilities would be provided between 8.30 am and 10 am was clearly both reasonable and useful. If the policy had been that, after 10 am, access would be arranged as soon as was reasonably practicable, having regard to the demands upon the police at any time, there would, in the absence of other circumstances not raised in this case, be no objection to the policy as such because it would not necessarily give rise to the likelihood of the denial of the right of a person in custody to access to legal advice. It is to be emphasised that the primary consideration is the right of the person in custody and the duty to give effect to it. The fact that the policy is not shown to have been erroneous when announced will not necessarily justify every decision made under it.

(xiv) To return to the events of 12 May, the evidence shows that there was available at 3.15 pm a sufficient number of officers to have enabled them to allow access by Mr Brierley to the applicant, and it seems clear to me that access was refused because the officer understood that he was, by the policy, required or entitled to refuse. The consequences of the refusal were, as I have said, of no great substance but not such as to be dismissed as of no significance at all.

(xv) I do not accept that, as submitted by the chief constable, any decisive effect can be given to the terms of the warrant, in common form as I understand it, by which the police are 'required to convey the accused to Cardiff Prison and there deliver the accused to the governor thereof together with this warrant'. It was contended that the warrant required, or authorised, the police to remove the accused forthwith from the court to prison and that, therefore, a request for access to a solicitor after a hearing and a remand in custody could not give rise to an obligation on the police at once to arrange it. If, after a hearing, the arrangements for transport reasonably required that an accused leave with others in a vehicle for the prison at once, or before access could be arranged, the police would not, in ordinary circumstances, be in breach of duty if they removed him, leaving the accused and his solicitor to arrange for access at the prison or on a later occasion at the court. If, however, after a hearing, it is reasonably practicable for access to be arranged when requested the police are, in the absence of some other explanation, in breach of duty if they do not permit it.

(xvi) As to the flexibility of the policy in practice, to which much effort and evidence were directed, for my part I found the evidence of no decisive effect upon the particular complaint of the applicant. The evidence, of course, did prove, as has been common ground throughout, not only that both the respondents and the junior officers have at all times wished and intended to respect and protect the rights of persons in custody and to meet the reasonable requirements of the solicitors, but also that they have, moreover, acted on all occasions with both care and courtesy. The flexibility in application of the policy was effective to ensure that the policy only caused denial or impairment of the right of a person in custody to consult a solicitor on few occasions, if more than the one considered in this case. That, in my judgment, is no answer to a complaint when the policy does cause denial of the right by failure to accede to a request when it is reasonably practicable to do so.

(xvii) The operation of such a 'flexible' policy, moreover, seems to me to give rise to difficulty in so far as it expects a solicitor to advance 'good reason' for seeking access to his client after 10 am. It is not generally the concern of police to assess the validity of the reasons for a request for permission to consult a solicitor, or for a solicitor's failure to attend at an earlier time; and it is objectionable, in my view, to base a policy for regulation of access to legal advisers on such a provision. No doubt, if the police cannot at once comply with a request for access, because of other unavoidable demands upon the police at the courts, a solicitor will assert the reason why high priority should be given to the request, and there can be no objection to the police trying to satisfy the special urgency of a particular request. Such matters must be left to the goodwill and good sense of those concerned.

In the result, I would make no order save to declare that the failure by the officers in charge of the cells at CMC at 3.15 pm on 12 May 1993 to permit the applicant to consult his solicitor constituted a breach of the right of the applicant when in custody to obtain legal advice as soon as it was reasonably practicable for access for that purpose to be permitted.

SMITH J. I agree.

Appeal allowed. Declaration accordingly.

Dilys Tausz   Barrister.

Deposit Protection Board v Dalia and another

HOUSE OF LORDS

LORD KEITH OF KINKEL, LORD GOFF OF CHIEVELEY, LORD BROWNE-WILKINSON, LORD MUSTILL AND LORD LLOYD OF BERWICK

8, 9 DECEMBER 1993, 19 MAY 1994

Bank – Deposit protection scheme – Deposit protection fund – Insolvent bank – Assignment of part of deposit after petition presented to wind up insolvent bank but before winding-up order made – Whether assignee of part of deposit entitled to compensation from deposit protection fund – Banking Act 1987, ss 5, 58, 59(1), 60, 61.

On 5 July 1991 the Bank of England presented a petition for a winding-up order against BCCI, an authorised institution under the Banking Act 1987, on the ground that it was insolvent. Under s 59(1)(a)[a] of the 1987 Act a body corporate wound up by the court became insolvent on the making of a winding-up order. Before the petition was heard on 30 July, certain depositors took steps to maximise the amount of payment they would be able to claim from the Deposit Protection Board under the compensation scheme contained in ss 58[b] and 60[c] of the 1987 Act. The board was required by ss 58 and 60 to pay out of the deposit protection fund to each depositor who had a protected deposit with a recognised bank or licensed institution which became insolvent an amount equal to three-quarters of his protected deposit, limited to a maximum deposit of £20,000. The depositors with BCCI accordingly assigned sums of £20,000 from their deposits to family members or close friends with the intent that they would each make a claim on the fund for payment of £15,000 in respect of the £20,000 share of the deposit assigned to them. BCCI was wound up on 14 January 1992. The question arose whether the assignees of deposits were entitled to payment out of the deposit protection fund pursuant to s 58(1) of the 1987 Act. Under s 5(1)[d] a 'deposit' was defined as a sum of money paid to an institution 'on terms [that] it will be repaid ... either on demand or at a time or in circumstances agreed by or on behalf of the person making the payment and the person receiving it'. The judge held that it was inconsistent with the purpose of s 58 to confine 'depositor' to the person who had made the original deposit and that an assignee under an assignment was to be treated as having made a deposit of an amount equal to that part. A bank which contributed to the scheme, supported by the board, appealed. The Court of Appeal dismissed the appeal, holding that entitlement to compensation out of the deposit protection fund was not restricted to original deposit makers and that legal and equitable assignees of original deposit makers were entitled to claim from the fund provided, in the case of equitable assignees, the assignment was unimpeachable and had taken place before the winding-up order was made against the bank. The appellant bank appealed to the House of Lords.

---

a   Section 59(1), so far as material, provides: 'For the purposes of this part of this Act a body corporate ... becomes insolvent—(a) on the making of a winding-up order against it ...'
b   Section 58, so far as material, is set out at p 582 b to d, post
c   Section 60, so far as material, is set out at p 582 e to p 583 c, post
d   Section 5, so far as material, is set out at p 581 f to j, post

Held – For the purposes of s 58(1) of the 1987 Act a 'depositor' who was entitled to compensation from the deposit protection fund meant a person who originally made the deposit to the insolvent institution since, having regard to the definition of 'deposit' in s 5(1) and the exclusion of sums paid by persons having certain characteristics from that definition, a 'depositor' prima facie meant a person whose characteristics at the time he paid the sum to the institution determined that the sum so paid was a 'deposit' within the meaning of the Act. An assignee of part of a deposit was not a 'depositor' since he lacked the necessary characteristics to show that the sum claimed was a 'deposit' under s 5 and unless the sum claimed was a 'deposit' he was not a depositor. There was nothing in the Act to displace the prima facie meaning, since although s 61[e] conferred a right to compensation on beneficiaries under bare trusts that did not indicate that an assignee was a depositor since a beneficiary's right was not automatic but depended on him being able to show that the sum claimed was a 'deposit' under s 5, and the fact that specific provision was made in s 60 for assignments of deposits evidenced by transferable certificates of deposit or other transferable instruments indicated that assignments of other deposits were not eligible for compensation from the fund. Accordingly, the appeal would be allowed and a declaration made that a person entitled to a debt by reason of the assignment of part of a deposit was not a depositor holding a protected deposit entitled to compensation pursuant to s 58(1) of the Act (see p 579 d e, p 583 j to p 584 c, p 585 d to j, p 586 b to e, p 587 a b d and p 588 b to d, post).

Decision of the Court of Appeal [1994] 1 All ER 539 reversed.

Notes

For compensation payments to depositors, see 3(1) *Halsbury's Laws* (4th edn reissue) paras 115–117.

For the Banking Act 1987, ss 5, 58, 59, 60, 61, see 4 *Halsbury's Statutes* (4th edn) (1987 reissue) 535, 589, 591, 592, 594.

Case referred to in opinions

Hanlon v Law Society [1980] 2 All ER 199, [1981] AC 124, [1980] 2 WLR 756, HL.

Appeal

The second defendant, Barclays Bank plc (Barclays), appealed from the decision of the Court of Appeal (Russell LJ and Sir Michael Fox; Simon Brown LJ dissenting in part) ([1994] 1 All ER 539) delivered on 6 May 1993 dismissing Barclays' appeal from the decision of Sir Donald Nicholls V-C ([1993] 1 All ER 599, [1993] Ch 243) on the application made by the plaintiff, the Deposit Protection Board (a body corporate established pursuant to the Banking Acts 1979 and 1987), by originating summons dated 15 April 1992 seeking the court's determination on the question whether a person entitled by reason of assignment of part of a deposit as defined by s 5(1) of the 1987 Act was a depositor holding a protected deposit entitled to a compensation payment from the board pursuant to s 58(1) of the 1987 Act. Sir Donald Nicholls V-C declared that for the purposes of Pt II of the 1987 Act an assignee of part of a deposit as defined in s 5 was to be treated as entitled to the assigned part of the deposit and as having made a deposit of an amount equal to that part so as to

---

[e] Section 61, so far as material, is set out at p 583 *e* to *j*, post

be a depositor in respect of that part. The first defendant, Varsha Dalia, was an assignee of part of a depositor's deposit and was joined in the proceedings to represent all such assignees. The facts are set out in the opinion of Lord Browne-Wilkinson.

Michael Brindle QC and *Bankim Thanki* (instructed by *Lovell White Durrant*) for Barclays.

Patrick Elias QC and *Philip Sales* (instructed by *Ashurst Morris Crisp*) for the claimant.

John Jarvis QC and *Jonathan Nash* (instructed by *Clifford Chance*) for the board.

Their Lordships took time for consideration.

19 May 1994. The following opinions were delivered.

LORD KEITH OF KINKEL. My Lords, for the reasons set out in the speech to be delivered by my noble and learned friend Lord Browne-Wilkinson, which I have read in draft and with which I agree, I would allow this appeal and make the declaration which he proposes.

LORD GOFF OF CHIEVELEY. My Lords, I have had the advantage of reading in draft the speech prepared by my noble and learned friend Lord Browne-Wilkinson. For the reasons he gives I, too, would allow the appeal.

LORD BROWNE-WILKINSON. My Lords, the Deposit Protection Fund, established under Pt II of the Banking Act 1987, is designed to provide compensation to depositors on the insolvency of an institution authorised to accept deposits under that Act. On the insolvency of the institution, a depositor is entitled to be paid three-quarters of the amount of his deposit, but limited to a maximum deposit of £20,000. Thus a depositor owed £20,000 can obtain compensation of £15,000. A depositor owed £100,000 is also entitled to compensation, but his claim, too, is limited to the same maximum of £15,000.

The facts

On 5 July 1991 the Bank of England presented a petition for the winding up of the Bank of Credit and Commerce International SA (BCCI). Provisional liquidators were appointed and depositors ceased to be able to withdraw their money. It was therefore clear that there was a substantial risk that depositors with BCCI would not recover the amount of their deposits and would have to look to the Deposit Protection Fund. A firm of accountants devised a scheme whereby a depositor would assign a part of his deposit to 'family members or close friends who can be trusted'. For example, in the case of a deposit of £100,000 the depositor would assign £20,000 out of it to each of four friends. In consequence, if the scheme is effective, instead of the compensation payable in respect of the deposit of £100,000 being limited to £15,000, the original depositor and each of the four assignees could claim compensation of £15,000 in respect of the £20,000 part of the deposit which belonged or had been assigned to him. In consequence, instead of £15,000 being the maximum compensation payable in respect of the original deposit of £100,000, the compensation payable would be increased to £75,000.

The accountants wrote to depositors in BCCI suggesting this scheme. A substantial number of depositors adopted the scheme. Before 30 July 1991 each depositor executed a deed of assignment which was in the standard form prepared by, or for, the accountants. It described the original depositor as 'the vendor' and the assignee as 'the purchaser'. After reciting the vendor's deposit with BCCI (which was identified by its number) the deed provided:

'... in consideration of the sum of £1 ... the vendor by this deed sells, assigns and transfers the sum of £ ... of the deposit to the purchaser.'

At the same time, the original depositor gave notice of the assignment to BCCI and instructed BCCI—

'that the above-mentioned sum is now held by the purchaser and that the purchaser should now be identified by you as a depositor. If, for administrative reasons, you are unable to arrange for the completion of formalities to designate a separate deposit account in the name of the purchaser, I/we confirm that I/we hold the above-mentioned sum on trust for the purchaser.'

It is common ground that such assignments were not statutory assignments of the debts owed by BCCI to the original depositors within the meaning of s 136 of the Law of Property Act 1925, since only part of the debt was assigned. However it is also agreed that they took effect as equitable assignments under which in equity, but not at law, BCCI became liable to pay each assignee the part of the debt assigned to him.

Whilst it is accepted by all parties that the scheme devised by the accountants was a device designed solely to increase the amount of compensation recoverable, it is for the purposes of these proceedings accepted that the assignments were genuine and that there was no arrangement that the assignee would hold any compensation received by him for the benefit of the assignor. However, the Deposit Protection Board has reserved the right in future proceedings to challenge the validity of the assignments if necessary.

These proceedings are designed to establish whether or not the scheme devised by the accountants is effective. Any future resort to such a scheme has now been counteracted by the Banking Act 1987 (Meaning of Deposit) Order 1991, SI 1991/1776, in such a way that any assignment of deposits made after 30 July 1991 and after a winding-up petition has been presented will not qualify for compensation. But the order does not affect this scheme which, if effective, will give rise to an additional £3·7m of compensation being payable out of the fund in respect of deposits with BCCI. The first defendant is an assignee of part of the debt owed to a Mr Dalia prior to the assignment: she is joined to represent all such assignees. The second defendant is Barclays Bank plc which is joined to represent all the authorised institutions which, under the 1987 Act, are responsible for providing the funds necessary to meet the compensation payments.

The issues

The question in this case is one of pure statutory construction. Under s 58(1), upon an authorised institution becoming insolvent compensation is payable 'to each depositor who has a protected deposit with that institution'. The question is whether an assignee of part of the deposit is a 'depositor'. No argument was advanced before the House based on the final words of the notice to BCCI referring to a declaration of trust.

The Act contains no relevant definition of the word 'depositor'. Broadly stated three possible constructions of 'depositor' have been put forward, viz:

(1) The deposit maker construction, ie the word 'depositor', means only the person who originally paid the sum to the insolvent institution. On this construction, no assignee of a deposit (other than a limited class of deposits under certificates of deposit) is a 'depositor'.

(2) The entitled-at-law construction, ie the person entitled in law (as opposed to equity) to the sum deposited. On this construction legal assignees of a deposit who acquire the whole legal and equitable right to the debts are 'depositors' but equitable assignees such as the present claimants are not.

(3) The entitlement construction, ie any person entitled to the deposit as against the institution whether or not he was the person who originally paid the sum to the institution. On this construction the present claimants and all other legal and equitable assignees are 'depositors'.

Sir Donald Nicholls V-C ([1993] 1 All ER 599, [1993] Ch 243) rejected the deposit maker construction as did, unanimously, the Court of Appeal ([1994] 1 All ER 539). The entitled-at-law construction was not fully advanced before Sir Donald Nicholls V-C and was rejected by the majority of the Court of Appeal (Russell LJ and Sir Michael Fox, Simon Brown LJ dissenting). Accordingly, Sir Donald Nicholls V-C and the majority of the Court of Appeal held in favour of the claimants. Barclays Bank appeal that decision to your Lordships' House.

Although the question raised is a simple one, the answer is far from simple and involves the very complicated interaction of a number of sections in the Act, not all of which were brought to the attention of the courts below.

The 1987 Act

Although the 1987 Act contains no definition of 'depositor' it does contain a definition of 'deposit' to which I attach considerable importance:

'**5.**—(1) Subject to the provisions of this section, in this Act "deposit" means a sum of money paid on terms—(a) under which it will be repaid, with or without interest or a premium, and either on demand or at a time or in circumstances agreed by or on behalf of the person making the payment and the person receiving it; and (b) which are not referable to the provision of property or services or for giving of security; and references in this Act to money deposited and to the making of a deposit shall be construed accordingly ...

(3) Except so far as any provision of this Act otherwise provides, in this Act "deposit" does not include—(a) a sum paid by the bank or an authorised institution; (b) a sum paid by a person for the time being specified in Schedule 2 to this Act; (c) a sum paid by a person, other than a person within paragraph (a) or (b) above, in the course of carrying on a business consisting wholly or mainly of lending money; (d) a sum which is paid by one company to another at the time when one is a subsidiary of the other or both are subsidiaries of another company or the same individual is a majority or principal shareholder controller of both of them; or (e) a sum which is paid by a person who, at the time when it is paid, is a close relative of the person receiving it or who is, or is a close relative of, a director, controller or manager of that person.'

That definition applies for all the purposes of the Act but, for the purposes of Pt II, certain amendments are made by s 60(9).

Part II of the Act provides for the payment of compensation on the insolvency of an authorised institution. Such payment is made out of a fund constituted under Pt II. Section 58(1) provides for compensation to be payable in the event of an authorised institution becoming insolvent, which, by s 59(1) is defined as the date of the winding-up order. Section 58(2) provides for the payment of compensation in the event of an administration order being made under s 8 of the Insolvency Act 1986. Section 58 provides:

'(1) Subject to the provisions of this section, if at any time an institution becomes insolvent and at that time—(a) it is an authorised institution; or (b) it is a former authorised institution ... the board shall as soon as practicable pay out of the fund to each depositor who has a protected deposit with that institution an amount equal to three-quarters of his protected deposit.

(2) Subject to the provisions of this section, if at any time an administration order is made under section 8 of the Insolvency Act 1986 in relation to an institution and at that time it is such an institution as is mentioned in subsection (1) above the board shall pay out of the fund to each depositor who has a protected deposit with that institution an amount equal to three quarters of his protected deposit ...'

These two subsections therefore require one to discover what is 'a protected deposit', a phrase defined by s 60:

'(1) Subject to the provisions of this section, in relation to an institution in respect of which a payment falls to be made under section 58(1) above any reference in this Act to a depositor's protected deposit is a reference to the total liability of the institution to him immediately before the time when it becomes insolvent, limited to a maximum of £20,000, in respect of the principal amounts of and accrued interest on sterling deposits made with the United Kingdom offices of the institution.

(2) Subject to the provisions of this section, in relation to an institution in respect of which a payment falls to be made under section 58(2) above any reference in this Act to a depositor's protected deposit is a reference to the liability of the institution to him in respect of—(a) the principal amount of each sterling deposit which was made by him with the United Kingdom office of the institution before the making of the administration order and which under the terms on which it was made is or becomes due or payable while the order is enforced; and (b) accrued interest on any such deposit up to the time when it is or becomes due and payable as aforesaid; but so that the total liability of the institution to him in respect of such deposits does not exceed £20,000 ...

(6) In determining the total liability of an institution to a depositor for the purposes of subsection (1) above, or liability or total liability of an institution to a depositor for the purposes of subsection (2) above, no account shall be taken of any liability in respect of a deposit if ... (c) the institution is a former authorised institution and the deposit was made after it ceased to be an authorised institution or a recognised bank or licensed institution under the Banking Act 1979 unless, at the time the deposit was made, the depositor did not know and could not reasonably

be expected to have known that it had ceased to be an authorised institution, recognised bank or licensed institution ...

(9) For the purposes of this section and sections 61 and 62 below the definition of deposit in section 5 above—(a) shall be treated as including—(i) any sum that would otherwise be excluded by paragraph (a), (d) or (e) of subsection (3) of that section if the sum is paid as trustee for a person not falling within any of those paragraphs; (ii) any sum that would otherwise be excluded by paragraph (b) or (c) of that subsection; (b) subject to subsections (10) and (11) below, shall be treated as excluding any sum paid by a trustee for a person falling within paragraph (e) of subsection (3) of that section; and (c) shall be treated as including any sum the right to repayment of which is evidenced by a transferable certificate of deposit or other transferable instrument and which would be a deposit within the meaning of section 5 as extended by paragraph (a) and restricted by paragraph (b) above if it had been paid by the person who is entitled to it at the time when the institution in question becomes insolvent.'

Section 61 has a sidenote 'Trustee deposits, joint deposits etc'. It provides, so far as relevant:

'(1) In the cases to which this section applies sections 58 and 60 above shall have effect with the following modifications.

(2) Subject to the provisions of this section, where any persons are entitled to a deposit as trustees they shall be treated as a single and continuing body of persons distinct from the persons who may from time to time be the trustees, and if the same persons are entitled as trustees to different deposits under different trusts they shall be treated as a separate and distinct body with respect to each of those trusts.

(3) Where a deposit is held for any person or for two or more persons jointly by a bare trustee, that person or, as the case may be, those persons jointly shall be treated as entitled to the deposit without the intervention of any trust.

(4) Subsection (3) above does not extend to Scotland and, in Scotland, where a deposit is held by a person as nominee for another person or for two or more other persons jointly, that other person or, as the case may be, those other persons jointly shall be treated as entitled to the deposit.

(5) A deposit to which two or more persons are entitled as members of a partnership (whether or not in equal shares) shall be treated as a single deposit.

(6) Subject to subsection (5) above, where two or more persons are jointly entitled to a deposit and subsection (2) above does not apply each of them shall be treated as having a separate deposit of an amount produced by dividing the amount of the deposit to which they are jointly entitled by the number of persons who are so entitled.'

I will deal first with the deposit maker argument since, if this is correct, no assignee can be a 'depositor' for the purposes of s 58.

The prima facie meaning of 'depositor'
Both Sir Donald Nicholls V-C and (to a lesser extent) the Court of Appeal considered that prima facie 'depositor' means a person who makes the deposit.

This view was challenged by Mr Elias for the claimants but, in the context of this Act, I agree with the courts below.

My view is strengthened by the definition of 'deposit' in s 5. To my mind, a depositor within the meaning of the Act must at least be entitled to a 'deposit' as defined in the Act. Section 5(3) excludes from the definition of 'deposit' certain sums 'paid' to the institution, such exclusions being formulated by reference to the personal characteristics of the payer. Thus, a sum paid to an institution by a person who at the time when it is paid is, for example, a close relative of a director (whom I will call a 'close relative') is not included in the definition of a deposit. One would assume therefore that the word 'depositor' prima facie means the person whose characteristics at the time he paid the sum to the institution determined whether or not the sum so paid is a 'deposit' within the meaning of the Act.

As the courts below appreciated, this prima facie meaning of depositor as being the deposit maker is much supported by sub-ss (2) and (6)(c) of s 60. Subsection (2) deals with the meaning of a 'depositor's protected deposit' in the event of an administration order being made. It is defined as the liability 'to him' (ie to 'the depositor') in respect of a sterling deposit 'which was made by him'. It is therefore clear that, in the context of administration orders, a 'depositor' for the purposes of Pt II means the person who originally made the deposit. Nobody has been able to suggest any reason why, in this respect, Parliament should have intended to treat compensation payable on the insolvency of a company differently from compensation in the event of an administration order being made in relation to a company.

Section 60(6)(c) points in the same direction. It deals with a case where a sum is deposited with an institution which was formerly authorised but at the date of deposit had ceased to be authorised. Such a person is entitled to compensation under s 58(2). The effect of sub-s (6)(c) of s 60 is to exclude compensation unless, *at the time the deposit was made*, the depositor did not have notice that the institution had ceased to be authorised. Thus 'the depositor' in this provision must be the person who originally paid the sums to the institution. If, as the claimants submit, 'depositor' includes an assignee, in the case of a claim made by an assignee either the state of knowledge of the original payer would have to be investigated or an assignee of the debt would be entitled to compensation even though he at all times (including the date of assignment) knew that the institution had ceased to be authorised. It seems improbable that Parliament intended either of these results.

Is the prima facie meaning displaced?

What, then, persuaded the courts below that an assignee of the debt was a depositor for the purposes of Pt II of the Act? In broad terms there were three reasons, viz (1) that since the provisions of s 61 confer a right to compensation on beneficiaries under bare trusts, it was inconceivable that statutory assignees should be treated less favourably; (2) that the 1991 order, being a legitimate aid to construction, only operates to negate assignments made after a winding-up petition is presented; therefore, by inference, assignments made before such presentation entitle the assignee to compensation; (3) that it would be surprising if statutory assignees of a debt were not entitled to compensation.

I can deal with the second of those reasons quite shortly. Although there are occasions on which regulations can be used as an aid to construction of the Act under which they are made (*Hanlon v Law Society* [1980] 2 All ER 199, [1981] AC

124) that is only where the regulations are roughly contemporaneous with the Act being construed. In my judgment regulations made by a government department and rushed through in order to counteract an identified mischief (viz the accountants' device which is the subject matter of this appeal) throw little if any light on the meaning of an Act passed by Parliament four years previously.

I turn then to the first reason urged, viz the provisions of s 61 relating to deposits held on trust. I fear that the proper construction of s 61 depends upon a complicated interaction between ss 5, 60(9) and 61. The courts below proceeded throughout on the basis that compensation is payable to a person who (a) is a 'depositor' and (b) is entitled to a sum deposited with an institution. On that basis, they treated it as being clear that since s 61(3) and (4) require one to treat the beneficial owner of deposits made by bare trustees or nominees as being 'entitled to the deposit' such person must be a 'depositor' for the purposes of Pt II. In their view, this was the result whether the nominee originally paid the sum as nominee or, after making the payment to the institution, subsequently declared himself to be a bare trustee or nominee. Therefore, they considered, it must have been the underlying purpose of the Act to provide compensation for a person who is beneficially entitled to the sum deposited. In particular, Parliament could not have intended to draw any distinction between a statutory assignee and a beneficiary entitled under a bare trust.

I cannot agree with this conclusion for the reasons which in outline can be stated as follows.

(1) The right of a beneficiary to compensation under s 61 depends on his entitlement to a 'deposit' within the meaning of Pt II of the Act: if there is no relevant 'deposit' he cannot be the 'depositor'. It is therefore impossible to draw any firm conclusion as to the rights of an assignee by comparison with those of a beneficiary absolutely entitled under a bare trust without considering the provisions of s 60(9) which vary the meaning of 'deposit' for the purposes, inter alia, of s 61.

(2) Section 60(9)(c) expressly modifies the definition of 'deposit' in relation to one type of assignment (those evidenced by a transferable instrument) but is significantly silent as to other assignments.

I will consider each of these reasons in turn.

(1) The meaning of 'deposit'

It is, in my view, clear that no one can be a 'depositor' unless he is entitled or deemed to be entitled to a 'deposit' within the statutory definition Under s 5(3) sums paid by someone who falls within the classes excluded by paras (a) to (e) of s 5(3) are not deposits within the meaning of the Act. Therefore, apart from the modifications introduced by s 60(9), in the case of a sum paid to the institution by a trustee, its status as a 'deposit' under s 5(3) depends upon the personal characteristics of the payer (the trustee) not the beneficiary. Thus, if A (who is a close relative of a director of the institution) pays a sum to an institution as bare trustee for B (who is not a close relative) under s 5(3)(e) the sum is not a deposit, since it was 'paid by' A, a close relative, and sums so paid are excluded from the definition of 'deposit'. The characteristics of B, the beneficiary, are irrelevant for the purposes of s 5(3).

When Parliament determined that compensation should be payable to certain beneficiaries under trusts, this necessarily required a modification of the definition of 'deposit' so as to determine whether or not a debt owed by an institution is a 'deposit' by reference to the characteristics of the beneficiary, B. This variation was effected by s 60(9)(a) and (b) under which the status of the sum as a 'deposit' is made to depend on the characteristics of the beneficiary, not those of the trustee. Thus, in the example given above, for the purposes of ss 60 and 61 of the Act, a sum which would have been excluded by s 5(3)(e) from being a 'deposit' falls to be treated as a deposit since it was paid by A, as trustee, for B who, not being a close relative, was not an excluded person under s 5(3)(e).

It follows that the provisions of s 61(3) which say that the nominee 'shall be treated as entitled to the deposit' do not, as the courts below consider, lead to the conclusion that he is a 'depositor'. A claimant who is a beneficiary under a bare trust also has to show that, within the definition in s 5(3) as amended by s 60(9), the sum falls to be treated as a 'deposit': unless it is a deposit he will not be the depositor.

Once the importance of the definition of 'deposit' is apparent, the analogy between the rights to compensation of a beneficiary under a bare trust and the right of an assignee to such compensation becomes very strained. A (a close relative) pays a sum to the institution as trustee for B (not a close relative): B is entitled to compensation since the sum is to be treated as a deposit (s 60(9)(*a*)). Compare the case where A (a close relative) assigns an existing deposit to B (not a close relative). B is not entitled to compensation: the sum is not a 'deposit' since its status falls to be determined according to the characteristics of A at the date of payment under s 5(3), there being nothing to modify that definition for the purposes of Pt II of the Act. Therefore the rights of an assignee to compensation would not be the same as a beneficiary under a bare trust.

Take another case. A (not a close relative) pays the sum to the institution as trustee for B (a close relative). The sum is not a 'deposit' (s 60(9)(b)): therefore no compensation is payable. Contrast the case where A, instead of declaring himself trustee, assigns the debt to B (a close relative). If assignees are to be treated as 'depositors', B would be entitled to compensation since there is nothing to link the definition of 'deposit' to the status of the assignee as opposed to that of the person who made the original payment. One would therefore have the remarkable result that close relatives who obtained assignments of debts would be entitled to compensation where, if they had made the original deposit themselves or were beneficiaries under a bare trust, they would have been expressly excluded.

For these reasons, in my judgment s 60 provides no clear guidance as to the meaning of the word 'depositor'.

(2) *'Negotiable deposits'*

In the courts below it was thought that the draftsman of the Act had probably overlooked the position of assignees. However, s 60(9)(c) deals specifically with one type of assignment, viz deposits evidenced by transferable certificates of deposit or other transferable instruments (CDs). Therefore the rights of assignees of at least one kind were in the mind of the draftsman.

It is interesting to see how Parliament dealt with the definition of 'deposit' in the context of CDs. The subject matter of a CD is to be included in the definition of 'deposit' 'if it had been paid by the person who is entitled to it at the time when the institution in question becomes insolvent'. There are two points to be noted. First, the assignee is to be deemed to have made the initial payment, ie he is deemed to be the deposit maker. This strongly suggests that Parliament was, throughout, considering a depositor to be the original payer and therefore had to deem an assignee to have paid the deposit. Second, unlike the personal characteristics of beneficiaries under a trust which are ascertained at the date of the original payment, it is the personal characteristics of the assignee at the date of insolvency which determines the status of the CD. As one would expect in the case of compensation for assignees, the entitlement to compensation is not made to depend on the personal characteristics of the original depositor.

However, the most significant feature of s 60(9)(c) is that it deals only with one type of assignment, viz assignments of sums deposited under CDs. If 'depositor' includes all assignees, this would lead to extraordinary results. If A (not a close relative) makes a CD deposit and then transfers it to B (a close relative), B is not entitled to compensation since the sum is not a deposit by virtue of s 60(9)(c). If, on the other hand, A were to make an ordinary deposit (not a CD) and then assign it to X (a close relative), X is entitled to compensation since there is nothing to exclude the debt from the definition of deposit. I find it impossible to accept that Parliament, having been to such lengths to exclude from compensation a close relative who was either the original depositor, or a beneficiary under a trust, or the holder of a CD, intended an assignee who is a close relative at the date of insolvency to receive compensation.

For these reasons I can find nothing in the provisions of s 61 which clearly indicate that an assignee is to be treated as a depositor and indications in s 60 that he is not to be so treated.

No compensation for assignees

There remains the final reason relied upon by the courts below for rejecting the prima facie meaning of the word depositor, viz that it would be odd if Parliament had not provided compensation for a statutory assignee: in the case of an assigned debt, the result would be that neither the original deposit maker nor the assignee would be entitled to compensation.

The Court of Appeal, but not Sir Donald Nicholls V-C, considered that unless assignees were 'depositors' neither the personal representatives nor the trustee in bankruptcy of the original deposit maker would be entitled to compensation. In my judgment this is not correct. Personal representatives and trustees in bankruptcy are, by operation of law, universal successors to those whom they represent. Therefore on any footing they are entitled to the compensation to which the persons they represent would have been entitled had they survived or not become insolvent.

That leaves the undoubted fact that, on the deposit maker construction, a legal assignee of the debt (apart from deposits under CDs) will not be entitled to compensation. Although I agree that it is difficult to see the reason for such exclusion, it may well be that the rarity of assignments of deposits provides an explanation. In the ordinary way, deposits with banks and other financial institutions are not assigned. The transfer of cash on deposit is normally achieved by drawing a cheque in favour of the transferee or drawing cash and paying it to the transferee. We were told that, apart from CDs and the assignments the subject matter of this action, the Deposit Protection Board had no experience of any statutory assignments and knew of only one

equitable assignment where trustees attempted to assign the deposit to
themselves. The view may well have been taken that, apart from CDs, in the
real world such assignments do not occur.

Conclusion

I therefore find nothing in the other provisions of the Act which is
inconsistent with the prima facie meaning of 'depositor' as being the person
who makes the deposit. I would therefore allow the appeal on this ground and
declare that a person entitled to a debt by reason of the assignment of part of a
debt is not a depositor holding a protected deposit entitled to compensation
pursuant to s 58(1) of the Act. In the circumstances it is unnecessary for me to
deal with the other arguments advanced.
It is agreed that there will be no order as to costs.

LORD MUSTILL. My Lords, I have had the advantage of reading in draft the
speech prepared by my noble and learned friend Lord Browne-Wilkinson. For
the reasons he gives I, too, would allow the appeal.

LORD LLOYD OF BERWICK. My Lords, I have had the advantage of reading
in draft the speech prepared by my noble and learned friend Lord
Browne-Wilkinson. For the reasons he gives I, too, would allow the appeal.

Appeal allowed.

Celia Fox   Barrister.

Balfour v Foreign and Commonwealth Office

COURT OF APPEAL, CIVIL DIVISION
RUSSELL, McCOWAN AND HIRST LJJ
17, 18, 19 NOVEMBER, 9 DECEMBER 1993

*Discovery – Production of documents – Privilege – Public interest – Disclosure
alleged to be injurious to public interest – Certificate signed by Secretary of State
claiming immunity from disclosure on ground of national security – Whether court
should inspect documents if ministerial certificate demonstrates actual or potential
risk to national security.*

The appellant, who was in the diplomatic service, was alleged to have issued a
visa to an Iranian businessman from whom he had accepted a gift of £5,000
while he was the vice-consul in Dubai. The appellant was instructed to return
to London and was dismissed following disciplinary proceedings. He made a
complaint to an industrial tribunal claiming that he had been unfairly
dismissed. He stated in his complaint that he was unable to provide details of
his grounds of appeal because they had been 'classified "secret" under the
Official Secrets Act' and applied for discovery of certain documents in the
possession of the Foreign Office, which claimed public interest immunity on
the grounds that disclosure of material in the documents relating to the

security and intelligence services would be contrary to the public interest. The Foreign Secretary and the Home Secretary both signed certificates claiming public interest immunity. The certificates set out particulars of the nature and content of the material attracting immunity and the reasons for the claim. The industrial tribunal refused to order the disclosure sought by the appellant and on appeal that decision was upheld by the Employment Appeal Tribunal. The appellant appealed to the Court of Appeal, seeking a direction that the industrial tribunal inspect the material in respect of which immunity was claimed so that it could rule upon its admissibility.

Held – Although the courts always had to be vigilant to ensure that public interest immunity of whatever kind was raised only in appropriate circumstances and with appropriate particularity, once there was an actual or potential risk to national security demonstrated by an appropriate certificate issued by a minister the court should not exercise its right to inspect the documents. Since the industrial tribunal had correctly recognised the constraints placed upon it by the terms of the certificates the appeal would be dismissed (see p 596 *e* to *h*, post).

Conway v Rimmer [1968] 1 All ER 874 and *Council of Civil Service Unions v Minister for the Civil Service* [1984] 3 All ER 935 applied.

Notes
For privilege where disclosure of documents is contrary to public interest, see 13 *Halsbury's Laws* (4th edn) paras 86–91, and for cases on the subject, see 18 *Digest* (2nd reissue) 203–219, 1822–1879.

Cases referred to in judgment
Conway v Rimmer [1968] 1 All ER 874, [1968] AC 910, [1968] 2 WLR 998, HL.
Council of Civil Service Unions v Minister for the Civil Service [1984] 3 All ER 935, [1985] AC 374, [1984] 3 WLR 1174, HL.
Duncan v Cammell Laird & Co Ltd [1942] 1 All ER 587, [1942] AC 624, HL.
Zamora, The [1916] 2 AC 77, PC.

Cases also cited or referred to in skeleton argument
Adams v West Sussex CC [1990] ICR 546, EAT.
Air Canada v Secretary of State for Trade (No 2) [1983] 1 All ER 910, [1983] 2 AC 394, HL.
Alister v R (1984) 154 CLR 404, Aust HC.
Asiatic Petroleum Co Ltd v Anglo Persian Oil Co Ltd [1916] 1 QB 822, [1916–17] All ER Rep 637, CA.
Birds Eye Walls Ltd v Harrison [1985] ICR 278, EAT.
Burmah Oil Co Ltd v Bank of England (A-G intervening) [1979] 3 All ER 700, [1980] AC 1090, HL.
Glasgow Corp v Central Land Board 1956 SC (HL) 1.
Henrie and Security Intelligence Review Committee, Re (1988) 53 DLR (4th) 568, Can Fed Ct.
Johnston v Chief Constable of the Royal Ulster Constabulary Case 222/84 [1986] 3 All ER 135, [1987] QB 129, CJEC.
Makanjuola v Comr of Police of the Metropolis (1989) [1992] 3 All ER 617, CA.
Neilson v Laugharne [1981] 1 All ER 829, [1981] QB 736, CA.

Pickering v Liverpool Daily Post and Echo Newspapers plc [1991] 1 All ER 622, [1991]
2 AC 370, HL.
R v Henderson (5 October 1992, unreported), Crown Ct.
R v Secretary of State for the Home Dept, ex p Ruddock [1987] 2 All ER 518, [1987]
1 WLR 1482.
R v Ward [1993] 2 All ER 577, [1993] 1 WLR 619, CA.
Rogers v Secretary of State for the Home Dept, Gaming Board for GB v Rogers [1972]
2 All ER 1057, [1973] AC 388, HL.
Thorburn v Hermon (Channel 4, third party) (1992) Times, 14 May.

Interlocutory appeal
The applicant, Andrew Balfour, appealed from the decision of the Employment Appeal Tribunal (Knox J, Mr A Ferry and Mr K Hack) ([1993] ICR 663) given on 29 January 1993 dismissing the applicant's appeal from the decision of the chairman of the London (South) Industrial Tribunal on 29 January 1992 refusing to order disclosure of certain documents by the respondent, the Foreign and Commonwealth Office, in his claim against the respondent, his employer, for unfair dismissal. The facts are set out in the judgment of the court.

Robin Allen and *Anthony Bradley* (instructed by *John Wadham*, Liberty) for the applicant.
Christopher Katkowski (instructed by the *Treasury Solicitor*) for the Foreign Office.

Cur adv vult

9 December 1993. The following judgment of the court was delivered.

RUSSELL LJ. This appeal raises once more the problem of public interest immunity, and in particular the function of the court when confronted with a certificate, signed by the Secretary of State, claiming immunity from disclosure of material on the ground of national security.
    The case has already generated a considerable volume of paper contained in a number of files, but for the purposes of this appeal it is necessary to refer to the facts only in the barest outline.
    The appellant began his career with the Foreign and Commonwealth Office in 1969. In 1985, whilst in Syria, he issued a visa permitting entry into the United Kingdom to a man called Hindawi. He was a terrorist. Much later the appellant was interrogated about the issue of the visa but no disciplinary charges were preferred.
    In 1986 the appellant was posted to Dubai as vice-consul and visa officer. There he had dealings with a man called Ansari. In early 1989 the appellant provided Ansari with the number of a bank account in the name of the appellant's brother-in-law, a Mr Broomhead, in the United Kingdom. On 16 April 1989 the appellant issued a visa to Ansari and in May 1989 Ansari transferred £5,000 into Mr Broomhead's account in the United Kingdom.
    On 27 May 1989 the appellant was instructed to return to London and he did so the following day. There he was interrogated and for a time was under arrest, detained pursuant to the Prevention of Terrorism (Temporary Provisions) Act 1984. No criminal proceedings ensued against the appellant.

However, on 16 March 1990 disciplinary proceedings against the appellant were commenced. The principal complaint was in the following terms:

'Mr Balfour approached an Iranian businessman in Dubai with a request to borrow £20,000. The businessman agreed to lend Mr Balfour £5,000. Subsequently £5,000 was paid into Mr Balfour's brother-in-law's bank account. Mr Balfour subsequently induced his brother-in-law to write three fictitious letters to the businessman purporting to show that the £5,000 was payment for a transaction between Mr Balfour's brother-in-law and the Iranian businessman, Mr Mehrdad Ansari Shirazi ... It cannot be proved why these considerable sums of money and gifts were received by Mr Balfour. But their receipt, unreported, and in one instance with an elaborate attempt at concealment, amounts ... to breaches of the following diplomatic service regulations:—(a) DSR 8 (General Principles of Conduct) and(b) DSR 9 (Acceptance of Gifts and Advantages).'

After some delay the disciplinary board recorded its decision on 20 September 1990. Inter alia it found that a sum of £5,000 had been transferred from Ansari's account to that of Mr Broomhead and that the appellant was aware that three fictitious letters had been written by Mr Broomhead in an endeavour to show that the £5,000 was paid pursuant to a legitimate commercial transaction. The board noted that no invoices had been issued for the £5,000 and concluded, contrary to the assertions of the appellant, that he had not arranged any legitimate business transaction with his brother-in-law but had been instrumental in obtaining the transfer of the money. Disciplinary offences had therefore been committed by the appellant and dismissal was recommended.

The appellant appealed unsuccessfully to the appeal board. Mr Broomhead declined an invitation to appear. The appellant's dismissal followed on 15 February 1991.

Meanwhile the appellant had submitted an application to an industrial tribunal on 11 January 1991 which contained the following observation:

'My grounds for appeal have been classified "secret" under the Official Secrets Act, and I am not yet able to provide details. The grounds for my dismissal are wrong and unfair.'

The Foreign Office's answer was to the effect that—

'the conduct in question was obtaining the transfer of £5,000 from an official contact, namely an Iranian businessman, to the account of the Applicant's brother-in-law in breach of Diplomatic Service Regulations ("DSR") 8 and 9, which, inter alia, require officers not to use their official position to further their private interests and not to accept gifts or advantages.'

Later in its response the Foreign Office observed:

'In relation to the transfer of £5,000 the Applicant, having set out the main substance of his arguments, included certain material of a secret nature, disclosure of which would be contrary to the public interest. For that reason the whole document was given a "secret" classification. In the proceedings before the Tribunal the FCO will resist disclosure of the material in question on grounds of public interest immunity, but will

consent to disclosure of the balance of the written submissions. For that
purpose the FCO will produce a copy of the written submissions from
which the material in question has been excised and will remove the
"secret" classification in respect of that copy.'

In amended grounds of application the appellant contended that he had been
requested by the United Kingdom security services to maintain contact with
Ansari and that the transfer of £5,000 was pursuant to a legitimate business
transaction between Ansari and the appellant's brother-in-law. The appellant
did not know that the £5,000 had actually been transferred and insofar as he
was involved in the writing of fictitious letters that was no more than an error
of judgment on his part.

Thus the battle lines were drawn and thus the Foreign and Commonwealth
Office defined its stance in relation to disclosure of sensitive material.

On 26 June 1991 the Secretary of State for Foreign and Commonwealth
Affairs signed the first of two certificates claiming public interest immunity.
His second certificate was dated 26 January 1992. A third certificate signed by
the Secretary of State for the Home Department was signed on 27 January
1992.

The three certificates are in similar terms. Each raised objection to the
production of any evidence, documentary or otherwise, about the organisation
of the security and intelligence services, their theatres of operation or their
methods. Express reference was made to foreign powers and terrorist
organisations and the threat to national security of disclosure. It has not been
suggested that the certificates lacked particularity either as to the nature and
content of the material which attracted immunity or as to the reasons for the
claim.

On 29 January 1992 the chairman of the London (South) Industrial Tribunal
conducted an interlocutory hearing and refused to order disclosure by the
Foreign Office of certain documents sought by the appellant. Her decision was
upheld by the Employment Appeal Tribunal (Knox J, Mr A Ferry and Mr K
Hack) and this appeal is against the judgment of Knox J, presiding, which he
delivered on 29 January 1993 ([1993] ICR 663).

It is right that we should record at this stage the precise ambit of this appeal.
Knox J did not deal in his judgment with the potential relevance of the material
in respect of which immunity is claimed, and we did not hear full argument
upon this aspect of the case. However, in his skeleton argument counsel for
the appellant recognised that disclosure of documents and inspection by the
court of such documents where public interest immunity is claimed can arise
only if the court is satisfied that the documents 'will contain material which
will give substantial support to the contentions of the parties seeking
disclosure'. We feel bound to observe that we have experienced great
difficulty in understanding how, in the instant case, the appellant could
overcome this first hurdle. The primary facts, the payment of £5,000 and the
appellant's complicity in the use of fictitious letters were admitted or
established to the satisfaction of the employers, and could be considered
sufficient to justify dismissal. Counsel never came anywhere near explaining
how matters involving national security could or might impinge upon these
findings. That said, however, and at the invitation of the Foreign Office as well
as the appellant we move on to consider what was identified by Knox J, as at
the heart of the appeal, namely—

'the proper approach to be adopted where, as here, there is a claim advanced that public interest immunity applies on grounds of national security in that the security and intelligence services are, or are claimed to be, involved.' (See [1993] ICR 663 at 665.)

Mr Allen for the appellant, whose basic submission was that we should direct the industrial tribunal to inspect the material in respect of which public interest immunity is claimed so that the tribunal could thereafter rule upon its admissibility in the appellant's claim, referred to and cited from a large number of authorities. We hope he will not regard it as a discourtesy if we do not refer to them all.

We take as our starting point *Duncan v Cammell Laird & Co Ltd* [1942] 1 All ER 587, [1942] AC 624, although there are cases of much greater antiquity. The case was concerned with the loss of the submarine Thetis in 1939, and subsequently actions for damages lodged by relatives of men who lost their lives in the disaster. Crown privilege was claimed in relation to technical documents concerned with the construction of the vessel.

Viscount Simon LC, having reviewed earlier authorities, said ([1942] 1 All ER 587 at 595, [1942] AC 624 at 626–643):

> 'Although an objection validly taken to production on the ground that this would be injurious to the public interest is conclusive, it is important to remember that the decision ruling out such documents is the decision of the judge. Thus, in the present case, the objection raised in the respondents' affidavit is properly expressed to be an objection to produce "except under the order of this honourable court." It is the judge who is in control of the trial, not the executive, but the proper ruling for the judge to give is as above expressed. In this connection, I do not think it is out of place to indicate the sort of grounds which would not afford to the minister adequate justification for objecting to production. It is not a sufficient ground that the documents are "state documents" or "official" or are marked "confidential." It would not be a good ground that, if they were produced, the consequences might involve the department or the government in Parliamentary discussion or in public criticism, or might necessitate the attendance as witnesses or otherwise of officials who have pressing duties elsewhere. Neither would it be a good ground that production might tend to expose a want of efficiency in the administration or tend to lay the department open to claims for compensation. In a word, it is not enough that the minister or the department does not want to have the documents produced. The minister, in deciding whether it is his duty to object, should bear these considerations in mind, for he ought not to take the responsibility of withholding production except in cases where the public interest would otherwise be damnified, e.g., where disclosure would be injurious to national defence, or to good diplomatic relations, or where the practice of keeping a class of documents secret is necessary for the proper functioning of the public service. When these conditions are satisfied and the minister feels it is his duty to deny access to material which would otherwise be available, there is no question but that the public interest must be preferred to any private consideration. The present opinion is concerned only with the production of documents, but it seems to me that the same principle must also apply to the exclusion of

verbal evidence which, if given, would jeopardise the interests of the community.'

Mr Allen contended that the view expressed in the House of Lords in 1942 was to the effect that wherever production would be injurious to the public interest and objection was taken on that ground, the objection 'was conclusive' although the executive must be selective in deciding to object to production.

In *Conway v Rimmer* [1968] 1 All ER 874 at 888, [1968] AC 910 at 951–952 Lord Reid said:

'LORD SIMON did not say that courts in England have no power to overrule the executive. He said in *Duncan's* case ([1942] 1 All ER 587 at 595, [1942] AC 624 at 642): "The decision ruling out such documents is the decision of the judge ... It is the judge who is in control of the trial, not the executive, but the proper ruling for the judge to give is as above expressed." I.e., to accept the Minister's view in every case. In my judgment, in considering what is "proper" for a court to do we must have regard to the need, shown by twenty-five years' experience since *Duncan's* case, that the courts should balance the public interest in the proper administration of justice against the public interest in withholding any evidence which a Minister considers ought to be withheld. I would therefore propose that the House ought now to decide that courts have and are entitled to exercise a power and duty to hold a balance between the public interest, as expressed by a Minister, to withhold certain documents or other evidence, and the public interest in ensuring the proper administration of justice. That does not mean that the court would reject a Minister's view: full weight must be given to it in every case, and if the Minister's reasons are of a character which judicial experience is not competent to weigh then the Minister's view must prevail ... I do not doubt that there are certain classes of documents which ought not to be disclosed whatever their content may be. Virtually everyone agrees that cabinet minutes and the like ought not to be disclosed until such time as they are only of historical interest; but I do not think that any people would give as the reason that premature disclosure would prevent candour in the cabinet. To my mind the most important reason is that such disclosure would create or fan ill-informed or captious public or political criticism. The business of government is difficult enough as it is, and no government could contemplate with equanimity the inner workings of the government machine being exposed to the gaze of those ready to criticise without adequate knowledge of the background and perhaps with some axe to grind. That must in my view also apply to all documents concerned with policy making within departments including it may be minutes and the like by quite junior officials and correspondence with outside bodies. Further, it may be that deliberations about a particular case require protection as much as deliberations about policy. I do not think that it is possible to limit such documents by any definition ...'

Earlier Lord Reid had identified the problem and the parameters of public interest immunity in these words ([1968] 1 All ER 874 at 880, [1968] AC 910 at 940):

'There is the public interest that harm shall not be done to the nation or the public service by the disclosure of certain documents, and there is the public interest that the administration of justice shall not be frustrated by the withholding of documents which must be produced if justice is to be done. There are many cases where the nature of the injury which would or might be done to the nation or the public service is of so grave a character that no other interest, public or private, can be allowed to prevail over it. With regard to such cases it would be proper to say, as LORD SIMON did, that to order production of the document in question would put the interest of the state in jeopardy; but there are many other cases where the possible injury to the public service is much less and there one would think that it would be proper to balance the public interests involved. I do not believe that LORD SIMON really meant that the smallest probability of injury to the public service must always outweigh the gravest frustration of the administration of justice.'

Lord Morris of Borth-y-Gest said ([1968] 1 All ER 874 at 890, [1968] AC 910 at 954–956):

'It is, I think, a principle which commands general acceptance that there are circumstances in which the public interests must be dominant over the interests of a private individual. To the safety or the well-being of the community the claims of a private person may have to be subservient. This principle applies in litigation. The public interest may require that relevant documents ought not to be produced. If, for example, national security would be or might be imperilled by the production and consequent disclosure of certain documents then the interests of a litigant must give way ... Though this case requires an answer to be given to the question whether in the last resort the decision rests with the courts or with a Minister, I see no reason to envisage friction or tension as between the courts and the executive. They both operate in the public interest. Some aspects of the public interest are chiefly within the knowledge of some Minister and can best be assessed by him. I see no reason to fear that the courts would not in regard to them be fully and readily receptive to all representations made in appropriate form and with reasonable sufficiency. If a responsible Minister stated that production of a document would jeopardise public safety, it is inconceivable that any court would make an order for its production. The desirability of refusing production would heavily outweigh the desirability of requiring it.'

Conway v Rimmer was clearly a landmark case of the highest authority and, in our view, the speeches delivered in that case, when applied to the instant case, dispose of this appeal. In more recent times the House of Lords has returned to the question of national security in a different context to *Conway v Rimmer*, but it has reinforced the views expressed a quarter of a century ago. In *Council of Civil Service Unions v Minister for the Civil Service* [1984] 3 All ER 935 at 944–945, [1985] AC 374 at 402 Lord Fraser said:

'The decision on whether the requirements of national security outweigh the duty of fairness in any particular case is for the government and not for the courts; the government alone has access to the relevant information, and in any event the judicial process is unsuitable for reaching decisions on national security. But if the decision is successfully challenged, on the ground that it has been reached by a process which is unfair, then the government is under an obligation to produce evidence that the decision was in fact based on grounds of national security. Authority for both these points is found in *The Zamora* [1916] 2 AC 77. The former point is dealt with in the well-known passage from the advice from the Judicial Committee delivered by Lord Parker (at 107): "Those who are responsible for the national security must be the sole judges of what the national security requires. It would be obviously undesirable that such matters should be made the subject of evidence in a Court of law or otherwise discussed in public."'

Further in the *CCSU* case Lord Diplock said ([1984] 3 All ER 935 at 952, [1985] AC 374 at 412):

'National security is the responsibility of the executive government; what action is needed to protect its interests is, as the cases cited by my noble and learned friend Lord Roskill establish and common sense itself dictates, a matter on which those on whom the responsibility rests, and not the courts of justice, must have the last word. It is par excellence a non-justiciable question. The judicial process is totally inept to deal with the sort of problems which it involves.'

In this appeal Mr Allen boldly invites this court to depart from these powerful dicta, contending that they were obiter and that in the society in which we now live, the time is ripe for what he described as a more open approach when issues of national security are raised by the appropriate ministers. Even if not constrained by authority we firmly decline to accept that invitation, for it seems to us to be contrary to principle and to good sense. In this case the court has not abdicated its responsibility, but it has recognised the constraints placed upon it by the terms of the certificates issued by the executive. There must always be vigilance by the courts to ensure that public interest immunity of whatever kind is raised only in appropriate circumstances and with appropriate particularity, but once there is an actual or potential risk to national security demonstrated by an appropriate certificate the court should not exercise its right to inspect. We recognise the importance of this case to the appellant, but in our judgment the uninhibited prosecution of his claim for unfair dismissal cannot prevail. We do not accept, as counsel submitted we should, that in such a situation a defendant should abandon his defence just as the Crown will abandon a prosecution where there exists a risk of the innocent being convicted.

We are satisfied that Knox J came to the right conclusion for the right reasons. We dismiss this appeal.

Appeal dismissed. Leave to appeal to the House of Lords refused.

24 *March 1994. The Appeal Committee of the House of Lords (Lord Keith of Kinkel, Lord Browne-Wilkinson and Lord Lloyd) refused leave to appeal.*

Raina Levy   Barrister.

Davidson v Chief Constable of North Wales and another

COURT OF APPEAL, CIVIL DIVISION
SIR THOMAS BINGHAM MR, STAUGHTON AND WAITE LJJ
20 APRIL 1993

False imprisonment – Elements of tort – Cause of false imprisonment – Information leading to wrongful arrest – Police officers lawfully arresting plaintiff on wrong information provided by informant – Whether informant merely giving information to properly constituted authority to act on – Whether informant instigator, promoter and active inciter of arrest – Whether informant liable for false imprisonment.

H, a friend of the plaintiff, purchased a cassette at a store and, having made the purchase, returned to the cassette counter where the plaintiff was waiting. They stood there talking before leaving the store. A store detective who had observed them standing at the cassette counter gained the impression that they had left without paying for the cassette and telephoned the police. When two police officers arrived the store detective told them that the plaintiff had taken the cassette without paying and pointed them out. The officers arrested the plaintiff and H on suspicion of shoplifting. H denied that he had taken anything dishonestly and produced the cassette but was unable to produce the receipt as he had thrown it away. The plaintiff remained silent. The plaintiff and H were taken to the police station but were released after two hours when the police received a message from the shop assistant who had served H confirming that he had paid for the cassette. The plaintiff brought an action against, inter alia, the store detective's employers for false imprisonment. At the trial of the action the police officers gave evidence that they had exercised their own judgment in arresting the plaintiff and H acting on the information received from the store detective. The judge withdrew the case from the jury on the grounds that the police officers were protected by s 24(6) of the Police and Criminal Evidence Act 1984 because they had had reasonable grounds to make the arrest and since they had acted independently of the store detective there was no case to answer. The plaintiff appealed.

Held – Since the police officers had been justified in arresting the plaintiff and H because they had had a reasonable suspicion, derived from the information supplied by the store detective, that the plaintiff and H had been shoplifting, the issue in relation to the liability of the store detective's employers for her actions depended on whether the store detective had merely given information to a properly constituted authority on which that authority could act or not as it saw fit or whether she herself was the instigator, promoter and active inciter of the arrest and imprisonment. On the facts, there was no evidence that the store detective's actions went beyond the giving of information to the police officers for them to take such action as they thought fit and that it amounted to some direction, or procuring, or direct request, or direct encouragement that they should act by arresting the plaintiff and H. In those circumstances the judge had been right to withdraw the case from the jury. The appeal would therefore be dismissed (see p 602 *d e*, p 603 *j*, p 604 *h* to p 605 *c f* to *j* to p 606 *a*, post).

Aitken v Bedwell (1827) M & M 68, Grinham v Willey (1858) 4 H & N 496 and Meering v Grahame-White Aviation Co Ltd (1920) 122 LT 44 applied.

Notes
For false imprisonment, see 45 Halsbury's Laws (4th edn) paras 1325–1338, and for cases on the subject, see 46 Digest (reissue) 307–311, 2675–2707.

Cases referred to in judgment
Aitken v Bedwell (1827) M & M 68, 173 ER 1084, NP.
Grinham v Willey (1858) 4 H & N 496, 157 ER 934, Exch.
Harnett v Bond [1925] AC 669, [1925] All ER Rep 110, HL.
Meering v Grahame-White Aviation Co Ltd (1920) 122 LT 44, CA.
Pike v Waldrum and Peninsula & Oriental Steam Navigation Co [1952] 1 Lloyd's Rep 431.

Appeal
The plaintiff, Marina Davidson, appealed against the decision of Judge Roberts sitting in the Llangefni County Court on 12 December 1991 withdrawing the plaintiff's claim against the second defendant, Frances Clarke Ltd, for damages for false imprisonment from the jury trying the action. At the outset of the trial the plaintiff had submitted to judgment against her in favour of the first defendant, the Chief Constable of North Wales. The facts are set out in the judgment of Sir Thomas Bingham MR.

Anthony Clover (instructed by *Patrick Blackmore*, Menai Bridge) for the plaintiff.
Andrew Lewis (instructed by *Ford & Warren*, Leeds) for the second defendant.

SIR THOMAS BINGHAM MR. This is an appeal against a decision of Judge Roberts given in the Llangefni County Court on 12 December 1991. The decision appealed against was made in the course of the hearing of a civil claim for false imprisonment which was proceeding before the learned judge and a jury and was to the effect that the case should be withdrawn from the jury. The plaintiff in one of the actions which was proceeding before the judge, then called Marina Davidson, now appeals against the learned judge's decision contending that there was an issue which the learned judge should properly have left to the jury.

The facts giving rise to the appeal fall within a small compass and they took place within a very short period of time. On 30 June 1988 the plaintiff, Marina Davidson (now called Mrs Astbury), was with a friend named Mr Robert Halford in Woolworths store at Bangor in North Wales where they were shopping. Mr Halford bought and paid for a cassette priced at £2·99. There is no doubt whatever that that was an entirely honest and bona fide transaction. Having paid for the cassette he and Miss Davidson did not leave the store at once. He returned to where she was standing by the cassette counter and they stood there for a period of some minutes talking together. While they were doing that a store detective, Mrs Jane Yates, who was employed by Frances Clarke Ltd as a store detective, observed them. It is important to note that she started observing them, so it would appear, at that stage and after the stage at which the cassette had been duly paid for. Having watched them she gained the impression that the cassette which she could see them handling had been obtained dishonestly and without paying. It is the case that Miss Davidson and

Mr Halford left the store without paying for the cassette during the period that Mrs Yates was watching them.

She followed them out of the store and saw them go into a cafe across the street where they had a cup of coffee. Mrs Yates herself went into a nearby branch of W H Smith to telephone the police as a result of which two police constables named Walker and Garland came on the scene. They saw Mrs Yates at or outside W H Smith and she told them what she had seen. When she came to give evidence she indicated she had told them that she was not 100% sure that she had seen Miss Davidson or Mr Halford take the cassette without paying but the police constables in their evidence denied that there had been any qualification at all about the information that she gave. Certainly, no qualification of that kind is to be found in the contemporary statement which she made in writing and signed. The learned judge concluded that probably there was no qualification such as she suggested and he dealt with the case on that basis.

Having received the information which Mrs Yates gave them the two police constables went into the cafe and Mrs Yates pointed out the plaintiff and Mr Halford. She then left and was not present when the next events took place.

The two police constables approached Miss Davidson and Mr Halford. Pc Walker told them that he was arresting them on suspicion of shoplifting. The plaintiff herself was silent. Mr Halford denied that he had taken anything dishonestly. There was further discussion in the course of which Mr Halford produced a cassette that no longer had its cellophane wrapping on, he having earlier removed that, and he was unable to produce the receipt which he had received on purchasing the cassette, having thrown it away. The fact that he could not produce a receipt but did, nonetheless, have the cassette confirmed the police officers' suspicions that the cassette had been taken unlawfully.

The plaintiff and Mr Halford were taken to the police station. They were detained and questioned but they were released after a period of about two hours. The reason for their release without charge was that a message was received from a shop assistant at Woolworths to the effect that Mr Halford had paid for the cassette and that the shop assistant who had served him remembered doing so and remembered his appearance. It is, therefore, quite clear that the plaintiff and Mr Halford were innocent of theft and it is right that should be made quite clear since they undoubtedly suffered some embarrassment and humiliation as a result of this incident.

Miss Davidson then instructed a solicitor. It appears that Mr Halford also instructed a different solicitor. Miss Davidson's solicitors wrote to the defendants on 5 July and received an answer by letter on 13 July which we have seen. It is correct to observe that the account of the matter given in the letter is not correct. Mrs Yates's employers say:

> 'She did not approach or arrest your client and there was no query on your client's behaviour. The police were not called, but happened to be passing. We must point out that your client's behaviour was in no way thought of as suspicious and all action taken was by the police.'

I observe in passing that it is very difficult to understand that letter since the police undoubtedly were called and the whole burden of Mrs Yates's statement was that she had been watching Mr Halford and the plaintiff and did consider their behaviour to be suspicious.

Proceedings were issued in May 1990 against (as first defendant) the Chief Constable of the North Wales Police and (as second defendant) the company who were the employers of Mrs Yates. A parallel action was brought by Mr Halford but since no appeal arises in that case it can be ignored.

At the outset of the trial before the learned judge the plaintiff submitted to judgment against her in favour of the chief constable. The learned judge gives his reason for the decision made when he said in the course of his ruling:

'At the beginning of the hearing, the plaintiffs submitted to judgment in favour of the chief constable on the ground that Constable Walker had been justified in arresting the plaintiff upon the reasonable suspicion that he had formed on the strength of the store detective's account of what she had seen. The authorities upon which Constable Walker acted in arresting the plaintiffs, as is apparent from his evidence as I have recited it and as he himself confirmed, is s 24(6) [of the Police and Criminal Evidence Act 1984] ... which provides as follows: "Where a constable has reasonable grounds for suspecting that an arrestable offence has been committed, he may arrest without a warrant anyone whom he has reasonable grounds for suspecting to be guilty of the offence."'

The police constable's evidence was recited by the learned judge in the course of his judgment. Pc Walker said of the incident:

'She [referring to Mrs Yates] said what she had witnessed. I then decided if I had reasonable suspicion. I did not need the store detective to tell me my job. I am not an agent. I act on information that witnesses give me. The store detective gave me information and I acted on it. What she did was to give me information and point them out. I was not acting under orders from her.'

The other officer, Pc Garland, also gave evidence which the learned judge recited, to this effect:

'We arrested them because of what the store detective said. It was Constable Walker who actually arrested them. We were acting on the information received. We act on information that we receive. If we are not satisfied with it we don't act upon it. We take the responsibility for an arrest that we make on information. The store detective did not say directly to us, "go and arrest them"; we don't take orders from her; we are not her agents. The information that she gave us led me to believe that an offence had been committed; we were acting on it.'

It is pertinent to observe that the evidence of the two police officers was adduced by the plaintiff at the hearing before the learned judge and was accordingly not the subject of cross-examination. It is plain on the facts that Mrs Yates herself did not arrest, imprison, detain or restrain the plaintiff's liberty directly in any way herself. She gave information to the police constables and according to their evidence they acted on it. If she is liable, therefore, it can only be through the police constables either as her agents or, as Mr Clover who appears for the appellants would prefer to put it, as persons whom she procured to act as they did. It is however plain, as I have indicated, that the police constables acted under s 24(6) of the Police and Criminal Evidence Act 1984. It was accepted that they had reasonable suspicion and acted in pursuance of that section and it is accepted that their action was proper. It, therefore, is correct, as the learned judge observed, that a somewhat anomalous situation arises if the appellant's case is correct, since the defendant would be liable for an act of persons who were not themselves liable in respect of what they had done.

The high watermark of the appellant's case derives from answers which Mrs Yates gave when she was cross-examined by counsel for the plaintiff. In the course of a series of answers she said that she expected information given by a store detective such as herself to carry weight with police officers. She intended and expected the police officers to act upon it. They had always done so in the past. She had never known of any occasion when they had failed to do so and accordingly she regarded the arrest as made on her behalf or for her.

We, nonetheless, as I repeat again, have a case in which the constables, according to them, exercised their own judgments and effected the arrest pursuant to s 24(6) of the 1984 Act.

Mr Clover complains that the judge wrongly withdrew the case from the jury but does not, I think, quarrel with the test which it was proper for the learned judge to apply, namely that he was certainly entitled and probably bound to withdraw the case from a jury if in all the circumstances, and on the evidence that had been given, a decision for the plaintiffs would be quashed upon appeal to this court as being either wrong in law or perverse.

The way in which the learned judge put it in the course of his judgment appears most clearly in two passages, the first of which is where he said:

'I was invited on behalf of the plaintiffs at the close of the evidence when submissions were being made to me to put an issue to the jury along these lines; did the officers make the arrests for the store detective on her behalf at her express or implied request? That issue is directed to the officers making the arrests. The arresting officer, Constable Walker, told the court that he was acting under s 24(6) and his colleague confirmed it. Of course, as I well appreciate, I have to look at the whole of the evidence, but I am unable to find any sufficient evidence upon which the jury could reasonably find otherwise than as the officers said.'

The learned judge then referred to the evidence again and to various authorities to which I will come and at the end of his judgment said this:

'In the circumstances which I have set out I am unable to put the suggested question, or indeed any other question, to the jury and I am therefore withdrawing the case from them Learned counsel for the plaintiffs put the ultimate question in the case in his opening to the jury in this way, whether the store detective is responsible in law for what the police did, namely arresting and detaining the plaintiffs; in my judgment that question must be answered in the negative. Accordingly, there will be judgment for the second defendants against each of the plaintiffs.'

The authorities to which the learned judge made reference have been the subject of consideration in this court. The first of them in order of time is the authority of *Aitken v Bedwell* (1827) M & M 68, 173 ER 1084. The case was one in which the master of an English merchant vessel lying in Odessa had procured that one of the members of his crew should be taken ashore and subjected to severe physical punishment at the hands of the Russian authorities. Lord Tenterden CJ summing-up to the jury put the issue in this way:

'The plaintiff contends that what was done on shore was the act of the captain, the defendant says it was the act of the Russian authorities only. The question for you is, Whether the punishment inflicted on shore was done by the constituted authorities, on the mere complaint of the defendant, or whether the defendant was the actor and immediate promoter of it? If you think the defendant merely preferred his complaint, and left the constituted authorities to act as they thought fit, the defendant is entitled to your verdict; if, on the other hand, you think he did more, and was active in promoting and causing the punishment to be inflicted, then he is answerable in this form of action.'

Following that direction the verdict was given for the plaintiff, the evidence having been very clear that when the punishment was administered the defendant was himself standing by and ordering the punishment and throughout taking an active part in the proceedings on shore. Accordingly, even in that early authority one sees the germ of a principle that what distinguishes the case in which a defendant is liable from a case in which he is not is whether he has merely given information to a properly constituted authority on which that authority may act or not as it decides or whether he has himself been the instigator, promoter and active inciter of the action that follows.

The second authority in course of time is *Grinham v Willey* (1858) 4 H & N 496, 157 ER 934. The case was one in which a barmaid was detained on an accusation that she was party to a theft or receiving of stolen property. The complaint was made against her by the defendant who, it appears, summoned the police and himself signed the charge sheet in which the details of the offence were set out. The question as to whether in those circumstances the defendant was liable for the false imprisonment of the plaintiff was the subject of consideration by a number of judges. Pollock CB himself ruled (4 H & N 496 at 499, 157 ER 934 at 934):

'A person ought not to be held responsible in trespass, unless he directly and immediately causes the imprisonment.'

Martin B opined that—

'there should be no rule, upon the ground that the policeman must be taken to have given a true account of the matter. If so, the mere writing of the defendant's name on the charge sheet does not make a defendant a trespasser.' (See 4 H & N 496 at 499, 157 ER 934 at 934.)

Bramwell B put it in this way (4 H & N 496 at 499–500, 157 ER 934 at 934):

'An offence was committed; the defendant sent for a policeman, who made inquiry, and on his own authority arrested the plaintiff. The defendant signed the charge sheet; but in doing so he did nothing but obey the direction of the police. It may have been hard upon the plaintiff that she was imprisoned, but it was the act of the constable.'

In that decision also the line seems to have been drawn at the point where the person actually effecting the arrest makes the decision to do so.

Taking the cases chronologically, the third case is *Meering v Grahame-White Aviation Co Ltd* (1920) 122 LT 44. Warrington LJ giving the first judgment said (at 47):

> 'I think that that evidence satisfies me that the officers of the defendant company did not give the plaintiff in charge, but that in that matter the Metropolitan Police acted on their own responsibility, and by virtue of the powers which were conferred upon them as police constables. That being so, the arrest of the plaintiff by them was not wrongful, because I think that they had at the time they arrested him sufficient reasonable ground for suspecting that a felony had been committed, and that the plaintiff had been involved in the commission of that felony. I think, therefore, that the arrest by the Metropolitan Police was not wrongful, was made on their own responsibility, and not as agents of the defendant company.'

Duke LJ said (at 50–51):

> 'The causes of action which were alleged were two: The first was a claim of damages for false imprisonment. In the statement of claim there was alleged a false imprisonment of the plaintiff by the officers of the Metropolitan Police, acting at the instance and under the direction or at the request of the defendants, and that was the ground of claim in respect of false imprisonment. To my mind it is very significant that there was no other ground of claim. So far as that matter of the alleged false imprisonment is concerned, it is necessary to consider whether the facts as they appear afford any proof of the allegation that the defendants requested or directed the officers of the Metropolitan Police to arrest the plaintiff. The police have specific duties and specific powers in the matter of arrest for the purpose of enforcement of the criminal law. In this case it was clear that the prosecution had been instituted by the defendants. It was not disputed that the defendants had left it to the police to do what they considered necessary. Nothing more than that was proved, as I think, and in that state of the case, my view of the matter is that the arrest on the part of the police which follows the placing of the case in their hands to do their duty is not an arrest by a private prosecutor, and is an arrest by the police.'

The third judgment was that of Atkin LJ. He said (at 55):

> 'But the main imprisonment that was complained of in the pleadings, and that which no doubt was that which gave rise to the substantial complaint, was the imprisonment which took the form of arrest by the detective officer, the plaintiff's removal—conveyance the police called it— to the railway station, and locking him up in a cell on a February night and bringing him before the justices the next morning. I think that can only be brought home to the defendants by establishing that the police acted under their direction and with their authority, which comes to the same thing.'

In that case, therefore, although somewhat different language is used, the essential test that is applied is the same, namely whether the defendant gave the information to a prosecuting authority so that what followed was the result of that prosecuting authority or whether the defendants themselves were responsible for the acts that followed.

The fourth of the cases that I should mention, and the most recent, is *Pike v Waldrum and Peninsula & Oriental Steam Navigation Co* [1952] 1 Lloyd's Rep 431. In that case the master of a vessel had in effect put a member of the crew ashore at Hobart in Australia and put strong pressure on the local authorities in Hobart to detain the crew member which they did, as it was held, unlawfully. There was, therefore, no question whatever but that the master of the vessel was calling for punishment of the crew member and that the local authorities acted improperly in acceding to that request. The test which was formulated by Barry J in the course of a lengthy judgment was put in this way (at 454):

> 'I must now turn to what I consider to be the more difficult problem which concerns the defendants' responsibility in law for the illegal arrest and imprisonment of the plaintiff that was carried out under the orders of the Naval Officer-in-Charge. Mr. Berryman contended that, under the Regulation, the Naval Officer-in-Charge had a discretion as to whether or not to order an arrest, and as this discretionary power was interposed between the acts of the first defendant and the arrest itself, the defendants are under no liability for the plaintiff's illegal arrest and imprisonment. He cited a number of authorities and relied in particular upon the case of *Harnett v. Bond and Another*,([1925] AC 669, [1925] All ER Rep 110). The order or warrant issued by the Naval Officer-in-Charge was, he submitted, equivalent to a warrant or other judicial order of a Court of Justice, which is clearly a *novus actus interveniens* absolving the person at whose instance it has been obtained from any action for false imprisonment.'

He then deals with an authority to which I need not refer and continues:

> 'I agree with the plaintiff's submission that the functions of the Naval Officer-in-Charge were more closely akin to those of a police officer or other executive official who is entitled to exercise some independent judgment, but not a judicial discretion, before taking an accused person into custody. The authorities cited to me, to which I need not refer in detail, establish quite clearly to my mind that a person who requests a police officer to take some other person into custody may be liable to an action for false imprisonment; not so if he merely gives information upon which the constable decides to make an arrest.'

That case was decided against the defendant on the facts but the principle upon which the learned judge relied appears plainly from that passage.

Accordingly, as it would seem to me, the question which arose for the decision of the learned judge in this case was whether there was information properly to be considered by the jury as to whether what Mrs Yates did went beyond laying information before police officers for them to take such action as they thought fit and amounted to some direction, or procuring, or direct request, or direct encouragement that they should act by way of arresting these defendants. He decided that there was no evidence which went beyond the giving of information. Certainly there was no express request. Certainly there was no encouragement. Certainly there was no discussion of any kind as to what action the police officers should take.

The crux of Mr Clover's submission is that this case is different from the case in which an ordinary member of the public gives information to a police officer because this is a store detective, somebody better informed than an ordinary member of the public as to what was likely to happen upon making a complaint, and somebody with a very clear intention and expectation as to what would happen. No doubt the store detective did have an intention and expectation as to what would happen. The fact remains that the learned judge to my mind quite correctly held that what Mrs Yates did and said in no way went beyond the mere giving of information, leaving it to the officers to exercise a discretion which on their unchallenged evidence they did as to whether they should take any action or not.

In those circumstances the learned judge was, as I think, entirely correct to withdraw the matter from the jury since it seems to me inevitable that had he left it to the jury, and had the jury found for the plaintiff, that verdict would have been open to challenge in this court which would have led to its being overruled. I, therefore, dismiss this appeal.

STAUGHTON LJ. Section 24(6) of the Police and Criminal Evidence Act 1984 provides that where a constable has reasonable grounds for suspecting that an arrestable offence has been committed he may arrest without a warrant anyone whom he has reasonable grounds for suspecting to be guilty of the offence. That applied to Pc Walker, who was the person who physically arrested Miss Davidson and Mr Halford. On that ground proceedings against the police were abandoned. That subsection could not apply to Mrs Yates, the store detective, because she was not a constable. In other circumstances she might have had the power of arrest under s 24(4), which enables any person to arrest without a warrant anyone whom he has reasonable grounds for suspecting to be committing such an offence. At the time of the arrest the offence, if there had been one, was no longer being committed.

Section 24(5) might have applied to Mrs Yates. That provides that when an arrestable offence has been committed a person may arrest without a warrant anyone whom he has reasonable grounds to suspect is guilty of it. But there had been no offence committed in this case. So Mrs Yates had no power of arrest by the time that these two persons were in the cafe.

Was there any evidence to go to the jury that she did arrest Miss Davidson and Mr Halford? It was not she who physically detained them. That was Pc Walker. She was not even there; but she had given information to the police officers and had pointed out Miss Davidson and Mr Halford to them.

In those circumstances, like Sir Thomas Bingham MR, I would refer to the passage in the judgment of Barry J in *Pike and Waldrum & Peninsular & Oriental Steam Navigation Company* [1952] 1 Lloyd's Rep 431 at 454:

'The authorities cited to me, to which I need not refer in detail, establish quite clearly to my mind that the person who requests a police officer to take some other person into custody may be liable to an action for false imprisonment; not so if he merely gives information upon which the constable decides to make an arrest.'

Whether a request by itself is sufficient to make a person liable does not arise in this case. What is clear in the passage I have read is that merely giving information is not enough. That does not give rise to false imprisonment. Mrs Yates did no more than that. However much one may look at evidence and analyse what possible consequences might or would arise from the information which she gave, the fact is that all she did was give the information.

I too would dismiss this appeal.

WAITE LJ. I agree the appeal should be dismissed for the reasons given by the Sir Thomas Bingham MR and Staughton LJ.

Appeal dismissed.

L I Zysman Esq   Barrister.

Martin v Watson

COURT OF APPEAL, CIVIL DIVISION
RALPH GIBSON, MCCOWAN AND HOBHOUSE LJJ
9 DECEMBER 1993, 21 JANUARY 1994

Decision of the Court of Appeal reversed.
[1995] 3 W.L.R. 318, H.L.(E.)

Malicious prosecution – Action – Essentials to action for malicious prosecution – Setting law in motion – Defendant providing false information to police – Police charging plaintiff with indecent exposure – Prosecution offering no evidence at hearing of charge – Plaintiff bringing action for malicious prosecution against defendant – Whether defendant setting law in motion – Whether defendant liable for malicious prosecution of plaintiff.

The plaintiff and defendant were neighbours between whom there had been a history of bad feeling for some 13 years culminating in the defendant making a complaint to the police that the plaintiff had indecently exposed himself to her. The plaintiff was arrested and charged with the offence of exposing his person with intent to insult, contrary to s 4 of the Vagrancy Act 1824. At the hearing of the charge the prosecution offered no evidence and the magistrates dismissed the charge. The plaintiff then brought an action against the defendant in the county court for malicious prosecution. The judge found that the defendant had maliciously made a false allegation against the plaintiff and held that the defendant, having been actively instrumental in setting the law in motion against the plaintiff, was to be regarded as a prosecutor in setting the law in motion against him. The judge awarded the plaintiff damages of £3,500. The defendant appealed to the Court of Appeal.

Held – (McCowan LJ dissenting) A person who made an allegation to the police knowing that the allegation was untrue with the intention that the police should act against the person accused was nevertheless not 'setting the law in motion' and was not the prosecutor for the purposes of the tort of malicious prosecution. For an action for malicious prosecution to succeed it was not sufficient for the plaintiff to show that the defendant maliciously provided false evidence with the intent that a prosecution should follow. Instead, it was necessary to show that the defendant had been actively instrumental in the application to the relevant judicial authority. The actual prosecution of the plaintiff had been undertaken by the police and the only steps in the prosecution had been taken by them. Accordingly, the defendant's involvement, which amounted to holding herself out as willing to give untruthful evidence in order to secure the conviction of the plaintiff, did not amount to the malicious prosecution of the plaintiff. The appeal would accordingly be allowed (see p 616 e, p 624 g to p 625 a h, p 629 b, p 631 d to f, p 633 d, p 634 c d, p 636 j to p 637 a and p 639 h to p 640 a f, post).

Notes
For malicious prosecution, see 45 Halsbury's Laws (4th edn) paras 1340–1369.

Cases referred to in judgments
Austin v Dowling (1870) LR 5 CP 534, CA.
Barber v Lesiter (1859) 7 CBNS 175, 141 ER 782.
Black v Mackenzie (1917) 36 NZLR 729, NZ SC.
Casey v Automobiles Renault Canada Ltd (1966) 54 DLR (2d) 600, Can SC.
Clements v Ohrly (1848) 2 Car & K 686, 175 ER 287.
Commercial Union Assurance Co of NZ Ltd v Lamont [1989] 3 NZLR 187, NZ CA.
Commonwealth Life Assurance Society Ltd v Brain (1935) 53 CLR 343, Aust HC.
Danby v Beardsley (1880) 43 LT 603.
Davidson v Chief Constable of North Wales Police [1994] 2 All ER 597, CA.
Dawkins v Lord Rokeby (1873) LR 8 QB 255.
Elsee v Smith (1822) 2 Chit 304.
Evans v London Hospital Medical College [1981] 1 All ER 715, [1981] 1 WLR 184.
Fanzelow v Kerr (1896) 14 NZLR 660, NZ CA.
Fitzjohn v Mackinder (1861) 9 CBNS 505, 142 ER 199.
Hargreaves v Bretherton [1958] 3 All ER 122, [1959] 1 QB 45, [1958] 3 WLR 463.
Harris v Warne (1879) 4 CPD 125, CA.
Hill v Anderton [1982] 2 All ER 963, [1983] 1 AC 328, [1982] 3 WLR 331, HL.
Lilley v Roney (1892) 61 LJQB 727, DC.
Lincoln v Daniels [1961] 3 All ER 740, [1962] 1 QB 237, [1961] 3 WLR 866, CA.
Malz v Rosen [1966] 2 All ER 10, [1966] 1 WLR 1008.
Marrinan v Vibart [1962] 1 All ER 869, [1963] 1 QB 234, [1962] 2 WLR 1224; affd [1962] 3 All ER 380, [1963] 1 QB 528, [1962] 3 WLR 912, CA.
Pandit Gaya Parshad Tewari v Sardar Bhagat Singh (1908) 24 TLR 884, PC.
R v Rowell [1978] 1 All ER 665, [1978] 1 WLR 132, CA.
Reid v Webster (1967) 59 DLR (2d) 189, Can SC.
Roy v Prior [1970] 2 All ER 729, [1971] AC 470, [1970] 3 WLR 202, HL.
Sewell v National Telephone Co Ltd [1907] 1 KB 557, CA.
Watson v M'Ewan [1905] AC 480, [1904–7] All ER Rep 1, HL.
Watters v Pacific Delivery Service Ltd (1964) 42 DLR (2d) 661, Can SC.

Cases also cited or referred to in skeleton arguments
Aitken v Bedwell (1827) M & M 68, 173 ER 1084.
Beckett v Walker [1986] CLY 129.
Johnstone v Sutton (1786) 1 TR 510, 99 ER 1225.
Palmer v Durnford Ford (a firm) [1992] 2 All ER 122, [1992] QB 483.
Soadwah v Obeng [1966] GLR 338, Ghana SC.

Appeal
The defendant, Ulka Watson, appealed with leave granted by Ralph Gibson LJ on 14 May 1993 from the order of Judge Goodman on 13 July 1992 whereby it was ordered that the defendant pay to the plaintiff, John Leonard Martin, damages of £3,500 in respect of the plaintiff's claim for malicious prosecution against the defendant and the plaintiff was ordered to pay the defendant £550 damages in respect of the defendant's counterclaim against the plaintiff of

malicious prosecution. The facts are set out in the judgment of Ralph Gibson
LJ.

Richard Christie (instructed by *C R Burton & Co*) for Mrs Watson.
Jonathan P Rose (instructed by *Wellers*, Bromley) for Mr Martin.

Cur adv vult

21 January 1994. The following judgments were delivered.

RALPH GIBSON LJ. This is an appeal by Mrs Ulka Watson, the defendant in proceedings in Bromley County Court, from the order of Judge Goodman made on 13 July 1992. By his order the judge gave judgment for the plaintiff, Mr John Martin, the respondent in this court, in the sum of £3,500 on the grounds that the defendant had maliciously prosecuted him for an offence of indecent exposure when to her knowledge he had not committed any such offence. I shall refer to the parties as defendant and plaintiff. By his order, the judge also gave judgment in favour of the defendant on her counterclaim for the sum of £550 on the grounds that the plaintiff had maliciously prosecuted her for an offence of assault when to his knowledge she had not committed that offence.

The defendant sought leave to appeal against the judge's order on many different grounds with reference to various issues of fact and of law. That application came before me, as a single judge of this court, on 18 May 1993. The order made by me was that leave to appeal was granted upon one point of law only, namely that the judge, in finding for the plaintiff, misdirected himself in that, on the facts found, it could not be said in law that the defendant set the law in motion against the plaintiff and was thus his prosecutor. It seemed to me then that the point of law was bad and essentially unarguable and I said so. I was wrong. The point of law is important, difficult and has been very well argued by Mr Christie. I gave leave to appeal because there was no decision of an appellate court in this country which dealt clearly with the question and it seemed, for that reason, right to grant leave.

Before describing the facts as found by the judge it is necessary to state in greater detail the point of law upon which the appeal turns and to place it in its context. It was common ground throughout the proceedings before the judge, and in this court, that the essential elements of the tort of malicious prosecution are as stated in *Clerk and Lindsell on Torts* (16th edn, 1989) para 19-05:

'In an action of malicious prosecution the plaintiff must show first that he was prosecuted by the defendant, that is to say, that the law was set in motion against him on a criminal charge; secondly, that the prosecution was determined in his favour; thirdly, that it was without reasonable and probable cause; fourthly, that it was malicious. The onus of proving every one of these is on the plaintiff.'

The main contentions of Mr Christie for the defendant have been (i) that, on the authorities, that which she was held by the judge to have done did not amount to 'setting the law in motion' against the plaintiff; and (ii) that, as a matter of public policy, to be derived from the principles of the law of tort in connected areas of the law, that which she was held to have done should not be held to amount to proof that she was 'the prosecutor'.

The history of the dispute

(1) The parties were at all material times neighbours. The plaintiff lives with his wife at 1 Denver Close, Orpington and the defendant lives with her husband at 231 Crofton Lane. The fence which is at the side of the plaintiff's back garden forms the boundary at the bottom of the defendant's garden. Each couple accused the other of unneighbourly conduct over much of the 13 years of their proximity. The plaintiff retired from work with British Telecom in April 1991. The defendant has long been a housewife living at home.

(2) The act of indecent exposure for which the plaintiff was prosecuted was said by the defendant to have occurred on 19 or 20 July 1989. She called the police. She made a statement to Pc Cratchley. On 21 July Det Con Haynes of CID took a further statement from her. In consequence of what she said, she was asked to, and did, attend at the magistrates' court on 27 July where Det Con Haynes obtained a warrant for the arrest of the plaintiff upon a charge that he had exposed his person with intent to insult the defendant contrary to s 4 of the Vagrancy Act 1824. (Reference is made in the judgment to 20 July. The charge sheet refers to 19 July. It is not suggested that anything turns on this discrepancy.) The plaintiff was arrested on 9 August and interviewed at the police station. He was bailed to appear at the magistrates' court on 10 August. On that day the Crown Prosecution Service appeared to conduct the proceedings. No evidence was offered and the case was dismissed.

(3) The allegation of assault made by the plaintiff against the defendant arose out of an incident on 18 August 1989. The incident was reported to the police by both sides. The police decided to 'leave them to their civil remedies'. Proceedings in the magistrates' court were, however, issued by both, each against the other. The plaintiff laid his information on 27 October 1989. On the hearing of the summons issued by the defendant against the plaintiff, he was on 4 May 1990 convicted and fined. He thereupon withdrew his information and summons by letter of 17 May 1990 and the defendant then advanced her counterclaim in the proceedings in respect of that malicious prosecution.

(4) The plaintiff had begun his action on 20 February 1990. His pleading alleged that the defendant had laid the information against him on 27 July 1989 and the particulars of malice included an assertion that she had repeatedly, within the last two years, made similar false allegations, the last having been made on 7 August 1989. He also alleged that the police officers who had arrested and interrogated him 'were acting as agents of the defendant pursuant to her information'. By her defence, the defendant first admitted that she had laid the information while denying malice, but by an amended defence she asserted that, as has been common ground, she had not laid the information and had not herself applied for the warrant which was obtained on 27 July. The plaintiff's claim was not amended to allege that she was, in law, to be treated as the prosecutor in the proceedings against him by reason of any other identified acts. No point has been taken for the defendant with reference to the pleading of the claim. At the outset of the trial before Judge Goodman, Mr Christie, for the defendant, applied for an order striking out the plaintiff's claim on the ground that she had not 'set the criminal proceedings in motion'. That application was rejected. Subsequent events have shown, in my view,

that it would have been useful if the plaintiff had been required to identify in
his pleading the facts and matters relied upon in support of his allegation that
the defendant had been the prosecutor against him.

(5) The action was complicated and lengthened by the investigation by the
parties of many peripheral facts by reference to which it was contended that
the veracity of each was to be tested. The first part of the hearing, in which the
judge heard the evidence and submissions upon the facts, took some seven
days spread over a month. The judge gave judgment upon the issues of fact on
5 December 1991. The hearing was then adjourned for further arguments on
the issues of law. The final judgment was given on 13 July 1992. The
judgments were, in my respectful opinion, prepared with conspicuous care and
skill in a case which presented difficulties with reference to the issues of fact
and law.

(6) Before turning to the facts found by the judge with reference to the
conduct of the defendant, it is right to refer briefly to the conduct of the parties
in this story which has been disgraceful for both of them. The judge called it
'an appalling history'. The plaintiff and his wife were 'largely responsible for
the trouble between the couples'. Further, of course, the plaintiff was
responsible for the incident in which the defendant was assaulted and for the
malicious prosecution by him of her with reference to that incident.

The findings of the judge

I take this account from the judge's judgment of 13 July 1992.

(1) The defendant first complained to the police that the plaintiff had
exposed himself to her in the summer of 1987, but nothing was done about it.
She made a further complaint to the police on 12 July 1988. However, after
discussing it with the police, she said that she did not wish to make a statement,
feeling it better to ignore the plaintiff's actions. Then, on 20 July 1989, the
defendant again called the police following a further alleged act of indecent
exposure by the plaintiff that day. Pc Cratchley called and took a statement
from her that was not before the court. Pc Cratchley returned to the police
station and handed over the defendant's complaint to the crime desk.
Normally this was a type of offence for investigation by the CID rather than by
the uniformed branch. On 21 July Det Con Haynes called on the defendant and
took a further statement from her which was before the court. Her statement
concluded with the words 'I am willing to attend court and give evidence if
required'. The defendant told Det Con Haynes about the alleged incident of
July 1988.

(2) On 27 July 1989 the defendant was asked to attend at the magistrates'
court when Det Con Haynes obtained a warrant for the plaintiff's arrest. The
defendant was not called into court and did not say anything to the magistrate.
The police did not take immediate steps to act on the warrant for reasons
which were not made clear to the court. Det Con Haynes was ill at the time of
the hearing and no evidence from him was before the court.

(3) On 7 August the defendant again called the police to make another
allegation of an act of indecent exposure by the plaintiff. Pc McKiernan called.
He found the defendant's complaint bizarre and unbelievable, and although
she made it clear that she wanted the matter to proceed and was willing to
attend court in respect of that serious allegation, Pc McKiernan reported to the
police station indicating that in his opinion no action should be taken, and no
statement was taken from her on that occasion.

(4) Finally, the defendant said that on the morning of 9 August another act of indecent exposure occurred. She telephoned the police and an officer called and said the matter would be reported. That officer may have taken a statement from the defendant, but that statement, if it existed, was not before the court.

(5) Later on 9 August the plaintiff was arrested and interviewed at the police station. The only record of interview about which evidence was before the court, and which was produced, concerned the alleged incident on 9 August. There were references in that record to 'further questions' and 'further allegation' which suggested that there had been an earlier interview about the alleged incident on 20 July. No witnesses were called about any earlier interview. Det Con Haynes, who was the officer who conducted the only recorded interview, was ill and unable to give evidence. No charge was made about the alleged incident on 9 August, and the plaintiff was only charged regarding the alleged incident of 20 July, for which the warrant had been obtained. He was bailed to appear at the magistrates' court the next day. On 10 August 1989, when he appeared, no evidence was offered and the case was dismissed.

(6) The judge summed up his view of the evidence by saying that, from the actions of the defendant, 'it was all clearly done to get the plaintiff arrested'.

The principles of law applied by the judge

Judge Goodman examined the authorities to which he was referred. They included passages from *Clerk and Lindsell on Torts* (16th edn, 1989) paras 19-05, 19-07, 19-12, *Clements v Ohrly* (1848) 2 Car & K 686, 175 ER 287, *Malz v Rosen* [1966] 2 All ER 10, [1966] 1 WLR 1008, *Danby v Beardsley* (1880) 43 LT 603, *Watters v Pacific Delivery Service Ltd* (1963) 42 DLR (2d) 661, *Casey v Automobiles Renault Canada Ltd* (1965) 54 DLR (2d) 600 at 614, *Reid v Webster* (1966) 59 DLR (2d) 189, *Pandit Gaya Parshad Tewari v Sardar Bhagat Singh* (1908) 24 TLR 884 and *Evans v London Hospital Medical College* [1981] 1 All ER 715, [1981] 1 WLR 184.

The judge stated the principles which he derived from those authorities as follows.

(1) It is not essential to prove that the defendant was herself the actual prosecutor in the sense that she personally applied for the warrant which was duly issued by the magistrate.

(2) The defendant may be liable if she was actively instrumental by representing herself as the prosecutor or by helping, influencing or urging some other person to set the law in motion. This does not necessarily involve signing a charge sheet or some overt act of that kind.

(3) On the other hand, it is not enough merely to show that she made a complaint to a police officer which is followed by an application for a warrant by the police officer, even if the complaint was, to her knowledge, quite untrue and the police officer was unaware that it was untrue. The fact that she was lying goes more to the question of reasonable and probable cause and malice.

(4) He noted the passage in *Clerk and Lindsell on Torts* para 19-12:

'*Deceiving tribunal.* A defendant who makes a maliciously false statement which causes a judicial act like the issue of a search warrant or an order for arrest to the prejudice of the plaintiff will be liable to the plaintiff even though he may not technically have been a prosecutor on the above reasoning.'

The word 'causes' is important, because there must be a continuous chain of causation between the maliciously false statement and the action of the police officer in applying for the warrant or order. That was the issue in this case. That statement was applicable to different torts although under the same generic heading of 'abuse of process'. Making a complaint may be regarded as part and parcel of setting the law in motion, but it depends on what was said, the circumstances in which it was said and the effect that it had.

The conclusion of Judge Goodman
The judge explained his conclusion as follows. The defendant was responsible for calling the police in to deal with her complaint, about which she felt very strongly. She told Pc Cratchley of a serious sexual incident involving her alone, as to which there were obviously no other witnesses, and she signed a written statement to that effect. She clearly wanted the plaintiff to be arrested and dealt with. She repeated her accusation to Det Con Haynes the following day, who took a further written statement from her. Moreover, she indicated to him that she was willing to attend court and give evidence. She did indeed attend court to assist him when he went to apply for the warrant although in the end she was not required to say anything.

The absence of evidence from Det Con Haynes as to the history of the matter leading up to his obtaining the warrant was unfortunate and had made the judge's task more difficult than it otherwise would have been. However, in the light of the defendant's further untruthful accusations about the plaintiff made to Pc McKiernan on 7 August, and to another officer about an alleged incident on 9 August, when nothing seemed to be happening about executing the warrant, as well as her wholly unfounded accusations to the police about earlier alleged incidents and her evidence generally, the judge held that she was clearly determined that action should be taken and he was therefore prepared to infer that that must have made such an impression on Det Con Haynes as to result in him applying for the warrant, notwithstanding the fact that the case depended on her word alone; and, she was willing to give evidence and to accompany Det Con Haynes to the magistrates' court on 27 July to assist him in obtaining the warrant.

The judge therefore held that the defendant was indeed actively instrumental in setting the law in motion against the plaintiff. To hold otherwise would, in his view, be an affront to a proper sense of justice. She wanted the plaintiff to be arrested and dealt with from the start, and that is what she achieved in causing Det Con Haynes to obtain the warrant from the magistrate. She was the only person who could testify about the alleged indecent exposure. She was therefore to be regarded as a prosecutor in setting the law in motion against him.

The submissions for the defendant
Mr Christie's submissions, were, in summary, as follows.

(1) The requirement of proof that the defendant prosecuted the plaintiff is a separate and independent requirement that is not satisfied merely by proving that she was malicious, and willing to give perjured evidence against him, and wished and intended that he be prosecuted.

(2) The law, as a matter of policy, denies any right to damages to someone who is a victim only of perjured evidence. The only sanction is a prosecution for the criminal offence of perjury (see *Watson v M'Ewan* [1905] AC 480 at 486, [1904–7] All ER Rep 1 at 3, *Hargreaves v Bretherton* [1958] 3 All ER 122 at 128, [1959] 1 QB 45 at 52, *Marrinan v Vibart* [1962] 1 All ER 869, [1963] 1 QB 234, on appeal [1962] 3 All ER 380, [1963] 1 QB 528 and *Evans v London Hospital Medical College* [1981] 1 All ER 715, [1981] 1 WLR 184).

(3) If a person in the position of this defendant makes an untrue and malicious allegation to the police with the intention of causing the police to pursue, if they so decide, prosecution of her victim, but the prosecution is not initiated, or is terminated before she gives perjured evidence, she may still be prosecuted for the offence of attempting to pervert the course of justice (see *R v Rowell* [1978] 1 All ER 665, [1978] 1 WLR 132 and *Archbold's Pleading, Evidence and Practice in Criminal Cases* (44th edn, 1992) vol 2, p 3028, para 28-119).

(4) By making her statements to police officers, with malicious intent, the defendant did not for the purposes of this tort prosecute the plaintiff: she did not 'set the law in motion' against him because that can only be done by an appeal to some person clothed with judicial authority (see *Clerk and Lindsell on Torts* para 19-07, as approved by Drake J in *Evans v London Hospital Medical College*; see also *Danby v Beardsley* (1880) 43 LT 603). Making a statement to a police officer, who is a ministerial and not a judicial officer, does not cause a prosecution to begin.

(5) The fact that such a statement is made falsely and maliciously is irrelevant to the question whether what is done constitutes setting the law in motion.

(6) Further, the defendant neither said nor did anything to show that she took responsibility for the prosecution, such as by laying the information or signing the charge sheet. The police exercised their discretion as to whether to prosecute or not. In what they did they were not acting at the behest of defendant: reference was made to *Davidson v Chief Constable of North Wales Police* [1994] 2 All ER 597. In particular, before the warrant was obtained, the allegations of this defendant were considered by a uniformed officer and by a detective constable. The further complaints made by this defendant, which were not pursued by the police, are irrelevant to the question.

(7) The policy of the law should cause the court not to expand the definition of 'prosecution' for this purpose. That course is required not for the protection of complainants who are, or who are held to have been, dishonest and malicious but for the protection of all complainants, in particular a complainant who, like most women victims of sexual offences, is the only direct witness of the alleged offence and who may reasonably fear civil proceedings against her if her evidence is not accepted by the prosecutor as sufficient to justify continuation of the prosecution or by the jury at trial.

The submissions for the plaintiff

For the plaintiff, Mr Rose, in substance, contended that the judge was right for the reasons which he gave. It was conceded for the plaintiff that it was the police officer who actually set the law in motion by obtaining the warrant from the magistrates' court but, it was submitted, a person who actively encourages a police officer to set the law in motion, as in this case, can be liable for malicious prosecution. The determination of whether a person is the prosecutor should be a question of fact, namely whether that person has been actively instrumental in setting the law in motion, and should not depend upon who technically has conduct of the prosecution.

Conclusion

We were referred in argument to additional authorities including *Austin v Dowling* (1870) LR 5 CP 534 and to decisions in the courts of Ghana and of Zambia which are cited and discussed in an article by Gilbert Kodilinye 'Setting in motion malicious prosecutions: the Commonwealth experience' (1987) 36 ICLQ 157. These decisions of Commonwealth courts have provided valuable assistance in emphasising the importance of policy in determining the formulation of the test for deciding whether a complainant is shown to have been the prosecutor and the relevance in that test of the fact that the complainant knows the allegation to be untrue. I have derived much assistance from the judgments in the Court of Appeal of New Zealand (Richardson, McMullen and Barker JJ) in *Commercial Union Assurance Co of NZ Ltd v Lamont* [1989] 3 NZLR 187, to which I shall refer later. This case was not cited to us but was mentioned in Clayton and Tomlinson *Civil Actions against the Police* (2nd edn, 1992) p 291, to which we were referred.

For many years the law has been stated in the books substantially as it now appears in *Clerk and Lindsell on Torts*, that is to say that the law must be shown to have been set in motion by the defendant, but there has been no clear statement of what conduct will suffice for that purpose. Thus, in 25 *Halsbury's Laws* (3rd edn) para 684:

'A prosecution exists [for the purposes of malicious prosecution] where a criminal charge is made before a judicial officer or tribunal, and any person who makes or is actively instrumental in the making or prosecuting of such a charge is deemed to prosecute it and is called the prosecutor.'

Reference is there made to cases including *Danby v Beardsley* (1880) 43 LT 603.

There is, I think, no decision of the courts of this country which clearly indicates the answer to the question raised in this case. There is certainly no decision binding upon this court.

Next, and if that is right, the question raised by this case is, in my judgment, to be answered by finding that answer which best serves the demands of conflicting principles of policy. It seems to me to be well stated in Fleming *The Law of Torts* (8th edn, 1992) p 609:

'The tort of malicious prosecution is dominated by the problem of balancing two countervailing interests of high social importance: safeguarding the individual from being harassed by unjustifiable litigation and encouraging citizens to aid in law enforcement. On one side, it needs no emphasis that the launching of scandalous charges is apt to expose the accused to serious injury, involving his honour and self-respect as well as his reputation and credit in the community. Malicious prosecution, therefore, bears close resemblance to defamation, both being infringements of essentially the same complex of interests on the part of the plaintiff. On the other side, however, is the competing interest of society in the efficient enforcement of the criminal law which requires that private persons who co-operate in bringing would be offenders to justice, no less than prosecutors, should be adequately protected against the prejudice which is likely to ensue from termination of the prosecution in favour of the accused. Moreover, there exist other sanctions against misconducting informants. [Making false statements to the police and perjury are crimes, and defamation is a tort.] So much weight has been attached to this consideration that the action for malicious prosecution is held on tighter reign than any other in the law of torts. Incidentally, it may also explain why this action was never absorbed into the law of defamation. For, though we have seen that the stringent liability of defamation is tempered by privileges when the importance of encouraging free speech outweighs the competing value of vindicating those unjustly defamed, it was probably felt that this would be an insufficient safeguard for the social interests here at stake. Thus, malicious prosecution has remained a distinct cause of action which, in several particulars, notably in the allocation of the burden of proof and the functions between judge and jury, affords greater protection to private persons who initiate criminal proceedings than is accorded by conditional privileges to publish defamation.'

Reference is also there made by Professor Fleming to other subsidiary policies including 'the desirability of letting the disposal of the principal litigation settle all collateral matters'. Thus, in this case, upon the making by the defendant of her deliberately false allegations, a police officer decided to initiate a prosecution for the summary offence. It was stopped at the first appearance of the plaintiff by the intervention of the Prosecution Service who, no doubt, judged that it would not be in the public interest to pursue a matter of that nature in which, by reason of the burden of proof, the prospects of success were small at best. If the rule of law is as the defendant contends that it is, and ought to be, that decision in the principal litigation would not settle all collateral matters: the defendant would not be prevented from pursuing her claim in civil proceedings if her false allegation gives rise to an arguable claim in tort; but the plaintiff would have no civil claim in respect of the prosecution and the question whether any action should be taken to punish the defendant for the making of her false allegation would be decided by a person able to bring objective judgment to bear with due regard to the public interest. It is very probable that the decision by any prosecuting authority would be against prosecution in the absence of independent evidence. The defendant, upon this supposition, would only have been exposed to the risk of civil proceedings for malicious prosecution if the police officer had decided not to initiate the prosecution and if the defendant had thereafter herself signed the charge sheet or laid the information, and if the court had permitted proceedings to issue

The question whether, if the defendant cannot be treated as having prosecuted the plaintiff so as to be liable for malicious prosecution, the defendant nevertheless would have been liable for the slander uttered by her in making her complaint to the police officer, was not separately examined in argument. It seems that it is only qualified privilege which applies to a statement made to a police officer by way of reporting a complaint (see *Gatley on Libel and Slander* (8th edn, 1981) p 205, para 484 and the cases there cited). A formal complaint which initiated proceedings under the Solicitors Act Rules 1889 was held to be absolutely privileged (see *Lilley v Roney* (1892) 61 LJQB 727); but a communication by a complainant sent to the Bar Council containing allegations against a barrister, with a view to the communication being sent to

the relevant Inn of Court, was not a step in proceedings and was therefore the
subject of qualified privilege at best (see *Lincoln v Daniels* [1961] 3 All ER 740 at
752–753, [1962] 1 QB 237 at 263 where Devlin J said):

'It is not at all easy to determine the scope and extent of the principle in
Watson v. *M'Ewan* ([1905] AC 480, [1904–7] All ER Rep 1). I have come to
the conclusion that the privilege that covers proceedings in a court of
justice ought not to be extended to matters outside those proceedings
except where it is strictly necessary to do so in order to protect those who
are to participate in the proceedings from a flank attack.'

If the laying down of the rule for which the defendant contends has the
result of decreasing the number of justiciable issues arising from a dispute
between neighbours which may require to be resolved at public expense, that
consequence may be regarded by many as in the public interest. If, however,
the law, in the terms in which it has been long defined, requires the court to
find that this defendant was the prosecutor of the plaintiff, then considerations
with reference to the public interest in not increasing the amount of litigation
must be reserved for assessment in an exercise of law reform. If the position is
that the rule of law is not clear, and must be decided by reference to the policy
of the law, such considerations are relevant to the main questions of policy to
which I have referred.

The test, as it has long been stated, is requirement of proof that the
defendant was 'actively instrumental in the making or prosecuting of a charge',
as derived from *Danby v Beardsley*. If the defendant, with the intention of
causing a police officer to initiate a prosecution against the plaintiff, makes an
allegation which (1) if believed is likely to cause the police officer to initiate the
prosecution; (2) is to her knowledge false; and (3) the police officer is thereby
caused to initiate the prosecution, then, in my judgment, there is nothing in the
test as formulated which obviously prevents a finding that such a defendant
has been 'actively instrumental in the making of the charge'. It is first
necessary to see whether the cases decided in our courts indicate that such a
view of the meaning of the words is not or should not be open to the court.

This inquiry can start, I think, with *Fitzjohn v Mackinder* (1861) 9 CBNS 505,
142 ER 199. The facts in the case were complicated. Mackinder sued Fitzjohn
in the county court for a debt. Fitzjohn claimed a set-off, in answer to which
Mackinder produced his ledger containing an acknowledgment signed, as he
swore, by Fitzjohn. Fitzjohn denied the signature which he averred to be a
forgery; but the judge, induced partly by the statement of Mackinder and partly
by the conduct of Fitzjohn before him, disbelieved Fitzjohn's denial and
committed Fitzjohn for trial for perjury under s 19 of the Criminal Justice
Administration Act 1851. The judge bound Mackinder over to prosecute.
Fitzjohn was accordingly tried for perjury and acquitted. Fitzjohn then
brought an action against Mackinder for maliciously and without probable
cause causing him to be prosecuted on an unfounded charge. It was held on
appeal in the Exchequer Chamber by Cockburn CJ, Bramwell and Channell
BB, Wightman and Blackburn JJ dissenting, that the action was maintainable
because the committal of Fitzjohn and his prosecution for perjury were the
result of the wrongful and malicious act of Mackinder.

After the county court judge committed the plaintiff for trial for perjury, the
defendant clearly took part in the further prosecution of the plaintiff before the
grand jury and, once the majority of the judges rejected the defence raised by

the defendant that he was acting pursuant to the order imposed upon him by
the judge that he prosecute the plaintiff, the defendant's liability was clear.
The first count against the defendant, however, alleged that the defendant had
by his false evidence before the judge caused and procured the judge to direct
that the plaintiff be prosecuted (which, I add, may be compared with the
allegation that this defendant in the present appeal caused the police officer to
initiate the prosecution). The answer to this point was seen by the minority as
being that the defendant had not intended to procure the prosecution: his
intention was simply to win the case and he was in fact greatly embarrassed by
the judge's direction to him to prosecute. It is to be noted that the answer to
the point was not that a prosecution cannot be commenced save by a formal
application such as by signing a charge or laying an information. Cockburn CJ,
whose decision was with the majority, said (9 CBNS 505 at 527–530, 142 ER 199
at 207–209):

'Upon these facts, I am of opinion that the defendant is liable in this
action. I do not feel it necessary to say that so much of the declaration as
charges the defendant with having maliciously procured the order of the
county court judge can be sustained, as it must be taken that the purpose
of the defendant's perjury was, not to cause the plaintiff to be prosecuted,
but simply to defeat the suit; but I am far from holding that it cannot. It is
enough to say that it appears to me that, at all events, the action may be
well maintained as to so much as charges the defendant with having
maliciously and without probable cause preferred an indictment against
the plaintiff, and prosecuted such indictment. It is beyond dispute, that,
independently of the order of the county court judge, the prosecution
would under the circumstances have been malicious. Called upon to
answer in damages for the injury inflicted by it on the plaintiff, the
defendant, in order to avoid the consequences of a proceeding on the face
of it otherwise clearly wrongful and actionable, seeks to protect himself by
shewing that he acted under the order of the county court judge. I am
disposed to [think] ... that it is not competent to the defendant to shelter
himself under this order, seeing that the judge was induced to make it
through his perjury and fraud. To suffer the judge to make such an order
without informing him of the truth, and disabusing his mind of the error
into which he had been led by wilful falsehood, was, as it seems to me, a
fraud upon the judge as well as a wrongful act towards the plaintiff and I
cannot bring myself to think that the defendant should be allowed to
shelter himself under an order having its origin in his own falsehood and
issuing through his own fraud ... But the main argument relied on in
favour of the defendant is that he did not originate the proceedings, or, as
the phrase is, set the law in motion,—the county court judge having,
without any complaint by the defendant with a view to that result, of his
own head directed the prosecution,—and the defendant's position is
compared to that of a stranger unwillingly bound over ... I do not feel at
all pressed by this argument. No doubt, under ordinary circumstances,
where the question of malice is still open, the fact that someone else set
the law in motion would be conclusive in favour of the defendant; or, if the
existence of reasonable and probable cause were in dispute, the fact that a
judge or magistrate had spontaneously bound over the defendant would
go very far to show that the prosecution was a proper one. But this

reasoning can have no application where the maliciousness of the prosecution and the absence of probable cause are necessarily implied in the fact that we have the guilty man pursuing the innocent.'

There is, I think, nothing in that decision to show that a defendant who makes a deliberately false allegation to a person who is able, if he thinks fit, to cause a prosecution to be initiated in respect of the alleged wrongdoing, with the intention of causing the prosecution to be initiated, and who does so, may not be treated as having thereby caused the prosecution to be initiated. There is also nothing in the decision to show that a defendant who so acts may be treated as prosecutor although he had made no application to the court by himself or his agent.

Some 19 years later came *Danby v Beardsley*. It is a puzzling and difficult case, a decision of Lopes and Lindley JJ in the Divisional Court of Common Pleas. Danby was employed by the defendant as groom and coachman and later as gardener but then left his employment. While employed as gardener he lent to his successor in the defendant's service two pairs of horse clippers which he took away with him. The defendant had seen the clippers in his stables and was under the impression that they belonged to him. Having noticed that they were missing, the defendant asked his groom and was told that the clippers belonged to Danby. The defendant, however, said to a policeman, for whom he had sent, 'I've had stolen from me two pairs of clippers and they were last seen in the possession of Danby'. The policeman then made further inquiries and, upon searching Danby's house, found two pairs of clippers which corresponded to the description given by the defendant. Without further communicating with the defendant, the policeman arrested Danby who was taken before the magistrates and committed for trial. The defendant gave evidence against Danby both before the magistrates and at quarter sessions. Danby, upon being acquitted, sued the defendant for false imprisonment and malicious prosecution. At the trial of his action, the judge directed a verdict to be entered for the defendant on the ground that there was no evidence that the defendant was the prosecutor. On appeal, the judge's ruling was upheld.

Before stating the reasons given for the decision, it is to be noted: (1) It was argued for the plaintiff that since there was no precise definition in the books of what is prosecution for this test, it must be a question of fact for the jury. The defendant had been told that the clippers belonged to Danby but he had not told the policeman of that fact. What he said to the policeman carried the inference that Danby had stolen the clippers and that must have been conveyed to the policeman's mind. If the defendant so acted that he intended the law to be put in motion, then, it was submitted, he is the prosecutor. The conduct of the constable was a rational consequence of the defendant's conduct. (2) For the defendant it was argued that it was the duty of any person to state the facts which he knows and the defendant had done no more. The policeman had then acted on his own discretion. There was nothing to show that the defendant did anything more than he was at liberty to do and what it was his duty to do. (3) It is thus clear that there was no reference in argument, as relevant to or sufficient for proof that the defendant was prosecutor, to the allegations which must have been made as foundation for the claim to damages for malicious prosecution, that there was no reasonable or probable cause for the prosecution and that it was malicious. The question of reasonable and probable cause was for decision by the judge but it would be for the jury to decide what were the facts known to the prosecutor before he made the charge including any inference to be drawn from them: see 25 *Halsbury's Laws* (3rd edn) para 698. The issue as to whether the defendant was actuated by spite or ill will, or by some indirect or improper motive, and was thus malicious was for decision by the jury. The defendant, however, may be malicious, without actually knowing or believing that the allegation which he has made against the plaintiff was false. The particular issue in this appeal, namely the relevance and effect of proof that the defendant knew the allegation made by her to be false was, thus, not raised in argument in *Danby v Beardsley* (1880) 43 LT 603.

The reasons given for the decision were as follows. Lopes J observed that there was in the books no express authority as to what a prosecution is. He then posed the question whether there was any evidence to show that the defendant was actively instrumental in putting the law in force. He stated the facts about the clippers and continued (at 604):

'No doubt the defendant thought that the clippers were his and that the plaintiff had stolen them. He sends for a constable and says "I've had stolen from me two pairs of horse clippers and when I last saw them they were in Danby's possession". Thereupon the constable makes enquiries from Gardener and elsewhere and searches the plaintiff's house where he finds two pairs of clippers ... I cannot see upon that state of facts that there is any evidence that the defendant was the prosecutor and the rules should be discharged.'

Lindley LJ agreed with Lopes J.

That which I have referred to as the particular issue in the present case, namely the relevance of the fact that the defendant knew her allegation to be false, was not only not raised but was expressly excluded by the reference by Lopes J to the fact that no doubt the defendant thought that the clippers were his and that the plaintiff had stolen them.

It is not clear from the report how Lopes J was able to proceed upon that presumption. The defendant was told by the groom that the clippers belonged to Danby but the defendant was not obliged to believe the groom. The authority of the decision, however, rests upon the reasons stated. There is nothing in that decision, in my view, which required the judge in this case to hold against this plaintiff on the ground that the defendant who knows that the allegation made by her is false, and who makes it with the intention that the police constable should initiate a prosecution against the plaintiff, cannot in law be held to be the prosecutor merely because she had not herself made direct application to the court. On the other hand, if either judge had thought that, although the defendant had done nothing else which was instrumental in setting the law in motion, yet he could be treated as prosecutor if he had known his allegation to be false, I would have expected reference to be made to the point if only to say that, assuming it to be the case, the plaintiff had not alleged knowledge of falsity.

The next case upon which Mr Christie relied is *Evans v London Hospital Medical College* [1981] 1 All ER 715, [1981] 1 WLR 184. The defendants were London Hospital Medical College and two lecturers in forensic medicine employed by the college. The five-month-old son of the plaintiff died. Post-mortem reports were provided through the Department of Forensic Medicine for the purpose of placing such reports before the police and the Director of Public Prosecutions. On the day that the child died, the post mortem on the infant was carried out during which organs and specimens were removed and examined for toxicological analysis by the defendants. As a result of reports made by the defendants to the police and the DPP the plaintiff was arrested and charged with the murder of her son by morphine poisoning. A further examination on behalf of the plaintiff by Professor Mant showed that it was not possible for there to have been morphine in the organs removed by the defendants at the time of such removal because the morphine would have contaminated all the organs in the body. On receipt of that information the defendants took no action to retract or amend the statements which they had previously made. No evidence was offered against the plaintiff and she was acquitted. The action as first commenced alleged negligence against the defendants. The claim so based was struck out. On appeal, leave was sought to make the alternative allegation of malicious prosecution by the defendants in that they made a false analysis and communicated it to the police and/or the DPP and procured the arrest and prosecution of the plaintiff. It was argued for the defendants that the statement of claim disclosed no basis for alleging malicious prosecution since the defendants had not initiated the prosecution but had merely passed on information to the police and/or the DPP. It was submitted for the plaintiff that it was because of the defendants' acts and omissions that the plaintiff had been charged and that the defendants, judged by their entire conduct, had in reality 'caused the law to be set in motion'.

Drake J applied the principle then stated in *Clerk and Lindsell on Torts* (14th edn, 1975) para 18-87:

'To prosecute is to set the law in motion, and the law is only set in motion by an appeal to some person clothed with judicial authority in regard to the matter in question ... If a charge is made to a police constable and he thereupon makes an arrest, the party making the charge, if liable at all, will be liable in an action for false imprisonment, on the ground that he has directed the arrest and therefore it is his own act and not the act of the law.'

Drake J continued ([1981] 1 All ER 715 at 718, [1981] 1 WLR 184 at 188–189):

'In my judgment the statement of claim in the present case makes it clear that all that is alleged against the defendants is that they provided reports "... for the purpose of placing such reports before the police and/or the Director of Public Prosecutions". It was for the police or the DPP ... to decide whether or not to prosecute and I think the proposed addition of a claim of malicious prosecution against the defendants or any of them is misconceived.'

I have no doubt that the decision of Drake J was right.

It does not, however, I think, clearly cover the point in this case but it is of assistance to Mr Christie's argument. There was no clear allegation that the defendants had known at the time that the reports were prepared and submitted that the allegations were false, and that is not surprising because the plaintiff's first allegation was of negligent contamination of the specimens. Further, it was not alleged by the plaintiff that the purpose of the defendants in preparing and sending the reports had been to procure the prosecution of the plaintiff. The fact that, when the report of Professor Mant was provided, the reports from the defendants were not withdrawn, provided the basis for asserting knowledge of falsity thereafter which could have been the basis for the continuation of a prosecution with malice, as in *Fitzjohn v Mackinder*, but the defendants in *Evans's* case were not in charge of the prosecution as was Mackinder.

I come now to *Commercial Union Assurance Co of NZ Ltd v Lamont* [1989] 3 NZLR 187, a decision of the Court of Appeal in New Zealand. The facts were complicated and, in my view, need not be examined. The headnote of the report reads (at 187–188):

'An action for malicious prosecution requires the balancing of two factors; one is the desirability of safeguarding individuals from unjustifiable litigation; the other is the need to recognise that the maintenance of the law depends on the co-operation of private citizens in reporting suspected crimes and supplying relevant information to the prosecuting authorities. In the modern New Zealand context, the police have the training and experience to investigate a possible offence impartially and with skill and in that process to assess whether the evidence justifies the invoking of the criminal process. Thus a cautious approach is required in determining whether a third party is responsible in an action for malicious prosecution for criminal proceedings instituted by the police. In some very special cases, a third party may be regarded as the prosecutor if, inter alia, he puts the police in possession of information which virtually compels an officer to lay an information; if he deliberately deceives the police by supplying false information in the absence of which the police would not have proceeded; or if he withholds information in the knowledge of which the police would not prosecute.'

It is not necessary to examine the case in detail to demonstrate to what extent the alternative—deliberate deception of the police by supplying false information—was necessary to the decision. The judgment of Richardson J contains a review of the authorities decided in the Privy Council, in our courts, and in the courts of New Zealand. His examination of the authorities in other jurisdictions included reference to the decision of the High Court of Australia in *Commonwealth Life Assurance Society Ltd v Brain* (1935) 53 CLR 343 at 379 where Dixon J stated the test thus:

'The rule appears to be that those who counsel and persuade the actual prosecutor to institute proceedings or procure him to do so by dishonestly prejudicing his judgment are vicariously responsible for the proceedings.'

Reference was also made to the *Corpus Juris Secundum* (1948) vol 54, para 14 published in the USA where the principle was stated as being:

'Was [the] defendant actively instrumental in putting the law in force? In order to sustain the action, it must affirmatively appear as a part of the case of the party demanding damages that the party sought to be charged was the proximate and efficient cause of maliciously putting the law in motion.' (See [1989] 3 NZLR 187 at 197–197.)

That was followed by reference to the *American Law Institute, Restatement of the Law, Torts* (2nd edn, 1977) p 409, para 653 where it was said (at 198):

'When a private person gives to a prosecuting officer information that he believes to be true, and the officer in the exercise of his uncontrolled discretion initiates criminal proceedings based upon that information, the informer is not liable under the rules stated in this section even though the information proves to be false and his belief was one that a reasonable man would not entertain. The exercise of the officer's discretion makes the initiation of the prosecution his own and protects from liability the person whose information or accusation has led the officer to initiate the proceedings. If, however, the information is known by the giver to be false, an intelligent exercise of the officer's discretion becomes impossible, and a prosecution based upon it is procured by the person giving false information. In order to charge a private person with responsibility for the initiation of proceedings by a public official, it must therefore appear that his desire to have the proceedings initiated, expressed by direction, request or pressure of any kind, was the determining factor in the official's decision to commence the prosecution, *or that the information furnished by him upon which the official acted was known to be false.*' (My emphasis.)

Richardson J also referred to the Canadian case of *Watters v Pacific Delivery Service Ltd* (1963) 42 DLR (2d) 661 to which, as stated above, Judge Goodman was referred. The conclusion of Richardson J was expressed as follows (at 199):

'It does not follow that there is any call for modifying the test which has been developed in the decisions of this Court for determining whether a third party is responsible in an action for malicious prosecution for criminal proceedings instituted by the police. What is required is a cautious application of that test where the police have conducted an investigation and decided to prosecute. The core requirement is that the defendant actually procured the use of the power of the State to hurt the plaintiff. One should never assume that tainted evidence persuaded the police to prosecute. In some very special cases, however, the prosecutor may in practical terms have been obliged to act on apparently reliable and damning evidence supplied to the police. The onus properly rests on the plaintiff to establish that it was the false evidence tendered by a third party which led the police to prosecute before that party may be characterised as having procured the prosecution.'

Mullin J said (at 207–208):

'A person may be regarded as the prosecutor if, inter alia, he puts the police in possession of information which virtually compels an officer to lay an information; if he deliberately deceives the police by supplying false information in the absence of which the police would not have proceeded; or if he withholds information in the knowledge of which the police would not prosecute.'

Barker J, in substance, agreed with the test as proposed by Richardson and McMullen JJ.

The reasoning of the judges in *Lamont's* case is persuasive. I agree with the approach in the emphasis placed upon policy. The judgments provide powerful support for the contention that the law should be held to admit the possibility that a defendant may be shown to have set the law in motion, so as to be liable as prosecutor in proceedings instituted by the police, if the defendant is shown to have provided information to the police upon which the police acted, with the intention of causing the police so to act and with knowledge that the information was false.

The decision of Diplock LJ in *Malz v Rosen* [1966] 2 All ER 10, [1966] 1 WLR 1008 presents no obstacle to that conclusion. The defendant there was held to be the prosecutor because he told the police sergeant that he was willing to prosecute and to prefer charges and later signed the charge sheet. He was also held to have given an honest account to the police. The issue raised in this case was not there addressed.

The officer who decided to initiate the prosecution against the defendant in this case is to be regarded as having exercised an independent judgment, in the sense that he made up his own mind what to do upon the basis of the information which had been given to him. But the effect of the interposition of an independent judgment by the police officer is not to be treated as the same as that given to the interposition of the opinion and judgment of a judicial officer: see *Clerk and Lindsell on Torts* para 19-07. In a claim of trespass by false arrest, if the act of the police officer in making an arrest is in fact caused by the defendant, then the defendant will be liable. In *Davidson v Chief Constable of North Wales Police* [1994] 2 All ER 597 a store detective employed by the defendants told a police officer that she had seen the plaintiff take a cassette from the store and leave the store without paying for it. She expected information given by her as store detective to carry weight with police officers. She intended and expected the police officers to act upon that information. They had always done so in the past and accordingly she regarded the arrest as made on her behalf. The police officers arrested the plaintiff, who was released without charge because it was quickly established that the plaintiff had in fact paid for the cassette. The plaintiff's claim against the employers of the store detective did not turn on proof of malice. The police constables had acted under s 24(6) of the Police and Criminal Evidence Act 1984 and, since they had reasonable grounds for suspecting that an arrestable offence had been committed, were not liable. The trial judge ruled that there was no case to go to the jury against the employers of the store detective. That decision was upheld on appeal. Sir Thomas Bingham MR said (at 604–605):

'... the question which arose for the decision of the judge in this case was whether there was information properly to be considered by the jury as to whether what [the store detective] did went beyond laying information before police officers for them to take such action as they thought fit and amounted to some direction, or procuring or direct request, or direct encouragement that they should act by way of arresting these defendants. He decided that there was no evidence which went beyond the giving of information. Certainly there was no express request. Certainly there was no encouragement. Certainly there was no discussion of any kind as to what action the police officers should take. The crux of [the submission for the plaintiff] is that this case is different from the case in which an ordinary member of the public gives information to a police officer because this is a store detective, somebody better informed than an ordinary member of the public as to what was likely to happen upon making a complaint, and somebody with a very clear intention and expectation as to what would happen. No doubt the store detective did have an intention and expectation as to what would happen. The fact remains that the learned judge ... correctly held that what [the store detective] did and said in no way went beyond the mere giving of information, leaving it to the officers to exercise a discretion which on their unchallenged evidence they did as to whether they should take any action or not.'

The questions arising from that decision, therefore, are, firstly, whether the giving of information by the defendant in this case to the two police officers should be held as falling within the principle there stated as 'the mere giving of information, leaving it to the officers to exercise a discretion', notwithstanding the fact that this defendant knew of the information so given to be false; and, secondly, whether the additional facts found by the judge as to the making of earlier and subsequent complaints would suffice as amounting to 'procuring or direct encouragement'.

I have no doubt that the act of giving false information, known to be false, with the intention of thereby causing the police officer to act against the plaintiff, is not within the principle stated. The giving of information known to be false is not the 'mere giving of information': see the passage from the *American Restatement, Torts* cited by Richardson J in *Lamont's* case [1989] 3 NZLR 187 at 198. The decision of this court in *Davidson v Chief Constable of North Wales Police* is, in my judgment, not clear authority which prevents the upholding by this court of the decision of Judge Goodman in this case.

The question, therefore, is whether the force of the point of policy is such that we should exclude as irrelevant, or find to be by itself insufficient, the fact that the defendant deliberately deceived the police by supplying false information in the absence of which the police would not have proceeded. There is in my judgment much to be said in favour of a rule which would confine a cause of action for malicious prosecution to claims against a defendant who has done by himself or by his agent some formal act by which he assumes responsibility for the prosecution, such as by laying an information. A point of form may be of the first importance (see Devlin LJ in *Lincoln v Daniels* [1961] 3 All ER 740 at 750, [1962] 1 QB 237 at 259). Such a rule would bring much increased certainty.

In my view it would not be right so to limit and define the concept of 'setting the law in motion' or of being 'actively instrumental in the making or prosecuting of the charge'. If that had been the meaning intended, it would, I think, have been so formulated long ago.

I am, however, persuaded that it would be wrong to accept that the concept of 'setting the law in motion' can be satisfied by proof that a defendant has done no more than to make an allegation to a police officer, with the intention that the police officer should act upon it against the party accused, and with knowledge that the allegation was untrue. The point of the rule of law as formulated, in my judgment, was to protect the person who goes to the police to complain and who leaves it to the police to decide what to do. Such a person is not the prosecutor for the tort of malicious prosecution. The purpose of the protection is that such a person should not have to face the anxiety and expense of being sued upon acquittal of the party accused. That protection would largely be destroyed if an arguable claim could be put forward against such a person by the addition of an allegation that he knew that his complaint to the police was untrue. I understand, and have much sympathy with, the opinion of Judge Goodman that for the law to deny to the plaintiff any cause of action against the defendant would be 'an affront to a proper sense of justice'. The importance, however, of the policy of the law in protecting from such proceedings the person who complains to the police, or who gives

information when asked, justifies the rule, as I am persuaded that it should be
held to be, notwithstanding the immediate and apparent unfairness to the
plaintiff. Such a plaintiff must be content with the fact that when the matter is
considered by the prosecution service, the prosecution is at once terminated.
In clear cases, no doubt, such a complainant may be prosecuted, as pointed out
by Mr Christie (see *R v Rowell* [1978] 1 All ER 665, [1978] 1 WLR 132).

Judge Goodman did not decide this case upon the basis that the making by
the defendant to the police of a complaint, with the intention that the police
should prosecute, and with knowledge that the complaint was false, could be
regarded as sufficient to justify treating the defendant as the prosecutor of the
plaintiff. He held that the defendant could properly be regarded as the
prosecutor of the plaintiff because of the additional acts of the defendant. They
are set out above in the account given of the conclusion of Judge Goodman.
They are not, in my judgment, arguably additional to the ordinary and
necessary consequences and concomitants of making a complaint to a police
officer. The judge noted that the defendant had made earlier and similar
complaints and made subsequent similar complaints with reference to which
no action, in the nature of commencing a prosecution, was taken by anybody.
Next, as the judge was able to infer, the defendant in making her complaint to
Det Con Haynes made such an impression upon him that, notwithstanding the
fact that the case depended on her word alone, Det Con Haynes decided to
apply for the warrant. Further, the defendant stated in her statement that she
was willing to give evidence and, when asked to do so, attended at court to be
available if called upon. The other matters mentioned by the judge seem to
me, for this purpose, to be of no distinctive force whatever, such as the fact that
the allegation was of a serious sexual incident involving her alone to which
there were no other witnesses, and that she felt very strongly about it. That
must be the situation in most if not all cases of complaints of sexual
wrongdoing.

The matters listed could not, in my judgment, justify taking this case out of
the ordinary rule so as to permit this defendant to be treated as prosecutor of
the plaintiff. The earlier and later complaints were merely complaints, and
they were regarded by the officers to whom the complaints were made as not
justifying the taking of any further action. Such impression as the defendant
was able to make on Det Con Haynes is not shown to have been more than, or
different from, that impression which any complainant must make if a police
officer is persuaded, upon the basis of the information given, and in the
absence of other evidence, to initiate a prosecution. As to the stated
willingness to give evidence, and the attendance at court when asked, such
factors seem to me to be no more than may be expected to be present in any
case of a complaint.

For these reasons, I would allow this appeal and set aside the judgment given
against the defendant.

McCOWAN LJ. I have found no English authority which is directly in point in
the present case. In particular, *Danby v Beardsley* (1880) 43 LT 603 is, in my
judgment, clearly distinguishable because the court accepted that the
defendant genuinely believed that the clippers were his and that the plaintiff
had stolen them. I do, however, obtain assistance from the judgment of Sir
Thomas Bingham MR in the Court of Appeal in *Davidson v Chief Constable of*

North Wales Police [1994] 2 All ER 597 at 604 in which he said (the claim being for false imprisonment)—

'the question which arose for the decision of the learned judge in this case was whether there was information properly to be considered by the jury as to whether what [the store detective] did went beyond laying information before police officers for them to take such action as they thought fit and amounted to some direction, or procuring, or direct request or direct encouragement that they should act by way of arresting these defendants.'

I bear in mind also that it is possible in English law for a defendant to commit, through the medium of another, not only a tort but a crime. Thus it is not necessary that a defendant in a criminal trial should have perpetrated the act with his own hands; he can be held guilty of an offence, though absent when the deed was done and though the agent, through the medium of whom he committed the offence, was innocent. (The principal in the present case was the defendant and the innocent agent the police officer who laid the information.)

In the Commonwealth, however, there have been a number of cases which posed similar problems to those in the present case and which lend powerful support to the argument on behalf of the plaintiff. It will suffice if I cite passages from the judgments in those cases.

In *Commonwealth Life Assurance Society Ltd v Brain* (1935) 53 CLR 343 at 379, a decision of the High Court of Australia, Dixon J said:

'The legal standard of liability for a prosecution which is instituted neither by the defendant nor by his servant is open to criticism on the ground of indefiniteness. It is clear that no responsibility is incurred by one who confines himself to bringing before some proper authority information which he does not disbelieve, even although in the hope that a prosecution will be instituted, if it is actually instituted as the result of an independent discretion on the part of that authority (*Danby v. Beardsley* ((1880) 43 LT 603); *Fanzelow v Kerr* ((1896) 14 NZLR 660)). But, if the discretion is misled by false information, or is otherwise practised upon in order to procure the laying of the charge, those who thus brought about the prosecution are responsible (*Pandit Gaya Parshad Tewari v Sardar Bhagat Singh* ((1908) 24 TLR 884); *Black v Mackenzie* ((1917) 36 NZLR 729)) ... The rule appears to be that those who counsel and persuade the actual prosecutor to institute proceedings or procure him to do so by dishonestly prejudicing his judgment are vicariously responsible for the proceedings.'

In the Canadian case of *Watters v Pacific Delivery Service Ltd* (1963) 42 DLR (2d) 661 at 669 Munroe J said:

'I reject this submission and hold that the defendant Sandover is liable because he instigated the proceedings that resulted in the arrest and imprisonment of the plaintiff, and did so maliciously and without reasonable cause. This is not a case of a person truthfully reporting the facts to a police officer and leaving the latter to determine whether or not such facts warranted prosecution. The bad faith of the defendant Sandover in deliberately deceiving Detective Cotter distinguishes this case from those cases relied upon by counsel for Sandover.'

Again, in the New Zealand case of *Commercial Union Assurance Co of NZ Ltd v Lamont* [1989] 3 NZLR 187 at 207–208 McMullin J said:

'But in some cases the person who supplied the information to the police may be regarded as the prosecutor even though the information was not laid by him. A person may be regarded as the prosecutor if, inter alia, he puts the police in possession of information which virtually compels an officer to lay an information; if he deliberately deceives the police by supplying false information in the absence of which the police would not have proceeded; or if he withholds information in the knowledge of which the police would not prosecute.'

I find myself in complete agreement with these views. Is there, however, some consideration of public policy which should lead me to a contrary conclusion? In Fleming *The Law of Torts* (8th edn, 1992) p 609 it is said:

'The tort of malicious prosecution is dominated by the problem of balancing two countervailing interests of high social importance: safeguarding the individual from being harassed by unjustifiable litigation and encouraging citizens to aid in law enforcement.'

There can surely be no wish to encourage citizens to make deliberately false charges against a fellow-citizen to the police. That can hardly be described as law enforcement. It is a perversion of the law and deserves no protection. I see no justification for the view that it would be harmful in those circumstances for such a false accuser to be sued for malicious prosecution. On the contrary, I think it would be very regrettable if the law were that a complainant could deliberately concoct an allegation of crime against an innocent man and persuade a police officer, in the absence of any other evidence against the man, to lodge a charge against him, knowing it to be false and malicious, but escape liability for malicious prosecution because the officer and not the complainant had laid the information. In the present case on the judge's findings this was plainly not a case where the complainant simply laid the facts before the police officer for him to take such action as he thought fit. Indeed, she did not lay the facts before him at all: she laid lies. She actively misled the police into taking criminal proceedings against the plaintiff by a series of false allegations against the plaintiff. There was no evidence against him other than hers. She actively misled and brought pressure to bear upon the police, and her only object in so doing can have been to cause them to prosecute him. She procured and directly encouraged the bringing of that prosecution, and she prejudiced the judgment of the actual prosecutor. On those findings of fact, in my judgment, the judge was entitled to hold that she played a sufficient role in the institution of the proceedings to be regarded as setting them in motion.

It will not of course be every case in which a complainant who has made a false allegation to the police, followed by the police laying the information, will be liable in malicious prosecution. There may for example be other evidence of the crime alleged which is taken into account by the police, or indeed the prosecution may not be brought about by her lies at all. In this case, however, the judge found, and was entitled to find, that—

'she was clearly determined that action should be taken and I am prepared to infer that that must have made such an impression on Det Con

Haynes as to result in him applying for the warrant, notwithstanding the fact that the case depended on her word alone, and of course, as I have said, she was quite willing to give evidence and to accompany Det Con Haynes to the magistrates' court on 25 July to assist him in obtaining the warrant. In the circumstances of this particular case, therefore, I find that the defendant was indeed actively instrumental in setting the law in motion against the plaintiff.'

I discern no fault in the judge's findings or reasoning. Accordingly I would dismiss the appeal.

HOBHOUSE LJ. There are four elements in the tort of malicious prosecution. The plaintiff must show, first, that he was prosecuted by the defendant, secondly, that the prosecution was determined in his favour, thirdly, that the defendant was acting maliciously, and fourthly, that no reasonable and probable cause existed for the prosecution. There is no dispute that these are the constituents of the tort nor is there any dispute in the present case that the trial judge, Judge Goodman, was entitled to decide the second, third and fourth points in favour of the plaintiff. The dispute on this appeal is the definition of the first element and whether, as a matter of law, the judge was entitled to decide the first point in favour of the plaintiff.

The third element, the element of malice, is the only point at which the mental state and intent of the defendant comes into the definition. The fourth element, reasonable and probable cause, is an objective assessment to be made by the judge. The first and second elements are questions of fact and relate to the prosecution. If there has been no prosecution, the tort of malicious prosecution cannot have been committed (see *Harris v Warne* (1879) 4 CPD 125). Thus, even if a defendant has maliciously and without any justification made false allegations that the plaintiff has committed a criminal offence with the intent that he should be prosecuted, the tort has not been committed; there must have been a prosecution.

In the present case, the relevant prosecution was a prosecution of the plaintiff before the Bromley Magistrates' Court for an alleged offence that he—

'on 19th July 1989 [sic] at the rear of 1 Denver Close Orpington Kent, did wilfully openly and lewdly expose his person with intent to insult a female contrary to section 4 of the Vagrancy Act 1824.'

This offence was triable summarily and was not an arrestable offence. The procedure for instituting such a proceeding is by laying an information before a justice of the peace that the person has, or is suspected of having, committed the offence and applying under s 1 of the Magistrates' Courts Act 1980 for the issue of a summons directed to that person requiring him to appear before a magistrates' court to answer to the information or for the issue of a warrant to arrest that person and bring him before a magistrates' court for the like purpose. Under sub-s (3) 'no warrant shall be issued under this section unless the information is in writing and substantiated on oath'.

The prosecution in the present case was instituted on 27 July 1989 when Det Con Haynes laid an information before the Bromley magistrates and the magistrates, on his application and on his oath, issued a warrant for the arrest of the plaintiff on the charge of the offence under s 4 of the Vagrancy Act 1824. The plaintiff did not put the warrant in evidence at the trial but it is clear that it must have recorded that it was Det Con Haynes who laid the information. The warrant was executed on 9 August when the plaintiff was arrested by Det Con Haynes. After interview he was formally charged by Det Con Haynes before Sgt Perrott at Bromley Police Station and bailed to appear at the magistrates' court the following day. At the hearing on 10 August the prosecution was represented by the Crown Prosecution Service and the proceedings were dropped and the plaintiff released.

This was the prosecution determined favourably to the plaintiff which is the subject matter of the alleged tort. There can be no question but that the actual prosecutor was Det Con Haynes and that the only steps in the proceedings were taken by him. There is no suggestion that he in any way acted improperly. The case of the plaintiff before us is succinctly summarised in the skeleton argument of Mr Rose, who appeared for the plaintiff:

'It is conceded by the plaintiff that it was the police officer who *actually* set the law in motion by obtaining a warrant from the magistrates' court, but submitted that a person who actively encourages a police officer to set the law in motion, as in this case, can be liable for malicious prosecution.'

In the course of argument before us the plaintiff's case was developed along two distinct lines. The first line involved the submission that the tort should be more widely defined and extended to a tort of maliciously causing or encouraging the prosecution of the plaintiff. The second line of argument amounted to an allegation that the defendant was liable as the party who committed the tort through the instrumentality of another.

Judge Goodman adopted formulations of the law from *Clerk and Lindsell on Torts* paras 19-05, 19-07, which have likewise been adopted by the parties before us:

'19-05 In action of malicious prosecution the plaintiff must show first that he was prosecuted by the defendant, that is to say, that the law was set in motion against him on a criminal charge ...

19-07 *What is a prosecution?* To prosecute is to set the law in motion, and the law is only set in motion by an appeal to some person clothed with judicial authority in regard to the matter in question, and to be liable for malicious prosecution a person must be actively instrumental in so setting the law in motion.'

Judge Goodman pointed out that this passage had been approved by Drake J in *Evans v London Hospital Medical College* [1981] 1 All ER 715 at 718, [1981] 1 WLR 184 at 188. The judge then went on to consider other authorities which might help in the understanding of the phrase 'actively instrumental'. He distinguished various of the English authorities and found support for the plaintiff in a Privy Council appeal from India and certain Canadian authorities. He gave a separate judgment upon the facts of the case, finding that the defendant had acted maliciously, and, in his judgment on the question of law whether the tort of malicious prosecution had been committed, he referred to and amplified his earlier findings of fact. Since these form the basis upon which the plaintiff supports the judge's conclusion of law it is necessary to set them out.

'In the present case the defendant said that she had actually seen the defendant commit the alleged offence and repeated that in two written statements, adding that she would attend trial and was willing to give evidence. It also appeared that she was the only witness to what had occurred. In this case I have also found that her allegation was false. Whether the fact that the defendant in the present case said she saw events being committed and was the only witness of it makes a difference to the question whether she set the law in motion is something that I shall have to consider later ...

The defendant was responsible for calling the police in to deal with her complaint about which she felt very strongly. She told Pc Cratchley (the police officer involved on 20 July) of a serious sexual incident involving her alone, as to which there were no other witnesses, and she signed a written statement to that effect. She clearly wanted the defendant to be arrested and dealt with, as I have found in my earlier judgment. She repeated her accusation to Det Con Haynes the following day, who took a further written statement from her when he investigated the matter on behalf of the CID. Moreover she indicated to him that she was willing to attend court and give evidence. She did indeed attend court to assist him when he went to apply for the warrant although in the end she was not required to say anything ...

In the light of the defendant's further untruthful accusations about the plaintiff made to Pc McKiernan on 7 August and to another officer about an alleged incident on 9 August when nothing seemed to be happening about executing the warrant, as well as her other wholly unfounded accusations to the police about earlier alleged incidents and her evidence generally, I consider that she was clearly determined that action should be taken and I am prepared to infer that that must have made such an impression on Det Con Haynes as to result in him applying for the warrant, notwithstanding the fact that the case depended upon her word alone ...

In the circumstances of this particular case, therefore, I find that the defendant was indeed actively instrumental in setting the law in motion against the plaintiff. To hold otherwise would, I consider, be an affront to a proper sense of justice. She wanted the plaintiff to be arrested and dealt with from the start, and that is what she achieved causing Det Con Haynes to obtain the warrant from the magistrate. She was, as I say, the only person who could testify about the alleged indecent exposure. I therefore find that the defendant is to be regarded as a prosecutor in setting the law in motion against the plaintiff.'

What the judge was therefore purporting to do was to apply the formulation in *Clerk and Lindsell on Torts* para 19-07 as approved by Drake J in *Evans*'s case.

On these findings of fact, what the defendant did was as follows. (1) On 20 July she made a false statement to Pc Cratchley that the plaintiff had exposed himself to her. (2) On 21 July she made a witness statement on Form 991 at the request of Det Con Haynes falsely stating that the plaintiff had exposed himself to her. This statement included a highly coloured description of what she said that the plaintiff had done. It did not suggest that the incident was trivial. The statement concluded with the words frequently included in such statements at the request of the police officer taking the statement, 'I am willing to attend court and give evidence if required'. Being on the standard form, this statement was entitled 'Statement of Witness' and referred to s 9 of the Criminal Justice Act 1967 and s 102 of the Magistrates' Courts Act 1980. The form also included the printed words:

'This statement ... is true to the best of my knowledge and belief and I make it knowing that if it is tendered in evidence I shall be liable to prosecution if I have wilfully stated in it anything which I know to be false or do not believe to be true.'

(3) She made this statement with the intention that Det Con Haynes should commence criminal proceedings against the plaintiff. (4) On 27 July she attended in the magistrates' court building at the request of Det Con Haynes prepared to give evidence if called upon to do so. She was not called to give evidence; she did not go into court; she took no part in the proceedings before the magistrates on that day. (5) Between 28 July and 9 August in connection with other incidents involving herself and the plaintiff, she made further separate allegations of indecent exposure against the plaintiff. No criminal proceedings were commenced in respect of any of those allegations. She was not herself concerned in the execution of the warrant or the charging of the plaintiff.

Thus, as regards the prosecutor, Det Con Haynes, and the prosecution which he instituted, her involvement was simply that she gave to Det Con Haynes, at his request, the signed witness statement and, again at his request, attended at the court building prepared to give evidence if called upon to do so. All that this shows is that she maliciously held herself out as willing to give untruthful evidence with a view to bringing about the arrest, prosecution and conviction of the plaintiff for a criminal offence which she knew he had not committed. The statement that she made was made to a police officer not to the court. She never herself made any appeal to any person clothed with judicial authority. The question of law is whether upon these facts she committed the tort of wrongful prosecution.

This question does not have to be answered as if there were no other remedies for such outrageous conduct. It is not appropriate that I should discuss what other tort or torts she may have committed at one time or another during this sequence of events. But it is clear, and not in dispute, that on these findings of fact she could have been prosecuted and convicted of the offence of attempting to pervert the course of public justice. This is a serious offence triable on indictment and for which the penalty is at large; anyone convicted of making a false allegation of crime is likely to receive a substantial prison sentence. To conclude that the defendant has not committed the tort of malicious prosecution, therefore, does not mean that she has been allowed to 'get away' with her behaviour or that a gap in the law has been exposed. Other and, it may be thought, more appropriate remedies are available. This feature overlaps with considerations of public policy regarding the status of witnesses to which I will have to return later in this judgment (see *Marrinan v Vibart* [1962] 1 All ER 869, [1963] 1 QB 234).

The expression 'the complainant' is commonly used to describe someone who has made an allegation to the police that she has been the victim of some offence of a sexual character and the defendant could be so described here. But the expression is not a term of art nor does it constitute the woman in question the prosecutor in the case. She is still no more than a witness, even if she is the only witness. Further, she is not to be confused with somebody who invokes the civil jurisdiction of a magistrates' court by making a complaint under s 51 of the Magistrates' Courts Act 1980.

In English law it is possible to bring a private prosecution and it would have been open to the defendant to do so had she so chosen. In the present case she did not so choose but she left it to the police whether or not an information should be laid before the magistrates. What is involved both in the decision of the person who chooses to lay an information and in the decision of the magistrates in deciding whether or not to issue a summons or warrant was discussed by the House of Lords in *Hill v Anderton* [1982] 2 All ER 963 at 971, [1983] 1 AC 328 at 342–343. To swear and lay a complaint is a step which the person who does so takes at his own choice and on his own responsibility and the issue of the summons or warrant is likewise a matter for the judicial responsibility of the magistrates. The present case is not in the rare category where a police officer can be required by a citizen to act in any particular way. His own judgment and choice and his willingness to swear the information intervene. Short of a conspiracy between the witness and the police officer to pervert the course of justice (which is not suggested in the present case), there is no legal or factual identification of the witness upon whose evidence the police officer relies in laying his information with the police officer nor with his decision to lay the information.

Part of the argument of the plaintiff before the judge and before us— encouraged, it must be recognised, by various dicta—has been that it follows from the finding that the defendant acted maliciously and made untruthful statements to the police officer that she was actively instrumental in setting the law in motion, whereas someone who had simply provided truthful evidence would not have been. In my judgment this argument involves an important and fundamental confusion between the *mental* element in the tort and what has to be proved as a matter of the *acts* of the defendant. The truth or falsity of the evidence provided is relevant to malice but does not assist to answer the question: 'Was the defendant the prosecutor?' That question should receive the same answer regardless of whether the person in question was acting maliciously or not and whether she was truthful or not. If it were to suffice that the defendant should have done no more than give dishonest evidence upon which the prosecutor relied, the first element in the definition of the tort of malicious prosecution becomes otiose; all that would need to be shown would be a causal connection between the provision of the dishonest evidence and the institution or the continuation of the prosecution. This is not the law of England. The extremity of the proposition becomes still more apparent if one is prepared to treat as a prosecutor someone who does no more than withhold information from the police which, if the police had had that information, would have led them to abandon the prosecution (see *Commercial Union Assurance Co of NZ Ltd v Lamont* [1989] 3 NZLR 187).

The argument of the plaintiff is inconsistent with the various cases which recognise the first element in the classical definition of the tort. This can be illustrated by the decision in *Evans v London Hospital Medical College*. In that case the relevant defendants were alleged to have maliciously fabricated false evidence that certain organs removed from the body of the deceased had contained large quantities of morphine. They had provided this evidence to the hospital authorities following a suspicious death and a post mortem (probably carried out at the request of the police). The matter having been reported to the police, the relevant defendants then made statements to the police to the same effect. The prosecution of the plaintiff for murder followed. The evidence of the relevant defendants, which was persisted in even after it was credibly contradicted, was fundamental to the prosecution case and the causal relationship between the provision of the evidence and the prosecution was clearly made out. The plaintiff was acquitted and she then brought civil proceedings against, among others, the relevant defendants for malicious prosecution. This claim was held to be demurrable by Drake J. The plaintiff submitted that it was because of the defendants' acts and omissions that the plaintiff had been charged and that the defendants, judged by their entire conduct, had in reality caused the law to be set in motion (see [1981] 1 All ER 715 at 718, [1981] 1 WLR 184 at 188). Drake J said:

'It was for the police or the DPP (in reality, clearly for the DPP) to decide whether or not to prosecute. I think the proposed addition of a claim of malicious prosecution against the defendants or any of them is misconceived.' (See [1981] 1 All ER 715 at 718, [1981] 1 WLR 184 at 189.)

It is not sufficient that the defendant, however malicious, should have merely provided the evidence upon which the prosecution case was founded. *Evans*'s case illustrates both the distinction between a witness and the prosecutor and the relevance of the independent judgment of the prosecutor who decided whether or not to bring criminal proceedings. *Evans*'s case also draws attention to the implications for the public policy which protects witnesses of any such extension of the law of tort which would make witnesses liable in tort for their false evidence.

There are other authorities which in my judgment are clearly in favour of the defendant upon the question of law and inconsistent with the conclusion of the judge. The first of these is *Danby v Beardsley* (1880) 43 LT 603. This was a decision of a Divisional Court composed of Lindley and Lopes JJ. The question before the court was whether Lindley J, who was the judge at the trial of the tort action, had correctly withdrawn the case from the jury and directed that a verdict be entered for the defendant on the ground that there was no evidence that the defendant was the prosecutor. The Divisional Court held that he had been right so to rule. The plaintiff had been employed by the defendant formerly as his groom, latterly as a gardener. The plaintiff lent two pairs of horse clipping machines to another servant of the defendant who had been engaged as his groom. The defendant having seen the clippers in his stables was under the impression that they belonged to himself, the defendant. Later, after the plaintiff had left the defendant's employ, the defendant inquired of the groom what had happened to the clippers. He was told that they belonged to the plaintiff. However, the defendant sent for a policeman and said: 'I have had stolen from me two pairs of clippers and they were last seen in the possession of [the plaintiff]'. When the clippers were subsequently found at the plaintiff's house, the plaintiff was arrested and charged with theft. Both before the magistrates and at the trial at Manchester Assizes the defendant gave evidence for the Crown against the plaintiff. The plaintiff was acquitted and the plaintiff then sued the defendant for (among other things) malicious prosecution.

It was upon this evidence that it was held, in the civil proceedings, that the action in tort could not lie because the defendant was not the prosecutor. It will be noted that the defendant was the sole source of the original allegation and the complaint to the police and that he thereafter gave evidence in the criminal proceedings. The test posed by Lopes J (at 604) was: 'Is there any evidence to show that the defendant was actively instrumental in putting the law in force?' Lindley J said (at 604):

> 'It has been said that he so acted that he intended the constable to arrest the plaintiff, or, as it has been said, to use a common phrase, he set the stone rolling. Now what stone has he set rolling? It is simply a stone of suspicion. There was no direction to the constable to arrest or prosecute. He, no doubt suspected Danby, and described the things to the constable; but there is not the slightest evidence that the defendant either prosecuted or directed anyone else to prosecute.'

This case again illustrates the distinction between the witness and the prosecutor and it is a strong case because the question was withdrawn from the jury despite the evidence to which I have referred. The case also illustrates the significance of the question whether or not the actual prosecutor was exercising an independent judgment or merely acting on the direction of the defendant. In my judgment, *Danby v Beardsley* is indistinguishable from the present case; it has for over 100 years been regarded as a leading English authority upon the constituents of this tort.

In *Malz v Rosen* [1966] 2 All ER 10, [1966] 1 WLR 1008 Diplock LJ was sitting as a judge of the High Court. The issues in the case included a denial by the defendant that he had prosecuted the plaintiff. The plaintiff had been tried at the magistrates' court for an alleged offence of using insulting behaviour likely to cause a breach of the peace. He was acquitted. The incident was reported to the police by the defendant. The police sergeant told the defendant that, according to what the defendant was telling him, the plaintiff had committed an offence but that the police could not proceed without the evidence of the defendant and another witness accompanying the defendant. The sergeant asked them whether they would be prepared to prosecute, prefer charges, and explained to them the responsibility of so doing. The defendant said he was willing to do this. Later in the presence of the plaintiff and the defendant the plaintiff was charged and the defendant signed the charge sheet. Diplock LJ said ([1966] 2 All ER 10 at 13, [1966] 1 WLR 1008 at 1012):

> 'It was, needless to say, never intended or thought by anyone that the defendant would conduct or have the actual conduct of the prosecution at the magistrates' court.'

Subsequently, the proceedings before the magistrates were conducted by a solicitor and counsel instructed by the Metropolitan Police. Diplock LJ continued ([1966] 2 All ER 10 at 13, [1966] 1 WLR 1008 at 1012–1013):

> 'On those facts I accept that the defendant was in the position of prosecutor and therefore, if it can be shown that he brought the accusation without reasonable or probable cause and with malice, an action for malicious prosecution will lie against him.'

Signing the charge sheet constitutes the person who does so the 'prosecutor' (see *Sewell v National Telephone Co Ltd* [1907] 1 KB 557 at 560). Diplock LJ clearly regarded it as necessary that the defendant should be more than a mere witness even though he was one of the two essential witnesses upon whose evidence any prosecution would have to be founded. In the case before him, the first element in the tort was made out because the defendant had taken the responsibility for initiating the prosecution, the police having expressly told him that he must make that choice and accept that responsibility. This case then is also an authority against the plaintiff's submissions.

The plaintiff relied upon *Clements v Ohrly* (1848) 2 Car & K 686, 175 ER 287. There the plaintiff had been acquitted at his trial before the Lord Mayor of London on a charge of having forged the acceptance of a bill of exchange with intent to defraud a firm of bankers, Messrs Fullers. The report is the report of the trial, before Lord Denman CJ and a jury, of the action brought by the plaintiff against the defendant for malicious prosecution. Lord Denman CJ directed the jury that it was open to them to return a verdict for the plaintiff and they did so. One of the issues at the civil trial was whether the defendant had been the prosecutor in the criminal proceedings. The defendant had been instructed by Messrs Fuller to go before the magistrates and obtain a warrant for the arrest of the plaintiff and it accordingly appears that he was acting as the agent of the bankers. However he had nevertheless personally appeared before the magistrates and applied for and obtained the warrant for the arrest of the plaintiff; the warrant expressly referred to the defendant by name. The defendant gave evidence at the criminal trial and allowed himself to be described as the prosecutor although he was not bearing the expense of the prosecution and solicitors and counsel had been instructed.

Lord Denman CJ approached the matter along the lines that the defendant had throughout the criminal proceedings held himself out as the prosecutor and that he could not subsequently, in the civil proceedings, resile from that position. However it is clear that the defendant was more than a mere witness. He had been directly instrumental in setting the prosecution in train and had done so on his own responsibility, himself making the application to the magistrates. This case therefore recognises the same distinction as the other cases and does not assist the plaintiff before us.

The other case mainly relied upon by the plaintiff and by Judge Goodman was *Pandit Gaya Parshad Tewari v Sardar Bhagat Singh* (1908) 24 TLR 884, an appeal to the Judicial Committee of the Privy Council from the Judicial Commissioner of Oudh. This case illustrates that in different jurisdictions prosecutions may be instituted or conducted in varying ways and therefore, when answering the question who can properly be described as the (or a) prosecutor, regard may have to be had to the particular character of the proceedings and the relevant procedural law. It is obvious that the question whether the defendant was the prosecutor must be answered taking into account the local law of criminal procedure; but it is also true that the definition of the tort of malicious prosecution (and other similar torts) has to take account of considerations of public policy which may vary in their importance from one jurisdiction to another (see *Lamont's* case and *Commonwealth Life Assurance Society Ltd v Brain* (1935) 53 CLR 343).

The question raised by *Pandit Gaya Parshad Tewari v Sardar Bhagat Singh* (1908) 24 TLR 884 at 885 was—

> 'whether a person may be sued for damages for malicious prosecution who makes a false report which results in a prosecution, or who instigates the police to send persons up for trial under section 170 of the Code of Criminal Procedure [of India], or who conducts the case against those persons when sent up for trial.'

It appears that the criminal procedure of India did not permit a private
prosecution but, under s 495 of the Code, a private person might, pro hac vice,
be allowed to represent the Crown and conduct the prosecution. That is what
had happened in the case with which the Privy Council were concerned. The
defendant had made malicious and false allegations against the plaintiff that he
had committed criminal offences but had not technically been himself the
prosecutor.

The Judicial Committee, having confirmed that 'the only person who can be
sued in an action for malicious prosecution is the person who prosecutes' and
having referred to the role of the police in India, said (at 884):

'If the charge was false to the knowledge of the complainant, if he misled
the police by bringing suborned witnesses to support it, if he influenced
the police to assist him in sending an innocent man for trial before the
Magistrate, it would be equally improper for him to escape liability
because the prosecution had not technically been conducted by him. The
question in all cases of this kind must be—Who was the prosecutor? And
the answer must depend upon the whole circumstances of the case. The
mere setting of the law in motion was not the criterion; the conduct of the
complainant before and after the charge must also be taken into
consideration. Nor was it enough to say the prosecution was instituted
and conducted by the police. That again was a question of fact.'

On the evidence in that case the defendant had directly intervened in the
criminal process to ensure that the plaintiff was arrested. He was 'directly
responsible for any charge at all being made against the plaintiff'. He took a
'principal part in the conduct of the case both before the police and in the
magistrates' court' and counsel for the prosecution had stated that he had
received certain 'instructions' from the defendant. Under these circumstances
and having regard to the procedural law in India at the time, the Judicial
Committee concluded that the commission of the tort had been made out
against the defendant.

This decision does not suffice for the plaintiff in the present case. It stresses
that one must have regard to the whole circumstances of the case and that it is
a question of fact. It also stresses the importance of considering what the
relevant procedure was and that it may be material to consider not only how
the proceedings were started but also how they came to be and were
continued: the tort can be committed by the malicious continuation of a
criminal prosecution even though it may not have been maliciously instituted
in the first place (see *Fitzjohn v Mackinder* (1861) 9 CBNS 505, 142 ER 199).

The cases relied upon by the plaintiff and *Malz* show that the question is one
to be considered on the actual facts of the case and is not solely concerned with
technicalities (see also *Clerk and Lindsell on Torts* para 19-12). However, all
cases confirm that what has to be shown is that the defendant was more than
a mere witness, more than merely somebody who has given false and
malicious evidence, and must be somebody who has been actually and directly
instrumental in the prosecution, that is, the judicial proceedings.

These authorities therefore do not assist the plaintiff's case before us nor do
they justify the conclusion that the tort can be committed by someone who,
although he has provided false and malicious evidence to the police, has not
himself taken any actual part in the actual process of prosecution. The
defendant must have been 'actively instrumental' in the application to the

relevant *judicial* authority. The defendant in the present case was not such a person. The first strand in the plaintiff's argument, which seeks to extend the scope of the tort to anyone who maliciously provides false evidence with the intent that a prosecution should follow, cannot be supported.

This leads on to the second strand in the plaintiff's argument. It is possible for a defendant to commit a tort through the agency or instrumentality of another. This is not a form of vicarious liability but is an illustration of the broader proposition that, in law, acts committed through the instrumentality of another are the acts of the principal and can give rise to a civil or criminal liability. (There is a general discussion of this aspect of the law in Atiyah *Vicarious Liability in the Law of Torts* Ch 27. The statement of Dixon J in *Commonwealth Life Assurance Society Ltd v Brain* (1935) 53 CLR 343 at 379 that 'those who counsel and persuade the actual prosecutor to institute proceedings or procure him to do so by dishonestly prejudicing his judgment are vicariously responsible for the proceedings' has to be justified in the same way despite the use of the word 'vicariously'.)

In the present context—the responsibility of individuals for judicial proceedings and judicial acts—a clear distinction has been drawn in the cases between those situations where the person interposed between the defendant and the consequence of which the plaintiff complains has acted ministerially or has acted on his own responsibility. This distinction has arisen most often in relation to the tort of false imprisonment (see e g *Austin v Dowling* (1870) LR 5 CP 534) but has also been recognised in relation to other similar torts including malicious prosecution (see e g *Barber v Lesiter* (1859) 7 CBNS 175 at 187, 141 ER 782 at 787). In the past, in certain situations, it has been possible for a private individual to bring about directly, without the intervention of any independent discretion, a particular legal consequence such as an arrest. In contrast there are the situations where, however clear the intent and well-founded and confident the expectation of the defendant, the relevant consequence only comes about on the responsibility of another. In such situations the tort has not been committed and the civil liability of the defendant has not been made out.

A clear illustration of this legal principle is the recent decision of the Court of Appeal in *Davidson v Chief Constable of North Wales Police* [1994] 2 All ER 597, to which, of course, Judge Goodman was not referred. The defendant company were the employers of a store detective who observed the plaintiff and another, as she thought, shoplifting. She informed two police officers who then arrested the plaintiff. Thereafter the store detective gave the police a written statement to the effect that the plaintiff had been shoplifting. The plaintiff was taken to the police station but subsequently released without being charged because information was received from others working at the store that the article in question had not in fact been stolen but had been paid for. The plaintiff sued the defendants for wrongful arrest.

The defendants' servant, the store detective, did not arrest, imprison or detain the plaintiff or restrain his liberty directly in any way herself. She gave information to the police constables and according to their evidence they acted on it. The store detective gave evidence in cross-examination that she expected information given by a store detective such as herself to carry weight with police officers; she intended and expected the police officers to act upon it; she regarded the arrest as made on her behalf or for her. The liability of the defendants was said to arise because the police constables acted 'as her agents' or because she 'procured them to act as they did'. However the fact was that the constables were, as was their duty, exercising their own judgment and making an arrest under s 24(6) of the Police and Criminal Evidence Act 1984.

Sir Thomas Bingham MR identified the principle which distinguishes a case in which a defendant is liable from a case in which he is not as being—

'whether he has merely given information to a properly constituted authority on which that authority may act or not as it decides or whether he has himself been the instigator, promoter and active inciter of the action that follows'. (See at 602.)

The question for the jury was therefore:

'Whether what [the store detective] did went beyond laying information before police officers for them to take such action as they thought fit and amounted to some direction, or procuring, or direct request, or direct encouragement that they should act by way of arresting these defendants.'

Accordingly, although the store detective had 'a very clear intention and expectation as to what would happen', what she did and said did not go beyond 'the mere giving of information, leaving it to the officers to exercise their discretion which on their unchallenged evidence they did as to whether they should take any action or not'. Under these circumstances the Court of Appeal held that there was no evidence upon which the defendants could be found liable in the tort of false imprisonment.

That was a case of an arrest by officers pursuant to their statutory powers of arrest. In *Roy v Prior* [1970] 2 All ER 729, [1971] AC 470, an action for 'malicious arrest', the arrest of the plaintiff occurred pursuant to the issue of a warrant by a court for his arrest. The defendant in the action was a solicitor who had been acting for a Mr Advani at his trial for a criminal offence. The defendant thought that the plaintiff could give evidence to assist the defence of Mr Advani and alleged that the plaintiff was evading the service of a witness summons upon him. The defendant instructed counsel for Mr Advani to apply to the judge at the criminal trial for the issue of a warrant for the arrest of the plaintiff and the defendant gave evidence in support stating on oath that the plaintiff was evading service. The judge ordered the issue of a warrant and the plaintiff was arrested and kept in custody until he was brought to court the following day. The plaintiff's case was that the defendant had acted maliciously and that the evidence which the defendant had given in support of the application for the warrant was false. The defendant applied to have the plaintiff's claim struck out as disclosing no cause of action. The primary point that was argued was whether to allow the action to proceed would infringe the principle that civil proceedings should not be brought in respect of evidence given to a court. Lord Morris of Borth-y-Gest said ([1970] 2 All ER 729 at 733, [1971] AC 470 at 477–478):

'It is well settled that no action will lie against a witness for words spoken in giving evidence in a court even if the evidence is falsely and maliciously given (see *Dawkins v Lord Rokeby* (1873) LR 8 QB 255 and *Watson v M'Ewan* [1905] AC 480, [1904–7] All ER Rep 1). If a witness gives false evidence he may be prosecuted if the crime of perjury has been committed but a civil action for damages in respect of the words spoken will not lie (see the judgment of Lord Goddard CJ in *Hargreaves v Bretherton*

[1958] 3 All ER 122, [1959] 1 QB 45). Nor is this rule to be circumvented by alleging a conspiracy between witnesses to make false statements (see *Marrinan v Vibart* [1962] 3 All ER 380, [1963] 1 QB 528). This, however, does not involve that an action that is not brought in respect of evidence given in court but is brought in respect of an alleged abuse of process of court must be defeated if one step in the course of the abuse of the process of the court involved or necessitated the giving of evidence. It must often happen that a defendant who is sued for damages for malicious prosecution will have given evidence in the criminal prosecution of which the plaintiff complains. The essence of the complaint in such a case is that criminal proceedings have been instituted not only without reasonable and probable cause but also maliciously. So also in actions based upon alleged abuses of the process of the court it will often happen that the court will have been induced to act by reason of some false evidence given by someone. In such cases the actions are not brought on or in respect of any evidence given but in respect of malicious abuse of process (see *Elsee v Smith* (1822) 2 Chit 304).'

This case illustrates that it is the malicious abuse of the process of the court which is the essence of such torts, not the giving of false evidence, and draws the distinction which corresponds to the public policy which protects those who provide evidence from civil suit as opposed to criminal prosecution. It also, in conjunction with cases such as *Davidson v Chief Constable of North Wales Police* [1994] 2 All ER 597, illustrates the difference between bringing about an arrest or other judicial consequence through an independent officer and doing so by the defendant's own direct intervention in the legal process.

It is tempting in such cases as the present to say that the defendant has maliciously intended to bring about the prosecution of the plaintiff and with that intention has given false information to the police and that she should therefore be tortiously liable for the criminal prosecution that follows. Thus it has been said that if the 'discretion' of the actual prosecutor is 'misled by false information' the fact that the defendant was not the prosecutor is immaterial (see per Dixon J in *Commonwealth Life Assurance Society Ltd v Brain* (1935) 53 CLR 343 at 379 and per McMullin J in *Commercial Union Assurance Co of NZ Ltd v Lamont* [1989] 3 NZLR 187). However, to say that such a cause of action should exist runs counter to both the identification of the role of the police officer who lays the information in the exercise of his own independent assessment and the principle that witnesses should be protected from civil proceedings in respect of evidence they have provided whether well founded or not.

In the present case the relevant police officer, Det Con Haynes, was under no obligation to lay the information. He had to form his own view and to decide whether or not he would swear the necessary oath. He was entitled to tell the defendant to bring a private prosecution if she thought fit, as in fact happened in respect of other incidents as between the plaintiff and the defendant. He was perfectly entitled not to be satisfied that the defendant was a reliable or creditworthy witness, as again happened in respect of another alleged incident. The plaintiff did not call Det Con Haynes to show that he was acting under some compulsion from the defendant nor to show that she was fulfilling the role of anything more than a witness from whom he had taken a statement which contained evidence which, if believed, showed that the plaintiff had committed a criminal offence. There was nothing in the present case to displace the discretion and judgment of Det Con Haynes whether or not to institute criminal proceedings against the plaintiff by laying a complaint.

The present case also demonstrates that the decision of Judge Goodman and the case of the plaintiff infringes the principle which requires that the provision of evidence should not be the subject of civil proceedings, as opposed to criminal prosecution. The principle exists for the protection of all witnesses, not merely those who have provided honest evidence. The reason for this is that if honest witnesses are to be protected from being harassed by allegations of perjury or malice, there must be a bar on all such actions. The public policy accepts that the protection from civil suit applies to the honest and dishonest alike; the policy is that such matters should be the province of the criminal not the civil law.

The line of argument which appealed to Judge Goodman, and was urged also upon us, was that it sufficed for civil liability to show that the purported information supplied to the police officer was dishonest and malicious and was supplied with the intent that a prosecution should follow. Dicta in the Canadian case *Watters v Pacific Delivery Service Ltd* (1963) 42 DLR (2d) 661 which suggested that deliberately misleading the police would suffice were also relied on (cf *Reid v Webster* (1966) 59 DLR (2d) 189). But these arguments do not meet the point or circumvent the principle of public policy. Indeed, if the present action was well conceived, I cannot see any distinction which would prevent an acquitted defendant to a rape or indecent assault prosecution from suing the 'complainant' for malicious prosecution. Her evidence will in most cases have been equally fundamental to the prosecution case and it will have been her allegations that formed the basis of the prosecution. Public policy requires that in such cases if there has been perjury or malice or other dishonest abuse of process on the part of the complainant that it be the subject of criminal not civil sanctions.

In my judgment this appeal must succeed.

Appeal allowed. Leave to appeal to the House of Lords granted.

Frances Rustin   Barrister.

Rastin v British Steel plc
and other appeals

COURT OF APPEAL, CIVIL DIVISION
SIR THOMAS BINGHAM MR, BELDAM AND SAVILLE LJJ
7, 8, 17 FEBRUARY 1994

County court – Practice – Striking out – Failure to request hearing date within time prescribed – Extension of time for requesting hearing date – Retrospective extension of time for requesting hearing date – Duty of plaintiff after close of pleadings to request fixing of hearing date within prescribed time limit – Automatic striking out of an action if plaintiff fails to request fixing of hearing date within prescribed time limit – Whether court having jurisdiction to extend time retrospectively and reinstate action – Principles on which court should exercise discretion to extend time to request fixing of hearing date – CCR Ord 17, r 11(3)(d), (9), Ord 13, r 4.

The county court has jurisdiction under CCR Ord 13, r 4[a] retrospectively to extend the time for requesting a hearing date following the automatic striking out of an action under Ord 17, r 11(9)[b] because of the plaintiff's failure to request the fixing of a hearing date within the time prescribed by Ord 17, r 11(3)(d)[c]. In exercising its discretion to do so the court should not grant a retrospective application to extend time unless the plaintiff (including his advisers) can show that, save for his failure (which must be excusable) to comply with r 11(3)(d), he has prosecuted his case with at least reasonable diligence and that overall he is innocent of any significant failure to conduct the case with expedition, having regard to the particular features of the case. However, if it appears that the defendant might be expected to suffer significant prejudice if the action were reinstated which he would not have suffered if the plaintiff had complied with the rules, that will always be a powerful and usually a conclusive reason for not exercising discretion in the plaintiff's favour. On the other hand, the absence of such prejudice is not a potent reason for exercising discretion in the plaintiff's favour (see p 646 a e and p 647 f j, post).

Notes

For the duty of a plaintiff in county court proceedings to request the fixing of a hearing date and the automatic striking out of the action if the plaintiff fails to do so within the time prescribed, see Supplement to 10 *Halsbury's Laws* (4th edn) para 257A.

Cases referred to in judgment

Allen v Sir Alfred McAlpine & Sons Ltd, Bostick v Bermondsey and Southwark Group Hospital Management Committee, Sternberg v Hammond [1968] 1 All ER 543, [1968] 2 QB 229, [1968] 2 WLR 366, CA.
Baxendale (Robert) Ltd v Davstone (Holdings) Ltd, Carobene v John Collier Menswear Ltd [1982] 3 All ER 496, [1982] 1 WLR 1385, CA.

---
a   Rule 4 is set out at p 645 e, post
b   Rule 11(9) is set out at p 645 c, post
c   Rule 11(3), so far as material, is set out at p 645 a, post

Birkett v James [1977] 2 All ER 801, [1978] AC 297, [1977] 3 WLR 38, HL.
Costellow v Somerset CC [1993] 1 All ER 952, [1993] 1 WLR 256, CA.
Leal v Dunlop Bio-Processes International Ltd [1984] 2 All ER 207, [1984] 1 WLR 874, CA.
Lewis v Wolking Properties Ltd [1978] 1 All ER 427, [1978] 1 WLR 403, CA.
Samuels v Linzi Dresses Ltd [1980] 1 All ER 803, [1981] QB 115, [1980] 2 WLR 836, CA.
Ward-Lee v Linehan [1993] 2 All ER 1006, [1993] 1 WLR 754, CA.

Cases also cited or referred to in skeleton arguments
Bernstein v Jackson [1982] 2 All ER 806, [1982] 1 WLR 1082, CA.
Caribbean General Insurance Ltd v Frizzell Insurance Brokers Ltd (1993) Times, 4 November, CA.
Dept of Transport v Chris Smaller (Transport) Ltd [1989] 1 All ER 897, [1989] AC 1197, HL.
Erskine Communications Ltd v Worthington (1991) Times, 8 July, CA.
Evans v Bartlam [1937] 2 All ER 646, [1937] AC 473, HL.
Grand Metropolitan Nominee (No 2) Co Ltd v Evans [1993] 1 All ER 642, [1992] 1 WLR 1191, CA.
Harwood v Courtaulds Ltd (1993) Times, 2 February, CA.
Heaven v Road and Rail Wagons Ltd [1965] 2 All ER 409, [1965] 2 QB 355.
Hornagold v Fairclough Building Ltd [1993] PIQR 400, CA.
Jokai Tea Holdings Ltd, Re (1989) [1993] 1 All ER 630, [1992] 1 WLR 1196, CA.
Kleinwort Benson Ltd v Barbrak Ltd [1987] 2 All ER 289, [1987] AC 597, HL.
R v Bloomsbury and Marylebone County Court, ex p Villerwest Ltd [1976] 1 All ER 897, [1976] 1 WLR 362, CA.
Restick v Crickmore [1994] 2 All ER 112, [1994] 1 WLR 420, CA.
Revici v Prentice Hall Inc [1969] 1 All ER 772, [1969] 1 WLR 157, CA.
Robinson v Fawcett & Firth [1901] 2 KB 325, DC.
Schafer v Blyth [1920] 3 KB 140.
Smith v Secretary of State for the Environment (1987) Times, 6 July, CA.
Waddon v Whitecroft-Scovill Ltd [1988] 1 All ER 996, [1988] 1 WLR 309, HL.
Whistler v Hancock (1878) 3 QBD 83.

Interlocutory appeals

Rastin v British Steel plc
The defendant, British Steel plc, appealed with the leave of the judge against the order of Judge Harris QC dated 2 April 1993 made in the Corby County Court whereby he dismissed the defendant's appeal against the order of District Judge Goodman dated 4 March 1993 reinstating the action brought by the plaintiff, Donald Rastin, after it had been automatically struck out pursuant to CCR Ord 17, r 11(9) on 4 October 1992 and granting the plaintiff an extension of time to request the fixing of a hearing date. The facts are set out in the judgment of the court.

Todd v Evans
The plaintiff, George Stephen Todd, appealed with the leave of the Court of Appeal granted on 28 July 1993 against the order of Judge Bates QC dated 17 June 1993 made in the Weymouth County Court whereby he allowed an appeal by the defendant, Gael Harley Evans, against the order of Deputy

District Judge Allin dated 9 February 1993 reinstating the action after it had been automatically struck out pursuant to CCR Ord 17, r 11(9) on 23 December 1992 and granting the plaintiff an extension of time to request the fixing of a hearing date. The facts are set out in the judgment of the court.

Adams v Geest plc

The defendant, Geest plc, appealed with the leave of the judge against the order of Judge Head dated 5 April 1993 made in the King's Lynn County Court whereby he allowed on technical grounds the defendant's appeal against the order of Deputy District Judge Rutherford dated 9 February 1993 granting the plaintiff, Paul Adams, an extension of time to request the fixing of a hearing date notwithstanding that the action had been automatically struck out pursuant to CCR Ord 17, r 11(9), but nevertheless reinstated the plaintiff's action. The facts are set out in the judgment of the court.

Byrne v Webber and anor

The plaintiff, Stella Byrne, appealed with the leave of the judge against the order of Judge Thompson QC dated 12 July 1993 made in the Bodmin County Court whereby he allowed an appeal by the first defendant, Terence Webber, against the order of District Judge Adam dated 11 May 1993 reinstating the plaintiff's action against the first defendant and the second defendant, George Hemmett, after it had been automatically struck out pursuant to CCR Ord 17, r 11(9) on 14 January 1993 and granting the plaintiff an extension of time to request the fixing of a hearing date. The facts are set out in the judgment of the court.

Donaldson v Canavan

The defendant, Herbert Canavan, appealed with the leave of the judge against the order of Judge Oppenheimer dated 15 June 1993 made in the Brentford County Court whereby he allowed an appeal by the plaintiff, Brian Donaldson, against the order of Deputy District Judge Sofaer dated 19 March 1993 dismissing the plaintiff's application to set aside the order of District Judge Gerlis dated 23 December 1992 confirming that the action had been automatically struck out pursuant to CCR Ord 17, r 11(9) on 3 December 1992, and reinstated the action, holding that an extension of time to request the fixing of a hearing date would have been granted, if sought. The facts are set out in the judgment of the court.

Ayres v British Steel plc

The defendant, British Steel plc, appealed with the leave of the Court of Appeal against the order of Judge Hywel ap Robert dated 18 May 1993 made in the Neath and Port Talbot County Court whereby he dismissed the defendant's appeal against the order of District Judge Moulson dated 19 April 1993 reinstating the action brought by the plaintiff, Henry Leyshon Ayres, after it had been automatically struck out pursuant to CCR Ord 17, r 11(9) on 25 March 1992 and granting the plaintiff an extension of time to request the fixing of a hearing date. The facts are set out in the judgment of the court.

Ronald Walker QC and *Paul Downes* (instructed by *Everatt & Co*, Evesham and *Cartwrights Adams & Black*, Cardiff) for the appellant British Steel plc.

Brian Leveson QC and *Gerwyn Samuel* (instructed by *Lawford & Co*, Richmond) for the respondent Rastin.
Anthony Coleman (instructed by *Howe & Shorter*, Weymouth) for the appellant Todd.
Edwin Glasgow QC and *Michael Pooles* (instructed by *Budd Martin Burrett*, Chelmsford) for the respondent Evans.
Quintin Tudor-Evans (instructed by *Roythorne & Co*, Spalding) for the appellant Geest plc.
John Beggs (instructed by *Ward Gethin*, King's Lynn) for the respondent Adams.
Alexander Dawson (instructed by *Stephens & Scown*, St Austell) for the appellant Byrne.
Christopher Russell (instructed by *Ford Simey Daw Roberts*, Exeter and *Veitch Penny*, Exeter) for the respondent Webber and the second defendant Hemmett.
Edwin Glasgow QC and *Michael Soole* (instructed by *Marshall & Galpin*, Oxford) for the appellant Canavan.
John Wilson (instructed by *Johnson Ryan Brady & Co*, West Drayton) for the respondent Donaldson.
John Cherry QC and *Matthias Kelly* (instructed by *Russell Jones & Walker*, Bristol) for the respondent Ayres.

Cur adv vult

17 February 1994. The following judgment of the court was delivered.

SIR THOMAS BINGHAM MR. The court has before it six appeals from county courts. All raise one common question of law and four of the appeals raise a second. The questions are: (1) if an action is automatically struck out under CCR Ord 17, r 11(9) on a plaintiff's failure to request the fixing of a hearing day, has the county court jurisdiction to extend the time for compliance retrospectively and so in effect to reinstate the action? (2) If a county court has jurisdiction so to act, on what principles should it exercise its jurisdiction? In five out of the six cases the county court judge held that there was jurisdiction to extend time retrospectively and so to reinstate the action. The sixth judge took the other view. There are a number of other cases, not before us, in which other judges have shared his opinion. On the second question, not surprisingly, a variety of views was expressed in the six cases. Four of the judges who held that the court had jurisdiction to extend time exercised their discretion in favour of the plaintiff. A fifth held that there was jurisdiction to extend time but that there was on the facts no good reason for doing so. It is desirable that the law on this subject should be clear, and that the discretion (if it exists) should be exercised on uniform principles. This is the judgment of the court, to which all members have contributed.

(1) *Jurisdiction*
CCR Ord 17, r 11 provides for the giving of automatic directions in default and fixed date actions, with some exceptions irrelevant for present purposes. When the pleadings are deemed to be closed (which is 14 days after delivery of a defence or 28 days after the delivery of a counterclaim: Ord 17, r 11(11)(a)), directions as to discovery and the reception of evidence take effect. Also, under Ord 17, r 11(3)(d):

'unless a day has already been fixed, the plaintiff shall within 6 months request the proper officer to fix a day for the hearing ...'

This six-month period is, however, capable of variation. Rule 11(4) provides:

'Nothing in paragraph (3) shall—(a) prevent the court from giving, of its own motion or on the application of any party, such further or different directions or orders as may in the circumstances be appropriate ...'

Rule 11(9) contains the provision central to these appeals:

'If no request is made pursuant to paragraph (3)(d) within 15 months of the day on which pleadings are deemed to be closed (or within 9 months after the expiry of any period fixed by the court for making such a request), the action shall be automatically struck out.'

Thus the plaintiff has six months from the close of pleadings to request a hearing date, and the action is automatically struck out if the plaintiff does not do so within nine months of the expiry of that six-month period (or of any other period which the court may have fixed for making the request).

The plaintiffs in these appeals rely in particular on CCR Ord 13, r 4:

'4.—(1) Except as otherwise provided, the period within which a person is required or authorised by these rules or by any judgment, order or direction to do any act in any proceedings may be extended or abridged by consent of all the parties or by the court on the application of any party.

(2) Any such period may be extended by the court although the application for extension is not made until after the expiration of the period.'

The plaintiffs argue that Ord 17, r 11(9) does not 'otherwise provide', and they contrast that provision with Ord 9, r 10 which also provides for an action to be struck out after 12 months but which carries the rider: '... and no enlargement of the period of 12 months shall be granted under Order 13, rule 4.' No such rider is found in the rule under consideration. More generally, the plaintiffs rely on decisions of this court in *Lewis v Wolking Properties Ltd* [1978] 1 All ER 427, [1978] 1 WLR 403, *Samuels v Linzi Dresses Ltd* [1980] 1 All ER 803, [1981] QB 115, *Robert Baxendale Ltd v Davstone (Holdings) Ltd*, *Carobene v John Collier Menswear Ltd* [1982] 3 All ER 496, [1982] 1 WLR 1385, *Lcal v Dunlop Bio-Processes International Ltd* [1984] 2 All ER 207, [1984] 1 WLR 874 and *Ward-Lee v Linehan* [1993] 2 All ER 1006, [1993] 1 WLR 754.

For the defendants it is argued that automatic striking out under Ord 17, r 11(9) amounts to a deemed dismissal of the action for want of prosecution. The action is then dead and there is no jurisdiction to revive it. Particular attention is drawn to the fact that striking out is a result which is under the rules to follow automatically and not as a result of judicial order. Attention is drawn to the *Civil Justice Review* (Cm 394 (1988), chairman Sir Maurice Hodgson) paras 220–228, and to the recommendation that the courts should be actively involved in monitoring the progress of actions. It is pointed out that Ord 17, r 11 contains no express provision, such as is found, for instance, in Ord 21, r 1(3), that the court may restore proceedings which have been struck out, on application or of its own motion. The time limits laid down are, it is submitted, generous; if a plaintiff cannot meet them he can apply under r 11(4) for the six-month period to be extended; but once the action has been automatically struck out that result must be intended to be final.

We see considerable force in the defendants' submissions, but we reject them for four reasons. (a) The authorities do in our view establish that the court's general power under Ord 13, r 4 will not be treated as excluded unless it is excluded expressly. There is here no express exclusion. (b) The contrast with Ord 9, r 10 is in our view persuasive. That is a very clear exclusion of Ord 13, r 4. We attach less significance to Ord 21, r 1(3), which applies where a plaintiff's action is struck out on his failure to appear at the hearing. The rule may exist to make clear that the court can act of its own motion. (c) While the *Civil Justice Review* may have envisaged an automatic and final striking out at a certain stage, it also envisaged that a plaintiff would be given express notice before this occurred. Order 17, r 11 provides for no such notice (other than through the rules themselves). It seems unlikely that the draftsman intended to provide an irrevocable penalty without also providing this important safeguard. (d) Hard cases are bound to arise in which plaintiffs, otherwise largely blameless, fail, perhaps through accident or mischance, to comply with the rule. We do not think it can have been intended to deprive the court of all power to give a remedy in appropriate cases. We accordingly agree with the majority of judges in the cases before us in holding that the court does have jurisdiction under Ord 13, r 4 retrospectively to extend time for requesting a hearing date following an automatic striking out of the action under Ord 17, r 11(9).

(2) The exercise of discretion

The proper approach to the exercise of any judicial discretion must be governed by the legal context in which the discretion arises. In considering the exercise of the court's discretion to extend time following an automatic striking out of the action the following matters are in our view relevant. (a) Delay has long been recognised as the enemy of justice. Order 17, r 11(9) is the latest in a long series of measures aimed to curb delay and promote the expeditious trial of cases. (b) Traditionally it has been assumed that a plaintiff's advisers can be relied on to serve his interests by driving his case forward to trial. Experience has shown this to be an unreliable assumption. Those acting for plaintiffs too often allow months and even years to pass with little or nothing done to press the case forward. Defendants are too often content to let matters rest, perhaps hoping that the claim will die a natural death, perhaps hoping that the time may come to dismiss for want of prosecution. Order 17, r 11 recognises that protection of the public interest in the expeditious trial of cases cannot be left exclusively to the plaintiff's advisers. A hearing date must either be requested within six months after the close of pleadings, or the court itself must grant, and control the period of, any deferment. Plainly the court is intended to control the timetable if the plaintiff for whatever reason seeks to delay the trial. Automatic striking out after 15 months is the sanction. (c) The duty to request the fixing of a hearing date is one which Ord 17, r 11(3)(d) lays squarely on a plaintiff. No corresponding duty is laid on a defendant. Under para (4) of the rule it is in theory open to a defendant to apply for, or the court of its own motion to order, an extension of the six-month period, but the first of these courses is not very likely and the second is very unlikely. In substance paras (3)(d) and (9) are aimed at plaintiffs and their advisers and the object is to ensure that they do not sleep on their oars. (d) The time limits provided by these paragraphs are generous, whether regarded as 15 months from the time when the duty to act arises or nine months from the time when the prescribed period for action expires. Failure to act within these periods will not ordinarily be explicable or excusable by sudden forgetfulness, temporary indisposition, pressure of work or the vagaries of the post. (e) In contrast with the familiar situation in which a defendant applies to dismiss an action for want of prosecution, it is plainly incumbent on a plaintiff seeking a retrospective extension of time to persuade the court that its discretion should be exercised in his favour. (f) In the six cases before the court, all personal injury claims, the limitation period had expired when the action was automatically struck out. This need not of course be so, but in cases where it is so the consequences of a refusal by the court to exercise its jurisdiction in the plaintiff's favour are likely to be more serious, at least to those acting for him.

These considerations lead us to reject the submission that the discretion to extend time after automatic striking out of the action should be exercised on principles similar to those which obtain where a party seeks an extension of time to cure a procedural default in the ordinary course of an action: see *Costellow v Somerset CC* [1993] 1 All ER 952, [1993] 1 WLR 256. That submission gives quite inadequate weight to the fact that in this instance the action has been struck out. To accede to it would deprive r 11(9) of its intended draconian effect. We also reject the submission that retrospective applications to extend time after automatic striking out should be treated as the obverse of applications to dismiss for want of prosecution, with particular attention paid to any prejudice suffered by the defendant. We would not readily extend the application of the rules laid down in *Allen v Sir Alfred McAlpine & Sons Ltd* [1968] 1 All ER 543, [1968] 2 QB 229 and *Birkett v James* [1977] 2 All ER 801, [1978] AC 297 into this new field, and it would in any event be strange to concentrate on the position of the defendant when the object of the rule is to ensure diligent prosecution of the case by the plaintiff.

This last point in our view gives a crucial pointer towards the way in which the discretion should be exercised. A retrospective application to extend time should not succeed unless the plaintiff (in which expression we include his advisers) is able to show that he has, save in his failure to comply with r 11(3)(d) and (4), prosecuted his case with at least reasonable diligence. That does not mean that there is no room to criticise any aspect of his conduct of the case but that overall he is innocent of any significant failure to conduct the case with expedition, having regard to the particular features of the case. The plaintiff's failure to comply with the rule can never be justifiable, but he must in all the circumstances persuade the court that it is excusable. If he is able to show that an extension of time for the requisite period, if sought prospectively, would in all probability have been granted, that will help him, and the more technical his failure the more readily it will be excused. If, but only if, the plaintiff can discharge these burdens should the court consider the interests of justice, the positions of the parties and the balance of hardship in a more general way. If it appears that the defendant might be expected to suffer significant prejudice if the action were reinstated which he would not have suffered if the plaintiff had complied with the rule, that will always be a powerful and usually a conclusive reason for not exercising discretion in the plaintiff's favour. The absence of such prejudice is not, however, a potent reason for exercising discretion in the plaintiff's favour. At this stage, but not before, it is relevant to consider matters such as the availability of an alternative remedy to the plaintiff if the action is not reinstated, the expiry of the limitation period and any admission of liability or payment into court that there may have been.

We now turn to the six appeals.

Rastin v British Steel plc

Mr Rastin suffered unpleasant burns in an accident at work on 14 December 1988. He issued proceedings in the Corby County Court on 2 May 1991. A defence was served on 19 June 1991. Pleadings closed on 4 July. The limitation period expired on 14 December. The six-month period prescribed by Ord 17, r 11(3)(d) expired on 4 January 1992. No request was made to fix a hearing date. The action was automatically struck out on 4 October 1992.

On 11 January 1993 the plaintiff applied for an extension of time which the district judge granted on 4 March. Judge Harris QC dismissed an appeal against that order on 2 April.

The judge gave a most helpful judgment. In this he held (rightly) that the court had jurisdiction to grant an extension and reviewed the grounds for exercising discretion. He pointed out that the rules were there to be observed, not disregarded. He characterised the plaintiff's solicitors' explanation for the delay as amounting to double negligence, since neither the six-month nor the 15-month limit had been observed. He regarded the explanation proffered as thin, insufficient and unacceptable. He inferred that the solicitor involved had simply forgotten all about, or had never known of, r 11(9). He found that the non-compliance was not intentional or contumacious, but accepted with evident reluctance the defendant's concession that the plaintiff's delay was not inordinate or inexcusable. He did, however, accept that the plaintiff's non-compliance had caused no prejudice to the defendant. He observed that the plaintiff could not by that stage issue a fresh writ against the defendant, but concluded that he would have an unanswerable claim against his solicitors, which it would not prejudice him greatly to have to pursue. He ended this section of his judgment:

'If Ord 17, r 11(9) is to be an effective sanction it must be clear that when a case is struck out pursuant to its provisions there will be no reinstatement unless fairness or justice call for it which, in some circumstances, they clearly might. I do not find it easy in common sense to conclude that they do so here. It is the plaintiff's solicitor's fault and he has no excuse, and I think that if I was making up my mind without assistance from authority I would conclude that the action should not be reinstated.'

The judge then referred to *Costellow v Somerset CC* [1993] 1 All ER 952, [1993] 1 WLR 256 from which he quoted at length, and concluded that it would not be consistent with the reasoning in that case if he were to refuse the plaintiff relief in the absence of any suggestion of prejudice to the defendant. He accordingly dismissed the appeal, although with obvious misgiving.

As we have made clear, the reasoning in *Costellow's* case is not applicable in a case such as this. We must therefore exercise our discretion afresh. The plaintiff's action was not, apart from r 11(3)(d) and (4), conducted diligently. Not until March 1992 (over three years after the accident, and nearly two years after the action began) was an expert engineer appointed by the plaintiff. No earlier application had been made to the court for facilities to inspect. When the report was received in August, counsel was asked to advise on evidence but nothing more was done. The judge did not regard the plaintiff's failure to comply with the rule as in any way excusable. On these facts the judge should have made the order which he himself favoured and not the order he felt obliged to make.

We therefore allow the defendant's appeal and set aside the order granting the plaintiff an extended period in which to request a hearing date. The result is that the plaintiff's action remains struck out.

Todd v Evans

On 2 August 1988 there was a motor accident in which Mr Todd was injured and his fiancée was killed. Mr Todd issued proceedings in the Weymouth County Court on 2 July 1991, just within the limitation period. Different solicitors were engaged to prosecute High Court proceedings on behalf of the fiancée's estate and dependants. A defence to Mr Todd's claim was served on 9 September 1991. Pleadings closed on 23 September. The six-month period under r 11(3)(d) expired on 23 March 1992. The action was automatically struck out on 23 December 1992. On 13 January 1993 the plaintiff issued and on 4 February he served an application to extend time. The district judge granted this on 9 February 1993. On 17 June Judge Bates QC allowed an appeal against this decision.

The judge's first reason for allowing the appeal, that the court had no jurisdiction to make the order sought, is one with which we do not agree, for reasons already given. But he went on to hold that even if, contrary to his view, there was jurisdiction, discretion should not be exercised in the plaintiff's favour. The plaintiff gave no adequate explanation of his failure to prosecute the action. The suggestion that the action should have been tried in conjunction with the High Court action is indeed formidable, but that should have been obvious years before. There was no excuse for the plaintiff's failure to comply with the rule. On the principles we have discussed the judge was bound to reach the decision he did. The appeal against his decision must be dismissed.

Adams v Geest plc

Mr Adams suffered an accident at work when he tripped over a pallet on 8 November 1989. He issued proceedings in the King's Lynn County Court on 29 August 1991. A defence was served on 19 September. Pleadings closed on 4 October. Under r 11(3)(d) the plaintiff should have requested the fixing of a trial date by 4 March 1992. He did not do so. The action was automatically struck out on 4 January 1993. But shortly before that date the plaintiff's solicitors wrote to the county court asking for a nine-month extension of time for applying for a hearing date.

On 9 February 1993 the district judge extended the plaintiff's time for applying for a hearing date. Judge Head, on appeal to him, allowed the appeal on technical grounds, but held that the court had jurisdiction to reinstate the action and exercised his discretion in favour of the plaintiff.

The judge's decision on jurisdiction was correct. His decision on the exercise of discretion has not been challenged on appeal. We therefore say nothing about it. The defendant's appeal must be dismissed.

Byrne v Webber and anor

On 24 August 1988 Mrs Byrne was a passenger in a car driven by Mr Hemmett when it collided with a car driven by Mr Webber. She was hurt. On 12 August 1991, just within the limitation period, she issued proceedings in the Liskeard County Court against both drivers. Both served defences, Mr Webber admitting liability and Mr Hemmett denying it. Pleadings closed on 14 October 1991. The six-month period prescribed by r 11(3)(d) expired on 14 April 1992. No request was made for a hearing date to be fixed.

In April 1992 Mr Webber's solicitors made an offer of £3,960 in settlement of the plaintiff's claim, which she rejected in July. The parties came very close to agreeing that the plaintiff should have judgment against Mr Webber for damages to be assessed, but failure to agree on payment of her costs and interest prevented a consent order being finalised. On 2 October 1992 an increased sum was paid into court. It was not accepted.

The plaintiff was resident in Wexford. Her direct instructions were accordingly given to Irish solicitors and she consulted an Irish orthopaedic surgeon. In April 1992 he advised that an MRI scan would, although expensive, throw valuable light on the plaintiff's medical condition.

On 14 January 1993 the plaintiff's action was automatically struck out. Her solicitor was advised of this on 25 January and an application for an extension of time and reinstatement was made which the district judge granted on 11 May. Mr Webber appealed to Judge Thompson QC who on 12 July allowed the appeal and affirmed the striking out of the action.

The judge gave a conspicuously clear and helpful judgment. First he held, rightly, that there was jurisdiction to extend time. Then he considered the exercise of discretion, drawing an analogy with the principles upon which the court extends the validity of a writ under RSC Ord 6, r 8. The judge was not told exactly when the Irish solicitors asked the surgeon to arrange an MRI scan, but he noted that no letter was written by the plaintiff's solicitors to Mr Webber's solicitors between the rejection of the offer in July 1992 and the striking out of the action in January 1993. He observed that it was the duty of the plaintiff to proceed timeously, that there was no agreement to extend time, that there was no difficulty created on Mr Webber's side which could have caused the plaintiff difficulty in applying to set down the case for trial and that there was admitted carelessness on the part of the plaintiff's English solicitors. He held that there was no justification for the delay and that the MRI scan could have been organised before April 1993, by which time the action had already been struck out.

The judge plainly took the view, which was inescapable, that the plaintiff (and her advisers) had not prosecuted her claim with reasonable diligence. He did not regard their failure to comply with the rules as excusable. He was accordingly right to reach the conclusion he did, and although his route to it was slightly different from ours we would not interfere with his exercise of discretion. This appeal is dismissed.

Donaldson v Canavan

Mr Donaldson, a serving soldier, was badly injured in a motor accident on 23 July 1988. He issued proceedings in the Brentford County Court on 11 July 1991, shortly before expiry of the limitation period, and a defence was served admitting liability on 20 August. Pleadings closed on 4 September 1991 and the six-month period provided by r 11(3)(d) ended on 3 March 1992. In August

1992 the plaintiff was discharged from the army. In the following month the plaintiff's solicitors indicated that they were ready for trial. There was however difficulty in attempting to assess the plaintiff's continuing loss of earnings so long as his employment prospects were uncertain and in October 1992 the defendant's solicitors indicated that they were not prepared to consider any claim for loss of earnings or continuing loss until they had considered the plaintiff's future earnings and employment prospects. On 3 December the action was automatically struck out. The district judge confirmed that that was so on 23 December. The plaintiff then applied to set aside that order. He failed before the district judge but succeeded before Judge Oppenheimer on 15 June 1993. The judge held that he had jurisdiction to reinstate the action and exercised his discretion in the plaintiff's favour. He held that an extension of time, if sought, would have been granted, and that there was no possibility of assessing the special damage until after the plaintiff had been discharged from the army. His future loss of earnings could not be considered until the latter part of 1992.

The judge's decision on jurisdiction was correct. His reasons for exercising his discretion as he did, explained in a clear and careful judgment, were not challenged. It follows that Mr Canavan's appeal is dismissed. Following an indication of our decision on jurisdiction the parties agreed, and we order, that the plaintiff should have his costs of and relating to this application and appeal in this court and in both courts below in any event.

Ayres v British Steel plc

Mr Ayres had an accident in the shower room at his place of work on 27 December 1989. He issued proceedings in the Neath and Port Talbot County Court on 14 November 1990. A defence was served on 11 December. Pleadings closed on Christmas Day. The six-month period limited under r 11(3)(d) expired on 25 June 1991. The action was automatically struck out on 25 March 1992.

The striking out of the action was not, it seems, appreciated at that stage by the plaintiff, the defendant or the county court. On 7 August 1992 the defendant made a without prejudice offer of £500 in settlement. On 29 October the district judge gave the plaintiff leave to amend the particulars of claim, and amended particulars were served on 15 November. On 12 January 1993 the plaintiff's solicitors asked the court to fix a date for trial and on 25 February the court gave notice to the plaintiff's solicitors that the action was fixed for hearing on 10 June. Meanwhile, however, in answer to a letter from the defendant's solicitors, the court had on 26 January 1993 told them that the action had been struck out. The defendant's solicitors passed this information on to the plaintiff's solicitors on 12 March. It came as a surprise to them, although the action had been struck out almost a year earlier.

On 7 April the plaintiff applied for an extension of time to request a hearing date to 13 January 1993. The district judge granted this application on 19 April and on 18 May 1993 Judge Hywel ap Robert upheld his decision. The judge first held, and we agree, that he had jurisdiction to grant the relief sought. On the exercise of discretion, the judge primarily considered prejudice: holding that the defendant had not been prejudiced by the plaintiff's non-compliance he regarded it as a strong and plain case for exercising discretion in the plaintiff's favour.

Had the judge applied what we hold to be the correct principles, he would have been bound to reach a different conclusion. This was a very straightforward case and it was not prosecuted with reasonable diligence. It appears that the plaintiff's solicitors had an efficient system for monitoring the progress of cases, and were aware of Ord 17, r 11(9), but that this case was inadvertently overlooked: this might excuse failure over a relatively short period, but can scarcely excuse a failure which lasted from 25 June 1991 when the six-month period expired until 12 January 1993 when the plaintiff's solicitors eventually requested a hearing date.

The defendant's appeal will be allowed, the judge's order set aside and an order made refusing an extension of time in which to apply for a hearing date. The consequence is that the action remains struck out.

Appeal in Rastin v British Steel plc allowed. Appeal in Todd v Evans dismissed. Appeal in Adams v Geest plc dismissed. Appeal in Byrne v Webber and anor dismissed. Appeal in Donaldson v Canavan dismissed. Appeal in Ayres v British Steel plc allowed. Leave to appeal to the House of Lords refused in all cases.

L I Zysman Esq   Barrister.

R v Secretary of State for Health and another, ex parte Furneaux and others

COURT OF APPEAL, CIVIL DIVISION
BUTLER-SLOSS, MANN AND PETER GIBSON LJJ
1 JULY 1993

Judicial review – Delay – Refusal of relief – Grant of relief likely substantially to prejudice rights of another person – Application to review decision of Secretary of State – Applicants applying for judicial review more than six months after Secretary of State's decision – Applicants guilty of undue delay – Whether court should refuse relief – Whether grant of relief likely substantially to prejudice rights of respondent – Whether causal connection required between prejudice and delay – Supreme Court Act 1981, s 31(6) – RSC Ord 53, r 4 (1).

The applicants, who were three doctors in a rural practice, applied to their local family practitioner committee for approval to provide pharmaceutical services at their surgery to patients in their practice area who resided more than one mile from a pharmacy providing National Health Service pharmaceutical services. The committee referred the application to the rural dispensing committee who granted outline consent in December 1990. Two pharmacists in the area appealed against that decision to the Secretary of State for Health who, without holding an oral hearing, allowed the appeal in July 1991 and refused the application. In January 1992 the applicants applied for judicial review of that decision on the ground that the Secretary of State had taken into consideration written evidence which the doctors had not seen and which they were therefore unable to comment upon. Leave to move for judicial review was granted and thereafter the Secretary of State conceded that he had taken into consideration in making his determination material of which the doctors were unaware. It was agreed by the applicants and the Secretary of State that the decision should be quashed and the matter remitted for redetermination by the Secretary of State. However, a company which had purchased the only pharmacy in the locality in reliance on the Secretary of State's decision to refuse the application was granted leave to intervene in the proceedings as the second respondent and applied for the application to be dismissed, contending that the court should exercise its discretion to dismiss the application either under RSC Ord 53, r 4(1)[a] on the ground that the applicants had been guilty of undue delay in applying for judicial review or under s 31(6)[b] of the Supreme Court Act 1981 on the ground that the grant of relief would 'substantially prejudice the rights' of the second respondent. The judge dismissed the application on the ground that there was no causal connection between the delay and any substantial prejudice to the rights of the second respondent which might have occurred. The second respondent appealed.

Held – If an applicant for judicial review failed to apply promptly he was guilty of undue delay even if the court was satisfied in the light of all the circumstances that there was good reason for the failure to apply promptly. In such circumstances the court retained a discretion under s 31(6) of the 1981 Act to refuse, on the grounds of undue delay, leave to make the application or the relief sought if it considered that the grant of relief would substantially prejudice the rights of another person. There was no requirement in s 31(6) of the 1981 Act that there had to be a causal connection between prejudice and undue delay for the refusal of relief; instead, what was required was a causal connection between prejudice and the grant of relief before the court could exercise its discretion to refuse leave or the relief sought. The judge had therefore misdirected himself and, considering the matter afresh, since there had been prejudice to the second respondent and unexplained delay the appeal would be allowed and the application for judicial review dismissed (see p 657 *e f* and p 658 *f g*, post).

Dictum of Ackner LJ in *R v Stratford-on-Avon, ex p Jackson* [1975] 3 All ER 769 at 774 applied.

Notes

For delay in applying for judicial review, see 37 *Halsbury's Laws* (4th edn) para 571.

For the Supreme Court Act 1981, s 31, see 11 *Halsbury's Statutes* (4th edn) (1991 reissue) 991.

Cases referred to in judgments

Caswell v Dairy Produce Quota Tribunal for England and Wales [1990] 2 All ER 434, [1990] 2 AC 738, [1990] 2 WLR 1320, HL.

R v Exeter City Council, ex p J L Thomas & Co Ltd [1990] 1 All ER 413, [1991] 1 QB 471, [1990] 3 WLR 100.

R v Stratford-on-Avon DC, ex p Jackson [1985] 3 All ER 769, [1985] 1 WLR 1319, CA.

R v Swale BC and Medway Ports Authority, ex p Royal Society for the Protection of Birds [1990] 2 Admin LR 790.

---

a   Rule 4(1) is set out at p 656 *e*, post
b   Section 31(6) is set out at p 656 *f*, post

Cases also cited or referred to in skeleton arguments
R v British Railways Board, ex p Great Yarmouth BC (1983) Times, 15 March, DC.
R v Independent Television Commission, ex p TV NI Ltd (1991) Times, 30 December, [1991] CA Transcript 1227.
R v Secretary of State for Transport, ex p Presvac Engineering Ltd (1991) 4 Admin LR 121, CA.
R v Tavistock General Comrs, ex p Worth [1985] STC 564.
With v O'Flanagan [1936] 1 All ER 727, [1936] Ch 575, CA.

Appeal
The second respondent, Elmfield Drugs Ltd, appealed from the order of Popplewell J on 10 July 1992 granting the applicants, Peter John Sidney Furneaux, Adam Skinner and Vivien Fox, judicial review by way of certiorari to quash the decision of the first respondent, the Secretary of State for Health, on 4 July 1991 to allow the appeal of Mr R Thomas and Mr D C Pay, who were pharmacists, against the decision of the Rural Dispensing Committee approving the applicants' application for outline consent for the provision of pharmaceutical services to patients resident within part of the applicants' practice area in Kent at a distance of more than one mile from any pharmacy providing National Health Service pharmaceutical services. The facts are set out in the judgment of Mann LJ.

Robert Carnwath QC and *Jonathan S Fisher* (instructed by *Charles Russell*) for the second respondent.
Nicola Davies QC (instructed by *Hempsons*) for the applicants.

MANN LJ. There is before the court an appeal from a decision of Popplewell J given on 10 July 1992. By his decision the judge granted the application for judicial review which had been made by Dr Peter Furneaux, Dr Adam Skinner and Dr Vivien Knox. The respondents to the application were the Secretary of State for Health and, by subsequent addition, Elmfield Drugs Ltd. The decision quashed by the judge was a decision of the Secretary of State for Health dated 4 July 1991. The present appeal is by the second respondent, that is to say, Elmfield Drugs Ltd. That company is a family company owning 11 pharmacies. The leading spirit is Mr N C Patel who is a registered pharmacist.

The way in which the matter has developed requires the consideration of two separate strands of events. The first strand concerns the applicants for judicial review. They are three doctors who are in practice at the Winterdon Surgery at Westerham in Kent. On 29 July 1989 they made an application to the Kent Family Practitioner Committee under reg 30A of the National Health Service (General Medical and Pharmaceutical Services) Regulations 1974, SI 1974/160. The purpose of the application was to enable the doctors to provide pharmaceutical services at their surgery to patients resident in the practice area in Kent but who reside at a distance of more than one mile from any pharmacy providing National Health services.

The Family Practitioner Committee referred the application to the Rural Dispensing Committee. That is a special health authority constituted by the Rural Dispensing Committee (Establishment and Constitution) Order 1983, SI 1983/312.

On 4 December 1990 the Rural Dispensing Committee granted an outline consent upon the doctors' application. There is provision for interested parties to appeal a decision of the Rural Dispensing Committee to the Secretary of State.

On respectively 12 and 13 December 1990 two pharmacists, Mr R Thomas and Mr D Pay, did so appeal. The appeal was determined by the Secretary of State without an oral hearing on 4 July 1991. By his decision the appeal was allowed and the doctors' application for outline consent was refused. The terms of the decision were as follows in a letter addressed to Mr Thomas:

'The Secretary of State for Health has now considered your appeal against the decision of the Rural Dispensing Committee (RDC) to approve the application from Dr P J S Furneaux and Partners for outline consent to provide pharmaceutical services to patients resident within part of their practice area in Kent at a distance of more than one mile from any pharmacy providing NHS pharmaceutical services. After studying all the documentary evidence, including evidence from Mr S J Brick of R H Ferris (Westerham) Ltd to which you drew attention, the Secretary of State concluded that your appeal could be properly determined without an oral hearing. He has given careful consideration to the facts and contentions upon which you relied, the observations of the RDC, the Kent and Bromley Family Health Services Authorities, the Kent and Surrey Local Medical Committees, the Kent and Bromley Local Pharmaceutical Committees and those others who provided written evidence. The question the Secretary of State had to consider was whether grant of the application would prejudice the proper provision of general medical or pharmaceutical services in the locality. The Secretary of State was satisfied that grant of application would not prejudice the proper provision of general medical services in the locality. With reference to the provision of pharmaceutical services, he considered that grant of the application would be such as to prejudice the proper provision of pharmaceutical services in the locality by reason of its effect upon the pharmacy in Westerham. I have to inform you, therefore, that the Secretary of State has upheld your appeal and that the application from Dr Furneaux and Partners for outline consent has been refused.'

That is the decision which was impugned by the doctors' application for judicial review. That application was made on 23 January 1992. The basis of the application was that the Secretary of State had regard to communications received which the doctors had not seen and were thus unable to comment upon. Leave to move was given by Macpherson J on a consideration of the documents on 4 February 1992. Thereafter the Secretary of State conceded that he had had regard to material of which the doctors were ignorant and that he had taken it into account in his determination. Accordingly as between the applicants and the Secretary of State a formal order was agreed under which the Secretary of State's decision would be quashed and the matter remitted for re-determination.

At that stage the second respondent came upon the scene and I must pick up the second strand. As I have said, the second respondent is a family company owning a number of pharmacies. In February 1991 Mr Patel, who was looking towards expansion of his business, saw an advertisement for the sale of a pharmacy which was in Westerham owned by R H Ferris (Westerham) Ltd of which company Mr S J Brick was a director. It was in fact the only pharmacy in Westerham. Mr Patel was interested in the purchase but learnt from a third party—not Mr Brick who had not revealed the position—that on 4 December the Rural Dispensing Committee had granted outline consent to the doctors for the provision of pharmaceutical services at their surgery. Mr Patel has deposed that on receiving that information he withdrew from negotiations for the acquisition of the pharmacy. However, he subsequently learnt of the Secretary of State's decision of 4 July. On the basis of that decision he returned to negotiations with R H Ferris (Westerham) Ltd, reached agreement with them, and on 19 September 1991 exchanged contracts for the purchase of the pharmacy. The sale was completed on 1 October 1991 for a price in excess of £550,000. He commenced to trade.

Late in February of 1992 Mr Patel learnt of the grant of leave by Macpherson J and in March learnt of the proposed settlement as between the Secretary of State and the doctors; a settlement to which apparently Mr Thomas and Mr Pay were willing to agree. That knowledge provoked Mr Patel's company to intervene in the proceedings and on 6 May Macpherson J gave leave for the company to be added as a second respondent.

Those then are the two strands which came together at the hearing before Popplewell J on 10 July. At that hearing there was no dispute between the applicant and the Secretary of State. The contention was as between the applicant and second respondent. The contention of the second respondent was that in discretion relief should be refused. The second respondent relied upon RSC Ord 53, r 4(1) and s 31(6) of the Supreme Court Act 1981. Order 53, r 4(1) provides:

'An application for judicial review shall be made promptly and in any event within three months from the date when grounds for the application first arose unless the Court considers that there is good reason for extending the period within which the application shall be made.'

Section 31(6) provides:

'... the court may refuse to grant—(a) leave for the making of the application; or (b) any relief sought on the application, if it considers that the granting of the relief sought would be likely to cause substantial hardship to, or substantially prejudice the rights of, any person or would be detrimental to good administration.'

The thrust of the second respondent's argument before the judge was that there had been undue delay in making the application for judicial review and that the granting of relief would be likely to cause substantial prejudice to the second respondent and that in discretion the court should refuse to grant the relief sought.

The judge rejected the second respondent's contention and he concluded in this way:

'I decide this simply on the basis that there is not established a causal connection between the delay which undoubtedly took place and any substantial prejudice which may have occurred to the rights of the applicant.'

Against that conclusion the second respondent now appeals. At the forefront of the appeal is the submission that the learned judge misdirected himself as to the mode of application of s 31(6).

The relationship between Ord 53, r 4 and s 31(6) is (as has been frequently observed) an uncomfortable one. The discomfort has to some degree been ameliorated by the decision of this court in *R v Stratford-on-Avon DC, ex p Jackson* [1985] 3 All ER 768, [1985] 1 WLR 1319 and the decision of the House of Lords in

CA   R v Secretary of State, ex p Furneaux (Mann LJ)   657

Caswell v Dairy Produce Quota Tribunal for England and Wales [1990] 2 All ER 434, [1990] AC 738.

In *R v Stratford-on-Avon DC, ex p Jackson* Ackner LJ, delivering the judgment of the court, said ([1985] 3 All ER 769 at 774, [1985] 1 WLR 1319 at 1325:

'... we have concluded that whenever there is a failure to act promptly or within three months there is "undue delay". Accordingly, even though the court may be satisfied in the light of all the circumstances, including the particular position of the applicant, that there is good reason for that failure, nevertheless the delay, viewed objectively, remains "undue delay". The court therefore still retains a discretion to refuse to grant leave for the making of the application or the relief sought on the substantive application on the grounds of undue delay, if it considers that the granting of the relief sought would be likely to cause substantial hardship to, or substantially prejudice the rights of, any person or would be detrimental to good administration.'

That passage was approved by Lord Goff of Chieveley in *Caswell* ([1990] 2 All ER 434 at 439, [1990] 2 AC 738 at 746) in a speech with which the other members of the House agreed. It is, therefore, plain that at the hearing of the application for substantive relief it is open to examination whether or not the application was made promptly and if not whether there are good reasons for delay.

The judge below directed himself in the way in which I have recited. I regret that I, with respect, cannot agree with his approach. In my judgment on the language of s 31(6) there is no requirement for a causal connection between prejudice and undue delay. What is required is a connection between prejudice and the grant of the relief sought. Accordingly I find here a misdirection and I indorse what Simon Brown J said in *R v Swale BC and Medway Ports Authority, ex p Royal Society for the Protection of Birds* [1990] 2 Admin LR 790 at 815 where he remarked that the statute clearly invites an approach based upon a relationship between prejudice and the relief sought.

The position being that I cannot agree with the judge's approach it is open to me to consider the matter afresh as a matter of my own discretion. The prejudice to the second respondent falls as it seems to me under two heads. First, uncertainty as to whether or not the doctors' surgery will be in operation. Secondly, the raising of the possibility that the premise upon which the pharmacy was purchased will be falsified sooner rather than later and will be falsified if upon remission an approval is granted. I say 'sooner rather than later' because the second respondent must accept that under reg 30E(12) of the 1974 regulations as amended it is open to the doctors to make a fresh application five years after a prior determination. That is to say, in this case in July 1996. If the premise was falsified then there would be financial loss to the pharmacy. The dimension of that loss is identified by Mr Patel at £26,000 p a but the applicants do not accept the correctness of that figure, albeit they concede there would be a financial detriment. Overall the applicants concede that there would be prejudice to the second respondent. There being prejudice identified, as I have said, the question arises as to how in the light of that prejudice discretion should be exercised. The matters which are material to an exercise of discretion are legion and cannot be listed. I would not, however, necessarily agree with Simon Brown J's observations in *R v Exeter City Council, ex p J L Thomas* [1990] 1 All ER 413 at 422, [1991] 1 QB 471 at 484 that the mere fact that the imperfection in the decision is a procedural irregularity is a matter of weight to take into account. What is after all a matter of weight to be taken into account is the quality of the delay by which I mean the reasons for the delay which by concession in this case are undue. This requires a more detailed examination of what occurred in relation to the application.

The mere narrative of the dates of 4 July 1991 and 23 January 1992 indicates that the application was not made promptly. What then occurred? It seems to have been this. After receiving the Secretary of State's decision the applicants consulted the British Medical Association. That was a natural thing to do. That consultation led to Messrs Hempsons being instructed on behalf of the doctors on 15 August 1991. That firm then did nothing until 10 October 1991 when they contacted the department and asked for copies of Mr Brick's representations. It will be recollected that Mr Brick was referred to in the decision below. A reply was received from the department on 22 October but that reply incompletely included the documentation. A request was made on 15 November for completion of the documentation and that request was complied with by letter dated 26 November 1991. At that date all relevant material was to hand.

On 12 December the solicitor in Hempsons having conduct of the matter left for holiday in Africa. Whilst on holiday he had the misfortune that two of his children were taken ill with appendicitis and he did not return to the office on 6 January as he had planned. On that day the file was looked at by a partner of his and the matter then proceeded in the light of instructions which had been received by Dr Furneaux on 16 December. It proceeded with a lodgment which resulted in the application for leave being dated 23 January. I regard, for my part, that chronology as being a dismal one in which substantial intervals of time are quite unexplained. The obligation under the rule is to proceed promptly. That obligation is of particular importance where third parties are concerned.

It is plain that this was a decision which affected third parties in that it was a decision affecting the only pharmacy in Westerham. The obligation to proceed promptly was simply not complied with. It is submitted by Miss Davies QC that we could have regard to the fact that the unexplained delay was not causative of loss. By that I think she means that the loss is no greater as a result of relief being granted on day A than it would have been if it had been granted on day A minus a considerable period. That may in an appropriate case be a matter to be taken into account in the exercise of discretion.

In my judgment it is an insignificant point in the context of this case where there is unexplained delay. I regard the existence of the unexplained delay as being decisive in exercising discretion against granting relief in this case, the foundation of the exercise of discretion having been laid by the conceded, and as I think, demonstrable prejudice to the second respondent. Accordingly I would allow this appeal.

PETER GIBSON LJ. I agree.

BUTLER-SLOSS LJ. I also agree.

Appeal allowed.

L I Zysman Esq   Barrister.

R v Canons Park Mental Health Review Tribunal, ex parte A

COURT OF APPEAL, CIVIL DIVISION
NOURSE, KENNEDY AND ROCH LJJ
26, 27 JANUARY, 16 FEBRUARY 1994

Mental health – Patient – Discharge from hospital – Psychopathic disorder – Treatability – Patient suffering from psychopathic disorder detained in hospital – Patient refusing to co-operate in appropriate treatment – Alternative treatment unlikely to alleviate or prevent deterioration of patient's condition – Mental health review tribunal refusing discharge – Whether patient suffering from psychopathic disorder entitled to be discharged if condition not able to be alleviated by treatment – Whether patient untreatable if unwilling to co-operate with suitable treatment – Mental Health Act 1983, ss 3, 16(2), 72.

The applicant was detained in a hospital pursuant to s 3[a] of the Mental Health Act 1983 on the ground of mental illness. Subsequently her condition was reclassified as psychopathic disorder. When the hospital managers refused to discharge her she applied to a mental health review tribunal under s 72[b] of the 1983 Act to be discharged. The tribunal refused to discharge her, on the grounds that it was necessary for her to be detained for nursing care under medical supervision in the interests of her own health and safety and for the protection of others. The tribunal further found that her condition was not being alleviated by the treatment she was receiving, that the appropriate treatment was group therapy, which depended on the voluntary co-operation of the patient, and that she was not willing to co-operate in that treatment but might be willing to do so later. The applicant applied for judicial review of the tribunal's decision on the ground, inter alia, that she had an absolute right to be discharged under s 16(2)[c] of the 1983 Act, which provided that, where a patient had been reclassified by a medical officer as having a psychopathic disorder and the medical officer's report stated that the patient's condition was not likely to be alleviated by further medical treatment in hospital, the authority of the hospital to detain the patient ceased. The applicant contended that because she had been reclassified as suffering from psychopathic disorder and her condition was not likely to respond to treatment in hospital she could not continue to be detained. It was contended on behalf of the respondent tribunal that, although treatability was necessary under other sections of the 1983 Act, such as ss 3, 16 and 20, the tribunal was entitled to decide under s 72(1)(b)(i) that a patient was liable to be detained if it was satisfied that he was suffering from, inter alia, psychopathic disorder of a nature or degree which

---

a Section 3, so far as material, is set out at p 670 j to p 671 a, post
b Section 72, so far as material, is set out at p 669 j to p 670 c, post
c Section 16(2) provides: 'Where a report ... in respect of a patient detained in a hospital is to the effect that he is suffering from psychopathic disorder or mental impairment but not from mental illness or severe mental impairment the appropriate medical officer shall include in the report a statement of his opinion whether further medical treatment in hospital is likely to alleviate or prevent a deterioration of the patient's condition; and if he states that in his opinion such treatment is not likely to have that effect the authority of the managers to detain the patient shall cease.'

made it 'appropriate for him ... to be detained' in a hospital irrespective of
whether or not he was treatable. The Divisional Court held that there was no
power to detain in hospital a psychopathic or mentally impaired person if he
could not be therapeutically or preventively treated and ordered that the
tribunal's decision be quashed and that it should direct the applicant's
discharge. The tribunal appealed, contending that under s 3(2) and s 20(4) of
the 1983 Act the respective criteria for admission for treatment and for
extension of authority to detain were, inter alia, (a) that a patient was 'suffering
from mental illness, severe mental impairment, psychopathic disorder or
mental impairment ... of a nature or degree which makes it appropriate for him
to receive medical treatment in a hospital' (the appropriateness test) and (b) 'in
the case of psychopathic disorder or mental impairment, such treatment is
likely to alleviate or prevent a deterioration of his condition' (the treatability
test) and that s 72(1)(b) contained the appropriateness test but not the
treatability test and the words 'appropriate for him to be liable to be detained'
in s 72(1)(b)(i) did not import the treatability test but if they did, the meaning
and scope of treatability was wider than that assumed by the Divisional Court
and covered the possibility of the applicant agreeing to co-operate in the future
in group therapy.

Held – The appeal would be allowed for the following reasons—

(1) (Roch LJ dissenting) – It was clear from the wording of s 72(1)(b) of the
1983 Act that, when deciding whether it must exercise its mandatory power to
discharge a patient under that section, a mental health review tribunal did not
have to have regard to the treatability test but only to the appropriateness and
safety tests that were expressly referred to in the section. The tribunal was
only required to direct the discharge of a patient if it was satisfied that the
patient was not then suffering from psychopathic disorder and hence the
function of the tribunal was different from the function of the doctors at the
admission or reclassification or renewal stages when the treatability test did
apply. If the tribunal was not required to discharge the patient pursuant to
s 72(1)(b) it had a discretion under s 72(2) whether or not to discharge and in
deciding whether to exercise that discretion the tribunal had to have regard to
the treatability test (see p 683 *b* to *e j* to p 684 *b* and p 685 *d* to *e*, post).

(2) The question that the mental health review tribunal should have
considered was not whether it was satisfied that treatment was likely to
alleviate or prevent deterioration of the patient's disorder but whether it was
satisfied that treatment was unlikely to have such an effect. If a tribunal
wished to direct the discharge of a patient contrary to the advice of the
responsible medical officer it ought to identify which of the matters set out in
s 72(1) of the 1983 Act it was satisfied did not exist and give reasons for that
decision. The Divisional Court had wrongly held that the tribunal had found
that it was unlikely that treatment would alleviate or prevent deterioration of
the patient's disorder. The tribunal had in fact indicated that it was not
satisfied that the applicant was not suffering from psychopathic disorder of a
nature or degree which made it appropriate for her to be liable to be detained
in hospital for medical treatment. The court had also wrongly sent the case
back to the tribunal with a direction to discharge the patient, since the proper
course would have been to send the case to a fresh tribunal with a direction
that if it was not satisfied that medical treatment would not alleviate the

condition it should direct that the patient be discharged (see p 676 *f* to *j* and p 677 *e* to *g*, post).

(3) For the purposes of the treatability test, what constituted medical treatment was not to be construed too narrowly. The tribunal had found that the only form of treatment likely to alleviate or prevent deterioration in the patient's condition was group therapy, that the patient was unwilling to co-operate in such treatment, but that continued detention and care might lead her to co-operate in time. The Divisional Court had been wrong to hold that in such circumstances the patient did not satisfy the treatability test, since Parliament could not have intended that a patient was to be deemed untreatable merely because she refused to co-operate with suitable treatment (see p 679 *c d* and p 680 *c*, post).

Decision of the Queen's Bench Divisional Court [1994] 1 All ER 481 reversed.

Notes
For the powers of a mental health review tribunal to direct discharge of non-restricted hospital patients, see 30 *Halsbury's Laws* (4th edn reissue) para 1360.

For the Mental Health Act 1983, ss 3, 16, 20, 72, see 28 *Halsbury's Statutes* (4th edn) 639, 653, 658, 712.

Cases referred to in judgments
Ainsbury v Millington [1987] 1 All ER 929, [1987] 1 WLR 379, HL.
Brind v Secretary of State for the Home Dept [1991] 1 All ER 720, [1991] 1 AC 696, [1991] 2 WLR 588, HL.
Pepper (Inspector of Taxes) v Hart [1993] 1 All ER 42, [1993] AC 593, [1992] 3 WLR 1032, HL.
R v Mental Health Review Tribunal, ex p Clatworthy [1985] 3 All ER 699.
R v Oxford Regional Mental Health Review Tribunal, ex p Secretary of State for the Home Dept [1986] 3 All ER 239, [1986] 1 WLR 1180, CA; *affd* [1987] 3 All ER 8, sub nom *Campbell v Secretary of State for the Home Dept* [1988] AC 120, [1987] 3 WLR 522, HL.
Wynne v Secretary of State for the Home Dept [1993] 1 All ER 574, [1993] 1 WLR 115, HL.
X v UK (1981) 1 BMLR 98, 4 EHRR 188, E Ct HR.

Cases also cited
Brutus v Cozens [1972] 2 All ER 1297, [1973] AC 854, HL.
Don Pasquale (a firm) v Customs and Excise Comrs (Practice Note) [1990] 1 WLR 1108, CA.
Padfield v Minister of Agriculture Fisheries and Food [1968] 1 All ER 694, [1968] AC 997, HL.
Poyser and Mills' Arbitration, Re [1963] 1 All ER 612, [1964] 2 QB 467.
R v Birmingham City Juvenile Court, ex p Birmingham City Council [1988] 1 All ER 683, [1988] 1 WLR 337.
R v Dartmoor Prison Board of Visitors, ex p Smith [1986] 2 All ER 651, [1987] QB 106, CA.
R v Hallstrom, ex p W (No 2), R v Gardner, ex p L [1986] 2 All ER 306, [1986] QB 1090.
R v Mental Health Review Tribunal, ex p Clatworthy [1985] 3 All ER 699.

R v Mental Health Review Tribunal, ex p Pickering [1986] 1 All ER 99.
R v Mersey Mental Health Review Tribunal, ex p D (1987) Times, 13 April, DC.
R v Nottingham Justices, ex p Davies [1980] 2 All ER 775, [1981] QB 38, DC.
R v Nottingham Mental Health Review Tribunal, ex p Secretary of State for the Home Dept (1988) Times, 12 October, CA.
R v Sunderland Juvenile Court, ex p G [1988] 2 All ER 34, [1988] 1 WLR 398, CA.
Sun Life Assurance Co of Canada v Jervis [1944] 1 All ER 469, [1944] AC 111, HL.
Vince v Chief Constable of the Dorset Police [1993] 2 All ER 321, [1993] 1 WLR 415, CA.
W v L [1973] 3 All ER 884, [1974] QB 711, CA.
Winterwerp v Netherlands (1979) 2 EHHR 387, E Ct HR.

Appeal
The Canons Park Mental Health Review Tribunal appealed from the decision of the Divisional Court of the Queen's Bench Division (Mann LJ and Sedley J) ([1994] 1 All ER 481) delivered on 28 July 1993 granting an order of certiorari quashing the decision of the tribunal dated 24 May 1993 that A, a patient detained under s 3 of the Mental Health Act 1983, should not be discharged from liability to be detained, and an order directing that the matter be remitted to the tribunal with a direction to discharge the applicant. By a respondent's notice filed on 20 September 1993 the applicant claimed that the Divisional Court had erred in rejecting her submissions that the decision of the tribunal not to exercise its discretionary power to discharge the applicant was irrational and in not finding that the reasons given by the tribunal for its decision were defective by reason of being neither adequate nor intelligible. The facts are set out in the judgment of Roch LJ.

Richard Gordon (instructed by *Steel & Shamash*) for the applicant.
Stephen Richards and *Rabinder Singh* (instructed by the *Treasury Solicitor*) for the tribunal.

Cur adv vult

16 February 1994. The following judgments were delivered.

ROCH LJ (giving the first judgment at the invitation of Nourse LJ). The applicant was born on 21 November 1964 and is now 29 years of age. She is a single mother of two children who are now aged 10 and 5 years respectively.

On 9 January 1992 the applicant was admitted to St Luke's Hospital as a voluntary patient. That occurred after she had seen Dr Hollander at the Friern Out-Patients Clinic, having shortly before that placed her two children in voluntary care because she was afraid she might harm them. The diagnosis on admission to St Luke's Hospital was reactive depression, suicidal ideation, deliberate self-harm, personality difficulties and abuse of alcohol.

On 2 October 1992 the applicant, to whom I shall refer as the applicant because she was the applicant before the mental health review tribunal and before the Divisional Court, was admitted to the Henry Rollin Unit at Horton Hospital under s 3 of the Mental Health Act 1983. The event which appears to have precipitated that admission was the departure of the psychotherapist who had been treating the applicant at St Luke's Hospital. Following that departure the applicant inflicted wounds on herself on several occasions, threatened to harm her children and had been heard to discuss her ideas for committing suicide with her elder child. The specific diagnosis at the time of the applicant's admission for treatment to what is a secure unit at Horton Hospital was reactive depression in an impulsive personality, which is a mental illness within the meaning of the 1983 Act.

At the beginning of April 1993, the authority to detain the applicant, being due to expire on 2 April under s 20(1) of the 1983 Act, was extended for a further period of six months under s 20(2)(a). The diagnosis at the time the authority to detain was renewed remained that of a reactive depression in an impulsive personality.

On 20 April 1993 the applicant was unsuccessful in an application for her discharge from detention in the secure unit made to the hospital managers under s 23 of the 1983 Act.

On 12 May 1993 Dr James, the consultant psychiatrist responsible for the applicant at Horton Hospital, and who was the appropriate medical officer, furnished to the managers of the hospital a report pursuant to s 16 of the 1983 Act to the effect that the applicant was suffering from a form of mental disorder other than the form specified in the application to admit her for treatment under s 3 and the application for renewal of the authority to detain her under s 20 of the Act. Dr James's report was made on the prescribed form, Form 22, and contained the following passages:

'It appears to me that this patient who is recorded on the application for admission to this hospital as suffering from mental illness is now suffering from psychopathic disorder. In my opinion further medical treatment in hospital is likely to alleviate or prevent a deterioration of the patient's condition.'

All those words were pro forma except the entries 'mental illness' and 'psychopathic disorder'. A marginal note appears against the third group of words which begin 'In my opinion further medical treatment ...', namely:

'Delete unless patient is reclassified above as suffering from psychopathic disorder or mental impairment.'

It would seem that the applicant had, prior to her application to the hospital managers for her discharge and prior to the reclassification by Dr James, applied for her discharge to the mental health review tribunal on 29 March 1993. I shall refer in this judgment simply to 'the tribunal'. The tribunal decided that the applicant should not be discharged. That decision was made on 24 May 1993. Prior to making the decision the tribunal received oral evidence from Dr James, Dr James's registrar Dr Duffield, Dr Frank, a consultant psychiatrist instructed by solicitors acting on behalf of the applicant for her application to the tribunal, and from the applicant herself. In addition, the tribunal had documentary evidence, being a psychiatric report of 11 May 1993 from Dr Duffield, a report from Dr Frank dated 21 May 1993, a supplementary report from Dr James dated 24 May 1993, the Form 22 completed by Dr James, a Pt A statement and an undated social circumstances report from a social worker with the Islington Council who had responsibility for the fostering and care of the applicant's children.

The tribunal's decision

The tribunal's decision is given in a document the first two pages of which contain eight paragraphs of the pro forma kind. The decision is contained in para 5 and reads simply: 'The patient shall not be discharged from liability to be detained.' The next relevant paragraph for the purposes of this appeal is para 7, which reads:

'Findings of the Tribunal Concerning the Statutory Criteria
The Tribunal is obliged to discharge the Patient if the answer to any of the following questions is "the Tribunal is so satisfied".

Question	Decision of the Tribunal
A Is the Tribunal satisfied that the patient is NOT now suffering from mental illness, psychopathic disorder, mental impairment, severe mental impairment or from any of those forms of disorder of a nature or degree which makes it appropriate for the patient to be liable to be detained in a hospital for medical treatment?	The tribunal is/is not so satisfied
B Is the Tribunal satisfied that it is NOT necessary for the health and safety of the patient *or* for the protection of others that the patient should receive such treatment?	The tribunal is/is not so satisfied

Note: If the patient has not been discharged under the Criteria above, the Tribunal has in any case a discretion to discharge the Patient.'

The answers to questions A and B were that the tribunal was not so satisfied.

Under para 8, which is to be completed only if the patient has not been discharged under para 7 and which is headed:

'Findings of the Tribunal concerning the main issues affecting the exercise of the Tribunal's discretion.'

'*Question:* Is it likely that medical treatment is alleviating or preventing a deterioration of the patient's condition? *Answer:* Yes/No ...'

The tribunal answered that question No.

Paragraph 9 is headed: 'Reasons for the Tribunal's decision.' There are then set out in manuscript five paragraphs of reasons for the decision in the applicant's case. Those paragraphs may be summarised in this way: (1) That the tribunal was satisfied that the applicant was suffering from psychopathic disorder. (2) That the only appropriate medical treatment which might alleviate the applicant's disorder would be psychotherapy in a group setting. Such treatment required the voluntary co-operation of the patient. The applicant was not at that time willing to co-operate. (3) That there was clear evidence of threats made by the applicant to a previous therapist and of a risk to the safety of that therapist if the applicant were not detained.

The fourth and fifth paragraphs of the reasons are the most important and I shall set them out in full:

'(4) We accept the view of the RMO [the responsible medical officer] that the patient's mental condition may deteriorate for a time and there is evidence that this has happened. There is also evidence that she deteriorated during a period of absconsion. However this deterioration may in due course give way to subsequent alleviation of her condition and she may then be willing to co-operate with appropriate therapy. Until then it is necessary that the patient should continue to be detained for nursing care under medical supervision. Consideration of her discharge is premature.

(5) It was argued that the patient's aggressive behaviour should have been subjected to criminal investigation rather than detention under the Mental Health Act. However the Tribunal takes the view that detention for medical treatment is appropriate for this patient. We are satisfied that it is in the interests of the patient's health and safety and for the protection of others that she should now be detained.'

The application for judicial review

Following the tribunal's decision, an application was made on behalf of the applicant to the High Court for orders of certiorari to quash the tribunal's decision and that the matter be remitted to the tribunal to reconsider it and reach a decision in accordance with the findings of the High Court. Alternatively orders of mandamus were sought requiring the tribunal to hear the applicant's application according to law and requiring the tribunal to give proper adequate and intelligible reasons for its decision. Two declarations were sought, first that where treatment is likely to result in a deterioration of a patient's condition, such a patient is entitled to be discharged under s 72(1)(b)(i) of the 1983 Act, and that where treatment is not likely to alleviate or prevent a deterioration of a patient's condition, such a patient is entitled to be discharged under the same subsection.

On 29 June Dr Michael James Raymond, a former consultant psychiatrist who was the medical member of the tribunal, swore an affidavit. In that affidavit Dr Raymond deposed first that the tribunal had accepted the view of the applicant's responsible medical officer that the applicant's mental condition might deteriorate for a time and that there was evidence that this had happened. The tribunal considered that the erosion of her condition was part of that deterioration. Second, that the tribunal considered that there was a likelihood of improvement in due course, and that view was expressed in para 4 of the tribunal's reasons, and that Dr Raymond's view to that effect was based on his own professional experiences and the evidence of Dr James.

The final paragraph of Dr Raymond's affidavit reads:

'I wish to dispel the impression which may be gained from reading the documents that it is highly unusual for patients suffering from psychiatric disorder who are detained in hospital to suffer a temporary deterioration in their condition. In my experience such patients dislike being subject to a controlled environment and are likely for a period to rebel against it, resulting in a deterioration of their condition.'

In the Divisional Court Sedley J expressed the view that Dr Raymond's affidavit was not admissible, but if it were he would reject it as inconsistent with the tribunal's expressed reasons. Sedley J said ([1994] 1 All ER 481 at 488):

'The tribunal have found very clearly indeed that it is unlikely that treatment in hospital will either alleviate or prevent deterioration of the applicant's psychopathic disorder. At best such an outcome is in the tribunal's view a hope or a possibility.'

On 28 July 1993 a Divisional Court consisting of Mann LJ and Sedley J granted an order of certiorari to quash the decision of the tribunal and further ordered that the matter be remitted to the tribunal with a direction that the applicant be discharged.

Events following the Divisional Court's decision

The tribunal, which is the Canons Park Mental Health Review Tribunal, appealed from the orders made by the Divisional Court on 6 August 1993 seeking that the orders made by the Divisional Court should be set aside. On 20 September a cross-notice was filed on behalf of the applicant that, despite the Divisional Court making two of the orders sought by the applicant, the Divisional Court had nevertheless erred in rejecting one of the applicant's submissions and not finding in the applicant's favour on another issue raised by the applicant before the Divisional Court. The error alleged in the cross-notice was the rejection of the applicant's submission that the decision of the tribunal not to exercise its discretionary power to discharge the applicant was irrational. The other issue raised by the applicant before the Divisional Court referred to in the cross-notice was that the reasons given by the tribunal for its decision were defective being neither adequate nor intelligible.

Following the decision of the Divisional Court, the respondent was discharged by the tribunal pursuant to the direction made by the court. It would seem that on 28 July the question of a stay of the Divisional Court's order was considered but that in the context of personal liberty no stay was imposed. Subsequently the applicant was readmitted to hospital pursuant to a fresh application for her detention for the purposes of treatment under s 3 of the 1983 Act. However, on that occasion the applicant was diagnosed as suffering from mental illness and not as having a psychopathic disorder. It was not therefore necessary for the application to show that medical treatment was likely to alleviate or prevent a deterioration of the applicant's condition.

The jurisdiction issue

These events raise the first issue which this court has to decide, namely is this a case in which this court should exercise or indeed has jurisdiction to hear the appeal? Mr Gordon says that the court does not have jurisdiction or alternatively that the court should not exercise its jurisdiction because the outcome of the appeal will not affect the applicant's liability to detention. The issues raised are truly hypothetical or academic. If the appeal were to be allowed, there is no effective order which this court could make. Further the decided cases show that the House of Lords would not entertain an appeal in this case, so that any decision by this court in this case could not be tested in their Lordships' House, or alternatively could not be authoritatively decided in their Lordships' House. Mr Gordon submitted that these were the results of the decisions of their Lordships in *Ainsbury v Millington* [1987] 1 All ER 929,

[1987] 1 WLR 379 and *Wynne v Secretary of State for the Home Dept* [1993] 1 All ER 574, [1993] 1 WLR 115.

It is true that if the Divisional Court's order quashing the tribunal's decision was held to have been wrongly made, the decision could not now be revived as a basis for the applicant's detention. But other consequences might flow from the quashing of the decision and, if the correct view is that it ought to have stood, declaratory relief ought to be granted accordingly. Moreover, as Mr Richards pointed out, the applicant might again be reclassified during her present admission to hospital or, on an application to the tribunal, the tribunal might find that she was suffering from a psychopathic disorder. Thus there is a real possibility that the same issue could arise in respect to the applicant. In all the circumstances, the issues raised are neither hypothetical nor academic and there is no impediment, in my judgment, to our hearing and disposing of the appeal.

The evidence before the tribunal

Before looking at the statutory provisions, the Divisional Court's decision and the submissions made to this court, the evidence received by the tribunal should be summarised. The report of Dr Duffield of 11 May recorded that on admission to the secure unit the applicant had seemed to settle into the ward environment well and had taken up a friendship with one of the other patients and spent much time with her. Subsequently the applicant had clearly settled into the very structured atmosphere of the ward. Her children had visited and the applicant began to talk about wanting to have them back at a future time. At one point the applicant asked not to be transferred out of the secure ward because of the friendship she had developed with another patient. The applicant became more sociable and overtly friendly. There had not been any episodes of self-harm whilst the applicant had been in the secure unit. The applicant had explained that by saying that she would not harm herself because she was afraid that Dr James would make her stay longer on the secure unit if she did harm herself. Dr Duffield's report records that the applicant absconded on 1 May and that on 7 May she had telephoned the ward to say that she had taken an overdose of a drug. That call was traced and resulted in her being treated at Wittingham Hospital for a drug overdose. There she told doctors she intended jumping off a building or in front of a train, and also said that she would follow her previous therapist for the next ten years. When returned to the secure unit that day the applicant was expressing suicidal ideas. In his report Dr Duffield expressed the following opinion:

'[The patient] is suffering from borderline personality disorder or psychopathic disorder as defined by the Mental Health Act 1983. Her recent behaviour and threatening correspondence suggests that she requires continued detention in hospital for the purposes of treatment. This is necessary both in the interests of her own safety and for the protection of others, namely her ex-doctor and her children.'

There is a very full note of the oral evidence given to the tribunal kept by the solicitor acting for the applicant before the tribunal. That note records that Dr Duffield added nothing to his report and the oral evidence of Dr James when he gave evidence to the tribunal.

The report of Dr James of 24 May was to the effect that in the view of the medical staff at the secure unit none of the criteria in s 72(1)(b) applied in the applicant's case. Specifically:

'1. [The patient] is clearly suffering from psychopathic disorder as defined in Section 1.
2. In our view her disorder is of a nature and degree which makes it appropriate for her to be detained in hospital for treatment. The treatment in question is psychotherapeutic rather than pharmacological. The current form of her disorder necessitates such treatment because of the risks that she poses to her own safety and to that of others.
3. It is necessary for the health and safety of the patient and for the protection of other persons that she should receive such treatment ...'

Dr James then went on to record that the applicant had told him as recently as that day (24 May) that there was nothing he could do to stop her killing herself and that she thought of suicide every day and the methods by which she could achieve it. He also recorded her recent absconding and overdosing. Dr James then set out the threats made by the applicant against her therapist at St Luke's Hospital.

Dr James gave evidence before the tribunal. Indeed he was the first witness. Dr James started by submitting to the tribunal that the criteria in s 3(2)(b) were not strictly relevant as they related to a renewal of the authority to detain and not to the tribunal's powers. It was s 72(2) which was the relevant provision and his submission on that was that the applicant's detention did prevent a deterioration of her condition and that was demonstrated by the fact that when she had absconded her condition had deteriorated because during that period of absconding she had again taken an overdose and made threats. In answer to questions by Dr Raymond, the medical member of the tribunal, Dr James stated that the applicant was suffering from a psychopathic disorder which was of a nature or degree which was appropriate for her treatment in hospital. The treatment that she was receiving was preventing deterioration in her condition and it was also necessary for her health and the safety and protection of others that she was detained. He agreed that the applicant's detention in the secure unit was not an ideal placement and that there was no ideal placement for her in the NHS system at present. He said that co-operation would be needed to make treatment by way of therapy practicable. The applicant did not want to co-operate and the task of the medical staff would be to change this attitude so that she became more amenable to a voluntary therapeutic environment. When questioned by the applicant's solicitor, Dr James stated that it was now evident that a group therapy rather than a single person therapy would be more beneficial for the applicant but that that required the applicant's consent. When asked about the applicant's progress on the ward since admission and whether she had improved, Dr James stated that he would expect her confinement initially to lead to a deterioration in her condition before an improvement. He said that sometimes patients reached a point of no return but he hoped that her condition would improve although he acknowledge she had deteriorated. He said that the absence of any facilities for group therapy did not necessarily mean that treatment, that is to say nursing care on the secure unit, might not offer an improvement. Dr James said that he believed that the applicant's detention was preventing a deterioration in her condition and that he could not recommend that she be discharged. If Dr Frank were to be correct that there would be deterioration, that was merely a stage her condition would go through before potential improvement.

Dr Frank in his report recorded that whilst in the secure unit the applicant had shown no further episodes of cutting herself and that the applicant had overdosed when she absconded from the secure unit. He reported that he agreed with Dr James that the applicant was unsuitable for any formal psychotherapy that relied on intense one to one work because of the applicant's tendency to act out in a dangerous way. Dr Frank agreed with Dr James's diagnosis of the applicant's mental disorder. He said that there was no evidence that the applicant was mentally ill and the applicant was fully responsible for her actions. Dr Frank reported that the most suitable form of treatment for borderline personality disorders such as the applicant's was what was often called milieu therapy. However any form of psychological treatment required the individual to act co-operatively and such treatments could not be applied in the context of a section of the Mental Health Act 1983. The only forms of treatment which would help the applicant required her active co-operation which at the moment she was not willing to give and it was likely that further deterioration would merely erode her already precarious confidence and ability to cope with the world. Dr Frank concluded his report by saying that it was obvious to him that the applicant did not meet the criteria in s 3(2)(b) of the 1983 Act and that it was therefore appropriate for the tribunal to discharge her.

When Dr Frank gave evidence he said that all the evidence showed that detention leads to a deterioration in this type of case. Since admitting herself voluntarily 18 months earlier the applicant had certainly deteriorated. Dr Frank said that the applicant was not suffering from a mental disorder of a nature which made it appropriate for her to be detained under the 1983 Act. In answer to Dr Raymond's question he agreed that the applicant was suffering from a severe example of borderline personality disorder. The word borderline did not mean that the applicant's case was unclear. If the applicant made threats to others or was violent to others then she was responsible for her own actions and would be answerable to the criminal justice system. It was not appropriate to use the 1983 Act to detain the applicant because that would not lead to a resolution of her problems.

The applicant gave evidence that she had deteriorated since coming into hospital and that she was not willing to engage in group therapy. She said that she had had no intention of harming her therapist at St Luke's and would not seek that doctor out if discharged. She confirmed that it was possible that she might harm herself again if she were to be discharged.

The Mental Health Act 1983

The crucial section of the 1983 Act in this case is s 72, which, so far as is material, reads:

'(1) Where application is made to a Mental Health Review Tribunal by or in respect of a patient who is liable to be detained under this Act, the tribunal may in any case direct that the patient be discharged, and ... (b) the tribunal shall direct the discharge of a patient liable to be detained otherwise than under section 2 above if they are satisfied—(i) that he is not then suffering from mental illness, psychopathic disorder, severe mental impairment or mental impairment or from any of those forms of disorder of a nature or degree which makes it appropriate for him to be liable to be detained in a hospital for medical treatment; or (ii) that it is not necessary for the health or safety of the patient or for the protection of other persons that he should receive such treatment; or (iii) in the case of an application by virtue of paragraph (g) of section 66(1) above, that the patient, if released, would not be likely to act in a manner dangerous to other persons or to himself.

(2) In determining whether to direct the discharge of a patient detained otherwise than under section 2 above in a case not falling within paragraph (b) of subsection (1) above, the tribunal shall have regard—(a) to the likelihood of medical treatment alleviating or preventing a deterioration of the patient's condition; and (b) in the case of a patient suffering from mental illness or severe mental impairment, to the likelihood of the patient, if discharged, being able to care for himself, to obtain the care he needs or to guard himself against serious exploitation ...'

Section 72 comes within Pt V of the 1983 Act, which deals with mental health review tribunals. Section 66 allows applications to be made to a tribunal in eight situations, the second of which is where a patient is admitted to a hospital in pursuance of an application for admission for treatment, the fourth of which is where a report has been furnished under s 16 of that Act in respect of a patient in which the appropriate medical officer makes a report to the managers of the hospital that the patient is suffering from a form of mental disorder other than a form or forms specified in the application for the patient's admission to the hospital for treatment. The sixth situation is where the authority for a patient's detention has been renewed under s 20 of the 1983 Act. Section 66(2) details the period in which applications have to be made with regard to each of the eight situations set out in subsection (1) of the section. Section 77(1) of the 1983 Act provides that no application shall be made to a tribunal by or in respect of a patient except in such cases and at such times as are expressly provided by the Act. Further, not more than one application is to be made within the specified period. Section 76 allows for registered medical practitioners to visit and examine patients for the purpose of furnishing information as to the patient's condition to the tribunal for the purpose of the application that is being made by or on behalf of the patient. Under s 68 the managers of hospitals have a duty to refer patients' cases to the tribunal if an application in respect of a patient has not been made. That section ensures that a patient's case is referred to the tribunal at least once in every three-year period.

The initial admission of a patient to a hospital for treatment is governed by s 3 of the 1983 Act. Section 3(2) of the Act lays down the criteria for admission for treatment in these terms:

'An application for admission for treatment may be made in respect of a patient on the grounds that—(a) he is suffering from mental illness, severe mental impairment, psychopathic disorder or mental impairment and his mental disorder is of a nature or degree which makes it appropriate for him to receive medical treatment in a hospital; and (b) in the case of psychopathic disorder or mental impairment, such treatment is likely to alleviate or prevent a deterioration of his condition; and (c) it is necessary for the health or safety of the patient or for the protection of other persons that he should receive such treatment and it cannot be provided unless he is detained under this section.'

Section 3(3) provides that an application for admission for treatment shall be founded on the written recommendations in the prescribed form of two registered medical practitioners, which include a statement that in the opinion of each of them the criteria in subsection (2) are satisfied. The four categories of mental disorder referred to in s 3(2) are defined in s 1(2).

Section 20 covers the extension of the authority to detain a patient in hospital admitted for treatment. Section 20(1) is in the form that such a patient shall not be detained for more than six months following his initial admission unless the authority for his detention is renewed under s 20. Section 20(4) lays down the conditions that the responsible medical officer must find satisfied before the responsible medical officer can furnish the managers of the hospital with a report which allows them to extend the period of the patient's detention for treatment. Section 20(4) provides:

'The conditions referred to in subsection (3) above are that—(a) the patient is suffering from mental illness, severe mental impairment, psychopathic disorder or mental impairment, and his mental disorder is of a nature or degree which makes it appropriate for him to receive medical treatment in a hospital; and (b) such treatment is likely to alleviate or prevent a deterioration of his condition; and (c) it is necessary for the health or safety of the patient or for the protection of other persons that he should receive such treatment and that it cannot be provided unless he continues to be detained; but, in the case of mental illness or severe mental impairment, it shall be an alternative to the condition specified in paragraph (b) above that the patient, if discharged, is unlikely to be able to care for himself, to obtain the care which he needs or to guard himself against serious exploitation.'

It can be observed that the alteration of the wording of s 3(2) of the 1983 Act made in s 20(4) of the Act would seem to indicate Parliament's intention that mentally disordered persons should not be detained in hospital beyond the initial six months' period unless medical treatment in the hospital is likely to alleviate or prevent a deterioration of the patient's condition unless the patient suffers from mental illness or severe mental impairment and would not be able to look after himself or be looked after in the community if discharged from hospital; that patients suffering from psychopathic disorders and mental impairment should cease to be detained once medical treatment in hospital is unlikely to alleviate or prevent deterioration in their conditions. That intention may owe as much to a policy that such patients should not occupy valuable hospital places and use scarce resources when no alleviation or stabilisation of their conditions was likely as to any concept of personal liberty.

Decision of the Divisional Court

The decision of the Divisional Court can be epitomised by the concluding words of Mann LJ in his short concurring judgment ([1994] 1 All ER 481 at 494):

'I am, however, persuaded for the reasons given by Sedley J that Parliament has enacted that an untreatable psychopath however dangerous cannot be detained.'

In his judgment Sedley J identified the issue before the tribunal in these terms (at 484):

'In the event the two doctors [Dr James and Dr Frank] did not disagree about the applicant's condition or prognosis. They differed only on the question, which is essentially a question of law, whether in the light of their view the applicant was entitled to be discharged.'

Sedley J went on to set out what he considered to have been the tribunal's clear finding on the outcome of treatment in hospital in the passage which has already been cited in this judgment. Sedley J observed (at 488):

'... the tribunal hoped that keeping the applicant in hospital would persuade her to agree to group therapy. Such an aim, though understandable, is not a lawful ground of detention.'

If the only reason for admission and detention in hospital is to coerce a person suffering from a psychopathic disorder into consenting to undergo group therapy, then I am wholly in agreement with this observation. Sedley J held (at 489) that the submission made on s 72(2) on behalf of the applicant by Mr Gordon was unsound, and that Mr Gordon's submission based on the inadequate reasons given by the tribunal was a fallback which was needed only if the reasons stated by the tribunal did not in law compel discharge without more. The judge then summarised the main arguments on both sides on the proper construction of s 72(1)(b). That for the applicant was that the detention of a person suffering from psychopathic disorder was lawful only if it was likely that medical treatment in hospital would alleviate or prevent a deterioration of the person's condition. The main submission on behalf of the tribunal was that s 3(2) of the 1983 Act in respect of those suffering from psychopathic disorder or mental impairment contained three tests, first that the mental disorder was of a nature or degree which made it appropriate for the patient to receive medical treatment in a hospital (the appropriateness test), second, that such medical treatment in hospital was likely to alleviate or prevent a deterioration in the patient's condition (the treatability test); third that detention was necessary for the health or safety of the patient or others. Section 72(1)(b) with regard to the tribunal's duty to discharge a patient contained the appropriateness test but did not contain the treatability test. The words 'appropriate for him to be liable to be detained' in s 72(1)(b)(i) of the 1983 Act did not and could not import the requirement in ss 3(2)(b) and 20(4)(b) that the treatment was likely to alleviate or prevent a deterioration of the patient's condition.

Sedley J preferred the construction of s 72(1)(b) urged upon him by Mr Gordon to that urged upon him by counsel for the tribunal. He said (at 490):

'Put simply, it is never "appropriate" under the provisions of the 1983 Act relating to admission, renewal or reclassification for a patient to be "liable to be detained in a hospital for medical treatment" for psychopathic disorder if he or she is not at that point in time treatable. The phrase "appropriate for him to be liable", while clumsy, picks up the language of ss 3 and 20 which include in their criteria for liability to detention the appropriateness of medical treatment as well as the likelihood of its being effective, and thus reasserts the role of expert assessment by the tribunal in its turn.'

Sedley J supported his conclusion by pointing out that the tribunal was a body
reviewing earlier decisions of others either to admit and detain the patient for
treatment or to extend the authority to detain or to reclassify the patient and
that in all those cases, for a decision to detain to be lawful under the 1983 Act
required, in the case of a patient diagnosed as having a psychopathic disorder,
that the treatability test was satisfied. Sedley J went on to say that if the matter
of construction were not as clear as in his judgment it was, then on first
principles any ambiguity in the statute would have to be resolved in favour of
personal liberty. Sedley J went on to consider the underlying policy of the 1983
Act as derived from dicta in a previous decision in *R v Oxford Regional Mental
Health Review Tribunal, ex p Secretary of State for the Home Dept* [1986] 3 All ER
239 at 245, [1986] 1 WLR 1180 at 1186 where Lawton LJ had said:

'It is clear that the intention of Parliament under s 72(1)(b) was that
people should not be detained in hospital when it was no longer
appropriate that they should be there for medical treatment.'

Sedley J looked also at a White Paper and the Report of the Percy
Commission (Royal Commission on the Law Relating to Mental Illness and
Mental Deficiency 1954–1957 (Cmd 169)) on the Mental Health Act 1959 as
throwing light on Parliament's intention that psychopaths should only be
detained in mental hospitals under compulsory powers where there was a
likelihood that they would benefit from medical treatment whilst detained in
hospital.

Finally, Sedley J referred to art 5 of the Convention for the Protection of
Human Rights and Fundamental Freedoms (Rome, 4 November 1950; TS 71
(1953); Cmd 8969) and the decision of the European Court of Human Rights in
X v UK (1981) 1 BMLR 98, 4 EHRR 188 as demonstrating that the construction
of s 72(1)(b) advanced on behalf of the tribunal would put the legislation into
conflict with the 1950 convention:

'It would mean that, far from being a court in which the lawfulness of a
patient's detention can be decided, a mental health review tribunal would
be a primary decision making body judging a patient's liability to be
detained on criteria different from and wider than those by which the
authorities whose decision is being reviewed were empowered to cause
the patient to be detained.' (See [1994] 1 All ER 481 at 493.)

The court in its judgment in that case had said ((1982) 4 EHRR 188 at 209–210):

'The review should, however, be wide enough to bear on those
conditions which, according to the Convention, are essential for the
"lawful" detention of a person on the ground of unsoundness of mind,
especially as the reasons capable of initially justifying such a detention
may cease to exist ... This means that in the instant case Article 5(4)
required an appropriate procedure allowing a court to examine whether
the patient's disorder still persisted and whether the Home Secretary was
entitled to think that a continuation of the compulsory confinement was
necessary in the interests of public safety.'

And then the court, in rejecting an argument that the existing mental health
review tribunals provided an independent review procedure, said (at 210):

'There is nothing to preclude a specialised body of this kind being considered as a "court" within the meaning of Article 5(4), provided it enjoys the necessary independence and offers sufficient procedural safeguards appropriate to the category of deprivation of liberty being dealt with. Nonetheless, even supposing Mental Health Review Tribunals fulfilled these conditions, they lack the competence to decide "the lawfulness of [the] detention" and to order release if the detention is unlawful, as they have advisory functions only ...'

That case was a case of a person detained in a mental hospital following his conviction of a criminal offence and the making of an order by the criminal court that he should be detained in a special secure mental hospital. The Home Secretary had authorised his conditional discharge but later as a result of information received the Home Secretary had issued a warrant for the convicted person's recall to mental hospital. X's complaints were that he had been recalled to the hospital unlawfully, and that he had not had the opportunity to have the lawfulness of his detention after recall decided by a court as guaranteed by para (4) of art 5 of the 1950 convention. The European Court rejected X's first complaint and upheld his second.

Submissions of counsel

The submissions of counsel to this court on the construction of s 72(1)(b)(i) and in particular of the words 'of a nature or degree which makes it appropriate for him to be liable to be detained', essentially followed the submissions made to the Divisional Court, with this important exception, that on behalf of the appellant tribunal, submissions were made by Mr Richards on the meaning and scope of the treatability test which were not made to the Divisional Court.

Construction of s 72(1)(b)

The submissions of Mr Richards on behalf of the tribunal can be summarised in this way: s 72(1) has to be read with s 72(2) and in the context of the 1983 Act as a whole. Read in that way there is no duty to discharge a patient suffering from psychopathic disorder just because the treatability test is not satisfied. It is clear from the examination of the earlier provisions in the Act such as ss 3, 16 and 20 that the appropriateness test and the treatability test are different. Where therefore the 1983 Act lays down only one of those tests and not the other, Parliament must be taken to have done that deliberately and intended that only the appropriateness test should apply and not the treatability test.

This reading is confirmed by the requirement that when exercising its discretionary power to discharge under s 72(2) the tribunal then has to have regard to the treatability test, although in that situation it is not bound to order discharge if the test is not satisfied. The Divisional Court's construction of s 72(1)(b) has the effect of transforming the tribunal's discretion under s 72(1) into a duty.

Mr Gordon's submissions on the construction of s 72(1)(b) follow broadly those points which found favour with the Divisional Court. If I do not summarise them in this judgment, it is not because those submissions were not presented clearly and persuasively. Indeed they were and I accept the construction of s 72(1) and (2) urged on us by Mr Gordon and accepted by the Divisional Court subject to an important qualification as to the proper approach of tribunals to the functions they must perform under s 72(1).

Parliament in ss 3, 16 and 20 of the 1983 Act has manifested its intention that persons suffering from psychopathic disorders or mental impairment are not to be admitted to or detained in hospitals for medical treatment unless such treatment is likely to alleviate or prevent deterioration of their condition. Put more shortly, Parliament's intention in those sections is that psychopaths cannot be detained once it is shown that they are untreatable. I accept Mr Richard's submission that s 72(1)(b) has to be read in the context of the 1983 Act as a whole and, therefore, I start from the position that in s 72(1)(b) it is unlikely that Parliament would have had a different intention with regard to the further compulsory detention of patients with psychopathic disorders.

The question is whether in s 72(1)(b)(i) Parliament was referring simply to the appropriateness test and was excusing the tribunal from a consideration of the treatability test in respect of applicants suffering from psychopathic disorders or mental impairment.

The first condition in ss 3(2)(a) and 20(4)(a) is in these terms—

'and his mental disorder is of a nature or degree which makes it appropriate for him to receive medical treatment in a hospital',

whereas s 72(1)(b)(i) reads—

'disorder of a nature or degree which makes it appropriate for him to be liable to be detained in a hospital for medical treatment ...'

The difference in the wording shows that Parliament did not intend to refer simply to the appropriateness test in s 3(2)(a) and s 20(4)(a). Had Parliament wished to do that, it would have omitted the words 'to be liable', and would have used the same wording as appears in both ss 3(2)(a) and 20(4)(a). Those words clearly refer in the case of psychopathic disorder and mental impairment to the treatability test, that is to say, to the terms of ss 3(2)(b) and 20(4)(b). They are words which are apt to deal with the four types of mental disorder that the 1983 Act recognises, and which are set out at the start of s 72(1)(b)(i) and to apply the treatability test to only two of those four categories of mental disorder. A psychopathic patient is not liable to be detained in hospital for medical treatment, unless the treatment is likely to be of some good to him. If his psychopathic disorder is untreatable then it is not of a nature which makes it appropriate for him to receive medical treatment in a hospital. The policy of the 1983 Act in relation to patients with psychopathic disorders is treatment not containment.

The provision in s 72(2)(a) is there with regard to the tribunal's discretionary power to direct a patient's discharge, because the tribunal's discretionary power has to apply to all four categories of mentally disordered patients, and no matter into which category the applicant patient comes, the tribunal must direct its mind to the likelihood of medical treatment alleviating or preventing a deterioration of the patient's condition. The tribunal has a discretionary power to discharge a patient who is psychopathically disordered even where it is likely that medical treatment in hospital will alleviate or prevent deterioration of his condition because the tribunal's discretionary power applies to any patient who is liable to be detained under the 1983 Act. Parliament by s 72(2)(a) is not introducing the treatability test as a pre-condition to the exercise by the tribunal of its discretionary power to direct a patient's discharge.

This construction of s 72(1)(b)(i) is consistent with the tribunal's role as an independent court which reviews the decisions to admit and detain a patient in a secure hospital and to extend the authority to detain him. It is correct that the tribunal reviews those decisions in the light of facts existing at the time of the tribunal's hearing. Section 72 was enacted to meet the criticisms which the European Court of Human Rights had made of the machinery and procedure for review which existed at the time of the decision in *X v UK* (1981) 1 BMLR 98, 4 EHRR 188. Those criticisms were twofold in the passages from the judgment which I have cited earlier. First, that a review of the lawfulness of the patient's detention was not in the hands of a court, that is to say, a body independent of the executive and the hospital authorities. Second, that that body did not have the power to order the patient's release if his detention was initially unlawful or the reasons capable of initially justifying such a detention had ceased to exist.

Parliament would have failed to meet those criticisms if a tribunal, despite being satisfied that medical treatment was not likely to alleviate or prevent deterioration in the psychopathic patient's condition and had never been likely to do so, was not then under a duty to direct the patient's discharge. The terms of s 66 of the 1983 Act make the tribunal's function under s 72 as a reviewing body, in my view, quite clear, and it cannot, I would suggest, be accepted that Parliament intended that a tribunal should when reviewing a decision under ss 3 or 20 apply only two of the three criteria laid down in the 1983 Act to justify the compulsory detention of patients suffering from psychopathic disorder or mental impairment.

The correct approach to s 72(1)(b)

I turn now to what is in my view the correct approach by a tribunal to the question whether they are under a duty to direct the discharge of a patient. The form in which the tribunal's duty to direct a patient's discharge under s 72(1)(b) is expressed is of the utmost importance. The tribunal will normally be considering a psychopathically disordered patient's case where the responsible medical officer has given a report that the patient is suffering from a psychopathic disorder of a nature or degree which makes it appropriate for him to receive medical treatment in hospital in that such treatment is likely to alleviate or prevent a deterioration of his condition; and that it is necessary for the health or safety of the patient or for the protection of other persons that he should receive such treatment and that the treatment cannot be provided unless he is detained in hospital. The duty to direct the patient's discharge arises if, but only if, the tribunal are satisfied that either the patient is not suffering from psychopathic disorder or that he is not suffering from psychopathic disorder of a nature or degree which warrants his detention in hospital for medical treatment or that it is not necessary for the health or safety of the patient or for the protection of other persons that he should receive such treatment. The question in this case was not, therefore, whether the tribunal was satisfied that the treatment was likely to alleviate or prevent a deterioration in the applicant's condition but whether the tribunal was satisfied that treatment was unlikely to alleviate or prevent a deterioration in her condition. That this is the correct approach is underlined by the Mental Health Review Tribunal Rules 1983, SI 1983/942, r 23 of which provides:

'The decision by which the tribunal determines an application shall be recorded in writing; the record shall be signed by the president and shall give the reasons for the decision and, in particular, where the tribunal relies upon any of the matters set out in section 72(1) or (4) or section 73(1) or (2) of the Act, shall state its reasons for being satisfied as to those matters.'

This is consistent with proper weight being given to the views of the responsible medical officer who will have had greatest contact with and knowledge of the patient. If the tribunal are to direct the discharge of a patient contrary to the report of the responsible medical officer, they have to identify which of the matters set out in s 72(1) they are satisfied do not exist and their reasons for being so satisfied. *R v Mental Health Review Tribunal, ex p Clatworthy* [1985] 3 All ER 699 was exceptional in that in that case the responsible medical officer had expressed the view that the applicant's condition was outside the scope of the 1983 Act and the tribunal refused to direct the discharge of the applicant from detention in hospital, giving as their reason a bare traverse of a circumstance in which discharge could be contemplated but not showing why the evidence of the responsible medical officer and of a consultant psychiatrist had not been accepted.

In the present case, in my judgment, the Divisional Court was in error to hold ([1994] 1 All ER 481 at 488)—

'The tribunal have found very clearly indeed that it is unlikely that treatment in hospital will either alleviate or prevent deterioration of the applicant's psychopathic disorder.'

In para 7 of the tribunal's decision the tribunal expressly said that it was not satisfied that the applicant was not suffering from psychopathic disorder of a nature or degree which made it appropriate for her to be liable to be detained in hospital for medical treatment. The tribunal's answer to question A in para 8 was an answer given in relation to the tribunal's discretionary power to direct the applicant's discharge. Sedley J pointed out that that question is phrased in the present tense and said that the use of the present tense was unfortunate. This criticism would be justified if the question related to the tribunal's duty to discharge. However it does not. To reflect the provisions of the 1983 Act accurately the question should be:

'Is there a likelihood of medical treatment alleviating or preventing a deterioration of the patient's condition?'

with pro forma answers of Yes/No.

The tribunal's answer No was consequently of limited value. Paragraph 4 of the tribunal's reasons show first that they accepted the view of the responsible medical officer. It must be remembered that the responsible medical officer's view was that the applicant was liable to be detained in hospital for medical treatment and that the terms of s 20 of the 1983 Act were satisfied. There was clear evidence that since being in the secure unit the applicant's drug abuse and episodes of self-harm had ceased and she had become more sociable and overtly friendly. The tribunal goes on to record that the applicant's mental condition might deteriorate for a time and that there was evidence that this had happened since her initial admission to hospital. The tribunal pointed out that there was evidence that the applicant's condition had deteriorated during her period of absconding from hospital. The tribunal then said:

'However, this deterioration may in due course give way to subsequent alleviation of her condition and she may then be willing to co-operate with appropriate therapy. Until then it is necessary that the patient should continue to be detained for nursing care under medical supervision.'

If the correct question for the tribunal was, were they satisfied that medical treatment would not lead to an alleviation or prevent a deterioration in the applicant's condition, then the tribunal in that paragraph of their reasons were answering that question, No, they were not so satisfied. If the correct question for the tribunal at that stage was, were the tribunal satisfied that medical treatment was not likely to alleviate or prevent deterioration in the applicant's condition, then at best the answer given in para 4 is unclear. In my view, it is this second question which the tribunal had to ask itself.

The orders of the Divisional Court

At this point, it is necessary to return to the affidavit sworn by Dr Raymond the medical member of the tribunal. I would agree that the decision of the tribunal is to be judged by the reasons given in the decision. When it comes to considering the order that should be made where a court is satisfied that the tribunal's decision should be quashed in a case of a patient in a mental hospital who is, on clear evidence, a potential danger to herself and others, especially where those others include children, then in my view the court should take into account the contents of an affidavit such as that of Dr Raymond. In my opinion the sending back of the matter to the tribunal with a direction that the tribunal direct the discharge of the applicant was not the order that should have been made in this case. The matter should have been sent back to be heard by a fresh tribunal with a direction that in this case if the tribunal were satisfied that the applicant was not suffering from a psychopathic disorder of a nature or degree which made it appropriate for her to be liable to be detained in hospital for medical treatment, because medical treatment in hospital was not likely to alleviate or prevent deterioration in her condition, they should direct her discharge. Put more shortly, the tribunal should have been directed that if they were satisfied that medical treatment in hospital was not likely to alleviate or prevent deterioration in the applicant's condition then they should direct her discharge from hospital.

Scope of the treatability test

The final matter is the question of the scope of the treatability test. This court heard submissions on that issue. Mr Gordon on behalf of the applicant pointed out that arguments on the scope and meaning of the treatability test had not been deployed by counsel for the tribunal before the Divisional Court. Mr Gordon went on to submit that this was not a live issue in this case because both Dr James and Dr Frank agreed that the only form of treatment for the applicant which was likely to alleviate or prevent a deterioration of her psychopathic disorder was that of group therapy, and that treatment to be effective required the willing co-operation of the patient. Mr Gordon accepted that medical treatment was, by reason of the terms of s 145 of the 1983 Act, wider than drugs, therapies or other treatment prescribed by doctors. He said:

'I accept that nursing care could be a step in the treatment of a mental disorder. But that was not the Tribunal's finding in this case.'

The tribunal's finding had been that group therapy was the only form of treatment likely to alleviate or prevent deterioration of the applicant's condition; that it required the applicant's willing co-operation in order to be likely to alleviate or prevent deterioration of her condition and that the applicant was unwilling to co-operate. Mr Gordon pointed out that the applicant would have co-operated with one-to-one therapy, but that the doctors were agreed that such therapy would have lead to a worsening of the applicant's condition and made her more dangerous.

Mr Richards's submissions were that the treatability test is concerned with the likely effect of treatment if such treatment were given, and is not concerned with the likelihood of the patient refusing such treatment. In this case there was a known treatment which was likely to alleviate or prevent deterioration of the applicant's condition, namely group therapy. Parliament could not have intended that a patient should be deemed untreatable simply because the patient withheld co-operation. That would place the key to the patient's being detained in hospital in the patient's own hands, and this would apply to cases where the patient was in hospital pursuant to an order of the Crown Court as well as to cases where the patient had been admitted under s 3 of the 1983 Act; s 37 of the Act also containing the treatability test. Further, such an interpretation would place a hitherto unnoticed constraint on the Secretary of State's discretion to make a transfer direction in respect of a prisoner under s 47 of that Act. Mr Richards's further submission was that the Divisional Court's conclusion on the meaning of treatability was not in accordance with medical experience of the treatment of those with psychopathic disorders. Here Mr Richards, in addition to passages in the reports and evidence of Dr James, relied on para 4 of Dr Raymond's affidavit. In such cases there may be an initial deterioration in the patient's condition, but detention in a secure environment with nursing care and medical supervision (medical treatment within the 1983 Act) can lead to the patient gaining an insight into his condition and the overcoming of the patient's initial refusal to co-operate. One of the skills of nurses and doctors in hospitals for the mentally disordered is to persuade their patients to accept treatment. A period of detention with nursing care and medical supervision is frequently a necessary prelude to treatment by way of therapy. If during such a period the patient is likely to gain an insight into his problem or is likely to change to being co-operative then that in itself is an alleviation of the patient's condition.

The Divisional Court, in my judgment, no doubt for the reason it did not have the advantage of the submissions addressed to this court on this aspect of the case, took too narrow a view of what could constitute medical treatment in hospital likely to alleviate or prevent a deterioration of the applicant's condition. I would suggest the following principles. First, if a tribunal were to be satisfied that the patient's detention in hospital was simply an attempt to coerce the patient into participating in group therapy, then the tribunal would be under a duty to direct discharge. Second, treatment in hospital will satisfy the treatability test although it is unlikely to alleviate the patient's condition, provided that it is likely to prevent a deterioration. Third, treatment in hospital will satisfy the treatability test although it will not immediately alleviate or prevent deterioration in the patient's condition, provided that alleviation or stabilisation is likely in due course. Fourth, the treatability test can still be met although initially there may be some deterioration in the patient's condition, due for example to the patient's initial anger at being detained. Fifth, it must be remembered that medical treatment in hospital covers nursing and also includes care, habilitation and rehabilitation under medical supervision. Sixth, the treatability test is satisfied if nursing care etc are likely to lead to an alleviation of the patient's condition in that the patient is likely to gain an insight into his problem or cease to be unco-operative in his attitude towards treatment which would potentially have a lasting benefit.

If the treatability test is given the wider scope which in my judgment it should be given, then it becomes clear that the tribunal was deciding that their duty to direct the discharge of the applicant did not arise because they were not satisfied that medical treatment in hospital was not likely to alleviate or prevent a deterioration of the applicant's condition. Such a finding is not surprising when it is appreciated that the applicant's detention in the secure unit for medical treatment had eliminated the symptoms in the diagnosis of her condition on her first admission to St Luke's Hospital of deliberate self-harm and alcohol abuse and reduced those of reactive depression and suicidal ideation.

KENNEDY LJ.

(1) Jurisdiction

On this issue I agree with Roch LJ so I pass at once to the two main substantive issues which we have to consider, namely treatability, and how to construe s 72(1) and (2) of the Mental Health Act 1983. In relation to both issues it is necessary to set out the statutory framework.

(2) Mental Health Act 1983

'Psychopathic disorder' means a persistent disorder or disability of mind (whether or not including significant impairment of intelligence) which results in abnormally aggressive or seriously irresponsible conduct on the part of the person concerned. That is the definition to be found in s 1(2) of the 1983 Act. A patient suffering from psychopathic disorder may not be admitted to hospital and detained for treatment unless three criteria are satisfied, namely: (1) his disorder is of a nature or degree which makes it appropriate for him to receive medical treatment in a hospital, and (2) such treatment is likely to alleviate or prevent a deterioration of his condition, and (3) it is necessary for his health or safety, or for the protection of others, that he should receive such treatment, and it cannot be provided unless he is detained.

Those three criteria which can, for convenience, be referred to as the appropriateness test, the treatability test and the safety test, are set out in s 3 of the 1983 Act, but when considering them it is important to remember that medical treatment includes nursing, and also includes care, habilitation and rehabilitation under medical supervision (see s 145).

If a patient detained in hospital, having been admitted on the grounds that he was suffering from mental illness, is to be reclassified as suffering from psychopathic disorder the doctor in charge of the treatment of the patient must include in his report a statement of his opinion whether further medical treatment in hospital is likely to alleviate or prevent a deterioration of the patient's condition. If he says it is unlikely to have that effect the patient cannot be detained (see ss 16 and 34(1)(a)). Neither the appropriateness test nor the safety test has to be reconsidered at that stage. They will, of course, have been considered on admission, but the treatability test at the classification stage is peculiar to cases of psychopathic disorder and mental impairment.

Not more than six months after admission, if a patient is to be detained further, the authority for his detention has to be renewed in accordance with s 20 of the 1983 Act. That section requires the responsible medical officer (which means the doctor in charge of the patient) to examine and if it appears to him that certain conditions are satisfied to report to the managers of the hospital in a prescribed form. The conditions are that the appropriateness test is satisfied, that the treatability test is satisfied, and that the safety test is satisfied, but for patients suffering from mental illness or severe mental impairment inability to cope in the community is an alternative to the treatability test. So, as Mr Richards points out, ss 16 and 20 do not simply mirror s 3. The tests are the same, but their application varies. The point can be further demonstrated by reference to s 37 which enables a Crown Court or a magistrates' court to make a hospital order in most cases where a person has been convicted before the court of an offence punishable with imprisonment. In all cases the appropriateness test has to be satisfied, and in cases of psychopathic disorder or mental impairment the treatability test has to be satisfied, but to fit the needs of a criminal case, the safety test is reformulated. In every case the court has to conclude that in all the circumstances the most suitable method of disposing of the case is by means of an order under s 37, but if it is necessary for the protection of the public from serious harm to do so the court may also make a restriction order under s 41. For present purposes it is unnecessary to detail the effects of a restriction order, but it is necessary to observe that under s 47 if the Secretary of State is advised by two doctors that a serving prisoner is suffering from mental disorder, that the appropriateness test is satisfied, and that (if it be a case of psychopathic disorder or mental impairment) the treatability test is satisfied, then the Secretary of State may order that the prisoner be removed to and detained in hospital. The safety test does not have to be satisfied before such a transfer direction can be made, but s 49 enables the Secretary of State to direct that the restrictions set out in s 41 shall apply to a person in respect of whom a transfer direction has been made.

Thus far I have been considering only the ways in which a person with a mental disorder can be admitted to and detained in hospital for treatment. The question is then considered in Pt IV of the 1983 Act of the extent to which such a patient can be treated without his consent. The approach adopted is that the most serious forms of treatment require at least a second opinion, and in some cases also require consent (see ss 57 and 58) but otherwise the consent of the patient is not required if the treatment is given by or under the direction of a responsible medical officer. Mr Richards argues that it would be curious if by refusing to co-operate a patient could bypass the statutory provisions which indicate when treatment can be given without his consent. Mr Gordon for his part recognises that some forms of treatment can be given without consent, but he submits that if a treatment requires co-operation and co-operation is not forthcoming the treatment cannot be administered.

That brings me to Pt V of the 1983 Act, which deals with mental health review tribunals. They came into existence under the Mental Health Act 1959 and their powers are dealt with in s 72. They must discharge a patient such as the present applicant if they are satisfied: (1) that she is not then suffering from

psychopathic disorder of a nature or degree which makes it appropriate for her
to be liable to be detained in a hospital for medical treatment, or (2) that it is
not necessary for her health or safety or for the protection of others that she
should receive such treatment.

If the tribunal is not satisfied as to either of those matters it is not obliged to
discharge the patient, but by virtue of s 72(2) it may do so and in making that
decision it must have regard 'to the likelihood of medical treatment alleviating
or preventing the deterioration of the patient's condition'. Sections 73 and 74
require the same approach to be adopted in relation to restricted patients, and
those subject to restriction directions.

(3) Treatability

Mr Richards submits that the approach adopted by the Divisional Court in
the present case shows that the court misunderstood the treatability test. In
order to satisfy that test it is not necessary to demonstrate a probability of short
term gain, and the fact that at present a patient demonstrates a fixed
determination not to co-operate in the administration of psychotherapy in a
group setting, which is the only form of therapy known to be beneficial, is not
decisive, even though such therapy cannot in practice be effective without her
consent. As I have already noted, nursing and care under medical supervision
are also 'medical treatment', and there was evidence before the tribunal from
which the tribunal was entitled to conclude that over a prolonged period
treatment, consisting at first of no more than nursing, care and gradual
persuasion to accept group therapy, followed by group therapy itself was likely
to alleviate or prevent deterioration of her condition, even if at first some
deterioration could not be avoided.

Mr Gordon emphasises, with justification, that treatability is a matter of
clinical judgment, and he submits that the tribunal found, and was entitled to
find, that the treatability test was not satisfied. There I consider that Mr
Gordon is mistaken. As was recognised in the Divisional Court, the tribunal
was not assisted by the unhappy formulation of question 8A on the form which
the tribunal had to use, and I agree that in its handwritten reasons the tribunal
seems to be at times focusing on the group therapy rather than considering the
whole spectrum of treatment that was proposed. It also stated that treatment
'might' alleviate the patient's condition, which may be said to leave open the
question whether it was likely to do so, or to prevent a deterioration, but when
the reasons are read as a whole together with the decision itself it seems to me
that the tribunal did envisage the treatment being likely to yield one or other
of those results. It is therefore unfortunate that the proper meaning of
treatability, which is now in the forefront of Mr Richards' case, was not
canvassed before the Divisional Court. Had it been canvassed, the court might
have considered it appropriate to send the matter back to the tribunal to be
reheard because, to my mind, unless the tribunal was to exercise its powers
under section 72(1)(b) without reference to treatability it was necessary to
know the tribunal's state of mind in relation to this topic. Was the spectrum
of treatment envisaged likely eventually to alleviate or prevent a deterioration
of the patient's condition? In answering that question the medical witnesses
and the tribunal itself would no doubt have regard to the patient's current
attitude of non-co-operation, but it would not be decisive if there was a
prospect that in time that attitude might change. Having regard to what has
happened since the applicant was discharged from hospital pursuant to the

order of the Divisional Court, I see no reason to say more about the treatability test, and I pass to the second substantive issue which Mr Richards asked us to consider, namely the proper construction of s 72(1) and (2).

(4) Construction of s 72

Mr Richards submits that when deciding whether it must exercise its mandatory power to discharge under s 72(1)(b) the tribunal does not have to have regard to the treatability test. It need only have regard to the appropriateness test and the safety test which are each expressly referred to in s 72(1)(b). If the tribunal is not required to discharge pursuant to s 72(1)(b), then it may discharge pursuant to s 72(2) and in deciding whether or not to exercise that statutory power the tribunal has to have regard to the treatability test. It comes in only, Mr Richards submits, at the discretionary stage.

Mr Gordon disagrees. He submits that in a non-criminal case it is only appropriate for a patient 'to be liable to be detained' if those conditions are satisfied which have to be met when a patient is admitted and detained (s 3), or reclassified (s 16) or when the period of his detention is extended (s 20), and in each of those cases the conditions include the treatability test. That approach commended itself to the Divisional Court, but in my judgment it is mistaken. The first thing to be noted about s 72(1)(b) is that the tribunal is only required to direct discharge if it is satisfied of a negative—first, that the patient is not then suffering from psychopathic disorder. If he may be, the obligation to discharge does not arise. The approach is not surprising, because the tribunal is not intending to duplicate the role of the responsible medical officer. His diagnosis stands until the tribunal is satisfied that it is wrong. If the diagnosis may be right, may the disorder be of a nature or degree which makes it appropriate for him to be liable to be detained in hospital for medical treatment? As Mr Richards concedes, that question may itself involve some consideration of treatability, in that if medical treatment can do nothing to alleviate or prevent a deterioration the tribunal may be the more easily satisfied that the patient is not then suffering from a disorder of a nature or degree which makes it appropriate for him to be liable to be detained in a hospital for medical treatment, but I see no reason why the words of s 72(1)(b)(i) should be read as a form of legal shorthand referring back to the three tests which have to be positively satisfied before a patient can be admitted and detained, and which are set out in section 3. If that was what Parliament intended to achieve when enacting s 72(1)(b) it could have said so, but I find it difficult to see how it could have done so without transferring the onus of proof and thus putting the tribunal in the same position as the responsible medical officer. If the respondent and the Divisional Court are right, then in relation to a patient not convicted of crime, s 72(1)(b) could read 'the tribunal shall direct the discharge of a patient liable to be detained otherwise than under section 2 above unless they are satisfied that the grounds relied upon when admitting or reclassifying the patient still exist'. There would be no need for the negative reflections of the appropriateness test which appears in s 72(1)(b)(i) and of the safety test which appears in s 72(1)(b)(ii). Indeed, if s 72(1)(b)(i) does by reference import all three tests set out in s 3, s 72(1)(b)(ii) would seem to be redundant.

If I am right in my approach to s 72(1) and (2), it necessarily follows that the function of the tribunal is different from the function of the doctors at the admission or reclassification or renewal stages, and no assistance as to the proper construction of s 72 can be gained from the fact that the patient would have had to be released if on reclassification the appropriate medical officer had said that further medical treatment in hospital was not likely to alleviate or prevent a deterioration of her condition, a matter which the Divisional Court considered to be of some relevance. I recognise, as Mr Gordon points out, that s 72(2) does not apply to restricted patients suffering from psychopathic disorders, but that does not enable me to read the treatability test into s 72(1).

Unlike the Divisional Court, I do not find the wording of s 72(1)(b) to be 'at best unclear', so I see no reason to resolve a doubt by resorting to the principle of construction which operates in favour of personal liberty. Indeed, I question whether that principle has any real part to play in the construction of a section which in terms seeks to have regard to the potentially conflicting interests of the health or safety of the patient on the one hand and the protection of other persons on the other. For the same reason I find it unnecessary to follow the Divisional Court's lead by considering the statute in its wider context. Mr Gordon invited us to look at *Hansard* and at the legislation which applies in Scotland, but I was unable to derive any real assistance from either of those sources. Unless the wording of the statute is ambiguous, obscure or absurd we should not be looking at *Hansard* (see *Pepper (Inspector of Taxes) v Hart* [1993] 1 All ER 42, [1993] AC 593), and the structure of the Scottish legislation is in some material respects quite different.

During the course of submissions we were invited to consider some of the provisions of the Mental Health Act 1959, together with White Papers and other material which can be regarded as part of the history of the present legislation. That was an interesting exercise and a useful approach, but I need not rehearse it. Both sides sought to draw support from the history, which tends to indicate, as I find, that it is not decisive either way. Mr Gordon also invited us to consider, as the Divisional Court did, art 5 of the 1950 convention, and the case of *X v UK* (1981) 1 BMLR 98, 4 EHRR 188. We could only invoke the assistance of the former if there was ambiguity or uncertainty in the 1989 Act, (see *Brind v Secretary of State for the Home Dept* [1991] 1 All ER 720, [1991] 1 AC 696). That I do not find to be case. In *X v UK* the court was critical of the United Kingdom government because at that time mental health review tribunals had only advisory powers, leaving the executive to take the final decision. That is not the position under the legislation with which we are concerned, and I cannot agree with the Divisional Court that the construction of s 72(1)(b) which I believe to be the right one puts the legislation in conflict with the convention. The tribunal has effective powers as defined in the statute.

(5) Irrationality

Mr Gordon, having served a respondent's notice, submitted that if on the facts the treatability test was not satisfied then, even if it was only to be found in s 72(2), it would be irrational for the tribunal not to be satisfied for the purposes of s 72(1)(b) that it was not appropriate for the patient to be detained in a hospital for medical treatment. That submission obviously cannot survive if in reality the tribunal found or on reconsideration might have found that the treatability test as formulated in s 72(2) was satisfied, and as I have already indicated that seems to be to me the case. I recognise, as I have said, that in some cases, perhaps in many cases, the tribunal will have some regard to treatability when deciding the matters set out in s 72(1)(b)(i) but, particularly having regard to the change of circumstances that has taken place since the

Divisional Court gave its decision, that is as much as I need to say about irrationality in the context of this case.

(6) Reasons

Finally, Mr Gordon attacked the tribunal's reasons. They were not, as I have said, well expressed, largely because question 8 on the form failed to reflect the statutory wording and so asked the wrong question, and if the factual situation was still as it was at the time when the matter before the Divisional Court I would order that the matter be remitted to a differently constituted tribunal so that clear findings could be made in relation to s 72(1)(b) and, if appropriate, in relation to s 72(2) in the light of the judgments of this court. To that extent I would have considered it appropriate to vary the order of the Divisional Court, but in the circumstances which prevail at the present time it seems to me inappropriate for any specific order to be made.

NOURSE LJ. I have had the advantage of reading in draft the judgments of Kennedy and Roch LJJ. On the true construction of s 72(1)(b) of the Mental Health Act 1983, the only point on which they differ, I prefer the view of Kennedy LJ to that taken by Roch LJ and the Divisional Court. There is nothing I can usefully add to the reasoning of Kennedy LJ on that question. On all other questions I agree with both the judgments in this court.

I too would allow the tribunal's appeal.

Appeal allowed.

27 April. The Appeal Committee of the House of Lords (Lord Jauncey of Tullichettle, Lord Browne-Wilkinson and Lord Nolan) refused leave to appeal.

Frances Rustin   Barrister.

El Ajou v Dollar Land Holdings plc and another

COURT OF APPEAL, CIVIL DIVISION
NOURSE, ROSE AND HOFFMANN LJJ
13, 14, 15 OCTOBER, 2 DECEMBER 1993

Company – Director – Company receiving improperly obtained money – Whether knowing receipt – Whether director having knowledge – Knowledge to be attributed to company – Directing mind and will of the company – Whether knowledge of agent could be imputed to company – Basis on which company liable to owner of money.

The plaintiff owned substantial funds and securities which were under the control of an investment manager in Geneva who was bribed to invest the plaintiff's money, without the plaintiff's authority, in fraudulent share selling schemes operated by three Canadians through the medium of two Dutch companies. The proceeds of the fraudulent share selling schemes were channelled through Geneva, Gibraltar, Panama and back through Geneva from where some of it was invested in a London property development project in conjunction with the first defendant ('DLH'), a property company which

was controlled by persons unconnected with the Canadians' fraud and which
had required financial backers for a speculative building project which it
proposed to enter into. DLH had been acquired by those persons on the advice
of S, who had been introduced to them by F, a Swiss fiduciary agent who also
acted for the Canadians. DLH's affairs were conducted by its controlling
shareholders and S, who was managing director of a subsidiary. F was the
chairman of DLH but played no active part in its management. S had
approached F for assistance in obtaining finance for the development project
and F had introduced S to the Canadians, who provided £270,000 as a deposit
for the purchase of a site by a DLH subsidiary, DLH London. The Canadians
through various companies controlled by them provided further funding of
£1,030,000 to DLH to develop the project. The Canadians had also deposited
money with a company controlled by F which F had misappropriated and was
unable to return. To resolve matters a meeting took place at DLH's
headquarters in London at which DLH agreed to guarantee F's indebtedness
to the Canadians subject to a specified limit. F later resigned as a director of
DLH in June 1987 for health reasons. The Canadians subsequently indicated
that they wished to withdraw from the property development project and S
was able to negotiate very favourable terms for the purchase by DLH of the
Canadians' interest in March 1988. The plaintiff when he discovered the fraud
perpetrated by the Canadians and his agent brought proceedings against DLH
to recover the money received by it from the Canadians on the grounds that
DLH had received the money with knowledge that it represented the proceeds
of fraud or, alternatively, sought to recover the value of the Canadians'
investment on the grounds that DLH had knowledge of the fraud before it
bought the Canadians out. The judge dismissed the plaintiff's claim, holding
that although the plaintiff was entitled in equity to trace his money to the DLH
venture, he could not succeed in his claim for knowing receipt because he had
failed to establish that DLH possessed the requisite degree of knowledge
through either F or S that the funds received by DHL from the Canadians were
the proceeds of fraud, because F had played only a minor role in the
management of DLH and his knowledge could not be attributed to the
company since he could not be considered the directing mind and will of the
company and the information he had acquired as to the Canadians' fraud had
been acquired by him in his capacity as an officer of another company and in
the case of S there was no evidence that he knew that the Canadians were using
money which they had obtained improperly. The plaintiff appealed,
contending that F's knowledge should be treated as the knowledge of DLH on
the ground that F was, in relation to DLH's receipt of the fraudulently acquired
assets, its directing mind and will and/or he was its agent in the transaction.

Held – The appeal would be allowed for the following reasons—
(1) The directing mind and will of a company was not necessarily that of the
person or persons who had general management and control of the company
since the directing mind and will could be found in different persons in respect
of different activities. It was therefore necessary to identify the person who
had management and control in relation to the act or omission in point. The
judge had been wrong to hold that a non-executive director such as F who was
responsible for formal paperwork but not for the business and who had played
no part in business decisions could not be for certain purposes the directing
mind and will of the company. On the facts, the transactions to be considered
were those by which DLH received assets representing the moneys

fraudulently misapplied and the crucial considerations were that F made all the arrangements for the receipt and disbursement of the £270,000 and the £1,030,000 and significantly, on 6 May 1986 signed the funding agreement whereby DLH obtained the £1,030,000 since it was those steps that caused DLH to become involved in the project and enabled it later to acquire the assets representing the moneys fraudulently misapplied. Each of those steps was taken without the authority of a resolution of the board of DLH, which showed that F had the de facto management and control of the transactions. The directing mind and will of DLH in relation to the relevant transactions was thus the mind and will of F and no one else, so that F's knowledge that the moneys were the proceeds of fraud could be attributed to DLH and therefore the claim to enforce a constructive trust on the basis of knowing receipt succeeded. That conclusion was not affected by the fact that F ceased to be a director of DLH in June 1987 or that DLH did not receive the asset representing the £1,030,000 until March 1988, since the steps that caused DLH to become involved in the project and enabled it later to acquire the asset were all taken when F and consequently DLH had the requisite knowledge. The subsequent acquisition was sufficiently connected with the original investment to be affected by the same knowledge (see p 696 *b j* to p 697 *f*, p 698 *a* to *d*, p 699 *j* to p 700 *e* and p 706 *f* to p 707 *b* , post).

(2) However, F's knowledge could not as a matter of law be imputed to DLH on the basis that he had acted as the agent of DLH in the transaction because DLH was under no duty to inquire as to the source of the offered money. Further, even if F, in his capacity both as broker and as chairman of DLH, was under a duty to inform DLH that the moneys in question were the proceeds of fraud, that duty alone was not a ground for imputing such knowledge to DLH. Moreover, as F had acquired the information about the fraud while acting for the Canadians and not in his capacity as agent for DLH, the principle that communication to an agent was deemed to be communication to the principal did not apply. Accordingly, F's knowledge could not be imputed to DLH on the ground of agency (see p 698 *f* to *j*, p 700 *f g* and p 703 *e* to p 704 *b*, post).

Decision of Millett J [1993] 3 All ER 717 reversed.

Notes

For following trust property, see 16 *Halsbury's Laws* (4th edn) paras 1460–1464 and 48 *Halsbury's Laws* (4th edn) para 941, and for cases on the subject, see 20 *Digest* (1982 reissue) 900, 6706 and 48 *Digest* (1986 reissue) 728–738, 6687–6751.

Cases referred to in judgments

Baldwin v Casella (1872) LR 7 Exch 325.
Blackburn Lowe & Co v Vigors (1887) 12 App Cas 531, HL.
Blackley v National Mutual Life Assurance [1972] NZLR 1038, NZ CA.
Carew's Estate Act, Re (No 2) (1862) 31 Beav 39, 54 ER 1054.
Dresser v Norwood (1864) 17 CBNS 466, 144 ER 188.
Fenwick Stobart & Co Ltd, Re, Deep Sea Fishery Co's Claim [1902] 1 Ch 507.
Gladstone v King (1813) 1 M & S 35, 105 ER 13.
Hampshire Land Co, Re [1896] 2 Ch 743.
Kelly v Cooper [1992] 3 WLR 936, PC.
Lennards Carrying Co Ltd v Asiatic Petroleum Co Ltd [1915] AC 705, [1914–15] All ER Rep 280, HL.

Montagu's Settlement Trusts, Re, Duke of Manchester v National Westminster Bank Ltd (1985) [1992] 4 All ER 308, [1987] Ch 264, [1987] 2 WLR 1192.
Payne (David) & Co Ltd, Re, Young v David Payne & Co Ltd [1904] 2 Ch 608, CA.
Powles v Page (1846) 3 CB 15, 136 ER 7.
R v Andrews Weatherfoil Ltd [1972] 1 All ER 65, [1972] 1 WLR 118, CA.
Regina Fur Co Ltd v Bossom [1957] 2 Lloyd's Rep 466.
Tesco Supermarkets Ltd v Nattrass [1971] 2 All ER 127, [1972] AC 153, [1971] 2 WLR 1166, HL.
Turton v London and North Western Rly Co (1850) 15 LTOS 92.

Appeal

The plaintiff, Abdul Ghani El Ajou, appealed from the judgment of Millett J ([1993] 3 All ER 717) delivered on 12 June 1992 whereby he dismissed the action brought by the plaintiff against the defendants, Dollar Land Holdings plc (DLH) and Factotum NV (Factotum), in which the plaintiff had claimed, inter alia, (i) damages from DLH, seeking to recover the sum of £1,300,000 being the property of the plaintiff or otherwise money traceable as money of the plaintiff in a development at 22–50 Nine Elms Lane, London SW8 on the ground that DLH received it with knowledge that it represented the proceeds of fraud, or, alternatively, the value of the investment of three Canadians whose interest in the joint venture at Nine Elms was bought out by DLH, the plaintiff alleging that DLH acquired such knowledge before it bought the Canadians out, (ii) a declaration that the said advance was at all times the property of the plaintiff, and/or was at all times held by DLH and Factotum upon trust for the plaintiff absolutely, (iii) a declaration that DLH had received the amount of the advance as a constructive trustee for the plaintiff absolutely and was liable to account to the plaintiff as such trustee, (iv) an order that there an account of all money paid or payable to or received or receivable by DLH (including any profits) in respect of the aforesaid development of the site be taken, (v) an order for the payment of the amount of the advance and all profits earned by DLH by the utilisation thereof and (vi) a declaration that the plaintiff was entitled to payment of all money found due on the taking of the accounts. The facts are set out in the judgment of Nourse LJ.

Michael Beloff QC, Roger Ellis and *Sarah Moore* (instructed by Bower Cotton & Bower) for the appellant.
Romie Tager (instructed by Kaufman Kramer Shebson) for the respondents.

Cur adv vult

2 December 1993. The following judgments were delivered.

NOURSE LJ.

Introduction
Of the questions that remain in dispute in this case, the most important is whether, for the purposes of establishing a company's liability under the knowing receipt head of constructive trust, the knowledge of one of its directors can be treated as having been the knowledge of the company. That is essentially a question of company law. There are or have been other questions on tracing and constructive trust.

The company is the first defendant, Dollar Land Holdings plc ('DLH'). The director is Mr Sylvain Ferdman, who was the chairman and one of the three directors of DLH between June 1985 and June 1987. The party who seeks to recover against DLH in constructive trust is the plaintiff, Abdul Ghani El Ajou. He has put his claim at £1·3m. On 12 June 1992, after a trial extending over some 11 days, Millett J delivered a reserved judgment dismissing the plaintiff's action (see [1993] 2 All ER 717). He held that the plaintiff had an equitable right to trace the money into the hands of DLH, but that Mr Ferdman's knowledge of their fraudulent misapplication could not be treated as having been the knowledge of DLH, either on the ground of his having been its directing mind and will or on the ground of his having been its agent in the transaction. The judge found that another person closely concerned with the affairs of DLH, Mr William Stern, did not have the requisite knowledge of the misapplication. The plaintiff now appeals to this court. He does not seek to upset the judge's finding in regard to Mr Stern. DLH has put in a respondent's notice whose primary purpose is to impugn the judge's finding as to one part of the tracing exercise.

Because the report sets out in full the judge's clear and necessarily lengthy statement of the facts and because the issues have narrowed in this court, the facts can now be stated relatively briefly. I will state them mainly in the judge's own words.

The facts

The plaintiff is a wealthy Arab businessman resident in Riyadh. He was the largest single victim, though only one of many victims, of a massive share fraud carried out in Amsterdam between 1984 and 1985 by three Canadians, Allan Lindzon (or Levinson), Lloyd Caplan and Harry Roth ('the Canadians'). Some of the proceeds of the fraud were passed from Amsterdam through intermediate resting places in Geneva, Gibraltar, Panama and Geneva (again) to London, where in 1986 they were invested in a joint venture to carry out a property development project at Nine Elms in Battersea in conjunction with DLH. The interest of the Canadians in the joint venture was bought out in 1988 by DLH, which is a public limited company incorporated in England but resident for tax purposes in Switzerland. It is a holding company. Its principal activities, carried on through its subsidiaries, are property dealing and investment. At the material time it was in a substantial way of business. It denies that in 1986 it had any knowledge that the money which the Canadians invested in the project represented the proceeds of fraud. Moreover, in buying out their interest in 1988 it claims to have been a bona fide purchaser for value without notice of the fraud.

Mr Ferdman is a Swiss national, resident in Geneva. He worked for many years for the Bank of International Credit in Geneva. In 1972 he left the bank and set up his own company, Société d'Administration et de Financement SA (SAFI), through which he acted as a fiduciary agent. SAFI was originally owned jointly by Mr Ferdman and an old-established Swiss cantonal bank of good reputation, but in 1982 Mr Ferdman became its sole proprietor. SAFI acted as a fiduciary agent for clients who did not wish their identities to be disclosed. Two of its clients were a Mr Singer and a Mr Goldhar, who were associates of the Canadians. Mr Ferdman was accustomed to accept funds from clients without questioning their origin, and to act for clients who were anxious to conceal their identity. He regarded the need to preserve his clients' anonymity as paramount—without it he would have had no business—and to this end he was willing on occasion to present himself or SAFI as a beneficial owner and to make false statements to that effect. The judge found that it must have been plain to Mr Ferdman by the end of October 1985 that Singer and Goldhar were implicated in a fraud. Moreover, Mr Ferdman admitted to the judge at the trial that he knew perfectly well that the Canadians were involved with Singer and Goldhar in the fraud and were not just behind them. The Canadians also had a fiduciary agent resident in Geneva who acted for them. He was Mr David D'Albis, an American citizen.

DLH is an English company which was formerly listed on the London Stock Exchange. In June 1985 its entire issued share capital was acquired by Keristal Investments and Trading SA (Keristal), a Panamanian company beneficially owned by a Liechtenstein foundation. In the annual reports of DLH Mr Ferdman described himself as the beneficial owner of Keristal, but that was not the case. He was simply preserving the anonymity of his principals, the founders and beneficiaries of the Liechtenstein foundation, who were two US citizens resident in New York ('the Americans'). The judge recorded that the plaintiff was satisfied that the Americans had no connection of any kind with the Canadians or their associates or any of the other persons involved in the fraud.

DLH was acquired as a vehicle for the Americans' property dealings in the United Kingdom. Its business activities were under the direction of Mr William Stern, described by the judge as a property dealer who suffered a spectacular and well-publicised bankruptcy as a result of the 1974 property crash. He was engaged in the business of identifying opportunities for property investment and introducing them to investors willing to pay him a fee or a share in the eventual profits. Mr Stern had lived in Geneva as a boy and was acquainted with Mr Ferdman. They became friends, though they lost contact with each other for some years. Mr Stern knew that he was a fiduciary agent and had established SAFI, which he believed still to be jointly owned by Mr Ferdman and a reputable cantonal bank. From time to time he suggested deals to Mr Ferdman and inquired of him whether he had any suitable investors among his clients.

Mr Ferdman introduced the Americans to Mr Stern, who was able to recommend a successful investment in a United Kingdom property. The Americans were willing to make further investments in the United Kingdom, and Mr Stern suggested that he should look for a suitable English vehicle, if possible a quoted company, which they could acquire and use as a medium for further investment. Mr Stern found DLH and Keristal acquired it as a pure cash shell in June 1985. Mr Ferdman and Mr Favre and Mr Jaton, two fellow directors of SAFI, were appointed to be the directors of DLH and Mr Ferdman its chairman. The judge described the three of them as nominee directors representing the interests of the beneficial owners. They played no part in the conduct of DLH's business which was carried on by Mr Stern in consultation with the Americans. Mr Stern was not a director of DLH, but he was appointed managing director of Dollar Land Management Ltd, one of its subsidiaries. DLH was in a substantial way of business and was able to raise very large sums on the security of its assets. At the end of 1986 it had secured bank loans and other mortgage creditors of more than £10m. By the end of 1987 that figure had risen to more than £30m.

Mr Stern asked Mr Ferdman if he could find an investor willing to put up equity finance for the Nine Elms project. Mr Ferdman, who was to receive from DLH an introductory commission of 5% of the funds obtained, brought one of the Canadians, Roth, to London in March 1986 and introduced him to Mr Stern, who provided him with a detailed investment proposal which included a profit forecast. All negotiations were conducted between Roth and Mr Stern. Mr Ferdman played no part. By a letter dated 20 March 1986 and addressed to Roth, care of SAFI in Geneva, the terms which had been agreed between him and Mr Stern were set out. Although that letter was signed by Mr Ferdman, it was composed entirely by Mr Stern. I will return to it later in this judgment.

On 25 March Mr Ferdman copied the letter of 20 March (with two variations which the judge inferred were made at the request of the Canadians) by telex to Mr D'Albis, who gave instructions on the same day for £270,000 to be transferred from Geneva to the Royal Bank of Scotland in London for the account of DLH's solicitors, Grangewoods. The judge found that that sum represented proceeds of the fraud and that finding has not been questioned in this court. Subsequently, Mr Ferdman despatched a duplicate of the telex in the form of a letter on DLH's headed paper, and over his own signature, to Yulara Realty Ltd (Yulara) in Panama. That letter was dated 7 April. Again, I will return to it later. Yulara was a Panamanian company owned by the Canadians, which Mr Ferdman knew was a vehicle for their investment in the Nine Elms project. Mr Ferdman retained on his own files a copy of the letter countersigned by a Panamanian lawyer on behalf of Yulara by way of acceptance.

Contracts for the purchase of the Nine Elms site were exchanged on 26 March. The purchaser was a subsidiary of DLH, Dollar Land (London) Ltd ('DLH London'). The £270,000 which Grangewoods had received on the previous day was used to pay the deposit. On 11 June 1986 DHL London assigned the benefit of the contract to DLH for £100,000 and on the same day DLH entered into a contract for the sale of the site to Regalian Properties (Northern) Ltd ('Regalian'). Completion took place on the same day at a price of £2·7m, £1m of which was recorded as being paid by DLH.

The further funding of the project was complex. Reduced to its essentials, the method adopted was as follows. On 6 May 1986 Keristal (expressed to be represented by Mr Ferdman) and Yulara (expressed to be represented by the Panamanian lawyer) entered into a written loan agreement which was signed by them on behalf of Keristal and Yulara respectively. The agreement recited that Keristal was the holding company of DLH and that Yulara and DLH had entered into an agreement as per the letter dated 7 April. Article 1 was in substance a further recital to the effect that Yulara was making available or had given to Keristal (it is not clear which) the amount of up to $US2·5m for as long as the agreement as per the letter of 7 April would be in force. By art 2 Keristal accepted that amount on terms that it undertook to use the funds (a) 'in order to make a joint venture in a certain real estate investment in London' in accordance with the terms contained in the letter dated 7 April and (b) 'in order to [obtain] a bank guarantee of £1,300,000 to be issued in favour of [DLH London] or another company owned by [DLH]'.

On 12 and 16 May respectively two sums of $US1,541,432 and $US1,143,000, making a total of $US2,684,432, were credited to an account of Keristal (the Keristal No 2 account) at Banque Scandinave in Geneva. The account was operated by SAFI and was used exclusively for the purpose of funding the Nine Elms project. The bank statement for the account shows that the first sum came from the Bank of America; the source of the second is not shown. The judge found that both sums were traceable to Panama as proceeds of the fraud. That is the finding which the respondent's notice seeks to impugn. I will return to it shortly.

Pursuant to arrangements made by Mr Ferdman, Scandinavian Bank Group plc in London then agreed to advance £1·3m to Factotum NV ('Factotum'), a shelf company previously incorporated by Mr Ferdman in the Netherland Antilles, which he decided to make use of as a convenient vehicle for channelling the money to DLH. (Factotum is the second defendant in the action, but it has no assets and has never been served.) The advance was supported by a guarantee given by Banque Scandinave secured on the moneys in the Keristal No 2 account. The whole of the loan from Scandinavian Bank in London to Factotum was drawn down and £1,030,000 was paid into Grangewoods' client account on 29 May. Of those moneys £745,598·60 were used to discharge the amount due from DLH on completion of the purchase of the site on 11 June. The balance was used to discharge obligations of DLH and to make various other payments at the direction of DLH, including payment to Mr Ferdman of his introductory commission of £65,000.

It is clear from the foregoing that the £1,030,000 paid to Grangewoods represented moneys that had been credited to the Keristal No 2 account. It is also clear that the moneys so credited belonged to the Canadians. What is in dispute is the judge's finding that they represented moneys which Mr D'Albis had sent to Panama from Gibraltar on 30 March and 1 April 1986, a fact that had to be established in order that they could be treated as proceeds of the fraud. It is convenient to deal with that question now.

Tracing through Panama

The question was dealt with by Millett J (see [1993] 3 All ER 717 at 734–736). He said that the plaintiff was unable, by direct evidence, to identify the moneys in the Keristal No 2 account with the money which Mr D'Albis had sent to Panama only a few weeks before. However, he thought that there was sufficient funds, though only just, to enable him to draw the necessary inference. He continued (at 734–735):

'One of the two sums received in the Keristal No 2 account was $1,541,432 received on 12 May 1986 from Bank of America. That corresponds closely with the sum of $1,600,000 transferred to Bank of America, Panama on 1 April 1986. In relation to the later transaction, Bank of America may, of course, merely have been acting as a correspondent bank in New York and not as the paying bank; and the closeness of the figures could be a coincidence. It is not much, but it is something; and there is nothing in the opposite scale. The source of the other money received in the Keristal No 2 account is not known, but from the way in which the Canadians appear to have dealt with their affairs, if one sum came from Panama, then the other probably did so, too.'

After considering other points on each side, the judge said that the fact remained that there was no evidence that the Canadians had any substantial funds available to them which did not represent proceeds of the fraud (see at 735). He concluded (at 736):

'In my judgment, there is some evidence to support an inference that the money which reached the Keristal No 2 account represented part of the moneys which had been transmitted to Panama by the second tier Panamanian companies some six weeks previously, and the suggestion that it was derived from any other source is pure speculation.'

Mr Tager, for DLH, submitted that neither of the routes followed by the judge led to the conclusion that he reached. He took us carefully through the bank statement for the Keristal No 2 account. He relied on the fact that there were two separate credits to it of very precise amounts, the second having been made four working days after the first. It had been impossible to identify the source of the second credit. All this suggested that the two credits had come from different sources. There was no necessary connection between the first and the sum of $US1·6m that had been sent from Gibraltar to the Bank of America in Panama on 1 April. Mr Tager argued that there were other very substantial funds available to the Canadians. He disputed the judge's view that there was no evidence that they had any substantial funds available to them that did not represent proceeds of the fraud. He submitted that the plaintiff had not discharged the evidential burden of establishing the necessary link.

Having carefully considered these and other arguments of Mr Tager, I remain unconvinced that the judge drew the wrong inference. I well appreciate both that the question is of critical importance to the plaintiff's case and that, since it depends almost entirely, if not exclusively, on documentary evidence and undisputed events, we in this court are, in theory at any rate, in as good a position to draw an inference as the judge himself. In practice, however, the judge, after an 11-day trial, was in a much better position than we are. From all that I have seen and heard of the case, I would feel no confidence at all in saying that the judge had drawn the wrong inference.

The assets received by DLH

On the footing that the moneys credited to the Keristal No 2 account were proceeds of the fraud, it becomes necessary to identify the assets received by DLH and the dates when it received them. The plaintiff's position is a simple one. He says that DLH received £270,000 on 25 March 1986 and a further £1,030,000 in June 1986 (though logically he ought to say on 29 May 1986, when the latter sum was paid into Grangewoods' client account; see further below). The judge considered these questions. He thought that the position was somewhat more complicated than the plaintiff would have had it.

As to the £270,000, the judge said (at 738):

'The sum of £270,000 was never received by DLH. It was paid into Grangewoods' client account, and their client at the time must be taken to have been DLH London. DLH London was not a nominee or agent for DLH. As had previously been agreed between Roth and Mr Stern, it was the intended contractual purchaser of the site, and the money was to be used exclusively for the payment of the deposit on exchange of contracts. In my judgment, DLH did not receive the money at all, and DHL London did not receive it beneficially but upon trust to apply it for a specific purpose. DLH London used the money, as it was bound to do, to pay the deposit on the site, and thereby acquired for its own benefit a corresponding interest in the site which it subsequently sold and transferred to DLH. The plaintiff can follow his money through these various transactions, but the relevant asset capable of being identified as having been received by DLH is an interest in the site corresponding to the payment of the deposit.'

This question depends on the true construction and effect of the letter of 20 March 1986. Both Mr Beloff QC, for the plaintiff, and Mr Tager for DLH referred to its terms at some length in order to determine whether DLH London had acted as principal or as agent for DLH. Although he was not greatly concerned either way, Mr Beloff submitted that DLH London had acted as agent and that the £270,000 was accordingly received by DLH on 25 March. But in my view the judge was right, as a matter of construction, to conclude that DLH London, and not DLH itself, was the principal, so that it was that company that was Grangewoods' client when the money was received. I therefore agree with the judge that DLH did not receive anything on 25 March, but that on the assignment of the benefit of the contract to it on 11 June it received an interest in the site corresponding to the payment of the deposit.

As to the balance of £1,030,000, the judge said (at 738):

'The sum of £1,030,000 was also paid into Grangewoods' client account, but by then their client had become DLH. The money was disbursed on the instructions and for the benefit of DLH. Only £745,598·60 was used to pay the money due to the vendor on completion, but this was the result of the arrangements which DLH had made with Regalian. So far as Yulara is concerned, the whole £1·3m must be taken to have been disbursed as agreed between them on the acquisition of a 40% interest in the project. Moreover, in my judgment, on a proper analysis of the transaction between Yulara and DLH, Yulara's money should be treated as having been invested in its share of the project, and not in or towards the acquisition of DLH's share. The investment proved highly successful. In itself it was not a breach of trust and caused the plaintiff no loss. Had he been able to intervene before the Canadians were bought out, he could have claimed the whole of Yulara's interest in the project; but whatever the extent of DLH's knowledge of the source of Yulara's funds, his claim would have been confined to Yulara's interest in exoneration of that of DLH. In the events which have happened, the plaintiff is in my judgment bound to treat his money as represented by Yulara's interest in the project, and must rely exclusively on the transaction on 16 March 1988 when Yulara's interest was bought out by DLH.'

For a reason which will become clear when I deal with the question whether Mr Ferdman was the directing mind and will of DLH, Mr Beloff expressed greater concern at the judge's decision of this question. However, subject to one point, I feel unable to differ from his reasoning on it.

I am puzzled by the judge's suggestion that by the time the £1,030,000 was paid into Grangewoods' client account their client had become DLH. He had found that that payment was made on 29 May, before the assignment of the benefit of the contract by DLH London to DLH on 11 June (see at 730). However, this point (which was not addressed in argument), though it may be of importance in relation to the date at which DLH must be treated as having had knowledge of the fraud (see below), does not affect the judge's view of the asset received by DLH in respect of the £1,030,000 and the date when it received it.

Knowledge

It having been established that DLH received assets representing proceeds of the fraud, I come to the question of knowledge. By the end of the hearing there could have been no doubt that Mr Ferdman himself had the requisite knowledge. The judge said of him (at 740):

'He freely admitted that he knew that the persons who were providing the money for the Nine Elms project were the persons who had been behind the fraud in Amsterdam; and that by 7 April 1986, when he signed the letter to Yulara, he knew (or assumed) that the money which he would be receiving into the Keristal No 2 account was part of the proceeds of the fraud.'

Thus arises the most important question remaining in dispute, which is whether Mr Ferdman's knowledge can be treated as having been the knowledge of DLH. The plaintiff contends that it can and ought to be, first, on the ground that Mr Ferdman was, in relation to DLH's receipt of the assets representing the moneys fraudulently misapplied, its directing mind and will; secondly and alternatively, on the ground that he was its agent in the transaction. Because a company's directing mind and will are often the mind and will of one or more of its directors and because a director is for many purposes an agent of the company, there is a danger of confusion between the two grounds on which the plaintiff relies. But they are, as the judge made clear, quite separate. The plaintiff can succeed on either. The convenient course is to deal with the law and the facts in regard to each of them in turn.

Directing mind and will

This doctrine, sometimes known as the alter ego doctrine, has been developed, with no divergence of approach, in both criminal and civil jurisdictions, the authorities in each being cited indifferently in the other. A company having no mind or will of its own, the need for it arises because the criminal law often requires mens rea as a constituent of the crime, and the civil law intention or knowledge as an ingredient of the cause of action or defence. In the oft-quoted words of Viscount Haldane LC in *Lennards Carrying Co Ltd v Asiatic Petroleum Co Ltd* [1915] AC 705 at 713, [1914–15] All ER Rep 280 at 283:

'My Lords, a corporation is an abstraction. It has no mind of its own any more than it has a body of its own; its active and directing will must consequently be sought in the person of somebody who for some purposes may be called an agent, but who is really the directing mind and will of the corporation, the very ego and centre of the personality of the corporation.'

The doctrine attributes to the company the mind and will of the natural person or persons who manage and control its actions. At that point, in the words of Millett J ([1993] 3 All ER 717 at 740): 'Their minds are its mind; their intention its intention; their knowledge its knowledge.' It is important to emphasise that management and control is not something to be considered generally or in the round. It is necessary to identify the natural person or persons having management and control in relation to the act or omission in point. This was well put by Eveleigh J in delivering the judgment of the Criminal Division of this court in *R v Andrews Weatherfoil Ltd* [1972] 1 All ER 65 at 70, [1972] 1 WLR 118 at 124:

'It is necessary to establish whether the natural person or persons in question have the status and authority which in law makes their acts in the matter under consideration the acts of the company so that the natural person is to be treated as the company itself.'

Decided cases show that, in regard to the requisite status and authority, the formal position, as regulated by the company's articles of association, service contracts and so forth, though highly relevant, may not be decisive. Here Millett J adopted a pragmatic approach. In my view he was right to do so, although it has led me, with diffidence, to a conclusion different from his own.

DLH contends that its directing mind and will in relation to its receipt of the assets representing the moneys fraudulently misapplied were either the mind and will of Mr Stern alone or of Mr Stern and the Americans together. They were not the mind and will of Mr Ferdman. The judge's acceptance of this contention is expressed (at 741):

'In 1986 [DHL's] directors were all officers of SAFI, but they were merely nominee directors representing the interests of the Americans. Mr Ferdman was a non-executive director. His only executive responsibilities were to act as a fiduciary agent, represent the interests of the Americans, and ensure that the necessary corporate documentation was in order. The witnesses agreed that, in the early days of DLH, Mr Ferdman played a bigger role than he did [later]; but I do not think that that was due to any change in his role. He was always responsible for the formal paperwork, but not for the business. As the business expanded, so his relative importance diminished. Even in 1986, he played no part in business decisions. These were taken by Mr Stern in consultation with the Americans. In my judgment, Mr Ferdman's position as chairman and non-executive director of DLH was insufficient by itself to constitute his knowledge ipso facto the knowledge of DLH. It has not been alleged, still less established, that the other two officers of SAFI, who with Mr Ferdman constituted the board of DLH in 1986, shared Mr Ferdman's knowledge of the source of the Canadians' money, but in my judgment it would make no difference if they did. Like Mr Ferdman, they were merely nominee directors with non-executive responsibility. They had no authority to take business decisions. In relation to its business affairs in 1986, neither Mr Ferdman alone nor the board as a whole can realistically be regarded as the directing mind and will of DLH.'

In disagreeing with the judge on this question, I start from the position that the transactions to be considered are those by which DLH received assets representing the moneys fraudulently misapplied. The responsibility for the management and control of those transactions is not to be determined by identifying those who were responsible for deciding that DLH would participate in the Nine Elms project and the nature and extent of that participation, far less by identifying those who were responsible for business decisions generally. Neither Mr Stern nor the Americans made any of the arrangements for the receipt or disbursement of the moneys by Grangewoods. Nor did they commit DLH to the obligations correlative to their receipt. None of them had the authority to do so. That was the responsibility of Mr Ferdman. The crucial considerations are that Mr Ferdman made all the arrangements for the receipt and disbursement of the £270,000 and the £1,030,000; that it was he who signed the letter of 20 March to Roth; that it was he who, on 25 March, copied that letter to Mr D'Albis; that it was he who signed and dispatched the letter of 7 April to Yulara; that it was he who, on 6 May, signed the agreement with Yulara; and that it was those steps that caused DLH to become involved in the project and enabled it later to acquire the assets representing the moneys fraudulently misapplied.

Each of the steps taken by Mr Ferdman was taken without the authority of a resolution of the board of DLH. That demonstrates that as between Mr Ferdman on the one hand and Mr Favre and Mr Jaton on the other it was Mr Ferdman who had the de facto management and control of the transactions. It may be that that state of affairs involved some breach of the directors' duties to DLH. But that would not enable DLH to say that Mr Favre and Mr Jaton were parties to its directing mind and will in any relevant respect. Mr Tager sought to show that they did perform duties as directors of DLH. No doubt they did. But there is no real evidence that they had any responsibility for the transactions in question. In my view the directing mind and will of DLH in relation to the relevant transactions between March and June 1986 were the mind and will of Mr Ferdman and none other. That means that DLH had the requisite knowledge at that time.

Next, I must consider whether the plaintiff's right to recover is affected by Mr Ferdman's having ceased to be a director of DLH in June 1987. This question is of significance only in relation to the £1,030,000. It has no bearing on the £270,000. Millett J, having repeated his view that, in regard to the £1,030,000, the relevant transaction was the acquisition by DLH of Yulara's interest in the joint venture on 16 March 1988, continued (at 743):

'By then Mr Ferdman had ceased to be a director of DLH for nine months, and he had nothing at all to do with the transaction. Even if, contrary to my judgment, Mr Ferdman's knowledge should be attributed to DLH in 1986, it would be quite wrong to treat DLH as still possessing that knowledge in 1988. As Megarry V-C pointed out in *Re Montagu's Settlement Trusts* [1992] 4 All ER 308 at 329, [1987] Ch 264 at 284, a natural person should not be said to have knowledge of a fact that he once knew if at the time in question he has genuinely forgotten all about it. In my judgment, where the knowledge of a director is attributed to a company, but is not actually imparted to it, the company should not be treated as continuing to possess that knowledge after the director in question has died or left its service. In such circumstances, the company can properly be said to have "lost its memory".'

While I might agree with the judge that the knowledge of a director, who had known of a misapplication of trust moneys at the time of their misapplication but had genuinely forgotten all about it by the time that they

were received by the company, could not be attributed to the company, I am
unable to see how that can assist DLH here. The steps that caused DLH to
become involved in the project and enabled it later to acquire the asset
representing the £1,030,000 were all taken between March and June 1986.
Moreover, although the judge held that the plaintiff was bound to treat the
£1,030,000 as represented by Yulara's interest in the project, he found that that
sum had been paid into Grangewoods' client account on 29 May 1986 and had
thereafter been wholly disbursed as directed by DLH, £745,000 approximately
in satisfaction of the purchase price (see at 730). In the circumstances, DLH
having had the requisite knowledge at the time that it became involved in the
project and when the £1,030,000 was disbursed as it directed, it would in my
view be unrealistic to hold that it ceased to have that knowledge simply
because the mind and will that had been the source of it played no part in the
receipt of the asset itself. I am therefore of the opinion that DLH is on this
ground liable to the plaintiff in constructive trust.

Agency

Although the views so far expressed are enough to dispose of the appeal in
favour of the plaintiff, I turn briefly to the alternative question whether Mr
Ferdman's knowledge ought to be imputed to DLH, on the ground that he
acted as DLH's agent in the transaction.

Millett J thought that it was not accurate to describe Mr Ferdman as having
acted as the agent of DLH in obtaining money from the Canadians. I am not
sure that I would agree with him on that question. The real question is
whether Mr Ferdman acted as the agent of DLH in the transactions by which
it received assets representing the moneys fraudulently misapplied. I find it
unnecessary to answer either question. That is because I agree with the judge
that, even if Mr Ferdman was DLH's agent, his knowledge could not, as a
matter of law, be imputed to it.

It is established on the authorities that the knowledge of a person who
acquires it as a director of one company will not be imputed to another
company of which he is also a director, unless he owes, not only a duty to the
second company to receive it, but also a duty to the first to communicate it: see
Re Hampshire Land Co [1896] 2 Ch 743 and *Re Fenwick Stobart & Co Ltd, Deep Sea
Fishery Co's Claim* [1902] 1 Ch 507.

Mr Ferdman acquired his knowledge of the fraudulent misapplication as a
director of SAFI. I do not doubt that he owed a duty to DLH to receive it. But
I agree with the judge that he owed no duty to SAFI to communicate it. I also
agree with him that the facts of this case are indistinguishable in any material
respect from those in *Re David Payne & Co Ltd, Young v David Payne & Co Ltd*
[1904] 2 Ch 608.

Conclusion

I would allow the appeal. On that footing, it becomes necessary to consider
the relief to which the plaintiff is entitled, a consideration so far made
unnecessary by the judge's dismissal of the action. Although it would be
possible for this court to deal with that question itself, I think it preferable to
remit it for consideration by the judge.

ROSE LJ. I gratefully adopt the recital of facts in the judgment of Nourse LJ. For the reasons which he gives, I agree that the appellant's submissions with regard to the payment of the deposit and the balance of the money fail. Millett J's conclusions, namely that the deposit was paid to Dollar Land Holdings London beneficially and that the balance was received by Dollar Land Holdings plc ('DLH') on trust to invest on behalf of Yulara Realty Ltd ('Yulara') pursuant to a joint venture agreement, were, on the evidence before him, correct. Equally, the judge's finding, which DLH seek to challenge, that the money can be traced to the proceeds of fraud by the Canadians, is, in my view, unimpeachable.

The submissions with regard to the role of Ferdman and whether his knowledge of the fraudulent origin of the invested funds should be attributed to DLH raise considerations of more general importance. In English law the concept of a company's directing mind and will has its origins in the speech of Viscount Haldane LC in *Lennards Carrying Co Ltd v Asiatic Petroleum Co Ltd* [1915] AC 705 at 713, [1914–15] All ER Rep 280 at 283. In *Tesco Supermarkets Ltd v Nattrass* [1971] 2 All ER 127 at 155, [1972] AC 153 at 200 Lord Diplock identified those who are to be treated in law as being the company as—

'those natural persons who by the memorandum and articles of association or as a result of action taken by the directors, or by the company in general meeting pursuant to the articles are entrusted with the exercise of the powers of the company.'

Lord Reid said ([1971] 2 All ER 127 at 132, [1972] AC 153 at 171):

'Normally the board of directors, the managing director and perhaps other superior officers of a company carry out the functions of management and speak and act as the company ... But the board of directors may delegate some part of their functions of management giving to their delegate full discretion to act independently of instructions from them.'

Lord Pearson said ([1971] 2 All ER 127 at 148, [1972] AC 153 at 190):

'There are some officers of a company who may for some purposes be identified with it, as being or having its directing mind and will, its centre and ego, and its brains ... The reference in s 20 of the Trades Descriptions Act 1968 to "any director, manager, secretary or other similar officer of the body corporate" affords a useful indication of the grades of officers who may for some purposes be identifiable with the company ...'

There are, it seems to me, two points implicit, if not explicit, in each of these passages. First, the directors of a company are, prima facie, likely to be regarded as its directing mind and will whereas particular circumstances may confer that status on non-directors. Secondly, a company's directing mind and will may be found in different persons for different activities of the company.

It follows that Millett J's unchallenged conclusion that Stern, although neither a director nor an employee, was the 'moving force' behind the company's activities does not preclude a finding that Ferdman was the company's directing mind and will in relation to some activities.

In the present case, the company's activity to which Ferdman's knowledge was potentially pertinent was the receipt of over £1m for investment.

Ferdman had been appointed by the Americans for two reasons in particular: first, as a Swiss resident operating the formal aspects of the company he was able to confer the tax advantages of non-resident status on DLH on the basis that its 'central management and control' was in Switzerland not England; and secondly because the Americans did not want Stern to be seen to have any official role in the company. Ferdman was a director and chairman of the board and his services were charged for at a higher rate than that for other directors. He instructed accountants and solicitors. He convened meetings. He claimed in the company's accounts to be its ultimate beneficiary. He was a necessary signatory of legal documents and signed the Yulara agreement without needing the authority of a board resolution to do so: by so doing he committed the company to that agreement.

Having regard to these matters, it seems to me to be plain that, for the limited purposes here relevant ie the receipt of money and the execution of the Yulara agreement, he was the directing mind and will of the company. In consequence, his knowledge of the fraud was DLH's knowledge and, in this respect, I differ from Millet J. It is immaterial that by March 1988, when DLH acquired Yulara's interest, Ferdman had ceased to be a director. That cessation did not deprive DLH of its continuing knowledge in relation to the transaction, which embraced both the initial receipt of the money in May 1986 and the ultimate acquisition of Yulara's interest.

If the appellant does not succeed on this point, Mr Beloff's alternative submission based on agency is, in my view, doomed to fail. This court is, in my judgment, bound to hold, on the authority of *Re David Payne & Co Ltd*, *Young v David Payne & Co Ltd* [1904] 2 Ch 608 that, qua agent, Ferdman was under no obligation to disclose his knowledge to DLH, there being no duty on DLH to inquire as to the source of the offered money. I agree with Hoffmann LJ's analysis of the three categories of agency cases to which he refers and with his conclusion that they have no application in the present circumstances.

To the extent indicated I would allow this appeal.

HOFFMANN LJ. This is a claim to enforce a constructive trust on the basis of knowing receipt. For this purpose the plaintiff must show, first, a disposal of his assets in breach of fiduciary duty; secondly, the beneficial receipt by the defendant of assets which are traceable as representing the assets of the plaintiff; and thirdly, knowledge on the part of the defendant that the assets he received are traceable to a breach of fiduciary duty.

There is no dispute that the first requirement is satisfied. The Canadians bribed the plaintiff's fiduciary agent to give them over $US10m of his money in return for worthless shares. The argument in this appeal has been over, first, which assets were received beneficially by Dollar Land Holdings plc ('DLH'); secondly, whether they are traceable as representing the plaintiff's money; and thirdly, whether the admitted knowledge of the frauds on the part of Mr Ferdman, chairman of DLH, can be imputed to the company.

1. IDENTIFYING THE ASSETS BENEFICIALLY RECEIVED

The judge has found as a fact that certain assets received by DLH, namely the benefit of the deposit paid under the contract for the purchase of the Nine Elms site and Yulara Realty Ltd's ('Yulara') interest in the development, were traceable in equity as proceeds of fraud. Both sides have challenged certain aspects of this finding.

(a) The deposit

The plaintiff says that the asset received by DLH was not the benefit of the deposit but the money used to pay it. This had been sent on 25 March 1986 to DLH's subsidiary Dollar Land (London) Ltd ('DLH London'), which entered into the contract to buy the site and afterwards assigned that contract (with the benefit of the deposit) to DLH. The plaintiff says that DLH London received the money as agent for DLH. The only evidence for this claim is that it was paid pursuant to an agreement between Roth and DLH. But that in my judgment is no reason why DLH London should not have received the money beneficially and this would be consistent with its having been the contracting party and subsequently assigning that contract for a substantial consideration to DLH.

(b) The main investment

The plaintiff says that the other asset received by DLH was not Yulara's interest in the project, which it acquired on 16 March 1988, but the £1,030,000 invested by Yulara on 29 May 1986. In my judgment the judge was right in holding that money was not received by DLH beneficially but on trust to invest on behalf of Yulara. DLH and Yulara were joint venturers. Yulara was making an equity investment by which it acquired a proprietary interest in half the share of profits due to DLH under its arrangements with Regalian Properties (Northern) Ltd (Regalian) and the benefit of a guarantee by DLH that its capital would be repaid. DLH received no part of this investment beneficially until it bought out Yulara's interest.

2. TRACING

DLH challenges the judge's finding that the money can be traced to the proceeds of fraud which the Canadians had remitted to Panama. In my view, this was a finding which the judge was entitled to make. Mr Tager says that it might have been the proceeds of frauds on other people or even the money realised by the Canadians when they sold the business. It might have been, but as against the plaintiff I do not think that the Canadians would have been entitled to say so. Nor is DLH. The mixed fund was impressed with an equitable charge in favour of the plaintiff which was enforceable against the Canadians and persons claiming under them.

3. KNOWLEDGE

The judge correctly analysed the various capacities in which Mr Ferdman was involved in the transaction between DLH and the Canadians. First, he acted as a broker, introducing the Canadians to DLH in return for a 5% commission. In this capacity he was not acting as agent for DLH but as an independent contractor performing a service for a fee. Secondly, he was authorised agent of DLH to sign the agreement with Yulara. Thirdly, he was at all material times a director and chairman of the board of DLH.

There are two ways in which Mr Ferdman's knowledge can be attributed to DLH. The first is that as agent of DLH his knowledge can be imputed to the company. The second is that for this purpose he *was* DLH and his knowledge was its knowledge. The judge rejected both.

(a) The agency theory

The circumstances in which the knowledge of an agent is imputed to the principal can vary a great deal and care is needed in analysing the cases. They fall into a number of categories which are not always sufficiently clearly distinguished. I shall mention three such categories because they each include cases on which Mr Beloff QC placed undifferentiated reliance. In fact, however, they depend upon distinct principles which have no application in this case.

(i) Agent's knowledge affecting performance or terms of authorised contract

First, there are cases in which an agent is authorised to enter into a transaction in which his own knowledge is material. So, for example, an insurance policy may be avoided on account of the broker's failure to disclose material facts within his knowledge, even though he did not obtain that knowledge in his capacity as agent for the insured. As Lord Macnaghten said in *Blackburn Lowe & Co v Vigors* (1887) 12 App Cas 531 at 542–543:

'But that is not because the knowledge of the agent is to be imputed to the principal but because the agent of the assured is bound as the principal is bound to communicate to the underwriters all material facts within his knowledge.'

In this category fall two of the cases upon which Mr Beloff relied, namely *Turton v London and North Western Rly Co* (1850) 15 LTOS 92 and *Dresser v Norwood* (1864) 17 CBNS 466, 144 ER 188. In the former case the agent was authorised to conclude a contract of carriage on behalf of the principal. The agent's knowledge of the carrier's standard terms of business was held sufficient to enable those terms to be treated as included in the contract. The agent, said Pollock CB, 'made the same contract in this case as if he had made it for himself'. In the latter case, the agent was authorised to enter into a contract for the purchase of wood. His knowledge that the vendor was a factor dealing for a principal was held sufficient to enable the contract to be treated as made with the principal and so preclude the purchaser from relying on a set-off against the factor. Neither are cases of imputation of knowledge. Rather, the agent's knowledge affects the terms or performance of the contract which he concludes on behalf of his principal.

These principles have no application in this case. We are not concerned with the contractual terms upon which DLH received the traceable assets but whether it had the knowledge which would impose a constructive trust. In other words, real imputation of knowledge is required.

(ii) Principal's duty to investigate or make disclosure

Secondly, there are cases in which the principal has a duty to investigate or to make disclosure. The duty to investigate may arise in many circumstances, ranging from an owner's duty to inquire about the vicious tendencies of his dog (*Baldwin v Casella* (1872) LR 7 Exch 325 at 326–327) to the duty of a purchaser of land to investigate the title. Or there may be something about a transaction by which the principal is 'put on inquiry'. If the principal employs an agent to discharge such a duty, the knowledge of the agent will be imputed to him. (There is an exception, the scope of which it is unnecessary to discuss, in cases in which the agent commits a fraud against the principal.) Likewise in cases in which the principal is under a duty to make disclosure (for example, to an insurer) he may have to disclose not only facts of which he knows but also material facts of which he could expect to have been told by his agents. So in *Gladstone v King* (1813) 1 M & S 35, 105 ER 13 a marine insurance policy was avoided because the master of the ship knew that it had suffered damage, even though he had not in fact communicated this information to the owner. *Regina Fur Co Ltd v Bossom* [1957] 2 Lloyd's Rep 466 upon which Mr Beloff strongly relied, also concerned the duty to make disclosure under an insurance policy and therefore falls within the same category.

None of these cases are relevant because in receiving the traceable assets, DLH had no duty to investigate or make disclosure. There was nothing to put it on inquiry.

(iii) Agent authorised to receive communications

Thirdly, there are cases in which the agent has actual or ostensible authority to receive communications, whether informative (such as the state of health of an insured: *Blackley v National Mutual Life Assurance* [1972] NZLR 1038) or performative (such as a notice to quit: *Tanham v Nicholson* (1872) LR 5 HL 561) on behalf of the principal. In such cases, communication to the agent is communication to the principal. These cases also have no application here. Mr Ferdman did not receive information about the frauds in his capacity as agent for DLH. He found it out while acting for the Canadians.

(iv) Agent's duty to principal irrelevant

What it therefore comes to is that Mr Ferdman, an agent of DLH, had private knowledge of facts into which DLH had no duty to inquire. Mr Beloff said that Mr Ferdman nevertheless owed DLH a duty to disclose those facts. He then submits that because he had such a duty, DLH must be treated as if he had discharged it.

I am inclined to agree that Mr Ferdman did owe a duty, both as broker employed by DLH to find an investor and as chairman of the Board, to inform DLH that the Yulara money was the proceeds of fraud. I reject Mr Tager's submission, based on *Kelly v Cooper* [1992] 3 WLR 936, that no term can be implied in a contract with a Swiss fiduciary agent which requires him to disclose that the money for which he is being paid a 5% procurement commission has been stolen. There is no evidence that Switzerland will enforce a confidence in iniquity any more than this country.

But Mr Beloff's submission that DLH must be treated as if the duty had been discharged raises an important point of principle. In my judgment the submission is wrong. The fact that an agent owed a duty to his principal to communicate information may permit a court to infer as a fact that he actually did so. But this is a rebuttable inference of fact and in the present case the judge found that Mr Ferdman did not disclose what he knew to anyone else acting on behalf of DLH. In some of the cases in the third of the categories I have mentioned, the fact that an agent with authority to receive a communication had a duty to pass the communication on to his principal is mentioned as a reason why the principal should be treated as having received it. I think, however, that the true basis of these cases is that communication to the agent is treated, by reason of his authority to receive it, as communication to the principal. I know of no authority for the proposition that in the absence of any

duty on the part of the principal to investigate, information which was
received by an agent otherwise than as agent can be imputed to the principal
simply on the ground that the agent owed to his principal a duty to disclose it.

On the contrary, I agree with the judge that *Re David Payne & Co Ltd, Young
v David Payne & Co Ltd* [1904] 2 Ch 608 at 611 is authority against such a
proposition. In that case the Exploring Land and Minerals Co Ltd lent £6,000
to David Payne & Co Ltd for 30 days on the security of a debenture. One
Kolckmann, a stockbroker who was concerned in an ambitious and somewhat
dubious scheme of flotation involving David Payne & Co Ltd, was also a
director of the Exploring Land Co. In his capacity as stockbroker he knew that
the money would not be applied to any authorised purpose of the company but
diverted to the use of its controlling shareholder. He actually signed the
cheque by which the money was advanced. David Payne & Co Ltd went into
liquidation and the liquidator challenged the validity of the debenture on the
ground that Kolckmann's knowledge of the ultra vires purposes for which the
money would be used should be imputed to the Exploring Land Co.

Buckley J appears to have assumed that, as a director of the Exploring Land
Co, Kolckmann owed a duty to disclose what he knew about the real purposes
for which the money would be used. But he regarded this as insufficient to
enable that knowledge to be imputed to the company. He said (at 611):

> 'I understand the law to be this: that if a communication be made to an
> agent *which it would be his duty to hand on to his principals* ... and if the agent
> has an interest which would lead him not to disclose to his principals the
> information that he has thus obtained, and in point of fact he does not
> communicate it, you are not to impute to his principals knowledge by
> reason of the fact that their agent knew something which it was not in his
> interest to disclose, and which he did not disclose.' (My emphasis.)

It is true that in the Court of Appeal, both Vaughan-Williams and Romer LJJ
said that Kolckmann owed no duty to impart his knowledge to the Exploring
Land Co. Thus Romer LJ said (at 619):

> 'I take it that in such a transaction the lending company was not bound
> to inquire as to the application of the money at all by the borrowing
> company. That being so, it appears to me that knowledge independently
> acquired by a director in his personal capacity in respect to a matter which
> was irrelevant so far as concerned the lending company is knowledge
> which cannot be imputed to the company, for it was knowledge of
> something which really did not concern the lending company as a matter
> of law. Therefore, you cannot imply a duty on the part of the director to
> have told these facts to the lending company, or a duty on the part of the
> lending company to have inquired into that question.'

It is however clear from the process of reasoning that what Romer LJ means is
that in the absence of a duty to inquire, there was no duty of disclosure on the
part of the director on which an outsider could rely for the purpose of imputing
his knowledge to the company. I do not think that it would have affected his
conclusion if the director had for some other reason (eg some internal
company rule) owed a duty of disclosure with which he did not in fact comply.
I agree with Buckley J that this would have been irrelevant.

It follows that in my judgment Millett J was right to hold that Mr Ferdman's position as agent or broker does not enable his knowledge to be imputed to DLH.

(b) The 'directing mind and will' theory

The phrase 'directing mind and will' comes from a well-known passage in the judgment of Viscount Haldane LC in *Lennards Carrying Co Ltd v Asiatic Petroleum Co Ltd* [1915] AC 705, [1914–15] All ER Rep 280 which distinguishes between someone who is 'merely a servant or agent' and someone whose action (or knowledge) is that of the company itself. Despite their familiarity, it is worth quoting the terms in which Viscount Haldane LC said that the directing mind could be identified ([1915] AC 705 at 713, [1914–15] All ER Rep 280 at 282):

'That person may be under the direction of the shareholders in general meeting; that person may be the board of directors itself, or it may be, and in some companies it is so, that that person has an authority co-ordinate with the board of directors given to him under the articles of association, and is appointed by the general meeting of the company, and can only be removed by the general meeting of the company. My Lords, whatever is not known about Mr. Lennard's position, this is known for certain, Mr. Lennard took the active part in the management of this ship on behalf of the owners, and Mr. Lennard, as I have said, was registered as the person designated for this purpose in the ship's register.'

Viscount Haldane LC therefore regarded the identification of the directing mind as primarily a *constitutional* question, depending in the first instance upon the powers entrusted to a person by the articles of association. The last sentence about Mr Lennard's position shows that the position as reflected in the articles may have to be supplemented by looking at the actual exercise of the company's powers. A person held out by the company as having plenary authority or in whose exercise of such authority the company acquiesces, may be treated as its directing mind.

It is well known that Viscount Haldane LC derived the concept of the 'directing mind' from German law (see Gower *Principles of Modern Company Law* (5th edn, 1992) p 194, n 36) which distinguishes between the agents and organs of the company. A German company with limited liability (GmbH) is required by law to appoint one or more directors (Geschäftsführer). They are the company's organs and for legal purposes represent the company. The knowledge of any one director, however obtained, is the knowledge of the company (see Scholz *Commentary on the GmbH Law* (7th edn, 1986), s 35). English law has never taken the view that the knowledge of a director ipso facto imputed to the company: see *Powles v Page* (1846) 3 CB 15, 136 ER 7 and *Re Carew's Estate Act (No 2)* (1862) 31 Beav 39, 54 ER 1054. Unlike the German Geschäftsführer, an English director may, as an individual, have no powers whatever. But English law shares the view of German law that whether a person is an organ or not depends upon the extent of the powers which in law he has express or implied authority to exercise on behalf of the company.

Millett J did not accept that Mr Ferdman was the directing mind and will of DLH because he exercised no independent judgment. As a fiduciary he acted entirely upon the directions of the American beneficial owners and their

consultant Mr Stern. All that he did was to sign the necessary documents and
ensure that the company's paper work was in order. This involved seeing that
decisions which had really been taken by the Americans and Mr Stern were
duly minuted as decisions of the board made in Switzerland.

But neither the Americans nor Mr Stern held any position under the
constitution of the company. Nor were they held out as doing so. They signed
no documents on behalf of the company and carried on no business in its name.
As a holding company, DLH had no independent business of its own. It
entered into various transactions and on those occasions the persons who
acted on its behalf were the board or one or more of the directors.

It seems to me that if the criterion is whether the candidate for being the
'directing mind and will' was exercising independent judgment, as opposed to
acting upon off-stage instructions, not even the board of directors acting
collectively would in this case have qualified. It also did what it was told. But
Mr Tager was inclined to concede that the board, acting as a board, could
properly be regarded as the directing mind and will. It was certainly held out
in certain quarters as such. DLH claimed non-resident status from the Inland
Revenue on the ground that its 'central management and control' was situated
in Switzerland.

The authorities show clearly that different persons may for different
purposes satisfy the requirements of being the company's directing mind and
will. Therefore the question in my judgment is whether in relation to the
Yulara transaction, Mr Ferdman as an individual exercised powers on behalf of
the company which so identified him. It seems to me that Mr Ferdman was
clearly regarded as being in a different position from the other directors. They
were associates of his who came and went. SAFI charged for their services at
a substantially lower rate. It was Mr Ferdman who claimed in the published
accounts of DLH to be its ultimate beneficial owner. In my view, however, the
most significant fact is that Mr Ferdman signed the agreement with Yulara on
behalf of DLH. There was no board resolution authorising him to do so. Of
course we know that in fact he signed at the request of Mr Stern, whom he
knew to be clothed with authority from the Americans. But so far as the
constitution of DLH was concerned, he committed the company to the
transaction as an autonomous act which the company adopted by performing
the agreement. I would therefore hold, respectfully differing from the judge,
that this was sufficient to justify Mr Ferdman being treated, in relation to the
Yulara transaction, as the company's directing mind and will. Nor do I think it
matters that by the time DLH acquired Yulara's interest in the Nine Elms
project on 16 March 1988, Mr Ferdman had ceased to be a director. Once his
knowledge is treated as being the knowledge of the company in relation to a
given transaction, I think that the company continues to be affected with that
knowledge for any subsequent stages of the same transaction. So, for example,
if (contrary to the judge's finding) the £1,030,000 sent by Yulara on 29 May 1986
had been received beneficially by DLH as a loan, but Mr Ferdman had resigned
or died a week earlier, I do not think that DLH could have said that it received
the money without imputed knowledge of the fraud. And in my judgment the

subsequent acquisition of Yulara's interest was sufficiently connected with the original investment to be affected by the same knowledge.

I would therefore allow the appeal. I do not regard this as an unsatisfactory outcome. If the persons beneficially interested in a company prefer for tax or other reasons to allow that company to be for all legal purposes run by off-shore fiduciaries, they must accept that it may incur liabilities by reason of the acts or knowledge of those fiduciaries.

Appeal allowed. Case remitted to judge to determine relief to which plaintiff was entitled.

16 May 1994. The Appeal Committee of the House of Lords (Lord Jauncey of Tullichettle, Lord Slynn and Lord Woolf) refused leave to appeal.

Frances Rustin   Barrister.

Marchant v Onslow

CHANCERY DIVISION
DAVID NEUBERGER QC SITTING AS A DEPUTY JUDGE OF THE HIGH COURT
14, 17 SEPTEMBER 1993

Education – School – Conveyance under School Sites Act 1841– Reverter – Cesser for use for purposes of Act – Land conveyed for full value – Provision for land to 'revert to and become a portion of ... Estate' – Whether provision capable of applying to freestanding land not part of an estate – Whether reverting to original grantor and successors – School Sites Act 1841, s 2 – Reverter of Sites Act 1987, s 1.

In 1848 the defendant's predecessors in title conveyed a piece of land to the plaintiffs' predecessors in title to be held by them on trust for use as a school pursuant to the School Sites Act 1841, s 2ª of which provided, inter alia, that any person seised of and having the beneficial interest in any land could grant or convey 'any Quantity [of that land] not exceeding One Acre ... as a Site for a School' provided that 'upon the said Land so granted ... ceasing to be used for the Purposes [of] this Act ... the same shall thereupon immediately revert to and become a portion of the said Estate'. By virtue of s 1ᵇ of the Reverter of Sites Act 1987, which was passed in order to amend the law with respect to the reverter of sites that had ceased to be used for particular purposes, the proviso to s 2 of the 1841 Act had effect as if the land, instead of reverting, vested in a trust to sell the land with the proceeds being held on trust for the persons otherwise entitled to the reversion. The land conveyed in 1848 ceased to be used for school purposes in 1984 and was sold in 1987, and the question arose whether the proceeds of sale were held on trust by the plaintiffs for the benefit of the successors in title to the grantors of the 1848 conveyance, as the defendant contended, or for the successors in title to the grantor's land of which the site once formed part.

---
a   Section 2, so far as material, is set out at p 709 *e* to *h*, post
b   Section 1, so far as material, is set out at p 709 *j* to p 710 *b*, post

Held – (1) On the true construction of s 2 of the 1841 Act, when a site which had been conveyed pursuant to that Act ceased to be used for school purposes the site reverted to the same ownership as that of the other land or estate of which it originally formed part. However, where the land conveyed was a freestanding site and did not form part of a larger estate or parcel of land, it reverted to the original grantor or his successors in title. Whether the site concerned formed part of other land or was freestanding was a question of fact in each case (see p 712 *b* to *f*, p 714 *g* and p 715 *c*, post); *Re Cawston's Conveyance, St Luke, Bromley Common (Vicar and Churchwardens) v Cawston* [1939] 4 All ER 140 distinguished.

(2) Since there was nothing in the conveyance which indicated that the land was part of other lands or of a manor owned by the grantors, as contemplated by s 2 of the 1841 Act, the onus of proof was on the plaintiffs to establish that it was part of some other land. However, there was insufficient evidence to show that the land conveyed in 1848 was anything other than freestanding and therefore it followed that the plaintiffs held the net proceeds of sale of the land pursuant to s 1 of the 1987 Act on trust for the defendant as the successor in title to the grantors of the conveyance (see p 712 *h j*, p 714 *a* to *c g* and p 715 *c*, post).

Notes

For the application and effect of the School Sites Act 1841, see 15 *Halsbury's Laws* (4th edn reissue) para 188, and for cases on the subject, see 19 *Digest* (reissue), 563–566, 4228–4235.

For s 2 of the School Sites Act 1841, see 15 *Halsbury's Statutes* (4th edn) (1990 reissue) 731.

For s 1 of the Reverter of Sites Act 1987, see 37 *Halsbury's Statutes* (4th edn) 460.

Cases referred to in judgment

Cawston's Conveyance, Re, St Luke, Bromley Common (Vicar and Churchwardens) v Cawston [1939] 4 All ER 140, [1940] Ch 27, CA.

Dennis v Malcolm [1933] All ER Rep 293, [1934] Ch 244.

Application

By originating summons of 9 August 1991 between the three plaintiffs, Iain William Marchant, Fred Harry Passant and Elaine Joy Frampton, and the defendant, Susan Margaret Onslow, the plaintiffs sought determination of two questions concerning the construction of s 2 of the School Sites Act 1841 and the effect thereof on certain land conveyed in 1848. The facts are set out in the judgment.

Nigel Gerald (instructed by *Treasures & Rivers, Wyatt*, Gloucester) for the plaintiffs.
Timothy Jennings (instructed by *Stoneham Langton & Passmore*) for the defendant.

Cur adv vult

17 September 1993. The following judgment was delivered.

DAVID NEUBERGER QC. This case raises a point of some difficulty as to the proper construction and effect of the Act 4 & 5 Vict c 38 (school sites 1841).

On 18 April 1848, Elizabeth Foley and Richard Onslow conveyed to the vicar and church wardens of the parish of Newent:

'[a] close piece or parcel of arable land or garden ground containing by admeasurement one rood and seven perches (be the same more or less) situate lying and being at Picklenash in the Parish of Newent ...'

The conveyance was expressly stated to be pursuant to the 1841 Act. The land thereby conveyed ('the premises') was to be held by the grantees—

'for the purposes of the [1841] Act and upon trust to permit the said premises and all buildings thereon erected or ... used as and for a School ... And for the residence of the Schoolmaster and Schoolmistress of the said School and for no other purpose ...'

The premises devolved from the original grantees presumably through various subsequent owners to the plaintiffs. The premises were continuously used as a school until the end of July 1984 when the school was closed down, the local authority having built a new school nearby.

On 3 September 1987 the plaintiffs sold the premises for conversion to residential use for £60,100. That sum has been deposited in an interest bearing account in a bank, and I am informed that the sum in that account is now in the region of £80,000. The issue between the parties is whether this money is, by virtue of the provisions of s 2 of the 1841 Act and s 1 of the Reverter of Sites Act 1987, the property of the defendant. The issue arises in this way.

Section 2 of the 1841 Act provides:

' ... any Person, being seised in Fee Simple, Fee Tail, or for Life, of and in any Manor or Lands of Freehold, Copyhold, or Customary Tenure, and having the beneficial Interest therein, ... may grant, convey, or enfranchise by way of Gift, Sale, or Exchange, in Fee Simple or for a Term of Years, any Quantity not exceeding One Acre of such Land, as a Site for a School for the Education of poor Persons, or for the Residence of the Schoolmaster or Schoolmistress, or otherwise for the Purposes of the Education of such poor Persons in religious and useful Knowledge; provided that no such Grant made by any Person seised only for Life of and in any such Manor or Lands shall be valid, unless the Person next entitled to the same in Remainder, in Fee Simple or Fee Tail, (if legally competent,) shall be a Party to and join in such Grant: Provided also, that where any Portion of Waste or Commonable Land shall be gratuitously conveyed by any Lord or Lady of a Manor for any such Purposes as aforesaid the Rights and Interests of all Persons in the said Land shall be barred and divested by such Conveyance: Provided also, that upon the said Land so granted as aforesaid, or any Part thereof, ceasing to be used for the Purposes in this Act mentioned, the same shall thereupon immediately revert to and become a Portion of the said Estate held in Fee Simple or otherwise, or of any Manor or Land as aforesaid, as fully to all Intents and Purposes as if this Act had not been passed, any thing herein contained to the contrary notwithstanding.'

The long title of the 1987 Act is 'An Act to amend the law with respect to the reverter of sites that have ceased to be used for particular purposes; and for connected purposes'. Section 1 is headed 'Right of reverter replaced by trust for sale'. The provisions of sub-ss (1) and (2) thereof are as follows:

'(1) Where any relevant enactment provides for land to revert to the ownership of any person at any time, being a time when the land ceases ... to be used for particular purposes, that enactment shall have effect ... as if it provided (instead of for the reverter) for the land to be vested after that time, on the trust arising under this section, in the persons in whom it was vested immediately before that time.

(2) Subject to the following provisions of this Act, the trust arising under this section in relation to any land is a trust to sell the land and to stand possessed of the net proceeds of sale ... upon trust for the persons who but for this Act would from time to time be entitled to the ownership of the land by virtue of its reverter.'

The issue between the parties may conveniently be taken from the originating summons as being:

'Whether upon the true construction of section 2 of the School Sites Act 1841 and in the events which have happened, the Plaintiffs hold the net proceeds of sale of the [premises] ... on trust for (a) the successors in title to the grantors of the said conveyance [as the defendant contends] or (b) the successors in title to the grantors' land of which the said site once formed part [as the plaintiff contends].'

It is common ground that if the answer to this question is in sense (a), then the moneys are held on trust for the defendant, and it is right to record that evidence has been put before the court which seems to show that the defendant is indeed the successor in title of the grantors, Elizabeth Foley and Richard Onslow. On the other hand, if the answer is in sense (b), then, pursuant to certain provisions of the 1987 Act to which I have not referred, the plaintiffs, having comprehensively advertised for any claimants to the proceeds of sale of the premises, and no one having come forward other than the defendant, the plaintiffs are entitled to approach the Charity Commissioners for the approval of a charitable scheme in relation to the moneys.

It is contended on behalf of the defendant that the premises should revert to her essentially on three different grounds. The first is that, as a matter of fact, the premises were in 1848 freestanding and not part of any manor or estate or any other land. The second ground is that, even if the premises were in 1848 part of any such manor, estate or other land, the proper construction of s 2 nonetheless leads to the conclusion that the premises should revert to the grantors' successors in title. Thirdly, it is said that, even if that result does not accord with the construction of s 2 as originally enacted, the effect of that section has been changed by the provisions of the 1987 Act.

I propose first to set out the relevant facts relied on by the parties and the inferences which I have been invited to draw from them. Then I propose to consider the proper construction and effect of s 2. I will then turn to the proper conclusion as to the effect of s 2 on the facts as I find them. Finally I will turn to the effect of the 1987 Act.

In the conveyance, the premises are described as being bounded in part by 'a garden belonging to the said Elizabeth Foley'. The Newent Parish Tithe Map 1841 and surveyor's report to the Tithe Commissioners apparently show that Elizabeth Foley was in 1841 the largest owner in the parish possessing at least 735 acres including three fairly large farms and dozens of smaller holdings as well as a number of very small plots, as well as a further 700 acres of woodlands described as 'in hand'. In the parish records of 1848 she was described as 'the Lady of the Manor'. Richard Onslow is shown in the 1841 records as owning 16 acres in the parish. The tithe map has a plot (numbered 1009) which seems to approximate to the premises, and is recorded as containing 1 rood and 12 perches, and is also recorded as being in the occupation of a Hannah Lewis and a Philip Owen. Immediately adjoining this site was another site, numbered 1008, containing nine perches, and described as a cottage in the occupation of John Guest, and the other side of parcel 1008 was a further site of 15 perches, described as 1007, a cottage in the occupation of Lydia Need. All three sites are recorded as owned by Elizabeth Foley. In the conveyance of 18 April 1848, the land is described as 'late in the several occupations of John Child and James Child or their undertenants and now in the possession of the ... vicar and church wardens of Newent'.

On the basis of this evidence, it is suggested on behalf of the plaintiffs that it would be right to conclude either that the premises formed part of the landholding or estate of Elizabeth Foley, possibly in her capacity as lady of the manor, or that it formed part of a landholding being site 1009 of 1 rood and 12 perches, or that it formed part of a landholding including site 1008 (and possibly 1007) and that accordingly the reverter provisions of s 2 lead to the conclusion that the reverter is not to the successor in title of the grantors, the defendant, but to the person or persons to whom the remainder of the landholding (be that all or some of the property owned by Elizabeth Foley in Newent in 1848) has devolved. It is suggested that the fact that Richard Onslow was a party to the conveyance of 18 April 1848 may well be explicable on the basis that the property held by Elizabeth Foley was enjoyed by her as tenant for life, and that Richard Onslow who, it is common ground, was her nephew, was the remainderman, and that therefore he had to join in the conveyance as required by s 2.

On behalf of the defendant, it is submitted that the evidence relied on by the plaintiffs is insufficient, and may well be inadmissible, in that, when considering whether the premises were part of an estate manor or another piece of land one must confine oneself to the four corners of the conveyance. Even if that is not right, it is said that the points relied on by the plaintiff are insufficient to establish that the premises were not, as it were, freestanding in 1848. There is no explanation why Richard Onslow was a party to the conveyance, and the plaintiffs' explanation for this is said to be conjecture. In addition, it is pointed out that there is no acknowledgement by the grantors in the conveyance of the grantees' right to production and delivery of copies of documents, (although the conveyance does contain covenants for type and for further assurances) which one would have expected if the premises were part of other land.

Section 2 is not a satisfactory piece of drafting, and its infelicity is particularly apparent in the final proviso, with which I am principally concerned in this case. The stipulation that on cesser of school use the site shall 'immediately revert to and become a Portion of the said Estate held in Fee Simple or otherwise or of any Manor or Land as aforesaid' is particularly obscure, not least because despite the 'said' there is no previous reference to an 'estate'. It seems to me that the strictures in the Law Commission's report *Property Law Rights of Reverter* (Law Com no 111 (1981)), para 29, are well founded; one finds the following:

'What Parliament actually had in mind is a matter of pure speculation but the phraseology ... suggests that it was expected that sites provided under the [Act] would always constitute small parts of landowners' existing estates; and, moreover, that it was not anticipated that those estates would be broken up. If those expectations had been fulfilled it would be a matter of substantial indifference whether the site reverted to the ownership of the *grantor* (or his successors) or was rejoined to the *grantor's neighbouring land*; and the fact that the [Act expressed itself] in the latter manner would not give rise to problems.

Unfortunately the conditions necessary for avoiding problems have not [been] satisfied.'

Considering the matter free of authority it seems to me that s 2 does indeed envisage that the site to be provided would be a small part of a substantial estate, and that if and when the site conveyed pursuant to the 1841 Act ceased to be used for school purposes, the site should revert to being part of the estate. In other words, subject to what I have to say about the precise formulation, I would have thought that the site, rather than reverting 'to the ownership of the grantor (or his successors)' would be 'rejoined to the grantor's neighbouring land'.

In the first place, that is how s 2 strikes me as a matter of impression. With such an ill-drafted provision, one is a little hesitant of entering into a more detailed analysis but I find it particularly difficult to give any meaning to the words 'or of any Manor or Land as aforesaid' in the second proviso to s 2 unless the reverter provisions have this meaning. Indeed, it is hard to see what the point of the reference at the very beginning of the section to 'any Manor or Lands of Freehold Copyhold or Customary Tenure' may be, unless it is to emphasise that when the site reverts pursuant to the second proviso, it reverts to being part of that manor or other lands.

Section 2 may well not have envisaged the possibility of a grantor conveying what I have called a freestanding site pursuant to the provisions of that Act. In those circumstances, still considering the matter free of authority, it seems to me that one would have to conclude that Parliament must have intended that the effect of the second proviso to the section was not that the site would simply fail to revert but that, there being no other land which it could, as it were, rejoin, it should revert to the original grantor or his successors in title. Indeed, I consider that one can read the second proviso to s 2 as having that express effect if one construes the reference therein to 'the said Estate' rather loosely as meaning the estate of the grantor. It does not appear to me, however, that such a result in relation to the reverter of the freestanding site vitiates the conclusion I have reached in relation to a site which is part of other land at the date of grant.

However, I think that it is also necessary to consider in what circumstances a site would be treated for the purposes of s 2 as part of 'any Manor or Lands of Freehold Copyhold or Customary Tenure'. In this connection, the mere fact that the grantor of the site happens to own other land in the vicinity, or even other land which adjoins the site, does not appear to me to be in any way conclusive that the site was, on the date of its conveyance pursuant to s 2, part of other land. Equally, the fact that the grantor has no other land which actually adjoins the site would not be conclusive that the site was not part of other land. In each case, it would be a question of fact as to whether or not the site was part of other land. I am conscious that in describing the site as being 'part of other land' I am departing from the express language of s 2 itself, but it seems to me to be a permissible way of describing in vernacular terms the sort of concept which the section has in mind particularly where it refers to a 'quantity of such land'. An obvious case where the site would be treated as part of other land might be where the site was included in a large self-contained parcel of agricultural land in one ownership farmed as a single farm by the owner. If, subsequent to granting such a site, the owner sold to a third party, and the site then ceased to be used as a school, it would seem at least as sensible that it should revert to the third party as to the original grantor. On the other hand where a site is one of two houses in their own grounds with a common boundary it would not, in the absence of other evidence, be right to describe it as a 'quantity of such land' on the basis of 'such land' being the two houses in their grounds.

It is suggested that one of the problems with such a construction of s 2 is that, in the event of the estate of which the unit formed part being sold off in lots, one would arrive at the site being owned beneficially by a large number of people in very small shares. While it would be wrong to reject such an argument wholly, I think that there are two answers to it. The first is that contained in the paragraph which I have cited from the Law Commission report, namely that it was not a situation envisaged in 1841. The second is that if the sort of practical approach I have suggested is applied in full, such a problem will not occur very frequently. If one acre of a 200-acre estate were the subject of a grant under s 2, and thereafter the estate owner conveyed, say, three five-acre plots for the purpose of building and selling off a number of houses, it seems to me that, if the site were to revert, a practical application of s 2 would result in the site reverting in full to the owner of the balance of the 184 acres on the basis that these are in reality the lands, the estate referred to in the proviso.

It is suggested that the decision and reasoning of the Court of Appeal in *Re Cawston's Conveyance, St Luke, Bromley Common (Vicar and Churchwardens) v Cawston* [1959] 4 All ER 140, [1940] Ch 27 is inconsistent with the conclusion that I have reached. I do not accept that. First, it was a case clearly concerned solely with what I have called a 'self standing' site: there was no question of the site being part of any manor or other lands at the date of grant. The only question, therefore, arising in relation to s 2 was that to which I have already referred, namely whether in those circumstances the reverter provisions contained in the second proviso to s 2 applied at all. Accordingly, any observations in the judgment of Sir Wilfred Greene MR (with whom the other members of the Court of Appeal agreed) on the instant point are strictly obiter. Secondly, I have come to the conclusion that, in any event, this is not a case where there is anything said, even obiter, in the Court of Appeal which is inconsistent with the conclusion which I reach in the absence of authority. It is true that there are one or two sentences in the judgment of the Master of the Rolls which, if taken on their own, might be said to indicate a view different from that which I have reached, but, when one reads his judgment as a whole, I find nothing in it which calls into question my conclusion. In particular, I consider that the last paragraph beginning 'Then came the next point ...' ([1939] 4 All ER 140 at 146, [1940] Ch 27 at 38) is, if anything, supportive of my conclusion. Further, as is pointed out in para 34 of The Law Commission in *Property Law of Reverter* (Law Com no 111 (1981)), Clauson LJ, who was party to the decision in *Cawston*, made observations when sitting at first instance in *Dennis v Malcolm* [1934] Ch 244 at 251, [1933] All ER Rep 293 at 296 which seem to indicate that, at any rate when he was hearing that case, he took the same view of the effect of the reverter provisions in s 2 as I do.

Having reached my conclusion as to the proper construction and effect of the second proviso to s 2, I turn to apply them to the facts of this case. There has been some argument about whether the onus of proof is on the defendant to establish that the premises were freestanding or whether it is on the plaintiffs to establish that it was part of some other lands. I am not at all sure this is a case which should be decided on the basis of the onus of proof, but, if it is, it seems to me that the defendant is entitled to say that there is nothing in the conveyance which indicates that the premises were part of other lands owned by the grantors, and that that is enough to shift the onus of proof, if it was initially on the defendant, to the plaintiffs.

Whatever the right analysis, I have reached the conclusion that, even bearing in mind the various indications on which the plaintiffs rely, there is insufficient evidence to satisfy me that the premises were, as at 18 April 1848, anything other than freestanding. On the basis of my construction of the effect of the proviso to s 2, it is not sufficient that the grantor owned other land in the parish, and even owned land which adjoined the site which is conveyed. The force of the plaintiffs' argument on the point is further weakened when one bears in mind that there were two grantors, and there is no evidence of any land in the parish being owned by both of them. Of course, it is quite possible that the premises, and some or all of the other land in the parish recorded as being owned by Elizabeth Foley, were held by her as tenant for life with Richard Onslow as remainderman. However, while that is one possible explanation, it is purely a matter of speculation. The fact, if it is one, that Elizabeth Foley was lady of the manor does not appear to be of great significance: there is no evidence either way as to whether the premises were part of the manor.

The fact that site 1009 is shown in the 1841 records as being somewhat bigger than it is recorded as being in the conveyance may be significant, but as counsel for the plaintiffs said, tithe records are not always particularly accurate, and I note that in the conveyance the area is described as being 'the same more or less'.

The fact that the conveyance contains no covenant for production is a mild factor supporting the defendant's contention that the land was freestanding; it may well be that the grantors took the view that, as the conveyance was a voluntary and charitable one, and they did not wish to have to produce their documents of title, they were not prepared to give such a covenant. That too is a matter of speculation.

Accordingly, there being nothing in the conveyance to show that the land was part of other lands or of a manor as contemplated by s 2, and there being insufficient evidence in the circumstances relied on by the plaintiffs to satisfy me that the premises were part of other lands or of the manor, I find in favour of the defendant and answer the question raised in the originating summons in sense (a).

I ought to refer briefly to the argument raised on behalf of the defendant to the effect that the provisions of the 1987 Act, and in particular the closing words of s 1(2) thereof, altered the effect of s 2 so that a site which reverts pursuant to the proviso to that section always reverts to the grantor or his successors in title irrespective of whether the site formed part of a manor or of other lands. It is suggested that, in this connection, the provisions of s 1(2) of the 1987 Act are ambiguous, and it is therefore open to me to have regard to what was said by Lord Hailsham of St Marylebone LC in the House of Lords when the 1987 Act was a bill before Parliament.

I reject that argument. First, I cannot see how s 1, in particular the closing words of sub-s (2) thereof, of the 1987 Act can be said to be ambiguous. It seems to me clear that all that it is purporting to do is to transfer the rights of reverter from the site to the proceeds of sale of the site. It virtually states in terms that it is not intending to alter the identity of the person to whom the site reverts, because it refers to the trust created by the 1987 Act as being 'for the persons who *but for this Act* would from time to time be entitled to the ownership of the land by virtue of its <u>reverter</u>' (emphasis added) . It seems to me that those words refer one straight back to the 1841 Act. If confirmation of this view were needed, I think that it is to be found in the long title of the 1987 Act and indeed the title of s 1 thereof. Secondly I do not think that what was said by the Lord Chancellor when introducing the bill is anything like clear enough to assist the defendant's argument on this point, even were I satisfied that there was some sort of ambiguity in s 1 of the 1987 Act which entitled me to look at what the Lord Chancellor had to say.

In these circumstances, I answer the first question in the originating summons in sense (a). The second question, which seeks a declaration that, if the answer to the first question is indeed in sense (a), whether the moneys are held on trust for the defendant, I answer in the affirmative.

Order accordingly.

Paul Magrath Esq Barrister.

R v Mandair

HOUSE OF LORDS
LORD MACKAY OF CLASHFERN LC, LORD TEMPLEMAN, LORD GOFF OF CHIEVELEY, LORD BROWNE-WILKINSON AND LORD MUSTILL
24, 25 JANUARY, 2 FEBRUARY, 19 MAY 1994

Criminal law – Grievous bodily harm – Causing and inflicting – Lesser offence – Defendant charged with causing grievous bodily harm with intent – Judge directing jury that they could return lesser verdict of 'causing grievous bodily harm' – Defendant convicted of 'causing' grievous bodily harm instead of 'inflicting' grievous bodily harm – Whether defendant convicted of offence not known to law – Whether causing grievous bodily harm wide enough to include inflicting grievous bodily harm – Whether judge entitled to leave lesser offence to jury – Offences against the Person Act 1861, ss 18, 20 – Criminal Law Act 1967, s 6(3).

Criminal law – Appeal – House of Lords – Powers of House of Lords in disposing of appeal – House of Lords having power not only to exercise all powers of Court of Appeal but also to remit case to Court of Appeal – Criminal Appeal Act 1968, ss 33, 35.

Criminal law – Appeal – Right of appeal – Effect of House of Lords decision – Further appeal on other grounds – Conviction restored by House of Lords – Whether open to Court of Appeal to set aside order made by House of Lords.

The defendant was charged with causing grievous bodily harm with intent, contrary to s 18[a] of the Offences against the Person Act 1861. Since there was room for doubt whether the defendant intended to inflict the serious injury suffered by the victim, the trial judge, applying s 6(3)[b] of the Criminal Law Act 1967, left to the jury the option of returning the lesser verdict of 'causing

---

a   Section 18, so far as material, is set out at p 726 *a b*, post
b   Section 6(3) is set out at p 729 *b c*, post

grievous bodily harm, contrary to s 20ᶜ of the 1861 Act' if they were satisfied
that he had caused the injury to the victim but without intent to cause serious
bodily harm. The jury acquitted the defendant of the s 18 charge but in
response to a request by the clerk of the court whether they had reached a
verdict on the alternative charge of 'causing grievous bodily harm, contrary to
s 20' purported to convicted him on that charge. The defendant appealed on
the grounds that he had been convicted of an offence not known to law, since
the offence under s 20 was 'inflicting', not 'causing', grievous bodily harm and
also that the judge had misdirected the jury. The Court of Appeal, without
dealing with the misdirection issues, allowed the appeal and quashed the
conviction on the ground that 'causing grievous bodily harm' was an offence
not known to law. The Crown appealed. The questions arose (i) whether the
judge was entitled to leave a conviction under s 20 to the jury as an alternative
to the charge under s 18, (ii) whether the jury had returned a valid verdict of
guilty in respect of an offence under s 20, and (iii) if so, what course should be
adopted in regard to the defendant's grounds of appeal not considered by the
Court of Appeal.

Held – (1) The expression 'causing grievous bodily harm' in s 18 of the 1861
Act was wide enough to include 'inflicting grievous bodily harm' under s 20
and therefore it was open to a jury to convict a defendant charged with causing
grievous bodily harm with intent, contrary to s 18, of the alternative offence of
inflicting grievous bodily harm, contrary to s 20. Accordingly, if the charge
against the defendant had been framed as 'inflicting' rather than 'causing'
grievous bodily harm, the judge would have been entitled under s 6(3) of the
1967 Act to leave the possibility of conviction under s 20 to the jury as an
alternative to the charge under s 18, as the charge under s 18 'include[d] ... an
allegation of another offence' (ie under s 20) for the purposes of s 6(3), and
therefore it would have been open to the jury to convict of the alternative
offence of inflicting grievous bodily harm, contrary to s 20 (see p 719 *f g*, p 724
b to *g*, p 725 *b* and p 730 *e* to *h*, post); *R v Wilson* [1983] 3 All ER 448 applied; *R v
Field* (1993) 97 Cr App R 357 overruled.

(2) (Lord Mustill dissenting) The jury's verdict of 'causing grievous bodily
harm, contrary to s 20' could only mean causing grievous bodily harm,
contrary to s 20 in that what the defendant did consisted of inflicting grievous
bodily harm on another person. Accordingly, the jury had not given a verdict
on an offence not known to law (see p 719 *h* to p 720 *c*, p 724 *b* to *f j* to p 725 *b*,
post).

(3) Where leave to appeal to the House of Lords had been granted, which
meant that a point of law of general public importance involved in the decision
of the Court of Appeal was to be considered by the House, the House had
power under ss 33ᵈ and 35ᵉ of the Criminal Appeal Act 1968 (relating to the
right of appeal to the House of Lords and the hearing and disposal of the appeal
by the House) not only to exercise all the powers of the Court of Appeal but
also to remit the case to that court for the purposes of disposing of the appeal.
Accordingly, where a ground of appeal remained undisposed of by the Court

---

c   Section 20, so far as material, is set out at p 726 *b*, post
d   Section 33 is set out at p 722 *d* to *f*, post
e   Section 35 is set out at p 722 *g* to *j*, post

of Appeal which was relevant to whether a conviction should stand, the House could either remit the matter to the Court of Appeal or itself exercise the powers of the Court of Appeal in relation to that ground. In the circumstances the appeal would be allowed and the case remitted to the Court of Appeal to consider the grounds of appeal not already disposed of and to decide whether or not the conviction of the defendant should stand or be quashed (see p 723 *e* to *j*, p 724 *c* to *f* and p 725 *b*, post).

Per curiam. (1) Where it is proposed that the jury should consider an alternative verdict on a lesser offence the better course is to add a new count to the indictment rather than the judge giving an oral direction to the jury that they may convict of the lesser offence (see p 721 *e f*, p 724 *d* to *f h* and p 725 *b*, post).

(2) When the House of Lords has decided that a conviction should be restored it is not open to the Court of Appeal to set aside that order of the House unless the case is remitted to the Court of Appeal by the Home Secretary under his statutory powers to consider the appeal afresh (see p 724 a *d* to *f*, p 725 *b* and p 736 *d*, post); *R v Berry (No 2)* [1991] 2 All ER 789 approved.

Per Lord Mackay LC. It is absolutely necessary that when an appeal to the House of Lords under the 1968 Act is being prepared for hearing the statement of facts and issues should state plainly whether any grounds of appeal have been undetermined by the Court of Appeal and in their written cases the parties should include submissions on these and on how the House of Lords should dispose of them (see p 723 *j*, post).

Notes

For the offences of causing grievous bodily harm with intent and inflicting grievous bodily harm, see 11(1) *Halsbury's Laws* (4th edn) paras 471, 469–472.

For the right of appeal from the Court of Appeal to the House of Lords in criminal cases, see 11(2) *Halsbury's Laws* (4th edn) paras 1537–1448

For the Offences against the Person Act 1861, ss 18, 20, see 12 *Halsbury's Statutes* (4th edn) 92, 94.

For the Criminal Law Act 1967, s 6, see 12 *Halsbury's Statutes* (4th edn) 332.

For Criminal Appeal Act 1968, ss 33, 35, see 12 *Halsbury's Statutes* (4th edn) 416, 418.

Cases referred to in opinions

A-G for Northern Ireland v Gallagher [1961] 3 All ER 299, [1963] AC 349, [1961] 3 WLR 619, HL.
R v Berry (No 2) [1991] 2 All ER 789, [1991] 1 WLR 125, CA
R v Clarence (1888) 22 QBD 23, [1886–90] All ER Rep 133, CCR.
R v Field (1993) 97 Cr App R 357, CA.
R v Gaston (1981) 73 Cr App R 164, CA.
R v Halliday (1889) 61 LT 701, [1886–90] All ER Rep 1028, CCR.
R v Jefferson [1994] 1 All ER 270, CA.
R v Lillis [1972] 2 All ER 1209, [1972] 2 QB 236, [1972] 2 WLR 1409, CA.
R v Martin (1881) 8 QBD 54, [1881–85] All ER Rep 699, CCR.
R v McCready [1978] 3 All ER 967, [1978] 1 WLR 1376, CA.
R v McVitie [1960] 2 All ER 498, [1960] 2 QB 483, [1960] 3 WLR 99, CCA.
R v Salisbury [1976] VR 452, Vic Full Ct.

R v Savage, R v Parmenter [1991] 4 All ER 698, [1992] AC 699, [1991] 3 WLR 914, HL.
R v Snewing [1972] Crim LR 267.
R v Springfield (1969) 53 Cr App R 608, CA.
R v Swift (31 July 1991, unreported), CA
R v Tyler (1992) 96 Cr App R 332, CA.
R v Wilson, R v Jenkins [1983] 3 All ER 448, [1984] AC 242, [1983] 3 WLR 686, HL.

Appeal

The Director of Public Prosecutions appealed with leave of the Appeal Committee granted on 8 July 1993 from the decision of the Court of Appeal (Nolan LJ, Swinton Thomas and Colman JJ) delivered on 18 February 1993 allowing the appeal of the defendant, Santokh Singh Mandair, against his conviction before Mr Recorder Higgs QC and a jury at the Central Criminal Court on 18 July 1991 of causing grievous bodily harm for which he was sentenced to four years' imprisonment. The Court of Appeal certified pursuant to s 33 of the Criminal Appeal Act 1968 that a point of law of general public importance was involved in the decision, namely '(1) whether it is open to a jury to convict a defendant indicted with causing grievous bodily harm with intent contrary to s 18 of the Offences against the Persons Act 1861 of a lesser offence contrary to s 20 or contrary to s 47 of the said Act by virtue of the provisions of s 6(3) of the Criminal Law Act 1967; and if so: (2) in what terms the jury may be directed as to the elements of the lesser offences. (3) Whether the construction of s 3 of the Criminal Appeal Act 1968 permits the Court of Appeal to substitute a conviction of an alternative offence where a jury has convicted the appellant of an offence unknown to law.' The facts are set out in the opinion of Lord Mustill.

Anthony Scrivener QC and *John Harvey* (instructed by the *Crown Prosecution Service*) for the Crown.
David Lederman QC and *David Harounoff* (instructed by *Howard Brown & Co*) for the defendant.

Their Lordships took time for consideration.

19 May 1994. The following opinions were delivered.

LORD MACKAY OF CLASHFERN LC. In this appeal the defendant was tried at the Central Criminal Court between 16 and 18 July 1991. The indictment contained a single count alleging causing grievous bodily harm with intent, contrary to s 18 of the Offences against the Person Act 1861. The particulars of offence were that the defendant on 31 January 1991 unlawfully caused grievous bodily harm to Amarjit Mandair with intent to do her grievous bodily harm.

The learned trial judge, applying s 6(3) of the Criminal Law Act 1967, left open to the jury the option of returning a lesser verdict under s 20 of the 1861 Act.. After sundry procedure the jury returned a verdict of not guilty on the charge against the defendant of causing grievous bodily harm with intent contrary to s 18 and a verdict of guilty on the alternative charge against the defendant of causing grievous bodily harm contrary to s 20. These verdicts were unanimous.

The defendant obtained leave to appeal on 25 November 1991. The Court of Appeal on 18 February 1993 allowed the defendant's appeal and quashed his conviction. On 2 April 1993 the Court of Appeal certified three questions as points of law of general public importance involved in the decision and on 8 July 1993 this House gave leave to the Crown to appeal against the judgment of the Court of Appeal. At the beginning of this appeal the parties were agreed that the issues in the appeal were:

'(i) Whether an allegation of causing grievous bodily harm with intent expressly or impliedly includes an allegation of inflicting grievous bodily harm and/or an allegation of assault occasioning actual bodily harm; (ii) whether a verdict of causing grievous bodily harm contrary to section 20 of the Offences against the Person Act 1861 is defective in form or in substance when the verdict is returned as a lesser verdict by virtue of the provisions of section 6(3) of the Criminal Law Act 1967; and (iii) whether section 3 of the Criminal Appeal Act 1968 permits the Court of Appeal to substitute a conviction for an alternative offence where a jury has purported to convict a defendant of causing grievous bodily harm contrary to section 20 of the Offences against the Person Act 1861.'

In the course of the argument before the Appellate Committee it became clear that in order that the appeal should be disposed of two grounds of appeal which had been before the Court of Appeal, but which they had not dealt with, required to be considered before a decision restoring the defendant's conviction could be made, assuming this House took the view that the Court of Appeal's decision of 18 February 1993 could not stand.

In my view 'cause' in s 18 is certainly sufficiently wide to embrace any method by which grievous bodily harm could be inflicted under s 20 and since causing grievous bodily harm in s 18 is an alternative to wounding I regard it as clear that the word 'cause' in s 18 is wide enough to include any action that could amount to inflicting grievous bodily harm under s 20 where the word 'inflict' appears as an alternative to 'wound'. For this reason, in my view, following the reasoning of this House in *R v Wilson, R v Jenkins* [1983] 3 All ER 448, [1984] AC 242, an alternative verdict under s 20 was open on the terms of this indictment.

The Court of Appeal in this case, following an earlier decision in *R v Field* (1993) 97 Cr App R 357, held that the jury has found the defendant guilty of an offence unknown to the law.

In my opinion, as I have said, the word 'cause' is wider or at least not narrower than the word 'inflict'. I consider that the verdict of causing grievous bodily harm contrary to s 20 must be construed as a whole. I leave out of account here the question of whether or not the jury were properly instructed in the ingredients of an offence under s 20 by the learned trial judge and shall return to this later but if one fills into that verdict the full wording of s 20 the verdict should read:

'causing grievous bodily harm contrary to the provision which states 'whosoever shall unlawfully and maliciously wound or inflict any grievous bodily harm upon any other person, either with or without any weapon or instrument, shall be guilty of a misdemeanour ...'

Since, as I said, causing grievous bodily harm is used in a sense which distinguishes it from wounding, I can read the verdict as a whole only as meaning that the causing of the grievous bodily harm was contrary to s 20 in that it consisted of inflicting grievous bodily harm upon another person. Obviously it is highly desirable in matters of this sort involving the liberty of the subject that the precise words of the statute, so far as relevant, should be used in the jury's verdict but where, as here, the jury has actually returned a verdict which to my mind read as a whole is capable of having a clear meaning it is a technicality to decline to give it meaning because the word 'cause' is not used in the section and thereby it is said that the defendant was convicted of an offence unknown to the law. A contravention of s 20 is certainly not an offence unknown to the law and I consider that in the circumstances in which the phrase was used 'causing grievous bodily harm contrary to s 20' is perfectly comprehensible as meaning that an infliction of grievous bodily harm in what the accused did in causing grievous bodily harm was a contravention of s 20.

This conclusion is challenged on two grounds. The first challenge is that this conclusion founds entirely on the proposition that the jury knew that s 20 calls for proof that the accused inflicted grievous bodily harm: for if the jury did not know this, there can be no justification in assuming that the response of guilty to the question posed by the clerk meant 'We find him guilty of an offence under section 20, namely of inflicting grievous bodily harm'.

This challenge to my mind, confuses the question whether the summing up was adequate with the effect of the jury's verdict. The question that arises is not whether the jury were correctly instructed but whether, in answering the question put by the clerk, 'Members of the jury, have at least ten of you agreed on your verdict on the alternative charge against the defendant of causing grievous bodily harm, contrary to section 20?' when the foreman replied, 'Yes', and the clerk then said, 'Do you find the defendant guilty or not guilty of that charge', the foreman replied 'Guilty', the jury found the defendant guilty of a crime unknown to the law. Whether the jury were properly instructed before they returned that answer is an important question but it is a quite different question.

The second challenge advanced against my conclusion is that what the jury was called upon to decide, when considering its verdict, was whether the elements of the offence had been proved. If the necessary elements of the offence are correctly stated in the count and are all found by the jury to be present, it is said to be doubtful whether the miscalling in the indictment of the statute which creates the offence and prescribes the necessary elements would invalidate the count; if the jury has not found the necessary elements to be proved, it is said to be difficult to see by what mechanism the identification of the right statutory provision can save it. In dealing with this challenge I first have to point out, that in terms of the Indictment Rules 1971, SI 1971/1253, r 6—

'Where the specific offence with which an accused person is charged in an indictment is one created by or under an enactment, then (without prejudice to the generality of r 5 of these Rules)—(a) The statement of offence shall contain a reference to—(i) the section of, or the paragraph of the Schedule to, the Act creating the offence in the case of an offence created by a provision of an Act ...'

This appears an essential part of the indictment and must be so since it is guilt of a contravention of the statute that gives the court power to impose punishment. In the present case the verdict of the jury is that the defendant caused grievous bodily harm contrary to s 20. This to my mind certainly satisfies the requirement for a statement of offence in the Indictment Rules and makes perfect sense when one realises that the word 'cause' is wide enough to include 'inflict'. Putting the matter another way, causing grievous bodily harm can mean either inflicting grievous bodily harm or causing it in some other way. The controlling words of reference to s 20, 'causing grievous bodily harm contrary to section 20', surely requires that the word 'cause' should have the meaning 'inflicting'. I cannot see why it is not correct to give every word in the verdict its full meaning and select the meaning of the word 'cause' which makes sense rather than selecting a meaning which does not make sense of the verdict as a whole. I cannot see why juries' verdicts should not be subject to the ordinary rules of construction that they be read in such a way as to give every word a meaning which it can reasonably bear and where more than one meaning is possible that meaning should be selected which makes sense of the verdict rather than one which makes a nonsense of it.

I have only to add that acceptance that s 6(3) of the 1967 Act renders competent a conviction under s 20 on the indictment in this case shows that the statement of offence modified to substitute s 20 for s 18 and using the same particulars of offence must be adequate notice of the alternative charge under s 20.

While I have no doubt that a simpler and more direct course would have been to add a count to the indictment based on s 20, your Lordships have to deal with the case as it has come to this House and, in my view, while the course followed here is not to be commended as a wise course for the future, the result is that the jury convicted the defendant of an offence known to the law, namely a contravention of s 20 of the 1861 Act which empowered the learned recorder to impose the appropriate punishment.

However, the Court of Appeal, having decided the case on the ground that the jury's verdict convicted the defendant of an offence unknown to the law, did not deal with grounds of appeal which had been stated by the defendant, namely that the learned trial judge had not adequately directed the jury on the necessary intent required by virtue of s 20 of the 1861 Act, nor the ground that the verdict of the jury should be set aside because in all the circumstances of the case the conviction was unsafe and unsatisfactory due to the alleged failure of the learned trial judge to direct the jury in the manner specified and because, as a result of that failure, the jury was left in a state of confusion as demonstrated by the course of events before the verdict was returned. When the application for leave to appeal was being considered the court seemed to have concluded that the argument on failure to direct the jury as to the necessary intent did not carry much prospect of success but that the argument about the course of events before the verdict had substance. The first matter was touched upon in the course of the argument before the Appellate Committee and is to some extent bound up with the question of the meaning of the verdict to which I have already referred. However I consider that the matter is so bound up with the second ground of appeal, which has not yet been dealt with, that it would be right to consider both of the outstanding grounds of appeal before coming to a conclusion upon whether or not the conviction of the defendant should stand.

This brings me to a question of wider importance than the present appeal. It is often the case that a number of grounds of appeal are urged before the Court of Appeal but having reached a clear conclusion upon one which determines the case, the Court of Appeal do not decide the other grounds since such decision is unnecessary to the disposal of the case on the view they have taken of it. It would obviously be highly undesirable and wasteful to require the Court of Appeal in every case to decide all the grounds of appeal before disposing of an appeal before them, on the basis that if a point of law of general public importance is raised in the appeal the House of Lords may take a different view of the point from that taken by the Court of Appeal if leave to appeal to the House of Lords is granted in respect of the decision. This necessitates a consideration of the statutory provisions under which the present appeal is brought. These are ss 33 and 35 of the Criminal Appeal Act 1968. Section 33 provides:

'*Right of appeal to House of Lords*

(1) An appeal lies to the House of Lords, at the instance of the defendant or the prosecutor, from any decision of the Court of Appeal on an appeal to that Court under Part 1 of this Act [or section 9 (preparatory hearings) of the Criminal Justice Act 1987].

(2) The appeal lies only with the leave of the Court of Appeal or the House of Lords; and leave shall not be granted unless it is certified by the Court of Appeal that a point of law of general public importance is involved in the decision and it appears to the Court of Appeal or the House of Lords (as the case may be) that the point is one which ought to be considered by that House.

(3) Except as provided by this Part of this Act and section 13 of the Administration of Justice Act 1960 (appeal in cases of contempt of Court), no appeal shall lie from any decision of the criminal division of the Court of Appeal.'

Section 35 provides:

'*Hearing and disposal of appeal*

(1) An appeal under this part of this Act shall not be heard and determined by the House of Lords unless there are present at least three of the persons designated Lords of Appeal by section 5 of the Appellate Jurisdiction Act 1876.

(2) Any order of the House of Lords which provides for the hearing of applications for leave to appeal by a committee constituted in accordance with section 5 of the said Act of 1876 may direct that the decision of that committee shall be taken on behalf of the House.

(3) For the purpose of disposing of an appeal, the House of Lords may exercise any powers of the Court of Appeal or may remit the case to the Court.'

Similar provisions were considered by this House in *A-G for Northern Ireland v Gallagher* [1961] 3 All ER 299, [1963] AC 349. In that case the House decided that the section before it did not limit the House to the question certified and matters consequential on its decision of that question but it was unnecessary to decide in that case whether it is open to an appellant to raise matters completely unrelated to the question certified. I refer particularly to the speeches of Lord Reid, Lord Goddard and Lord Denning (see [1961] 3 All ER 299 at 304, 305 and 314, [1963] AC 349 at 368, 369 and 383). In my opinion the statutory provisions under which this appeal is brought make it necessary that a point of law of general public importance is involved in the decision of the Court of Appeal before it can competently be considered by this House but where leave to appeal has been granted which means that the point is to be considered by the House, the House has power not only to exercise all the powers of the Court of Appeal but also to remit the case to that court for the purposes of disposing of the appeal. In his speech in *A-G for Northern Ireland v Gallagher* [1961] 3 All ER 299 at 303, [1963] AC 349 at 366 Lord Reid says, after referring to the authorisation in the statute before him of a remit to the Court of Appeal:

'... but that is only for the purpose of disposing of the appeal to this House. I can find nothing to authorise a remit to the court below directing it to re-open and re-hear the case and come to a fresh decision.'

He took the view that where a ground of appeal remained undisposed of by the Court of Appeal which was relevant to whether a conviction should stand this House had to go beyond the point certified and decide upon that ground which might have no connection at all with the first. In my opinion it is perfectly reasonable to conclude that where as in this case a decision must ultimately be taken whether the defendant's conviction should stand or be set aside, the appeal to this House cannot be completely disposed of without that question being resolved and I believe that it is natural to read the statutory provisions as enabling this House either to remit the matter to the Court of Appeal or to itself to exercise the powers of the Court of Appeal in relation to grounds of appeal not disposed of by the Court of Appeal.

In the present case while the first ground of appeal is very closely related to the matters which your Lordships have required to decide, I consider that the second ground is much more a matter for the Court of Appeal and that it would therefore be appropriate in this case to remit both to the Court of Appeal for their decision. No doubt in considering the first point they will have regard to the views expressed by your Lordships in deciding whether the Court of Appeal's judgment of 18 February 1993 should stand.

In these circumstances my motion to your Lordships would be that your Lordships should allow this appeal, set aside the judgment of the Court of Appeal of 18 February 1993 and remit the case to the Court of Appeal to dispose of the grounds of appeal not already disposed of by that Court and to decide whether or not the conviction of the defendant should stand or be quashed. I would answer the first certified question in the affirmative, in view of the remit to the Court of Appeal decline to answer the second question and the third question does not arise on the view I have taken.

I would add that it is absolutely necessary that when an appeal under the provisions of the Criminal Appeal Act 1968 is being prepared for hearing in this House the statement of facts and issues should state plainly whether any grounds of appeal have been undetermined by the Court of Appeal and in their written cases the parties should include submissions on these and on how this House should dispose of them.

I should also state my view that, as decided in *R v Berry (No 2)* [1991] 2 All ER 789, [1991] 1 WLR 125, when this House has decided that a conviction should be restored it is not open to the Court of Appeal to set aside that order of this House unless the case is remitted to the Court of Appeal by the Home Secretary under his statutory powers to consider the appeal afresh.

LORD TEMPLEMAN. My Lords, the criminal law is already overburdened with technicalities. In my opinion: (1) An allegation of causing grievous bodily harm includes an allegation of inflicting grievous bodily harm. (2) A jury may convict of an offence under s 20 of the Offences against the Person Act 1861 as an alternative to a charge of convicting of an offence under s 18 of that Act. (3) The Court of Appeal may substitute a conviction under s 20 for a conviction under s 18. (4) In the present case the defendant was convicted of an offence under s 20. (5) Under s 35 of the Criminal Appeal Act 1968 this House is entitled but not bound to consider and determine any question or argument which might result in a conviction being upheld or quashed and may remit the case to the Court of Appeal for determination of any question. (6) It is not open to the Court of Appeal to set aside an order of this House. (7) The present case should be remitted to the Court of Appeal to determine the questions which were not disposed of by the Court of Appeal.

I agree therefore with the order proposed by my noble and learned friend the Lord Chancellor.

LORD GOFF OF CHIEVELEY. My Lords, I have had the opportunity of reading in draft the speech of my noble and learned friend the Lord Chancellor, and I agree with him that, for the reasons he gives, the appeal should be allowed, the judgment of the Court of Appeal set aside, and the case remitted to the Court of Appeal to dispose of the grounds of appeal not already disposed of. In particular, in agreement with my noble and learned friend, I do not consider that in the present case the jury, by their verdict, purported to convict the defendant of an offence not known to law since, having regard to the wording of s 20 of the Offences against the Person Act 1861, the verdict of causing grievous bodily harm contrary to s 20 can only be read as meaning causing grievous bodily harm in the sense of unlawfully and maliciously inflicting grievous bodily harm. Of course, like my noble and learned friend, I think it highly desirable that the precise words of the statute should be used; moreover I agree with my noble and learned friend Lord Mustill (whose speech I have also had the opportunity of reading in draft) that, if only an alternative count under s 20 had been included in the indictment, the present problem would almost certainly not have arisen. But I do not, with all respect, agree with the reasons given by him for not accepting the solution of the Lord Chancellor to the central problem arising on the appeal. As I read the first of those reasons, it raises certain possible questions as to the adequacy of the direction given to the jury by the learned recorder (which is a matter for consideration by the Court of Appeal when the case is remitted to them) but does not impugn the conclusion that, in the present case, it is clear beyond doubt of what offence, known to the law, the jury by their verdict convicted the defendant. As to the second reason, viz that it is not right to accept that the verdict was dominated by the reference to s 20, I agree with my noble and learned friend the Lord Chancellor that, since the expression 'causing grievous bodily harm' is wide enough to include 'inflicting grievous bodily harm', it must follow that the only sensible construction of the verdict, giving effect to all the words used, is that which I have described.

LORD BROWNE-WILKINSON. My Lords, I have read in draft the speech prepared by my noble and learned friend the Lord Chancellor. I agree with it and for the reasons which he gives I would make the order which he proposes.

LORD MUSTILL. My Lords, on the third day of a trial at the Central Criminal Court the following exchanges took place between the clerk of the court and the foreman of the jury:

'*Clerk of the court*: Members of the jury, have at least ten of you agreed on your verdict on the alternative charge against the defendant of causing grievous bodily harm, contrary to section 20 ? *Foreman*: Yes.

Clerk of the court: Do you find the defendant guilty or not guilty of that charge? *Foreman*: Guilty.'

Later a court official indorsed on the back of the indictment:

'Guilty of causing grievous bodily harm (sec. 20). Not guilty of causing grievous bodily harm with intent (sec. 18).'

From this brief episode stems the present appeal, for the section called up by the clerk, namely s 20 of the Offences against the Person Act 1861, makes it an offence to 'inflict' grievous bodily harm: not to 'cause' it, which is the word used in s 18 of the Act. The present respondent, Santokh Singh Mandair, the defendant at the trial, contends that in consequence the verdict which led to the imposition of a sentence of four years' imprisonment was not a verdict at all, since it purported to convict him of an offence not known to the law.

The reappearance of s 20 before your Lordships' House barely two years after it was minutely examined in *R v Savage, R v Parmenter* [1991] 4 All ER 698, [1992] AC 699 demonstrates once again that this unsatisfactory statute is long overdue for repeal and replacement by legislation which is soundly based in logic and expressed in language which everyone can understand. Meanwhile we must make of ss 18 and 20, those staples of the Crown Court, the best that we can.

The story may be quite briefly told. The case for the prosecution was that on the evening in question the defendant came home in a bad temper. He brought with him a plastic container in which was a quantity of dilute sulphuric acid intended for use in clearing a drain. In his annoyance he kicked the refrigerator and some milk spilled out. As the defendant's wife was bending over to mop up the milk he threw the container and the acid at his wife and badly injured her face. From the start the defendant denied all this. He said that he was nowhere near the event. Through some accident the acid must have fallen on to the floor, so that when his wife bent down to clear up the milk she must have come into contact with it. At the trial each side was to call expert evidence on the probabilities of each story, in the light of various acid splash marks on the walls and appliances.

I pause to establish the statutory context within which the trial was to take place.

The following are the material provisions of the 1861 Act as amended:

'18. Whosoever shall unlawfully and maliciously by any means whatsoever would or cause any grievous bodily harm to any person ... with intent ... to do some ... grievous bodily harm to any person, or with intent to resist or prevent the lawful apprehension or detainer of any person, shall be guilty of felony, and being convicted thereof shall be liable ... to imprisonment for life ...

20. Whosoever shall unlawfully and maliciously wound or inflict any grievous bodily harm upon any other person, either with or without any weapon or instrument, shall be guilty of a misdemeanour, and being convicted thereof shall be liable ... to imprisonment not exceeding five years ...

29. Whosoever shall unlawfully and maliciously ... cast or throw at or upon, or otherwise apply to any person, any corrosive fluid ... with intent in any of the cases aforesaid to burn, maim, disfigure, or disable any person, or to do some grievous bodily harm to any person ... shall be liable to imprisonment for life.'

Resuming the story, the defendant was committed for trial by the justices on charges under ss 18 and 29. The indictment as originally drawn contained counts under these two sections, but the latter was quashed on the first day of the trial by order of the judge and the case proceeded on the basis of only one count which read as follows:

'Causing grievous bodily harm with intent, contrary to section 18 of the Offences against the Person Act, 1861.'

When casting the particulars of offence the draftsman could do no better than state that the defendant on 31 January 1991 unlawfully caused grievous bodily harm to his wife with intent to do her grievous bodily harm. Whether this exiguous count complied with the Indictment Rules 1971 need not be pursued. The important point is that the indictment did not include an alternative count under s 20. If it had done so it is almost certain that the present problems would not have arisen.

This was the basis on which the trial began and continued until the conclusion of the evidence. By this time it had become clear from the evidence of the defendant and from the conflicting opinions of the expert witnesses that even if the jury rejected the defendant's account of the incident, and accepted that the container and its contents had been deliberately thrown, there was room for a conclusion that he had not intended to cause the really serious injury which his wife had suffered. Accordingly the learned recorder very properly raised with counsel the possibility of inviting the jury to consider an alternative verdict under s 20; and counsel agreed. It will be necessary to consider later whether this course was open to the recorder in law, but from a practical point of view it was entirely sensible. Unfortunately, there was no discussion of how the jury should be directed in respect of the alternative offence and no suggestion that the recorder should reduce to writing the issue which the jury would have to consider. Hindsight must be avoided, and it is easy to understand how the learned recorder came to make what now seems an obvious mistake and why it was that none of those present drew it to his attention. Still, a mistake it was, and one which had unfortunate consequences.

After an unexceptionable opening statement of the law on the functions of judge and jury, the burden of proof and the meaning of grievous bodily harm the recorder continued:

'The question for you to decide, therefore: firstly, did this defendant cause those injuries which I have no doubt, in your judgment, amount to grievous bodily harm? Secondly, if you are satisfied, so that you are sure that he caused those injuries deliberately and intentionally—did he do so intending at the time he inflicted the injury, did he intend at the time he did it—to cause her really serious bodily harm? Those are the two factors. One, did he do it? Did he cause her grievous bodily harm? If the answer to that is Yes; at the time he did it, did he intend to cause grievous bodily harm? If you are satisfied, members of the jury, that he caused the injuries but he did not do it with the intent to cause really serious bodily harm, it would be open for you to find him guilty of the lesser charge, an alternative charge, of causing grievous bodily harm contrary to s 20 of the Offences against the Persons Act. So that is a second possibility. The third possibility, of course, is that you find him not guilty because you are not satisfied that he, in fact, deliberately and intentionally caused these injuries at all. There are three possibilities, are there not? If you have any reasonable doubt as to how she sustained these injuries, you will find the defendant not guilty. If you are satisfied that he did, in fact, cause them and did so with the intention of causing grievous bodily harm, then guilty on count 1 as charged. If you are satisfied he did it, but did not do it with the accompanying intent, then, members of the jury, guilty of causing grievous bodily harm contrary to s 20.'

After a short summary of the factual and expert evidence, the fairness and accuracy of which has not been challenged, the jury retired to consider its verdict. After two and a half hours the jury sent a note asking for an account of what the defendant's wife had said about the events before she suffered injury. With some amplification by counsel the recorder recounted the evidence and the jury retired again. After a further interview the jury sent another note. Evidently there was some difference of opinion within the jury on the question of intent and some confusion in the mind of the foreman. In the absence of the jury there followed a discussion between counsel, the clerk of the court and the recorder on the problems arising where some jurors favoured a conviction on one count and others a conviction on another. Ultimately this was solved in a satisfactory way. Meanwhile the jury sent another note which appears once again to have indicated that they were agreed upon a conviction on the alternative charge but that they were not satisfied on the intent called for by s 20. By now five hours had passed. The jury returned to court once again and the recorder asked the following question:

'Can you indicate to me if that means that all of you have concluded that this defendant caused grievous bodily harm to his wife, but you disagree as to whether or not that was accompanied by the intent to cause grievous bodily harm?'

The foreman replied in the affirmative. After a further retirement during which counsel and the recorder discussed the familiar but difficult practical and theoretical problems which arise where the jury cannot bring in a verdict on a more serious count but are agreed upon a lesser it was decided to put the two charges to the jury in the light of an indication by the recorder that a verdict of not guilty of the offence under s 18 ought to be returned. There then took place the exchange between the clerk and the foreman of the jury which I have already recounted, followed by the sentence of four years' imprisonment founded on the jury's verdict on the lesser charge.

The defendant then applied for leave to appeal against conviction. His application having been rejected by the single judge it was renewed to the full court on two grounds. First, that the direction to the jury gave no guidance on the element of intention required by s 20. Second, that the transcript of the dialogue between the jury and the court during the long interval between their first retirement and the return of the verdicts shows them to have been so confused that the conviction cannot safely be allowed to stand. The full court was evidently unimpressed by the first argument but saw enough force in the second to grant leave to appeal.

In the event when the appeal was heard the court concentrated on a different question, namely whether it had been open to the recorder to offer the jury the possibility of a conviction under s 20 even though no count laid under this section appeared on the indictment. For this purpose the court examined the previous decision of *R v Field* (1993) 97 Cr App R 357, a case for all material purposes identical to the present. It was relevant for two reasons. First, because the court decided, as I understand it, that a verdict under s 20 is not in principle available as an alternative to a conviction under s 18, unless a separate count is included in the indictment, the words of s 6(3) of the Criminal Law Act 1967 being inapt to cover such a case; and second because the judgment of the Court of Appeal (delivered by Russell LJ) in *R v Field* (1993) 97 Cr App R 357 at 359–361 stated on three occasions that 'causing grievous bodily harm' is an offence not known to the law. Rightly treating itself as bound by *R v Field* the Court of Appeal in the present case concluded that the conviction was void. Arguments that the conviction could be upheld by the use of the proviso to s 2(1) of the Criminal Appeal Act 1968 and that an effective verdict of guilty in respect of the s 20 offence could, under the powers conferred by s 6(3) of the 1967 Act, be substituted for the ostensible conviction recorded at the trial were rejected on the ground that neither power was available in a case where there had been no conviction in the court of trial—as was the case if the purported verdict was void. Accordingly the appeal was allowed and the defendant's conviction quashed.

The Crown now appeals pursuant to leave granted by this House. Three questions of law were certified by the Court of Appeal as being of general public importance. In the event the argument before your Lordships ranged more widely and it is convenient to consider the appeal by reference to the following groups of issues. First, was the recorder entitled to leave a conviction under s 20 to the jury as an alternative, should they be unable or unwilling to return a verdict of guilty in respect of the only charge on the indictment? If not, the verdict cannot stand. Second, by virtue of the exchange between the clerk and the foreman did the jury return a valid verdict of guilty in respect of an offence under s 20, and if not what is the consequence? Third, if the verdict withstands the attacks on its validity embraced in the first two questions, what should be done about the other grounds of complaint raised but not ruled upon in the Court of Appeal? Has the House power to remit these grounds for decision by the Court of Appeal? If it has a choice, should the House retain these questions and decide them itself, or send them to the Court of Appeal?

Turning to the first question, the power of the trial court to invite an alternative verdict rests on s 6(3) of the 1967 Act:

'Where, on a person's trial on indictment for any offence except treason or murder, the jury find him not guilty of the offence specifically charged in the indictment, but the allegations in the indictment amount to or include (expressly or by implication) an allegation of another offence falling within the jurisdiction of the court of trial, the jury may find him guilty of that other offence or of an offence of which he could be found guilty on an indictment specifically charging that other offence.'

The unsystematic language of the 1861 Act has made the application of this power to the gamut of criminal violence, from s 18 wounding to common assault, a constant source of difficulty. But for the decision of your Lordships' House in R v Wilson, R v Jenkins [1983] 3 All ER 448, [1984] AC 242 there would have been cause to examine minutely both the mental and physical elements of the offences under ss 18 and 20, and to decide in the light of the reported cases whether the allegations in an indictment under s 18 amount to or include (expressly or by implication) an allegation of an offence under s 20. This task is no longer necessary. Although R v Wilson was directly concerned with a verdict of guilty under s 47 of the 1861 Act left to the jury as an alternative response to an indictment under s 20, and although the relationship between these two offences is undoubtedly different from that which exists between s 18 and 20, the statement of general principle by Lord Roskill, with whose speech the remainder of the House concurred, is of general application. His Lordship said ([1983] 3 All ER 448 at 453, [1984] AC 242 at 258):

'My Lords, the right approach to the solution of the present problem must first be to determine the true construction of s 6(3), bearing in mind the observations of Lawson LJ in R v Lillis ([1972] 2 All ER 1209, [1972] 2 QB 236) as to its purpose and as to the position before its enactment. Ignoring the reference to murder or treason, there seem to me to be four possibilities envisaged by the subsection. First, the allegation in the indictment expressly amounts to an allegation of another offence. Second, the allegation in the indictment impliedly amounts to an allegation of another offence. Third, the allegation in the indictment expressly includes an allegation of another offence. Fourth, the allegation in the indictment impliedly includes an allegation of another offence. If any one of these four requirements is fulfilled, then the accused may be found guilty of that other offence. My Lords, if that approach to the construction of the subsection be correct, it avoids any consideration of "necessary steps" or of "major" or "lesser" offences, and further avoids reading into the subsection words which were never used by the draftsman. I am unable to find that this approach to the construction of the subsection was ever advanced in R v Springfield, (53 Cr App R 608). If it were, there is no reflection of such an argument in the judgment. I would add the observation that although s 6(3) is often spoken of as permitting conviction for a less serious offence upon a count charging a more serious offence, the maximum penalties for offences against both s 20 and s 47 are the same—five years' imprisonment.'

After analysing various reported decisions his Lordship continued, [1983] 3 All ER 448 at 455, [1984] AC 242 at 260-261:

'The critical question is, therefore, whether it being accepted that a charge of inflicting grievous bodily harm contrary to s 20 may not necessarily involve an allegation of assault, but may none the less do so, and in very many cases will involve such an allegation, the allegations in a s 20 charge "include either (expressly or by implication)" allegations of assault occasioning actual bodily harm. If "inflicting" can, as the cases show, include "inflicting by assault", then even though such a charge may not necessarily do so, I do not for myself see why on a fair reading of s 6(3) these allegations do not at least impliedly *include* "inflicting by assault". That is sufficient for present purposes though I also regard it as also a possible view that those former allegations *expressly* include the other allegations.' (Lord Roskill's emphasis.)

His Lordship therefore held that an offence under s 47 could properly be left as an alternative to a count under s 20, and that the decision in *R v Springfield* (1969) 53 Cr App R 608 to the contrary effect should be overruled.

My Lords, it was not submitted to the House that the decision in *R v Wilson, R v Jenkins* [1983] 3 All ER 448, [1984] AC 242 should be re-examined under *Practice Statement (Judicial Precedent))* [1966] 3 All ER 77, [1966] 1 WLR 1234 and indeed it scarcely could have been, given the recent indorsement by this House in *R v Savage, R v Parmenter* [1991] 4 All ER 698, [1992] AC 699 of both the decision and the statements of principle. Accordingly there is no need to do more than apply those statements to the case of ss 18 and 20. The answer is I believe quite plain. Causing grievous bodily harm may not amount to inflicting grievous bodily harm, in the sense that the two expressions are identical; and the elements of intent in the two offences are of course critically different. But the s 18 offence 'includes' the lesser offence, at least in the sense that I believe the word to have been understood by Lord Roskill. Thus, although I would not endorse the practice of giving an oral direction to the jury that they may convict of the lesser offence in preference to adding a new count which the jury can take away and study, the existence of s 6(3) shows that this is a permissible course and in the light of *R v Wilson, R v Jenkins* [1983] 3 All ER 448, [1984] AC 242 it was one which the recorder was entitled to adopt. Accordingly I would hold, here differing from the Court of Appeal in the present case and following *R v Swift* (31 July 1991, unreported), that if the words of s 20 had been accurately reproduced in the additional charge the defendant would have no ground of complaint.

I now turn to the second question, whether the interchange between the clerk and the foreman of the jury amounted to a conviction under s 20, or at least something which an appellate court can cause to be treated as such a conviction. Before examining the grounds upon which the Crown proposed an affirmative answer it is convenient to deal with a number of reported cases. The first is *R v McVitie* [1960] 2 All ER 498, [1960] 2 QB 483. The appellant was convicted on a count which, so far as material read as follows:

'Statement of Offence: Possessing explosives contrary to section 4(1) of the Explosive Substances Act, 1883.

Particulars of offence: You had in your possession a certain explosive substance ... to wit a four ounce slab of plaster gelatine and four electric detonators under such circumstances as to give rise to a reasonable suspicion that it was not in your possession for a lawful object.'

The words of the statute were in fact '... knowingly has in his possession or under his control ...' It was argued on appeal that the conviction was void since, in the absence of the word 'knowingly', it related to an offence not known to the law. Counsel for the prosecution (F H Lawton QC) conceded that for this reason the indictment was defective or imperfect, but maintained that the case was one for the application of the proviso. The Court of Criminal Appeal dismissed the appeal, saying ([1960] 2 All ER 498 at 502, [1960] 2 QB 483 at 495):

'In our opinion this did not make the indictment a bad indictment, but simply a defective or imperfect one. A bad indictment would be one disclosing no offence known to the law, for example, where it was laid under a statute which had been repealed and not re-enacted. In the present case the indictment described the offence with complete accuracy in the "Statement of Offence". Only the particulars, which merely elaborate the "Statement of Offence", were incomplete. The question of applying the proviso is to be considered, therefore, not upon the basis that the indictment disclosed no known offence but that it described a known offence with incomplete particulars.'

The next case is *R v Gaston* (1981) 73 Cr App R 164. One of the counts on which the appellant was convicted read as follows:

'Statement of Offence: Attempted Rape.
Particulars of Offence: Daniel Gaston on November 25, 1979 attempted to rape Lynette Rogers per anum.'

After pointing out that there is no offence of rape 'per anum' the court in a judgment delivered by O'Connor LJ proceeded directly to the question whether the court could substitute a conviction for indecent assault under s 6(3) of the 1967 Act:

'Before this can be done there has to be "an offence specifically charged in the indictment". Here there was none.'

The appeal was allowed. The report makes no reference to *R v McVitie*.

Next, there is *R v Tyler* (1992) 96 Cr App R 332 which arose under s 1(1) of the Public Order Act 1986. As judicially interpreted this falls into two parts. The first creates a condition precedent to the possible existence of the offence, and does so by stipulating that (inter alia) there must be twelve or more persons present together who use or threaten unlawful violence. The second part of the subsection actually creates the offence and does so solely by reference to the use of unlawful violence. The statement of offence correctly identified the offence as 'Riot, contrary to s 1(1) of the Public Order Act 1986', but incorrectly employed in the particulars of offence the words 'used or threatened' unlawful violence, whilst the crucial second part of the subsection makes no reference to threatening violence. When the defect was pointed out the prosecution

obtained leave to amend the count by deleting the words 'or threatened'. The
jury convicted on the amended count, and on appeal it was contended that the
amendment was impermissible since the count was wholly void, so that there
was nothing to which the amendment could relate. In a judgment delivered by
Farquharson LJ the appeal was dismissed. It was said (at 336):

> 'The statement of offence clearly and accurately referred to riot. The
> particulars disclosed the correct offence but widened its ambit to include
> "threaten" as well as the "use" of violence. In our judgment, that is not in
> the same category as alleging an offence which does not exist, as in *Gaston*.
> It gives an imperfect description of one that does. In those circumstances,
> the defect is capable of amendment on the basis laid down in *McVitie*.'

Next, there is *R v Swift* (31 July 1991, unreported), where the trial judge
decided to add an extra written count under section 20, rather than rely on
s 6(3) of the 1967 Act but unfortunately did so in the following terms—

> 'Statement of Offence: Inflicting grievous bodily harm contrary to
> section 20 of the Offences against the Person Act 1861.
> Particulars of Offence: Craig Alan Swift on the 30th day of May 1990
> unlawfully and maliciously caused grievous bodily harm to Simon
> Mallett.'

Refusing an application for leave to appeal based on the use of 'caused' in the
particulars, Taylor LJ (delivering the judgment of the court) said:

> '... if anybody had asked the question "how caused?" (because there are
> various ways grievous bodily harm may be caused) the answer would
> inevitably have been: "Look at the Statement of Offence—'inflicted', that
> is how it was caused. It was inflicted." Indeed the whole of the case here
> was concerned with an assault ... There was therefore no other way in
> which the grievous bodily harm here could have been caused other than
> by infliction, even if there were not that word governing the whole of the
> count at the beginning of the statement of offence.'

Finally there is *R v Jefferson* [1994] 1 All ER 270 where the indictment was in
the same form as in *R v Tyler* and suffered from the same vice. The case differed
from *Tyler* in that there the judge declined to amend the indictment and the
jury retired with a copy of the count in its defective form. On appeal it was
held that if the defect was to be regarded as an irregularity it was not a material
irregularity because the judge's direction had made it clear that the jury were
to look for participation in unlawful violence so that the jury could not have
been misled by the reference to 'threatened'. Alternatively the irregularity
could be cured by applying the proviso.

From these authorities and from *R v Field* (1993) 97 Cr App R 357 I collect the
following propositions.

(1) For the purpose of deciding whether an indictment charges an offence
not known to the law what matters is the statement of offence.

(2) If the statement of offence purports to charge the defendant under a
statute in language which does not reflect the terms of the relevant statute it is
nullity and the defendant cannot properly be put in charge of the jury upon it.

(3) If the statement of offence correctly identifies an offence which does exist but the particulars of offence do not accurately reproduce the words of the statute the count is not a nullity but is irregular.

(4) If the count is a nullity: (a) a verdict of guilty returned upon it is not a conviction; (b) the purported conviction cannot be upheld on appeal by the use of the proviso since there is no conviction to uphold; (c) even if the appellate court is sure that the jury would have convicted of an offence that does exist, the court cannot substitute a conviction for that offence in place of the invalid verdict.

(5) If the count is irregular because of an error in the particulars of offence: (a) it may be cured by amendment; (b) the verdict returned in respect of it is not void; (c) if the circumstances of the case, including the evidence adduced and the direction given to the jury, are such that the irregularity has not misled the jury the proviso may properly be applied.

I should add, since the cases above-mentioned, apart from *Field*, were not cited in argument, that I would even without them have considered these propositions to be sound.

I now turn to the arguments advanced for upholding the conviction in the present case. They are four-fold.

First, it is said that the words 'cause' and 'inflict' are synonymous and that the exchange between the clerk and the foreman of the jury amounted to a valid verdict of inflicting grievous bodily harm under s 20. This argument involved two propositions, with both of which I am unable to agree. In the first place I am unable to accept that the two words mean the same, although there will of course be many states of fact to which they can both be accurately applied. The point is very short and I cannot develop it beyond submitting that whereas in the case of both words there must be a causal connection between the defendant's act and the injury, in the case of the 'cause' the nature of the connection is immaterial (provided the chain of events is short enough to satisfy the criminal law of causation), but the word 'inflict' conveys the idea of a direct and immediate doing of harm. It is true that in *R v Martin* (1881) 8 QBD 54, [1881–85] All ER Rep 699 and *R v Halliday* (1889) 61 LT 701, [1886–90] All ER Rep 1028 injuries suffered when the frightened victim was attempting to escape were assumed to bring the case within s 20; but the point was not raised. On the other hand *R v Clarence* (1888) 22 QBD 23, [1886–90] All ER Rep 133, *R v McCready* [1978] 3 All ER 967, [1978] 1 WLR 1376 (which on this point I believe to have survived *R v Wilson, R v Jenkins* [1983] 3 All ER 448, [1984] AC 242) and *R v Salisbury* [1976] VR 452, an Australian decision which (if I correctly read his speech) was approved by Lord Roskill in *R v Wilson*, support the narrow reading of 'inflict'. Opinions to the same effect are contained in 14th Report of the Criminal Law Revision Committee, *Offences against the Person* (1980, Cmnd 7844), pp 69–70, para 153; the Report of the Law Commission on Offences against the Person (1993, Law Com No 218) p 18, para 12.15, fn 12; *Archbold, Criminal Pleading Evidence and Practice* (1994 edn), para 19-208, Smith and Hogan, *Criminal Law* (7th edn, 1992), pp 425–426; and a case note by Professor J C Smith on *Snewing* [1972] Crim LR 267. In addition, this reading was taken for granted by the court in *R v Field*, in the passage already quoted. Thus, although the distinction is undoubtedly very narrow and often of no practical significance I believe that it is none the less real, and therefore reject the submission that the words used by the clerk 'causing grievous bodily harm' have exactly the same meaning as 'inflicting grievous bodily harm', and that the hypothetical verdicts conveyed by the response of 'Guilty' to the two versions of the clerk's question will not have exactly the same meaning.

I would however go further. When sending the defendant to prison the recorder purported to exercise powers created by s 20. These powers were exercisable only upon the conviction of the defendant of an offence under that section, by a plea or verdict of guilty. If the indictment had contained from the outset a count intended to allege an offence under s 20 but using the same incorrect words as the clerk was later to use, and if the error had been noticed before arraignment an application to quash the count would have been irresistible, since the defendant would otherwise have been called on to plead guilty or not guilty to an offence which did not exist; and it could not, in my opinion, be an acceptable response to say that since everyone knew that the words had the same meaning as those of the statute the count as drawn would do perfectly well. This is not a technicality, but a reflection of the fact that the court has no power to put the accused person in peril of punishment unless expressly authorised by statute so to do. The case is not the same as where the words of the count include surplusage, or mis-spellings, or other matters which do not go to the identification of the offence to which the person arraigned must respond. No doubt even where the offence is incorrectly stated in the indictment practical means could readily be devised in such a situation for putting matters right if detected early enough. But here the error persisted to the moment when the verdict was taken, and I can see no alternative to the view that the sentence of four years' imprisonment was imposed in circumstances where, although in the press of the trial understandably nobody realised it, there was no power to do so.

The second argument is that even if the two words have different meanings the supposed offence on which the verdict was brought in must by the way it was formulated necessarily have comprised an offence under s 20, albeit in unnecessarily wide terms, and that accordingly there was an effective conviction concealed by inapt words. For the reasons already stated I question whether it is right in principle to treat a verdict which says one thing as if it meant another. There is, however, no need to pursue this path for, assuming the difference in meaning to exist, 'cause' is the wider word; so a verdict of 'causing' can embrace a set of facts which does not amount to 'inflicting'. In other words, although the verdict was wide enough to cover a kind of causing injury which did fall within the statute, it also comprised a form of injury which did not.

The third argument is similar to the second, but adapts it to the individual facts of the case. The only contest on the evidence was whether the defendant deliberately brought the can of fluid into contact with his wife or whether he had nothing at all to do with it. The possibility that he caused the injury in a manner which did not amount to 'inflicting' cannot have been in the contemplation of the jury. Thus, so the argument runs, the jury's finding that the defendant had caused grievous bodily harm to his wife must be translated into 'caused in such a manner as to have inflicted' such harm. The words 'caused in such a manner as to have' would then be surplusage which could be discarded, leaving an accurate verdict under s 20. Notwithstanding the attractions of this argument I am constrained to reject it. This is not a case of correcting a written record which does not accurately reflect the verdict actually brought in; or of rejecting immaterial words used by the jury when returning its verdicts; or even of correcting, before the close of the trial, some verbal discrepancy between what the jury had been asked and what they had replied, so as to make clear what they had really meant. Here the jury was asked by the clerk whether they found the defendant guilty of causing grievous bodily harm, which was the question which the recorder's directions had instructed them to consider. There is no reason to read the verdict as anything but an answer to this question. What the argument requires is that after the trial is over and the jury discharged, an appellate court can re-write the verdict so as to substitute for it the verdict which the jury would have returned if it had been asked the right question. This proposition entails that if there had been on the indictment from the outset a count under s 20 framed by reference to 'caused', and the jury had returned a verdict of guilty upon it, the count could be rectified by the Court of Appeal so as to sustain the conviction and sentence by reference to a verdict which had never in fact been rendered. I cannot believe this to be the law (see *Archbold*, at para 1-213.)

The fourth and final way of putting the Crown's case is founded on the reference to s 20 in the question put by the clerk. The answer given by the foreman shows that the jury intended to find the defendant guilty of an offence under s 20. Since s 20 creates an offence referable only to inflicting grievous bodily harm the jury must have intended to find that the defendant did just that, and the verdict should be read accordingly. The additional finding that the defendant had caused grievous bodily harm should either be disregarded as a mistaken gloss on the true verdict, or clarified by notionally adding the words 'in such a manner as to inflict' before the reference to grievous bodily harm.

Whilst this is much the most convincing account of the Crown's case I must, with proper respect to your Lordships who consider otherwise, reject it on two grounds. In the first place the argument founds entirely on the proposition that the jury knew that s 20 calls for proof that the accused inflicted grievous bodily harm: for if the jury did not know this there can, to my mind, be no justification in assuming that the response of 'Guilty' to the question posed by the clerk meant 'We find him guilty of an offence under s 20, namely of inflicting grievous bodily harm'. In fact there is no reason to suppose that the jury had in mind the correct words of s 20. Plainly, an uninstructed jury could not have any idea of what s 20 required, and such instruction as was conveyed by the recorder directed attention to 'cause' and not to 'inflict'; and the jury's attention was diverted further from the right direction because the question to which the answer guilty was returned made use of the wrong word.

Quite apart from this, however, I cannot accept that the verdict was dominated by the reference to s 20. What the jury was called upon to decide, when considering its verdict, was whether the elements of the offence had been proved. If the necessary elements of the offence are correctly stated in the count and are all found by the jury to be present I would doubt whether the miscalling in the indictment of the statute which creates the offence and prescribes the necessary elements would invalidate the count; and if the jury has not found the necessary elements to be proved I do not see by what mechanism the identification of the right statutory provision can save it. In reality, as it seems to me, the verdict rendered in the present case made no sense, and it cannot be validated by concentrating on one part to the exclusion of the other.

I have given my reasons for rejecting the argument for the Crown at some length because I recognise that in the particular circumstances of this case the outcome is unattractive. Nevertheless, I see the case being concerned not with a mere technicality but rather with the important principle that a defendant can be punished for a statutory offence only if he has been properly convicted of that offence. As it seems to me the defendant was not so convicted, and it is no answer to say that if matters had taken a different course an unassailable verdict of guilty would very probably have ensued. For these reasons I would have dismissed the prosecutor's appeal.

For these reasons I would have dismissed the appeal. Since, however, your Lordships are of a different opinion I will proceed to the third question, which concerns the steps now to be taken with regard to the grounds which led the Court of Appeal to grant leave to appeal, but which have not yet been dealt with.

Two questions arise. First, does the House have jurisdiction to remit the two outstanding grounds for consideration by the Court of Appeal. For the reasons stated by my noble and learned friend, the Lord Chancellor, I have no doubt that it does, and that upon such remission the court has power, notwithstanding *R v Berry (No 2)* [1991] 2 All ER 789, [1991] 1 WLR 125, to re-list and hear the appeal.

Secondly, what course should the House now adopt? In my opinion the better course will be to return the matter to the Court of Appeal. It is true that the issue on the adequacy of the direction on the necessary element of content for the purposes of s 20 is to some extent linked to the matters now decided by the House, but neither of the outstanding issues raises any question of general principle. Moreover the Court of Appeal has particular experience of forming a judgment on whether circumstances are such that a verdict cannot safely be allowed to stand. Absent the issues debated before your Lordships the case would be very typical of those regularly decided by the Court of Appeal and may now most conveniently be remitted to that Court.

For my part therefore I would have dismissed the appeal, but since your Lordships are of a different opinion, I agree with the order proposed.

Appeal allowed.

Celia Fox   Barrister.

Presentaciones Musicales SA v Secunda and another

COURT OF APPEAL, CIVIL DIVISION
DILLON, NOLAN AND ROCH LJJ
26, 27, 28 OCTOBER, 12 NOVEMBER 1993

Agent – Ratification – Solicitor – Proceedings commenced by solicitor without authority – Ratification after expiry of limitation period – Whether plaintiff entitled to adopt action after expiry of limitation period.

Solicitor – Authority – Action begun without authority – Ratification by or on behalf of plaintiff – Expiration of limitation period applicable to cause of action – Whether plaintiff entitled to adopt action after expiry of limitation period.

In April 1988 a firm of English solicitors issued a writ on the instructions of a director of the plaintiff company, PMSA, which had been incorporated in Panama. The writ claimed relief against the first defendant for alleged infringements of copyright in certain sound recordings. In 1991 the defendants discovered from a search in the Panama Companies Register that PMSA had been 'dissolved' under Panamanian company law in 1987, ie before the writ had been issued. Under Panamanian law a dissolved corporation was entitled for a period of three years after dissolution to initiate and defend legal proceedings and the directors were empowered to initiate proceedings in the corporation's name and represent it in such proceedings. In May 1991 the three directors appointed as liquidators of the company purported to ratify the instructions to the English solicitors to initiate the proceedings. The first defendant issued a notice of motion seeking an order that proceedings in the action be stayed and/or that the claim against the first defendant be struck out as an abuse of process. PMSA and the solicitors accepted that PMSA had been dissolved in 1987 but claimed that the writ had been issued within three years of the company's dissolution and that the liquidators of the company had ratified the issue of proceedings, albeit after the expiration of the three-year limitation period. On the hearing of a preliminary issue as to whether the liquidators could, after the expiration of the three-year limitation period, ratify the commencement or conduct of an action commenced without authority within the limitation period, the judge held that the liquidators were entitled to ratify the issue of the writ. The first defendant appealed, contending that proceedings commenced without a plaintiff's authority could not be ratified after the expiration of a limitation period which afforded a defence to the action.

Held – In accordance with the doctrines of agency and ratification, where a solicitor commenced proceedings in the name of a plaintiff, whether a company or an individual, without authority, the plaintiff could ratify the act of the solicitor and adopt the proceedings and thereby cure the original defect in the proceedings, but only if the act of ratification was done at a time and in circumstances when the ratifying party could himself have lawfully done the act which was ratified. Moreover (per Dillon and Nolan LJJ), if a time was fixed for doing a particular act the doctrine of ratification did not apply if it had the effect of extending that time, or (per Roch LJ) the putative principal was not allowed to ratify the acts of his assumed agent, if such ratification would affect adversely rights of property in either real or personal property, including intellectual property, which had arisen in favour of a third party or others claiming through him since the unauthorised act of the assumed agent. A writ issued without authority was not a nullity and accordingly the plaintiff in an action raising a single cause of action which had been begun by solicitors without authority was entitled to adopt the action notwithstanding the expiration of the limitation period applicable to that cause of action. A fortiori the liquidators were entitled to ratify the issue of the writ where the causes of action pleaded and the claims made were not statute-barred by May 1991. The appeal would therefore be dismissed (see p 743 f to j, p 745 a, p 746 d e j and p 751 d to j, post).

Bird v Brown (1850) 4 Exch 786 applied.
Bolton Partners Ltd v Lambert (1889) 41 Ch D 295 and Pontin v Wood [1962] 1 All ER 294 considered.

Notes
For the doctrine of ratification, see 1(2) Halsbury's Laws (4th edn reissue) paras 72, 78.

Cases referred to in judgments
Ainsworth v Creeke (1868) LR 4 CP 476.
Audley v Pollard (1597) Poph 108, 79 ER 1216.
Bird v Brown (1850) 4 Exch 786, 154 ER 1433.
Bolton Partners v Lambert (1889) 41 Ch D 295, CA.
Dalmia Dairy Industries Ltd v National Bank of Pakistan [1978] 2 Lloyd's Rep 223, CA.
Danish Mercantile Co Ltd v Beaumont [1951] 1 All ER 925, [1951] Ch 680, CA.
Dibbins v Dibbins [1896] 2 Ch 348.
Doe d Mann v Walters (1830) 10 B & C 626, [1842–34] All ER Rep 428, 109 ER 583.
Holland v King (1848) 6 CB 727, 136 ER 1433.
Keighley, Maxsted & Co v Durant [1901] AC 240, HL.
Pontin v Wood [1962] 1 All ER 294, [1962] 1 QB 594, [1962] 2 WLR 258, CA.
Walter v James (1871) LR 6 Exch 124.

Cases also cited or referred to in skeleton arguments
Alexander Ward & Co Ltd v Samyang Navigation Co Ltd [1975] 2 All ER 424, [1975] 1 WLR 673, HL.
Tiedemann and Ledermann Frères, Re arbitration between [1899] 2 QB 66.
Banco de Bilbao v Sancha [1938] 2 All ER 253, [1938] 2 KB 176, CA.
Bank of America National Trust and Savings Association v Chrismas [1994] 1 All ER 401.
Bank of Ethiopia v National Bank of Egypt and Liguori [1937] 3 All ER 8, [1937] Ch 513.
Banks v CBS Songs Ltd (1992) 19 FSR 278, CA.
Bedford Insurance Co Ltd v Instituto de Resseguros do Brasil [1984] 3 All ER 766, [1985] 1 QB 966.
Brook v Hook (1871) LR 6 Exch 89.
Bumper Development Corp v Comr of Police of the Metropolis [1991] 4 All ER 648, [1991] 1 WLR 1362, CA.

Carl Zeiss Stiftung v Rayner & Keeler Ltd [1966] 2 All ER 536, [1967] AC 853, HL.
Central Insurance Co Ltd v Seacalf Shipping Corp [1983] 2 Lloyd's Rep 25, CA.
Chatenay v Brazilian Submarine Telegraph Co Ltd [1891] 1 QB 79, [1886–90] All ER Rep, CA.
Davison v Vickery's Motors Ltd (1925) 37 CLR 1, Aust HC.
Employers' Liability Assurance Corp v Sedgwick, Collins & Co [1927] AC 95, [1926] All ER Rep, HL.
First Russian Insurance Co (in liq) v London and Lancashire Insurance Co Ltd [1928] Ch 922.
Fleming v Bank of New Zealand [1900] AC 577, PC.
Foster Yates & Thom Ltd v H W Edgehill Equipment Ltd (28 November 1978, unreported).
Gloucester Municipal Electoral Petition 1900, Ford v Newth [1901] 1 KB 683.
Hooper v Kerr, Stuart & Co Ltd (1900) 83 LT 729.
Infabrics Ltd v Jaytex Ltd [1981] 1 All ER 1057, [1982] AC 1, HL.
Janred Properties Ltd v Ente Nazionale Italiano per il Turismo [1989] 2 All ER 444, CA.
Ketteman v Hansel Properties Ltd [1988] 1 All ER 38, [1987] AC 189, HL.
Kleinwort Benson Ltd v Barbrak Ltd [1987] 2 All ER 289, [1987] AC 597, HL.
Lazard Bros & Co v Midland Bank Ltd [1933] AC 289, [1932] All ER Rep, HL.
LRT Pension Fund Trustee Co Ltd v Hatt [1993] PLR 227.
Lucy v Henleys (WT) Telegraph Works Co Ltd (ICI Ltd, third parties) [1969] 3 All ER 456, [1970] 1 QB 393, CA.
Mabro v Eagle Star and British Dominions Insurance Co Ltd [1932] 1 KB 485, CA.
Maspons Y Hermano v Mildred (1882) 9 QBD 530, CA.
Mitchell v Harris Engineering Co Ltd [1967] 2 All ER 682, [1967] 2 QB 703, CA.
Portuguese Consolidated Copper Mines Ltd, Re, Badman's case, Bosanquet's case (1890) 45 Ch D 16, CA.
Ransburg-Gema AG v Electrostatic Plant Systems Ltd (1990) 18 FSR 508, CA.
Ruby Steamship Corp Ltd v Commercial Union Assurance Co (1933) 150 LT 38, CA.
Russian Commercial and Industrial Bank v Comptoir d'Escompte de Mulhouse [1925] AC 112, [1924] All ER Rep 381, HL.
Sardinia Sulcis, The [1991] 1 Lloyd's Rep 201, CA.
Sinfra AG v Sinfra Ltd [1939] 2 All ER 675.
Von Hellfeld v E Rechnitzer and Mayer Freres & Co [1914] 1 Ch 748, CA.
Warehousing & Forewarding Co of East Africa Ltd v Jafferali & Sons Ltd [1963] 3 All ER 571, [1964] AC 1, PC.

Interlocutory appeal

The first defendant, Daniel Secunda, appealed with leave of the judge against the decision of Mervyn Davies J given on 14 January 1992 whereby it was ordered on the trial of a preliminary issue, namely: 'Where an English action has been commenced and conducted in the name of a Panamanian corporation without its authority within the three-year period after its dissolution prescribed by Article 85 of the Panamanian Corporation Law, can the liquidators or trustees of the corporation ratify the commencement or conduct of the action after the expiration of that three-year period?', that the question be answered in the affirmative. The respondents to the appeal were (i) the plaintiff, Presentaciones Musicales SA, in an action brought against the first defendant Daniel Secunda and CBS United Kingdom Ltd for breach of copyright of some sound recordings called 'The Jimi Hendrix Tapes', (ii)

Cameron Markby Hewitt, the plaintiff's present solicitors, and (iii) Goodman Derrick & Co, the solicitors who issued the writ in the action. The facts are set out in the judgment of Dillon LJ.

John McDonnell QC and *John Eidinow* (instructed by *Compton Carr*) for the second defendant.
Michael Burton QC and *Henry Carr* (instructed by *Cameron Markby Hewitt*) for the plaintiff and for Cameron Markby Hewitt.
Christopher Nugee (instructed by *Goodman Derrick & Co*) for *Goodman Derrick & Co*.

Cur adv vult

12 November 1993. The following judgments were delivered.

DILLON LJ. This is an appeal by the first defendant in the action, Mr Daniel Secunda, against the order of Mervyn Davies J made on 14 January 1992 after he had heard a preliminary issue in the action directed by an earlier order. The general field of law with which the appeal is concerned is that of the ratification and adoption by the nominal plaintiff of an action started by English solicitors in the name of that plaintiff without proper authority.

The writ was issued on 19 April 1988 by English solicitors, Messrs Goodman Derrick & Co, in the name of Presentaciones Musicales SA ('PMSA'), a company which had been incorporated in the Republic of Panama. Goodman Derrick supposed that they had authority, derived indirectly from a Mr Van Walsum, to issue the writ on behalf and in the name of PMSA. Subsequently another firm of solicitors, Messrs Cameron Markby Hewitt, succeeded Goodman Derrick as the solicitors on the record in the action for PMSA. Both firms of solicitors are respondents to the present appeal, as is PMSA itself, if it still exists.

The writ claimed relief against the first defendant for alleged infringement of copyright in some sound recordings called 'The Jimi Hendrix Tapes'. The relief claimed was the usual relief in a copyright action brought under the Copyright Act 1956, viz an injunction, damages for infringement of copyright or an account of profits, and delivery up of offending copies. It has to be borne in mind that, where successive copies are published in breach of copyright, the publication of each gives rise to a fresh cause of action.

On 11 March 1991, however, the defendants learned from a search in the Companies Registry in Panama that PMSA had been 'dissolved' under the Panama Corporations Law on 17 June 1987—some ten months before the writ was issued. Therefore the first defendant on 18 April 1991 issued a notice of motion seeking an order that all proceedings in the action be stayed and additionally or alternatively that the claims in the action against the first defendant be struck out as an abuse of process.

As against that it is claimed for the two firms of solicitors and for PMSA that the commencement of the action was ratified and the action was adopted by PMSA acting by its directors as its liquidators in May 1991.

The issue directed to be tried as a preliminary issue was the issue as to ratification of the issue and conduct of the action.

In the course of the hearing before Mervyn Davies J and in the light of certain provisions of Panamanian law to which I shall come, that issue was expanded to read:

'Where an English action has been commenced and conducted in the name of a Panamanian corporation without its authority within the three-year period after its dissolution prescribed by Article 85 of the Panamanian Corporation Law, can the liquidators or trustees of the Corporation ratify the commencement or conduct of the action after the expiration of that three-year period.'

Moreover, for the purpose only of the hearing of the preliminary issue, certain assumptions were agreed viz: (1) that PMSA was 'dissolved' by means of the registration on 17 June 1987 of an earlier shareholders' resolution, (2) that three particular individuals were directors and were appointed to be the liquidators of PMSA on 17 June 1987, (3) that the writ in this action was issued and the proceedings were carried on down to May 1991 without the authority of PMSA or the liquidators and (4) that the liquidators have on dates in May 1991 ratified (or, as the first defendant would assert, have purportedly ratified) the instructions given by Mr Van Walsum.

The essential question is whether by May 1991 it was possible in law for the three liquidators to ratify or adopt the action as they purported to, or whether that was not possible. That raises issues of Panamanian law and also one issue of possibly much greater importance under English law. I propose to deal with the Panamanian issues first.

The Panamanian issues

The key provisions of the law of Panama are arts 85 and 86 of the Panama Corporations Law. These provide as follows:

'*Acts of dissolution*

Article 85. Every corporation existence of which ends by expiration of the term established in the articles of incorporation or by dissolution, will continue, nevertheless, for a period of three years from that date for the specific purpose of initiating the special proceedings deemed necessary, defend its interests as defendant, settle its affairs, transfer and dispose of its assets and divide its corporate capital: but in no case it may continue the business for which it was organised.

Powers of the directors after dissolution

Article 86. When the existence of a corporation ends by expiration of its term of duration or by dissolution, the directors shall act as trustees of the corporation with power to settle its affairs, collect its credits, sell and transfer its assets of all kinds, distribute its properties among its shareholders, once the debts of the corporation have been paid; and they shall also be empowered to initiate judicial proceedings in the name of the corporation with respect to its credits and assets, and to represent it in the proceedings that may be brought against it.'

These raise, very obviously, two points which have never been resolved by the Panamanian courts but remain the subject of discussion and disagreement between eminent Panamanian jurists.

The first of these points is whether the reference to 'dissolution' in art 85 means, as it would in English law, that the corporation ceases to exist as a

separate corporate entity and its assets are automatically vested in the directors
as trustees and liquidators to wind up the corporation's affairs, or whether it
means that the corporation continues to exist as a somewhat shadowy
corporate entity in liquidation which continues to have its assets vested in it
while its directors proceed with the winding up of its affairs, bringing and
defending proceedings in the corporation's name wherever necessary.

The second point is as to the effect of the expiration of the three-year period
under art 85. In the present case, that period of three years from the dissolution
on 17 June 1987 expired in June 1990, which was nine months before the
defendants in this action discovered that PMSA had been 'dissolved', and even
longer before any ratification. The question is whether, even if the
'dissolution' of PMSA did not automatically cause it to cease to exist as a
corporate entity at the date of dissolution, the expiration of the three years
from the date of dissolution did have that effect, leaving the assets thenceforth
vested in the trustees or liquidators personally or possibly claimable by the
state as bona vacantia.

Besides these two points, a further issue has been discussed by Panamanian
lawyers, which is whether art 557 of the Commercial Code of Panama applies
to corporate bodies which are subject to the Panama Corporations Law.
Article 557 provides that:

> 'The document of final approval of the liquidation and partition
> accounts, or the judicial sentence in respect thereof, shall be published and
> registered at the Mercantile Register and shall fix the end of the juridical
> existence of the company.'

The judge had evidence from two Panamanian lawyers—Mr de Puy, called
by the appellant, and Mr Patton, called by the respondents. Mr de Puy held the
view that a company ceased to be a corporate entity at the moment of its
dissolution under art 85 or at the latest at the end of the three-year period
specified in art 85. In the latter view he was supported by an authoritative
textbook written by Mr R A Durling.

Mr Patton held the view that dissolution came at the end of liquidation when
all of the obligations were satisfied, all judicial and administrative affairs were
resolved and the net assets were distributed among the members. The views
held by Mr Patton had also been expressed by Professor Ozores, highly
respected in Panama, in a prologue to Mr Durling's book, and by influential
commentators, Mr A V Herrera and Mr Guillero Endara, who at the time of the
hearing before Mervyn Davies J had become President of Panama.

One point, however, on which everyone, including Mr de Puy, agreed was
that proceedings could be started by the liquidators in the name of the
company in a court in Panama during the three-year period under art 85, and
if they had not been concluded by the end of the three-year period they could
be continued in the name of the company after the expiration of the three-year
period, at any rate in a court in Panama. That of course led to questioning as
to what the position would be if an inchoate sale of a property had not been
completed by the end of the three-year period.

It appears that there has been only one decision of a Panamanian court
which relates at all to the question—a decision in a case of *Portillo* in May 1961.
That decision would not bind any other Panamanian court. It is said that Mr
Patton accepted that that decision indorsed the view of Mr Durling. I have not
myself derived any assistance from that decision; the only passage to which we

were referred (in translation) is very brief and appeared to me to be non-committal.

The judge preferred the views of Mr Patton and Professor Ozores and the others with whom Mr Patton agreed to the views of Mr de Puy and Mr Durling. The judge also said that he found support for Mr Patton in some of the answers given by Mr de Puy in his evidence. Mr McDonnell QC for the appellant asserted that the judge was unjustifiably devising a synthesis of the views of Mr Patton and Mr de Puy. I doubt if the judge was entitled to find support for Mr Patton's views in Mr de Puy's answers; with many of his answers it is difficult to be sure what Mr de Puy was trying to say. But I do not regard the judge's reliance on some of Mr de Puy's answers as invalidating his preference for Mr Patton's evidence.

Our function in this court is, as stated by Megaw LJ in *Dalmia Dairy Industries Ltd v National Bank of Pakistan* [1978] 2 Lloyd's Rep 223 at 286, to consider the evidence afresh and form our own view of the cogency of the rival contentions, while remembering that the trial judge had the undoubted initial advantage of having seen and heard the witnesses.

For my part I agree with the judge that Mr Patton's views on Panamanian law are to be preferred to Mr de Puy's. I reach this conclusion for two reasons. Firstly I find the conception that a company is dissolved when it goes into liquidation and its affairs have yet to be wound up inherently difficult, and Mr de Puy's alternative that the company is dissolved at the end of the three years and there is a vesting of assets in mid-stream in the liquidators for them to conclude the liquidation equally difficult. In the second place, although Mr de Puy is a graduate of Cambridge University, I have considerable doubts over his command of English, and I often did not find his answers, as recorded in the transcript, at all clear—at times, he appeared on the transcript to be saying the opposite of what I would have expected him to have meant.

The point on English law

It is well-recognised law that where a solicitor starts proceedings in the name of a plaintiff—be it a company or an individual—without authority, the plaintiff may ratify the act of the solicitor and adopt the proceedings. In that event, in accordance with the ordinary law of principal and agent and the ordinary doctrine of ratification, the defect in the proceedings as originally constituted is cured: see *Danish Mercantile Co Ltd v Beaumont* [1951] 1 All ER 925, [1951] Ch 680, since approved by the House of Lords. The reason is that by English law ratification relates back to the unauthorised act of the agent which is ratified; if the proceedings are English proceedings, the ratification which cures the original defect, which was a defect under English law, must be a ratification which is valid by English law.

There is, however, a qualification to this rule of English law as to the effect of ratification, for which the leading authority is the case of *Bird v Brown* (1850) 4 Exch 786, 154 ER 1433. (Lord Macnaghten points out in *Keighley, Maxsted & Co v Durant* [1901] AC 240 at 248 that in each of the three reports in which the case is reported the single judgment is attributed to a different member of the court, but the case is well established.) What is said in *Bird v Brown* (1850) 4 Exch 786 at 799, 154 ER 1433 at 1439 is that the doctrine of ratification 'must be taken with the qualification, that the act of ratification must be taken at a time, and under circumstances, when the ratifying party might himself have lawfully done the act which he ratifies'.

The point taken by Mr McDonnell for the appellant is that, as he submits, there can be no ratification of an action started without authority if at the time of the purported ratification the cause or causes of action on which the unauthorised action was founded would have been wholly or partly statute-barred, with the result that the plaintiff could not effectively have issued a fresh writ, raising the same claims, at the date of the purported ratification.

It is therefore necessary to look at the basis on which the qualification in *Bird v Brown* is founded.

In *Ainsworth v Creeke* (1868) LR 4 CP 476 the question was whether a certain person was entitled to have his name kept on the list of voters for a certain township. That depended on whether his name had been entered on the list of ratepayers before a certain date. It had been entered on the list before that date by his landlord without his authority, and he purported, after that date, to ratify the entry. It was held that the ratification was of no effect; as Brett J put it (at 487), agreeing with the other members of the court, 'this case comes within the rule that a person cannot effectually ratify an act at a time when he could not do the act himself.'

In *Audley v Pollard* (1597) Poph 108, 79 ER 1216, as explained in (1613) 9 Co Rep 106a, 77 ER 886, the position under a statute of Henry VII was that an entry to dispute a fine had to be made not more than five years after the proclamation of the fine. Therefore an unauthorised entry by a stranger on behalf of a claimant during the five years could not be ratified by the claimant after the five years had expired. To allow subsequent ratification would be to give the claimant longer to decide whether or not to make his claim than the five years Parliament had allowed.

Bird v Brown (1850) 4 Exch 786, 154 ER 1433 itself was a case of stoppage in transitu. The right of stoppage was only exercisable during the continuance of the transitus, ie, on the facts, until formal demand for the goods had been made by the assignees of the consignees. Before such demand, notice of stoppage in transitu had been given without authority on behalf of the shipper of the goods in New York. That was ratified by the shipper, but only after the transitus had been ended by the formal demand by the assignees. It was therefore held that the purported ratification was too late and ineffective.

In *Dibbins v Dibbins* [1896] 2 Ch 348, a decision of Chitty J, the same principle was applied. Under a partnership agreement, on the death of a partner the surviving partner had an option of purchasing the share of the deceased partner upon giving notice in writing of his intention to do so within three calendar months from the death. Notice was given within three months by the solicitor of the surviving partner, purportedly on his behalf but without authority. The solicitor's action was ratified pursuant to an order of the court made after the expiration of the three months, but it was held that the ratification came too late to have any effect.

So again, in cases in the last century, it was held that if a notice to quit to terminate a tenancy at a particular date had been given by the agent on behalf of the landlord, but without authority, the notice could not be validly ratified by the landlord, even before the date for which the notice had been given, if at the date of the purported ratification it would have been too late for the landlord to have given a fresh notice to quit for the date for which the unauthorised notice had been given. See eg *Doe d Mann v Walters* (1830) 10 B & C 626, [1824–34] All ER Rep 428 esp per Littledale and Parke JJ.

The ratio of all these cases seems to be that, if a time is fixed for doing an act, whether by statute or by agreement, the doctrine of ratification cannot be allowed to apply if it would have the effect of extending that time (see also the observation of Maule J in *Holland v King* (1848) 6 CB 727 at 740, 136 ER 1433 at 1439).

As against those cases, there is the decision of this court in *Bolton Partners Ltd v Lambert* (1889) 41 Ch D 295. An offer was made by the defendant to an agent of the plaintiff to purchase a property of the plaintiff. The agent purported to accept the offer on behalf of the plaintiff, but in fact he had no authority to do so. Within a reasonable time the plaintiff ratified the acceptance, but in the meantime the defendant had withdrawn the offer. It was held that the ratification was effective notwithstanding the withdrawal of the offer.

The judgments give various explanations for distinguishing *Bird v Brown*. Cotton LJ said ((1889) 41 Ch D 295 at 307) that an estate once vested could not be divested by the application of the doctrine of ratification. But the wider interpretation, as I see it, is that there was no final date for acceptance in *Bolton Partners v Lambert* and there was, before the withdrawal of the offer, an acceptance by the agent which was valid subject to ratification, and so after the acceptance it was not open to the defendant to withdraw the offer. I refer to this further below. Lopes LJ ((1889) 41 Ch D 295 at 310) considered that to hold otherwise would be to deprive the doctrine of ratification of its retrospective effect—ie (as I understand him) if it did not apply in that case it would not apply in any case where the retrospective effect was necessary to make the ratification valid.

What then, in the light of the authorities above discussed, is the effect of the Limitation Act 1980, and the passage of time between the issue of the writ without authority in April 1988 and the ratification in May 1991?

The judge seems to have felt that that was a matter which could be left to the trial, where it might be held that PMSA would not be entitled to relief in respect of some of the earlier copy recordings made by the first defendant.

He considered the limitation point in the particular context of the proviso to s 18 of the Copyright Act 1956. That adds the twist that s 18 was repealed by the Copyright Designs and Patents Act 1988, and, under the transitional provisions of that Act, can only apply for the purposes of proceedings begun before the commencement of that Act, 1 August 1989. But, as I see it, the point can best be tested by considering the simple case of an action begun by solicitors in the name of a plaintiff without authority, raising a single cause of action which would not have been barred by the Limitation Act 1980 if the issue of the writ had been duly authorised in advance, but would have been barred if the nominal plaintiff had issued a fresh writ at the much later date of his adoption or ratification of the unauthorised action.

I note that in *Pontin v Wood* [1962] 1 All ER 294, [1962] 1 QB 594, where a writ had been issued which was defective because it failed to comply with certain requirements of the Rules of the Supreme Court, but the defects could be cured by the plaintiff by further pleading or other procedural steps which did not require leave from the court, it was held that the writ was not a nullity, and the defects were cured by the appropriate steps notwithstanding that the limitation period applicable to the intended cause of action had expired after the issue of the writ and before the remedial steps to cure the defects were taken. Davies LJ distinguished between such a case and cases of seeking to add a new party or add a new cause of action after the expiration of a limitation

period, where the plaintiff was seeking the leave of the court to do something
to the detriment of the defendants which, without such leave, the plaintiff had
no right to do (see [1962] 1 All ER 294 at 302, [1962] 1 QB 594 at 616).

In *Bird v Brown* and the various other cases cited above where ratification
after a time limit had passed was held to be too late, the act done by the
self-appointed agent, before the crucial date, had no effect in law unless
ratified. By contrast in *Bolton Partners Ltd v Lambert* the acceptance by the
agent, without authority, of the defendant's offer to purchase the plaintiff's
property was not without legal effect. As is apparent from the judgment of
Lindley LJ (1889) 41 Ch D at 308–309, it was an acceptance which precluded the
defendant from withdrawing his offer. He added 'that the acceptance by the
assumed agent cannot be treated as going for nothing [ie as a nullity] is
apparent from the case of *Walter v. James* ((1871) LR 6 Ex 124)'. Lopes LJ held
that there was a contract made directly the agent on behalf and in the name of
the plaintiff accepted the defendant's offer.

Where a writ is issued without authority, the cases show that the writ is not
a nullity. For the nominal plaintiff to adopt the writ, or ratify its issue, does not
require any application to the court. Accordingly, on the same general
principle that justifies *Pontin v Wood*, the plaintiff, in the simple example of an
action raising a single cause of action which has been begun by solicitors
without authority, must be entitled to adopt the action notwithstanding the
expiration of the limitation period applicable to that cause of action.

That must a fortiori be so in a case like the present where the causes of action
pleaded, and the claims made, were not all statute-barred by May 1991.

Accordingly I would dismiss this appeal.

As Holroyd Pearce LJ said in *Pontin v Wood* [1962] 1 All ER 294 at 299, [1962]
1 QB at 612:

'The defendant was at all times perfectly aware of the nature of the
action which the writ was intended to initiate and the defect has caused
him no difficulty whatever.'

I would add this. I have had the advantage of reading the judgment of Roch
LJ. I do not, for my part, accept that the *only* justification for the *Bird v Brown*
line of cases is to regard them as an aspect of property law, viz that an interest
in property which has become vested or indefeasible cannot be divested by the
retrospective effect of a subsequent ratification of a previously unauthorised
act, as mentioned by Cotton LJ in *Bolton Partners Ltd v Lambert* (1889) 41 Ch D
295 at 307. It has seemed to me that Lindley and Lopes LJJ took a wider view,
and that the narrow explanation relating to not divesting property rights
retrospectively does not explain *Ainsworth v Creeke* (1868) LR 4 CP 476. On the
one hand it is well-established that ratification is retrospective; on the other
hand there are authorities decided over a long period which show that in
certain circumstances 'ratification' may come too late to be effective. What
the logic of the dividing line between the two should be is not easy to discern.
Mr McDonnell submitted that *Bolton Partners Ltd v Lambert* was wrongly
decided and ought to be overruled; but that is not a course open to this court.

NOLAN LJ. I agree that the appeal should be dismissed, for the reasons given
by Dillon LJ.

ROCH LJ. The plaintiff company is incorporated in Panama. It claims to own the copyright in all the musical works of the late Jimi Hendrix and, in particular, in a collection of certain of his performances in album form entitled 'The Jimi Hendrix Concerts'. The plaintiffs further claim to have employed Mr Secunda, the first defendant, as their sole and executive sales agent for the album throughout the world apart from the US and Canada. The appointment is said to have been made in November 1981. Since that time, it is alleged, Mr Secunda has been in breach of his agency agreement and Mr Secunda and the second defendants have been in breach of the plaintiffs' copyright in the album.

Proceedings were commenced against the defendants on 19 April 1988 by a specially indorsed writ. On 5 January 1989 the first defendant entered a defence and counterclaim to which there was a reply and defence to the counterclaim served on behalf of the plaintiffs on 10 April 1989. That elicited a reply from the first defendant on 16 June 1989. A defence on behalf of the second defendants had been served on 10 June 1988. On 27 November 1990 Hoffmann J ordered that paras 14 to 16 of Mr Secunda's counterclaim and paras 1 to 4 of the prayer for relief in that counterclaim be struck out on the ground that they were frivolous or vexatious. There were also orders restraining Mr Secunda from infringing the plaintiffs' copyright in the album entitled 'The Jimi Hendrix Concerts'.

On 11 March 1991, the first defendant's solicitors discovered, as a result of instructing Panamanian attorneys to do a search of the Companies Register in Panama, that the plaintiff company had been 'dissolved' on 4 June 1987. On 15 March Mr Secunda's solicitors wrote to the plaintiffs' present solicitors, Cameron Markby Hewitt, informing them of the result of that company search. A month later on 18 April 1991 Mr Secunda's solicitors took out a notice of motion seeking to have the writ and statement of claim against Mr Secunda struck out pursuant to RSC Ord 18, r 19 or alternatively under the court's inherent jurisdiction, as an abuse of process, the point being that the writ and statement of claim had been issued and served without the plaintiffs' authority.

The solicitors who had issued and served the writ were Goodman Derrick. The individual who had instructed them was a Mr Van Walsum who was or had been a director of the plaintiff company. For the purposes of this appeal it is to be assumed that Mr Van Walsum did not have actual authority from the plaintiff company to instruct Goodman Derrick to commence proceedings on behalf of the company in England and Wales. By 31 May 1991 the three persons who are either the trustees of the plaintiff company or the liquidators of the plaintiff company had all purported to ratify the act of Mr Van Walsum in instructing Goodman Derrick to act as the plaintiffs' solicitors in this country and Goodman Derrick's act of commencing proceedings on the plaintiffs' behalf against the defendants. Under RSC Ord 5, r 6 a body corporate may not begin or carry on proceedings in the High Court otherwise than by a solicitor.

In January 1992 the following issue came before Mervyn Davies J:

'Where an English action has been commenced and conducted in the name of a Panamanian Corporation without its authority within the three-year period after its dissolution prescribed by Article 85 of the Panamanian Corporation Law, can the liquidators or trustees of the corporation ratify the commencement or conduct of the action after the expiration of that three-year period?'

Counsel before Mervyn Davies J agreed that certain assumptions should be made for the purpose of resolving the preliminary issue, namely: (1) the plaintiffs were dissolved by means of the registration on 17 June 1987 of the shareholders' resolution of 3 June 1987; (2) that the three named persons (none of whom was Mr Van Walsum) were directors and were appointed to be the liquidators of the plaintiffs on 17 June 1987; (3) that proceedings were issued against the defendants in the name of PMSA on 19 April 1988 and carried on down to May 1991 as a result of instructions to Goodman Derrick and thereafter Cameron Markby Hewitt by Mr Van Walsum through Mr Branton without the authority of PMSA or the liquidators; (4) the liquidators have (or as the first defendant would assert 'have purportedly') ratified the instructions by Mr Van Walsum through Mr Branton on 17, 27, and 31 May 1991.

The conclusions reached by Mervyn Davies J were these:

'(a) that [PMSA] continues to exist in the eyes of Panamanian law and (b) that its liquidators were entitled to ratify the issue of the writ; and that whether the ratification is referable to English or Panamanian Law. Thus on the assumptions I have to make I answer in the affirmative the question raised in the preliminary issue.'

I agree that the judge's findings in relation to the law of Panama were sound for the reasons given by Dillon LJ.

Mr McDonnell QC on behalf of the appellant accepts that the writ issued in this case was not a nullity, albeit it was issued on behalf of the plaintiffs without proper authority from them. His submission is that the plaintiffs cannot ratify the unauthorised act of commencing proceedings because the law applicable is English law and the principles of English law relating to ratification preclude ratification in the present case.

Counsel for the respondents make two submissions in answer to this submission by Mr McDonnell: first that the question of Mr Van Walsum's authority is governed by the law of Panama and under Panamanian law the acts of the liquidators in May 1991 had the effect of putting the plaintiffs and Mr Van Walsum in the position they would have been in had Mr Van Walsum had prior authority to commence proceedings on behalf of the plaintiffs in April 1988. Second, that if the issue is governed by the law of England, the English principles of ratification serve to cure the defect in the writ as from 19 April 1988.

In my judgment the respondents are wrong on their first submission. I do not doubt that if the issue had been whether Mr Van Walsum had actual authority to instruct Goodman Derrick to issue proceedings in April 1988, that question could only have been resolved by the court examining the law relating to corporate bodies in the Republic of Panama and, probably, the constitution of the plaintiff corporation. In the present case there is no dispute, for the purposes of resolving the preliminary issue, that Mr Van Walsum did not have actual authority in April 1988.

What has to be considered, in my view, is first the effect of the contract apparently entered into between the plaintiffs and Goodman Derrick and of the act of Goodman Derrick in issuing proceeding against the defendants. The law which should apply to that contract and to that act, in my opinion, is the law which has the closest connection with that contract and with that act, namely English law. Dicey and Morris *The Conflict of Laws* (12th edn, 1993) at p 1459 under the heading 'English conflicts rules' says:

> 'Where A [the agent] lacks actual authority from P [the principal], it seems right, in principle, that the law applicable to the contract between A [the agent] and T [a third party] should determine whether P [the principal] is bound (or entitled). In effect in this situation, one is asking whether A [the agent] had apparent or ostensible authority to bind the P [principal] ... As between P [the principal] and A [the agent], the scope of A's [the agent's] authority to bind P [the principal] and to confer rights upon him is necessarily determined by the law which governs their relationship, but third parties must be able to assume, at least where A [the agent] has no actual authority from P [the principal], that A's [the agent's] authority covers everything which would be covered by the authority of an agent appointed under the law applicable to the contract made between the agent and the third party.'

The correct analysis of the facts of this case, in my judgment, is that the agents whose authority really has to be considered are Goodman Derrick and the act, the validity of which has to be considered is their act of commencing proceedings. Goodman Derrick are English solicitors retained, ostensibly on behalf of a Panamanian company, to perform legal services for that company in England. On that analysis the validating of the act of commencing proceedings by later ratification by those who clearly have authority under Panamanian law to do so on behalf of the plaintiffs must be a matter for English law.

Mr Nugee on behalf of the second respondents in his skeleton argument submits:

> 'In general the question whether a person who purports to act as an officer of a foreign corporation is authorised to do so must be determined by the law of the place of incorporation ... The whole notion of ratification is that when it takes place it is the equivalent of an express prior authority.'

Both those statements are correct, with this qualification, that although ratification when it takes place is the equivalent of an express prior authority that does not mean that for the purposes of the conflict of the laws it is the same thing as express prior authority. Once it is shown by the law of Panama that neither Mr Van Walsum nor the second respondents were authorised to act, the consequences of that lack of authority are matters for the law of the place where the unauthorised act was performed. Thus despite the clear and vigorous submissions of Mr Nugee, I conclude that the issue of ratification is governed by English law.

If ratification is permitted in this case, it will mean that the plaintiffs will be able to sue Mr Secunda for alleged breaches of his contractual obligations as the plaintiff's selling agents going back to 19 April 1982, and for breaches of copyright committed by the defendants going back to the same date, which would include the principal infringement alleged, namely the agreement between Mr Secunda and the second defendants on 1 August 1982 and the initial sales of the album between that date and 31 May 1985. Further the plaintiffs will be able to rely on provisions in the Copyright Act 1956 which may well be more advantageous to them than the provisions of the Copyright Designs and Patents Act 1988. On the other hand, if the purported ratification is ineffective to save the writ of 19 April 1988, then the plaintiffs will not be able to recover compensation for breaches of contract or copyright which occurred before 1 June 1985, nor will they be able to rely on the provisions of the Copyright Act 1956.

Mr McDonnell's submission is that proceedings commenced without a plaintiff's authority can never be ratified after the expiration of a limitation period which would afford a defence as at the date of ratification. Mr McDonnell argues that the correct statement of the principle of ratification is that ratification is retroactive and because it is retroactive 'the act of ratification must take place at a time, and under circumstances, when the ratifying party might himself have lawfully done the act which he ratifies'. (*Bird v Brown* (1850) 4 Ex Ch 786 at 799, 154 ER 1433 at 1439.) It is then said that on 31 May 1991 the plaintiffs could no longer have commenced proceedings against Mr Secunda in England for breaches of his selling agency agreement committed prior to 1 June 1985, nor could the plaintiffs have commenced proceedings against Mr Secunda based on the Copyright Act 1956, or for breaches of copyright committed by Mr Secunda prior to 1 June 1985. Thus the plaintiffs will not be permitted to ratify Mr Van Walsum's instructions to the second respondents or the second respondents' issuing of proceedings. There can be no partial ratification so that the plaintiffs' only course was to start fresh proceedings on or after 31 May 1991 with the authority of the liquidators.

I would accept that there can be no partial ratification. Either what the liquidators have done ratifies the writ issued on 19 April 1988 or it does not. If it does not then that writ should be struck out as an abuse of process.

The conclusion that I have reached is that the dictum cited from the case of *Bird v Brown* (1850) 4 Ex Ch 786 at 799, 154 ER 1433 at 1439 is not a correct statement of the exceptions to the principles of ratification. In my view the correct statements of principle are contained in the judgment of Cotton LJ in *Bolton Partners v Lambert* (1889) 41 Ch D 295, first at 306:

> 'The rule as to ratification by a principal of acts done by an assumed agent is that the ratification is thrown back to the date of the act done, and that the agent is put in the same position as if he had had authority to do the act at the time the act was done by him',

and then at 307:

> 'The rule as to ratification is of course subject to some exceptions. An estate once vested cannot be divested, nor can an act lawful at the time of its performance be rendered unlawful, by the application of the doctrine of ratification.'

In this part of his judgment, as I read it, Cotton LJ was giving examples of exceptions to the general principle of ratification rather than setting out an exhaustive list of exceptions. The Court of Appeal in that case treated the decision in *Bird v Brown* as an instance of the first exception, namely that ratification could not operate to divest ownership, in that case of goods, which had previously vested in the purchaser, the purchaser's ownership of the goods being rendered free of any qualification by the termination of the transit of the goods. Another exception is that in the case of *Walter v James* (1871) LR 6 Ex 124. There the defendant was indebted to the plaintiff. The amount of the debt was disputed. S, who had acted as the defendant's attorney in the matter of the plaintiff's claim, but after his authority had been withdrawn by the defendant, paid the plaintiff £60 in discharge of the disputed claim. Later S requested the plaintiff to repay him the £60, which the plaintiff did. The plaintiff then sued the defendant for debt. The defendant pleaded as to £60 of the alleged debt that that sum had been paid by S and the defendant was then entitled to ratify that payment. The court, consisting of Kelly CB, Martin B, and Cleasby B, decided that the plaintiff and S had, prior to any purported ratification by the defendant been entitled to cancel what they had done and that consequently the plea of payment was not proved. In the course of his judgment Kelly CB said (1871) LR 6 Ex 124 at 127:

'And now the question is, whether the defendant can by his plea of payment adopt and ratify the act of Southall, although before action that act had, by arrangement between the plaintiff and Southall, been undone?'

Thus if the act which the putative principal later seeks to ratify has been undone or cancelled by the assumed agent there can be no effective ratification.

It follows in my view that where the putative principal seeks to ratify not a contract but an act done by an assumed agent (in this case the issuing of the writ) the first question is whether that act still existed at the moment of the purported ratification. In *Walter v James* it did not because the £60 had been repaid. In the present case the writ came into existence on 19 April 1988 and remains in existence unless and until it is struck out as being an abuse of process. It was still in existence in May 1991 when the liquidators purported to ratify it. I would conclude that ratification in this case has been effected, unless another exception established by the case law to the general principle applies.

The other exception which has to be considered in the present case is that indicated by Cotton LJ in the passage cited by the words 'an estate once vested cannot be divested'. I would suggest that exception ought to be stated in these terms: that the putative principal will not be allowed to ratify the acts of his assumed agent, if such ratification will affect adversely rights of property in either real or personal property, including intellectual property, which have arisen in favour of the third party or others claiming through him since the unauthorised act of the assumed agent. The expiry of the limitation period in the present case does not create any such right in the defendants; if applicable it would merely bar the plaintiffs' remedies. I would not extend this exception to cases such as the present where a defendant would receive a windfall defence in a case where the vice against which the Limitation Acts are designed to protect defendants, namely the bringing of claims at a time so far after the occurrence of the cause of action that a defendant is put at a disadvantage in defending the claim, does not exist. In this case Mr Secunda cannot claim to be in that position. The principle in *Bird v Brown* on which Mr McDonnell relies is, in my opinion, too widely stated and that case should be considered as it was by Cotton LJ in *Bolton Partners v Lambert* as an example of the 'vested property right' exception.

I too would dismiss the appeal.

Appeal dismissed. Leave to appeal to the House of Lords refused.

Celia Fox   Barrister.

R v Rossiter

COURT OF APPEAL, CRIMINAL DIVISION
RUSSELL LJ, ROCH AND WRIGHT JJ
2, 3 APRIL 1992

Criminal law – Murder – Provocation – Direction to jury – Wife killing husband following matrimonial altercation – Provocation not raised as defence at trial – Facts implying possible loss of self-control – Judge not leaving issue of provocation to jury – Whether sufficient evidence for question of provocation to be left to jury – Whether issue of provocation should be left to jury whenever there was material, however tenuous, capable of amounting to defence of provocation – Homicide Act 1957, s 3.

In the course of a domestic altercation the appellant inflicted on her husband two fatal knife wounds together with 4 serious wounds, 17 superficial wounds and 'defence injuries' on his wrists and hands. Her account of the altercation to the police and in evidence was confused but it was clear that she had been exposed to a degree of verbal abuse and physical violence from her husband on the day in question. She herself sustained injuries consistent to a limited extent with her account that the incident had been 'a ghastly accident' or that she had for the most part been defending herself, except when she had struck the fatal blows. At no stage did she accept that she had deliberately inflicted injury on her husband thus inhibiting defence counsel from putting forward the defence of provocation. She was convicted of murder. She appealed on the ground, inter alia, that the judge had failed to leave the question of provocation to the jury as required by s 3[a] of the Homicide Act 1957, which provided that 'Where on a charge of murder there is evidence on which the jury can find that the person charged was provoked ... to lose his self-control, the question whether the provocation was enough to make a reasonable man do as he did shall be left to be determined by the jury'.

Held – Whenever there was material which was capable of amounting to the defence of provocation, however tenuous it might be, the issue had to be left to the jury. On the facts, although the appellant had never conceded that she had deliberately stabbed her husband and had never actually said that she had lost her self-control, it was possible to infer from the circumstances of the killing and the number of wounds inflicted that she had in fact lost her self-control and therefore the jury should have been given the opportunity to consider, as required by s 3 of the 1957 Act, whether the provocation had been sufficient to make a reasonable individual act as the appellant had. Since the judge had failed to leave that issue to the jury the conviction for murder was unsafe and unsatisfactory. The appeal would therefore be allowed and a verdict of guilty of manslaughter substituted (see p 758 d and p 759 h to p 760 a, post).

Dictum of Lord Tucker in *Bullard v R* [1961] 3 All ER 470n at 470–471 applied.

---

a   Section 3 is set out at p 758 b c, post

Notes
For provocation as a defence to a charge of murder, see 11(1) *Halsbury's Laws* (4th edn reissue), paras 438–439, and for cases on the subject, see 14(2) *Digest* (2nd reissue) 33–48, 5260–5409.

For the Homicide Act 1957, s 3, see 12 *Halsbury's Statutes* (4th edn) (1994 reissue) 280.

Cases referred to in judgment
Bullard v R [1961] 3 All ER 470n, [1957] AC 635, PC.
Palmer v R [1971] 1 All ER 1077, [1971] AC 814, PC.
R v Hopper [1915] 2 KB 431, [1914–15] All ER Rep 914, CCA.

Appeal against conviction
Ethel Amelia Rossiter appealed against her conviction on 16 February 1988 in the Crown Court at Maidstone before Boreham J and a jury of murder for which she was sentenced to life imprisonment. The facts are set out in the judgment of the court.

James Wood (who did not appear below) (assigned by the *Registrar of Criminal Appeals*) for the appellant.
Geoffrey Nice QC and *Simon Browne* (instructed by the *Crown Prosecution Service*, Maidstone) for the Crown.

RUSSELL LJ (delivering the judgment of the court). Ethel Amelia Rossiter is now nearing her late sixties. She was a woman who was, prior to the events I am about to relate, of good character. On 16 February 1988 in the Crown Court at Maidstone before Boreham J and a jury she was convicted of murder and sentenced to the mandatory term of life imprisonment. She appeals against that conviction with the leave of the Full Court (Watkins LJ, Rose J and Pill J).

The case arises out of matrimonial discord and, before we deal with it in any detail, perhaps some preliminary observations would not be out of place. Matrimonial disharmony does not in itself and cannot entirely excuse, let alone justify, extreme violence. The other observation we make relates to this particular case. The members of this court have all read transcripts of the evidence given by this appellant as well as a transcript of the summing up. The impression we have all gained is that the appellant was a very unsatisfactory witness and, making all allowances for the stress of her predicament, her various versions of events, as given first to the police and later to the court, led to a confused and confusing picture. It created enormous difficulties for those charged with the responsibility of defending Mrs Rossiter and it also created problems for the learned judge.

Counsel had to follow their client's instructions and at no stage did she concede that she had deliberately inflicted injury upon her husband who was the victim of the charge. Her case was that the death of her husband at her hands was a ghastly accident. Alternatively, as she suggested during the course of the hearing, she had been defending herself, though let it be plainly understood not defending herself when striking the fatal blows.

The absence of any concession by the appellant to a deliberate stabbing of her husband inhibited the defence in the way of running before the jury the defence that it is suggested should have been left for the jury's consideration, namely provocation. More of that later.

We now endeavour to rehearse the facts in summary form. As we have indicated, the victim of the killing was one Leslie Thomas Rossiter, the appellant's husband, who at the date of his death was a little older than the appellant; he was 64 years of age. The couple had married in 1969. It is plain that the marriage was a turbulent one. It was common ground that between the years 1979 and 1983 there had been a separation and that later, after a reconciliation, there was correspondence with solicitors whom the appellant had instructed with a view to obtaining a divorce. Nothing came of that however and the parties continued to cohabit.

They lived together at a small flat in Whitstable, Kent. It was on any view somewhat cramped accommodation. On 23 July 1987 at about 4.30 pm the appellant telephoned the police from 4 The Saltings, Whitstable, the adjoining flat to that which she and her husband occupied. She was obviously in a very distressed condition and she told the authorities on the emergency call that she had stabbed her husband. Ambulance men and police officers were soon on the scene. They found the body of Mr Rossiter lying in the flat close by the outer door and close by a door leading into the bathroom and what was described as the 'cubby-hole'. Clearly, Mr Rossiter had sustained very serious injuries to his chest. The appellant was arrested and thereafter interviewed, being questioned about what had occurred on at least two separate occasions: on the night of the killing, and during the following day.

Before going to that part of the case, we deal with the post-mortem findings. Mr Rossiter was killed by two knife wounds of great depth that had penetrated the chest and passed through the heart. One was 10 cm in depth; the other was 4 to 7 cm in depth. In addition to those wounds, which were fatal and would have caused death within about a minute, Mr Rossiter had also suffered four other wounds, described by the judge in summing up as being 'three on the left side and one on the right side'. They had each penetrated the skin and had gone as far as the rib. They were therefore significant but played no part in the death.

There were 17 other superficial wounds all, it was acknowledged, caused by a knife. Twelve of them were on the right side of the chest, four on the left side of the chest and one in the region of the armpit. Mr Rossiter also bore injuries commonly known as 'defence injuries', in particular to his hands and wrist, no doubt caused as he attempted to ward off the knife that was being used as a weapon.

As for the appellant, she too had sustained some injuries consistent, at least to a limited extent, with what she was subsequently to tell the police. She had some bruising that was consistent with a blow from a hard object on her arm and she was to tell the police that, shortly before the killing, her husband had indeed struck her a blow aiming at her head, which she had warded off at the time the deceased was wielding a rolling pin.

During the day of the killing, the appellant's brother had visited the flat and the threesome, namely the appellant, her brother Frank, and the deceased, had had lunch together. We now gratefully adopt what is conceded by counsel as being an accurate record of what happened thereafter in the words of the learned judge. Referring to the appellant, the judge said:

'She said: "We ate our dinner quietly, only a few words between Frank, my brother, and Leslie. I spoke to Frank a bit. My husband was looking very depressed, he hardly spoke a word. He asked me what I had spent." She said that is not unusual. I do not know, ladies and gentlemen, you all live your own lives, is it very unusual for people to check up and see how the family finances are going? She said: "We never quarrelled before about money but we did this day, and about half past three Frank went out for a walk and made my husband a cup of tea which he drank in the living room, and he started an argument about Simon leaving the Air Force, as my husband thought prematurely, and I told him he is 22 years of age, he has a mind of his own, and there is no point in getting angry about it. [I interpose to observe that Simon was of course the son of the appellant.] I suggested that we washed up before Frank returned from his walk. He washed and I dried. We both put away. He started being abusive to me whilst he was at the sink. The knives were by the bread bin, but I could see only two of the steak knives, we had had three out for lunch." She said the bread bin is under a cabinet to the right-hand side of the sink. She said: "I went to the lounge to put cutlery and plates in the sideboard. I put the knives in the drawer. Leslie", I think she said, "was doing something with the dishes. He suddenly went quiet." She said: "When I went back into the kitchen he hit me with a rolling pin. He aimed at my face but I warded off the blow with my left arm. It was quite a hard blow. He was mumbling, he was incoherent. As I recall", she said, "he gave no reason for attacking me in that way. So I took the rolling pin from him and struck him with it. I don't know where. I think it was on his left shoulder. I told him to calm down. Then", she said, "I dropped the rolling pin on the floor. I thought, well, I better leave the kitchen until he has calmed down. I knew he was angry and depressed. So I went back to the living room and folded the tablecloth. I had put two steak knives away. Then I put the rest of the cutlery and the plates away. I went back to the kitchen." She said: "He came out of the kitchen towards me and stared at me wildly and he raised his hands to my throat and put his thumbs in front of my throat, one thumb on my neck. I put my hands up and flung his hands away. My nails went down the side of his face when that happened." She said: "He was wearing a blue shirt open at the front because it was hot in the kitchen. He had stared at me before. He seemed to go blank. I said to him: 'Don't be stupid', but he seemed not to hear me. Suddenly he came out of his daze and said, 'Don't call me stupid'. It seemed to enrage him and he turned and went back in the kitchen. I felt very shocked. He put away the aluminium dishes, and I was in the kitchen now trying to calm him down by speaking reasonably to him. I saw the third knife by the bread bin, about two feet away from him. I was going to put that knife away and he turned and picked up a tea towel lying near the cooker and in his hands he twisted it as if he was going to go after me: I had nothing in my hands so I picked up the knife to defend myself. I jabbed quickly with that knife, short jabs twice. I could see he intended to kill me and I recall jabbing him on the left side near the nipple, only a slight touch, the knife did not enter his body. He dropped the tea towel then and he went back and hit the handle of the oven door. He seemed to stumble and fell flat on the floor on his back. I put down the knife immediately. I said to him, 'I am going to call the ambulance or the police', and he told me 'to piss off'." She said:

"I stood there and suddenly he got to his feet unaided, still swearing. He told me to leave him alone. There was just a trickle of blood coming from near his left nipple." She said: "I went to the living room again to leave him to calm down. No sign of serious hurt on him." She had a look at the tea towel, you remember. She said: "That's the one or one like it. He tried to twist it into a garrotte. I could hear him banging and crashing about in the kitchen, mumbling incoherently. So I went to the corner of the kitchen and asked if I should call the ambulance because there was blood. He said: 'No, there's no need.' Then I suggested calling the police. He said: 'The police do not want to be involved in a domestic quarrel.' He must have been in the kitchen anything from three to eight minutes." That is after the jabbing of the knife, do you understand? "I was saying to him, 'we are too old to argue'." Then she talked about the knife being nearer where he was, and then she said she got that out of order so I will try and put it into order. She said: "I stood in the kitchen doorway and I spoke about our being compatible. I couldn't see the knife. I told him 'we are too old to argue' and he just became abusive. He did not answer me so I went and looked out to sea. He came out of the kitchen, his shirt was wrapped round his chest. I couldn't see any marks on his shirt and he went down to the hall cupboard which is half-way down the hall opposite where his clothes are kept. I saw him clutching his blue shirt and he had a white shirt on now." [We interpose to say that it was common ground that the deceased did change his shirt.] He had changed his shirt in other words. She said: "On his way towards the cubby-hole", and you know where the cubby-hole is, "I still had nothing in my hand. I had gone to the kitchen to look for the missing knife and I found it. I picked it up and I was going to put it away in the living room drawer. The next thing I saw him in the cubby-hole." That is his little place where he does his painting. "I suddenly wanted to go to the toilet. I had got the knife in my hand and I could not get into the bathroom because the cubby-hole door was open." You know how the thing works, one door is open, you cannot get into the other. She said: "He was in the cubby-hole doorway and I had the knife down by my side, by my hip. I calmly said to him 'I'll call the ambulance'. He said, 'I don't want the ambulance', and I said to him again that we ought to be compatible as we have no more worries because the family has grown up. At that he went berserk, going on about my not seeing my family often enough. He wasn't making sense, he was just mumbling. He had a long-handled paint brush in his hand." [The jury were reminded by the judge of the picture of the paint brush.]'

Finally, the judge said:

'She said that he had that long-handled paint brush. "He went to strike me in the face and I stepped back, said to him suddenly: 'Can I use the toilet?' Now he had a mitre block in his hand. [That was a piece of carpentry equipment that the husband used.] That is normally in the cubby-hole. I still had my knife in my right hand down by my right hip. He raised the mitre block and aimed it at my face and he came towards me, brought the knife up near waist height. I don't recall where the blade was pointing. He seemed to stumble and the knife went into him. I don't know where it went. I cannot say how far it went in. He gave two horrible screams. I think he was in pain. I stepped back still having the knife in my hand and he toppled towards the ground."'

During the police interviews the appellant added that at some stage during this prolonged altercation the deceased had called her 'a fucking cow' and at some earlier stage he had said, 'You bastard, kill me. I don't want to live'. In other words, the general tenor of the interviews that the appellant had had with the police was to the effect that on the day of the killing she was exposed to verbal abuse as well as a measure of physical violence.

The ground of appeal that has been pursued before us with not quite so much force, if we may say so, as the other ground of appeal was that the judge misdirected the jury upon the issue of self-defence. We have been taken to material passages in the transcript of the appellant's evidence. Complaint is made of a short passage in the summing up where the judge said:

'No-one, not even she, suggests that she struck with that knife or that on doing so to defend herself. Do you understand?'

Mr Wood, to whom this court is greatly indebted for the care displayed by him in the preparation of this appeal as well as for his lucid submissions to us, submits that that was a misdirection upon the facts and, further, that once self-defence was raised the judge failed to give a direction along the lines of the well-known authority of *Palmer v R* [1971] 1 All ER 1077, [1971] AC 814. That case, of course, is authority for the proposition that a jury should be careful to have regard to all the circumstances of the case when somebody is acting in self-defence and should not be too critical of what is done in the agony of the moment. The court is very familiar with that proposition.

Having examined the passages to which our attention has been directed, we agree with the judge that the appellant never at any stage seriously contended that what she did to her husband in the way of killing him was done in self-defence. We go so far as to say that any realistic view of this case must necessarily dismiss self-defence as a viable proposition. The wounds, as we have described, were multiple; the degree of violence used, even on the appellant's own story, by the husband toward her was out of all proportion to that which happened to him. We find no justification whatever for the complaint that in relation to self-defence there was either a misdirection or a failure to leave it properly for the jury's consideration.

We are fortified in that view by a passage to which Mr Nice QC directed our attention toward the end of the summing up, when the judge said:

'On behalf of the defence [counsel] asks you to take a very different approach. He accepts you may think realistically that if Dr Heath is correct in his conclusions then her account to the court cannot be correct, but he asks you to take the view that she is not lying to you, she is not deliberately putting up a smokescreen, she is an honest witness but her account, it is submitted you should find, is just incomplete, not a smokescreen. He asks you to take the view that you cannot dismiss the possibility she was defending herself when she was in the kitchen.'

The judge then went on to deal with one or two pieces of evidence and invited the jury, if they thought it right, and there was a real possibility of self-defence, to acquit entirely of the charge of murder. The jury declined to do so and in so doing it is manifestly plain to this court that they inevitably rejected the evidence of the appellant and, rightly so, in so far as it raised self-defence if, in reality, it did, which we very much doubt.

Much more compelling is the submission made by Mr Wood that the judge failed to leave for the jury's consideration the issue of provocation. Mr Wood acknowledges that, so far as he is aware, it was not raised by counsel for the defence; we should have said at an earlier stage that Mr Wood did not represent this appellant at her trial. The starting point for this submission is s 3 of the Homicide Act 1957. That section, as is well known, reads as follows:

'Where on a charge of murder there is evidence on which the jury can find that the person charged was provoked (whether by things done or by things said or by both together) to lose his self-control, the question whether the provocation was enough to make a reasonable man do as he did shall be left to be determined by the jury; and in determining that question the jury shall take into account everything both done and said according to the effect which, in their opinion, it would have on a reasonable man.'

The emphasis in that section is very much on the function of the jury as opposed to the judge. We take the law to be that wherever there is material which is capable of amounting to provocation, however tenuous it may be, the jury must be given the privilege of ruling upon it.

The judge in this case did not leave provocation to the jury. Mr Wood submits, in our judgment with force, that there was some evidence to support that defence. There was the appellant's version of events which had to be left to the jury in relation to the provocation to which she was subjected. There was no evidence that she 'lost her self-control' (coming from the lips of the appellant herself) but, so submits Mr Wood, one need look no further than the circumstances of the killing and the number of wounds that were inflicted to draw the inference that it would have been open to the jury that this was indeed a killing which took place when the appellant was under great stress and she, indeed, must have gone, so it is submitted, virtually berserk, something like 50-odd wounds being inflicted. The rest of the statutory definition contained in s 3 of the 1957 Act would have been a matter for the jury and the jury was never given the opportunity of considering it.

In support of those legal propositions, Mr Wood helpfully drew our attention, not only in his skeleton argument but in a helpful bundle of authorities, to a number of cases where the question of provocation has been considered both before and after the passing of the Homicide Act 1957. We propose to refer to only two such authorities.

In *R v Hopper* [1915] 2 KB 431 at 435, [1914–1915] All ER Rep 914 at 916 Lord Reading CJ had this to say:

'We do not assent to the suggestion that as the defence throughout the trial was accident, the judge was justified in not putting the question as to manslaughter. Whatever the line of defence adopted by counsel at the trial of a prisoner, we are of opinion that it is for the judge to put such questions as appear to him properly to arise upon the evidence even although counsel may not have raised some question himself. In this case it may be that the difficulty of presenting the alternative defences of accident and manslaughter may have actuated counsel in saying very little about manslaughter, but if we come to the conclusion, as we do, that there was some evidence—we say no more than that—upon which a question ought to have been left to the jury as to the crime being manslaughter only, we think that this verdict of murder cannot stand. We desire to add further that we do not accept the argument addressed to us by counsel for the Crown, and relied upon by the judge in his summing-up, that because the appellant said that he was not angry at the time, that must be taken against him as negativing the proposition that the crime could be manslaughter. In saying that he was not angry the appellant was trying to shelter himself behind the plea of accident, and it was open to the jury to say that the statement he made was not true. Other views of the facts than those given by him in his evidence cannot be excluded. In a Court of justice it is for the Court, with the assistance of the jury, to arrive at the true view of the facts without paying too much attention to whether a particular witness is called by one side or the other. Having arrived at the conclusion that the question whether the crime was manslaughter and not murder should have been left to the jury, this Court has power ... to substitute for the verdict found the verdict which might have been found if the jury had been properly directed. We cannot possibly say that a verdict of manslaughter would have been found by the jury, but as the question should have been left to them the appellant is entitled to the benefit of a verdict for the lesser offence. We direct accordingly that the verdict of murder be quashed and a verdict of manslaughter entered.'

The other case to which Mr Wood directed our attention was *Bullard v R* [1961] 3 All ER 470n, [1957] AC 635. Mr Wood in his skeleton argument cites this passage from the speech of Lord Tucker ([1961] 3 All ER 470 at 470–471, [1957] AC 635 at 642–644):

'It has long been settled law that if on the evidence, whether of the prosecution or of the defence, there is any evidence of provocation fit to be left to a jury, and whether or not this issue has been specifically raised at the trial by counsel for the defence and whether or not the accused has said in terms that he was provoked, it is the duty of the judge, after a proper direction, to leave it open to the jury to return a verdict of manslaughter if they are not satisfied beyond reasonable doubt that the killing was unprovoked ... Every man on trial for murder has the right to have the issue of manslaughter left to the jury if there is any evidence on which such a verdict can be given. To deprive him of this right must of necessity constitute a grave miscarriage of justice and it is idle to speculate what verdict the jury would have reached.'

In our judgment, those observations are particularly applicable to this instant appeal.

We are firmly of the view that, however well-intentioned in what was otherwise a full and careful direction to the jury, on this occasion Boreham J fell into error in failing to leave the issue of provocation for the jury's determination. There was, in our judgment, sufficient evidence in the case taken as a whole to demand that that course be taken. It follows that this conviction for murder cannot stand. We cannot be sure, if the issue of provocation had been left to the jury, what the verdict would have been. We are therefore satisfied that the verdict in fact returned must be regarded as unsafe and unsatisfactory. We quash that verdict. We are however abundantly satisfied that the killing was unlawful and, accordingly, exercising our powers under s 3 of the Criminal Appeal Act 1968, we shall substitute for the verdict of guilty of murder a verdict of guilty of manslaughter, that being on the ground of provocation. We shall hear submissions before deciding what is the appropriate sentence for that offence.

[The court then heard submissions from counsel on sentence. His Lordship continued:] The circumstances of this case have been fully related in the judgment which we have just delivered allowing this appeal. In all those circumstances, bearing in mind that this appellant, as we indicated, was a woman of good character, we consider that an appropriate sentence would have been, if passed in February 1988, a term of six years' imprisonment. That is the sentence which we now impose. Its effect, we are told, is that it will lead to the appellant's immediate release.

Appeal allowed. Conviction of murder quashed. Conviction of manslaughter substituted. Sentence varied.

N P Metcalfe Barrister.

R v Cambridge

COURT OF APPEAL, CRIMINAL DIVISION
LORD TAYLOR OF GOSFORTH CJ, AULD AND MITCHELL JJ
31 JANUARY, 14 FEBRUARY 1994

Criminal law – Murder – Provocation – Direction to jury – Victim killed in struggle with appellant or persons unknown – No witnesses of killing – Provocation not raised by defence – Issue of provocation not left to jury – Circumstances in which provocation must be left to jury – Evidence required before provocation can be left to jury – Homicide Act 1957, s 3.

The appellant, the deceased and their respective girlfriends spent an evening drinking in a public house. In the course of the evening there were several arguments. After one such argument the appellant, the deceased and another man, D, left the bar and went into the foyer where the deceased was fatally stabbed. The appellant was charged with his murder. At his trial there was no evidence that anyone had seen the knife or an actual stabbing movement but the Crown relied on the evidence of D and his girlfriend that when they went into the foyer they saw the appellant on top of the deceased. There was no evidence that anyone other than the appellant had attacked or been involved in a struggle with the deceased. The defence was that the killing had not been done by the appellant but by persons unknown. There was no suggestion that the appellant had been provoked into attacking the deceased. The appellant was convicted of murder. He appealed on the ground that the judge ought to have left the issue of provocation to the jury as required by s 3[a] of the Homicide Act 1957, which provided that 'Where on a charge of murder there is evidence

---

a Section 3, so far as material, is set out at p 765 *e*, post on which the jury can find that the person charged was provoked ... to lose his self-control, the question whether the provocation was enough to make a reasonable man do as he did shall be left to be determined by the jury'.

Held – The trial judge was required to leave the defence of provocation to the jury if there was material capable of amounting to provocation even though the defence did not rely on provocation but maintained that the defendant was not at the scene of the crime or that he did not kill the deceased. However, for the purposes of the defence of provocation under s 3 of the 1957 Act it was for the judge to decide whether there was evidence on which the jury could find that the defendant was in fact provoked to lose his self-control. While there need only be a slight or tenuous possibility that the acts or words in question or both together amounted to provocation the evidence itself on which the jury could find that the defendant was in fact provoked to lose his self-control had to be more than slight or tenuous and it was not for the judge to conjure up a speculative defence which was not relied on and which was unrealistic. If the judge concluded that there was sufficient evidence of provocation he was obliged to leave to the jury the question whether the things done or said might have caused a reasonable man to have reacted similarly to the defendant, even if the judge himself believed the circumstances to be such that no reasonable man would have reacted as the defendant did. On the facts, the issue of provocation should have been left to the jury and since it was impossible to determine what the outcome would then have been the conviction for murder would be quashed and a verdict of guilty of manslaughter substituted. The appeal would therefore be allowed (see p 764 *j* to p 765 *d f g j* and p 766 *b*, post).

Notes
For provocation as a defence to a charge of murder, see 11(1) *Halsbury's Laws* (4th edn reissue), paras 438–439, and for cases on the subject, see 14(2) *Digest* (2nd reissue) 33–48, *5260–5409*.

For the Homicide Act 1957, s 3, see 12 *Halsbury's Statutes* (4th edn) (1994 reissue) 280.

Cases referred to in judgment
Bullard v R [1961] 3 All ER 470n, [1957] AC 635, PC.
DPP v Camplin [1978] 2 All ER 168, [1978] AC 705, [1978] 2 WLR 679, HL.
Fazal Mohammed v The State [1990] 2 AC 320, PC.
Mancini v DPP [1941] 3 All ER 272, [1942] AC 1, HL.
R v Hopper [1915] 2 KB 431, [1914–15] All ER Rep 914, CCA.
R v Porritt [1961] 3 All ER 463, [1961] 1 WLR 1372, CCA.
R v Rossiter [1994] 2 All ER 752, 95 Cr App R 326, CA.

Cases also cited
R v Bonnick (1978) 66 Cr App R 266, CA.
R v Cascoe [1970] 2 All ER 833, CA.
R v Newell (1980) 71 Cr App R 331, CA.
R v Williams (Winston Anthony) (1993) Times, 11 November, CA.

Appeal against conviction
David John Cambridge appealed against his conviction on 13 February 1992 in the Crown Court at Bristol before Macpherson J and a jury of murder for which

he was sentenced to life imprisonment. The facts are set out in the judgment of the court.

Gilbert Gray QC and *Michael Roach* (assigned by the *Registrar of Criminal Appeals*) for the appellant.
Roderick Denyer QC and *Ian Bullock* (instructed by the *Crown Prosecution Service*, Bristol) for the Crown.

Cur adv vult

14 February 1994. The following judgment of the court was delivered.

LORD TAYLOR OF GOSFORTH CJ. On 13 February 1992 in the Crown Court at Bristol the appellant was convicted of murder by a majority verdict of 10 to 2. He was sentenced to life imprisonment. He now appeals against conviction by leave of the single judge.

On 20 April 1991 at about 11.15 pm Martin Hopes (known as 'Dot') was fatally stabbed in a Bristol public house called The Portcullis. There had been several arguments earlier in the evening. One had involved the deceased and his girlfriend whom he had slapped and pushed to the floor. Another involved the appellant's girlfriend, Marie Casswell. She had been called a slag by another man. She became irate and asked the appellant if he was going to let the other man get away with it. At that stage the appellant did not rise to her incitement. There were then words between the appellant and the deceased. According to two witnesses, the deceased said: 'If it were me, I would have hit her.' The appellant replied: 'If it just comes down to me and you then, Dot ...'

After that the appellant, the deceased and a man called Davies left the bar and went into the foyer. There was evidence that as he left, the appellant shouted to Davies: 'I'll have you, Davies, when you are by yourself.'

It is clear that the deceased was stabbed while in the foyer, but no one claimed to have seen the knife or an actual stabbing movement. The Crown relied principally on the evidence of Davies and his girlfriend Samantha Tucker. Davies said that when he went into the foyer, he saw the deceased crouched in a ball and the appellant on top. He, Davies, struck the appellant several times from behind to try to get him off the deceased. Samantha Tucker pulled him away. She gave evidence to similar effect, save that she said the deceased was flat on his back. There was no evidence that anyone other than the appellant attacked or was in a struggle with the deceased. However, there were three significant wounds: one to the left temple, one just below the hip-bone, but most importantly, one below the left collar-bone which penetrated the pulmonary artery causing an ultimately fatal haemorrhage.

After being stabbed, the deceased managed to get up and go outside the public house where he collapsed. The appellant and his girlfriend got into a taxi. The taxi driver overheard their conversation. Marie Casswell was complaining that the appellant had not backed her up. The appellant said: 'Don't worry babe, it's not over yet, he's dead.' In cross-examination, the taxi driver agreed that he understood that comment as a threat for the future rather than an admission of murder.

The appellant and Marie Casswell were arrested in the early hours of the morning when they were in bed. The appellant's clothes were found soaking in the bath, but analysis of the bath water and its contents found no trace of blood. The appellant answered no questions in interview, but read a prepared statement denying the offence. In evidence, he said that when the mood in the public house changed, he decided to leave with his girlfriend. He went out, thinking she was following him. She was not, so he returned to the foyer where he was met by a tidal wave of people who bundled him to the floor and tried to attack him. Thus, his defence was, 'Not me', and there was no suggestion that he was provoked into attacking the deceased.

The first ground of appeal is that the judge failed to sum up the evidence in sufficient detail and that he summarised only those prosecution witnesses who supported the Crown's case.

It is true that the judge reviewed most fully the evidence of Davies and Samantha Tucker, and that there were a number of other witnesses from the public house to whom he did not refer except in passing. However, Davies and Samantha Tucker were the only two who actually saw the deceased being attacked. They were therefore crucial. Mr Gray QC complains that the judge did not review the evidence of Nicola Peacock and Adrian Bryer. In fact, the judge did refer to Miss Peacock's evidence in the course of his summing up, and Mr Gray raised one point of her evidence before the jury retired, the judge accepting fully Mr Gray's reminder. Adrian Bryer gave no evidence as to what had happened to the deceased and although Nicola Peacock said that Bryer had pulled the appellant up and in effect rescued him from attack, Bryer himself gave no such evidence.

Mr Gray also complains that the judge did not adequately remind the jury of the taxi driver's understanding of the appellant's remark, 'He is dead'. However, Mr Gray raised that point at the end of the summing up. The judge agreed with what he said and it was clearly before the jury.

There is no obligation on a judge to repeat or refer to the evidence of every witness. He must of necessity be selective and the judge here followed the accepted practice of telling the jury the facts were for them and that although he was not going to refer to all the witnesses, they should bear in mind all the evidence and draw their own conclusions. The judge put the defence clearly to the jury and summarised the rival contentions succinctly and fairly at the end of his summing up. In our judgment, his treatment of the evidence was well balanced and cannot justly be criticised. Accordingly, the first ground of appeal fails.

A further ground complains of non-disclosure. It has emerged since the trial that there was evidence from a forensic scientist who examined the taxi in which the appellant and his girlfriend left the public house. His examination revealed no sign of blood or the knife. That information was not disclosed. Clearly it should have been, and Mr Denyer QC on behalf of the Crown concedes that the scientist's report ought to have been provided to the defence. Having said that, it was clear that the prosecution could adduce no evidence that the appellant had smeared blood anywhere as he left the scene or indeed that there was any blood on his clothing, nor was there any evidence to connect him with the knife. Mr Gray concedes that he was able to address the jury on this basis, but he argues that had he been provided with the scientist's report, he could have pursued the point with greater confidence. In our judgment, regrettable as the non-disclosure was, it did not make any difference to the outcome of the case.

We turn to the third and more substantial ground of appeal. Mr Gray submits that the judge ought to have left provocation to the jury as an issue for their consideration. As already noted, provocation was not raised on behalf of

the defence. Indeed, it would have been inconsistent with the appellant's
contention that he was not the assailant. Notwithstanding this, Mr Gray
submits that a clear line of authority required the judge to leave provocation to
the jury on the evidence in this case.

The line of authority goes back to *R v Hopper* [1915] 2 KB 431, [1914–15] All
ER Rep 914, *Mancini v DPP* [1941] 3 All ER 272, [1942] AC 1 and *Bullard v R*
[1961] 3 All ER 470n, [1957] AC 635. In *R v Porritt* [1961] 3 All ER 463, [1961] 1
WLR 1372, this court approved a passage from the opinion of the Privy Council
in *Bullard v R* [1961] 3 All ER 470 at 470, [1957] AC 635 at 642 delivered by Lord
Tucker, as follows:

'It has long been settled law that if on the evidence, whether of the
prosecution or of the defence, there is any evidence of provocation fit to
be left to a jury, and whether or not this issue has been specifically raised
at the trial by counsel for the defence and whether or not the accused has
said in terms that he was provoked, it is the duty of the judge, after a
proper direction, to leave it open to the jury to return a verdict of
manslaughter if they are not satisfied beyond reasonable doubt that the
killing was unprovoked.'

It is necessary to refer to only two other cases. In *DPP v Camplin* [1978] 2 All
ER 168 at 173, [1978] AC 705 at 716 Lord Diplock, having cited s 3 of the
Homicide Act 1957, went on:

'... it makes it clear that if there was any evidence that the accused
himself at the time of the act which caused the death in fact lost his
self-control in consequence of some provocation however slight it might
appear to the judge, he was bound to leave to the jury the question, which
is one of opinion not of law, whether a reasonable man might have reacted
to that provocation as the accused did.'

In *R v Rossiter* [1994] 2 All ER 752 at 758 Russell LJ said:

'We take the law to be that wherever there is material which is capable
of amounting to provocation, however tenuous it may be, the jury must
be given the privilege of ruling upon it.'

For the Crown, Mr Denyer sought to limit the situation in which a judge is
required to leave provocation to the jury, although it has not been raised by the
defence. He submits that in all the cases cited above it was common ground
that the defendant had caused the death. The issues before the jury were
therefore concerned with the defendant's state of mind and in those
circumstances, whether he was running accident, self-defence, no intent, or
even diminished responsibility, it was appropriate, if any evidence of
provocation existed, that the judge should also leave that issue to the jury.
Where, however, the defendant's case is that he was not there or it was not his
hand which killed the deceased, Mr Denyer submits different considerations
apply. There, if the defence did not rely upon provocation, the judge need not
leave that issue to the jury.

We cannot agree. The authorities cited above draw no such distinction.
Moreover, by way of example, a defendant may rely on an alibi whilst the
prosecution witnesses identifying him as the killer may describe provocative
acts or words followed by an apparent loss of self-control on the defendant's
part. In such a case, it would manifestly be wrong, if the alibi were rejected,

for the jury to convict of murder without considering provocation. So, even though the defence may prefer provocation not to be raised, in the fear that it may be a distraction offering the jury a possible compromise verdict, the judge must leave it to the jury if there is evidence.

But what sort of evidence gives rise to the duty? Clearly, it is not for the judge to conjure up a speculative possibility of a defence which is not relied on and is unrealistic. (See *Fazal Mohammed v The State* [1990] 2 AC 320 at 332.) There must be some evidence, but of what strength? In *Bullard v R* [1961] 3 All ER 470n, [1957] AC 635 the phrase used was, 'any evidence ... fit to be left to a jury'. It is true that in *DPP v Camplin* Lord Diplock used the phrase 'however slight', but he used it to describe the measure of the provocative acts or words, not the strength of the evidence that such acts or words in fact occurred and caused the defendant to lose his self-control. Likewise in *Rossiter,* when Russell LJ referred to 'material capable of amounting to provocation, however tenuous it may be', the word 'tenuous' described the provocative acts and words, not the evidence of their existence.

There are the two limbs of provocation: first, whether things said or done or both caused the defendant to lose his self-control; and secondly, whether those things might have caused a reasonable man to have reacted similarly. Section 3 of the Homicide Act 1957 provides:

'Where on a charge of murder there is evidence on which the jury can find that the person charged was provoked (whether by things done or by things said or by both together) to lose his self-control, the question whether the provocation was enough to make a reasonable man do as he did shall be left to be determined by the jury ...'

The starting point, therefore, is whether there is evidence on which the jury can find the defendant was in fact provoked to lose his self-control. That is a question for the judge. In our judgment, therefore, there must be evidence on the first limb from which a reasonable jury might properly conclude that the defendant was in fact provoked to lose his self-control or may have been so by some words or acts or both together. If the judge decides that there is not such evidence, he ought not to leave provocation to the jury. If, on the other hand, he concludes there is such evidence on the first limb of the two-stage test, the statute obliges him to leave provocation to the jury, even if he himself believes the circumstances to be such that no reasonable man would have reacted as the defendant did.

In the present case Mr Gray submits there was evidence from which a reasonable jury might have concluded that the appellant was in fact provoked to lose his self-control. He was incited by Marie to take up her cause, but at that stage her attempts to wind him up were unsuccessful. Then the deceased goaded the appellant further by saying: 'If it were me, I'd have hit her'. The appellant's riposte seems to have been: 'If it just comes down to you and me then, Dot ...', followed by his threat to 'have' Davies when he was on his own. Thus, there was evidence to suggest that the appellant had in fact been roused or provoked. He, the deceased, and Davies then went into the foyer where the fatal blows were struck. The jury found that the appellant struck them. That being so, something must have prompted him to do so. In our judgment there was clearly material from which the jury might reasonably have concluded that the appellant lost his self-control as a result of things said and done in the bar and possibly in the foyer.

We well understand the judge's reluctance to leave to the jury an issue which had not been canvassed, which was contrary to the defence contentions and where counsel on both sides had accepted that the jury's only possible verdicts were not guilty or guilty of murder. However, in the course of argument before us, Mr Denyer conceded that had the defence of provocation been run, it would 'probably have succeeded'. Without necessarily going that far, we are clearly of the view that it was an issue which ought to have been left to the jury. It is not possible, in our view, to say what the outcome would then have been. In those circumstances, the verdict of murder cannot stand, and the conviction for that offence must be quashed. On the other hand, the jury clearly found that the appellant had unlawfully killed the deceased. Accordingly, we substitute a verdict of manslaughter.

The court now has to consider what is the appropriate sentence to impose upon the appellant, having substituted the conviction for manslaughter on the grounds of provocation. It is trite to say that sentences for manslaughter can vary enormously depending on the circumstances.

The appellant was exposed to some verbal taunting and provocation in the course of the evening which preceded the killing, but this court takes the view that the measure of the provocation offered, certainly so far as the evidence went, was not intense. It would appear from the appellant's record that he is of a somewhat explosive nature. He is 28 years of age. He has previous convictions for violence and the threat of violence, although none as serious as this. In 1982, when he was a juvenile, he was convicted of possessing an offensive weapon. The court clearly took a mild view of that offence, fining him only £10. However, he was subsequently convicted of assault occasioning actual bodily harm in 1984, for which a community service order was imposed. That related to his being a member of an unruly crowd which was being dispersed by police officers. He assaulted an off-duty policeman, punched him in the mouth, cut his lip and split a tooth. In 1986, he was convicted of using threatening and insulting words or behaviour for which he was fined. There, the circumstances were that he spat at a disc jockey and, whilst being ejected, head-butted a doorman.

We take the view that the provocation about which we have heard was by way of incitement to take a more active part in the arguments that were taking place. It was not of the greatest gravity. Bearing in mind the appellant's record and age and the fact that he has for two years laboured under the threat of a life sentence hanging over him, we consider that the proper sentence here is one of six years' imprisonment. That is the sentence which we impose.

Appeal allowed and conviction of murder quashed. Conviction of manslaughter substituted.

N P Metcalfe Esq   Barrister.

Re Seagull Manufacturing Co Ltd (in liq) (No 2)

CHANCERY DIVISION (COMPANIES COURT)

MARY ARDEN QC SITTING AS A DEPUTY JUDGE OF THE HIGH COURT

24, 25 FEBRUARY, 1, 2 MARCH, 7 APRIL 1993

Disqualification of director – Unfit conduct – Jurisdiction – Territorial limitation on jurisdiction – Director of insolvent company a British subject resident outside jurisdiction – Official Receiver seeking disqualification order and serving proceedings on director outside jurisdiction – Whether court having jurisdiction to disqualify director resident overseas – Whether jurisdiction extending to activities by director conducted overseas – Company Directors Disqualification Act 1986, s 6(1).

On 4 April 1990, following an inquiry under s 447 of the Companies Act 1985, a compulsory winding-up order was made in respect of an English company. From that time S, a director of the company from January 1986 to July 1988, resisted every effort by the Official Receiver to investigate the company's affairs. In particular, S refused to provide information to the Official Receiver, contending that he could not be compelled to co-operate since, although a British subject, he was resident in Alderney and therefore outside the jurisdiction of the English courts. The Official Receiver was subsequently unable to trace the proceeds of a rights issue amounting to some £599,000. The Secretary of State later concluded that it was expedient in the public interest that S be disqualified from holding office as a director of the company and directed the Official Receiver to apply to the court for an order under s 6(1)[a] of the Company Directors Disqualification Act 1986, which enabled the court to make a disqualification order against a person in any case where it was satisfied (a) that he was or had been a director of a company which had at any time become insolvent and (b) that his conduct as a director of the company or any other company made him unfit to be concerned in the management of a company. The originating summons was served on S out of the jurisdiction pursuant to r 5(2)[b] of the Insolvent Companies (Disqualification of Unfit Directors) Proceedings Rules 1987. S sought a declaration that the court had no jurisdiction over him in respect of the disqualification proceedings on the ground that at all material times he was resident and domiciled in Alderney. He contended, inter alia, that under s 6(1) of the 1986 Act the activities which rendered a director unfit to manage a company could only be those which had taken place in England and Wales or had been directed from abroad and had some effect in the jurisdiction. The Official Receiver contended that s 6(1) applied to any person (whether a British subject or a foreigner) irrespective of their presence within the jurisdiction or at the time the alleged activities took place.

---

a   Section 6(1) is set out at p 771 *a b*, post
b   Rule 5(2), so far as material, provides: 'Where any process or order of the court ... is required under proceedings subject to these Rules to be served on any person who is not in England and Wales, the court may order service on him of that process or order ... in such manner as it thinks fit ...'

Held – (1) On its true construction, s 6(1) of the 1986 Act did not place any jurisdictional limitation on the court's power to make a disqualification order against a director of an insolvent company. Having regard to the fact that the word 'company' in s 6(1) (by virtue of the s 22(2)[c] definition) included any company which might be wound up under the Insolvency Act 1986 and therefore included companies incorporated in other jurisdictions and because modern methods of communication enabled companies to be controlled across borders, Parliament was presumed to have legislated not merely for British subjects and foreigners who happened to be in the jurisdiction at the time when the conduct relied on as rendering a director unfit to manage a company took place, but also for other foreigners who were out of the jurisdiction at the critical time. Any distinction in s 6(1) between foreigners based on presence would lead to anomalous results, since it would entail that disqualification proceedings could be brought against a London-based director who had caused a company to do acts overseas which had no effect on the British public, but not against a foreign director who conducted his company's business in London from outside the jurisdiction as his activities would be outside the scope of s 6(1). Parliament could not have intended such anomalous results, which would also preclude disqualification of a foreign director whose activities overseas had shown him to be unfit to manage a company but who sought to act as a director in England, when the very purpose of s 6 was to protect the public and potential creditors from losing money through companies becoming insolvent due to incompetent management. It followed that the court had jurisdiction to make a s 6(1) disqualification order against S and therefore to serve proceedings on him out of the jurisdiction (see p 771 *e* and p 777 *d* to p 778 *a c d*, post); dicta of Dillon LJ in *Re Sevenoaks Stationers (Retail) Ltd* [1991] 3 All ER 578 at 583, of Sir Donald Nicholls V-C in *Re Paramount Airways Ltd* [1992] 3 All ER 1 at 8–11 and of Peter Gibson J and Hirst LJ in *Re Seagull Manufacturing Co Ltd (in liq)* [1993] 2 All ER 980 at 985, 990 applied.

(2) However the court also had a discretion under r 5(2) of the 1987 rules not to order service of disqualification proceedings out of the jurisdiction where it was not convinced that there was a good arguable case for satisfaction of the conditions in s 6(1). On the facts, there were a number of grounds which could form the basis of a disqualification order if proved at trial, subject, of course, to evidence which S, as the director sought to be disqualified, might place before the court. S's request for a declaration that the court had no jurisdiction over him with regard to the disqualification proceedings brought by the Official Receiver and served on him in Alderney would accordingly be refused (see p 779 *b d j*, post); dictum of Sir Donald Nicholls V-C in *Re Paramount Airways Ltd* [1992] 3 All ER 1 at 13 applied.

Notes

For disqualification of company directors, see 7(2) *Halsbury's Laws* (4th edn reissue) paras 2113–2115.

For the Company Directors Disqualification Act 1986, ss 6, 22, see 8 *Halsbury's Statutes* (4th edn) (1991 reissue) 786, 798.

---

c   Section 22(2), so far as material, is set out at p 771 *d*, post

For the Insolvent Companies (Disqualification of Unfit Directors) Proceedings Rules 1987, r 5, see 4 *Halsbury's Statutory Instruments* (1992 reissue) 540.

Cases referred to in judgment

Bishopsgate Investment Management Ltd (in prov liq) v Maxwell, Cooper v Maxwell, Mirror Group Newspapers plc v Maxwell [1992] 2 All ER 856, [1993] Ch 1, [1992] 2 WLR 991, CA.

Clark (Inspector of Taxes) v Oceanic Contractors Inc [1983] 1 All ER 133, [1983] 2 AC 130, [1983] 2 WLR 94, HL.

Eurostem Maritime Ltd, Re [1987] PCC 190.

Levitt (Jeffrey S) Ltd, Re [1992] 2 All ER 509, [1992] Ch 457, [1992] 2 WLR 975.

Paramount Airways Ltd, Re [1992] 3 All ER 1, [1993] Ch 223, [1992] 3 WLR 690, CA.

Sawers, Re, ex p Blain (1879) 12 Ch D 522, [1874–80] All ER Rep 708, CA.

Seagull Manufacturing Co Ltd (in liq), Re [1993] 2 All ER 980, [1993] Ch 345, [1993] 2 WLR 872, CA.

Sevenoaks Stationers (Retail) Ltd, Re [1991] 3 All ER 578, [1991] Ch 164, [1990] 3 WLR 1165, CA.

Theophile v Solicitor General [1950] 1 All ER 405, [1950] AC 186, HL.

Application

By summons dated 8 July 1992 Colin John Slinn sought a declaration that the court had no jurisdiction over him in respect of proceedings brought by the Official Receiver for his disqualification as a director and served on him outside the jurisdiction pursuant to r 5(2) of the Insolvent Companies (Disqualification of Unfit Directors) Proceedings Rules 1987, SI 1987/2023, on the ground, inter alia, that although he was a British subject he was not resident in the jurisdiction, being at all material times resident and domiciled in Alderney, the Channel Islands. The facts are set out in the judgment.

Paul Teverson (instructed by *Rose & Birn*) for Mr Slinn.
Nigel Davis QC (instructed by the *Treasury Solicitor*) for the Official Receiver.

Cur adv vult

7 April 1993. The following judgment was delivered.

MARY ARDEN QC. These are proceedings brought by the Official Receiver for the disqualification as a director of the respondent, Colin John Slinn. Mr Slinn is a British subject but he is not resident in England. Accordingly, on 24 March 1992 Mr Registrar Buckley made an order for service of the originating summons on him, out of the jurisdiction, pursuant to r 5(2) of the Insolvent Companies (Disqualification of Unfit Directors) Proceedings Rules 1987, SI 1987/2023.

By a summons dated 8 July 1992 Mr Slinn sought relief arising out of that order including by para 3, the only paragraph with which I am concerned, a declaration that the court has no jurisdiction over Mr Slinn in respect of the subject matter of the proceedings or the relief or remedies sought in the proceedings. The only ground on which this application is now pursued is ground 3. The remaining grounds have been abandoned or, in the case of

ground 4, reserved for a higher court. I should add that there is some dispute as to whether Mr Slinn can properly reserve ground 4.
Ground 3 reads:

'(3) The said order dated 24th March 1992 was made without jurisdiction since, at all material times, the respondent was resident and domiciled in Alderney.'

On this summons Mr Teverson represented Mr Slinn. The Official Receiver has been represented by Nigel Davis QC.

There is an affidavit of Mr Slinn in support of his summons. The only part to which I need refer is para 11 in which Mr Slinn states that from January 1979 to July 1986 he was resident in and domiciled in Alderney in the Channel Islands. The application made for leave to serve out of the jurisdiction which culminated in the order of 24 March 1992, was supported by an affidavit of John Charles Youdell, a solicitor employed by the Treasury Solicitor. Paragraphs 3 and 4 of that affidavit state as follows:

'3. I am informed by the applicant and verily believe that the respondent was a director of Seagull Manufacturing Company Ltd. That company was wound up on 4th April 1990 by order of the court upon the petition of the Secretary of State for Trade and Industry on public interest grounds. Since that time the respondent has resisted every effort of the Official Receiver to investigate the affairs of Seagull. He has refused to render up books and papers concerning the company in his possession before compelled to do so by a court order obtained in Alderney. He has failed to provide a Statement of Affairs. He has refused to provide information to the Official Receiver and has sought to frustrate the Official Receiver by contending that he cannot be compelled to cooperate on the basis that he is resident outside the jurisdiction of the English Court. The Official Receiver has been unable to trace the proceeds of a rights issue amounting to some £599,000. 4. The Secretary of State has concluded that it is expedient in the public interest that the respondent be disqualified from holding office as a director of the company and has directed the Official Receiver to make application to the court for such an order. It is my belief that the applicant has a good cause of action'.

The arguments on which this application has been principally based revolved around ss 1, 6 and 22 of the Company Directors Disqualification Act 1986 and I will start by reading the relevant parts of those sections. Section 1 provides:

'(1) In the circumstances specified below in this Act a court may, and under section 6 shall, make against a person a disqualification order, that is to say an order that he shall not, without leave of the court—(a) be a director of a company, or (b) be a liquidator or administrator of a company, or (c) be a receiver or manager of a company's property, or (d) in any way, whether directly or indirectly, be concerned or take part in the promotion, formation or management of a company, for a specified period beginning with the date of the order ...'

Section 6 provides:

'(1) The court shall make a disqualification order against a person in any case where, on an application under this section, it is satisfied—(a) that he is or has been a director of a company which has at any time become insolvent (whether while he was a director or subsequently), and (b) that his conduct as a director of that company (either taken alone or taken together with his conduct as a director of any other company or companies) makes him unfit to be concerned in the management of a company.

(2) For the purposes of this section and the next, a company becomes insolvent if—(a) the company goes into liquidation at a time when its assets are insufficient for the payment of its debts and other liabilities and the expenses of the winding up, (b) an administration order is made in relation to the company, or (c) an administrative receiver of the company is appointed; and references to a person's conduct as a director of any company or companies include, where that company or any of those companies has become insolvent, that person's conduct in relation to any matter connected with or arising out of the insolvency of that company.'

Section 22(2) states:

'The expression "company" ... (b) elsewhere [ie other than in s 11], includes any company which may be wound up under Part V of the Insolvency Act.'

There is no express statement in the 1986 Act of any jurisdictional requirements which must be satisfied before the court can make an order under s 6(1). For example, there is no statement as to whether the conduct complained of must have occurred in England. However, it is well established that English legislation is prima facie territorial: see *Re Sawers, ex p Blain* (1879) 12 Ch D 522, [1874–80] All ER Rep 708. Accordingly, it was held in that case that an adjudication order in bankruptcy could not be made under the Bankruptcy Act 1869 against a foreigner who was neither resident nor domiciled here unless the act of bankruptcy which was relied upon occurred here. This was so notwithstanding that the Bankruptcy Act 1869 did not contain an express limitation to that effect. The court reached its decision by reference to the principle that legislation is prima facie territorial.

The principle in question was recently considered by two members of the House of Lords in *Clark (Inspector of Taxes) v Oceanic Contractors Inc* [1983] 1 All ER 133, [1983] 2 AC 130. The members of the House of Lords in question were Lord Scarman and Lord Wilberforce with whom Lord Roskill agreed. After citing from the judgment of Cotton LJ in *Re Sawers, ex p Blain* Lord Scarman said ([1983] 1 All ER 133 at 139, [1983] 2 AC 130 at 145):

'Put into the language of today, the general principle being there stated is simply that, unless the contrary is expressly enacted or so plainly implied that the courts must give effect to it, United Kingdom legislation is applicable only to British subjects or to foreigners who by coming to the United Kingdom, whether for a short or long time, have made themselves subject to British jurisdiction. Two points would seem to be clear: first, that the principle is a rule of construction only and, second, that it contemplates mere presence within the jurisdiction as sufficient to attract the application of British legislation. Certainly there is no general principle that the legislation of the United Kingdom is applicable only to

British subjects or persons resident here. Merely to state such a
proposition is to manifest its absurdity. Presence, not residence, is the
test.'

Lord Wilberforce put the matter thus ([1983] 1 All ER 133 at 144, [1983] 2 AC
130 at 152):

> 'In my opinion [the taxpayer's] contention is erroneous, because it is
> based on a mistaken application or understanding of the "territorial
> principle". That principle, which is really a rule of construction of statutes
> expressed in general terms and which, as James LJ said, is a "broad
> principle", requires an inquiry to be made as to the persons with respect to
> whom Parliament is presumed, in the particular case, to be legislating.
> Who, it is to be asked, is within the legislative grasp, or intendment, of the
> statute under consideration? The contention being that, as regards
> companies, the statute cannot have been intended to apply to them if they
> are non-resident, one asks immediately: why not?'

From these passages it is clear that the question whether and, if so, what
territorial restriction applies to s 6 of the Company Directors Disqualification
Act 1986 is a question of construction. The general principle is that legislation
applies only to British subjects or foreigners who come to England. The
general principle is subject to any express enactment to the contrary or to any
plain implication to the contrary. The court must inquire as to the person with
respect to whom Parliament is presumed in this particular case to have been
legislating.

I have been referred to two recent cases in which these principles have been
applied to the Insolvency Act 1986 and they are both of considerable assistance
to me because, as Mr Davis points out, that Act and the Company Directors
Disqualification Act 1986 should be treated as part of a single statutory scheme
(see *Re Jeffrey S Levitt Ltd* [1992] 2 All ER 509 at 522–523, [1992] Ch 457 at 473–
474 per Vinelott J). The cases in question are *Re Seagull Manufacturing Co Ltd
(in liq)* [1993] 2 All ER 980, [1993] Ch 345 and *Re Paramount Airways Ltd* [1992] 3
All ER 1, [1993] Ch 223.

Re Seagull Manufacturing Co Ltd (in liq) concerned the question whether an
order for public examination of Mr Slinn could be served on him in Alderney.
After citing *Re Sawers, ex p Blain* and *Clark (Inspector of Taxes) v Oceanic
Contractors Inc*, Peter Gibson J, with whom Hirst and Lloyd LJJ agreed, said
([1993] 2 All ER 980 at 985, [1993] Ch 345 at 354):

> 'In considering Lord Wilberforce's question as to who comes within the
> legislative grasp of the section, one must look to the policy of the
> legislature in enacting the section in question. Where a company has
> come to a calamitous end and has been wound up by the court, the
> obvious intention of this section was that those responsible for the
> company's state of affairs should be liable to be subjected to a process of
> investigation and that investigation should be in public. Parliament could
> not have intended that a person who had that responsibility could escape
> liability to investigation simply by not being within the jurisdiction.
> Indeed, if the section were to be construed as leaving out of its grasp
> anyone not within the jurisdiction, deliberate evasion by removing oneself
> out of the jurisdiction would suffice. That seems to me to be a wholly
> improbable intention to attribute to Parliament. Further, s 133 must be

construed in the light of circumstances existing in the mid-1980s when the legislation was enacted. By use of the telephone, telex and fax machines English companies can be managed perfectly well by persons who need not set foot within the jurisdiction. There is no requirement that an officer of an English company must live in England, nor of course need an officer of an overseas company which may be wound up by the court. Such a company is very likely to have officers not within the jurisdiction.'

I would emphasise that the question before this court is one of the scope of the Company Directors Disqualification Act 1986 and I am not concerned with whether the order for public examination can be effectively enforced against a person out of the jurisdiction (see *Theophile v Solicitor General* [1950] 1 All ER 405 at 407, [1950] AC 186 at 195).

When Parliament enacted s 133 of the Insolvency Act 1986 it was very likely that it did so against the background of what Dillon LJ in *Bishopsgate Investment Management Ltd (in prov liq) v Maxwell, Cooper v Maxwell, Mirror Group Newspapers plc v Maxwell* [1992] 2 All ER 856 at 871, [1993] Ch 1 at 24, described as 'The public worry and concern over company failures on a large scale and the need to safeguard the public against such failures ...' Both public and private examinations have a significant role to play in the investigation of a company failure. The particular purposes that can be served by public examination were instructively set out in the *Report of the Review Committee on Insolvency Law and Practice* (Cmnd 8558) (June 1982).

I will pause there and turn to the judgment of Hirst LJ in *Re Seagull Manufacturing Co Ltd (in liq)* [1993] 2 All ER 980 at 990, [1993] Ch 345 at 360:

'In my judgment the key to this appeal lies in the determination of the question "who ... is within the legislative grasp, or intendment, of [s 133 of the Insolvency Act 1986]?": (per Lord Wilberforce in *Clark (Inspector of Taxes) v Oceanic Contractors Inc* [1983] 1 All ER 133 at 144, [1983] 2 AC 130 at 152). Section 133 is headed "Public examination of officers" and each class of persons referred to in s 133(1)(a) to (d) is or has been personally involved in that capacity in the direction or management of the company in liquidation. The purpose of the public examination is to enable the Official Receiver in the fulfilment of his duty under s 132 of the 1986 Act to investigate inter alia the causes of failure of the company, and its business dealings and affairs, for which the officer in question is or may have been wholly or partly responsible, and therefore personally and directly accountable for what has gone wrong. The efficient and thorough conduct of such investigation by the Official Receiver is of great public importance, as several recent and notorious cases have demonstrated. This process would be frustrated if, for example, a director who had with the aid of modern methods of communication run the company entirely from abroad, was immune from public examination, as he or she would be if Mr Teverson's submissions were correct. The same applies to a director who has defrauded the company in England and then absconded abroad shortly before the liquidation. These are by no means fanciful illustrations in the world of the 1980s and 1990s, and many similar ones could be given. It follows that, in my judgment, all officers as described in s 133(1)(a) to (d), whether inside or outside the jurisdiction, are within the legislative grasp and intendment of s 133, which on its proper construction has no territorial limits.'

Accordingly, the Court of Appeal held that s 133 of the Insolvency Act 1986 applied to persons such as Mr Slinn notwithstanding his absence from the jurisdiction.

The second case from which I have derived particular assistance is *Re Paramount Airways Ltd* [1992] 3 All ER 1, [1993] Ch 223. In that case the question was whether a transaction with a bank in Jersey was justiciable under s 238 of the Insolvency Act 1986 as a transaction at undervalue. The relevant parts of s 238 are as follows:

'... (2) Where the company has at a relevant time (defined in section 240) entered into a transaction with any person at an undervalue, the office-holder may apply to the court for an order under this section.

(3) Subject as follows, the court shall, on such an application, make such order as it thinks fit for restoring the position to what it would have been if the company had not entered into that transaction ...'

The Court of Appeal held that it was not possible in construing the expression 'any person' in s 238 to identify any particular jurisdictional limitation and accordingly that those words had to be given their literal and unrestricted meaning so as to apply to foreigners.

The Court of Appeal went on to hold that in the exercise of the discretion which the court had as to the relief to be given if a transaction at an undervalue was proved (see sub-s (3)) the court would need to be satisfied that the defendant was sufficiently connected with England for it to be just and proper to make an order against him despite the foreign element. There is no room for a similar exercise of discretion under s 6 of the Company Directors Disqualification Act 1986, but it has not been suggested by counsel that that diminishes the assistance to be gained from the Court of Appeal's judgment in that case as to the question of construction of s 238.

The approach to that question of Sir Donald Nicholls V-C, with whom Farquharson and Taylor LJJ agreed, was as follows ([1992] 3 All ER 1 at 8–11, [1993] Ch 223 at 235–239):

'It will be seen from the above summary that, on its face, the legislation is of unlimited territorial scope. To be within the sections a transaction must possess certain features. For instance it must be at an undervalue and made at a time when the company was unable to pay its debts, the company must be in the course of being wound up in England or subject to an administration order, and so on. If a transaction satisfies these requirements, the section applies, irrespective of the situation of the property, irrespective of the nationality or residence of the other party, and irrespective of the law which governs the transaction. In this respect the sections purport to be of universal application. The expression "with any person" merely serves to underline this universality. It is, indeed, this generality which gives rise to the problem. In these circumstances one is predisposed to seek for a limitation which can fairly be read as implicit in the scheme of the legislation in such all-embracing terms. Parliament may have intended that the English court could and should bring before it, and make orders against, a person who has no connection whatever with England save that he entered into a transaction, maybe abroad and in respect of foreign property and in the utmost good faith, with a person who is subject to the insolvency jurisdiction of the English court. Indeed, he might be within the sections and subject to orders even though he had not entered into a transaction with the company or debtor at all. Such an intention by Parliament is possible. But self-evidently in some instances such a jurisdiction, or the exercise of such a jurisdiction, would be truly extraordinary. The difficulty lies in finding an acceptable implied limitation. Let me say at once that there are formidable, and in my view insuperable, objections to a limitation closely modelled on the formula enunciated in *Ex p Blain* as explained by Lord Scarman in *Clark (Inspector of Taxes) v Oceanic Contractors Inc* [1983] 1 All ER 133, [1983] 2 AC 130. The implied limitation for which Hambros Jersey contended is riddled with such serious, glaring anomalies that Parliament cannot be presumed to have intended to legislate in such terms. In the first place, to treat presence of the other party within England and Wales as the factor which determines whether a transaction is within the ambit of the sections would be to adopt a criterion which would be capricious in the extreme. A transaction with a foreigner who is resident here would be outside the embrace of the legislation if he happened to be abroad, or chose to be abroad, at the time the transaction was effected. Conversely, a foreign national resident abroad would find that the transaction with him was within the 1986 Act if, but only if, he was physically present in this country at the time of the transaction. Secondly, this criterion would leave outside the scope of the legislation a transaction by a debtor with an overseas company wholly controlled by him. Siphoning money abroad in this way is a typical case to which the new legislation must have been intended to apply. Thirdly, this test would draw a distinction between the position of British subjects and others on a matter of substantive law affecting property transactions. It would be surprising if Parliament had such an intention today. Fourthly, this test would mean that there was no remedy under the 1986 Act in respect of a transaction with an overseas company, or a foreigner living here but abroad at the crucial moment, even if the subject matter was English land. Mr Davis felt constrained to accept that such a case might be within the purview of the legislation. This concession betrays the weakness of the respondent's argument. If a transaction relating to English land is within the legislation regardless of the identity or whereabouts of the other party to the transaction, why should not this equally be so with regard to a transaction relating to shares in an English company? Or United Kingdom government stocks? Or money in an English bank account? What this shows is that the physical absence or presence of the other party at the time of the transaction by itself bears no necessary relationship to the appropriateness of the transaction being investigated and made the subject of an order by an English court. As a sole touchstone it is useless. The oddities do not end there. Hambros Jersey's contention, if correct, would mean that the jurisdiction of the English court under the sections would be much more restricted than the circumstances in which an individual may be adjudged bankrupt or a company may be wound up by an English court. Under s 246 the English court has jurisdiction, for example, over a debtor who is a foreign national who has never lived or been here so long as, at a time within the last three years, he was a member of a firm which carried on business in this country. As to companies, under s 221 the court has jurisdiction to wind up overseas companies, a subject to which I shall return. Given the width of the ambit of these basic provisions, it would be surprising if Parliament is to be taken to have intended to limit the sections now under consideration as the respondent contended. Particularly, perhaps, since English law provides for the distribution of the assets of the insolvent among all the creditors worldwide. English law does not erect a "ring fence" so as to exclude creditors living abroad. For completeness I mention one further small pointer in the same direction, if one be needed. It is of a linguistic nature. As already seen, the sections make special provision for transactions with persons who are connected with the company or are associates of the debtor. For example a company which has given a preference to a person connected with the company is rebuttably presumed to have been influenced by a desire to prefer that person. Under the statutory definitions one of the circumstances in which a person is connected with a company is where the person is a company which is under common control (see ss 249 and 435(6)). Section 435(11) provides that for this purpose "company" includes any body corporate, whether incorporated in England or elsewhere. These provisions do not sit happily with the implied limitation for which the respondent contended ... In the end I am unable to discern any satisfactory limitation. I am unable to identify some other class. The case for some limitation is powerful, but there is no single, simple formula which is compelling, save for one expressed in wide and loose terms (eg that the person, or the transaction, has a "sufficient connection" with England) that would hardly be distinguishable from the ambit of the sections being unlimited territorially and the court being left to display a judicial restraint in the exercise of the jurisdiction. I mention, to dismiss, some examples of unacceptable simple tests. One possibility might be that the section applies only to transactions with persons who are available to be served with process in England and Wales. Such a limitation would have similar defects to those discussed above. Another possibility is that the transactions are confined to those governed by English law. But the remedies given by the sections include personal remedies, such as an order that the recipient of property transfer it back to the company, or an order that the other party to a transaction pay a sum of money to the trustee of the bankrupt's estate. It would be odd if a transaction were outside the section in all circumstances solely because it was governed by a foreign law even though, for instance, all the parties were in this country at all times. The same objection applies to a third possibility, namely that the sections apply only to dealings with property, immovable or movable, situate in England and Wales at the relevant time ... In my view the solution to the question of statutory interpretation raised by this appeal does not lie in retreating to a rigid and indefensible line. Trade takes place increasingly on an international basis. So does fraud. Money is transferred quickly and easily. To meet these changing conditions English courts are more prepared than formerly to grant injunctions in suitable cases against non-residents or foreign nationals in respect of overseas activities. As I see it, the considerations set out above and taken as a whole lead irresistibly to the conclusion that, when considering the expression "any person" in the sections, it is impossible to identify any particular limitation which can be said, with any degree of confidence, to represent the presumed intention of Parliament. What can be seen is that Parliament cannot have intended an implied limitation along the lines of *Ex p Blain, re Sawers* (1879) 12 Ch D 522, [1874–80] All ER Rep 708. The expression must therefore be left to bear its literal, and natural, meaning: any person.'

In the present case, the positions taken by counsel in their submissions on jurisdiction have been widely different. Mr Teverson for Mr Slinn, while reserving, he said, the right to argue elsewhere that the Company Directors Disqualification Act 1986 applied only to directors present within the jurisdiction, submitted before me that the limitation which ought fairly to be implied into that Act is that the activities which it is said rendered him unfit to be a director should either take place in the jurisdiction or be directed from abroad. Thus, the activities of a director would only be relevant to the extent that they had some effect here.

Mr Davis, on the other hand, submitted on behalf of the Official Receiver that s 6(1) applied to any person, that is to a British subject or a foreigner, irrespective of their presence here at the time the activities took place.

Section 6 of the Company Directors Disqualification Act 1986 contains no express statement of any jurisdictional requirement. Indeed, on its face it applies to any person and to any conduct. However, when it is analysed in a manner similar to that undertaken in *Re Paramount Airways* it is, in my judgment, clear that it too has no jurisdictional limitation as a matter of plain implication. The word 'company' in s 6(1) includes any company which may be wound up under the Act (see s 22(2)). In this way companies incorporated in other jurisdictions are included (see ss 220 and 221 of the Insolvency Act 1986). In the case of foreign companies the likelihood is that some of the directors will not be persons resident here, or even foreigners present here, when the conduct relied upon as rendering them unfit takes place.

Accordingly, in my judgment, Parliament must be presumed to have been legislating not simply for British subjects and foreigners who happened to be here at the relevant time, but also for other foreigners who were out of the jurisdiction at the critical time. Likewise, in relation to conduct, s 6(1) contains no territorial restriction. Accordingly, the court must ask what is the conduct in respect of which Parliament must have been presumed to have been legislating?

There are two factors which, in my judgment, indicate that the conduct in question in s 6(1) need not be conduct which occurred within the jurisdiction. The first such factor is the definition of 'company' to which I have already referred. This includes foreign companies and the acts of the directors of those companies are likely to have taken place abroad, and Parliament must have been presumed to have been legislating with that in mind. Secondly, in these days of modern communications a person may conduct himself as a director in such a way as to affect persons within the jurisdiction without himself ever entering the jurisdiction. Again, in my judgment, Parliament must be presumed to have been legislating with this in mind and, accordingly, by plain implication to be taken to have been referring to conduct wherever committed.

Were there a distinction in s 6(1) between foreigners based on presence, the results would be anomalous. For example, proceedings could be brought under that section against a director who from his office in London had caused a company to do acts in a foreign country which had no effect on the British public. Yet, on the other hand, a director who was a citizen of another country and who conducted the company's business here from abroad could not be proceeded against under s 6(1) since his activities would be outside the scope of s 6. In my judgment, Parliament cannot have intended those anomalous results. They are significant because as Dillon LJ, with whom Butler-Sloss and Staughton LJJ agreed, said in *Re Sevenoaks Stationers (Retail) Ltd* [1991] 3 All ER 578 at 583, [1991] Ch 164 at 176 in a passage to which Mr Teverson referred me:

'It is beyond dispute that the purpose of s 6 is to protect the public, and in particular potential creditors of companies, from losing money through companies becoming insolvent when the directors of those companies are people unfit to be concerned in the management of a company.'

Accordingly, as a matter of construction, I prefer Mr Davis's approach on behalf of the Official Receiver to that of Mr Teverson for Mr Slinn. Moreover, it seems to me that Mr Teverson's construction would lead to anomalous results. It would mean that disqualification proceedings could not be brought against a foreign director whose activities, which had been exclusively conducted abroad, had shown him to be unfit to be a director even though he might seek to expand his activities and to act as a director in England.

Mr Davis submitted that as a result of an order under s 6(1) a director would be disqualified from acting as a director in any part of the world. I express no view upon this proposition since I am not called upon to decide either the scope of an order under s 1 or the acts which may be justiciable under s 13 which creates a criminal offence.

It was submitted to me that my conclusion in this case would be consistent with a decision on s 300 of the Companies Act 1985 of Mervyn Davies J in *Re Eurostem Maritime Ltd* [1987] PCC 190. However, in my view it is not clear from the report of that case whether the director in question was within the jurisdiction when the conduct complained of occurred.

Mr Davis for the Official Receiver submitted to me that there were limitations on the court's power under s 6 which I accept have relevance in an inquiry as to Parliament's presumed intention as to the persons to whom this section should apply. Firstly, Mr Davis drew my attention to the fact that the class of persons in respect of whom a disqualification order can be made is limited to those mentioned in s 6(1)(a). Secondly, Mr Davis relied on the fact that s 6 may only be invoked where the company has become insolvent. Thirdly, Mr Davis relied on the fact that the application can be made only by the Secretary of State or the Official Receiver: see s 7(1). In my judgment, that is a particularly important point since the Official Receiver is an officer of the court and responsible to the Secretary of State and the Secretary of State is, in turn, responsible to Parliament.

Mr Davis also relied on a fourth limitation on s 6, namely that in the case of foreign persons the court retains a residual discretion in the context of deciding whether to give leave to serve out. This involved the construction of r 5 of the Insolvent Companies (Disqualification of Unfit Directors) Proceedings Rules 1987. Mr Davis contended, but Mr Teverson disputed, that that rule gave the court a discretion not to order service out if it is not satisfied that there was a good arguable case.

In *Re Seagull Manufacturing Co Ltd (in liq)* [1993] 2 All ER 980, [1993] Ch 345, a decision of the Court of Appeal, it was held that the discretion in the parallel insolvency rule, r 12.12(3) of the Insolvency Rules 1986, SI 1989/1925, extended only to the time and manner of service since the court could not refuse to make an order for public examination.

In my judgment, where the court is ordering service of disqualification proceedings out of the jurisdiction, the situation is different from where it is ordering public examination because there are certain important conditions which must be fulfilled before a disqualification order can be made and which are set out in s 6 itself.

However, in my judgment, the court has a discretion not to order service out and should not do so where it is not satisfied that there is a good arguable case for satisfaction of the conditions in s 6(1) (see *Re Paramount Airways Ltd* [1992] 3 All ER 1 at 13, [1993] Ch 223 at 241).

Finally, on this aspect of the case, as I have already stated, Mr Slinn is a British subject. He is, therefore, a person to whom s 6 applies on the *Re Sawers, ex p Blain* test. However, in my view, s 6 applies to anyone, British subject or not, and irrespective of where the conduct occurs.

Mr Teverson submitted for Mr Slinn that there were no sufficient grounds for service shown in the affidavit in support of the application for leave to serve out. I have already cited the relevant passage of the affidavit of Mr Youdell. In the light of my conclusion as to the absence of a territorial limitation in s 6(1) I consider that that passage sets out a number of grounds which could form the basis of a disqualification order if proved at trial and subject, of course, to any evidence on behalf of the director sought to be disqualified which that director seeks to place before the court.

Finally, Mr Teverson sought to rely on a Charter of Queen Elizabeth I, which had been given to the people of Alderney and which provides in these terms:

'Moreover, our royal pleasure is that we grant for ourselves our heirs and successors by these presence of the said bailiffs and jurists and all other inhabitants and sogenies in the said isles and maritime places that for the time to come none of them be cited or summonsed or drawn by any lawsuit or forced in any manner by any writs of process issued from any of our courts of the Kingdom of England to appear and answer before any judges courts or other offices of justice out of any of these islands and maritime places touching or concerning any thing dispute causes or matters in controversy whatsoever arising in the said islands.'

However, the Court of Appeal dealt with a similar argument in *Re Seagull Manufacturing Co Ltd (in liq)* [1993] 2 All ER 980 at 989–990, [1993] Ch 345 at 360. There is no evidence before me as to the law of Alderney or which shows that the matters arose within the islands. Accordingly, in my judgment, Mr Slinn cannot rely on that charter in this court.

I should add that I have not dealt with Mr Teverson's submission based on the in-aid procedure in s 426 of the Insolvency Act 1986, since Mr Teverson informed me that he was merely reserving the right to argue that point elsewhere.

In the circumstances, I decline to make the declaration sought.

Declaration refused.

Paul Magrath Esq   Barrister.

R v Kelt

COURT OF APPEAL, CRIMINAL DIVISION
KENNEDY LJ, WATERHOUSE AND EBSWORTH JJ
23, 25, 26 NOVEMBER, 3 DECEMBER 1993

Criminal evidence – Intimate sample taken from defendant – Use as evidence – Use as evidence in unrelated trial – Blood sample obtained from defendant during murder inquiry – Sample matching blood found at scene of robbery unconnected with murder – Whether sample admissible at defendant's trial for robbery – Whether sample taken from defendant in course of criminal investigation admissible as evidence at trial of defendant on unrelated charge – Police and Criminal Evidence Act 1984, s 62.

At the trial of the appellant on a charge of robbery the Crown sought to adduce scientific evidence to show that a sample of blood found at the scene of the robbery matched a sample of the appellant's blood. The blood sample from the appellant had been obtained by the police under s 62[a] of the Police and Criminal Evidence Act 1984 in the course of a murder inquiry unconnected with the robbery. Section 62 provided for the taking of an intimate sample from a person suspected of being involved in a serious arrestable offence. The judge allowed the evidence to be admitted and the appellant was convicted. He appealed, contending that an intimate sample obtained pursuant to s 62 could only be used for the purposes of the inquiry in connection with which it had been obtained and therefore the judge had erred in admitting the evidence of the blood sample.

Held – It would not be in the public interest if an intimate sample lawfully obtained in the course of one investigation could not be compared with a sample obtained at the scene of another serious crime and it could not have been the intention of Parliament that the use of a sample would be restricted to the inquiry in connection with which it had been obtained, since otherwise the 1984 Act would have specifically stated that to be the case. Accordingly, the judge had been right to admit the scientific evidence of the matching blood samples. The appeal would be therefore dismissed (see p 783 *g* to p 784 *a*, post).

Notes
For intimate samples and the destruction thereof see 11(1) *Halsbury's Laws* (4th edn reissue) paras 779, 781.
For the Police and Criminal Evidence Act 1984, s 62, see 12 *Halsbury's Statutes* (4th edn) (1994 reissue) 910.

Appeal against conviction
Stephen Kelt appealed with the leave of the full court against his conviction on 20 March 1990 at the Central Criminal Court before Judge Capstick QC and a jury of robbery and possessing a firearm with intent to endanger life, for which he was sentenced to a total of 15 years' imprisonment. The facts are set out in the judgment of the court.

---
a Section 62, so far as material, is set out at p 782 *c*, post

Stephen Batten QC and *Alexander Cameron* (assigned by the *Registrar of Criminal Appeals*) for the appellant.
David Bate (instructed by the *Crown Prosecution Service*, Central Courts Branch) for the Crown.

Cur adv vult

3 December 1993. The following judgment of the court was delivered.

KENNEDY LJ. On 20 March 1990 at the Central Criminal Court Desmond Patrick Cunningham, James Stevens and Stephen Kelt were each convicted of robbery and firearms offences, and they were each sentenced to substantial terms of imprisonment. They now appeal against conviction by leave of the full court.

There were five armed robberies committed between 28 May 1987 and 29 September 1987, and on each occasion one of the robbers was a man named James Watts. On 20 October 1987 he fled to Gibraltar, but was taken into custody there, and then not only admitted what he had done but also told the police, at considerable length, who else had been involved. At that stage the information which he gave was, however, incomplete. He was repatriated and on 8 December 1987 he was granted bail so that he could continue to assist the police as an informer, but in fact he continued to offend and on 18 April 1988 he was re-arrested. On 1 July 1988 Watts's girlfriend, Christine Vincent, made a statement to the police about his criminal activities since being granted bail in December 1987. On 3 August 1988 that statement was put to Watts, who says that he decided to tell the police the whole truth as to all of the crimes he had committed. In November 1988 he was granted residential informer status, and in March 1989 there began a series of raids to arrest those whom Watts had incriminated.

The first of the five robberies with which we are at present concerned was committed at Poole, Dorset on 28 May 1987 when a Security Express vehicle was attacked outside the Midland Bank. Watts identified the appellant Kelt as one of the robbers, and asserted that it was he who was injured in the struggle with the guard. Undoubtedly, the blood of an injured robber was on a bag of money which was left behind, and there was a sufficient amount of blood for it to be analysed.

In November 1988 Kelt was arrested in the course of a murder inquiry, and gave a sample of blood for the purposes of that inquiry, but a comparison was then made with the sample from the bag of money, and it was found to match. At the trial with which we are concerned, counsel for Kelt sought unsuccessfully to exclude the scientific evidence, and Kelt was convicted of robbery and possessing a firearm with intent to endanger life, for which he received a total of 15 years' imprisonment.

The sole point now being taken on behalf of Kelt in this appeal is that the judge was wrong to admit the scientific evidence. Mr Batten QC realistically does not seek to go behind the trial judge's finding that the police and the prosecuting authorities acted in good faith, but he submits that when intimate samples are obtained, as Kelt's sample was obtained, in accordance with the provisions of s 62 of the Police and Criminal Evidence

Act 1984, such a sample can only be used for the purposes of the inquiry in connection with which it is obtained.

Mr Batten began by reminding us that at common law the citizen is under no duty to provide evidence against himself. That right was first restricted by the road traffic legislation, and then by s 62 of the 1984 Act, but the latter restriction was carefully confined by means of a statutory scheme which extends to photographs and fingerprints as well as to blood samples. Such a sample cannot be taken unless a police officer of at least the rank of superintendent authorises it, and the person detained consents (see s 62(1)), and s 62(2) provides:

'An officer may only give an authorisation if he has reasonable grounds—(a) for suspecting the involvement of the person from whom the sample is to be taken in a serious arrestable offence; and (b) for believing that the sample will tend to confirm or disprove his involvement.'

Clearly the inference is that the serious arrestable offence in the mind of the police officer will be one which both he and the person detained know to be under investigation. Indeed, the person detained must be told the officer's grounds for giving authority (see s 62(5)), and Mr Batten submits that if a sample once obtained can be used for any purpose the safeguard that such a sample can only be required during the investigation of a serious arrestable offence will be devalued.

Next, Mr Batten points to the sanction which s 62(10) provides for use against those who refuse to provide a sample. It provides:

'Where the appropriate consent to the taking of an intimate sample from a person was refused without good cause, in any proceedings against that person for an offence—(a) the court, in determining—(i) whether to commit that person for trial; or (ii) whether there is a case to answer; and (b) the court or jury, in determining whether that person is guilty of the offence charged, may draw such inferences from the refusal as appear proper; and the refusal may, on the basis of such inferences, be treated as, or as capable of amounting to, corroboration of any evidence against the person in relation to which the refusal is material.'

Mr Batten submits that the value of the sanction will be reduced if a person who refuses a sample can say that he did so lest the sample might be used in some other inquiry, and clearly the refusal could only be regarded as corroborative in relation to the offence being investigated when the sample was demanded. Mr Batten also drew our attention to the wording of the *Code of Practice for the Identification of Persons by Police Officers* (Code D), which came into existence under the provisions of the 1984 Act, but that wording does not seem to us to add significantly to this part of his argument.

Finally, Mr Batten invited our attention to s 64, which, so far as relevant, provides:

'(1) If—(a) ... samples are taken from a person in connection with the investigation of an offence; and (b) he is cleared of that offence, they must be destroyed as soon as is practicable after the conclusion of the proceedings.

(2) If—(a) ... samples are taken from a person in connection with such an investigation; and (b) it is decided that he shall not be prosecuted for the offence and he has not admitted it and been dealt with by way of being cautioned by a constable, they must be destroyed as soon as is practicable after that decision is taken.

(3) If—(a) ... samples are taken from a person in connection with the investigation of an offence; and (b) that person is not suspected of having committed the offence, they must be destroyed as soon as they have fulfilled the purpose for which they were taken.

(4) Proceedings which are discontinued are to be treated as concluded for the purposes of this section ...'

The whole purpose of s 64 is, submits Mr Batten, to assure the detainee that the samples will not be used otherwise than in relation to the inquiry in the course of which they are being obtained, and thus to deprive the detainee of any reasonable excuse for failing to provide a sample. Under para 5.7 of Code D a detainee must be told not only the reason why a sample is required, but also the circumstances under which it will be destroyed. Mr Batten complains that the statutory scheme says nothing about destruction of written data, but he submits that the intention of Parliament clearly was that such data should be destroyed, otherwise s 64 would be of very limited effect.

In the context of the present case, Mr Batten submits that once it became clear in the course of the murder inquiry that the blood was all from the deceased, the sample obtained from Mr Kelt should have been destroyed, and thus this sample should have been destroyed before it was compared with the blood on the money bag from the robbery. But, as Mr Bate for the Crown points out, the evidence shows that Mr Kelt was still a murder suspect in March 1990, long after all relevant blood comparisons had been made, so according to the Crown the statutory duty to destroy the sample had even then not yet arisen.

In any event, we are satisfied for the purposes of this appeal that, despite the warnings of Mr Batten as to the danger of undermining the statutory scheme, the words of the statute should not be interpreted as he contends. Of course, the police must act in good faith, but the public interest would not be served if a sample lawfully obtained in connection with one investigation could not be compared with blood left at the scene of another serious crime. As Mr Bate in the course of his argument has pointed out, if a serial rapist were to be arrested and were to give a sample in the course of an inquiry into an offence which he did not commit, it can hardly have been the intention of Parliament that the sample which he gave could not then be compared with a whole series of specimens obtained from rapes which he had committed. Of course, there is force in the arguments which Mr Batten has advanced, but if Parliament had intended that a sample obtained in connection with one inquiry could only be used in evidence in connection with that inquiry, as opposed to envisaging that generally it would only be so used, it could have said so, and it did not. In our judgment the trial judge was right to admit the evidence which established the match between the

sample of blood provided by Stephen Kelt, and the blood left at the scene of the robbery. His appeal is therefore dismissed.
[The court then dealt with the appeals of the co-accused.]

Appeal dismissed. The court refused leave to appeal to the House of Lords but certified under s 33(2) of the Criminal Appeal Act 1968 that the following point of law of general public importance was involved in the decision: whether the results of analysis of an intimate sample taken under s 62 of the Police and Criminal Evidence Act 1984 for the purpose of one investigation are properly admissible in proceedings resulting from a separate investigation into a different offence.

Kate O'Hanlon   Barrister.

R v Secretary of State for the Home Department, ex parte Schmidt

QUEEN'S BENCH DIVISION
ROCH LJ AND SEDLEY J
15, 16, 17, 26 NOVEMBER 1993

Applied.
R. v. Comr. of Police of the Metropolis, Ex p. Bennett
[1995] 2 W.L.R. 598, D.C.

Extradition – Judicial review – Authority to proceed – Applicant tricked by police into returning to jurisdiction – Applicant alleged by German authorities to have committed drug smuggling offences – Applicant tricked into entering United Kingdom from Eire – Applicant arrested and remanded in custody to await extradition to Germany – Secretary of State issuing authority to proceed with extradition at request of German authorities – Home Office having no details of events leading up to applicant's arrest – Applicant seeking leave to apply for judicial review of Secretary of State's decision to issue authority to proceed – Whether decision subject to judicial review – Extradition Act 1989, s 7(4).

Extradition – Discharge of fugitive – Jurisdiction of High Court – Conditions under which court may entertain application to release fugitive – Whether jurisdiction of court limited to conditions laid down by Parliament – Whether court having residual supervisory jurisdiction to entertain application to release fugitive – Extradition Act 1989, s 11(3).

Between 1989 and 1991 the applicant, S, a German national, was alleged to have committed drug smuggling offences in Holland and Germany which, if proved, would amount to extradition crimes for the purposes of the Extradition Act 1989. In 1989 S left Germany and moved to the Republic of Eire where he set up a kite and model airplane business. In 1991 the Metropolitan Police received a request from Interpol that S be located and arrested under an international arrest warrant which had been issued by a German court. The Interpol request included information that S had stayed in the United Kingdom. Initial police inquiries failed to locate S but in 1992 the German authorities contacted the Metropolitan Police with information that they had traced S to Waterford and that they intended to apply for his extradition from Eire. The officer of the Metropolitan Police in charge of the case, posing as an officer investigating cheque fraud offences, subsequently contacted S and persuaded him to attend an interview on one of his regular visits to the United Kingdom so that he could be excluded from the inquiry. As a result of that ruse S was enticed into visiting the United Kingdom, where he was arrested on a provisional warrant and remanded in custody. The German authorities then submitted the necessary documents in support of the extradition request to the Home Office. Following consideration of those documents the Secretary of State issued an authority to proceed under s 7(4)[a] of the 1989 Act. S was later committed to custody pursuant to s 9(8)[b] of the Act to await the Secretary of State's decision as to his return. S applied for leave to seek judicial review of the Secretary of State's decision to issue an authority to proceed and a writ of habeas corpus. He contended that the events preceding his arrest and the deception practised by the police amounted to an abuse of power and/or process, that the Secretary of State's decision to issue the authority to proceed had been taken in ignorance of the material circumstances and that consequently the court should quash the Secretary of State's decision and issue a writ of habeas corpus effecting his release. The Secretary of State, the German government and the governor of the prison where S was being held contended (i) that the application for leave to seek judicial review of the Secretary of State's decision was inappropriate and should be refused and (ii) that the application for habeas corpus should also be dismissed on the ground that the facts relied on by S did not fall with s 11(3)[c] of the 1989 Act, which gave the court power to discharge an individual in circumstances where it would be unjust or oppressive to return him to the requesting state because of (a) the trivial nature of the offence, (b) the passage of time since the offence was allegedly committed or (c) the fact that the accusation was not made in good faith in the interests of justice, and that the court did not retain any supervisory jurisdiction to consider an application for habeas corpus which fell outside the scope of s 11(3).

Held – (1) In the absence of any dispute that the Home Office was unaware of the events leading up to S's arrest or assertion that knowledge of the deception practised by the police could be attributed to the Secretary of State, it was clear that, at the time when the Secretary of State issued the authority to proceed, he was to be treated as having no reason to think that an order for committal could not lawfully be made in respect of S or that such an order could not in fact be made in accordance with the 1989 Act. It followed that the Secretary of State had power under s 7(4) of that Act, if not a duty, to issue the authority to proceed. S's application for judicial review of the Secretary of State's decision to issue the s 7(4) authority therefore had no prospect of success. Moreover,

---

a Section 7(4), so far as material, provides: 'On receipt of [an extradition request] the Secretary of State may issue an authority to proceed unless ... an order for ... return ... could not lawfully be made, or would not in fact be made ...'

b Section 9(8), so far as material, provides: 'Where an authority to proceed has been issued ... and the court of committal is satisfied ... that the offence to which the authority relates is an extradition crime ... the court ... shall commit him to custody ...'

c Section 11(3), so far as material, provides: 'Without prejudice to any jurisdiction of the High Court apart from this section, the court shall order the applicant's discharge if it appears ... that—(a) by reason of the trivial nature of the offence; or (b) by reason of the passage of time since he is alleged to have committed it ... or (c) because the accusation against him is not made in good faith in the interests of justice, it would ... be unjust or oppressive to return him.'

the application was premature since all the steps available to S other than judicial review had not been exhausted. In particular, it was too early to know whether the facts relied on by S would persuade the Secretary of State not to make the order for return when the time came to make representations under s 13^d of the Act, following notification that an order for return was contemplated. S's application for judicial review would accordingly be dismissed (see p 793 e to h, p 794 b and p 799 d f, post).

(2) The supervisory jurisdiction of the High Court under s 11(3) of the 1989 Act to order the discharge of a person who had been committed to prison in the course of extradition proceedings was confined to the three specific cases set out in the subsection, namely where it would be unjust or oppressive to return him to the requesting foreign state because of the trivial nature of the offence of which he was accused or had been convicted, or because of the time which had elapsed since he was alleged to have committed the offence, or because the accusation against him had not been made in good faith in the interests of justice. Further, the opening saving clause of s 11(3), 'Without prejudice to any jurisdiction of the High Court apart from this section', was to be read as referring to other parts of the 1989 Act, such as s 13(6)^e, which (per Roch LJ) conferred jurisdiction on the court or (per Sedley J) merely acknowledged a jurisdiction of the court to review the Secretary of State's decision to make an order for return, and not as indicating some residual supervisory jurisdiction of the High Court. Any residual unfairness in returning a fugitive to the requesting state was a matter for the Secretary of State. Since S's case did not fall within s 11(3) of the 1989 Act, the court had no jurisdiction to entertain his application for a writ of habeas corpus, which would accordingly be dismissed (see p 796 j, p 797 b, p 799 d, p 801 d to f, p 803 h to p 804 a c to f j to p 805 a h, post); *Atkinson v US Government* [1969] 3 All ER 1317 and *Sinclair v DPP* [1991] 2 All ER 366 followed.

(3) In the event that the High Court did have an inherent supervisory jurisdiction to stay extradition proceedings on the ground of abuse of process, there would have to be a serious or grave abuse of power by the executive before the court would intervene, such as kidnapping or forcible abduction in the territory of the foreign state as a means of circumventing the extradition procedure which the executive could and should have used. That principle would not be confined to cases where there had been an application of physical force to the person of the detainee in the foreign country, but would also embrace cases where there had been threats or inducements of a serious and grave nature. On the facts (Sedley J dissenting) and taking account of the fact that no legal process existed by which S could have been brought from Eire to the jurisdiction of England and Wales for the purpose of being extradited to Germany, the conduct of the police was not so grave or serious that the court should intervene in the extradition process. That did not mean that the conduct of the police might not be a good ground for the Secretary of State to refuse to make an order for the return of S to Germany. The Secretary of State

---

d   Section 13, so far as material, provides: '... (2) The person to whom [an order for return] would relate shall have a right to make representations [against return], at any time before the expiration of the period of 15 days commencing with the date on which the notice [in writing informing him that an order for return is contemplated] is given ...'

e   Section 13(6) provides: 'At any time within [the seven-day period provided for by the order for return], the person to whom the order applies] may apply for leave to seek judicial review of the Secretary of State's decision to make the order.'

was in a position to know and would be able to take into consideration the attitude of the Irish authorities to the case, a matter of which the court could have no knowledge (see p 798 *c* to *e*, p 799 *b* to *d* and p 802 *e h*, post); *Bennett v Horseferry Road Magistrates' Court* [1993] 3 All ER 138 considered.

Notes

For committal, habeas corpus and order for return of a fugitive offender, see 18 *Halsbury's Laws* (4th edn) para 203A.

For the Extradition Act 1989 ss 7, 9, 11, 13, see 17 *Halsbury's Statutes* (4th edn) (1993 reissue) 568, 572, 576, 579.

Cases referred to in judgments

Atkinson v US Government [1969] 3 All ER 1317, [1971] AC 197, [1969] 3 WLR 1074, HL.

Bennett v Horseferry Road Magistrates' Court [1993] 3 All ER 138, [1994] AC 42, [1993] 3 WLR 90, HL.

Hunter v Chief Constable of West Midlands [1981] 3 All ER 727, [1982] AC 529, [1981] 3 WLR 906, HL.

Liangsiriprasert v US Government [1990] 2 All ER 866, [1991] 1 AC 225, [1990] 3 WLR 606, PC.

M v Home Office [1993] 3 All ER 537, [1993] 3 WLR 433, HL.

Osman, Re [1992] Crim LR 741, DC.

Sinclair v DPP [1991] 2 All ER 366, [1991] 2 AC 64, [1991] 2 WLR 1028, HL.

State (Quinn) v Ryan [1965] IR 70, Ir SC.

Trimbole v Governor of Mountjoy Prison [1985] IR 550.

Cases also cited

Denton Road, No 56, Twickenham, Re [1952] 2 All ER 799, [1953] Ch 51.

Governor of Australia v Harrod [1975] 2 All ER 1, [1975] 1 WLR 745, HL.

Union of India v Narang [1977] 2 All ER 348, [1978] AC 247, HL.

Application

Norbert Schmidt, by a notice of motion dated 4 March 1993, applied for a writ of habeas corpus ad subjiciendum directed to the Governor HM Prison, Brixton, whereto he had been committed to custody pursuant to an order made under s 9(8) of the Extradition Act 1989 on 18 February 1993 by the metropolitan stipendiary magistrate at Bow Street to await the Secretary of State's decision as to his return to Germany as a person accused of drug smuggling offences. On the same day the applicant applied for leave to seek judicial review of the Secretary of State's decision made on 7 January 1993 to issue an authority to proceed under s 7(4) of the 1989 Act. The grounds for the applications were that the events leading up to the applicant's arrest in the United Kingdom on 17 November 1992 amounted to an abuse of power and an abuse of the process of the courts of England and Wales and that the decision to issue the authority to proceed had been taken in ignorance of material facts. The facts are set out in the judgment of Roch LJ.

Clive Nicholls QC and *James Lewis* (instructed by *Reynolds Dawson*) for the applicant.

R Alun Jones QC and Clare Montgomery (instructed by the Crown Prosecution Service, International Branch) for the government of Germany and the governor of Brixton Prison.
Richard McManus (instructed by the Treasury Solicitor) for the Secretary of State for the Home Department.

Cur adv vult

26 November 1993. The following judgments were delivered.

ROCH LJ. On 17 November 1992 the applicant, Norbert Schmidt, was arrested by Det Sgt David Jones at the Charing Cross police station. The applicant was arrested on a provisional warrant which had been issued that morning by the metropolitan stipendiary magistrate at Bow Street under s 8(1)(b) of the Extradition Act 1989. The applicant appeared at the Bow Street Magistrates' Court on the following day and was remanded in custody. On 21 December 1992 the extradition unit at the Home Office received from the German government via diplomatic channels the documents which are required under s 7 of the 1989 Act. Those documents satisfied the officials at the extradition unit that the German government had requested the extradition of the applicant as a person accused of serious drug offences; that a court at Mannheim in the Federal Republic of Germany had issued a warrant for the applicant's arrest; that the applicant had been arrested in the United Kingdom on 17 November 1992 on a provisional warrant of that date and had appeared at the Bow Street Magistrates' Court on 18 November 1992 where he was remanded in custody; that the German government had provided the necessary supporting documentation as required by s 7 of the 1989 Act and art 12 of the European Convention on Extradition (which had the force of law in the United Kingdom by virtue of art 2 of the European Convention on Extradition Order 1990, SI 1990/1507, and was set out in Sch 1 thereto); and that on the evidence of the supporting documentation supplied by the German government, the German offences were extraditable under s 2 of the 1989 Act. Consequently on 7 January 1993 the minister of state issued an authority to proceed on behalf of the Home Secretary under s 7(4) of the Act.

At that time the Home Office were unaware of the events which had led to the applicant being in the United Kingdom and in the Charing Cross police station on 17 November 1992.

The applicant seeks two remedies. First, a writ of habeas corpus ordering his release and second leave to move for judicial review and, if leave is granted, judicial review of the minister of state's decision of 7 January 1993 to issue an authority to proceed to the metropolitan stipendiary magistrate.

Shortly put, the applicant's case is that the events which led up to his being in this country and to his arrest on 17 November 1992 amount to an abuse of power and an abuse of the process of the courts of England and Wales. Further, the decision of the minister to issue the authority to proceed was taken in ignorance of the events which preceded the applicant's arrest and was therefore taken without regard to material matters which should have led the minister to decide not to issue such authority. Consequently an order for certiorari should issue to quash the minister's decision and a writ of habeas corpus should issue to effect the release of the applicant.

What is said on the applicant's behalf is that he was tricked and deceived into coming to this country by Det Sgt Jones; that but for such conduct the applicant would not have been in this country on 17 November; that the conduct of that officer was a breach of the law of another country, namely the Republic of Eire, a deliberate evasion of the extradition procedures of the Republic of Eire and a breach of international law; and therefore there has been such a serious abuse of power by the police that this court must take cognisance of such conduct and should order the release of the applicant.

Between 1987 and 1991, so the German authorities allege, the applicant, who is a German national, committed drug offences in Holland and Germany involving the importation of cannabis into Germany from Holland. It is common ground that the conduct alleged by the German authorities, if proved against the applicant, would amount to extradition crimes for which the applicant might be arrested in this country and returned to Germany under s 1 of the 1989 Act.

The applicant left Germany in 1989 and moved to the Republic of Eire. There he set up a business in kites and model airplanes based in Waterford. His business flourished to such an extent that he retained an Irish solicitor, Mr Dermot Coyne of 46, North Circular Road, Dublin, to advise him.

On 12 August 1991 the applicant was arrested in Dublin by the drug squad of the Irish police for being in possession of controlled drugs. On the following day, 13 August 1991, an international arrest warrant was issued by the Mannheim local court in respect of the applicant for violation of the German Narcotics Act. On the following day the German authorities asked the Irish authorities to procure a provisional warrant for the arrest of the applicant. The applicant pleaded guilty to being in possession of controlled drugs before the Dublin court and was released from custody in Eire in October 1991. On 29 October the German authorities were told by the Irish authorities that the documents in support of the provisional arrest warrant were not in order. No further step was taken by the German authorities in Eire to extradite the applicant. Mr Jones QC, who appeared for the German government, told the court that he had no instructions as to the reason why the German authorities took no further step to extradite the applicant from Eire.

Two months later, in December 1991, a despatch letter was received at New Scotland Yard from Interpol at Wiesbaden arising out of the international arrest warrant which had been issued on 13 August 1991 by the Mannheim local court. That letter requested that the applicant be searched for and arrested. It stated that in the case of arrest the public prosecutors' office at Mannheim would request the applicant's extradition through diplomatic channels. The letter also contained specific information that the applicant had stayed in the United Kingdom. It was that part of that letter which led to the extradition squad of the international and organised crime branch of the Metropolitan Police being contacted and being given the investigation. The particular officer in that squad charged with the investigation was Det Sgt David Jones. He contacted Det Insp Mulligan of the Irish Drug Squad and discovered the events of August and October 1991 in Ireland but was told that Det Insp Mulligan could not assist with regard to the applicant's then whereabouts. Further investigation by Det Sgt Jones failed to disclose any trace of the applicant and consequently he returned the file to Interpol in London on 3 February 1992, the inquiry at that stage being closed.

On 14 April 1992 information was received from the German authorities that they had traced the applicant to Waterford and that they intended to apply for his extradition from Eire. During the subsequent six months the extradition squad in London were told by intelligence sources that the applicant was entering and leaving the United Kingdom, and had entered this country on numerous occasions using false British and EEC passports to conceal his true identity. The information also suggested that the applicant had travelled to Italy and Belgium in 1992 using false travel documents. Such behaviour was characteristic of a fugitive seeking to avoid detection. Further Det Sgt Jones deposes that that information caused him to be concerned that the applicant might be involved in terrorist activities and might be committing offences in this country as a result of his use of forged documents, particularly passports. It has to be observed that counsel for the respondents conceded that there is no evidence that the applicant has been involved in terrorist activities.

On 10 September 1992 Det Sgt Jones received information that the applicant was believed to be attending a kite festival in Bristol. Inquiries by the Bristol police led them to the Bristol Kite Store and inquiries at those premises showed that the owner of those premises knew of the applicant and had seen him practising with a kite on Durdham Downs, Bristol, during the festival weekend. Some six weeks later the officer who made those inquiries, Det Con Gregory, received a phone call at the Redland police station in Bristol from a man purporting to be the applicant. That officer gave the caller the name of Det Sgt Jones and his number and asked the caller to phone Det Sgt Jones saying he was the officer who wished to trace the applicant. The caller gave Det Con Gregory a telephone number in Eire where he could be contacted.

Det Sgt Jones in his affidavit says that on 10 September 1992 he had decided to investigate whether the applicant had committed offences in connection with forged passports. Det Sgt Jones believed that it would be very difficult to trace the applicant whilst he was in England and Wales, and consequently he approached his superior, Det Chief Insp Alan Wright, who is the officer in charge of the extradition squad, for permission to adopt the ruse of passing himself off as an officer investigating cheque fraud offences in the hope of persuading the applicant to meet him on one of the applicant's visits to the United Kingdom. Det Sgt Jones deposes that both he and the detective chief inspector had experience of how difficult it is to arrest those concerned in the international trade in prohibited drugs and that they therefore believed that if Det Sgt Jones could tempt the applicant into meeting him in England or Wales the applicant could be arrested on a provisional warrant and, if the German government were to make a request for his extradition he could be extradited to Germany. Det Sgt Jones adds that he did not believe that the ruse he was suggesting would circumvent any extradition arrangements between the Republic of Eire, Germany and the United Kingdom as he was not intending to tempt the applicant to enter the United Kingdom in circumstances where he would never otherwise have come here. He was simply trying to persuade the applicant to get in touch with him when he came to the United Kingdom for his own purposes. The German authorities were not told of Det Sgt Jones's intentions or any of the steps that Det Sgt Jones was taking. Nor were the German authorities told that Det Sgt Jones was taking steps until after the applicant had been arrested. Det Chief Insp Wright gave Det Sgt Jones permission to adopt the stratagem.

On 20 October 1992 Det Sgt Jones telephoned the number the applicant had given to Det Con Gregory. The applicant was not available but the detective sergeant left the number of his message pager and a request that the applicant contact him on that number. The detective sergeant used the paging answering system in order that the applicant would not realise that he was a member of the extradition squad. The detective sergeant says he was careful not to mention that he was attached to any particular squad because it would have been easy for someone to check whether that was or was not correct. The following day the detective sergeant was paged by the applicant. He phoned the applicant back at the Irish number. There is some disagreement between the affidavits of the applicant and his solicitor Mr Coyne on the one hand and that of Det Sgt Jones on the other hand about the number of calls and precisely what was said during the calls. In my view those differences are not material to the issues this court has to decide. What emerges from the affidavits is that Det Sgt Jones told the applicant and his solicitor that he was investigating a cheque fraud which had allegedly been committed by a Mr N Schmidt and that the detective sergeant had in his possession documents, some with handwriting by the perpetrator of the offence upon them, and photographic evidence of the perpetrator of the offence committing cheque frauds; and that Det Sgt Jones was anxious to exclude the applicant from his inquiries. Det Sgt Jones asked the applicant both directly and through his solicitor whether the applicant could come to this country to be interviewed so that the matter could be resolved. Det Sgt Jones told the applicant's solicitor that he, Det Sgt Jones, was not able to go to Eire to interview the applicant about these matters. Det Sgt Jones offered to interview the applicant at the ferry port at Holyhead or Fishguard if that would prove more convenient to the applicant. At some stage the applicant's solicitor asked Det Sgt Jones specifically what would happen if the applicant did not attend for interview and was told by Det Sgt Jones that it would be the normal practice to circulate the applicant on the police national computer as being suspected of these offences and he would then be arrested when he first came to the notice of the authorities in the United Kingdom. Ultimately it was agreed that the applicant and his solicitor would come to London on 17 November 1992. The applicant's solicitor was to fly to Heathrow and was to meet Det Sgt Jones at Green Park tube station in Piccadilly. The time was to be arranged when the applicant's solicitor arrived at Heathrow Airport and phoned the police officer.

Det Sgt Jones deposes to the fact that his contact with the applicant was mainly through the applicant's solicitor because he, Det Sgt Jones, took the view that it was better to deal through the solicitor so as not to deter the applicant from coming to this country.

The evidence makes it clear that the applicant and his solicitor travelled separately to London, the solicitor coming by air to Heathrow, and the applicant by car ferry through Fishguard. The applicant's solicitor was met by two police officers, Det Sgt Jones and Det Con James, and that there then followed a series of phone calls and moves from one location to another, manoeuvres probably designed to give the applicant a chance to observe the police officers who wished to speak to him. In the event the applicant met Det Sgt Jones, got voluntarily into a police car and was taken to the Charing Cross police station where the provisional warrant obtained by Det Sgt Jones earlier that morning was executed.

The applicant deposes that he was enticed into the United Kingdom by means of the deceit and manipulation practised by Det Sgt Jones. His main reason for coming to this country was to be interviewed by Det Sgt Jones in respect to alleged cheque frauds, and but for the prospect of that interview he would not have come to this country on that particular occasion. The applicant had on him a return ticket, which showed that he intended to remain in this country for two days, and £1,000 in currency. The applicant admits in his affidavit that he would have taken advantage of his journey to London to see other people in connection with his business.

The remaining history can be briefly told. On 17 November the extradition unit at the Home Office was informed of the issuing of the provisional warrant for the arrest of the applicant. On 18 November the applicant appeared before the Bow Street Magistrates' Court and was remanded in custody. The court informed the extradition unit of the applicant's arrest, appearance and remand. On 17 December 1992 the applicant appeared again before the Bow Street Magistrates' Court, Det Sgt Jones gave evidence and was cross-examined by the applicant's solicitor and admitted the stratagem by which the applicant's presence in this country had been obtained. An application for bail on behalf of the applicant was unsuccessful.

On 21 December the extradition unit received the documents required under s 7 of the 1989 Act from the German authorities via diplomatic channels. Following consideration of those documents the minister of state issued an authority to proceed on behalf of the Secretary of State on 7 January 1993. None of the documents which the Home Office then had contained any details of the events leading up to the applicant being arrested under the provisional warrant, nor at any time prior to the issue of the authority to proceed were the allegations made by the applicant of deceit and malpractice on the part of the police raised with the extradition unit at the Home Office. On 18 February 1993 the metropolitan stipendiary magistrate sitting at Bow Street made a committal order pursuant to s 9(8) of the Extradition Act 1989. On 4 March 1993 an application for habeas corpus was made on behalf of the applicant and on the same day an application for leave to apply for judicial review of the Secretary of State's decision to issue an authority to proceed on 7 January 1993 was made.

The court has before it two affidavits by Michael Forde, a practising barrister in Ireland who is an expert in the extradition law and constitutional law of the Republic of Eire. In those affidavits Mr Forde deposes that under the relevant legislation in Ireland, namely, the Extradition Act 1965, the applicant could be extradited from Eire to Germany in respect of one or more of the offences set out in the documentation provided by the German authorities, because the offences set out in those documents fall within the definition of 'extraditable offence' in s 10 of the 1965 Act, and they do not appear to fall within any of the exceptions contained in ss 11 to 21 of that Act. The applicant had certain rights and liberties guaranteed him by the constitution of the Republic including a right to liberty and a right of access to the courts of the Republic. Mr Forde says: 'I have no doubt that the English police authorities have contravened Mr Schmidt's constitutional rights to personal liberty and to access to the courts in Ireland.' Mr Forde further deposes that a trick of the type practised upon the applicant in this case by Det Sgt Jones constitutes a deceit in the law of tort in the Republic and is unlawful. If done by the police authorities of a foreign state it is also unconstitutional, at least if done to achieve an objective which apparently could be achieved through existing legal machinery.

There are four questions which counsel for the parties have raised on the facts of this case. First, does the High Court have the supervisory jurisdiction which the House of Lords held existed in *Bennett v Horseferry Road Magistrates' Court* [1993] 3 All ER 138, [1994] AC 42, that is to say, where a person is brought to England and Wales to stand trial, jurisdiction to examine the means by which that person was brought here and to prevent the trial proceeding on the ground that to proceed would be an abuse of the process of our courts, in the case of extradition proceedings in England and Wales for a person to be surrendered to another foreign sovereign state? Second, if such an inherent supervisory jurisdiction does exist, then do the facts of this case bring it within the statement of principle in *Bennett's* case? Has there been such an abuse of power to amount to an abuse of process so that this court should intervene to prevent the process of extradition advancing any further and to order the release of the applicant? Third, should the court grant leave to the applicant to move for judicial review of the Secretary of State's decision and act of 7 January 1993 of issuing an authority to proceed? Fourth, if the court should grant leave, should an order of certiorari issue to quash the Secretary of State's decision and act of 7 January 1993 of issuing an authority to proceed to the magistrate? The fourth question will arise if leave is granted because all parties through their counsel agreed that if the court decided to grant leave, the hearing should be considered as the hearing of the application for judicial review.

It is convenient to start by considering the third question.

The conclusion that I have reached is that leave, which is a matter of discretion, should not be granted in this instance. There is no dispute in this case that the extradition unit at the Home Office were unaware of the events leading up to the applicant's arrest under the provisional warrant on 17 November 1992. It was not submitted on behalf of the applicant that the extradition squad at New Scotland Yard were the agents of the Secretary of State or that knowledge of the members of that squad could be attributed to the Secretary of State. Consequently at the time the Secretary of State issued an authority to proceed, the Secretary of State has to be treated as having no reason to think that an order for committal of the applicant could not lawfully be made or that such an order would not, in fact, be made in accordance with the provisions of the 1989 Act. The Secretary of State therefore had power under s 7(4) of the Extradition Act 1989, if not a duty, to issue an authority to proceed. I say 'if not a duty' because under the European Convention on Extradition the contracting parties are under an obligation to extradite, by virtue of art 1 of the convention, which provides:

'The Contracting parties undertake to surrender to each other, subject to the provisions and conditions laid down in this Convention, all persons against whom the competent authorities of the requesting Party are proceeding for an offence ...'

Further, before the Secretary of State makes an order for the return of the applicant to Germany, under s 13 of the 1989 Act the Secretary of State has to give the applicant notice in writing that he is contemplating making such an order, and the applicant will have the right to make representations and a period of 15 days in which to do so commencing with the date of the notice given to him by the Secretary of State. It is the duty of the Secretary of State

under s 13(4) to consider such representations. Further, if after considering
such representations the Secretary of State makes an order for the return of the
applicant, the applicant under s 13(6) can apply to this court for judicial review
of the Secretary of State's decision.

Thus in my view, on the particular facts of this case the application for
judicial review is premature and all the steps available to the applicant other
than judicial review have not yet been exhausted. Further, on the particular
facts of this case an application to quash the Secretary of State's decision to
issue an authority to proceed has no prospect of success.

I turn now to the question of the application by the applicant for his
discharge under a writ of habeas corpus. Two propositions were accepted by
the parties to these proceedings. First, that the committal court has no
jurisdiction under s 11(3) to entertain an application for habeas corpus. This
would seem to follow from the terms of s 9(8) of the 1989 Act which obliges the
court of committal to commit the person arrested if it is satisfied as to certain
matters, and the wording of s 11(1) which contemplates the court of committal
informing the person arrested in ordinary language of his right to make an
application for habeas corpus. That suggests that the matter will go to another
court. Second, that the jurisdiction of the High Court under s 11(3) would not
enable this court to discharge the applicant on the facts relied on by him
because those facts do not come within s 11(3)(a), (b) or (c).

The dispute here has been whether the High Court has any residual
supervisory jurisdiction of the type which was held to exist in *Bennett's* case
where a person has been brought within the jurisdiction for the purposes of
being tried here.

Mr Nicholls QC has submitted that such a jurisdiction exists. First,
extradition involves a process of the court which abuse of power by the
executive abuses. Second, there is persuasive judicial authority that such a
jurisdiction exists, namely the observations of Woolf LJ in *Re Osman*, noted in
[1992] Crim LR 741, where having set out the terms of s 11(3) of the 1989 Act
he said:

'Quite clearly in view of the opening words of sub-s (3), the fact there is
a statutory right to apply for habeas corpus on limited and specified
grounds does not have the effect of restricting the applicant's right to
apply for judicial review or habeas corpus on other grounds.'

Mr Nicholls relies upon the opening words of s 11(3), 'Without prejudice to
any jurisdiction of the High Court apart from this section ...' to show that there
must be some further jurisdiction in the High Court.

Finally Mr Nicholls submits that the authorities on which the respondents
rely are distinguishable and in any event predate *Bennett's* case.

Mr Jones for the first two respondents and Mr McManus for the third
respondent submit that the High Court does not have any residual supervisory
jurisdiction for these reasons: first, extradition is a different procedure from
trial. It is an executive act, in which the executive is discharging an obligation
it has assumed in relation to other states and parties to the convention. The
role of the courts is limited, and Parliament intended that the role of the courts
should be limited to those matters set out in the Act. By way of illustration—
and the example is mine and not counsel's—Mr Forde, the expert in Irish
constitutional law, says in his second affidavit:

'Accordingly, in my view, what may be described as the extradition by trick which caused Mr. Schmidt to come to London will not help the cause of extradition in Ireland because it will suggest that the English police cannot be fully trusted; that they are prone to deception.'

Such a factor, it is submitted, is a matter for the Secretary of State and not for the courts. It is a question of policy and not of law. Second, two decisions of their Lordships' House are to the effect that no such residual supervisory jurisdiction exists and in *Bennett's* case their Lordships did not cast doubt on, far less overturn, these decisions. They are *Atkinson v US Government* [1969] 3 All ER 1317, [1971] AC 197 and *Sinclair v DPP* [1991] 2 All ER 366, [1991] 2 AC 64.

These are necessarily brief summaries of the cogent and well-researched submissions made by counsel, which do not do justice to counsel's labours.

Atkinson's case concerned the Extradition Act 1870. Section 10 of that Act provided:

'In the case of a fugitive criminal accused of an extraditional crime, if ... such evidence is produced as ... would, according to the law of England, justify the committal for trial of the prisoner if the crime of which he is accused had been committed in England, the police magistrate shall commit him to prison, but otherwise order him to be discharged.'

The appellant had escaped from prison in Louisiana having been sentenced to 18 years' imprisonment on charges of attempted armed robbery. He had entered pleas of guilty as a result, so he alleged, of a plea bargain with the prosecutor that if he pleaded guilty to attempted armed robbery no further action would be taken on charges of attempted murder. Attempted armed robbery and escape from prison were not extraditable crimes. The authorities in Louisiana revived the charges of attempted murder and, in addition, a charge of aggravated burglary, which were extraditable crimes. The chief metropolitan magistrate committed the appellant on the charges of attempted murder but refused to commit on the charge of aggravated burglary.

One of the issues which came before the House of Lords was stated by Lord Reid in his speech in this way ([1969] 3 All ER 1317 at 1321, [1971] AC 197 at 231):

'The question is whether, if there is evidence sufficient to justify committal, the magistrate can refuse to commit on any other ground such as that committal would be oppressive or contrary to natural justice. The appellant argues that every court in England has power to refuse to allow a criminal case to proceed if it appears that justice so requires.'

Lord Reid came to the conclusion that although it was by then well recognised that the court has power to expand procedure laid down by statute if that is necessary to prevent infringement of natural justice and is not plainly contrary to the intention of Parliament, the 1870 Act did provide a safeguard ([1969] 3 All ER 1317 at 1322–1323, [1971] AC 197 at 232):

'The Secretary of State always has power to refuse to surrender a man committed to prison by the magistrate. It appears to me that Parliament must have intended the Secretary of State to use that power whenever in his view it would be wrong, unjust or oppressive to surrender the man. Section 10 of the Act of 1870 provides that when a magistrate commits a man to prison "... he shall forthwith send to a Secretary of State a

certificate of the committal and such report upon the cases as he may think
fit." So the magistrate will report to the Secretary of State anything which
has come to light in the course of proceedings before him showing or
alleged to show that it would be in any way improper to surrender the
man. Then the Secretary of State is answerable to Parliament, but not to
the courts, for any decision he may make. If I had thought that Parliament
did not intend this safeguard to be used in this way, then I would think it
necessary to infer that the magistrate has power to refuse to commit if he
finds it would be contrary to natural justice to surrender the man. But in
my judgment Parliament by providing this safeguard has excluded the
jurisdiction of the courts.'

It is to be noticed that s 13 of the 1989 Act expressly requires the Secretary of
State to give notice in writing that he is contemplating making an order for the
return of that person to the foreign state, to afford that person 15 days within
which to make representations, and the Secretary of State is under a duty to
consider any representation made before the Secretary of State decides
whether or not to make an order for the person's return. That decision is
subject to judicial review. Further, by s 11(3) Parliament has expressly
conferred on the High Court a supervisory jurisdiction in three particular cases
where it would be unjust or oppressive to return the individual to the
requesting state. In *Atkinson's* case all their Lordships reached the same
conclusion on this issue.

In *Sinclair v DPP* [1991] 2 All ER 366, [1991] 2 AC 64 the court was again
concerned with the terms of the Extradition Act 1870. Their Lordships applied
the decision in *Atkinson's* case and held that the question whether the
extradition proceedings might be an abuse of the process of the court was not
one for the magistrate. Lord Ackner in his speech, having set out the terms of
s 11(1) and (3) of the Extradition Act 1989, said ([1991] 2 All ER 366 at 377,
[1991] 2 AC 64 at 80):

'By this section a radical alteration has been made by giving to the *High
Court* in part at least, the same kind of discretion, as to whether or not to
discharge an applicant, as the Secretary of State has in deciding whether or
not to order a fugitive criminal to be returned to a requesting state. It is
the clearest possible recognition by the legislature that hitherto no such
discretion existed in the courts and in particular in the magistrates' court.'
(Lord Ackner's emphasis.)

The other members of the House of Lords all agreed with the speech of Lord
Ackner.

These decisions are referred to in *Bennett's* case by Lord Griffiths in his
speech and by Lord Lowry (see [1993] 3 All ER 138 at 151, 168, [1994] AC 42 at
62, 82). I do not understand either of those passages to cast doubt upon the
decisions in *Atkinson's* case and *Sinclair's* case that prior to the 1989 Act the
High Court had no power to order the discharge of a detainee if it would be
unjust or oppressive to surrender him to the requesting state. If that is so, then
the power of the High Court at the present time must be limited to the power
conferred by s 11(3) of the 1989 Act. There is a sharp distinction between cases
where the individual is being extradited from this country to a foreign state
where the extradition legislation of this country will apply, and the case where
the individual has been either extradited or brought from a foreign state to this

country for the purposes of being tried here, where the extradition legislation of this country will have no application at all. Thus Parliament's intention as manifested in the extradition legislation and in particular Parliament's intention as to the jurisdiction and powers the High Court should have will not be relevant in the latter case but will be highly relevant in the former case.

After some hesitation I have reached the conclusion that the submissions made by the respondents on this issue are correct and that the jurisdiction of the High Court is that conferred by s 11(3) of the 1989 Act and no more. This court is bound to follow the decisions in *Atkinson*'s case and *Sinclair*'s case. The opening words to the subsection must be read, in my judgment, as referring to other parts of the Act, for example s 13(6), which confer jurisdiction on the High Court.

In view of my conclusion on this issue the fourth question does not arise. Nevertheless if the conclusion I have reached on the third question is wrong and the case goes further it may be of some value to express my view on the fourth question.

The first matter is to determine the scope of the general principle expressed by their Lordships in *Bennett*'s case [1993] 3 All ER 138 at 163, [1994] AC 42 at 77 where Lord Lowry said:

'I regard it as essential to the rule of law that the court should not have to make available its process and thereby indorse (on what I am confident will be a very few occasions) unworthy conduct when it is proved against the executive or its agents, however humble in rank.'

Lord Lowry went on to say that he would not expect a court to stay proceedings of every trial which had been preceded by 'a venial irregularity'. That is a very broad expression of the principle and is perhaps at variance with the passage earlier in Lord Lowry's speech (see [1993] 3 All ER 138 at 163, [1994] AC 42 at 76) which speaks of 'kidnapping and a grave contravention of international law, the comity of nations and the rule of law generally' and ([1993] 3 All ER 138 at 161, [1994] AC 42 at 74):

'I agree that prima facie it is the duty of a court to try a person who is charged before it with an offence which the court has power to try and therefore that the jurisdiction to stay must be exercised carefully and sparingly and only for very compelling reasons.'

Lord Bridge said ([1993] 3 All ER 138 at 155–156, [1994] AC 42 at 68):

'Since the prosecution could never have been brought if the defendant had not been illegally abducted, the whole proceeding is tainted ... By parity of reasoning, if the authorities, instead of proceeding by way of extradition, have resorted to abduction, that is the effective commencement of the prosecution process and is the legal foundation on which it rests. It is apt, in my view, to describe the circumstances ... as a "degradation" of the court's criminal process. To hold that in these circumstances the court may decline to exercise its jurisdiction on the ground that its process has been abused may be an extension of the doctrine of abuse of process but is, in my view, a wholly proper and necessary one.'

Lord Griffiths said ([1993] 3 All ER 138 at 151, [1994] AC 42 at 62):

'In my view your Lordships should now declare that where process of law is available to return an accused to this country through extradition procedures our courts will refuse to try him if he has been forcibly brought within our jurisdiction in disregard of those procedures by a process to which our own police, prosecuting or other executive authorities have been a knowing party. If extradition is not available very different considerations will arise on which I express no opinion.'

Earlier Lord Griffiths had spoken of 'a serious abuse of power' and of the court refusing to countenance 'behaviour that threatens either basic human rights or the rule of law' (see [1993] 3 All ER 138 at 150, [1994] AC 42 at 62).

In my opinion what has to exist before the court will intervene on the grounds of abuse of process is a serious or grave abuse of power by the executive as typified by kidnapping or forcible abduction in the territory of the foreign state as a means of circumventing extradition procedures which the executive could and should have used. The principle will not be confined to cases where there has been an application of physical force to the person of the detainee in the foreign country, but will embrace cases where there have been threats or inducements of a serious and grave nature.

Turning to the facts of this case, the trick employed by Det Sgt Jones was a breach of the protection conferred on the applicant by the Irish constitution whilst he was in the Republic of Eire on the evidence of Mr Forde and also a civil wrong, namely the tort of deceit. The device was not, however, a breach of Irish criminal law.

No legal process existed by which the applicant could have been brought from Eire within the jurisdiction of this court for the purpose of being extradited to Germany. In my view it can hardly be said that the telephone conversations between Det Sgt Jones and the applicant and between the officer and the applicant's solicitor were the effective commencement of the process of extraditing the applicant from this country to Germany. On the other hand, extradition processes exist between Germany and the Republic of Eire and this court does not know why the German authorities did not pursue extradition in Eire.

The applicant was in the habit of coming to this country from time to time for his own purposes, both recreational and business. Initially Det Sgt Jones's purpose was to arrest him on one of those visits and the reason for the subterfuge was to find out when and where the applicant would next be within the jurisdiction. There was no question of forcible abduction in this case nor was there any physical act committed within the Republic of Eire.

If there has to be a balancing between the gravity of the alleged offences for which the applicant is wanted by the German authorities and the improper conduct of the police, then the smuggling of substantial quantities of drugs across borders is a serious matter indeed. As Lord Griffiths observed in *Liangsiriprasert v US Government* [1990] 2 All ER 866 at 871–872, [1991] 1 AC 225 at 242, a decision of the Privy Council:

'As to the suggestion that it was oppressive or an abuse of process [that the applicants had been lured to Hong Kong for the purposes of being extradited to the United States by the authorities in Hong Kong acting in concert with the American Drug Enforcement Agency, members of which had penetrated the applicants' drug ring, on the basis that the applicants would be paid in Hong Kong for quantities of drugs illegally exported from

Thailand] the short answer is that international crime has to be fought by international co-operation between law enforcement agencies. It is notoriously difficult to apprehend those at the centre of the drug trade; it is only their couriers who are usually caught. If the courts were to regard the penetration of a drug dealing organisation by the agents of a law enforcement agency and a plan to tempt the criminals into a jurisdiction from which they could be extradited as an abuse of process it would indeed be a red-letter day for the drug barons.'

My conclusion on the fourth question would be that the conduct of the police, against the background that no legal process existed whereby the presence of the applicant could have been secured from Eire within this jurisdiction, was not so grave or serious that this court should intervene in the extradition process. This is not to say that the conduct of the police in this case may not be a good ground for the Secretary of State to refuse to make an order for the return of the applicant to Germany. The Secretary of State will be able to take into consideration such matters as relations between the authorities in this country and those in the Republic of Eire and the effect on those relations of the applicant being returned to Germany as opposed to being released and allowed to return to Eire. The Secretary of State is in the position of being able to know the attitude of the Irish authorities to this case, a matter of which this court can have no knowledge.

For these reasons I would not grant either relief sought by the applicant.

SEDLEY J. I have reached the same conclusions as Roch LJ, but because I have done so by different routes, and because in the field of public law we labour under the Chinese curse of living in interesting times, I will set out my reasons.

Judicial review

I agree that the application for leave to seek judicial review of the Secretary of State's decision of 7 January 1993 is inappropriate and should be refused in the exercise of the court's discretion. It comes both too late and too early: too late to prevent the authority to proceed from being acted on, and too early for it to be known whether the facts relied on by the applicant will yet persuade the Secretary of State not to return him to Germany.

I too would wish to reserve to a case where the point is taken the question whether the Home Secretary can plead ignorance of what the Metropolitan Police have done. Although the minister and the police officer represent distinct functions of the Crown, both are today executive limbs of the state, and it is arguable that in a real as well as a constitutional sense the state cannot be heard to say that its left hand does not know what its right hand is doing. To allow such a plea is to shift on to the individual the burden of risk of failures of co-ordination or communication in public administration and law enforcement. Even if such a broad proposition is incorrect, there remains the fact that the Home Secretary is the police authority for the metropolitan district and that the Metropolitan Police act in aid of his department in response to diplomatic requests for extradition, so that special considerations may arise in the present situation.

Habeas corpus

In order to decide whether the *Bennett* principle (see *Bennett v Horseferry Road Magistrates' Court* [1993] 3 All ER 138, [1994] AC 42) can come to the applicant's aid it is necessary to decide first what the principle is and secondly whether it applies to the facts of the applicant's situation. Only if these two questions are answered in the applicant's favour can the final question of the applicability of the principle to extradition proceedings become material. I will state briefly, since I agree with Roch LJ about the last question and hence about the outcome, why I consider that the applicant's situation comes both potentially and factually within the *Bennett* principle.

Question 1: What is the Bennett principle?

The House of Lords in *Bennett*'s case were considering as an assumed fact the removal of the appellant to the United Kingdom against his will from a place outside the jurisdiction of the United Kingdom's courts. In at least one place the statement of principle is framed accordingly. Lord Griffiths said ([1993] 3 All ER 138 at 151, [1994] AC 42 at 62):

> 'In my view your Lordships should now declare that where process of law is available to return an accused to this country through extradition procedures our courts will refuse to try him if he has been forcibly brought within our jurisdiction in disregard of those procedures by a process to which our own police, prosecuting or other executive authorities have been a knowing party.'

Lord Griffiths' views have the express concurrence of Lords Bridge, Lowry and Slynn. But it is to be observed that the certified question is not confined to the use of physical coercion: it asks in general terms whether the court has power to inquire into the circumstances by which a person has been brought within the jurisdiction. Their Lordships' reasoning is correspondingly large, and it may be noted in particular that Lord Bridge, although postulating the question in terms of forcible abduction, answers it in terms which make not physical force but executive lawlessness the critical factor ([1993] 3 All ER 138 at 155, [1994] AC 42 at 67–68):

> 'There is, I think, no principle more basic to any proper system of law than the maintenance of the rule of law itself. When it is shown that the law enforcement agency responsible for bringing a prosecution has only been enabled to do so by participating in violations of international law and of the laws of another state in order to secure the presence of the accused within the territorial jurisdiction of the court, I think that respect for the rule of law demands that the court take cognisance of that circumstance. To hold that the court may turn a blind eye to executive lawlessness beyond the frontiers of its own jurisdiction is, to my mind, an insular and unacceptable view ... Since the prosecution could never have been brought if the defendant had not been illegally abducted, the whole proceeding is tainted.'

This, it seems to me, is also the key to Lord Griffiths' reasoning where he crystallises it in a notable passage before focusing it on the use of force in the passage I quoted earlier ([1993] 3 All ER 138 at 150, [1994] AC 42 at 61–62):

> 'Your Lordships are now invited to extend the concept of abuse of process a stage further. In the present case there is no suggestion that the appellant cannot have a fair trial, nor could it be suggested that it would have been unfair to try him if he had been returned to this country through

extradition procedures. If the court is to have the power to interfere with the prosecution in the present circumstances it must be because the judiciary accept a responsibility for the maintenance of the rule of law that embraces a willingness to oversee executive action and to refuse to countenance behaviour that threatens either basic human rights or the rule of law. My Lords, I have no doubt that the judiciary should accept this responsibility in the field of criminal law. The great growth of administrative law during the latter half of this century has occurred because of the recognition by the judiciary and Parliament alike that it is the function of the High Court to ensure that executive action is exercised responsibly and as Parliament intended. So also should it be in the field of criminal law and if it comes to the attention of the court that there has been a serious abuse of power it should, in my view, express its disapproval by refusing to act upon it.'

This passage provides, too, the foundation for Lord Griffiths' concluding answer to the certified question, which is in the same broad terms as the question itself.

What then is the possible ambit of such executive lawlessness? I accept the submission of Mr Jones that Lord Lowry's phrase 'unworthy conduct' is not, and is not intended to be, the threshold. But I do not accept his argument that only the use of physical force passes the threshold. Lawlessness can take many forms. In my judgment what the doctrine of *Bennett* strikes at is an act on the part of the executive government of the United Kingdom: (a) which violates the laws of the foreign state, international law or the legal rights of the individual within that state, and thus offends against the principle of comity; (b) which circumvents extradition arrangements made with that state; (c) which instead brings the suspect by coercion into the jurisdiction of the United Kingdom's courts, and (d) but for which the domestic proceedings could not have been initiated. The last of these requirements, a 'but for' test of causation, emerges clearly from the language used by Lord Bridge and Lord Lowry and is implicit in the reasoning of Lord Griffiths.

In total, the decision of the House enlarges the concept of abuse of process to embrace serious abuses of power where it is only by the abuse of power that legal process has become possible. It articulates the supervisory obligation of the High Court to maintain the rule of law as something different from and greater than the maintenance of individual rules of law. In constitutional terms the decision, it seems to me, is of the highest importance, establishing a principle which will take time to be worked out in our jurisprudence.

Question 2: Force or fraud?

In the present case, the uncontroverted expert evidence, that of Mr Michael Forde, a well-known academic commentator in the field of Irish constitutional and extradition law and a member of the Bars both of Ireland and of England and Wales, is to the following effect.

(a) Ireland, Germany and the United Kingdom are all parties to the same extradition treaty, the European Convention on Extradition, so that in law the same extradition procedures (subject to any differential reservations) are available to the German government in Ireland as are available to it in the United Kingdom.

(b) To deny by a trick the protection of Irish law to which a person resident in Ireland is constitutionally entitled is itself an unconstitutional act whether the trick is that of officials of the Irish state or of a foreign state. In *Trimbole v Governor of Mountjoy Prison* [1985] IR 550 the subterfuge of an arrest on bogus grounds was held to vitiate subsequent extradition proceedings, however well founded these might substantively be. (The reasoning of the Irish High Court and Supreme Court bears striking resemblances in places to that of the House of Lords in *Bennett's* case.)

(c) Among the rights enjoyed by the applicant under Irish law are rights to personal liberty within the law and of access to the courts: see arts 34.1, 40.3 and 40.4.1 of the Constitution. In *State (Quinn) v Ryan* [1965] IR 70 the continued use under nineteenth century legislation of removal to England without a hearing in Ireland was struck down as unconstitutional because it deprived the individual of his right of access to the courts to question the legality of his removal. (The reasoning of the Irish court in this case marches in places with that of their Lordships' House in *M v Home Office* [1993] 3 All ER 537, [1993] 3 WLR 433.)

(d) The tricking of the applicant by the British police amounts to the tort of deceit in Irish law.

(e) The law of Ireland, at least in actions for trespass, rejects consent obtained by fraud or unlawful means.

In my view the way in which the applicant was induced to come to England, for the detail of which I gratefully rely on Roch LJ's judgment, is within the mischief to which the principle in *Bennett's* case is directed. But for the deception practised on him, the applicant would not have come to England and so made his arrest and extradition possible. This deception amounted to more than temptation (to use Det Sgt Jones's word) or inducement: it amounted to coercion, because it deliberately led the applicant to believe that Det Sgt Jones had sufficient evidence to justify his arrest for cheque frauds if and when he next entered the United Kingdom, but that by coming here voluntarily and surrendering himself to Det Sgt Jones he could clear himself. Since Jones knew that the whole cheque fraud story was bogus, he knew too that this was an offer that the applicant could not refuse: either he could come and establish what both he and Jones knew was his innocence of cheque frauds, or he could (so Jones led him to believe) face the prospect of arrest and possible trial for the frauds whenever he next chose to come to the United Kingdom, as he periodically did.

To offer an ostensible choice between a serious limitation on movement (whether by having to stay away from the United Kingdom or by facing arrest for cheque frauds on entry) and a simple and certain way of removing that bogus limitation was in my judgment coercive both in intention and in effect. It was a baited trap, but it was a trap into which the applicant was driven by a mendacious threat of adverse consequences if he did not take the bait. To change the metaphor, without the use of the stick the carrot would have been of no help. The subterfuge was intended precisely to ensure that the applicant believed he had no worthwhile choice but to come to the United Kingdom and deliver himself to Det Sgt Jones, and that is what he did.

There is no need in my judgment to cast around in the law of England and Wales for an exact precedent equating fraud with force in such a situation, and no attempt has been made to do so in argument. There are, as it happens, however, good analogies in common law and equity: with apologies to counsel for citing sources of law not canvassed in argument, I refer to 18 *Halsbury's Laws* (4th edn), para 332 (undue influence); 9 ibid, para 297 (duress in contract); and 16 ibid, para 679, esp n 4 (duress in equity). According to *Clerk and Lindsell on Torts* (16th edn, 1989) para 18-02: 'Public policy usually demands that nobody be permitted to found an action on an illegal act.' What is objectionable about fraud, actual or constructive, is that it robs the victim of the power of autonomous decision and action as surely as does physical coercion. In my judgment a fraud practised in and contrary to the law of a sovereign state, as this fraud was, and but for which the applicant would not and could not have been arrested on a provisional warrant as and when he was, would entitle this court to intervene to stay consequent criminal proceedings by parity of reasoning with *Bennett*'s case.

Comparably, if the applicant were to have been present in the United Kingdom for another reason—including an invitation, true *or* false, from Det Sgt Jones to meet him in order, say, to discuss kites—the objection would fall away because the element of coercion would be absent. Whatever the moral objections to the use of pure subterfuge, they have to be matched against the reality of police work in a dangerous and complex world, as the Privy Council has memorably recognised in *Liangsiriprasert v US Government* [1990] 2 All ER 866, [1991] 1 AC 225. But the limit placed upon this by the House of Lords in *Bennett*'s case, on grounds of constitutional principle, is that the use of subterfuge must not be such as to violate the rule of law by substituting coercion for established extradition procedures.

Question 3: Are extradition proceedings included?

Does a principle which would in my judgment have entitled this court to stay a prosecution of the applicant in the United Kingdom for dealing in cannabis extend to staying proceedings designed to extradite him to another state for trial on similar charges? If it were not for the decisions of the House of Lords in *Atkinson v US Government* [1969] 3 All ER 1317, [1971] AC 197 and in *Sinclair v DPP* [1991] 2 All ER 366, [1991] 2 AC 64, I would have little hesitation in acceding to the submission of Mr Clive Nicholls QC that the *Bennett* principle must apply to extradition as to domestic criminal process.

I would in any event unhesitatingly reject the contention of Mr Jones that extradition is essentially an executive act. Even under the truncated procedures introduced by the 1989 Act the courts and the executive have discrete, though in places overlapping, roles: see eg s 6(1), (2) and (3) and the definition of 'appropriate authority' in s 6(9). In my view a court of law entrusted with the conduct of a distinct stage of the extradition process retains the obligation of all courts to prevent abuse of their process (see *Hunter v Chief Constable of West Midlands* [1981] 3 All ER 727 at 729, [1982] AC 529 at 536) unless the power and hence the obligation is plainly excluded. I am not persuaded by Mr Jones that s 11(3) of the 1989 Act can have had this dramatic effect by means of an inferred limitation of the saving of 'any jurisdiction of the High Court apart from this section' to other powers of the High Court set out elsewhere in the Act itself. Section 11(3), it will be recalled, begins: 'Without prejudice to any jurisdiction of the High Court apart from this section, the court shall order the applicant's discharge if …' and the subsection then goes on to list three situations in which discharge comes as of right if in the court's judgment it would in all the circumstances be unjust or oppressive to return the person claimed. I much prefer the view expressed by Woolf LJ in *Re Osman* noted in [1992] Crim LR 741 at 748:

> 'Quite clearly in view of the opening words of subsection (3) the fact that there is a statutory right to apply for habeas corpus on limited and specified grounds does not have the effect of restricting the applicant's right to apply for judicial review or habeas corpus on other grounds ... it is possible to imagine circumstances where there could be grave unfairness which would certainly justify the interference of the court by way of judicial review not covered by section 11. It is no doubt for this reason that the legislation itself expressly makes clear that the statutory application for habeas corpus is not to be the only remedy available to a person who is the subject of a committal order.'

But it remains the case, at least for the present, that this court is bound by the holding of the House of Lords in *Atkinson's* case that any residual unfairness in returning a person claimed to the requesting country is a matter for the Secretary of State. Although s 8(3) of the Fugitive Offenders Act 1967 did not include the important words of reservation with which s 11(3) of the 1989 Act begins, to treat those words as opening extradition proceedings to the wider supervisory jurisdiction of the High Court may be to negate Lord Reid's words about the provision in both Acts of an executive discretion to refuse removal: 'Parliament by providing this safeguard has excluded the jurisdiction of the courts.' (See [1969] 3 All ER 1317 at 1322, [1971] AC 197 at 232.) Public law has today moved so far and so fast, largely under the impetus given to it by Lord Reid, that it is doubtful whether the exclusion of judicial by executive power which he was prepared to deduce from the legislation in 1969 (the year when *Atkinson's* case was actually decided) is a result which would at all readily be arrived at today if the matter were free of authority, especially in an Act passed as recently as 1989. I would in particular respectfully doubt whether in its context s 13(6), to which Roch LJ has briefly referred in this context, confers rather than simply acknowledges a jurisdiction of this court. But Mr Jones is entitled to and does rely on the much more recent decision of their Lordships' House in *Sinclair v DPP* [1991] 2 All ER 366, [1991] 2 AC 64. There Lord Ackner, with whom the other members of the House concurred in full, said ([1991] 2 All ER 366 at 377, [1991] 2 AC 64 at 80):

> 'Since the decision in *Atkinson's* case the Extradition Act 1989 has been enacted ... By [s 11] a radical alteration has been made by giving to the *High Court*, in part at least, the same kind of discretion, as to whether or not to discharge an applicant, as the Secretary of State has in deciding whether or not to order a fugitive criminal to be returned to a requesting state. It is the clearest possible recognition by the legislature that hitherto no such discretion existed in the courts and in particular in the magistrates' court.' (Lord Ackner's emphasis.)

By 'discretion' I take Lord Ackner to mean the power to judge whether it would be unjust or oppressive on any of the three grounds set out in s 11(3) to return the fugitive. Lord Ackner cannot, I would respectfully think, have meant that the words of reservation with which s 11(3) opens themselves give any new discretion to the High Court. Moreover, on one possible reading of Lord Ackner's words, their Lordships were deciding in *Sinclair's* case that although the magistrate lacked, and had always lacked, the power to decide whether extradition proceedings were an abuse of process, the 1989 Act had put that issue within the jurisdiction of the High Court.

This, however, does not appear to have been the reading of it made by their Lordships in *Bennett's* case. Lord Griffiths referred to the prosecutor's submission, based on the decisions in *Sinclair's* case and *Atkinson's* case, that examining magistrates have no power to stay proceedings on the ground of abuse of process. These two authorities, Lord Griffiths pointed out—

'established that in extradition proceedings a magistrate has no power to refuse to commit an accused on the grounds of abuse of process. But the reason underlying those decisions is that the Secretary of State has the power to refuse to surrender the accused if it would be unjust or oppressive to do so; and now under the Extradition Act 1989 an express power to this effect has been conferred upon the High Court.' (See [1993] 3 All ER 138 at 151, [1994] AC 42 at 63.)

Lord Lowry pointed out, as Lord Ackner had done, that Lord Reid's view of the magistrate's inability to adjudicate on an abuse of process in an extradition proceedings was obiter. He added ([1993] 3 All ER 138 at 168, [1994] AC 42 at 82):

'None the less a view expressed by such a high authority commands respect, and Lord Reid was making his point as an integral link in his argument, to show that in extradition proceedings a magistrate had no such power.'

The problem, which I accept may be more technical than substantive, is that the 'express power' to which Lord Griffiths refers must be the power to discharge the applicant on one of the three grounds set out in s 11(3), although this was not in fact a new provision in the 1989 Act. The opening saving clause in s 11(3), which *was* new, confers no express power but preserves unspecified extant powers which—and this is the stumbling block—have still to be treated as limited by Lord Reid's allocation of jurisdiction to the Home Secretary.

This is a profoundly unsatisfactory basis on which to decide an issue as important as the present. It may well be that Lord Ackner in *Sinclair's* case and Lord Griffiths in *Bennett's* case were intending to recognise exactly that supervisory jurisdiction to which Woolf LJ referred in *Re Osman* as a statutory inroad into Lord Reid's proposition, opening not only the Secretary of State's own decision on removal but the initiation of process itself to the supervisory jurisdiction of the court. It is therefore with reluctance that I agree with Roch LJ that it is not open to this court, recent decisions notwithstanding, to hold that by reason of the wording of s 11(3) of the Extradition Act 1989 alone the logic of *Atkinson's* case has fallen to the logic of *Bennett's* case. Any such decision must be for their Lordships' House.

Motion dismissed. Application for leave to appeal to the House of Lords refused.

Dilys Tausz   Barrister.

Re Goldcorp Exchange Ltd (in receivership)

PRIVY COUNCIL

LORD TEMPLEMAN, LORD MUSTILL, LORD LLOYD OF BERWICK AND SIR THOMAS EICHELBAUM

23, 24, 25, 29, 30 NOVEMBER 1993, 25 MAY 1994

Sale of goods – Title – Unascertained goods – Generic goods – Purchasers buying gold bullion for future delivery from company dealing in bullion– Dealer holding non-allocated stocks of bullion for customers – Company becoming insolvent and having insufficient stocks of bullion to satisfy debt owed to secured creditor – Non-allocated claimants asserting proprietary interest to bullion held by company – Whether non-allocated claimants entitled to proprietary interest in company's bullion stocks in priority to secured creditor – Whether contract for sale of unascertained goods conferring equitable title to goods.

The respondents (the 'non-allocated claimants') were customers of a New Zealand company which dealt in gold and other precious metals. They purchased bullion for future delivery on terms that they were purchasing 'non-allocated metal' which would be stored and insured free of charge by the company. An investor who purchased non-allocated metal received a certificate of ownership and had the right on giving seven days notice to take physical delivery of the metal purchased. It was explained or represented by and on behalf of the company that bullion purchased was not set aside as a customer's metal, but was instead stored in safe-keeping as part of the company's overall stock of bullion and was insured by the company and that the stock of bullion held by the company from which customers could call for delivery if they so wished would always be sufficient to meet the company's obligations under all outstanding contracts of sale. The company became hopelessly insolvent and a bank holding a debenture from the company appointed receivers. At the date of the appointment of the receivers, when the bank's floating charge crystallised, the company held stocks of bullion but the debt secured by the bank's debenture and floating charge exceeded the entire assets of the company, including the stocks of bullion. No appropriation of specific and segregated parcels of bullion to the individual purchase contracts of non-allocated claimants had been made and, faced with the prospect of obtaining nothing in the company's insolvency, the respondents brought claims of a proprietary nature claiming to be entitled to trace their proprietary interest to the remaining stock of bullion. They later asserted claims to the moneys paid under the various purchase contracts, or to a proportion of the company's general assets which represented the moneys so paid. The receivers applied to the High Court for directions concerning the disposal of the remaining bullion. At first instance the judge rejected the claims of the non-allocated claimants. On appeal, the New Zealand Court of Appeal held that the non-allocated claimants had no proprietary rights to the bullion but by a majority allowed their appeal, holding that the entire amount of the purchase moneys could be traced into the general assets of the company on the basis that the company stood in a fiduciary relationship to the non-allocated claimants and from the moment of payment of the purchase price received those monies on trust, and accordingly the non-allocated claimants had a charge over

Applied.
Bishopsgate
Investment
Management Ltd. *v.*
Homan
[1995] Ch. 211,
C.A.

the company's assets ranking in priority to the bank's charge. The receivers and the bank appealed to the Privy Council.

Held – The appeal would be allowed for the following reasons—
(1) An equitable title could not pass under a simple contract for the sale of unascertained goods merely by virtue of the sale, since the buyer could not acquire title until it was known to what goods the title related. Accordingly, where customers of a company purchased goods for future delivery and the company became insolvent before there was any appropriation of specific and segregated parcels of goods to the individual purchase contracts the customers could not assert a proprietary interest in the non-allocated goods. It followed that property in non-allocated metal held by the company did not pass to the non-allocated claimants simply by virtue of the contract of purchase (see p 813 *h j*, p 814 *b d h j* and p 815 *b*, post).

(2) The bullion purchased by the non-allocated claimants was unascertained goods in the nature of generic goods sold on terms that the company as the seller was free to decide for itself how and from what source it would obtain goods answering the contractual description. On that basis it could not have been intended by the parties that the company would create an interest in its general stock of bullion which would inhibit any dealings with it otherwise than for the purpose of delivery under the non-allocated sale contracts or that a customer's rights would be fixed by reference to a shifting proportion of a shifting bulk, depending on the quantity of bullion held by the company at any one time and the number of purchasers who happened to have open contracts at that time for goods of that description. It followed that, the remaining stocks of bullion being generic goods, it was not possible to impose a declaration of trust over that bullion arising out of the collateral promises made by or on behalf of the company as to storage, safe keeping, insurance and the maintenance of a separate stock of bullion. Nor could the collateral promises give rise to a title based on estoppel since although the company may have represented to its customers that they had title to bullion held by the company, a representation could not confer a deemed title by estoppel over generic goods when there was never a fixed bulk of goods from which an individual title could be carved out. In any event, it was doubtful whether an estoppel could ever confer title to goods which were the subject matter of the estoppel but it certainly could not against a third-party creditor possessing a real proprietary interest in the subject matter. Furthermore, the collateral promises made by or on behalf of the company did not impress on the bullion, as and when it was acquired by the company, either a trust in favour of each purchaser or a trust arising out of a floating bailment in respect of the constantly changing undifferentiated bulk of bullion which should have been set aside to back the customers' contracts, since that could not be reconciled with the fact that the purchases were of generic goods and not purchases ex-bulk and the body of potential beneficiaries and the pool of available bullion was constantly changing (see p 815 *d* to *j*, p 816 *c*, p 817 *d e h*, p 818 *e f* and p 820 *d e g* to *j*, post); dictum of Brett LJ in *Simm v Anglo-American Telegraph Co, Anglo-American Telegraph Co v Spurling* (1879) 5 QBD 188 at 206–207 applied; *Knights v Wiffen* (1870) LR 5 QB 660 distinguished.

(3) The non-allocated claimants were not entitled to assert any proprietary rights over the remaining stocks of bullion arising out of a so-called fiduciary relationship since any such relationship was no different from the contractual relationship between the parties. The company's failure to carry out its

obligations was a breach of contract, not a breach of a fiduciary relationship giving rise either to obligations different from its contractual obligations or to equitable remedies. Furthermore, the company's stock of bullion was merely another of the company's assets and had no connection with the claimants' purchases. In those circumstances it would not be right to impose a remedial constructive trust or a restitutionary proprietary interest over the bullion held by the company as a means of affording the claimants priority over the secured creditor (see p 821 *f* to *j* and p 822 *d* to *j*, post).

(4) Nor were the non-allocated claimants entitled to assert any proprietary rights arising out of the moneys originally paid by them under the contracts of sale, since there was no mutual intention that the moneys would not fall within the general fund of the company's assets but would be applied for a special designated purpose; on the contrary, there was nothing express or implied in the sale by the company to the customer which limited in any way the company's freedom to spend the purchase money how it chose, or to establish the stock of bullion from any source and with any funds as it thought fit. In those circumstances the purchase price was not impressed with a continuing beneficial interest in favour of the customer enabling the purchase moneys to be traced into other assets. Nor, given that the company's default was the simple contractual breach of failing to deliver goods ordered and paid for before it became insolvent, were the contracts vitiated by misrepresentation, mistake or total failure of consideration so that the customer in some way retained a beneficial proprietary interest in the purchase moneys which would otherwise have passed to the company when the money was paid, or which re-vested the moneys in the customer in a way which attached to the moneys an interest superior to that of the bank. Furthermore, notwithstanding the scale of the claimants' losses it would not be right for the court to create after the event a remedial restitutionary right superior to the security created by the bank's charge (see p 823 *j* to p 824 *e*, and p 825 *b* to p 827 *d*, post).

Notes

For contracts for the sale of unascertained goods, see 41 *Halsbury's Laws* (4th edn) para 709.

Cases referred to in judgment

A-G for Hong Kong v Reid [1994] 1 All ER 1, [1994] AC 324, [1993] 3 WLR 1143, PC.
Barclays Bank Ltd v Quistclose Investments Ltd [1968] 3 All ER 651, [1970] AC 567, [1968] 3 WLR 1097, HL.
Carlos Federspiel & Co SA v Charles Twigg & Co Ltd [1957] 1 Lloyd's Rep 240.
Chase Manhattan Bank NA v Israel-British Bank (London) Ltd [1979] 3 All ER 1025, [1981] Ch 105, [1980] 2 WLR 202.
Commonwealth of Australia v Verwayen (1990) 95 ALR 321, Aust HC.
Diplock's Estate, Re, Diplock v Wintle [1948] 2 All ER 318, [1948] Ch 465, CA; affd sub nom *Ministry of Health v Simpson* [1950] 2 All ER 1137, [1951] AC 251, HL.
Dublin City Distillery Ltd v Doherty [1914] AC 823, HL.
Eastgate, Re, ex p Ward [1905] 1 KB 465, [1904–7] All ER Rep 890.
Holroyd v Marshall (1862) 10 HL Cas 191, [1861–73] All ER Rep 414, 11 ER 999.
Indian Oil Corp Ltd v Greenstone Shipping SA, The Ypatianna [1987] 3 All ER 893, [1988] QB 345, [1987] 3 WLR 869.
Kayford Ltd, Re [1975] 1 All ER 604, [1975] 1 WLR 279.
Knights v Wiffen (1870) LR 5 QB 660.

Laurie and Morewood v Dudin & Sons [1926] 1 KB 223, [1925] All ER Rep 414, CA.
London Wine Co (Shippers) Ltd, Re [1986] PCC 121.
Mac-Jordan Construction Ltd v Brookmount Erostin Ltd (in receivership) [1992] BCLC 350, CA.
Napier and Ettrick (Lord) v Hunter, Napier and Ettrick (Lord) v R F Kershaw Ltd [1993] 1 All ER 385, [1993] AC 713, [1993] 2 WLR 42, HL.
Neste Oy v Lloyds Bank plc, The Tiiskeri, The Nestegas, The Enskeri [1983] 2 Lloyd's Rep 658.
Roscoe (James) (Bolton) Ltd v Winder [1915] 1 Ch 62.
Savage v Salem Mills Co (1906) 85 Pacific Rep 69
SEC v Chenery Corp 318 US 80, 85-86 (1943)
Sharpe (a bankrupt), Re, ex p the trustee of the bankrupt v Sharpe [1980] 1 All ER 198, [1980] 1 WLR 219.
Simm v Anglo-American Telegraph Co, Anglo-American Telegraph Co v Spurling (1879) 5 QBD 188, CA.
Sinclair v Brougham [1914] AC 398, [1914–15] All ER Rep 622, HL.
South Australian Insurance Co v Randell (1869) LR 3 PC 101.
Space Investments Ltd v Canadian Imperial Bank of Commerce Trust Co (Bahamas) Ltd [1986] 3 All ER 75, [1986] 1 WLR 1072, PC.
Spence v Union Marine Insurance Co Ltd (1868) LR 3 CP 427.
Wait, Re [1927] 1 Ch 606, [1926] All ER Rep 433, CA.
Waltons Stores (Interstate) Ltd v Maher (1988) 164 CLR 387.
Whitehouse v Frost (1810) 12 East 614, 104 ER 239.

Appeal

The appellants, namely (1) Bryan Norreys Kensington and John Joseph Cregten, the receivers of Goldcorp Finance Ltd, and (2) the Bank of New Zealand, appealed from the decision of the New Zealand Court of Appeal (Sir Robin Cooke P and Gault J; McKay J dissenting in part) ([1993] 1 NZLR 257) delivered on 30 April 1992 allowing the appeal of the first and second respondents, namely (1) a class known as 'the non-allocated claimants', and (2) Steven Paul Liggett, from the judgment of Thorp J in the High Court delivered on 17 Octber 1990 in which, on the hearing of an application by the receivers for directions, he dismissed the claims of the first and second respondents but upheld in part the claims of the third respondents, a class known as 'the Walker & Hall claimants' represented by James William Heppleston. The facts are set out in the judgment of the Board.

Jonathan Sumption QC and *Anthony Patterson* (of the New Zealand Bar) (instructed by *Dibb Lupton Broomhead*) for the receivers.
Jonathan Sumption QC and *John Moody* (of the New Zealand Bar) (instructed by *Dibb Lupton Broomhead*) for the bank.
Patrick Finnegan and *Julie Maxton* (both of the New Zealand Bar) (instructed by *Alan Taylor & Co*) for the non-allocated claimants.
David Baragwanath QC, William Akel and *Tracey Walker* (all of the New Zealand Bar) (instructed by *Alan Taylor & Co*) for the second respondent.
David Knight (of the New Zealand Bar) (instructed by *Alan Taylor & Co*) for the third respondent.

25 May 1994. The following judgment of the Board was delivered.

LORD MUSTILL. On 11 July 1988 the Bank of New Zealand Ltd (hereafter 'the bank') caused receivers to be appointed under the terms of a debenture issued by Goldcorp Exchange Ltd (hereafter 'the company'), a dealer in gold and other precious metals. The company was then and still remains hopelessly insolvent. Amongst its assets is a stock of gold, silver and platinum bullion. Even if the company had not been brought down by dealings unconnected with bullion this stock would have been far short of what was needed to satisfy numerous contracts under which members of the public had purchased precious metals for future delivery. The discovery that not only was there a shortfall in available bullion but also that the stock of bullion had been dealt with internally in a manner quite different from what had been promised by the vendors in their promotional literature has aroused great indignation amongst the members of the public (more than one thousand) whose faith in the promises made by the vendors has proved to be misplaced. These feelings were exacerbated when it was realised that the debt secured by the debenture and the floating charge which it created were in excess of the entire assets of the company, including the stocks of bullion, so that if the secured interest of the bank is satisfied in preference to the claims of the purchasers, the latter will receive nothing at all. This has impelled the private investors (hereafter collectively referred to as 'the customers') to assert in the liquidation of the company, not their unanswerable personal claims against the company for damages or for the repayment of sums paid in advance, but claims of a proprietary nature; in the first instance as regards the remaining stock of bullion, and at a later stage of the litigation asserted by reference to the moneys paid under the various purchase contracts, or to a proportion of the company's general assets seen as representing the moneys so paid.

In response, the receivers applied to the High Court under s 345 of the Companies Act 1955 for directions concerning the disposal of the remaining bullion. They have pursued proceedings of great complexity, very skilfully marshalled by Thorp J in such a manner as to enable decisions to be given in principle with regard to various categories of customer and thus to minimise the inevitable cost and delay involved in the investigation of so many and diverse claims. The outcome has been the settlement, or disposal by court decisions against which there is no appeal, of claims by several types of customer. There remain three categories, forming the subject matter of the present appeal. The first and largest category comprises those customers who have come to be known as 'non-allocated claimants'. These were customers who had purchased bullion for future delivery. At the time when the bank's floating charge crystallised upon the appointment of receivers, there had not been any appropriation of specific and segregated parcels of bullion to the individual purchase contracts. The second category of claimant has only one member, namely Mr S P Liggett, whose case resembles that of the non-allocated claimants but has certain additional features upon which he relies to contend that his claim will succeed even if the rights of the non-allocated claimants are subordinated to those of the bank. The third category of claimant consists of those who had made contracts for the purchase of bullion from Walker & Hall Commodities Ltd before the business of that company was acquired by the company in 1986.

In the High Court all the claims were founded on the proposition that the customers had, or must be deemed to have, proprietary interests in bullion which could be traced into the stock remaining on liquidation. Thorp J rejected the claims of the non-allocated claimants and of Mr Liggett (save in one respect which is not directly before the Board), but allowed the claims of the Walker & Hall claimants. In the case of the latter Thorp J limited the amount of the remedy by reference to a question of tracing to which their Lordships must later refer. On appeal, the Court of Appeal ([1993] 1 NZLR 257) agreed with Thorp J in holding that the first two categories of customer had no proprietary rights to the bullion. The scope of the debate was, however, enlarged to embrace a new claim to a proprietary remedy related directly or indirectly to the original payments of price by the customers under the purchase contracts. On this part of the appeal the court was divided in opinion. Sir Robin Cooke P and Gault J found in favour of the non-allocated claimants and Mr Liggett, albeit for reasons which were not identical, and went on to hold that the entire amount of the purchase moneys could be traced into the general assets of the company. McKay J rejected this basis of claim. The position as regards the Walker & Hall claimants was the subject of procedural complications which their Lordships must later describe. The receivers and the bank have appealed to the Board in relation to all three categories of customer.

I. NON-ALLOCATED CLAIMANTS

The facts

Dealings in gold coins and ingots as consumer products are a comparative innovation in New Zealand. In the forefront of developing the market was a predecessor of Goldcorp Exchange Ltd. (Details of the alterations in the management and corporate structure of the concerns which acted as vendors in the transactions giving rise to the present litigation are complex, but they are not material to the issues now before the Board, and it is convenient to refer simply to 'the company').

Although the course of business between the company and the non-allocated claimants was not wholly consistent, and the documents varied somewhat from time to time, the general shape of the business was always as follows. Sales were promoted in various ways, particularly through glossy, illustrated brochures. So far as presently material the brochures offered two methods of purchasing bullion: 'The first is what we call physical delivery and the second is non-allocated metal.' After explaining how purchases of granules, ingots and coins could be made for physical delivery a typical brochure described the procedure for purchasing non-allocated metal, which (it was said) was 'preferred by the majority of investors and ... recognised as the most convenient and safe way of purchasing metal'. According to this brochure:

> 'Basically, you agree to buy metal at the prevailing market rate and a paper transaction takes place. [The company] is responsible for storing and insuring your metal free of charge and you are given a "Non-Allocated invoice" which verifies your ownership of the metal. In the case of gold or silver, physical delivery can be taken upon seven days notice and payment of nominal delivery charges.'

A later version of the brochure said that—

> 'Basically, you agree to buy and sell as with physical bullion, but receive a certificate of ownership rather than the metal. The metal is stored in a vault on your behalf ...

What protection have I that Goldcorp will deliver? The metal stocks of Goldcorp are audited monthly by Peat Marwick, to ensure there are sufficient stocks to meet all commitments.'

If a member of the public decided to make a purchase on the non-allocated basis he or she received a certificate stating:

'This is a certificate for Non-Allocated Metal stored and insured by [the company]. Delivery may be taken within seven days upon payment of delivery charges.'

Later, the certificate was altered so as to read:

'This is to Certify that is the registered holder of **** [quantity] FINE GOLD ****. The above metal is stored and insured *free of charge* by Goldcorp Exchange Ltd on a non-allocated basis. Delivery may be taken upon seven days notice and payment of delivery charges. The owner shall be entitled to the collection of the bullion, or funds from the sale of bullion, only upon presentation of this Certificate.'

In addition to the documentation there were of course preliminary discussions between the customer and the company. Whilst these varied in detail from one occasion to another, the following general description by McKay J was accepted as correct for the purposes of argument ([1993] 1 NZLR 257 at 296–297):

'The wording makes it clear that the investor is not merely depositing money or acquiring a contractual right to be supplied at some later date after giving seven days' notice. The wording describes an actual purchase of gold or silver which will then be stored free of charge and insured by Exchange [i e the company]. Delivery is available on seven days' notice and on payment of a small fee for ingotting. This suggests that although there will be physical bullion held in storage for the investor and insured for him, it will be part of a larger bulk and will require ingotting before he can take delivery of his specific entitlement. In the meantime, he will have an interest, along with other investors, in the bulk which is being held and stored by Exchange for him and for other investors. That certainly was the perception of investors. As the Judge said: "No one could read the claimants' affidavits, still less hear the evidence given by them on cross-examination, without being convinced of the depth and genuineness of their belief that by accepting the invitation to purchase on a non-allocated basis they were not simply buying 'gilt edged investments', but gold itself. The speed and strength of their reaction to advice that Exchange had not stored bullion sufficient to cover their 'bullion certificates' made that plain." In an appendix to his submissions on behalf of the non-allocated claimants Mr Finnigan collected numerous extracts from the affidavits filed on their behalf. These amply support the Judge's finding. They depose to the various statements made to them on behalf of Exchange, all emphasising the absence of security problems, the fact that their bullion would be stored in safe keeping and would be safer than if they took delivery of it, the risks of storing bullion at one's own home, and the safety and security offered by storage with Exchange. Verbal assurances were also given that not only was the bullion insured, but the metal stocks were audited monthly by a large and respected firm of chartered accountants. Some deponents relied particularly on this factor as a guarantee that there would always be sufficient bullion to cover all the certificates issued by Exchange as was indicated in its brochures. Others refer to correspondence with Exchange which reinforced their belief that their metal was physically stored in vaults on their behalf. A number of investors received letters in connection with Exchange's audit asking them to confirm "the amount of non-allocated bullion we hold on your behalf as at 31 March" ... Exchange's evidence as to what investors were told is more consistent with Exchange's brochures and with the evidence of investors. Mr Campbell, who was bullion manager from January 1984 until the receivership, said at para 7.2 that it was invariably explained to the non-allocated investors that the bullion purchased "was not set aside as that person's metal, but instead was stored as part of the company's overall stock of bullion", that "the bullion was stored and insured by the company", and as to safe keeping that "they would not have to worry about security problems of storing the bullion in their own homes". This suggests that the bullion would be stored in bulk rather than on an allocated basis, but that it would be physically stored and held safely for the investor.'

II. THE ISSUES

As already seen, by the time the judgment in the Court of Appeal had been delivered the proprietary claims of the customers had been widened to comprise not only bullion but also the general assets of the company, to an extent representing the sums originally paid by way of purchase price. The following issues now arise for consideration.

(i) Did the property in any bullion pass to the customers immediately upon the making of the purchases (a) simply by virtue of contract of purchase itself, or (b) by virtue of the written and oral statements made in the brochures and by the company's employees? (Although these were referred to in argument as representations their Lordships believe them to be more in the nature of contractual undertakings, and therefore call them 'the collateral promises').

(ii) Did the property in any bullion subsequently acquired by the company pass to the customer upon acquisition?

(iii) When the customers paid over the purchase moneys under the contract of sale did they retain a beneficial interest in them by virtue of an express or constructive trust?

(iv) Should the court now grant a restitutionary remedy of a proprietary character in respect of the purchase moneys?

If the answer to any of these questions is in the affirmative it will be necessary to consider the extent to which the customer's rights in the relevant subject matter can be applied to the bullion or other assets now in the possession of the company.

III. TITLE TO BULLION: THE SALE CONTRACTS

Their Lordships begin with the question whether the customer obtained any form of proprietary interest, legal or equitable, simply by virtue of the contract of sale, independently of the collateral promises. In the opinion of their Lordships the answer is so clearly that he did not that it would be possible simply to quote s 18 of the Sale of Goods Act 1908 (New Zealand) (corresponding to s 16 of the Sale of Goods Act 1893 (UK)) and one reported case, and turn to more difficult issues. It is, however, convenient to pause for a moment to consider why the answer must inevitably be negative, because the reasons for this answer are the same as those which stand in the way of the customers at every point of the case.

It is common ground that the contracts in question were for the sale of unascertained goods. For present purposes, two species of unascertained goods may be distinguished. First, there are 'generic goods'. These are sold on terms which preserve the seller's freedom to decide for himself how and from what source he will obtain goods answering the contractual description. Secondly, there are 'goods sold ex-bulk'. By this expression their Lordships denote goods which are by express stipulation to be supplied from a fixed and a pre-determined source, from within which the seller may make his own choice (unless the contract requires it to be made in some other way) but outside which he may not go. For example, 'I sell you 60 of the 100 sheep now on my farm'.

Approaching these situations a priori common sense dictates that the buyer cannot acquire title until it is known to what goods the title relates. Whether the property then passes will depend upon the intention of the parties and in particular on whether there has been a consensual appropriation of particular goods to the contract. On the latter question the law is not straightforward, and if it had been decisive of the present appeal it would have been necessary to examine cases such as *Carlos Federspiel & Co SA v Charles Twigg & Co Ltd* [1957] 1 Lloyd's Rep 240 and other cases cited in argument. In fact, however, the case turns not on appropriation but on ascertainment, and on the latter the law has never been in doubt. It makes no difference what the parties intended if what they intend is impossible: as is the case with an immediate transfer of title to goods whose identity is not yet known. As Lord Blackburn wrote in his *Treatise on the Effect of the Contract of Sale* (1st edn, 1845), pp 122–123, a principal inspiration of the Sale of Goods Act 1893:

> 'The first of [the rules] that the parties must be agreed as to the specific goods on which the contract is to attach before there can be a bargain and sale, is one that is founded on the very nature of things. Till the parties are agreed on the specific individual goods, the contract can be no more than a contract to supply goods answering a particular description, and since the vendor would fulfil his part of the contract by furnishing any parcel of goods answering that description, and the purchaser could not object to them if they did answer the description, it is clear there can be no intention to transfer the property in any particular lot of goods more than another, till it is ascertained which are the very goods sold. This rule has existed at all times; it is to be found in the earliest English law books ... It makes no difference, although the goods are so far ascertained that the parties have agreed that they shall be taken from some specified larger stock. In such a case the reason still applies: the parties did not intend to transfer the property in one portion of the stock more than in another, and the law which only gives effect to their intention, does not transfer the property in any individual portion.'

Their Lordships have laboured this point, about which there has been no dispute, simply to show that any attempt by the non-allocated claimants to assert that a legal title passed by virtue of the sale would have been defeated, not by some arid legal technicality but by what Lord Blackburn called 'the very nature of things'. The same conclusion applies, and for the same reason, to any argument that a title in equity was created by the sale, taken in isolation from the collateral promises. It is unnecessary to examine in detail the decision of the

Court of Appeal in *ReWait* [1927] 1 Ch 606, [1926] All ER Rep 433 for the facts were crucially different. There, the contract was for a sale ex-bulk. The 500 tons in question formed part of a larger quantity shipped on board a named vessel; the seller could supply from no other source; and once the entire quantity had been landed and warehoused the buyer could point to the bulk and say that his goods were definitely there, although he could not tell which part they were. It was this feature which prompted the dissenting opinion of Sargant LJ that the sub-purchasers had a sufficient partial equitable interest in the whole to found a claim for measuring-out and delivery of 500 tons. No such feature exists here. Nevertheless, the reasoning contained in the judgment of Atkin LJ ([1927] 1 Ch 606 at 625–641, [1926] All ER Rep 433 at 441–448), which their Lordships venture to find irresistible, points unequivocally to the conclusion that under a simple contract for the sale of unascertained goods no equitable title can pass merely by virtue of the sale.

This is not, of course, the end of the matter. As Atkin LJ himself acknowledged ([1927] 1 Ch 606 at 636, [1926] All ER Rep 433 at 446):

'[The rules in the statute] have, of course, no relevance when one is considering rights, legal or equitable, which may come into existence dehors the contract for sale. A seller or a purchaser may, of course, create any equity he pleases by way of charge, equitable assignment or any other dealing with or disposition of goods, the subject-matter of sale; and he may, of course, create such an equity as one of the terms expressed in the contract of sale.'

Their Lordships therefore turn to consider whether there is anything in the collateral promises which enables the customers to overcome the practical objections to an immediate transfer of title. The most direct route would be to treat the collateral promises as containing a declaration of trust by the company in favour of the customer. The question then immediately arises: what was the subject matter of the trust? The only possible answer, so far as concerns an immediate transfer of title on sale, is that the trust related to the company's current stock of bullion answering the contractual description; for there was no other bullion to which the trust could relate. Their Lordships do not doubt that the vendor of goods sold ex-bulk can effectively declare himself trustee of the bulk in favour of the buyer, so as to confer pro tanto an equitable title. But the present transaction was not of this type. The company cannot have intended to create an interest in its general stock of gold which would have inhibited any dealings with it otherwise than for the purpose of delivery under the non-allocated sale contracts. Conversely the customer, who is presumed to have intended that somewhere in the bullion held by or on behalf of the company there would be stored a quantity representing 'his' bullion, cannot have contemplated that his rights would be fixed by reference to a combination of the quantity of bullion of the relevant description which the company happened to have in stock at the relevant time and the number of purchasers who happened to have open contracts at that time for goods of that description. To understand the transaction in this way would be to make it a sale of bullion ex-bulk, which on the documents and findings of fact it plainly was not.

Nor is the argument improved by reshaping the trust, so as to contemplate that the property in the res vendita did pass to the customer, albeit in the absence of delivery, and then merged in a general equitable title to the pooled stock of bullion. Once again the argument contradicts the transaction. The customer purchased for the physical delivery on demand of the precise quantity of bullion fixed by his contract, not a shifting proportion of a shifting bulk, prior to delivery. It is of course true that a vendor may agree to retain physical possession of the goods on behalf of his purchaser after the sale has been completed, and that there may be a constructive delivery and redelivery of possession, so as to transform the vendor into a bailee or pledgee without the goods actually changing hands: see per Lord Atkinson in *Dublin City Distillery Ltd v Doherty* [1914] AC 823 at 844. Lord Atkinson was there contemplating a situation, such as existed in the *Dublin City* case itself, where the goods held in the warehouse were already identified (by numbers on the casks: see at 825), so that the contract was one for the sale of specific goods under which the property would pass at once to the vendee. The case is, however, quite different where the sale is of generic goods. Even if the present contract had been a sale ex-bulk, in the sense that the contractual source was the bulk of bullion in the store, s 18 of the 1908 Act would have prevented the property from passing on sale: see *Laurie and Morewood v Dudin & Sons* [1926] 1 KB 223, [1925] All ER Rep 414 and *Whitehouse v Frost* (1810) 12 East 614, 104 ER 239. The present case is even more clear, since the customers contracted to purchase generic goods without any stipulation as to their source.

The next group of arguments for the non-allocated claimants all turn on an estoppel, said to derive from the collateral promises. Their Lordships derive no assistance from cases such as *Waltons Stores (Interstate) Ltd v Maher* (1988) 164 CLR 387 and *Commonwealth of Australia v Verwayen* (1990) 95 ALR 321 which show that on occasion a party may estop himself from relying on the protection of the statute. No such estoppel could assist the customers here, for the problem facing them at every turn is not s 18, but the practical reality underlying it which Lord Blackburn called 'the very nature of things': namely that it is impossible to have a title to goods, when nobody knows to which goods the title relate. The same objection rules out reliance on cases such as *Re Sharpe (a bankrupt), ex p the trustee of the bankrupt v Sharpe* [1980] 1 All ER 198, [1980] 1 WLR 219 concerning what is called a proprietary estoppel.

A more plausible version of the argument posits that the company, having represented to its customers that they had title to bullion held in the vaults, cannot now be heard to say that they did not. At first sight this argument gains support from a small group of cases, of which *Knights v Wiffen* (1870) LR 5 QB 660 is the most prominent. Wiffen had a large quantity of barley lying in sacks in his granary, close to a railway station. He agreed to sell 80 quarters of this barley to Maris, without appropriating any particular sacks. Maris sold 60 quarters to Knights, who paid for them and received in exchange a document signed by Maris addressed to the station master, directing him to deliver 60 quarters of barley. This was shown by the station master to Wiffen who told him that when he got the forwarding note the barley would be put on the line. Knights gave a forwarding note to the station master for 60 quarters of barley. Maris became bankrupt, and Wiffen, as unpaid vendor, refused to part with the barley. Knights sued Wiffen in trover, to which Wiffen pleaded that the barley was not the property of the plaintiff. A very strong Court of Queen's Bench found in favour of the plaintiff. Blackburn J explained the matter thus (at 665–666):

'No doubt the law is that until an appropriation from a bulk is made, so that the vendor has said what portion belongs to him and what portion belongs to the buyer, the goods remain in solido, and no property passes. But can Wiffen here be permitted to say, "I never set aside any quarters?" ...

The defendant knew that, when he assented to the delivery order, the plaintiff, as a reasonable man, would rest satisfied ... The plaintiff may well say, "I abstained from active measures in consequence of your statement, and I am entitled to hold you precluded from denying that what you stated was true."'

There may perhaps be a shadow over this decision, notwithstanding the high authority of the court: see the observations of Brett LJ in *Simm v Anglo-American Telegraph Co, Anglo-American Telegraph Co v Spurling* (1879) 5 QBD 188 at 212. Assuming that the decision was nevertheless correct the question is whether it applies to the present case. Their Lordships consider that, notwithstanding the apparent similarities, it does not. The agreement for sale in *Knights v Wiffen* was a sale ex-bulk, or at least it must have been seen as such, for otherwise Blackburn J's judgment would have contradicted his treatise in the passage above quoted.

On this view, the bulk was the whole of the stock in Wiffen's warehouse. This stock was therefore committed to the purchase to the extent that Wiffen could not properly have sold the whole of it without making delivery of part to his buyer. Another and more important aspect of the same point is that the bulk actually existed. The effect of Wiffen's representation was to preclude him from denying to the sub-purchaser, Knights, that he had made a sufficient appropriation from the fixed and identified bulk to give the intermediate purchaser, and hence Knights himself, the proprietary interest sufficient to found a claim in trover. The present case is quite different, for there was no existing bulk and therefore nothing from which a title could be carved out by a deemed appropriation. The reasoning of *Knights v Wiffen* does not enable a bulk to be conjured into existence for this purpose simply through the chance that the vendor happens to have some goods answering the description of the res vendita in its trading stock at the time of the sale—quite apart, of course, from the fact that if all the purchasers obtained a deemed title by estoppel there would not be enough bullion to go around.

All this aside, there is another reason why the argument founded on estoppel cannot prevail. The answer is given by Mellor J in *Knights v Wiffen* itself, where quoting from *Blackburn's Contract of Sale* p 162–163, he says (LR 5 QB 660 at 666–667):

'This is a rule [ie the estoppel], which within the limits applied by law is of great equity; for when parties have agreed to act upon an assumed state of facts their rights between themselves are justly made to depend on the conventional state of facts, and not on the truth. The reason of the rule ceases at once when a stranger to the arrangement seeks to avail himself of the statements which were not made as a basis for him to act upon. They are for a stranger, evidence against the party making the statement, but no more than evidence which may be rebutted; between the parties they form an estoppel in law.'

Later, Brett LJ was to observe in *Simm v Anglo-American Telegraph Co* (1879) 5 QBD 188 at 206–207:

'... it seems to me that an estoppel gives no title to that which is the subject-matter of estoppel. The estoppel assumes that the reality is contrary to that which the person is estopped from denying, and the estoppel has no effect at all upon the reality of the circumstances ... a person may be estopped from denying that certain goods belong to another; he may be compelled by a suit in the nature of an action of trover to deliver them up, if he has them in his possession and under his control; but if the goods, in respect of which he has estopped himself, really belong to someone else, it seems impossible to suppose that ... he can be compelled to deliver over another's goods to the person in whose favour the estoppel exists against him ... that person cannot recover the goods, because no property has really passed to him, he can recover only damages. In my view estoppel ... only creates a cause of action between the person in whose favour the estoppel exists and the person who is estopped.'

Similar statements can be found in several texts, such as for example Palmer *Bailment* (2nd edn, 1991), p 1374.

To this the customers respond that they are not obliged to assert the same proprietary interest against the bank as they would do if their opponents were strangers to the entire relationship. By taking a floating rather than an immediate fixed charge the bank accepted the risk of adverse dealings by the company with its assets, and when the charge crystallised the bank 'stood in the shoes' of the company, taking those assets with all the detrimental features which the company had attached to them. If the estoppel binds the company, then it must bind the bank as well.

Attractive as this argument has been made to seem, their Lordships cannot accept it. The chargee does not become on the crystallisation of the charge the universal successor of the chargor, in the same way as the trustee in bankruptcy or personal representative, who is as much subject to the personal claims of third parties against the insolvent as he is entitled to the benefit of personal claims of which the insolvent is the obligee. Rather, the chargee becomes entitled to a proprietary interest which he asserts adversely to the company, personified by the liquidator and all those general creditors who share in the assets of the company. The freedom of the chargor to deal with its assets pending the crystallisation of the charge does not entail that the chargee's right to the assets is circumscribed by an indebtedness of a purely personal nature. The most that the *Knights v Wiffen* line of authority can give to the purchaser is the pretence of a title where no title exists. Valuable as it may be where one party to the estoppel asserts as against the other a proprietary cause of action such as trover, this cannot avail the purchaser in a contest with a third-party creditor possessing a real proprietary interest in a real subject matter, whereas the purchaser has no more than a pretence of a title to a subject matter which does not actually exist.

Similar obstacles stand in the way of a more elaborate version of the same argument. This seeks to combine two principles: the first that a person who represents (by attornment or otherwise) that he has goods in his possession which he holds for a third party is in certain circumstances precluded from denying to that third party that he does so possess and hold the goods even if in fact he does not; the second that a bailee of goods is precluded, as against the bailor, from denying that the bailor has a good title. The result is said to be that by acknowledging itself to be a bailee the company gave its customers a good title to that which they had agreed to purchase. Whilst acknowledging the ingenuity of this argument their Lordships are unable to accept it. If correct, it would entail that a customer, who chose to bring a proprietary action (such as trover, under the former law) rather than simply claiming damages for non-delivery would be entitled to an order for delivery-up of the goods which he had purchased. But which goods? Not a portion of the goods in store, for there was no representation and the customers cannot have believed that it was from these goods alone that by a process of separation their own orders would be fulfilled. And if not these goods, there were no others to which the title could attach since the source of supply was completely at large.

Their Lordships must also reject a further variant of the argument, whereby a trust in respect of bullion came into existence as an aspect of a bailment, so that even if title stricto sensu did not pass nevertheless the fruits of the breach of trust may be traced into the existing stock of bullion. In other circumstances it might be necessary to look more closely at those elements of the argument which seek to attach the characteristics of a trust to a relationship of bailment, which does not ordinarily have this character, and also at the feasibility of tracing. There is no need for this, however, since there was never any bailment, and no identifiable property to which any trust could attach.

IV. TITLE TO AFTER-ACQUIRED BULLION

Having for these reasons rejected the submission that the non-allocated claimants acquired an immediate title by reason of the contract of sale and the collateral promises their Lordships turn to the question whether the claimants later achieved a proprietary interest when the company purchased bullion and put it into its own stock. Broadly speaking, there are two forms which such an argument might take.

According to the first, the contracts of sale were agreements for the sale of goods afterwards to be acquired. It might be contended that quite independently of any representation made by the company to the non-allocated claimants, as soon as the company acquired bullion answering the contractual description the purchaser achieved an equitable title, even though the passing of legal title was postponed until the goods were ascertained and appropriated at the time of physical delivery to the purchaser. In the event this argument was not separately pursued, and their Lordships mention it only by way of introduction. They will do so briefly, since it was bound to fail. The line of old cases, founded on *Holroyd v Marshall* (1862) 10 HLCas 191, [1861–73] All ER Rep 414 and discussed in *Benjamin's Sale of Goods* (3rd edn, 1987), pp 80, 218–219, paras 106, 357 which might be said to support it, was concerned with situations where the goods upon acquisition could be unequivocally identified with the individual contract relied upon. As Lord Hanworth MR demonstrated in *Re Wait*, the reasoning of these cases cannot be transferred to a situation like the present where there was no means of knowing to which, if any, of the non-allocated sales a particular purchase by the company was related. Since this objection on its own is fatal, there is no need to discuss the other obstacles which stand in its way.

The second category of argument asserts, in a variety of forms, that the collateral promises operated to impress on the bullion, as and when it was acquired by the company, a trust in favour of each purchaser. Before looking at the arguments in detail it is necessary to mention a problem which is very little discussed in the judgments and arguments. It will be seen that the analysis to date has involved two markedly different assumptions. The first relates to the expectation of the customer in the light of the collateral promises. The customer is assumed to have believed that it would make no difference whether he took immediate delivery of the bullion and put it in a bank, or left it with the company—except that in the latter case he would avoid the trouble, risk and expense of storage. In law this expectation could be fulfilled only by a system under which the company obtained bullion either by an outside purchase or by transfer from its own stock, and immediately stored it separately in the name of the customer, leaving it untouched until the moment of delivery or re-purchase. The second assumption relates to the obligations which the company actually undertook. It has not been suggested that this matched the customer's expectation, for there is nothing in the collateral promises, either written or oral, entitling the customer to separate and individual appropriation of goods. Instead, as shown by the passage already quoted from the judgment of McKay J, the arguments proceed on the basis that the company promised to maintain bullion, separate from its own trading stock, which would in some way stand as security, or reassurance, that the bullion would be available when the customer called for delivery. But what kind of security or reassurance? If the scheme had contemplated that, properly performed, it would have brought about a transfer of title to the individual customer before that customer's appropriated bullion was mixed in the undifferentiated bulk, analogies could have been drawn with decisions such as *Spence v Union Marine Insurance Co Ltd* (1868) LR 3 CP 427, *South Australian Insurance Co v Randell* (1869) LR 3 PC 101, *Indian Oil Corp Ltd v Greenstone Shipping SA, The Ypatianna* [1987] 3 All ER 893, [1988] QB 345 and the United States silo cases of which *Savage v Salem Mills Co* (1906) 85 Pacific Rep 69 is an example. Since, however, even if the company had performed its obligations to the full there would have been no transfer of title to the purchaser before admixture, these cases are not in point. The only remaining alternative, consistently with the scheme being designed to give the customer any title at all before delivery, is that the company through the medium of the collateral promises had declared itself a trustee of the constantly changing undifferentiated bulk of bullion which should have been set aside to back the customers' contracts. Such a trust might well be feasible in theory, but their Lordships find it hard to reconcile with the practicalities of the scheme, for it would seem to involve that the separated bulk would become the source from which alone the sale contracts were to be supplied: whereas, as already observed, it is impossible to read the collateral promises as creating a sale ex-bulk.

This being so, whilst it is easy to see how the company's failure to perform the collateral obligations has fuelled the indignation created by its failure to deliver the bullion under the sales to non-allocated purchasers, their Lordships are far from convinced that this particular breach has in fact made any difference.

Let it be assumed, however, as did McKay J in his dissenting judgment, that the creation of a separate and sufficient stock would have given the non-allocated purchasers some kind of proprietary interest, the fact remains that the separate and sufficient stock did not exist.

The customers' first response to this objection is that even if the concept of an immediate trust derived from a bailment arising at the time of the original transactions cannot be sustained, the collateral promises created a potential or incomplete or (as it was called in argument) 'floating' bailment, which hovered above the continuing relationship between each purchaser and the company, until the company bought and took delivery of bullion corresponding to the claimant's contract, whereupon the company became bailee of the bullion on terms which involved a trust in favour of the purchaser. Their Lordships find it impossible to see how this ingenious notion, even if feasible in principle, could be put into practice here, given that the body of potential beneficiaries was constantly changing as some purchasers called for and took delivery whilst others came newly on the scene, at the same time as the pool of available bullion waxed and waned (sometimes to zero as regards some types of bullion) with fresh deliveries and acquisitions. Even if this is left aside, the concept simply does not fit the facts. True, there is no difficulty with a transaction whereby B promises A that if in the future goods belonging to A come within the physical control of B he will hold them as bailee for A on terms fixed in advance by the agreement. But this has nothing to do with a trust relationship, and it has nothing to do with the present case, since in the example given A has both title to the goods and actual or constructive possession of them before their receipt by B, whereas in the present case the non-allocated claimants had neither. The only escape would be to suggest that every time the company took delivery of bullion of a particular description all the purchasers from the company of the relevant kind of bullion acquired both a higher possessory right than the company (for such would be essential if the company was to be a bailee) and a title to the goods, via some species of estoppel derived from this notional transfer and re-transfer of possession. Their Lordships find it impossible to construct such a contorted legal relationship from the contracts of sale and the collateral promises.

Next, the claimants put forward an argument in two stages. First, it is said that because the company held itself out as willing to vest bullion in the customer and to hold it in safe custody on behalf of him in circumstances where he was totally dependent on the company, and trusted the company to do what it had promised without in practice there being any means of verification, the company was a fiduciary. From this it is deduced that the company as fiduciary created an equity by inviting the customer to look on and treat stocks vested in it as his own, which could appropriately be recognised only by treating the customer as entitled to a proprietary interest in the stock.

To describe someone as a fiduciary, without more, is meaningless. As Frankfurter J said in *SEC v Chenery Corp* (1943) 318 US 80 at 85–86 cited in *Goff and Jones, The Law of Restitution* (4th edn, 1993) p 644:

'To say that a man is a fiduciary only begins analysis; it gives direction to further inquiry. To whom is he a fiduciary? What obligations does he owe as a fiduciary? In what respect has he failed to discharge these obligations? And what are the consequences of his deviation from duty?'

Here, the argument assumes that the person towards whom the company was fiduciary was the non-allocated claimant. But what kind of fiduciary duties did the company owe to the customer? None have been suggested beyond those which the company assumed under the contracts of sale read with the collateral promises; namely to deliver the goods and meanwhile to keep a separate stock of bullion (or, more accurately, separate stocks of each variety of bullion) to which the customers could look as a safeguard for performance when delivery was called for. No doubt the fact that one person is placed in a particular position vis-à-vis another through the medium of a contract does not necessarily mean that he does not also owe fiduciary duties to that other by virtue of being in that position. But the essence of a fiduciary relationship is that it creates obligations of a different character from those deriving from the contract itself. Their Lordships have not heard in argument any submission which went beyond suggesting that by virtue of being a fiduciary the company was obliged honestly and conscientiously to do what it had by contract promised to do. Many commercial relationships involve just such a reliance by one party on the other, and to introduce the whole new dimension into such relationships which would flow from giving them a fiduciary character would (as it seems to their

Lordships) have adverse consequences far exceeding those foreseen by Atkin LJ in *Re Wait*. It is possible without misuse of language to say that the customers put faith in the company, and that their trust has not been repaid. But the vocabulary is misleading; high expectations do not necessarily lead to equitable remedies.

Let it be assumed, however, that the company could properly be described as a fiduciary and let it also be assumed that notwithstanding the doubts expressed above the non-allocated claimants would have achieved some kind of proprietary interest if the company had done what it said. This still leaves the problem, to which their Lordships can see no answer, that the company did not do what it said. There never was a separate and sufficient stock of bullion in which a proprietary interest could be created. What the non-allocated claimants are really trying to achieve is to attach the proprietary interest, which they maintain should have been created on the non-existent stock, to wholly different assets. It is understandable that the claimants, having been badly let down in a transaction concerning bullion should believe that they must have rights over whatever bullion the company still happens to possess. Whilst sympathising with this notion their Lordships must reject it, for the remaining stock, having never been separated, is just another asset of the company, like its vehicles and office furniture. If the argument applies to the bullion it must apply to the latter as well, an obviously unsustainable idea.

Finally, it is argued that the court should declare in favour of the claimants a remedial constructive trust, or, to use another name, a restitutionary proprietary interest, over the bullion in the company's vaults. Such a trust or interest would differ fundamentally from those so far discussed, in that it would not arise directly from the transaction between the individual claimants, the company and the bullion, but would be created by the court as a measure of justice after the event. Their Lordships must return to this topic later when considering the Walker & Hall claimants who, the trial judge has held, did acquire a proprietary interest in some bullion, but they are unable to understand how the doctrine in any of its suggested formulations could apply to the facts of the present case. By leaving its stock of bullion in a non-differentiated state the company did not unjustly enrich itself by mixing its own bullion with that of the purchasers: for all the gold belonged to the company. It did not act wrongfully in acquiring, maintaining and using its own stock of bullion, since there was no term of the sale contracts or of the collateral promises, and none could possibly be implied, requiring that all bullion purchased by the company should be set aside to fulfil the unallocated sales. The conduct of the company was wrongful in the sense of being a breach of contract, but it did not involve any injurious dealing with the subject matter of the alleged trust. Nor, if some wider equitable principle is involved, does the case become any stronger. As previously remarked the claimants' argument really comes to this, that because the company broke its contract in a way which had to do with bullion the court should call into existence a proprietary interest in whatever bullion happened to be in the possession and ownership of the company at the time when the competition between the non-allocated claimants and the other secured and unsecured creditors first arose. The company's stock of bullion had no connection with the claimants' purchases, and to enable the claimants to reach out and not only abstract it from the assets available to the body of creditors as a whole, but also to afford a priority over a secured creditor, would give them an adventitious benefit devoid of the foundation in logic and justice which underlies this important new branch of the law.

V. CONCLUSION ON PROPERTY IN BULLION

For these reasons their Lordships reject, in company with all the judges in New Zealand, the grounds upon which it is said that the customers acquired a proprietary interest in bullion. In the light of the importance understandably attached to this dispute in the courts of New Zealand, and the careful and well-researched arguments addressed on this appeal, the Board has thought it right to approach the question afresh in some little detail. The question is not, however, novel since it has been discussed in two English authorities very close to the point.

The first is the judgment of Oliver J in *Re London Wine Co (Shippers) Ltd* [1986] PCC 121. The facts of that case were not precisely the same as the present, and the arguments on the present appeal have been more far-reaching than were there deployed. Nevertheless their Lordships are greatly fortified in their opinion by the close analysis of the authorities and the principles by Oliver J, and in other circumstances their Lordships would have been content to do little more than summarise it and express their entire agreement. So also with the judgment delivered by Scott LJ in *Mac-Jordan Construction Ltd v Brookmount Erostin Ltd (in receivership)* [1992] BCLC 350 which is mentioned by Gault J ([1993] 1 NZLR 257 at 284), but not discussed since it was not then reported in full. This was a stronger case than the present, because the separate fund which the contract required the insolvent company to maintain would have been impressed with a trust in favour of the other party, if in fact it had been maintained and also because the floating charge which, as the Court of Appeal held, took priority over the contractual claim, expressly referred to the contract under which the claim arose. Once again, their Lordships are fortified in their conclusion by the fact that the reasoning of Scott LJ conforms entirely with the opinion at which they have independently arrived.

VI. PROPRIETARY INTERESTS DERIVED FROM THE PURCHASE PRICE

Their Lordships now turn to the proposition, which first emerged during argument in the Court of Appeal, and which was not raised in the *London Wine* case, that a proprietary interest either sprang into existence on the sales to customers, or should now be imposed retrospectively through restitutionary remedies, in relation not to bullion but to the moneys originally paid by the customers under the contracts of sale. Here at least it is possible to pin down the subject matter to which the proprietary rights are said to relate. Nevertheless, their Lordships are constrained to reject all the various ways in which the submission has been presented, once again for a single comparatively simple reason.

The first argument posits that the purchase moneys were from the outset impressed with a trust in favour of the payers. That a sum of money paid by the purchaser under a contract for the sale of goods is capable in principle of being the subject of a trust in the hands of the vendor is clear. For this purpose it is necessary to show either a mutual intention that the moneys should not fall within the general fund of the company's assets but should be applied for a special designated purpose, or that having originally been paid over without restriction the recipient has later constituted himself a trustee of the money: see *Barclays Bank Ltd v Quistclose Investments Ltd* [1968] 3 All ER 651 at 656, [1970] AC

567 at 581–582. This requirement was satisfied in *Re Kayford Ltd* [1975] 1 All ER 604, [1975] 1 WLR 279 where a company in financial difficulties paid into a separate deposit account money received from customers for goods not yet delivered, with the intention of making withdrawals from the account only as and when delivery was effected, and of refunding the payment to customers if an insolvency made delivery impossible. The facts of the present case are, however, inconsistent with any such trust. This is not a situation where the customer engaged the company as agent to purchase bullion on his or her behalf, with immediate payment to put the agent in funds, delivery being postponed to suit the customer's convenience. The agreement was for a sale by the company to, and not the purchase by the company for, the customer. The latter paid the purchase price for one purpose alone, namely to perform his side of the bargain under which he would in due course be entitled to obtain delivery. True, another part of the consideration for the payment was the collateral promise to maintain separate cover, but this does not mean that the money was paid for the purpose of purchasing gold, either to create the separate stock or for any other reason. There was nothing in the express agreement to require, and nothing in their Lordships' view can be implied, which constrained in any way the company's freedom to spend the purchase money as it chose, or to establish the stock from any source and with any funds as it thought fit. This being so, their Lordships cannot concur in the decision of Cooke P that the purchase price was impressed with a continuing beneficial interest in favour of the customer, which could form the starting point for a tracing of the purchase moneys into other assets.

The same insuperable obstacle stands in the way of the alternative submission that the company was a fiduciary. If one asks the inevitable first question—what was the content of the fiduciary's duty?—the claimants are forced to assert that the duty was to expend the moneys in the purchase and maintenance of the reserved stock. Yet this is precisely the obligation which, as just stated, cannot be extracted from anything express or implied in the contract of sale and the collateral promises. In truth, the argument that the company was a fiduciary (as regards the money rather than the bullion) is no more than another label for the argument in favour of an express trust and must fail for the same reason.

Thus far, all the arguments discussed have assumed that each contract of sale and collateral promises together created a valid and effective transaction coupling the ordinary mutual obligations of an agreement for the sale of goods with special obligations stemming from a trust or fiduciary relationship. These arguments posit that the obligations remain in force, albeit unperformed, the claimants' object being to enforce them. The next group of arguments starts with the contrary proposition that the transactions were rendered ineffectual by the presence of one or more of three vitiating factors: namely, misrepresentation, mistake and total failure of consideration. To these their Lordships now turn.

It is important at the outset to distinguish between three different ways in which the existence of a misrepresentation, a mistake or a total failure of consideration might lead to the existence of a proprietary interest in the purchase money or its fruits superior to that of the bank.

(1) The existence of one or more of these vitiating factors distinguished the relationship from that of an ordinary vendor and purchaser, so as to leave behind with the customer a beneficial interest in the purchase moneys which would otherwise have passed to the company when the money was paid. This interest

remained with the customer throughout everything that followed, and can now be enforced against the general assets of the company, including the bullion, in priority to the interest of the bank.

(2) Even if the full legal and beneficial interest in the purchase moneys passed when they were paid over, the vitiating factors affected the contract in such a way as to re-vest the moneys in the purchaser, and, what is more, to do so in a way which attached to the moneys an interest superior to that of the bank.

(3) In contrast to the routes just mentioned, where the judgment of the court would do no more than recognise the existence of proprietary rights already in existence, the court should by its judgment create a new proprietary interest, superior to that of the bank, to reflect the justice of the case.

With these different mechanisms in view, their Lordships turn to the vitiating factors relied upon. As to the misrepresentations these were presumably that (in fact) the company intended to carry out the collateral promise to establish a separate stock and also that (in law) if this promise was performed the customer would obtain a title to bullion. Whether the proprietary interests said to derive from this misrepresentation were retained by the customers from the moment when they paid over the purchase moneys, or whether they arose at a later date, was not made clear in argument. If the former, their Lordships can only say that they are unable to grasp the reasoning for, if correct, the argument would entail that even in respect of those contracts which the company ultimately fulfilled by delivery the moneys were pro tempore subject to a trust which would have prevented the company from lawfully treating them as its own. This cannot be right. As an alternative it may be contended that a trust arose upon the collapse of the company and the consequent non-fulfilment of the contracts. This contention must also be rejected, for two reasons. First, any such proprietary right must have as its starting point a personal claim by the purchaser to the return of the price. No such claim could exist for so long as the sale contract remained in existence and was being enforced by the customer. That is the position here. The customers have never rescinded the contracts of sale, but have throughout the proceedings asserted various forms of proprietary interest in the bullion, all of them derived in one way or another from the contracts of sale. This stance is wholly inconsistent with the notion that the contracts were and are so ineffectual that the customers are entitled to get their money back. As a last resort the non-allocated claimants invited the Board to treat the contracts as rescinded if their claims for a proprietary interest in bullion were rejected. There is however no mechanism which would permit the claimants to pause, as it were, half-way through the delivery of the present judgment and elect at last to rescind; and even if such a course were open, the remedies arising on rescission would come too late to affect the secured rights of the bank under its previously crystallised floating charge.

Furthermore, even if this fatal objection could be overcome, the argument would, in their Lordships' opinion, be bound to fail. Whilst it is convenient to speak of the customers 'getting their money back' this expression is misleading. Upon payment by the customers the purchase moneys became, and rescission or no rescission remained, the unencumbered property of the company. What the customers would recover on rescission would not be 'their' money, but an equivalent sum. Leaving aside for the moment the creation by the court of a new remedial proprietary right, to which totally different considerations would apply, the claimants would have to contend that in every case where a purchaser is misled into buying goods he is automatically entitled upon rescinding the contract to a proprietary right superior to those of all the vendor's other creditors, exercisable against the whole of the vendor's assets. It is not surprising that no authority could be cited for such an extreme proposition. The only possible exception is *Re Eastgate, ex p Ward* [1905] 1 KB 465, [1904–7] All ER Rep 890. Their Lordships doubt whether, correctly understood, the case so decides, but if it does they decline to follow it.

Similar objections apply to the second variant, which was only lightly touched upon in argument: namely, that the purchase moneys were paid under a mistake. Assuming the mistake to be that the collateral promises would be performed and would yield a proprietary right, what effect would they have on the contracts? Obviously not to make them void ab initio, for otherwise it would mean that the customers had no right to insist on delivery. Perhaps the mistake would have entitled the customers to have the agreements set aside at common law or under statute, and upon this happening they would no doubt have been entitled to a personal restitutionary remedy in respect of the price. This does not, however, advance their case. The moneys were paid by the customers to the company because they believed that they were bound to pay them; and in this belief they were entirely right. The situation is entirely different from *Chase Manhattan Bank NA v Israel-British Bank (London) Ltd* [1979] 3 All ER 1025, [1981] Ch 105, to which much attention was given in the Court of Appeal and in argument before the Board. It may be—their Lordships express no opinion upon it—that the *Chase Manhattan* case correctly decided that where one party mistakenly makes the same payment twice it retains a proprietary interest in the second payment which (if tracing is practicable) can be enforced against the payees' assets in a liquidation ahead of unsecured creditors. But in the present case, the customers intended to make payment, and they did so because they rightly conceived that that was what the contracts required. As in the case of the argument based on misrepresentation, this version conceals the true nature of the customers' complaint: not that they paid the money, but that the goods which they ordered and paid for have not been delivered. As in the case of the misrepresentation, the alleged mistake might well have been a ground for setting aside the contract if the claimants had ever sought to do so; and in such a case they would have had a personal right to recover the sum equivalent to the amount paid. But even if they had chosen to exercise this right, it would not by operation of law have carried with it a proprietary interest.

Their Lordships are of the same opinion as regards the third variant, which is that a proprietary interest arose because the consideration for the purchase price has totally failed. It is, of course, obvious that in the end the consideration did fail, when delivery was demanded and not made. But until that time the claimants had the benefit of what they had bargained for, a contract for the sale of unascertained goods. Quite plainly a customer could not on the day after a sale have claimed to recover the price for a total failure of consideration, and this at once puts paid to any question of a residuary proprietary interest and distinguishes the case from those such as *Sinclair v Brougham* [1914] AC 398, [1914–15] All ER Rep 622, where the transactions under which the moneys were paid were from the start ineffectual; and *Neste Oy v Lloyds Bank plc, The Teeskeri, The Nestegas, The Enskeri* [1983] 2 Lloyd's Rep 658, where to the knowledge of the payee no performance at all could take place under the contract for which the payment formed the consideration.

There remains the question whether the court should create after the event a remedial restitutionary right superior to the security created by the charge. The nature and foundation of this remedy were not clearly explained in argument. This is understandable, given that the doctrine is still in an early stage and no single juristic account of it has yet been generally agreed. In the context of the present case there appear to be only two possibilities. The first is to strike directly at the heart of the problem and to conclude that there was such an imbalance between the positions of the parties that if orthodox methods fail a new equity should intervene to put the matter right, without recourse to further rationalisation. Their Lordships must firmly reject any such approach. The bank relied on the floating charge to protect its assets; the customers relied on the company to deliver the bullion and to put in place the separate stock. The fact that the claimants are private citizens whereas their opponent is a commercial bank could not justify the court in simply disapplying the bank's valid security. No case cited has gone anywhere near to this, and the Board would do no service to the nascent doctrine by stretching it past breaking point.

Accordingly, if the argument is to prevail some means must be found, not forcibly to subtract the moneys or their fruits from the assets to which the charge really attached, but retrospectively to create a situation in which the moneys never were part of those assets. In other words the claimants must be deemed to have a retained equitable title (see *Goff and Jones*, p 94). Whatever the mechanism for such deeming may be in other circumstances their Lordships can see no scope for it here. So far as concerns an equitable interest deemed to have come into existence from the moment when the transaction was entered into, it is hard to see how this could co-exist with a contract which, so far as anyone knew, might be performed by actual delivery of the goods. And if there was no initial interest, at what time before the attachment of the security, and by virtue of what event, could the court deem a proprietary right to have arisen? None that their Lordships are able to see. Although remedial restitutionary rights may prove in the future to be a valuable instrument of justice they cannot in their Lordships' opinion be brought to bear on the present case.

For these reasons the Board must reject all the ways in which the non-allocated claimants assert a proprietary interest over the purchase price and its fruits. This makes it unnecessary to consider whether, if such an interest had existed, it would have been possible to trace from the subject matter of the interest into the company's present assets. Indeed it would be unprofitable to do so without a clear understanding of when and how the equitable interest arose, and of its nature. Their Lordships should, however, say that they find it difficult to understand how the judgment of the Board in *Space Investments Ltd v Canadian Imperial Bank of Commerce Trust Co (Bahamas) Ltd* [1986] 3 All ER 75, [1986] 1 WLR 1072, on which the claimants leaned heavily in argument, would enable them to overcome the difficulty that the moneys said to be impressed with the trust were paid into an overdrawn account and thereupon ceased to exist: see, for example, *Re Diplock's Estate, Diplock v Wintle* [1948] 2 All ER 318, [1948] Ch 465. The observations of the Board in *Space Investments* were concerned with a mixed, not a non-existent, fund.

VII. THE POSITION OF THE BANK

The claimants have sought to contend that if they fail on everything else they are still entitled to an equitable right founded on wrongful dealing on the part of the bank. Thorp J was prepared to go this far with the argument that the bank knew at least by June 1988, and probably before, that the company's obligations to supply bullion far exceeded its ability to do so. But the learned judge could not see, any more than the Board can see, how this could prevent the bank from claiming the normal benefits of its security. Much more than this would be required, and nothing has so far been forthcoming. Quite apart from the practical impossiblity of founding any conclusion on the fragmentary written material now available, it would be quite impossible for the Board to conclude any enquiry on its own account without the benefit of an investigation by the courts in New Zealand, in the light of the full discovery and extensive oral evidence which would be essential to doing justice in the matter. Understandably, Thorp J did not consider an application by the receivers for directions to be a suitable vehicle for such an enquiry. All that the Board can say is that if there is material in support of the more serious allegations, nothing in this opinion will prevent its deployment in a proper manner.

VIII. NON-ALLOCATED CLAIMANTS: CONCLUSIONS

Their Lordships fully acknowledge the indignation of the claimants, caught up in the insolvency of the group of which the company formed part, on finding that the assurances of a secure protection on the strength of which they abstained from calling for delivery were unfulfilled; and they understand why the court should strive to alleviate the ensuing hardship. Nevertheless there must be some basis of principle for depriving the bank of its security and in company with McKay J they must find that none has been shown.

IX. THE CLAIM BY MR LIGGETT

The claim by Mr Liggett differs in only three respects from those of the non-allocated claimants as a whole. First, it is very much larger. He agreed to purchase 1,000 gold maple coins at a price of $732,000. While this entirely explains his special indignation at the conduct of the company, and his consequent decision to pursue a separate claim, it plainly makes no difference to the outcome.

The second ground of distinction concerns the circumstances of the purchase. In brief, what happened was this. On 11 February 1988 Mr Liggett made a purchase for 52 maple coins. He handed over a cheque and was told that seven days would be needed to clear it before he could collect the coins. In the meantime, he decided to make a larger purchase and with this in mind he hired a safe deposit box from another company to store the 52 maples and the further maples which he proposed to purchase. He then called again at the offices of the company and was given a description of the method of making unallocated purchases on the same general lines as those given to the other claimants. This caused him to change his mind about taking physical delivery of the coins already bought and those which he intended to add. Instead, he made an agreement for the purchase of a further 1000 maples and did not call for delivery, relying on the collateral promises. He did not personally receive a certificate of deposit referring to the goods as unallocated, since he was abroad at the relevant time.

These facts are more favourable to Mr Liggett's claim than those of the non-allocated claimants as a whole. Mr Liggett was at least shown 52 coins in respect of which the court was later to find that there was an ascertainment and appropriation sufficient to pass the property, and the fact that the two transactions were closely linked could certainly have given Mr Liggett the impression that their legal effect would be the same. Acknowledging this, their Lordships cannot find that the distinction makes any difference. Whatever Mr Liggett may have thought, and whatever the special features of the transaction, the fact remains that it was an agreement for the purchase of generic goods. For the reasons already given such contract even when accompanied by the collateral promises could not create a proprietary interest of any kind.

The third ground of distinction from the case of the non-allocated claimants is as follows. Mr Liggett's purchase was so large by comparison with the company's ordinary retail bullion transactions that the company felt it prudent to reduce its 'short' position in maples by buying in a substantial quantity of extra coins. It was argued on behalf of Mr Liggett that the coins so purchased were earmarked for Mr Liggett's purchases and hence through ascertainment and appropriation became his immediate property, only afterwards being wrongfully admixed with the bulk of the bullion in the vault. If this argument were correct, it would follow that not only was the company not entitled to deal with the coins in any other way than to deliver them to Mr Liggett when called, but also that it could not supply him with coins from any other source. No doubt if the facts were strong enough the court would be able to conclude that this was what the company had done with the implied consent of Mr Liggett. In the event, however, the evidence of the bullion manager and clerk, upon which Mr Liggett relied before Thorp J to prove the appropriation, was (as the learned judge put it) 'demonstrably against the proposition that the maples purchased by Exchange were purchased expressly for Mr. Liggett and therefore appropriated to his contract'. The learned judge went on to give reasons for this opinion, and nothing in the analysis of the facts presented to the Board gives their Lordships any reason to doubt that the learned judge's conclusion was correct.

In these circumstances their Lordships are constrained to allow the appeal of the bank in respect of Mr Liggett for the same reasons as those already given in relation to the non-allocated claimants.

X. THE WALKER & HALL CLAIMS

These claims are on a different footing. It appears that until about 1983 the bullion purchased by customers of the predecessor of Walker & Hall was stored and recorded separately. Thereafter, the bullion representing purchases by customers was stored en masse, but it was still kept separate from the vendor's own stock. Furthermore, the quantity of each kind of bullion kept in this pooled mass was precisely equal to the amount of Walker & Hall's exposure to the relevant categories of bullion and of its open contracts with customers. The documentation was also different from that received by the customers who later became the non-allocated claimants. The documents handed to the customer need not be quoted at length, but their general effect was that the vendor did not claim title in the bullion described in the document and that the title to that bullion, and the risk in respect of it, was with the customer. The document also stated that the vendor held the bullion as custodian for the customer in safe storage. These arrangements ceased when the shares of Walker & Hall were purchased by the company, and the contractual rights of the customers were transferred.

The features just mentioned persuaded Thorp J at first instance to hold, in contrast to his conclusion in relation to the non-allocated claimants and Mr Liggett, that there had been a sufficient ascertainment and appropriation of goods to the individual contracts to transfer title to each customer; and that thereafter the customers as a whole had a shared interest in the pooled bullion, which the vendors held on their behalf. The *Dublin City Distillery* case [1914] AC 823 was cited in support of this conclusion. It followed that when the company

absorbed the hitherto separated bullion into its own trading stock upon the
acquisition of Walker & Hall's business, and thereafter drew upon the mixed
stock, it wrongfully dealt with goods which were not its own.

Thus far, the decision of Thorp J was favourable to the Walker & Hall
claimants. There remained, however, the question of relief. Here, the learned
judge applied conventional principles of tracing and concluded that the
proprietary recoveries of the Walker & Hall claimants and those in a similar
position could not exceed the lowest balance of metal held by the company
between the accrual of their rights and the commencement of the receivership:
see *James Roscoe (Bolton) Ltd v Winder* [1915] 1 Ch. 62 and the passages from *Ford
and Lee's Principles of the Law of Trusts* (2nd edn, 1990), pp 738–768, paras 1716–
1730 and *Goff and Jones, The Law of Restitution* (3rd edn, 1986), p 74, cited by the
learned judge.

Although the Walker & Hall claimants had succeeded on liability the bank was
not unduly concerned, since the limitation of the claim to the lowest
intermediate balance meant that it was of comparatively small financial
significance. The bank therefore did not appeal against this part of Thorp J's
judgment when the unsuccessful claimants appealed to the Court of Appeal
against other aspects of that judgment. A rather confusing situation then arose.
Because the bank had not appealed in relation to the Walker & Hall claimants the
Court of Appeal had no occasion to consider whether these claimants really
were, as the judge had held, in a different position from the non-allocated
claimants and Mr Liggett, although some brief observations by Gault J in his
judgment ([1993] 1 NZLR 257 at 277) appeared to indicate some doubt on this
score. When, however, the court had turned to the question of quantum, and
ordered that the non-allocated claimants and Mr Liggett were entitled to charges
on the remaining bullion assets of the company in priority to the charge of the
bank, it concluded its declaration with the words 'and the successful claimants in
the High Court are in the same position as the present appellants to the extent
they cannot recover under the judgment of His Honour Mr. Justice Thorp'. This
enhancement of the remedy available to the Walker & Hall claimants made
Thorp J's adverse judgment much more serious for the bank, and accordingly the
bank desired to appeal to this Board not only on the ground that the Court of
Appeal had wrongly enlarged the remedy but also (in case it should be held that
in principle the decision of the court on the availability of a remedy should be
upheld) on the ground that Thorp J had been in error when holding that the
Walker & Hall claimants had any proprietary rights at all. To this the Walker &
Hall claimants objected, on the ground that since the bank had never appealed to
the Court of Appeal on the issue of liability it could not appeal to the Board. The
bank responded that it was not they but the claimants who had set the appellate
procedure in motion and if the judgment of Thorp J was to be reopened at all, it
ought to be reconsidered in full.

In the event, a lengthy investigation by the Board of what had happened in the
Court of Appeal was avoided by a sensible arrangement between the parties,
whereby the bank accepted its willingness to abide by the decision of Thorp J on
liability (although without making any concession upon it) in the event that the
Board restored the learned judge's decision on the measure of recovery. To this
issue, therefore, their Lordships will immediately turn.

On the facts found by the learned judge the company as bailee held bullion
belonging to the individual Walker & Hall claimants, intermingled the bullion of
all such claimants, mixed that bullion with bullion belonging to the company,

withdrew bullion from the mixed fund and then purchased more bullion which was added to the mixed fund without the intention of replacing the bullion of the Walker & Hall claimants. In these circumstances the bullion belonging to the Walker & Hall claimants which became held by the company's receivers consisted of bullion equal to the lowest balance of metal held by the company at any time: see *James Roscoe (Bolton) Ltd v Winder* [1915] 1 Ch 62.

The Walker & Hall claimants now seek to go further and ask the court to impose an equitable lien on all the property of the company at the date of the receivership to recover the value of their bullion unlawfully misappropriated by the company. Such a lien was considered by the Board in *Space Investments Ltd v Canadian Imperial Bank of Commerce Trust Co (Bahamas) Ltd* [1986] 3 All ER 75, [1986] 1 WLR 1072. In that case the Board held that beneficiaries could not claim trust moneys lawfully deposited by a bank trustee with itself as banker in priority to other depositors and unsecured creditors. But Lord Templeman considered the position which would arise if a bank trustee unlawfully borrowed trust moneys. He said ([1986] 3 All ER 75 at 76–77, [1986] 1 WLR 1072 at 1074):

'A bank in fact uses all deposit moneys for the general purposes of the bank. Whether a bank trustee lawfully receives deposits or wrongly treats trust money as on deposit from trusts, all the moneys are in fact dealt with and expended by the bank for the general purposes of the bank. In these circumstances it is impossible for the beneficiaries interested in trust money misappropriated from their trust to trace their money to any particular asset belonging to the trustee bank. But equity allows the beneficiaries, or a new trustee appointed in place of an insolvent bank trustee to protect the interests of the beneficiaries, to trace the trust money to all the assets of the bank and to recover the trust money by the exercise of an equitable charge over all the assets of the bank.'

These observations were criticised by Professor Goode in his Mary Oliver Memorial Address published in (1987) 103 LQR 433 at 445–447 as being inconsistent with the observations of the Court of Appeal in *Re Diplock's Estate, Diplock v Wintle* [1948] 2 All ER 318 at 347, [1948] Ch 465 at 521 where it was said:

'The equitable remedies presuppose the continued existence of the money either as a separate fund or as part of a mixed fund or as latent in property acquired by means of such a fund. If, on the facts of any individual case, such continued existence is not established, equity is as helpless as the common law itself. If the fund, mixed or unmixed, is spent on a dinner, equity, which dealt only in specific relief and not in damages, could do nothing. If the case was one which at common law involved breach of contract, the common law could, of course, award damages, but specific relief would be out of the question. It is, therefore, a necessary matter for consideration in each case where it is sought to trace money in equity, whether it has such a continued existence, actual or notional, as will enable equity to grant specific relief.'

In the case of a bank which employs all borrowed moneys as a mixed fund for the purpose of lending out money or making investments, any trust money unlawfully borrowed by a bank trustee may be said to be latent in the property acquired by the bank and the court may impose an equitable lien on that property for the recovery of the trust money.

The imposition of such an equitable lien for the purpose of recovering trust money was more favourably regarded by Professor Peter Birks in *An Introduction* to the *Law of Restitution* (1989) 377–401 and by *Goff and Jones, The Law of Restitution* (4th edn) esp at pp 73–75.

The law relating to the creation and tracing of equitable proprietary interests is still in a state of development. In *A-G for Hong Kong v Reid* [1994] 1 All ER 1, [1994] AC 324 the Board decided that money received by an agent as a bribe was held in trust for the principal who is entitled to trace and recover property representing the bribe. In *Lord Napier and Ettrick v Hunter, Lord Napier and Ettrick v R F Kershaw Ltd* [1993] 1 All ER 385 at 397, [1993] AC 713 at 738–739 the House of Lords held that payment of damages in respect of an insured loss created an equitable charge in favour of the subrogated insurers so long only as the damages were traceable as an identifiable fund. When the scope and ambit of these decisions and the observations of the Board in *Space Investments* fall to be considered, it will be necessary for the history and foundations in principle of the creation and tracing of equitable proprietary interests to be the subject of close examination and full argument and for attention to be paid to the works of Paciocco in (1989) 68 Can Bar Rev 315, Maddaugh and McCamus *The Law of Restitution* (1990), Emily L Sherwin's article *Constructive Trusts in Bankruptcy* (1989) U Ill L Rev 297 at 335 and other commentators dealing with equitable interests in tracing and referring to concepts such as the position of 'involuntary creditors' and tracing to 'swollen assets'.

In the present case it is not necessary or appropriate to consider the scope and ambit of the observations in *Space Investments* or their application to trustees other than bank trustees because all members of this Board are agreed that it would be inequitable to impose a lien in favour of the Walker & Hall claimants. Those claimants received the same certificates and trusted the company in a manner no different from other bullion customers. There is no evidence that the debenture holders and the unsecured creditors at the date of the receivership benefited directly or indirectly from the breaches of trust committed by the company or that Walker & Hall bullion continued to exist as a fund latent in property vested in the receivers.

In these circumstances the Walker & Hall claimants must be restored to the remedies granted to them by the trial judge.

Their Lordships will accordingly humbly advise Her Majesty that the appeal ought to be allowed, the judgment of the Court of Appeal of New Zealand of 30 April 1992 set aside and the judgment of Thorp J of 17 October 1990 restored. Their Lordships were informed that the parties had been able to agree the matter of costs in any event and therefore make no order in that regard.

Appeal allowed.

Celia Fox   Barrister.

Re ELS Ltd

CHANCERY DIVISION
FERRIS J
16–19 NOVEMBER 1993, 16 FEBRUARY 1994

Company – Distress – Rates – Business rates – Unpaid rates – Local authority – Company creating floating charge over all its undertaking and assets by debenture in favour of bank – Bank appointing applicants as joint administrative receivers – Floating charge crystallising on appointment – After appointment bailiffs acting for local authorities attempting to levy distress over property of company – Whether local authorities entitled to levy distress over company's goods after floating charge has crystallised – Non-Domestic Rating (Collection and Enforcement) (Local Lists) Regulations 1989, reg 14.

The crystallisation of a floating charge on the appointment of administrative receivers completes the assignment to the debenture holder of the goods which are the subject of the charge with the consequence that the goods are no longer 'goods of' the company over which distress for rates may be levied under reg 14[a] of the Non-Domestic Rating (Collection and Enforcement) (Local Lists) Regulations 1989 (see p 845 *f g*, post).

Notes

For distress for rates, see 13 *Halsbury's Laws* (4th edn) paras 397–433, and for cases on the subject, see 18 *Digest* (2nd reissue) 557–591, 5450–5713.

For the Non-Domestic Rating (Collection and Enforcement) (Local Lists) Regulations 1989, reg 14, see 16 *Halsbury's Statutory Instruments* (1994 reissue) 216.

Cases referred to in judgment

Adolphe Crosbie Ltd, Re (1910) 74 JP 25.
Barker (George) (Transport) Ltd v Eynon [1974] 1 All ER 900, [1974] 1 WLR 462, CA.
Biggerstaff v Rowatt's Wharf Ltd [1896] 2 Ch 93, CA.
Carreras Rothmans Ltd v Freeman Mathews Treasure Ltd (in liq) [1985] 1 All ER 155, [1985] Ch 207, [1984] 3 WLR 1016.
French's (Wine Bar) Ltd, Re [1987] BCLC 499.
Marriage Neave & Co, Re, North of England Trustee Debenture and Assets Corp v Marriage Neave & Co [1896] 2 Ch 663, [1895–9] All ER Rep 393, CA.
Metropolitan Life Assurance Co of New Zealand Ltd v Essere Print [1991] 2 NZLR 197; *affd* [1991] 3 NZLR 170, NZ CA.
National Mutual v National Capital Development Commission (1975) 37 FLR 404, ACT SC.
Robbie (N W) & Co Ltd v Witney Warehouse Co Ltd [1963] 3 All ER 613, [1963] 1 WLR 1324, CA.
Roundwood Colliery Co Ltd, Re [1897] 1 Ch 373, [1895–9] All ER Rep 530, CA.
Taggs Island Casino Ltd v Richmond upon Thames BC [1967] RA 70.

---

a   Regulation 14, so far as material, is set out at p 836 *b c*, post

Cases also cited
Cassell & Co Ltd v Broome [1972] 1 All ER 801, [1972] AC 1027, HL.
Opera Ltd, Re [1891] 3 Ch 260, CA.
Pound (Henry) Son & Hutchings, Re (1889) 42 Ch D 402, Ch D and CA.
Power v Sharp Investments Ltd [1994] 1 BCLC 111, CA.
Richards v Kidderminster Overseers [1896] 2 Ch 212.
Sowman v David Samuel Trust Ltd (in liq) [1978] 1 All ER 616, [1978] 1 WLR 22.
Tancred v Delagoa Bay and East Africa Rly Co (1889) 23 QBD 239.
Westminster City Council v Haymarket Publishing Ltd [1981] 2 All ER 555, [1981] 1 WLR 677, CA.

Originating summons
By an originating summons dated 11 June 1993 the applicants, Philip Ramsbottom and Alan Athol Elmslie Benzie, the joint administrative receivers of ELS Ltd (the company), applied to the court for directions as to the following matters: (1) whether the crystallisation of a floating charge upon the appointment of administrative receivers completed the assignment of the goods of a company covered by a floating charge to the debenture holder with the consequence that such goods were no longer 'goods of' the company for the purposes of reg 14(1) of the Non-Domestic Rating (Collection and Enforcement) (Local Lists) Regulations 1989, SI 1989/1058; (2) whether administrative receivers appointed under a floating charge who had a statutory duty pursuant to s 40 of the Insolvency Act 1986 to pay preferential creditors were entitled to a declaration that a charging authority was not entitled to levy distress on the goods of the debtor for non-domestic rates pursuant to reg 14(1) of the 1989 regulations unless and until all preferential debts (within the meaning given to that expression by s 86 of the 1986 Act) had been paid out of the assets coming to the hands of administrative receivers. The respondents were the Luton Borough Council and the Wrekin District Council. The facts are set out in the judgment.

Gabriel Moss QC and *Peter Havey* (instructed by *Addleshaw Sons & Latham*, Manchester) for the applicants.
Christopher Brougham QC and *Lexa Hilliard* (instructed by *Iqbal Javed*, Luton and *PJ Roscoe*, Telford) for the respondents.

Cur adv vult

16 February 1994. The following judgment was delivered.

FERRIS J. Can a local authority having a power of distress in order to recover business rates exercise that power over the goods of a company which are subject to a floating charge after that floating charge has crystallised? This case has been brought in order to determine the answer to that question.

The facts are agreed and are set out in an agreed statement. It is not necessary for me to set out the whole of that statement in this judgment. It will suffice to summarise the salient facts as follows.

(1) At all material times ELS Ltd (ELS), formerly English Lifestyle Ltd, carried on the business of retailing furniture from premises in the districts for which the Luton Borough Council and the Wrekin District Council are respectively the local authorities.

(2) Each of these authorities is the charging authority in relation to non-domestic rates in its area.

(3) By a debenture dated 15 October 1990 ELS created in favour of National Westminster Bank Ltd (the bank) charges over all its assets including a charge by way of floating security over its undertaking and all its property not charged by way of specific charge. The debenture was to secure all money covenanted to be paid by ELS to the bank.

(4) Clause 8 of the debenture conferred an express power to appoint a receiver who, if appointed as an administrative receiver within the meaning of the Insolvency Act 1986, was to have all the powers of an administrative receiver specified in Sch 1 to the Act. These include power to take possession of and to sell the property of ELS.

(5) On 14 February 1992 the bank appointed the applicants, Philip Ramsbottom and Alan Athol Elmslie Benzie (the receivers), to be joint administrative receivers under the debenture.

(6) On 19 September 1991, on the application of the Luton Borough Council, the South Bedfordshire Magistrates' Court made a liability order against ELS in the sum of £191,644·48 in respect of unpaid non-domestic rates. Before the appointment of the receivers ELS made payments which reduced the amount due to the council to £151,644·48. After the appointment of the receivers bailiffs appointed by the council endeavoured to levy a distress over property of ELS at its premises in that council's district in respect of this unpaid liability, but they were restrained by injunctions from continuing to levy such distress.

(7) On 17 March 1992 Telford Magistrates' Court made a liability order against ELS in the sum of £65,654·61 in respect of unpaid non-domestic rates. In late March 1992 bailiffs acting for the Wrekin District Council endeavoured to levy a distress over property of ELS at its premises in that council's district. The completion of such distress has been suspended by agreement pending the determination of the point of principle which is at issue in this case

(8) For the purpose of this application it is agreed that the court should proceed on the assumption that the goods over which the two councils have respectively sought to levy distress were, until the appointment of the receivers, goods of owned by and belonging to ELS.

In contrast to the right of a landlord to levy distress for unpaid rent, which is a common law right, the right of an authority to levy distress in respect of unpaid rates is entirely statutory. By the Poor Relief Act 1601 (43 Eliz 1 c 2) provision was made for the churchwardens and overseers of the poor of every parish to levy and assess a rate for certain prescribed statutory purposes. By s 4 of that Act, so far as it is material, it was provided that it should be lawful for the churchwardens and overseers to levy the sums due—

'from every one that shall refuse to contribute according as they shall be assessed, by Distress and Sale of the Offender's Goods.'

In default of such distress the non-payer was liable to be committed to prison by the justices. No power was given to sue for unpaid rates in debt.

The legislation has, of course, changed from time to time over the years and the reference to a non-payer as 'the offender' has been dropped. But throughout successive enactments the goods in respect of which distress may be levied have been defined, in one way or another, as the non-payer's goods.

The current provisions are contained in Pt III of the Non-Domestic Rating (Collection and Enforcement) (Local Lists) Regulations 1989, SI 1989/1058. The procedure can be summarised as follows. (i) A billing authority must, before taking other enforcement steps, serve a reminder notice on the ratepayer. (ii) If the relevant rates remain wholly or partly unpaid seven days after a reminder notice has been served the billing authority may apply to a magistrates' court for a liability order. (iii) By reg 14(1), which is the material provision for present purposes:

> 'Where a liability order has been made, the authority which applied for the order may levy the appropriate amount by distress and sale of the goods of the debtor against whom the order was made.'

It will be noted that the relevant words are 'the goods of the debtor'. (iv) Provision is made for committal to prison (reg 14); for a creditor's petition in bankruptcy or for a winding-up order on the basis that the amount due under an unsatisfied liability order is a debt (reg 18); and for recovery by means of a money judgment obtained from an appropriate court (reg 20). Committal is available only when distress has been attempted and has been unsuccessful. The insolvency remedies and the ability to seek a money judgment are available whether or not distress has been attempted.

There is one further part of statute law which it is convenient to deal with at this stage. Under s 32 of the Bankruptcy Act 1869 (32 & 33 Vict c 71), rates due within 12 months next before a bankruptcy were (together with certain other debts) made preferential debts in the bankruptcy. The bankruptcy rule was applied to company liquidations by s 10 of the Judicature Act 1873. Preference for one year's rates was reaffirmed by s 1 of the Preferential Payments in Bankruptcy Act 1888 (51 & 52 Vict c 62). A similar principle was applied in the case of receiverships arising pursuant to a floating charge by the Preferential Payments in Bankruptcy Act 1897 (60 & 61 Vict c 19, 20). It is not necessary to trace the development of the legislation in full. The preference was retained in a winding up by s 319 of the Companies Act 1948 and in receivership under a floating charge by s 94. This situation was changed when the Insolvency Act 1986 came into force. Although, under s 40 of that Act, a receiver appointed under debentures secured by a charge which, as created, was a floating charge remains liable to pay the company's preferential debts in priority to the principal and interest in respect of debentures, preferential debts, which are defined in s 386 and Sch 6, no longer include rates. The existence of a preference in respect of the rates until 1986 and its abolition in that year may provide a partial explanation why the extent of the power of distress for rates has not been the subject of litigation during this century although, as will be seen, there were a number of decisions in this field in the 1890s. While unpaid rates were preferential there may have been little reason for the remedy of distress to be resorted to in the case of insolvent companies.

The originating summons in this case seeks the decision of the court on the question—

> 'Whether the crystallisation of a floating charge upon the appointment of Administrative Receivers completes the assignment of the goods of a company covered by a floating charge to the debenture holder with the consequence that such goods are no longer "goods of" the company for

the purposes of Regulation 14(1) of the Non-Domestic Rating (Collection and Enforcement) Regulations 1989 (SI 1989/1058).'

There is a second substantive question which I will come to later.

The receivers accept that where goods owned by a company are subject to a floating charge which has not crystallised they are 'goods of the company'. Thus where the company is a debtor against which a liability order has been made, those goods are 'goods of the debtor' for the purposes of reg 14(1) and distress can be levied. The receivers argue, however, that once the floating charge has crystallised, whether by the appointment of administrative receivers or for any other cause, the goods cease to be 'goods of the debtor' because crystallisation completes the assignment of title to the chargee which was made when the debenture was created.

The difference between the operation of a charge created as a floating charge before crystallisation and its operation after crystallisation has been recognised for 100 years, if not longer (see the reasoning in *Biggerstaff v Rowatt's Wharf Ltd* [1896] 2 Ch 93). In *N W Robbie & Co Ltd v Witney Warehouse Co Ltd* [1963] 3 All ER 613, [1963] 1 WLR 1324 it was considered in relation to a claim that a debtor of a company in receivership could set off against the debt owed by it to the company a debt owed by the company which had been assigned to it after the commencement of the receivership. One issue in the case was whether a sum which had become due to the company from the debtor during the receivership fell to be treated in the same way as a debt due from the debtor prior to the receivership. A majority of the Court of Appeal (Sellers and Russell LJJ; Donovan LJ dissenting) held that it did. In respect of these combined debts Russell LJ said ([1963] 3 All ER 613 at 622, [1963] 1 WLR 1324 at 1338):

'It was next argued that, if the charge in favour of the debenture-holder existed on such future assets, it was really of the same quality as a floating charge, since the debenture-holder, by procuring the agreement of the [company] that the receiver and manager should be agent for the [company], permitted the [company] to continue to trade through [its] agent without immediate regard to the debenture charge; therefore, it was argued, such charge no more precluded set-off than did the original charge while floating, as to which see *Biggerstaff v. Rowatt's Wharf, Ltd.* I confess that I do not find this argument easy to follow. Why does it not apply equally to the charge upon the assets existing at the time of the appointment? And what then is meant by crystallisation of a floating charge in such a case? I venture to think that in rejecting this argument I would have the whole hearted support of the members of this court who decided the *Biggerstaff* case and who were at such pains to point out the radical difference produced by crystallisation. Thus far, in my judgment, by force of the debenture charge an equitable charge attached in favour of the debenture-holder, not only on the £95 debt existing at the date of the appointment of the receiver and manager, but also upon the other debts constituting the total of £1,346 6s. 1d. as they came into existence on delivery of goods to the defendant after such appointment. These choses in action belonging to the [company] became thus assigned in equity to the debenture-holder, at times when the defendants had no cross-claim of any kind against the [company] and consequently no right of set-off. Before the defendants acquired by assignment this cross-claim the defendants must be fixed with knowledge of this equitable assignment to the debenture-holder (by way of charge) of the debt owed by the defendants to the [company]. A debtor cannot set off his claim against X against a claim by X against him which the debtor knows has been assigned by X to Y before the debtor has acquired a right of set-off. Just as an assignee of a chose in action takes subject to an already existing right of set-off, so a debtor with no existing right of set-off cannot assert set-off of a cross-claim which he first acquires after he has notice of the assignment of the claim against him: here, for instance, no part of the £852 18s. 4d. could have been set off against the £95.'

This accords with the reasoning of Sellers LJ.

In *George Barker (Transport) Ltd v Eynon* [1974] 1 All ER 900, [1974] 1 WLR 462 the point arose in relation to a lien. In that case a road haulage company was owed money for haulage by a meat importing company which had charged all its goods to its bank by way of floating security. The road haulage company asserted a general lien over goods transported after the appointment of a receiver under the debenture in respect of money which had become due to it before the appointment of the receiver. The precise reasoning by which this claim was resolved is not relevant for present purposes but in the Court of Appeal there were some observations as to the effect of a floating charge and its crystallisation. Edmund Davies LJ said ([1974] 1 All ER 900 at 905, [1974] 1 WLR 462 at 467):

'A floating charge is ambulatory and hovers over the property until some event occurs which causes it to settle and crystallise into a specific charge ... One of the events which causes crystallisation is the appointment of a receiver, which, as we know, occurred in the present case on 31st August 1971 ... One consequence of the receiver's appointment by the debenture holders was that the incomplete assignment constituted by the 1970 deed became converted into a completed equitable assignment to them of the assets charged and of the company's rights ...'

Stamp LJ said ([1974] 1 All ER 900 at 908–909, [1974] 1 WLR 462 at 471):

'The appointment of a receiver operates as an equitable assignment (by way of charge) of the property of the company to the debenture holder ... and so in this case operated as an equitable assignment (by way of charge) of (a) the company's property in the goods, and (b) the company's rights under the contract of carriage.'

Sir Gordon Willmer observed ([1974] 1 All ER 900 at 912, [1974] 1 WLR 462 at 475):

'On the appointment of the defendant as receiver the rights of the debenture holder crystallised, and they became equitable assignees of the rights of the company.'

Similar reasoning, applying the English authorities, is to be found in Australia in *National Mutual v National Capital Development Commission* (1975) 37 FLR 404 at 408–410 and in New Zealand in *Metropolitan Life Assurance Co of New Zealand Ltd v Essere Print* [1991] 2 NZLR 197. (There was an appeal in the last mentioned case and the decision at first instance was upheld, but without reference to the principle with which I am concerned (see [1991] 3 NZLR 170).)

The importance of whether a floating charge has or has not crystallised has been recognised in relation to distress in *Re Roundwood Colliery Co Ltd* [1897] 1 Ch 373, [1895–9] All ER Rep 530. In that case a mining company was lessee of two adjoining coal mines, A and B. There was no shaft on mine B, both mines being worked by the shaft on mine A. In both leases the landlord reserved a right of distress, not only upon chattels upon the demised premises but also upon chattels 'belonging to the lessees' in or about adjoining or neighbouring collieries. The landlord of mine B levied a distress upon chattels on mine A. The proceedings were brought to determine the validity of this distress. At first instance the case was decided against the landlord on a point under the Bills of Sale Acts on which the Court of Appeal reversed the judge. The Court of Appeal had then to determine whether the distress was good against the debenture holders of the mining company. It was held that the distress, having been levied before the commencement of the winding up and before a receiver was appointed by the debenture holders, was valid against the debenture holders.

Lindley LJ said ([1897] 1 Ch 373 at 393, [1895–9] All ER Rep 530 at 535):

'This ground [ie the Bills of Sale Acts point] being, in my opinion, erroneous, it becomes necessary to consider the respective rights of the landlord and of the debenture-holders to the goods seized. These rights depend upon the question whether the landlord distrained while the debentures were still a floating security, or whether the debentures are to be regarded as having definitively attached to the goods seized, so that, as between the landlord and the debenture-holders, those goods had become the property of the latter before the landlord seized them. It is not contended that the landlord could distrain off the property on goods which were not the goods of the company, both at law and in equity. The debenture-holders contend that the goods seized were not the goods of the company, except subject to the ˙equitable charge created by the debentures. As between the debenture-holders and the company this proposition is true; but it does not decide the respective rights of the lessor and the debenture-holders, which is what we have to consider. The goods seized by the lessor were seized under a power conferred either before the debentures were issued or whilst they were clearly a floating security, and in either case that power could be exercised before the debentures ceased to be floating securities. They did not cease to be so before the distress was put in. The winding-up did not commence until after that date, nor was any effectual order for a receiver made until after the same date. The order of October 7 was never really effective. It was never drawn up, the lessor had no notice of it, and before the receiver could take possession he had to give security. The distress, having been made before the commencement of the winding-up of the company, and before a receiver was effectively appointed, was, in my opinion, valid as against the debenture-holders.'

The other two members of the Court of Appeal, AL Smith LJ and Rigby LJ, agreed.

The decision in the *Roundwood Colliery* case is relied upon by Mr Moss, on behalf of the receivers, as being, in substance, the converse of the present case. The decision of the Court of Appeal in favour of the landlord was that the chattels over which distress had been levied remained chattels 'belonging to the lessees' at the time of the distress. The reason why this was so was that the charge in favour of the debenture holder was a floating charge which had not crystallised at the relevant time. The clear implication of the passage cited from Lindley LJ is that, if the floating charge had crystallised when the distress was levied, the chattels would no longer have been chattels 'belonging to the lessees' and the distress would have been held to be bad. The present case, it was argued, is precisely covered by this implication.

However another case in the Court of Appeal, decided some six months earlier by a court of which Lindley and Rigby LJJ were both members, is said to stand in the way of this conclusion. The case is Re Marriage Neave & Co, North of England Trustee Debenture and Assets Corp v Marriage Neave & Co [1896] 2 Ch 663, [1895–9] All ER Rep 393. There, on the face of it, the Court of Appeal allowed a distress for unpaid rates to be levied notwithstanding the existence of a charge in favour of debenture holders, the appointment of receivers on behalf of those debenture holders and a resolution for the voluntary winding-up of the company. In order to see whether this is indeed the effect of the decision it is necessary to consider the facts, arguments and judgments in that case in some detail.

In the Marriage Neave case the company had, on 30 June 1890, executed two debenture trust deeds to secure issues of first and second mortgage debentures respectively. Each deed constituted a floating security. The report then goes on to state:

> 'The company, by each debenture, charged with the payment of the principal sum and interest thereby secured "all its property whatsoever and wheresoever, both present and future, not comprised in or subject to the trusts of or effectually charged by" the trust deed.' (See [1896] 2 Ch 663 at 664.)

It appears, therefore, that there were potentially three different assignments or charges to be considered, namely (i) that contained in the first mortgage debenture trust deed; (ii) that contained in the second mortgage debenture trust deed; and (iii) that contained in the debentures. In 1896 the company became insolvent. On 6 February 1896 receivers and managers were appointed under the second mortgage debenture trust deed; on 17 February 1896, in a debenture holders action brought by the first mortgage debenture holders, the court appointed the same persons to be receivers and managers under the first mortgage debenture; and on 19 February 1896 the company passed an extraordinary resolution to wind up, one of the receivers and managers being appointed liquidator. On 12 November rates for the half year which was to end on 25 March 1896 had been demanded of the company and, when these remained unpaid, steps were taken to enforce payment. On 2 March 1896 a distress warrant for the unpaid rates was issued by the justices. It was accepted that, in view of the existence of court appointed receivers and managers, distress could not be levied without the leave of the court. Such leave was sought by a summons which came before Kekewich J.

The argument presented to Kekewich J appears to have been that a 'change of occupation' for the purposes of the relevant rating legislation had taken place when receivers and managers were appointed by the court on 17 February. Kekewich J upheld this argument, with the consequence that rates could not be levied after that date in respect of rates which became due partly before and partly after that date. The receivers and managers subsequently paid the part of the rates which was apportioned to the period after the commencement of the receivership. An appeal was brought to determine whether the power of distress could be exercised after that time in order to recover rates due for the period preceding that time.

The first argument on behalf of the first debenture holders was that, notwithstanding the subsequent reversal of an authority on which Kekewich J had relied, there was indeed a change of occupation when the receivers and managers were appointed by the court. This argument, which failed, need not be explored further. The second argument, which is relevant for present purposes, was that the goods over which it was sought to levy the distress were not the goods of the company but the goods of the debenture holders, by reason of the assignment contained in the first mortgage debenture trust deed or the charges contained in the debentures. As reported, it appears that the argument was that the assignment or the charges by themselves caused the goods to cease to be the goods of the company, no reliance being placed upon the crystallisation of the floating charge which had been created by the first mortgage debenture trust deed.

In his judgment Lindley LJ dealt first with the change of occupation point, holding that there had been no change of occupation. He went on ([1896] 2 Ch 663 at 672, [1895–9] All ER Rep 393 at 395):

'The next point is this. These rates can only be distrained for upon goods of the person assessed and who has made default; that is the "offender", I agree. The "offender" here is the company. The company is assessed: the company has made default; and the only goods which can be taken under the distress warrant are the goods of the company. Then, are there any goods of the company on these premises which are liable to distraint? It is said, No. It is said, first of all, that the goods belong in point of law to the trustees for the debenture-holders. That turns upon the true construction of the trust deed ...'

He then considered the first mortgage debenture trust deed and concluded that it was not in terms which caused the goods to pass to the trustees for the debenture holders. Then he said ([1896] 2 Ch 663 at 673, [1895–9] All ER Rep 393 at 395):

'The next point is this. The debentures appear to be expressed in language so large as to include the goods of the company although the trust deed does not, but their only effect is to give the debenture-holders an equitable charge upon these goods. That is all the debenture-holders want. They do not require to take possession, and they have no right even to take possession. Their only right is to institute an action and get a receiver appointed. The goods are not theirs: they are the goods of the company, subject to the equitable charge created by the debentures.'

Lindley LJ then considered the duties of the bailiff in respect of the proceeds of sale of the goods distrained and concluded that the bailiff's duty—

'does, in effect, give these rates priority with regard to the proceeds of the goods when seized and sold under that distress.' (See [1896] 2 Ch 663 at 674, [1895–9] All ER Rep 393 at 396.)

The second member of the court, Lopes LJ, dealt similarly with the change of occupation point. He dealt with the effect of the trust deed and the debentures as follows ([1896] 2 Ch 663 at 675–676, [1895–9] All ER Rep 393 at 396–397):

'Then it is said that these goods which it is sought to seize were not the goods of the company—that they passed under a certain deed of trust. When that trust deed is examined, it appears that these goods were excepted, and did not pass under the deed at all: they cannot therefore be said to belong to the debenture-holders. The position with regard to the goods is really this, that they belong to the company subject to an equitable charge in favour of the debenture-holders. Then another question was raised as to the effect of the equitable charge. It was said that these goods have been subjected to this equitable charge of the debenture-holders, and that therefore no distress can be issued against them or is enforceable against them ... I am conversant with the practice as to enforcing the payment of rates such as these, and I never heard of this point being raised before. However, when the point is looked into, it really comes to this, that there is a preferential charge in favour of rates— that rates are to be paid in preference to any equitable charge such as this. What leads me to that conclusion is, amongst other things, this, that there is power given by statute to distrain for rates, and no action can be brought to recover them.'

Rigby LJ, the third member of the court, agreed with the others as to change of occupation. On the other main point he said ([1896] 2 Ch 663 at 677–678, [1895–9] All ER Rep 393 at 397):

'I have nothing to add respecting the construction of the debenture trust deed, which to my mind did not carry the goods and chattels; but there is a charge given by the debentures. Does that prevent the goods from being the goods of Marriage, Neave & Co? I apprehend not. Putting aside the Bills of Sale Act, and, considering the state of the law before the Bills of Sale Act was passed, can it be said that because a man writes on a piece of paper, "I charge my household furniture with the payment of 5l. favour of So-and-so," that the man is thereby securing himself practically from the payment of rates? The argument put forward virtually goes as far as that, for the contention is that furniture so charged becomes the property of the person in whose favour the charge is made, and that it cannot be seized by way of distress. I think that the construction of the statute is really this, that the overseers take the goods of the "offender" as they find them, that they must distrain and sell, and pay the rates first. When they have paid the rates, I apprehend that they may be called upon in a proper way to account for the surplus, it may be to the equitable mortgagee, if any, or, if there is no equitable mortgagee, then to the owner of the goods. They have to pay the rates, and that practically gives them a preferential charge on the goods.'

These extensive quotations from the judgments in the *Marriage Neave* case demonstrate, to my mind, two points. First they seem to confirm what appears from the report of the argument that what was being contended on behalf of the debenture holders was that it was the charge itself, as executed in

1890, which had caused the goods to cease to be the goods of the company, not the events of 1896. Secondly, going hand in hand with the first point, there is nothing in any of the judgments to suggest that crystallisation of a floating charge had anything to do with the case.

The *Marriage Neave* case, apart from being referred to in argument in the *Roundwood Colliery* case, has been followed in one reported case, namely *Re Adolphe Crosbie Ltd* (1910) 74 JP 25. There the relevant power of distress arose under the Gasworks Clauses Act 1871. The relevant charge was undoubtedly created as a floating charge and had crystallised on the appointment of receivers before there was any distress. Neville J held that the case was covered by the *Marriage Neave* case, but added no reasoning of his own.

Mr Brougham QC for the respondent councils accepted that the decision in *Marriage Neave* did not depend in any way on crystallisation. He argued that what the *Marriage Neave* case establishes is not the proposition that crystallisation of a floating charge over goods makes no difference to liability to distress but the wider proposition that an equitable charge over a company's goods does not cause them to cease to be 'goods of the company' for the purposes of the law of distress in respect of unpaid rates. As a charge over goods to be acquired after the date of the charge must, of necessity, be only an equitable, not a legal, charge this would mean that few, if any, debentures created in the usual form could ever cause goods to cease to be the goods of the company until such goods are actually sold to a third party.

Mr Brougham argued that expressions such as 'goods of the debtor', 'chattels of any person' or 'the company's property' are not terms of art which have an invariable or even a prima facie legal meaning. Thus in the New Zealand case of *Metropolitan Life Assurance Co of New Zealand Ltd v Essere Print* [1991] 3 NZLR 170 the New Zealand Court of Appeal had regarded as finely balanced the question whether a statutory limitation precluding the levying of distress by a landlord on any chattels save those of the tenant required that, in order to be liable to distraint, the goods must belong to the tenant in equity as well as law. (The actual decision of the court was that where both the tenant and a debenture holder under a debenture created by the tenant had substantial interests in the chattel, it was not the chattel of the tenant for the purpose of the statute.) In *Re French's Wine Bar Ltd* [1987] BCLC 499 there was serious argument whether property which, at the time when a company went into liquidation, was subject to a contract of sale which could be enforced by specific performance was 'the company's property' for the purposes of s 522 of the Companies Act 1985. Vinelott J held that it was not, so that the completion of the contract after the commencement of the winding up did not require validation under the section (now s 127 of the Insolvency Act 1986)

Mr Brougham sought to obtain some assistance from a passage in the judgment of Peter Gibson J in *Carreras Rothmans Ltd v Freeman Mathews Treasure Ltd (in liq)* [1985] 1 All ER 155, [1985] Ch 207. One of the issues in that case was whether a particular agreement created a charge on the book debts of a company which was registrable under s 95 of the Companies Act 1948. Peter Gibson J said ([1985] 1 All ER 155 at 169, [1985] Ch 207 at 227):

'"Charge" is not defined for the purpose of section 95 (save to extend its meaning to include a mortgage) and so must, in the absence of any indication to the contrary (and none is suggested), bear its ordinary meaning. The type of charge which it is said was created is an equitable charge. Such a charge is created by an appropriation of specific property to the discharge of some debt or other obligation without there being any change in ownership either at law or in equity, and it confers on the chargee rights to apply to the court for an order for sale or for the appointment of a receiver, but no right to foreclosure (so as to make the property his own) or take possession.'

As I understood the argument, it was that an equitable charge over chattels, including the charge under consideration in the *Marriage Neave* case and the charge created by the debenture in this case, was of this character. However I cannot accept, if it was intended so to suggest, that the description of Peter Gibson J is to be taken to apply to every case in which a charge operates in equity, so making the term 'equitable charge' appropriate. It will be recollected that in the present case the charge arises under a formal debenture executed under seal, there is an express power to appoint a receiver without any application to the court, and a receiver who is an administrative receiver is expressly given the powers specified in Sch 1 to the Insolvency Act 1986, including the power to take possession of and sell the assets charged.

I do not find the *Marriage Neave* case a particularly easy case to understand. On the language used by all the members of the court it does seem that what was being said was that a mere equitable charge did not prevent the goods subject to the charge from being 'goods of the company'. But if that were so as a general proposition it is difficult to see why, some six months later, a division of the Court of Appeal which included two of those who had decided the *Marriage Neave* case gave the reasons which were given for the decision in the *Roundwood Colliery* case. The actual decision in the *Roundwood Colliery* case, like that in the *Marriage Neave* case, was in favour of the distress. But if the fact that the debenture holders were only equitable assignees was sufficient to prevent them from challenging the distress it is difficult to see why Lindley and Rigby LJJ did not simply refer to their earlier judgments in the *Marriage Neave* case and say that this was sufficient to dispose of the appeal in the *Roundwood Colliery* case. If the *Marriage Neave* case had decided what Mr Brougham contended that it decided it is surprising, to say the least, that Lindley LJ should have said in the *Roundwood Colliery* case that the rights of the landlords and the debenture holders to the goods seized—

'depend upon the question whether the landlord distrained while the debentures were still a floating security, or whether the debentures are to be regarded as having definitively attached to the goods seized, so that, as between the landlord and the debenture-holders, those goods had become the property of the latter before the landlord seized them.'

Indeed the way in which the court dealt with the argument on the debenture trust deed in the *Marriage Neave* case is somewhat surprising if Mr Brougham is correct. It would have been different if the debenture trust deed had carried the chattels. But if Mr Brougham is right the result would have been the same, because the debenture trust deed created only an equitable charge.

Mr Brougham's argument concerning the scope of the decision in the *Marriage Neave* case is also, to my mind, impossible to reconcile with what has been said about the effect of the crystallisation of a floating charge in *Biggerstaff v Rowatt's Wharf Ltd* [1896] 2 Ch 93 (to which Lindley LJ was a party); or in the passages from *N W Robbie & Co Ltd v Witney Warehouse Co Ltd* [1963] 3 All ER

613, [1963] 1 WLR 1324 and *George Barker (Transport) Ltd v Eynon* [1974] 1 All ER 900, [1974] 1 WLR 462 which I have quoted above. This argument would also lead to the conclusion that the abolition of preferential status for unpaid rates which was brought about by the passing of the Insolvency Act 1986 was to a large extent irrelevant because, by resorting to the remedy of distress, an authority entitled to receive rates can establish a de facto preference ranking above that accorded to debts which remain preferential.

I cannot accept that what was said in the *Marriage Neave* case applies to every type of equitable charge, whatever the formality of its creation, whether or not effected by means of an assignment or created as a floating charge and, if created as a floating charge, whether or not it has crystallised. In my judgment the decision applies only to a mere charge which does not operate by way of assignment and which, like the type of charge described by Peter Gibson J in the *Carreras* case, confers no power, without the assistance of the court, to appoint a receiver, take possession or sell. This view of the decision would, I think, avoid conflict between the *Marriage Neave* and *Roundwood Colliery* cases and with the description of the effect of crystallisation in the other case I have cited. Viewed in this way the decision lends no support to the argument that in the present case the goods over which Luton Borough Council and Wrekin District Council seek to levy distress remain the property of ELS notwithstanding crystallisation of the floating charge.

If, however, the *Marriage Neave* case is not to be confined in this way then it is, in my view, in conflict with the reasoning in the later decisions in the *Roundwood Colliery*, *Robbie* and *George Barker* cases. These are all decisions of the Court of Appeal and I am, I think, entitled to follow them in preference to the *Marriage Neave* case.

I therefore answer the question posed by para 1 of the originating summons by declaring that the crystallisation of the bank's floating charge in this case completed the assignment of the goods of ELS effected by the floating charge contained in the debenture dated 15 October 1990, with the consequence that such goods were thereafter no longer the goods of ELS for the purpose of reg 14 of the 1989 regulations. So expressed the declaration relates to this particular case rather than following the generalised proposition put forward in the originating summons, but in my view that is as far as I ought to go.

Paragraph 2 of the originating summons raises a separate question, albeit one designed to arrive at the resolution of the same point of substance as the first. In its original form the paragraph sought the determination of the question—

'Whether Administrative Receivers appointed under a floating charge who have a statutory duty to pay preferential creditors are entitled in principle to an injunction to restrain the levy of distress for non-domestic rates by a Charging Authority which would have the effect of giving the Charging Authority levying distress priority over preferential creditors of the company.'

After I had expressed some concern about the court being asked to declare that a party is 'entitled in principle to an injunction' Mr Moss formulated a different question, which I gave the applicants leave to add to the originating summons by amendment. This question is in the following terms:

'Whether Administrative Receivers appointed under a floating charge who have a statutory duty pursuant to Section 40 of the Insolvency Act 1986 to pay preferential creditors are entitled to a declaration that a Charging Authority is not entitled to levy distress for non-domestic rates pursuant to Regulation 14 (1) of the Non-Domestic Rating (Collection and Enforcement) (Local Lists) Regulations 1989 (SI No. 1058 of 1989) unless and until all preferential debts (within the meaning given to that expression by Section 386 of the Insolvency Act 1986) have been paid out of the assets coming to the hands of the Administrative Receivers.'

Both the original and the amended question sought, so far as the applicants are concerned, to take advantage of the decision of Ungoed-Thomas J in *Taggs Island Casino Ltd v Richmond upon Thames BC* [1967] RA 70. In that case a debenture holder had appointed a receiver and manager under the debenture. After the appointment the rating authority sought to levy a distraint over property on the company's premises in respect of rates which had become due before the receiver and manager was appointed. An application was then made to the court for an interlocutory injunction to restrain completion of the distress. Much of the argument was concerned with the question of occupation, which the judge held to be largely irrelevant. There was, however, an alternative argument which was that ss 94 and 319(1) of the Companies Act 1948, whose effect was to require the receiver to pay certain rates and taxes as preferential debts, was inconsistent with the existence of a power of distress. On this Ungoed-Thomas J referred to the relevant sections and continued (at 80–81):

'It therefore appears to me prima facie to follow that, when provision is made as it is under s 94 for the application of assets in the receiver's hands, none of the persons in whose favour those assets are to be administered can levy distress and, in effect, obtain priority over other creditors, who, according to the Act, are to rank pari passu with the creditor levying the distress. It may be that it is so, but it seems to me to be a matter which requires the consideration and investigation which is proper for the trial of the action. This consideration appears to me to govern quite a number of arguments and submissions which were made to me with regard to the receiver's liability to pay these rates and the consequential, so it was said, liability of the goods in his hands to be available for distress. These were powerful considerations submitted on behalf of the rating authority, but, as I have indicated, there appeared to me to be powerful considerations on the other side too'

Ungoed-Thomas J then turned to the balance of convenience and, finding this to be in favour of restraining the distress, granted an injunction until trial.

Clearly Ungoed-Thomas J did not himself decide the point at the interlocutory stage in that case and there is no record of the matter ever having gone to trial. The precise argument which was presented then is no longer available since the abolition of preference for rates. Nevertheless it was submitted by Mr Moss that the essential point is still a good one, if not indeed now reinforced. Whereas at the time of the decision in the *Taggs Island* case the law was that one year's rates were to be paid pari passu with certain taxes and other specified debts and in preference to the debt due to the debenture holder, the law is now that rates no longer have any preference. If, however, distress can be levied notwithstanding the appointment of a receiver the practical result is that, to the extent of the value of goods distrained, a charging authority can obtain preference even over preferential debts. This, argued Mr Moss, cannot be the law. Section 40 of the Insolvency Act 1986, like s 94 of the Companies Act 1948, should therefore be treated as having impliedly excluded the levying of distress after the appointment of a receiver under a floating charge.

This argument certainly has some attraction, but I am not wholly convinced by it. If I am right in my conclusion on the arguments under question 1 of the originating summons there is no need to uphold this alternative argument as a means of avoiding conflict with the statutory provisions as to priority. In any event it is an argument which, if correct, benefits only the preferential creditors, not the bank as debenture holder. In all the circumstances I do not propose to answer either of the questions raised by para 2 of the originating summons.

Declaration accordingly.

Jacqueline Metcalfe   Barrister.

R v Ananthanarayanan

COURT OF APPEAL, CRIMINAL DIVISION
STEYN LJ, ROUGIER AND LAWS JJ
5, 11 MARCH 1993

Criminal evidence – Corroboration – Similar fact evidence – Risk of contamination – Complaints of indecent assault – Complaints not spontaneous – Complaints prompted by common source – Whether real risk that one complainant's evidence contaminated by another complainant – Whether judge wrongly directing jury that complainants' evidence capable of mutual corroboration.

The appellant, a consultant psychiatrist, was convicted of five offences of indecent assault on four women. The complaints were all made at the same time, the majority of them many months after the alleged incidents complained of. There was evidence to suggest that certain of the complaints were not spontaneous but were prompted by a common source in that the local social services department had sought potential complainants who might make allegations of indecency against the appellant. The appellant appealed against his conviction on the ground, inter alia, that the judge should not have directed the jury that the evidence of the women was capable of offering mutual corroboration because on the facts there was a real risk that any one of the complainant's accounts might have been 'contaminated' by any other and that because of the risk of contamination the possibility of mutual corroboration should not have been left to the jury.

Held – Since the value of potentially corroborative evidence critically depended upon its being independent of the complaint sought to be

Considered.
R. v. H.
[1995] 2 W.L.R.
737, H.L.(E.)

corroborated, if there existed a real risk that the evidence might have been contaminated by the evidence of another complainant there could be no mutual corroboration between them and the evidence was therefore not admissible as corroboration. It was the judge's function to decide what evidence was admissible and the jury's function to decide what facts to find on the evidence; accordingly where a question of admissibility depended upon the resolution of an issue of fact such as contamination it was for the judge to resolve it. Where the judge formed the view that there was a real, as opposed to merely speculative, risk that the evidence was not independent, the evidence was not admissible as corroboration and he had a duty to direct the jury that no possibility arose of corroboration between the witnesses in question. In the circumstances, since there was a real possibility that the complaints were not truly independent of each other, the judge should not have directed the jury that the evidence of the women was capable of being mutually corroborative. The appeal would therefore be allowed and the convictions quashed (see p 854 b c f g and p 858 j to p 859 c, post).

Boardman v DPP [1974] 3 All ER 887 and DPP v Kilbourne [1973] 1 All ER 440 considered.

R v Johannsen (1977) 65 Cr App R 101 distinguished.

Notes

For corroboration, see 11(2) *Halsbury's Laws* (4th edn reissue) paras 1140, 1141, and for cases on the subject, see 15(2) *Digest* (2nd reissue) 106–107, *19059–19065*.

For admissibility of similar fact evidence see 11(2) *Halsbury's Laws* (4th edn reissue) paras 1091–1098, and for cases on the subject, see 15(1) *Digest* (2nd reissue) 587–595, *17731–17784*.

Cases referred to in judgment

Boardman v DPP [1974] 3 All ER 887, [1975] AC 421, [1974] 3 WLR 673, HL.
DPP v Kilbourne [1973] 1 All ER 440, [1973] AC 729, [1973] 2 WLR 254, HL.
R v Bedford (1991) 93 Cr App R 113, CA.
R v Brooks (1991) 92 Cr App R 36, CA.
R v Johannsen (1977) 65 Cr App R 101, CA.
R v P [1991] 3 All ER 337, [1991] 2 AC 447, [1991] 3 WLR 161, HL.
R v Scarrott [1978] 1 All ER 672, [1978] QB 1016, CA.
R v Sims [1946] 1 All ER 697, [1946] KB 531, CCA.
Selvey v DPP [1968] 2 All ER 497, [1970] AC 304, [1968] WLR 1494, HL.

Appeal against conviction

Tinnevely Subramanian Ananthanarayanan appealed against his conviction on 16 October 1991 in the Crown Court at Stoke on Trent before Judge Orrell and a jury of five counts of indecent assault in respect of which he was conditionally discharged for 12 months in respect of each count. The facts are set out in the judgment of the court.

Anthony Barker QC and *Bernard Thorogood* (instructed by *Sankeys*, Stoke on Trent) for the appellant.
David Seconde (instructed by the *Crown Prosecution Service*, Stoke on Trent) for the Crown.

Cur adv vult

5 March 1993. The following judgment of the court was delivered.

LAWS J. This appeal requires the court to revisit an area of law which has been the subject of much judicial authority and academic analysis in the past, namely the use as corroboration of what used to be called 'similar fact' evidence.

In October 1992 the appellant faced his trial at the Crown Court at Stoke on Trent upon an indictment alleging seven offences of indecent assault. He was convicted on five counts, counts 2 to 6, and he was acquitted on the two remaining counts, counts 1 and 7. He was conditionally discharged for 12 months in respect of each count on which he had been convicted.

The facts may be described as follows. The appellant was, at the material time, practising as a consultant psychiatrist in the Staffordshire area. He specialised in the mental illnesses of old age. His work took him to two hospitals and a number of old people's homes.

The four complainants were nurses or care assistants with whom he came into contact at these different establishments. One was P. She was a senior care assistant at an institution known as The Grove. She alleged that on about 15 June 1989 the appellant indecently touched her breasts; that was the subject of count 1 on which he was acquitted; later he touched her leg; that was the subject of count 2. Staff Nurse L worked at the Bucknall Hospital. She said that on a number of occasions between February 1990 and July 1991 the appellant had pressed his hand or legs against hers. On one occasion, she said, he brushed his hand against her breast and once tried forcefully to put his hand between her legs. Her complaints formed the subject of counts 3 and 4. The third complainant was B who was an assistant officer in charge of The King George V Home. She said that on a date in February 1991 the appellant had rubbed her legs with his. The last complainant was F. She was a deputy officer at another home and her allegation was that on 12 August 1991 the appellant had pressed his knees against hers and put his hand on her leg; that was count 6. She also said that he had touched her left breast. That formed the subject of count 7 of which he was acquitted. It was only after she made a formal complaint that the other complainants came forward and, as will be seen, this is of some importance in the light of the issue which the appeal raises.

The appellant denied all the allegations. He said that he could not remember touching the nurses at all, but that if he had done so there was nothing indecent in it; it would have been done in the same way that he touched patients. He was, it was said, a tactile person. The judge had told the jury that there was no evidence capable of amounting to corroboration of the allegations made in counts 1 and 7, those of which the appellant was, in due course, acquitted, but that there was evidence capable of amounting to corroboration on the other counts. It seems reasonable to assume that the jury attached considerable importance to what they were told about corroboration.

It is necessary to look at the details a little further. P said that the appellant first touched her knees when they were sitting at a table talking to a patient. They went back to the office for a private discussion. It was there, according to her, that he twice touched her breast and did so again when they visited the residents' lounge; that was count 1. Back in the office she said that he pulled her chair next to his and spoke of their work and other matters and that whilst he was talking he slowly moved his leg over hers. She said she told him to stop it and tried to move away. When someone knocked at the door, he moved his

chair and then she made an excuse to leave the room. There was a witness who
said that she saw P after the appellant had left the building and that at that time
she appeared angry and upset. However, she made no specific complaint. The
appellant's evidence was that P's account could not be correct as to certain
details she had given and he recalled nothing remarkable about any occasion
when he had visited the home in question. He had certainly never been told
by anyone to stop it.

L said that the appellant changed the pattern of his visits in order that he
might see her. He and she would discuss patients in an office that had windows
on to the wards and corridor and it was in May 1990 that there was an occasion
when he began to move his chair closer to hers little by little. He did not touch
her at first, but there were similar incidents and increasing physical contact
took place in the months which followed. She said he frequently touched her
knees and once brushed his arm against her breast. There was an occasion
when she was squashed against the desk and had her legs crossed firmly. He
tried forcibly to put his hand between them. She resisted and suffered a bruise.
When she was cross-examined she agreed that she had asked the appellant for
a reference; that was because there was friction between herself and the sister.
The appellant invited her out for a meal, she said, shortly before she left for the
new job, but she did not go. She accepted that she made no complaints to the
appellant about the bruise.

Three of her colleagues gave evidence that on looking through the window
at her request they had seen the appellant touching her knees. The appellant
denied any impropriety with this witness just as he denied any with any of the
others. He said he had been shown a bruise but had understood that it was
caused when she fell playing squash. He had not visited the hospital more
frequently deliberately in order to see her. In fact, he said, his visits to the
hospital had decreased. He had advised her to apply for a new job because
there was some difficulty between her and the sister. There was some medical
evidence about the bruise, but it is not necessary to say more about that.

B, the next complainant, told the jury of an occasion when she sat with the
appellant and a patient. The appellant moved his chair closer to hers little by
little. He put one of his legs between hers and brought the other leg up to
touch her knees. She got up and asked what treatment he would be ordering
for the patient. He said he would put it in writing to the general practitioner
and then left, but he came back unexpectedly an hour or so later. He said he
had decided to leave the prescription himself. He began to speak about
Alzheimer's disease and again moved his chair towards her and put his leg next
to hers. As he spoke to her he brushed her leg. This went on for some minutes.
She said nothing to him about it but made an excuse to leave the room. When
she was cross-examined she agreed there was no record of the appellant
coming back to the home in the report book, but insisted that he had done so.

F was the last complainant, though the first to complain. She gave evidence
that after seeing a patient the appellant had discussed the case with her in a
medical room and shuffled his chair towards her as he spoke. The incident was
interrupted by the arrival of another person, but the appellant continued to
edge forward until his knees were pressed against her. As the appellant turned
away to get his notes she took the opportunity to cross her legs and he then
pressed the back of his hand against her left breast; that was count 7, one of the
counts of which he was acquitted. The appellant continued to talk about
depression among elderly patients and as he did so, he again edged his chair

towards her. He started to pat her leg. He put his palm quite firmly on the inside of her knee. She knocked his hand away and told him not to do it. He said 'OK' in a defensive manner. There was some evidence from other witnesses who said that they saw this complainant afterwards and she appeared to them to be upset. Some conversation took place. It is not necessary to recite the details of that. F reported the incident to the officer in charge the next day. She then saw Mr Carter from the Stoke on Trent social services department, and it will be seen later that that event may be of some significance.

The appellant gave evidence not only about the complaints made against him but about his own family and professional background. He say that he was shocked when he heard that the complaints had been made. He received a letter to that effect from the health authority. He had no recollection, as we have said, of touching any of these nurses and certainly had not done so indecently. There was a formidable body of character evidence called in his support: seven consultants, a nursing manager, a matron in a private home, a professor of psychiatry, four nurses, two occupational therapists, a clinical psychologist and a senior probation officer. Their evidence was much to the same effect. He was, it was said, a man of the highest integrity, both professional and personal, courteous to women, and none of the witnesses could believe the allegations which had been made. None had heard any rumours about any such behaviour on his part. A number spoke about his dedication and enthusiasm for his work. That is a picture of the case which the jury had to try.

The first point argued before us by Mr Barker QC was that the judge should have severed the indictment, so that the allegations made by the individual complainants would be tried separately. However, it quickly became apparent that severance as such was not the true issue. The reason is this: if any of the women's complaints was capable of corroborating that of any other, and it was correct for the judge so to direct the jury, there could have been no question of severance. Clearly, in such an event, the indictment had to be tried as one. If, on the other hand, it was impermissible for the judge to direct the jury that the women's accounts were capable of corroborating one another, the appeal would have to be allowed since that is what he did; and ex hypothesi it would amount to a material misdirection. This would be so irrespective of any decision as to severance. Thus the question raised by the principal ground argued by Mr Barker comes to this: was it right on the facts for the judge to direct the jury that the evidence of the women was capable of amounting to corroboration inter se or not?

Before addressing that issue, however, which, as will be seen, has ramifications travelling wider than the facts of the instant case, we should notice another question which is not expressly addressed in the grounds and indeed was suggested to Mr Barker by the court in the course of argument. If it were to be answered in favour of the appellant it would dispose of the appeal without the necessity to navigate the turbulent but much travelled waters of similar fact evidence. The question is whether the judge's direction to the jury as to what is meant by 'contamination' in a context such as this was correct. He said:

'... go on to ask yourselves, "Are we sure that the evidence of all the women is free from ... contamination", by which I mean that you are sure

that they have not put their heads together to make false allegations or to
exaggerate allegations or to put a sinister connotation on an incident
which does not deserve a sinister connotation or they have been
influenced by hearing of other people's allegations or they have been
influenced by the suggestion by some third person, such as a person
carrying out the preliminary investigation in this case. You have to be
satisfied that all these women are independent witnesses when they make
these allegations.'

Had the judge only directed the jury that the possibility of contamination
could be excluded if they were sure that the witnesses had not conspired to
give false evidence, that, we think, would have been a misdirection. The
reason is that for the evidence of one complainant to be admissible as
corroborative of the evidence of another it is a necessary condition that each
be truly independent of the other; and a witness's account may be infected by
what another complainant has said without there being even a suspicion of a
deliberate intention to tell a false story. One witness may be unconsciously
influenced by what she has heard from another: she may adopt details of which
she has been told as if they were details of what had happened to her, and may
do it in all innocence, and so it is not enough to direct the jury that they must
negative perjury or conspiracy to perjure. But the judge did not limit his
direction in that way. He told the jury that they must also be sure that none of
the women was 'influenced by hearing of other people's allegations or ... by
the suggestion of some third person'. This was a proper direction, so that on
examination there is nothing in this point and we return to Mr Barker's
principal argument.

His submissions proposed two reasons why we should hold that the judge
ought not to have directed the jury that the evidence of the women was
capable of offering mutual corroboration. The first was that on the facts there
was a real risk that any one of the complainant's accounts might have been
'contaminated' by any other. The second was that, even leaving aside any
possibility of contamination, the evidence given by any of the women was not
in law capable of corroborating that of any other. He referred us to passages
in the summing up in which the judge summarised the essential evidence of, at
any rate, three of the complainants, P, L, and B.

We can deal with this latter submission shortly. There is of course a good
deal of learning about the circumstances in which evidence of one offence can
corroborate evidence of another. The succession of cases which discuss what
used to be called the 'similar fact' rule culminates in the decision of the House
of Lords in *R v P* [1991] 3 All ER 337, [1991] 2 AC 447, but the nature of Mr
Barker's submission on this aspect of the case makes it unnecessary to rehearse
this jurisprudence. His argument was that the evidence of indecent touching
by the appellant disclosed such trivial acts as not, in law, to amount to indecent
assault at all and the jury ought to have been told that any corroborating
material would have to be evidence of indecent assault. In his perfected
grounds he submitted that the jury should have been given a direction that if
they felt that any particular incident was 'de minimis' that would not amount
to indecent assault.

In our judgment this would have been a pernicious approach for the judge
to take. It would amount to saying that so far as the law is concerned women
have to put up with minor indecent assaults. Of course there may be cases

where the circumstances of an alleged indecent assault are such that a real question arises whether the public interest requires prosecution, but in principle there should be no doubt that under the modern law any deliberate and non-consensual touching accompanied by circumstances of indecency constitutes the criminal offence of indecent assault. There is no room in this area of the law for any 'de minimis' exception.

Leaving that argument aside, it is quite plain that the account of each woman would have probative value in relation to the account of any other, assuming there was no 'contamination', and so Mr Barker's first argument, namely that there was a risk of contamination such that the possibility of mutual corroboration should not have been left to the jury, discloses the only point of substance in the case and we turn to that now.

The basis upon which Mr Barker submits on the facts that there was a risk of contamination between the witnesses' accounts is, essentially, twofold, and the two considerations in question interlock. The first is that in large measure the women's complaints were first made at the same time, one with another, and that, save in the case of F, they were made at a considerable distance of time after the events were alleged to have taken place. Thus the complaint of P was made in August 1991 but the assault which she alleged took place was in June 1989. L alleged acts of indecency between February 1990 and July 1991 but she too complained no earlier than August 1991. B's complaint related to an episode said to have taken place in February 1991 but again she did not complain until August or September. Indeed, none of these three complainants made their allegations until after the complaint made by F in August 1991.

Alongside these facts runs Mr Barker's second point, namely that there was evidence to show, or at the least to suggest, that the complaints (at any rate those made after that of F) were not spontaneous but prompted by a common source: in the summer of 1991 the social services department of Stoke on Trent were actually seeking potential complainants who might make allegations of indecency against the appellant. He said that in cross-examination B told the court that in August 1991 the social services department were looking for persons who might make an allegation against him, and P said that she made her statement in 1991 because her superior, a Miss Tempest, telephoned and asked her to do so.

In our judgment these circumstances give rise, at least, to a real possibility that the complaints which ultimately emerged, and which formed the basis of the prosecution case before the jury, were not truly independent one of another. The fact that some of them may have been prompted obviously suggests this. It is not necessary to speculate upon what precisely might have been said, for example, over the telephone to P or to B, to conclude that there must at any rate have been a suggestion that there already existed a basis for suspecting the appellant of crimes of indecency which was sought to be bolstered by the active collection of further complaints.

Given that the judge's direction as to what would constitute contamination of one witness's evidence by that of another cannot itself be impeached, the true question here is whether he should have left the possibility of mutual corroboration to the jury at all.

In a series of authorities it has been held that if there is a 'real chance' that there has been collusion between the makers of two or more complaints one cannot be corroborative of the other: see per Lord Reid in *DPP v Kilbourne*

[1973] 1 All ER 440 at 456, [1973] AC 729 at 750; per Lord Cross in *Boardman v DPP* [1974] 3 All ER 887 at 910, [1975] AC 421 at 459. Other authorities such as *R v P* [1991] 3 All ER 337, [1991] 2 AC 447 and *R v Brooks* (1991) 92 Cr App R 36 use such expressions as 'real danger' or 'real possibility'.

There is no doubt that if there exists a 'real risk' or 'real possibility' that the evidence of one complainant may have been contaminated by that of another, there can be no mutual corroboration between them. The question starkly raised in this case is whether it is for the judge or the jury to decide whether the risk exists. That being so, one can see at once that the answer depends upon a correct analysis of their respective roles. Elementarily it is always the judge's function to decide what evidence is admissible before the jury, and the jury's function to decide what facts to find on that evidence. In principle, therefore, where a question of admissibility depends upon the resolution of an issue of fact, it is for the judge to resolve it. Thus if, for example, it is suggested that a confession has been obtained through a process of questioning by the police in which there have been breaches of the codes made under the provisions of the Police and Criminal Evidence Act 1984, and the breaches are denied, the judge must find the necessary facts himself. In the days before the contemporaneous electronic recording of police interviews there were frequently disputes as to what had passed between the defendant and the interviewing officers, and where an issue of admissibility turned on the dispute the judge would hold a voire dire to decide it. All this is basic and uncontentious. Is there any reason why the same approach should not apply when the question is whether there is a real risk that 'similar fact' evidence might not be truly independent of the evidence which otherwise it might corroborate?

Unassisted by authority, we would conclude that the same principle applies. The value of potentially corroborative evidence of this kind critically depends upon its being independent of the complaint sought to be corroborated. If it is not independent it cannot qualify as corroboration, and the test of independence for this purpose is not whether contamination is proved but whether there is a real risk of contamination. It follows that where such a risk exists the evidence is not admissible as corroboration. It must, therefore, be the judge's task to decide whether the risk exists. In carrying out that task he is doing no more nor less than deciding a question of admissibility.

In our judgment the balance of authority favours this view. It is first to be noted that in *DPP v Kilbourne* [1973] 1 All ER 440, [1973] AC 729 the trial judge had directed the jury that the evidence of any of the complainant boys belonging to one particular group could not be used to reinforce the evidence of any boy in the same group. Lord Hailsham LC said ([1973] 1 All ER 440 at 444, [1973] AC 729 at 737):

> 'He evidently had in mind that the boys of each group were respectively well known to one another and wished thereby to exclude the possibility that they might have put up within each group, but not between groups, a concocted tale.'

The issue in *Kilbourne* was whether evidence, which itself requires corroboration, can be used to support other evidence also requiring corroboration. The House was not concerned to rule upon the respective functions of judge and jury in relation to the assessment of the risk of contamination between witnesses, so that the correctness of the trial judge's implicit view that the existence of such a risk in relation to the evidence of the

boys within either group was a matter for him, not the jury, did not fall for
scrutiny. However, in *Boardman v DPP* [1974] 3 All ER 887 at 897, [1975] AC 421
at 444 Lord Wilberforce said:

> 'The basic principle must be that the admission of similar fact evidence
> (of the kind now in question) is exceptional and requires a strong degree
> of probative force. This probative force is derived, if at all, from the
> circumstances that the facts testified to by the several witnesses bear to
> each other such a striking similarity that they must, when judged by
> experience and common sense, either all be true, or have arisen from a
> cause common to the witnesses or from pure coincidence. The jury may,
> therefore, properly be asked to judge whether the right conclusion is that
> all are true, so that each story is supported by the other(s). I use the words
> "a cause common to the witnesses" to include not only (as in *R v Sims*
> [1946] 1 All ER 697, [1946] KB 531) the possibility that the witnesses may
> have invented a story in concert but also that a similar story may have
> arisen by a process of infection from media of publicity or simply from
> fashion. In the sexual field, and in others, this may be a real possibility;
> something much more than mere similarity and absence of proved
> conspiracy is needed if this evidence is to be allowed. This is well
> illustrated by *DPP v Kilbourne* [1973] 1 All ER 440, [1973] AC 729 where the
> judge excluded "intra group" evidence because of the possibility, *as it
> appeared to him*, of collaboration between boys who knew each other well.
> This is, in my respectful opinion, the right course rather than to admit the
> evidence unless a case of collaboration or concoction is made out.' (Lord
> Wilberforce's emphasis.)

In the opening paragraph of his speech in *Boardman v DPP*, Lord Cross makes
some broad observations about the ordinary rule that the prosecution are not,
as a general rule, permitted to adduce evidence of acts done by the accused
other than those with which he is charged in order to show a propensity to
commit the crime in question, and describes the 'similar fact' rule as an
exception to this principle based on the dictates of commonsense. He said
([1974] 3 All ER 887 at 909, [1975] AC 421 at 457):

> 'In the end—although the admissibility of such evidence is a question of
> law not of discretion—the question as I see it must be one of degree.'

Later he said this ([1974] 3 All ER 887 at 910, [1975] AC 421 at 459):

> 'In such circumstances the first question which arises is obviously
> whether his accusers may not have put their heads together to concoct
> false evidence and if there is any real chance of this having occurred the
> similar fact evidence must be excluded. In *DPP v Kilbourne* [1973] 1 All ER
> 440, [1973] AC 729 it was only allowed to be given by boys of a different
> group from the boy an alleged offence against whom was being considered
> ... When in a case of this sort the prosecution wishes to adduce "similar
> fact" evidence which the defence says is inadmissible, the question
> whether it is admissible ought, if possible, to be decided in the absence of
> the jury at the outset of the trial and if it is decided that the evidence is
> inadmissible and the accused is being charged in the same indictment with
> offences against the other men the charges relating to the different persons
> ought to be tried separately.'

It is true that *Boardman* was no more directly concerned than was *Kilbourne* with the distinct question whether the risk of contamination in a case concerning mutual corroboration was a matter for the judge to decide as an issue going to the admissibility of evidence. So the closing words of Lord Wilberforce and the passage from Lord Cross, which we have cited, are obiter. Clearly, however, they lend strong support, from a source of high authority, for the view which we believe to be correct in principle. We should notice the fact that while the decision of the House of Lords in *R v P* [1991] 3 All ER 337, [1991] 2 AC 447 deprecates the use of the rubric 'striking similarity' as the touchstone in every kind of case for allowing evidence of one offence to be relied on as corroboration of evidence of another, there is nothing in Lord Mackay LC's speech (with which their other Lordships concurred) to call into question these remarks of Lord Wilberforce and Lord Cross.

In *R v Scarrott* [1978] 1 All ER 672, [1978] QB 1016 Scarman LJ, while recognising that a decision before arraignment as to whether the indictment should be severed is truly one for the judge's discretion, makes it clear that when during the trial on (say) one count, the others having been severed, the judge is invited by the prosecution to allow evidence relating to the other counts to be adduced as 'similar fact' evidence, 'it will then be for the judge to rule, *in accordance with the laws of evidence*, whether the evidence is *admissible* or not' (see [1978] 1 All ER 672 at 681, [1978] QB 1016 at 1028; our emphasis).

In *R v Johannsen* (1977) 65 Cr App R 101, which was also a sexual case, Lawton LJ, having cited from *Kilbourne* and *Boardman*, said this (at 104-105):

'If the defendant alleges, as in this case, that there is a real chance that the alleged victims conspired to give false evidence, how is [the judge] to determine that issue? His only source of information is the depositions. The depositions may, as in this case, show that the alleged victims knew each other ... Is the judge to infer in every such case that acquaintance with one another may have resulted in a conspiracy to give false evidence? If he is, many sexual molesters of the young will go free. What if prosecuting counsel says that the police officer in charge of the case is satisfied that there has been no conspiracy? Experienced police officers do try to find out whether there has been. Is the speculative possibility which occurs to the judge to be preferred to the assertions of the prosecution? How is any conflict to be resolved? The answer must surely be—by the jury. This has long been the practice of the Courts. Judges know of the possibility. That is why it is common practice to direct juries about it. In this case the trial judge followed the common practice. In our judgment their Lordships' comments should not be understood as meaning that if the depositions contain no evidence of a conspiracy to give false evidence the judge can use his imagination to decide that there may have been one and in consequence sever the indictment so as to provide for separate trials in respect of each victim. Problems of severance and the admissibility of evidence should be decided on the facts known to the Court, not on speculation as to what the facts may turn out to be. A trial judge, however, has a discretion to exclude evidence tendered by the prosecution if its prejudicial effect outweighs its probative value: see *Selvey v. Director of Public Prosecutions* [1968] 2 All ER 497, [1970] AC 304. In our judgment their Lordships' comments were directed to the exercise of judicial discretion but if such discretion is to be exercised there must, in our judgment, be a factual basis disclosed in the depositions to show there is a 'real chance'—we adopt the words of Lord Reid and Lord Cross—that there has or may have been a conspiracy.'

A number of observations fall to be made as to the reasoning in *Johannsen*.

First, the remarks of Lawton LJ are directed to the possibility of collusion between witnesses to concoct a false story. It is clear that that was the basis on which the case was argued, and Lawton LJ plainly did not intend to suggest that it is only in such a case that corroboration between witnesses asserting similar facts ought to be excluded.

Secondly, the court was concerned with the trial judge's ruling upon an application to sever the indictment after arraignment; hence the remarks of Lawton LJ to the effect that the judge's only source of information as to the possibility of collusion would be the depositions. The present appeal is, of course, not such a case. However, that seems to us to make no difference to the question of principle, namely whether it is for the judge or the jury to decide that there is a real risk of contamination between witnesses. Where the issue is raised before any evidence is given, it is of course true that the judge would have to arrive at his decision on the papers. Later in his judgment Lawton LJ indicated that defending lawyers 'who wished to protect their clients against a possibility of conspiracy' could seek a committal with the witnesses called. That is clearly right, but whether or not that recourse is resorted to cannot, in our judgment, be material to the issue of whether it is for the judge or the jury to decide that a real risk of contamination exists.

Thirdly, the observations of Lawton LJ to the effect that the possibility of a conspiracy is to be decided by the jury have to be viewed in the light of the fact that the court clearly considered, in that case, that the possibility was no more than a speculative one. In a case where an assertion by the defence to the effect that potentially corroborative evidence is contaminated depends in truth on speculation only, the judge will be right to leave the evidence to the jury as capable of amounting to corroboration, since ex hypothesi he will not have found that there is a 'real risk' that the evidence is not independent.

The distinction between a real risk and a speculative possibility is well recognised in the law. It arises, for instance, in relation to the administration of s 2 of the Contempt of Court Act 1981 and the provisions of the Bail Act 1976. It is unnecessary to enter into the details of those provisions. The short point for present purposes is that there is nothing in *Johannsen* to contradict the view which we have formed that, whether immediately after arraignment or in the course of the evidence, the judge forms the view that there is indeed a real risk of contamination, he is to act on that view and direct the jury that no possibility of corroboration between the witnesses in question arises. At most the judgment in *Johannsen* offers this gloss: that in a case where there is a *possibility* but not a *real risk* of contamination the judge should leave the matter to the jury, but in fairness direct them that if they consider the possibility of contamination to be substantial and not merely speculative (despite the judge's own view) they should not treat the evidence as corroborative. It may be said that such a direction would be a departure from the strict logic inherent in the proposition that questions of admissibility are always for the judge, but logic is the handmaid and not the mistress of the law and this position does no more nor less than put in the hands of the jury the right and duty to protect the defendant against a residual possibility of injustice.

There is, however, one aspect of *Johannsen* from which we would respectfully depart. It consists in Lawton LJ's remarks to the effect that the question of whether evidence of this kind should be left to the jury is a matter for judicial discretion. We have already explained that the risk of contamination in potentially corroborative evidence goes to the admissibility of that evidence. Questions of admissibility are not matters for the discretion of the judge, since by definition the existence of a true discretion means that the judge may in principle lawfully decide the point either way. But if evidence is inadmissible, nothing is more obvious than that the judge cannot properly admit it. If a trial judge concludes that a real risk of contamination exists in circumstances of the kind raised by this case, he possesses no discretion to admit it. This consideration offers no quarrel with the result in *Johannsen*, which is readily explained by the fact that the assertion there of a conspiracy to give false evidence was no more than speculative.

There is a dictum in another case which also uses the language of discretion. In *R v Bedford* (1991) 93 Cr App R 113 at 116 Stuart-Smith LJ said this:

'It was not suggested in the present case that there had been any concoction or collaboration between the boys to put up a false story. Nor was it suggested that their evidence might have been affected by media publicity. If there is a real possibility of either occurring the judge must exercise his discretion to exclude the evidence.'

Nothing critical to the decision in *Bedford* turns on this choice of language. The case was not concerned with any question as to the respective functions of judge and jury and we certainly do not consider that Stuart-Smith LJ was intending to hold, by implication, that the exercise on which the judge would be engaged in the circumstances contemplated would not involve an issue as to the admissibility of evidence. In our judgment this dictum should not deflect us from the view we have formed as to the principle upon which this appeal ought to be decided, and likewise, nothing in *Johannsen* offers a basis for departing from that view.

There is some material to show that this court has recently considered it to be an open question whether potential corroboration, where there is a real risk of its being contaminated, falls to be excluded as a strict matter of inadmissibility. In *R v Brooks* (1991) 92 Cr App R 36 at 42 Mustill LJ, in a judgment which comprehensively deals with many of the problems relating to similar fact evidence, said this:

'The judge should be particularly cautious about admitting evidence of similar facts where there is a real possibility that the evidence relied upon to prove those facts has been concocted ... Whether it is the law that where collusion is seriously in issue the evidence must always be ruled out is at present debatable, although there is authority for this view in *Boardman v DPP* [1974] 3 All ER 887, [1975] AC 421. See also *Cross on Evidence* (6th edn 1985) p 333. Perhaps this goes too far, but the risks are so obvious that the judge should hesitate long before admitting the evidence and if he does, should give the jury the plainest possible warning.'

In our judgment it should now be made clear that the question whether such evidence should be ruled out or not is one which goes to the legal admissibility of that evidence. The test for the trial judge to apply is that vouchsafed all through the cases: he must ask himself whether there is a real (as opposed to a merely speculative or fanciful) risk that the evidence is not independent. The risk can arise not only when there may have been deliberate concoction, but, as has been said, from media publicity or because one witness may have been innocently influenced by his or her knowledge of another's account. Where the judge finds that the risk exists, he has no discretion to let the evidence go to the jury as corroboration.

It follows that in the present case the judge should not have allowed the jury to proceed to their task on the basis that the evidence of the women was capable of being mutually corroborative. That being so, the convictions cannot stand. The appeal will be allowed, and they will be quashed.

Appeal allowed. Convictions quashed.

N P Metcalfe Esq   Barrister.

R v Ryder

COURT OF APPEAL, CRIMINAL DIVISION
LORD TAYLOR OF GOSFORTH CJ, POPPLEWELL AND LAWS JJ
21 DECEMBER 1992, 1 FEBRUARY, 12 MARCH 1993

Considered.
R. v. H.
[1995] 2 W.L.R.
737, H.L.(E.)

Criminal evidence – Corroboration – Similar fact evidence – Possibility of collusion – Direction to jury – Circumstances in which similar fact evidence should not be permitted to be led.

The appellant was convicted on eight counts of offences including rape, attempted rape, buggery, and attempted buggery against five prostitutes. There were various features in common between the incidents. At his trial the judge directed the jury that if they found that shared features between the evidence of one woman and that of another were so strikingly similar that it would be against common sense for that to be a coincidence or invention then the evidence of each of the two woman was capable of corroborating that of the other, but that if they found that the evidence of either was tainted by discussion between them, either deliberately or innocently, no corroboration was possible. The appellant appealed, contending, inter alia, that since there was the possibility of collusion between certain of the prostitutes the similar fact evidence should either not have been admitted or should not have been left to the jury, and that in relation to two of the counts the judge had failed to give any direction to the jury as to the absence of corroborative evidence as to lack of consent.

Held – (1) Where the prosecution sought to admit similar fact evidence which was challenged by the defence on the ground of collusion between witnesses, whether deliberate or through the unconscious influence of one witness's evidence on that of another, there were four possible situations which might confront the court. First, if a real possibility of collusion was apparent to the judge on the face of the documents, he ought not to allow the similar fact evidence to be led. Secondly, if a submission was made raising the suggestion of collusion the judge might find it necessary to hold a voire dire. Thirdly, if the evidence was admitted but at the end of the case the judge took the view that there was a real possibility of collusion he should direct the jury in summing up not to use the evidence as corroboration. Fourthly, even if the judge himself was of the view that there was no real possibility of collusion, but the matter had been argued, he should leave the issue to the jury to decide whether the evidence was tainted by collusion and therefore incapable of providing corroboration. On the facts, the likelihood of collusion between the women was no more than fanciful and the judge had been correct in admitting the similar fact evidence and in directiing the jury as to how to approach such evidence. However, since in the case of two of the counts a direction as to the absence of corroborative evidence as to lack of consent to intercourse was essential and had not been given, the conviction on those counts would be quashed. The appeal against conviction on the remaining six counts would be dismissed (see p 868 *d* to *h*, p 869 *f* to *j*, p 870 *e* and p 871 *f* to *j*, post).

R v Ananthanarayanan [1994] 2 All ER 847 applied.

Notes
For admissibility of similar fact evidence, see 11(2) *Halsbury's Laws* (4th edn reissue) paras 1091–1098; and for cases on the subject, see 15(1) *Digest* (2nd reissue) 587–595, 17731–17784.

Cases referred to in judgment
Boardman v DPP [1974] 3 All ER 887, [1975] AC 421, [1974] 3 WLR 673, HL.
DPP v Kilbourne [1973] 1 All ER 440, [1973] AC 729, [1973] 2 WLR 254, HL.
Hoch v R (1988) 81 ALR 225.
Makin v A-G for New South Wales [1894] AC 57, PC.
R v Ananthanarayanan [1994] 2 All ER 847, (1994) 98 Cr App R 1, CA.
R v Bedford (1991) 93 Cr App R 113, CA.
R v Brooks (1991) 92 Cr App R 36, CA.
R v Inder (1977) 67 Cr App R 143, CA.
R v P [1991] 3 All ER 337, [1991] 2 AC 447, [1991] 3 WLR 161, HL.
R v Scarrott [1978] 1 All ER 672, [1978] QB 1016, CA.
R v Sims [1946] 1 All ER 697, [1946] KB 531, CCA.
R v Smith (1915) 84 LJKB 2153, 11 Cr App R 229, [1914–15] All ER Rep 262, CCA.
R v Straffen [1952] 2 All ER 657, [1952] 2 QB 911, CCA.
R v Turnbull [1976] 3 All ER 549, [1977] QB 224, [1976] 3 WLR 445, CA.

Cases also cited
R v Chance [1988] 3 All ER 225, [1988] QB 932, [1988] 3 WLR 661, CA.
R v Johannsen (1977) 65 Cr App R 101, CA.
R v Mills [1992] Crim LR 802, CA.
R v Wilmot (1989) 89 Cr App R 341, CA.

Appeal against conviction and sentence
David Ryder appealed against his conviction on 24 May 1989 in the Crown Court at Bristol before Jowitt J and a jury on three counts of rape, one count of attempted rape, one count of buggery, one count of attempted buggery, one count of theft and one count of assault occasioning actual bodily harm. On 20

July 1989 he was sentenced to two years' imprisonment for the theft, five years' imprisonment for the assault occasioning bodily harm and life imprisonment on the other counts, all concurrent. The facts are set out in the judgment of the court.

Anthony Arlidge QC and *Richard Guy* (assigned by the *Registrar of Criminal Appeals*) for the appellant.
Christopher Leigh QC for the Crown.

Cur adv vult

12 March 1993. The following judgment of the court was delivered.

LORD TAYLOR OF GOSFORTH CJ. On 24 May 1989 at the Crown Court at Bristol before Jowitt J this appellant was convicted of three counts of rape, one count of attempted rape, one count of buggery, one count of attempted buggery, one count of theft and one count of assault occasioning actual bodily harm. On 20 July 1989 he was sentenced to a term of two years' imprisonment for the theft, five years' imprisonment for the assault occasioning actual bodily harm and life imprisonment on the other counts, all concurrent.

He appeals against the convictions by leave of the Full Court and seeks leave to appeal against the sentence.

On count 1 the appellant was convicted of raping Miss M, a prostitute from Swindon. On counts 2, 3 and 4 he was convicted of rape, attempted buggery and theft from Miss S, a prostitute from Bournemouth. On counts 5 and 6 he was convicted of rape and buggery of Miss W, a prostitute from Bournemouth, and on counts 7 and 8 he was convicted of attempted rape and of assault occasioning actual bodily harm on Miss C, a prostitute from Swindon. A fifth prostitute, Mrs W from Bournemouth, gave evidence of rape, her evidence being admitted on the basis of similar fact.

The offence against Miss M was alleged to have taken place between 1 January 1986 and 31 December 1986; the offences against Miss S between 1 to 31 January 1988; the offences against Miss W on 3 February 1988 and the offences against Miss C on 1 May 1988. The incident involving Mrs W occurred in March 1988.

It was the appellant's case at trial that the evidence given by Miss M was a fabrication and that she had a motive for telling lies. He admitted that he had had sexual intercourse with Miss S consensually several times but denied rape and the other allegations. He denied that he had ever met Miss W and he produced alibi evidence to support that. He denied that he had ever met Miss C and produced alibi evidence. He made a similar denial in respect of Mrs W.

At the hearing before this court leading counsel on his behalf handed to the court a document signed by him at Wakefield Prison in the presence of his solicitor in which he admitted, contrary to the evidence which he had given at trial, (1) that on 3 February 1988 he had sexual intercourse with Miss W, (2) that on 22 March 1988 he had sexual intercourse with Mrs W and (3) that on 1 May he had picked up Miss C and driven her in his car. Those admissions effectively destroyed a number of submissions which had originally appeared in the appellant's grounds.

Mr Arlidge QC on behalf of the appellant nevertheless made three substantive submissions. (1) The counts alleging the incidents in

Bournemouth should have been severed from the counts alleging incidents at Swindon and/or that the evidence in relation to the Bournemouth incidents should not have been treated as similar fact evidence in relation to the Swindon incidents and vice versa. (2) That there should in relation to Miss M have been a *Turnbull* direction (see *R v Turnbull* [1976] 3 All ER 349, [1977] QB 224). (3) That in relation to Miss S, where his defence at trial and before this court was consent, there was no proper direction as to corroboration.

Application was made to sever the indictment by leading counsel who was then appearing on behalf of the appellant. The judge declined to accede to that application. The appellant then sacked his counsel and himself made a similar application to sever. The judge reconsidered the application but did not change his mind. Mr Arlidge has argued the case on the basis that the judge misdirected the jury in relation to the existence of and force of similar fact evidence and that he misdirected the jury that a series of commonplace features could in combination be treated as probative when on the facts of this case they could not.

The factual background to the case is this. When the appellant was interviewed by the police he was firm in his assertion that he had never used or sought to use the services of prostitutes and he had never driven around looking for them. He repeated those assertions when he gave evidence before the jury. This was contrary to evidence given at trial. On 6 October 1987 his blue Volvo, registration No OAP, was seen by a woman police officer to be driving round and round the red light area in Bournemouth. On 30 October 1987 a detective sergeant saw the same car some seven times in the red light area. On 2 November 1987 a woman police officer acting as a decoy spoke to the appellant in the red light area when he was plainly making enquiries. He was also seen during the course of that evening some nine times in the red light district in the space of about an hour and a half. On 15 November 1987 a woman police sergeant saw the appellant driving slowly around the red light area, this time in Swindon, several times. He was seen again driving in Bournemouth in the red light area on 17 November 1987. On 4 January 1988 he picked up Miss S in Bournemouth and on 23 February 1988 he was again seen in his Volvo in the red light district of Bournemouth.

Miss M

One Sunday evening in 1986 she was picked up by a man from her beat in a left-hand drive estate car. He took her to Blunsdon some miles outside Swindon where she gave him her prices and asked what he wanted. He said: 'How much for rape?' She said: 'About 3 or 4 years'. He said he was going to fuck and kill her. She screamed and tried to fight him off but he had sexual intercourse with her and then said he was going to kill her. She told him that his registration number had been taken; he laughed. He did not use a condom. He also said that they could make a deal and she could earn lots of money. He threatened her if she should report the matter.

Miss S

In January 1988 the appellant picked her up in Bournemouth; they had normal sexual intercourse using a condom. She agreed to accept a cheque and she allowed the appellant to take some photographs of her before they had sexual intercourse. The bank refused to cash his cheque. Some four or five days later he telephoned her and asked her to meet him. She did. She got into his car and he told her not to worry as he was going to buy the Dorset Yacht

Club for £300,000 and she was going to manage it for him. They drove around for about 20 minutes and then drove into some forestry commission land and parked. The time was between 10.30 and 11 pm. He became aggressive and told her to take off her clothes. She said she was desperate for money and he just laughed. He put his forearm across her throat. He removed her clothes; he then had intercourse against her will; he did not use a condom. After it was over he laughed. He then forced her head onto his penis and photographed her in the act of oral intercourse. After that he tried to bugger her six times, ejected her from the car and gave her another cheque for £200 saying: 'You don't seem to realise I am in love with you'. He threatened to show the photographs to her parents if she made a complaint.

Miss W

She gave evidence that on 3 February 1988 she was looking for business in the red light district of Bournemouth. At 9.30 pm she saw a blue Volvo estate registration No OAP. It stopped and she got in. She stated her terms and the man agreed to them. He told her he was a rapist; he asked her to take all her clothes off and threatened to kill her. They had oral sex, he repeating that he would make her a rich woman. He made her lie on her stomach and buggered her. He then had sexual intercourse with her in different positions on the back and front seat. He laughed at her. He gave her a cheque for £100 and asked her to meet him the next night. The cheque was returned.

Miss C

She was in the red light district of Swindon on 1 May 1988. About 8.15 pm a Rover car stopped and she got into the front passenger seat. He drove towards Blunsdon and parked at the back of a church. She asked him what he wanted and he said he was going to rape her. She told him she didn't do that. He said she had no choice. He was not going to use a condom. She tried to get out. He grabbed her hair, pulled her head down and scratched her face with what looked like to her a broken bottle. She managed to get away and stopped a car driven by a Mr Pothecary who gave evidence of her making a complaint.

Mrs W

She was visiting her sister in March 1988 when she was picked up by a man driving a Rover. She did not know where they drove to. When they stopped she became frightened and tried to get out. He stopped her by grabbing her arms. He sat on her lap, took off her clothes and removed his own clothes. He had sexual intercourse with her. He said: 'You know this is rape, don't you'. He gave her a cheque and told her his name. He did not use a condom.

The judge gave this direction to the jury:

'The prosecution say that when you look at these five incidents and I am including [Mrs W] there are certain common features. We shall have to look at the evidence about that later. In other words the evidence about the common features. Not every feature said to be common to another incident or other incidents is common to every incident. For example [Miss M] does not say she was given a cheque. But if there are shared features between the account of one woman and another woman and you say of those shared features when looked at in combination (can I stress that: in combination) that they are so strikingly similar that it would fly in the face of common sense to regard the striking similarity as coincidence or as being the result of invention by one or both of the women independent of the other and that the striking similarity indicates that each of the women is talking about the same man, then the evidence of each of the two women so far and so far only as it relates to the features which create the striking similarity between their accounts is capable of corroborating the evidence of the other.'

To assist the jury a grid was prepared.

Feature	Miss M Swindon	Miss S B'Mouth	Miss W B'Mouth	Miss W B'Mouth	Miss C Swindon
Prostitute	X	X	X	X	X
Picked up by car from her beat	X		X	X	X
The man chooses the place	X Blunsdon	X	X	X	X Blunsdon
Speaks of Rape	X		X	X	X
No condom	X	X	X	X	Says he won't use one
Laughs at the woman	X	X	X		
Hands over a cheque		X	X	X	
Suggests association with him will provide opportunity to make money	X	X	X		
Oral sex		X	X		
Threatens her if she should tell (not the same threat)	X	X			
Words suggesting this is how he achieves satisfaction			X	X	
Buggery as well		X Attempt	X		

The judge said this:

'Now may I ask you to take this grid in front of you. I hope the form of it is self-explanatory. There you have across the top the names of the women and I have put in the towns in which they operate. Then down on the left are the various features that you will be wanting to consider and I put in [crosses] in the boxes to indicate when there is evidence of that feature in the evidence of the particular woman. There are a number of features about the grid I want to draw to your attention. First of all, its purpose. It is an aide memoire to remind you where there is evidence of similar features and where there is not because it would be unfortunate if there was confusion and you were saying there is a similar feature when there is not one. Secondly, whether some of the features referred to in the grid really are similar may be open to argument and it is for you to say whether they are similar. In other words, you do not say they are similar just because you see [crosses] in the boxes. You decide. Thirdly, the fact that features are similar does not mean necessarily that there is any significance in those similarities. That is for you to say. The fact there is evidence of a similar feature does not mean that evidence is true. Again that is for you to say. The appearance of a [cross] in a box does not mean the fact of that similarity is proved. It simply reminds you there is evidence in relation to that particular woman of that feature as I hope is made clear on the typed sheet you have. What you are looking at is not individual similarities but the combination of similarities common to two cases to discover whether the comparison is significant. Use the grid as an aide memoire to remind you of the evidence you will have to think about and come to a conclusion about. Your consideration of significance of similarities that you find to be established must be guided by the direction you have on the typed sheet of paper. Members of the jury, in deciding whether one woman's evidence corroborates the evidence of another on account of the similar features of their respective accounts do not go outside the list you have on the grid. Do not, in other words, say, 'The judge has missed off this feature, we will take this into account'; look at these and these only. If you look at the boxes on the grid for [S and C] (you will be able to check my arithmetic later) there are only three common features. I direct you as a matter of law that these two women cannot corroborate one another because the similar features are not sufficient to produce the striking similarity you have to find before one woman's evidence can corroborate another woman's. That does not mean that I am saying to you you should find striking similarity between other accounts; that is for your decision.'

Mr Arlidge complains that none of the acts taken individually were sufficiently striking to be the basis of similar fact evidence and that a combination of commonplace details is insufficient to mount a similar fact argument. Thus it is said that the fact that someone who is a prostitute is picked up by a car from her beat and is taken by a man to a place of his choice is so commonplace as not to arouse any sort of comment.

We were referred to the decision in *R v P* [1991] 3 All ER 337, [1991] 2 AC 447. Lord Mackay LC, after referring to the decisions of *Makin v A-G for New South Wales* [1894] AC 57 and *Boardman v DPP* [1974] 3 All ER 887, [1975] AC 421, said ([1991] 3 All ER 337 at 346, [1991] 2 AC 447 at 460):

'As this matter has been left in *Boardman v DPP* I am of opinion that it is not appropriate to single out "striking similarity" as an essential element in every case in allowing evidence of an offence against one victim to be heard in connection with an allegation against another. Obviously, in cases where the identity of the offender is in issue, evidence of a character sufficiently special reasonably to identify the perpetrator is required ... From all that was said by the House in *Boardman v DPP* I would deduce the essential feature of evidence which is to be admitted is that its probative force in support of the allegation that an accused person committed a crime is sufficiently great to make it just to admit the evidence, notwithstanding that it is prejudicial to the accused in tending to show that he was guilty of another crime. Such probative force may be derived from striking similarities in the evidence about the manner in which the crime was committed and the authorities provide illustrations of that, of which *R v Straffen* [1952] 2 All ER 657, [1952] 2 QB 911 and *R v Smith* (1915) 84 LJKB 2153, [1914–15] All ER Rep 262, provide notable examples. But restricting the circumstances in which there is sufficient probative force to overcome prejudice of evidence relating to another crime to cases in which there is some striking similarity between them is to restrict the operation of the principle in a way which gives too much effect to a particular manner of stating it, and is not justified in principle ... Once the principle is recognised, that what has to be assessed is the probative force of the evidence in question, the infinite variety of circumstances in which the question arises demonstrates that there is no single manner in which this can be achieved. Whether the evidence has sufficient probative value to outweigh its prejudicial effect must in each case be a question of degree. The view that some feature of similarity beyond what has been described as the pederast's or the incestuous father's stock-in-trade before one victim's evidence can be properly admitted upon the trial of another seems to have been stated for the first time in those terms in *R v Inder* (1977) 67 Cr App R 143. Although that case also contains a reference to a warning not to attach too much importance to Lord Salmon's vivid phrase "uniquely or strikingly similar" I think in the context this is what has occurred. This trend has been followed in later cases ... In so far as these decisions required, as an essential feature, a similarity beyond the stock-in-trade I consider they fall to be overruled.'

Later Lord Mackay LC said ([1991] 3 All ER 337 at 348, [1991] 2 AC 447 at 462):

'When a question of the kind raised in this case arises I consider that the judge must first decide whether there is material upon which the jury would be entitled to conclude that the evidence of one victim, about what occurred to that victim, is so related to the evidence given by another victim, about what happened to that other victim, that the evidence of the first victim provides strong enough support for the evidence of the second victim to make it just to admit it, notwithstanding the prejudicial effect of admitting the evidence. This relationship, from which support is derived, may take many forms and while these forms may include "striking similarity" in the manner in which the crime is committed, consisting of unusual characteristics in its execution the necessary relationship is by no means confined to such circumstances. Relationships in time and circumstances other than these may well be important relationships in this connection. Where the identity of the perpetrator is in issue, and evidence of this kind is important in that connection, obviously something in the nature of what has been called in the course of the argument a signature or other special feature will be necessary. To transpose this requirement to other situations where the question is whether a crime has been committed, rather than who did commit it, is to impose an unnecessary and improper restriction upon the application of the principle.'

In the instant case the Crown point out that this is not simply a case of a prostitute being picked up by car from her beat and the man choosing a particular place, which are no doubt commonplace features. There were the added factors of a prostitute to whom the man speaks of rape and with whom he does not use any form of protection. These four factors taken together were unusual and showed an intention to rape the prostitutes in question. Those matters seem to us to be sufficiently similar and significant to entitle the judge to admit the evidence even if there were no other 'similar features'. In addition, the admissions which the appellant has now made obviously and substantially strengthen the prosecution argument on this limb of the case.

In support of his first ground, Mr Arlidge further argued that there may have been collusion within each group of prostitutes and that accordingly the similar fact evidence should either not have been admitted or not have been left to the jury because if there is any suggestion of collusion it is for the Crown to negative that possibility. The rationale of similar fact evidence is that two or more people do not make up or mistakenly make similar allegations against the same person independently of each other. As Lord Goddard CJ said in *R v Sims* [1946] 1 All ER 697 at 701, [1946] KB 531 at 540:

'The probative force of all the acts together is much greater than one alone; for, whereas the jury might think one man might be telling an untruth, three or four are hardly likely to tell the same untruth unless they were conspiring together. If there is nothing to suggest a conspiracy their evidence would seem to be overwhelming.'

In *DPP v Kilbourne* [1973] 1 All ER 440 at 456, [1973] AC 729 at 750 Lord Reid said:

'We must be astute to see that the apparently corroborative statement is truly independent of the doubted statement. If there is any real chance that there has been collusion between the makers of the two statements we should not accept them as corroborative.'

Similar dicta are to be found in *Boardman v DPP* [1974] 3 All ER 887 at 897, 910, [1975] AC 421 at 444, 459, per Lord Wilberforce and Lord Cross. More recent dicta to like effect are to be found in *R v Bedford* (1991) 93 Cr App R 113 at 116 per Stuart-Smith LJ and in *R v Brookes* (1991) 92 Cr App R 36 at 42 per Mustill LJ.

Professor Cross in *Cross on Evidence* (7th edn, 1990) p 364 notes that Lord Wilberforce said in *Boardman v DPP* [1974] 3 All ER 887 at 897, [1975] AC 421 at 444 that the right course was for the judge to exclude the evidence if there was a 'possibility', as it appeared to him, of collaboration.

Professor Cross went on as follows (at p 365):

'Although Lord Cross agreed on this point, the other members of the House were more equivocal, and in *R v Scarrott* [1978] 1 All ER 672 at 680, [1978] QB 1016 at 1027 the Court of Appeal was content to leave the matter to the discretion of the judge. The court was prepared to accede to the trial judge's view that the question could be ventilated in summing up and decided by the jury. It is submitted that the question is so important that the procedure suggested by Lords Cross and Wilberforce should be adopted in all cases where there are grounds for suspecting concoction. The admissibility of similar fact evidence of this type is likely to be just as damaging to the accused as that of a disputed confession, and it is appropriate to pursue an analogous course. So if the defence alleges some such concoction and adduces some credible evidence of it, the prosecution should be required to satisfy the judge on a *voire dire* that there is no real possibility that such concoction has occurred. Such an approach was endorsed by the High Court of Australia in *Hoch v. R* (1988) 81 ALR 225. If the prosecution succeed on the *voire dire* the evidence should be admitted, but the defence remain free to attack its cogency, in much the same way as it remains free to attack the cogency of a confession admitted after a contested *voire dire*.'

We agree with that view. There are thus four possible situations. In identifying them, we refer to collusion but we use that word to encompass not only deliberate but also unconscious influence of one witness by another. First, where a real possibility of collusion is apparent to the judge on the face of the documents, he should not allow the similar fact evidence to be led. Secondly, if a submission is made raising the suggestion of collusion he may find it necessary to hold a voire dire. Thirdly, if the evidence is admitted but at the end of the case he takes the view there is a real possibility of collusion he should tell the jury in summing up not to use the evidence as corroboration. Finally, even if the judge himself is of the view there is no real possibility of collusion, but the matter has been argued, he should leave the issue to the jury. That view of the law is in accord with the judgment of another division of this court in *R v Anantharanayanan* [1994] 2 All ER 847.

We turn to the circumstances of the present case. It is not suggested here that there was or could be any collusion between the Bournemouth group of prostitutes and the Swindon group. Secondly, Mr Arlidge submitted that the possibility of collusion was now confined to consent, identity no longer being an issue. Thirdly, we are entitled to look at the matter as it now stands following the admission by the appellant that he did have sexual intercourse with Miss W, that he did have sexual intercourse with Mrs W and that he had indeed picked up Miss C and driven her in his car. Since it is now clear that there was no collusion falsely to identify the appellant, it is difficult to argue on his behalf that there was a real chance of collusion in relation to consent.

No suggestion was made to the witnesses either in the Bournemouth group or in the Swindon group that they had indeed put their heads together. The only suggestion was to Miss M that she had colluded with a police officer. Miss C told the court that she had spoken about her experience to Miss M, that she knew Miss M although they were not best friends, and that Miss M had asked her what she had done to her face. Miss C told her, described the car and warned Miss M not to get into it. Miss M replied that she already knew who the man was, that he had done it to her and that she, Miss C, ought to report it to the police. Miss C told the jury she had heard that Miss M had been attacked but had not known by whom. According to Miss M she had told Miss C in the past that the defendant had raped her and kept trying to get different girls into his car and that he was always changing cars. She thought she had given Miss C a description. The result was that Miss M spoke to a policeman on the beat and Miss C went to the police station where she made a statement. Three days later she picked out the defendant on an identification parade.

It was submitted that the women were involved in drugs, that the offences had not been reported in good time, that they were used to talking about clients, that they themselves were arrested and told that someone else had made a statement and that they had actually discussed the identity of the attacker between them.

Turning to the prostitutes from Bournemouth, Miss W was arrested for soliciting. She made a statement to the police. She had learnt from the police that Miss S had also made a statement. She had not known about that until then. She was further told that the police had been looking for her because one or two months earlier she had told Miss S the same thing had happened to her, Miss W. She agreed to make a statement.

In our judgment it is extremely doubtful whether, had identity remained in issue, there would have been any significant force in the argument that any of these women, consciously or unconsciously, influenced any other in picking out the appellant. As we have said, there was no question of collusion between the Bournemouth group and the Swindon group, so that the submission would have had to be that there may have been collusion in one group, even though, by the merest coincidence, similar allegations were made against the same man by the other, which is admittedly entirely independent of the first. Alternatively, it might have been suggested that there was collusion in both groups, in each case wholly unknown to the other. The fact is that the independent existence of the two sets of similar accusations tends strongly to disprove the possibility that the account given by any one of the women was tainted by any of the others. Since it is now clear that there is no question of any collusion in relation to identification, the possibility that nevertheless it may have happened in relation to the issue of consent may be seen to be still more fanciful. We are in effect being asked to contemplate the chance that within either or even both of these two independent groups of women, every one of whom correctly and without collusion identified the appellant as having been with her, a pair of them may have put their heads together, or one influenced another, so as to produce a false story of non-consensual intercourse. Moreover, the exchanges that did take place, certainly between Miss M and Miss C, were concerned with identity of the attacker rather than the fact of the attack.

In the result, we are not persuaded that the judge should have severed, or excluded the similar fact evidence, on the ground of any perceived possibility of collusion. Indeed, given what we have said and the fact that the only collusion suggested by counsel at the time of trial went to identity, which is no longer in issue, his direction to the jury was more favourable to the appellant than justice required. After directing them as to how the women might corroborate one another, he said:

'There is an important qualification, though, to what I have just said, and it is this: you must consider what chances there existed for discussion in relation to the evidence between the two women. By the women, I mean any pair of women when you are asking if the one supports the other. When you consider the chances for discussion, whether directly or through intermediaries, and despite any striking similarity, neither woman can corroborate the other unless you are sure that the account each of them has given is untainted by discussion. If you think there was or may have been discussion of any kind which has tainted a woman's evidence, then so far from enabling her evidence to lend support to the evidence of another woman, it would be damaging to her own evidence. If you think the other woman tried, or may have tried, to taint that evidence, this would be damaging to that other woman's evidence. Members of the jury, evidence can become tainted through discussion in two ways. The first and the obvious way is if the purpose of the discussion is a dishonest one to collude about evidence and to trim or fabricate evidence. The second, less obvious one, may occur when, quite innocently, some idea is put into someone's mind as a result of discussion, with the result that his evidence, without him realising, is influenced by something that he does not really remember, or does not really remember clearly, or something that he has not seen. Or, he may speak with an apparent conviction which his own independent, unaided and unprompted recollection may not really justify.'

In our judgment, the judge was right to admit this evidence and his directions as to the way in which the jury should approach the 'similar features' cannot be faulted.

We turn next to Mr Arlidge's second ground, which is the failure of the judge to give a *Turnbull* direction. This criticism relates now to count 1, namely, Miss M, there now being no dispute in relation to the others that an incident had taken place. The incident took place both in the dark and for a short period. She did not report the matter until May 1988. The appellant denied that Miss M was ever in his car and alleged that her evidence was a fabrication. It was his case that sometime in 1985 he had been visiting his former wife when there had been some altercation with a youth. Miss M came out into the street, intervened and began to argue. The appellant told her that it was none of her business. She threatened that she would get her friends to come and knife him.

There was a dispute about this incident but the appellant contended that after that incident, on occasions when he drove along Manchester Road in the evening on his way to and from home, Miss M seemed always to be there and she would recognise his car and make abusive and obscene gestures to him. On one or two occasions it was his evidence that he would stop to tell her what he thought of her and there was an exchange of words which, as the judge said, was not in the least friendly. According to him, there had been some seven, eight or nine times when his temper got slightly the better of him. Accordingly he had stopped in Manchester Road and told Miss M what he thought of her. Again there was a dispute as to whether there had been this campaign of abuse or not.

The identification of the appellant by Miss M did not occur for nearly two years. On 9 May 1988 she was at the magistrates' court in Swindon to answer a charge of soliciting together with another prostitute called Miss Iles. She was sitting in the back of one of the courts and she saw the appellant brought into court. She looked at him, she recognised him as the man who had raped her.

'My God', she thought, and walked straight out. She told the jury 'I'll never forget him' and she told Miss Iles that the appellant was in court.

This was not a 'fleeting glance' case but it was a case of recognition. It accordingly required a *Turnbull* direction. None was given nor hinted at. However, the defence was not one of mistaken identity in the sense of honest mistake. It was that Miss M had deliberately falsified her evidence because of her animosity. We have considered this point with great care. We have come to the conclusion that the credibility of the witness was the fundamental issue. Accordingly, notwithstanding the failure by the judge to give the *Turnbull* direction, no miscarriage of justice has in fact occurred.

We turn to the third of Mr Arlidge's points, namely, the absence of any direction as to corroboration in relation to counts 2, 3 and 4 involving Miss S. The appellant always accepted that intercourse took place, and contended that it was with consent. The photograph which he took showing her in the act of oral intercourse was before the court as it was before the jury. There was no evidence to corroborate the allegation of attempted buggery. The judge gave the jury the proper direction in sex cases that: 'It can be very dangerous to convict a man upon the evidence of the complainant alone unless her evidence is supported by corroboration'. He further properly directed them that they could convict without corroboration provided that they could say: 'Nevertheless, we are sure in this case that we can exclude those dangers and we are sure in this case it is safe to convict without corroboration'. The judge further properly told the jury that it was his task to tell them what evidence was capable of corroborating the complainants' evidence. He pointed out that in S's case sexual intercourse was admitted and that they would be looking for corroboration of the issue of whether there was consent for that intercourse.

Corroboration of lack of consent was particularly important because shortly before the incident complained of the appellant had picked her up, taken her to a place of her own choosing, and she had had consensual intercourse with him using a condom. On that occasion she had been paid by cheque, she had agreed to be photographed and she had given the appellant her parents' phone number. It is accepted by the Crown that there was in truth no corroborative evidence either of non-consent to intercourse or of the attempted buggery. The judge unhappily in a detailed summing up omitted so to tell the jury.

The result was that they may have thought the other evidence in the case was corroborative of her story. The Crown contended that she was such a convincing witness that the jury were bound to believe her. We regret we cannot accept that submission. A proper direction as to the absence of corroborative evidence of non-consent in Miss S's case was vital for the reasons we have already indicated.

Accordingly the convictions on counts 2 and 3 relating to rape and attempted buggery must be quashed. Count 4, which relates to the theft charge, is unaffected by the misdirection on corroboration. The appeal against conviction on counts 1, 4, 5, 6, 7 and 8 is dismissed.

Appeal allowed in part. Convictions on counts 2 and 3 quashed.

N P Metcalfe Esq   Barrister.

R v W

COURT OF APPEAL, CRIMINAL DIVISION
LORD TAYLOR OF GOSFORTH, CJ, FRENCH AND HARRISON JJ
13 JANUARY, 17 FEBRUARY 1994

Criminal evidence – Corroboration – Similar fact evidence – Sexual offences – Trial 20 to 30 years after alleged offences – Possibility of contamination or collusion – Whether sufficient to warrant holding of a voire dire – Direction to jury on whether evidence capable of mutual corroboration.

The appellant was convicted of a number of sexual offences, including indecent assault and attempted rape, against his nieces and nephews and step-daughter. The offences were alleged to have occurred between 10 and 20 years before the trial and it emerged during the trial that at various times within that period there had been discussions concerning the allegations between some of the complainants. At the start of the trial the defence had applied to the judge to hold a voire dire on the ground that there was a real possibility of concoction between the complainants. The judge declined to do so, holding that the possibility of concoction was no more than speculative. The appellant appealed contending, inter alia, that as there was a possibility of deliberate collusion between the complainants or contamination as between their stories the judge should have held a voire dire to investigate such possibility.

Held – A bare assertion on behalf of the defence that there may have been collusion or contamination did not oblige the judge to hold a voire dire and only if the judge believed that it was necessary to hear evidence to enable him properly to consider an issue raised in the committal papers or put before him by way of credible evidence on behalf of the defence, ought he to hold a voire dire. On the facts, whereas at the start of the trial the assertion of concoction was mere speculation, by the end of the prosecution case the situation had changed in that cross-examination had elicited a number of facts raising a real possibility of collusion or at least contamination and the judge should have directed the jury not to use the evidence as corroboration. For that reason and in view of the fact that the judge had taken over the prosecution's role in a manner which might have resulted in unfairness to the appellant and against the background of the unusually long delay before the complaints were made there was doubt whether the verdicts were safe and satisfactory. The appeal would therefore be allowed (see p 878 *e* to *g*, p 879 *d* to *g* and p 880 *h j*, post).

Notes

For corroboration in sexual offences, see 11(2) *Halsbury's Laws* (4th edn reissue) para 1142, and for evidence of complainants in sexual cases, see ibid para 1142. For cases on corroboration see 15(2) *Digest* (2nd reissue) 106–107, *19059–19065*.

For admissibility of similar fact evidence, see 11(2) *Halsbury's Laws* (4th edn reissue) paras 1091–1098, and for cases on the subject, see 15(1) *Digest* (2nd reissue) 587–595, *17731–17784*.

Cases referred to in judgment
R v P [1991] 3 All ER 337, [1991] 2 AC 447, [1991] 3 WLR 161, HL.
Hoch v R (1988) 81 ALR 225.
R v Ananthanarayanan [1994] 2 All ER 847, CA.
R v Johannsen (1977) 65 Cr App R 101, 98 Cr App R 1, CA.
R v Ryder [1994] 2 All ER 859, CA.

Cases also cited or referred to in skeleton arguments
DPP v Kilbourne [1973] 1 All ER 440, [1973] AC 729, [1973] 2 WLR 254, HL.
R v Bainbridge (1991) 93 Cr App R 32, CA.
R v Bedford (1991) 93 Cr App R 113, CA.
R v Brooks (1991) 92 Cr App R 36, CA.
R v Cohen (1990) 91 Cr App R 125, CA.

Appeal against conviction
On 21 October 1992 in the Crown Court at Leicester before Judge Young and a jury the appellant, CW, was convicted after an eight-day trial of attempted rape and other sexual offences against children to all of whom he was related and stood in loco parentis, the alleged offences having taken place between 10 and 20 years before the trial. The complainants were all children who, as adults, had given evidence. He was sentenced to terms totalling 12 years' imprisonment. He appealed on the grounds that the trial judge had (1) erred in law in refusing to order severance of the indictment as between counts of indecency against each complainant, and wrongly decline to hold a voire dire in order to decide whether there was a real risk of collusion between the witnesses and ruled that the question of collusion was one which fell to be decided by the jury; and (2) erred in law in ruling that the probative effect of admitting the evidence of each complainant outweighed its prejudicial effect, and exercised his discretion in favour of the prosecution without hearing any submissions on admissibility; (3) misdirected the jury in relation to corroboration; (4) misdirected the jury in relation to the character of the appellant; and (5) given the impression that he was biased in favour of the prosecution; so that, in all the circumstances, the convictions were unsafe and unsatisfactory. The facts are set out in the judgment of the court.

David Bate (assigned by the *Registrar of Criminal Appeals*) for the appellant.
Robert Brown (instructed by the *Crown Prosecution Service, Leicester*) for the Crown.

Cur adv vult

17 February 1994. The following judgment of the court was delivered.

LORD TAYLOR OF GOSFORTH CJ. On 21 October 1992 at the Crown Court at Leicester the appellant was convicted, after an eight-day trial, of a number of sexual offences. He was sentenced as follows: on count 1, for buggery, six years' imprisonment; on count 3, for indecent assault on a male person, three years' imprisonment; on count 4, for a similar offence, three years' imprisonment; on each of counts 5 to 8 inclusive, which charged indecent assault on a female, five years' imprisonment; on counts 11 to 13 inclusive, being further counts of indecent assault on a female person, five years' imprisonment; on count 14, for attempted rape, six years' imprisonment; and on count 15, for indecent assault on a female, five years' imprisonment. The sentences on all those counts, except for the last four, were concurrent. The sentences on counts 12, 13, 14 and 15 were concurrent inter se but consecutive to the six years on count 1. The total sentence was therefore one of 12 years' imprisonment.

Not guilty verdicts were entered by direction of the judge in respect of counts 2 and 10, and a charge of rape on count 9, which was severed from the rest, was ordered on 12 November 1992 to lie on the file.

The appellant renewed his application for leave to appeal against conviction, after refusal by the single judge, and we granted him leave.

Each of the charges concerned sexual abuse by the appellant of children to whom he was related. Counts 1 to 11 concerned offences against his nephews and nieces, the children of his sister. They were committed between January 1969 and December 1975. The appellant went to live with his sister after his first marriage broke down. Originally, he was to stay a few weeks, but he remained until 1975. He then left to live with a woman whom he married in 1982. She already had a daughter, J, who was the victim of counts 12 to 15 on the indictment. The appellant left his second wife finally in March 1983.

Count 1 related to a single incident in which the appellant was alleged to have buggered his nephew S. (All the other counts were said to be specimen offences.) S said that when he was about eight years old he went to stay at the address where the appellant lived before he moved in with his sister. The appellant joined him in bed, put his arms around him and buggered him. S said it was painful and he passed out.

The other offences against the sister's children occurred often when the appellant was taking a bath. It was his practice to ask one of the children to run it for him and to get his towel for which he would give them 10p. He would then have an erection whilst standing in the bathroom, and the sexual abuse occurred in that situation. In brief, count 3 charged the appellant with inserting his erect penis into S's mouth when he was about nine or ten years old. Count 4 charged the appellant with compelling another nephew, D, to masturbate him when D was about eight or nine. Counts 5 to 8 inclusive were indecent assaults on his niece T by compelling her to masturbate him (count 5) by inserting his fingers into her vagina (count 6) by masturbating himself over her abdomen (count 7) and by putting his erect penis in her mouth when she was about eight, sometimes in the bathroom, sometimes in the bedroom. Ejaculation was usually onto some lavatory paper. The appellant was a lorry driver, and on occasions took T with him to Sheffield, forcing her to masturbate him or suck his penis whilst they were away together. Count 11 charged indecent assault against the appellant's other niece W by inserting his fingers into her vagina.

Counts 12 to 15 involved abuse of J between 1975 and 1983. Counts 12, 13 and 15 were similar to earlier counts, but count 14 alleged attempted rape. J said the appellant was a strict disciplinarian. He had treated her mother badly and had ruined her childhood. In addition to sexual abuse in the home, there were occasions when he took J to Scotland in his lorry and abused her in bed-and-breakfast establishments.

From the dates already mentioned, it will be apparent that all these offences were alleged to have occurred between 10 and 20 years before the trial. By the time the complainants came to describe them, they were mature adults aged between 20 and 32.

When asked about the allegations, and in evidence at his trial, the appellant totally denied any impropriety. He admitted that he used to masturbate in the bathroom or bedroom, but not so that anyone could see. He admitted having a bath most nights and paying one or other of the children 10p or 20p to run it. He had slept in the same room as J in Scotland and it could be that, on other occasions too, the children had seen him naked, but that was all. He admitted he was a strict disciplinarian.

On 15 January 1992 an application was made to the judge that the proceedings were an abuse of process and that the indictment should be stayed. Defending counsel pointed to the very long delay. Further, unless the complainants were capable of corroborating each other, there was no corroboration in respect of any of the charges. On the authorities, it was submitted that the evidence of the complainants was not capable of amounting to mutual corroboration.

The delay in reporting the offences was said by the complainants to be due to a reluctance on their part since they did not think they would be believed, or if believed, they might be sent away. The judge, in a cogently reasoned ruling, rejected the contention that to proceed after such delay would be an abuse of process. He also held, following *R v P* [1991] 3 All ER 337, [1991] 2 AC 447, that the evidence of each of the children was capable as similar facts of corroborating that of the others. All the children were related to the appellant. He was in loco parentis to all five. The allegations were similar in that he was said to have offered money as a reward, to have told each of them to keep it a secret, and to have committed similar acts in the bathroom context. The judge concluded—

'that it would be wrong on the material contained in the witness statements to suspect that there had been anything more than discussion in a family circle about what had gone on and that there is not enough material here (and I remind myself that I must approach this with caution) which would justify a suspicion of conspiracy.'

The judge also said that if asked, he would rule the counts should be tried together (apart from count 9) but he acknowledged that he might have to reconsider the matter if the situation changed.

At the start of the trial in October 1992 the defence applied to the judge to sever the various counts on the grounds that there was a real possibility of concoction between the complainants. Defence counsel invited the judge to hold a voire dire. He declined to do so and held that on the material before him nothing more than a speculative possibility that there might have been concoction had been raised.

Mr Bate relied upon a number of grounds of appeal. Among them were two which we can dispose of at the outset.

One relates to the judge's direction about the appellant's character. He had minor convictions in the past, one for dishonesty and one for indecent exposure. The defence were concerned that if nothing were said about character, the jury might infer that the appellant had committed acts of sexual abuse previously. It was therefore agreed between counsel that the jury would be told the appellant had never been in any trouble 'for this type of offence in the past'. The prosecution undertook not to apply to put the appellant's character in. On the other hand, the defence did not hold the appellant out as a man of good character, nor was any submission made on his behalf to the judge that he should be treated as a man of good character.

Against this background, the judge said in his summing up:

'You know that the defendant has never been in trouble for this type of offence and has now reached the age of 50. What effect should that play in your deliberations? Simply this, it is a factor which you are entitled to take into consideration in his favour since it is uncharacteristic of him. That is all it is. It is obviously not a passport to acquittal; it is simply a matter which you are entitled to take into account in his favour when asking yourselves in this case: has he been telling us the truth or not?'

The complaint made is that the judge did not specifically deal with the two possible benefits of good character, namely its effect on his credibility and its negation of any propensity. In our judgment however, since this was not a case in which the appellant was truly a man of good character, and no submission was made that it should be treated as such, the judge's direction was adequate and cannot be criticised.

Secondly, Mr Bate criticises the judge's direction on corroboration. He began by submitting that it was muddled, that it did not sufficiently explain why corroboration was necessary, or what considerations the jury should have in mind in deciding whether they regarded the evidence of one complainant as corroborating that of another.

The judge dealt generally with corroboration, stating:

'Judges are required to tell juries, for obvious reasons—because we know that false complaints could be made for reasons which are never discovered—it is dangerous to act on the unconfirmed evidence of one who makes an allegation of a sexual nature and it is important ... to consider whether that evidence is corroborated in any way, that is to say, confirmed or supported by evidence from another source, not from the mouth of a complainant, which confirms the complainant's allegation that she was sexually assaulted.'

It is true that the judge made two false starts in seeking to explain how one complainant might corroborate another. However, after those false starts, he gave a direction which Mr Bate ultimately conceded was 'just about correct, the bare minimum'. He then went on to indicate the similarities in the evidence of the complainants which were relied upon by the Crown and which the judge suggested were capable of amounting to corroboration. He also indicated the dissimilarities between the complainants' evidence relied upon by the defence. Whilst the judge's directions on corroboration were by no means as clear as could be wished, we do not think that they amounted to a misdirection.

However, we turn to more fundamental criticisms of the judge's approach. Mr Bate submits that he ought to have severed the indictment since the complainants' evidence was not capable of affording mutual corroboration. He also submits that the judge should have held a voire dire to investigate whether there was a risk of deliberate collusion between the complainants or contamination as between their stories.

In our view, the judge's approach at the beginning of the trial cannot be faulted. As already mentioned, there were features common to the evidence of the various complainants which, whether strikingly similar or not, were capable of amounting to probative and corroborative evidence in accordance with the principles laid down in *R v P* [1991] 3 All ER 337, [1991] 2 AC 447. Moreover, at that stage of the trial there was no evidence to show any collusion or contamination. In *R v Johannsen* (1977) 65 Cr App R 101 at 104 Lawton LJ said:

'If the defendant alleges, as in this case, that there is a real chance that the alleged victims conspired to give false evidence, how is [the judge] to determine that issue? His only source of information is the depositions. The depositions may, as in this case, show that the alleged victims knew each other ... Is the judge to infer in every such case that acquaintance with one another may have resulted in a conspiracy to give false evidence? If he is, many sexual molesters of the young will go free ... Problems of severance and the admissibility of evidence should be decided on the facts known to the Court, not on speculation as to what the facts may turn out to be.'

That view was echoed by this court in *R v Ananthanarayanan* [1994] 2 All ER 847. Laws J, dealing with the judge's duty to consider the risk of contamination between witnesses, said (at 857):

'Where the issue is raised before any evidence is given, it is of course true that the judge would have to arrive at his decision on the papers.'

Mr Bate has sought to rely on the judgment of this court in *R v Ryder* [1994] 2 All ER 859 which was given the day after the judgment in *Ananthanarayanan* and which made reference to that case. The judgment in *R v Ryder* cited a passage from *Cross on Evidence* (7th edn 1993) p 365, which included the following:

'"So if the defence alleges some such concoction and adduces some credible evidence of it, the prosecution should be required to satisfy the judge on the *voire dire* that there is no real possibility that such concoction has occurred. Such an approach was endorsed by the High Court of Australia in *Hoch* v. *R* (1988) 81 ALR 225. If the prosecution succeed on the *voire dire* the evidence should be admitted, but the defence remain free to attack its cogency, in much the same way as it remains free to attack the cogency of the confession admitted after a contested *voire dire*."'

The judgment of this court in *R v Ryder* continued (at 868):

'We agree with that view. There are thus four possible situations. In identifying them, we refer to collusion but we use that word to encompass not only deliberate but also unconscious influence of one witness by another. First, where a real possibility of collusion is apparent to the judge on the face of the documents, he should not allow the similar fact evidence to be led. Secondly, if a submission is made raising the suggestion of collusion, he may find it necessary to hold a voire dire. Thirdly, if the evidence is admitted but at the end of the case he takes the view there is a real possibility of collusion, he should tell the jury in summing-up not to use the evidence as corroboration. Finally, even if the judge himself is of the view there is no real possibility of collusion, but the matter has been argued, he should leave the issue to the jury.'

Mr Bate relies upon the second situation of the four envisaged. He suggests that where the defence raise the possibility of collusion or contamination, the judge is under an obligation to hold a voire dire. We cannot agree. The words used in the passage above as to holding a voire dire are that the judge 'may find it necessary'. The passage in Professor Cross's book predicates that the defence must adduce some credible evidence of concoction to give rise to the requirement of a voire dire. Mr Bate's suggestion is contrary to the dicta cited above from *R v Johannsen* and from *R v Ananthanarayanan*. Even in *Hoch v R* (1988) 81 ALR 225, the Australian case upon which Mr Bate relied, the judgment reads (at 233):

'Was it incumbent on the trial judge to examine the evidence on a *voir dire*? It is not always necessary for a trial judge to do so. Whether a *voir dire* is necessary depends upon the state of the evidence disclosed on the depositions and on the issue for the judge's determination.'

In our view, the judge should only hold a voire dire if something contained in the committal papers or something put before him by way of credible evidence on behalf of the defence raises an issue for him to consider and he believes it is necessary to hear evidence to enable him properly to consider it. A bare assertion on behalf of the defence that there may have been collusion or contamination would not warrant the holding of a voire dire.

In the present case, at the start of the trial there was nothing but speculation to suggest either collusion or contamination.

However, by the end of the prosecution case, the situation was different. By then, cross-examination of the prosecution witnesses had elicited a number of facts bearing on the possibility of collusion or at the very least contamination. It is true that the complainants and their parents denied there had been any deliberate concoction or collusion. However, it emerged that all the complainants and their mothers strongly disliked the appellant. Indeed, a number of them professed to hate him, and not only because of the alleged abuse but on other grounds. For example, it was said that he was too strict a disciplinarian and that he was violent towards his second wife.

It also emerged that T and W had discussed the alleged abuse before May 1980 and had mentioned it together to their parents at that time. In November 1987 there was a family gathering at the appellant's sister's for the 21st birthday party of the youngest sibling. On that occasion, T and W told their parents what had happened. So did D and S. S also said that before his 21st birthday he had told W and she had told him of the appellant's sexual abuse when he visited her in Germany. T said that disclosure to the parents at the birthday party was preceded by a discussion among the complainants. In his summing up, the judge put it thus:

'At that time, [W] disclosed that [the appellant] had sexually abused her over a number of years. [T] said that [W] had spoken to her before but it was the first time she had disclosed it to all of us together. They all said it had happened to them as well, apart from the youngest sibling.

She said that after [the birthday] party she remembered going to her mum and dad's house.'

It was then that the matter was raised en famille.

There was also evidence that when the police were finally brought into the matter in 1991 it was the complainants' mother, the appellant's sister, who took the initiative. There was some pressure on the complainants to make statements. W and T spoke together about the abuse although, according to W, 'nothing specific'. D made a statement unwillingly and only because his mother wanted him to and told him the others had made statements. At court, they were given their statements to read. They were handed the whole bundle, but said that each only read his or her own. As to whether J was insulated from contact with the appellant's sister's children, it was said that they had been apart for some years but, in the childhood period in question, they had lived very close and visited each other's houses to play and to babysit.

Thus, the alleged abuse was said to have occurred during the period between 10 and 20 years before the police were involved. Since then, at various times, especially in 1979/1980, at the 21st birthday party in 1987 and prior to the taking of statements in 1991, it became clear from cross-examination that there had been discussions concerning the allegations between the complainants or some of them. Towards the end, there was evidence of some pressure upon them from their mother. In our judgment, this altered situation called for a review of the judge's original ruling with regard to possible concoction or contamination. The judge had, in his original ruling, quite rightly stated that it was not final and that the situation might change. It did. However, no such review seems to have taken place. Had it done so, in our view, the judge ought to have concluded there was a real possibility at least of contamination of the witnesses' evidence from mutual discussions which had taken place intermittently. After 10 to 20 years, especially in the case of a witness who was then a young child, now an adult, it would be very difficult to disentangle individual recollection of incidents from recollection of shared discussions about the alleged conduct. On the evidence here, there was clearly the possibility of contamination. Accordingly, in our view, this case had, by the end of the prosecution, reached the third situation of the four posed in *R v Ryder* [1994] 2 All ER 859.

When summing up to the jury, the judge directed them that the complainants could be mutually corroborative. All he said by way of warning was—

'but you must have ruled out any possibility of an untruthful concoction between witness B and witness A.'

There was no reference to the possibility of innocent contamination.

We turn to the final ground of appeal. Mr Bate contends that in the course of the evidence, the judge intervened in a way which was or may have seemed biased. At the end of T's examination-in-chief, the judge questioned T, saying:

'I shall have to ask some questions so we can understand the detail of this …'

In the course of his questioning, he elicited from T evidence of rapes of her by the appellant which had not been charged and which were not included in her statements. Having done so, he said to counsel for the Crown:

> 'With other witnesses can you, please, extract the detail rather than leave it to me because I really should not have to be doing that.'

The next witness was W. At the end of her re-examination, the judge picked up something the girl had said in cross-examination to the effect that there was a time when she thought something 'might be happening between [T] and [the appellant].' He invited W to expand on this. Mr Bate objected and there followed some discussion in the course of which the judge asked prosecuting counsel why he had not re-examined on the point and pressed him for an answer.

The judge then said that it was not appropriate that he, the judge, should be seen to be either the defence or the prosecution. He suggested that counsel for the prosecution might consider whether he wished to re-examine the witness and whether in that event, to meet the objections of Mr Bate, W might be interviewed on the particular point the judge had raised and a short statement might then be served on the defence. Mr Bate objected to this course, but the judge adjourned after inviting counsel for the Crown to 'consider [his] situation'. When the court re-convened in the absence of the jury, counsel for the Crown said it would not be proper for him to have the witness re-interviewed, but he sought leave to re-open his re-examination so as to ask W whether she had actually seen anything between T and the appellant. However, the judge refused to allow further re-examination. The jury returned and the judge said:

> 'I have decided it would not be right for counsel for the prosecution to re-open the re-examination. You heard the witness's reply and that will be the totality of the evidence you will hear from her.'

Mr Bate complains that the judge ought not to have questioned T so as to introduce allegations never levelled at the appellant by the prosecution. Furthermore, the effect of the exchanges at the end of W's re-examination and the judge's final announcement to the jury were prejudicial to the appellant. The jury may well have thought that the defence was seeking to exclude relevant and probative evidence and the judge had protectively refused to allow the prosecution to pursue it. The true position, it is submitted, was that the judge, while recognising that he ought not to do so, took over a prosecuting role in a manner which may well have resulted in unfairness to the appellant. We consider there is force in Mr Bate's submission.

Putting together the possibility of contamination and the possibly unfair effect of the way the evidence of T and W was handled, against the background of such an unusually long delay before official complaint was made, each member of this court feels doubtful as to whether the verdicts can be regarded as safe and satisfactory. In those circumstances, this appeal must be allowed.

Appeal allowed. Conviction quashed.

N P Metcalfe Esq   Barrister.

R v H

COURT OF APPEAL, CRIMINAL DIVISION
RUSSELL LJ, FRENCH AND HARRISON JJ
24 JANUARY, 18 FEBRUARY 1994

Criminal evidence – Corroboration – Similar fact evidence – Risk of contamination – Sexual offences – Risk of contamination in mutually corroborative evidence – Whether contamination going to admissibility or quality of evidence – Whether evidence capable of amounting to corroboration.

The appellant was convicted of sexual offences carried out against his adopted daughter and stepdaughter between 1987 and 1989. They confided in the appellant's wife in May 1992 and the complaints to the police were made on the same day. The judge directed the jury that if they found similarities between the girls' accounts and if they were sure that they had not collaborated to concoct a false story against the appellant it was open to them to conclude that the evidence of one girl was related to the evidence given by the other so as to be capable of mutually supporting each other. The appellant appealed, contending that in view of the risk of collusion between the girls, in that they had been living under the same roof and had complained to their mother together long after the alleged offences had occurred, the judge had erred in directing that the evidence of one girl could corroborate that of the other.

Held – The possible contamination of a witness's evidence by his contact with other witnesses or complainants was, save in extreme cases, relevant not to the admissibility of the evidence but to its weight and probative value, and like any other feature which might taint evidence the assessment of its effect was a fact-finding exercise for the jury, not the judge. Accordingly, if there was a risk of contamination evidence could not be used as corroboration but it did not necessarily follow that the evidence became wholly inadmissible. Furthermore, it would be wrong for a judge to direct a jury that because there was a real risk of contamination a witness's evidence was not capable of amounting to corroboration. Provided the jury received the appropriate warnings and directions from the judge they had to assess for themselves the dangers of relying on it and had to decide for themselves whether the evidence of one complainant corroborated the evidence of the other. Contamination by collusion did not call for any different treatment in that regard since it was the degree of contamination that mattered. In an extreme case where the judge concluded that there had been collusion between witnesses he could either sever the indictment or stop the trial and direct an acquittal. On the facts, although there was a risk of collusion, the question whether the jury could regard one girl as corroborating the other had properly been left by the judge to the jury. The appeal would therefore be dismissed (see p 886 *b* to *g j* to p 887 *b*, p 888 *f* to *j* and p 889 *a*, post).

DPP v Hester [1972] 3 All ER 1056 and *R v Johannsen* (1977) 65 Cr App R 101 applied.

R v Ananthanarayanan [1994] All ER 847 not followed.

Decision of the Court of Appeal (Criminal Division) affirmed. [1995] 2 W.L.R. 737, H.L.(E.)

Notes
For corroboration, see 11(2) *Halsbury's Laws* (4th edn reissue) paras 1140, 1141, and for evidence of complainants in sexual cases, see ibid para 1142. For cases on the subject, see 15(2) *Digest* (2nd reissue) 106–107, *19059–19065*.

For admissibility of similar fact evidence, see 11(2) *Halsbury's Laws* (4th edn reissue) paras 1091–1098; and for cases on the subject, see 15(1) *Digest* (2nd reissue) 587–595, *17731–17784*.

Cases referred to in judgment
Boardman v DPP [1974] 3 All ER 887, [1975] AC 421, [1974] 3 WLR 673, HL.
DPP v Hester [1972] 3 All ER 1056, [1973] AC 296, [1972] 3 WLR 910, HL.
DPP v Kilbourne [1973] 1 All ER 440, [1973] AC 729, [1973] 2 WLR 254, HL.
R v Ananthanarayanan [1994] 2 All ER 847, 98 Cr App R 1, CA.
R v Brooks (1991) 92 Cr App R 36, CA.
R v Galbraith [1981] 2 All ER 1060, [1981] 1 WLR 1039, CA.
R v Johannsen (1977) 65 Cr App R 101, CA.
R v P [1991] 3 All ER 337, [1991] 2 AC 447, [1991] 3 WLR 161, HL.
R v Ryder [1994] 2 All ER 859, CA.
Selvey v DPP [1968] 2 All ER 497, [1970] AC 304, [1968] WLR 1494, HL.

Appeal against conviction
The appellant H appealed against his conviction on 4 February 1993 in the Crown Court at Winchester before Tucker J and a jury of four counts of an indictment charging him with indecent assault on his adopted daughter (count 1), gross indecency towards the same child (count 2), unlawful sexual intercourse with the same girl when she was under 14 years of age (count 3), and indecent assault on his stepdaughter (count 4), for which he was sentenced to four years' imprisonment in all. The facts are set out in the judgment.

Stanley Best (assigned by the *Registrar of Criminal Appeals*) for the appellant.
Jeremy Gibbons (instructed by the *Crown Prosecution Service*, Portsmouth) for the Crown.

Cur adv vult

18 February 1994. The following judgment of the court was delivered.

RUSSELL LJ. On 4 February 1993 in the Crown Court at Winchester this appellant was convicted before Tucker J and a jury of four counts contained in a single indictment. Count 1 charged indecent assault upon the appellant's adopted daughter. Count 2 charged an act of gross indecency towards the same child. Count 3 alleged sexual intercourse with the child when she was under the age of 13 years, and count 4 charged indecent assault with another girl who was the appellant's stepdaughter.

The offences were all alleged to have taken place over a period of about two years between 1987 and 1989 when one girl was about nine years of age and the other about 14 years of age.

The younger girl complained that the appellant put his finger in her vagina, handled her breasts and made her kiss his penis. Eventually sexual intercourse took place. Hence the first three counts in the indictment. The appellant's stepdaughter made similar complaints, though in her case the indecency fell short of sexual intercourse. There were, however, plainly similarities in the accounts that were ultimately given by the two alleged victims.

Neither confided in the appellant's wife until May 1992. The complaints were made on the same day. This led to the appellant's arrest, whereupon he consistently denied that he had been responsible for any indecency with either of the children concerned. He suggested that the younger girl had formed an association with a boy of which he did not approve. She wanted the boy to move in and, when the appellant was arrested and forced to leave home, this is what the boy did at the girl's invitation.

At trial no application for severance was made by counsel appearing for the appellant. It was and is conceded that there were features of the evidence given by the girls which, subject to one reservation, fell within the concept of 'similar fact' evidence, and that therefore the jury were entitled to regard one girl's evidence as corroborating the other (*R v P* [1991] 3 All ER 337, [1991] 2 AC 447).

The one reservation which we are told was put by counsel to the girls was to the effect that they had had their heads together and had collaborated in concocting a false story. The suggestion was denied by the girls, and there the matter rested save that in his closing address to the jury Mr Best, who appeared in the court below and who has argued the appeal before this court, submitted that the case was one of 'collaboration not corroboration'.

In his advice on the prospects of an appeal against conviction, dated 20 February 1993, Mr Best is on record as saying:

'The trial judge [Tucker J] ruled correctly that C and S's evidence as to indecency involved in three of the four counts could be treated as corroboration, but he accepted my submission that so far as sexual intercourse with S was concerned there was no corroboration. It was simply her word against that of the defendant. The judge so directed the jury and I should say at this stage (as I indicated to the defendant at the time) that in my view no criticism could be advanced in respect of the summing up which was entirely fair.'

For the purposes of this judgment it is necessary to refer to only two passages in the summing up. The judge said:

'In the present case there are two girls who complain of the defendant's indecent attentions on separate occasions. The defendant was in the position of a father to both of them. Their complaints, you may think, are very similar in several respects. All the matters complained of took place in the home, and partly during the same period of time. In other words, the offences overlap. Both girls allege that the defendant put his finger up their vaginas. They both allege that he put their hands on his penis and then moved their hands up and down, and they both allege that he tried to get them to kiss his penis. If you find that there are those similarities in the girls' accounts and, in particular, if you are sure that they have not collaborated to concoct a false story against the defendant, then it would be open to you to conclude that the evidence of one girl about what occurred to her is so related to the evidence given by the other girl about what happened to the other girl, that the evidence of the first girl provides support for the evidence of the

second girl, and visa versa. In other words, their evidence on those
matters is capable of mutually supporting each other. But there is one
matter at least which is spoken of by one girl and not mentioned by the
other. I refer in particular to the evidence of S that the defendant had
sexual intercourse with her. There is no corroboration for that
allegation in the evidence of C, or anywhere else. Nevertheless, despite
the absence of independent confirmation that sexual intercourse took
place, and provided you bear in mind the danger of convicting without
it, you may rely on S's evidence if you are sure that she is telling the
truth.'

Later the judge commented:

'Members of the jury, is it possible that these girls have made it up
because of some resentment towards the defendant, or because S knew
he disapproved of her relationship with her boyfriend and would not
have allowed her boyfriend to come and live in the house, as he has done
since shortly after the defendant's departure, apparently sleeping in
what was formerly the matrimonial bedroom? The defence say this is
the key to the matter, and that this story, as they allege it to be, of her
father assaulting her is a scenario that S conceived as an excuse for
rejecting her boyfriend's overtures, and that when her boyfriend pressed
her about it out came this story, and the boyfriend, it is suggested,
insisted that the matter went further. The defence, in other words, as
expressly stated to you, is that these girls have told a pack of lies, have
put their heads together, have collaborated in concocting a false story
against their father. Alternatively, may the girls have fantasised about
all this? I emphasise it is not for the defendant to prove either of those
matters but for the prosecution to satisfy you so that you are sure that
the girls are telling the truth.'

On 11 March 1993 another constitution of this court gave judgment in *R v
Ananthanarayanan* [1994] 2 All ER 847. This was followed by another
judgment of another constitution of this court, *R v Ryder* [1994] 2 All ER 859.
Mr Best submits that these two cases have radically altered the law and,
relying upon them, he now submits that Tucker J should not have directed
the jury that the evidence of one girl could corroborate the other, that in so
doing the summing up was fatally flawed, and that the verdicts returned
were unsafe and unsatisfactory. It is necessary for this court, therefore, to
examine the authorities in order to decide whether there is substance in
counsel's submissions.

R v Ananthanarayanan was a case involving seven alleged offences of
indecent assault by a consultant psychiatrist. There were four complainants
who were nurses or care assistants with whom the defendant came into
contact at different establishments. The defendant was convicted on five
counts but acquitted on two. He denied all the allegations. The submission
was made that the judge was wrong to direct the jury that the evidence of
the women was capable of amounting to corroboration because, so it was
submitted, there was a possibility of contamination.

Laws J, giving the judgment of the court, said (at 853–854):

'The basis upon which Mr Barker submits on the facts that there was a risk
of contamination between the witnesses' accounts is, essentially, twofold, and

the two considerations in question interlock. The first is that in large measure the women's complaints were first made at the same time, one with another, and that, save in the case of F, they were made at a considerable distance of time after the events were alleged to have taken place. Thus the complaint of P was made in August 1991 but the assault which she alleged took place was in June 1989 ... Indeed, none of these three complainants made their allegations until after the complaint made by F in August 1991. Alongside these facts runs Mr Barker's second point, namely that there was evidence to show, or at the least to suggest, that the complaints (at any rate those made after that of F) were not spontaneous but prompted by a common source: in the summer of 1991 the social services department of Stoke on Trent were actually seeking potential complainants who might make allegations of indecency against the appellant. He said that in cross-examination B told the court that in August 1991 the social services department were looking for persons who might make an allegation against him, and P said that she made her statement in 1991 because her superior, a Miss Tempest, telephoned and asked her to do so. In our judgment these circumstances give rise, at least, to a real possibility that the complaints which ultimately emerged, and which formed the basis of the prosecution case before the jury, were not truly independent one of another. The fact that some of them may have been prompted obviously suggests this. It is not necessary to speculate upon what precisely might have been said, for example, over the telephone to P or to B, to conclude that there must at any rate have been a suggestion that there already existed a basis for suspecting the appellant of crimes of indecency which was sought to be bolstered by the active collection of further complaints. Given that the judge's direction as to what would constitute contamination of one witness's evidence by that of another cannot itself be impeached, the true question here is whether he should have left the possibility of mutual corroboration to the jury at all. In a series of authorities it has been held that if there is a "real chance" that there has been collusion between the makers of two or more complaints one cannot be corroborative of the other: see per Lord Reid in *DPP v Kilbourne* [1973] 1 All ER 440 at 456, [1973] AC 729 at 750; per Lord Cross in *Boardman v DPP* [1974] 3 All ER 887 at 910, [1975] AC 421 at 459. Other authorities such as *R v P* [1991] 3 All ER 337, [1991] 2 AC 447 and *R v Brooks* (1991) 92 Cr App R 36 use such expressions as "real danger" or "real possibility". There is no doubt that if there exists a "real risk" or "real possibility" that the evidence of one complainant may have been contaminated by that of another, there can be no mutual corroboration between them. The question starkly raised in this case is whether it is for the judge or the jury to decide whether the risk exists. That being so, one can see at once that the answer depends upon a correct analysis of their respective roles. Elementarily it is always the judge's function to decide what evidence is admissible before the jury, and the jury's function to decide what facts to find on that evidence. In principle, therefore, where a question of admissibility depends upon the resolution of an issue of fact, it is for the judge to resolve it. Thus if, for example, it is suggested that a confession has been obtained through a process of questioning by the police in which there have been breaches of the codes made under the provisions of the Police and Criminal Evidence Act 1984, and the breaches are denied, the judge must find the necessary facts himself. In the days before the contemporaneous electronic recording of police interviews there were frequently disputes as to what had passed between the defendant and the interviewing officers, and

where an issue of admissibility turned on the dispute the judge would hold a
voire dire to decide it. All this is basic and uncontentious. Is there any reason
why the same approach should not apply when the question is whether there
is a real risk that "similar fact" evidence might not be truly independent of the
evidence which otherwise it might corroborate? Unassisted by authority, we
would conclude that the same principle applies.'

For our part we pause and venture to suggest that in the passage cited
from *R v Ananthanarayanan* [1994] 2 All ER 847 the court was confusing the
admissibility of evidence with the quality of evidence, that is, *the role that the
evidence, once admitted, plays in the jury's deliberations*. If there is a risk of
contamination the evidence cannot be used as corroboration. It does not
necessarily follow that the evidence becomes wholly *inadmissible* as is the
case when the judge excludes evidence because of breaches of the code made
under the provisions of the Police and Criminal Evidence Act 1984. In our
judgment the two situations are quite different and the one is not an analogy
of the other.

In our judgment and experience, in almost every case where two or more
daughters are living under the same roof and complain of molestation by
their father it is virtually inevitable that at some stage the daughters will
have talked between themselves and usually with their mother. Whether
this contaminates their evidence is very much a fact-finding process. Active
collaboration will invariably be denied. There may be extreme cases where
the judge concludes, having seen and heard the witnesses, that collaboration
has taken place, and in such a case he may exercise his powers to stop the
trial and direct an acquittal on *Galbraith* principles (*R v Galbraith* [1981] 1
WLR 1039) or abort the trial and sever the indictment. But these exceptional
cases apart, we take the view that a jury, having seen and heard the
witnesses, should form its own assessment of the dangers and, provided it
receives the warnings and directions to be found in the summing up of
Tucker J in the instant case, the jury can properly decide whether the
evidence of one complainant corroborates the evidence of the other. In our
view, to deny the jury the responsibility of this fact-finding exercise is to
usurp the function of the jury and we do not believe that the long line of
authority to which reference was made in *R v Ananthanarayanan* was ever
intended to assert the contrary. The judgment of *R v Ananthanarayanan*
continues (at 854):

'The value of potentially corroborative evidence of this kind critically
depends upon its being independent of the complaint sought to be
corroborated. If it is not independent it cannot qualify as corroboration,
and the test of independence for this purpose is not whether
contamination is proved but whether there is a real risk of contamination.
It follows that where such a risk exists the evidence is not admissible as
corroboration. It must, therefore, be the judge's task to decide whether
the risk exists. In carrying out that task he is doing no more nor less than
deciding a question of admissibility.'

Again, with respect, we find ourselves unable to agree. The judge is not
deciding a question of admissibility when he considers whether evidence can
be used as corroboration. The evidence of the individual complainant
remains admissible even if it is contaminated. Contamination goes not to

admissibility but to the part to be played by the evidence after it is admitted. The proper role of the evidence, once admitted, can be left to the jury, who will receive appropriate directions from the judge. It must depend, in our judgment, upon the degree of contamination.

The court in *Ananthanarayanan* sought to derive support from what it described as the 'balance of authority', but in our judgment the only citation which is directly in point is the judgment of Lawton LJ in *R v Johannsen* (1977) 65 Cr App R 101. He said (at 104):

'If the defendant alleges, as in this case, that there is a real chance that the alleged victims conspired to give false evidence, how is [the judge] to determine that issue? His only source of information is the depositions. The depositions may, as in this case, show that the alleged victims knew each other. In the cases of this class which are the most common, namely those against schoolmasters and others who have dealings with the young, the depositions will almost certainly reveal that the alleged victims knew each other. Is the judge to infer in every such case that acquaintance with one another may have resulted in a conspiracy to give false evidence? If he is, many sexual molesters of the young will go free. What if prosecuting counsel says that the police officer in charge of the case is satisfied that there has been no conspiracy? Experienced police officers do try to find out whether there has been. Is the speculative possibility which occurs to the judge to be preferred to the assertions of the prosecution? How is any conflict to be resolved? The answer must surely be—by the jury. This has long been the practice of the Courts. Judges know of the possibility. That is why it is common practice to direct juries about it. In this case the trial judge followed the common practice. In our judgment their Lordships' comments should not be understood as meaning that if the depositions contain no evidence of a conspiracy to give false evidence the judge can use his imagination to decide that there may have been one and in consequence sever the indictment so as to provide for separate trials in respect of each victim. Problems of severance and the admissibility of evidence should be decided on the facts known to the Court, not on speculation as to what the facts may turn out to be. A trial judge, however, has a discretion to exclude evidence tendered by the prosecution if its prejudicial effect outweighs its probative value: see *Selvey v. Director of Public Prosecutions* [1968] 2 All ER 497, [1970] AC 304. In our judgment their Lordships' comments were directed to the excise of judicial discretion but if such discretion is to be exercised there must, in our judgment, be a factual basis disclosed in the depositions to show there is a "real chance"—we adopt the words of Lord Reid and Lord Cross—that there has or may have been a conspiracy.'

Further, in *DPP v Hester* [1972] 3 All ER 1056, [1973] AC 296 (not referred to in *Ananthanarayanan*) the House of Lords had to consider whether the unsworn evidence of a child could corroborate evidence given on oath by another child. Lord Morris of Borth-y-Gest, in the course of his speech, said ([1972] 3 All ER 1056 at 1065, [1973] AC 296 at 316):

'If child A gave sworn evidence of having been assaulted by X then only if the jury, after having applied their minds to a proper warning, were absolutely sure, could there be a conviction in the absence of the support of corroborative evidence. If child B was allowed to give evidence, not on oath, of having seen X assault A there could, in my view, be a conviction if the jury, regarding the evidence of A and of B with great care, were satisfied that each was telling the truth. It was argued that this conclusion would lead to the result that A would be corroborating himself. The argument, is in my view, fallacious. If A and B were independent of each other then clearly what B said would be separate from and independent of what was said by A. If A and B were not independent of each other either for the reason that they had agreed together to concoct a story or for some other reason such as that they had (although with no wrong motive) closely collaborated then their evidence would be either discredited or of little value. Any warning to a jury of the need to examine the evidence of children with care would no doubt in a suitable case include mention of any circumstances affecting the independence of their testimony. But as to this no general rule could be laid down. According to the infinite variety of differing sets of circumstances a judge would exercise his judgment as to the style and language of the guidance that it would be helpful and wise for him to give. For reasons which I have given I consider that the point of law as formulated should be answered by saying the evidence of an unsworn child (admitted pursuant to s 38(1)) can amount to corroboration of evidence given on oath by another child (a complainant) provided that the unsworn evidence is corroborated as required by the proviso. In terms of the present case the evidence of June could corroborate the evidence of Valerie and that of Valerie could corroborate that of June provided that the jury after suitable adequate guidance and warning were satisfied that each child was a truthful and satisfactory witness.'

In so far as these observations are in conflict with *Ananthanarayanan*, as we believe them to be, we prefer *Johannsen* and we are bound by *Hester*. In our view the problem unearthed by *Ananthanarayanan* arises because repeatedly the court in that case dealt with the admissibility of evidence when in fact that is not the problem once the risk arises that there is contamination. Contamination, save in extreme cases, does not go to admissibility. It goes to weight and probative value. Like any other feature which might taint evidence, such as jealousy or overt hostility or exaggeration, the assessment of its effect is for the jury and not for the judge. In our view contamination by collusion does not call for any different treatment.

Upon the facts of this appeal we are satisfied that, although because the complainants were living under same roof and complained to their mother together long after the alleged offence, there must have existed a risk of collusion, that question whether the jury could regard one girl as corroborating the other (in the offences other than unlawful sexual intercourse) were properly left to the jury by Tucker J whose summing up we find to be unimpeachable.

During the course of the hearing of this appeal, it was suggested that the judge could have held a voire dire. This process can prolong hearings inordinately. It is not always in the interests of an accused. It can prolong the ordeal of witnesses who may be of tender years. In our judgment there was no place for a voire dire in this case, had counsel applied for it.

The appeal must be dismissed.

Appeal dismissed. Leave to appeal to House of Lords granted. The court certified under s 33(2) of the Criminal Appeal Act 1968 that the following point of law of general public importance was involved in the decision: how should the trial judge deal with a similar fact case (R v P [1991] 3 All ER 337, [1991] 2 AC 447) where the Crown proposes to call more than one complainant and to rely on each as corroborating the evidence of the other or others, and the defence demonstrates that there is a risk that the evidence is contaminated by collusion or other factors?

N P Metcalfe Esq   Barrister.

Singh v Duport Harper Foundries Ltd

COURT OF APPEAL, CIVIL DIVISION
NEILL, FARQUHARSON AND HENRY LJJ
4 OCTOBER, 3 NOVEMBER 1993

Writ – Extension of validity – Discretion – Failure to serve writ – Exercise of discretion to extend validity of writ – Principles on which discretion to be exercised – RSC Ord 6, r 8(2)(2A).

On 5 April 1991 the plaintiff issued a writ against the defendant, his employer, claiming damages for personal injuries sustained in his employment on 29 April 1988. The plaintiff's solicitors failed to serve the writ on the defendant within the initial period of the writ's validity under RSC Ord 6, r 8[a], namely four months from the date of issue of the writ, because of an error by the solicitors in erroneously believing that the writ could not be served without an accompanying medical report. On 10 January 1992, ie some five months after the expiry on 5 August 1991 of the initial four month period of the writ's validity, the plaintiff applied for an extension of the writ's validity. On 4 March 1992 the district judge granted the application and extended the writ's validity for a period of approximately seven months from 5 August 1991 to 11 March 1992. The defendant appealed to the judge who upheld the district judge's decision on the ground that Ord 6, r 8(2A) conferred on the court a discretion to extend the validity of the writ for up to 12 months from the expiry of its initial period of validity on 5 August 1991. The defendant appealed to the Court of Appeal contending (1) that r 8(2A) did not in the circumstances confer a discretion to extend the writ's validity for a period of up to 12 months from its expiry on 5 August 1991, and (2) that under r 8(2) a writ's validity could be extended at any one time only for a period of four months and then only if the application for extension was made within the initial four month period of validity or at most within the following period of four months, with the result that the district judge had no jurisdiction under r 8(2) to grant an extension of the writ's validity.

---

a RSC Ord 6, r 8, so far as material, is set out at p 892 *d* to *f*, post

Held – The appeal would be allowed for the following reasons—
(1) RSC Ord 6, r 8(2A) gave the court discretion to extend the validity of a writ for up to 12 months only in the specific circumstances that despite all reasonable efforts it might not be possible to serve the writ on the defendant within four months. Rule 8(2A) was designed to meet a situation where the defendant could not readily be served because for example he had gone abroad or could not be traced, and did not apply where it had not been shown that there was any difficulty in serving the writ on the defendant. Since there was no difficulty in serving the defendant and there was no evidence of any need to make all reasonable efforts to do so, r 8(2A) did not apply (see p 892 g to j and p 896 j to p 897 a, post).

(2) The intention of Ord 6, r 8 was to provide a code to avoid undue delay in the service of writs and an application under r 8(2) to extend the validity of a writ usually had to be made during the initial four month period of the writ's validity or at least within the four months following the expiry of the initial four month period of validity. Only one extension for a period not exceeding four months could be granted on any one application and then only for a period not exceeding four months. The applicant had to show good reason for the grant of any extension and, where the application was made after the expiry of the initial four month period of validity, he had to give a satisfactory explanation for the failure to apply for an extension within the initial four month period. Since the application to extend the writ's validity had been made some five months after the expiry of the initial four month period of validity and there was no sufficient explanation for the delay the appeal would be allowed and the order extending the validity of the writ set aside (see p 893 a to e, p 896 d to p 897 a, post)

Per curiam. Normally where a litigant seeks an extension of the validity of a writ RSC Ord 6, r 8 will apply, but the court will entertain an application to extend the validity of a writ under Ord 2, r 1 (whereby failure to comply with the rules of court may be treated as a mere irregularity) and Ord 3, r 5 (which empowers the court to extend the period within which a person is required to do any act in proceedings) in exceptional circumstances and where the interests of justice so require (see p 896 f g j to p 897 a, post); *Chappell v Cooper, Player v Bruguiere* [1980] 2 All ER 463 and *Rolph v Zolan* [1993] 4 All ER 202 applied;*Ward-Lee v Linehan* [1993] 2 All ER 1006 explained; *Caribbean Gold Ltd v Alga Shipping Co Ltd* [1993] 1 WLR 1100 disapproved.

Notes
For renewal of a writ, see 37 *Halsbury's Laws* (4th edn) para 124.

Cases referred to in judgments
Baxendale (Robert) Ltd v Davstone (Holdings) Ltd, Carobene v John Collier Menswear Ltd [1982] 3 All ER 496, [1982] 1 WLR 1385, CA.
Bernstein v Jackson [1982] 2 All ER 806, [1982] 1 WLR 1082, CA.
Caribbean Gold Ltd v Alga Shipping Co Ltd [1993] 1 WLR 1100.
Chappell v Cooper, Player v Bruguiere [1980] 2 All ER 463, [1980] 1 WLR 958, CA.
Kleinwort Benson Ltd v Barbrak, The Myrto (No 3) [1987] 2 All ER 289, [1987] AC 597, HL.

Leal v Dunlop Bio-Processes International Ltd [1984] 2 All ER 207, [1984] 2 WLR 874, CA.
Lewis v Wolking Properties Ltd [1978] 1 All ER 427, [1978] 1 WLR 403, CA.
Rolph v Zolan [1993] 4 All ER 202, [1993] 1 WLR 1305, CA.
Ward-Lee v Linehan [1993] 2 All ER 1006, [1993] 1 WLR 754, CA.

Appeal

The defendant, Duport Harper Foundries Ltd (the appellant), appealed from the order of Judge Black QC, sitting as a High Court judge on 17 July 1992, whereby he dismissed the appellant's appeal against the order of District Judge Merriman made on 4 March 1992 on the application of the plaintiff, Joginder Singh (the respondent), extending to 11 March 1992 the validity of a writ issued by the plaintiff on 5 April 1991 claming damages for personal injuries in the course of his employment against the appellant, his employer. By his notice of appeal the appellant sought an order setting aside the district judge's order and purported service of the writ on the appellant on 5 March 1992 following the district judge's grant of an extension of the writ's validity. The facts are set out in the judgment of Farquharson LJ.

J Pendlebury (instructed by *William Hatton*, West Midlands) for the appellant.
M Conry (instructed by *Peter J Edwards & Co*, Birmingham) for the respondent.

Cur adv vult

3 November 1993. The following judgments were delivered.

FARQUHARSON LJ. This is an appeal from an order made by Judge Black QC, sitting as a High Court judge on 17 July 1992 when he upheld the decision of District Judge Merriman made on 4 March 1992 granting the application of the plaintiff (now the respondent) for an extension of the validity of the writ in this action.

On 29 April 1988 the respondent claims that he suffered personal injuries in the course of his employment and that the injury was due to the negligence and breach of statutory duty of his employer, the present appellant. There followed a considerable delay and it was not until 5 April 1991, almost at the end of the limitation period that the respondent issued a writ. The writ was not served and its validity expired on 5 August 1991. It was not until 10 January 1992 that an application was made to the court ex parte on behalf of the respondent for the validity of the writ to be extended, and that application was granted on 4 March 1992 when the district judge extended the time for service of the writ until 11 March 1992, a period of some seven months. The writ was duly served on 5 March 1992.

In support of his application the respondent filed an affidavit by Mr Joginder Singh, an employee of his solicitors. The explanation given in that affidavit for the delay was that another of the employees of the solicitor, a Mr Biggerstaff, who was responsible on his principal's behalf for the conduct of the action, was erroneously under the impression that the writ could only be properly served if accompanied by a relevant medical report. Mr Biggerstaff admitted that he was at fault in making this error. It appears further from the affidavit that Mr Biggerstaff had become unwell in June

1991 but had continued to work at the office until 3 November 1991 when he suffered a heart attack. The affidavit does not reveal when Mr Biggerstaff's colleagues became aware that the writ had expired, nor whether there was any further delay from that time until the application was made to the court in January 1992. Nor is there any explanation why a medical report dated 6 September 1990 from a consultant accident surgeon, Mr Irshad Ahmed (which is among the Court of Appeal papers) was not available for service with the writ.

The argument both here and below has turned on the meaning of RSC Ord 6, r 8. Rule 8(1)(b) provides that the writ in this case was valid in the first instance for a period of four months, beginning with the date of issue. As already observed that meant this writ expired on 5 August 1992.

RSC Ord 6, r 8(2) gives the court power to extend the validity of the writ and is in these terms:

> 'Subject to paragraph (2A), where a writ has not been served on a defendant, the Court may by order extend the validity of the writ from time to time for such period, not exceeding 4 months at any one time, beginning with the day next following that on which it would otherwise expire, as may be specified in the order, if an application for extension is made to the Court before that day or such later day (if any) as the Court may allow.'

RSC Ord 6, r 8(2A) provides:

> 'Where the Court is satisfied on an application under paragraph (2) that, despite the making of all reasonable efforts, it may not be possible to serve the writ within 4 months, the Court may, if it thinks fit, extend the validity of the writ for such period, not exceeding 12 months, as the Court may specify.'

The learned judge based his decision on Ord 6, r 8(2A) saying:

> 'I am satisfied that the words of Ord 6, r 8 at sub-rule (2A) do give the court a discretion to extend the validity of the writ for up to 12 months.'

In my judgment the learned judge was in error in his interpretation of the sub-rule. While it undoubtedly does give the court a discretion to extend the validity of the writ for up to 12 months it does so only in specifically defined circumstances, viz where despite the making of all reasonable efforts, it may not be possible to serve the writ within four months. It is a provision designed to meet a situation where the defendant cannot readily be served because, for example, he has gone abroad or cannot easily be traced. In the present case there was no difficulty in serving the appellant and there was no evidence of any need to make all reasonable efforts to do so. Accordingly if the respondent is to succeed in this appeal he must do so by virtue of the provisions of Ord 6, r 8(2).

Mr Pendlebury for the appellant submits that the district judge had no jurisdiction to extend the validity of the writ in the terms he did on two grounds; (1) because he had no power to extend the period of validity for a period in excess of four months, at any one time and (2) because any application under Ord 6, r 8(2) must be made either during the period of the original validity of the writ, or during the period of four months next following.

Dealing with the first submission Mr Pendlebury points to the words of Ord 6, r 8(2):

' ... the court may by order extend the validity of the writ from time to time for such period, not exceeding 4 months at any one time ... '

In the present case the district judge granted what was in effect an extension of seven months, ie from 5 August 1991 to the 11 March 1992. Counsel argues that such an order was in direct conflict with the rule. He fortifies this submission by reference to *The Supreme Court Practice 1993*, vol 1 para 6/8/3 where it is stated:

'The application for renewal should ordinarily be made before the writ has expired. The court has power to permit a later application but it *must* be made within the appropriate period of the first expiry. The laxer practice of allowing two or more successive renewals to bring the writ up to date is no longer available ... '

For my part I can see no answer to this submission. The words in RSC Ord 6, r 8(2) 'from time to time' refute the suggestion that more than one renewal can be granted on the same day. Furthermore Ord 6, r 8(2) says in terms that the extension granted is to be for such period not exceeding four months at any one time. Yet the district judge purported to order an extension of seven months under this rule. In my judgment counsel is right in his submission that the district judge exceeded his jurisdiction.

Counsel also relies on the statement in *The Supreme Court Practice* above referred to in support of his further submission that the application for an extension of the validity of the writ must be made within the appropriate period after the first expiry. The authority relied upon in the Annual Practice to support that proposition is *Chappell v Cooper, Player v Bruguiere* [1980] 2 All ER 463, [1980] 1 WLR 958.

At the time that case was heard the appropriate period for the validity of the writ was 12 months and not four. After quoting Ord 6, r 8(2) Roskill LJ said ([1980] 2 All ER 463 at 469, [1980] 1 WLR 958 at 966):

'The writ in the action of *Player v Bruguiere* was issued on 6th December 1974. The 12 months therefore expired on 5th December 1975, and the second period of 12 months, which would be the maximum for which a timeous extension might be allowed, would have run out on 5th December 1976. But the affidavit in support of this application was not sworn until 13th June 1979, some 3½ years after that last date. In view of those dates it seems to me clear, with all respect to council for the plaintiff, beyond doubt that we have no power under the rules to grant the extension sought.'

j Thus Roskill LJ held that the power of renewal could only be exercised during the period of 12 months next following the primary period of validity. If that be right District Judge Merriman in the present case would clearly have exceeded his jurisdiction, but Mr Pendlebury has very properly drawn our attention to a more recent authority which appears at first sight to cast doubt on that decision: *Ward-Lee v Linehan* [1993] 2 All ER 1006, [1993] 1

WLR 754. The facts of that case were unusual; the tenant of business premises applied to the county court under s 24 of the Landlord and Tenant Act 1954 for the grant of a new tenancy. The tenant provided a copy of the originating application for the landlord and requested the issue of a summons which had to be served within two months. Unfortunately the court failed to serve the proceedings upon the landlord as required by the County Court Rules. When the oversight was discovered the landlord refused to consent to an extension of time for service of the summons. It was not until a period of over four months had expired that the tenant applied to the court for an extension. The landlord opposed the application and it was dismissed by the judge. The tenant was accordingly in the same difficulty as the respondent in the present appeal in that not only had the period of original validity expired namely two months, but a further two months had elapsed. If the decision in *Chappell v Cooper, Player v Bruguiere* [1980] 2 All ER 463, [1980] 1 WLR 958 is correct, the learned judge would have had no jurisdiction to entertain the application but he in fact dismissed it in the exercise of his discretion.

The tenant appealed relying on CCR Ord 7, r 20 which is the corresponding provision to RSC Ord 6, r 8(2). The argument that the court had no jurisdiction under that rule was rejected, notwithstanding the time which had elapsed. The Court of Appeal pointed out that notwithstanding the expiry of the period or periods in CCR Ord 7, r 20 the time for service could be extended under CCR Ord 13, r 4 which gives the court power to extend the period within which a person is required to do any act in any proceedings, and/or under CCR Ord 37, r 5 whereby a failure to comply with the rules is to be treated as an irregularity and does not nullify the proceedings. The corresponding provision in the Rules of the Supreme Court are Ord 3, r 5 and Ord 2, r 1.

The judgment of the court was given by Sir Thomas Bingham MR. He said ([1993] 2 All ER 1006 at 1014, [1993] 1 WLR 754 at 762):

'This review of the authorities and the rules leads us to conclude that, even where an originating application of this type is not served within two months of the date of issue and application to extend is not made within four months of the date of issue, the county court has jurisdiction on proper grounds being shown (i) to extend the time for service under CCR Ord 13, r 4 of the CCR Ord 13, r 4 and (ii) to treat the failure to extend and serve as an irregularity and order the action to proceed under Ord 37, r 5. Counsel for the landlord did not press a contrary argument. Although the opening words of CCR Ord 13, r 4 differ from those considered in *Lewis's* case, we have already indicated that in our view the difference, if significant at all, strengthens the tenant's argument.'

Chappell v Cooper, Player v Bruguiere [1980] 2 All ER 463, [1980] 1 WLR 958, does not appear to have been cited.

An alternative submission was addressed to the court to the effect that CCR Ord 7, r 20 and RSC Ord 6, r 8 were of a special character and could not be overridden by the provisions in the rules which have been referred to above. Sir Thomas Bingham MR rejected that argument in these terms ([1993] 2 All ER 1006 at 1014, [1993] 1 WLR 754 at 763):

CA   Singh v Duport Harper Foundries Ltd (Farquharson LJ)   895

'It was argued for the landlord that although the court had a discretion to extend time in this case it was one which could only properly be exercised by refusing an extension. This was because CCR Ord 7, r 20, like RSC Ord 6, r 8 (and Ord 11, r 1), were of a special character such that it was impermissible to override them ... So far as Ord 7, r 20 and Ord 6, r 8, are concerned, the submission is in our judgment unsound. It is not consistent with *Lewis v Wolking Properties Ltd* ([1978] 1 All ER 427, [1978] 1 WLR 403), *Robert Baxendale Ltd v Davstone (Holdings) Ltd, Carobene v John Collier Menswear Ltd* ([1982] 3 All ER 496, [1982] 1 WLR 1385) or *Leal v Dunlop Bio-Processes International Ltd* ([1984] 2 All ER 207, [1984] 2 WLR 874) and it is not supported by *Bernstein v Jackson* ([1982] 2 All ER 806, [1982] 1 WLR 1082) as explained in *Leal*. It is not supported by the wide terms of RSC Ord 2, r 1 and Ord 3, r 5 and CCR Ord 13, r 4 and Ord 37, r 5. And it is not in our view consonant with the requirements of justice in some cases.'

In the later case of *Rolph v Zolan* [1994] 4 All ER 202, [1993] 1 WLR 1305 the plaintiff instituted proceedings in the County Court in July 1991 shortly before the expiration of the limitation period. Service of the summons upon the defendant was irregular and so ineffective. The plaintiff applied to the court in June 1992 for an extension of time for service which was granted. On appeal the court held that under CCR Ord 7, r 20 of the, a first application for the renewal of a summons which had not been served could not be made more than eight months after the date of the issue of the summons. The relevant period of validity was like the High Court one of four months. Dillon LJ in giving the judgment of the court relied upon the judgment of Roskill LJ in *Chappell v Cooper, Player v Bruguiere* [1980] 2 All ER 463, [1980] 1 WLR 958. The case of *Ward-Lee v Linehan* [1993] 2 All ER 1006, [1993] 1 WLR 754 which had been decided only two months previously was not cited. Neither does there appear to have been any reliance placed on CCR Ord 13, r 4 or Ord 37, r 5.

In my judgment the decision in *Ward-Lee v Linehan* can be reconciled with *Rolph v Zolan* in that in the former the Sir Thomas Bingham MR was saying in the first of the two passages cited above that even if the two periods of two months had expired the court still had jurisdiction under CCR Ord 13, r 4 and Ord 37, r 5 to extend time. In the latter case Dillon LJ was not dealing with these rules but with the provisions of CCR Ord 7, r 20.

In the present appeal no reliance was placed by the respondent on RSC Ord 3, r 5 or Ord 2, r 1 although reference was made to them in argument by the court.

It would appear therefore that the case should be decided on the same basis as *Rolph v Zolan*. There is however a further complication. In November 1992 in the case of *Caribbean Gold Ltd v Alga Shipping Co Ltd* [1993] 1 WLR 1100 Potter J considered the decision in *Chappell v Cooper*. He said ([1993] 1 WLR 1100 at 1110–1111):

> Mr. Picken has relied on the passage emphasised and its derivative references in *The Supreme Court Practice* as establishing that, in every case, whether or not it raises an issue of limitation, in order to qualify for relief from a failure to make application for renewal of the writ the party applying must apply not later than the end of the appropriate

period of the first period of extension which the court could have granted under sub-rule (2) or (2A). I do not think that is right. I consider that such a submission places an undue restriction upon the meaning and operation of the words "or such later day (if any) as the court may allow" which appear in sub-rule (2). The sub-rule itself contains nothing to indicate such an overall restriction on the discretion of the court.'

Although it was heard before either *Ward-Lee v Linehan* [1993] 2 All ER 202, [1993] 1 WLR 754, CA or *Rolph v Zolan* [1993] 4 All ER 202, [1993] 1 WLR 1305, *Caribbean Gold Ltd v Alga Shipping Ltd* [1993] 1 WLR 1100 was not reported until July 1993 so that it was not cited in either of those cases.

Chappell v Cooper was cited to Potter J and he considered that case in considerable depth in his judgment distinguishing it from the case before him.

RSC Ord 6, r 8 was intended to provide a code whereby undue delay in the service of writs is avoided. It is for this reason that the period for the validity of a writ was recently reduced from 12 months to four. Only in the most exceptional circumstances as described in para 5 below will the court allow a further extension beyond that permitted by the rule. For that reason I am unable to agree with the interpretation put upon it by Potter J in *Caribbean Gold Ltd v Alga Shipping Ltd*.

It is difficult to reconcile the authorities cited above but the following propositions should be applied: (1) Where a litigant seeks an extension of the validity of a writ the provision of RSC Ord 6, r 8 will apply. (2) An application under that rule must be made during the validity of the writ, ie four months in the usual case, or during the four months next following. (3) Only one extension of time can be granted on a particular application and that must be for a period not exceeding four months. (4) If the litigant has not conformed with the requirements of the Rule he cannot be granted relief under Ord 6,r 8. (5) In exceptional circumstances and where the interests of justice so require the court will entertain an application to extend the validity of the writ under the provisions of Ord 2, r 1 and Ord 3, r 5. Before the court will extend the validity of the writ the applicant must show that there is good reason for such an extension, and where appropriate provide a satisfactory explanation for the failure to apply during the period of the original validity (see *Kleinwort Benson Ltd v Barbrak Ltd, The Myrto (No 3)* [1987] 2 All ER 289, [1987] AC 597).

In the present case it would not be possible to say that the respondent has satisfied the court that there was good reason for the delay. The explanation given that the respondent's legal representative had made an error in not serving the writ at the appropriate time is insufficient to discharge the burden on the respondent. Furthermore the unsatisfactory nature of the affidavit which was referred to earlier in this judgment does not assist him.

Even if RSC Ord 3, r 4 or Ord 2,r 1 had been relied on, there could have been no question of the test set out in proposition 5 being satisfied.

For these reasons I would allow the appeal.

HENRY LJ. I agree.

NEILL LJ. I also agree.

Appeal allowed. Appellant to pay costs of the appeal and the application before judge below.

Wendy Shockett   Barrister.

R v Liverpool City Magistrates' Court, ex parte Pender (No 2)

QUEEN'S BENCH DIVISION

WATKINS LJ AND LEONARD J

20 JULY 1993

Legal aid – Criminal cases – Revocation of legal aid for non-payment of contributions – Fresh application for legal aid made to trial court after revocation of legal aid order – Whether application may be made at pre-trial proceedings – Legal Aid in Criminal and Care Proceedings (General) Regulations 1989, reg 10.

The court (which includes a magistrates' court) may exercise its power under reg 10[a] of the Legal Aid in Criminal and Care Proceedings (General) Regulations 1989 to make a legal aid order, and an applicant whose legal aid has been refused or revoked may apply for legal aid, in respect of pre-trial proceedings, including remands, bail applications and arrangements for trial, since such proceedings are 'other proceedings' in respect of which an application for legal aid may be made under reg 10. Accordingly, a magistrates' court may entertain an application for legal aid under reg 10 made in the course of proceedings to make arrangements for trial, notwithstanding that a previous legal aid order has been revoked for non-payment of contributions (see p 900 j, p 902 j to p 903 a g to j, post).

R v Liverpool City Magistrates' Court, ex p Shacklady, R v Liverpool City Magistrates' Court, ex p Pender [1993] 2 All ER 929 considered.

Notes

For applications for legal aid in criminal cases and withdrawal or revocation of legal aid orders, see Supplement to 37 *Halsbury's Laws* (4th edn) paras 982–983.

For the Legal Aid in Criminal and Care Proceedings (General) Regulations 1989, SI 1989/344, reg 10, see 11 *Halsbury's Statutory Instruments* (1991 reissue) 82.

Cases referred to in judgments

R v City of Cambridge Justices, ex p Leader (1980) 144 JP 148, DC.
R v Liverpool City Magistrates' Court, ex p Shacklady, R v Liverpool City Magistrates' Court, ex p Pender [1993] 2 All ER 929, DC.

---

a   Regulation 10 is set out at p 898 *f g*, post

R v Macclesfield Justices, ex p Greenhalgh (1980) 144 JP 142, DC.

Case also cited
R v Greater Manchester Coroner, ex p Tal [1984] 3 All ER 240, [1985] QB 67, [1984] 3 WLR 643, DC.

Application for judicial review
Kevin Michael Pender applied, with the leave of Laws J given on 26 April 1993, for judicial review by way of (1) an order of certiorari to quash the decision of Mr D R G Tapp, a stipendiary magistrate sitting in the Liverpool City Magistrates' Court on 5 January 1993 that he had no power to grant him legal aid under reg 10 of the Legal Aid in Criminal and Care Proceedings (General) Regulations 1989, SI 1989/344, and (2) an order of mandamus requiring the magistrate to reconsider whether the applicant should be granted legal aid in accordance with the Legal Aid Act 1988 and the Legal Aid in Criminal and Care Proceedings (General) Regulations 1989, SI 1989/344. The facts are set out in the judgment.

Andrew Nicol (instructed by *R M Broudie & Co*, Liverpool) for the applicant.
Ian Burnett (instructed by the *Treasury Solicitor*) for the respondents.

WATKINS LJ. Kevin Michael Pender applies for judicial review of a decision of the stipendiary magistrate sitting at Liverpool Magistrates' Court on 5 January 1993, which was to the effect that the court had no power to grant legal aid to him under reg 10 of the Legal Aid in Criminal and Care Proceedings (General) Regulations 1989, SI 1989/344. That regulation states:

> '*General power to grant legal aid* Subject to the provisions of section 21(2), (3) and (5) of the Act and to regulation 23, nothing in Part II or in regulation 36 shall affect the power of a court, a judge of the court or of the registrar to make a legal aid order, whether an application has been made for legal aid or not, or the right of an applicant whose application has been refused or whose legal aid order has been revoked under section 24(2) to apply to the court at the trial or in other proceedings.'

Section 21 of the Legal Aid Act 1988 (as material) states:

> '(2) Subject to subsection (5) below, representation may be granted where it appears to the competent authority to be desirable to do so in the interests of justice; and section 22 applies for the interpretation of this subsection in relation to the proceedings to which that section applies.
>
> (3) Subject to subsection (5) below, representation must be granted ... (c) where a person charged with an offence before a magistrates' court— (i) is brought before the court in pursuance of a remand in custody when he may be again remanded or committed in custody, and (ii) is not, but wishes to be, legally represented before the court (not having been legally represented when he was so remanded), for so much of the proceedings as relates to the grant of bail ...
>
> (5) Representation shall not be granted to any person unless it appears to the competent authority that his financial resources are such as,

under regulations, make him eligible for representation under this Part ...'

The competent authority is clearly defined in s 20(1), which states:

'Subject to any provision made by virtue of subsection (10) below, the following courts are competent to grant representation under this Part for the purposes of the following proceedings, on an application made for the purpose.'

Later in the section there is set out a description of the courts, each of which can be said for the purposes of the 1988 Act to be a competent authority for the purposes of granting legal aid. Those courts seem to be just about every court save the House of Lords.

I refer also to reg 36 of the 1989 regulations, which states:

'*Refusal to pay contribution* (1) Where any sums which are due under a contribution order before the conclusion of the proceedings have not been paid by the legally assisted person, the court or the proper officer of that court may ...'

There follow provisions for the service of notice upon a person who has been given legal aid, reminding him of his liability to make a contribution and notifying him of what might happen if he does not deal with arrears and continue to make contributions.

'(3) The court shall consider any representations made under paragraph (1)(b) and, if satisfied that the legally assisted person—(a) was able to pay the relevant contribution when it was due; and (b) is able to pay the whole or part of it but has failed or refused to do so, may revoke the grant of representation ...'

Finally, s 24(2) of the 1988 Act states:

'Where a legally assisted person fails to pay any relevant contribution when it is due, the court in which the proceedings for the purposes of which he has been granted representation are being heard may, subject to subsection (3) below, revoke the grant.'

The relief which is sought on behalf of the applicant is an order of certiorari to quash the learned magistrate's decision that the court had no power to grant legal aid to the applicant under reg 10, and an order of mandamus requiring him to reconsider whether the applicant should be granted legal aid in accordance with the 1988 Act and the regulations.

The grounds upon which this relief is sought are, briefly stated, these. The applicant had been summonsed to attend before the magistrates' court by the Department of Trade and Industry for a number of offences which included failing to keep proper accounts contrary to ss 221 and 222 of the Companies Act 1985, obtaining a pecuniary advantage from Barclays Bank contrary to s 18 of the Theft Act 1968, and falsifying documents contrary to s 17 of that Act.

Initially, the applicant was granted legal aid for representation in the proceedings which were to have ensued as a result of being charged with the aforementioned offences, but he failed to make the requisite contributions under the legal aid order, so that was revoked. There was subsequently an oral application made to a stipendiary magistrate sitting at the Liverpool

Magistrates' Court for a fresh legal aid order. That application was made on the basis that the applicant's financial position had changed; he was, it was so said, then unemployed. The court, in a written judgment on 1 July 1992, refused that fresh application on the basis that reg 41(2) of the regulations precluded it from entertaining a second application. The applicant was dissatisfied with that. So proceedings were commenced for judicial review. The matter came before this court and judgment was given on 27 November 1992 (see *R v Liverpool City Magistrates' Court, ex p Shacklady, R v Liverpool City Magistrates' Court, ex p Pender* [1993] 2 All ER 929). The headnote reads:

> 'A defendant in criminal proceedings whose grant of legal aid has been revoked for non-payment of contributions cannot make a fresh application to the clerk of the justices under reg 11(1) of the [1989 regulations] to renew his legal aid but must reapply for legal aid to the trial court under reg 10 thereof, which vests a general power in the court or a judge to make a legal aid order in favour of an applicant notwithstanding that an earlier legal aid order has been revoked. There is a clear distinction in the 1989 regulations between renewal of an application for legal aid after refusal under Pt II thereof and a fresh application following revocation or withdrawal of a legal aid order under Pt IV ...'

In the course of his judgment, with which Tudor Evans J agreed, Beldam LJ stated quite clearly that though it was not competent for the court to entertain the applicant's application under reg 11 ([1993] 2 All ER 929 at 935):

> 'The applicant Pender may still apply to the court for a grant of representation under reg 10.'

It is quite clear, therefore, that that court entertained no doubt that in respect of the proceedings which up to that time had been before the court it was competent for that court to entertain that application from the applicant, notwithstanding the fact that his previous legal aid order had been revoked. It is appropriate to refer to an earlier part of the judgment where Beldam LJ stated (at 932):

> 'The two applications for judicial review of the decisions to refuse legal aid by the clerk to the Liverpool city magistrates raise the common question whether, under the terms of the 1989 regulations, an accused whose grant of legal aid has been revoked for non-payment of contributions can make a fresh application to the clerk to the justices under reg 11(1) of Pt II of the 1989 regulations, or whether in such a case an accused must apply under the provisions of reg 10 to the court at the trial.'

Thus it is that recent authority clearly tends to support the view that reg 10 is a regulation which gives, as indeed it states, a general power to the court to grant legal aid and, so it would appear from the observations of Beldam LJ, to entertain an application following revocation in respect of proceedings held prior to trial.

A contrary view could be said to have been expressed in two cases which were before the magistrate when he reached the decision now under review, the first of them being *R v Macclesfield Justices, ex p Greenhalgh* (1980) 144 JP 142. The regulation then in force, to which reg 10 bears a close resemblance, was reg 5 of the Legal Aid in Criminal Proceedings (General) Regulations 1968, SI 1968/1231, and that read:

> 'Subject to the provisions of reg 4 of these regulations, nothing in reg 1, 2 or 3 of these regulations shall affect the power of a court or a judge of the court or the registrar (subject to the provisions of s 75 of the Criminal Justice Act 1967) to make a legal aid order, whether an application has been made for legal aid or not, or the right of an applicant whose application has been refused to apply to the court at the trial or other proceedings.'

In the course of his judgment—it was agreed to by the other two members of the court—Roskill LJ said as to the meaning of 'other proceedings' (at 143):

> 'Counsel for the applicant has strenuously argued that in that context the words "or other proceedings" include appearances on remand at committal proceedings before the trial. I do not think that that is the right construction of that phrase in this context. I think probably those words "or other proceedings" are added there to cover the case of an appeal, having regard to the references to the registrar of the Criminal Division of the Court of Appeal earlier in that regulation. Accordingly I do not think that the applicant has any right under that regulation to apply when appearing on remand. That disposes of that point.'

Later in the same year *R v City of Cambridge Justices, ex p Leader* (1980) 144 JP 148 was heard in this court, presided over by Waller LJ. In that case the phrase 'other proceedings' was referred to in the judgment of Waller LJ, a judgment with which Park J agreed. He stated (at 150):

> 'I would accept that at the trial, which after all is the last opportunity, there is a duty on the court to give fresh consideration to an application for legal aid. Of course if the circumstances are exactly the same as those that were considered when the original refusal was made, it is unlikely that the court will come to a different conclusion, but, the grant of legal aid being a matter of wide discretion, it is perfectly possible that three magistrates sitting may take a different view from one, even though the circumstances were the same. But in this particular case, whatever may be said about other proceedings (and, in my judgment, no duty arises in those circumstances unless they are final proceedings), this was not the trial and these were not 'other proceedings' which imposed on the magistrates a duty of giving reconsideration to this application.'

Later, he added (at 151):

> 'I would just add one further point, that, while there is clearly no legal duty to do so at the time when the plea is being taken and the case is not being tried, I would have thought that as a matter of practical politics that was perhaps the best time to give further consideration to the application. But all of that is by the way.'

Those two cases have caused a footnote, so we are informed by Mr Burnett, to appear in *Stone's Justices' Manual* (125th edn, 1993), p 1-5439 which is to the effect that 'other proceedings' in reg 10 refer only to proceedings after trial, for the reasons stated by Roskill LJ.

I return to the grounds which the applicant relies upon, to see how the decision complained of arose.

After the decision in *R v Liverpool City Magistrates' Court, ex p Shacklady, R v Liverpool City Magistrates' Court, ex p Pender* [1993] 2 All ER 929 the matter of legal aid returned to the Liverpool Magistrates' Court for consideration. There were some appearances there on behalf of Pender and eventually the crucial decision came to be taken by the stipendiary magistrate, Mr Tapp. He had become concerned at the delay which had clearly taken place in holding committal proceedings and on one if not more occasions he remonstrated with those appearing for the defendants and the prosecution (if not remonstrated, commented sharply about the fact) that there had been such delay and urged everyone to, so to speak, get on with it.

Eventually, on 5 January 1993 the parties appeared before him with the object of arrangements being made for the mode of trial and so on, but with the clear expectation, as I understand from the affidavit of Mr Tapp, that there would also be an application made on behalf of Pender for a fresh legal aid order (the previous one having been revoked).

Mr Tapp informs us that he had well in mind *R v Macclesfield Justices, ex p Greenhalgh* (1980) 144 JP 142 and *R v City of Cambridge Justices, ex p Leader* (1980) 144 JP 148 and of course the provisions of reg 10, he had reminded himself of the contents of those judgments and of the regulation before the parties appeared before him on 5 January. Certain submissions were made to him by solicitors on behalf of both the prosecution and the defence, but, without stating his reasons therefor in any sort of judgment, he informed the parties that he had read the cases referred to and had come to the clear conclusion that he had no power to deal with the application which was before him, and so he dismissed it.

On that day, neither the prosecution nor the defence sought to advance the proceedings to committal, and there was an application for yet another adjournment; that was granted. Nothing has happened further, plainly for the reason that this application was made and has taken some time to come to this court to be resolved.

I understand the magistrate as having come to his decision because he was clearly of the view, persuaded by what had been said by Roskill LJ, that there were no other proceedings before him such as would give him the power which is contained in reg 10. If that be right, as I say, as I assume it to be, the question is: was the magistrate right in coming to a conclusion that 'other proceedings' (as that phrase appears in the regulation) refers only to proceedings post-trial and can have no reference whatsoever to anything which takes place pre-trial, such as remand proceedings?

We have had the benefit of, if I may say so, an excellent submission from both Mr Burnett for the prosecution and Mr Nicol for the applicant. I feel greatly indebted to both of them, not only for their oral submissions but for the high quality of their skeleton arguments. They will, I am sure, not take it amiss if I go to the heart of the matter and my conclusion as to it without dealing in a great deal of detail with the arguments advanced.

Initially, argument ranged around the point as to whether reg 10 can properly be said to refer at all to proceedings in the magistrates' court or, conversely, is concerned only with proceedings in the Crown Court and the Court of Appeal, and so on. I had, before hearing the argument, a feeling that reg 10 was confined to the higher courts, but I am now under no doubt at all that the word 'court' in the regulation undoubtedly embraces the magistrates' court. Therefore reg 10 is to be regarded, as its heading plainly states, as a general power to be resorted to by an applicant who has been refused legal aid by justices or a magistrate or whose order has been revoked under s 36 and, of course, the general power of revocation under s 24.

Therefore, clearly the application made before the magistrate here was one which, putting aside the question of other proceedings for the moment, he was competent to entertain. He was competent to entertain it for the reason that, on the one hand, the regulation gives him the power to entertain an application and, indeed, gives him the further power to grant legal aid when no application at all has been made to him; and on the other because in the second part of the regulation the applicant, his first order having been revoked, was plainly entitled, as the regulation states, to make a fresh application for legal aid. Therefore, what the regulation does is to grant the power to the court and a right to an applicant subject, of course, in both instances to certain reservations which are expressed in the regulation itself. Those reservations are of no significance for the present purposes.

Therefore, as I see the matter, the question is as I posed it earlier on: were the proceedings before the magistrate in the present case 'other proceedings' for the purposes of reg 10? We are invited by both learned counsel to say either that we are bound by the two cases of 1980 or that we should say that we disagree with the relevant parts of the judgments in those cases. Or, in the further alternative, we should express a view that there are differences between reg 5 and reg 10 which allow this court to come to the conclusion that the construction of reg 10 leads to a different conclusion than the construction placed in the cases I have referred to upon reg 5. Of course, the main difference is obvious, namely that reg 5 makes no reference whatsoever to revocation of a legal aid order, whereas reg 10 plainly does. On that basis alone, the contention is that we may put aside the earlier authority and in so doing, come to the conclusion that there has been no other authority. The field is open for us to consider and so construe for ourselves the meaning of the relevant words in reg 10.

It is of significance in my judgment that the court presided over by Beldam LJ seemed clearly to be of the view that the magistrate was competent to entertain the application which is now under review. In any event, I have reached the clear conclusion, in regarding the provisions of reg 10 on their own, that it would be straining the language of that regulation beyond endurance to come to the conclusion that 'other proceedings' refer only to proceedings which take place after the trial, whether it is in the magistrates' court or in the Crown Court.

However one would put a comma here or a comma there, as Mr Burnett entices us into thinking we might, it seems to me that to deny that 'other proceedings' refers to pre-trial matters only is to strip away from the general power given by Parliament, unwarrantably, vital proceedings in which defendants very often have to take part in and to be represented. Apart altogether from the matter of pure construction, that would in my view be an unjust conclusion. Therefore, I would say that the footnote in *Stone's Justices' Manual* must be eliminated for the simple reason that 'other proceedings' refers not only to proceedings post-trial, but proceedings pre-trial, and those latter proceedings must obviously include such proceedings as remands, bail applications and arrangements for trial, and so forth.

Having reached that decision, I look back upon what happened on the day in the magistrates' court. Were they proceedings at all? In my view they clearly were. The magistrate was concerned to make arrangements for a stay of the case. Those representing the applicant were concerned that legal aid be granted so that the applicant had representation for future proceedings for the trial.

For those reasons, I have reached the conclusion that the magistrate was wrong in his decision. I should add, however, that he did not appear to have the assistance which would have enabled him to consider the matter of construction of reg 10 with anything approaching the excellent way in which we have been assisted.

For those reasons, I would let certiorari go and order mandamus.

LEONARD J. I agree.

Application allowed.

Kate O'Hanlon Barrister.

Re Dent (a bankrupt)
Trustee of the property of the bankrupt v Dent and another

CHANCERY DIVISION
FERRIS AND ARDEN JJ
18, 19 OCTOBER, 10 NOVEMBER 1993

Bankruptcy – Avoidance of settlement – Application to set aside deed of gift – Application made subsequent to donor's discharge from bankruptcy – Husband executing deed of gift of property in favour of wife in 1985 – Husband adjudicated bankrupt in 1986 but later obtaining discharge order – Trustee in bankruptcy applying to set aside deed of gift nearly two years after discharge order – Whether trustee entitled to make application – Whether order operating to vest interest in property for benefit of husband's creditors – Bankruptcy Act 1914, ss 38(a), 42(1).

On 2 August 1985 D executed a deed of gift of a property in favour of his wife. In 1986 D applied for bankruptcy on his own petition and in the course of the proceedings made full disclosure of the deed of gift and the circumstances relating to it. D was adjudicated bankrupt in December 1986 and on 29 December 1989 he obtained a discharge from the bankruptcy. On 24 September 1991, nearly two years after D's discharge, the trustee in bankruptcy began proceedings to set aside the deed of gift under s 42[a] of the Bankruptcy Act 1914, which provided that any settlement of property, not being a settlement made before and in consideration of marriage, or made in

---

a   Section 42, so far as material, is set out at p 907 *h j*, post

favour of a purchaser or incumbrancer in good faith for valuable consideration, was void against the trustee in bankruptcy if the settlor became bankrupt within two years after the date of settlement. D and his wife applied to the court to determine whether a trustee in bankruptcy could maintain proceedings for the avoidance of a settlement under s 42 of the 1914 Act after the bankrupt had been discharged from his bankruptcy. They contended (i) that s 42 did not render a settlement void, merely voidable, and as a consequence, property comprised in the settlement only became property of the bankrupt passing to his estate as and when s 42 was invoked and (ii) that since property acquired by a bankrupt after his discharge did not constitute property which might 'belong to or be vested in the bankrupt at the commencement of the bankruptcy' or might 'be acquired by or devolve on him before his discharge' within s 38(a)[b] of the 1914 Act, such property could not be treated as part of the bankrupt's estate and was not therefore divisible among his creditors. The judge held that the order of discharge had no effect on s 42 or the right of the trustee in bankruptcy to invoke that section, on the grounds that once s 42 had been invoked it operated as against the donee to treat the transfer of property as if it had not been made, thereby rendering the subject matter of the settlement part of D's property as at the commencement of the bankruptcy, with the result that the subject matter of the avoided settlement became property vested in the trustee in bankruptcy as part of D's estate by virtue of s 38(a). D and his wife appealed.

Held – The appeal would be dismissed for the following reasons—

(1) Although s 42 of the 1914 Act treated a settlement before bankruptcy as voidable, the effect of an order of the court rescinding a settlement under s 42 was to avoid the settlement from at least the date of adjudication, which meant that the subject matter of the avoided settlement then became property of the bankrupt within s 38(a) of that Act. It followed that a s 42 order operated to treat the property as vesting in the trustee in bankruptcy and as becoming divisible among the creditors in the same way as other property of the debtor (see p 909 *j* to p 910 *a* and p 912 *d*, post); *Re Farnham (a lunatic)* [1895–9] All ER Rep 897 and *Re Gunsbourg* [1920] All ER Rep 492 considered.

(2) Alternatively, where a donee of property acquired title to property under a deed of gift, he did so subject to defeasance in favour of the donor's creditors in the event that the donor became bankrupt and his trustee in bankruptcy obtained an order under s 42 of the 1914 Act. A s 42 order was merely a fulfilment of those events. The contingent liability to defeasance was always present and it represented a flaw in the donee's title from the outset. The corresponding right vested in the donor was a right which would only become of value for the benefit of the donor's creditors in the event of his bankruptcy and the operation of s 42. That right was nevertheless in existence from the outset and, on bankruptcy, it became vested in the trustee in bankruptcy as part of the bankrupt's estate by virtue of s 38(a) of the 1914 Act. In effect, s 42 operated to give value to what, without such operation, would be only a nominal interest (see p 910 *a* to *e*, post).

---

b   Section 38(a) is set out at p 908 *a b*, post

(3) It was immaterial that the application to set aside the transaction and/ or the decision of the trustee to take such proceedings was not made until after the bankrupt's discharge. Moreover, in the event that the trustee succeeded in his claim that s 42 of the 1914 Act was applicable, the former bankrupt would not himself recover the property in question. If, on the substantive application, the court were to make a declaration that the deed of gift was void by reason of s 42 it would, in effect, declare and validate the entitlement which was already vested in the trustee in bankruptcy under s 38(a) of the 1914 Act. That was why the usual order consequential on a successful s 42 application was an order vesting the property directly in the trustee without any need for it to be revested in the former bankrupt as an interim measure. It followed that there was no reason why s 42 should operate differently when the bankrupt had, before the section was invoked, obtained his discharge (see p 910 *e* to *h*, post).

Notes

For conditions of forfeiture on settlor's bankruptcy, see 3(2) *Halsbury's Laws* (4th edn reissue), para 398.

For cases on property void against the trustee, see 5(2) *Digest* (2nd reissue) 165–167, 13600–13617.

Cases referred to in judgment

Carter and Kenderdine's Contract, Re [1897] 1 Ch 776, CA.
Debtor, Re a, (No 12 of 1958), ex p the trustee of the property of the debtor v Clegg [1968] 2 All ER 425, [1968] 1 WLR 788, DC.
Elgindata Ltd (No 2), Re [1993] 1 All ER 232, [1992] 1 WLR 1207, CA.
Farnham, Re (a lunatic) [1895] 2 Ch 799, [1895–9] All ER Rep 897, CA.
Gunsbourg, Re [1920] 2 KB 426, [1920] All ER Rep 492, CA.
Hart, Re, ex p Green [1912] 3 KB 6, CA.
Holden, Re (1887) 20 QBD 43.
Sanquinetti v Stuckey's Banking Co [1895] 1 Ch 176.
Tankard, Re, ex p the Official Receiver [1899] 2 QB 57.
Vansittart, Re, ex p Brown [1893] 2 QB 377, [1891–4] All ER Rep 1111.

Appeal

Judith Anne Dent and her husband, Graham John Dent, appealed from the affirmative determination made by Judge Maddocks on 7 May 1993 on the trial of the following preliminary issues on their application: (a) whether the trustee in bankruptcy of Mr Dent was entitled to make an application to set aside a deed of gift of property known as 9 South Road, Bowden, Cheshire in favour of Mrs Dent by Mr Dent under s 42 of the Bankruptcy Act 1914; and, if so, (b) whether the order sought under s 42 could operate to vest any interest in the property in the trustee for the benefit of the bankruptcy's creditors. The trustee in bankruptcy did not initiate the s 42 proceedings until nearly two years after Mr Dent's discharge from bankruptcy. The facts are set out in the judgment of the court.

James W Bonney (instructed by *Neil Myerson & Co*, Altringham) for the appellants, Mr and Mrs Dent.

Mark Halliwell (instructed by Aaron & Partners, Chester) for the respondent trustee.

Cur adv vult

10 November 1993. The following judgment of the court was delivered.

ARDEN J. We have before us an appeal on a preliminary issue which primarily raises the apparently novel question whether a trustee in bankruptcy can maintain proceedings for the avoidance of a settlement under s 42 of the Bankruptcy Act 1914 after the bankrupt has been discharged from his bankruptcy. We should point out at the outset that we have not been concerned with the Insolvency Act 1986. The particular point in issue on this appeal could not arise under that Act.

The material facts are that on 2 August 1985 the second respondent (Mr Dent) executed a deed of gift of a property known as 9 South Road, Bowden, Cheshire in favour of the first respondent (Mrs Dent). In December 1986 Mr Dent was adjudicated bankrupt on his own petition. It is accepted that, during the course of the bankruptcy, Mr Dent made full disclosure of the deed of gift and the circumstances relating to it. On 29 December 1989 Mr Dent was discharged from his bankruptcy. It was not until 24 September 1991, nearly two years after the discharge, that the trustee in bankruptcy, David Alistair Thomas Wood (Mr Wood) began these proceedings to set aside the deed of gift under s 42 of the Bankruptcy Act 1914.

On 27 April 1992, on the application of Mr and Mrs Dent, an order was made for the determination of the issues whether—

'(a) the Trustee in Bankruptcy is entitled to make this application; and, if so, (b) whether the order sought under s 42 of the Bankruptcy Act 1914 could now operate to vest any interest in 9 South Road in the trustee for the benefit of the bankruptcy's creditors.'

After a hearing on 6 and 7 May 1993 Judge Maddocks determined both these issues in the affirmative. Mr and Mrs Dent appealed from this determination. They have been represented before us and below by Mr Bonney. Mr Wood (the respondent to this appeal) has been represented before us and below by Mr Halliwell.

On this appeal we are not concerned with reasons for Mr Wood's delay in commencing the proceedings or with the merits or otherwise of the substantive application.

Section 42 provides in material parts as follows:

'(1) Any settlement of property, not being a settlement made before and in consideration of marriage, or made in favour of a purchaser or incumbrancer in good faith and for valuable consideration ... shall, if the settlor becomes bankrupt within two years after the date of the settlement, be void against the trustee in the bankruptcy ...'

In giving his decision on the preliminary issue Judge Maddocks set out the relevant parts of the statutory scheme for bankruptcy under the 1914 Act. In particular, he referred to s 18 of the 1914 Act which provides that upon adjudication in bankruptcy the property of the bankrupt becomes divisible among his creditors and vests in his trustee. He also referred to s 38 of the

1914 Act which defines what is meant in the 1914 Act as the property of the bankrupt. Such property includes:

> '(a) All such property as may belong to or be vested in the bankrupt at the commencement of the bankruptcy, or may be acquired by or devolve on him before his discharge.'

As the judge pointed out, it follows from s 38, and this is a main plank in Mr Bonney's argument, that assets acquired by a bankrupt after his discharge do not fall into the bankrupt's estate and are not divisible among his creditors. A further important element in the statutory scheme, as the judge pointed out, is s 26(9), which deals with the obligations of a discharged bankrupt. It provides that he shall—

> 'notwithstanding his discharge, give such assistance as the trustee may require in the realisation and distribution of such of his property as is vested in the trustee ...'

Reference was also made by the judge to s 28 of the Bankruptcy Act 1914 which provides inter alia that an order of discharge in general releases a bankrupt from debts provable in the bankruptcy. It is common ground on this appeal that the administration of a bankrupt's estate may continue after the bankrupt has been discharged from his bankruptcy, and that the powers of the trustee continue for that purpose.

The judge then set out the argument for Mr and Mrs Dent, which has been repeated and developed also before us. We can summarise it at this point by adopting the words used by the judge:

> 'The case for the respondent, as ably deployed by Mr Bonney, is shortly as follows: s 42, as interpreted by the court, does not render a settlement void but only voidable. As a consequence, the property comprised in the settlement only becomes property of the bankrupt passing to his trustee as and when the section is invoked. In order to become divisible among creditors, it must fall within the description in s 38(a) under one limb or the other. It cannot fall within the first limb of (a) because at the commencement of the bankruptcy the property was not vested in the bankrupt but in his wife, the section not having been invoked so as to disturb the transfer to her at that time.'

We would interpolate that it is common ground on this appeal that the effect of the words 'void against the trustee' in s 42 is to render a settlement within the section voidable rather than void. Accordingly an order is only made under s 42 subject to the rights of third parties acquired bona fide and for value from the donee under the settlement (see *Re Carter and Kenderdine's Contract* [1897] 1 Ch 776). This is so whether the donee acquires his rights before any act of bankruptcy (as in *Re Carter and Kenderdine's Contract*) or subsequent thereto (*Re Hart, ex p Green* [1912] 3 KB 6). As a result, an order under s 42 may operate to accelerate a subsequent incumbrance created by the donor over the balance of property remaining vested in him after a gift of a partial interest which is avoided as against his trustee in bankruptcy (see *Sanquinetti v Stuckey's Banking Co* [1895] 1 Ch 176). Mr Bonney cited other cases illustrating this point (see *Re Holden* [1887] 20 QBD 43 and *Re Vansittart, ex p Brown* [1893] 2 QB 377, [1891–4] All ER Rep 1111). However we consider that the proposition is so well established as not to require us to refer to the earlier authorities.

Mr Bonney criticised a passage in the judgment of the judge which is based on these authorities:

> 'The effect of a settlement becoming void as against the trustee is that the trustee is able to treat the property transferred as not having been transferred. If nothing more has happened then, so far as the trustee is concerned, it remains, on adjudication, property of the bankrupt and can be treated as becoming divisible among the creditors and vesting in the trustee in the same way as other property of the debtor. That, as I see it, is the way s 42 operates.'

Mr Bonney argued that property the subject of an avoided settlement does not 'remain' property of the bankrupt but only becomes such property on the declaration of avoidance being made. This point lies at the heart of this appeal and we return to it below.

The judge then expressed his conclusion on the preliminary point in these terms:

> 'The principle of these cases is quite plain, that a bona fide purchaser prior to the time when the trustee has invoked s 42 will obtain a good title. That, however, does not touch upon the effect of the operation of the section as against the donee once the section has been invoked. As to that, it is, in my judgment, quite clear—and clear from the judgments—that the effect is to treat the transfer as if it had not been made so as to render the subject matter of the settlement part of the property of the bankrupt as at the commencement of the bankruptcy. The fallacy in the argument as I see it lies in equating the process by which s 42 is invoked with the consequences of the section once it has been invoked. So far as a purchaser is concerned, the position remains open until the trustee invokes the section and in that sense the adjective "voidable" is apt. That does not, however, affect the consequence of the section being applied in favour of the trustee as against a donee, who has no such protection. That, it seems to me, is the fundamental fallacy in the reasoning which seeks to apply the decisions relating to a bona fide purchaser to this case. However, I would add that I cannot see how property which is the subject of an avoided disposition could be viewed as after acquired property. Section 47(1) makes it plain that after acquired property is something the bankrupt himself acquires after the time of the bankruptcy. Section 42 does not produce that result; it merely treats a settlement before the bankruptcy as void and the fact that it is necessarily invoked only after the bankruptcy does not affect its operation as being upon what is an antecedent transaction. For these reasons, in my judgment, the order of discharge has no effect upon s 42 or upon the right of the trustee to invoke the section.'

We agree with the conclusion of the judge and we will endeavour to explain in our own words why we do so. Even though settlements within the section are not void but merely voidable, the effect of an order of the court rescinding a settlement under s 42 will be to avoid the settlement from (at least) adjudication. (It is unnecessary for us to decide whether avoidance takes effect from any earlier date.) This means that the subject matter of the avoided settlement becomes property to which s 38(a) applies. We do not think that the use of the word 'remain' in the passage from the judgment which we earlier referred to was inappropriate.

There is an alternative analysis by which in our view the same result is achieved. When Mrs Dent, the donee of the property, acquired title to the property under the deed of gift, she did so subject to defeasance in favour of Mr Dent's creditors in the event that Mr Dent became bankrupt and his trustee in bankruptcy obtained an order under s 42 of the 1914 Act. An order under s 42 is merely a fulfilment of those events. The contingent liability to defeasance was always present: it represented a flaw in Mrs Dent's title from the outset. Accordingly there must always have been a corresponding right vested in Mr Dent. This right did not give him anything which he would enjoy personally because the deed of gift was fully binding against him. It was, in effect, a right which would only become of value for the benefit of Mr Dent's creditors in the event of his bankruptcy and the operation of s 42. It was, nevertheless, in existence from the outset and, on the bankruptcy, it became vested in his trustee as part of his estate by virtue of s 38(a) of the 1914 Act. We do not accept Mr Bonney's submission that the only asset which falls to be considered in these circumstances is the actual property transferred and that as this was in Mrs Dent it could not be in the bankrupt's estate. The definition of property in s 167 of the 1914 Act expressly includes things in action and is therefore sufficiently widely drawn to include a right of the kind we have described. The operation of s 42 is to give value to what, without such operation, would be only a nominal interest.

It is thus immaterial that the application to set the transaction aside and/or the decision by the trustee to take such proceedings is not made until after the bankrupt's discharge. It also follows that in the event of the trustee succeeding in his claim that s 42 is applicable the former bankrupt will not himself recover the property in question. It appears to us that if, on the substantive application, the court were to make a declaration that the deed of gift is void by reason of s 42 it would, in effect, declare and validate the entitlement which is already vested in the trustee in bankruptcy under s 38(a). This is the reason why, as we understand it, the usual order consequential upon a successful application based on s 42 is an order vesting the property directly in the trustee without any need for it to be revested in the former bankrupt as an interim measure. We see no reason why s 42 operates differently when the bankrupt has, before the section is invoked, obtained his discharge.

Mr Bonney placed considerable reliance on two cases in the Court of Appeal, *Re Gunsbourg* [1920] 2 KB 426, [1920] All ER Rep 492 and *Re Farnham (a lunatic)* [1895] 2 Ch 799, [1895–9] All ER Rep 897, which are, of course, binding on us. *Re Gunsbourg* concerned a settlement which was absolutely void because it constituted an act of bankruptcy. The question was whether a bona fide purchaser for value and without notice could take a good title from the donee. The Court of Appeal (Lord Sterndale MR and Warrington LJ, with Younger LJ dissenting) held that he could not. A distinction was drawn between a disposition which was absolutely void and one which was only voidable, such as a settlement to which s 42 of the 1914 Act applies. The latter case was governed by the earlier decisions of the Court of Appeal in *Re Carter and Kenderdine's Contract* [1897] 1 Ch 776 and *Re Hart, ex p Green* [1912]

3 KB 6. In the course of his judgment in *Re Gunsbourg*, Lord Sterndale MR said that the situation in *Re Hart, ex p Green* was—

> 'an ordinary case of a voluntary settlement, and when the trustee avoided it his title accrued from the avoidance, and there was no relation back so far as that transfer was concerned.'

(See [1920] 2 KB 426 at 442, [1920] All ER Rep 492 at 497, see also [1920] 2 KB 426 at 438 and [1920] All ER Rep 492 at 495–496 for a passage to the same effect.)

The other member of the majority, Warrington LJ, did not say in terms at what time the trustee's title accrues to property the subject of a settlement under s 42. For the answer to this question we must return to *Re Carter and Kenderdine's Contract* and *Re Hart, ex p Green*.

In *Re Carter and Kenderdine's Contract* the Court of Appeal expressly considered the time from which avoidance under the predecessor of s 42 took effect. They were unanimous in rejecting the contention that the settlement was void ab initio and held that the trustee's title could not predate his appointment (per Lindley LJ) or the commencement of the bankruptcy (per A L Smith and Rigby LJJ; see also per Wright J obiter in *Re Tankard, ex p the Official Receiver* [1899] 2 QB 57 at 60). In the later case of *Re Hart, ex p Green*, the Court of Appeal followed the view of Lindley LJ. We do not consider that *Re Gunsbourg* is authority for the view that avoidance dates only from when the trustee elects to avoid the settlement (or obtains an order to that effect) because the remarks of Lord Sterndale which were relied upon by Mr Bonney are inconsistent with the decisions in *Re Hart, ex p Green* and *Re Carter and Kenderdine's Contract*.

That conclusion deals with a further submission of Mr Bonney based on *Re Farnham* [1895] 2 Ch 799, [1895-9] All ER Rep 897. In that case it is said that upon the making of an order avoiding a settlement under s 42 property 'reverts' to the donor and thereupon 'became vested' in him or 'came to the trustee' (see [1895] 2 Ch 799 at 808, 810, 812, [1895-9] All ER Rep 897 at 899, 901 per Lindley, Lopes and Rigby LJJ). We think that these expressions have to be read in the light of the later decisions of the Court of Appeal in *Re Carter and Kenderdine's Contract* and *Re Hart, ex p Green*. Moreover the decision in *Re Farnham* was that property the subject of a settlement avoided by an order under (the predecessor of) s 42 vested in the bankrupt with retrospective effect, and that, as the bankrupt's affairs were subject to jurisdiction in lunacy when he was adjudicated bankrupt, such property went to his committee in lunacy and not to his trustee in bankruptcy. On analysis, therefore, we consider this case is against Mr Bonney. It supports the conclusion of the judge, with which we agree, that the effect of an order under s 42 is that the property transferred—

> 'can be treated as becoming divisible among the creditors and vesting in the trustee in the same way as other property of the debtor.'

We therefore reject Mr Bonney's criticism of this passage. We also likewise reject his submission that the property the subject of an order under s 42 would be after-acquired property.

Mr Bonney's alternative submission was that after the bankrupt has been discharged, the trustee no longer has any locus standi to commence proceedings under s 42. But his argument rapidly runs into difficulty. If it be said that the trustee had no locus because the property the subject of the avoided settlement is after-acquired property which does not vest in the trustee this argument depends on the correctness of Mr Bonney's first submission and adds nothing to it. If, however, it is contended that, even though the property becomes vested in the trustee, he has no locus standi to take proceedings to collect such property this would reveal a strange lacuna in the 1914 Act. It would mean that there would be property which forms part of the bankrupt's estate but yet which cannot be realised for the benefit of creditors. We agree with Mr Halliwell that if such was the intention of the 1914 Act it would have required clear wording. Such wording is not in our view present in s 26(9) of the 1914 Act, and we do not consider that the decision in *Re a Debtor (No 12 of 1958), ex p the trustee of the property of the debtor v Clegg* [1968] 2 All ER 425, [1968] 1 WLR 788, on which Mr Bonney relied and which concerned property of a former bankrupt allegedly not disclosed until after discharge, provides any support for his submission.

In the circumstances we consider that the judge's determination of the preliminary point was correct.

Now we turn to the appeal against the judge's decision that Mr and Mrs Dent should pay the costs of the preliminary issue in any event. The gist of Mr Bonney's argument was that these costs should have been reserved to trial because if the issue had been dealt with at trial and the result of the trial was a victory for Mr and Mrs Dent on the substantive issues, notwithstanding a ruling against them on the points now raised by way of preliminary issue, they ought not to have been ordered to pay any part of the trustee's costs unless they had acted improperly or unreasonably, of which there is no suggestion. In support of his submission, Mr Bonney referred us to the recent decision of the Court of Appeal in *Re Elgindata Ltd (No 2)* [1993] 1 All ER 232, [1992] 1 WLR 1207.

Although the preliminary issues concern the trustee's claim, not some special defence raised by Mr and Mrs Dent, the fact that they fall to be determined as preliminary issues is attributable to the initiative of Mr and Mrs Dent. Moreover, if they had not raised the points on which they have failed there may have been no argument on them at all and if there had been argument on them by the trustee at the request of the court it may well have taken less time. We do not consider that *Re Elgindata Ltd (No 2)* is authority for the proposition that, where the determination of a preliminary issue does not dispose of the entire proceedings, it is wrong in principle for a court hearing a preliminary issue to refuse to reserve the costs to the substantive trial. That case concerned the costs incurred in the action arising out of issues of fact relevant to the relief which the successful party obtained. The case did not concern the costs of a preliminary issue and in our view is distinguishable. Accordingly we consider that the judge had a discretion to decide where the burden of costs should fall. It is not suggested that in these circumstances the conclusion he reached is one which can be challenged by way of appeal.

Accordingly we also dismiss the appeal against the judge's order on costs. It has not been suggested that *Re Elgindata Ltd (No 2)* applies to the costs of this appeal. We direct that they should follow the result of this appeal and be paid by the respondents in any event.

Appeal dismissed.

Jacqueline Metcalfe   Barrister.

R v Berry (No 3)

COURT OF APPEAL, CRIMINAL DIVISION
LORD TAYLOR OF GOSFORTH CJ, OTTON AND KAY JJ
20, 21, 28 SEPTEMBER 1993

Explosives – Offence – Making explosive substance for unlawful object – Mens rea – Whether necessary for Crown to prove that defendant knew that what he was making or had in his possession or under his control was an explosive substance – Explosive Substances Act 1833, s 4.

The appellant, an exporter of electronic appliances to the Middle East, was convicted in May 1983 of making an explosive substance, namely electronic timers, in such circumstances as to give rise to a reasonable suspicion that they had not been made for a lawful object, contrary to s 4[a] of the Explosive Substances Act 1883. The Crown contended that the appellant was an accessory to the manufacture by his co-accused of electronic timers which were designed and intended for use by terrorists in making time bombs, and that he had exported them to the Middle East. The appellant contended that the timers had been made for a lawful object and that he was supplying them not to terrorists but to the Syrian government. He appealed against his conviction on the grounds, inter alia, that the offence under s 4 of the 1883 Act required proof of mens rea and that the judge had failed so to direct the jury, that the judge had not adequately directed the jury as to the law relating to the appellant's defence that he had made the timers for a lawful object, and that fresh expert evidence cast doubt on the expert evidence adduced by the Crown at trial.

Held – The appeal would be allowed and the conviction quashed, for the following reasons—

(1) For the purposes of an offence under s 4 of the 1883 Act the Crown had to prove that the defendant knew that what he was making or had in his possession or under his control was an explosive substance in that it was a piece of apparatus intended to be used for causing an explosion. Accordingly, the judge should have identified mens rea as a specific ingredient of the offence which the Crown had to prove and his failure to do so was a material misdirection (see p 918 *g* to *j* and p 919 *c d g h*, post).

(2) Under s 4 of the 1883 Act the burden was on the defendant to establish that he had made the explosive substance for a lawful object and since

---

[a] Section 4, so far as material, is set out at p 917 *g* to *j*, post

supplying the timers to the Syrian government was a lawful object, whatever their subsequent use might be, it was incumbent on the judge to direct the jury that if they found that the appellant had so acted that was a good defence. To the extent that the judge had not dealt adequately with that issue his summing up was defective (see p 920 *f g*, post).

(3) The fresh expert evidence presented to the court cast doubt on the expert evidence adduced by the Crown at the trial, which had been largely unchallenged and had been emphasised by the judge as being the most vital evidence in the case, and on that ground alone the jury's verdict was unsafe and unsatisfactory (see p 922 *g h*, post).

Per curiam. In any case in which the Court of Appeal is minded to allow an appeal on one ground, leaving others unresolved, the Crown should inform the court before judgment if there is any reason to believe it would seek to have the decisive point certified for consideration by the House of Lords. The Court of Appeal can then decide whether, out of caution, the other grounds ought to be considered there and then (see p 924 *a b*, post).

Notes
For possessing explosive substances etc, see 11(1) *Halsbury's Laws* (4th edn reissue) para 482.

For the Explosive Substances Act 1833, s 4, see 12 *Halsbury's Statutes* (4th edn) (1994 reissue) 145.

[Editor's note. In *R v Mandair* [1994] 2 All ER 715 the House of Lords considered the question of the disposal by the House of grounds of appeal not dealt with by the Court of Appeal.]

Cases referred to in judgment
A-G for Northern Ireland v Gallagher [1961] 3 All ER 299, [1963] AC 349, [1961] 3 WLR 619, HL.
R v Berry [1984] 3 All ER 1008, [1985] AC 246, [1984] 3 WLR 1274, HL; *rvsg* [1984] 2 All ER 296, [1984] 1 WLR 824, CA.
R v Berry (No 2) [1991] 2 All ER 789, [1991] 1 WLR 125, CA.
R v Hallam [1957] 1 All ER 665, [1957] 1 QB 569, [1957] 2 WLR 521, CCA.
R v Stewart and Harris (1959) 44 Cr App R 29, CCA.
R v Ward [1993] 2 All ER 577, [1993] 1 WLR 619, CA.

Cases also cited
R v Maguire [1992] 2 All ER 433, [1992] QB 936, CA.
R v Guildhall Justices, ex p DPP (1983) 78 Cr App R 269, DC.

Appeal against conviction
Following a reference by the Home Secretary under s 17 of the Criminal Appeal Act 1968 John Rodney Francis Berry appealed against his conviction in the Crown Court at Chelmsford on 24 May 1983 before Judge Greenwood and a jury of making an explosive substance for which he was sentenced to eight years' imprisonment. An earlier appeal against his conviction had been allowed by the Court of Appeal ([1984] 2 All ER 296, [1984] 1 WLR 824) but on appeal by the Crown on a point of law certified as of general public importance the House of Lords ([1984] 3 All ER 1008, [1985] AC 246) directed that his conviction be restored. A subsequent application to the Court of Appeal ([1991] 2 All ER 789, [1991] 1 WLR 125) inviting the court to

determine grounds of appeal which had been argued before, but not decided by, the Court of Appeal on the hearing of the first appeal was refused, the court ruling that it had no power to re-list the appeal following the order of the House of Lords. His sentence was however reduced to six years' imprisonment on 10 October 1990. The facts are set out in the judgment of the court.

Geoffrey Robertson QC and *Edward Fitzgerald* (assigned by the *Registrar of Criminal Appeals*) for the appellant.
David Cocks QC and *Jonathan Fisher* (instructed by the *Crown Prosecution Service*, Headquarters) for the Crown.

Cur adv vult

28 September 1993. The following judgment of the court was delivered.

LORD TAYLOR OF GOSFORTH CJ. This case has had a long and chequered history. It is a source of great regret to this court that the prosecution arising from events in 1981 and leading to a conviction in 1983, should not be finally decided until 1993.

The history of the proceedings

The appellant was jointly charged, together with one Geoffrey Smith, with making in 1981 an explosive substance, namely a quantity of electronic timers, in such circumstances as to give rise to a reasonable suspicion that they had not made them for a lawful object, contrary to s 4 of the Explosive Substances Act 1883. At a late stage, a second count was added charging both men with an offence contrary to s 68(2) of the Customs and Excise Management Act 1979. However, that count was withdrawn from the jury by the judge and needs no further mention.

After a trial at the Crown Court at Chelmsford, the appellant was convicted on 24 May 1983 by a majority of ten to one and was sentenced to eight years' imprisonment. The jury was unable to agree in Smith's case. On his retrial, the judge directed Smith's acquittal on a point of jurisdiction. On appeal, the appellant raised a number of grounds. However, his conviction was quashed on 26 March 1984, solely on a ground raising the same point of jurisdiction as had availed Smith (see [1984] 2 All ER 296, [1984] 1 WLR 824). On application by the Crown, the Court of Appeal certified that a point of law of general public importance was involved on the issue of jurisdiction, but refused leave to appeal to the House of Lords. The appellant was granted bail on surrendering his passport.

The House of Lords granted leave and on 29 November 1984 allowed the Crown's appeal and ordered that the appellant's conviction be restored (see [1984] 3 All ER 1008, [1985] AC 246). The appellant had attended the hearing in the House of Lords but, fearing an adverse result, left the country for Spain, his passport having been returned to him in error. On 18 December 1984 this court implemented the decision of the House of Lords and restored the conviction.

There was then a gap in the chronology until 24 February 1989, when the appellant was returned to the United Kingdom from Spain to continue to serve his sentence of imprisonment. It is right to say therefore that the absence of any progress towards redress in those four years was due to the appellant himself. During October 1989 an application was made on his behalf inviting this court to adjudicate upon grounds of appeal which had not been determined in the court's judgment of 26 March 1984. The application was refused, this court ruling that it had no power to re-list the case following the order of the House of Lords. However, on 10 October 1990 another constitution of this court reduced the sentence imposed upon the appellant from eight years to six years.

The appellant, being aggrieved that some of his original grounds of appeal had never been determined, petitioned the Home Secretary and invited him to refer the case back to this court pursuant to his powers under s 17 of the Criminal Appeal Act 1968.

On 20 January 1992 the Home Secretary sought the opinion of this court under s 17(1)(b) of the 1968 Act as to whether the court would be competent to entertain an appeal by the appellant were a reference to be made under s 17(1)(a) of that Act, and if so, to treat his letter as such a reference.

On 3 April 1992 this court ruled that it was competent to entertain such an appeal on a reference by the Home Secretary. Fresh counsel were instructed for the appellant and, after some months, fresh grounds of appeal were lodged. The appeal came on before us on 20 September 1993.

The facts

The appellant was a businessman engaged in exporting electronic appliances to Middle Eastern countries. The co-accused, Smith, was a manufacturer of electronic appliances. The case for the Crown was that a quantity of electronic timers, designed and intended for use by terrorists in the construction of time bombs, had been made by Smith's company with the connivance of the appellant who had then exported them to the Middle East.

A Mr Aspin, a licensed arms dealer, gave evidence that he was approached by the appellant in October 1981. They discussed the sale of detonating and transmitting equipment for export. On one occasion the appellant was in the company of two officials from Oman and he produced a timer. Its use in the demolition of buildings was, according to Mr Aspin, discussed. Mr Aspin was worried. He took legal advice from his solicitor, who happened also to be the appellant's solicitor, and, as a result, handed the timer to the police. It was sent to be examined by Mr Fereday, a forensic science officer with great experience of explosive devices. He concluded that the timer had been designed for attachment to an explosive device in terrorist operations.

The appellant was questioned by police officers on 20 October 1981. He said the timers had numerous applications, such as for runway lighting and garage doors. He was interviewed in the presence of his solicitor on 16 November and made a statement. He said that timers were first discussed in Beirut whilst he was there transacting other business with Syrian government officials. As a result, he supplied 1000 of the timers, together with some ultra-high frequency (UHF) equipment. He added that during recent visits to Beirut, he had seen the timers still in the possession, as he put it, of the Beirut government department. In a later interview on 11 December the appellant gave a fuller account of the supply of 1000 timers. He said he and Smith had been in Beirut and had been introduced to some businessmen who were interested in buying equipment. In particular, a man named Monser had a dummy plastic box as a model and although the performance of the timer was discussed, its purpose was not mentioned. He denied that there had been any mention of user for aircraft landing lights.

In evidence, the appellant said Mr Monser was one of several contacts he had in the Middle East. In December 1980 he went to Beirut with Smith and in the course of discussions at which Mr Monser was present a timer was produced, but no mention was made of its purpose. It was agreed that Smith would manufacture timers and the appellant would sell them to Monser. The timers were duly made pursuant to contract by Smith's firm. They were collected by Berry who delivered them at Monser's direction to a Syrian official in London.

Mr Monser was called for the defence to confirm that the timers were delivered to the Syrian government. He said that subsequently they were returned to him because they were unsatisfactory. He, like the appellant, did not inquire what they were to be used for, but he believed there had been mention of landing lights.

Dr Hanka, a scientific consultant, was called on behalf of the defence to rebut Mr Fereday's opinion as to the intended terrorist use of the timers. Dr Hanka said the article was simply a timing device which could be used for a number of purposes. However, he conceded he had no experience of terrorist equipment and had to defer to Mr Fereday's expertise in that field.

Grounds of appeal

Before this court, Mr Robertson QC rightly abandoned two of his lodged grounds of appeal—that which was based on an alleged inconsistency of verdicts as between the appellant and Smith, and that which sought to re-argue the point of jurisdiction decided by the House of Lords. He relies, however, on four main grounds. The first two relate to the judge's directions to the jury. It is right to say that they were raised for the first time in a skeleton argument helpfully provided by Mr Robertson, but only on the morning of the hearing.

Mens rea

He submits first that the offence charged under s 4 of the 1883 Act requires proof of mens rea and the judge failed so to direct the jury.

Section 4(1) provides as follows:

'Any person who makes or knowingly has in his possession or under his control any explosive substance, under such circumstances as to give rise to a reasonable suspicion that he is not making it or does not have it in his possession or under his control for a lawful object, shall, unless he can show that he made it or had it in his possession or under his control for a lawful object, be ... liable to ... imprisonment for a term not exceeding 14 years ...'

Section 9 provides that unless the context otherwise requires—

'The expression "explosive substance" shall be deemed to include any materials for making any explosive substance; also any apparatus, machine, implement, or materials used, or intended to be used, or adapted for causing, or aiding in causing, any explosion in or with any explosive substance; also any part of any such apparatus, machine, or implement.'

Clearly, the relevant phrases in s 9 were, 'Any apparatus ... intended to be used ... for causing ... any explosion.'

Mr Robertson argues that to be guilty of the offence under s 4 of the 1883 Act, the appellant had to be proved to have known that what was being made was an explosive substance in that it was a piece of apparatus intended to be used for causing an explosion. The need to prove such guilty knowledge is underlined, he submits, because the appellant was charged on the basis of being an accessory to the making of the timers by Smith. Section 5 of the 1883 Act provides, so far is relevant, as follows:

> 'Any person who ... by the supply of ... money ... or in any manner whatsoever, procures ... or is accessory to, the commission of any crime under this Act ... shall be liable to be tried and punished for that crime, as if he had been guilty as a principal.'

Mr Robertson relies upon two authorities. *R v Hallam* [1957] 1 All ER 665, [1957] 1 QB 569 was a case under the same section, but the defendant was charged with knowingly having in his possession or under his control an explosive substance. Lord Goddard CJ, giving the judgment of the court, said ([1957] 1 All ER 665 at 666, [1957] 1 QB 569 at 572–573):

> 'The section says he must knowingly have in his possession an explosive substance; therefore, it does seem that it is an ingredient in the offence that he knew it was an explosive substance. If evidence is given that the [accused] had the substance in his possession, and some evidence of circumstances which give rise to a reasonable suspicion that he had not got it for a lawful purpose is given, the jury are then entitled to infer that he knew it was an explosive substance.'

That decision was followed in *R v Stewart and Harris* (1959) 44 Cr App R 29, which was also a case alleging that the defendant knowingly had in his possession an explosive substance. His appeal was allowed because, as Lord Parker CJ said (at 31):

> '... the only direction given was in regard to possession and not in regard to the knowledge that the thing possessed was an explosive.'

The section applies to a person who makes, or has in his possession, or has under his control, an explosive substance. It is true that the word 'knowingly' qualifies only the second and third of those categories. However, in our judgment all three categories of person must be shown to have known that the substance was an explosive substance. We cannot read the section as requiring proof of such knowledge in a possessor or controller, but not in the maker. The word 'knowingly' simply emphasises that where possession or control is relied upon, the defendant must know the substance is in his possession, for example in his house or his car. No person who makes the substance can be unaware that he had done so.

Mr Cocks QC accepted this view of the law at the trial. He also accepted it in his argument before the House of Lords: see *R v Berry* [1985] AC 246 at 248. However, he has sought to rely upon a passage in the speech of Lord Roskill which he suggests is to contrary effect. Lord Roskill said ([1984] 3 All ER 1008 at 1012, [1985] AC 246 at 254):

> 'In the present case the guilty conduct was shown by proof of the making of what was beyond peradventure an explosive substance

within the definition. A guilty state of mind was shown by proof that that making was under such circumstances as to give rise to a reasonable suspicion that that making did not have a lawful object.'

We cannot read that passage as indicating that the maker does not have to be proved to have known it was an explosive substance. It may be that Lord Roskill, in the passage quoted, was following the line of reasoning adopted by Lord Goddard CJ, ie that proof of circumstances giving rise to a reasonable suspicion that the making did not have a lawful object can lead to the inference that the maker knew he was making an explosive substance. However that may be, the issue for the House of Lords concerned solely the jurisdiction point and the argument did not focus upon whether mens rea needed to be established.

In our judgment, Mr Robertson's contention is correct and accordingly the judge ought to have identified mens rea as a specific ingredient of the offence requiring to be proved by the Crown. It was particularly important in the present case because, unlike gunpowder or gelignite which were substances found in R v Hallam, a timer is not so obviously an explosive substance within the definition in s 9 of the 1883 Act.

Given that mens rea was a necessary ingredient which the judge had to identify, Mr Cocks relies upon two passages in the summing up. The judge read the whole of s 9, without filleting out for the jury the words relevant to this case. He then went on as follows:

'So the prosecution have to prove that these timers come within that section and they go about it in this way: they say to you—and this is something they must prove so that you are sure about it—that the real purpose of these timers comes within that definition.'

Later, having again read out the whole of s 9 unselectively, the judge went on:

'So before you can decide whether these timers were an explosive substance, you have to consider most carefully what was their real purpose.'

We do not think that the use of the phrase 'real purpose' was sufficient to convey that the jury had to be sure the maker intended the timer to be used to cause explosions. The phrase might be taken to mean simply the objective function of such a timer, or even the purpose which the ultimate purchaser had in mind. Whether the appellant intended the timers for a use within s 9 was an issue specifically raised by the defence. Accordingly, we consider that the summing up was flawed in this respect and there was a material misdirection.

Lawful object

The second ground of appeal is that the judge did not give an adequate direction to the jury as to the law relating to the appellant's defence of 'lawful object'. The section puts the burden on the defendant to establish that he made the explosive substance for a lawful object. The appellant's case was that he was supplying the timers, not to terrorists, but to the Syrian government. Mr Cocks accepts the case was conducted on the basis that a sale of the timers to the Syrian government would have been lawful whatever the subsequent use, or further transfer of them, may have turned out to be. It was therefore incumbent on the judge to make clear to the jury that if, on a balance of probability, the defendant showed he was party to the making of the timers with the object of selling them to the Syrian government, he should be acquitted.

The judge dealt with the matter at three points in his summing up. He said:

> 'Their defence is ... they had a lawful object in mind that they were going either to Syria to be used for aircraft landing lights, or to be exported properly, says [the appellant], as far as he was concerned, in the latter stage, to the Oman or somewhere like it.'

Later, the judge said:

> 'So we have the situation of the Syrian government, if that is where they were going, getting ... two somewhat different timers, ten-minute and thirty-minute cycle. The Crown say, and this is their case, that that would not matter if they were really for bombs—to set off bombs. Remember, Mr Fereday said it is his experience that such devices as timers are normally placed near the bombs so that they are blown up at the same time. So the Crown say that that would not matter. But it would if they were to be used for lawful civilian or military purposes. That is a matter for you, not for me.'

Later still, he merely repeated that the burden was on the defence to show that the timers were made for a lawful object.

In our judgment, these passages fail to deal adequately with the defence. The first passage may well have conveyed that the defendant's case was export to Syria for landing lights and if, for example, the Syrian government was going to use them to cause explosions, the defence failed. This erroneous implication was repeated in the muddled passage quoted above, suggesting the jury should draw a distinction between setting off bombs and 'lawful civilian or military purposes'. What was lacking was a clear direction that if the timers were probably being supplied to the Syrian government, that was a good defence and the jury should not concern itself with how they were to be used by that government.

Non-disclosure

The third ground of appeal concerns non-disclosure. It was learnt only a few days before this hearing, both by the Crown's lawyers and through them by the defence, that a memorandum from the Israeli security service had been received on 11 February 1982 at the Forensic Explosives Laboratory. The document was marked 'Secret' and revealed that Fatah terrorist squads operating in Israeli-administered territory, were using UHF transmitters manufactured by Mr Smith's company. However, the timers in use by Fatah were not the same as those concerned in the indictment. The information was clearly relevant to these proceedings and Mr Cocks accepts that even before the decision in *R v Ward* [1993] 2 All ER 577, [1993] 1 WLR 619, and pursuant to the Attorney General's guidelines at the time, the document or its information ought to have been disclosed to the defence. However, it is obvious that the impact of that information on the jury would probably have been more damaging than helpful to the defence. The UHF equipment and the timers were both contained in the same written order. To reveal to the jury that even part of that order found its way to terrorist squads would have been prejudicial to the defence. It is highly unlikely that defending counsel would have used it. Our view is, therefore, that whilst the document ought to have been disclosed, the failure to disclose it had no material impact on the trial.

Expert evidence

The final ground of appeal turns upon fresh evidence. At the trial, Mr Fereday's expert evidence stood effectively unchallenged. The only expert for the defence, Dr Hanka, lacked experience of terrorist weaponry. The Home Secretary's reference adverted specifically to fresh expert evidence casting doubt on Mr Fereday's opinion, and application was made to us to admit the evidence of four expert witnesses. It might have been possible to have called such evidence at the trial, although it may well have been hard to find, and some of the witnesses were serving army officers at the time. However, we admitted the evidence pursuant to s 23(1) of the Criminal Appeal Act 1968, as we considered it was in the interests of justice to do so.

Mr Fereday expressed it as his strong and firm conclusion that these timers could only have been designed for use by terrorists to cause explosions. Thus he said:

'As a result of an examination of the timing device, I came to the conclusion that it was specifically designed and constructed for a terrorist purpose, that is to say to be attached to an explosive device ... I came to the conclusion that it could only be designed and manufactured for a terrorist operation.'

He excluded the possibility of any non-explosive use such as for surveillance or lighting. He also excluded use by a legitimate army because of the lack of any inbuilt safety device. He contended that terrorists did not trust them and preferred to improvise their own visual and external safety devices. The military, on the other hand, he said, were concerned for the lives and limbs of their squaddies, and always had safety devices built in.

The witnesses called before us were highly experienced and, in our view, impressive experts. Colonel Wyatt had served for 23 years in the Royal Engineers. He was concerned with bomb disposal and counter-terrorist operations. He now runs a company advising governments on counter-terrorism. Major Lewis served in the Royal Signals for 22 years, acquiring specialist knowledge of electronic warfare, triggers, improvised explosive devices, surveillance and the marking of dropping and landing zones. He had experience of practices in the Middle East. Dr Borer is a highly qualified chemist with experience of explosive devices used by terrorist organisations in the United Kingdom. Finally, Dr Scott, senior lecturer at Dublin City University, is an expert in electronics with experience of electronic devices used by terrorists.

It is unnecessary to lengthen this judgment by summarising in detail the evidence of these witnesses. It is sufficient to say that each of them disagreed with the extremely dogmatic conclusion expressed by Mr Fereday in his evidence at the trial. The effect of their evidence was that the timer in question is indeed a timer and nothing more. It could be used for a variety of purposes, especially in surveillance. Perhaps most significantly, these witnesses disagreed with Mr Fereday's evidence at the trial that a legitimate military user for demolition or explosive purposes could be excluded due to the absence of built-in safety devices. Whereas Western armies would require built-in safety devices, as Mr Fereday testified, in the Middle East this was not so. When recalled before this court, Mr Fereday conceded that in the Middle East it might be difficult to separate terrorists from military use. He also conceded that he had no experience of the operational use of surveillance devices and he expressly deferred to Colonel Wyatt's experience.

It is submitted that, if the expert evidence before this court had been before the jury, they may well have rejected the uncompromising and incriminating conclusions expressed to them by Mr Fereday. All four of the experts called before us concluded that these timers were less likely to be used for explosive than for other purposes. As it was, the judge highlighted Mr Fereday's largely unchallenged evidence, making it central to the case. He described Mr Fereday as 'the principal and most vital witness for the prosecution'. He took the unusual step of obtaining a transcript of Mr Fereday's evidence and reading passages from it verbatim in his summing up.

Mr Cocks pointed to other evidence upon which the prosecution relied as being sufficient to sustain the verdict. The appellant's own testimony was in some respects at variance with what he told the police and with what Smith had said. Mr Aspin said he discussed with the appellant the use of the timers for blowing up buildings. The appellant denied this. Mr Cocks submitted that if the appellant did not discuss the purpose of the timers, that in itself was indicative of guilt, since any supplier would want and need to know the purpose for which the timer was required. No doubt these matters would have been supportive to any cogent primary evidence of guilt which the prosecution could adduce. Here, however, there was no direct evidence of supply to terrorists, or use by terrorists, of the timers in question. The Crown therefore had to rely heavily upon the opinion of the explosives expert.

In our judgment, Mr Fereday's conclusions, which he no doubt honestly held, were, as he himself has now partially conceded, open to doubt at the very least. The dogmatic terms in which they were expressed, the absence of challenge to them at the trial and the judge's emphasis of them as the most vital evidence, makes it likely that they played a crucial part in the jury's deliberations. In our view, on this ground alone, the verdict of the jury could not be regarded as safe and satisfactory. Having regard also to our conclusions on the first two grounds argued before us, we have no doubt that our duty is to allow this appeal.

Before parting with the case, we repeat our regret that it has taken so long for the matter to be concluded and that, in the interim, the appellant has served the sentence imposed. We also wish to consider how such protraction of proceedings can be avoided in future.

If one of a number of grounds of appeal appears well-founded, this court not infrequently indicates that it will allow the appeal on that ground without hearing argument on the others. This is a desirable option in the interests both of the speedy and economical disposal of the instant case and of enabling other appellants' cases to come on. If the Crown then appeals successfully to the House of Lords, what should happen to the other unresolved grounds of appeal?

This matter was considered but left open by the House of Lords in *A-G for Northern Ireland v Gallagher* [1961] 3 All ER 299 at 303–304, [1963] AC 349 at 365–367 where Lord Reid said:

'To make the issue clearer, let me suppose a case where the respondent in this House argued two points in the court below either of which, if right, entitled him to succeed. The court below, having decided one in his favour, might well say it was unnecessary to consider the second. Then, the first point having been certified, this House holds that the court below was wrong. What is then to happen? It cannot reasonably be supposed that Parliament intended that the respondent is to have no opportunity of having his second point considered so that his conviction must stand. So it must either be considered by this House or by the court below. It is true that sub-s. (4) [of s 1 of the Administration of Justice Act 1960, now s 35(3) of the Criminal Appeal Act 1968] authorises a remit to that court, but that is only for the purpose of disposing of the appeal to this House. I can find nothing to authorise a remit to the court below directing it to re-open and re-hear the case and come to a fresh decision. So in that case at least this House must go beyond the point certified and heard and decide the second point which may have no connection at all with the first. If in such a case this House must exercise the whole of its ordinary functions on appeal, what is there to show that, in some other class of case, it is not to do so? ... As the proper construction of this section raises a new and important issue, I do not wish to go further than is necessary to decide this case. Others regarding it in the light of different facts may be more successful than I have been in finding in the terms of the section some basis for an implication that, in hearing an appeal under it, the powers of this House are in some way limited.'

Lord Goddard and Lord Denning said that if it were necessary to do so the House of Lords had power to consider points other than that certified. Lord Tucker said it was a matter for the exercise of discretion as to whether other points could be argued and it should not be assumed that they could be raised as of right. Lord Morris of Borth-y-Gest expressed no view on this issue.

The views of the majority in *Gallagher*'s case were applied by the Court of Appeal in the present case (see [1991] 2 All ER 789, [1991] 1 WLR 125) holding that once an appeal reached the House of Lords, the party to the appeal had a final opportunity to bring such points as he wished to make to the notice of the House, and the House had power in its discretion to deal with other grounds. Since, in the present case, the House of Lords was not invited to deal with the unresolved grounds, there was no residual jurisdiction for the Court of Appeal to re-list the case.

It may well be that the House of Lords would have been reluctant to consider other grounds, particularly any turning on questions of fact, or involving fresh evidence. We can well understand counsel's disinclination to raise these matters, but, in the result, the unresolved grounds fell between two courts and finally redress was available only through the exercise of the Home Secretary's powers.

In our view, it is desirable that Parliament clarify the position by giving the House of Lords power, either to consider any unresolved grounds additional to the certified point, or to remit them for consideration by this court. Consideration should also be given to granting this court power to reserve argument on unresolved grounds with liberty to apply when allowing an appeal on one point and certifying it for the House of Lords. Meanwhile, in any case in which this court is minded to allow an appeal on one ground, leaving others unresolved, the Crown should inform the court before judgment if there is any reason to believe they would seek to have the decisive point certified for consideration by the House of Lords. Then this court could decide whether, out of caution, the other grounds ought to be considered there and then.

Appeal allowed. Conviction quashed.

Kate O'Hanlon Barrister.

Yip Chiu-cheung v R

PRIVY COUNCIL
LORD JAUNCEY OF TULLICHETTLE, LORD GRIFFITHS, LORD BROWNE-WILKINSON, LORD MUSTILL AND LORD SLYNN OF HADLEY
20, 21 APRIL, 16 JUNE 1994

Criminal law – Conspiracy – Mens rea – Mens rea of co-conspirator – Co-conspirator an undercover drug enforcement agent acting to break up drug ring – Co-conspirator not to be charged if plan to export heroin from Hong Kong carried out – Whether co-conspirator having mens rea to commit offence, albeit he would not be prosecuted.

Criminal law – Defence – Defence of superior orders or Crown or Executive fiat – Whether defence available in English or Hong Kong criminal law – Whether Executive having power to authorise breach of law.

The appellant met one N in Thailand and arranged that he would act as a courier to carry five kilos of heroin from Hong Kong to Australia. N was to fly to Hong Kong under an assumed name, where he would be met by the appellant and he was then to fly on to Australia with five kilos of heroin supplied by the appellant, for which he was to be paid $US16,000. In fact, unknown to the appellant, N was an undercover drug enforcement officer of the United States and the Hong Kong and Australian authorities were prepared to permit him to carry the drugs from Hong Kong to Australia in the hope of breaking the drug ring of which the appellant was a member. However, on the subsequent advice of the Hong Kong authorities the plan was not carried through and N did not fly to Hong Kong. The appellant was nevertheless arrested in Hong Kong and charged with conspiring with N to traffic in heroin. At his trial the judge directed the jury that if they found that N intended to export the heroin out of Hong Kong he was in law a co-conspirator and they could convict the appellant of a conspiracy with him. The appellant was convicted and sentenced to 15 years' imprisonment. He appealed to the Court of Appeal of Hong Kong which dismissed his appeal. He appealed to the Privy Council, contending that N could not in law be a co-conspirator because he lacked the necessary mens rea for the offence and therefore there could be no conspiracy.

Held – There was no general defence of superior orders or of Crown or Executive fiat in English or Hong Kong criminal law and the Executive had no power to authorise a breach of the law. Accordingly, the fact that N would not have been prosecuted if he carried out the plan to carry the drugs from Hong Kong to Australia as intended did not mean that he did not intend to commit the criminal offence of trafficking in drugs by exporting heroin from Hong Kong, albeit as part of a wider scheme to combat drug dealing. N intended to commit that offence by carrying the heroin through the customs and on to the aeroplane bound for Australia. It followed that there had been a conspiracy and that the appellant had been properly convicted. The appeal would therefore be dismissed (see p 928 *d* to *j*, post).

R v Anderson [1985] 2 All ER 961 distinguished.

Notes

For the mental element in conspiracy, see 11(1) *Halsbury's Laws* (4th edn) paara 65, and for cases on the subject, see 14(1) *Digest* (2nd Reissue) 175, 1417–1418.

Cases referred to in judgment

A v Hayden (No 2) (1984) 156 CLR 532, Aust HC.
R v Anderson [1985] 2 All ER 961, [1986] AC 27, [1985] 3 WLR 268, HL.

Appeal

Yip Chiu-cheung appealed against the decision of the Court of Appeal of Hong Kong (Silke V-P, Power JA and Kaplan J) delivered on 15 May 1992 dismissing his appeal against his conviction on 27 March 1991 before Duffy J and a jury of conspiracy to traffic in heroin, contrary to the to the common law and s 4 of the Hong Kong Dangerous Drugs Ordinance, for which he was sentenced to 15 years' imprisonment. The facts are set out in the judgment of the Board.

Lord Hoosen QC and *Robert Britton* (instructed by *Edwin Coe*) for the appellant.
James Guthrie QC and *Stephen Wong* (assistant principal Crown Counsel of Hong Kong) (instructed by *Macfarlanes*) for the Crown.

The Board took time for consideration.

16 June 1994. The following judgment of the Board was delivered.

LORD GRIFFITHS. On 27 March 1991 the appellant was convicted of conspiracy to traffic in heroin and sentenced to 15 years' imprisonment. His appeal was dismissed by the Court of Appeal of Hong Kong on 15 May 1992 and he now appeals from that decision.

The indictment charged the appellant as follows:

> 'STATEMENT OF OFFENCE Conspiracy to traffic in a dangerous drug, contrary to Common Law and section 4 of the Dangerous Drugs Ordinance, Cap. 134.

PARTICULARS OF OFFENCE Yip Chiu-cheung, between the 19th day of August, 1989 and the 15th day of November, 1989 in Thailand and Hong Kong, conspired with Philip Needham and another person unknown to traffic in a dangerous drug, namely salts of esters of morphine commonly known as heroin.'

The relevant provisions of the Dangerous Drugs Ordinance are as follows:

'2(1) In this Ordinance, unless the context otherwise requires—"Director" means the Director of Health, Deputy Director of Health or an assistant director of health; "export" means to take or cause to be taken out of Hong Kong or any other country, as the case may be, by land, air or water; "trafficking", in relation to a dangerous drug, includes importing into Hong Kong, exporting from Hong Kong, procuring, supplying or otherwise dealing in or with the dangerous drug ... and "traffic in a dangerous drug" shall be construed accordingly; "unlawful" or "unlawfully", in relation to trafficking in or manufacturing or storage of a dangerous drug, means otherwise than under and in accordance with this Ordinance or a licence issued thereunder ...

4(1) Save under and in accordance with this Ordinance or a licence granted by the Director hereunder, no person shall, on his own behalf or on behalf of any other person, whether or not such other person is in Hong Kong—(a) traffic in a dangerous drug; (b) offer to traffic in a dangerous drug or in a substance he believes to be a dangerous drug; or (c) do or offer to do an act preparatory to or for the purpose of trafficking in a dangerous drug or in a substance he believes to be a dangerous drug.'

The prosecution case was based primarily on the evidence of Philip Needham who was an undercover drug enforcement officer of the United States of America and named in the indictment as a co-conspirator. The other conspirator, referred to in the indictment as a person unknown, was introduced to Needham by the appellant under the name of Hom.

In outline Needham's evidence was that he had a series of meetings in Thailand with the appellant, at one of which Hom also took part, at which it was arranged that Needham would act as a courier to carry five kilos of heroin from Hong Kong to Australia, travelling by air. The arrangement was that Needham would fly to Hong Kong on 22 October under the name of Larsen, where he would be met by the appellant. He would then stay at the Nathan Hotel in Kowloon for a few days and then fly on to Australia with five kilos of heroin supplied by the appellant. For this service he would be paid $US16,000. In fact Needham did not fly to Hong Kong on 22 October because the flight was delayed and he missed the rescheduled flight. Needham said he had no way of contacting the appellant in Hong Kong and had been advised by the Hong Kong authorities that the Nathan Hotel would be a dangerous place for him to stay. Needham therefore proceeded no further with the plan, and did not go to Hong Kong.

The appellant was arrested in Hong Kong on 15 November, a piece of paper with the name 'Larsen' was found in the appellant's possession and it was admitted that he had come to the airport to meet Needham's flight on 22 October. Needham said that throughout his dealings with the appellant and Hom he kept the authorities in Hong Kong and Australia informed of the plans and they agreed that he would not be prevented from carrying the heroin out of Hong Kong and into Australia. It was obviously the intention to try to identify and arrest both the suppliers and the distributors of the drug.

The defence was that there had been no arrangement to carry any drugs, and the appellant was to assist Needham to buy travellers cheques that had been reported lost. He agreed that on one occasion Hom had been present when he met Needham.

In his summing up the judge directed the jury that, if they accepted Needham's evidence, it was open to them to convict the appellant of a conspiracy with Hom, and if they were sure that Needham had intended to carry the heroin out of Hong Kong he was in law a co-conspirator and they could convict the appellant of a conspiracy with Needham.

The jury found the appellant guilty, but they were not asked to bring in separate verdicts in respect of conspiracy with Hom and Needham.

The appellant raised a number of grounds of appeal before the Court of Appeal all of which failed, and only one of which is now pursued before the Board, which is that Needham, the drug enforcement officer, cannot in law be a co-conspirator because he lacked the necessary mens rea for the offence.

Before, however, turning to consider this ground of appeal, it will first be convenient to deal with a further ground of appeal arising out of a concession made by the prosecution in the Court of Appeal. The prosecution told the Court of Appeal that, if the appeal succeeded, they would not seek to uphold the conviction by relying upon a conspiracy between the appellant and Hom. The appellant submitted that this concession was fatal to the conviction, the argument being that the jury might have convicted only on the conspiracy with Hom and might not have been satisfied that Needham ever had the necessary intent to carry the heroin to make him a conspirator; therefore, it is said, if the conspiracy with Hom is not upheld the conviction cannot stand.

Their Lordships are satisfied that this argument is based on a misunderstanding of the nature of the concession made by the prosecution. There was no attack in the Court of Appeal upon the judge's direction that the jury could on the evidence find a conspiracy between Hom and the appellant. But if the appeal succeeded in establishing that Needham was not in law a co-conspirator, there was no way of knowing whether the jury had convicted on the basis of the conspiracy with Hom or with Needham. In these circumstances the prosecution rightly said they would not seek to rely on the conspiracy with Hom if the conspiracy with Needham failed, because the jury might have founded their verdict on the conspiracy with Needham. If, however, Needham was capable in law of being a co-conspirator with the appellant there was ample evidence to support the jury's verdict of guilty either on the grounds of conspiracy with Hom or Needham or both of them. As, for the reasons that follow, Needham was rightly held to be capable of being a conspirator this ground of appeal fails.

On the principal ground of appeal it was submitted that the trial judge and the Court of Appeal were wrong to hold that Needham, the undercover agent, could be a conspirator because he lacked the necessary mens rea or guilty mind required for the offence of conspiracy. It was urged upon their Lordships that no moral guilt attached to the undercover agent who was at all times acting courageously and with the best of motives in attempting to infiltrate and bring to justice a gang of criminal drug dealers. In these circumstances it was argued that it would be wrong to treat the agent as having any criminal intent, and reliance was placed upon a passage in the speech of Lord Bridge of Harwich in *R v Anderson* [1985] 2 All ER 961 at 965, [1986] AC 27 at 38–39; but in that case Lord Bridge was dealing with a different situation from that which exists in the present case. There may be many cases in which undercover police officers or other law enforcement agents pretend to join a conspiracy in order to gain information about the plans of the criminals, with no intention of taking any part in the planned crime but rather with the intention of providing information that will frustrate it. It was to this situation that Lord Bridge was referring in *Anderson*. The crime of conspiracy requires an agreement between two or more persons to commit an unlawful act with the intention of carrying it out. It is the intention to carry out the crime that constitutes the necessary mens rea for the offence. As Lord Bridge pointed out, an undercover agent who has no intention of committing the crime lacks the necessary mens rea to be a conspirator.

The facts of the present case are quite different. Nobody can doubt that Needham was acting courageously and with the best of motives; he was trying to break a drug ring. But equally there can be no doubt that the method he chose and in which the police in Hong Kong acquiesced involved the commission of the criminal offence of trafficking in drugs by exporting heroin from Hong Kong without a licence. Needham intended to commit that offence by carrying the heroin through the customs and on to the aeroplane bound for Australia.

Neither the police, nor customs, nor any other member of the executive have any power to alter the terms of the Ordinance forbidding the export of heroin, and the fact that they may turn a blind eye when the heroin is exported does not prevent it from being a criminal offence.

The High Court of Australia in *A v Hayden (No 2)* (1984) 156 CLR 532 declared emphatically that there was no place for a general defence of superior orders or of Crown or Executive fiat in Australian criminal law. Gibbs CJ said (at 540):

'It is fundamental to our legal system that the executive has no power to authorize a breach of the law and that it is no excuse for an offender to say that he acted under the orders of a superior officer.'

This statement of the law applies with the same force in England and Hong Kong as it does in Australia.

Naturally, Needham never expected to be prosecuted if he carried out the plan as intended. But the fact that in such circumstances the authorities would not prosecute the undercover agent does not mean that he did not commit the crime albeit as part of a wider scheme to combat drug dealing. The judge correctly directed the jury that they should regard Needham as a conspirator if they found that he intended to export the heroin.

Their Lordships will humbly advise Her Majesty that the appeal should be dismissed.

Appeal dismissed.

Celia Fox   Barrister.